July 3–5, 2017
Bologna, Italy

I0036696

**Association for
Computing Machinery**

Advancing Computing as a Science & Profession

ITiCSE'17

Proceedings of the 2017 ACM Conference on
Innovation and Technology in Computer
Science Education

Sponsored by:
ACM SIGCSE

Supported by:
Universita di Bologna

Association for Computing Machinery

Advancing Computing as a Science & Profession

The Association for Computing Machinery
2 Penn Plaza, Suite 701
New York, New York 10121-0701

ISBN: 978-1-4503-4704-4 (Digital)

ISBN: 978-1-4503-5592-6 (Print)

Additional copies may be ordered prepaid from:

ACM Order Department
PO Box 30777
New York, NY 10087-0777, USA

Phone: 1-800-342-6626 (USA and Canada)
+1-212-626-0500 (Global)
Fax: +1-212-944-1318
E-mail: acmhelp@acm.org
Hours of Operation: 8:30 am – 4:30 pm ET

Foreword

Benvenuti a Bologna—welcome to ITiCSE 2017 in Bologna!

The Università di Bologna was founded in 1088 and is the oldest university in continuous operation worldwide. Bologna itself has a rich history going back at least 3,000 years, and among other things boasts a well-preserved historical town center, many porticoes and towers. The city is ranked at the top on the list of Italian cities in terms of quality of life and quality of food.

The conference continues to be a truly international conference with 241 submissions with a total of 554 authors from 40 countries on all continents: the authors came from Africa (5), Asia (33), Europe (232), the Middle East (11), North America including Central America and the Caribbean (189), Oceania (34), and South America (50). In total, a total of 175 papers, one panel, and 16 working groups were submitted. Additionally, there were 31 posters and 18 tips & techniques submissions.

All research papers were double blind reviewed by at least six reviewers. This year, 56 papers (32%) were selected for presentation and inclusion in the proceedings. All posters and tips & techniques submissions were also reviewed by two reviewers. 24 posters and nine Tips and Techniques submissions were accepted.

The nine accepted working groups will address a diverse section of topics, including student engagement, game development, integrating international students, assessment development, code quality perceptions, a holistic understanding through research papers, effects of lecturer intervention on student behaviour, the Internet of Things and early developmental activities leading to computational thinking skills. Participating in a working group is probably one of the most efficient ways to become part of the ITiCSE community. It provides participants a unique opportunity to work with people from different countries who are interested and knowledgeable in the area of the working group.

This conference will have two keynote speakers. Stefano Zacchiroli from the University of Paris, Diderot will present the Software Heritage project; its goals, challenges, and potential scholarly and educational uses. Sana Odeh will discuss her work in broadening participation in computer science in the Arab world. In particular, Dr. Odeh will present the achievements of her annual Hackathon for Social Good in the Arab world.

In addition to the tradition conference banquet, which will be held at a traditional Italian trattoria, conference delegates will have the opportunity to explore Bologna's sights, smells, and tastes.

We hope you will be intellectually challenged, gastronomically sated, and culturally fulfilled. Furthermore, our most fervent hope is that you will return home with new ideas to try in your classroom, and new friends and colleagues with whom you can collaborate.

Benvenuti a Bologna

Renzo Davoli and Mikey Goldweber
ITiCSE 2017 Conference Chairs

Irene Polycarpou and Guido Rößling
ITiCSE 2017 Program Co-Chairs

Table of Contents

Keynote Addresses

Session 1A: Providing a Good Start

Session 1B: Software Engineering and Design

Session 2A: CS 1

Session 2B: Off the Beaten Path

Session 2C: Tool, Tips, and Courseware

Session 3A: Educational Tools: Programming Support

Session 3B: Code Maturity

Session 3C: Selecting / Training the Teaching Staff

Session 4A: Exams and Exam Preparation

Session 4B: K-12 Computing Education

Session 4C: Educational Tools

Session 5A: CS Learning

Session 5B: K-12 Computing Education II

Session 5C: Panel

Session 6A: Academic Integrity

Session 6C: Panel

Session 7A: Gender & Diversity in Computing

Session 7B: Non-Majors

Session 7C: Feedback

Session 8A: Programming

Session 8B: Enhancing CS Instruction

Session 8C: Gamification

Poster Session I

Working Groups Session

ITiCSE 2017 Conference Organization

Conference Co-Chairs: Renzo Davoli *(University of Bologna, Italy)*
Michael Goldweber *(Xavier University, USA)*

Program Co-Chairs: Guido Rößling *(Technische Universität Darmstadt, Germany)*
Irene Polycarpou *(University of Central Lancashire, Cyprus)*

Treasurer & Registration Chair: Cary Laxer *(Rose-Hulman Institute of Technology, USA)*

Working Groups: Ari Korhonen *(Aalto University, Finland)*
Judithe Sheard *(Monash University, Australia)*

Proceedings Chair: Stan Kurkovsky *(Central Connecticut State University, USA)*

Tips, Techniques & Courseware: Judith Gal-Ezer *(The Open University, Israel)*

Posters and Panels: Jacqueline Whalley *(Auckland University of Technology, New Zealand)*
Panayiotis Andreou *(University of Central Lancashire, Cyprus)*

Database Coordinator: Simon *(University of Newcastle, Australia)*

Webmaster: Simon *(University of Newcastle, Australia)*

Evaluations: Bruce Scharlau *(The Universitee of Aberdeen, UK)*

Associate Program Chairs: Dennis Bouvier *(Southern Illinois University Edwardsville, USA)*
Yingjun Cao *(University of California San Diego, USA)*
John Dougherty *(Haverford College, USA)*
Petri Ihantola *(Tampere University of Technology, Finland)*
Carsten Kleiner *(University of Applied Sciences & Arts, Hannover, Germany)*
Daniel Krutz *(Rochester Institute of Technology, USA)*
David Levine *(St Bonaventure University, USA)*
Andrew Luxton-Reilly *(University of Auckland, New Zealand)*
James Paterson *(Glasgow Caledonian University, UK)*
Andrew Petersen *(University of Toronto, Canada)*
Samuel Rebelsky *(Grinnell College, USA)*
Cliff Shaffer *(Virginia Tech, USA)*
Mark Sherriff *(University of Virginia, USA)*
Ian Utting *(University of Kent, UK)*
Troy Vasiga *(University of Waterloo, Canada)*
Henry Walker *(Grinnell College, USA)*

Reviewers:

Pedro Henriques Abreu	Lawrence D'Antonio
Rajeev Agrawal	Sayamindu Dasgupta
Ibrahim Al-Bluwi	Debzani Deb
Hend Al-Khalifa	Adrienne Decker
Meghan Allen	Leigh Ann DeLyser
Vicki L Almstrum	Yuli Deng
Carl Alphonce	Aaron Dingler
Christine Alvarado	Zachary Dodds
Sven Anderson	John Dooley
Barbara Anthony	Mohsen Dorodchi
Vaibhav Anu	Toby Dragon
Michal Armoni	J Philip East
Doug Baldwin	Samuel Ekundayo
John Barr	Yasmine El-Glaly
Austin Bart	Kiran Eranki
Ashok Basawapatna	Katrina Falkner
Lina Battestilli	Nick Falkner
Aaron Bauer	Mohammed Farghally
Brett Becker	Pedro Guillermo Feijóo García
R Scott Bell	Alan Fekete
Moti Ben-Ari	Georgios Fesakis
Luciana Benotti	Gene Fisher
Marc Berges	Kathi Fisler
Bradley Beth	Pamela Flores
Marie Bienkowski	Daniel Fokum
William Billingsley	Matthew Forshaw
Charles Boisvert	Eric Fouh
Grant Braught	Mohammad Fuad
Bo Brinkman	Alexandra Funke
Michael Brinkmeier	Alessio Gaspar
Andrej Brodnik	Katharina Geldreich
Kevin Buffardi	James Geller
David Bunde	Paul Gestwicki
Barry Burd	Anurag Goswami
Matthew Butler	Jean Goulet
Ricardo Caceffo	Ronald I Greenberg
Jennifer Campbell	Dahai Guo
Lillian Cassel	Margaret Hamilton
Francisco Enrique Vicente Castro	Brian Harrington
Veronica Catete	Christopher Harris
Juan Chen	Matthias Hauswirth
Jacqui Chetty	Scott Hawker
John Cigas	Sarah Heckman
Alison Clear	Michelle Craig
Stephen Cooper	Quintin Cutts

Reviewers (continued):

Scott Heggen	Lester I McCann
Arto Hellas	Sean McCulloch
Cay Horstmann	António José Mendes
David Hovemeyer	Susan Mengel
Brian Howard	Larry Merkle
Helen Hu	José Carlos MM Metrôlho
Janet Hughes	Joe Miró Julià
John Impagliazzo	Shitanshu Mishra
Cruz Izu	Mattia Monga
Jana Jackova	Michael Morgan
Bill Joel	Srikanth Mudigonda
Chris Johnson	Brandon D Myers
Colin Johnson	Robert Noonan
Anthony Joseph	Darragh O'Brien
Sarah Judd	Edward Okie
Viggo Kann	Michael Oudshoorn
Beth Katz	Myung Ah Park
David Kay	Young Park
Petros Kefalas	Miranda Parker
Hassan Khosravi	Vijay Parmar
Michael Kirkpatrick	Allen Parrish
Antti Knutas	Elizabeth Patitsas
Peter Komisarczuk	Raymond Pettit
Eileen Kraemer	Matthew Peveler
Martin Kropp	Vreda Pieterse
Jan Kruger	Ian Pollock
Stephan Krusche	Wayne Pollock
Martina Kuhn	Leo Porter
Bastian Küppers	Thomas Price
Stan Kurkovsky	Binsen Qian
Zachary Kurmas	Yizhou Qian
Yesem Kurt Peker	Saquib Razak
Clifton Kussmaul	Chuck Riedesel
Lisa Lacher	Adrián Riesco
Dieter Landes	Susan Rodger
Joan Langdon	Jennifer Rosato
David Largent	Miguel Rubio
Eric Larson	Daniel Russo
Gilliean Lee	Dobrila Lopez
Chi-Un Lei	Shawn Lupoli
Juho Leinonen	Francesco Maiorana
Dan Leyzberg	Dario Malchiodi
Justin Li	Martin Malchow
Yanyan Li	Chao Mbogo
Soohyun Nam Liao	John Russo

Reviewers (continued):

Ian Sanders	William Turner
André Santos	Hakan Tuzun
Suzanna Schmeelk	Tammy Vandegrift
Stephanie Elzer Schwartz	J Ángel Velázquez Iturbide
Andreas Seitz	David Voorhees
Cynthia Selby	Sally Wahba
Sue Sentence	Charles Wallace
Amit Shesh	Andrew Watkins
Robert Sloan	Thomas Way
Gina Sprint	Joshua Levi Weese
Bernhard Standl	Victor Winter
Ben Stephenson	Steve Wolfman
Chris Stephenson	Anna Xambó
Kalpathi Subramanian	Jeong Yang
Claudia Szabo	Lan Yang
Anya Tafliovich	Arthur Yanushka
Burcin Tamer	Chen-Hsiang Yu
Charles Thevathayan	Timothy Yuen
Neena Thota	Zhen Zeng
Daniel Toll	Jian Zhang
Peter Tucker	

ITiCSE 2017 Sponsor & Supporter

Sponsor:

Supporter:

ALMA MATER STUDIORUM
UNIVERSITÀ DI BOLOGNA

Broadening Participation in the Arab World

Sana Odeh
New York University
New York, USA
sao1@nyu.edu

ABSTRACT

In my talk, I will present two important projects that I've been leading during the past several years focusing on increasing diversity and innovation in computer Science education. I will first focus on the research that I have been leading for the past few years on the Representations, Challenges and Opportunities for Women in Computing in the Arab World. Women in Computing is an important and timely topic. Despite the remarkable progress that women made in almost all professions in the US, Canada, Australia, and several countries in Europe, however, their under-representation in the fields of computing raises an on-going societal concern. Very few women are in senior-level positions and the number of women technology-entrepreneurs is scarce. Various international studies have documented the underrepresentation of women at every level of science and technology.

The Arab world, however, presents a hopeful exception to these depressing trends. Our research indicates that women dominate STEM and sciences in the Arab world, in very stark contrast to trends in the US, Canada, Australia and Germany. On average, females comprise the majority of undergraduate students studying Computer Science in Arab countries including Algeria, Egypt, Jordan, Morocco, Saudi Arabia, and the UAE, whereas in the United States female enrolment in Computer Science and Engineering has fallen from 37% in the early 80's to a dismal rate nearing 20% in the first years of the 21th century. I will present our research findings focusing on the representation, challenges, and opportunities for Arab Women in Computing and also present motivation factors for enrolling in CS and technology fields. We hope that this study can shed some light and also contribute to the international debate and discourse on women enrolment and participation in the CS and technology fields.

Secondly, I will present ways in which "The Annual NYUAD International Hackathon for Social Good in The Arab World", an event that I have been organizing at New York University Abu Dhabi have focused on increasing diversity (close to 50% women and students from more than 30 countries participate every year) and innovation in Computer Science. The goal of the NYUAD Hackathon is to promote creativity in computer science, tech startups and entrepreneurship, and the development of innovative

technology for the social good. This event provides an opportunity for students from the Arab region and the world (we usually have participants from more than 30 countries) to experience the full cycle of creating a tech startup (sharing and generating ideas, pitching ideas, learning new platforms and programming languages, CS cutting edge trends such AI, Machine learning and Data Science, designing and developing mobile and web applications, hardware hacks, VR, and working with a team). Aside from learning top practices in software development, and CS research trends, students get a rare opportunity to be mentored by top leaders in both industry and academia. Also, students create innovative and solution-based technology for social good, which is becoming an important goal for computer scientists worldwide, as the field is now viewed as having created revolutionary innovations in many areas. This type of Hackathon creates opportunities for future international project collaboration, launching startups, and undertaking academic research among students in top trends such as AI, Machine learning and Data Science. I will present how the NYUAD Hackathon fosters diversity and innovation and off a creative way to teach Computer Science.

Author Keywords

Computing education; computing education programs; collaborative and social computing; empirical studies in collaborative and social computing; collaborative learning.

BIOGRAPHY

Professor Sana Odeh, is a Clinical Professor, and Faculty Liaison for Global Programs of Computer Science at Courant Institute of Mathematical Sciences, New York University, and an Affiliated Faculty of Computer Science, New York University Abu Dhabi (NYUAD). A proponent of women in technology, professor Odeh is the founder and chair of the Conference on Women in Computing in the Arab world (held at NYUAD in Abu Dhabi during Spring 2012, May 2013, May 17, and 18, 2015, February 12 in Algeria, and 2017 will be held in Lebanon at the American University of Beirut (AUB) on August 10-12), founder and chair of the Arab Women in Computing (arabwic.org), founder and chair of the Annual NYU Abu Dhabi International Hackathon for the Social Good in the Arab World (Held in 2017,

ITiCSE '17, July 03-05, 2017, Bologna, Italy
© 2017 Copyright is held by the owner/author(s).
ACM ISBN 978-1-4503-4704-4/17/07.
http://dx.doi.org/10.1145/3059009.3080530

2016, 2015, 2014, 2013, 2012, and 2011), chair of the annual New York City Girls Computer Science and Engineering Conference (sponsored by Google, NYU's Courant Women in Computing (WinC) and Princeton University Graduate Women in Science and Engineering (GWISE, and the faculty advisor for NYU's Courant Women in Computing (WinC) at NYU NY. She is a member of the leadership committee of the Grace Hopper Celebration of Women in Computing (GHC), the world's largest conference for women technologists, and also a member of the steering committee of the Association for Computing Machinery Council on Women in Computing (ACM-W). Also, on May 8th, 2016, Professor Odeh was selected by Facebook for her work on Arab Women in Technology (ArabWIC) as one of six stories to feature in honor of International Women's Day. Also, made the final list for the prestigious "2016 WORLD TECHNOLOGY AWARD" http://www.wtn.net/summit-2016/finalists.

She is also an Affiliated Faculty of Computer Science at New York University Abu Dhabi (NYUAD) where she spent three years (from 2010 to 2013) setting up the Computer Science department at New York University Abu Dhabi (NYUAD) and also created successful international collaboration projects in Computer Science.

Her research focuses on Programming Languages and Web and Mobile Technologies, Developing information technologies for the developing world, E-Learning, and Arab Women in Computing" http://cs.nyu.edu:~odeh

Software Heritage: Scholarly and Educational Synergies with Preserving Our Software Commons

Stefano Zacchiroli
University Paris Diderot and Inria
Paris, France
zack@irif.fr

ABSTRACT

The Software Commons is the vast body of human knowledge embedded in software source code, that is publicly available and can be freely altered and reused. Free and Open Source Software (FOSS) constitutes the bulk of it. Sadly we seem to be at increasing risk of losing this precious heritage built by the FOSS community over the paste decades: code hosting sites shut down when their popularity decreases, tapes of ancient versions of our toolchain (bit-)rot in basements, etc.

The ambitious goal of the Software Heritage project is to contribute to address this risk, by collecting, preserving, and sharing *all* publicly available software in source code form. Together with its complete development history, as captured by state-of-the art version control systems.

For how long? Forever, of course.

By pursuing this mission Software Heritage will serve the needs of:

- **Society**, by preserving our collective technological heritage;

- **Industry**, by building the largest software provenance and licensing open database and offering the equivalent of "part numbers" for FOSS components;

- **Science**, by assembling the largest curated archive for software research and a much needed source code archival service to improve over the current state of scientific reproducibility when it comes to software-backed experiments;

- **Education**, by laying the groundwork for permanent source code anthologies and collectively curated "source books" for programming curricula.

Although still in Beta, Software Heritage has already archived more than 3 billion unique source code files and 700 million unique commits, spanning more than 50 million software development projects from major code hosting sites, distributions, and upstream software collections.

In this talk we will give a general overview of Software Heritage, its design principles and current status, with a particular focus on the scholarly and educational use cases that might be supported by the project.

Author Keywords

Software preservation; source code; free and open source software; software commons; source book; reproducibility.

BIOGRAPHY

Stefano Zacchiroli is Associate Professor of Computer Science at University Paris Diderot on leave at Inria. His research interests span formal methods, software preservation, and Free/Open Source Software engineering. He is co-founder and current CTO of the Software Heritage project. He is an official member of the Debian Project since 2001, where he was elected to serve as Debian Project Leader for 3 terms in a row over the period 2010-2013. He is a former director of the Open Source Initiative (OSI) and recipient of the 2015 O'Reilly Open Source Award.

ITiCSE '17, July 03-05, 2017, Bologna, Italy
ACM ISBN 978-1-4503-4704-4/17/07.
http://dx.doi.org/10.1145/3059009.3059066

Learning to Program – Choose your Lecture Seat Carefully!

Aidan McGowan
Queen's University Belfast
Malone Rd, Belfast
Northern Ireland
+44 (0)28 9097 1185
aidan.mcgowan@qub.ac.uk

Philip Hanna
Queen's University Belfast
Malone Rd, Belfast
Northern Ireland
+44 (0)28 9097 4634
p.hanna@qub.ac.uk

Des Greer
Queen's University Belfast
Malone Rd, Belfast
Northern Ireland
+44 (0)28 9097 1190
des.greer@qub.ac.uk

John Busch
Queen's University Belfast
Malone Rd, Belfast
Northern Ireland
+44 (0)28 9097 1188
j.a.busch@qub.ac.uk

ABSTRACT

Much previous research has indicated that where a student sits in a university lecture theatre has a correlation with their final grade. Frequently those students that sit regularly in the front rows have been reported to achieve the highest grades. However most of the research restricted student seat movement, which is both unnatural and may have adversely influenced the research results. A previously reported unique unrestricted seat tracking investigation by the authors of this paper used a web and mobile software tracking application (*PinPoint*) to investigate student seating related performances in a 12 week Java programming university module. The *PinPoint* investigation concluded that the best assessment results were achieved by the students in the front rows and that assessment scores degraded the further students sat from the front. Additionally while the most engaged students were found to regularly sit at the front the same was not true for the most academically able or those with the greatest prior programming experience. This paper presents a further analysis of the *PinPoint* data, focusing on assessment performances within similar groups (academic ability, engagement and prior programming experiences) and additionally presents results of a temporal movement study and a qualitative analysis of the group and individual student seating decisions. It concludes that a comparison of student assessment performances within each of the peer groups, in every instance, found that the front row students outperformed their peers sitting further back. This strongly suggests that there is a benefit to sitting at the front regardless of academic ability, engagement or prior subject knowledge. It also points to other untested factors that may be positively influencing the front row performances.

Keywords

Computing; Attitudes; Assessment performance; Seating Lecture theatre; Temporal movement

ITiCSE '17, July 03-05, 2017, Bologna, Italy. Copyright is held by the owner/author(s). Publication rights licensed to ACM.
ACM 978-1-4503-4704-4/17/07...$15.00
DOI: http://dx.doi.org/10.1145/3059009.3059020

1. INTRODUCTION

Students that regularly sit at the front of the lecture theatre tend to achieve higher grades than those students sitting elsewhere, has been commonly concluded by much of the research in the area ([6]; [15]; [24]).

The common causation factor being that the best students tend to sit in the front rows and therefore this directly influences why the best grades come from there.

The definition of best students tends to involve both academic ability and engagement. Giles [13] found a direct relationship between test scores and seating distance from the front with students in the front, middle and back rows of class scored on average 80.0%, 71.6%, and 68.1% respectively on course exams. However, the theory of enhanced performance from the front row students due to academic clustering was challenged by Perkins [25]. In that study, students were randomly allocated seats to exclude any potential natural bunching of the academically best students at the front of the lecture theatre. Nevertheless, the study concurs with the majority of other findings that grades dropped the further the students sat from the front. This would suggest that there are other untested factors that affect the relationship between performance and seating than simply student subject ability or positive attitudes.

Attitudes and abilities

Other studies have sought to identify these factors. These studies have included an analysis of the attitudes of the students including attendance [27], attention [26] and motivation [9]. Generally they suggest that those that sit at the front are indeed the best attenders, most attentive and motivated.

Better learning experience

The students that sit at the front may simply have a better learning experience and consequently end up with better grades. Part of this better experience may involve better note taking. Traditional lecturing involves the presenter speaking almost continuously for an extended period of time with the students' job to listen and take notes [5]. The importance of accurate notes is not lost on students with Brown [8] and Kierwa [17] reporting that the majority of test questions on college exams come from the lectures and that students who take better class notes get better course grades. This in turn places demands on students' ability to listen carefully and take notes that are accurate and complete. Conventional wisdom would suggest the note taking is better done at the front rather than the back of the lecture theatre due to better sight lines and being easier to hear the lecturer.

Participation

Marx [22] links the active participation of students in a lecture with a more positive learning experience which results in a strong positive influence on attention and long-term memory storage. Students that sit up front are generally less inhibited at asking questions and are able to make better eye contact with the lecturer and are regularly the most participative [11]. The ability to interact [2] and participate [10] in the lecture are important factors influencing the learning experience during the lecture. Traditional lecturing would tend to offer better participation opportunities at the front. It would follow then that if active participation opportunities are extended beyond the traditional front rows of the lecture hall by using active learning approaches then this would negate the perceived advantage to sitting up front. Perkins study [25] included an analysis of active teaching styles and seating effect. However, even with lectures that employ active learning activities the results also displayed grade degradation from front to back. This would suggest that even with active learning styles there are still performance gains to be made by sitting at the front.

There are some other obvious logistical reasons a student may opt to sit at the front. These include where their friends are sitting or if the student was late to class and the front happens to be all that is available [20] or better visibility and improved ability to hear at the front [21].

Counter argument and issues with previous research

While most studies report a correlation between seating position and performance a small number of studies including Kalinowski [16] and York [3] suggest that seating position has no effect on student attainment. In both studies the authors conclude that the negligible effect on assessment scores and associated seating position may have been influenced by the confined nature of the lecture hall coupled with small sample sizes.

However the methodology employed by many of the seating studies is also questionable. Many studies required students to either self-select their seats or be allocated to seats at the beginning of the course. The students were then restricted to the same seat for the remaining number of lectures. Other studies randomly grouped students into seating zones and asked the groups to switch zones during the module. These control measures do not reflect the natural or the usual occurrence on university courses. It is perhaps the case that the restrictions improperly influenced the research outcomes. Other studies sourced their positional data from a self-completed student questionnaire at the end of the module, by simply asking the students where they predominantly sat.

It also follows that any temporal factors that may influence a student to change seats could not be accessed or reported in these studies. For instance if a student that normally sits towards the back receives a low in-term grade, does this influence them to start sitting at the front? Other unanswerable questions from these restricted movement studies include analysis of natural migrations over time, for example do those that sit at the front at the start of the course remain there throughout? What would cause a student to move? Do students tend to move towards the front as exam or submission dates approach in the hope to glean exam hints from the lecturer?

PinPoint - accurate tracking

In this research and in [23] during a series of lectures in a twelve week university Java programming module the students were allowed to sit wherever they wished and were free to move seats throughout. In order to record each session's seating arrangements a mobile application (*PinPoint*) was developed by the researchers. This methodology provided a unique platform to accurately and authentically track student seating positions. To the best of the authors' knowledge this extent of unrestricted tracking has not been conducted before.

Previous PinPoint research findings

In summary, the previous PinPoint study [19] found that:

- The best assessment results were achieved by the students in the front row and that assessment score degraded the further students sat from the front (Figure 1).
- The most engaged were found to regularly sit at the front.
- The most academically able or those with the greatest prior programming experience were not found to regularly sit at the front.

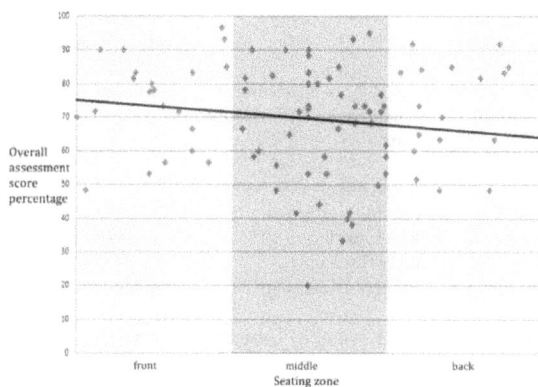

Figure 1 – Overall student assessment scores and average seating position and trend line illustrating degradation in assessment score from front to back.

2. RESEARCH OBJECTIVES

This focus of this paper was to build on and extend the understandings gained from xxx [23] by answering the following questions.

1. Does the performance of students with similar standard academic ability remain consistent regardless of seating position?
2. Does the performance of students with similar standard course engagement remain consistent regardless of seating position?
3. Does the performance of students with previous programming experience remain consistent regardless of seating position?
4. Are there significant changes in seat positions during the course?
5. What are the main factors influencing student seating decisions?

The answers to these questions will gain further insights in the effects of seating on student academic performance, especially between peer groups. This has possible consequences for teaching delivery styles, class sizes, lecture venues, the physical design of lecture theatres and recommendations of where to best sit in the lecture theatre to maximise assessment performance.

3. METHODOLOGY

The study was conducted with a cohort of 91 post graduate students taking a compulsory module in Java programming in semester one of a one year conversion Masters course in Software Development. Table 1 details the demographics of the students in the study.

Category	Subcategories and frequency
Gender	Male (78), Female (13)
Previous Degree type	1st (17), 2.1 (48), 2.2 (26)
Previous programming experience	None (50), Some (41), Considerable (0)

Table 1 – Demographics of students in the study

Other data collection areas

The assessment of other factors that may affect seating position was grouped into several thematic areas (Table 2).

Theme	Data type	Source
Student performance	Assessment results	Summative assessments at weeks 6 and 12
Course Engagement	Attendance at lectures	PinPoint App
	Engagement with weekly tests	VLE
	Engagement with online module resources	VLE
Academic ability	Previous degree classification	University records
Programming experience	Subject knowledge	Student survey (week 1)

Table 2 - Thematic areas of investigation with data types and data source.

Student seating tracking – PinPoint

The students were encouraged to use PinPoint (Figure 2), a mobile and web app to register their selected seating zone at the start of each lecture. To ensure authenticity each student's profile was initially registered and authenticated with the PinPoint system. Subsequently each student simply selected the zone they were sitting in during each lecture. It was not possible for a student to select outside of the lecture time, nor was it possible to submit more than once per lecture. The zones were front, middle and back further subdivided into left, centre and right.

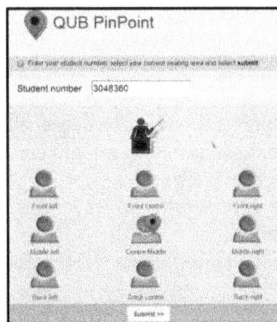

Figure 2 – PinPoint mobile app user interface

3. RESULTS AND CONCLUSIONS

The use of PinPoint was on a voluntary basis and all the 91 students actively participated in its use throughout the course. While PinPoint recorded exactly the seating positions in nine zones the results presented here are accurately aggregated into front, middle and back rows. In addition to enable comparisons

with other studies, in instances where previous research attention has been focused on front row versus other seating locations, the results were further aggregated in front row and other rows (middle and back).

1. Does the performance of students with similar standard academic ability remain consistent regardless of seating position?

Regardless of seating position the students with the highest previous degrees First Class Honours group (1st) performed best with an overall average of 78.93% compared to those with the Second Class Honours classifications (2.1) (69.13%) and 2.2 (65.00%).

Comparing like-for-like abilities on assessment scores

An analysis of the assessment scores for like-for-like academic ability groups (based on previous degree classifications) was made between the front rows and the other (middle and back) rows. It highlights that those sitting in the front rows scored better in the assessments than those sitting further back within the same academic grouping (Figure 3).

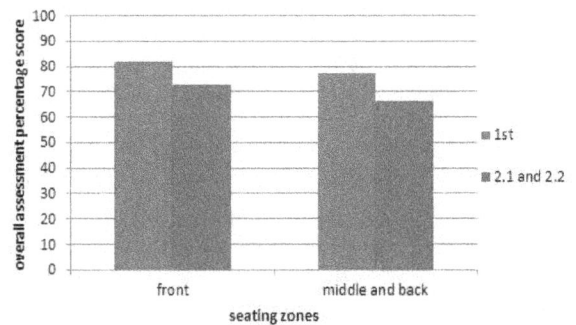

Figure 3 – Overall assessment scores in comparison with seating zones and previous degree classifications.

The students at the front in the First Class Honours group (1st) achieved an average of 81.67% whereas the remaining First Class Honours students sitting further back averaged of 77.42%. A similar pattern emerges with the Second Class Honours students, with front row students averaging 72.66% in comparison to 66.42%.

The difference in overall average assessment scores between the two groups indicates that academic ability is clearly a factor influencing performance. However the difference in assessment averages between seating zones within each similar academic grouping indicates that it is not the only determining factor. Accordingly it can be concluded that in this case the performance of students with similar standard academic ability did not remain consistent regardless of seating position, with the front row students performing better than their peers further back.

2. Does the performance of students with similar course engagement remain consistent regardless of seating position?

A like-for-like comparison of engagement groups was also conducted. The analysis of assessment scores of the top 25% of engaged students (highest engaged group) (mean=75.18, SD=17.62) and the remaining 75% of students (less engaged group) (mean=68.05, SD=22.10) showed a statistically significant difference (p=0.049, t=1.984, df=180). The difference in overall average assessment scores between the two groups indicates that engagement is also a factor influencing assessment performance.

A comparison within each group found that the students in the highest engaged group that sat in the front rows (n=4) achieved 81.94% in the overall assessment, whereas the remaining students in the same group (n=17) sitting further back achieved 72.79%. The comparison of the less engaged group showed that those that sat in the front row (n=17) achieved an average of 74.61% with the other remaining students sitting elsewhere (n=51) scored 65.87%.

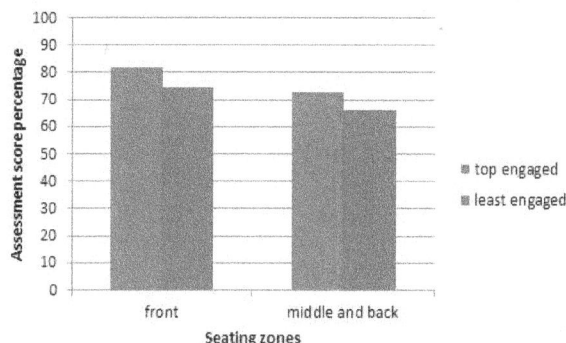

Figure 4 – The top and least engaged student groups' seating overall assessment score.

In a similar vein to the performance pattern, within the same peer academic groupings the front row students of similar engagement out performed those sitting further back. It is also notable that the less engaged students in the front rows actually outperformed the more engaged students that sat further back. In that regard it can be concluded that in this case the performance of students with similar engagement did not remain consistent regardless of seating position, with the front row students performing better than their peers at the back.

3. Does the performance of students with previous programming and those without programming experience remain consistent regardless of seating position?

A comparison was made regarding the assessment scores and seating position within the two separate programming experience groups namely, 1.) some prior programming experience and 2.) no prior programming experience. The group with some prior subject experience outperformed the group with no prior knowledge. As shown in Table 3 within both groups the best assessment scores emanated from those students that opted to sit in the front rows.

	Some prior programming experience group	No prior programming experience group
Front rows	79.58% (8)	70.49% (12)
Other rows	70.06% (33)	67.46% (38)

Table 3 – Overall assessment scores for the some and no prior programming experience groups.

Again the pattern of better performance from front row students within similar groups emerges. It is notable that the students at the front with no prior experience performed to a level just below the level of the students with some experience that sat at the back. In that regard it can be concluded that in this case the performance of students within the separate programming experience groups did not remain consistent regardless of seating position, with the front row students performing better than their peers at the back.

4. Are there significant changes in seat positions during the course?

The PinPoint app enabled an accurate tracking of seating position, thereby exposing potential seating positional changes never before available in previous similar studies. The results are presented of the early stages (weeks one – two) and the midpoint (week six) and the end of the module (week twelve). Each lecture theatre used in the study had sufficient capacity to afford the opportunity for movement. Figure 5 illustrates that there were some movement shifts between seating zones. By the end of week twelve the front row had reduced by 15.35% of its original numbers (as initially recorded at week two), an overall shift of four students, whereas the middle row and back rows finished with an overall increase of two students each.

Week six showed an increase in students sitting at the back at the expense of both the front and middle rows but the middle row recovered its numbers by week twelve. The students that moved from the front never returned.

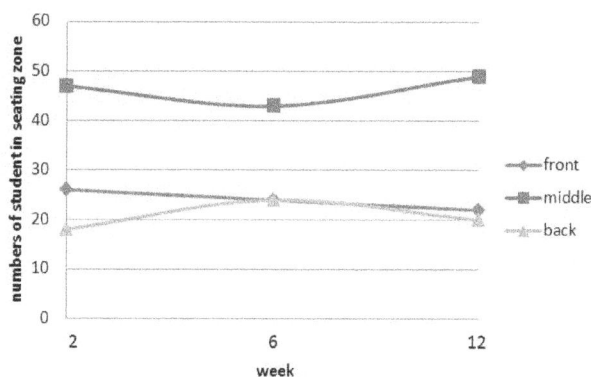

Figure 5 – movement between seating zones as sampled as weeks 2, 6 and 12.

Movement within academic ability groups

Figure 6 shows a more detailed breakdown of movement between zones per undergraduate degree classification.

Week		two	six	twelve	two	six	twelve	two	six	twelve
		front row			middle row			back row		
Previous degree	1st	6	6	6	9	8↓	8	2	3↑	3
	2.1	11	11	11	29	23↓	26↑	8	14↑	11↓
	2.2	9	7↓	5↓	9	12↑	15↑	8	7↓	6↓
total in row at end of week		26	24↓	22↓	47	43↓	49↑	18	24↑	20↓

Figure 6 – position of students per degree classification at the end of weeks 2, 6 and 12

Only one student in the First Class Honours student group moved during the module, specifically from the middle to the back from week six onwards. That student's shift was only by a small number of rows and he continued to score highly in the assessments. The other group of students with Second class honours were also generally constant in seating zones showing proportionally similar frequency of zone movements. Of the students that averaged over 70% (n=53) in the assessments there was some limited movement recorded (n=5). There were no consistent patterns discernible for these movements or reasons given by these students in the seating position questionnaire. The failing students stayed in same zones throughout the module, which indicates that the feedback result from the first assessment (week 6) did not prompt the students to move.

5. Survey results – qualitative views

To attempt to better comprehend the decisions that influence seat selection the seating position questionnaire was given to all the students at the end of the course.

The majority of the lectures in this study involved some individual and paired coding activities and all lecture notes where provide online before the lecture. 98.1% of the responding students (n=65) stated they brought and used their own laptop to follow along with the notes and for the coding activities during the lecture. Consequently, some students felt that the physical environment and having their own laptop reduced their need to sit towards the front, with the following quote being reasonably representative of those that expressed that opinion, "*multiple screens, having the notes on your laptop, and typing you own code along with the lecturer reduces the importance of sitting close to the front*". In that sense the active learning experiences should have been reasonably homogenised irrespective of seating position.

However 78.3% of the responding students stated they had a strong preference of where they sat. The front row students that responded (n=18) stated that their preference to that zone was either due to physical reasons, for example being able to see the screen and hear better, or to better engage with the lesson "*I sit in that seat so I can stay focused, engaged and to get the best bang for my buck during teaching time*".

Interestingly a large portion of those that sat in the middle rows also stated that they could see the screen better in the middle. For the most part that was in relation to the banked seating used in one of the lecture theatres, "*my preference depends on the lecture theatre, but generally if the seats are elevated it is uncomfortable to sit at the front because you need to strain your neck and eyes to see the projector. The sound is never an issue so sitting further back does not affect hearing the lecture*". Additional common reasons for the sitting in the middle were "*habit*" and "*to sit with friends*".

Style of teaching came up as a strong influence in seating choice for those at the back. With some responding that they actively avoided the front rows to actively avoid having to engage with the lecturer, "*by sitting near the back it's probably less likely for me to be involved in a demonstration in front of the class*". The majority stated they sat at the back because of where friends sat or because they were late to the lecture and did not want to disturb others. A small portion stated "*I feel more comfortable not being surrounded by people*", and there was evidence to indicate in this study and in [23] that this was a particularly strong influence for students with diagnosed anxiety issues.

In that regard it would appear that seating decisions are determined by a mixture of common themes; the ability to see and hear better, the willingness or lack of willingness to interact with the lecturer, wanting to sit with friends or simply being late to the lecture. Either way most are personal decisions that considering the assessment performance results presented in this study may well have influenced on final mark attained.

4. DISCUSSION AND FUTURE WORK

General conclusions

Looking separately at the influence of academic ability, engagement and prior subject exposure indicates that students at the top end of each group generally outperformed in assessments the other students in the group. However, further to these findings a comparison of student assessment performances within each of these groups in every instance found that the front row students outperformed their peers sitting further back. This strongly suggests that there is a benefit to sitting at the front regardless of academic ability, engagement or prior subject knowledge. It points to other untested factors that may be positively influencing the front row performances. The dependence on each of the considered factors was tested using a linear multiple regression. It revealed that engagement (p<0.05) and academic ability (p<0.05) were both highly significant factors related to assessment scores. The positional seating and prior programming knowledge were of influence, with (p=0.151) and (p=0.191) respectively. Taking that into consideration along with the overall group average score differences would suggest that it would be unwise to ignore the potential influence seating position has in influencing assessment scores.

Better experience – hearing, seeing and doing

There were a number of physical factors highlighted in the Seating position questionnaire, including a large portion of students that sat in the front and middle to hear and see better. Additionally many in the front and to a lesser extent in the middle rows sat in those zones specifically to increase individual engagement with the lecture. If engagement translates to a better cognitive experience, than it would be of considerable interest to be able to measure responses to cognitive events during the lecture. As far back as the 1970s a series of experiments by Lacey([18],[19]) demonstrated that tasks requiring increased cognitive processing are associated with Heart Rate (HR) acceleration. Numerous clinical experiments have been conducted measuring HR and cognitive tasks, including a reported increase in HR for computer gamers performing complex gaming tasks and by subjects performing difficult mental arithmetic [28]. However there have been a very limited number of studies in the use of HR as a measure of student cognitive engagement in university lectures. Bligh[5] carried out a series of classroom lecture studies showing that student HR decreased over the course of a 50-minute lecture [7]. The decline in HR was interpreted as a measure of decreasing arousal, which Bligh considered as one component of cognitive engagement. Darnell and King [12] expanded on this work, and concurred with Bligh that there appears to be a decrease in average HR across a 50 minute lecture class and a temporary increase in HR in response to student questions. The recent proliferation of wearable biometric devices may enable future research to test cognitive stimuli performance in a mass education environment. An investigation of cognitive activity during lectures between seating zones could potentially link sitting up front with cognitive and potentially assessment performance benefits.

Mitigation of the effects of seat location

It would appear that having more students regularly sitting at the front may be of benefit to their assessment score. Where a lecture theatre does not facilitate the majority of students sitting close to the front, then a reduction in class size would enable more students to sit there. Decreasing class sizes would effectively increase the ability of the front rows to potentially seat more students. Considering the continuing demand for graduate computing professionals ([1] [14]) it is reasonable to expect that a reduction in class sizes is unlikely to happen any time soon.

Perhaps it may be as simple as the lecturer encouraging the students to sit at the front or if the benefits of sitting at the front were explained then they may choose to sit there. Although in this research it should be noted that even with the lecture theatre at half capacity the front row regularly had some empty seats. It would appear that given the option some students will still likely chose to sit elsewhere. The decision of where to sit is personal and generally consciously made. Additionally, Armstrong [3] concluded "that changing seating position from choice to assigned seating can have an adverse effect on student output and performance which is associated with decreased perceived competence and increased tension". This finding and the responses in this study from students with anxiety issues would suggest that prudence in encouraging students to move to the front would be advisable. To exemplify this, one of the highest assessment scores came from a back row student whose preference to that seating zone was stated as, *"I find it's easier to ask for quick explanations from peers when sitting at the back rather than the front"*. Encouraging that individual to move to the front would likely inhibit his learning style and possibly to the detriment of his assessment score.

Limitations and future work

Replication of the study using the same methodology would test the repeatability of the results and it would be of interest to re-examine this issue with a more traditional, less interactive, style lecture. As is common in many programming modules in universities there were a limited number of females in the cohort. This inhibits the study of any potential gender influences other than to report in this instance that there was normal distribution of the females throughout the lecture theatre. While the study concentrated on highlighting differences between front, middle and back rows there would be merit in a further analysis of the zonal areas to include the left, middle and right areas of the lecture theatre. The cohort in this study were generally regarded to be highly motivated, it would be if interest to extend the study to a less motivated group. While this study was with a cohort of programming students the authors feel that the accuracy of the data collection methods used could easily be transferrable to other subject areas.

5. REFERENCES
[1] eskills, (2013). e-Leadership:e-Skills for Competitiveness and Innovation Vision, Roadmap and Foresight Scenarios Vision Report.
[2] Adams, R. and Biddle B. (1970). Realities of teaching: Explorations with video tape. New York: Holt, Inc.
[3] Armstrong, N. and Chang, S. (2007) Location, Location, Location? Journal of College Science Teaching 37 (2), 54-58.
[4] Becker, F. D., R. Sommer, J. Bee, and B. Oxley. (1973). College classroom ecology. Sociometry 36 (4): 514–25
[5] Bligh, D. (2000), What's the Use of Lectures? San Francisco: Jossey-Bass.
[6] Benedict, M.E., and J. Hoag. (2004). Seating location in large lecturesJournal of Economic Education 35 (3): 215–31.
[7] Bligh D.A. (1998) What's the Use of Lectures? Jossey-Bass Publishers, SF (2000).
[8] Brown, R. D. (1988). Self-quiz on testing and grading issues. Teaching at UNL, 10(2), pp. 1-3. The Teaching and Learning Center, University of Nebraska-Lincoln
[9] Burda, J. M., and Brooks, C. I. (1996). College classroom seating position and changes in achievement motivation over a semester. Psychological Reports, 78, 331-336.
[10] Cinar,A.(1999) Classroom geography: who sit where in the traditional classroom? J Int Sco Res. 2010;3:200–12.
[11] Cuseo, J., Fecas, V. S., & Thompson, A. (2007). Thriving in College & Beyond: Research-Based Strategies for Academic Success and Personal Development. Dubuque, IA: Kendall/Hint.
[12] Darnell, D., and Krieg, P. (2014) Use of heart rate monitors to assess student engagement in lecture. The FASEB Journal vol. 28 no. 1 Supplement 721.25.
[13] Giles, R. M. et al. (1982). Recall of lecture information: A question of what, when, and where. Medical Education, 16(5), 264-268.
[14] Higher Education Statistics Agency: Home - HESA (2016), Available at: https://www.hesa.ac.uk/ (Accessed: 6/12/2016).
[15] Holliman, W.B., and H.N. Anderson. (1986). Proximity and student density as ecological variables in a college classroom. Teaching of Psychology 13 (4): 200–03.
[16] Kalinowski, S., Taper, M. (2007) The Effect of Seat Location on Exam Grades and Student Perceptions in an Introductory Biology Class. Journal of College Science Teaching, v36 n4 p54-57 Jan-Feb 2007
[17] Kierwa, K. A. (2000). Fish giver or fishing teacher? The lure of strategy instruction. Teaching at UNL, 22(3), pp. 1-3. Lincoln, NE: University of Nebraska-Lincoln.
[18] Lacey, J., Obrist, B., Black, P, Brener, A., DiCara, L. (1974). Studies of HR. Cardiovascular psychophysiology, Chicago.
[19] Lacey, J, Lacey, B., Black, P. (1970). Some autonomic-central nervous system interrelationships Physiological correlates of emotion, Academic Press, New York
[20] Mastrine, J. (2012) Does where you sit in the classroom say a lot about you? Available at http://college.usatoday.com/2012/01/05/does-where-you-sit-in-class-say-a-lot-about-you/
[21] Martin, J (2012) It doesn't matter where I sit does it? Online Educational Research Journal. Available at : http://www.oerj.org/View?action=viewPDF&paper=51
[22] Marx, R. W. (1983). Student perception in classrooms. Educational Psychologist, 18, 145-164.
[23] McGowan, A., Hanna, P., Greer, D. and Busch, J. (in press). Learning to program-does it matter where you sit in the lecture theatre? (2017) MIPRO 2017.
[24] Pedersen, D.M. (1994). Personality and classroom seating. Perceptual and Motor Skills 78 (33): 1355–60.
[25] Perkins, K., and C. Wieman. (2005).The surprising impact of seat location on student performance. The Physics Teacher 43 (1): 30–33
[26] Schwebel, A.L. and Cherlin, D.L. (1972) Physical and social distancing in teacher pupil relationships. J. Educ. Psychol. 63, 543-550.
[27] Stires, L. (1980) Classroom seating location, Environment or self-selection. Environ. Behaviour, 12, 241-254.
[28] Turner J., Carroll D. (1985) Heart rate and oxygen consumption. Psychophysiology, 22 (1985), pp. 261–267

First Year Computing Students' Perceptions of Authenticity in Assessment

Roger McDermott, Mark Zarb
School of Computer Science and Digital Media
Robert Gordon University
Scotland, United Kingdom
+44 1224 262717
roger.mcdermott@rgu.ac.uk,
m.zarb@rgu.ac.uk

Mats Daniels
Dept. of Information Technology
Uppsala University
Uppsala, Sweden
+46 18 4713160
mats.daniels@it.uu.se

Ville Isomöttönen
Dept. of Mathematical Information Technology
University of Jyväskylä
FIN-40014, Finland
+35 8400608130
ville.isomottonen@jyu.fi

ABSTRACT

The problem of how best to assess student learning is a fundamental one in education. Changes to computer science curricula seek to emphasise teaching practices that promote deep learning through direct, contextual examination of student performance on tasks that resemble those of practitioners, rather than more traditional methods. This kind of "authentic assessment" is becoming more popular as it appears to incorporate employability skills associated with professional practice into the curriculum in a natural way.

In this paper, we report on an investigation into how computing students themselves understand the terminology of authentic assessment. We give a brief summary of some of the salient points of the theory before using a simple qualitative methodology to analyse responses from a cohort of first year students on their understanding of the term. We produce a learner characterisation of the concept and compare this to those found in educational models of this assessment approach. We comment on the similarities and differences that emerge and draw inferences about its use and the necessary scaffolding that should accompany it in order for it to be successful.

CCS Concepts

• Social and professional topics~Student assessment   • Social and professional topics~CS1

Keywords
Authentic Learning; Authentic Assessment; Situated Learning; First Year Computer Science

1. INTRODUCTION

One of the most striking features of research into educational theory and practice in the past two decades is a reaffirmation that the learning process is an integrated whole, and that elements such as teaching, assessment, the social context of learning, and the learning environment, form a network of interrelated, interdependent concepts which cannot be disentangled, e.g. [1, 2, 3]. This is especially evident in the relationship between learning and assessment.

Boud [1] noted that learning is influenced by assessment in three ways. Firstly, the nature of the assessment itself has an impact on what is learned; qualitatively different types of assessment promote different responses in students. Secondly, the way in which the teacher presents the material to be assessed in a given format and selects the tasks deemed appropriate for the subject and the specific learning goals is significant. Thirdly, and most importantly when considering the depth of learning [4] is the way that the student interprets the task in the context of the assessment. When students perceive the assessment as measuring recall of factual information, they tend to rely on surface learning strategies that seem suitable for remembering factual information [5] rather than those aimed at more comprehensive understanding of the material [6].

Curricular changes which emphasise constructivist and student-centred pedagogies such as problem-based learning [7], inquiry-based learning [8], active learning [9], project-based learning [10], etc., all require non-traditional methods of assessment in which students are examined on their performance in the context of meaningful tasks. The requirement that courses begin to include employability as an explicit feature of the curriculum [11], and the need to ensure that skills for lifelong/lifewide learning [12] are incorporated into the university education, are also driving changes to the student experience that find expression in new forms of assessment. The inclusion of professional competencies [13, 14] as a fundamental part of the computing curriculum also promotes this change.

Given these developments, it is to be expected that teachers have looked for educational ideas that can motivate and underpin the changes that are perceived to be necessary. One such concept is that of "authenticity", which is used to describe the alignment of educational aspects of a course of study with those of the professional environment into which the graduate emerges, and has been applied to a variety of educational settings and practices. It fits naturally into the network of ideas about student-centred pedagogies and has a solid conceptual base in philosophical and psychological discourse, e.g. [15, 16].

Unfortunately, the positive implication of the word, together with the widespread conventional application of the term, has led to a situation where meaning tends to become diluted. Researchers and practitioners speak about the need for students to undertake authentic tasks, for them to be assessed by authentic assessments which appraise their authentic learning, all of this being done in an authentic learning environment. Moreover, the positive connotation tends to dominate: who, after all, would wish for "inauthentic learning" or to be assessed in an inauthentic manner? One useful exercise would be to focus on the way the concept is being used in practice within the CSEd community. However, as noted by Gulikers et al. [17, 18, 19], there may be a difference between the understanding of authenticity expressed by teachers and that expressed by students.

This paper investigates student perceptions of authentic assessment in the context of an elementary programming course. We start by giving an overview of relevant aspects of authentic learning theory found in the educational literature, before focussing on authenticity applied to assessment. In particular, we describe the five-dimensional framework of Gulikers et al, before considering the four-component model of "thick" authenticity developed by Shaffer and Resnick [20]. We then describe an investigation into student perceptions of authentic assessment in the context of a first year programming course and classify these the results according to the thick authenticity schema. The results show that students are strongly focused on a subset of the four components in the model. We discuss these findings and consider the implications of the "missing" components in student views of the concept. Finally, we draw conclusions concerning the impact that this has on student attitudes to assessment and make suggestions for further work in this area.

2. BACKGROUND

2.1 Situated Learning

The concept of authenticity, considered as a specific quality of a particular pedagogical approach, arose out of work done on situated knowledge and cognitive apprenticeships by Brown, Collins and others, e.g. [21, 22]. It was argued that the assimilation of useable, robust knowledge was facilitated by the use of approaches which embedded the learning activities in their appropriate social context [23]. In order to successfully use the cognitive tools of a particular community of practice, the novice acquires the behaviour and values of the culture in which the community subsists. This is essentially an apprenticeship model in which the student is enculturated into the attitudes and practices of the community (the language, modes of communication, professional epistemology, problem-solving methodologies, disciplinary priorities, etc.) by progressive identification with its more skilful members. In this context, Collins [24] defined situated learning as "the notion of learning knowledge and skills in contexts that reflect the way the knowledge will be useful in real life". This approach later found a central place in the work of Lave and Wenger on the social context of learning, e.g. [25, 26].

2.2 Authentic Assessment

Lave and Wenger's work on the social context of learning and the situated learning models described above have clear implications for educational praxis, not least for assessment practices. The key pedagogical components of these models, e.g. as described in [27], include such elements as the didactic use of stories, the articulation by learners of skills and reflection on the learning process, mentoring as a key part of the apprenticeship experience, collaboration and the repeated experience of practice, often using technology. While these may claim to assess the learning that students put into practice outside the classroom, showing that this is the case is not straightforward. Wiggins [28] suggested that important indicators of authenticity following on from the apprenticeship model included a correspondence with professional or work-based situations, appraisal of skill through observable performance and the capacity to deal with ill-defined problems with complex behaviour.

2.3 Models of Authentic Assessment

While the need to use some kind of performance-based assessment may follow from the work on situated learning and the apprenticeship model, one difficulty with authentic assessment

was that the meaning of authenticity was not clearly defined and appeared to subsume a variety of related, but different concepts. From a pedagogical perspective, this was problematic as the term was applied to a range of assessment practices which were only tenuously linked to the original conception. Since authenticity is defined by its correspondence to something else, it was important to state precisely of what this consisted. For example, it was argued that correspondence to real-world situations need not be a factor if the real world played no part in the assessment goals.

Because of these considerations, a number of models were developed which sought to abstract the key elements of authentic assessment and construct a logical framework in which their operation could be analysed. Two important models are the five-dimensional framework of Gulikers et al, and the "Thick" Authenticity model of Shaffer and Resnick.

Gulikers et al [29, 17, 18, 19] argued that the degree of authenticity of an assessment depends upon five situational factors or dimensions. These were:

- the task that defines the content of the assessment,
- the physical context in which students have to perform the assessment task,
- the social context, which tracked the degree of interaction that was possible during the assessment,
- the form or mode of assessment,
- the value criteria that constitute the measure of performance.

It is claimed that these five characteristics correspond to the parameters of professional practice.

Shaffer and Resnick [20] also argued for a more nuanced approach to the application of the concept. They suggested that a learner perception of authenticity is essentially tied to an experience of consonance or harmony between different features of the learner experience. Students perceive authenticity in terms of an alignment between some important aspect of the learning process and some other element of the educational experience that they perceive to be meaningful.

They identified four distinct uses of the term which appears in educational contexts. The first of these is a learning experience that was personally meaningful to the student, while the second is one that is related to a "real-world" context outside the immediate educational environment. The third type of authenticity relates to learning that provides an opportunity for students to "think in the modes of a particular discipline" and lastly there is an operational view of authenticity in which the assessment process reflects the learning process.

Shaffer and Resnick argued for what they called a "thick" view of authenticity which subsumed all these descriptions and recognised the "interdependent and mutually-supporting" nature of the concept.

This brief tour of the educational theory surrounding authenticity informs the experimental method used in our investigation of learner perceptions of authentic assessment. It provides the terminology as well as the broader categories employed in the content analysis of student responses described below.

3. METHOD

We wished to investigate concepts of authenticity in assessment in the context of first year students on a computing programme. Specifically, we wished to see what students understood by the term and to compare this with the range of meaning that modern educational researchers ascribe to it. We also wished to see whether the concept was something that students would prioritise as an essential part of the assessment process.

3.1 The Participants

Our study used data obtained from a group of seventy-eight first-year undergraduate students in Robert Gordon University, Scotland, UK. RGU is a "post-92", former polytechnic institution with a strong focus on professional and vocational education, which is reflected in very high employment rates for graduates. The students in the investigation were aged between 17 and 27 with the majority having entered university directly from secondary school. They were registered on two degrees within the School: the largest group was studying BSc. Computer Science, with a smaller cohort studying BSc. Computing for Graphics and Animation. Students on these courses undertook identical course units in the first year. The students had completed about three quarters of the first semester course when the data was collected.

The course unit that the students were studying was a first semester introductory procedural programming course unit using Javascript as the coding language. It consisted of a nine-week block with six hours of class time each week, comprising two one-hour lectures immediately followed by two two-hour labs. The students were not assumed to have any prior knowledge of either the specific language or of programming in general, although there was a range of previous experience within the group and a minority of students had studied some procedural languages at secondary school. The summative assessment for the course unit consisted of a short coursework assignment, which was handed out to the students to complete in their own time, and an assessed programming lab. The assessment was held in week 9 of the twelve-week semester.

A further relevant factor is that the majority of students entered the course from the Scottish secondary education system. They would therefore have studied for a number of years under the Scottish "Curriculum for Excellence" (CfE). This is a national, primary and secondary educational framework which applies to pupils from ages 3 in (pre-School) to 18 year olds who are just about to enter the university system. CfE recognises four key purposes for education: that students become "*successful learners, confident individuals, responsible citizens and effective contributors.*"[29]. It aims to provide a coherent and flexible *enriched curriculum* where this term is understood to mean "*everything that is planned for children and young people throughout their education, not just what happens in the classroom*". It includes four contexts for learning, specifically curriculum areas and subjects, interdisciplinary learning, ethos and life of the school, and opportunities for personal achievement. This is an important point in the context of this study because the CfE makes specific reference to a greater focus on skills development including skills for learning, skills for life and skills for work [30], which has been reflected in a general attempt to embed skills-based assessments as a major component of secondary school practice. This, in turn, has resulted in the language of authenticity being used by staff who teach within the educational system and it is not unreasonable to suggest, therefore, that the terminology was not unknown to the students. We return to this point in the Discussion section.

3.2 The Questions

The students were asked to write a short paragraph (150 - 200 words) on the topic: What does it mean for an assessment to be 'authentic'?" In addition, they were instructed to write a question for a hypothetical assessed programming lab on the subject of arrays. They were told that the total assessment was graded out of 60 marks and that the student's question would contribute 10 marks to this total. They were also given a duration for the hypothetical assessment. As well as being required to devise a question on arrays, they were asked to supply a solution to the question and a marking scheme containing a justification for why they chosen to assign the marks they did.

It was decided to use this approach, together with the qualitative method described below for a number of reasons. Although a quantitative questionnaire has been developed by Gulikers et al. [31] and has provided the empirical data which underpins the theoretical basis of their five-dimensional framework, we wished to use a qualitative methodology as it was felt that this would give more insightful results due to the sample size. While N = 78 is not a very small sample, it was felt that the validity of the inferences based on the questionnaire data would tend to be quite weak, due in part to the likelihood of low reliability scores.

Some initial preparation for the topic was delivered on a class-wide basis. This took the form of a series of exploratory, non-directive question-and-answer sessions which examined student perceptions of the broad purposes of higher education and the ways in which evidence of achievement could be provided. One topic in this series was the purpose of assessment and the relative merits of different assessment mechanisms used within the School.

3.3 The Experimental Method

A qualitative content analysis approach [32] was employed to analyse the data. The method was a combination of three forms: inductive content analysis was used to generate a set of codes based on student responses. These were then grouped into larger thematic areas based on a directed (i.e. theory-informed) content analysis of the codes. Finally, frequency information was used to draw out conclusions (summative content analysis).

In the initial stage, each student response was examined and a series of code words generated based on a conceptual analysis of what the respondent thought was important in the definition of authenticity. A total of 253 codes were abstracted from the 78 respondents which resulted in 33 different terms. These were then analysed and assigned to one of five general categories, the assignment being based on a broad thematic analysis informed by the range of theoretical considerations described in section 2.

The general themes chosen were "Cognitive" which included the cognitive elements which the assessment should contain, "Content", which included the broad characteristics of the content on which the assessment was based, "Context", i.e. the wider educational or social context of the assessment question(s), "Form", which included operational factors, and a final theme, "Outcome" which students reported as part of the description of authenticity but appeared to be based on outcomes that they thought should follow from the assessment. Two data tables were constructed from consideration of the mapping between students and the reported code categories. The first was a frequency chart of occurrences of a particular code category (i.e. the column sums of the spreadsheet) which is given as Table 1. The second is a table of the relative frequency of a code occurring in a student response (Table 2).

4. RESULTS

The tabulated results of the classification exercise are given below. The table gives the frequencies of 253 incidences of the codes among the responses. For the "Cognitive" group, the codes should be read as indicative of the type of learning behaviour that the students say the assessment should promote (e.g. deep learning, critical thinking, problem solving, opportunity for reflection) and are relatively self-explanatory. The code "Demonstrates Flexibility" referred to a desire for the assessment to provide students with the opportunity to demonstrate multiple approaches to the solution of a problem. "Potential for development" refers to the assessment giving the opportunity for the student to develop a solution in an innovative way.

Table 1. Frequency of Codes associated with Authenticity

Code	%	Code	%
Cognitive		Form	
• Demonstrate Flexibility	0.8	• Presentation Style	0.4
• Depth of Understanding	2.0	• Clear Question	2.0
• Potential for Development	4.3	• Summative	1.6
• Opportunity for Reflection	1.2	• Personalised	1.6
• Problem-solving	5.1	• Not time-limited	0.8
• Critical Thinking	2.4	• Transparent (marking)	1.2
		• Focussed	0.8
Content		• Allows Choice	0.8
• (Appropriately) Challenging	13.0	• Novel/Original (Questions)	4.0
• Fairness	8.7	• Attributable	3.6
• Multifaceted/ Graduated	0.8		
• Relevant	4.7	Outcome	
• Not just memorisation	2.4	• Motivating/ Engaged	2.0
• Open-ended	1.2	• Satisfying/Sense of Accomplishment	0.4
• Creativity	3.2	• Confidence-building	0.4
• Discriminating	0.4	• Allow best work	1.2
• Comprehensive	5.1		
Context			
• Knowledge used in future	5.1		
• Application to Real-World	18.6		
• Collaborative	0.4	Total Number of Codes = 253	
• Scenario-based	0.8	Total Number of Categories = 33	

The "Content" codes are adjectives that students thought should describe an authentic assessment. They divide roughly into those concerned with the syllabus being assessed and those concerned with how the content is assessed. In the former sub-category, "Fairness", i.e. that the assessment should be on content that was clearly delineated by the syllabus, showed comparatively high score. "Relevance", like fairness, is a curricular variable, but differed in that it sought to ensure that only material at an appropriate level was assessed. A third factor, "Comprehensiveness", which sought to track the proportion of the syllabus, was also reported. Essentially these factors delimited the assessment content to the curriculum of the course unit involved and nothing else. The most frequent code in this section referred to the level of academic challenge, which students thought should be set at the "Goldilocks" level of being "just right". Other codes that were placed with "Content" describe the nature of the question, e.g. open-ended, not just memorisation. "Multifaceted/Graduated" refers to an assessment having elements which are either of range of different types or else graduated in difficulty in some way. Creativity referred to the questions being framed in a creatively engaging way.

The third general theme was "Context" and this referred to the way in which the assessment related to the wider social context

outside the classroom. Authentic assessment criteria included "Application to the real world", the perception that the "Knowledge [was] to [be] used in the future", as well as codes for "Collaborative" within the assessment and "Scenario-based" questions.

The fourth theme abstracted from the responses dealt mainly with operational aspects of the assessment, including its style of presentation, textual clarity, the time-limited nature of the regulations, the summative nature of the assessment and the transparency of the marking procedures. The code for "Personalised" learning referred to whether the questions were tailored to the individual student taking the test. "Focussed" and "Allows Choice" were converse codes which tracked whether the student had any freedom to choose particular elements of the assessment. The "Attributable" code was surprising but there appeared to be a number of students who thought that the word "authentic", taken in the sense of this paper, was synonymous with attributable (perhaps confusing it with "authenticated") and therefore derived a primary meaning for the concept based on ideas about academic integrity. A similar confusion may have led to the "Novel/Original" code which appeared to be concerned with some kind of security/data assurance property for the questions (e.g. ensuring that students did not have access to the question beforehand).

Table 2. Relative Frequency of Codes in Student Responses

Code	%	Code	%
Cognitive		Form	
• Demonstrate Flexibility	3	• Presentation Style	1
• Depth of Understanding	6	• Clear Question	6
• Potential for Development	14	• Summative	5
• Opportunity for Reflection	4	• Personalised	5
• Problem-solving	17	• Not time-limited	3
• Critical Thinking	8	• Transparent (marking)	4
		• Focussed	1
Content		• Allows Choice	1
• (Appropriately) Challenging	42	• Novel/Original (Questions)	13
• Fairness	28	• Attributable	12
• Multifaceted/ Graduated	3		
• Relevant	15	Outcome	
• Not just memorisation	8	• Motivating/ Engaged	6
• Open-ended	4	• Satisfying/Sense of Accomplishment	1
• Creativity	10	• Confidence-building	1
• Discriminating	1	• Allow best work	4
• Comprehensive	17		
Context			
• Knowledge used in future	17		
• Application to Real-World	60		
• Collaborative	1	Total Number of Codes = 253	
• Scenario-based	3	Total Number of Students = 78	

Finally, codes were recorded for a fifth theme which appear to describe outcome-based effects rather than qualities of the assessment itself. So, for example, some students reported that authentic assessments should be motivating, boost their confidence in the subject, provide them with a sense of accomplishment or allow them to showcase their best work.

5. DISCUSSION

The results show some agreement with the theoretical models described in section 3. The most obvious point is that the tabular data given above state that application to the real-world (which contributed about 19% of the codes) is mentioned by at 60% of the students. This indicates that a significant proportion of the cohort do, in fact, agree that application to real world situations plays a significant role in the identifying characteristics of authentic assessment. This is important since, historically, it has been the generating idea for interest in the concept, as well as its continued development. However, it clearly also means that 2 out of 5 students did not think that the real world application is naturally part of the definition of the concept.

It perhaps should also be remembered that, in addition to providing a description of authentic assessment, students were also asked to create an assessment question on arrays. These questions were analysed and classified according to whether they used some kind of real-world scenario as opposed to a purely formal question with no contextualisation of the problem. Of the 47 students who mentioned that real world application code in their description of authenticity, 30 devised a scenario-based question. This shows some degree of corroboration that those students did indeed think that real world assessment context was important, but the relative proportions involved are perhaps not as high as would be expected.

The second most common code mentioned in student responses was "(Appropriately) Challenging" which made up 13% of the codes and was mentioned by 42% of the students. This perhaps has some correspondence with the thick authenticity classification of Shaffer and Resnick since it could be considered an example of an assessment which is personally meaningful. However, examination of the correlation between the two codes over the student cohort indicates that it is not more likely that a respondent who states that authentic assessment needs to find application in the real world, also states that such an assessment needs to be appropriately challenging.

The code with the third highest frequency is "Fairness" which contributed ~9% of the codes and was listed by 28% of students as important to the description of an authentic assessment. This might also be interpreted in terms of the fourth thick authenticity item, namely the assessment process reflecting the learning process.

However, a notable omission from the codes is an explicit reference to Shaffer and Resnick's third type of authenticity, which relates to learning that provides an opportunity for students to "*think in the modes of a particular discipline*". We would see this as an extremely important educational experience and, from an employability perspective, it is perhaps even more important than the real-world component. The absence of this aspect of authenticity from the responses indicates that students do not appear to recognise a key component of the rationale for including performance-based activities and assessments. Previous studies, e.g. [33], suggest that awareness of being part of a discipline, with its own modes of discourse and communication, may be more prevalent in interdisciplinary teams. The subject-based homogeneity of the class may therefore partially explain this lack of appreciation of disciplinary speciality.

Although there were some codes which were reproduced by a relatively high number of students in the cohort, analysis of the results suggested that there was substantial variation between students. There are indications of some dependencies between codes within a particular category, e.g. the code for "Knowledge used in future" is only given by students who also give "Application to Real-World" which is, perhaps to be expected, since they are similar although not identical concepts. However, for the most part, the responses do not appear to be reproduced from one student to another. We could interpret this as indicating that authenticity in assessment is not necessarily a primary concept for students on this course and one question that may be raised is whether first year students would have any appreciation of the conceptual category of authentic assessment in a subject such as programming. We would argue that there had been some preliminary exposure at least to the conceptual precursors of authenticity if not to the concept itself. Furthermore, we would claim that there is a practical element which is essential to the discipline and which is something that is irreducible in the courses taught at a university such as RGU. This inevitably informs student views of the subject and how it is taught and assessed. There are significant implications for questions of student identity and epistemology here, but these will be explored elsewhere.

It is worth noting some limitations of this study. The qualitative methodology used here is based on an analysis of codes allocated to the student responses. There is always some degree of subjectivity in the process by which text is reduced to the codes, both in the choice of words that were considered important enough to warrant being given code status, and the identification of sentences within the text that can be labelled with these codes. First year students were describing a reasonably unfamiliar concept and this led to some degree of ambiguity in the language they used. Once this list was decided, a minimalist approach was taken, which allocated single codes to each significant concept within the authenticity paragraphs, without seeking to multiply them by inferring hidden codes.

It should also be pointed out that despite its utility in some situations, the robustness of the concept of authenticity also presents some problems from an educational perspective. While authenticity may be an attractive quality to track when considering assessments, it suffers from the disadvantage that it is not a completely objective construct [34]. People can genuinely differ in their perception of the authenticity of the same assessment for a variety of reasons. If, as claimed, the authenticity of the assessment is a measure of its alignment with the professional practice, this will partly be a function of how the learner perceives that correspondence and may depend on a number of factors, including the validity of previous experience of that professional practice, as well as the student's personal history. Perceptions of authenticity could therefore not just vary from person to person, but from one time to another. Furthermore, as mentioned by Gulikers et al., [19], student learning is often influenced more by perception of assessment characteristics than by the more objective features of the assessment themselves. This suggests that a poor or ill-informed comparison between an assessment task may be dangerous if trying to promote learning.

6. CONCLUSIONS

From the results of the investigation, it appears that students, considered at the cohort level, have a reasonable perception of authentic assessment being linked to real world situations, and therefore to a range of student-centred pedagogies that propose such practices. However, this is not necessarily the case at the level of individual students. This fact, if replicated in other studies, should give some concern. It appears that, for students, the relationship between authenticity and real-world problems may be one of practical definition rather than a natural one. If this is the case, then students require some scaffolding to more fully understand the link between authenticity, the form of the assessment and the professional context in which the question is set, in order to derive the associated educational benefits.

This is a preliminary study and further analysis needs to be done to gain a more coherent understanding of the concept and its perception by students. Following Gulikers et al., [17, 18] it would also be interesting to investigate the views of academic staff and contrast them with student views. This will the subject of subsequent work.

7. REFERENCES

[1] Boud, D., 1995. Assessment and learning: contradictory or complementary. In P. Knight (Ed.) Assessment for learning in higher education, pp.35-48, London: Kogan.

[2] Biggs, J. B. (1999). Teaching for Quality Learning at University. Buckingham: Open University Press.

[3] Entwistle, N., 2000, November. Promoting deep learning through teaching and assessment: conceptual frameworks and educational contexts. In TLRP conference, Leicester.

[4] Marton, F. and Säljö, R., 1976. On qualitative differences in learning: I—Outcome and process. *British journal of educational psychology*, *46*(1), pp.4-11.

[5] S Scouller, K., 1997. Students' perceptions of three assessment methods: Assignment essay, multiple choice question examination, short answer examination. Research and Development in Higher Education, 20, pp.646-653.

[6] Laurillard, D., 2013. Rethinking university teaching: A conversational framework for the effective use of learning technologies. Routledge.

[7] Boud, D. and Feletti, G., 1997. *The challenge of problem-based learning.* Psychology Press.

[8] Salovaara, H., 2005. An exploration of students' strategy use in inquiry-based computer-supported collaborative learning. *Journal of computer assisted learning*, *21*(1), pp.39-52.

[9] Hazzan, O., Lapidot, T. and Ragonis, N., 2015. Guide to teaching computer science: An activity-based approach. Springer.

[10] Bilgin, I., Karakuyu, Y. and Ay, Y., 2015. The Effects of Project Based Learning on Undergraduate Students' Achievement and Self-Efficacy Beliefs Towards Science Teaching. *Eurasia Journal of Mathematics, Science & Technology Education*, *11*(3), pp.469-477.

[11] Yorke, M. and Knight, P., 2006. *Embedding employability into the curriculum* (Vol. 3). York: Higher Education Academy.

[12] Jackson, N.J., 2014. Lifewide Learning and Education in Universities & Colleges: Concepts and Conceptual Aids. *Lifewide Learning and Education in Universities and Colleges.*

[13] Daniels, M., 2016, July. Professional Competencies for Real?: A Question about Identity!. In *Proceedings of the 2016 ACM Conference on Innovation and Technology in Computer Science Education* (pp. 2-2). ACM.

[14] Cajander, Å., Daniels, M. and von Konsky, B.R., 2011, October. Development of professional competencies in engineering education. In *2011 Frontiers in Education Conference (FIE)* (pp. S1C-1). IEEE.

[15] Wrathall, M.A. and Malpas, J.E. eds., 2000. *Heidegger, authenticity, and modernity* (Vol. 1). MIT press.

[16] Snyder, C.R. and Lopez, S.J., 2009. *Oxford handbook of positive psychology.* Oxford University Press, USA.

[17] Gulikers, J., Bastiaens, T. and Kirschner, P., 2006. Authentic assessment, student and teacher perceptions: the practical value of the five-dimensional framework. Journal of Vocational Education and Training, 58(3), pp.337-357.

[18] Gulikers, J.T., Bastiaens, T.J., Kirschner, P.A. and Kester, L., 2008. Authenticity is in the eye of the beholder: student and teacher perceptions of assessment authenticity. Journal of Vocational Education and Training, 60(4), pp.401-412.

[19] Gulikers, J.T., Kester, L., Kirschner, P.A. and Bastiaens, T.J., 2008. The effect of practical experience on perceptions of assessment authenticity, study approach, and learning outcomes. *Learning and Instruction*, *18*(2), pp.172-186.

[20] Shaffer, D.W. and Resnick, M., 1999. " Thick" Authenticity: New Media and Authentic Learning. Journal of interactive learning research, 10(2), p.195.

[21] Brown, J.S., Collins, A. and Duguid, P., 1989. Situated cognition and the culture of learning. Educational researcher, 18(1), pp.32-42.

[22] Collins, A., Brown, J. s., & Newman, s. E.(1989). Cognitive apprenticeship: Teaching the crafts of reading, writing, and mathematics. Knowing, learning, and instruction: Essays in honor of Robert Glaser, pp.453-494.

[23] Honebein, P.C., Duffy, T.M. and Fishman, B.J., 1993. Constructivism and the design of learning environments: Context and authentic activities for learning. In *Designing environments for constructive learning* (pp. 87-108). Springer Berlin Heidelberg.

[24] Lave, J., 1988. The culture of acquisition and the practice of understanding. Palo Alto. CA: Insititute for Research on Learning (No. 88-0007). Tech. Rep.

[25] Collins, A. (1988). Cognitive apprenticeship and instructional technology (Technical Report No. 6899): BBN Labs Inc., Cambridge, MA.

[26] Lave, J. and Wenger, E., 1991. Situated Learning: Legitimate Peripheral Participation. Cambridge University Press.

[27] McLellan, H., 1996. Situated learning: Multiple perspectives. Situated learning perspectives, pp.5-17.

[28] Wiggins, G.P., 1993. Assessing student performance: Exploring the purpose and limits of testing. Jossey-Bass.

[29] Scottish Government, 2008, Curriculum for Excellence. Building the Curriculum 3 – A Framework for Learning and Teaching, ISBN: 978-0-7559-5711-8

[30] Working Group on Assessment and National Qualifications, 2017, Assessment and National Qualifications Group Changes to The National Qualifications, http://www.gov.scot/Topics/Education/Schools/WorkingGro uponAssessmentandNQs/ANQGDoc

[31] Gulikers, J.T., Bastiaens, T.J. and Kirschner, P.A., 2004. A five-dimensional framework for authentic assessment. Educational technology research and development, 52(3), pp.67-86.

[32] Hsieh, H.F. and Shannon, S.E., 2005. Three approaches to qualitative content analysis. *Qualitative health research*, *15*(9), pp.1277-1288.

[33] Heikkinen, J. and Isomöttönen, V., 2015. Learning mechanisms in multidisciplinary teamwork with real customers and open-ended problems. *European Journal of Engineering Education*, *40*(6), pp.653-670.

[34] Petraglia, J., 1998. Reality by design: The rhetoric and technology of authenticity in education. Routledge.

Analyzing How Interest in Learning Programming Changes During a CS0 Course: A Qualitative Study with Brazilian Undergraduates

Pasqueline Dantas Scaico
Federal University of Pernambuco
Av. Anibal Fernandes, Cidade
Universitária, Recife, Brazil
+558398814-3078
pds@cin.ufpe.br

Ruy José G. B. de Queiroz
Federal University of Pernambuco
Av. Anibal Fernandes, Cidade
Universitária, Recife, Brazil
+558199998-2374
ruy@cin.ufpe.br

José Jorge Lima Dias Jr
Federal University of Paraíba
R. da Mangueira, Campus IV
Rio Tinto, Brazil
+558398873-7384
jorge@dcx.ufpb.br

ABSTRACT

In this paper, we present the preliminary findings of a study proposed to understand how interest of novices in learning programming changed during a CS0 course. This in-depth qualitative study, based on a longitudinal design, was performed over four months. Observing the learning experience of ten Brazilian freshmen students, the authors could obtain a dynamic view about how their interest in learning programming changed and why changes occurred. Six trajectories of interest were identified and the factors that had influence on them. As an example, the sense of being completing same tasks again when working on similar problems as before but in more detail was revealed as an inhibitor aspect to develop their interest. The Four-Phase Model of Interest Development was used as a theoretical framework to identify these trajectories. Looking at interest under this perspective was important to better understand how novices engage with introductory computer science and what might nurture and inhibit their interest in learning this content. This knowledge is something that CS educators could take into account when planning instructional strategies, course material and tasks.

Keywords

Interest development; trajectories of interest; programming education; CS0 course; qualitative research.

1. INTRODUCTION

Despite the increasing demand for developers, undergraduate students are not choosing a major in computer science. In Brazil, CS enrollments are not on increase either. Programming courses face considerable dropout and failure rates all over the world [24]. One reason for this is connected to the lack of motivation to learn programming [11]. Learning to code can be difficult, frustrating and time-consuming. These aspects turn the context of learning programming into something discouraging.

Interest is an important motivational factor for learning because of its potential to "energize" the engagement with the learning setting [5, 7]. The level of interest drives how individuals define goals, stay focused, persist and realize the effort required to succeed [4, 16]. In

this sense, it is important to cultivate interests to keep beginners engaged while learning programming. Over the years, substantial efforts have been employed in the teaching setting to develop motivational resources and promote experiences that raise students' interest, such as games, robotics and new pedagogical strategies [3, 11, 14]. However, it is unclear what really impacts students and promotes longer term changes in their interest in learning programming [13]. In part, this lack of knowledge can be a consequence of a research culture that overvalues technical aspects and quantitative research questions, underestimates empirical studies and stands aloof from theories from other fields [10, 20]. As Sheard and colleagues [23] expressed: in computing education, "there are not many studies that investigated learning within a theoretical framework." Also, concerns with weak methodological rigor and propagation of anecdotal evidence are issues to be aware of, according to [11]. In this way, some questions remain open, especially those related to why some circumstances occur in experiences of learning programming. In this scenario, it still remains unknown how the interest in learning programming changes across the learning process and what factors might nurture or inhibit its development. Accomplishing more successful experiences requires studying well-known questions through a new research lens.

We perceive interest development as a complex phenomenon which cannot be understood through a diminished view of its complexity. Very few studies have been undertaken in regard to it in the context of programming education. To help overcome this knowledge gap, we have been observing this phenomenon in a situated way, grounded by knowledge from the research on interest and a qualitative design. In this study, we have been pursuing the following research question: "How and why do interests in learning programming change across an introductory course?". Aiming to reach a deeper comprehension about the nature of beginners' interest and why changes occur over time, a set of exploratory case studies have been conducted with undergraduates in CS0 courses in Brazil. In this paper, the preliminary findings obtained from one of those studies are presented and discussed. The text is structured as following: in section 2 we present the theoretical framework we adopted. In section 3, the methodological design is detailed, as well as, the context where the study was run. In sections 4 and 5, the findings are reported and an initial discussion is presented, respectively.

2. THEORETICAL FRAMEWORK

The way people give attention to things, perform tasks, make an effort and set learning goals derives from how interested they are in those things [19]. Interest is a key to long-term learning

ITiCSE'17, July 3–5, 2017, Bologna, Italy.
© 2017 ACM. ISBN 978-1-4503-4704-4/17/07...$15.00.
DOI:http://dx.doi.org/10.1145/3059009.3059015

processes and domain expertise [7]. Despite multiple interpretations, some scholars define interest as the psychological state of being willing to (re)engage with certain objects, activities or content [18]. Interest is a variable built under emotional and cognitive components. While emotions frame and follow the engagement with the object, cognition brings meaning, value and knowledge about it [22].

For many, interest is not considered a personality trait, whereas other motivational variables like motivation or self-efficacy are [18]. For them, the notion of "interested people" does not exist because people just get interested in specific objects. This relation of *person-object* was central to build this research field as it is. The source of interest is the object itself instead of any other kind of reward which might come with it. In other words, the motive to engage with something is intrinsic. However, even if it is internalized, the nature of interest is primarily situational which means that the stimulus is external. Then, the primary nature of an interest is *situational* and manifests itself as an affective reaction to something interesting that comes from outside and catches someone's attention, putting a person in a "state of interest" [12]. At this stage, the engagement is unstable. Further, as long as proper conditions exist, its nature can change thereby becoming *individual*, when the disposition of engaging is settled.

Interests can be developed. Hidi and Renninger have built the Four-Phase Model of Interest Development (4PM) [10]. From an educational perspective, they explain how interests can be cultivated. Triggering a situational interest is the first phase of this process and represents when the connection with the object first happens. At this point, interest is almost an emotion because knowledge and meaning do not exist yet. If the focus remains on the object, the interest can evolve into the second phase. In this case, it is said that a situational interest is maintained. At this stage, learners are capable of making some effort to keep themselves engaged but since there is still little knowledge and value, the involvement can be lost whether it requires autonomous behavior or tasks that are meaningless or unattractive. Hidi and Renninger stated that depending on circumstances or conditions, an interest can stay inert at a point, regress or even disappear. Distinct attitudes, emotions, expectations and needs can be expected in each stage.

When interest reaches the third phase its nature is changing. As the interest develops, learners become less dependent on support and stimuli from their environment. At the third phase, learners already have more knowledge and can engage with the object of their own accord. They also develop curiosity about it, which helps them to pursue *what-if* questions. This is a clue about how much interest is developed. In phase 4, learners are capable of demonstrating self-regulated behavior and a self-directed attitude, persistence in the face of challenging situations and adjustment of their own learning agenda. Individual interests take time to be developed. It represents a more permanent state of motivation and is more valued as a learning outcome [12].

Measuring interest is a major issue for this research field [17]. Realizing its expressions can be challenging, even more in formal settings, once engagement is mandatory. In our research, the 4PM was used as a framework to guide this process. Because this study addresses a comprehension of interest from a dynamic point of view, observing learning experiences in programming was a

suitable way to understand its expressions. And due to its explanatory potential, the characteristics described by the 4PM for each stage of the development process were taken as indicators in our measurement process.

3. RESEARCH METHOD

The question that drives our research required a qualitative approach of inquiry so the phenomenon could be understood through a holistic, systematic and participant-centered approach. As it will be shown further, due to immersion into the context, this study has also ethnographic traits. As stated previously, a set of case studies have been conducted at Brazilian universities which offer different majors in computing. In this paper, we detail one of them.

3.1 The context

As Pears and colleagues [15] stated: "three decades of active research on the teaching of introductory programming has had limited effects on classroom". This scenario is particularly real in Brazil. Thus, as the reader will notice, we chose to study a case where neither educational technology nor motivational strategies are planned as part of the instructional agenda. We decided that not only because this is the typical setting of Brazilian CS0 courses, but also for the reason that observing interest this way brings power to influence the existing local practice.

We observed the experience of freshmen students majoring in information systems at a public university located in a small town in Brazil. After a recruitment process, four females and six males attending an introductory programming course volunteered as participants (the only requirement was that they had to be attending a CS0 course for the first time). They did not earn any kind of reward. They had no previous experiences with programming. Most of them came from public schools[1]. The average age was 20 years old. Some reasons reported for choosing this major were pleasant experiences with games, social media and technology, and influence of relatives. Most of them were not sure about their choices and defined their background in Math as weak.

Regarding the instructional setting, the instructor was an experienced coder. He used to lecture on advanced programming courses for the last ten years. Because he expected a certain level of autonomy from students, he did not adopt a structured system of tasks or assignments, neither kept an attendance record. Python was adopted as the programming language. The instructional context was based on a top-down approach within which students were provided an overall view of content without explanation of all components that make up the subject. Classes ran in a computer lab containing one machine per student. Students practiced new concepts in programming after a lecture. Most of the time, by solving simple problems assigned by the instructor. Pedagogical practices such as group work, challenge-based activities, use of educational technology or constant feedback were not observed. A mentoring system was provided as an elective activity: those interested were assigned to mentoring sessions that ran twice per week. Observing the learning atmosphere, any discourse reinforced perceptions about programming being a difficult content.

3.2 Data collection

Measuring interest is challenging. It is even more difficult when the goal involves observing interest as an ongoing process. Although other studies in CS education found some perceptions surrounding

---

[1] In general, in Brazil, the public education system is known for producing poorer learning outcomes than the private one.

what students consider interesting in their learning environment, until now, this construct had not been studied in such level of detail and depth. In our study, participants' experiences were observed according to a longitudinal design (data were collected from February to June of 2016). Even if there are not specific instruments to measure stages of interest development [17], since 4PM is a descriptive model, we could build a set of variables of measurement from it.

The process of measuring interest requires assessing cognitive and emotional components. In our study, to assess the cognitive dimension, engagement became a central construct to interpret its expressions. Accordingly, we observed how participants were interested in learning programming by noticing: their reasons to engage with it; frequency of engagement; sense of effort and passage of time when engaged in tasks, and, also, participation (including their willingness to meet and exceed tasks). Knowledge acquisition and changes in goals in programming were also taken into account. Emergence of self-regulated behavior; persistency; desire of pursuing exploratory questions and new learning strategies were indicators of changes in their interests as well. Because the instructional approach expected a sort of autonomous behavior by students, this made it easier for us to understand episodes when the engagement happened by choice (and that was another indicator of the stage of a participant's interest).

To make sense of the emotional component that constitutes their interest, we considered what feelings emerged during some interaction with the learning setting. The Genova Emotion Wheel was used so the participants could report them over time [21]. Interviews, field observation, diaries, grades and reflective field notes were used as instruments of data collection. Three semi-structured interviews were conducted with each participant. Through these mechanisms, it was possible to build an awareness of how participants were realizing the experience of learning programming. The same subset of questions was repeated to participants in all of the interviews which included self-reports of changes in their interests, perceptions about disposition to be engaged with programming by their own volition, and changes in knowledge and goals in programming. The interviews produced about 25 hours of audio that was transcribed for purposes of data analysis.

We have closely followed the classes, performing almost 50 hours of observation. On a two-week basis, participants were asked to complete diaries in two different contexts to understand engagement: a) in classes: emotions that emerged from interaction with the learning context; realization by participants how time passed; perceptions about the cognitive effort required to perform tasks and interesting elements around the learning setting and b) out of classes: reports of engagement with programming in the forms of assignments, reading, participation in study groups or mentoring sessions and time spent with these forms. The number of diaries returned per participant varied from 9 to 18. In this way, the sense of how interested they were over time was built from different datasets which constituted a rich qualitative data corpus.

3.3 Data analysis
The process of data analysis occurred in two steps. First, to answer "How does interest change over time?", the data corpus was structured in separate clusters based on three points in time: at the

beginning of the course; two months later; and at the end. We based 'this subject is missing' on the indicators that we mentioned in section 3.2 in order to proceed measuring interest and its changes.

As we stated, understanding characteristics of engagement was the central strategy for building a map of expressions of interests, something that was achieved through different ways. From the researchers' observation notes, aspects such as attendance and participation in class activities were observed. From diaries, what emotions were predominant. When participants decided to engage with programming, we observed how long, and what was the cognitive effort perceived from it. From grades and interviews (based on the vocabulary used), we examined if learning was progressing from domain to specific knowledge. Changes in attitude, study strategy and goals were also taken into account. Likewise, participants were asked to self-report changes in their interest in learning programming each time they were interviewed and what made them believe in that. These data were also used for triangulation purposes.

To clarify the process of analysis, we present a small number of examples of phrases uttered by a participant and characteristics of her engagement with programming: "Before Maria[2] begins college, she mentioned some of her attempts of learning programming for her own sake, looking for online courses and friends that could help her to get started (researcher's field note).[3]" This participant turned your attention to programming before starting college. So, when the course began, her situational interest in learning this content was already triggered. Along the experience, she did not increase the amount of time studying programming nor diversify learning strategies. Her motivation to be engaged was mostly based on reaching good grades. According to 4PM, at the initial phases of interest development, the source of engagement with the object relies on external aspects. Also, we realized that she did not develop an autonomous behavior with regard to her learning process or set *what-if* questions to pursue. These aspects are expected on later stages of interest.

However, unlike other participants, Maria did not disconnect from learning programming completely, even when some difficulties took place: "Even not knowing how to code very well, I see programming as an amazing thing. I persist because it's impossible to give up. It's fascinating, even if it's something so tough to learn (excerpt from her first interview)." After a while, frustration became a constant emotion pointed out in her diaries: "I'm interested in programming at the same way, but I feel discouraged when I don't know how to apply content that I thought I had learned by myself at classes (excerpt from the second interview)." As the time went by, she kept recognizing value for learning programming but she lacked technical knowledge and basic skills. As Maria expressed, she missed support and guidance to learn. These circumstances adversely affected her engagement, and, consequently, her interest.

At the end of the course, her interest did not reach the individual dimension, but she was still interested in learning programming. In part because of a personal effort of being connected to it: most of time, Maria was reframing her expectations about what in programming could please her in the future. The nature of her interest remained as situational all over the semester (staying at the phase 2 - in Figure 1, this is represented by the trajectory labeled as B). This said much about how she took action during the course.

---

[2] Fictional name.

[3] All the excerpts were translated from Brazilian Portuguese to English by the authors.

After analyzing the experience of each participant in those three points in time, we grouped the stages of her/his interest on individual timelines. Six patterns of trajectories were identified (they will be described in the next section). The second step of analysis was targeted to answer the question: "Why does interest change?". Looking at similar transitions[4] in those trajectories (as an example, looking at all participants who had moved from a stage of "no interest" to a "triggered situational interest"), we examined what students were mentioning about their motivational states and reasons to be (or not) engaged with programming. This effort allowed the identification of what influenced changes on the nature of their interest. Data from interviews and diaries were analyzed using techniques from the Grounded Theory as they are systematic. Using these techniques, data are constantly compared which helps to identify patterns. We open-coded data segments and a coding scheme emerged. This approach helped to identify the categories that represent the influential factors for those trajectories of interests. Because we assumed an interpretative method to build knowledge, the analysis demanded several iterations in the data corpus such that it was constantly revisited and discussed by researchers.

4. PRELIMINARY FINDINGS

According to our process of measurement, participants' interest unfolded in six different ways. These were named as trajectories of interest, they are labeled using letters from A to F (Figure 1). In these trajectories it was observed how participants' state of interest changed: evolving to a more developed state; regressing to a lesser developed one and remaining at the same state over a long period of time. In the figure, a lighter color represents a return to a lesser developed state of interest.

Trajectories A, E and F were observed in the experience of one participants; both trajectories B and C in two, and trajectory D in three participants. Considering the four phases described by Hidi and Renninger's framework, until the end of the course, we observed that the interest of five participants evolved to phase 2 and two to phase 1. Three beginners lost the interest at all. Besides other evidences, because participants did not develop abundant knowledge in programming and their reasons to learn was founded on external aspects (such as earning good grades or doing well in the course to apply for a scholarship), we realized that in none of these trajectories interest evolved to an individual level.

Six participants did not demonstrate any signs of interest for learning programming before initiating the course. They never had any curiosity or tried to engage by themselves. Four others had. Maria, for instance, whose path is reflected through the trajectory B, started an online course of algorithms couple of months before starting college. Due to this factor, in trajectories B and C the starting point of interest fell in phase 1 (triggered situational interest).

a) Evolving from "*no interest*" to "*triggered situational interest*"

In trajectories A, D, E and F this movement was observed mostly due to three circumstances that acted as triggers:

- Listening to a successful experience of a peer. At the first class, the instructor Skyped in a former student to speak to the class. This student was working at The New York Times as a developer and shared that "he had been in their shoes once". Because participants have come from public schools and a small town with few career opportunities, they did not realize how far they could get being a

coder. Being aware that "one of them" achieved this provided a large impact to move them to a "state of interest" for learning programming. That moment was an opportunity to show this content as something possible and fire their curiosity about it;

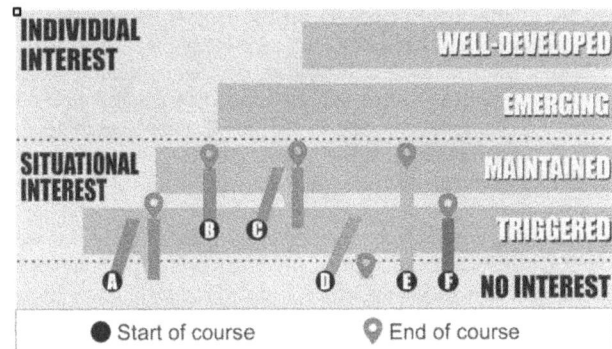

Figure 1. Participants' trajectories of interest development

- Novelty. Due to not having experiences with computing in high school, the participants were excited to attend the programming classes. As we noticed from reports, the nature of programming itself was a positive element to spark interest;
- Completing the first code. Coding a "Hello world" program was frequently reported as a trigger to their interest in learning programming (instructor taught it during the second class). Many of them not only reported being "inspired" to learn because of this, but also, engaged with it. Some of them borrowed books from the library and others tried to improve their domain knowledge about programming and Python by searching specialized information on the Internet.

b) Regressing from "*triggered situational interest*" to "*no interest*"

We also observed that in trajectories A and D, interest regressed from a triggered situational interest to no interest after a while. When investigating what might have influenced this decline, some circumstances revealed themselves. We realized that they functioned on a "waterfall" effect. Looking at the environment, we noticed that some circumstances were not appealing and engaging for the setting:

- Lack of novelty. Using the top-down approach to teach programming was not effective with some beginners. The sense of always being exposed to the same thing, in matter of content and tasks, was an inhibitor to engaging with programming. Because participants were taught about all the leading structures in the beginning, they may have missed the fact that new structures were still coming in. As the instructor moved deeper into each structure and brought new information related to syntax, participants felt that nothing new was forthcoming. Participants were not motivated to engage with classes and this was reflected in their engagement out of class;
- Disinteresting tasks. Besides the fact that participants did not expect novelty in terms of new content, the instructor used the same pattern of tasks in classes. For example, the instructor worked on trivial domains, solving small problems in the context of restaurants and banks. The codes progressed, class by class, to larger and more complex systems. Participants often noted they were working on the "same tasks" even though they were not. Because the teaching environment became something predictable, it was no longer

---

[4] A transition represents a change in the nature of an interest.

interesting to them and by then a disposition to engage with programming was being lost;

- Demand for an autonomous behavior. The absence of a structured system of tasks and assignments was another negative circumstance for participants. We noticed that engagement relied heavily on personal effort did not happen frequently, not only because they did not have substantial knowledge in programming to set an agenda for learning by themselves, but also, because without external stimulus, participants were not encouraged to engage with the content. As long as participants did not develop a routine for studying programming, it was realized too late that some difficulties were encountered.

In these trajectories, there were very few reports that associated non-engagement with difficulty to perform a task of programming. This means that difficulty by itself did not appear as a strong inhibitor of their interest, compared to the weight that other contextual factors had. However, we also noticed that their culture of studying also played a relevant role to explain why engagement went away little by little;

- Lack of competence for developing new habits. By being aware that the participant's habits of studying should change, the practices acquired from high school could not be replaced immediately. Moreover, all participants reported problems with time management. This lack of competency impacted how other courses disturbed the experience in programming;
- Generational traits. Curiously, some features were frequently self-reported. Participants mentioned, for example, issues on focusing attention for long periods of time. Thus, if a situation is not capable of gathering their attention or challenging them in an interesting way, the engagement was easily lost. We also observed that participants did not handle frustration well. Instead of trying to overcome problems, boredom or lack of support, they chose to give up.

Hidi and Renninger explain that interest development is influenced by external and individual factors. In this study, it was observed that two traits of personality influenced those trajectories:

- External locus of control. This construct is understood as the belief people have about how results are influenced by their own behaviors [20]. It is an expectation related to how our capacity to control the results that follow our actions. When the locus is external, people believe that they have little control about it. Even when not using specific instruments to measure this construct, we realized that some participants had an external locus of control. The participants attributed their disengagement with programming to other concerns, such as personal issues, lack of time, or other classes/events that needed to be attended. Participants felt that they could not do anything to change what was happening in programming. In our understanding, this was a factor with influence on how they engaged with programming;
- Self-efficacy beliefs. Self-efficacy represents a conviction about our abilities to successfully perform a task. It is not about what we know, but how we perceive our capability to do it [1]. Observing the learning experience, we noticed as the course moved forward, that some beginners had diminishing self-efficacy, which also influenced their disposition of engaging. The worst case scenario occurred through trajectory D. The only participant in this trajectory lost confidence in his being able to learn programming and as a result, his interest for learning it.

c) Evolving from *"triggered situational interest"* to *"maintained situational interest"*

We noticed two conditions that pushed participants' interest from phase 1 to phase 2, especially in trajectories B, C and E:

- A mentoring system. Students were offered this model of support two months after the course began. As soon as participants started attending mentoring sessions, novelty came up in the form of a new pedagogical design, based on group discussions, and a structured system of tasks. All of it contributed positively to return interest back to the learning context and guidance. These two features are defined by the 4PM as conditions to leverage interest;
- Developing a final project. This opportunity was presented almost at the end of the course and carried different meanings to participants, whether it was authorship, a challenge or a sense of working on something meaningful. Many participants referred to the project as noteworthy and also as a mechanism of self-assessment which influenced their disposition of engaging with programming. Furthermore, the project created a new practical experience that provided learning by doing.

d) Remaining at a stage of *"maintained situational interest"*

We observed these trajectories where participants' interest reached phase 2 and stayed steady. Those participants were more skilled in programming than the classroom average. In addition to the group of negative factors related to the teaching setting, lack of challenge was another inhibitor for participants whose interest was not boosted on an individual level. This happened in trajectories B and E.

When we analyzed why interest in trajectories B and E did not regress as in other pathways, we found that participants who owned those trajectories were somehow capable of self-regulating behavior. Facing difficulties, participants looked for new forms of support (attending other programming classes on campus or trying to help classmates as a way to learn by teaching). Some participants adjusted their goals in programming to keep engaging (by planning to work with front-end tasks instead being on the logic layer which demands more technical skills).

5. CONCLUSION

In this paper, we presented a glance of how interest of Brazilian students in learning programming changed through a CS0 course. One important aspect to be noticed is that all participants had some level of interest in learning programming at some point. However, circumstances discouraged them to be more engaged which affected, consequently, how they felt interested in learning this content. We illustrated, for instance, that lack of novelty and use of a top-down approach created an unpleasant setting for learning. Also, that the instructional design demanded competencies that they have not developed yet, like being independent and autonomous through the whole learning process.

The multiple changes (transitions) observed in some trajectories reflect how interest can be volatile at the initial phases of its development and responsive to what comes from the environment. Since programming is a brand new content to many, it is important to pay attention to what should be balanced in the learning experience to sustain interest in its primary forms of development, and, mainly, what can inhibit it from growing.

Understanding interest from this perspective brought more context to make us understand how beginners experienced learning programming. Also, it took us through the diversity in a classroom and how some circumstances might contribute to build a disinteresting environment to novices who never experienced coding before. As an example, the willingness of some students to be engaged with programming was negatively influenced when their sense of self-efficacy of learning it was diminished, which prevented their interest to raise.

Looking at these trajectories, we realized how complex is the phenomenon of developing a new interest. Because many of us are interested in contributing with possibilities that raise students' interest in programming, it is important to acknowledge that relying on one-off solutions is not enough for achieving this complex goal. And, especially for "audiences" like those we have been studying, this is a process that requires meaningful interactions that make beginners create a connection with this content and, consequently, sustain their engagement with it. Also, it demands conditions that allow them to overcome the initial struggles and feel empowered to learn. This is certainly something that educators need to take into account when planning material, strategies, tasks and use of technology to a CS0 course.

Using the 4PM, we could investigate how and why students felt interested in programming over time. The way we have been operating it is an unprecedented perspective to scrutinize interest in this context. Especially if we consider how simplistically some previous studies handled this intricate construct, these preliminary findings are something to be aware of, especially, if it is intended to achieve long-term impacts. This research is part of an effort to improve the theoretical basis for the motivational research in the context of programming education. Building this theoretical base is necessary so more effective motivational and teaching strategies can be designed. After a set of exploratory studies, we have improved our approach of measuring interest, using existing instruments to assess cognitive effort and self-efficacy as the NASA Task Load Index and The Situational Motivation Scale as well.

6. REFERENCES

[1] Bandura, A. 1982. Self-efficacy mechanism in human agency. *American psychologist*, 37,2 (Feb. 1982), 122.

[2] Bennedsen, J. and Caspersen, M. E. 2005. An investigation of potential success factors for an introductory model-driven programming course. In *Proc. of the first intern. workshop on Comp. education research*, 155–163.

[3] Burguillo, J. C. 2010. Using game theory and Competition-based Learning to stimulate student motivation and performance. *Computers & Education*. 55, 2 (Sep. 2010), 566–575.

[4] Edelson, D. C and Joseph, D. M. 2004. The Interest-Driven Learning Design Framework: Motivating Learning through Usefulness. In *Proceedings of the 6th international conference on Learning sciences*. 6 (2004), 166–173.

[5] Ely, R. B. W., Ainley, M. and Pearce, J. 2010. Identifying the dimensions of interest to support engagement and learning. In *6th Global Conference for Creative Engagements - Thinking with children*. (2010), 10.

[6] Hazzan, O., Dubinsky, Y., Eidelman, L., Sakhnini, V., and Teif, M. 2006. Qualitative Research in Computer Science Education. In *Proceedings of the 37th SIGCSE technical symposium on Computer science education*. 38,1, 408–412.

[7] Hidi, S. 1990. Interest and Its Contribution as a Mental Resource for Learning. *Review of Educational research*. 60, 4, 549–571.

[8] Hidi, S. and Harackiewicz, J. M. 2000. Motivating the Academically Unmotivated: A Critical Issue for the 21st Century. *Education & Educational Research*. 70, 2, 151–179.

[9] Hidi, S. and Harackiewicz, J. M. 2000. Motivating the Academically Unmotivated: A Critical Issue for the 21st Century. *Review of Educational Research*. 70, 2, 151–179.

[10] Hidi, S. and Renninger, K. A. 2006. The Four-Phase Model of Interest Development. *Educational psychologist*. 41, 2, 111–127.

[11] Konecki, M., Kadoic, N., and Piltaver, R. 2015. Intelligent assistant for helping students to learn programming. In *8th International Convention on Information and Communication Technology, Electronics and Microelectronics (MIPRO)*, 924–928.

[12] Krapp, A. 2002. *An Educational-Psychological Theory of Interest and Its Relations to SDT*. Handbook of Self-Determination Research. (E. L. Deci and Richard M. Ryan, Eds. University of Rochester Press, 2002), 405.

[13] Lakanen, A. J., Isomöttönen, V., and Lappalainen, V. 2014. Understanding differences among coding club students. In *Proceedings of the 2014 conference on Innovation & technology in computer science education*. (2014), 159–164.

[14] McGill, M. M. 2012. Learning to Program with Personal Robots: Influences on Student Motivation. *ACM Trans. Comput. Educ.* 12, 1 (Mar. 2012), 1–32.

[15] Pears, A., Seidman, S., Malmi, L., Mannila, L, Adams, E., Bennedsen, J., Devlin, M., and Paterson, J. 2007. A survey of literature on the teaching of introductory programming. In *Working group reports on ITiCSE on Innovation and technology in computer science education*. 39,4 (December, 2007), 204.

[16] Renninger, K. A., Ewen, L., and Lasher, K. 2002. Individual interest as context in expository text and mathematical word problems. *Learn. and Instr.* 12, 4 (Aug. 2002), 467–491.

[17] Renninger, K. A. and Hidi, S. 2011. Revisiting the Conceptualization, Measurement, and Generation of Interest. *Educational Psychologist*. 46, 3 (July. 2011), 168–184.

[18] Renninger, K. A. Working with and cultivating the development of interest, self-efficacy, and self-regulation. 2010. In *Innovations in educational psychology. Perspectives on learning, teaching, and human development*. (Springer Publishing Co, 2010), 107–138.

[19] Renninger, K. A., Bachrach, J. E., and Posey, S. K. E. 2008. *Learner Interest and Achievement Motivation*. Social Psychological Perspectives, 2008, p. 559.

[20] Rotter, J. B. 1966. Generalized expectancies for internal versus external control of reinforcement. *Psychological monographs: General and applied, 80*,1 (1966), 1–28.

[21] Sacharin, V., Schlegel, K., and Scherer, K. R. Geneva Emotion Wheel rating study. Geneva, Switzerland, 2012.

[22] Schiefele, U. 1991. Interest, learning and Motivation. *Educational Psychologist*. 26, 3 (Nov. 1991), 299–323.

[23] Sheard, J., Simon, S., Hamilton, M., and Lönnberg, J. 2009. Analysis of research into the teaching and learning of programming. In *Proceedings of the fifth international workshop on Computing education research workshop (ICER '09)*. ACM, New York, NY, USA, 93-104.

[24] Watson, C., Frederick, L., "Failure rates in introductory programming revisited," in Proceedings of the 2014 conference on Innovation & technology in computer science education, 2014, pp. 39–44.

Comparing Remote and Co-located Interaction in Free and Open Source Software Engineering Projects

Kevin Buffardi
Computer Science Department
California State University, Chico
Chico, California, USA 95929-0410
(+1) 530-898-5617
kbuffardi@csuchico.edu

ABSTRACT

By working on open source software projects, software engineering students can benefit from working on more realistic products than traditional, educational programming assignments. However, careers in software engineering demand learning how to work within a professional environment and how to follow software development processes. We studied the impact of students' interactions with external collaborators on open source projects and found many similar outcomes between those who communicated remotely and those who communicated face-to-face. However, we also discovered that face-to-face interactions with local software professionals following the Localized Free and Open Source (LFOSS) model had particular advantages in teaching Agile methods, holding students accountable, and introducing professional networking opportunities.

CCS Concepts

• **Social and professional topics~Software engineering education**   • Social and professional topics~Project and people management   • **Software and its engineering~Open source model**

Keywords

Software engineering, interaction, communication, remote, co-located, Agile, Localized Free and open source software (LFOSS)

1. INTRODUCTION

Software engineering education needs real-life experiences to help foster students' transition from academic to professional software development environments. One remedy suggested to move from "throw-away" projects to real product development is to involve students in Free and Open Source Software projects (FOSS)[1]. Among other advantages, FOSS projects introduce opportunities for students to maintain existing, larger scale, and more sophisticated products that have real "customers" [14].

However, the study of software engineering does not only

concentrate on *what* is built, but also *how* a team of developers go about building it. *Agile* became a leading software development framework since its emergence in the turn of the century and it stresses continuous delivery of software in short intervals [11]. In particular, the *Agile Manifesto* emphasizes frequent and close communication with the specific principle that "The most efficient and effective method of conveying information to and within a development team is face-to-face conversation" [2].

On the other hand, it is common for FOSS projects to rely on developers to volunteer their time and effort rather than having a dedicated, full-time team of developers. Consequently, a key mechanism for FOSS products' success is their open access, which empowers software developers from around the world to collaborate. As a result, interaction usually takes place online, and often asynchronously. Therefore, the traditional FOSS model is not conducive to face-to-face interaction and may not provide learning experience of co-located collaboration. To understand the affect of remote or co-located interaction, we investigated the learning experiences of students' interactions with open source projects.

2. BACKGROUND

Software engineering courses often group students to collaborate and experience the software development lifecycle in small teams. It is reasonable to believe that students may be more highly motivated to work on projects of their own creative invention. However, without having to create software that will be used and maintained in the real world, students may not appreciate the onus of producing maintainable and extensible software. In particular, Martin warns that "toy" projects—without implications of real world use—may be harmful to students' education since "Students know their code matters only as much as they might find our assignments interesting, or as much as it counts toward their grades" [12].

In a study concentrating on how to improve realism of software engineering education, Nurkkala and Brandle [14] identify six key gaps between education and real software development in industry: "No product, short duration, high turnover, low [sophistication], no maintenance, and no customer." They attribute many of the problems to the lack of external pressures and the absence of having to adapt to changes and stakeholders' needs. Meanwhile, immersing students in maintaining Free and Open Source Software (FOSS) *products* with real users (*customers*) is an emerging trend to address some of these shortcomings [1][7][8]. However, given the inherent, global distribution of FOSS collaboration, difficulties may arise when teaching *Agile* techniques that emphasize frequent and face-to-face communication and reliable, prompt feedback [2].

In the Fall of 2014, *California State University, Chico*'s Computer Science Department co-founded the Chico Open Source Consortium (COSC) with local software professionals to foster collaboration with students on open source projects [5]. Although located in a small city with no major software development companies, the COSC gathered twelve core members representing several local businesses and began weekly meetings to design and develop BossyUI [4], a collection of reusable, data-driven widgets for AngularJS web applications. During the school year, undergraduate students in software engineering and usability engineering teams became principal contributors to the project under the guidance of the professional, core members of COSC. We distinguished this co-located approach from the traditionally remote Free and Open Source Software (FOSS) model as *Localized* FOSS, or LFOSS.

In our preliminary investigations, we observed anecdotes of LFOSS students adopting software development habits and communication styles from their face-to-face interactions with COSC mentors. In addition, the collaboration even lead to COSC business sponsors hiring students [5]. As the project continued and spanned multiple semesters, we compared student teams who worked on the LFOSS project to others who worked on student-lead entrepreneurial software products or who worked on proprietary products for a remote software company. We found that LFOSS students were more motivated to continue working on the project after the end of the semester than those who worked for the industry project and benefitted from having an external stakeholder, unlike the self-contained entrepreneurial projects [6]. Instead, in this study, we compare LFOSS to traditional FOSS projects.

Additionally, others have adopted a variation of the FOSS model in which students work on humanitarian (HFOSS) projects to serve social good [8]. Although HFOSS projects also collaborate remotely, they exhibited some promise to appeal more to under-represented minorities (URM) in computing and provide tangible ways to learn about social impact of software. Consequently, in our previous study, we investigated student preferences when choosing software engineering projects. We found no significant differences in preference between racial/ethnic URM, but females preferred HFOSS more than males at a difference approaching statistical significance [6]. Accordingly, in this study, we continued our formative exploration of what motivates students to choose their software engineering projects.

3. METHOD
3.1 Course Organization
To investigate the differences between *localized* (LFOSS), *humanitarian* (HFOSS), and general free and open source software (FOSS) projects, we observed students' opinions and experiences as they worked on semester-long assignments to contribute to and help maintain existing open source software products. In Spring 2016—the fourth sequential semester that the COSC has collaborated with students on BossyUI—we studied the interactions of a graduate-level Software Engineering class, a required course for a Masters degree in Computer Science at California State University, Chico. The degree is oriented toward preparing students for careers in industry.

The course involved in-depth study of software testing and quality assurance with overviews of tools for automated testing, coverage analysis, build automation, and continuous integration. The semester-long project to contribute to an existing open source software product accounted for 75% of students' final grades.

Credit earned for contributions emphasized code maintenance but also acknowledged secondary accomplishments such as improvements to documentation, bug verification and logging, and development operations (DevOps) management. To gather insights into students' experiences, pre- and post-semester surveys (described in the following subsections) were collected and 36 of 37 (97%) students consented to include their responses in data analysis.

3.2 Project Identification and Assignment
Following a description of course expectations, the instructor summarized FOSS along with popular examples (Firefox [13] and *nix operating systems) as well as HFOSS and LFOSS projects. The instructor provided links to directories of: FOSS projects specifically indicating interest in mentoring students [15], HFOSS communities [10], Open HUB [3] for a extensive list of FOSS projects, and the active LFOSS project [4]. Students were asked to review the projects outside of class and contact the instructor with projects that interested them. The instructor reviewed the proposed projects and vetted them to make sure they met the criteria: projects must be free and open source software with an existing repository for version control; projects must be existing products of non-trivial size; projects must be active with evidence of updates and/or community interactions within the past 30 days; and projects must have documented resources for common activities including logging bugs and communicating with other developers

After the vetting process, the instructor compiled a list of 8 approved projects along with their respective websites for students' reference. Altogether, there were two (2) HFOSS options, one (1) LFOSS option, and the remaining five (5) were FOSS projects that fit neither of the aforementioned categories. During the second week of class, students completed a survey to rank their top three preferred projects from the reference list. In addition to identifying the projects they preferred, they were also surveyed to rate their general computing interests on: serving {school, local, and national/international} communities, contributing to "products I will use," and contributing to "products that are well-known" with 5-point Likert-type items. The survey also asked them to explain in free response form: "What other motivations do you have for choosing a project to contribute to?"

The free response explanations were analyzed qualitatively using Grounded Theory by coding responses for the common themes identified: using familiar technologies/languages; learning new technologies; working on a product that helps others; working with an active, helpful community; working on a product with widespread use; and availability of ways to contribute (e.g. many unresolved bug reports).

The course instructor assigned students to projects based on their top-three rankings and to ensure that projects had at multiple students working on them so that they had peers to support one another. Although student teams were formed for projects, grading was based strictly on individuals' contributions. The projects with teams for this project included: Akka (n=3), Apache Spark (n=6), BossyUI (n=7), KDevelop (n=7), MouseTrap (n=3), Mozilla (n=7), RethinkDB (n=4). MouseTrap is a HFOSS project for accessibility features for the GNOME desktop environment.

3.3 Interaction Assessment
During the final week of the semester, students were asked to complete the *post-semester* survey to report their experiences. The

survey was given as a graded assignment based on participation where content of their responses had no bearing on the grade. Students received 100% credit for the assignment by submitting the survey but were offered the option to write a journal entry that described their experience for equal credit if they opted to *not* consent to include their responses in this research. Only one student (n=1, 3%) opted out of the survey.

For the *post-semester survey*, we adopted the HFOSS Student Survey with content questions for Software Engineering [9]. This instrument has been used to evaluate student experiences with HFOSS in studies since 2008 [8] including a multi-institutional study [7]. The survey includes questions about student demographics as well as 5-point Likert-type items (with additional options for "not applicable" and "don't know") for measuring students' opinion of HFOSS projects and their confidence and perspectives of computing. The Software Engineering content question items include ratings for:

SE01. I am comfortable that I could participate in the planning and development of a real-world software project;

SE02. I can list the steps in the software process we used in the HFOSS project;

SE03. I can use a software process to develop an HFOSS project;

SE04. I am sure that I can actively participate in an HFOSS community to develop a software project;

SE05. I have gained some confidence in collaborating with professionals from a variety of locations and cultures;

SE06. I can describe the impact of project complexity on the approaches used to develop software;

SE07. I can describe the impact of project size on the approaches used to develop software;

SE08. I am confident that I can maintain an HFOSS project;

SE09. I can describe the drawbacks and benefits of FOSS to society;

SE10. I can use all tools and techniques employed in my HFOSS project;

SE11. I can participate in an HFOSS development team's interactions; and

SE12. Participation in an HFOSS project has improved my understanding of how to behave like a computing professional.

The entire instrument is available on Foss2Serve's website [9]. Since our students participated in different types of FOSS projects (and not only humanitarian), we edited all references of "HFOSS" to more general "FOSS." We also supplemented the survey with additional questions pertaining to their interaction with the project (5-point Likert-type items, unless otherwise noted with response options in *italics*):

INT01. Outside of lecture and lab, estimate how many hours you spent per week on your project *(free response)*

INT02. I directly communicated with the mentor/customer for my project...
Choose one: {I didn't have a mentor or customer; I had a mentor or customer but only other team members directly communicated with them; Less than once a month; Each month; Each week; Each day}

INT03. My predominant contact with my mentor/customer was...
Choose one: {I didn't have a mentor or customer; I had a mentor or customer but only other team members directly communicated with them; In person; Synchronous communication (Phone, video messaging, instant messaging, etc); Asynchronous communication (Email, bulletin boards, messaging at different times, etc); Other}

INT04. My mentor/customer was prompt in replying to me

INT05. My mentor/customer's communication was helpful to my progress on the software development project

INT06. My mentor/customer held me accountable to completing my work well and on time

INT07. Interacting with my mentor/customer was valuable for my professional networking

INT08. I believe my project can help serve my school (and/or affiliated groups)

INT09. I believe my project can help serve the local community

INT10. I believe my project can help serve national or international communities

INT11. I believe Computer Science and Software Engineering are fields that help people

HFOSS projects have the overt goal of serving a social good so we predicted the subject of students' work would impact their perceptions of the project and of computing in general, as addressed in items {INT08, INT10, INT11}. Consequently, we hypothesized:

*(H1) Students who worked on **humanitarian** open source projects will **have greater appreciation of computing as a social good** than those who worked on other types of projects.*

However, the LFOSS project involved direct interaction specifically with members of the local community so for INT09, we hypothesized:

*(H2) Students who worked on **either humanitarian or localized** open source projects will **believe their projects can help serve the local community** more so than those who worked on other projects.*

Identifying unique characteristics in students' experiences when collaborating with local software professionals on an LFOSS project was the primary motivation for this study. Consequently, we investigated the difference between *co-located* (LFOSS) projects and other projects that involve *remote* collaboration from geographically distributed contributors. Because students working on an LFOSS project should have more direct exposure to professional software developers and their environments, we hypothesized:

*(H3) Students who worked on **local** projects will be **more confident working as a software engineer** than those who worked on a remote project.*

To evaluate this hypothesis, we compared average responses of LFOSS projects to the software engineering content questions in the *post-semester* survey to those of students who worked on remote FOSS projects. The survey contained the twelve Likert-type items listed earlier in this section so we first tested the reliability of all the items for describing general confidence in software engineering. Cronbach's alpha (α) tests a group of items' internal consistency. **Table 1** shows the descriptive statistics and Cronbach's alpha score for each item.

As shown, the items scored with consistent reliability (α=87). Therefore, as a comprehensive measurement of all the software engineering items, we averaged individual students' responses as a *SE Aggregate* score (M=4.0, sd=0.49) to compare overall confidence working as a software engineer. However, we recognized that the mentors in our LFOSS project roughly fit the status quo for demographics in the field: predominantly males of Caucasian and Asian ethnicities. Therefore, we hypothesized:

*(H4) Students who worked on **remote** open source projects will have **more appreciation for diversity** in the software development community than those who worked on local projects.*

For this hypothesis, we compared students' responses to SE05: "*I have gained some confidence in collaborating with professionals from a variety of locations and cultures*" between local and remote projects. On the other hand, in our previous study [6], we observed that LFOSS students have the unique opportunity to interact with professionals face-to-face so we hypothesized:

*(H5) Students who worked on **local** open source projects will have **more meaningful communication** with other members of the project than those who worked on remote projects.*

*(H6) Students who worked on **local** open source projects will **feel greater responsibility** for contributing to their projects than those who worked on remote projects.*

*(H7) Students who worked on **local** open source projects will have **better professional networking experiences** with other members of their project than those who worked on remote projects.*

We addressed these final three hypotheses using the supplementary interaction ratings {INT01...INT07}. Responses to frequency (INT02) of contact with mentors were on an ordinal scale so responses were ranked from (1) "Each Day" to (5) "I had a mentor or customer but only other team members directly communicated with them" and those who abstained (n=1) or reported to have no mentor (n=10)—and therefore had no interaction to report—were excluded from questions regarding those interactions. Shapiro-Wilk test found that the ranked responses for INT02 (M=2.36, sd=0.91) were not normally distributed (p<.0001).

Similarly, predominant mode of contact with mentors (INT03) were ranked as (1) In Person, (2) Synchronous, (3) Asynchronous and those without mentors or reported "Other" were excluded. Shapiro-Wilk test found that the ranked responses for INT03 (M=2.56, sd=0.79) were not normally distributed (p<.0001).

Table 1. Software Engineering Item Reliability

Item	M	sd	α
SE01 Plan	4.5	0.65	0.87
SE02 List	4.1	0.69	0.86
SE03 Process	4.0	0.77	0.85
SE04 Participate	4.2	0.76	0.85
SE05 Collaborate	4.3	0.72	0.85
SE06 Complexity	4.0	0.77	0.85
SE07 Size	4.1	0.63	0.86
SE08 Maintain	3.6	0.93	0.85
SE09 Society	3.8	0.96	0.85
SE10 Tools	3.5	0.89	0.86
SE11 Interactions	4.2	0.75	0.87
SE12 Behave	4.2	0.71	0.86
SE Aggregate	4.0	0.49	0.87

Likewise, the remaining interaction responses were tested for normality using Shapiro-Wilk. INT01 Hours outside of class (M=10.93, sd=9.24) were not normal (p<.0001); INT04 Prompt reply (M=3.74, sd=1.20) was not normal (p<.01); INT05 Helpful communication (M=4.00, sd=1.12) was not normal (p<.001); INT06 Accountability (M=3.23, sd=1.34) was not normal (p<.05); and INT07 Networking (M=3.74, sd=1.16) was not normal (p<.01); consequently, non-parametric tests were used to compare responses for each of these items.

4. RESULTS
4.1 Project Preference and Motivations
After students ranked their top three project choices, we compared preferences for different types of projects: localized (LFOSS), humanitarian (HFOSS), and other Free and Open Source Software (FOSS). First, we reviewed each student's top choice and found that FOSS (27, 75%) projects were most popular, followed by LFOSS (7, 19%) and HFOSS (2, 6%). However, there were more FOSS options than either LFOSS or HFOSS so these percentages should not be generalized as inherent differences between types of projects. Furthermore, while the most popular top choice projects were Apache Spark and Mozilla (n=8 each), the seven students identified the LFOSS project as their top choice, which was at least as popular than the remaining three FOSS and two HFOSS projects.

In addition, we reviewed all students' free-response explanations for their preferences and identified common themes. Subsequently, we compared frequency of mentions of the following motivations for choosing projects: using *familiar technologies*/languages; *learning new* technologies/languages; working on a product that *helps others*; working with an active, helpful *community*; working on a product with *widespread use*; and *availability* of ways *to contribute*. **Table 2** summarizes the responses.

Two students abstained from indicating their sex so the final column is *not* the sum of the preceding columns. Percentages provided represent the proportion of members represented *by that column*. Since the motivations were described in free response, many descriptions included more than one motivation and therefore the percentages do not sum 100%.

Contrary to our expectations, students did not explicitly state that an opportunity to network with local professionals as a motivating factor for choosing LFOSS. However, it is also noteworthy that 17% of students expressed a desire for projects with supportive communities with whom they wish to interact and collaborate, even though they were not specifically asked about how project communities influence their preferences. Some of these comments may have been alluding to LFOSS local professionals, but for the sake of objectivity, we do not make that assumption.

Table 2. Frequency and Proportion of Students' Motivations

Motivation	Female (n=5)	Male (n=29)	All (n=36)
Familiar technologies	0 (0%)	10 (34%)	10 (28%)
Learning new	2 (40%)	9 (31%)	12 (33%)
Helps others	0 (0%)	3 (10%)	4 (11%)
Community	1 (20%)	4 (14%)	6 (17%)
Widespread use	1 (20%)	7 (24%)	9 (25%)
Availability to contribute	1 (20%)	5 (17%)	6 (17%)

There is no indication females were more interested than their male counterparts in humanitarian projects. In fact, no females described *helping others* as a motivation for their project even though 11% of all other students (including those who abstained from identifying gender) did. However, a sample size of only five females should not be generalized for the entire population.

4.2 Interaction Assessment

We investigated our hypothesis *(H1)* "*Students who worked on humanitarian open source projects will have greater appreciation of computing as a social good than those who worked on other types of projects*" by comparing *post-semester* responses to the Likert-type items: INT08 *I believe my project can help serve my school (and/or affiliated groups)*; INT10 *I believe my project can help serve national or international communities*; and INT11 *I believe Computer Science and Software Engineering are fields that help people.* Wilcoxon-Mann-Whitney test found that HFOSS (M=4.67, sd=0.57) approaches significantly stronger agreement that the project can help serve the school (p=.17) than other projects (M=3.71, sd=1.23); HFOSS (M=5.00, sd=0.00) has borderline significantly stronger agreement (p=.0501) that the project can help serve the (inter)national communities than other projects (M=3.67, sd=1.36); but there is no significant difference (p=.34) between HFOSS (M=5.00, sd=0.00) and other projects (M=4.63, sd=0.70) that Computer Science and Software Engineering are fields that help people.

These results are not conclusive given the borderline significance for HFOSS students' higher expectations of their products serving an international, social good. At the advanced stages of the graduate students' educations, they appear to have relatively positive outlook of the field's potential to help others. Consequently, HFOSS projects did not demonstrate a significant impact of their broad perceptions of the field as a whole.

To test the second hypothesis *(H2)*, "*Students who worked on either humanitarian or localized open source projects will believe their projects can help serve the local community more so than those who worked on other projects*" we compared responses to INT09 *I believe my project can help serve the local community*. We grouped mutually exclusive categories for HFOSS (n=3), LFOSS (n=6), and other FOSS (n=27). Students who worked on HFOSS (M=5, sd=0) and LFOSS (M=5, sd=0) projects had the same (p=NaN; no variance from identical means and no deviation within either group) strong confidence that they served the local community. HFOSS (M=5, sd=0) students were significantly more confident (p<.05) in serving the local community than FOSS students (M=3.6, sd=1.1). Likewise, LFOSS (M=5, sd=0) students were significantly more confident (p<.01) than FOSS students (M=3.6, sd=1.1). Hypothesis *(H2)* is supported because both HFOSS and LFOSS students showed stronger confidence in serving the local community than did other students.

We tested *(H3)* "*Students who worked on local projects will be more confident working as a software engineer than those who worked on a remote project*" by comparing Software Engineering Aggregate scores (*SE Aggregate* in **Table 1**) of students who worked on the LFOSS project to all others who did not. The Wilcoxon-Mann-Whitney test found no significant difference (p=.71) between LFOSS students' confidence as software engineers (M=4.08, sd=0.71) and that of other students (M=4.03, sd=0.45). Hypothesis *(H3)* is rejected because students of all project types reported comparable confidence in their software engineering abilities.

Since the LFOSS project did not draw from a diverse, global community, we hypothesized that *(H4)* "*Students who worked on remote open source projects will have more appreciation for diversity in the software development community than those who worked on local projects.*" Wilcoxon-Mann-Whitney test of ratings for SE05 *I have gained some confidence in collaborating with professionals from a variety of locations and cultures* found no difference (p=.47) between remote (M=4.43, sd=0.68) and local (M=4.67, sd=0.51) projects. Hypothesis *(H4)* is rejected because students gained confidence in working with diverse software development communities regardless of whether the project was remote or local.

Finally, we tested hypotheses {H5…H7} on project interaction by compared responses to the supplementary interaction items {INT01…INT07}. Wilcoxon-Mann-Whitney tests revealed that the remote group (M=11.67, sd=9.89) approached significantly more weekly hours (p=.15) outside of class than the local group (M=7.15, sd=3.03). There was no significant difference (p=.32) between how often remote (M=2.45, sd=1.00) and local (M=2.00, sd=0.00) directly communicated with their mentors (lower values indicates more frequent contact). However, local (M=1.60, sd=0.89) predominantly used more direct forms of communication (p<.01) than remote projects (M=2.83, sd=0.51), where lower values indicate more direct communication.

According to Wilcoxon-Mann-Whitney tests, students in local projects (M=4.40, sd=0.89) received replies from mentors approaching significantly quicker (p=.16) than remote projects (M=3.59, sd=1.22). Mentors' communication was borderline significantly more helpful (p=.056) for local (M=4.80, sd=0.44) than remote (M=3.80, 1.15).

Students reported that interacting with local mentors (M=5.00, sd=0.00) was significantly more valuable for professional networking (p<.01) than remote (M=3.45, sd=1.10). Most notably, students reported that mentors held them significantly more accountable (p<.01) for local (M=4.80, sd=0.45) than remote (M=2.86; sd=1.20) projects. In addition, we performed post-hoc analysis across all projects to investigate the relationship between students feelings of accountability (M=3.29, sd=1.37) and the ordinal levels of primary communication (M=2.56, sd=0.79): (1) in person, (2) synchronous online, and (3) asynchronous online. Spearman's rho (ρ) indicated a moderate, negative correlation (ρ=-0.46, p<.05), suggesting that closer forms of communication (i.e. in person) may instill a greater sense of accountability in students. **Table 3** summarizes all statistically significant results along with the hypotheses to which they correspond. Note that *(H5)* concerned how meaningful the communication students experienced with FOSS project communities. While we tested the hypothesis with regards to helpfulness, promptness, frequency, and modes of communication, only the last was found to have statistically significant differences between local and remote.

Table 3. Summary of Significant Results

Hypothesis	Significant Result(s) [*](p<.01)
H2 Local Impact	LFOSS > FOSS[*] HFOSS > FOSS[*]
H5 Communication	Local > Remote[*] *(directness of communication only)*
H6 Accountable	Local > Remote[*]
H7 Networking	Local > Remote[*]

5. CONCLUSIONS

In this study, we explored how working on open source projects with either co-located or remote collaborators/mentors impacted software engineering students' experiences. From analyzing responses to pre- and post-term surveys, we discovered that students involved in remote and co-located projects shared several common outcomes.

Students showed no difference in their confidence as software engineers regardless of whether their collaborators were local or globally dispersed. In the same notion, students across both groups gained comparable confidence in their abilities to collaborate with software professionals from a variety of locations and cultures. However, our study also discovered some unique advantages to co-located teams.

The Localized Free and Open Source Software (LFOSS) model [5] affords face-to-face interaction between students and software professionals, which is otherwise rare in FOSS projects. Consequently, students involved in the LFOSS project could adhere more closely to the Agile principles [2] and associated techniques [11] that require frequent, in-person communication. That unique experience may offer benefits for students' pursuit of software engineering careers in industry, where Agile methods are widely adopted. In future studies, we plan to explore and elaborate on the specific outcomes from practicing Agile methods within co-located projects. In the meantime, LFOSS students also reported that their interaction on the project was more valuable for professional networking by working side-by-side with software professionals from local employers.

Furthermore, we found that students who worked on the co-located LFOSS project felt that they were held more accountable for producing quality work on time. Accordingly, our post-hoc analysis investigated students' predominant mode of communication (e.g. in person discussion, synchronous remote conversation, or asynchronous online contact) with their project mentors and demonstrated that more direct forms of communication had a moderate correlation with greater sense of accountability. Since previous research identified external pressures—such as those from project stakeholders—as a necessity to bridge the gap between academic and professional software projects [14], the factor of accountability should not be underestimated.

The study also yielded some promising but inconclusive results that warrant further investigation with a larger sample size. For example, LFOSS students reported that communication with their mentors was more helpful, at borderline significance (p=.056) and that mentors' replies approached significantly quicker (p=.16) than those who worked on remote projects. In future work, we plan to incorporate data from mentors for more robust insights into their communication and assessments of the students' work.

Furthermore, our formative exploration of students' reasons for preferring particular types FOSS projects revealed that (1) the programming language and platform technologies required in a project and (2) the expectation for the product to have popular end-user adoption were two primary motivating factors. However, several students specifically sought a helpful project community.

At the end of the semester, students perceive that both HFOSS and LFOSS have a stronger *local* impact than other FOSS projects. The combination of a project that collaborates local professionals *and* serves a humanitarian purpose might be even more impactful and effective in appealing to under-represented groups in computing. It warrants further research to identify opportunities to promote social responsibility in computing while also appealing to and empowering diverse student populations in software engineering.

6. REFERENCES

[1] Auer, L., Juntunen, J. and Ojala, P., (2011) "Open Source Project as a Pedagogical Tool in Higher Education," Proc. of the 15th Intern'l Academic MindTrek conf. ACM, 207-213

[2] Beck, K., Grenning, J., Martin, R.C., et al.: 2001. Principles behind the Agile Manifesto. http://agilemanifesto.org/. Accessed August 2016

[3] Black Duck: 2006. Open HUB, the open source network. http://www.openhub.net. Accessed August 2016

[4] BossyUI. http://bossyui.io/. Accessed August 2016

[5] Buffardi, K., (2015) "Localized Open Source Collaboration in Software Engineering Education." Proc. of IEEE Frontiers in Education

[6] Buffardi, K., (2016) "Localized open source software projects: Exploring realism and motivation." Proc. of IEEE Int'l conf. on Computer Science & Education

[7] Ellis, H. J., Hislop, G. W., Pulimood, S. M., Morgan, B., & Coleman, B., (2015) "Software Engineering Learning in HFOSS: A Multi-Institutional Study." Proc. of the 122nd Annual ASEE Conference and Exhibition, Seattle, WA.

[8] Ellis, H.J.C. and Morelli, R.A. (2008) "Support for Educating Software Engineers Through Humanitarian Open Source Projects." Proc. of the 2008 21st IEEE-CS Conf. on Software Engineering Education and Training Workshop. IEEE Computer Society, Washington, DC, 1-4. doi: http://dx.doi.org/10.1109/CSEETW.2008.5

[9] Foss2Serve. Evaluation Instruments. http://foss2serve.org/index.php/Evaluation_Instruments. Accessed August 2016.

[10] Foss2Serve. HFOSS Communities. http://foss2serve.org/index.php/HFOSS_Communities. Accessed August 2016.

[11] Fraser, S., Astels, D., Beck, K., et al, (2003) "Discipline and practices of TDD: (test driven development)." Companion of the 18th annual ACM SIGPLAN conference. Anaheim, CA, USA, ACM: 268-270

[12] Martin, F., (2006) "Toy projects considered harmful." Communications of the ACM 49, 7, 113-116. doi: 10.1145/1139922.1139958

[13] Mozilla: 2002. Firefox. http://www.mozilla.org/en-US/firefox/products/. Accessed August 2016

[14] Nurkkala, T. and Brandle, S. 2011. Software studio: teaching professional software engineering. In Proc. of the 42nd ACM technical symposium on Computer science education. ACM, New York, NY, 153-158. doi: http://dx.doi.org/10.1145/1953163.1953209

[15] Teaching Open Source: FOSS Mentor Projects Interested in Mentoring Students. http://teachingopensource.org/index.php/FOSS_Mentor_Proj ects. Accessed January 2017.

Learning Agile with Tech Startup Software Engineering Projects

Kevin Buffardi
Computer Science Department
California State University, Chico
Chico, California, USA 95929-0410
(+1) 530-898-5617
kbuffardi@csuchico.edu

Colleen Robb
Department of Management
California State University, Chico
Chico, California, USA 95929-0011
(+1) 786-229-9760
ccrobb@csuchico.edu

David Rahn
Department of Management
California State University, Chico
Chico, California, USA 95929-0011
(+1) 530-588-5907
drahn@csuchico.edu

ABSTRACT

The Tech Startup model is an approach to learning software engineering methods by partnering with students studying entrepreneurship to collaborate on real software products. Agile software development methods align with Lean Startup practices so that students in sister classes experience leading contemporary practices in their respective fields. This paper describes a pilot study of interdisciplinary Tech Startup projects with a heuristic evaluation of software engineering realism and formative assessment of students' surveyed experiences. The study found several similar student outcomes to other project models; however, it also identified limitations in the pilot with corresponding recommendations for future implementations.

CCS Concepts

• **Social and professional topics~Software engineering education** • *Social and professional topics~Computing and business* • **Software and its engineering~Agile software development**

Keywords

Software engineering; Agile software development; Lean Startup; interdisciplinary collaboration; entrepreneurship; team projects

1. INTRODUCTION

As many computer science students shift from academic to professional software development careers, upper-division software engineering courses may provide a unique opportunity to usher a smooth transition. Educational programming assignments often have limited scope and rigid designs for each individual student to complete in the matter of a couple weeks while real software development projects involve teamwork to design and produce more sophisticated products. Consequently, software engineering courses can expose students to development methods and skills that they will need if they choose to pursue the popular career path of software engineering.

Since its emergence during the turn of the century, Agile software development has grown as a prominent approach to building

ITiCSE '17, July 03-05, 2017, Bologna, Italy
© 2017 ACM. ISBN 978-1-4503-4704-4/17/07...$15.00
DOI: http://dx.doi.org/10.1145/3059009.3059063

software in industry. Agile emphasizes incremental development with continuous delivery of the product to the customer with feedback that drives future revisions [2]. This quick cycle accentuates the ability to rapidly adapt to changing needs, especially in contrast to Agile's predecessors that rely on rigidly documented requirements.

Following the Agile process and learning associated tools techniques can logically fit in software engineering courses meant to prepare students with contemporary software development skills. In particular, software engineering courses commonly incorporate semester-long team projects to approach emulating the real world software development process and environment. However, while students may enjoy the freedom of defining their own software products, studies [19] have recognized that such "toy projects" lack the pressure of delivering well-designed and tested software to real users and consequently, "Students know their code matters only as much as they might find our assignments interesting, or as much as it counts toward their grades" [18]. To properly learn Agile development, students' team projects require business people (or customers) as external stakeholders.

Meanwhile, the United States Bureau of Labor Statistics projects that software publishers will be among the fastest growing industries through 2024 [14]. In the USA alone, fifteen to twenty technology companies are founded each year that eventually surpass over $100 million dollars in revenue [15]. Correspondingly, there is potential for computer science students to pursue technology startup business (tech startups) and follow in the footsteps of the founders of Google and Facebook, whose entrepreneurial ideas and development began while they were studying at university [13][21].

In this paper, we introduce a "Tech Startup" approach to teaching Agile software development in a software engineering course by leveraging collaboration with an entrepreneurship class. We outline the partnership between the sister courses and explain strategies to address challenges such as managing intellectual property. Finally, we evaluate initial findings from students' experiences from the first semester of implementing the tech startup model and compare the outcomes to other contemporary approaches to software engineering education.

2. BACKGROUND

2.1 Lean Startup

Lean Startup methodology arose from principles of Toyota's innovative Lean manufacturing and supply chain management which eliminated risk by shortening development cycles and testing business hypotheses by regularly producing new releases and measuring results to drive business decisions [25]. Specifically, Lean Startup methodology encourages releasing a version of the product that provides the greatest opportunity to discover and validate information about customers that also takes the least amount of effort to produce, known as the Minimum Viable Product (MVP) [23]. By releasing MVPs, studying customer response, and adapting to the observations for the next MVP, Lean Startups enter a "build-measure-learn" loop and continuously optimize both the business model and product.

2.2 Agile Software Development
Similarly to principles of Lean Startup, Agile software development focuses on continuous delivery of software products in small increments with the ability to respond and adapt quickly to changes in requirements [2]. Moreover, Agile asserts that self-organized teams of "Business people and developers must work together daily throughout the project [and] the most efficient and effective method of conveying information to and within a development team is face-to-face conversation." To also continually refine the team's practices, "At regular intervals, the team reflects on how to become more effective, then tunes and adjusts its behavior accordingly" [2]. The Agile paradigm does not prescribe specific methods; instead, various tools and techniques have established widespread use based on their compatibility with Agile philosophies.

For example, Scrum [24] is a framework that facilitates face-to-face conversation by arranging scrums—or *daily standup* meetings—and organizes intervals of rapid, incremental development and deployment into *sprints*. In correspondence with Lean Startup's emphasis on MVP's, Scrum sprints can focus on creating working functionality that delivers the most value with the least effort required.

Instead of dedicating a distinct phase to verifying software functionality, Test-Driven Development (TDD) involves writing unit tests—automated tests that exercise a small unit (e.g. function) of code to check that it produces the correct functionality—incrementally as small units of code are developed [12] so they can be verified immediately and errors can be corrected before moving on. However, while methods and techniques like Scrum and TDD are commonplace in industry, Agile software development methods usually reflect a significant departure from how students are accustomed to working on programming assignments.

2.3 Software Engineering Projects
Accordingly, understanding and experiencing the process of software development is vital to software engineering education. Consequently, Problem-Based Learning (PBL) is a popular constructivist approach by which students discover issues and learn about a subject through the process of solving a problem [8]. By working on designing and developing a novel software product, students can follow PBL by exploring and discovering software engineering techniques that help them deliver quality software. Therefore, semester-long team projects are common in software engineering courses to expose students to experiential learning.

However, when software engineering students generate their own ideas for their assignment, their projects are often "thrown away," and never used by real customers nor maintained by a development team beyond the end of the semester. Without the pressure to produce well-designed code that will have a longer lifespan and have to satisfy customers, students' software development experience will not be particularly realistic.

Specifically, Nurkkala and Brandle [19] identify six ways academic software engineering projects differentiate from real, professional projects, including: the lack of a real product, relatively short duration, high personnel turnover, low sophistication of software, no software maintenance, and no customer. They explain that external pressures from customers also help address projects focus on creating a real product.

An emerging remedy to engage students in more realistic projects is to involve them in Free and Open Source Software (FOSS) [1]. FOSS is a model for software development where the product's code is publicly available online and licensed permissively so that anyone can use or modify it. Consequently, people from across the world may contribute to the same project. Meanwhile, others have leveraged the FOSS model to engage students in projects for social good by contributing to humanitarian (HFOSS) software [10].

Nevertheless, FOSS model's strength in gathering remotely distributed collaborators also makes it impractical for applying Agile principles of frequent face-to-face communication. In acknowledging both the advantages and disadvantages of the traditional FOSS model, in Fall 2014, we founded the Chico Open Source Consortium (COSC), an organization to foster collaboration between local software professionals and computer science students on a FOSS project.

Since its inception, COSC has worked on BossyUI [3] each semester and organized weekly face-to-face meetings. Because the team's co-location differs from the traditionally remote-located FOSS model, we distinguish it as a *localized* (LFOSS) model [4]. A previous study found advantages to LFOSS in its ability to adhere more closely to the Agile paradigm and by providing professional networking and employment opportunities for students [5]. Likewise, more direct modes of communication are positively correlated with software developers' perceptions of being held accountable [6].

On the other hand, we previously compared FOSS and LFOSS projects to students working on propriety software sponsored by industry (hereafter referred to as industry for brevity) and self-contained (SE-only) projects. While the vast majority of SE-only projects lacked external clients, we observed that students dedicated more hours [5] outside of class to SE-only projects. While increased hours worked on a project could possibly be attributed to a number of different factors, based on our anecdotal observations, we believe it may be at least partially credited to students' greater motivation.

Others have involved external customers in software engineering projects, such as for service-learning projects [17], but doing so is difficult to scale for large software engineering courses with multiple teams. On the other hand, there is no literature on software engineering projects collaborating with entrepreneurship students to create viable commercial software products.

3. METHOD
3.1 Course Organization & Collaboration
In the Fall, 2016 semester at California State University, Chico, professors from the Computer Science and Management departments planned and implemented a collaboration between students in upper-division courses in their respective programs: Software Engineering and Web Entrepreneurship. The latter course concentrated on acquiring experience and skills for running e-businesses, including: *Lean Startup* methodology; minimum viable products (MVP); customer and market development; web-

based sales and marketing; social media; search engine optimization; and web analytics [7].

Before the semester began, we reached out to the entrepreneurship students to introduce them to the opportunity to collaborate with software engineering students. Those who expressed interest provided a brief questionnaire to describe their project idea, agree to dedicate at least 2 hours per week for interacting with and providing feedback to the software developers, and arrange a time for them to pitch their idea to the software engineering class. In addition, contacts from an industry partner, a local LFOSS collaborative project, and a remote FOSS project (as represented by a student who had interned with active development leads for the project) each pitched their projects.

Likewise, software engineering students with their own entrepreneurial ideas were given the opportunity to pitch their idea to the Web Entrepreneurship class to solicit a (student) client to focus on the business needs of the software product. Before approving any ideas, professors from both departments vetted the projects to make sure they were appropriate for the courses.

All projects that garnered interest from both courses were compiled into a list along with brief descriptions and posted on the learning management system website for students' reference. At the beginning of the second week of class, all software engineering students completed a *pre-project survey,* which included identifying students' top three preferences (in order) for projects. The software engineering professor reviewed student preferences and assigned students to teams according to their preferences, while keeping into account students' schedules and team sizes. As a result, the software engineering students (n=58) were divided into ten teams—one LFOSS (n=7), two industry (n=12), one FOSS (n=6), and six Tech Startup (n=33) teams.

Software engineering students had two, one-hour lectures and two, one-hour labs per week. Lab hours were dedicated to project teamwork where teams began each lab with a scrum (daily standup meeting) and occasionally reported team progress to the professor in a "scrum-of-scrums." Meanwhile, teams coordinated with their respective clients outside of class.

Software engineering lectures covered the Agile paradigm first, but also included learning applicable skills: collaborative version control with Git and GitHub, scrum, test-driven development (TDD), developer operations (DevOps) for continuous integration, software design patterns, and analyzing software quality using software tools and metrics. The team projects accounted for 75% of the course grade while the remaining 25% included assessments of mostly in-class assignments to practice the aforementioned skills.

Software engineering students performed an end-of-term team presentation that demonstrated their product and reported their self-assessment of the software's quality and adherence to Agile. In lieu of a final exam, teams (along with some of their clients) exhibited and discussed their work in a public "tech showcase," where teams set up booths to show their work to the general public. External, impartial judges—recruited by the professors to represent tech and business professionals—rated each group for technical innovation and market viability; prizes (sponsored by local companies) were awarded to the highest-rated teams in each category.

3.2 Evaluation

For formative assessment of the Tech Startup model [7], we evaluated the different categories of projects using a mixed-methods approach. First, we assessed how the Tech Startup model

compared to other forms of project collaborations relative to how they address the six gaps between academic and realistic professional software engineering [19]. Specifically, comparisons were made based on the following needs: real product, long duration, continuity, design/program sophistication, software maintenance, and real customer. We refer to "sophistication" rather than Nurkkala and Brandle's "complexity" to avoid confusion with cyclomatic complexity, the software metric.

Likewise, we compared the Tech Startup model to LFOSS as well as remote FOSS and Industry projects with regards to their compatibility with Agile principles. Specifically, we addressed the needs: iterative development, frequent delivery and feedback, face-to-face communication, business people and developer interaction, and reflective adaptation. We combined both assessments to form a set of criteria for heuristic evaluation.

Separately, we evaluated the execution of the Tech Startup model's pilot semester based on surveys of students' attitudes and experiences. Along with with *pre-project survey* that collected students' project preferences, students also completed the Foss2Serve pre-course instrument [11], a questionnaire with Likert-type items regarding computing and software engineering that has been used by multiple institutions [9] to evaluate students' experiences with FOSS projects. Items exclusive FOSS projects were omitted and any questions that referred to FOSS or HFOSS were reworded to address "software engineering projects" more broadly. The following 5-point (1 "Strongly Disagree" to 5 "Strongly Agree") Likert-type items were included in the instrument specifically to address students' confidence in a breadth of software engineering topics (as adapted for wording):

SE01. I am comfortable that I could participate in the planning and development of a real-world software project;

SE02. I can list the steps in the software process we used in the software engineering project;

SE03. I can use a software process to develop a software engineering project;

SE04. (omitted as HFOSS-specific question)

SE05. I have gained some confidence in collaborating with professionals from a variety of locations and cultures;

SE06. I can describe the impact of project complexity on the approaches used to develop software;

SE07. I can describe the impact of project size on the approaches used to develop software;

SE08. I am confident that I can maintain a software engineering project;

SE09. I can describe the drawbacks and benefits of software engineering to society;

SE10. I can use all tools and techniques employed in my software engineering project;

SE11. I can participate in a software development team's interactions; and

SE12. Participation in a software engineering project has improved my understanding of how to behave like a computing professional.

However, we also wanted to gauge student confidence in applying specific skills taught in lecture as they applied them to software engineering projects. Consequently, we supplemented the questionnaire with the following software engineering skill items:

SK01. I can write automated software tests to verify that the software reliably behaves as was intended;

SK02. I can set up and manage a development environment and development operations (DevOps) tools for collaborating on a software development team;

SK03. I can identify and use software design patterns appropriately;

SK04. I can analyze and evaluate the design of large software projects for strengths and weaknesses

Accordingly, we collected a *post-project survey* that used Foss2Serve's post-semester evaluation instrument along with the supplementary software engineering skill items {SK01...SK04}. To investigate the impact of the students' projects on their confidence in software engineering, we categorized students by project category {Tech Startup, LFOSS, FOSS, Industry} and compared the changes in their responses from *pre-* to *post-project surveys.*

The *post-project survey* also included items for students to report their ratings on their project interactions, as previously used to evaluate FOSS project interaction [5] (5-point Likert-type items, unless otherwise noted with response options in *italics*):

INT01. Outside of lecture and lab, estimate how many hours you spent per week on your project *(free response)*

INT02. I directly communicated with the mentor/customer for my project...
Choose one: {I didn't have a mentor or customer; I had a mentor or customer but only other team members directly communicated with them; Less than once a month; Each month; Each week; Each day}

INT03. My predominant contact with my mentor/customer was...
Choose one: {I didn't have a mentor or customer; I had a mentor or customer but only other team members directly communicated with them; In person; Synchronous communication (Phone, video messaging, instant messaging, etc); Asynchronous communication (Email, bulletin boards, messaging at different times, etc) }

INT04. My mentor/customer was prompt in replying to me

INT05. My mentor/customer's communication was helpful to my progress on the software development project

INT06. My mentor/customer held me accountable to completing my work well and on time

INT07. Interacting with my mentor/customer was valuable for my professional networking

Finally, the students answered two free response questions to provide qualitative feedback: "Explain what was most helpful about working with your mentor/customer" and "Explain what was most difficult about working with your mentor/customer."

Software engineering students received participation credit for completing each survey but their responses were not reviewed until after credit was awarded. As an option to opt-out of including their responses in this research, students were offered an opportunity to write a short essay instead but 100% of students (n=58) consented to include their responses in this research.

4. RESULTS
4.1 Heuristic Evaluation
We have incorporated LFOSS, FOSS, and Industry projects in the Software Engineering course for multiple semesters, since Fall 2014. Meanwhile, each project category continued during the Fall 2016 semester, when we piloted the Tech Startup model in the same course. Based on our each project category's inherent design as well as our observations of them in practice, we evaluated the Tech Startup in comparison to the others according to the software engineering project realism and adherence to Agile paradigm principle criteria outlined in the methods section of this paper.

4.1.1 Real Products and Customers
The Tech Startup model evolved from exclusively software engineering student (SE-only) projects that often had no contact with customers and their software was usually discarded and unused at the end of the semester. Through collaboration with entrepreneurship students, Tech Startup projects are designed to benefit from external stakeholders who focus their attention on the product's market as well as business and end-user needs. Even though these projects begin from scratch like SE-only, the entrepreneurship clients should help steer products with clearer goals of real world use.

LFOSS and FOSS projects have arguably more tangible evidence for having real products and real customers as long as their software is already published and adopted by users. However, the LFOSS project began (in Fall 2014) in a similar manner to Tech Startups, where target customers and products had been identified but the execution was yet to be seen. Likewise, our Industry-mentored projects have always begun with comparable *ideas* for products and customers but no evidence of either until the product has been released. In terms of project realism, though, external pressure from a client to create a real, functional product provides an element of real world realism. In this perspective, each project category is similar but the biggest difference is that Tech Startups have business-minded students as clients while other projects tend to have professional, technology-minded mentors.

4.1.2 Project Duration and Continuity
Real software is not complete within the limited timespan of a semester. Therefore, any project that begins and ends along with the semester lacks that element of realism. FOSS benefits from an open and public design that allows for projects to be continued, even when there is turnover in the development team. Likewise, by leveraging the FOSS model and the momentum of local software professionals carrying the project from semester-to-semester, LFOSS has also demonstrated strength in this dimension. On the other hand, none of the Industry projects we have observed lasted for more than a semester. Granted, the short duration is not inherent to Industry-supervised projects; it has just been the decision of our industry sponsor to change projects each semester.

By its design and dependence on teams comprised entirely of students, continuity of Tech Startup projects may be its biggest challenge. However, we believe the challenge can at least partially addressed by involving entrepreneurship students, who are motivated to gain experience and success with a real startup business. Even if software engineering students become inactive at the end of the semester, we have required their work to be maintained on an online repository, which could then be passed on to new developers who will continue development.

In cases of continuing with an entrepreneurial project despite team member turnover, intellectual property should be addressed to avoid legal repercussions of inadvertent partnerships [16]. In anticipation of this concern, the entrepreneurship professor held an intellectual property workshop for all Tech Startup teams at the beginning of the semester. Dynamic equity sharing, such as the Slicing Pie model, establishes a flexible relationship where different contributions—such as developing a particular feature—earn pre-defined amounts, as agreed upon by the entire team [22]. Consequently, if a contributor leaves a Tech Startup project that continues and later earns revenue, they still receive compensation, as previously agreed upon.

During this preliminary investigation of the Tech Startup model, it would be premature to report on whether it is conducive to project continuation and realistic software duration. However, it is worth noting anecdotally that three of the pilot Tech Startup teams expressed interest in recruiting more developers from the following semester and one team reported (unsolicited) that they plan to legally incorporate the business in the immediate future.

4.1.3 Software Sophistication and Maintenance

Sophistication follows product continuity and maturation. While designing a product from scratch exercises useful software design skills, understanding, maintaining, and extending other programmers' design and implementation is a distinct software engineering skill of its own. Given that software development jobs at established employers (with existing software) probably outnumber those for startup businesses, class projects that begin with pre-existing, sizable software generally expose students to more common real-world experience. FOSS and LFOSS projects again have an advantage in this dimension. However, if Tech Startup projects manage to continue for multiple semesters, the difference in sophistication and maintenance may become trivial for continuing projects of any category.

4.1.4 Agile Iteration

The Agile process of developing in small intervals, delivering and receiving feedback, and adapting to changes is not particularly inherent to FOSS projects. However, from our observations, most active FOSS projects review code via pull requests—submissions of developers' requested software revisions, such as bug patches or addition of new features. Accordingly, those reviewing pull requests usually do not want a laborious task of reviewing a lot of changes at once. Small, iterative pull requests are encouraged and the feedback (as comments or pull request rejections) establishes a sort of *de facto* Agile-like process. However, this iteration usually requires students to be more proactive about seeking feedback from FOSS projects, unless there is a dedicated mentor actively managing students (as we had for our FOSS project). In that regard, LFOSS tends to foster iterative development more naturally since local software professionals mentor the students in person with weekly meetings. Industry projects operate similarly.

By design, Tech Startup projects coordinate Agile iterations via interactions between the software engineering and entrepreneurship students. Since both groups of students are taking classes that guide the process, adhering to Agile should come more naturally. However, by our observations in practice, this may take more hands-on involvement from the instructors because, unlike the other categories, the Tech Startup model does not involve software professional mentors.

4.1.5 Agile Interaction

The Agile paradigm encourages developers and business people to work together daily. Since our students can only be considered "part-time" software engineers given their other school (and other) responsibilities, any sort of expectation of daily work is impractical. However, the Tech Startup model has a distinct advantage over the other categories since the entrepreneurship students serve as the "business people" while interactions in most other projects involve exclusively developers. Frequent, interdisciplinary collaboration of Tech Startups reflect closer adherence to Agile principles. In addition, the experience should also uniquely help those students develop the soft skills to "communicate effectively with [non-technical] vendors and [technical] colleagues alike" [20].

Likewise, the Agile paradigm emphasizes face-to-face communication. While all projects encounter face-to-face communication with other developers within their lab scrums,

only Tech Startup and LFOSS models inherently involve in-person meetings between students and their clients, by design. The analysis of student surveys also shed light into project interactions in practice.

4.2 Survey Analysis

In the *post-project survey*, students identified their predominant form of communication with their client (INT02), which we ranked from 1 (*Asynchronous communication*) to 3 (In Person). To compare ordinal data from the Tech Startup group to those of other groups, we performed Wilcoxon-Mann-Whitney tests and used the Bonferroni method to adjust the critical value (α=.017) to account for multiple one-way tests. Despite the Tech Startup (M=2.38, sd=0.86) design for intended face-to-face communication, many students communicated most often through online messaging and only one team's members unanimously reported face-to-face as the primary method of communication (n=3, M=3.0, sd=0.0). Even so, the Tech Startup group used more direct forms of communication approaching significance (p=.04) than Industry (M=2.0, sd=0.0) and FOSS (p=.12, M=2.0, sd=0.0), while less direct forms on average than LFOSS (p=.06, M=3.0, sd=0.0) approaching significance. For more nuanced understanding of combination of modes of communication, we plan to use survey items that report frequency of use for each level of communication in future studies.

Likewise, we ranked the reported frequency of communication from 1 "*I had a mentor or customer but only other team members directly communicated with them*" to 5 "*Each day*" and compared Tech Startup to other groups using Wilcoxon-Mann-Whitney one-way tests with Bonferroni-corrected critical value (α=.017). Tech Startup (M=3.19, sd=.91) groups reported less frequent communication with their clients than Industry (p<.01, M=4.0, sd=0.0), and LFOSS (p<.017, M=4.0, sd=0.0), while approaching significance in comparison to FOSS (p=.09, M=3.83, sd=0.41).

Next, we compared the impact of the projects on students' confidence in software engineering. Cronbach's alpha finds the internal consistency of a series of item data for and we found that responses to items {SE01…SE12} have good consistency for both pre- (α=.87) and post-project (α=.90) data. Consequently, we calculated *SEall* as an aggregate average for each individual student's general confidence in software engineering and compared the change in scores (ΔSE) from pre- to post-project surveys between project categories. Overall changes were slight, but Tech Startup (M=-0.02 sd=0.41) approached significantly (α=.017) less improvement than Industry (p=.05, M=0.27, sd=0.49), but no difference from FOSS (p=.36, M=0.26, sd=0.41) nor LFOSS (p=.90, M=0.19, sd=0.80).

Similarly, we compared changes in individuals' aggregate average (ΔSK) of software engineering-specific skill confidence {SK01…SK04} since Cronbach's alpha found good internal consistency for pre- (α=.89) and post-project (α=.85) data. Tech Startup (M=0.36, sd=0.79) showed no significant (α=.017) difference from FOSS (M=0.5, sd=0.91), but approached significantly smaller gains than Industry (p=.13, M=0.71, sd=0.93) and LFOSS (p=.10, M=1.04, sd=0.93).

Finally, to examine the relationships between mode of communication and Tech Startup team outcomes {INT04…INT07}, we performed Spearman correlations with adjusted critical value (α=.0125) and found ranked mode directness (INT02, M=2.38, sd=0.86) showed moderately positive correlation (ρ=.53, p<.01) with client feedback promptness; weakly positive correlation (ρ=.39) approaching significance (p=.04) for client feedback helpfulness; weak and insignificant

(ρ=.22, p=.24) correlation with clients holding students accountable; and borderline significant (p=.0144) moderate correlation with gaining professional networking.

5. CONCLUSIONS

Primarily, this paper outlines pedagogical and practical rationales as well as the novelty of adopting the Tech Startup model for learning Agile development in software engineering courses. Our pilot study revealed that while the interdisciplinary design of Tech Startup projects intended to promote Agile-like frequent face-to-face communication between developers and business people, additional mechanisms are necessary to hold students accountable to meeting regularly in-person. We recommend and intend to dedicate time and space specifically for interdisciplinary collaboration to take advantage of face-to-face interactions [6].

In comparison to Industry, FOSS, and LFOSS projects, Tech Startup students performed comparably on some outcomes, but slightly weaker on others. Students' inconsistent adherence to in-person meetings may have influenced these outcomes. However, we also do not take the deficits as an indictment on the Tech Startup model, which is still in its infancy. Stronger outcomes from projects that incorporate mentoring from software professionals should be expected. However, finding active and invested mentors has not been as easy as pairing interdisciplinary teams for the Tech Startup model. Meanwhile, the heuristic evaluation and formative assessment of the Tech Startup model identified ways to address shortcomings in its pilot semester. In the spirit of Agile, adapting the model to address weaknesses in its pilot semester will foster improvements in future implementations and evaluations.

6. REFERENCES

[1] Auer, L., Juntunen, J. and Ojala, P. (2011) "Open Source Project as a Pedagogical Tool in Higher Education," Proc. of the Intern'l Academic MindTrek Conf., ACM, pp. 207-213.

[2] Beck, K., Grenning, J., Martin, R.C., et al. (2001). Principles behind the Agile Manifesto. http://agilemanifesto.org/. Accessed August 2016

[3] BossyUI. https://bossyui.io/ Accessed January 2017.

[4] Buffardi, K., (2015) "Localized Open Source Collaboration in Software Engineering Education." Proc. of IEEE Frontiers in Education

[5] Buffardi, K., (2016) "Localized open source software projects: Exploring realism and motivation." Proc. of IEEE International conference on Computer Science & Education

[6] Buffardi, K., (2017) "Comparing Remote and Co-located Interaction in Free and Open Source Software Engineering Projects." Proc. of conf. on Innovation & technology in computer science education

[7] Buffardi, K., Robb, C., Rahn, D., (2017) "Tech Startups: A Model for Realistic Software Engineering Project Collaboration." The Journal of Computing Sciences in Colleges

[8] Dos Santos, S.C., et al. (2009). "Applying PBL in software engineering education." Software Engineering Education and Training, IEEE

[9] Ellis, H. J., Hislop, G. W., Pulimood, S. M., Morgan, B., & Coleman, B. (2015). "Software Engineering Learning in HFOSS: A Multi-Institutional Study." In Proc. of the 122nd Annual ASEE Conf. and Exhibition, Seattle, WA.

[10] Ellis, H.J.C. and Morelli, R.A. (2008). "Support for Educating Software Engineers Through Humanitarian Open Source Projects." Proc. of the 21st IEEE-CS Conf. on Software Engineering Education and Training Workshop. IEEE Computer Society, Washington, DC, 1-4. DOI= http://dx.doi.org/10.1109/CSEETW.2008.5

[11] Foss2Serve. Evaluation Instruments. http://foss2serve.org/index.php/Evaluation_Instruments. Accessed August 2016.

[12] Fraser, S., Astels, D., Beck, K., et al. (2003). "Discipline and practices of TDD: (test driven development)." Companion of the 18th annual ACM SIGPLAN conference, Anaheim, CA, USA, ACM: 268-270

[13] Google: Our History in Depth. https://www.google.com/about/company/history/ Accessed January 2017.

[14] Henderson, R. (2015). "Industry employment and output projections to 2024." Monthly Lab. Rev. 138: 1.

[15] Kedrosky, P. (2013). The Constant: Companies that Matter. Available at SSRN 2262948.

[16] Litton, J., Patterson, R., & Little, A. (2014) "Business organization legal issues arising from ideas generated by university students." Southern Law Journal. Fall, 24(2) 267-280.

[17] Liu, C., (2005) "Enriching software engineering courses with service-learning projects and the open-source approach." Proc. of the 27th intern'l conf. on Software engineering. ACM, New York, NY, DOI=http://dx.doi.org/10.1145/1062455.1062566

[18] Martin, F., (2006). Toy projects considered harmful. Commun. ACM 49, 7, 113-116. DOI=10.1145/1139922.1139958

[19] Nurkkala, T. and Brandle, S. (2011). "Software studio: teaching professional software engineering." In Proc. of the 42nd ACM technical symposium on Computer science education. ACM, New York, NY, USA, 153-158. DOI=http://dx.doi.org/10.1145/1953163.1953209

[20] Orsted, M. (2000). "Software development engineer in Microsoft. A subjective view of soft skills required. Proc. of the 2000 Intern'l Conference on Software Engineering, IEEE

[21] Phillips, S. (2007). A brief history of Facebook. The Guardian, 25(7).

[22] Rahn, D., Schakett, T., & Tomczyk, D. (2016). "Building an Intellectual Property and Equity Ownership Policy for Entrepreneurship Programs." Journal of Entrepreneurship Education, 19(1), 51-67.

[23] Ries, E. (2009). Minimum viable product: a guide. Startup Lessons Learned.

[24] Sutherland, J, (2004). "Agile Development: Lessons learned from the first Scrum" Scrum Alliance.

[25] Trimi, S., & Berbegal-Mirabent, J. (2012). "Business model innovation in entrepreneurship." International Entrepreneurship and Management Journal, 8(4), 449-465

Student Software Designs at the Undergraduate Midpoint

Lynda Thomas
Department of Comp Science
Aberystwyth University
Aberystwyth, Wales
ltt@aber.ac.uk

Chris Loftus
Department of Comp Science
Aberystwyth University
Aberystwyth, Wales
cwl@aber.ac.uk

Carol Zander
Computing & Software Systems
University of Washington Bothell
Bothell, WA USA
zander@u.washington.edu

Anna Eckerdal
Department of Information Technology
Uppsala University
Uppsala, Sweden
annae@it.uu.se

ABSTRACT

We replicate a study and extend previous research that examined graduating students' achievement and understanding when asked to 'produce a design'. In this paper, we examine software designs produced by students at an earlier stage in their undergraduate studies – the midpoint. We were looking for characteristics of the development of skill at software design as students progress through the curriculum. These students did about as well as graduating students from the same institution in terms of the quality of their software designs, although they failed to produce as many complete designs. In addition to attributes uncovered in previous research, a new design attribute was noticed – meaningful links between static components. We raise the question of where GUI designs fit in the area of software design.

We were also looking for evidence that mastering software design is a Threshold [8] that could be seen in development in this earlier cohort. There was some evidence for this, and the identified design attributes provide an indication of the sub-skills that need to be mastered.

The paper concludes with some implications for the teaching of software design.

Categories and Subject Descriptors

Software and its engineering → Software creation and management → Designing software
Software and its engineering → Software notations and tools → System description languages → Unified Modeling Language (UML) ; Applied computing → Education

Keywords

Software design; Software engineering; Replication; UML; Threshold Concepts; Threshold Skills.

ITiCSE '17, July 03-05, 2017, Bologna, Italy
© 2017 ACM. ISBN 978-1-4503-4704-4/17/07...$15.00
DOI: http://dx.doi.org/10.1145/3059009.3059016

1. INTRODUCTION

As a group, the authors of this paper have an ongoing interest in how students design software. This has evolved over a series of papers. Initially the emphasis was on how successful graduating students are at designing software [4,7]. More recently, the question of students' understanding of what it means to 'produce a design' was examined by looking at the artifacts produced in the designs and determining their attributes [12].

This links to another of the group's interests - Threshold Concepts and Skills [8,10]. We have theorized that being able to produce a software design is a Threshold Skill for computer scientists. That is, that it is a skill that is *troublesome, semi-irreversible* (requires review and practice), *integrative*, and serves to indicate the *boundaries of a field*. There has been some debate about the existence of such Thresholds [11], but we consider that the theory provides a useful structure for understanding student learning. If software design *is* a Threshold skill, it is certainly a big topic, and it would be informative to see if it could be broken down further. By examining students at the midpoint, halfway through their studies, we were looking for possible development of design sub-skill and understanding.

This paper reports on a study that considered these two ideas. It looks at students at the midpoint of their undergraduate computing studies in order to examine the overarching theme: *As students progress through the curriculum, what can be observed about the development of their software design skills?*

In particular we consider the following questions:

- Is there evidence that students at the midpoint of their studies can (or cannot) design in a similar fashion to graduating students?
- Can we confirm the original attributes and/or find additional attributes within these software designs from those discovered in [12] – given a different scenario with different level students at the same institution?

And, in addition:

- Can we see evidence that software design exhibits the characteristics of a Threshold Skill as outlined above [10], and if so
- Can we compare the designs of less advanced students with those of graduating students to observe what sub-skills may be seen to be developing?

2. BACKGROUND

This work builds upon several studies of student software designs. The first, [4], asked the question "Can graduating students design software systems?" The authors of the paper looked at 149 designs for a 'super alarm clock' produced by students nearing graduation in multiple countries and institutions, and found that 62%, "the majority of graduating students cannot design a software system." This was followed by a study that looked at students in one institution designing in groups [7], and using the same 'alarm clock' problem, that confirmed these findings. The authors noted that it was possible that the social dynamics of the groups may have had an effect on the designs submitted, but a positive facet of that work was that students could recognize a good design. The successor of that study [12], looked again at graduating students, who were fairly uniform in their preparation, and using the same problem found more encouraging results. Of the 35 students included in the study, 26 achieved at least a first step toward a reasonable software design. The main emphasis in that work was the examination of the artifacts of the designs in order to discover attributes of student designs.

There have been other studies of software design. In [3], Box examined the variation in approaches that professionals use to do analysis and design. Most of the students looked at in [12] appeared to understand analysis and design as Box's category that produces "artifacts with the intention of showing that analysis/design has taken place". In [1], Boustedt reports on a study of students' understanding of UML class diagrams. Class diagrams were seen as specification of classes, and in a more advanced view, as showing relationships between classes.

Petre, [9], put into question the use of UML by students since its use by actual practicing software engineers was found to be limited. A total of 35 out of the 50 she surveyed did not use it. Of the ones who did, use was selective '..a number of informants in this group remarked that they had studied and used UML within formal education. One informant, who summarized that "UML does things we already had ways of doing. The notation doesn't really matter" '. As Petre points out, however, students typically don't already have "… a repertoire [of techniques]. …One might conjecture that UML is effective in software engineering education, because of what it captures, and where it directs attention, rather than as a prescription for design actions."

3. METHODOLOGY
3.1 Data Collection
We collected data in a class of students who were exactly halfway through their undergraduate 3-year computing degree, and who had been studying an intense and fairly uniform computing curriculum including courses on Java programming, software design, database, and data structures[1]. In their first year, the students had been introduced to UML diagrams: use case, class, object, and sequence. In addition, they had looked at software development methodologies with an emphasis on the waterfall method. In their second year, they were in the process of studying more advanced data structures and design patterns and had just finished the 'coding week' of a group software engineering project that required documentary evidence of design such as user interaction diagrams, a deployment diagram,

class diagrams, and sequence diagrams. In all modules, students are expected to document their software projects with formal UML notation for requirements, classes, and behaviour.

In the first lecture of the second semester, the students were asked to 'produce a design' (see Figure 1). A different problem was used from that in previous research [4,7,12] because the 'super alarm-clock' was deemed to be dated, but we used a problem that appeared to require about the same level of design skill. The students were told that, while they could submit their design anonymously if they wished, if they included their email address they would be given feedback. Students were given about 50 minutes to produce their design. All students finished before the time was up.

There were 161 students registered for the module; only 107 attended this ungraded activity (which took place at 9am on a Monday morning) and we only collected 96 designs. It is estimated that about 20 students were in the process of withdrawal from the degree. This still leaves more than 30 students who did not do the exercise, and, in addition there were 11 students who took their designs home with them. We guess these students were weak, but we have no evidence of that. At a later date, for comparison, we collected a design from a non-computer scientist.

The task: The Parking Garage - You are asked to produce a design for the software system that runs a parking garage. Drivers will have a mobile app that allows them to register the license plate, and whether the car is compact and/or qualifies for disabled parking. The system should then inform the user whether there is a space and direct them to it. When the user returns to the garage they will be told how much to pay and be reminded where their car is.

Alternatively, drivers can drop off their car at the front door and give their car to a garage employee. In that case, the employee uses the same mobile app to enter the relevant information. In addition to finding a space as outlined above, the garage employees are allowed to 'roam' the garage and find an empty parking space: they enter the spot's ID into the system, check its availability, and if it is free register that they have occupied the space. They are also able to indicate that the customer has arrived back and requested their car and that they have gone to get it; and then that it has been delivered to the customer and parking paid for.

You only have 50 minutes, so produce the best design that you can in this amount of time – you are producing an initial solution that someone (not necessarily you) could work from. Include as many artefacts (for example, list of classes, object diagrams, class diagrams, sequence diagrams, use-case diagrams, flowcharts, user-interface design, pseudocode etc.) as needed, and as time permits, so someone could fill in the details for your design and implement it.

Figure 1: The problem that students were asked to design

3.2 Data Analysis
The analysis was done in several phases. To gain familiarity with the data, we read the designs individually and in groups. Using software engineering concepts and influenced by previous studies, we created a spreadsheet that tagged the artifacts used (for example, use case diagram, GUI, class diagram, etc.).

---

[1] This was possible due to the nature of the degree organisation in the UK in general and this institution in particular.

There were two parts to the analysis – one in which the designs were compared to the categories determined, using inductive content analysis, from the initial study of graduating seniors, [4] (nicknamed the 'Skumtomte' categories). The designs were initially examined by two researchers independently, using deductive content analysis to place in the categories. Then the researchers resolved discrepancies by discussion. Representatives of each category were then given to the other two researchers for verification. See Section 4.1 for results.

In addition, we were seeking to gain an understanding of what it means to students to be asked to 'produce a design' by using the designs that students produce as our raw data, as was done in [12] where we were primarily interested in artifacts produced. This analysis was also a time-consuming iterative process of reading and comparing the designs, seeking to elicit attributes that differentiated the various ways students understood producing a design. The findings of [12] influenced us to some extent, but we approached the analysis with open minds looking for new as well as previously identified attributes. We eventually reached consensus and confirmed the previous result, while also discovering further refinements (see Section 4.2).

4. RESULTS

4.1 'Skumtomte' categories[2]

We examined these midpoint student designs using the categories developed in our first study of graduating seniors [4], the 'Skumtomte' categories. We then compared the results of the analysis of the present data with the results obtained from the group of graduating students from the same institution [12]. We had to add a category 'unknown' since students were allowed to simply remove their designs from the study. We could assume that such designs were weak but have no evidence. The distribution, seen in Figure 2, was in line with the previous study, particularly for the first three categories. Unsurprisingly, the graduating students produced more partial and complete designs. This is discussed further in Section 5.

In terms of what the current designs contained, we noted that no design included an overall architecture diagram. These were present in a few of the graduating students' designs. Otherwise, they contained the same type of artifacts, with more GUIs than the graduating students' designs, however.

Artifacts that students produced in this study were mapped to the Skumtomte categories, typically as follows:

- Restatement: Use case diagrams or re-writing the problem statement or restating as an unadorned graphical user interface (GUIs). We discuss GUIs in Section 4.3.
- Skumtomte[1]: One or more UML diagrams or other diagrams that make little sense from a design viewpoint.
- First step: A single class diagram that might or might not have internal static links, or a single sequence diagram or flow chart.
- Partial: Several design diagrams such as a class diagram and sequence diagram, or a class diagram and database table. However, these were not linked.
- Complete: Has linked static and dynamic elements, such as a class diagram, a sequence diagram and associated design-related text. Ready for implementation.

---

[2] 'Skumtomte' is a Swedish word which refers to a pink-and-white marshmallow Santa Claus, a traditional Christmas confection – it appears substantial, but is only colored marshmallow fluff.

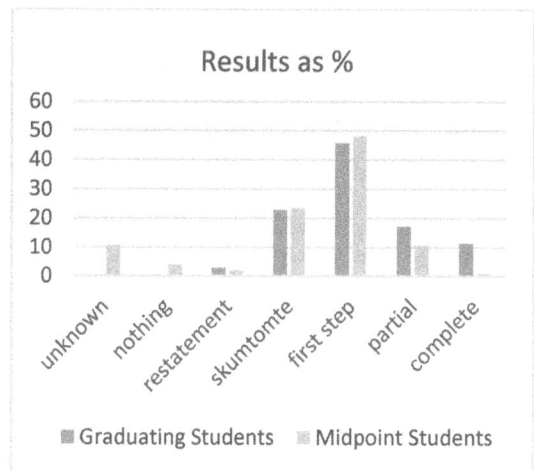

Figure 2: Comparison of midpoint and graduating students at the same university of [12] using 'Skumtomte' categories

4.2 Design Attributes Found

In the previous study of graduating studentss at the same institution, [12], we noted that some students produced very little, and used no formal notation. Some students used *formal notation* such as a use case diagram, adding almost nothing to the problem statement, and no more. At the next level were designs that exhibited *structural decomposition*, i.e., static information in the form of class diagrams, although often the diagrams were non-standard. Stronger designs showed *dynamic information* in addition to the static relationships. Here also, many diagrams were non-standard. The strongest designs expressed *both* structural components alongside some dynamic behaviour using notations like sequence diagrams or flowcharts, and the static and dynamic were *linked*.

In the current analysis, we found designs exhibiting the same characteristics. In addition, we identified that many designs showed *meaningful links between the static components* (inheritance, association etc. although often expressed non-standardly). Others did not – the static components were either not linked at all, or lines that appeared to have no meaning were drawn between all components. The meaningful links were included in some designs that had only static information (see Figure 4) and also in some of those that also included dynamic information. In the strongest designs, we saw that students related static and dynamic and also showed meaningful links between static components (for example Figure 5).

4.3 GUIs and GUI-based design

One of the most challenging aspects of the analysis was the consideration of GUIs. When students handed in a design like that of Figure 3, was that evidence that they understood decomposition in a static or dynamic sense? In some sense, the arrows could be said to represent behaviour, but what do the screens indicate that the original requirements do not, and how are these designs different from those that might be completed by a non-computer scientist? To check, we gave the problem to a non-computer scientist who produced just this kind of design. In fact it is a fragment of her design that we show in Figure 3.

In the area of Threshold concepts, researchers discuss the 'boundaries' of the field [8]. If a design such as that in Figure 3 can be created by a non-computer scientist, then a purely GUI design (with no software at all indicated) was considered to be outside the boundaries of computing.

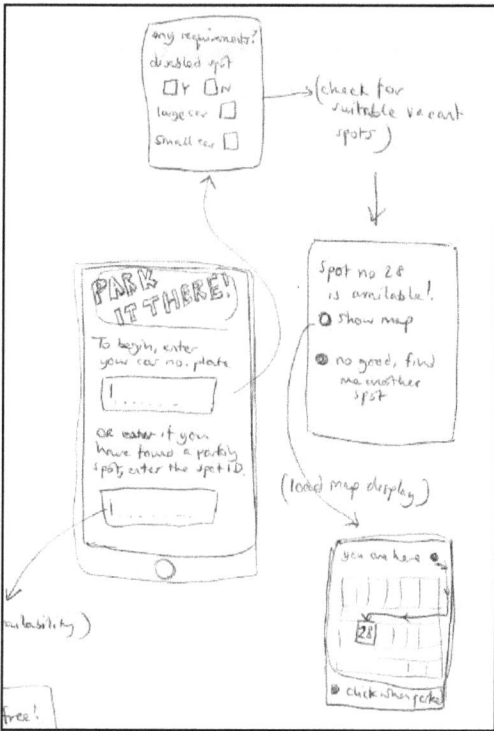

Figure 3: An informal design (no formal notation) by a non-Computer Scientist

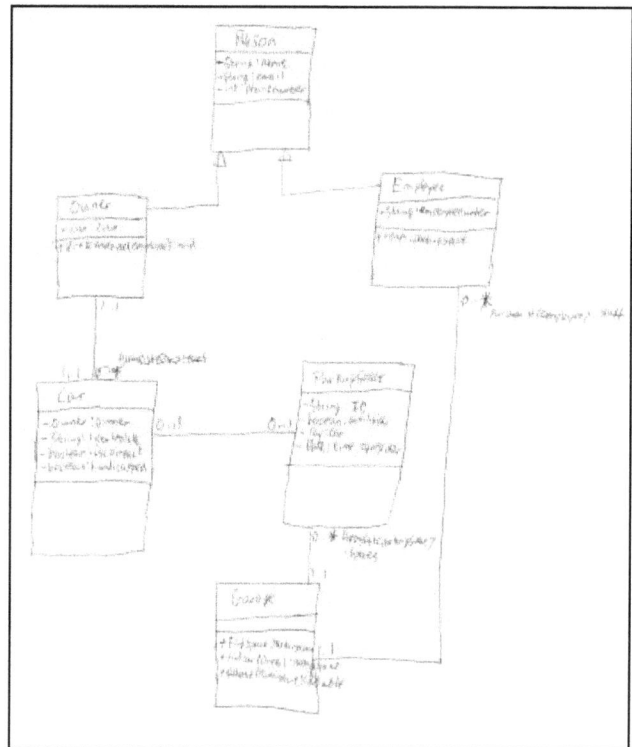

Figure 4: An example exhibiting an understanding of meaningful links in static relationships

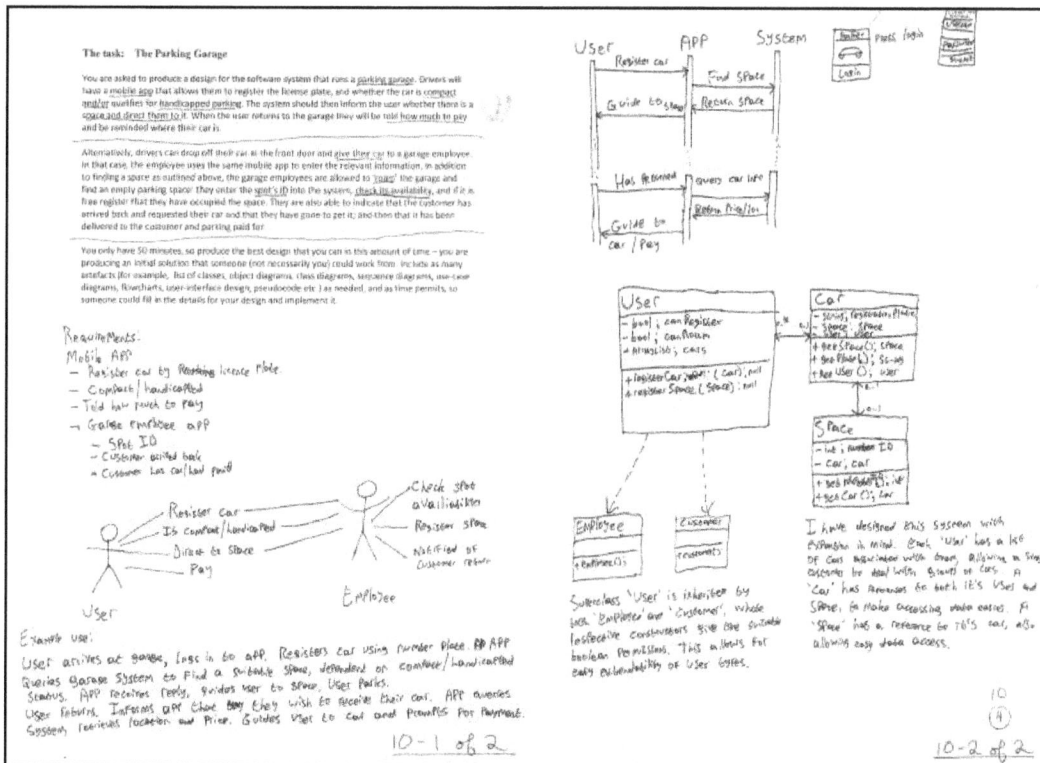

Figure 5: A design that exhibits static and dynamic information and relationship between the two (plus a very sketchy GUI)

That said, even just considering GUIs, different levels of understanding were exhibited. The design in Figure 3 was at the highest level in a hierarchy (from exhibiting *least* understanding to *most*):

- superficial understanding – a single screen with boxes for data entry;
- multiple screens but no sense of movement between them;
- separate screens which express movement between them based on clicking buttons;
- separate screens which express movement between them and also indicate different users;

Given that different levels of understanding exist even at the GUI level, while we stand by our contention that computing students should produce designs that include software, we recognize that the whole area of GUI design requires further consideration.

4.4 Trustworthiness of the research

In this study we used a different problem from that used in previous work. This was necessary because the 'super alarm clock' used in [4,7,12] was too dated to use, but it means that comparisons such as that of Figure 2 are somewhat problematic. On the other hand, the kinds of understanding demonstrated and the artifacts submitted are very similar to those previously noted.

In terms of the dependability of the comparison in Figure 2, we note that there was overlap in evaluators between the two studies. Moreover, inter-rater consensus was established. We believe that our analysis is less suspect than the standard marking of designs that Computer educators complete as routine.

It is likely that the weakest students did not complete, or did not hand in, the exercise, skewing the results. A couple of students wrote negative things on their designs. This may be an indication that they did not try. One wrote "I learnt nothing from this", but even that student seemed to have made a reasonable attempt. These issues are discussed further in the next section.

5. DISCUSSION

In this section we go on to discuss the research questions, but first we must note that in some ways the most worrying result of this study resides in the data collection statistics. There were 161 students registered for the module; it is estimated that about 20 students were in the process of withdrawal from the degree. More than 30 students missed the session, and there were 11 students who took their designs home with them. Five students submitted blank papers.

Some of the 30 students may be perfectly competent software designers who just slept in. Some of the 11 students who took designs home may have just been shy about submitting good designs! But we worry that about 1/3 of the students registered for this module are likely to be very weak at software design. This is a result that needs further examination.

In relation to the overarching question: *As students progress through the curriculum, what can be observed about the development of their software design skills?* Apart from the fact that more Graduating students linked static and dynamic components, we were unable to see specific sub-skills that existed in the Graduating students, but not in these midpoint students. We were, however, able to gain deeper understanding of student design in relation to the specific research questions.

5.1 Research questions

The first two research questions related to previous work:

- Is there evidence that students at the midpoint of their studies can (or cannot) design in a similar fashion to graduating students?
- Can we confirm the original attributes and/or find additional attributes within these software designs from those discovered in [12] – given a different scenario with different level students at the same institution?

The most significant finding here, which can be seen in Figure 2, is the similarity in the distributions of the two cohorts at the same university (from [12] and this work): the majority of the designs from both cohorts were in the categories *first step*, followed by *skumtomte* (includes little more than a restatement). The graduating students produced a few more *partial* and *complete* designs, but the numbers were relatively low.

One way of looking at this is encouraging, in that as many graduating students exhibited a basic level of design expertise, and more produced better designs. This suggests that students improve between the half way and the final point of their studies, and that a basic level of expertise is not fragile - graduating students are still able to continue to access it. However, less positively, the improvement was minimal. It appears that many students reach a basic level of design capability and no more. Since the groups of students were different, a longitudinal study is needed to confirm this.

The second question related to the characteristics of the software designs. The designs of the midpoint students, who were at an earlier level of their studies and were completing a different problem, exhibited broadly the same attributes as noted in [12]. In addition, a further characteristic of good student design was noted- meaningful links between static components. (These may have been present in [12] but not noted). Designs that exhibit this occurred both with and without behavioural information.

The other two research questions related to Threshold Skills:

- Can we see evidence that software design exhibits the characteristics of a Threshold Skill as outlined above [10], and if so
- Can we compare the designs of less advanced students with those of graduating students to observe what sub-skills may be seen to be developing?

This study has taken us only a little way in answering the first of these questions. We already knew that software design was *troublesome*. In this study we saw students who failed to understand the *boundaries of the field* and turned in designs that were 'non-computer-science-like'. In terms of *semi-irreversibility*, it appears that the graduating students were at least at the same level of competence, as students at the midpoint. The students had just been practicing the production of software design artifacts, but students continue to practice design skills throughout their education. One could only really evaluate the influence of practice if students were removed from any design activity for several years before reassessing.

The last question relates to an attempt to break down the large skill – 'produce a software design' – into smaller sub-skills. We wondered if it would be possible to identify sub-skills which needed to be gained in order to gain complete mastery. In a sense, that is what the identified design attributes represent. The previous attributes were confirmed, with the identification of the need for meaningful links as a new observation from this study.

5.2 Teaching Implications

The majority of students whom we examined still have a long way to go to create complete software designs. This is in line with previous research - in [5], Hu also presents an assessment of second-year students' software design abilities and reaches the same conclusion. He suggests broad ways to improve teaching design, such as using test-driven development and design-in-the-small, and those techniques may be helpful.

Our analysis concentrated more specifically on specific attributes of student software designs. These aspects of design should be emphasized in teaching and practice and are those identified in Section 4.2.

There is a **formal language** of computing. As educators, we can help students to understand this. For example, using a GUI such as the one given by the non-Computer Scientist as a comparison can help students to distinguish between informal and formal notation in software design.

A good design should describe **static decomposition, with meaningful links** between the components. Many introductory programming textbooks show examples of simple class diagrams, and in our experience students grasp these quite readily. But students also need to be exposed to interaction between objects of different classes (this is also noted in [2]). Asking students what the lines between the components in designs *mean* should help focus on these ideas. While software engineering texts include larger problems, they are beyond beginning students, so more intermediate problems are needed.

A good design should also describe the **behaviour** of the system in question. Behaviour appears to be the most difficult step in software design for most students. Students generally understand that software *does* something, but have a hard time showing this formally. To focus on behaviour, students can be given extensive static designs and asked to add behaviour or asked to role play systems in operation. In [6], Kurkovsky shows the effectiveness of using LEGO Serious Play by "creating tangible objects". This 'play' in tandem with traditional software design notation may help more students understand the place of behaviour in software design. Further work needs to be undertaken in this area.

For a more complete discussion, from a phenomenographic viewpoint, of improving teaching by using patterns of variation on identified attributes. see [12].

6. CONCLUSIONS AND FUTURE WORK

This study tells us again that things are not as bad in the area of students' design skills as first thought in [4]. We have replicated our previous research and these students (who had a fairly uniform preparation) performed better than those in [4]. In fact, the students who handed in the exercise performed comparably to those in [12]. However, the students who skipped the session, or who took their designs, or who wrote nothing are a worrying indication that some students are not developing software design skill as we hope.

We were able to confirm the student understanding of 'produce a design', while noting a further attribute – that some students understand the need to have meaningful links between static components. Furthermore, the study has cast some light on the use of GUIs within software design and highlighted the need for more investigation. For example, can we distinguish between truly informal GUIs and those that exhibit human computer interaction principles, the latter showing computer science skill?

There was some evidence that software design is a Threshold skill, and the identified attributes of the student designs indicate sub-skills that develop with time and experience. Further work needs to be done in order to test students longitudinally. None of our studies have interviewed students to obtain more nuanced information on design skills. Such interviews associated with a design exercise would provide valuable insight into the thought processes involved during the exercise.

Finally, we provide some teaching implications of this research, including an emphasis on ways of helping students understand behaviour in a software design.

7. ACKNOWLEDGEMENTS

The authors which to thank the students of Aberystwyth University's Software Development Lifecycle module 2014-15 and Saoirse Morgan for their participation. An initial hierarchy of GUIs was produced by Kate Sanders – thank you!

REFERENCES

[1] J. Boustedt. 2014. Students' different understandings of class diagrams. *Computer Science Education*, 22(1), 29-62.

[2] J. Börstler, M. S. Hall, M. Nordström, J. H. Paterson, K. Sanders, C. Schulte, and L. Thomas. 2010. An evaluation of object oriented example programs in introductory programming textbooks. *SIGCSE Bull.* 41, 4 (January 2010), 126-143.

[3] I. Box. 2009. Toward an understanding of the variation in approaches to analysis and design. *Computer Science Education*, 19(2), 93-109.

[4] A. Eckerdal, R. McCartney, J. E. Mostrom, M. Ratcliffe, and C. Zander. 2006. Categorizing student software designs: Methods, results, and implications. *Computer Science Education*, 16(3):197-209.

[5] C. Hu. 2016. Can Students Design Software?: The Answer Is More Complex Than You Think. In *Proc. SIGCSE '16*. ACM, New York, NY, USA, 199-204

[6] S. Kurkovsky. 2015. Teaching Software Engineering with LEGO Serious Play. In *Proc. ITiCSE'15*. ACM, New York, USA, 213-218.

[7] C. Loftus, L. Thomas, and C. Zander. 2011. Can graduating students design: Revisited. In *Proc. SIGCSE '11*, ACM, New York, NY, USA, 105-110.

[8] J.H.F. Meyer, and R. Land, 2003. Threshold concepts and troublesome knowledge: linkages to ways of thinking and practising, In: Rust, C. (ed.), *Improving Student Learning - Theory and Practice Ten Years On.* Oxford: Oxford Centre for Staff and Learning Development (OCSLD), 412-424.

[9] M. Petre. 2013. UML in practice. In *Proc. ICSE 2013*. 722-731, San Francisco, CA, USA.

[10] K. Sanders, J. Boustedt, A. Eckerdal, R. McCartney, J.E. Mostrom, L. Thomas, and C. Zander. 2012. Threshold concepts and Threshold skills in computing. In *Proc. ICER '12*. ACM. New York, NY, USA, 23-30.

[11] D. Shinners-Kennedy and S. A. Fincher. 2013. Identifying threshold concepts: from dead end to a new direction. In *Proc. ICER '13*. ACM, New York, NY, USA, 9-18.

[12] L. Thomas, A. Eckerdal, R. McCartney, J.E. Mostrom, K. Sanders, and C. Zander. 2014. Graduating students' designs: through a phenomenographic lens. In *Proc. ICER '14*. ACM, New York, NY, USA, 91-9.

Initial Experiences with a CS + Law Introduction to Computer Science (CS 1)

Robert H. Sloan
Dept. of Computer Science
University of Illinois at Chicago
sloan@uic.edu

Cynthia Taylor
Dept. of Computer Science
University of Illinois at Chicago
cynthiat@uic.edu

Richard Warner
IIT Chicago-Kent College of Law
rwarner@kentlaw.iit.edu

ABSTRACT

We present the curriculum, pilot offering, and initial evaluation of a CS + Law based CS 1 course that was team taught by a Computer Science professor and a law school professor. Relevant legal topics were interwoven through the course. The results from this initial offering suggest that this sort of highly interdisciplinary offering can be successful both in computing education and in making students realize the relevance of Computer Science to the broader world beyond IT.

Keywords

CS + X; Contextualized CS; CS 1; CS + Law

1. INTRODUCTION AND MOTIVATION

Should the FBI be able to force Apple to circumvent the cryptography on an iPhone? Should any government be able to force decryption by any computing company? What rights to use copyrighted digital media do students, professors, and the public have? Did Russia attempt to influence the 2016 US Presidential election by hacking the US Democratic party? Questions at the boundary of Computer Science and Law have never been more pertinent than they are right now.

Within Computer Science education, there has been growing interest in CS + X approaches. Two of the US's largest and most well known CS departments, Stanford and University of Illinois at Urbana Champaign, have introduced a whole series of CS + X majors ranging from CS + Anthropology to CS + Spanish [11,13].

There have also been several CS + X versions of CS 1 introduced. Guzdial's Media Computation course is at least implicitly a CS + X approach [5,6], and Harvey Mudd's CS 5 Green [4] is explicitly a CS + Biology CS 1. However, there have been very few who have looked at the intersection of *law* and Computer Science (outside of narrow coverage in a Computer Ethics class or a Computer Ethics unit of a senior design course), and as far as we know, none who have looked

ITiCSE '17 July 03-05, 2017, Bologna, Italy

© 2017 ACM. ISBN 978-1-4503-4704-4/17/07...$15.00

DOI: http://dx.doi.org/10.1145/3059009.3059029

at CS + Law in the context of an introduction to Computer Science.

We report here on our initial experiences with a CS + Law CS 1 course after its first offering, and give student-generated evidence of its strong and weak points. This course covered as much *computing* material as our other sections of CS 1, but not precisely the *same* material. In particular, there was significant coverage of data analytics, and only light coverage of object orientation and no coverage of recursion. The complete curriculum and materials are available at https://www.cs.uic.edu/CS111Law. The CS + Law section of CS 1 was one of three sections of CS 1 offered in Fall 2016; all three are treated simply as different sections of "CS 1 for CS majors and other interested students."

Some key findings on this course's first offering include:

- On the overlapping Computer Science material, students in the CS + Law section performed roughly as well, and in some cases better, as students in our other two sections (based on common final exam questions).
- The CS + Law section drew a *much* higher percentage students from majors outside of Computer Science or Engineering than our other two sections of CS 1.
- The CS + Law section drew a mildly lower percentage of women than our other two sections of CS 1.
- In a post-course survey, students in the CS + Law section were more likely to respond positively to the statement, "I understand how the material covered in this course relates to society".

2. CS + LAW BACKGROUND

There are longstanding deep connections between law and technology. Patents are explicitly mentioned in the US Constitution, and the first US patent law was enacted by the first Congress in 1790. Today there are several dozen strong journals of law and technology. A bibliography of books written in the past ten years about the intersection of legal and highly technical computing issues in intellectual property, computer security, cryptography, privacy, computer crime, net neutrality, use of data analytics for policing, etc., would surely run to many thousands of titles.

2.1 Why CS + Law is a Good Idea

A law-themed CS course meets two needs. First, the twenty-first century economy needs most, perhaps even all, college educated workers and citizens to know something of college-level CS. Second, addressing critical ethical and public policy questions requires input from people who understand CS and the related ethical, social, and political questions.

A law-themed course introduces students to both CS and policy issues in a natural and forceful way in the very first CS course.

Almost every CS program says (and generally means) that it wants its students to consider such policy issues very seriously, but it is often difficult to work them into the curriculum any way except with a dedicated course. Not only are some programs reluctant to dedicate a whole course to ethical, social, and public policy issues, but also a separate course isolates those issues from the arts of problem solving and coding. In a law-themed course in contrast, students write and then discuss code that raises public policy questions. This brings the issues alive in a way that can be difficult to do in a separate course.

Bringing the issues alive in this way should make the CS 1 course appealing to a more diverse group of students. Many students enter college with at least some interest in the law as it applies to technology-focused public policy issues, but US law degree is a post-graduate professional degree. At most schools, there are one or two undergraduate courses in Political Science that truly truly cover substantive legal topics. A law-themed CS 1 can draw in majors and prospective majors in Communications, Criminology, Political Science, Management, and Public Health, some pre-law, and some not. It will be doubly useful to them because it provides *two* useful lenses through which to view the world. Just as "[c]omputation is widely accepted as a lens for looking at the world" [3], so too law is a useful lens for looking at public policy questions in general, and public policy questions in electronic security and privacy in particular.

The broader appeal should make CS more welcoming to women. Law school students have been close to gender balanced for decades now. Total US law school enrollment has been at least 40 percent female since the 1985–1986 school year, and has been consistently running between 45 and 49 percent female since 1997–1998 [1]. Fewer women than expected may have enrolled in the Law section because was only added to the course offerings in the Summer, which limited advertising to pre-law students.

3. CURRICULUM

The setting for this curricular experiment is the University of Illinois at Chicago, a large, diverse, public research university. During Fall 2016, we offered three sections of our CS 1 course: The law-focused section, a new biology-focused section inspired by Harvey Mudd's CS 5 Green [4], and a section using media computation that previously had been our only offering of CS 1. Our CS 1 targets Computer Science majors but is open to all; our school also offers other introductory CS courses that are strictly for non-CS majors. For this pilot offering, the law section was capped at 45 students; the new biology section had around 30 students; the media computation section had 160 students. All three sections had the same structure: Two 75 minute lectures a week, and one weekly 50-minute closed lab. All three sections used Python and made some use of peer instruction [2, 7, 9, 10]. The CS + Law section made heavy use of peer instruction.

There is no textbook that covers the precise blend of problem solving, Python programming, and data science that we wanted to cover, much less one with examples coming from law. We used substantial portions of the open source online textbook *How To Think Like A Computer Scientist* [8], and a host of ad hoc materials for other bits and pieces of com-

topics	Law	CS	Highlights student HW
wks 1-3	4th Am. Search 5th Am. & govt. compulsion of disclosure	functions, variables, data, strings, debugging	Build two historically important cryptosystems
wks 4-6	Open Access, Web Crawlers and Open Access	program design, loops, lists intro	find and print all links on a web page
wks 7-9	Supreme Court Data Analytics Use in the Law	complexly nested control structures Pandas module and data science	Analysis of Justices' voting from Wash U Supreme Court Database
wks 10-12	Copyright Computer Fraud and Abuse Act (CFAA)	modules more generally more on lists abstraction, hierarchical decomposition	Complete Web Crawler
wks 13-15	Predictive Policing, its pros and cons surveillance in 21st century	basic graph theory network analysis Python modules for network analysis	network analysis of real data geolocated crime prediction (real data)

Figure 1: Summary of syllabus, law and computational topics, and a sample of student assignments.

puting not covered in that text and for all the legal content.

For this pilot offering, we wanted to make sure that the legal material was treated as a first-class citizen. Therefore, the course was team taught by a Computer Science professor and a law school professor, who each have some very basic knowledge of the other's discipline. In the first week or two of the course legal material took up almost as much time as computing material; thereafter legal material took up roughly 20 to 30 percent of class time.

Most weeks the closed lab consisted of a simple three question multiple-choice quiz followed by some simple programming task that perhaps half of the students would finish in the lab. There were eight longer out-of-lab homework assignments; most built on top of one of the labs.

Figure 1 presents an overview of our syllabus, broken up into five modules, together with a small sample of the lab and homework assignments.

3.1 Combining Law with CS

Our primary goal was to teach a CS 1 oriented around creative problem solving, and a sampling of legal topics with connections to computing. There were no legal topics that we "had" to cover, except that, as we discuss in Section 3.2, we wanted to include some data science partially because of the law theme and partially because we believe it is a very important contemporary computing topic.

Three assignments combining law and CS were particularly successful. First, early in the course, after an introduction to strings, students had to write a Caesar and a Vigenère cipher. The related law discussion concerned Fourth Amendment protections against government searches and Fifth Amendment protections against government demands for encryption keys. Both discussions can easily enter legal thickets of interest primarily to legal experts, but the assignment tied the discussion to students' work, and that gave the discussion a very useful concreteness. In this way, the assignment illustrated early on how the law and coding themes go together.

Those two cryptosystems are lovely assignments for several weeks into any Python-based based CS 1 that chooses to start with strings. The Vigenère cipher is built on top of the Caesar cipher in a moderately complex way that makes an excellent example of building more complicated functions out of simpler ones. In general, we believe that assignments that produce actual working software that can do something real (though not necessarily at scale or in a 21st century way), such as matching encrypt and decrypt functions, are particularly appealing to students.

The second assignment was to write a web crawler that harvested email addresses. The task is a complex one for a CS 1 targeting both majors and non-majors. We covered a bit of the material right after the cryptosystems, and then spread the remainder over a few weeks in the second half of the course. This provided a unifying theme and gave ample time to discuss the related legal issues of unauthorized access under the Computer Fraud and Abuse Act (CFAA) and copyright violations. We were discussing these issues while students wrote code that could potentially be used to commit both CFAA violations and copyright violations. (We cautioned students to use that crawler *only* on the test website we specially constructed for them). The class discussion around the issues owas particularly robust.

The third assignment concerned data analysis using the Supreme Court database (http://scdb.wustl.edu/). We introduced the Pandas module (http://pandas.pydata.org/), which provides R-style ability to analyze very large dataframes in Python, for this purpose. Data analysis is rapidly growing in importance and acceptance in the legal world, so the assignment showed students they had acquired skills that they could put to real world use, and it underscored the connection of technological choices and public policy issues.

The mix of law and computer science underscored and illustrated the importance of each topic and made the teaching experience particularly satisfying.

3.2 (Other) Differences from a Classic CS 1

We made a deliberate decision to introduce some elements of beginning data science into our course. Data science is a field of growing importance, with strong roots in computer science, so it is, in our opinion, a natural fit in any CS 1 course. Additionally, data science is of interest to a growing minority of practicing lawyers—it seemed right to introduce our students to a tool that the most tech-oriented lawyers will use. Finally, data science is really impressive to beginning students, in that they are able to read in a data set with a million rows and dozens of columns and process it on their laptops. Seeing a data set that Excel can open only after 5 minutes, if at all, be read in by a Python program using the Pandas module in 5 seconds is a very forceful lesson about the power of being able to code, instead of always having to rely on other people's code. We also believe it is really powerful to work with real data in a first course, instead of "toy" data.

We had a total of three assignments that were heavily or exclusively data science. One was the analysis of the Supreme Court database. A second was a module on predictive policing. Students used a very large, real-world database of urban crime and made their own predictions based on it. A third was a classic (very simple) network analysis.

There were trade-offs in what we covered. The network analysis meant we had to introduce basic ideas of graph theory. Of course presenting legal material took up some of

the course's time that would be spent on problem solving and coding in a traditional CS 1 course. We did not cover recursion at all, and we did not cover the design of classes at all, and touched on object orientation only lightly in terms of using methods from built-in classes such as strings. However, research by Tew et al. suggest that even when exposed to different material in CS 1, students' knowledge of introductory topics is likely to converge after completing the same CS 2 course [12].

Additionally, our evaluation, discussed in the next section, showed that students found our section to be considerably more work than the other sections of CS 1. As a result, we may have to reduce the total amount of material we give to students in future offerings of this course.

4. EVALUATION

As mentioned, during Fall 2016, we offered three sections of our CS 1 course: The law-focused section, a new biology-focused section, and a section using media computation that previously had been our only offering of CS 1.

We surveyed students in all three courses before and after the course, and had five identical common short questions across all three final exams, and one similar in spirit, different in details, longer coding question across all three final exams. We also had access to the regular end-of-term course evaluations for our law-focused section, and demographic information for all three courses.

4.1 Student Learning

We asked five identical multiple-choice questions on all three sections' final exams: three on control structures, and two on function calls and parameters. The students in the CS + Law section did significantly better over all, averaging 77 percent correct responses to the five questions, versus 61 and 62 percent correct in the other two sections.

We also asked one broadly similar coding question on all the sections' final exams. It asked students to produce a weighted sum of two sequences, with some sort of limiting rule of the form, "If the weighted sum is greater than x in absolute value, use x with the appropriate sign as the value." For the law section, this was posed as two hash tables with the same set of keys, and the values being different indicators for predictive policing. For this question, students in the law section performed the worst, earning on average 61 percent of the points, versus 71 percent in both of the other sections.

A tentative conclusion would be that the CS + Law section was at least as effective as the other sections in teaching Computer Science concepts, but because the CS + Law section had students spending a fair amount of time on data science explorations, time taken from programming, that students were somewhat weaker at writing code.

4.2 Student Comments

Students generally found the instructional approach worthwhile. Here is a selection of comments in response to "Please comment on specific characteristics of the course that were most beneficial to you" in our institution's regular post-course course evaluation:

- "Understanding of Python in an exciting way."
- "It was a good use of Python, and it was interesting in building a web crawler."
- "It was interesting to see real world data implemented with the course assignments'."

Table 1: Ethnicity, gender, and CS major data in percentages, compared to two other Fall 2016 sections of CS 1, and the Fall 2015 single CS 1 (media computation) section.

	Law	Media	Bio	Fall 15
Asian	31	30	29	39
Black	4	6	11	6
Hispanic	20	22	30	15
International	2	5	11	6
Multiracial	7	2	4	2
White (non-Hispanic)	33	34	15	30
Female	18	22	22	25
Male	82	78	78	75
CS Majors	53	87	74	NA

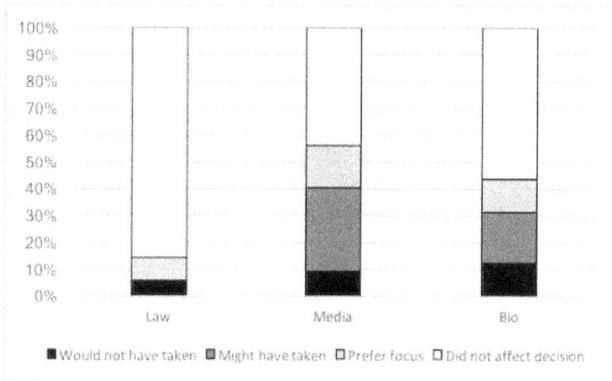

Figure 3: Responses to the statement "I plan to major in Computer Science", before and after taking the course. "-Pre" indicates responses from the pre-course survey, and "-Post" indicates responses from the post-course survey.

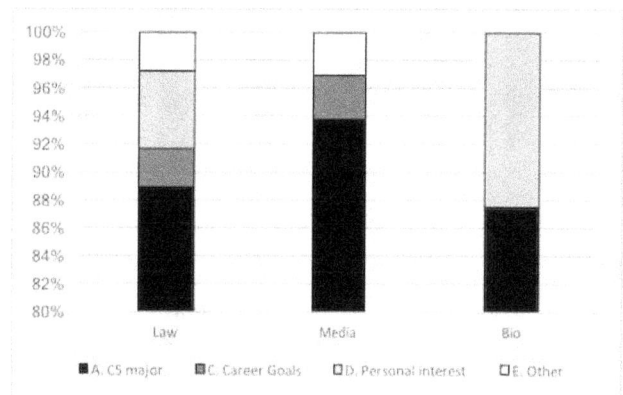

Figure 2: Answers to the question "How important was the Law/Media Computation/Biology focus in you deciding to take this course? A. Would not have taken an introductory computer science course with a different focus B. Might have taken a different introductory computer science course, but focus was the deciding factor C. Would have taken a different introductory computer science course, but prefer one with this focus D. Did not factor into decision to take an introductory computer science course."

- "Very lively, had very interesting ideas, and was very interactive with the class."
- "Working with real data and making a web crawler."

4.3 Course Demographics

We obtained complete demographic information for the students from our institution. As shown in Table 1 the ethnicity distribution of the students enrolled in the Law section was very similar to that of Media Computation section. The Law section stands out for having *many* more non-majors, and mildly fewer women.

4.4 Pre-course Survey

Before the course started, we surveyed the students to see why they were taking the course, and what their initial perceptions of computer science were.

Reasons For Taking Course.

We surveyed students on how important the particular fo-

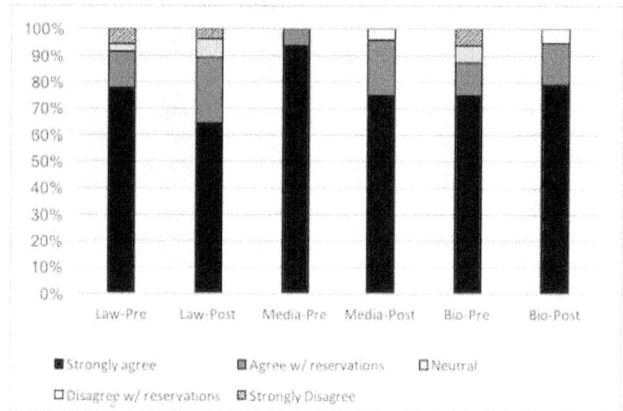

Figure 4: Responses to the question "Reason for taking course: A. Interest in CS major, B. Relevant to non-CS major, C. Relevant to career goals unrelated to major, D. Personal interest, E. Other."

cus of the course (law, biology or media computation) was to their decision to take a CS 1 course. As shown in Figure 2, the Law focus was significantly less important to students than the Media Computation or Biology focus. This was a statistically significant difference from the Media Computation course (p-value = .0008). (All p-values were calculated using a two-sample t-test.) This may be partly because the Law section was added as a new course over the summer, and we were unable to advertise it to pre-law and other students as much as we would have liked.

The Law section of CS 1 had both fewer students who had already declared a CS major (see Table 1) and significantly fewer students who entered planning to major in Computer Science than in the traditional Media Computation section (see Figure 3). Using a 5 point Likert scale, with "Strongly Agree" coded as a 1, and "Strongly Disagree" coded as a 5, Law had a mean of 1.42 versus Media Computation's mean of 1.06 (p-value = .046). (A similar difference is also observed in our other targeted section, Biology, which had a mean of 1.5.) This difference may be due to the Media Com-

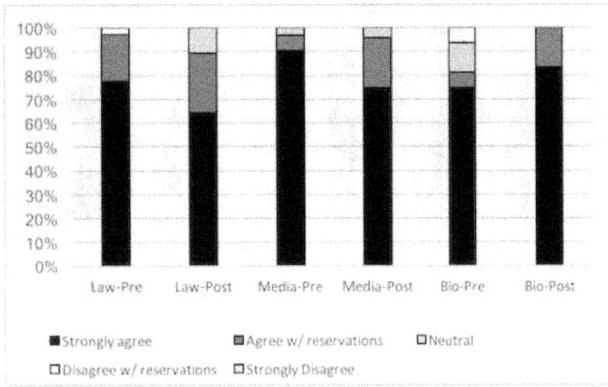

Figure 5: Responses to the statement "Knowing programming will help me earn a living."

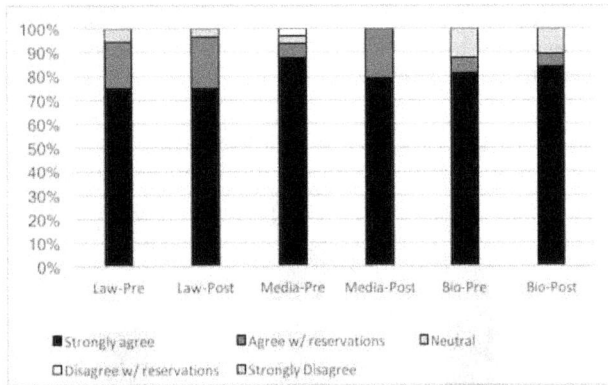

Figure 6: Responses to the statement "Computer science is a worthwhile and necessary subject."

putation section being the traditional section for our majors to take, or our new targeted sections appealing to students who were less certain they wanted to major in CS. As shown in Figure 4, both targeted sections had more students taking the course for reasons other than planning to major in CS.

Student Opinions on Computer Science, Pre-Course.

Students in the Law section were consistently less likely to agree with statements like "Knowing programming will help me earn a living" (Figure 5, mean of 1.28 vs 1.13), "I'll need programming for my future work" (mean of 1.306 vs 1.25), "Computer science is a worthwhile and necessary subject" (Figure 6, mean of 1.31 vs 1.22), and "I will use programming in many ways throughout my life" (mean of 1.44 vs 1.31), although not to a statistically significant extent. This may indicate students in the Law section came into the course feeling less positive about Computer Science in general than students in the Media Computation section. Students in the Biology section were also less likely to agree with these statements, indicating that our alternative focused sections attracted a population of students who were less sure about Computer Science.

4.5 Post-Course Survey

After the course completed, we surveyed all three sections on their perceptions of computer science and feelings about the course.

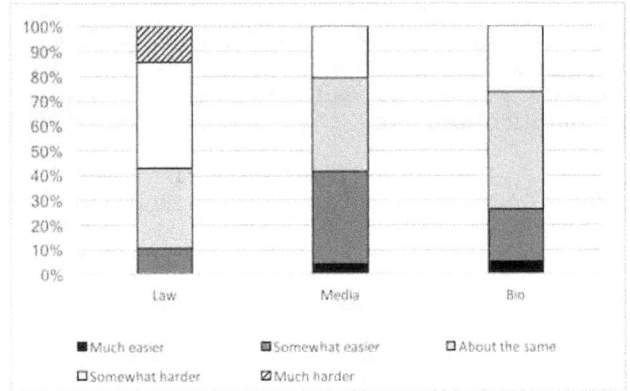

Figure 7: Student responses to the question "Compared to other classes, how difficult do you find this class?"

Likelihood to Major, Post Course.

While before the course students in the Law section were significantly less likely to agree with the statement "I plan to major in Computer Science" than students in the Media Computation section, after the course there was not a statistically significant difference between responses from the students in the Law section, and responses from the students in the other sections (shown in Figure 3, Law mean of 1.54, Media computation mean of 1.33, Biology mean of 1.31). In both the Media Computation and the Law section students had more reservations about majoring after taking the course than before taking it, possibly due to many of them being exposed to what Computer Science actually involves for the first time.

Student Reactions to Assignments.

The Law section found their assignments significantly more difficult than the Media Computation or Biology sections, as show in Figure 7. Using a 5 point Likert scale to answer the question "Compared to other classes, how difficult do you find this class?", with "Much harder" coded as a 5, and "Much easier" coded as a 1, the Law section had a mean of 3.61, the Media Computation section had a mean of 2.75 (p-value = .0008), and the Biology section had a mean of 2.95 (p-value= .014). This may be related to the high proportion of Law students entering the course with non-engineering majors, or students entering the course less sure of their intention to be Computer Science majors. However, as this is the first offering of this course, assignments may have genuinely been more challenging or time consuming than the equivalent assignments in the Media Computation or Biology sections.

Students in the Law section agreed with the statement "I understand how the material covered in this course relates to society" more than students in either the Media Computation or the Law section. On a 5-point Likert scale with "Strongly agree" coded as a 1, students in the law section had a mean of 1.5, versus 2.09 in Media Computation (p-value = .051), and 2.11 in Biology (p-value = .16) (shown in Figure 8). This seems likely due to the fact that one of the main focuses of the Law section was the impact of Computer Science on society and the law, and many of the assignments looked at socially relevant problems.

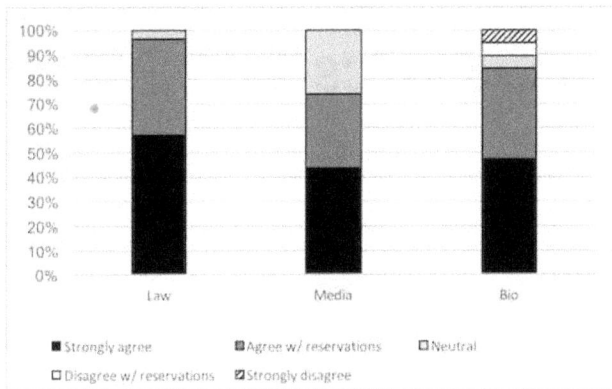

Figure 8: Student responses to the statement "I understand how the material covered in this course relates to society."

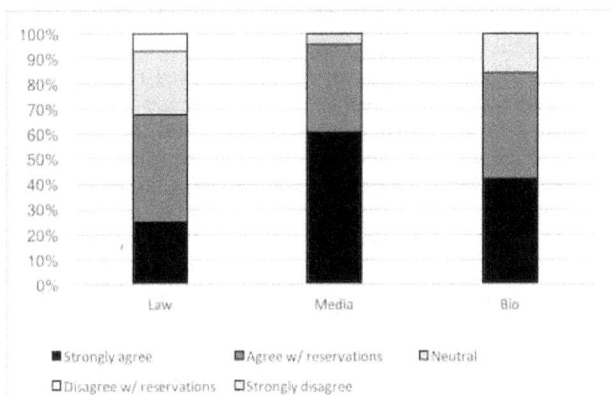

Figure 9: Student responses to the statement "Assignments increased my interest in the subject matter of computing."

In both of our specialized sections, students agreed less with the statement "Assignments increased my interest in the subject matter of computing". The Law section had a mean of 2.54, while Biology had a mean of 1.90 (p-value = .089) and Media Computation had a mean of 1.48 (p-value = .002). It may be that the application of Computer Science to a specific topic resulted in students feeling less focused on CS as its own subject. Alternatively, it may be that the students in the Media Computation class, who were overwhelmingly planning on a CS major when they entered, were simply more positive on any measure of interest in computing.

5. CONCLUDING THOUGHTS

A law-themed introduction to computer science can be successful both in computing education, and in making students realize the relevance of Computer Science to current social and public policy issues. Our initial data suggests that students find seeing the relevance interesting and that it motivates some of them to take more computer science courses. We plan to more heavily advertise future offerings to pre-law students, and hope as a result to have a greater percentage of women in the course.

6. ACKNOWLEDGMENTS

This material is based upon work supported by the National Science Foundation under Grant No. DUE-1612455.

7. REFERENCES

[1] American Bar Association. First year and total J.D. enrollment by gender 1947 - 2011. Online at http://www.americanbar.org/content/dam/aba/administrative/legal_education_and_admissions_to_the_bar/statistics/jd_enrollment_1yr_total_gender.authcheckdam.pdf.

[2] C. H. Crouch and E. Mazur. Peer Instruction: Ten years of experience and results. *American Journal of Physics*, 69(9):970–77, 2001.

[3] P. J. Denning. The profession of IT: Beyond computational thinking. *Communications of the ACM*, 52(6):28–30, 2009.

[4] Z. Dodds, R. Libeskind-Hadas, and E. Bush. When CS 1 is Biology 1: crossdisciplinary collaboration as CS context. In *Proceedings of the 15th Annual Conference on Innovation and Technology in Computer Science Education*, ITiCSE '10, pages 219–223, 2010.

[5] A. Forte and M. Guzdial. Computers for communication, not calculation: Media as a motivation and context for learning. In *Proc. 37th Hawaiian International Conference of Systems Sciences*, 2004.

[6] M. Guzdial. A media computation course for non-majors. In *Proceedings of the 8th Annual Conference on Innovation and Technology in Computer Science Education*, ITiCSE '03, pages 104–108, 2003.

[7] C. B. Lee and B. Simon. Peer Instruction for computer science website. Online at http://www.peerinstruction4cs.org/.

[8] B. Miller, D. Ranum, J. Elkner, P. Wentworth, A. B. Downey, C. Meyers, and D. Mitchell. *How to Think Like a Computer Scientist: Interactive Edition*. Runestone, 3rd edition, 2014. Online at http://interactivepython.org/runestone/static/thinkcspy/index.html.

[9] B. Simon, M. Kohanfars, J. Lee, K. Tamayo, and Q. Cutts. Experience report: Peer Instruction in introductory computing. In *Proceedings of SIGCSE 2010*, pages 341–45, 2010.

[10] J. Spacco, J. Parris, and B. Simon. How we teach impacts student learning: Peer Instruction vs. lecture in CS0. In *Proceedings of SIGCSE 2013*, pages 41–46, 2013.

[11] Stanford University. Joint majors: CS + X. Online at https://majors.stanford.edu/more-ways-explore/joint-majors-csx.

[12] A. E. Tew, W. M. McCracken, and M. Guzdial. Impact of alternative introductory courses on programming concept understanding. In *Proceedings of the First International Workshop on Computing Education Research*, ICER '05, pages 25–35, 2005.

[13] University of Illinois at Urbana Champaign. CS + X degree programs. Online at http://www.cs.uiuc.edu/academics/undergraduate/degree-program-options/cs-x-degree-programs.

A Hybrid Open/Closed Lab for CS 1

Timothy Urness
Drake University
2507 University Ave
Des Moines, IA 50311
timothy.urness@drake.edu

ABSTRACT

In this paper we introduce hybrid labs, an alternative to open or closed labs for CS 1, in which a set of written instructions, demonstration of techniques, and code examples are provided to students in lieu of a lecture. The hybrid lab also consists of several challenges which require students to write code or answer questions based off the concepts introduced in the document. Students are presented with the lab two days prior to a class period and are given an option of submitting solutions to the challenges on their own time (similar to an open lab) or attending the class in which an instructor is available to provide additional help as needed (similar to a closed lab). We compare a section of CS 1 that utilized a combination of hybrid labs and lectures against a section that utilized only lectures. We found no statistical significance between the abilities of the students of the two sections, but surveys show that students found the hybrid labs to be more engaging and preferred the hybrid labs over lectures as means of instruction. Furthermore, instructors found that the hybrid labs allowed for more tailored, individualized instruction for a variety of student abilities.

Keywords

CS 1; Open Labs; Closed Labs

1. INTRODUCTION

The primary goals of a CS 1 course typically involve introducing the fundamental components of algorithm design and development. Many of the objectives common to CS 1 courses are articulated by the ACM/IEEE curriculum guidelines and include if statements, loops, simple I/O, files, methods, and object oriented programming [1].

There are many factors, however, that influence *how* an institution teaches the introductory computing sequence and achieves the desired objectives. These factors include the size of the program, the number of students per instructor, the course load of the faculty, the availability of teaching assistants or adjunct instructors, physical resources, students'

ITiCSE '17, July 3–5, 2017, Bologna, Italy.

© 2017 Copyright held by the owner/author(s). Publication rights licensed to ACM.
ISBN 978-1-4503-4704-4/17/07. . . $15.00

DOI: http://dx.doi.org/10.1145/3059009.3059014

access to laptops, and a tradition or history of offering labs. A combination of these issues often dictate whether or not a formal, hands-on instructional element (a "lab") is included as part of a course.

In cases where a lab is a formal component of the CS 1 course, the lab is implemented as either a *closed* lab or an *open* lab. A closed lab consists of a required timeframe in which students are all present in a computer lab or classroom that is equipped with the necessary hardware. The students work through guided exercises individually or in groups and are supervised by an instructor or teaching assistant. An open lab is an unconstrained time in which the required resources (e.g. computers) are made available to students. In an open lab, attendance at specific times is optional, and the lab may or may not be monitored by tutors or teaching assistants.

In this paper, we describe an alternative to an open or closed lab for CS 1, which we refer to as a *hybrid* open/closed lab (or simply *hybrid* lab). We introduce and assess the advantages of a hybrid lab and describe an experiment in which two sections of CS 1 were given the same instructional resources; however, one section utilized a combination of lectures and a weekly hybrid lab while the other section was only instructed via lectures.

2. RELATED WORK

Although the implementation details of labs may vary greatly among institutions, the main idea behind the utilization of labs is that students learn more by doing than by listening to lectures [5]. The use of a lab changes the instructional approach of a "standard" classroom and allows instructors to have a different perspective on student progress and understanding [8].

The literature regarding the use of labs in CS 1 (open or closed) with an explicit assessment of the lab experience vs. a non-lab control group is rather sparse. References [10, 14] postulate that this is due to all sections of a course typically being taught the same for pragmatic reasons. In this case, newly-adopted approaches must be compared to previously taught sections in which multiple variables have changed from the initial offering. As such, there are few simultaneous non-lab baseline sections in which to compare experimental lab sections. In addition, cases in which open labs are directly compared to closed labs are limited. In a study from 1994, which compared open labs against closed labs, Thweat et. al reported that students in a closed laboratory performed better on a comprehensive CS 1 exam than students in open labs [13]. A more recent study has reported that benefits of open labs in computer science include an improved performance on exams, but also resulted in a decreased performance on extended homework assignments [14].

While many studies have not found a significant correlation between labs and student performance, the use of closed labs have been found to have several positive effects. Closed labs have helped students better prepare for online tests [7] and have been noted to have a qualiative effect on student learning [6]. Soh et. al conducted a study on closed CS 1 labs and concluded that motivated students found value in lab activities, and student performance in labs correlates to performance on exams and homework assignments [12]. Furthermore, structured exploration activities in the form of a lab have been shown to help novice programmers overcome common misconceptions regarding computing [9].

Previous work on self-guided labs has proven to have positive results in the introductory computer science sequence. Students who have participated in self-guided labs in a learn-as-you go fashion (abductive learning) have been shown to have decreased failure rates [11].

There are many published works (e.g. [4]) that provide excellent exemplar studies for computer science courses that utilize labs in a variety of areas, and the hands-on approach of education has been widely accepted.

3. HYBRID LABS

3.1 Introduction

The hybrid lab is a set of written instructions, demonstration of techniques, and examples of code presented in a walkthrough format. The lab also consists of several challenges in which students must write original code or answer questions that are based off the concepts introduced in the written components of the lab. Students are presented with the lab two days prior to a class period and are given the option of completing the challenges in lieu of attending a class period (simiar to an open lab). Students must submit working solutions to the challenges in order to be excused from attending the class period. If the student does not have time or is unable to complete the lab, he or she is expected to attend the class session to get the necessary help from the instructor or spend time working through the material (similar to a closed lab). Participation can be strongly encouraged by using attendance at the class periods or completed lab submissions as a component of the final grade.

3.2 Theoretical Advantages of Hybrid Labs

The lecture-based instruction format is not ideal for individual learning. A significant disadvantage of a standard lecture-based instruction format is that material is presented at the same rate for all students in attendance. It is the responsibility of the instructor to present the material at an appropriate pace for most of the students. Unfortunately, lectures will likely be to too fast for some students and too slow for others. The motivating factor behind the hybrid labs is to allow students to practice the components of the course on their own and learn at an individual pace.

The hybrid lab will reward students who are proactive in their studies by allowing them to complete the lab on their own time and not attend a class period. Furthermore, this will reduce the number of students in the classroom on lab days, making the answering of individual questions more manageable for the instructor. In our study, we found approximately 50% of students would typically submit the challenges to the labs prior to class on Fridays.

As the lab on Friday must be attended by students who found the lab too challenging to complete on their own or didn't have sufficient time to complete it prior to class, the instructor has a smaller class size and can give more focused individual attention to the students who need it. Thus, the hybrid labs have multiple advantages: students are able to work at their own pace, and students who need additional help attend a lab session that is smaller and more intimate, in which the instructor can effectively answer individual questions as needed. This experience is in contrast to a regular lecture class period, in which the instructor must present the material at one pace to the entire class.

4. METHODOLOGY

4.1 Hybrid Labs in Practice

In the fall of 2016, we conducted an experiment to assess the effectiveness of the hybrid labs as compared to a completely lecture-based course. The CS 1 course at Drake University, a small private liberal arts college, is typically taught via 50 minute courses on Mondays, Wednesdays, and Fridays over a 15-week semester term. In the hybrid lab approach, the lab occurs on the Friday of each week of the term. The walkthrough lab is supplied to the students on Wednesday afternoon. The students have the choice of completing the lab on their own, submitting solutions to the challenges, and not attending the Friday session. Or, if the student does not have time or is unable to complete the lab, the student must attend the class session on Friday where the instructor is available for individual assistance.

We taught one section (the *lecture* section) as a standard, lecture-only course that met for 50 minutes on Mondays, Wednesdays, and Fridays. The experimental section (the *lab* section) met on Mondays and Wednesdays, and was presented the same material via lecture as the classroom-only section. The lab section, however, was given the hybrid lab on Wednesdays afternoons with the option of completing it prior to the class time on Friday. The lecture section was required to attend the class on Friday, and the material was presented in a traditional lecture-style with frequent breaks to allow for students to complete short in-class exercises on their own laptops. This was consistent with how the course was taught on non-lab days throughout the semester. Both sections were taught by the same instructor.

The CS 1 sections at Drake University are capped at 45 students. In recent years, this course has filled to capacity with several sections. In our case, the size of each of the sections makes a closed lab experience difficult to manage by a single instructor in a classroom that is limited on space.

Students use their own laptops which are not supplied by the university. The software tools used, Python using the Pycharm IDE, are reliable and platform independent which enables all of the students to participate in all of the required activities of the course without the need for a dedicated computer lab.

4.2 Survey Questions

The goals and objectives for CS 1, inspired by the 2013 ACM/IEEE curriculum guidelines [1], include mastery of data structures, if-statements, loops, files, methods, and

Table 1: Survey Questions Measuring Attitudes Related to Computer Science

#	Question
1	Errors generated by computers are random, and when they happen there's not much I can do to understand why.
2	I find the challenge of solving computer science problems motivating.
3	If I want to apply a method used for solving one computer science problem to another problem, the problems must involve very similar situations.
4	Tools and techniques from computer science can be useful in the study of other disciplines (e.g., biology, art, business).
5	I enjoy solving computer science problems.
6	Learning computer science is just about learning how to program in different languages.
7	A significant problem in learning computer science is being able to memorize all the information I need to know.
8	The subject of computer science has little relation to what I experience in the real world.
9	There is usually only one correct approach to solving a computer science problem.
10	I worry that mistakes I make when writing a program may damage my computer.
11	I am interested in learning more about computer science.
12	I prefer a classroom lecture format for learning.
13	I prefer a hands-on lab format for learning.

Table 2: Survey Questions for Self-Reported Abilities Related to Computer Science Content

#	Question
14	Write a computer program that uses a variety of data types (e.g. int, float, string).
15	Write a computer program that effectively uses if statements and if-else statements.
16	Write a computer program that uses loops and nested loops.
17	Write a computer program that uses a method or function, passes parameters to the function, and returns a value.
18	Write a computer program that uses a file to read or write information.
19	Write a computer program that creates a class, including accessor and mutator methods, and creates an object of this new class type.
20	Write a computer program that helps solve a problem that you are working on for another course or research area.

Table 3: Coding Questions that Appeared on the Pre-Semester Survey and the Final Exam

#	Question
21	Write the code that will prompt a user for an integer and a float value. Add the two numbers together and print out the result.
22	Write the code that will print out "within range" if the value of the variable score is between the numbers 60 and 100 (including both 60 and 100).
23	Use a loop to print out the integers 1 thru 10 followed by the square of the number.
24	Write a function called double that returns 2 times the input parameter.
25	Assume that there exists a file named temps.txt that consists of a sequence of temperatures measured over the past several weeks. Open the file and determine the maximum temperature in the file. Print this value in a separate file called result.txt.
26	Write the code to define a class called Student. The class should inherit from a class called Person. The Student class should contain a data attribute called gpa. Write the Student class to include an initializer method, accessor method, mutator method.

object oriented programming. We were particularly interested in measuring students' attitudes and abilities related to these objectives prior to the start of the semester so that exposure to programming and computer science concepts could be controlled for in the assessment of the effect of the hybrid labs vs. the lecture-only instructional methodology. These survey questions are designed to assess the exposure and abilities students have acquired before the course. The surveys are repeated after the course to assess the effectiveness of the instructional techniques.

Student attitudes play an important role in shaping how students learn from their experiences [2]. To assess the attitudes and perceptions of computer science, we utilized survey questions from the CAS (Computing Attitudes Survey) [3] on the first day of the course, and again on the last day of the course. The questions ask students to rate their attitudes to various statements on computer science on a Likert-like scale: Strongly Disagree (0), Disagree (1), Neutral (2), Agree (3), and Strongly Agree (4).

In addition to questions designed to measure attitudes related to computer science (questions 1 through 11), we also asked questions related to a preferred learning style (lecture vs. hands-on lab) on questions 12 and 13. The questions presented to the students are listed in Table 1.

In the pre-semester survey, we asked two different kinds of questions related to student's abilities: the first had the students rate on a scale from 0 to 5 how confident they felt they could answer questions related to the objectives for the course (Table 2). The second method asked them to answer basic programming questions as part of the survey (Table 3).

The self-confidence survey was repeated on the last day of the course, and the programming questions were a part of the final exam.

5. RESULTS

5.1 Assessment of Student Attitudes

The lecture section consisted of 44 participating students whereas the lab section consisted of 41 participating students. In addition to being the entry-level course in the computer science major, the CS 1 course at Drake University satisfies a category in the general-education curriculum. As a result, a majority of the students entered the course

Table 4: Survey Results Measuring Attitudes Related to Computer Science

#	Lecture Pre-Term	Lab Pre-Term	Lecture Post-Term	Lab Post-Term
1	0.95	0.70	0.50	0.44
2	2.73	3.20	2.98	3.47*
3	1.75	1.87	1.64	1.63
4	3.34	3.58	3.41	3.44
5	2.34	2.85	3.00	3.37*
6	1.74	1.78	1.72	1.81
7	2.00	1.60	1.91	1.38
8	1.16	1.18	0.89	0.91
9	0.72	0.58	0.77	0.44
10	1.35	0.95	0.64	0.54
11	3.34	3.56	3.25	3.56*
12	2.32	2.23	2.47	2.35
13	2.89	2.55	2.98	2.84

Table 5: Survey Results of Self-Reported Abilities of Entire Class

#	Lecture Pre-Term	Lab Pre-Term	Lecture Post-Term	Lab Post-Term
14	0.57	1.23	4.70	4.72
15	1.05	1.78	4.74	4.70
16	0.43	1.08	4.38	4.56
17	0.45	1.28	4.34	4.43
18	0.50	1.05	3.95	4.07
19	0.18	0.55	4.27	4.37
20	0.39	0.93	3.78	3.70

Table 6: Survey Results of Self-Reported Abilities of Novice Students

#	Lecture Pre-Term	Lab Pre-Term	Lecture Post-Term	Lab Post-Term
14	.057	0.57	4.70	4.73
15	1.05	1.07	4.74	4.76
16	0.43	0.41	4.38	4.58
17	0.45	0.57	4.34	4.39
18	0.50	0.47	3.95	4.03
19	0.18	0.07	4.27	4.39
20	0.39	0.33	3.78	3.67

as novice programmers without any computer science background.

The results of the pre-semester and post-semester survey, which correspond to the questions listed in Table 1, are presented in Table 4. Note that the post-semester responses for the lab section on questions 2 (*I find the challenge of solving computer science problems motivating*), 5 (*I enjoy solving computer science problems*), and 11 (*I am interested in learning more about computer science*), are statistically significant with $p < 0.05$, as indicated (*) in Table 4.

A majority of the differences between the pre-term survey and the post-term survey indicate a favorable influence of the course on the attitudes and beliefs students have regarding computer science. However, the results also indicate potential areas of improvement for our future courses, such as emphasizing the variety application areas for computer science and the ability to implement solutions in a number of different ways. We noticed a slight decrease in agreement from the lab section in question 4 (*Tools and techniques from computer science can be useful in the study of other disciplines*) and a slight increase in agreement for the lecture section in question 9 (*There is usually only one correct approach to solving a computer science problem.*). Further conclusions are discussed in the final section of the paper.

5.2 Assessment of Self-Reported Abilities

On the first day of the course, we asked students to rate their confidence levels on their ability to answer questions related to the primary goals for the course (if-statements, loops, files, methods, object oriented programming) as listed in Table 2. This allowed us to identify several students in the lab section who had previous programming experience. We classified the experienced students with self-reported average scores above 2.0 (on a scale from 0 to 5) on the pre-term survey, which consisted of 7 students in the lab section. All other students were considered novice programmers.

Table 5 indicates the average pre- and post- semester self-evaluation scores for the entire class, including the students with a self-reported knowledge of some of the material. Table 6 displays the average scores of only the novice programmers from both sections, which are demonstrably similar amongst both sections. We can use the results of the novice programmers as a standard baseline for students in both sec-

tions to help determine any difference that the hybrid labs make in comparison to the lecture instructional format. All of the post-term scores are statistically significant with $p < 0.01$, indicating that the course had a significant impact on students' confidence regarding the course objectives.

5.3 Assessment of Abilities

In addition to students' self-assessment of abilities, the pre-term survey also contained questions asking them to demonstrate abilities related to the course objectives (Table 3). The average score for all of the questions in the pre-term survey was below 0.2. This indicates that while some students had a self-reported confidence in the material, many students were not able to (or chose not to) demonstrate it on the pre-semester survey. Each of the questions was repeated on the final exam to measure any difference in specific programming skills between the sections of the course. Table 7 displays the individual scores (out of 5) for each of the programming questions which were a component of the final exam.

The average final exam scores as well as the average individual question scores were very similar between the two sections, regardless of programming experience. The average final exam score for the lecture section was 84.90% whereas the average final exam score for the lab section was 86.64%.

Table 7: Exam Results of Students for Coding Questions

#	LecturePost-Term	LabPost-Term
21	4.83	4.90
22	4.72	4.50
23	4.45	4.63
24	4.00	4.28
25	3.94	4.07
26	4.49	4.65

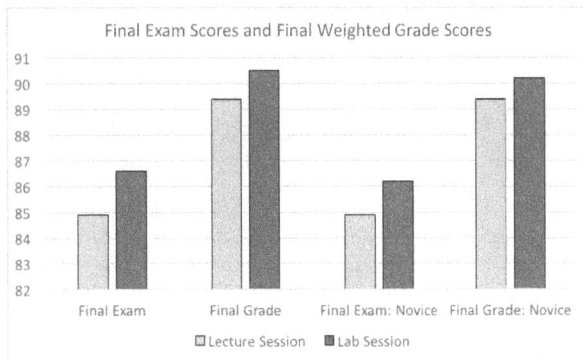

Figure 1: Final exam scores and semester grades for both the lecture and lab sections. The left half of the figure represents the scores for all students in each section. The right half of the figure represents the scores for students who had no prior programming experience.

If we consider only those students with no self-reported previous programming experience, the final differences are also not significant (84.9% for the lecture section and 86.2% for the lab section). The scores for the final grade, which were calculated as a weighted average amongst programming assignments, two midterm exams, and a final exam, were also similar (89.4% for the lecture section and 90.5% for the lab section) as shown in Figure 1. While the lab section outperformed the lecture section by one to two percent on each of the midterm and final exams, no statistically significant differences were found when comparing the two sections and controlling for gender, year of study, or programming experience.

6. CONCLUSIONS

In the self-reported and demonstrated metrics related to skills developed during the course, we did not detect any statistically significant differences between to two sections. This indicates that both the lecture format and the hybrid-lab format are justifiable, acceptable methods for instruction. However, there are several results from the study that are noteworthy.

Result #1: Students appreciate the hybrid lab format.

We can determine to what extent students' perceptions changed by comparing the responses to questions from the pre-semester survey to the post-semester survey. In the case of questions 12 and 13, the extent students agree with the statements "I prefer a classroom lecture format for learning" and "I prefer a hands-on lab format for learning" can indicate the appreciation for the different formats. In our study, both the lecture section and the lab section responses increased for both statements. The lecture section responses for the classroom lecture format increased from 2.32 to 2.47 (increase of 0.15), and for the lab format from 2.89 to 2.98 (increase of 0.09) as shown in Figure 2. The lab section responses for the classroom lecture format increased from 2.23 to 2.35 (increase of 0.12) whereas the responses for the lab format jumped from 2.55 to 2.83 (increase of .28). The

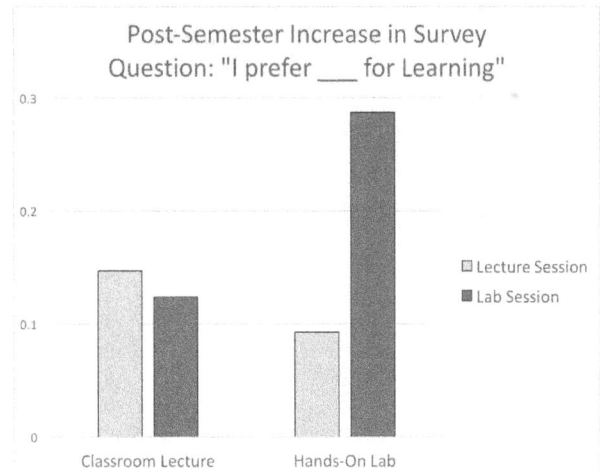

Figure 2: The pre-semester to post-semester increase in the average agreement to the survey question "I prefer (blank) for learning". The relative increase for the lab session's change of preference to the hands-on lab was much greater than all others.

large relative change indicates that students' appreciation for hands-on learning greatly increased over the semester.

Result #2: Students are more engaged with the hybrid lab format.

We obtained statistically significant differences between the sections on three of the post-semester survey questions measuring attitudes towards computer science: "I find the challenge of solving computer science problems motivating.", "I enjoy solving computer science problems.", and "I am interested in learning more about computer science." Each of these statements were more strongly agreed with by the lab section. In particular, the notion of "I am interested in learning more about computer science" drops slightly for the lecture group from the pre-semester to post-semester survey (3.34 to 3.25) whereas the interest remains consistent for the lab section (3.51 to 3.51) between the pre-semester and post-semester surveys.

These questions are related to students' attitudes and engagement regarding the problem solving aspects of the course. Indeed, the lab section was given more freedom to explore and solve problems (and make mistakes) as part of the hybrid lab that the lecture section didn't directly experience. One of the main advantages of the hybrid lab format is the unstructured nature of the lab, which allows for more hands-on exploration and engagement with the material.

Result #3: The labs allowed for a more tailored, individualized instruction for a variety of student abilities.

The most significant drawback with the lecture format of delivering information to a group of students is that not all students learn at the same pace. Undoubtedly, the speed in which the content of the course is being covered will be too fast for some and too slow for others. This dilemma can be articulated best by a selection of student comments from the end-of-semester course evaluations from the lecture section:

> "sometimes information was rushed."

> "class was a bit slow..."

> "I wish I was in the Friday lab section so I could practice more rather than sit in a lecture."

The hybrid lab allowed for a tailored, individually-paced instruction. For students who were able to complete the lab challenges at home, they were not forced to sit in a lecture while others caught up. For the students who needed more time or more help, the lab provided an opportunity to get more focused attention from the instructor. The following selected comments from the lab section end-of-semester course evaluation articulates this advantage:

> "I liked the hands-on, in-class examples and Friday labs. I think they really helped me try to learn it on my own with hands on work."

> "I really enjoyed how the labs could be done outside of class. The detailed instructions basically counted as a lecture, but I was able to work at my own pace rather than getting distracted while waiting for others."

> "The combination of lecture and hands-on learning helped to understand both concepts and applications of the material."

Result #4: The lecture section students learned the material and had a better rapport with the instructor.

As the collected data demonstrates, the lecture section learned the same material to a comparable degree as the students from the lab section. Anecdotally, we noticed that the class dynamics and interactions amongst students and the instructor were more lively during the lecture section than during the lab section. While the lab students have expressed feeling more engaged with the material, the class dynamics were different. An explanation for this result is that the lecture students had more time collectively with the professor and each other in the lecture format. The attendance on Fridays during the lab section was smaller due to students completing the lab at home. As such, the group dynamics were not as consistent, and the lecture section seemed to benefit from a better sense of comradery.

In conclusion, while we found no statistical significance between the abilities of the students of the two sections, the surveys show that students found the hybrid labs to be more engaging and preferred the hybrid labs over lectures as means of instruction. Furthermore, instructors found that the hybrid labs allowed for a more tailored, individual instruction for a variety of student abilities. In the future, we plan to offer all sections of CS 1 using hybrid labs and will consider extending the use of hybrid labs to additional courses.

7. ACKNOWLEDGMENTS
Thank you to the students that took part of the study as well as Kevin Moenkhaus for his assistance in the data analysis.

8. REFERENCES
[1] ACM/IEEE-CS Joint Task Force on Computing Curricula. Computer science curricula 2013. Technical report, ACM Press and IEEE Computer Society Press, 2013.
[2] B. Dorn and A. Elliott Tew. Becoming experts: Measuring attitude development in introductory computer science. In *Proceedings of the 44th ACM Technical Symposium on Computer Science Education (SIGCSE '13)*, pages 183–188, 2013.
[3] B. Dorn and A. E. Tew. Empirical validation and application of the computing attitudes survey. *Computer Science Education*, 25(1):1–36, 2015.
[4] W. Du, K. Jayaraman, and N. B. Gaubatz. Enhancing security education with hands-on laboratory exercises. In *Proceedings of the 5th Annual Symposium on Information Assurance (ASIA'10)*, pages 56–61, 2010.
[5] D. A. Kolb. *Experiential learning: Experience as the source of learning and development*. FT press, 2014.
[6] A. N. Kumar. The effect of closed labs in computer science i: An assessment. *Journal of Computing Sciences in Colleges*, 18(5):40–48, May 2003.
[7] A. N. Kumar. Closed labs in computer science i revisited in the context of online testing. In *Proceedings of the 41st ACM Technical Symposium on Computer Science Education (SIGCSE '10)*, pages 539–543, 2010.
[8] D. Laurillard. *Rethinking university teaching: A conversational framework for the effective use of learning technologies*. Routledge, 2013.
[9] R. Lischner. Explorations: Structured labs for first-time programmers. In *Proceedings of the Thirty-second SIGCSE Technical Symposium on Computer Science Education (SIGCSE '01)*, pages 154–158, 2001.
[10] R. P. Mihail and K. Roy. Closed labs in programming courses: A review. In *Proceedings of the International Conference on Frontiers in Education: Computer Science and Computer Engineering (FECS)*, pages 104–109, 2016.
[11] A. Radenski. Digital support for abductive learning in introductory computing courses. In *Proceedings of the 38th SIGCSE Technical Symposium on Computer Science Education (SIGCSE '07)*, pages 14–18, 2007.
[12] L.-K. Soh, A. Samal, S. Person, G. Nugent, and J. Lang. Analyzing relationships between closed labs and course activities in cs1. In *Proceedings of the 10th Annual SIGCSE Conference on Innovation and Technology in Computer Science Education (ITICSE '05)*, pages 183–187, 2005.
[13] M. Thweatt. Csi closed lab vs. open lab experiment. In *Proceedings of the Twenty-fifth SIGCSE Symposium on Computer Science Education (SIGCSE '94)*, pages 80–82, 1994.
[14] N. Titterton, C. Lewis, and M. Clancy. Benefits of lab-centric instruction. *Computer Science Education (Ed. Y. Ben-David Kolikant)*, 20(2):79–102, 2010.

Opening a (Sliding) Window to Advanced Topics

Orna Muller
Software Engineering and
Teaching Departments
ORT Braude College of
Engineering
Karmiel, Israel
+972504041364
ornamu@braude.ac.il

Ayelet Butman
Computer Science Department
Holon Institute of Technology
Holon, Israel
+972526887016
ayeletb@hit.ac.il

Moshe Butman
Computer Science School
The College of Management
Academic Studies
Rishon Lezion, Israel
+97236902092
moshebu@colman.ac.il

ABSTRACT

It is widely agreed that an introductory computer science (CS) course should be about more than just programming. Other aims are acquainting students with concepts and principles of CS and developing students' problem-solving skills. In this paper we propose an early introduction of a term often used by computer scientists: the Sliding Window (SW). The term has evolved over time among professionals to simplify the description of algorithms and can be used as well to support beginners when solving algorithmic problems. This metaphoric term enables abstracting and communicating ideas and at the same time it is easy to implement with elementary programming tools. We illustrate a set of stimulating problems in contemporary CS topics that use the SW and may be introduced in an introductory course.

1. INTRODUCTION

Various approaches to teaching an introductory Computer Science (CS) course, frequently called CS1, are discussed in the Computer Science Education literature; nevertheless, it is widely agreed that a CS1 course should be about more than learning to program. Among other aims of a CS1 course are acquainting students with concepts and principles of CS and developing students' critical and problem-solving skills. It is desirable that the course help students grasp the essence of the discipline they have chosen to study, stimulate their interest, and prepare them for the advanced courses that lie ahead.

As part of this view of an introductory course goals, we suggest looking at concepts that are used by computer scientists when solving contemporary problems and introduce them at early stages of the CS and software engineering (SE) programs. The main concept we discuss here is the Sliding Window (SW); a mechanism for traversing a data sequence.

The advanced terms we introduce are frequently used by computer scientists to simplify the development and description of algorithms; these concepts may likewise be used to support novices when solving problems that are within the scope of a CS1 course.

ITiCSE '17, July 03-05, 2017, Bologna, Italy
© 2017 ACM. ISBN 978-1-4503-4704-4/17/07…$15.00
DOI: http://dx.doi.org/10.1145/3059009.3059041

The concepts are simple to understand and can be implemented with basic programming tools (e.g., do not require knowledge of data structures). These concepts may be introduced in the context of contemporary tasks that students meet in daily life, thus making the problems introduced in the course interesting and motivating.

The advantages we see and experience in the early introduction of these concepts are the following:

a. Exposing students to the nature and the essence of the discipline of CS or SE develops some sense of the kinds of real issues and ways of tackling problems that exist in these domains. Curricula should deliver an appreciation of computer science fundamentals that underlie much of what software engineers do. Students need to understand both practical and theoretical motivations behind what they are taught. "Many SE concepts, principles, and issues should be taught as recurring themes throughout the curriculum to help students develop a software engineering mindset"[9]. "It is important that students do not perceive CS as only learning the specifics of particular programming languages. Care must be taken to emphasize the more general concepts in computing within the context of learning how to program"[8].

b. Interesting problems, such as a search for a pattern in text or image processing that students meet in daily life add interest and create motivation to study CS [12,14]. Routine problems are frequently introduced to practice programming, and the addition of attractive contexts is desirable. Although advanced topics and real-world experience are usually introduced at advanced stages of the curriculum, some exposure to up-to-date topics may be introduced earlier, even during the first year [9].

c. Advanced concepts may help students reach solutions that are easier to develop, simple to understand, elegant, and in many cases more efficient. Elegance of a solution is frequently achieved by simplifying an idea. Consequently, advanced concepts may serve as scaffolding tools for solving problems among novices who tend to write cumbersome and erroneous code [16]. Advanced approaches are those that beginning programmers usually do not grasp by themselves. Learning these concepts may help students develop an appreciation of elegant solutions for which computer scientists and software developers strive. Furthermore, our experience shows that succeeding to solve problems in a straightforward and elegant way increases satisfaction and enjoyment among students.

d. The pedagogical approach described here puts an emphasis on explicit learning of problem-solving strategies and heuristics, which were found to have a significant contribution to learning [11,15].

e. Early exposure to abstract ideas in an introductory course in addition to learning to program allows reducing the gap between CS1 and later courses on advanced algorithmic topics, which tend to be much more theoretical. The student learns the relationships and transitions between abstraction and implementation of ideas. The study of concepts and problem-solving approaches promotes students' abilities to abstract and acquire general ideas, and underlines similarities between problems in different contexts. Curricula should include exposure to aspects of professional practice including abstraction and implementation of ideas, analysis skills and critical thinking, problem-solving and written and oral communication skills [9].

The problems we introduce are from several fields of CS such as text processing, image processing, and computer vision, which are highly relevant in the context of the rapidly evolving areas of data analytics, data mining, big data and machine learning. These sciences have become highly prominent in research, industry, and organizations that examine data with the purpose of drawing conclusions about information, sorting through huge amounts of data, discovering new patterns, and more.

As the Curriculum Guidelines for Undergraduate Degree Programs in CS argue, there are no well-described list of topics that appear in virtually all introductory courses, not everything that is relevant can be taught right in the beginning, rather choosing what to cover in the course depends on various parameters including students' characteristics and on subsequent courses [8].

Our guidelines for a CS1 course incorporate problem solving and implementation of algorithms in code, so by the end of the course, students are expected to develop programs "from scratch". These guidelines suit the profile of students who are enrolled in either a CS or SE program and have some background in CS and programming, usually from high school. The main difficulties perceived by students with this profile are how to approach a problem, develop an algorithm, reach a solution in an effective manner, and implement ideas with well-written code [16,17].

The paper first introduces the Sliding Window concept and its metaphorical strength, then it illustrates a set of stimulating problems in contemporary CS topics that use the SW and several other advanced terms. Finally, we propose a way to integrate the presented concepts, ideas, and examples in a CS1 course in accordance with our experience so far.

2. SLIDING WINDOW

A well-known term in various fields of CS is the sliding window. It is used in string matching, object detection in images, image processing, data mining, online algorithms [3,7,18] and other areas. The main benefit of using the term *sliding window* (SW) is to simplify the description of algorithms.

A SW refers to scanning data of length n, where in each step we look only at m successive characters of the data, meaning that we are using a window of size m. The window is first placed at the beginning of the data so it captures the characters from location 1 to location m on the data. In the next iteration, the window captures the characters from location 2 to location m+1, and so on. Therefore, sliding a window means advancing the window by one character at each step.

The term *last window* refers to the window whose last character is the last character of the data.

The sliding window mechanism (D, f, k)
1. Initial window of size k at the beginning of the data D
2. While not *last window*:
   2.1 Operate a function f on the window data D
   2.2 Slide the window

Following is a description of the SW mechanism on the input data D and specific function f applied to k values:

2.1 Simple Use of SW

A simple demonstration of using the term SW may be introduced in the context of processing a sequence of elements, such as in the Peaks Problem:

The Peaks Problem

Input: A string S of real numbers of length n.

Output: All the triples (substrings of size 3) of S such that the middle number is the largest of the three.

A motivation for the Peaks Problem may be identifying local peaks on a topographic map.

Figure 1 illustrates an example of the Peaks Problem where the input string is numerical characters. The triples marked in the figure are substrings that satisfy the problem requirements.

Figure 1: Peaks Problem

It is easy to describe the algorithm solution to the Peaks Problem by the SW mechanism: slide a window of size 3 and check if the middle number in the window is bigger than the other two.

Figure 2 describes the four steps of running the Peaks algorithm on the input 2,3,4,2,3,1. While scanning the text, the algorithm "sees" at a given time only the information that is inside the window and the rest of the text is "hidden". In the first step the window is located from the first to the third index, "seeing" (2,3,4). In each iteration, the window advances one index; therefore, in the second iteration the window is placed from the second to the fourth index, "seeing" (3,4,2), and so on. When the middle value is greater than its neighbors, the window is marked with light blue. The output is (3,**4**,2), (2,**3**,1).

2.2 Strength of Metaphorical Terms

A metaphor is a cognitive process that occurs when we seek to understand an idea (the target domain) in terms of a different, already known idea (the source domain). We create a conceptual mapping between the properties of the source and the target, thereby gaining new understanding about the target [10].

Metaphors are frequently used in everyday life, in science, and in teaching and learning. Metaphors facilitate the development of new conceptual structures, new mental models and abstractions. A simple example is the term *loop* to describe a repetitive structure. We suggest here that borrowing terms from advanced levels and applying them to beginning stages may be powerful and supportive. The use of suitable metaphors may help students understand and visualize abstract concepts and ideas behind algorithm development. In addition, our thinking is limited by the language we use, therefore a more powerful language allows us to be more efficient in thinking and in communicating ideas [19].

Empirical evidence for the help of metaphors in CS education was found by Chee [5].

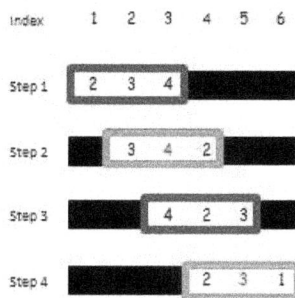

Figure 2: Sliding Window for solving the Peaks Problem

The concept of Sliding Window is actually a metaphor. Similarly, to a real window where the view of the observer is limited to what can be seen through the window while the rest is hidden behind walls, using a SW in algorithm description means looking at each stage only on a fixed-size sub-sequence of the input. As the window slides, we progressively look at different parts of the input.

The term SW simplifies the explanation of algorithms since it allows an upper-level view of a mechanism and hides the details of implementation in code (such as manipulating indices). The main code development details that the use of the term SW captures are the number of elements we process at each iteration (the size of the window); which elements belong to the examined sub-sequence; the number of iterations calculated by the [length of text] − [size of window] + 1, and what characterizes the last window. As a CS1 course strives to improve students' skills in algorithm development and writing code, such terms may help them move from the abstract to the practical.

2.3 Evolution of the SW Term

In the early 1970s algorithm descriptions did not make use of the term SW for more than another 20 years. The term SW has gradually developed over the years in the description of algorithms. As an example, we discuss the evolution of the SW in the string matching world. The basic problem in this field is the exact string matching problem:

For a text T (of length n) and pattern P (of length m), find all the locations in T where P matches exactly.

In the book "Computer Algorithms" by Baase (1983, p. 173) [1], the algorithm describes the mechanism of SW without using the term, and the result is a rather complicated description:

"Starting at the beginning of each string, we compare characters, one after the other, until either the pattern is exhausted or no match is found... In the latter case we start over again, comparing the first pattern character with the second subject character...".

In a more recent publication of the book [2], p. 485, the algorithm description uses "sliding" but there is no use of "window":

"In general, when a mismatch is found, we (figuratively) slide the pattern one more place forward over the text and start again comparing the first pattern character with the next text character".

Therefore, the description became less complicated.

In "Introduction to Algorithms" by Cormen, Leiserson, and Rivest [6], first published in 1989 (with no change in wording in the following editions), on p. 855, the algorithm description uses

"sliding" but does not use "window"; but the Rabin-Karp algorithm description in this book, p. 860, uses "window" but not "sliding".

Later on, in "Handbook of Exact String-Matching Algorithms" by Charras and Lecroq, published in 2004 [4], p.12, they describe the algorithm using the SW: *"scan the text with the help of a window, repeat the same procedure again until the right end of the window goes beyond the right end of the text. This mechanism is usually called the sliding window mechanism".*

Nowadays, SW has become very popular in different fields of computer science in algorithm descriptions. Moreover, in some programing languages there is built-in functionality of the SW, such as the built-in function nlfilter in MATLAB [13].

3. PROBLEM SOLVING IN CONTEMPORARY CONTEXTS

We further introduce several problems that make use of the SW term, suitable for an introductory CS1 course. The problems are taken from various CS and SE topics, simplified and adjusted to novices; they exemplify approaches to solving problems in the areas of pattern matching, pattern recognition, machine learning, and image processing. Some of the examples are categorized as detection and classification problems, while others belong to the processing problems field.

The term SW is used alone as well as with the *histogram* and *convolution* terms, explained later. These examples may serve CS educators when choosing and developing examples and assignments for a CS1 course.

3.1 SW with a Histogram

Numerical Expressions Detection Problem
Input: A string comprised of a textual and numerical expression.
Output: The locations (with high probability) of mathematical

The Numerical Expressions Problem is an example of a detection problem, and may be used, for example, when processing a digital document, automatically applying an italic-style font to all the numerical expressions.

Two methods are frequently used for solving the Numerical Expressions Problem. They assume that the characters in the text are represented in ASCII code. ASCII codes of numerical values are between 33 to 57 while only few values in this range are non-numeric.

The first method is based on histogram calculations. Later in the paper we present a second method based on convolution.

The histogram-based solution runs a SW of size k and for each window calculates a two-bucket histogram, where the first bucket is for ASCII values in the range of 33 to 57 and the second is for the other values. If the value of the first bucket is k then the location of the window is added to the output.

This method does not give an exact solution; rather, a solution with high probability. Solutions of this type are common and highly important in the world of big data. These problems usually require "good enough" solutions: very fast (running time) solutions with high probability of correctness. These demands frequently occur when the exact solution is not known, e.g., in face recognition problems or where the running time complexity for the exact solution is "expensive".

Figure 3 presents the result of the algorithm on a specific text. The algorithm output is two expressions (marked with a frame) although the second output is a non-numerical expression.

The first is an example of a numerical expression: 1+2-(34*10) while the second is an example of a non-numerical expression: 1+2"&"34*10

Figure 3: Numerical Expressions Detection Problem

3.2 Adding Convolution to SW

The term *convolution* in CS means running a SW on an input vector v (of length n) with vector g (of length m, smaller than v). We denote g as a *mask*, and at each step calculate the dot product between the vector that is captured in the window and the mask. The output of the convolution is the vector of the dot products.

Convolution is used as a mechanism for solving many CS problems. The only difference between one solution and another in the use of convolution is the size of the mask and its values.

The term *mask* is another example of a metaphor: a mask is "worn" on a window and may change some attributes of the elements it covers.

Note that the output vector of the convolution on input vector v of length n with mask g of length m has only n-m+1 result values. There are various ways to avoid the size mismatch when necessary, such as padding the input. This issue may be mentioned or ignored in the context of an introductory level.

We present another solution to the Numerical Expressions Detection Problem that is based on convolution. This solution makes a naïve way of using the convolution (a *naïve mask*). Later we present various visual problems that require less naïve masks.

3.2.1 Convolution-based Solution to the Numerical Expressions Classification Problem

Run a convolution on the input vector with the naïve mask [1...,1,1] of length k. The meaning of this mask is summing the values in the window. For each window if the value product is between k×33 to k×57 then a location with the desired output is "found".

Similarly to the histogram-based method, it doesn't give an exact solution; rather, a solution with high probability.

3.3 SW and Convolutions in 2D

Use of the terms we have discussed allows relatively simple expansion and natural transition from one-dimensional to two-dimensional problems. We have chosen to present examples from image processing and detection & classification in images because they are visually illustrated.

The following is an example of a 2D image processing problem.

Blurring Image Problem

Input: An n×n image I.

Output: A new image, which is a blurred version of the image.

A motivation for the Blurring Image Problem is noise reduction, such as Salt & Pepper noise, which is noise that sparsely occurs in white and black images. Figure 4 demonstrates Salt & Pepper noise.

Figure 4: Image with Salt & Pepper noise

We show two methods for reducing the noise. The first method uses a blurring process and is based on convolution. Different algorithms may use masks that differ in values and size. A simple mask is of size 5×5 where all values are 1/25; this mask computes a windowed average by replacing each entry with the average of that entry and its neighbors.

A more sophisticated mask for blurring an image is the following Gaussian mask:

$$\begin{bmatrix} 1 & 4 & 6 & 4 & 1 \\ 4 & 16 & 24 & 16 & 4 \\ 6 & 24 & 36 & 24 & 6 \\ 4 & 16 & 24 & 16 & 4 \\ 1 & 4 & 6 & 4 & 1 \end{bmatrix} \times \frac{1}{256}$$

Actually, the idea of using the mask is to replace every pixel of the image with its weighted averaging, giving the central pixel a higher weight.

The second method for reducing the noise replaces the central pixel in each window with the median of the window. The convolution method has a better complexity running time but gives less effective result.

The images in figure 5 demonstrate the effect of running each of the two methods on the Salt & Pepper noise image in figure 4.

Figure 5: Left: result of averaging masks on the noisy image, Right: result of the median SW

Another example of an image processing problem is the Edge Detection Problem; a motivation for the problem could be to sharpen an image (described later).

Edge Detection Problem

Input: An n×n image I.

Output: A new image that includes only the edges of I.

The Edge Detection Problem requires identifying points in the image where brightness changes sharply, which means a rapid change from a dark pixel to a bright one. A simple solution uses a convolution such as this mask:

0	-1	0
-1	4	-1
0	-1	0

The basic idea of this mask is that every pixel with a similar value to its neighbors is replaced with a close-to-zero value, while a pixel that is very different from its neighbors is replaced with a high value.

The following figure demonstrates the result of running an edge detection mask of size 5X5.

Figure 6: Left: original image, Right: result of edge detection

Now we present the sharpening image problem that uses the edge detection algorithm.

Sharpening Image Problem

Input: An n×n image I.

Output: A sharpened version of the input image.

A motivation for the sharpening image problem is image enhancement. One way to sharpen an image is to add the edges detection image to every pixel of the image. This can be done by convolution with the following mask:

$$\begin{bmatrix} 0 & -1 & 0 \\ -1 & 4 & -1 \\ 0 & -1 & 0 \end{bmatrix} + \begin{bmatrix} 0 & 0 & 0 \\ 0 & 1 & 0 \\ 0 & 0 & 0 \end{bmatrix} = \begin{bmatrix} 0 & -1 & 0 \\ -1 & 5 & -1 \\ 0 & -1 & 0 \end{bmatrix}$$

The idea of this mask is to take the edges of the image and add them to the image itself. Here, convolving with a mask with 1 at the center and 0 elsewhere results in the same image.

The following image demonstrates the effect of running a sharpening process on the image.

Figure 7: Left: original image, Right: the sharpened image

All the 2D problems we have presented so far come from the world of image processing, where the input and output are both images. Next, we present a problem from the field of detection and classification.

The darker patches problem is the detection and classification of darker patches in an image, such as detection of snow thawing in Alaska or penguins on snow in Antarctica.

Here we use a simple mask to mark the penguins in the following image.

Figure 8: Darker Patches Problem: penguins on snow

Darker Patches Classification Problem

Input: An n×n image I.

Output: Locations (with high probability) of dark patches.

Similarly to the numerical expression classification problem, a two-dimensional window is used, and the same two methods are possible: histogram-based (small value and high value buckets) SW, and convolution-based SW (mask of ones of the window size).

Here we use a mask of size 80 x 20, since we know that a penguin has a rectangular shape. We use a two-step algorithm: in the first step we run the mask of ones (summing the pixels' values) and marking as white every pixel above a threshold (see Figure 9).

Then we run the edge detection mask (discussed above) to mark with pink the penguin's contours (see Figure 10).

Figure 9: First step: output of convolving with one's mask and marking as white/black every pixel above/below a threshold

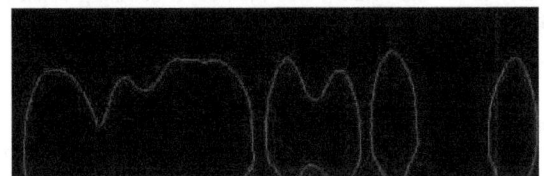

Figure 10: Second step: results of the edge detection mask

In each of the above problems, several aspects can be discussed such as the size of the mask and the complexity.

The implementation of convolution in programming allows students to use the mathematical knowledge they acquire when studying an algebra course in parallel to CS1 (including the dot product of vectors and matrices). There is added value to showing the close links between math and CS.

4. SUMMARY AND RECOMMENDATIONS

A CS1 course seeks to build students' skills in developing correct, efficient, and understandable computer programs. It interleaves theoretical and practical aspects of problem solving and programming. In accordance with this approach the course moves back and forth from abstract descriptions of ideas to the details of their implementation in code. The course is designed to set the foundations for the following courses in the algorithm-programming chain, with regard to basic CS concepts and principles. It also strives to acquaint students with issues that confront computer scientists and software engineers.

We propose early introduction of the SW concept that describes an algorithmic-programming mechanism often used in different CS topics. The term appears in scientific articles as well as in programming packages and helps simplify the description of algorithms. We argue that this term may also be a supporting tool for beginner students when solving problems often included in a CS introductory course, especially when more than one element needs to be observed at each step (even in classical problems such as checking if a sequence of numbers is sorted).

The use of general terms expands the language and supports analysis of a problem, formulating an idea for a solution, and communicating ideas. Using a phrase such as "scanning the text with a SW of size 3" hides the details of implementation such as how to go through the text and which elements are processed.

We illustrate a set of stimulating problems taken from contemporary CS topics that use the SW and several other advanced terms that allow solving many problems with the tools acquired in an introductory course. The problems may be introduced early in CS and SE programs since they are simple to understand and do not require programming knowledge that is beyond many introductory courses. They may be integrated in the study of programming structures such as arrays, matrices, and strings. The set of problems may serve CS educators in choosing and developing other examples and assignments for a CS1 course.

Familiarity with the concept and its implementation exercises the transition between different abstraction levels required for high-level formulation of ideas and their implementation in code. Early introduction of advanced concepts prepares students for subsequent courses that tend to be more theoretical.

We recommend the integration of various problems from daily life to raise students' interest and motivation, and introduce common approaches to solving problems in contemporary topics of CS and SE, such as looking for fast solutions "with high probability", common in the big data world (i.e., a Google search).

We suggest that following the demonstration of a problem and its solution, some of the challenges in similar real-life problems will be mentioned as well as other similar problems in other contexts. In this way, the students may get some sense of what computer scientists and software engineers deal with, and, therefore, the nature of the discipline they have chosen to study.

We have integrated the SW concept in CS1 over the last two years when teaching arrays, strings, and matrices. Problems such as those described above were discussed, solved, and implemented in code. These examples have replaced more routine problems, practicing the same subjects in the context of modern and more stimulating contexts. The problems, even when reducing the complexity of real problems, have generated considerable interest. The concept of the SW was adopted without difficulty by students during discussion of ideas for problems' solutions, in documentation of programs, and in written assessment tasks. Animations of traversing sequences and matrices (figures 1 & 2 are their snapshots) were placed in the course site, and students indicated their usefulness in illustrating the SW mechanism and how problems are approached.

There was evidence of a considerable reduction of common coding errors and cumbersome solutions for sequence problems, compared to previous years, yet further comparative study is required to verify this result.

5. REFERENCES

[1] Baase, S. (1983), Computer Algorithms: Introduction to Design and Analysis, Addison-Wesley.

[2] Baase, S., & Van Gelder, A. (2000), Computer Algorithms: Introduction to Design and Analysis, Addison-Wesley.

[3] Beame, P., Clifford, R., & Machmouchi, W. (2013). Element distinctness, frequency moments, and sliding windows. *FOCS 2013*: 290-299.

[4] Charras, C., & Lecroq, T. (2004). Handbook of Exact String Matching Algorithms. King's College Publications.

[5] Chee, Y. S. (1993). Applying Gentner's theory of analogy to the teaching of computer programming. *Int. J. Man Mach. Stud. 38*(3), 347–368.

[6] Cormen, T. H, Leiserson, C. E., & Rivest, R. L. (1985). Introduction to Algorithms, MIT Press, (1st ed.).

[7] Lu, C., Lu, Y., Chen, H., & Tang, C. (2015). Square localization for efficient and accurate object detection, *ICCV 2015.*

[8] Curriculum Guidelines for Undergraduate Degree Programs in Computer Science (2013). IEEE Computer Society, ACM. https://www.acm.org/education/CS2013-final-report.pdf

[9] Curriculum Guidelines for Undergraduate Degree Programs in Software Engineering (2015). IEEE Computer Society, ACM. https://www.acm.org/education/se2014.pdf

[10] Forišek, M. & Steinová, M. (2013). Explaining Algorithms Using Metaphors. Springer, London.

[11] Govender, I., Govender, D. W., Havenga, M., Mentz, E., Breed, B., Dignum, F. & Dignum, V. (2014). Increasing self-efficacy in learning to program: exploring the benefits of explicit instruction for problem solving. *Journal for Transdisciplinary Research in Southern Africa,10*, 187-200.

[12] Hunt, K. (2003). Using image processing to teach CS1 and CS2. *SIGCSE Bulletin, 35*(4), 86-89.

[13] MathWorks: https://www.mathworks.com/help/images/ref/nlfilter.html

[14] Matzko, S., & and Davis, T. A. (2006). Teaching CS1 with graphics and C. In *Proceedings of the 11th annual SIGCSE conference on innovation and technology in computer science education*, 168-172.

[15] Muller, O., & Haberman, B. (2008). Supporting Abstraction Processes in Problem Solving through Pattern-Oriented Instruction. *Computer Science Education, 18*(3), 187-212.

[16] Muller, O., & Haberman, B. (2010). A non-linear approach to solving linear algorithmic problems. *The 40th ASEE/IEEE Frontiers in Education (FIE) Conference.*

[17] Robins, A., Rountree, J., & Rountree, N. (2003). Learning and teaching programming: A review and discussion. *Computer Science Education, 13*(2), 137-172.

[18] Sermanet, P., Eigen, D., Zhang, X., Mathieu, M., Fergus R., & LeCun, Y. (2014). OverFeat integrated recognition, localization and detection using convolutional networks. *International Conference on Learning Representations, 2014.*

[19] Tishman, S., & Perkins, D. N. (1997). The language of thinking. *Phi Delta Kappan, 78*(5), 368-374.

Media Literacy as a By-Product of Collaborative Video Production by CS Students

Anna Vasilchenko[1], David Philip Green[2], Haneen Qarabash[1], Anne Preston[3],
Tom Bartindale[1], Madeline Balaam[1]

[1]Newcastle University,
Newcastle, UK
{initial.last name}@newcastle.ac.uk

[2]Northumbria University,
Newcastle, UK
d.p.green@northumbria.ac.uk

[3]Kingston University,
London, UK
a.preston@kingston.ac.uk

ABSTRACT

Understanding, promoting, and teaching media literacy is an important societal challenge. STEM educators are increasingly looking to incorporate 21st century skills such as media literacy into core subject education. In this paper we investigate how undergraduate Computer Science (CS) students can learn media literacy as a by-product of collaborative video tutorial production. The paper presents a study of 34 third-year CS undergraduates who, as part of their learning, were each asked to produce three video tutorials on Raspberry Pi programming, using a collaborative video production tool for mobile phones (Bootlegger). We provide results of both quantitative and qualitative analysis of the production process and resulting video tutorials, and conclude that the student cohort demonstrated a clear development of media literacy skills. The paper's contribution is twofold. First, we add to the understanding of how the use of mobile collaborative video production technology by non-professionals can help them learn to create meaningful media messages with little scaffolding. Second, we present an alternative pedagogical approach that can help CS students acquire 21st century skills such as media literacy.

Keywords

media literacy; mobile video; co-production; user-generated content

1. INTRODUCTION

Computer Science educators, and STEM educators in general, are increasingly concerned about teaching "soft skills" to their students. Today, a successful graduate has to demonstrate not only solid core subject knowledge, but also a set of additional 21st century skills. These include, among others, communication and critical thinking, as well as information and media literacies [28]. It has been argued that 21st century skills should be taught across the curriculum in both secondary [4] and higher education [7]. Besides, "it can be integrated into nearly any subject area" [4].

There is a growing demand for the ability to understand and create multimedia messages. We encounter media on-the-go, in our workplaces and at home; via TV, public display screens, phones, tablets, and computers. Elections and referendums are fought, won,

and lost on media battlegrounds, and our social lives are increasingly entwined within media-rich social platforms. Public discourses play out in the 'comments' of publications by powerful media organizations and many of us are now habitually representing our own lives in media forms [2].

It is widely accepted that media is a kind of *language* [11]. Like English or Mandarin, the language of media allows people to 'encode' and 'decode' meanings in various ways, from the highly *poetic* to the relatively *prosaic*. Like spoken or written languages, the language of the media requires certain *literacies* in order to encode and decode the meaning it represents, enabling people to both understand and engage critically with media [1, 14].

Furthermore, in the Web 2.0 era, where all of us gradually become *prosumers* (i.e. both producers and consumers) [20], educators need to prepare their students to be capable producers. Production of multimedia messages is no longer a prerogative of artists and journalists. Modern technical professions require the ability to produce creative solutions, powerful portfolios, and video presentations, and graduates must be equipped with these skills.

The SIGCSE community is driving the innovation in teaching soft skills as part of CS education, with substantial efforts dedicated to improving student communication skills [5], fostering team building and collaboration [26], as well as empowering students with entrepreneurial skills [19]. However, there is little research on developing media literacy of CS students, and we address this gap.

In this paper we present an empirical study of a pedagogical approach that facilitates the emergence of *media literacy skills as a by-product of collaborative video production* by third year undergraduate CS students during their coursework on a core subject module. We recorded student behaviour through the use of a collaborative video production tool and analysed it with respect to three key components of media literacy, namely: *access*, *analysis* and *production* of meaningful information. The study contributes to learning design and classroom practice for CS courses that aim to teach media literacy as a by-product of innovative pedagogy.

2. RELATED WORK

In this section, we: 1) critique the fragmented conceptualisation of "media literacy" within existing discourses and call for an applied model that is more suitable for use in empirical contexts; 2) introduce "student-generated content", the central empirical dataset from our study; and 3) outline why student-generated content can be considered a key indicator of student media literacy.

2.1 Definition of Media Literacy

Media literacy has been discussed and approached by educators in Europe, North America, and Australasia for nearly three decades. Many studies, including white papers (e.g., [14]) and national reports (e.g., [27]), have been dedicated to this important component of 21st century life. It is also a component of an effective pedagogical approach, which attracts increasing attention from STEM educators. Yet there are gaps in understanding media literacy as both a research area and as an educational concept [17].

Hobbs [15] suggests that defining media literacy is not an easy task due to the variety of global education systems and fast changing nature of the media itself. For the purpose of this study, we adopted one of the most accepted general definitions: media literacy is *"the ability of a citizen to access, analyse, and produce information for specific outcomes"* [1]. Aufderheide [1] suggested that each component of this definition could be articulated in a number of ways. Among others, Hobbs [14] and Churchill [8] have developed models of media literacy. These models share the components of *analysis, evaluation,* and *creation,* but differ with respect to other factors (e.g. access, question, reflect, act, etc.) as well as in their structure (linear or circular). The relatively abstract nature of these models limits their utility for theoretical application. Thus, building on the flexibility of Aufderheide's definition and drawing on other media literacy research, we have derived our own cyclical model of media literacy, including definitions of the key components of media literacy as following:

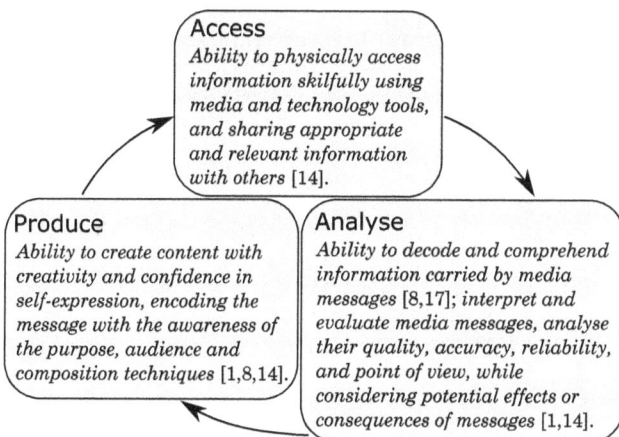

Access
Ability to physically access information skilfully using media and technology tools, and sharing appropriate and relevant information with others [14].

Produce
Ability to create content with creativity and confidence in self-expression, encoding the message with the awareness of the purpose, audience and composition techniques [1,8,14].

Analyse
Ability to decode and comprehend information carried by media messages [8,17]; *interpret and evaluate media messages, analyse their quality, accuracy, reliability, and point of view, while considering potential effects or consequences of messages* [1,14].

Figure 1: Media literacy model

Our model largely echoes Hobbs's scheme and inevitably preserves the *creation* component, which is almost always present in such models. As Gilmor reasons, "being literate in today's world means more than just smarter consumption, however actively you do that. Being literate is also about creating, contributing, and collaborating" [10]. This perspective resonates with pedagogical theory, and particularly *Constructionism,* which theorises that the best learning happens through application of the knowledge in the form of learning artefact creation [13, 21].

2.2 Student-generated content

Let us discuss the 'produce' component of media literacy in detail from the educational perspective. It has been argued that today's students use technology more creatively and efficiently outside of the education system than they do within classrooms [24]. Multiple studies proposed that schools should take into consideration learners' passion for technology and their naturally developed media literacy to enhance their learning experience. The development of Web 2.0 technologies emphasises user-generated content along with user interaction and collaboration [20] and powers another growing trend: yesterday's *audience members* increasingly become content *creators* and *communicators* [30]. "Producing, commenting, and classifying are just as important as

the more passive tasks of searching, reading, watching, and listening" [16].

Asking students to create class content is not new. Indeed, instructors asked students to create multiple-choice questions to build interaction and support excitement in the classroom in the 1980's [6], long before Web 2.0. However, with an abundance of technological tools available today, we see more studies demonstrating learning improvements for students who engage in content creation. For example, Hamer *et al.* [12] studied the concept of Contributing Student Pedagogy, which is grounded on student-generated content, and evaluated its benefits with regards to CS education. On reviewing numerous studies, the authors concluded that Contributing Student Pedagogy fosters learning of course content and promotes the development of a wide range of skills such as research, communication, interdependence, individual accountability, and interpersonal skills [12]. In addition to multiple-choice questions, other examples of student-generated content introduced into the curriculum include: editable wiki-pages [30], narrated animations [13], video vignettes [23], and tutorials [12].

In addition to linking the creation of digital products with deeper learning of subject knowledge and improved academic performance, evidence suggests further benefits: i) multi-media production helps students to better engage with the subject and to look at it under a different angle [13]; ii) it stimulates the development of creativity and critical thinking skills [20]; and iii) produced materials become tangible objects for student learning portfolios [20]. Furthermore, when tasked with creating digital products for the purpose of teaching, students are encouraged to reflect on how to communicate their learning to others, which further embeds their own learning [9].

In summary, the current settings of CS education are favourable for innovating with digital media and collaborative content production. Today's students are "digital natives" [22]; they are born and raised in the Internet era and expect (or at least positively accept) a curriculum that involves working with digital multimedia and content creation. Similarly, educators report numerous benefits of student-generated content and incorporation of multimedia materials into teaching and learning activities. This paper contributes a study of digital content creation as part of an undergraduate CS curriculum. Through studying the process by which students created these products, as well as their experiences doing so, we show how a model of media literacy needs to evolve to take into account the complexity of the content creation process.

3. STUDY METHODOLOGY

We ground our stance for the overall study on Constructionism theory, which advocates *learning through making* [21]. Although this paper does not evaluate the improvement in student core subject learning, it does focus on the investigation of the *making* process and evaluates the *learning* of additional skills facilitated by this process. In other words, we look at how media literacy skills were learnt by students through the process of making digital artefacts.

A mixed methods approach was chosen for the study as media message creation is a complex concept, which is better analysed from multiple angles. We investigated it a) quantitatively through analysis of video creation data; and b) qualitatively through inquiring about student experience and examining the artefacts they produced. Data were collected and analysed with the following research questions in mind:

RQ1: What is the process by which students collaboratevly create meaningful multimedia message about their own learning?

RQ2: What is the student acceptability and experience of creating media as a form of assessment within an undergraduate CS module?

3.1 Study Context

The study took place within a semester-long 3rd year undergraduate module on Ubiquitous computing (Ubicomp) at the School of Computing Science, Newcastle University, UK (module website: https://openlab.ncl.ac.uk/ubicomp). The learning objectives of the module were to introduce students to the field of Ubicomp and develop practical skills in building interactions with a prototyping toolkit (Raspberry Pi). The module was delivered in a flipped classroom format. The class comprised 34 students (85% male). All of them agreed for their final products and records of the creation process of these products to be included into the study.

As part of module assignments (30% of the total mark) students created three short video tutorials of their practical, or lab, sessions, which explained how to program Raspberry Pi and the Grove Pi kit in different scenarios, such as how to detect light or proximity. The activity was designed so that it would not require any more time or effort from students than usual report writing. Besides, tutorial making was incorporated into the existing practical sessions within the course and it did not considerably interfere with the normal running of the sessions. The teaching team used Bootlegger [3], a collaborative video production tool, to facilitate video production as described below.

The production of video tutorials comprised two phases. In the first phase, all students created short video *clips* during practical sessions to document their work, and uploaded these clips to the Bootlegger.tv platform. The uploaded clips would then become available for all other students to use in their own video; students could use clips produced by all their peers. In the second phase, students combined clips into *edits*, to individually create their tutorials. (See: https://openlab.ncl.ac.uk/ubicomp/?page_id=502)

3.2 Bootlegger and Class Integration

Bootlegger is an open source platform consisting of a web and mobile component for commissioning the creation of videos. It supports non-professionals in generating high production value content in situated locations such as concerts, marathons, and ethnography fieldwork. Participants use their mobile phones to capture short video clips, the framing and description of which are defined and requested by the producer, which can be later used to make video for the event. Bootlegger has previously been used for a variety of scenarios, including education [3, 25].

The following aspects influenced the choice of Bootlegger:

i. *A collaborative environment:* Bootlegger is designed to allow users to share video footage, providing different points of views on the same step at a practical session. The students can therefore work together to make a comprehensive coverage of different steps of their work. Video clips can be used by all students in making the final edits to submit for assessment. This approach provides students an opportunity to examine how other students convey technical details and create learning materials.

ii. *Ease of use:* the Bootlegger mobile app and the web platform are designed to be used by non-professionals, thus they are easy to use and require no prior skills in video capturing and editing.

iii. *It is a mobile application:* this allowed the students to use their own familiar devices rather than to worry about acquiring video cameras and learning how to use them.

iv. *The shoot templates:* Bootlegger provides a "shoot template", a set of suggested shots that the teacher (producer) can choose from to help guide students on what to shoot, and aid framing it

better. The students are free to ignore the template and make their own choices.

3.3 Data Collection and Processing

Our dataset comprised both qualitative and quantitative data. Our quantitative data included system logs from the Bootlegger platform, which detailed the clip production and edit 'lifecycle' for all six practical sessions. The data comprised: i) for each created clip: id, author, time of creation, length, practical session id, file path; ii) for each created edit: id, name, author, description, path, time of creation, practical session id, number of clips used, clips ids. This provided us with a large dataset that we analysed with R, a programming language and environment for data analysis.

The qualitative set of the data included the following:

i. Semi-structured face to face interviews (about 30 minutes long) conducted at the end of the module focusing on student general experience of the module and including questions about digital media creation as a form of assessment. The participation was voluntary, 8 out of 34 students were recruited. The transcripts were analysed using inductive thematic analysis.

ii. Student artefacts: a sample of the 10% most popular clips used in student edits (50 clips, with 6 to 18 uses each); and all student final tutorials submitted for assessment along with their marking criteria – all analysed using inductive thematic analysis.

iii. Our preliminary analysis of quantitative data and the student artefacts revealed a number of further questions we wished to investigate. A questionnaire with 6 closed- and 2 open-ended questions was created, tested, and distributed to the students electronically, with two £10 vouchers as an incentive; 10 students responded. The questionnaire covered: the impact of access to clips created by other students; most important factors for clip choice for edits; and perception of overall activity outcome. The answers to open-ended questions were analysed using a deductive approach.

4. FINDINGS

The module comprised eight practical sessions. In six of these sessions students were asked to document their work with the Raspberry Pi to generate footage for the tutorials. Students could choose any three practical sessions for their final submissions. The first three sessions, however, were significantly more popular with 88%, 82%, and 71% of students choosing them for their final submissions. The fact that the majority of students chose the same sessions contributed to a high degree of video clip sharing and facilitated student collaboration (e.g. 50% of students had their clips reused by other students 10 times and more). 102 tutorials were submitted in total (see Table 1).

Table 1: Summary of student contribution for each tutorial

Week	Tutorial	# of clips made	# of clip uses	# of submitted tutorials	% of total class
1	Pi is alive	177	745	30	88%
2	Proximity detector	221	699	28	82%
3	Context awareness	165	397	24	71%
4	Interactive surface	90	295	13	38%
5	Natural user interface	87	224	6	18%
6	Responsive LCD	66	62	1	3%
	Total:	806	2422	102	

By the end of the module the students captured 806 clips; 657 were successfully uploaded to the system (some were lost due to connectivity issues). The total number of clips used for edits by unique users was 500. Many clips were used multiple times by the same and different students, and the overall number of clip uses for all edits was 2,422.

All students enrolled to the module had successfully completed the video creation assignment. The average mark for the class was 19.9 out of 30 (66.3%, equivalent to 2.1 classification), and 13 out of 34 students earned the first class mark (70% or above). The marking criteria for the assignment emphasised the clarity of video tutorials and their fitting to the purpose – showing all necessary steps to complete a task with enough details for another student to follow the tutorial and produce the same output. Therefore, we consider that the student artefacts were *meaningful multimedia messages*.

4.1 Media Literacy Model vs Student Behaviour

To answer **RQ1** we use Aufderheide's definition [1] of media literacy and our description of its three key components (see Section 2.1) as a framework for classifying our findings into categories of student behaviour. Below we describe how students *access*, *analyse* and *produce* a media message and demonstrate the necessary literacies using examples from the collected data.

4.1.1 Ability to Access

Access is the ability to physically access the information by skilfully using media and technology tools, and sharing appropriate and relevant information with others [14]. In terms of interactions with Bootlegger this is the ability to use mobile phones and PCs with the Bootlegger application; and to access the clips stored in the cloud that were created with Bootlegger.

Student behaviour:
Students used the Bootlegger mobile and online applications with shot planning and templates for shooting the clips, documenting the process of their work with Pis. They were also able to access and see all the clips uploaded into the Bootlegger system and participate in sharing the clips with others.

Activity outcome:
5 interview and 7 survey respondents said they liked the idea of using video for assessments, and 4 students said they preferred video tutorials to written reports. By possessing the required technology (mobile phones and PC), being able to download and install the tool (Bootlegger), and agreeing to do so, the students demonstrated their "ability to physically access information".

4.1.2 Ability to Analyse

Analyse/Decode is the ability to decode and comprehend information carried by media messages [8, 18]; interpret and evaluate media messages, analyse their quality, accuracy, reliability, and point of view, while considering potential effects or consequences of messages [1, 14]. In terms of interactions with Bootlegger this translates to 1) decoding the clips from the cloud to interpret their meaning and decide what they are good for; 2) evaluating the quality of the clips to select the best ones for the final video.

Student behaviour:
Students decoded the information carried by clips in Bootlegger to determine which clips they could use in their own tutorials.

Activity outcome:
The Bootlegger platform allows the user to sort clips connected with a shot by the time of creation, author, and other preselected characteristics, such as association of the clip with a particular step, shot overlay, or subject focus; it also has a thumbnail preview with metadata. The Bootlegger log data demonstrates that all students (even those whose final videos contained only their own clips) tried

to create edits using clips made by others. This is also confirmed by student answers in the interviews and survey.

> *"I first looked at my own clips, as I just wanted to use my own resources. Only when I didn't find something in my clips I went looking for others' clips. I also did use Lea's 'title' clips because they're good, she just nailed it."*

Qualitative analysis of 10% of most popular clips used in student edits gave us a list of most common features preferred by the students, including genre and cinematic qualities apparent in clips. We took this further and asked survey participants to rate these features with regards to their importance for student choice of the required clip, see Fig. 2.

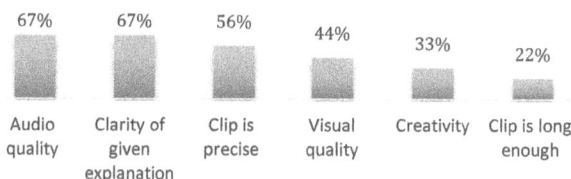

Figure 2: Most important factors for selecting clips for final edits (percentage of survey responses)

Further analysis of most used clips also revealed the following clip genres were most popular: 1) Title; 2) Close up, connecting things; 3) Code explanation; 4) Head shot (introduction); 5) Head shot (explanation); 6) Demonstrating how something is working; 7) Code and output demonstration; 8) Graph explanation, close up; 9) Objects, details, close up. See Fig. 3 for a correlation between the number of popular clips per genre and the number of their total uses among the 10% most used clips. 64% of most popular clips were short and concise, focusing on only one thing (e.g. titles for tutorial steps; connecting something to the Pi), which suggests that elementary clips were more reusable.

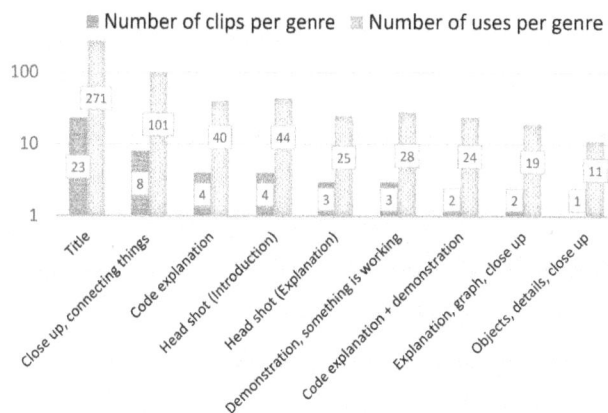

Figure 3: Clip genres (X-axis); number of clips and number of total uses (Y-axis) as seen from analysis of 50 most popular clips

4.1.3 Ability to Produce

Produce/Encode is the ability to create content with creativity and confidence in self-expression, encoding the message with the awareness of the purpose, audience and composition techniques [1, 8, 14]. In terms of interactions with Bootlegger this translates to: 1) at clip level: generation of clips documenting each step of student work; 2) at edit level: editing the clips into the film (tutorial) in order to create a meaningful narrative for a specific purpose.

Student behaviour:
Video production through Bootlegger consisted of two steps:

Clip level: students recorded clips showing the steps of their work. They were given some tips via the assignment brief, Bootlegger templates (suggested steps of the tutorial, clip lengths, a collection of possible shot overlays), and an example tutorial prepared by the instructor, but were free to experiment and demonstrate creativity.

Edit level: recorded clips needed to be composed into a tutorial, creating a meaningful narrative for i) demonstration of learning outcomes of the course; ii) instruction of other students.

Activity outcome:
Although students were tasked to produce clips during the class time, nearly half of the interview and survey respondents admitted that they were unhappy with the quality level of recorded clips and spent additional time to reshoot and improve most of the clips. By analysing time stamps of the clips uploaded to the cloud we can see that, for example, many clips related to Practical 1 were shot substantially later in the semester (see Fig. 4). In the interview and survey responses students also admitted that attempts to create an edit made them reconsider which clips had to be recorded:

> *"When we actually did that first video, like maybe a couple of weeks before the deadline, we kind of realised that there is all this content that we needed that we haven't actually been recording for all of the weeks, so in the end we had to go back and basically just record everything from scratch again."*

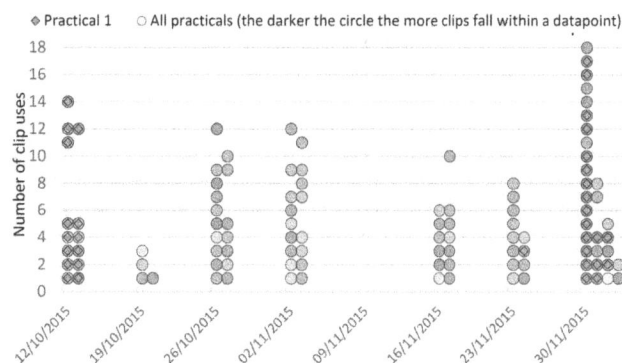

Figure 4: Number of clip uses (Y-axis) and production timeline (X-axis) during the module

Students acknowledged that access to clips shot by their peers had a positive impact on their video creation (8 survey respondents), inspired them, and made them rethink their clips (6 respondents).

> *"It got me thinking about things I never considered before and also on ways to improve it."*

> *"On seeing other's clips I realized mine featured only code and the Pi, however some students had introduced the project and gave explanations with the camera focused on themselves. I thought this was a much more personal and friendly approach so I incorporated this into my own videos."*

9 survey participants said they used clips shot by others because they did not capture those clips themselves. Also, 4 respondents admitted that clips made by others were of better quality.

On the other hand, 6 respondents preferred to use their own clips for the final edits as they thought they were of better quality. 3 respondents said they wanted to use only their own clips as they were shot in the same style so the edits would look homogeneous.

4.2 Student experience
Half of the students who took part in the interviews and survey reported that they had previous experience of creating video

tutorials. As mentioned above, 12 out of 18 respondents said that they liked the idea of alternative way of assessment for a CS module. Moreover, students reported that this assignment did not take them any longer to do than a regular written report.

When students were asked if they thought they had learned anything extra from creating the tutorials, 3 answered that they had improved their instructional videos creation skills. While 2 respondents reported that the task also improved their subject learning.

> *"It did force me to gain an understanding of the task thoroughly so that I knew I had the knowledge to explain precisely what to do."*

Although the students mostly liked the idea of using videos instead of written reports, there were a lot of complaints due to some technical issues with Bootlegger. Until asked, the students did not realise the benefits the tool provided them.

> *"Bootlegger coursework - I didn't think it really test the knowledge of the actual course content. I like the idea of making videos through the practicals but I thought having 30% of the coursework on just ordering other people's videos was worth a bit too much...whereas you could've had another coursework kind of more programming based or an essay, which would've tested the knowledge a bit more... Also I just didn't like the software we had to use."*

Yet, some respondents still reflected positively on Bootlegger.

> *"I thought that was really great, since everyone had different videos particularly because not everyone knew exactly what to shoot, and so some people would have like a really great clip of what the outcome was, someone would do a really good like speech on how to set up the code, and so it all just pieced together really nicely."*

To summarise, student experience with video creation in general was mainly positive. However, their attitude to the used tool was mixed due to its instability and bugs.

5. DISCUSSION
We have explored the process of media message creation in student-generated content through a novel framework of media literacy. In doing so, we observed each of the three main components of media literacy (*access*, *analyse* and *create*), in the process of student learning to engage in the practice of producing a video. Like Weilenmann *et al* [29], we assume that the demonstration of these skills is a candidate step for the manifestation of an emerging media literacy trajectory.

In addition, there are further takeaways about student behaviour:

i. The students realised certain problems with their video footage (e.g. the lack of different perspectives or poor audio quality) only when they encountered them as part of the final video editing. Thus, student media literacy emerged and developed through the process, prompting them to redo the clips or to search for alternatives among clips produced by their peers.

In its essence, the production at clip and edit levels is very different: the former is to record what is happening here and now; the latter is to construct a storyline where each component/clip is in the right place and appropriate for the whole story. While in everyday life many of us create clip-level videos (recording events that are happening around us and catch our attention or interest), not everyone is familiar with video editing techniques, when the author has to bear in mind the ultimate purpose and hence the content and shape of the final product [29]. So the fact that our students had to redo most of their recordings after trying to construct the final edits suggests that their media literacy emerged on the go.

ii. The fact that students moved back and forth between the media literacy components when they decided to redo the video to improve it, implies that the process of media message creation is neither linear nor cyclic (as suggested in Section 2.1). We believe that the three main components are interdependent and may occur in different sequences, which is an important consideration in updated media literacy models.

iii. Students took advantage of the possibility to see contributions uploaded by others. They *learned from each other*, as evidenced by their clip reshooting after watching clips by others (seen from Bootlegger log data, confirmed by interviews and survey). Students also developed an understanding of *reusability of media components* with such factors as the clip authorship, its visual and audio quality, as well as clip genre, and time of creation.

iv. The collaborative environment of Bootlegger in its nature is similar to crowdsourcing (something familiar to many CS practitioners). Thus, students looking at and selecting clips from the cloud have demonstrated the pattern of *deconstruction*, where the more elementary component is, the easier it is to reuse it. Such clips as 'title' and 'connecting things' are less personal, more elementary, and have limited capacity for misconception or presentation of a wrong point of view. Hence, they were popular for reuse among students. On the other hand, 'intro' and 'demo' clips display more individuality and present deeper levels of information, so there was a greater risk of being misinterpreted or provide incorrect details, thus most students preferred to shoot these clips themselves.

v. Returning to **RQ2** we can say that modern CS students are ready and mainly willing to deal with media creation as a form of learning and assessment, however they can easily become demotivated when they encounter technical issues with the tools used.

5.2 Limitations and Future Work

At the time of the study Bootlegger was still under development and it has been used in this specific context for the first time. Hence, the students and the teaching team faced several difficulties during the process, such as mobile application bugs, connectivity issues and scalability problems due to the rapid uptake of editing. These problems led to a mixed attitude of students to the tool.

The sample of this study is not suitable for generalisation due to its size. However, we hope that our results provide insights on innovative classroom practice. In our future work we plan to repeat the study with a larger student cohort to further validate our current findings and to focus on evaluation of the *learning through making* multimedia artefacts for CS subjects. We also intend to examine the student artefacts in more detail, from different perspectives, e.g. a professional videographer and other learners.

7. CONCLUSION

The purpose of this study was to report on innovative learning design and classroom practice for a CS course that aimed at teaching media literacy as a by-product of video tutorial production. We also presented how the use of mobile collaborative video production technology by non-professionals can help them learn to create meaningful media messages with little scaffolding.

8. REFERENCES

[1] Aufderheide, P. 1993. *Media Literacy: A Report of the National Leadership Conference on Media Literacy*. Aspen Institute.

[2] Aylett, M.P. et al. 2016. My Life On Film. *CHI EA' 16*, 3379-3386

[3] Bartindale, T. et al. 2016. Scaffolding Community Documentary Film Making using Commissioning Templates. *CHI'16*, 2705–2716.

[4] Bergsma, L. et al. 2007. *The Core Principles of Media Literacy Education*. Denver, CO: Alliance for a Media Literate America

[5] Blume, L. et al. 2009. A "Communication Skills for Computer Scientists" Course. *ACM SIGCSE Bulletin*. 41, 3 (Aug. 2009), 65.

[6] Bonwell, C.C. and Eison, J.A. 1991. *Active Learning: Creating Excitement in the Classroom*. The George Washington University.

[7] Christ, W.G. 2004. Assessment, Media Literacy Standards, and Higher Education. *American Behavioral Scientist*. 48, 1, 92–96.

[8] Churchill, D. 2010. New Literacy in the Digital World: Implications for Higher Education. *ALSR 2010: Conference towards Future Possibilities*.

[9] Dale, E. 1946. *Audio-Visual Methods in Teaching*. Dryden Press.

[10] Gillmor, D. 2010. *Mediactive*. Creative Commons.

[11] Hall, S. 1980. Encoding/decoding. *Culture, media, language*, 128–138.

[12] Hamer, J. et al. 2008. Contributing Student Pedagogy. *inroads - SIGCSE Bulletin'08*, 194–212.

[13] Hoban, G. et al. 2010. Articulating constructionism: Learning science though designing and making "slowmations" (student-generated animations). *ASCILITE'10*, 433–443.

[14] Hobbs, R. 2010. *Digital and Media Literacy: A Plan of Action*. Aspen Institute.

[15] Hobbs, R. 2016. Literacy: Understanding media and how they work. *What Society Needs from Media in the Age of Digital Communication*. R.G. Picard, ed. Media XXI. 131–160.

[16] Horizon Report 2007. *http://www.nmc.org/pdf/2007_Horizon_ Report.pdf*. Accessed: 2016-06-23.

[17] Jolls, T. and Wilson, C. 2014. The Core Concepts: Fundamental to Media Literacy Yesterday, Today and Tomorrow. *Journal of Media Literacy Education*. 6, 62, 68–78.

[18] Livingstone, S. and Thumim, N. 2003. Assessing the media literacy of UK adults: a review of the academic literature. *Seminar on Media Literacy*. March (2003), 54.

[19] McGee, O. et al. 2016. Out of the Comfort Zone: Embedding Entrepreneurship in a Cohort of Computer Science Doctoral Students. *ITiCSE'16*, 83–88.

[20] Mcloughlin, C. and Lee, M.J.W. 2008. The Three P's of Pedagogy for the Networked Society. *International Journal of Teaching and Learning in Higher Education*. 20, 1, 10–27.

[21] Papert, S. and Harel, I. 1991. Situating Constructionism. *Constructionism*. Ablex Publishing Corporation.

[22] Prensky, M. 2001. Digital Natives, Digital Immigrants Part 1. *On the Horizon*. 9, 5, 1–6.

[23] Read, D. and Lancaster, S. 2012. Unlocking video: 24/7 learning for the iPod generation. *EDUCATION IN CHEMISTRY*. July 2012

[24] Rodriguez, P.M. et al. 2012. Examining Student Digital Artifacts During a Year-Long Technology Integration Initiative. *Computers in the Schools*. 29, 4, 355–374.

[25] Sarangapani, V. et al. 2016. Virtual.Cultural.Collaboration. *MobileHCI'16*, 341–352.

[26] Soundarajan, N. et al. 2015. Collaborative and Cooperative-Learning in Software Engineering Courses. *ICSE'15*, 319–322.

[27] Thoman, E. 2004. Media Literacy - A National Priority for a Changing World. *American Behavioral Scientist*. 48, 1, 18–29.

[28] Trilling, B. and Fadel, C. 2012. *21st Century Skills*. *Learning for Life in Our Times*. Jossey-Bass.

[29] Weilenmann, A. et al. 2014. Mobile video literacy: Negotiating the use of a new visual technology. *Personal and Ubiquitous Computing*. 18, 3, 737–752.

[30] Wheeler, S. et al. 2008. The good, the bad and the wiki: Evaluating student-generated content for collaborative learning. *British Journal of Educational Technology*. 39, 6, 987–995.

Raspberry Pi as a Platform for the Internet of Things Projects: Experiences and Lessons

Stan Kurkovsky, Chad Williams
Central Connecticut State University
Department of Computer Science
{kurkovsky,cwilliams}@ccsu.edu

ABSTRACT

The Internet of Things (IoT) represents a new computing paradigm that may soon add a new dimension to the skillset expected from a well-rounded computing professional. Computer Science education is addressing these demands by adding IoT-centric courses to the curriculum and including relevant content into a broad range of existing courses. This paper presents the experience of incorporating IoT projects into an existing Systems Programming course. We examine several suitable hardware platforms, provide a sampling of student projects implemented using the Raspberry Pi with a variety of sensors, and discuss a number of lessons learned that could benefit other educators planning to incorporate the IoT material into their coursework.

CCS Concepts

• **Social and professional topics ~ Computer science education** • **Computer systems organization ~ Embedded and cyber-physical systems**

Keywords

Internet of Things; Raspberry Pi; sensors; student projects.

1. INTRODUCTION

The term 'Internet of Things' (IoT) became truly prominent in 2005 when the International Telecommunication Union published a report on this subject [12]. The IoT concept encompasses devices, sensors, and services existing within an interconnected infrastructure with an efficient access to ample computational facilities. This paradigm enables tangible objects to gather and transmit information about the physical world, thus creating usable services and interfaces allowing these objects to intelligently interact with their users and other systems [28]. The IoT systems have been successfully implemented in many areas, including home automation, surveillance, transportation, and healthcare.

An IHS report from March 2016 indicates that the number of installed IoT devices will grow from 15.4 billion in 2015 to 30.7 billion devices in 2020 and to 75.4 billion in 2025 [11]. Consequently, the number of IoT devices is expected to exceed the number of mobile phones by 2018 becoming the largest category of connected devices [4]. A McKinsey report estimates that IoT has a potential economic impact between $3.9 trillion to $11.1 trillion

ITiCSE '17, July 03-05, 2017, Bologna, Italy
© 2017 ACM. ISBN 978-1-4503-4704-4/17/07...$15.00
DOI: http://dx.doi.org/10.1145/3059009.3059028

a year by 2025 [19]. It is unsurprising that many major industry players, including IBM, Samsung, Intel, and ARM, to name just a few, are showing a very significant interest in the IoT market showcasing their relevant products at many recent technology exhibitions.

Unlike a new technology or a framework du jour, the IoT represents a new paradigm of computing, much like mobile computing did a decade ago. Given such a tremendous growth in the number of deployed devices and services, the IoT is positioned to make a significant impact on the skillset of professionals working in the software and hardware industries. Computer Science educators began to respond to these demands by adding IoT-centric courses in the curriculum and including relevant content into a broad range of existing courses. This paper reviews a number of such initiatives and describes the authors' experiences of incorporating IoT projects into an existing Systems Programming course. We examine several hardware platforms suitable for student projects, provide a brief sampling of the projects completed by the students, and conclude by discussing a number of our experiences and lessons that could benefit other educators planning to incorporate the IoT material into their coursework.

2. BACKGROUND WORK

A draft version of Computer Engineering Curricula 2016 does mention the IoT in the Computer Engineering Body of Knowledge (Strategies for Emerging Technologies unit, Applied Emerging Technologies area) as a core outcome: *"Describe the internet of things (IoT) and its effect on computer engineering."* We believe that the role of the IoT is significantly downplayed here because other items in the same list of outcomes also include *"Describe the manner in which a 3D printer would reproduce a miniature model sailboat in a bottle"* and *"Explain ways in which Web 2.0 and social networks might affect the field of computer engineering."*

Lacking specific guidance from the current Computer Science Curricula [7], colleges and universities have begun to introduce IoT topics in many different ways, some of which are sampled below.

Jeong et al [13] describe an IoT-centric course designed around the Lab of Things platforms developed by Microsoft Research [3]. With the IoT being the main topic of the course, the authors used a project-based learning approach to provide students with a solid experience of building IoT systems using industry-standard frameworks such as Microsoft Azure.

Osipov and Riliskis [21] conducted a 'triple-run experiment,' in which three quarter-long graduate and undergraduate courses were taught in parallel to provide a holistic view on the IoT concept. The work in each of these three network-centric courses covered network applications, programming, and wireless sensor networks. It was rooted in different aspects of the same research project for non-intrusive detection and monitoring of motor vehicles traveling along the motorways equipped with a road sensor network.

Perhaps the largest course to introduce the IoT concepts has been My Digital Life offered by the Open University in the UK [15]. First offered in 2011 and scheduled to be discontinued in 2017, this 9-month introductory course attracted many thousands of students. Each student in this course received a SenseBoard, a custom-designed device based on the Arduino microcontroller, along with a collection of sensors that can be attached to the SenseBoard. SenseBoard runs Sense, a visual programming environment based on MIT's Scratch that has been extended with special features to interact with the sensors.

Given that many existing CS programs have little or no room for adding another required course into their curriculum, integrating IoT topics into other existing courses is a viable option. He et al [9] describe a broad framework of laboratory modules for an embedded systems design course, which incorporates many elements of IoT systems, their design and programming. Using Arduino and Raspberry Pi kits, each module is designed for using independently from others, but the courses in which they can be adopted are greatly limited by their embedded systems context.

Zhong and Liang developed an IoT-focused course for Computer Science majors using the Raspberry Pi as the hardware platform [29]. The course focuses on a series of progressively complex projects, in which student teams design and prototype devices constructed by pairing Raspberry Pi with a range of sensors.

Whether educators used IoT systems built out of a single device [2,15,29] or as a part of a larger infrastructure combining cloud-based services with local hardware [9,13,21], there is a strong consensus that Computer Science graduates need more exposure to the IoT concepts and that IoT systems offer an excellent foundation for hands-on student projects.

Incorporating IoT studies in the Computer Science curriculum may have a number of additional positive impacts. Using tangible toolkits for physical computing that incorporate tinkering with processor boards, wires, sensors, and other devices support pedagogies of production and collaboration [5]. In general, as a constructionist activity, creating tangible objects has been shown to help develop critical thinking skills and solidify the learners' understanding of the subject matter [22]. Not being constrained to a single computing environment, such as a desktop computer, tangible components used to build IoT devices embedded in everyday objects provide learners with ample opportunities to construct and share their mental models through design and prototyping of interactive objects.

3. IOT HARDWARE PLATFORMS

There is an ongoing debate aimed to standardize the reference architecture common to all IoT systems [27]. As shown in Figure 1, generally, the architecture of most IoT systems is comprised of four functional layers: a *sensing layer* to collect the data about the physical world, which may also include actuators that make a tangible impact on the environment or other objects; an *access layer* to collect and transmit the data; a *service layer* to create and handle usable value-added services and applications, and an *interface layer* to interact with the users and other systems.

As a rule, the sensing and networking layers of most IoT systems are implemented within the hardware, while the load of the service and interface layers may be balanced between the device itself and the related infrastructure of various web-based services. A

framework that supports designing, building, and experimenting with an IoT system in any setting, including student learning, must support some, if not all of the above layers inside of a hardware device rather than being implemented entirely on a desktop computer or any other general purpose computing device. Therefore, studying, let alone building an IoT system, requires a dedicated hardware platform capable of implementing some of the four layers within a relatively small physical form factor.

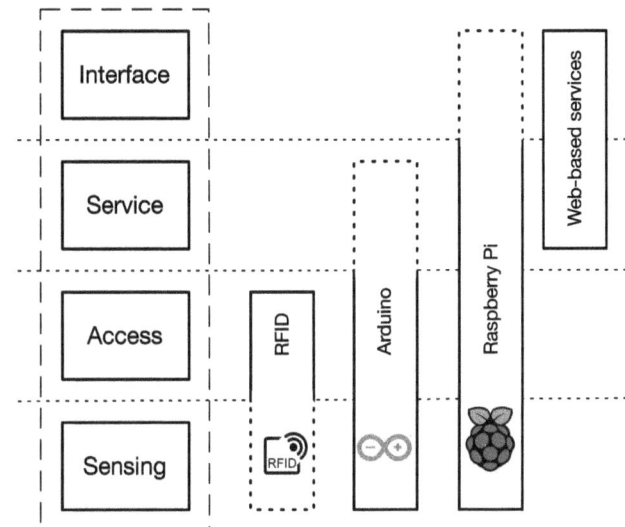

Figure 1. Hardware platforms for the Internet of Things systems and functional layers of their architecture.

Some educators pioneering the use of IoT paradigm in education as early as a decade ago, started experimenting with radio-frequency identification (RFID) technology to communicate the physical proximity of tangible objects to each other. RFID tags store and transmit identification numbers of physical objects they are embedded in or attached to, which can be read by RFID readers using radio communication [8]. Although today RFID is widely adopted in transportation, logistics, supply chain management, pharmaceutical, medical, and many other industries, RFID technology only supports the networking layer of the IoT paradigm. In a way, RFID also implements the sensing layer, but only to the extent of being able to detect the presence of the tagged object, without the possibility to collect any information about the environment. The functionality of all other layers typically must be implemented on a separate computing system equipped with one or more RFID readers.

Arduino, originally introduced in 2005, is a programmable microcontroller board that can be extended by connecting to other devices, sensors, or special purpose expansion boards ('shields'). Low cost, flexibility, and the ease of programming quickly made Arduino a popular choice for hobbyists, individual learners, and educators seeking a platform for teaching concepts ranging from introductory programming to embedded computing [10]. All Arduino boards can be programmed with a language based on C/C++ using a cross-platform IDE. WiFi networking has been added to recent versions of Arduino boards, while Ethernet ports were supported early on. Given the open architecture of Arduino to connect virtually any possible sensors, actuators, or networking interfaces, Arduino makes a great choice for building an IoT system with the full support for the sensing and networking architectural. However, given its limited processing power, Arduino may not be able to efficiently support the implementation of the service and interface layer components.

Raspberry Pi is an inexpensive credit-card sized computer originally developed to promote teaching computer science basics to school children [25]. Like Arduino, the Raspberry Pi encourages experimenting with its hardware configuration. The purpose behind the development of the Raspberry Pi project was to create a replacement for an increasingly complex 'closed box' computer that would encourage kids to code and tinker with it. The Raspberry Pi includes a processor, system memory, network interfaces, and a memory card slot, along with the ports for attaching sensors, peripherals, and other devices. A number of add-on board, including the Sensorian shield [18] and the Sense HAT (http://www.raspberrypi.org/products/sense-hat), combining several types of sensors have been developed for the Raspberry Pi. Typical setups include connecting Raspberry Pi to the same kind of peripherals that can be attached to a traditional desktop, or remotely logging in to it from another computer, in which case Raspberry Pi does not need to be connected to anything other than a power supply and a wired or wireless network. Raspberry Pi runs Linux-based Raspbian, which includes a number of programming environments such as Python, Scratch, BlueJ, and Greenfoot [14]. The Raspberry Pi platform is a natural fit for implementing the sensing and access layers of the IoT system architecture. In the case of designing a single-device IoT system, Raspberry Pi has enough flexibility and processing power to implement the service layer by running data- and sensor-driven applications on the device. At the same time, its IO and networking capabilities would easily allow one to extend it in order to implement the interface layer to make these applications easily accessible by the users and its services accessible by remote systems.

Many commercially available IoT devices and IoT projects described in the literature increasingly rely upon a cloud-based middleware infrastructure partially or fully implementing the functionality of the service and interface layers. This infrastructure can enable IoT devices to access a broad range of web services that can leverage much higher processing power, provide access large data sets, and enable a rich interaction with other systems and services [20]. For example, ThingSpeak enables collection, storage, analysis, and visualization of data received from sensors connected to Arduino, Raspberry Pi and other IoT hardware platforms [23]. ThingSpeak provides APIs for a number of programming languages including C, Java, and Python, as well as MATLAB support for data analytics and visualization. A survey of other middleware platforms for IoT can be found in [26].

4. IOT AND SYSTEMS PROGRAMMING

Our Systems Programming course has been a required component in our ABET-accredited undergraduate program in Computer Science for many years. The course originated as a low-level programming course aimed to study the inner workings of Linux while writing system-level programs in C. It is a 3-credit semester long course with a typical class size of 25 students. With Data Structures being the only prerequisite for this course, it is aimed mainly at sophomores and juniors.

We made a decision to add IoT material to this course to achieve the following objectives: expose students to the basics of programming hardware/software interfaces; review recent trends in IoT applications, especially in home automation; and provide students with an opportunity to design their own IoT system using the Raspberry Pi as the hardware platform.

At the same time, we had to operate within a number of constraints. All IoT material had to fit into the existing course without compromising its integrity. We needed to continue using C as the main programming language for Linux systems programming. Given the target audience, we had to assume that in many cases student experience beyond Data Structures may be limited. We also needed to present a substantial amount of sample IoT applications while leaving enough room for students to suggest their own ideas for the course project.

Raspberry Pi was chosen as the hardware platform for this course because its operating system is Linux-based and it comes equipped with the tools needed for programming in C making it an excellent fit for teaching all Systems Programming concepts. For the duration of the semester, each student received their own Raspberry Pi kit, which included Raspberry Pi 3 model B with WiFi and Bluetooth connectivity, a USB power supply, a 16GB Micro SD card with Raspbian OS, an enclosure case, two heatsinks, and an HDMI cable.

5. IOT PROJECTS

A semester-long project is an integral part of our Systems Programming course. With the IoT topics being integrated into the course, it only became natural to give the course project the focus on building an IoT system. Given the possible complexity of the resulting system, the importance of early design choices in shaping the structure and features of the system, and given a possibly limited student exposure to hardware design and advanced topics, we structured the course project into the following three incremental phases.

Simple IoT device/sensor. Students were first asked to design and implement a system that would enable the Raspberry Pi to interact with one or more sensors. This would help students break the barrier of designing a system comprised of both hardware and software, something that most of them likely have never done before. This phase implemented the sensing and access layers of the IoT system architecture outlined in Section 3. It was also important to ensure that the logic of interfacing and communicating with the sensors or other hardwired devices was implemented and debugged before moving to the next phase. For example, consider creating a single-device system to monitor the weather. This device can be designed using the Raspberry Pi with several sensors (such as temperature, pressure, and humidity) or a Sense HAT attached to it. This phase would involve enabling the Raspberry Pi to read the data from the sensors.

Smart IoT device. At this phase, students focused on the logic of processing the data received from the sensors. Based on this logic, students also implemented any value-added service that this system would be able to provide if it were implemented on a single device. This phase implemented the service and interface layers of the architecture. In the weather monitoring example, this phase would involve programming the Raspberry Pi to query the sensors on schedule or on demand, storing the readouts, and developing an interface (perhaps with an attached touchscreen monitor) to display the current readout values and, possibly, reviewing the readout history.

Networked IoT device. Once the main functionality of the previous phase is implemented, the students are ready to distribute the logic of this functionality across the network so that the services of this IoT system can be accessed from multiple locations, aggregated with data and/or services provided by other systems. This phase would extend or provide a new implementation of the service and interface layers. For example, instead of storing historical sensor readouts locally, the weather monitoring system could transfer them to a cloud-based service such as ThingSpeak [23], which can provide more advanced computational tools and data visualization capabilities and combine the data from multiple weather monitoring IoT nodes.

The remainder of this section provides a brief sampling of student projects implementing IoT systems with the Raspberry Pi on our course. All of them were implemented following the three incremental phases described above.

5.1 Smart Camera

This system implements a motion-activated camera that takes a picture any time when a motion of a warm body is detected. The system is configurable so that the photo can be stored locally in the Raspberry Pi's memory, sent to an email address, and/or uploaded securely to a remote server. A system of this nature may have a number of application areas including security/surveillance cameras, wildlife/game photography, motion detection for home automation systems, license plate capture at gate/toll, baby monitoring, etc.

The Raspberry Pi Camera Module is attached via a ribbon cable to a camera serial interface (CSI) included on board of the Raspberry Pi. The case provided with the Raspberry Pi kit used in this project has a special cutout for the camera lens, so the camera module can be securely enclosed. The camera draws power from the Raspberry Pi, so no additional power cables are needed. The passive infrared sensor (PIR) is a simple device that sends a high (3V) signal when infrared radiation is detected. The sensor hardware itself controls sensitivity and delay settings for detection of motion and can be adjusted as needed. The PIR uses pulse width modulation (PWM). The PWM wires can be connected directly to the Raspberry Pi's general-purpose input/output (GPIO) pins as shown in Figure 2.

Figure 2. Design and implementation of the Smart Camera project.

5.2 Automatic Door Lock

A prototype of an automatic door lock was developed to unlock a door whenever a user of the previously approved mobile device is in the vicinity. This system used Bluetooth addresses associated with every Bluetooth-enabled mobile device as a label uniquely identifying its owner. Each approved device must be enrolled into the system, either locally, or remotely. When a Bluetooth-enabled device is in the vicinity of the lock, the Bluetooth module onboard the Raspberry Pi can identify its presence, compare it with a list of approved devices, and unlock the door if there is a match.

This device should be located behind the locked door to prevent tampering. Enrollment of approved Bluetooth devices and logging of unlocking attempts can be done locally, as well as remotely via a network connection to an external server. Remote operation also enables building this system without any additional devices attached to the Raspberry Pi. A solenoid-based linear actuator driving the door lock (http://www.adafruit.com/products/1512) requires an additional power supply to activate the electromagnet inside the actuator.

5.3 NFC Tracking

All student and faculty IDs at our university have a built-in RFID tag, which is used to unlock office doors and access parking garages. A device built with the Raspberry Pi connected to an appropriate RFID reader and placed at a room entrance could inconspicuously register all people entering or leaving the room. Such a system may be particularly useful in a computer lab to gather statistics about the utilization of the facility. At the very minimum, the collected data could show the amount of through traffic and its distribution over time. A minimal analysis of the data could tell how much time each individual spends in the lab. Connecting the system with the university's LDAP server would enable getting the names of individuals associated with their ID tags. Similar systems employing near field communication (NFC) technologies such as RFID for tracking people and objects are currently among the most broadly deployed implementations of IoT systems in the industry.

6. LESSONS LEARNED

Choice of the hardware platform. As shown in Section 2, both Raspberry Pi and Arduino have been successfully used to build IoT devices and systems in student projects. With the costs of the boards and sensors aside, both platforms are fully capable of implementing rich functionality for the sensing and access layers of the IoT system architecture shown in Figure 1. The choice between the two platforms, in our opinion, should be dictated mainly by the complexity of the other two layers: how much data processing and other logic is needed at the service layer to implement a meaningful application, and what are the requirements for the system's interaction with the users and, possibly, with other networked systems at the interface layer. The Raspberry Pi is very capable of implementing all four layers of functionality on the device itself. However, both platforms can be extended with web-based services such as ThingSpeak to fully implement the service and interface layers of functionality.

Teamwork. Given the target audience of sophomores and juniors, students may have a varied and possibly limited exposure to different Computer Science topics. Special care must be taken when forming the project teams to ensure that each team is comprised of students with a varied knowledge background and skillsets that include some computer networking, databases, and distributed computing. Our experience also shows that it was much easier to debug the hardware issues when students were working on it as a team, which resulted in a division and exchange of responsibilities related to hardware.

Version control. As with any team environment, it is crucial to ensure that all team members are working with the same code base. Once the Raspberry Pi devices were added to the mix, this created an additional layer where mistakes could be made as many students chose to mix development on their computers and then transfer code to the Raspberry Pi devices. To help alleviate this issue, basic Git version control instruction was embedded in lessons and GitHub repositories were created for student teams to assist with distributed version control. Instructing students how to integrate Git version control into their workflow and distribute code between environments via GitHub rather than direct file transfer smoothed out this complexity that many students were initially encountering. Similar to the experience of other programs, this exposure also helped students see first-hand how versioning issues can arise in practice and the benefit of using tools to manage them [17].

Regression testing. A common issue students encountered in their debugging were small differences in hardware configuration of sensors from device to device causing code to execute differently between devices. One of the trends that emerged from this was that, without prompting, students started developing simple regression test suites to allow them to quickly verify that the problematic areas of code still worked with their configuration. This demonstrates that while students might have experienced frustration related to these scenarios, it also led to the highest level of understanding in Bloom's taxonomy – reflection, and a far deeper understanding of what the issue was and how to create basic regression testing in real systems [1].

Connection logistics. Raspbian does not properly support WiFi networking with enterprise-level certificate-based encryption, which is deployed on our campus. For classroom use, we chose to use a 'headless' setup for each individual Raspberry Pi, in which it would connect to a student's laptop via an Ethernet cable. The only other connection required is power, which can be supplied via a USB cable connected to the same laptop. This setup enables a straightforward terminal connection to the Raspberry Pi via SSH. While a terminal connection to Raspberry Pi is sufficient for writing C code with the *GNU nano* editor and *gcc* compiler, some students chose to use a VNC (virtual network computing) client to have full access to the Raspbian graphical desktop on their laptops.

Importance of design. Although we provided every student with a Raspberry Pi kit, we made a decision not to provide students with sensors or sensor kits. By doing so, we encouraged students to be more thorough in investigating the hardware features of the IoT systems they designed. Because of the time constraints of the project, these design decisions were crucial for a successful implementation of the project.

Real-world hardware. Hardware can sometimes break, wired connections may fail (especially if the entire Raspberry Pi plus sensors assembly is handled without a special care), sensors are not always precise, and the sensors may behave differently depending on the external factors such as network infrastructure and physical environment. These issues can add a lot of frustration and difficulty to debugging the code. As a result, students eventually learn to resolve these situations, which brings them closer to the real-world

experiences that are much different compared to many traditional classroom projects.

Big data. By their very nature, IoT systems are designed to collect the data about their environment, their users, and the surrounding objects. Cloud-enabled IoT systems are capable of aggregating and analyzing this data. It would seem natural to add a discussion about big data analytics into an IoT-centric course. Similarly, any course focusing on big data would also benefit from added coverage of the IoT systems, their architecture, as well as the kinds and amounts of data they can generate.

Security and privacy. Proliferation of IoT devices naturally leads to an increased number of incidents where their possible security weaknesses are exploited. For example, in October 2016, a massive distributed denial of service attack was launched against Dyn, an Internet infrastructure company that provides critical services to many top companies, such as Amazon, Twitter, Netflix, and Spotify. This attack was launched using thousands of compromised IoT devices, such as digital video recorders and video cameras [16]. The IoT paradigm offers an excellent context for discussions about the tradeoffs between convenience and added value of the IoT services vs their possible threats to security and privacy. A summary addressing many aspects of security, privacy, and trustworthiness of many existing and plausible IoT system is presented in [24].

Ethical and societal issues. Related to security and privacy are the issues of eavesdropping and surveillance enabled by the IoT devices and services, the data they collect, and the resulting possibly compromising information that could be mined out of that data. These issues offer a fertile ground for discussions about the impact that the proliferation of IoT systems will have on the society and the individuals.

7. SUMMARY

As a computing paradigm, the IoT has already made very significant inroads in the industry. This is resulting in new demands on Computer Science programs to prepare graduates ready to build and work with the IoT systems, create tools to process and analyze the data they generate, and understand and address many aspects of the societal impact of the IoT ecosystem. Furthermore, IoT-centric projects offer an excellent framework for exposing students to many issues of hardware/software design, implementation, and testing. Students seem to embrace this approach, which is reflected in their feedback:

It was very beneficial to be able to learn what we did and see it in action in the IoT projects on the Raspberry Pi and devices. It really helped to understand the material better than just writing "ordinary" programs. I honestly can't say one bad thing about using the Raspberry Pi, it was a lot of fun and very educational.

Experimenting with IoT and RPi gave me a true understanding that computing systems can be built and used not only for personal computers and mobiles.

Raspberry Pi works well for introducing students to software/hardware interaction. Forces students to collaborate.

While students did note that additional complexity was added by incorporating the Raspberry Pi, the types of challenges reported related to requiring a more in depth knowledge of the operating system and hardware integration. Thus, while some additional effort may need to be made to simplify certain aspects of this type of IoT project to be incorporated in other courses to avoid adding overhead to the curriculum; for a Systems Programming class, these challenges actually further emphasized the curriculum and led to deeper student learning. Our goal in future work will be to build upon these successes and recognize potential problem areas so that Raspberry Pi IoT project-based learning can be integrated into other existing courses in our curriculum.

8. ACKNOWLEDGMENTS

Providing each student in our course with a Raspberry Pi kit was made possible by a CCSU AAUP Curriculum Development grant.

9. REFERENCES

[1] Anderson, L.W., Krathwohl, D.R. and Bloom, B.S. 2001. *A taxonomy for learning, teaching, and assessing: A revision of Bloom's taxonomy of educational objectives.* Allyn & Bacon.

[2] Bruce, R.F., Brock, J.D. and Reiser, S.L. 2015. Make space for the Pi. In *SoutheastCon 2015*. IEEE.

[3] Brush, A.J., Filippov, E., Huang, D., Jung, J., Mahajan, R., Martinez, F., Mazhar, K., Phanishayee, A., Samuel, A., Scott, J. and Singh, R.P. 2013. Lab of things: a platform for conducting studies with connected devices in multiple homes. In *Proceedings of the 2013 ACM conference on Pervasive and ubiquitous computing adjunct publication* (pp. 35-38). ACM.

[4] Cerwall, P., Ed. 2016. *Ericsson Mobility Report*. June 2016. https://www.ericsson.com/res/docs/2016/ericsson-mobility-report-2016.pdf.

[5] Charlton, P. and Avramides, K. 2016. Knowledge Construction in Computer Science and Engineering when Learning Through Making. *IEEE Transactions on Learning Technologies*, 9(4), pp.379-390.

[6] Computer Engineering Curricula 2016. Curriculum Guidelines for Undergraduate Degree Programs in Computer Engineering. ACM/IEEE CS, October 2015. https://www.computer.org/cms/Computer.org/professional-education/curricula/ComputerEngineeringCurricula2016.pdf.

[7] Computer Science Curricula 2013. Curriculum Guidelines for Undergraduate Degree Programs in Computer Science. ACM/IEEE CS, December 2013. https://www.acm.org/education/CS2013-final-report.pdf.

[8] Gubbi, J., Buyya, R., Marusic, S. and Palaniswami, M. 2013. Internet of Things (IoT): A vision, architectural elements, and future directions. *Future Generation Computer Systems*, 29(7), pp.1645-1660.

[9] He, J., Lo, D.C.T., Xie, Y. and Lartigue, J. 2016. Integrating Internet of Things (IoT) into STEM undergraduate education: Case study of a modern technology infused courseware for embedded system course. In *Frontiers in Education Conference (FIE), 2016 IEEE* (pp. 1-9). IEEE.

[10] Hodges, S., Taylor, S., Villar, N., Scott, J., Bial, D. and Fischer, P.T. 2013. Prototyping connected devices for the internet of things. *Computer*, 46(2), pp.26-34.

[11] IHS Markit. 2006. *IoT platforms: enabling the Internet of Things*. March 2016. https://www.ihs.com/Info/0416/internet-of-things.html.

[12] International Telecommunication Union. 2005. The Internet of Things. *ITU Internet Reports*. November 2005. https://www.itu.int/net/wsis/tunis/newsroom/stats/The-Internet-of-Things-2005.pdf

[13] Jeong, G.M., Truong, P.H., Lee, T.Y., Choi, J.W. and Lee, M. 2016. Course design for Internet of Things using Lab of Things of Microsoft Research. In *Frontiers in Education Conference (FIE), 2016 IEEE*.

[14] Kölling, M. 2016. Educational programming on the Raspberry Pi. *Electronics*, 5(3), p.33.

[15] Kortuem, G., Bandara, A.K., Smith, N., Richards, M. and Petre, M. 2013. Educating the Internet-of-Things generation. *Computer*, 46(2), pp.53-61.

[16] Krebs, B. 2016. Hacked Cameras, DVRs Powered Today's Massive Internet Outage. Krebs on Security, October 21, 2016. https://krebsonsecurity.com/2016/10/hacked-cameras-dvrs-powered-todays-massive-internet-outage/

[17] Lawrance, J., Jung, S., and Wiseman, C. 2013. Git on the Cloud in the Classroom. In *Proceedings of the 44th ACM Technical Symposium on Computer Science Education (SIGCSE '13)*. ACM, pp. 639-644.

[18] Mahmoud, Q.H., Qendri, D. and Lescisin, M. 2016, February. The Sensorian Shield: Transforming the Raspberry Pi into an IoT Platform. In *Proceedings of the 47th ACM Technical Symposium on Computing Science Education*, p.162. ACM.

[19] Manyika, J., Chui, M., Bisson, P., Woetzel, J., Dobbs, R., Bughin, J., and Aharon, D. 2015. The Internet of Things: Mapping the Value Beyond the Hype. June 2015. http://www.mckinsey.com/business-functions/digital-mckinsey/our-insights/the-internet-of-things-the-value-of-digitizing-the-physical-world.

[20] Mashal, I., Alsaryrah, O., Chung, T.Y., Yang, C.Z., Kuo, W.H. and Agrawal, D.P. 2015. Choices for interaction with things on Internet and underlying issues. *Ad Hoc Networks*, 28, pp.68-90.

[21] Osipov, E. and Riliskis, L. 2013. Educating innovators of future internet of things. In *2013 IEEE Frontiers in Education Conference (FIE)*, pp. 1352-1358. IEEE.

[22] Papert, S. 1980. *Mindstorms: Children, computers, and powerful ideas*. Basic Books, Inc.

[23] ThingSpeak API. http://thingspeak.com, accessed January 12, 2017.

[24] Voas, J. 2016. Demystifying the Internet of Things, *Computer*, vol. 49, no. 6, pp. 80-83, June 2016.

[25] Vujović, V. and Maksimović, M. 2015. Raspberry Pi as a Sensor Web node for home automation. *Computers & Electrical Engineering*, 44, pp.153-171.

[26] Wang, F., Hu, L., Zhou, J., Wu, Y., Hu, J. and Zhao, K. 2015. Software toolkits: practical aspects of the internet of things—A survey. *International Journal of Distributed Sensor Networks*, 2015.

[27] Weyrich, M. and Ebert, C. 2016. Reference Architectures for the Internet of Things. *IEEE Software*, 33(1), pp.112-116.

[28] Xu, L. D., He, W., and Li, S. 2014. Internet of Things in Industries: A Survey, *IEEE Transactions on Industrial Informatics*, vol. 10, no. 4, pp. 2233-2243. 2014.

[29] Zhong, X. and Liang, Y. 2016. Raspberry Pi: An Effective Vehicle in Teaching the Internet of Things in Computer Science and Engineering. *Electronics*, 5(3).

An Experience-based Comparison of Unity and Unreal for a Stand-alone 3D Game Development Course

Paul E. Dickson, Jeremy E. Block, Gina N. Echevarria, and Kristina C. Keenan
Ithaca College
Computer Science Department
953 Danby Rd.
Ithaca, NY 14850, USA
(pdickson, jblock, gecheva1, kkeenan)@ithaca.edu

ABSTRACT

Students' interest in game development often leads departments to attempt to put together a stand-alone game development course. We have used both Unity and Unreal for just such a course. Unity and Unreal are discussed here in the context of how viable they are and how they compare in terms of usefulness for teaching game development. We also present them in context of high level overviews of other game engines and discuss which factors add to a more effective game engine for teaching game development. This paper is intended to help answer some of the questions asked by those without experience in the field who find themselves developing stand-alone game development courses.

CCS Concepts

•Social and professional topics → Computer science education;

Keywords

Unity; Unreal; Game Development; 3D Games

1. INTRODUCTION

Computer games are fun to play and because of this there is a thriving industry to build them [24]. Playing games is a way of life for many current college students as most were exposed to computer games before they were exposed to the internet [3]. Therefore both playing and creating games can be a great motivator for students both in terms of single assignments and game development (game dev) courses [1, 3, 5, 11, 21, 26, 27]. Like many institutions we have enough student interest to support a course on game dev but not the resources, budget, or interest to put together an entire major. We therefore built a stand-alone game development course (GDC) to give students a taste of game dev. We have taught this course using two different game dev engines (or game engines [GEs]): Unity [23] and Unreal [17]

ITiCSE '17, July 03-05, 2017, Bologna, Italy

© 2017 ACM. ISBN 978-1-4503-4704-4/17/07...$15.00

DOI: http://dx.doi.org/10.1145/3059009.3059013

The goal of the GDC being discussed here is to give students a chance to take a concept for a game and turn it into a playable game while experiencing the game dev process. The three major student learning objectives (SLOs) for the course are learning how to build a game, improving ability to learn material on their own (through learning how to implement mechanics of games on their own), and learning how to work in teams. The course is taken by major and non-major students (non-major students are required to have a minimal programming background) in any of their 4 years and therefore designed to be generally accessible.

One way to offer such a course is to build it around a GE: the same technology that the game industry uses to facilitate the creation of video games [18]. GEs are a series of components and standard tools that make implementing games more efficient. GEs simplify game dev by handling complex computations such as object physics, 3D primitive shape creation, animation, sound, collision detection, and trigger events. They provide an IDE suited for handling assets as well as populating the environment of the game space. Use of a GE for a stand-alone course makes sense because without it students will spend an entire semester building a GE instead of a game.

Although building a GE is a valuable learning experience for students, our experience is that students who can only take a single GDC generally want to build games and not the GE [6]. As the course will be used to emphasize points that the department thinks are important for student development, there is no reason that the course cannot be focused more directly where student interest lies.

Our stand-alone GDC spends about 1/3 of the semester teaching students the GE and 2/3 having students building a single game as part of a team. This motivation helps students to achieve all three SLOs. They learn the details of building a game and build a game as as part of a team. Each team decides the subject of their game, and the variation in the types of games created means that every team learns how to implement different game mechanics on its own. This is covered in greater detail in a previous publication about using Unity for this course [7].

We originally settled on using Unity because a misunderstanding of the licensing agreement led us to believe that using the scaled-down personal version of the software in an academic setting was acceptable. With our misunderstanding, the opportunity to use a professional GE at no cost made sense. As of March 2015 the licensing agreement to use the Unreal [17] GE was modified to make it free for personal use and in an academic setting. Many of our students began asking if our GDC would now be taught in Unreal after the licensing agreement change and in Spring 2016 we decided to teach our stand-alone GDC using Unreal. As of the publication of this paper, both engines now allow for free personal development and academic licenses and only begin to have a cost associated with them for special options or for selling games developed using the GE.

2. RELATED WORK

A lot of work has been published about using games and GEs in computer science courses [1, 3, 9, 11, 26, 27]. Most of this work relates to how games can be highly motivational for teaching computer science topics, especially in the fields of software engineering, virtual reality, and computer languages, and does not specifically relate to using GE to teach game dev. We addressed this previously in greater detail [7].

Of greater interest here is work that relates to using GEs to teach game dev or that consider modern GEs in more detail. When deciding to use a GE in class, most faculty appear to determine a key needed feature and chose an GE on that basis. These features vary from wanting cross-platform and mobile compatibility [5] to being inexpensive and having good documentation [21]. Some papers create benchmarks and compare various GEs [19, 26, 27]. Our experience when first building a stand-alone course was that without experience building games, it was hard to pick an appropriate GE based on features because of our ignorance [7].

The work of Petridis et al. [19] illuminates the problem for the novice. They created a framework for choosing a GE to use for building serious games. They focused chiefly on the features and quality of graphics for the games created. This work appears perfect as they discuss CryEngine [4], Source [15], Unreal [17], and Unity [23], all of which are professional GEs. Unfortunately, these criteria are not appropriate for deciding what to use when teaching a course because how quickly students are able to learn the GE is more important than graphics quality for a stand-alone GDC.

Wang and Wu [26, 27] made comparisons that are far more useful for deciding on a teaching GE. Their guidelines are useful for anyone trying to build a stand-alone GDC. They followed with a review article on GE literature[27] that covers what was freely available in 2009 and 2012; however, in 2017 many more GEs are available. Wang and Wu cover none of the GEs covered by Petridis et al., which are the more modern GEs used to build more of the games our students are likely to see on a daily basis.

3. TEACHING GE FACTORS

To compare Unity and Unreal we will first discuss what factors to consider when choosing a teaching GE. We begin with the framework presented by Wang and Wu [26], which is mostly in line with our previous experience teaching GDCs [7], and that of Ritzhaupt [21], who similarly approached creating a stand-alone GDC with no background in game dev. We address Wang and Wu's 7 guidelines in the context of 7 factors we believe are important for deciding which GE to choose. Each section begins with a direct quote from Wang and Wu on the GE.

3.1 Shallow Learning Curve

"It must be easy to learn and allow rapid development."

In stand-alone GDCs [7, 21] and other courses that use GEs [26], the purpose of the course is not learning the GE but instead using it. The time set aside to learn the GE is generally 3-5 weeks and not the ˜15 weeks of a full semester. If students are unable to learn and implement mechanics on their own within 3-5 weeks, the GE cannot work for a stand-alone course that requires students to work independently for the rest of the semester. Additionally, if faculty members with little to no experience with the GE cannot learn the GE sufficiently well within a couple of weeks, they are unlikely to have enough time to learn it to prepare for a new course.

3.2 GE Popularity

"It must provide an open development environment to attract students' curiosity." We interpret this liberally to mean GE popularity because we focus on attracting students' curiosity. Many modern GEs have open environments that allow for the development of a large variety of games. With this being the case, the most important aspect to attracting students' curiosity is to get them excited to use a particular GE. How often students see a particular GE's logo on games they play can help generate student excitement as we saw when Unreal changed it's licensing.

3.3 Available Programming Languages

"It must support programming languages that are familiar to the students." Partially this relates to a shallow learning curve in that requiring students to learn a new language or programming paradigm will add to the time it takes to learn a GE. Similarity to languages they are familiar with or something that students can pick up relatively quickly can help to mitigate this. According to Hewner et al. [14], game dev companies are looking for graduates who have experience using C++, so having students spend the time to learn a language (like C++ in Unreal) may have positive consequences.

3.4 Cross-platform Development

"It must not conflict with the educational goals of the course." This is most applicable in the context of using games to teach concepts in non-GDCs, for example, when a GE uses a programming paradigm that conflicts with course material. In the context of GDCs, almost any GE will enable students to achieve our SLOs for the course. More important is that students need to be able to run the GE on their personal computers. The GE must run cross-platform because the old model of forcing students to use a specific computer lab to do work for a course is breaking down now that students generally have laptops that they bring with them and expect to use for class.

3.5 Stability

"It must have a stable implementation." The reality is that many GEs are not stable. We have seen multiple instances where the GE crashes for no reason, requires a restart to run correctly, or fails to compile for reasons unrelated to student code. While this can be found with any software, our experience is that it is more prevalent in GEs. Discussions with an invited speaker during our class suggested that such problems are equally common in industry and that to be successful you need to know how to remain productive in your part of a game dev team even if the GE itself requires up to a week to repair. So, while no GE is stable, the level of stability of a given GE should be considered.

Also important is how often the GE is updated with code base changes. Whether you want students to constantly update the GE to learn about the issues involved with updates or to stick to a particular version must be considered.

3.6 Community and Documentation

"It must have sufficient documentation." This factor is about how easily students can find help on their own. A good teaching GE must have thorough easy-to-follow documentation and a large, active community of online support to answer questions. These are important because the professor teaching the course is likely to only use the GE for the GDC and will not have the depth of knowledge required to answer all student questions.

3.7 Affordability

"It should be inexpensive (low costs) to use and acquire." Academic institutions do not have the funds to pay for expensive software to be installed in computer labs for a single elective course. With the rising cost of higher education, students have less money than ever before. Unless there is an inexpensive or free option for using a GE, it is not feasible to use it for a single course.

4. GE COMPARISON

To put Unity and Unreal in a greater context, we compare them and other professional GEs for how they fit some of the factors described above (Table 1). The information found here does not cover all of the factors and is compiled from company releases and websites and not verified through experience using the GEs. It is a sample of available comparable GEs, not a complete list of current professional GEs.

Blender [2] is open-source 3D modeling software that includes a GE. A large community uses Blender but it is not often used for major game dev. Blender is free under the GNU general public license.

CryEngine [4] is the only GE in Table 1 that has a cost associated with it in the form of a monthly subscription fee (roughly $10 at time of publication) to use the GE. CryEngine is only available for Windows machines, which limits its usefulness for teaching. CryEngine is well known and can be used with many computer languages.

Frostbite is a proprietary GE produced by Electronic Arts [16]. In terms of games produced, it is sufficiently popular to use for comparison but it is not available for download.

Lumberyard [22] was released by Amazon Web Services, Inc. in February 2016 and is built on CryEngine. It is free to use and sell games that are built using it and Amazon only charges a fee if you decide to use their integrated web services (for example making a multiplayer game). It currently only allows development under Windows and is so recent that there are few active users.

Source 2 [15, 20] is proprietary software of Valve Software[25]. It was released to the public at the end of 2015 with a cost associated with publishing games created with it similar to Unity and Unreal. It runs only on Windows. The original Source GE had an active community and was popular with people who modified the game Half-life.

Torque 3D [12] lacks many of the features found in more modern GEs. It is open source, a lot of helpful documentation is available, and the support community is large.

The Torque 3D GE is available for Mac, Windows, and Linux, making it strong candidate for classroom environments. Ritzhaupt et al. [21] used Torque3D as a successful teaching GE in 2009. Torque 3D has potential as a teaching GE but tends to be less interesting to students as fewer of the games they play are created with it.

5. UNITY VS. UNREAL

We have used both Unity and Unreal for our stand-alone GDC: Unity 3 times and Unreal once. They are very similar GEs providing a full range of features, content, and a complete development environment. A study by Develop Economics [10] described the two as being largely the same except that Unreal was "massively more expensive" for equivalent licensing. In 2015 this changed when Unreal's licensing agreement was changed. Anecdotally, professionally Unity is used more for mobile games while Unreal is used in more major title releases.

We used the same class model for both GEs, approximately 1/3 of the semester teaching the GE and 2/3 with students working on group games. In the final 2/3, students spend most of their time researching how to make the GEs do what they need for their games and then implementing what they have learned.

5.1 Learning Curve

The learning curve of the GEs largely depends on background knowledge. To give a fuller picture, we describe it from both a faculty and student perspective. Authors on this paper include students who took the course in Unity, Unreal, and Unreal while learning Unity on their own.

5.1.1 Faculty Perspective

Our experience learning Unity [7] was that it was easy to learn from a good introductory text [13]. It was easy to get up to speed to teach a course using it and to update notes as the GE developed and the book went out of date.

Learning Unreal was also facilitated by finding a good introductory text [8]. Unreal was equally easy to pick up despite it being a more complex GE with many more features. One reason is that layout and design seems to be more logical and standardized across tools with Unreal than with Unity. For example, objects are by default linked into the physics controllers in Unreal but the connection needs to be added in Unity. Another factor that cannot be ignored is that Unreal is similar to Unity, so our 3 years of experience with Unity definitely made it easier to learn Unreal.

We believe that Unity is easier to learn. What we saw in class was that students seemed to be more frustrated while learning Unreal but also seemed to have a greater sense of accomplishment when they got things to work. We believe that some of this sense of accomplishment is because default objects and lighting in Unreal are higher resolution than those in Unity and therefore the results look better with less work.

Both GEs are viable options for a stand-alone GDC in terms of learning curve, though from our experience Unreal is close to the maximum level of complexity for a course like this.

5.1.2 Student Perspective

Students who learned Unity then Unreal, Unity and Unreal simultaneously, and only Unreal provided perspective on

GE	Available Programming Languages	Dev OS	Help Community	Price
Blender	Python	macOS, Windows, Linux	Large	Free
CryEngine	C++, Flash, ActionScript, Lua	Windows	Medium	Subscription
Frostbite	C++	Windows	Medium	Proprietary
Lumberyard	C++, Lua	Windows	Small	Free
Source 2	C++	Windows	Medium	Free
Torque3D	C++, TorqueScript	macOS, Windows, Linux	Large	Free
Unity	C#, JavaScript, Boo	macOS, Windows	Large	Free
Unreal	C++, Blueprint	macOS, Windows, Linux	Large	Free

Table 1: GEs and How They Fit Our Criteria

learning each GE and coauthor this paper. Opinions were also gathered from many of the other students who have taken this course. In terms of ease of learning, the student who learned Unity first believed that each GE had about the same learning curve and that any perceived greater difficulty learning Unreal came from the fact that the student learned it on his own. The student who learned both at the same time found Unity to be far easier to learn and that Unreal was far more daunting; this was despite the fact that she was learning Unity on her own while taking the course in Unreal. The student who learned only Unreal found it to be daunting but doable with available resources.

General feelings on scripting, gleaned from observing student struggles, are that scripting in Unity and Unreal is roughly equivalently hard to learn. In both cases students found learning scripting to be easier in the semesters after the one in which the GE was introduced, when the professor had a far better intuition for scripting in the GE and was able to pass that intuition along. This course is being taught with Unreal for the second time concurrently with the writing of this paper. It is worth noting that scripting in Unreal refers to using Blueprints and not C++.

The student coauthors who used both GEs found the help community resources available for Unity to be far better than those for Unreal. The student coauthor who only had the perspective of learning Unreal found navigating through online resources to be a great challenge though ultimately sufficient for learning the GE. Unreal was far more difficult to debug because the error messages were usually not as clear as those in Unity.

5.2 GE Popularity

Both Unity and Unreal are used professionally and in general students have played games produced using both. Students were more excited about using Unreal because in their minds it was linked to more of the games they usually play.

5.3 Available Programming Languages

Unity and Unreal both have good but very different options for scripting. Unity has JavaScript, which is fairly universal, and C#, which is not uncommon in game dev. Unreal has both the industry standard C++ and a visual language called Blueprints.

Unity comes packaged with the MonoDevelop IDE, which fully integrates with the GE. We never experienced any difficulties when developing code in either JavaScript or C# and the tight integration made for stable scripting. JavaScript and C# scripts can be used interchangeably within a game.

The Blueprint scripting language used by Unreal is fairly easy to learn and follows patterns that are easy for a pro-

grammer to grasp. Blueprints are a visual programming language in which modules are linked together. Students seemed to pick it up quickly. It is tightly integrated into Unreal and there is no way to create a game without at least some use of Blueprints. Our experience with C++ for scripting in Unreal was a complete disaster. Xcode is used for development on Mac and Visual Studio is used for development on Windows and neither is tightly integrated. It is hard to get compilation working correctly through the IDE and the simplest way to compile is through Unreal itself. One of the many problems with this is compile time, which could run to 5 minutes for even a simple a script that printed "Hello World" to screen. Also, small errors that could not be identified cropped up often with students sometimes being unable to get examples from the Epic Games' (manufacturer of Unreal) website to work. Many students in the class also experienced problems when trying to move their games between machines because a C++ script that worked with game files under macOS would not compile under Windows.

Our experiences in class showed that Unity is a viable option using either C# or JavaScript for scripting. Unreal is only a viable option using Blueprints. During our second time teaching the course in Unreal, we are only using Blueprints and the course has gone noticeably smoother. We intend to leave it up to students to try scripting with C++ on their own when developing their group games if they determine that there is some behavior they can only get by using C++.

5.4 Cross-platform Development

Both Unity and Unreal allow development under both macOS and Windows, which are the platforms used by most students in the class, so either is a viable option. There appear to be efforts by users to make it possible to develop both Unity and Unreal games under Linux. The Unreal effort looks to be further along but neither appears to be a viable option.

5.5 Stability

Both Unity and Unreal update the code base and basic feature base often and multiple new versions appear within the course of a semester. No update has proved crippling to our students existing code, but it is worth considering that Unity once rewrote the entire way they created menus in a manner that was not backward compatible between version 4.6 and 4.7 instead of waiting 2 months for version 5.0.

Unity was better for overall GE stability but neither was truly stable. With Unity some students frequently had to restart the program to get their scripts to run correctly. Nothing indicated that this was the problem: they just learned to restart during debugging as sometimes it was not errors with their scripts. A couple of students had to reinstall Unity weekly to keep it running smoothly, though they tended to be running on less powerful laptops.

Unreal's stability problems concerned bugs in the GE itself. An example is that a script written with a filename of maximum length will not compile while the exact same code cut and pasted into a file with a smaller filename will; this was discovered with a name equivalent to inClassCollisionExampleDay2.cpp. Unreal also tended to take a long time to perform tasks like compiling lighting (over 30 minutes was not uncommon), which broke up work flow. Some of this is related to the system requirements of each GE (Table 2). Unity is less computationally expensive and can run on older machines, making it the better option for classrooms and students who cannot afford advanced hardware. Unreal can run on systems below the recommended requirements, just with some noticeable performance issues. One way of boosting Unreal's performance is to lower the quality of lighting build, which can lower build times during development.

5.6 Community and Documentation

Unity and Unreal both have active community forums to answer questions. As with all community forums, they suffer from GE updates resulting in out-of-date articles and answers.

Unity forums lack any method of identifying the knowledge level of the person posting an answer. The forums contain a lot more information because Unity has been free for personal use for a lot longer, leading to a lot more answered questions. Students generally were able to find answers in the forums and online video tutorials.

Unreal's forums appear to have a higher response rate from staff members and also a higher proportion of out-of-date articles. The forums definitely suffer from the fact that Unreal has not been free for personal use for as long and has not yet had time to build the same level of knowledge base. Students often had trouble finding good answers on the forums. It also appears that the most of Unreal users use Blueprint for scripting so it is a lot harder to find C++ information. We assume that more professional developers use C++ in larger titles because it is faster but these developers rarely write tutorials or forum posts.

5.7 Affordability

Unity currently offers the GE with a personal license for free and a professional license with some additional features for $75/month or a flat fee of $1500. The one useful feature that is missing from the personal license is version control. Free access includes a fully functional royalty-free GE with the ability to build on a multitude of platforms. Unity now has free academic licenses available and is free to use for personal development.

Unreal is available for free and includes all its features. The only cost associated with the Unreal GE license is royalties. When you publish a game or application, Epic Games collects a 5% royalty on your gross revenue beyond $3,000 per product per quarter. This makes the GE perfect for educational settings that do not plan on making much revenue from their games. Unreal also comes with access to its source code (written in C++), giving students more control over how the GE works.

6. GE DISCUSSION

Comparison by teaching GE factors does not capture all of the differences experienced using the two GEs in class. The default higher quality assets and lighting in Unreal made the projects that students were working on look better and more like production games than those developed by students using Unity. Also, Unreal has better tools for building objects in scenes and students found it easier to import models and animations.

Like most IDEs, GEs have starting templates and this was a stark difference. For Unity the template is a first person game. For Unreal there are a dozen templates including first person, third person, top down, and puzzle games. The added features are nice but also come with multiple downsides. The complexity steepens the learning curve. Times for compiling scripts and lighting are extremely long. Students who were running Unreal on older hardware had significantly more trouble with GE crashes than were experienced with Unity. Despite the fact that Unreal was installed on more powerful machines in a computer lab, students developed exclusively on their personal machines and simply joked about lag times and crashes on older hardware.

A final point of comparison is the group projects that students worked on for 2/3 of the semester. The games created by the students using Unreal were better in terms of look and overall playability on average than those created during the most successful semesters using Unity. The weakest game from the Unreal semester would have been middle of the road to upper half for any Unity semester. Also, with Unreal we saw a game that was networked and multi-player for the first time. This could be because it is easier in Unreal or because the right tutorial was found. Another factor is that students were more technically sound during the semester Unreal was taught than during the other semesters of this course. Another caveat, however: all Unity games were compiled into stand-alone games for Mac, Windows, and the web. Two of the 4 games from the Unreal semester could only be played in the GE and only 1 was compiled cross-platform. None is playable on the web because all require a level of server-side support beyond what we could easily provide. The Unity games can be played online with a browser plugin.

7. CONCLUSIONS

Unity and Unreal are both viable options for teaching a stand-alone GDC. They both fit the criteria necessary for students to learn easily and use to build games in a limited time. They have similar interfaces. Unity is a little less complicated to learn while Unreal can create more professional-looking results more easily. Unity currently has better online resources. Unreal is more unstable. Students found Unreal to be more frustrating to learn than Unity, but when students in the Unreal course were asked at the end of the semester whether the course should be taught in Unity or Unreal the next time (after being told that learning went more smoothly with Unity), 2/3 of the students thought it should be taught in Unreal again. Only one student thought Unity would be a better choice and the rest were undecided. While learning Unreal is more daunting, it also seems to be more satisfying. From the faculty perspective, it was easier to teach the course in Unity but more satisfying to teach it in Unreal. Unity always has felt like a toy environment and

	Unity 5.5.2 Requirement	Unreal 4.15 Requirement
Operating System	Windows 7, 8, 10; Mac OS X 10.8+	Windows 7, 8 64-bit; Mac OS X 10.9.2; (Ubuntu 15.04)
CPU	1 GHz or faster	Quad-core Intel or AMD, 2.5 GHz or faster
Memory	2GB RAM	8GB RAM (16GB RAM)
Video Card	Graphics Card with DirectX9+	DirectX 11, OpenGL 4.1 (NVIDIA GeForce 470 GTX)

Table 2: Recommended System Requirements for Development in Current Unity vs. Unreal

Unreal does not. With limited background it was easy to create quality results in Unreal. We are now teaching the course in Unreal for a second semester.

8. REFERENCES

[1] K. Bierre, P. Ventura, A. Phelps, and C. Egert. Motivating oop by blowing things up: An exercise in cooperation and competition in an introductory java programming course. In *Proceedings of the 37th SIGCSE Technical Symposium on Computer Science Education*, SIGCSE '06, pages 354–358, New York, NY, USA, 2006. ACM.

[2] Blender.org. Introduction to game engine. https://www.blender.org/manual/game_engine/introduction.html. Accessed: 2015-08-26.

[3] R. Coleman, M. Krembs, A. Labouseur, and J. Weir. Game design & programming concentration within the computer science curriculum. In *Proceedings of the 36th SIGCSE Technical Symposium on Computer Science Education*, SIGCSE '05, pages 545–550, New York, NY, USA, 2005. ACM.

[4] Crytek. The complete solution for next generation game development. http://cryengine.com. Accessed: 2015-08-27.

[5] D. V. de Macedo and M. A. Formico Rodrigues. Experiences with rapid mobile game development using unity engine. *Comput. Entertain.*, 9(3):14:1–14:12, Nov. 2011.

[6] P. E. Dickson. Experiences building a college video game design course. *J. Comput. Small Coll.*, 25(6):104–110, 2010.

[7] P. E. Dickson. Using unity to teach game development: When you've never written a game. In *Proceedings of the 2015 ACM Conference on Innovation and Technology in Computer Science Education*, ITiCSE '15, pages 75–80, New York, NY, USA, 2015. ACM.

[8] J. P. Doran. *Unreal Engine Game Development Cookbook*. Packt Publishing, 2015.

[9] K. Doss, V. Juarez, D. Vincent, P. Doerschuk, and J. Liu. Work in progress: A survey of popular game creation platforms used for computing education. In *Frontiers in Education Conference (FIE), 2011*, pages F1H–1–F1H–2, Oct 2011.

[10] D. Economics. State of the developer nation q3 2014. Vision Mobile.

[11] M. S. El-Nasr and B. K. Smith. Learning through game modding. *Comput. Entertain.*, 4(1), Jan. 2006.

[12] GarageGames. Torque 3d | products | garagegames.com. http://www.garagegames.com/products/torque-3d. Accessed: 2014-12-16.

[13] W. Goldstone. *Unity 3.x Game Development Essentials*. Packt Publishing, 2011.

[14] M. Hewner and M. Guzdial. What game developers look for in a new graduate: Interviews and surveys at one game company. In *Proceedings of the 41st ACM Technical Symposium on Computer Science Education*, SIGCSE '10, pages 275–279, New York, NY, USA, 2010. ACM.

[15] ign. Gdc 2015: Valve announces source 2 engine. http://www.ign.com/articles/2015/03/04/gdc-2015-valve-announces-source-2-engine. Accessed: 2015-08-27.

[16] E. A. Inc. Electronic arts home page - official ea site. https://www.ea.com/. Accessed: 2017-01-05.

[17] E. G. Inc. Unreal engine technology | home. https://www.unrealengine.com/. Accessed: 2015-08-27.

[18] J. Kasurinen, J.-P. Stranden, and K. Smolander. What do game developers expect from development and design tools? In *Proceedings of the 17th International Conference on Evaluation and Assessment in Software Engineering*, EASE '13, pages 36–41, New York, NY, USA, 2013. ACM.

[19] P. Petridis, I. Dunwell, S. Arnab, A. Protopsaltis, M. Hendrix, and S. de Freitas. Game engines selection framework for high-fidelity serious applications. *International Journal of Interactive worlds*, 2012:1–19, 2012.

[20] Polygon. Valve announces source 2 engine, free for developers. http://www.polygon.com/2015/3/3/8145273/valve-source-2-announcement-free-developers. Accessed: 2015-08-27.

[21] A. D. Ritzhaupt. Creating a game development course with limited resources: An evaluation study. *Trans. Comput. Educ.*, 9(1):3:1–3:16, Mar. 2009.

[22] A. W. Services. Amazon lumberyard - free aaa game engine. https://aws.amazon.com/lumberyard/. Accessed: 2017-01-04.

[23] U. Technologies. Unity - game engine. http://unity3d.com/. Accessed: 2014-07-24.

[24] D. Trenholme and S. P. Smith. Computer game engines for developing first-person virtual environments. *Virtual Real.*, 12(3):181–187, Aug. 2008.

[25] Valve. Valve. http://www.valvesoftware.com. Accessed: 2015-08-27.

[26] A. I. Wang and B. Wu. An application of a game development framework in higher education. *Int. J. Comput. Games Technol.*, 2009:6:1–6:12, Jan. 2009.

[27] B. Wu and A. I. Wang. A guideline for game development-based learning: A literature review. *Int. J. Comput. Games Technol.*, 2012:8:8–8:8, Jan. 2012.

Curriculum Mapping as a Tool for Improving Students Satisfaction with the Choice of Courses

Vangel V. Ajanovski
Faculty of Computer Science and Engineering
Ss. Cyril and Methodius University
ul. Rugjer Boshkovikj 16, P.O. Box 393
Skopje 1000, Macedonia
vangel.ajanovski@finki.ukim.mk
orcid.org/0000-0002-6789-0111

ABSTRACT

Computing is a field that is constantly evolving and as a result curricula at the universities are frequently under reconstruction. The number of curricula reconstructions at the author's institution produced multitude of options and sometimes confusingly similar choices that the students can have. This is considered as one of the main problems in improving student guidance and the primary objective behind the structured solution presented in this paper that enables the tracking of all the variances and inter-dependencies produced by all the curricula changes and helps the students make the most relevant choices towards specialization.

Keywords

curricula guidelines; curriculum development; curriculum analysis; course enrollment; virtual guidance

1. INTRODUCTION

Constant change in curricula is a necessity and goal of many higher-education institutions in order to align to new scientific and technological development. As an example, at the author's department, full curricula reconstruction occurred 5 times in the last 20 years, resulting in new or revised study programs. The frequency of change and flexibility of studying (requirements from the introduction of ECTS and adherence to the Bologna process), created situations where study programs from different student generations can run in parallel, creating many confusions especially when students have to choose elective courses.

The problem of continuous curriculum reconstructions has been one of the topics of research of the long-term project – "Integrated Study Information System of the Next Generation (ISISng)"[1]). This is an open-source software that is envisioned as a complement to an official institutional student information system and intended to be used within departments to better support everyday tasks of students

ACM ISBN 978-1-4503-4704-4/17/07.

DOI: http://dx.doi.org/10.1145/3059009.3072978

and teachers. Recently developed tools that are part of this system, that use the results of the process of curriculum mapping and apply them in guiding students towards better and more informed choices, are presented in this paper.

2. CURRICULA COVERAGE MAPPING

The vision behind coverage mapping of curricula implementation is to be able to: track the quality of implementation of newly developed study programs as compared to model curricula guidelines defined by world-renown organizations and standards (as in the case of the ACM Guidelines [2]); compare curricula among several study programs within the same institution (in order to check progress or check for redundancies); and, compare and distinguish between similarly entitled study programs across institutions. The mapping includes a list of topics within a curriculum, each of them associated to a specific topic from the Body of Knowledge as defined in the relevant curricula guidelines. For each topic, the details are added – lecture hours, objectives, homework and testing/exam targets.

The mapping process itself is to be performed in advance, during the development of new curricula. But it can also be performed for existing curricula in order to investigate the breadth of coverage of the implemented curricula and compare it to model curricula, so that we can find topics that are not fully covered, or not covered with enough detail.

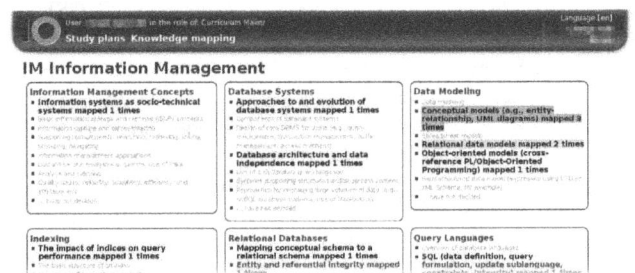

Figure 1: Coverage of knowledge units. Bold colors indicate topics that are covered in many curricula.

Fig. 1, shows a web-based report which can be used to investigate the status of the overall curriculum development effort. All the knowledge areas are shown, together with the list of units in each area, and proposed topics in each unit. The report is a heat map, using colors to indicate extent of

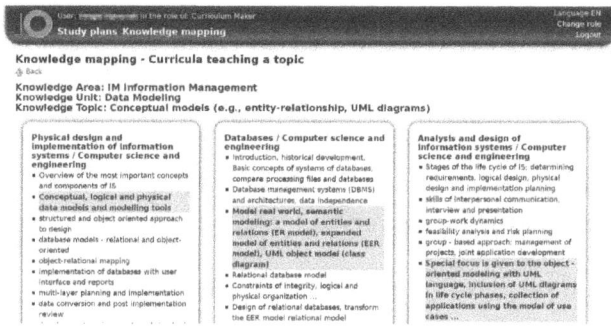

Figure 2: Side-by-side comparison of curricula covering the same knowledge topic.

Figure 3: The "Virtual academic adviser" with the auto-generated study plan for a student.

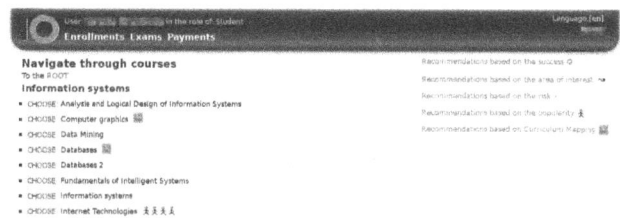

Figure 4: The "Virtual academic adviser" integrates curriculum mapping recommendations.

coverage, varying the saturation and intensity of the colors depending on the number of mapping associations between the guidelines and the implementation of a topic.

The report in Fig. 2 focuses on one chosen knowledge area, and specific unit and topic. It shows all the teaching topics in an implemented curriculum that cover the same chosen knowledge unit and topic. It can be used as a side-by-side comparison to find-out about differences and similarities among curricula.

Such reports certainly help during curricula development, but it is more important that the resulting mapping can also be of benefit to students, during enrollment.

3. MAPPING COURSE OFFERINGS

The "Virtual academic adviser" sub-system of the ISISng was built with the goal to define a general structure able to alleviate some problems the students have during the term enrollment processes, such as:

- Choosing the most suitable course according to their personal wishes and inclination

- Getting information about possible other choices (especially from other departments within the university)

- Getting recommendations based on their peers' choices (this is something that is usually asked via external web-sites, social networks and online forums)

- Getting information on the consequences to the whole study process of making wrong choices

By using the virtual academic adviser the student can experiment with an automatically generated estimation of their future study plan, from the day being until graduation. The tool uses the average speed of studying, past course success and curricula inter-dependencies to generate a possible future scenario according to the chosen study plan (see Fig. 3). This enables the student to perform what-if analysis and change the loads, reorder courses, switch to other study programs or departments, even try a migration to a new institution[3].

As part of the latest efforts within the framework of the project, the "Virtual academic adviser" was extended to also give recommendations based on the curriculum mapping data. During enrollment, the students can consult the adviser's recommendation lists, and check which courses would be most beneficial – in terms of the topics of the course and it's mapping to model curricula.

During enrollment, the students are able to browse the whole tree of course offerings, using both the organizational structure of the study programs themselves, and the inherited mapped curricula recommendations. As can be seen in Fig. 4, the student can navigate through the lists of available courses, where some of them have annotation icons. Each icon represents a recommendation issued by the system. If a student is enrolled to a study program in a certain knowledge area, the courses that have topics in that area will be marked as recommended.

The result is that we can guide the student through a set of courses and prerequisites, that would be relevant for the specialization in the chosen field.

4. ACKNOWLEDGMENTS

This work is part of the ISISng project[1], partially supported by the Faculty of Computer Science and Engineering.

5. REFERENCES

[1] V. V. Ajanovski. ISISng: Integrated Student Information System of the Next Generation – Official Project Website. https://develop.finki.ukim.mk/projects/isis, Apr. 2017.

[2] A. f. C. M. A. Joint Task Force on Computing Curricula and I. C. Society. *Computer Science Curricula 2013: Curriculum Guidelines for Undergraduate Degree Programs in Computer Science.* ACM, 2013.

[3] V. V. Ajanovski. A personal mobile academic adviser. In F. Daniel, G. A. Papadopoulos, and P. Thiran, editors, *Mobile Web Information Systems: 10th International Conference, MobiWIS 2013, Paphos, Cyprus, August 26-29, 2013. Proceedings*, pages 300–303, Berlin, Heidelberg, 2013. Springer Berlin Heidelberg.

When the Robot meets the Turtle: A Gentle Introduction to Algorithms and Functions

Elizabeth Vidal Duarte
Universidad La Salle
Arequipa - Perú
evidal@ulasalle.edu.pe

Eveling Castro Gutierrez
Universidad Nacional de San Agustín
Arequipa - Perú
ecastro@unsa.edu.pe

Marco Aedo
Universidad Nacional de San Agustín
Arequipa - Perú
maedo@unsa.edu.pe

ABSTRACT

Educators have long been trying to motivate students in their introductory programming courses. Games help students to practice formulas, facts and processes, motivating learning by adding fun. This work describes our experience in the use of Lightbot and the graphic library Turtle to introduce students to the concepts of algorithm and function. This approach has been implemented in two Universities in Arequipa. We present the assignments used in the first and second session of CS1. Our experience has shown us that students get a clear understanding of algorithm and functions that are later implemented with Python (Universidad La Salle) and Java (Universidad Nacional de San Agustin). We believe that the visual nature of games and the graphical component to teaching anything is more effective for students. Results were measured by students' perception in 2016.

CCS Concepts

Social and professional topics→Computing Education

Keywords

First Programming Course, Teaching, Motivation, Game-Oriented. Pedagogical Tool, specific assignments.

1. INTRODUCTION

Piteira and Haddad[4] point that the difficulty in understanding abstract concepts and the current teaching method based on traditional lectures with low interaction between students generate low motivation and consequently the lack of interest in learning computer programming. Several approaches to overcome this problem have been used. Some of these approaches are based on well-designed educational games that can be a valuable way to engage students with topics in computer science [2]. Lightbot [3] can be used to introduce two concepts from the ACM Software Development Fundamentals (SDF), namely, fundamental programming concepts and algorithms and design [4].

The main advantage of Lighbot is that it is independent from the programming language. In a previous work we detailed the impact of using Lightbot to introduce students to abstraction,

function, and reuse [5]. But there is the need to show how to move to the programming language. We decided to use the graphic library Turtle.

2. THE EXPERIENCE
2.1 Overview

The LightBot-Turtle approach has been implemented in two Universities in CS1. Both of them use a different programming language. Universidad La Salle uses Python, and Universidad Nacional de San Agustín uses Java. CS1 has 8 hours a week (4 theoretical and 4 laboratory hours). Lightbot and Turtle have been used in both of them since 2015 as tools to introduce two programming concepts: algorithm and function. Lightbot is used in the first laboratory session and Turtle in used in the second one.

2.2 Assignment 1: Lightbot

Lightbot is a programming puzzle game. Its properties make it have a relationship with the programming concepts. Lightbot's objective is to program a small robot to light up all the blue blocks on a board. This objective is achieved by giving the robot a series of instructions from a limited set of commands (Fig. 1a) and in a finite instruction space referred to as Main Method (Fig. 1b) As the levels progress, the Lightbot challenge level increases, requiring more sophisticated combinations of commands like functions (Fig. 2).

Fig 1. Lightbot's Instructios and Main Method Space

ITiCSE'17, July 3–5, 2017, Bologna, Italy.
© 2017 Copyright is held by the owner/author(s).
ACM ISBN 978-1-4503-4704-4/17/07.
DOI: http://dx.doi.org/10.1145/ 3059009.3072974

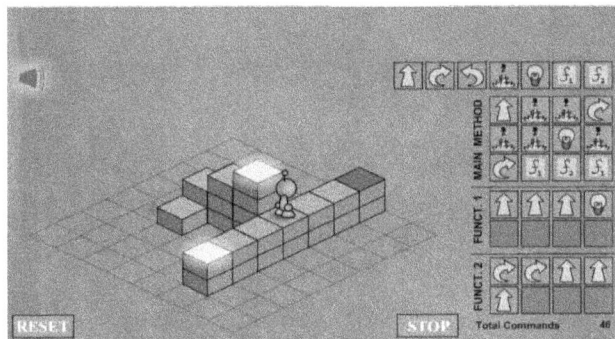

Fig 2. Calling Functions

2.3 Assignment 2: Meet the Turtle

In order to give students a gentle introduction to their respective programming language, in the second CS1 session, we decided to use Python's [6] and Java's [7] Turtle graphic library. Turtle library has a simple syntax, it is easy to use and its methods are quite intuitive and very similar to LightBot's instructions. (Because of the limited space we will only show Python's Turtle code). In Fig. 3, we show the second assignment: Students are required to create three squares. They use some standard functions like `forward(distance)`, `left(angle)` and `right(angle)`. Students create the function square (lines 14 to 22).

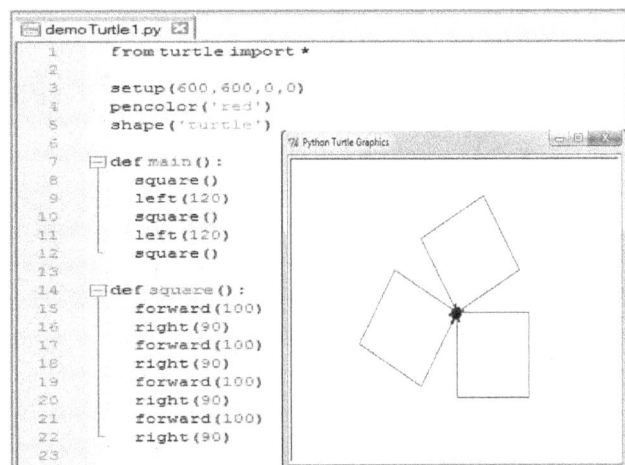

Fig. 3. Python's Turtle First Assigment

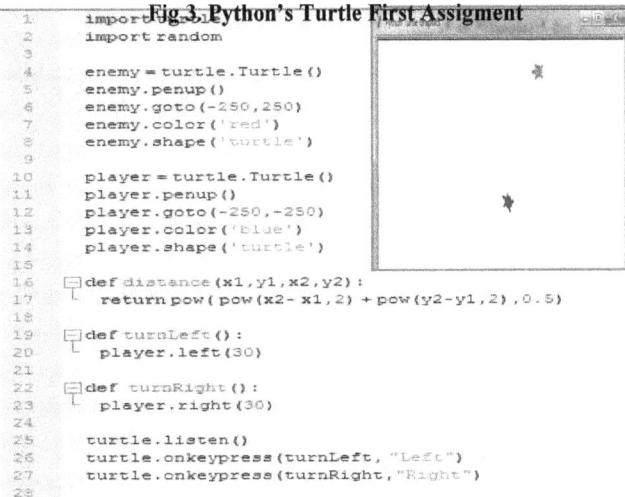

Fig 4. Python's Turtle First Game Assigment

Then, students program the simulation of a basic game with two turtles. The red one moves horizontally at the top of the screen and the blue one moves at the bottom of the screen and is controlled by using the arrow keys. The objective of the game is to hit the red turtle. The partial code is shown in Fig 4

One of the tasks that the students have to perform is the implementation of the functions `turnLeft()` and `turnRight()` to control the arrow keys. The function `distance()` implements the collision detection between the turtles.

3. RESULTS AND CONCLUSIONS

Students in both Universities, (30 students from Universidad La Salle and 90 students from Universidad Nacional de San Agustin), were given a survey regarding their experience with LightBot and Turtle. The survey had four questions, shown in Table 1. Students had five options a) Totally agree, b) Mostly agree, c) Sometimes agree, d) Mostly disagree and e) Completely disagree. The results are shown in Table 1.

Table 1: Survey: Students' perceptions about LightBot and Turtle

Survey Question:	a	b	c	d	E
1. Lightbot helped me to better understand the concept of an algorithm.	77.5%	18.33%	4.17%	0%	0%
2. Lightbot allowed me to better understand the concept of functions.	88.33%	8.33%	3.33%	0%	0%
3. Turtle allowed me to better understand how to program functions.	66.67%	20.83%	10%	2.5%	0%
4. The use of Lightbot allowed me to better understand how to program functions with Turtle.	85%	8.33%	6.67%	0%	0%

The overall feedback received from students was very positive. Students seemed to enjoy Lightbot and the challenge to finish the game. The transition to the programing language seems to be very smooth since students are already familiar with an algorithm and with the idea of a function. From the survey, we highlight the fact that it seems that LigthBot helped more to teach the concept of functions than the concept of an algorithm. Another interesting finding is that students pointed out that the prior use of Lightbot was helpful to understand programing functions with Turtle later.

4. REFERENCES

[1] Piteira, M. and Haddad, S.R. 2011. Innovate in your program computer class: an approach based on a serious game. In *Proceedings of the 2011 Workshop on Open Source and Design of Communication* ACM, 49-54..

[2] Gibson, B. and Bell, T. 2013. Evaluation of games for teaching computer science. *In Proceedings of the 8th Workshop in Primary and Secondary Computing Education* ACM, 51-60.

[3] Lightbot. https://lightbot.com/

[4] ACM Curriculum Guidelines for Undergraduate Degree Programs in Computer Science. Available https://www.acm.org/education/CS2013-final-report.pdf

[5] Aedo, M., Vidal, E., Castro, E., and Paz, A. 2016. Teaching Abstraction, Function and Reuse in the first class of CS1: A Lightbot Experience. In *Proceedings of the 2016 ACM Conference on Innovation and Technology in Computer Science Education*, 256-257.

[6] Turtle Python. https://docs.python.org/2/library/turtle.html,

[7] Turtle Java http://sites.asmsa.org/java-turtle/documentation,

Immersive Algorithms: Better Visualization with Less Information

Philip Bille
Technical University of Denmark
phbi@dtu.dk

Inge Li Gørtz
Technical University of Denmark
inge@dtu.dk

ABSTRACT

Visualizing algorithms, such as drawings, slideshow presentations, animations, videos, and software tools, is a key concept to enhance and support student learning. A typical visualization of an algorithm show the data and then perform computation on the data. For instance, a standard visualization of a standard binary search on an array shows an array of sorted numbers and then illustrate the action of the algorithm in a step-by-step fashion. However, this approach does not fully capture the computational environment from the perspective of the algorithm. Specifically, the algorithm does not "see" the full sorted array, but only the single position that it accesses during each step of the computation. To fix this discrepancy we introduce the *immersive principle* that states that at any point in time, the displayed information should closely match the information accessed by the algorithm. We give several examples of immersive visualizations of basic algorithms and data structures, discuss methods for implementing it, and briefly evaluate it.

Keywords

Algorithms; Visualization; Immersiveness

1. INTRODUCTION

Visualizing algorithms, with drawings, slideshow presentations, animations, videos, or software tools, is a basic teaching concept used to enhance and support student learning. Software tools that support visualization have been extensively studied over the past few decades [?, ?]

A typical visualization shows the underlying data and a step-by-step computation on top of the data. For instance, a standard visualization of a binary search on a sorted array shows the array and then exeuctes the search on top of the array, while keeping track of the state of the algorithm (a constant number of pointers in the array). However, this visualization does not fully capture the computational environment from the "perspective" of the algorithm. Specifically, the algorithm does not "see" the full sorted array, but

ITiCSE '17 July 03-05, 2017, Bologna, Italy

© 2017 Copyright held by the owner/author(s).

ACM ISBN 978-1-4503-4704-4/17/07.

DOI: http://dx.doi.org/10.1145/3059009.3072972

only the single position that it accesses during each step of the computation. Indeed, if students see the entire array a somewhat reasonable objection is that they do not need an algorithm to search since they can immediately see if the element is there or not. In this paper, we propose a principle for visualizing algorithms, called *immersive visualization*, that addresses this discrepancy between the perspective of the computational environment of the algorithm and information shown in the visualization. The principle is stated succinctly as follows:

> At any point in time, the displayed information should closely match the information accessed by the algorithm.

The name comes from the idea that students have to "immerse" themselves in the computational perspective of the algorithm. For instance, in a binary search the principle dictates that the visualization should only reveal contents of the array as the algorithm accesses it (see Sec. 2.1).

In this paper, we argue that immersive visualization can enhance student understanding and reasoning about introductory algorithms and data structures, and present several examples of immersive visualizations. We also consider variants of the immersive principle, discuss methods for implementing it in teaching, and briefly evaluate a simple case.

2. EXAMPLES

2.1 Searching

Consider a standard binary search in a sorted array A (see e.g. Sedgewick and Wayne [?]). A typical non-immersive visualization of this shows the contents of the A and the pointers `low`, `high`, and `mid` indicating the current range of the search and midpoint of the range, respectively. To enhance immersion we propose to only show the contents at the position accessed by the algorithms ($A[\texttt{mid}]$) and the pointers `low` and `high` (see Fig. 1(a)). This reveals precisely the information used by the algorithm. This also exposes the key property that the array must be sorted for the algorithm to work and thus helps students to reason about the correctness of the computation. Finally, the approach encourages interaction with students (selecting inputs and participation in execution) if the setup supports it (see Sec. 3).

The approach easily extends to other simple algorithms on arrays, e.g., linear search, merging, insertion sort, bubble sort, etc. We leave it as an open problem whether more difficult to visualize algorithms such as merge-sort can be effectively (or should be?) visualized according to the immersive principle.

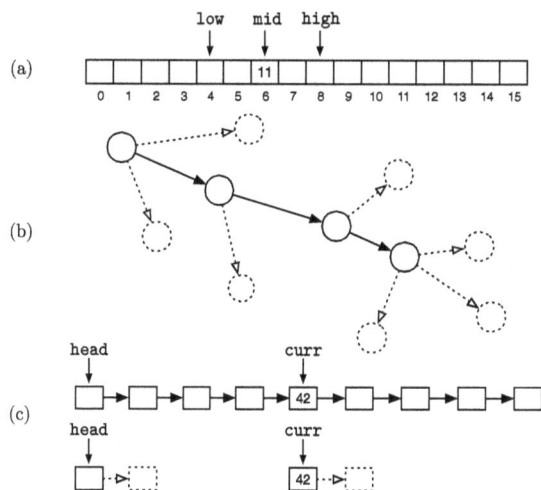

Figure 1: (a) Binary search. (b) Graph search. (c) Partial and fully immersive linked lists.

2.2 Graph Search

Consider a standard textbook depth-first search on a directed graph G [?, ?]. A typical non-immersive visualization shows the full graph and colors on nodes (or marks, labels) as the algorithm explores the graph. We propose an immersive approach, where only the explored nodes and their outgoing edges are visible during search (see Fig. 1(b)). The node coloring can also be updated since this always only affect the explored nodes. Note how this visualization captures the common "maze exploration" analogy for depth-first search [?]. If depth-first search (or it's many variants) is studied later in implicit graph contexts, such as searching game-trees or exploring state-spaces, the immersive visualization already emulates this context.

Breath-first search is slightly more involved, since the algorithm also maintains a queue of nodes during the execution. We propose an immersive visualization that reveals the graphs as it is explored, exactly like depth-first search, but explicitly shows the full queue. The idea is to apply the immersive principle on the graph search part of the algorithm, while viewing the queue as information available to the algorithm.

We leave it as an open problem whether more advanced graph algorithm (shortest-paths, minimum spanning trees, maximum-flow) can be visualized effectively using the immersive principle.

2.3 Linked Lists

Consider a singly linked linked list data structure. A standard non-immersive visualization depicts the linked list as a sequence of nodes each containing data and a pointer to the next element, and a single pointer head to access the front the list. We propose two different immersive visualizations depending on learning objectives, students level, and algorithmic focus. The *fully immersive* approach reveals only the node currently accessed by the algorithm and the *partially immersive* approach reveals all nodes and pointers but hides the data stored in each node (see Fig. 1(c)). The fully immersive approach is useful for both teaching basic concepts of pointers, and for teaching advanced manipulation

of linked-lists, e.g., constant space reversing or Floyd's cycle-finding algorithm [?]). The partially immersive approach is useful for algorithms that primarily use the data stored in the nodes, e.g., searching the list.

The above approach easily extends to other simple pointer-based data structures or abstract data structures, such as doubly linked list, binary search trees, heaps, stack, queue, tries, etc. For instance, we suggest that the partially immersive approach can be effective in teaching the basic ordering properties of binary search trees and heaps.

3. VISUALIZATION METHODS

We can produce immersive visualization with several methods. Most visualizations made with presentation software (e.g., PowerPoint, Keynote, etc.) can easily be adapted to the immersion principle by hiding and revealing information in each step of the visualization. For classic black-board lectures with drawings we have had significant success with applying immersion in a few cases. For instance, to visualize binary search as described in Sec. 2 we have used cards with numbers attached to a black-board using magnets such that flipping cards reveals or hides the number. This allows for a very simple setup that easily supports interaction with students. We can also imagine simple pointer-based data structures visualized using small cardboard boxes containing hidden pieces of paper (the data) and connected by of strings (the pointers). Numerous software tools for visualizing algorithm have been studied. We are not aware of any software tool that uses the immersive principle. A promising direction for future research is to adapt some of the tools to use immersion.

4. EVALUATION

We conducted a short survey on the interactive binary search visualization on a black-board as described in Sec. 3 in our introductory algorithms courses at the Technical University of Denmark in 2017. Out the 385 students, 215 students responded ($\approx 56\%$). For the question "The visualization helps me understand which data the algorithm accesses" 190 students agreed ($\approx 88\%$), (124 strongly ($\approx 58\%$)). For the question "The visualization helps me understand how the algorithm works" 201 ($\approx 93\%$) students agreed, (134 strongly ($\approx 62\%$)).

5. REFERENCES

[1] T. H. Cormen, C. E. Leiserson, R. L. Rivest, and C. Stein. Introduction to algorithms, 3rd edition, 2009.

[2] D. E. Knuth. *The Art of Computer Programming, Vol 2: Seminumerical Algorithms*. Addison Wesley, 1969.

[3] R. Sedgewick and K. Wayne. *Introduction to programming in Java: an interdisciplinary approach*. Addison-Wesley Publishing Company, 2007.

[4] R. Sedgewick and K. Wayne. Algorithms, 4th edition, 2011.

[5] C. A. Shaffer, M. L. Cooper, A. J. D. Alon, M. Akbar, M. Stewart, S. Ponce, and S. H. Edwards. Algorithm visualization: The state of the field. *Trans. Comput. Educ.*, 10(3):9, 2010.

[6] J. Urquiza-Fuentes and J. A. Velázquez-Iturbide. A survey of successful evaluations of program visualization and algorithm animation systems. *Trans. Comput. Educ.*, 9(2):9:1–9:21, 2009.

GIT: Pedagogy, Use and Administration in Undergraduate CS

Arnold Rosenbloom
University of Toronto
Mississauga
arnold@cs.toronto.edu

Sadia Sharmin University
of Toronto Mississauga
s.sharmin@mail.utoronto.ca

Andrew Wang
University of Toronto
Mississauga
andrew.wang@mail.utoronto.ca

ABSTRACT

A pedagogical and technical HOW-TO for the git version control system, including administration, applications in class, for student collaboration, and assignment submission.

Keywords

Version control, course management, software engineering

1. INTRODUCTION

Git (git-scm.com) is a very powerful, modern version control system. Students have heard of commercial products such as github.com, and so are motivated to learn and use git. Git allows users to collaborate on projects, supporting remote, distributed, simultaneous, development. It provides a historical record of development as well as naturally backing up software. It allows students to work on projects from multiple systems. From the educational perspective, git is an integral part of software development so is naturally the subject of Computer Science courses. More than that, it is a useful tool in teaching Computer Science.

This document outlines how to effectively use git as a teaching tool, for software development, and for assignment submission and feedback. Resources related to this document can be downloaded from [7].

2. ADMINISTRATION

We describe our best practices for setting up git for use by instructors, students and TAs. It will be used for software development as well as a teaching tool. We will outline the repositories created and used for CSC207, Software Design, as run in the Fall of 2016. Full details, references, and download-able examples can be found on [7].

We suggest the setup consist of at least two servers. The first server is an instructor only server (**i-server**) with ssh access. The second server (**s-server**) will house student repos as well as lecture repos. For technical reasons, this server

will serve git via Apache. The repos created include the following:

course.git on **i-server** The instructor repo on an instructor only server, secured with unix permissions. Each member of the instructor group has read and write access to the repo. Each instructor has ssh access to **i-server**.

lecture1.git, lecture2.git, ... on **s-server**. One repo for each lecture section taught. Each one of these is world readable, writable by the instructors. These repos will allow instructors to interact with students in real time during lectures.

student1.git, ... on **s-server** and **group1.git, ...** on **s-server** One repo for each student or project group with Apache permissions set to allow the student, the instructors and the TAs read and write access. This allows students to work on individual projects from multiple systems, provides backup, and allows students to revert to earlier versions of developed work. Finally, it gives instructors and TAs an easy way to review students work, when helping them with their work, and a way for students to submit their work.

Each of the instructor repos under control of **i-server** is accessed via ssh, for example, via a command line of the form

```
git clone ssh://user@host/path/course.git
```

Repos that live on **s-server** and are under control of Apache. Apache must be prepared to enable smart HTTP git integration, see [1], [2] and [7]. In the end, each repo will be owned by the Apache process, and have its own `LocationMatch` directive in the Apache config file. Each `LocationMatch` directive will restrict access to the repo to only appropriate students, the instructors and the TAs.

3. GIT AND ECLIPSE

Git is integrated into IDEs such as Eclipse, NetBeans, and IntelliJ. For Eclipse, a single repo can contain many projects. Each repo is added once, and each project in the repo is separately imported. For lectures, students add their **lectureN.git**, then import the weeks live code projects. Additionally, Eclipse provides interesting views of the project repositories, integrating graphical views of projects branches and commit histories, enabling simple point and click through commits and tracking individual file histories. Instructors may find this useful to determine group cooperation and participation.

4. USE DURING LECTURES

Git can very effectively be used during lecture. In 2016, when running CSC207, each instructor prepared and then committed and pushed to their **lectureN.git** repo. Lectures were organized so that by week 3, **lecture2.git** consisted of directories week01, week02, week03. For a software development course like csc207, week03 could consist of notes as well as one or more Eclipse projects. Students would `git clone` the repo once at the start of the course, then would `git pull` the latest lecture updates.

In CSC207, we used git for collaboration during lectures, demonstrating concepts and live coding examples. At key moments during presentations, instructors would add, commit and push to their **lectureN.git** resulting in an evolutionary record of lecture progress, for example, step by step refactoring Java code to use a Design Pattern. Students could pull, branch, experiment, explore and annotate the code. Additionally, instructors could pose exercises for student pull and work during lecture.

This process allows students to play a more active role during lecture. Instead of passively watching the instructor write code, students are given the opportunity to pull the lecture notes onto their personal laptops during lecture time and interact with the code for themselves. The integration of git can thus contribute to a more active learning environment. Several studies have found active learning techniques to be beneficial to student learning in lecture class settings [4][5][3][6]. Git provides us with a potential tool to work toward this goal of changing the role of a lecturer from a transmittor of knowledge to a facilitator of learning [8].

5. GIT AND ASSIGNMENTS

Students in CSC207 were required to work in groups and develop using git. Students were organized into groups and associated group repos created. Projects were broken down into user stories. Each group member would participate by branching and owning a project user story. Work on the user story was added, committed and pushed back to the remote student or group repo. For easy tracking, branches were named after their user stories. Completed user stories would merge back to the master branch. This allows instructional staff, by viewing the git history, to attribute work to students, and understand how well they coordinated on the project.

When students need help with their work, instructional staff can now git clone student repos, add their projects, and quickly understand and investigate issues with their code. To support this, we enabled separate `tester` accounts on our systems, to secure against questionable student code.

When students are finished with their assignments, we have a couple of options to enable submission via git. One option is to have students specifically `git tag` a commit for submission. Instructional staff later script the cloning and checking out of the tagged commit. Alternatively, a script can be written to clone repos and checkout the last commit before a specified date. For example, using

```
COMMIT_ID='git rev-list -n 1 \
    --before="$DUE_DATE" master'
git checkout $COMMIT_ID
```

Once the correct commit is checked out, the marker branches, creating an "Assignment 2 Feedback" branch, for example.

This branch contains the specific commit marked for the assignment as well as additional files added to the commit as marker feedback. Once marking of this commit is complete, the marker simply adds, commits and pushes the feedback to the remote repo. The student then picks up their marks by checking out the head of the "Assignment 2 Feedback" branch. Markers are advised to maintain copies of the repos to avoid questions of repo tampering.

6. PROBLEMS

Throughout the course, there were many instances when students "corrupted" their local repos, requiring intervention to get them back on track. This was usually due to group members not correctly recognizing when there were merge conflicts, forgetting to push, or forgetting to pull before working. In the end, we adopted a general principle, which was, if the problem was not fixable in short order, we had students re-clone the repo, with the possibility that they would loose their most recent work and then advise them to pull, work, add, commit and push, verifying that all went as planned.

7. CONCLUSIONS

We found git to be an exciting and useful tool for instructor collaboration, for communicating with students during lecture, and as a tool for student software development and assignment submission.

8. REFERENCES
[1] S. Chacon. Apache git integration. https://git-scm.com/book/en/v2/Git-on-the-Server-Smart-HTTP, Mar. 2017.

[2] S. Chacon. git-http-backend. https://git-scm.com/docs/git-http-backend/2.9.1, Mar. 2017.

[3] V. S. Gier and D. S. Kreiner. Incorporating active learning with powerpoint-based lectures using content-based questions. *Teaching of Psychology*, 36(2):134–139, 2009.

[4] M. Huxham. Learning in lectures: Do 'interactive windows' help? *Active learning in higher education*, 6(1):17–31, 2005.

[5] B. O. Omatseye. The discussion teaching method: An interactive strategy in tertiary learning. *Education*, 128(1):87–94, 2007.

[6] A. Revell and E. Wainwright. What makes lectures 'unmissable'? insights into teaching excellence and active learning. *Journal of Geography in Higher Education*, 33(2):209–223, 2009.

[7] A. Rosenbloom. Iticse git resource page. http://www.cs.toronto.edu/~arnold/iticse2017/git, Mar. 2017.

[8] Q. C. Vega and M. R. Tayler. Incorporating course content while fostering a more learner-centered environment. *College Teaching*, 53(2):83–88, 2005.

Machine Learning Modules for All Disciplines

Thomas Way, Mary-Angela Papalaskari, Lillian Cassel,
Paula Matuszek, Carol Weiss and Yamini Praveena Tella
Villanova University
800 Lancaster Avenue
Villanova, PA 19803, USA
+1 610-519-7307
thomas.way@villanova.edu

ABSTRACT

Recognizing that the changing nature of science and its reliance on massive amounts of data has led to the integral use of machine learning approaches in just about every discipline, we present the results of a multi-year research effort entitled "Broader and Earlier Access to Machine Learning." For this project, we explored teaching strategies for introducing machine learning topics to non-technical students in discipline-relevant ways, culminating in a large collection of ready-to-use learning modules suitable for use in a wide variety of academic fields. We present a roadmap to our online repository of module materials, a detailed walk-thru of the contents of an example module, ideas and approaches for incorporating modules into a class or assisting non-technical colleagues in doing the same, and a summary of results of using these modules in course settings.

CCS Concepts

• **Computing methodologies** → **Machine learning** • **Social and professional topics** → **Computational thinking** • **Applied computing** → **Digital libraries and archives.**

Keywords

Machine learning; Big data; Computer science education; Learning modules; Computing in the humanities.

1. INTRODUCTION

In this age of Big Data, the nature of science is changing [3]. Research is rarely the work of a single scientist doing experiments, gathering data and single-handedly drawing conclusions. The data now may come from the combined results of distributed experiments by people who may or may not have any direct connections with each other. Machine learning is becoming an integral part of how science (and just about everything else) is done. However, the typical undergraduate is unlikely to see any introduction to machine learning. Some courses exist, but are rarely accessible outside of majors in mathematics, computer science or computer engineering. In fact, the appropriateness of introducing machine learning to undergraduates reaches well beyond students of science and mathematics [1]. This project addresses the way undergraduates gain access to the necessary intellectual content for doing science in the modern world, and for productive careers in a variety of

fields, from astrophysics to music to zoology, and for an informed life in a world where decisions may well be made by intelligent, but not infallible, machines, and where students increasingly need to be active participants in steering the use of data in a computational setting.

The work reported here follows up on significant progress made since our ITiCSE 2016 poster presentation [4]. We provide a roadmap to accessing the machine learning modules that we have created, a walk thru of some examples of the various materials in an example module, and suggestions on how to incorporate the materials into one's own classes or those of others. In particular, we discuss how to offer machine learning content to colleagues in disciplines outside of computer science, either as a guest lecturer or content advisor. Results of use in course settings are presented, as well.

2. MACHINE LEARNING MODULES

Identifying, creating, improving and disseminating multi-discipline-friendly educational materials is the briefly stated objective of our NSF-funded project "Broader and Earlier Access to Machine Learning." First, we review the three goals of our project. Next, we present a high level roadmap of our material as a guide to identifying and selecting an appropriate module, all of which is available via the Ensemble Computing Portal (ComputingPortal.org). Then, we discuss illustrative examples of module content and their many instructor- and student-friendly features. Finally, we present examples and practical ideas for incorporating modules into courses both inside and outside of computer science while providing some concrete results of recent classroom experiences with the material.

2.1 Project Goals

The goals of the project are threefold: (1) gain experience and document findings regarding the effective packaging of materials for teaching machine learning to undergraduates, particularly non-majors in computer science or related areas, (2) produce stand-alone modules that can be adapted for relevant learning experiences for students in a variety of fields, and (3) disseminate the knowledge gained about module development and propagation to the wider computing education community. The project is in the third and final dissemination phase, although we continue to maintain and refine existing content.

2.2 Learning Module Roadmap

Modules are available for 12 topics in an online repository. Some are introductory and require no previous experience while others expect one or more of the other modules as background. Module content is being disseminated via ComputingPortal.org, a digital archive created as part of the Ensemble Project [2]. The content is organized hierarchically with elements available for individual download or as a zipped package.

The hierarchy of modules in the Machine Learning group on Ensemble is organized into three categories, with the "Machine Learning Introduction" topic in the first category serving as a pre-requisite for most others. Note that other introductory modules work as stand-alone modules but may not be sufficient as a pre-requisite for later modules. Modules are organized like this:

- Introduction and Background
  - Machine Learning Introduction
  - Kinds of Machine Learning
  - Choosing Inputs for Machine Learning
  - Introduction to WEKA for Text Classification
  - Introduction to Classification and Clustering
- Supervised Methods
  - Evaluating Classifiers
  - Decision Trees
  - Support Vector Machines (SVMs)
  - Neural Networks
  - Naive Bayes
- Unsupervised Methods
  - K-Means Clustering
  - Dimensionality Reduction

2.3 Module Content Walk Thru

The structure for a typical module consists generally of most or all of the following components:

- An overview description of the topic,
- A one page topic summary,
- A lesson plan for an instructor,
- PowerPoint slides and accompanying notes,
- Student learning exercises targeted to the topic,
- Appropriate software tools for the topic, if applicable,
- Other resources as needed such as references, videos, visualizations and URLs, and
- For selected modules, pre- and post-tests that are suitable to get a measure of student learning and thus the effectiveness of the module as a learning tool.

For example, the "Introduction to Classification and Clustering" module take half of a class meeting and consists of a summary, lesson plan, hands-on activity, slides, and a quiz. The more advanced "Support Vector Machines" module assumes experience with an introductory module and a WEKA software tutorial with data sets for exploring topics in a variety of disciplines.

2.4 Suggestions and Results

These modules are designed for use in a variety of educational scenarios. Results of pre- and post-tests to measure student learning show that students experience solid learning that is retained and non-technical students generally gain more than technical students. Scenarios we suggest include:

- Computer science courses designed for Arts majors
- Interdisciplinary courses combining computer science with another discipline
- Data and information science courses for any major
- Machine learning courses for majors
- Non-science courses that have a connection to machine learning in some way

Example 1: Computer Evolution and Learning

In this computer science lab course for Arts majors, the Classification and Clustering module has been used for three semesters. Student engagement and learning were enthusiastic and measureable, supported by results of a pre- and post-tests. [5]

Example 2: French Writing and Stylistics

The Classification and Clustering module was used in an interdisciplinary setting by French Literature students in a French Writing and Stylistics course who collaborated with computer science students studying Machine Translation. Selected content was presented and explored by French students to develop approaches for "teaching" a computer program to analyze and compare the style of selected works of French literature. The full module was not used, so no pre- and post-test was given.

Example 3: Machine Learning

In this elective course for computer science majors, nearly all of the modules have been test-driven to measure effectiveness in a more technically sophisticated student population. Results comparing pre- and post-tests indicate that students benefit from use of the modules, though the degree of learning tends to be less marked as would be expected since students often come into the course with at least some familiarity of the subject matter.

Example 4: Information Retrieval

As part of studying analysis techniques for working with Big Data, including the theory and practice of locating, organizing, and rendering of meaningful content from largely unorganized sources, students in this computer science elective course used the Introduction to WEKA for Text Classification module. Student and instructor feedback was positive.

Ideal Course Topics

Many other class configurations are suitable for using one or more of these modules. The ideal course topics will have some component of data that is integral to that topic and which can be analyzed and "learned from" using one or more machine learning technique. As an instructor in your own course or as a content advisor to a colleague teaching a suitable course in a non-technical discipline, modules can be used to briefly introduce, significantly discover or deeply explore a machine learning topic.

3. ACKNOWLEDGMENTS

This project is funded in part by NSF DUE award 1141033.

4. REFERENCES

[1] Domingos, P. "The Master Algorithm: How the Quest for the Ultimate Learning Machine Will Remake Our World." Basic Books, New York, NY, 2015.

[2] Hislop, Gregory W., et al. "Ensemble: creating a national digital library for computing education." Proceedings of the 10th ACM conference on SIG-information technology education. ACM, 2009.

[3] Tansley, S, and Tolle, K. M., eds. The fourth paradigm: data-intensive scientific discovery. Vol. 1. Redmond, WA: Microsoft Research, 2009.

[4] Way, T., Cassel, L., Matuszek, P., Papalaskari, M., Bonagiri, D. and Gaddam, A. "Broader and Earlier Access to Machine Learning." Poster presentation. 21st Annual Conference on Innovation and Technology in Computer Science Education (ITiCSE 2016), Araquipa, Peru, July 11-13, 2016.

[5] Way, T., Matuszek, P., Cassel, L., Papalaskari, M. and Weiss, C.. "Machine Learning for Everyone: Introduction to Classification and Clustering." Educational module content and presentation. Seventh AAAI Symposium on Educational Advances in Artificial Intelligence (EAAI-17), San Francisco, Feb. 5-6, 2015.

A 12 Week Full Stack Web Course in 2017

Arnold Rosenbloom
University of Toronto Mississauga
arnold@cs.toronto.edu

Larry Yueli Zhang
University of Toronto Mississauga
ylzhang@cs.toronto.edu

ABSTRACT

Taught and continually evolved since 2001, we discuss the critical path through a full stack, single term web development course including a discussion of topics and academic content. Our course design addresses the challenge of selecting a small collection of topics, technologies and classroom examples that provide the best pedagogical value in the rapidly changing area of web development. With the solid understanding of the fundamental Web/CS concepts learned in this course, the students are able to adapt to the favorite web frameworks of their employers and solve problems on the web.

Keywords

computer science education, web development, course outline

1. INTRODUCTION

CSC309, Programming on the Web [2], has been in constant development by the authors since 2001. The intense 2017 full stack version is the result of this experience. It is a balance between latest technologies, frameworks, academic content, and available time and workload and follows many of the best practices as outlined in [4]. This document provides a high level outline of the course, and discusses its philosophy and implementation. The reader will find our extensive collection of examples, exercises, labs and demonstrations valuable. Please feel free to review and download them at [2].

2. PHILOSOPHY

Instructors for web development courses in 2017 face the same challenges as authors of web applications, the choice of the few topics/tools/technologies/platforms that provide best (longevity, power, simplicity) value, in an area of rapid change. Each of the over 120 items in Wikipedia's comparison of web frameworks [5] claimed to provide a valuable

ITiCSE '17 July 03-05, 2017, Bologna, Italy

© 2017 Copyright held by the owner/author(s).

ACM ISBN 978-1-4503-4704-4/17/07.

DOI: http://dx.doi.org/10.1145/3059009.3072977

model of computation simplifying web development with long term applicability. Each has been, or will be, replaced by subsequent versions and alternatives. For example, in comparison with earlier version of CSC309, and similar courses in 2006[3] and 2011[1] CSC309 now covers more and more current concepts, tools and techniques.

The course philosophy guides the choices and direction of CSC309 and consists of the following:
- Focus on CS Concepts, with examples drawn from current technology. Students grasp the common design principles shared by various technologies.
- Rapid exposure to all layers of the current web development stack, modern API and framework concepts.
- Careful choice of an exemplar technology from each layer. The examples are chosen so that students could "easily" pick up alternates at the same level.
- Treat each technology as a model of computation. Lectures focus on the difficult model concepts with pointers for later exploration.
- Encourage the students to learn to explore and learn by themselves. This ability is necessary in rapidly changing areas.
- Demo/play with working code and problem-solve in lecture to model human understanding of topics. We model the conceptual and technical challenges faced when applying tools to solve problems.
- Repeat examples on multiple platforms. This approach works nicely for saving time and contrasting platform capabilities.
- Tutorials focus on the difficult 'show stopping' issues, with TAs running hands on labs, pushing students one on one, through conceptual and technical issues.

3. LECTURE SCHEDULE

We outline the schedule of topics covered in CSC309H at the University of Toronto Mississauga. Each week consists of two lecture hours and one lab hour.

Weeks 1-3 cover web fundamentals, and one-page-at-a-time style web applications. Topics include basic networking, sufficient to understand HTTP, HTML + forms, cookies and how they are used to implement sessions. We also cover the association between HTML, forms, URLs and HTTP. We next switch to server side programming using PHP, covering language basics as well as sessions and request parameters. PHP is covered by a sequence of increasingly complex example scripts, each introducing a few new PHP language features. The first three weeks conclude with a discussion of MVC frameworks, and the problems they solve. Instead of using a standard framework, such as Django or Ruby on Rails, we code and play with a simple, home grown PHP based MVC framework. Ours is quick to learn, easy to understand and has no hidden details. We believe it is a good stepping stone to all other similar frameworks. Students in the most recent CSC309, have commented that their favorite web technology was this MVC framework. We also cover PHP+PostgreSQL, stressing prepared statements, for security. Lectures include an abundance of in-class coding and examples (see the website to download). Demonstrations include hand simulating an HTTP request by pulling apart a URL, `dig` the domain name, `telnet/nc` an HTTP/1.1 request, inspect the response's header and body. Another Week 1-3 demonstration includes coding a "guess-the-number" game in class using our MVC framework.

Weeks 4-7 focus on more modern technologies and architectures. We start with dynamic front end content, covering JavaScript, OO JavaScript, the DOM, and event-driven programming. In class, we code click event handlers for forms and images, and explain or write simple JavaScript games. We next cover AJAX and JQuery, including the idea of web services and asynchronous computation. JQuery provides a nice preview to CSS selectors as well as simplifies AJAX coding. In class, we show how a PHP script can implement a service, and again implement the "guess-the-number" game as an AJAX application. Other demos include implementing a chat room app using JQuery, AJAX and PHP. We use JSON to encode AJAX request messages and PHP responses. Week 6 tightens the notion of web service and introduces RESTful API. We cover routing, HTTP verbs GET, POST, PUT and DELETE, and demonstrate a RESTful PHP service, connecting to it via Firefox and the developer console. The final week in this part of the course introduces CSS, the box model, simple selectors and properties, div vs span, positioning, location and precedence. During the lecture, we style a website, including navigation, content positioning, and borders.

Weeks 8-12 focus on advanced HTML5 and a JavaScript-only web stack. For advanced HTML5 we cover the canvas and mobile API such as touch, the accelerometer, GPS, and the gyroscope. In class, we demonstrate and discuss code animating balls falling under gravity, and flies chasing your finger as it touches a mobile devices screen. Week 9 covers Node.js, including its event driven, asynchronous I/O model of computation. We demonstrate a Node.js "guess-the-number" game, then re-implement it with our own home grown notion of sessions. We briefly point out template engines such as Pug, and finally use Express to create a simple RESTful API. We cover WebSockets, addressing some of the shortcomings of standard HTTP connectionless applications. This is done by demonstrating a Node.js chat room application and a collaborative scribble application. The remaining weeks address a selection of topics from responsive design and Bootstrap, to web security and scalability, to usability. It should be noted that we have a separate course covering information security, so do not focus on it in this one.

4. ASSIGNMENTS

The three course assignments are completed by teams of two. Submissions must include a setup script and run on our lab systems. Each assignment allocates 10% to student cre-

ated extra features. TAs use a shared Google document to rank extra features by difficulty. So a Level 3 extra feature contributes a maximum of 3 additional points. The extra feature totals are used to rank students against each other resulting in the extra features mark. Examples of assignments include:

A1 Weeks 1-3: An MVC Database backed page at a time web application. Requirements include: use of our MVC PHP framework, correct page life cycle, PostgreSQL DB back-end, authentication and authorization, user profile management, proper use of sessions, and interesting forms and inputs.

A2 Weeks 4-7: Single page, OO JavaScript, JQuery + CSS 2-D game. Skeleton code introduces a game framework. Students complete the game and extend it, using JavaScript inheritance, to include additional "monsters" and features. User profile management is done through AJAX to a RESTful PHP API backed by a PostgreSQL database. Some exposure to .htaccess.

A3 Weeks 8-12: Convert A2 to a Node.js + WebSocket multi-player game with a RESTful Node.js + Express.js + MongoDB user profile management system. This game includes mobile features for play on tablets and phones. Examples include: chat with local players by GPS, tilt to move, and shake to launch an attack.

5. CONCLUSIONS

By the end of this 12-week course, a typical student with little prior knowledge of web development is able to implement a fully functional web service with reasonably well-organized front-end and back-end, as well as creating more advanced web applications such as mobile, multi-player online games (students actually organize game showcases after this course). After CSC309, our students are able to adapt to the favorite web frameworks of their employers, whether it is AngularJS, React, Django or Ruby on Rails, and solve problems on the web.

6. REFERENCES

[1] Y. Liu and G. Phelps. Challenges and professional tools used when teaching web programming. *Journal of Computing Sciences in Colleges*, 26(5):116–121, 2011.

[2] A. Rosenbloom. Csc309h course page. http://www.cs.toronto.edu/~arnold/iticse2017/webProgramming, Mar. 2017.

[3] X. Wang. A practical way to teach web programming in computer science. *Journal of Computing Sciences in Colleges*, 22(1):211–220, 2006.

[4] X. Wang and J. C. McKim. The opportunities and challenges to teach web programming in computer science curriculum cs2013. *Journal of Computing Sciences in Colleges*, 29(2):67–78, 2013.

[5] Wikipedia. Comparison of web frameworks. https://en.wikipedia.org/wiki/Comparison_of_web_frameworks, Mar. 2017.

TetrisOS and BreakoutOS: Assembly Language Projects for Computer Organization

Michael Black
Department of Computer Science
Bridgewater State University
Bridgewater, MA 02325
m1black@bridgew.edu

ABSTRACT

TetrisOS and BreakoutOS are projects developed for a sophomore-level computer organization course. Each project teaches a wide range of x86 assembly language topics, including iteration, function calls, data storage, segmentation, communication with devices, and polling-based and interrupt-based I/O. They run "bare-metal" and avoid system calls. Each game can run natively on any PC and boot from a USB stick. The projects were tested on six classes of students over three semesters at two universities, and though rigorous, had a high completion rate.

CCS CONCEPTS

• **Social and professional topics** → Computer science education

KEYWORDS: computer organization, assembly language, x86

1 INTRODUCTION

This paper describes two projects, based on the well-known games Tetris and Breakout, developed from the ground-up by the author for the assembly language component of computer organization. The author tested the projects on five classes of Computer Organization: Tetris at American University and Breakout at Bridgewater State University.

These projects are novel because students build them from scratch to run on the bare-metal on their own PCs. Students follow detailed tutorials that walk them through each component of the game and are completed entirely in two weeks. In the process students learn to communicate directly to the video memory and keyboard ports, construct simple device drivers and interrupt handlers. Additionally, students experience

ACM Reference format:
Michael Black. 2017. TetrisOS and BreakoutOS: Assembly Language Projects for Computer Organization. In *Proceedings of the 2017 ACM Conference on Innovation and Technology in Computer Science Education (ITiCSE '17).* ACM, New York, NY, USA

the basic mechanics of x86 assembly: register usage, memory variables, segments, iteration, conditionals, subroutine calls and parameter passing. Because no system calls are made, students can run their project in place of an operating system. The final step in each project is to set up a bootable USB stick and use it to boot their own computers. The projects are called BreakoutOS and TetrisOS, as they effectively create a miniature operating system.

TetrisOS and BreakoutOS take advantage of the state of a PC at the point the BIOS calls the bootloader. Modern laptops are backward compatible to the 1981 IBM 5150 at this stage. They run in 16-bit mode, with directly addressable memory, unprotected I/O, and 80x25 text-mode video. Students used the author's Emumaker86 PC emulator [2], along with a 10MB hard disk image with FreeDOS and a legacy version of Turbo Assembler and Linker.

Students convert projects into bootable images with minimal modifications. They create an empty image file, extract the machine code and transfer it to the image, put a bootloader at the top of the image, and transfer the image to a USB drive.

2 BREAKOUTOS

The BreakoutOS project is a simplified version of the 1970's Atari game. A ball moves and bounces off walls; blocks disappear when the ball collides; and a paddle responds to left and right arrow keys (Figure 1). Students learn to 1) set up segments, 2) write to video, 3) handle 16-bit variables, 4) poll the keyboard and flush its buffer, 5) construct assembly loops and conditionals. Students completed seven steps, each teaching specific material (Table 1).

Table 1: BreakoutOS Project Steps

Step	Task	Learning
1	Initial screen with ball, paddle, and blocks	Write to video memory
2	Variables for ball position and velocity	Segments; translate variables to assembly
3	Ball moves	Loops
4	Ball bounces off sides of screen	Conditionals, variable manipulation
5	Paddle moves in response to arrow keys	Keyboard I/O, subroutines
6	Ball bounces off paddle	Conditionals
7	Bootable from a USB drive	

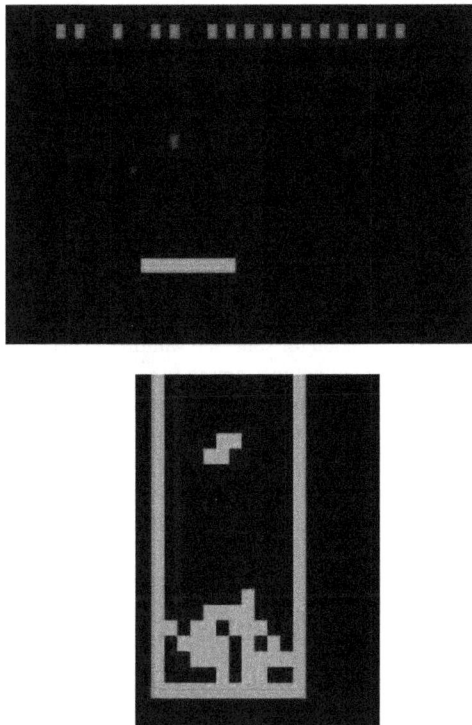

Figure 1: Screenshots of student submissions.

3 TETRISOS

TetrisOS implements the key rules of the Tetris puzzle game. A completed project alternates through seven pieces, draws pieces at the top of the screen, moves a piece down until it reaches an obstacle, responds to left and right keystrokes, and clears completed rows. Students learn to 1) handle multiple segments, 2) write to video, 3) handle 8 bit variables, 4) perform integer multiplication and division, 5) poll the keyboard, 6) create subroutines and pass parameters, 7) construct nested while loops and if-else statements, and optionally: 8) respond to keyboard interrupts, 9) initialize the timer and respond to timer interrupts. The project is broken into ten steps (Table 2).

Table 2: TetrisOS Project Steps

Step	Task	Learning
1	Initialize screen and draw border	Write to video memory, iteration
2	Functions setPixel and getPixel	Subroutines, parameters, stack, arithmetic
3	Select a piece and draw it	Segments, arrays and pointers
4	Check if a piece can move down	
5	Main game loop	Iteration and conditionals
6	Piece moves in response to arrow keys	Keyboard I/O
7	Clear completed rows	Nested iteration
8	Keyboard interrupt	Interrupt vectors and routines
9	Timer interrupt	Timer I/O, interrupt-driven code
10	Bootable from a USB drive	

4 STUDENT EXPERIENCE

Each project is designed with progressive steps to demonstrate understanding of specific concepts. Students can do the bare minimum to prove their knowledge of the material; can produce a playable game; or can go beyond with optional bonus steps. More than 1/3 of the students (40 of 115) completed the projects in entirety, including bonus steps. Sixty-six out of 115, a majority of students, produced a playable game, with video responding to keyboard. This proportion was consistent across both projects, and it suggests these projects are well within the capability of second-year undergraduate computer science students.

Each class had a journal requirement where students gave their own written feedback at the end of the course. Forty-one students commented specifically on the TetrisOS and BreakoutOS projects. These 41 students were evenly distributed across the five classes. Figure 2 shows these comments, categorized by general theme.

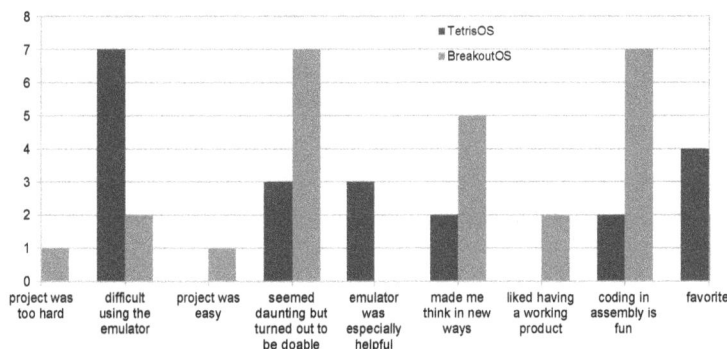

Figure 2: Student Comments

ACKNOWLEDGMENTS

The author thanks the students for their feedback and the use of their project submissions.

REFERENCES

[1] John Aycock. 2015. Applied Computer History: Experience Teaching Systems Topics through Retrogames. In *Proceedings of the 2015 ACM Conference on Innovation and Technology in Computer Science Education* (ITiCSE '15). ACM, New York, NY, USA, 105-110. DOI: http://dx.doi.org/10.1145/2729094.2742583
[2] Michael Black and Nathaniel Waggoner. 2013. Emumaker86: a hardware simulator for teaching CPU design. In *Proceedings of the 44th ACM technical symposium on Computer science education* (SIGCSE '13). ACM, New York, NY, USA, 323-328. DOI: http://dx.doi.org/10.1145/2445196.2445294
[3] Erik Brunvand. 2011. Games as motivation in computer design courses: I/O is the key. In *Proceedings of the 42nd ACM technical symposium on Computer science education* (SIGCSE '11). ACM, New York, NY, USA, 33-38. DOI=http://dx.doi.org/10.1145/1953163.1953178
[4] Jalal Kawash and Robert Collier. 2013. Using video game development to engage undergraduate students of assembly language programming. In *Proceedings of the 14th annual ACM SIGITE conference on Information technology education* (SIGITE '13). ACM, New York, NY, USA, 71-76. DOI=http://dx.doi.org/10.1145/2512276.2512281

Courseware: HFOSS Project Evaluation

Heidi J. C. Ellis
Western New England University
Springfield, MA, USA
ellis@wne.edu

Gregory W. Hislop
Drexel University
Philadelphia, PA, USA
hislop@drexel.edu

Darci Burdge
Nassau Community College
Garden City, NY, USA
darci.burdge@ncc.edu

ABSTRACT

Many instructors are excited by the potential learning that occurs via student participation in Humanitarian Free and Open Source Software (HFOSS) projects. However, one of the main challenges for instructors desiring to support such participation is identifying an appropriate project. There are a vast number of HFOSS projects with varying sizes, complexities, domains and community cultures. This presentation describes a guided approach to evaluating an HFOSS project for someone trying to pick a project to which they will contribute. The activity is designed with particular attention to instructors who need to identify an HFOSS project that they will use in a class. The characteristics evaluated include the pattern of contributions, pattern of commits, programming languages used, and more. This activity uses OpenMRS as a sample project to evaluate.

CCS CONCEPTS

• **Applied computing** → *Collaborative learning*;

KEYWORDS

Open source software, HFOSS, computing education

ACM Reference format:
Heidi J. C. Ellis, Gregory W. Hislop, and Darci Burdge. 2017. Courseware: HFOSS Project Evaluation. In *Proceedings of ITiCSE'17, July 3–5, 2017, Bologna, Italy, , 2 pages.*
DOI: http://dx.doi.org/10.1145/3059009.3072975

1 INTRODUCTION

The use of free and open source software (FOSS) is becoming widely used by instructors to provide students with experience with real-world projects. Student learning ranges from software engineering skills to soft skills to domain knowledge. Humanitarian FOSS (HFOSS) has the added incentive for students to be able to "do good". However, there are some challenges inherent in this approach including large complex code bases, new programming languages and tools, and differing cultures and schedules between academia and the HFOSS project. This presentation will discuss an approach for evaluating an HFOSS project for use in the classroom. The approach is an update and refinement of earlier efforts [1], [2]. and is drawn from http://foss2serve.org/index.php/Project_Evaluation_(Activity).

1.1 Background

The activity begins by providing background on project selection. Not all projects are equally good for someone wanting to become a contributor. Some projects are not welcoming to new contributors, or are not well organized to support getting new people up to speed. Other projects are welcoming to new contributors and provide clear pathways to join the community. Anyone considering becoming a contributor to a project should have some idea what to look for in evaluating whether a project is a good choice for becoming a contributor. While these evaluation criteria are not foolproof, they provide a starting point and framework of things to consider.

1.2 Directions

There are many criteria that should be looked at when determining if a project is appropriate to use in a class. These criteria are prioritized and explored below:

Licensing - An important first step is to identify the license used by the project. An open source project must specify that others are free to use it, redistribute it, change it, and redistribute modified versions too. An extensive list of open source licenses can be found at https://opensource.org/licenses/alphabetical. A list of free software licenses can be found a https://www.gnu.org/licenses/license-list.html#GPLCompatibleLicenses. A project without a license is not open source and therefore not usable in the classroom.

Language - The language(s) used in the project is an essential consideration for students. If the project is written in a language(s) with which students are already familiar, or better yet, well versed in, this is one less hurdle to overcome.

Activity - To support student participation, a project should be reasonably active. The number of commits can be used as an indicator of activity. Little to no activity over a year, for example, may indicate that the project is dead, or mature and not being actively developed.

Number of contributors - A common fossism states that "It's all about community," so a suitable project should have an active user community. The community members are great resources for both faculty and students as they learn about a new project, its culture, and norms.

Size - The size of the project is likely to be a factor depending on the level of students. A large project that is built using many various technologies is likely to seem overwhelming to a CS2 student, for example, but may be a perfect fit for a senior capstone course. A simple first step is to determine how large the project is, additional research could be done to ascertain complexity.

Issue tracker - The issue tracker can provide insight into the health of a project. An active issue tracker should highlight issues that clients/developers have logged as well as an indication that these issues are being addressed.

ITiCSE'17, , July 3–5, 2017, Bologna, Italy.

Heidi J. C. Ellis, Gregory W. Hislop, and Darci Burdge

New contributor - The project should appear welcoming to new contributors. Some clear examples of this would be links to "getting started" pages or information on ways to become involved. These pages, in turn, should include additional detail about how to become involved, as well as information about how to connect with the community.

Community norms - The way in which community members interact with one another is equally important, especially for student involvement. You do not want to point students to a project that advocates or permits lewd and unprofessional behavior. Some projects provide a "Code of Conduct", yet others do not.

User base - A project will not thrive without a core user-base. The user-base consists of clients, people who use the product on a day-to-day basis. They provide the development team with necessary feedback about the project, what works, what doesn't and what new features they might like to see. If no one is using the product then developers are likely to abandon it.

1.3 Observations

The criteria defined above are general, but the specific ways of evaluating each criterion will vary by project. OpenMRS provides a good example for evaluating each criterion for projects on GitHub. Projects on other forges will require different approaches to evaluating many of the criteria.

There tend to be similarities in the way HFOSS projects are structured. Repeating this evaluation for a series of candidate projects will likely get easier with each successive project. The situation is similar to the time it takes to learn a first or second programming language vs a sixth or seventh programming language. After doing a few, you know what to look for.

2 PRESENTATION

The presentation briefly walks through the application of the criteria to the OpenMRS project as a guided tour. The presenter explains how the criteria are applied and key features to examine during evaluation.

ACKNOWLEDGMENTS

This material is based on work supported by the National Science Foundation under Grant Nos. DUE-1525039, DUE-1524877, and DUE-1524898. Any opinions, findings and conclusions or recommendations expressed in this material are those of the author(s) and do not necessarily reflect the views of the National Science Foundation (NSF).

REFERENCES

[1] Heidi J.C. Ellis, Michelle Purcell, and Gregory W. Hislop. 2012. An Approach for Evaluating FOSS Projects for Student Participation. In *Proceedings of the 43rd ACM Technical Symposium on Computer Science Education (SIGCSE '12)*. ACM, New York, NY, USA, 415–420. DOI: http://dx.doi.org/10.1145/2157136.2157260

[2] Heidi J. C. Ellis, Gregory W. Hislop, Michelle Purcell, and Lori Postner. 2013. Project Selection for Student Participation in Humanitarian FOSS. *J. Comput. Sci. Coll.* 28, 6 (June 2013), 16–18. http://dl.acm.org/citation.cfm?id=2460156.2460162

Automatic Grading and Feedback using Program Repair for Introductory Programming Courses

Sagar Parihar   Ziyaan Dadachanji   Praveen Kumar Singh

Rajdeep Das   Amey Karkare   Arnab Bhattacharya

{sparihar, ziyaand, pravsin, rajdeepd, karkare, arnabb}@cse.iitk.ac.in

Dept. of Computer Science and Engineering, Indian Institute of Technology, Kanpur, India.

ABSTRACT

We present *GradeIT*, a system that combines the dual objectives of automated grading and program repairing for introductory programming courses (CS1). Syntax errors pose a significant challenge for testcase-based grading as it is difficult to differentiate between a submission that is almost correct and has some minor syntax errors and another submission that is completely off-the-mark. GradeIT also uses program repair to help in grading submissions that do not compile. This enables running testcases on submissions containing minor syntax errors, thereby awarding partial marks for these submissions (which, without repair, do not compile successfully and, hence, do not pass any testcase). Our experiments on 15613 submissions show that GradeIT results are comparable to manual grading by teaching assistants (TAs), and do not suffer from unintentional variability that happens when multiple TAs grade the same assignment. The repairs performed by GradeIT enabled successful compilation of 56% of the submissions having compilation errors, and resulted in an improvement in marks for 11% of these submissions.

Keywords

CS1; Programming Assignments; Automated Grading

1. INTRODUCTION AND MOTIVATION

Graded assignments are an important component of any course. For a student, the grades are a kind of feedback about her learning of the concepts (and also a motivating factor to do well among her peers). For a teacher, the grades are a measure to track the performance and learning achievements of the students in the class. An introductory programming course (CS1) is an integral part of any curriculum, and is a compulsory course during the first year of undergraduate program in most of the universities. As a result, large number of students enroll for CS1 in any institute. Effective and efficient grading of programming assignments in CS1 is important to maintain the effectiveness and quality of the course.

Due to the large number of students enrolled in the course, grading of programming assignments requires a significant amount of effort and time that is typically beyond the capacity of a single in-structor. Thus in CS1, two common approaches are used for grading: (a) manual grading by teaching assistants (TAs) or, (b) automated testsuite-based grading. We next describe them in details.

1.1 Manual Grading

For manual grading, a course generally employs a team of human teaching assistants (TAs). Each TA is assigned a subset of the submissions for grading. A TA decides the grade of a submission based on its performance on a testsuite as well as manual inspection of the code. Manual inspection is important in introductory programming courses such as CS1 since it is very common that students grasp the logic but fail to code a syntactically correct program. Thus, the TAs award partial marks on codes that are close to the correct solution, but fail on the testsuite due to minor mistakes (syntax or run time errors). In some cases, the TAs repair these mistakes by hand and then run the testsuite. For submissions that successfully compile, TAs also provide feedback on the reason for failing cases. Two major drawbacks of this approach are:

1. *Time:* A large number of students (typically first-year undergraduate students) are enrolled in CS1. Since manual grading takes a considerable amount of time, TAs cannot provide immediate feedback for the submissions, which is necessary to understand the later concepts.

2. *Variability:* The TAs are typically postgraduate students who had done their undergraduate studies (including programming courses) from different institutes. There is, thus, a large variation in their knowledge and experience of programming. Although detailed instructions and policies related to grading are provided, it is nearly impossible to avoid human bias and ensure consistency, thereby causing unintentional variability in grading of similar submissions.

1.2 Automated Grading

Simple automated grading systems (such as the ones used by programming contest sites [7, 22]) evaluate a submission against a suite of testcases. Each testcase is assigned a weight based on its perceived difficulty. The grade is computed as the sum of the weights of the passing testcases. Recent approaches improve this process in two ways in order to generate better feedback for submissions that fail some testcases in the testsuite:

1. Clustering of similar submissions [11, 15, 16]: Submissions that are semantically similar are grouped together. The instructor provides feedback (or grade) for one representative in the group. The feedback can be repeated (after appropriate customization) for the remaining submissions.

2. Finding "semantic distance" from correct solutions [12, 13, 21]: Each erroneous submission is compared with a set of correct solutions to find the minimum distance (number of changes) from

ITiCSE '17, July 03-05, 2017, Bologna, Italy

© 2017 ACM. ISBN 978-1-4503-4704-4/17/07...$15.00

DOI: http://dx.doi.org/10.1145/3059009.3059026

Table 1: An example of improved feedback by GradeIT.

Error Type	Missing & before a variable in scanf
Compiler Message	format specifies type 'int *' but the argument has type 'int'

GradeIT Feedback	You have not put an & before 'b' in the scanf statement on this line. Whenever you use scanf to input a value, you must put an & before the variable (except for pointers and strings).
	
	Valid statements:
	1. `scanf("%d",&a);`
	2. `char st[20];`
	   `scanf("%s",st);`
	
	Invalid statements:
	1. `scanf("%d",a);`
	2. `char st[20];`
	   `scanf("%s",&st);`

a correct solution. The distance is used as a metric for grading, and the changes determine the feedback provided to the student.

These tools work on an abstract representation of programs (Abstract Syntax Tree, Control Flow Graphs, etc. [1]) generated by a compiler and, therefore, require that the program compiles successfully. Programs having syntax errors do not compile successfully, and are awarded zero marks. While acceptable for programming contests, this, in our view, is not a good solution for CS1, especially at the beginning of the course. A student who is programming for the first time expects better feedback (and grade) for a submission that is logically close to a correct solution, but fails to compile than a submission that is far from the correct solution, but compiles successfully (say, an empty program!).

1.3 Program Repairing

Another issue with CS1 is that novice programmers struggle to understand the compiler error messages. This is because the error messages are targeted towards experienced programmers, and mention concepts that may not have been covered in the class. An example is shown in Table 1. The error of a missing '&' happens frequently in the first few labs, much before the pointers are covered for a C like language. However, the error message uses "int *", and it is impossible for a beginner to comprehend that the problem is of missing '&' by looking at the error message. For similar reasons, students find it difficult to fix even simple syntax errors, such as a missing semicolon or an unmatched parenthesis, especially towards the beginning of the course.

In our experience, TAs read the code and typically deduct only a small penalty for such minor mistakes and tend to grade more based on the logic of the submitted code. Automated testing fails since it assumes programs without any compilation errors. A complementary tool to the automatic grading is, therefore, a *program repairing* system that can identify and correct simple syntax errors.

In addition to fixing the program, program repairing can be used to improve the error messages and generate feedback to help the students write better code. An example feedback by GradeIT is also shown in Table 1. The details are presented in Sec. 2.4.

1.4 Contributions

In this paper we present *GradeIT*, a system that combines the dual objectives of automated grading and program repairing for introductory programming courses. For a program having minor syntax errors, GradeIT repairs the program before grading it automatically, albeit with a suitable penalty in marks. For a program that compiles successfully, GradeIT also uses features other than the number of passing testcases to determine the grade.

In sum, our main contributions are:

1. We present GradeIT, a grading system that uses program repair to grade programs with syntax errors. Unlike programming contest judge systems that use only number of passing testcases as the grading criterion, GradeIT uses a combination of features to decide the final grade for a submission.
2. We present a study of GradeIT over 15613 submissions in a CS1

Table 2: Statistics for CS1 (2015-16 Spring offering).

Count of	Lab	Exam
Students	410	410
TAs	40	40
Events	12	2
Problems	141	10
Submissions	12,872	2,741

course. We show that grades computed by GradeIT are comparable to manual grading by TAs (less than 20% difference on 88% of the submissions). In a controlled study, where grades of multiple TAs for similar assignments were compared with those by GradeIT, we found that the later were more consistent and closer to the final marks. The repairs done by GradeIT could enable successful compilations of 798 submissions out of 1417. Out of these, marks were improved for 90 submissions, with the maximum improvement being as high as 80% of the total marks.

3. GradeIT includes a feedback system that generates better feedback messages to help students identify errors. A user study found the feedback more useful than compiler messages (average rating 2.43 out of maximum 3).

2. GradeIT

Our institute, Indian Institute of Technology, Kanpur, has adapted *Prutor (PRogramming tUTOR)* [9] to conduct introductory programming course using C (called CS1 in the rest of the paper).[1] Prutor is a software system for managing programming assignments in CS1. It allows plugins to analyze submissions and provide feedback. We have developed GradeIT as a plugin for Prutor. CS1 is offered to all first-year students (400–450 students per offering) in the undergraduate program across all branches.

CS1 conducts compulsory weekly labs of 3 hours where students are assigned programming problems. The students are required to code solutions to the assignments and then submit them within the lab duration. About 40 TAs are employed in each offering to grade the submissions. They test the solutions against a set of preset testcases, read the code, and then award the marks. Two lab examinations (one mid-term and one end-term) are also conducted; they generally have much higher weight than the weekly lab sessions.

2.1 Automated Grading

We studied the data collected by Prutor for 4 offerings (2014-15 autumn, 2014-15 spring, 2015-16 autumn and 2015-16 spring semesters). Table 2 summarizes the offering of CS1 in 2015-16 spring semester.

We found that the major factors that contribute to higher grades for a submission are: (a) number of testcases passed, (b) inverse of time taken to solve, (c) fraction of successful compilations, (d) better coding discipline including indentation and modularity, (e) better comments, and (f) more readable programming logic. Although an ideal autograding tool should capture all the above factors, the last three factors require extensive program analysis and natural language processing. Hence, we decided to concentrate on the first three factors for the current version of our tool.

2.1.1 Testcases Passed

The primary and most important factor to determine the correctness of a solution program is the number of testcases passed out of all the testcases. These testcases are preset by the problem setter

---

[1] While the study reported in this paper is for C language on Prutor platform, GradeIT can be easily adapted for other languages, like C++, Java, Python; and for other platforms that can communicate using JSON (JavaScript Object Notation) format.

and consists of an input and the corresponding correct output. A testcase is deemed to pass if the output of the program matches the expected output (a numeric match is done such that 42 and 42.0 are considered equal).

If, for a solution S, k testcases pass out of a preset set of n testcases, the *partial score* of S is the fraction of testcases passed: $f_p(S) = k/n$.

2.1.2 Correctness of the Solution

A solution S is deemed to be *correct* only if *all* the testcases pass. Hence, the *correctness score* is defined as an indicator function that is either 0 or 1 based on whether all the testcases pass: $f_c(S) = 1$ iff *all* the testcases have passed; 0 otherwise. The correctness score is essentially a binary variable that checks whether the solution is correct. Even if one test case fails, the solution cannot be deemed to be correct and, therefore, the correctness score falls to 0. If, on the other hand, all the testcases set by the instructor passes, the solution can be considered to be *correct*.

2.1.3 Time Taken to Solve

Another indicator of a better program is the time taken to solve the problem. All other parameters being equal, TAs generally give higher marks to solutions that are submitted earlier. Also, from the training data, it was inferred that students who code better submit early. To capture this, the *time score* of a solution S is computed as $f_t(S) = (t_{end} - t_S)/(t_{end} - t_{start})$ where t_S is the timestamp when the solution S was submitted and t_{start} and t_{end} denote the starting and ending timestamps of the programming lab session when the solution was attempted. The score $f_t \in [0, 1]$ essentially captures the fraction of time that is unspent.

2.1.4 Fraction of Successful Compilations

For students just being introduced to programming, successful compilation can be a challenge. Hence, TAs tend to award higher marks to programs that at least compile successfully. To capture this, we compute the *compilation score* of a program S as $f_e(S) = 1 - (e_S/e_{max})$ where e_S is the number of compilation errors for S and e_{max} is the maximum over all such programs.

2.2 Grading Function

The final grade awarded to a submission is a *linear* function of the 4 types of scores described above:

$$g(S) = w_c.f_c(S) + w_p.f_p(S) + w_t.f_t(S) + w_e.f_e(S)$$

where w's are the weights attributed according to the importance of each type of score. The weights are learned by a *linear regression* model. We constrain the weights to be such that their sum is equal to 1, i.e., $w_c + w_p + w_t + w_e = 1$.

Note that the grade $g(S)$ is between 0 and 1. To obtain the marks for a particular programming question, the grades are scaled by the total marks for that question.

It is important to note that if a factor (such as time to solve) is irrelevant for the final grade, its corresponding weight will be very low since an empirical learning is done. However, as we see later in Sec. 3, none of the weights were very low, thereby empirically proving a correlation between the factor and the final grade. Similarly, if other attributes are deemed more important, they can be incorporated in the learning.

A second important point is that while the above function (and the corresponding learned weights) may be too specific for our institute, the methodology is generic. Given a set of such parameters and the corresponding set of final grades, the linear regression function can learn these weights for the particular situation.

Table 3: Top categories of syntax errors/warnings of student submissions for CS1 2015-16 Spring offering.

#	Error Type	Count
1	Use of undeclared identifier(s)	122375
2	Control may reach end of non-void function	49016
3	Missing '&' before variable name in scanf	
4	Use of wrong format specifier in scanf and printf	48327
5	Extra '&' before variable name in printf	
6	Use of uninitialized variable	43767
7	Expected ';' after expression	20578
8	Expected ')' ,']',',}'	18558
9	Use of '=' instead of '=='	9823
10	Type specifier missing, defaults to 'int'	9427
11	Subscripted value not an array, pointer, or vector	6633
12	Redefinition of variable 'var'	5642
13	Extraneous closing brace ('}')	5589
14	Use of undeclared identifier 'varr'; did you mean 'var'?	5264
15	Missing declaration for a function	4454
16	Multi-character character constant	3804
17	Empty body for `for`, `while` or `if`	3598
18	Expected ';' in 'for' statement specifier	2928
19	Use of '.' instead of '->' for pointer dereference	1917
20	Invalid conversion specifier '.'	1519
21	Use of '->' instead of '.' for struct dereference	1304
22	Missing size or initializer for array declaration	1094
23	Missing terminating '"' character	1041
24	Returning value from a void function	656

2.3 Automated Program Repairing

As mentioned earlier, a major limitation of any testcase based grading is handling of submissions that do not compile. If a student's submission is close to the correct solution, but does not pass any testcase due to some compilation error (say a missing semicolon), she will get extremely low marks with an autograding tool.

To alleviate this problem, GradeIT uses an automated repair tool to fix simple compile time errors before running the tests. The repairing tool targets simple but frequent compile time errors and warnings. It uses simple re-write rules to fix these errors. If the program gets corrected and some (or all) of the testcases pass, the student gets the corresponding marks for the passing testcases, albeit with a penalty for repairing of compilation error(s). The details of the repair system are given in [20].

We used Prutor compilation logs to identify frequent errors committed by the students. Table 3 lists the frequent errors/warnings as produced by the Clang [6] compiler along with their frequencies (errors with similar compiler messages are grouped together).

2.4 Automated Feedback

Compiler messages form the basic feedback for programming assignments. However, these messages are generally geared towards professional programmers and may refer to advanced concepts not covered in class. For example, consider the error message provided by Clang when a student misses the '&' while reading user input in an `int` variable (Table 1). This type of error is very common at the beginning of an introductory programming course when the students have little idea about pointers or format specifiers. Therefore, the error message does not make any sense to them. Table 1 shows how the feedback provided by GradeIT explains the issue more lucidly along with examples.

We created such simplified feedback for the most frequent errors. The feedback messages are displayed when students encounter compile errors. Our system handles 55 types of syntax errors covering 404,848 compilation warnings and errors out of a total of 514,585 (78.67% coverage). The details are in [8].

For each error/warning, the feedback is formatted as follows.

Table 4: Automated repair system statistics.

Status	#Submissions	
	Lab	Exam
Total Submissions	12872	2741
Before Repair		
Compile time warnings only	2359	724
Compile time errors and warnings	881	536
Errors Fixed By Repair		
Removed both errors as well as warnings	323	185
Removed errors, but warnings remaining	138	152
Total number of successful compilations	461	337
Unsuccessful compilations even after repair	420	199
Warnings Fixed By Repair		
Removed all warnings only	241	136

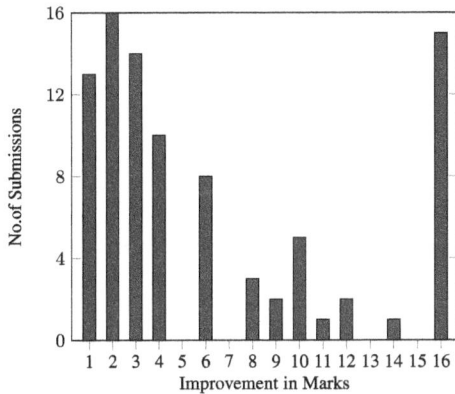

Figure 1: Frequency of submissions with improvement in marks.

First, we use a fixed set of *rewrite rules* to reformat the compiler error message into a simple message suitable for a novice programmer. Along with the message, we provide examples of two types: (a) valid code fragments to explain the student how to correct the error, and (b) invalid code fragments to show the common variations of the error.

3. EXPERIMENTS AND RESULTS

We present our results for the offering of CS1 in 2015-16 spring semester (Table 2). The course had 12 weekly lab assignments and 2 examinations. The labs were graded by 40 TAs, where each submissions was assigned to a TA randomly. The examinations had higher weightage and problems were more difficult than the weekly labs. Therefore, 2 TAs were asked to grade each submission independently. If their marks were similar (difference less than 5% of the total marks for the question), the higher value was finally awarded. Otherwise, instructor's intervention was needed and the final marks were awarded by the instructor. For both the labs and the examinations, students were allowed to request re-grading, in which case the instructor re-graded the submission.

3.1 Effectiveness of Program Repair

Table 4 shows the statistics for the repair subsystem of GradeIT. It attempted to repair 3240 (2359 + 881) submissions for the labs and 1260 (724 + 536) submissions for the exams. While not every repair was successful, we could reduce the number of unsuccessful compilations by 52% for the labs and by 62% for the exams.

For 90 of the repaired submissions, the grades were improved compared to when GradeIT was used on the original submission without repairing, with maximum improvement being as high as 80% of the total marks. The average improvement was 5.97/20

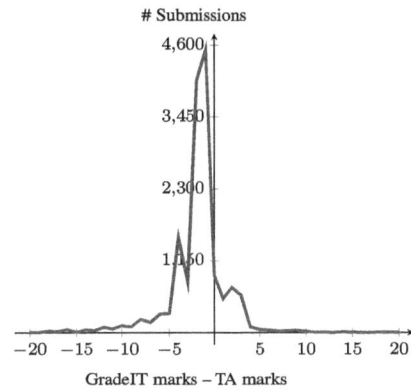

Figure 2: Comparing GradeIT with TAs.

marks per submission over these 90 submissions. Fig. 1 shows the statistics for the improvement in marks due to repair. Since the program repairing system presently targets only simple syntactic repairs without any semantic analysis, the total number of improvements was low. Still, program repair is important as it allows to award partial marks to submissions that do not compile due to minor mistakes.

3.2 GradeIT versus TA Grading

The linear regression function for GradeIT was trained using the lab marks from a previous offering of CS1. The weights of the different scores learned were: (i) partial: 0.75, (ii) correctness: 0.05, (iii) time: 0.05, and (iv) compilation: 0.15. Thus, although the number of testcases passed was the most important factor, the other factors also contributed to the final grade[2].

The main goal of GradeIT is to grade similar to a TA, albeit more consistently and more objectively. Thus, to compare the performance of GradeIT with respect to that of TAs, we computed the difference between the TA marks and GradeIT marks (using the learned weights as mentioned above) for all the lab and exam submissions. For uniformity, we set the maximum marks for all problems to 20, and scaled the submission grades accordingly. The counts of number of submissions corresponding to each value of difference between the GradeIT marks and the TA marks are shown in Fig. 2. We make two important observations:

1. Approximately 88% (13787 out of 15613) of the submissions are in the difference range -4 to 4, which shows that the GradeIT marks are close to that of a TA. For ~69% (10759/15613) of the submissions, the marks difference is ≤ 2.

2. For ~80% (12473/15613) of the submissions, TAs gave more marks than GradeIT, while for ~14% (2223/15613) of submissions, the reverse happened. This tells us that GradeIT is a more conservative grader than a human.

Some of the reasons for the differences in marks are:

1. TAs awards partial marks to submissions that capture the logic somewhat even if they do not compile. GradeIT, on the other hand, awards 0 marks to submissions that do not compile even after autorepair.

2. TAs typically deduct only a few marks when students make mistakes in output format. For example, if a submission prints result of some computation in an unsorted order where sorted order was expected. TAs generally penalize only a small fraction of marks corresponding to the testcase. However, GradeIT considers this a failure and deducts all marks assigned for the testcase.

---

[2]Due to operational issues, Prutor did not capture the fraction of successful compilations for lab examination 2. GradeIT used $f_e = 1$ and, thus, awarded marks on the higher side.

Problem: Write a program to determine if a year (int) given as input is a leap year or not. **[20 Marks]**	
Submission 1	**Submission 2**
| ```
#include <stdio.h>
int main(){
  int a,b;
  scanf ("%d",&a);
  b=(a%4);
  if (b==0)
    printf ("Leap");
  else
    printf ("Not Leap");
  return 0;
}
``` | ```
#include <stdio.h>
int main(){
  int y;
  scanf("%d",&y);
  if (y%4==0)
    printf("Leap");
  else
    printf("Not Leap");
  return 0;
}
``` |
| **TA Marks: 19** | **TA Marks: 5** |

Figure 3: Very different TA marks for similar submissions.

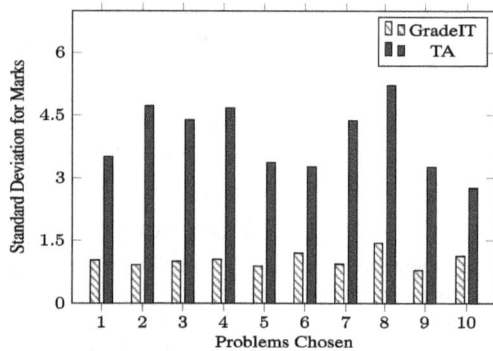

Figure 4: Comparing consistency of TA grading with GradeIT.

3. There exists inconsistency in grading of similar submissions by TAs, as explained next in Sec. 3.3.

3.3 Inconsistency in TA Grading

Due to the large number and varying backgrounds of TAs it is difficult to maintain consistency in grading across them. TAs are humans and have their own biases (such as favorite loop constructs, use of recursion versus iteration, formatting, etc.). Even in the presence of detailed grading policies, these factors cause different grades being given to similar submissions.

Consider, for example, two submissions for the same problem statement in Fig. 3. (Note that these are real submissions, and are formatted here only for readability.) The problem is to determine whether a given year is a leap year or not. Both the submissions make the simplistic assumption that every year divisible by 4 is a leap year and are, therefore, not fully correct. Submission 1 was awarded 19 marks by one TA while submission 2 was awarded 5 marks by another TA. It is obvious that the submissions are identical, the only difference being the variable names and the use of an extra variable to hold an intermediate computation. In a large class, it is difficult to detect such inconsistencies, unless reported by the students themselves. The GradeIT system effectively removes such inconsistencies. It awarded 12 marks to both the submissions.

To study this issue further, we randomly selected 10 problem statements and created 10 clusters of similar submissions for each. The clustering was done manually by looking at the code. Each cluster consisted of 10-20 submissions. Ideally, we expected the marks for submissions within each cluster to be close to each other. Fig. 4 shows the standard deviations for the grades assigned by GradeIT and by TAs for each problem. It is clear that the grades assigned by the TAs deviated a lot more than those by GradeIT. We infer that grading by GradeIT is consistent when compared to TAs.

Table 5: Interpretations of scores for GradeIT feedback messages.

#	Interpretation
0	The feedback is incorrect or poorly written.
1	The feedback is no better than the compiler message.
2	The feedback is somewhat better than the compiler message.
3	The feedback is substantially better than the compiler message.

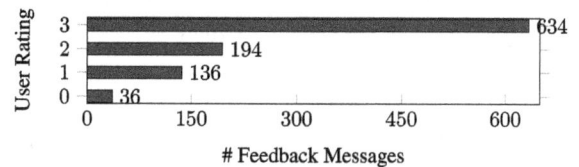

Figure 5: User ratings for the feedback messages.

3.4 Response Time of GradeIT

Since GradeIT is used as a real-time system, we measured the average time to grade a submission against the number of lines of code for the various lab and exam events. The time varies from 118 ms per submission (for lab 1) to 2033 ms per submission (for end-term exam). Some important observations are:

1. The response time is never more than 2 sec, thereby confirming the real-time nature of GradeIT.
2. The average SLOC for the labs and exams remain between 30-60 lines. The average SLOC generally increases since problems involving more complex concepts are asked in later labs.
3. Lab exams ask problems that require more thinking than coding, i.e., the problems are more algorithmic in nature. Thus, the average SLOC for exams decrease.
4. The time taken by GradeIT increases during exam events since students make more mistakes during exams (compile time warnings and errors, see Fig. 1).

Such detailed analyses is possible only with the aid of GradeIT like systems. This helps the instructors to understand at what pace the course is advancing and how well the students are coping with the various concepts introduced in each week. Continuing the analysis further, some of the reasons why students make more mistakes during exams were found to be the following:

1. The problems during exams are more challenging as the connection between the statement and the expected program is not as obvious as in case of the labs.
2. The exams cover the entire range of concepts (or C constructs) taught so far. A lab, on the other hand, is typically tuned to test only the major concept covered in class during the week.
3. Since the weightage on exams are more, the testsuite for exams consists of a substantially larger number of testcases including tricky corner cases.

Larger number of mistakes increases the response time of GradeIT as larger number of repairs are applied.

3.5 Effectiveness of Our Feedback Messages

To evaluate the effectiveness of our feedback messages, we performed a user study with 8 students and 1000 erroneous programs. These students were given a web interface, where they could see a program along with the errors/warnings generated by Clang [6] as well as the feedback from GradeIT. Each student was shown 125 unique submissions, and was asked to compare GradeIT feedback with Clang messages and then rate the feedback on a scale of 0 to 3, where the ratings had the interpretations as listed in Table 5.

Fig. 5 shows that the students found GradeIT feedback useful for a large number of cases (average rating 2.426/3). The main reason for low ratings (0 and 1) was that GradeIT handles only 55 types of errors for generating feedback. For any other error, the

```
int main(){
  int ans, ...;
  ...
  printf(%d, ans);
  ...
}
```
(a) Program snippet

```
error: expected expression
       printf(%d, ans);
              ^
error: use of undeclared identifier 'd'
       printf(%d, ans);
               ^
```
(b) Compiler Messages

You have not declared the variable 'd' that is used on this line.
Please declare it before using it. ...

(c) GradeIT Feedback

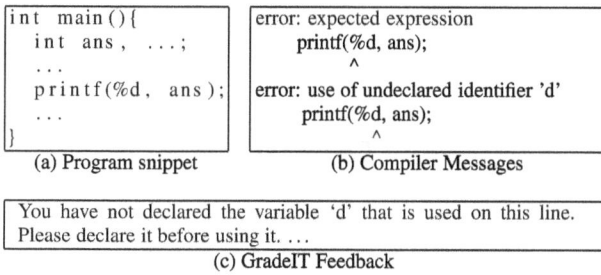

Figure 6: Incorrect GradeIT feedback.

compiler message is repeated. Also, presence of multiple errors or possibility of multiple (unrelated) repairs in the same submission confuses GradeIT sometimes, causing an incorrect feedback. Fig. 6 shows such an example.

4. RELATED WORK

Due to popularity of Massive Open Online Courses (MOOC), automated grading and feedback generation for programming assignments are receiving a lot of attention. Section 1.2 described some popular approaches [11–13, 15, 16, 21]. However, all these approaches work only on submissions that compile successfully. Several programming assignment submission systems have been proposed recently (for example, [2, 10, 18]) that allow automated grading of the submissions. However, the grading is based on the test cases only. Gao et al. [10] and Earle et al. [2] improve the quality of the grading by generating the testsuite automatically.

Recent works [3, 14, 19] use neural networks to "learn" the correct sequence of tokens from submissions that compile successfully, and use this knowledge to repair syntax errors in other submissions. In contrast, our technique uses a fixed set of rewrite rules and compiler hints to generate repairs for simple, but frequent, syntax errors. The study by [17] involving two groups of students using different styles of error messages concluded that the location and structure of error messages play an important role in understanding errors and developing coding skills. Another study by [23] analyzes cryptic compiler error messages and suggest possible measures to improve them to help the programmers.

5. CONCLUSIONS AND FUTURE WORK

We presented GradeIT, a program repair based feedback and grading tool. For students, GradeIT improves upon the compiler messages to help them fix syntax errors. For instructor, GradeIT helps grade student submissions automatically. It uses features of submitted programs to decide the grade. Further, it repairs the submissions that do not even compile to award them partial grades.

GradeIT performed close to human TAs on 15,613 submissions. The difference in marks was less than 20% of the total marks for ~88% of submissions. The main cause of the difference is the variability in TA grading. We found that GradeIT is more consistent than TAs when awarding marks for similar submissions.

We believe that the consistency and the quick response time of GradeIT can help instructors in understanding the students' learning patterns better. Specifically, the students who tend to struggle with programming can be identified quickly and helped better.

GradeIT is still in a prototype stage. The repair tools work on simple syntax errors only, but can be improved by using more sophisticated algorithms [3, 14, 19]. Our grading model can be improved by considering more features of the submitted program. Even with these limitations, GradeIT can be used for a large CS1 class to augment the TAs. GradeIT can be easily adapted to languages like C++, Java, Python since it is not strongly tied to the semantics of a language, but depends on the syntactic features of the program, the testsuite, and the error/warning messages generated by a compiler.

Testsuite-based grading process is sensitive to the tests employed for grading. If an expected feature is not covered by the testsuite, the tools cannot distinguish between a submission that implements it and one that does not implement it.[3] Automated testsuite generation tools [4, 5] can be used to improve the coverage of testsuite and improve the grading for programs that compile successfully.

6. REFERENCES

[1] A. V. Aho, M. S. Lam, R. Sethi, and J. D. Ullman. *Compilers: Principles, Techniques, and Tools.* 2006.

[2] C. Benac Earle, L. Fredlund, and J. Hughes. Automatic grading of programming exercises using property-based testing. In *ITiCSE*, 2016.

[3] S. Bhatia and R. Singh. Automated correction for syntax errors in programming assignments using recurrent neural networks. *CoRR*, abs/1603.06129, 2016.

[4] J. Burnim and K. Sen. Heuristics for scalable dynamic test generation. In *Automated Software Engineering*, 2008.

[5] C. Cadar, D. Dunbar, and D. Engler. Klee: Unassisted and automatic generation of high-coverage tests for complex systems programs. In *OSDI*, 2008.

[6] Clang. http://clang.llvm.org/.

[7] Codechef. https://www.codechef.com/.

[8] Z. Dadachanji. Automated feedback and grading for programs in introductory programming courses. M. Tech. thesis, Indian Institute of Technology Kanpur, India, 2016.

[9] R. Das, U. Z. Ahmed, A. Karkare, and S. Gulwani. Prutor: A system for tutoring CS1 and collecting student programs for analysis. *CoRR*, abs/1608.03828, 2016.

[10] J. Gao, B. Pang, and S. S. Lumetta. Automated feedback framework for introductory programming courses. In *ITiCSE*, 2016.

[11] E. L. Glassman, J. Scott, R. Singh, P. J. Guo, and R. C. Miller. Overcode: Visualizing variation in student solutions to programming problems at scale. *ACM Trans. Comput.-Hum. Interact.*, 2015.

[12] S. Gulwani, I. Radicek, and F. Zuleger. Feedback generation for performance problems in introductory programming assignments. *CoRR*, abs/1403.4064, 2014.

[13] S. Gulwani, I. Radicek, and F. Zuleger. Automated clustering and program repair for introductory programming assignments. *CoRR*, abs/1603.03165, 2016.

[14] R. Gupta, S. Pal, A. Kanade, and S. Shevade. DeepFix: Fixing common C language errors by deep learning. In *AAAI*, 2017.

[15] S. Kaleeswaran, A. Santhiar, A. Kanade, and S. Gulwani. Semi-supervised verified feedback generation. In *FSE*, 2016.

[16] A. Nguyen, C. Piech, J. Huang, and L. Guibas. Codewebs: Scalable homework search for massive open online programming courses. In *World Wide Web*, 2014.

[17] M.-H. Nienaltowski, M. Pedroni, and B. Meyer. Compiler error messages: What can help novices? *SIGCSE Bull.*, 2008.

[18] M. Peveler, J. Tyler, S. Breese, B. Cutler, and A. Milanova. Submitty: An open source, highly-configurable platform for grading of programming assignments. In *SIGCSE*, 2017.

[19] Y. Pu, K. Narasimhan, A. Solar-Lezama, and R. Barzilay. sk_p: a neural program corrector for MOOCs. *CoRR*, abs/1607.02902, 2016.

[20] P. K. Singh. Automated repair of programs in introductory programming courses. M. Tech. thesis, Indian Institute of Technology Kanpur, India, 2016.

[21] R. Singh, S. Gulwani, and A. Solar-Lezama. Automated feedback generation for introductory programming assignments. In *PLDI*, 2013.

[22] Topcoder competitive programming. https://www.topcoder.com/community/competitive-programming/.

[23] V. J. Traver. On compiler error messages: What they say and what they mean. *Adv. in Hum.-Comp. Int.*, 2010.

---

[3]"Program testing can be used to show the presence of bugs, but never to show their absence!" – E. W. Dijkstra

An Automated System for Interactively Learning Software Testing

Rebecca Smith
Rice University
rjs@rice.edu

Terry Tang
Rice University
terry.tang@rice.edu

Joe Warren
Rice University
jwarren@rice.edu

Scott Rixner
Rice University
rixner@rice.edu

ABSTRACT

Testing is an important, time-consuming, and often difficult part of the software development process. It is therefore critical to introduce testing early in the computer science curriculum, and to provide students with frequent opportunities for practice and feedback. This paper presents an automated system to help introductory students learn how to test software. Students submit test cases to the system, which uses a large corpus of buggy programs to evaluate these test cases. In addition to gauging the quality of the test cases, the system immediately presents students with feedback in the form of buggy programs that nonetheless pass their tests. This enables students to understand why their test cases are deficient and gives them a starting point for improvement. The system has proven effective in an introductory class: students that trained using the system were later able to write better test cases — even without any feedback — than those who were not. Further, students reported additional benefits such as improved ability to read code written by others and to understand multiple approaches to the same problem.

Keywords

Computer science education; Interactive learning; Software testing; Automated assessment

1. INTRODUCTION

Testing is an important part of software development that can take up to half of the total development time [3]. Thus, it is critical to teach students how to test software [4, 5, 6, 19]. Yet, computer science education focuses primarily on software development — including topics such as languages, tools, and design principles — and not on testing. This is particularly true at the introductory level.

Further, many students do not want to test their code, often viewing it as an unpleasant afterthought [23]. While students often derive a great deal of satisfaction from seeing a program that they wrote solve a problem, they do not derive that same sense of satis-

faction from exposing flaws in their own programs. However, there is evidence that learning to test helps students to write better code and to do so more quickly [14, 24]. Therefore, it is crucial to design and develop strategies to expose students to testing early in their computer science education [18, 32].

This paper presents an automated and interactive system designed to help students learn how to write better test cases. The system was evaluated through a study that was conducted in an introductory computer science class. In our system, students are given a specification for a program and asked to submit a test suite for that program. Note that they do not need to write the program; rather, they must think about what inputs would stress an implementation of the given specification. After submitting their tests and receiving feedback from the system, students can iteratively improve their tests and resubmit. We believe that several key elements of the system that contribute to its effectiveness.

First, students are not testing their own code. When testing their own code, students are less motivated to find bugs, as bugs expose their own failure to develop a correct program [8, 21]. When there is no personal investment in the code being tested, students are able to view testing as a rewarding activity and are driven to find as many bugs as possible. Second, the submitted tests are evaluated based on the number of buggy programs they detect from a large corpus of buggy programs, not their code coverage. This approach is motivated by the fact that techniques such as mutation analysis and all-pairs testing have been shown to be more effective than code coverage at identifying weak test sets [2, 16], and thus give students a a far more accurate view of the quality of their test cases.

Finally, and perhaps most importantly, the system provides immediate feedback that not only tells students how well their tests perform, but also gives clear examples of buggy implementations that their tests do not detect. It is often difficult for a student to reason about all possible edge cases in a program. Our system provides multiple example implementations with similar bugs, allowing students to understand *why* their test suite is not comprehensive by seeing the type(s) of bugs that their tests do not catch. This feedback not only helps students to develop better test cases, but also gives them practice reading, understanding, and debugging code written by others. Further, it has the added benefit of exposing students to a diverse set of solution strategies to the same problem.

The system has proven to be successful at teaching introductory students how to write better test cases. After using the system, students were able to think about testing in a more comprehensive way and to develop better test cases without continuing to need to see example implementations. With no other training, students that used the system were able to score nearly a standard deviation higher on a testing assessment than students who had not — a statistically significant result ($p < 0.0001$). Furthermore, over 73% of the students reported that the system improved their ability to write comprehensive test cases, to read code written by other people, and to understand multiple approaches to the same problem.

The paper proceeds as follows. Section 2 places our contributions in the context of past work. Section 3 describes our system for teaching students to write better tests. Section 4 describes the study used to evaluate this system, and Section 5 presents the results of this study. Last, Section 6 concludes the paper.

2. RELATED WORK

Much of the past work on teaching software testing has focused on broad structural changes to place greater emphasis on testing within computer science curricula [4, 5, 6, 14, 18, 19], touting the importance of integrating testing into the curriculum early and often. Such work is largely orthogonal to the methodological techniques presented in this paper. Several other papers have proposed highly formal approaches to teaching software testing in upper-level courses which require devoting roughly half of the instructional time to teaching software testing [9, 10, 19]. While appropriate in an advanced context, these approaches are too heavyweight for an introductory course where testing is not the primary focus.

Of the past work that has investigated techniques for integrating testing into introductory courses, the most closely-related work focuses on mutation analysis and all-pairs testing. DeMillo et al. helped popularize mutation testing [12], in which students simultaneously submit an implementation and set of test cases; the submitted implementation is mutated in various ways, and the mutants are used to determine how effective the test suite is as finding bugs. However, their approach does not assess students consistently, as the mutants presented to each student are highly personalized.

More recently, Aaltonen et al. demonstrated the superior ability of mutation analysis, as compared to code coverage, to identify weak test suites [2]. Like DeMillo et al., they used the student's own implementation to generate mutants on the fly. However, they noted a flaw in their approach: students could exploit the grading system by introducing dead code into their solution, which would result in an artificially-inflated score. In contrast to our interactive framework, both Aaltonen et al. and DeMillo et al. performed mutation analysis after-the-fact to evaluate students' final submissions.

Another popular approach to testing in introductory courses is pairwise testing, which requires that students submit both an implementation and a test suite, and scores the test suite by running it on one or more implementation(s): traditionally, submission(s) of one [21] or more [17, 20, 22, 26] classmates. Such approaches require students to submit a final test suite "blindly", with no opportunity to interact with the implementation(s) on which their tests will be evaluated. Similar work has used alternate implementations including an instructor-provided reference implementation [11], or even a corpus of instructor-provided buggy implementations [29], posing less challenges to interactivity. Still, this past work largely required blind submissions and after-the-fact evaluation.

Recent work has improved pairwise testing by proving the feasibility of applying it synchronously, enabling students to see their scores progress as they develop their test cases [31]. This work required students to develop implementations and test suites simultaneously, and built up a corpus of student implementations to run the tests against as students submitted their work. However, this work faces several challenges. First, as the corpus of student implementations grows, the score associated with a given test suite will decrease, which may frustrate students. Additionally, the quality of the evaluation relies on the diversity of the student submissions, which is unpredictable. Last, the paper does not indicate that students receive any feedback beyond the score to help them complete the exercises, nor does it provide any evaluation of the effectiveness of the tool in improving the students' testing capabilities.

In contrast, our system emits consistent, deterministic scores for a given test suite. Further, it ensures a diverse and thorough pool on which to evaluate students' test suites by using a pre-existing corpus of programs that melds instructor-provided solutions, student solutions from prior iterations of the course, and prefabricated mutants. Additionally, we have experimentally proven the success of our system by performing a thorough evaluation its effectiveness within a controlled experimental environment.

3. INFRASTRUCTURE

Many studies have cited limited time (both preparation time and instruction time) as one of the major barriers to teaching software testing [15, 25]. This motivates the use of an automated system to help students develop testing abilities. Yet, an even larger body of work demonstrates the value of active learning [7, 28, 30]. To balance these concerns, we created a system that evaluates students' test suites immediately and automatically, but fosters interactive learning by creating a constant cycle of formative feedback. This system was implemented for Python programs, but the pedagogical principles underlying it transcend any particular language.

At a high level, students are given a natural language specification for a function and tasked with developing a test suite: a list of test cases, where each test case is a tuple of inputs that adheres to the specification. As students develop tests, they can submit them to the system at any time and receive feedback. This feedback is designed not only to evaluate the quality of the submitted tests, but also to help students to recognize subsets of the input domain that their tests do not cover. They can then iteratively improve their tests based on this feedback until they are satisfied with their results.

In greater detail, the system runs the submitted test suite against a corpus of incorrect implementations of the function, and provides the student with two pieces of feedback. First, they receive a score based on the number of incorrect implementations that were "caught" by the submitted test suite, i.e. that failed one or more test. Second, they are shown the source code for one or more incorrect programs that were not caught by their tests. Specifically, the system outputs up to three programs that share the same "test signature", i.e. that exhibit the same set of bugs. Limiting the feedback to a single test signature scaffolds the students' progress without immediately revealing all uncaught bugs. At the same time, providing multiple examples of implementations that exhibit that single signature exercises students' pattern-matching skills, facilitating the process of identifying weaknesses in their current test suite.

As Figure 1 shows, our system consists of four key phases: creating a corpus of implementations, identifying bugs within these implementations, developing a scaffolded progression through these implementations, and an interface through which students can interact with the scaffolded exercises as they develop their test suites.

3.1 Corpus Constructor

There are many viable means of building a corpus of implementations; we chose to combine two. First, we extracted student solutions S from CodeSkulptor [33], an online interactive development environment (IDE) that automatically stores version history as stu-

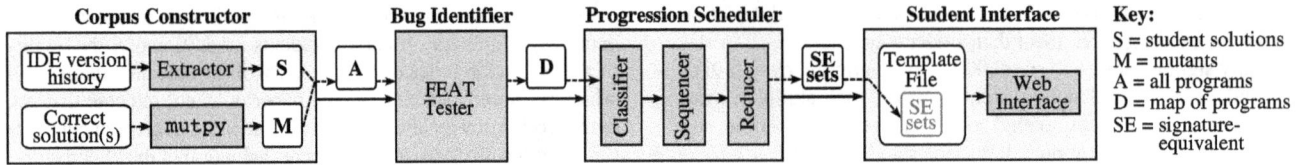

Figure 1: System Infrastructure

Table 1: Corpus Sizes for Training & Test Functions

Function	|S|	|M|	|A|	|SE sets|
blackjack3	156	110	266	71
format	2295	235	2530	76
stringtime	115	263	378	97

Figure 2: Sample Function Specification

The blackjack3() function takes as its input three cards, each of which is represented as a single character from the string "23456789TJQKA". For instance, one valid tuple of inputs might be ("A", "K", "5"). In blackjack, number cards (including "T", which represents 10) are worth their value, and face cards ("JQK") are worth 10. Aces can be worth either 1 or 11; the choice between these is made such that the value of the hand is as high as possible without going over 21. (Note that there are some cases in which it is impossible to stay under 21.) Returning to the example of ("A", "K", "5"), the expected output would be 16. Your input file should contain a single Python definition:

- A list TEST_CASES containing at most **12 test cases** for the function blackjack3().
- Each test case in this list should be a list of tuples of length three whose entries are characters in "23456789TJQKA".

dents develop their code. This IDE has been used by many students across multiple MOOCs and physically co-located classes, and thus has amassed a large corpus of student solutions to the programming exercises posed by these courses. By mining implementations directly from the IDE's version history rather than using final submissions, we capture a broader — and thus more interesting for testing — spectrum of buggy and incomplete solutions.

Second, we ran mutpy [13], a mutation testing tool, on correct solutions to introduce a set of additional faulty implementations M, giving us an aggregate set of implementations $A = S \cup M$. As a supplement to S, M serves two purposes. First, it introduces new test signatures for students to face as they develop their tests. Second, it increases the number of implementations with the same test signature, allowing the system to provide students with more detailed feedback for debugging. M is also effective in the absence of S, rendering our system viable for small classes, new classes, and other scenarios in which a large corpus of student implementations may not yet exist. Table 1 shows the corpus sizes and number of unique signatures for the training functions (blackjack3, format) and the test function (stringtime) used in the evaluation.

3.2 Bug Identifier

Identifying bugs within A is necessary in order to identify unique test signatures and choose which programs should be displayed as feedback. For this, we used FEAT [34], an existing tool for test case generation and automated programming assessment. FEAT begins by creating an expansive "base test set" through a combination of exhaustive and random generation. For the functions used in our experiment, the input domains were sufficiently constrained to use fully-exhaustive base test sets. FEAT outputs a mapping D associating each $a \in A$ with the set of test cases that it failed on. This set of failed tests is its test signature; implementations that share the same test signature typically have the same or very similar bugs.

3.3 Progression Scheduler

For the third component of our system, we extended FEAT with a new module that classifies and sequences programs based on their signatures. This module first creates a mapping of each signature to the set of programs with that signature ("signature-equivalent" or SE sets). It eliminates the empty test signature, as this represents programs that have no bugs. Next, it sequences the SE sets in order of descending signature size. As students work through the testing exercise, they will be provided with feedback in this order. The intuition for this is that it will be easier for students to create test

suites that catch programs that fail on a larger number of cases than on those that fail in only one or two specific scenarios.

Each signature-equivalent set may be arbitrarily large. However, presenting students with a large number of programs may be overwhelming. So, the module selects a maximum of three programs to represent each signature in the feedback provided to the students. To choose these three programs, it uses the radon package [1] to compute the McCabe cyclomatic complexity metric [27] for each program. The module then selects those programs that have the lowest complexity, with the goal of making the feedback maximally approachable for the students. Thus, at the end of this process, the module outputs a list of sets of programs, where each element in the outer list is a signature-equivalent set of size at most three.

3.4 Student Interface

To enable students to interact with these signature-equivalent sets, we used our existing auto-grading system, which requires instructors to upload a file defining how student submissions are processed and scored. We created a template file that imports the submitted test suite, runs a validation function to ensure that it meets the specification, and then runs each of the submitted tests on one representative program from each signature-equivalent set. During this process, it makes note of the first signature that the student's tests fail to catch, as that signature will be used for feedback. It then computes a score based on the proportion of signatures caught.

Last, this file generates feedback: the score and the source code of the program(s) in the first SE set that the submitted tests failed to catch. This scaffolds the exercise such that students receive some direction regarding which cases they're missing, but are not immediately given full "white-box" knowledge. For each function to be tested, the template need only be modified to import the correct SE sets and to provide a specification for the function being tested, a

Figure 3: Assessment: Final Scores

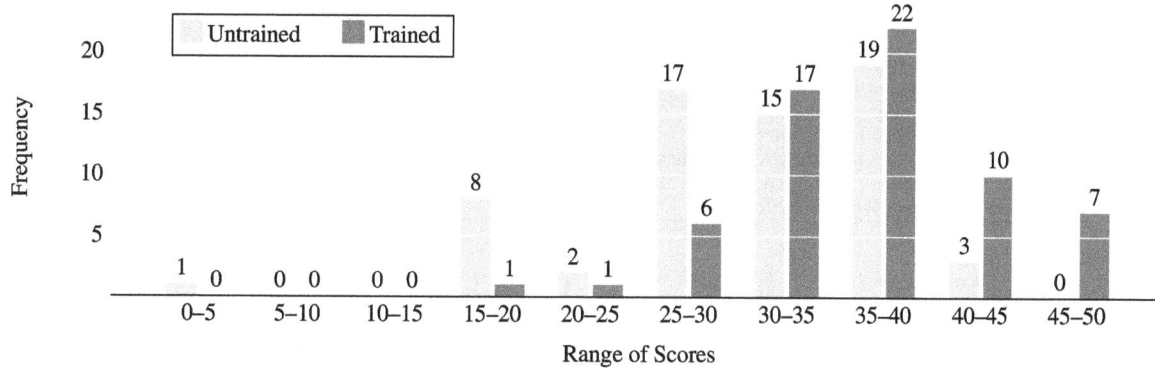

reference solution, and a validation function for the test suite. Optionally, the grading scale may also be customized.

4. METHODOLOGY

We evaluated the framework described in Section 3 within the fall 2016 iteration of an introductory computer science course that teaches students how to solve problems in a computational way and how to implement their solutions in Python. This course has no prerequisites and is taken by a mix of majors and non-majors.

We ran a study consisting of a training exercise, an assessment, and two surveys. Students were randomly assigned to a control or experimental group. Both groups completed the assessment simultaneously; however, the experimental group completed the training exercises beforehand, while the control group did not complete the training until afterwards. Training the control group after-the-fact was not necessary for the study, but preserved fairness in workload and ensured that both groups reaped the benefits of the training. Neither group received any other training in testing prior to the assessment. Due to random assignment, we would expect both groups to perform equally on the assessment, all else being equal. Thus, since the only difference between groups was whether they had completed our training, inter-group differences on the assessment are likely due to that training. Last, both groups completed surveys before the training and after the test, in which they reported their level of confidence in their software testing abilities.

The training exercise was a mandatory homework assignment in which students used the framework described in Section 3 to develop test cases for two training functions. Students were given five days in which to complete these training exercises. The assessment was a mandatory in-class assignment, but was not counted towards the students' course grades for the sake of fairness. On the assessment, students were given a natural language specification for a function and asked to construct a list of at most 12 test cases for this function. To eliminate any potential advantages due to familiarity with the interface discussed in Section 3, the assessment was completed by hand. Students were given 15 minutes in which to complete the assessment. They were also asked to write down their partial solutions after five and ten minutes to provide greater insight into their process as they progressed through the exercise.

The pre-survey asked the students about their attitudes toward testing and confidence in their testing abilities. The post-survey asked the same questions, so that the delta might show the effectiveness of the training exercises. However, we hypothesized that students might not recognize their lack of testing capabilities un-

Table 2: Assessment: Summary Statistics
($p < 0.0001$)

	Min	Average	Max	Stdev	N
Untrained	0	30.65	43.2	7.81	68
Trained	17.7	36.53	50	6.34	66
Aggregate	0	33.54	50	7.69	134

til after they completed the training assignment, so the post-survey also included explicit questions about the effectiveness of the training.

5. EVALUATION

In fall 2016, 196 students were enrolled in the course in which we evaluated our system. 141 of these students consented to participate in the study. Students were randomly assigned to the control and experimental groups; of the consenting students, 70 were assigned to the control group and 71 to the experimental group. Due to absences, 134 students ultimately took the assessment, of which 68 belonged to the control group and 66 to the experimental group. We ran this study approximately halfway through the semester, at which point students had gained basic familiarity with Python and had likely written some test cases on their own, but had received no formal instruction on software testing within the course.

We used three pieces of data to assess the effectiveness of the training exercises. First, we compared the distributions of assessment scores of the experimental (trained) and control (untrained) groups. Second, we compared the students' self-reported confidence in their abilities before and after completing the training exercises. Last, we examined the students' perceptions of the effectiveness of the training exercises.

Assessments were scored out of 50, where the score was proportional to the number of unique signatures caught; Table 2 presents the summary statistics for each group, and Figure 3 shows the full distribution of scores. While both groups' scores were roughly normally distributed, the trained group outperformed the untrained group by nearly a full standard deviation, with an average score of 36.53 as compared to 30.65 for the untrained group. A one-tailed unpaired t-test yielded a p-value of < 0.0001, which is regarded as statistically significant. Note that students received no feedback during assessment; the fact that the trained students performed better on the test even in the absence of feedback indicates that, while the feedback during training likely helped them to improve, they did not become dependent on it for future success in writing tests.

Table 3: Implicit Feedback

"I am confident in my ability to..."	% Agree (Pre-survey)	% Agree (Post-survey)	Delta
Identify distinct logical categories of input (corresponding to unique code paths) for a particular problem	59.3%	77.6%	+18.3%
Write comprehensive test cases	34.5%	55.2%	+20.7%
Write comprehensive test cases for my own code	51.4%	71.6%	+20.2%
Write comprehensive test cases for code written by other people	28.6%	62.7%	+34.1%
Write comprehensive test cases based on a description of a function, without seeing the implementation (code)	32.9%	36.6%	+3.7%

Table 4: Assessment: Intermediate Results

	Average (5 minutes)	Average (10 minutes)	Average (Final)
Untrained	21.80	26.90	30.65
Trained	26.80	32.55	36.53
Delta	+5.00	+5.66	+5.87

Table 5: Explicit Feedback

"The training exercises improved my ability to..."	% Agree
Write comprehensive test cases	73.1%
Read code written by other people	82.1%
Understand multiple approaches to the same problem	91.0%

Interestingly, examining the scores from the five- and ten-minute checkpoints revealed that the gap between groups increased with time. As Table 4 shows, the trained group averaged a 5.00 point advantage at five minutes; by ten minutes, this had grown to 5.66 points, and by fifteen it had expanded to 5.87 points. One possible explanation is that the untrained students more quickly approached a point of diminishing returns, while the trained students were able to continue reasoning productively about the input domain.

Further, students reported increased confidence on a variety of testing-related skills. For each statement in Table 3, students rated their confidence using a four-point Likert scale (Strongly Disagree, Disagree, Agree, Strongly Agree) at the beginning and end of the study. In every case, the percentage of students who responded with Agree or Strongly Agree increased. Most notably, the percentage of students who felt confident in their ability to write comprehensive test cases increased from 34.5% to 55.2%, those who felt confident in their ability to test their own code increased from 51.4% to 71.6%, and those who felt confident in their ability to write comprehensive test cases for code written by others more than doubled, from 28.6% to 62.7%. Students also indicated notably higher confidence in their ability to reason about the input domain.

Surprisingly, a fairly small percentage of students felt improved confidence in their ability to write test cases without actually seeing the code they were testing. However, the results of the assessment, which asked students to do exactly that — develop a black-box test suite —, indicate that this lack of confidence was unfounded.

When asked to provide explicit feedback on the training exercises using the same four-point Likert scale, the students strongly corroborated their effectiveness. Over 73% of students agreed that the exercises improved their ability to write comprehensive test cases. Moreover, students reported auxiliary benefits of the training exercises. Over 82% of students felt increased confidence in their ability to read code written by others, and over 91% of students felt better equipped to understand multiple approaches to the same problem — both hugely valuable skills in software development.

6. CONCLUSION

This paper has presented an interactive system for helping students learn to develop better test suites. The system was evaluated within an introductory class, and has been shown to improve students' testing abilities by a statistically significant degree. Given the benefits the students derived from the system, we plan to continue to use it in our introductory class in the future to teach testing.

Three key features contribute to the system's effectiveness. First, students are not testing their own code. This allows them to focus on developing test cases, rather than worrying about bugs in their own code. Second, the submitted test suites are evaluated based on how many buggy programs they detect from a large corpus of programs. This gives a more objective measure of test quality than many other metrics such as code coverage. Finally, students are given instantaneous feedback on their submitted test cases in the form of programs that contain bugs which are undetected by their tests. This enables students to reason about the quality of their test cases and to understand why they are not sufficient.

Students who trained with our system were able to construct better test cases than those who had not: on an assessment that required students to develop black-box tests for a natural language specification, the average performance of the trained group was nearly a full standard deviation higher than that of the untrained group. This indicates that our system teaches students to think about testing in a more comprehensive way without continuing to need to see example implementations. Further, the students recognized the improvements in their abilities, reporting increased confidence in their ability to write comprehensive test cases.

The nature of the feedback system also provides additional benefits. Examining buggy programs not only helps students to develop better test cases, but also gives them practice reading, understanding, and debugging code written by others. Similarly, being exposed to these buggy programs helps students to reason about a variety of different solution strategies to the same problem. These are both extremely valuable skills for software developers to have.

Testing is a critical part of the software development process. Despite this, most computer science curricula devote little time to teaching students how to test. Therefore, it is essential to develop new systems and techniques for integrating testing into the curriculum. This paper has introduced one such system and evaluated it within an introductory course, demonstrating how the combination of automation and interactive feedback can quickly and effectively yield striking improvements in student testing capabilities.

7. ACKNOWLEDGEMENTS

This material is based upon work supported by NSF Award CCF-1320860: "Computer-Aided Grading, Feedback, and Assignment Creation in Massive Online Programming Courses" as well as an NSF Graduate Research Fellowship under Grant No. 1450681.

8. REFERENCES

[1] radon. https://pypi.python.org/pypi/radon.

[2] K. Aaltonen, P. Ihantola, and O. Seppala. Mutation analysis vs. code coverage in automated assessment of students' testing skills. In *Proceedings of the ACM SIGPLAN Conference on Systems, Programming, Languages, and Applications: Software for Humanity*, 2010.

[3] D. S. Alberts. The economics of software quality assurance. In *Proceedings of the 1976 National Computer Conference and Exposition*, 1976.

[4] E. F. Barbosa, J. C. Maldonado, R. LeBlanc, and M. Guzdial. Introducing testing practices into objects and design course. In *Proceedings of the 16th IEEE Conference on Software Engineering Education and Training*, 2003.

[5] E. F. Barbosa, M. A. G. Silva, C. K. D. Corte, and J. C. Maldonado. Integrated teaching of programming foundations and software testing. In *Proceedings of the 38th ASEE/IEEE Frontiers in Education Conference*, 2008.

[6] E. G. Barriocanal, M.-A. S. Urban, I. A. Cuevas, and P. D. Perez. An experience in integrating automated unit testing practices in an introductory progamming course. *ACM SIGCSE Bulletin*, 34(4), 2002.

[7] C. C. Bonwell and J. A. Eison. *Active Learning: Creating Excitement in the Classroom*. ASHE-ERIC Higher Education Report No. 1., Washington, D.C.: The George Washington University, School of Education and Human Development, 1991.

[8] D. Carrington. Teaching software testing. In *Proceedings of the 2nd ACM SIGCSE Australasian Conference on Computer Science Education*, 1997.

[9] D. Carrington. Teaching software design and testing. In *Proceedings of the 28th ASEE/IEEE Frontiers in Education Conference*, 1998.

[10] T. Y. Chen and P.-L. Poon. Experience with teaching black-box testing in a computer science/software engineering curriculum. *IEEE Transactions on Education*, 47(1), 2004.

[11] D. M. de Souza, S. Isotani, and E. F. Barbosa. Teaching novice programmers using progtest. *International Journal of Knowledge and Learning*, 10(1), 2015.

[12] R. A. DeMillo, R. J. Lipton, and F. G. Sayward. Hints on test data selection: Help for the practicing programmer. *IEEE Computer*, 11(4), 1978.

[13] A. Derezinska and K. Halas. Experimental evaluation of mutation testing approaches to python programs. In *Proceedings of the 7th IEEE International Conference on Software Testing, Verification, and Validation Workshops*, 2014.

[14] S. H. Edwards. Improving student performance by evaluating how well students test their own programs. volume 3, 2003.

[15] S. H. Edwards. Using software testing to move students from trial-and-error to reflection-in-action. In *Proceedings of the 35th SIGCSE Technical Symposium on Computer Science Education*, 2004.

[16] S. H. Edwards and Z. Shams. Comparing test quality measures for assessing student-written tests. In *Companion Proceedings of the 36th International Conference on Software Engineering*, 2014.

[17] S. H. Edwards, Z. Shams, M. Cogswell, and R. C. Senkbeil. Running students' software tests against each others' code: New life for an old "gimmick". In *Proceedings of the 43rd*

ACM Technical Symposium on Computer Science Education, 2012.

[18] M. Felleisen, R. B. Findler, M. Flatt, and S. Krishnamurthi. *How to Design Prorgams: An Introduction to Programming and Computing*. MIT Press, 2010.

[19] S. Frezza. Integrating testing and design methods for undergraduates: Teaching software testing in the context of software design. In *Proceedings of the 32nd ASEE/IEEE Frontiers in Education Conference*, 2002.

[20] M. H. Goldwasser. A gimmick to integrate software testing throughout the curriculum. In *Proceedings of the 33rd ACM Technical Symposium on Computer Science Education*, 2002.

[21] N. B. Harrison. Teaching software testing from two viewpoints. *Journal of Computing Sciences in Colleges*, 26(2), 2010.

[22] M. Hauswirth, D. Zaparanuks, A. Malekpour, and M. Keikha. The javafest: A collaborative learning technique for java programming courses. In *Proceedings of the 2008 International Conference on Principles and Practices of Programming on the Java Platform*, 2008.

[23] T. B. Hilburn and M. Townhidnejad. Software quality: A curriculum postscript? *ACM SIGCSE Bulletin*, 32(1), 2000.

[24] J. J. Li and P. Morreale. Enhancing cs1 curriculum with testing concepts: A case study. *Journal of Computing Sciences in Colleges*, 31(3), 2016.

[25] H. Liu, F. Kuo, and T. Chen. Teaching an end-user testing methodology. In *Proceedings of the 23rd International IEEE Conference on Software Engineering Education and Training*, 2010.

[26] W. Marrero and A. Settle. Testing first: Emphasizing testing in early programming courses. In *Proceedings of the 10th Annual ACM Conference on Innovation and Technology in Computer Science Education*, 2005.

[27] T. J. McCabe. A complexity measure. *IEEE Transactions on Software Engineering*, 4, 1976.

[28] C. Meyers and T. B. Jones. *Promoting Active Learning: Strategies for the College Classroom*. Jossey-Bass Inc., Publishers, 350 Sansome Street, San Francisco, CA 94104, 1993.

[29] J. G. Politz, S. Krishnamurthi, and K. Fisler. In-flow peer review of tests in test-first programming. In *Proceedings of the 10th International Computing Education Research Conference*, 2014.

[30] M. Prince. Does active learning work? a review of the research. *Journal of Engineering Education*, 93(3), 2004.

[31] Z. Shams and S. H. Edwards. Toward practical mutation analysis for evaluating the quality of student-written software tests. In *Proceedings of the 9th International Computing Education Reseach Conference*, 2013.

[32] T. Shepard, M. Lamb, and D. Kelly. More testing should be taught. *Communications of the ACM*, 44(6), 2001.

[33] T. Tang, S. Rixner, and J. Warren. An environment for learning interactive programming. In *Proceedings of the 45th ACM Technical Symposium on Computer Science Education*, 2014.

[34] T. Tang, R. Smith, S. Rixner, and J. Warren. Data-driven test case generation for automated programming assessment. In *Proceedings of the 21st Annual ACM Conference on Innovation and Technology in Computer Science Eduation*, 2016.

DevEventTracker: Tracking Development Events to Assess Incremental Development and Procrastination

Ayaan M. Kazerouni, Stephen H. Edwards, T. Simin Hall, and Clifford A. Shaffer

Dept. of Computer Science, Virginia Tech, Blacksburg, VA 24061

ayaan|s.edwards|simin.hall|shaffer@vt.edu

ABSTRACT

Good project management practices are hard to teach, and hard for novices to learn. Procrastination and bad project management practice occur frequently, and may interfere with successfully completing major programming projects in mid-level programming courses. Students often see these as abstract concepts that do not need to be actively applied in practice. Changing student behavior requires changing how this material is taught, and more importantly, changing how learning and practice are assessed. To provide proper assessment, we need to collect detailed data about how each student conducts their project development as they work on solutions. We present DevEventTracker, a system that continuously collects data from the Eclipse IDE as students program, giving us in-depth insight into students' programming habits. We report on data collected using DevEventTracker over the course of four programming projects involving 370 students in five sections of a Data Structures and Algorithms course over two semesters. These data support a new measure for how well students apply "incremental development" practices. We present a detailed description of the system, our methodology, and an initial evaluation of our ability to accurately assess incremental development on the part of the students. The goal is to help students improve their programming habits, with an emphasis on incremental development and time management.

CCS Concepts

•**Social and professional topics** → Computer science education; •**Software and its engineering** → *Software creation and management;*

Keywords

Incremental development; procrastination; interactive development environment; educational data mining; project management practice

1. INTRODUCTION

Tools for automatic assessment of programming assignments enable students to gain more programming practice with less active grading effort for instructors [11]. These tools are able to automatically grade on metrics like code style and thoroughness of testing in addition to correctness [3, 9]. Many such systems are designed to support small-scale programming exercises. At that scale, there is little concern for the development process, and procrastination generally relates only to getting started with the assignment. Mid-level computer science courses often involve major programming projects, in which students are writing many hundreds or even thousands of lines of code, with life cycles measured in weeks. In this situation, support systems such as Web-CAT [3] can help with managing project submissions, evaluating code style, automated grading through unit testing, and assessment of artifacts such as student tests in terms of code coverage.

None of these aspects directly address a major concern that too many students are unable to complete programming projects at this scale. This often is a result of inadequate skill by the student in good project management techniques, including time management and fundamental development processes such as incremental development. Procrastination has proven to be a pervasive problem among students working toward project completion. Previous work has shown that students who start their projects early and practice good time management receive better grades than students who start late [4].

Unfortunately, to date there have not been tools to help instructors assess and evaluate student adherence to good development practice. This is in large part because the necessary data about the details of the student's development process have not been available. For example, incremental development with regular testing is a known best practice of software development [2]. Existing tools are generally unable to assess incremental development and time management as students work on their solutions. In this paper we present *DevEventTracker*, a system designed to collect fine-grained data about the student development process. With these data in hand, the next step is to analyze the data to detect procrastination and whether students employ good development practices like incremental development and effective testing procedures. If that could be done, then suitable interventions to encourage good practices could be devised.

Section 2 presents related work in data tracking and procrastination assessment systems and strategies. A detailed description of DevEventTracker's functionality is given in

Section 3. Sections 4, 5, and 6 present preliminary findings obtained from using the system over the course of two semesters, and the results of a series of student interviews.

2. RELATED WORK

Web-based Center for Automated Testing (Web-CAT) [3] is a web-based automated grading system that allows students to make multiple submissions to an assignment and receive immediate feedback. This feedback can be about correctness, code style, or code coverage by student-written tests. Web-CAT interacts with a custom Eclipse plugin that allows students to make submissions and download starter projects directly from within the IDE.

This model of multiple submissions affords us the ability to gather information about the student's development process, such as when a student started submitting it to get feedback and when they finished. It also provides an opportunity for analysis of the differences between submissions, giving a rough idea of a project's development trajectory. What it does *not* do is give us enough insight to assess whether or not students are practicing incremental development. To accurately assess this, we would need more granular data collected *during development*, rather than after submissions; in the latter state, we would invariably receive data about projects already in varied degrees of completion.

To this end, an addition was made to Web-CAT's Eclipse plugin, called the DevEventTracker Addition. The plugin continuously collects development event data as students program, giving us unique insight into the development process of the typical student. Benefits are twofold: 1) Our data are no longer limited by when a student decides to make a submission. 2) Since we are collecting data directly from the IDE, we have access to events that were not available through Web-CAT alone.

The Test My Code (TMC) plugin [10] for NetBeans behaves in a similar fashion to our Eclipse plugin. It records events whenever the student saves, runs, or tests code using instructor-provided tests. Hosseini, et al [5] make use of this plugin in an attempt to achieve goals similar to ours, but with some differences in the type of data collected. For example, in terms of detecting student testing, the TMC plugin collects data on runs of pre-written tests provided by the instructor, while DevEventTracker collects data about students writing and running their own tests. This provides information about the student's autonomous software development habits, which is ultimately what we wish to assess.

Hackystat [6] is an open-source project from the University of Hawaii that provides product and process measurements in software engineering situations in education and industry. DevEventTracker builds upon Hackystat, using Hackystat's client-side protocols and preexisting sensors in conjunction with our own extensions to send data to the server. Unlike Hackystat, DevEventTracker also collects event data for program and test launches from within the IDE. These additional events provide valuable information for assessing development patterns.

Marmoset [9] is an automated grading system developed at the University of Maryland. It uses an Eclipse plugin to collect student code and store it in a Concurrent Versioning System (CVS) repository each time a file is saved. Marmoset inspired us to capture repositories of student code, since event data alone might not capture enough of a student's work-flow to properly assess incremental development.

Researchers at the University of West Georgia [1] mined student revision histories from the Mercurial version control system to assess the state of incremental development in a CS2 course. Incremental development was defined in terms of the size and scope of commits, including checking for commits related to integrated test-writing. In answer to the question *Are students properly incorporating testing as part of their iterative development?*, the researchers found that there was room for improvement.

A previous study [4] collected five years of data from the first three programming courses at Virginia Tech. Assignment results were partitioned into two groups: scores above 80% (A/B), and scores below 80% (C/D/F). Analysis yielded important results. When students received A/B scores, they started earlier and finished earlier than when the same students received C/D/F scores. After normalizing for program length, there was no significant difference in the amount of time spent on each project stemming from starting earlier vs. later. This study provided convincing evidence that procrastination was correlated with lower project scores.

These findings led to another study [8] that administered three different types of interventions to prevent procrastination. That study found that of the three interventions (short reflection essays after each project, a requirement to set and track scheduling information and progress throughout the assignment, and e-mail alerts regarding progress toward completion), only e-mail alerts were associated with significantly reduced rates of late program submissions and significantly increased rates of early program submissions. The promise shown by this method was credited to the fact that the emails were relevant to individual students, generated using data from that student's latest submission to Web-CAT. However, we note that the emails were quite non-specific as to how much progress the student had actually made. More detailed feedback about progress and class standing could potentially have a greater impact.

We believe that interventions that provide students with feedback about their own programming practices should encourage the practice of incremental development and self-checking behavior. When a student makes a submission to Web-CAT, Web-CAT is able to give the student a percentage of code covered by their test cases, but is unable to tell with accuracy *when* the testing takes place: students could be practicing regular testing and development like they are supposed to, or they could be churning out tests right before the deadline. The reality is probably somewhere in the middle, and a rough idea can be gleaned from looking at the differences between submissions. Unfortunately, the information is not granular enough to accurately assess incremental development, especially since some students submit frequently to Web-CAT, while others prefer to do a lot of work between submissions. Some students make their first Web-CAT submission early in the development cycle with the goal of initially passing only a few tests, while others wait until much later in the development cycle to make their first submission. While early submission might seem to be more indicative of incremental development, we can't know that those whose initial submissions are made relatively late are not doing a lot of incremental development and testing without feedback from Web-CAT. We should ideally generate feedback from data that is generated directly from the student's edit-and-run process within their IDE.

3. THE *DEV EVENT TRACKER*

In this section we present a detailed description of the DevEventTracker subsystem. We use a custom Eclipse plugin to allow students to make submissions to Web-CAT and to download starter projects provided by the instructor. An addition was made to the plugin that allows the continuous collection of data from the IDE, not limited by when a student decides to make a submission. This continuous stream of data will provide instructors and researchers with a real-time understanding of a typical student's programming process. We collect timestamped development events as well as Git snapshots of the project as the student develops it. The development events capture a number of activities from within the student's IDE, and are used in the development of automatic assessment. The Git snapshots are used primarily for verification and evaluation of these assessments.

Edit Events: DevEventTracker collects Edit events in real time as a student programs. An Edit event is recorded each time a student saves their work. For each event, some meta-data is included. We know the size of the edit in statements or methods added or removed, and we know if the edit was within *solution code* or *test code*. Analysis of an ordered sequence of edits containing this information yields an understanding of how and when a student approaches writing tests for their program. These time-stamped events also provide insight into a student's procrastination habits, using a method described in Section 5.

Launch Events: Often, especially in the early stages of a project and for small changes, testing mainly consists of launching a program and examining its behavior. DevEventTracker monitors launches within Eclipse, collecting and recording meta-data about each launch. It records the type of the launch (execution of test cases vs. a regular interactive execution of the program); whether the launch terminated normally or with an error code; and for unit test runs, how many test case successes, failures, and errors resulted. This functionality does not limit our knowledge of a student's testing behavior to when they create *new* tests; it also records when they are running *existing* tests.

The sequence of tests passing or failing over the course of development provides a representation for how testing aides the successful implementation of a project. This information can be provided to students, who will benefit from an external view of how regular testing would help them successfully complete projects.

Other events: When students encounter build errors, we receive events containing the error message and information about the Java file that caused it. Data such as this can be used to analyze the types of problems most commonly encountered by students with different levels of programming expertise.

DevEventTracker also saves data about a student's use of the Eclipse debugger. It records when breakpoints are added or removed, when a debug session is started, and a student's actions during that session (*step into*, *step over*, etc.). The plugin collects data about code-refactoring activities within Eclipse. It records renaming and moving activities, with the plugin collecting information about old and new names and locations of units as they are refactored. Refactoring data do not star in the initial analysis we present in this paper, but they open up avenues for further research that depends on this type of analysis.

Git snapshots: Every student's project has a git repository associated with it, with the remote repository residing on the Web-CAT server. Whenever a student makes a change and saves a file, a Git snapshot is captured and sent to the server. This provides us with the ability to make further fine-grained observations about the changes to a project over time. More importantly, it allows us to evaluate the assessments made using development events.

4. METHOD

DevEventTracker was used by students in five sections of a post-CS2, junior level Data Structures and Algorithms course over two semesters. On the first day of class, we collected informed consent from the students. Students who did not give consent (less than 4% of the total) were excluded from data analysis. Once the number of students enrolled had stabilized, this made for a total of 370 students, generating data each time they worked on their projects. The course had four assigned projects, and data were collected for each one.

The class syllabus required students to program all of their projects in the Eclipse IDE, using the Web-CAT submission plug-in to submit assignments and download starter code. This setup has been the standard for many programming courses at our university for several years. The only difference for this project is that the plugin was augmented with data-collection functionality. The act of downloading starter code or making a submission creates a link between Web-CAT and a specific project in a student's Eclipse workspace, and this allows Web-CAT to begin receiving data for that project. To ensure that we received data from the moment work began on a project, we provided starter code for each project. In other words, we did not wait until the first submission to begin receiving data. The starter files provided for each project did not contain any stubbed out code except a `main()` method (with the correct file and class names) that printed the string 'Hello world!' and a test method invoking it. This is because we wanted unadulterated information about how students approach assigned projects, from start to finish. An added benefit of this approach was that students did not have to worry about the semantics of structuring and naming the project so that Web-CAT would accept it; that was already provided via the starter project. While we attempted to minimize the impact our data collection had on the students' programming experience, students were aware that it was taking place, and they sometimes experienced some delays due to data transmission.

If a connection to the Web-CAT server was unavailable, event data was logged locally until a connection became available. This ensured that we did not miss out on event data generated when students programmed without an internet connection, or if the Web-CAT server went down for a period of time.

5. ASSESSMENT MODEL

Our modeling process involved taking in a large volume of data for each student's project and reducing it to a vector of four metrics that we designed to cover the various dimensions of incremental development.[1] We focused on having each metric represent an item that—when presented to the

---

[1] See https://github.com/ayaankazerouni/sensordata

student—provides a concrete course of action aimed at improving their programming practice.

At this stage of our project, each metric is intentionally kept separate from the project grade. Students were not informed about any of these results (except for the students interviewed as described in Section 6.1), since at this stage we were only trying to judge our ability to recognize the level of incremental development. Note that the metrics as described below are *raw indices*, meaning that lower numbers might be better for some of them.

Early/Often Index: A measure of how early and how often a student works on a project, defined in relation to the due date for the project. We add up each edit's size in statements, with each size being weighted by the number of days until the project deadline. Then we divide this total by the total edit size. If E is the set of all edits, then the early/often index is defined as:

$$\text{earlyOften} = \frac{\sum_{e \in E} \text{size}(e) \cdot \text{daysToDeadline}(e)}{\sum_{e \in E} \text{size}(e)}$$

This produces an average that is weighted by how many days from the deadline—and how often—a student tends to work on their project. Therefore, if a student tends to work several weeks or days before the deadline, this metric will have a larger value; and if a student tends to procrastinate until the project deadline is close, this metric will have a smaller value (or possibly negative, depending on course policies). This metric is used as a quantitative assessment of procrastination, and **a larger value is better**.

Incremental Checking: A measure of how well a student self-checks their code by launching it. Here, 'launches' are defined as either regular program executions or test executions. For many students, simple launching with diagnostic print statements is a valuable method of testing and debugging. To focus on unit test launches only would be to ignore a common testing strategy for many. We add up each edit's size, with each size being weighted by the number of hours until the next project launch. Then we divide this total by the total number of edits:

$$\text{incrementalChecking} = \frac{\sum_{e \in E} \text{size}(e) \cdot \text{hoursToNextLaunch}(e)}{\sum_{e \in E} \text{size}(e)}$$

This gives a value governed by the amount of the code a student writes and the time that passes before they next launch their code. For this metric, **smaller values are better**.

Incremental Test Checking: A measure of how well a student self-checks their code using automated tests. Unlike the previous metric, here we focus only on test executions. The metric is calculated in a similar way: we add up each edit's size, with each size being weighted by the number of hours until the next test launch. Then we divide this total by the number of edits:

$$\text{incTestChecking} = \frac{\sum_{e \in E} \text{size}(e) \cdot \text{hoursToNextTestLaunch}(e)}{\sum_{e \in E} \text{size}(e)}$$

The main benefit from this metric over the previous one is that it gives us an indication of whether the student is practicing progressive regression testing [7] or not. It also gives an indication of the role that formalized testing plays in the student's development process. For these first two metrics, if a student tends to write a lot of code before checking that

it works, they would have larger values, and vice-versa, so **smaller values are better**.

Incremental Test Writing: A measure of how regularly a student writes tests. To successfully practice incremental development, students should regularly write unit tests to verify the correctness of the functionality they have recently implemented. We calculate Early/Often indices separately for *solution code* and *test code*. Then we find the difference between these two metrics. The result is a metric whose value is governed by the average amount of time that passes between the writing of solution code and test code, and by the amount of code written for each. Let SE be the set of all solution edits, and let TE be the set of all test edits. Then we calculate this as:

$$\text{incTestWriting} = \text{earlyOften}(SE) - \text{earlyOften}(TE)$$

Therefore, if a student writes a lot of code before writing tests for it, this metric would have a larger value. Similarly, if a student writes test code a long time after writing solution code, a larger value would be produced; for example, students who do their testing at the end of the project life cycle will receive a higher value for this metric. Therefore, **smaller values are better**.

It is important to note that this score is not related to procrastination. A student can do the entire the project on the last day and still receive a good score for this metric; it depends on when solution code and test code were written in relation *to each other*, rather than in relation to the deadline.

6. EVALUATION

With the data collection process in hand, our main concern now is whether we can accurately determine if the student is using good time management practice, and if the student is using incremental development practice. Assessing these are difficult. The four measures proposed in the previous section are models, and they might or might not, singly or in combination, provide reliable results. A primary concern is that there is no readily available 'ground truth' against which we can test our metrics. Validating our models against grades could potentially lead to inaccuracies. It is possible for students with good grades to follow poor incremental development, and vice-versa.

6.1 Interviews

In order to evaluate the validity of our models, we decided to use individual interviews to gather student opinions. As we neared the end of the semester, we generated incremental development scores for students on the projects they had worked on until that point. Scores were generated by running the raw event data through in-house Python processing scripts written to calculate the metrics described in Section 5. Ten students representing a range of scores on the different metrics were selected and invited to participate in interview sessions. Of those ten, seven agreed to participate.

The students were interviewed in depth about their programming practices. Specifically, we asked about their testing habits: How often did they write/run tests on the specified projects? What is their preferred method of testing? What do they think of Web-CAT's testing requirements? The interviewers were not involved in grading students in any way, to avoid the possibility of students thinking that their answers would somehow affect their grade. The students were shown our model's assessment of their programming practice, and were asked what they thought about its accuracy, usefulness, and potential efficacy in helping them change their programming habits in the future.

Accuracy: Six of the seven students found our assessment accurate. The descriptions that follow use feminine pronouns, regardless of the gender of the participant.

- **Interviewee 1** stated that she found the model's assessment to be accurate.
- **Interviewee 2** mentioned that she had been ill and started Project 1 late and worked past the deadline. When the assessment was revealed, we saw that our model had been able to detect this and had given her a low Early/Often score. When the interviewee saw the scores, she agreed with the overall assessment.
- **Interviewee 3** acknowledged that she and her partner had gotten a late start on Project 1, but that she had worked alone on Project 2 and started relatively earlier. Our model was able to detect this—the interviewee was given a low Early/Often score for one project, and a higher score for the next.

  The student also mentioned that she "didn't write the best tests during the beginning of [Project 1]"; she relied mostly on simple diagnostic print statements for testing and "wrote tests at the end". This is in contrast to Project 2, where she "[brought] in formal testing", since she now had some experience with it. The model's assessment recognized this difference—the student received a poor score for Incremental Test Writing on the first project, but a much better score for the second project.
- **Interviewee 4** received a much lower score for Incremental Test Writing on Project 2 than she did on Project 1. Project 2 was almost universally cited as the hardest project that the students worked on this semester (at the time of the focus group, they were starting work on Project 4). The student mentioned that, because the project was so hard, she found herself getting caught up in trying to implement it correctly and ended up writing "more code before testing" than she did on Project 1. This was reflected in our assessment. Also seen was a lower score for Incremental Test Checking, which intuitively makes sense—if she was not writing tests until the end, she was not running them, either. An interesting thing to note here is that, on a hard project where testing would be most useful, the student brushed it aside in favor of going straight ahead with the implementation.
- **Interviewee 5** thought the model was *mostly* accurate. Her answers to questions about writing tests did not agree with her failing score for Incremental Test Writing on Project 2. After initially expressing surprise, she backtracked on what she had said earlier by saying that the project involved a lot of recursion, and she tends to test recursive algorithms using iterative print statements rather than formalized testing strategies. This was the only occurrence of a student volunteering new information to explain a score provided by our metric.
- **Interviewee 6** was the only student who did not find the metrics accurate. The interview revealed disconnects between our assessment and the student's description of her programming practice. However, further investigation revealed transient issues with this student's data reaching the server, which would lead to inaccuracies during metric calculation.
- **Interviewee 7** received high scores on all metrics, except Incremental Test Writing for Project 2. She expressed surprise at her low score for this. The remaining scores were in keeping with her description of her programming practices.

Usefulness and future efficacy: Only one of the seven students did not see value in the model. This was the student who had received an inaccurate assessment due to data transmission errors. Of the remaining six students, five found the model to be useful and stated unconditionally that they would try to change their programming practice if they were given this feedback between projects. The final student said that while the model could be useful to "somebody coming into their best practices", it was not particularly useful to her since she already knows about and follows incremental development. This student received high scores on nearly all metrics.

Overall, the model was mostly accurate with students generally finding the information interesting and useful. The interviews confirmed the model's ability to detect differences in programming practices *between students* as well as *within students and between projects*. The model also has benefits in that it is clear what kinds of actions students should pursue to increase their scores on any of the metrics.

6.2 Git Snapshots

While our focus group provided student validation of the measures, we also wanted to directly investigate the edits students were performing in their projects. A second type of evaluation was carried out by manually inspecting the Git repositories maintained by DevEventTracker. Twelve projects were randomly sampled from the pool of submissions. The inspection focused on checking whether our assessment of incremental development matched the "actual programming process" of the student (as seen in the Git revision histories). Eight of the twelve projects had low scores (< 80 on a normalized 100-point scale) for **working early and often**. Stepping through commit histories showed that seven of these projects had multiple breaks of several days where no work was done, leading to the project being completed within the last few days before the due date. The remaining project with a low Early/Often score was worked on the day before the project deadline, in a marathon session taking up most of the day. One out of the remaining four projects received a surprisingly high Early/Often score, since the project was started within the last two days. However, it was worked on steadily without breaks, possibly contributing to its high Early/Often score.

Incremental checking and **incremental test checking** were evaluated using a combination of raw DevEvent data and Git snapshots. For two consecutive 'Launch' events, we stepped through revisions for commits made between the two launches. Doing this for several random pairs of launches gives an idea of the usual amount of work done by that student before the program is launched. Most projects received middling or good scores (> 80 on a normalized 100-point scale) for these metrics, but one project received a low score. This project was not launched for the first 10 days in its life-cycle, and launches took place after large amounts of code were written.

Five projects received failing scores (< 70) for **incremental test writing**. Inspecting the file changes over time showed that a majority of testing was done on the last few days of work. Three projects received middling scores (70 to 90) for this metric. Inspection of their commit histories showed that regular testing began after a few days of regular work on the project, but was fairly regular for the rest of the project. The remaining four projects received high scores ($\geq$ 90) for this metric. Their commit histories showed that testing began on the first day of work and continued consistently until the end of the project. Also clear was the fact that test classes were usually created and edited within a few minutes of their corresponding solution class.

This method of validation, carried out on a separate set of projects by manually inspecting the code edits of students through Git snapshots, produced a similar result as the interviews: Our metrics do track the incremental development behaviors they were designed to capture, although there is certainly room for improvement of accuracy.

7. CONCLUSIONS AND FUTURE WORK

In this study, we analyzed data for 370 students working on four large projects in a Data Structures and Algorithms course over the course of two semesters. We collected detailed development event data using custom event-tracking software integrated into an Eclipse plugin. In order to accurately assess abstract concepts like incremental development and procrastination, we developed a set of four metrics we believe cover the different dimensions of both concepts. Development of these easy-to-understand metrics allowed us to gather feedback from students on the accuracy of our model.

Six out of seven students interviewed found the model accurate and useful, stating that the feedback provided might encourage them to change their programming behavior from one project to the next. Further, a separate manual investigation of code snapshots in student projects confirmed the measures track intended behaviors. Together, these represent encouraging results in an effort to turn qualitative ideas that are difficult to assess into quantitative measures that can be systematically and repeatedly applied.

An important benefit of DevEventTracker is that it affords us the ability to conduct further work toward answering questions about student programming behaviors. Such questions include:

- How does incremental development (as measured by our metrics) affect project grades?
- How does providing students with their incremental development scores affect their programming practice from one project to the next?
- Are there meaningful patterns in the ways partners work together on projects?
- Are there meaningful patterns of behavior related to early vs. late Web-CAT submission practices?

8. ACKNOWLEDGEMENTS

This work is supported in part by the National Science Foundation under grant DUE-1245334. Any opinions, findings, conclusions, or recommendations expressed in this material are those of the authors and do not necessarily reflect the views of the National Science Foundation.

9. REFERENCES

[1] L. Baumstark, Jr. and M. Orsega. Quantifying introductory cs students' iterative software process by mining version control system repositories. *J. Comput. Sci. Coll.*, 31(6):97–104, June 2016.

[2] K. Beck, M. Beedle, A. Van Bennekum, A. Cockburn, W. Cunningham, M. Fowler, J. Grenning, J. Highsmith, A. Hunt, R. Jeffries, et al. *The Agile Manifesto*, 2001.

[3] S. H. Edwards and M. A. Perez-Quinones. Web-cat: Automatically grading programming assignments. In *Proceedings of the 13th Annual Conference on Innovation and Technology in Computer Science Education*, ITiCSE '08, pages 328–328, 2008.

[4] S. H. Edwards, J. Snyder, M. A. Pérez-Quiñones, A. Allevato, D. Kim, and B. Tretola. Comparing effective and ineffective behaviors of student programmers. In *Proceedings of the Fifth International Workshop on Computing Education Research Workshop*, ICER '09, pages 3–14, 2009.

[5] R. Hosseini, A. Vihavainen, and P. Brusilovsky. Exploring problem solving paths in a java programming course. In *Psychology of Programming Interest Group Conference, PPIG 2014*, pages 65–76, 2014.

[6] P. M. Johnson, H. Kou, J. M. Agustin, Q. Zhang, A. Kagawa, and T. Yamashita. Practical automated process and product metric collection and analysis in a classroom setting: Lessons learned from Hackystat-UH. In *Proceedings of the 2004 International Symposium on Empirical Software Engineering, ISESE'04*, pages 136–144, 2004.

[7] H. K. N. Leung and L. White. Insights into regression testing [software testing]. In *Proceedings. Conference on Software Maintenance - 1989*, pages 60–69, Oct 1989.

[8] J. Martin, S. H. Edwards, and C. A. Shaffer. The effects of procrastination interventions on programming project success. In *Proceedings of the Eleventh Annual International Conference on International Computing Education Research*, ICER '15, pages 3–11, 2015.

[9] J. Spacco, J. Strecker, D. Hovemeyer, and W. Pugh. Software repository mining with Marmoset: an automated programming project snapshot and testing system. In *ACM SIGSOFT Software Engineering Notes*, volume 30, pages 1–5, 2005.

[10] A. Vihavainen, T. Vikberg, M. Luukkainen, and M. Pärtel. Scaffolding students' learning using test my code. In *Proceedings of the 18th ACM Conference on Innovation and Technology in Computer Science Education*, ITiCSE '13, pages 117–122, 2013.

[11] C. Wilcox. The role of automation in undergraduate computer science education. In *Proceedings of the 46th ACM Technical Symposium on Computer Science Education*, SIGCSE '15, pages 90–95, 2015.

Code Quality Issues in Student Programs

Hieke Keuning
Open University of the Netherlands
and Windesheim University of
Applied Sciences
hw.keuning@windesheim.nl

Bastiaan Heeren
Open University of the Netherlands
bastiaan.heeren@ou.nl

Johan Jeuring
Utrecht University and Open
University of the Netherlands
j.t.jeuring@uu.nl

ABSTRACT

Because low quality code can cause serious problems in software systems, students learning to program should pay attention to code quality early. Although many studies have investigated *mistakes* that students make during programming, we do not know much about the *quality* of their code. This study examines the presence of quality issues related to program flow, choice of programming constructs and functions, clarity of expressions, decomposition and modularization in a large set of student Java programs. We investigated which issues occur most frequently, if students are able to solve these issues over time and if the use of code analysis tools has an effect on issue occurrence. We found that students hardly fix issues, in particular issues related to modularization, and that the use of tooling does not have much effect on the occurrence of issues.

KEYWORDS

Code quality, programming education

ACM Reference format:
Hieke Keuning, Bastiaan Heeren, and Johan Jeuring. 2017. Code Quality Issues in Student Programs. In *Proceedings of ITiCSE'17, July 03-05, 2017, Bologna, Italy,*, 6 pages.
DOI: http://dx.doi.org/10.1145/3059009.3059061

1 INTRODUCTION

Students who are learning to program often write programs that can be improved. They are usually satisfied once their program produces the right output, and do not consider the quality of the code itself. In fact, they might not even be aware of it. Code quality can be related to documentation, presentation, algorithms and structure [11]. Fowler [7] uses the term 'code smells' to describe issues related to algorithms and structure that jeopardise code quality. A typical example is duplicated code, which could have been put in a separate method. Another example is putting the same code in both the true-part and the false-part of an if-statement, even though that code could have been moved outside the if-statement. Low quality code can cause serious problems in the long term, which affect software quality attributes such as maintainability, performance and security of software systems. It is therefore imperative to make students and lecturers aware of its importance.

For a long time, researchers have been interested in how students solve programming problems and the mistakes that they make. Recently, large-scale data mining has made it possible to perform automated analysis of large numbers of student programs, leading to several interesting observations. For example, Altadmri and Brown [3] investigated over 37 million code snapshots and found that students seem to find it harder to fix semantic and type errors than syntax errors.

Although many studies have investigated the errors that students make, little attention has been paid to code quality issues in student programs. While Pettit et al. [10] looked at code quality aspects and found that several metrics related to code complexity increased with each submission, their study does not elaborate on the causes of these high metric scores. Aivaloglou and Hermans [1] analysed a large database of Scratch projects by measuring complexity and detecting different code smells. Although the complexity of most Scratch projects was not high, the researchers found many instances of these code smells.

In this study we analyse a wider range of code quality issues, and observe their appearance over time. Our data set, taken from the Blackbox database [6], contains over two million Java programs of novice programmers recorded in four weeks of one academic year. First, we investigate the type and frequency of code quality issues that occur in student programs. Next, we track the changes that students make to their programs to see if they are able to solve these issues. Finally, we check if students are better at solving code quality issues when they have code analysis tools installed.

The contributions of this paper are: (1) a selection of relevant code quality issues for novice programmers, (2) an analysis of the occurrence and fixing of these issues, and (3) insight into the influence of code analysis tools on issue occurrence.

The remainder of this paper is organised as follows: Section 2 elaborates on related studies on student programming behaviour. Section 3 describes the research questions, the data set we used, the code quality issues we have selected to investigate, and the automatic analysis. Section 4 shows the results for each research question, which are discussed in Section 5. Section 6 concludes and describes future work.

2 RELATED WORK

This section discusses previous research into student programming habits related to code quality. We also consider studies that have analysed student programming behaviour on a large scale.

Pettit et al. [10] have analysed over 45,000 student submissions to programming exercises. The authors monitored the progress that students made over the course of a session, in which students submit their solutions to an automated assessment tool that provides feedback based on test results. For each submission they computed several metrics: lines of code, cyclomatic complexity, state space (number of unique variables) and the six Halstead complexity measures (calculations based on the number of operators and operands of a program). The authors also distinguish between sessions in which the number of attempts within a specific time frame is restricted. The main conclusion from the study is that although the metric scores increase with each submission attempt, restricting the number of attempts has a positive influence on the code quality of students. Second, the authors argue that instructors should also consider coding style and quality, because focusing solely on testing may result in inefficient programs. The study does not elaborate on the particular problems that cause high complexity scores.

Aivaloglou and Hermans [1] analysed a database of over 230,000 Scratch projects. Scratch is a block-based programming language that is often used to teach children how to program. Besides investigating general characteristics of Scratch programs, the authors also looked at code smells, such as cyclomatic complexity, duplicate code, dead code, large scripts and large sprites (image objects that can be controlled by scripts). Translating to the object-oriented domain, a large script is comparable to a large class and a large sprite to a large method. In 78% of over 4 million scripts the cyclomatic complexity is one. Only 4% of the scripts has a complexity over four. In 26% of the projects the researchers identified code clones (12% for exact clones), consisting of at least five blocks. It should be noted that Scratch only supports procedure calls within sprites, leaving copy-pasting code as the only option. Dead code occurs in 28% of the projects. Large scripts (with at least 18 blocks) are present in 30% of the projects and large sprites (with at least 59 blocks) in 14% of the projects.

Breuker et al. [5] investigated the differences in code quality between first and second year students in approximately 8,400 Java programs in 207 projects, using a set of 22 code quality properties. They found that for half of the properties there were no major differences. For the remaining properties, some differences could be attributed to increased project size and complexity for second year students. Finally, second year students performed better because their code had smaller methods, fewer short identifiers, fewer static methods and fewer assignments in while and if-statements.

Much more research into code smells exists for professional code. For example, Tufano et al. [12] investigated the repositories of 200 software projects, answering the question when and why smells are introduced. They calculated five metrics related to the size and complexity of classes and methods, and proper use of object-orientation. They found that most smells first occur when a file is created and that, surprisingly, refactorings may introduce smells.

Altadmri and Brown [3] used data from one academic year of the Blackbox database to investigate what common student mistakes are, how long it takes to fix them, and how these findings change during an academic year. Although there are various other studies that look at these aspects, it had not been done on such a large scale before. Individual source files were tracked over time by checking them for 18 mistakes, and calculating how much time had passed before the mistake disappeared from the source file. One important observation from the study is that students seem to find it harder to fix semantic and type errors than syntax errors.

3 METHOD

This study addresses the following research questions:

RQ1 Which code quality issues occur in student code?
RQ2 How often do students fix code quality issues?
RQ3 What are the differences in the occurrence of code quality issues between students who use code analysis extensions compared to students who do not?

3.1 Blackbox database

Our data set is extracted from the Blackbox database [6], which collects data from students working in the widely used BlueJ IDE[1] for novice Java programmers. BlueJ, used mostly in first year programming courses, has a simplified user interface and offers several educational features, such as interacting with objects while running a program.

The Blackbox database stores information about events in BlueJ triggered by students, such as compiling, testing and creating objects. Blackbox stores data on sessions, users, projects, code files and tests, which are linked to these events. A *source file* is a file of which there may be multiple versions called *snapshots*, which are unique instances of the source file at a certain *event*.

The database has been receiving data constantly since June 2013, and contains millions of student programs to date. BlueJ users have to give prior consent (opt-in) to data collection, and all collected data is anonymous. Permission is required to access the database. In this study we have investigated programs submitted in four weeks of the academic year 2014–2015 (the second week of September, December, March and June). From the Blackbox database we extracted data on source files, snapshots, compile events, extensions and startup events, which we stored in a local database. We only extracted data on programs that are compilable.

3.2 Data analysis

We performed an automatic analysis of all programs in our data set that compiled successfully. To enable replication and checks, we have published the code online.[2] We counted the source lines of code (SLOC) for each file using the cloc tool.[3] Although this metric is sensitive to style and formatting and therefore not very accurate, it provided us with an indication of the size of a program.

3.2.1 Issues (RQ1). Stegeman et al. [11] have developed a rubric for assessing code quality, based on their research into professional code quality standards from the software engineering literature and interviews with instructors. The rubric is based on a model with ten categories for code quality. We omit the categories that deal with documentation (the names, headers and comments categories) and presentation (the layout and formatting categories). Our study focuses on the remaining five categories that deal with algorithms and structure, because they are the most challenging for students:

Flow Problems with nesting and paths, code duplication and unreachable code.
Idiom Unsuitable choice of control structures and no reuse of library functions.

---

[1]http://www.bluej.org
[2]https://github.com/hiekekeuning/student-code-quality
[3]https://github.com/AlDanial/cloc

Expressions Expressions that are too complex and use of unsuitable data types.

Decomposition Methods that are too long and excessive sharing of variables.

Modularization Classes with an unclear purpose (low cohesion) and too many methods and attributes, and tight coupling between classes.

For each category, we selected a number of issues to investigate by applying the PMD tool to a limited set of student programs to identify the issues that occur most frequently. PMD[4] is a well-known static analysis tool that is able to detect a large set of bad coding practices in Java programs. We also used the Copy/Paste Detector tool (CPD)[5] included with PMD for duplicate detection. In PMD a *rule* defines a bad coding practice, and running PMD results into a report of rule violations. In this paper we use the term *issue* to refer to a rule in PMD. The PMD version we used offers 26 sets consisting of issues that all deal with a particular aspect.

We discarded sets of issues using the following criteria:

- An issue is too specific for Java, such as issues that apply to Android, JUnit and Java library classes.
- An issue is too advanced, strict or specific for novice programmers, such as exceptions, threads, intermediate-level OO concepts (abstract classes, interfaces) and very specific language constructs (e.g. the final keyword).
- An issue falls under the documentation or presentation categories.
- An issue points at an actual error.

Our first selection consisted of 170 issues in 12 sets. We used the default value for issues with a minimal reporting threshold, such as the value 3 for reporting an if-statement that is nested too deeply. Additionally, we added 'code duplication' as three issues that fire for duplicates of 50, 75 and 100 tokens. Our initial analysis was applied to a smaller set of programs from four different days throughout the academic year 2014–2015. For each unique source file we recorded for each issue if it occurred in some snapshot of that file.

For a more detailed analysis we made a selection of the 170 issues. For each issue we decided whether it should be included or not, based on the criteria mentioned above. We also discarded all issues in the 'controversial' set, 'import statements' set and the 'unused code' set, and issues that occurred in fewer than 1% of the unique files. Table 1 shows our final set of issues, now grouped according to the categories of Stegeman et al.

We ran PMD for these 24 issues on all compilable programs in the final data set of four weeks and stored the results in our local database. We cleaned the database by removing all data of the files that could not be processed and files with 0 LOC. For each of these 24 issues, we counted in how many unique source files it occurred at least once, and how often. We also calculated the differences in occurrence over time.

3.2.2 Fixing (RQ2). For RQ2 we examine the changes in a source file over time. For each issue we calculated the number of *fixes* and the number of *appearances*. As an example, let us assume that source file X has 6 snapshots in which the occurrences of issue Y

Table 1: Selected issues (report level) per category

Flow	
CyclomaticComplexity (10)	Strict version that counts boolean operators as decision points.
ModifiedCyclomaticComplexity (10)	Counts switch statements as a single decision point.
NPathComplexity (200)	
EmptyIfStmt	
PrematureDeclaration	
Idiom	
SwitchStmtsShouldHaveDefault	
MissingBreakInSwitch	
AvoidInstantiatingObjectsInLoops	
Expressions	
AvoidReassigningParameters	
ConfusingTernary	
CollapsibleIfStmts	
PositionLiteralsFirstInComparisons	
SimplifyBooleanExpressions	
SimplifyBooleanReturns	
Decomposition	
NCSSMethodCount (50)	Counts Non-Commenting Source Statements, report level in statements.
NCSSMethodCount (100)	
SingularField	The scope of a field is limited to one method.
CodeDuplication (50)	Only identified in single files, not over projects.
CodeDuplication (100)	
Modularization	
TooManyMethods (10)	Excludes getters and setters.
TooManyFields (15)	
GodClass	
LawOfDemeter	Call methods from another class directly.
LooseCoupling	Use interfaces instead of implementation types.

are 2 1 3 0 4 2. The number of fixes is 6: the total number of issues that were solved in a subsequent snapshot (1 + 0 + 3 + 0 + 2). The number of appearances is 8: the total number of issues that were introduced in a subsequent snapshot (2 + 0 + 2 + 0 + 4 + 0). These metrics are simplified measures to investigate fixing: we cannot be sure the student really fixed the problem, or simply removed the problematic code.

3.2.3 Extensions (RQ3). BlueJ users may install various extensions to support their programming, such as UML tools, submission tools and style checkers. We generated a list of all extensions used in the selected four weeks of the year 2014–2015. We selected extensions related to code quality from the 29 that were active in at least 0.05% of all BlueJ-startups in those weeks:

- Checkstyle[6] (9,626 start-ups), a static analysis tool for checking code conventions.
- PMD (3,751 start-ups), the tool used for our analysis.
- PatternCoder[7] (507 start-ups), which helps students to implement design patterns.

Findbugs[8] translates Java code into bytecode, and then performs static analysis to identify potential bugs. It is a relevant tool, but with 242 start-ups not used often enough. We also excluded a small number of extensions that we could not find information about.

For RQ3, we calculated the occurrence of issues for each of the extensions, and for source files for which no extensions were used.

4 RESULTS

Table 2 shows some general information on the data sets taken from the academic year 2014–2015.

Table 2: Data set summary

Initial data set (4 days)	Unique source files	90,066
	Snapshots	439,066
Final data set (4 weeks)	Unique source files	453,526
	Snapshots	2,661,528
	Avg events per source file	5.87
	Median events per source file	2
	Max events per source file	700
	Average LOC per source file	52.75
	Median LOC per source file	27

4.1 All issues (RQ1)

Table 3 shows the summary of checking the initial data set of four days for 170 issues. For each unique source file we recorded for each issue if it occurred in some snapshot of that file. In total we found 574,694 occurrences of 162 different issues (8 issues did not occur in any file). The top 10 issues is shown in Table 4.

In the controversial set, seven issues were found in at least 5% of the unique source files. DataFlowAnomalyAnalysis is at the top of the list with 38.6%. This issue deals with redefining variables, undefinitions (variables leaving scope) and references to undefined variables, which may not always be a serious problem. AvoidLiteralsInIfCondition is second with 14.0%. For other issues such as AtLeastOneConstructor and OnlyOneReturn it is also questionable whether they are problematic in novice programmer code, therefore we decided to further omit all issues in this set.

The top 10 also includes issues that we omit in the remainder of this study. The two issues that occur in the most files, 84.2% for MethodArgumentCouldBeFinal and 61.3% for LocalVariable-CouldBeFinal, are both in the optimization set and point at the possibility to use the final keyword to indicate that a variable will not be reassigned. A reason for these high percentages may be that this language construct is not being taught to novice programmers. UseVarargs deals with the 'varargs' option introduced in Java 5, allowing parameters to be passed as an array or as a list of arguments. UseUtilityClass points at the option to make a class with only static methods a utility class with a private constructor. ImmutableField detects private fields that could be made final.

4.2 Selected issues (RQ1)

We now focus on the selection of 24 issues in five categories (Flow, Idiom, Expressions, Decomposition, Modularization), which we applied to our final data set of four weeks. In total we found over 24 million instances of these issues. Table 5 shows in how many unique source files an issue occurs at least once, and the average number of occurrences per KLOC. To calculate this last value, we first calculated the average for each source file, and then the overall average, so the number of snapshots of a source file does not influence the total.

LawOfDemeter stands out as an issue with a very high number of occurrences. Upon closer inspection, it was not always clear why this issue was reported, and it has been suggested online that there

Table 3: Summary of running PMD on the initial data set, showing per PMD set the number of issues that were seen, the percentage of unique files in which at least one issue from that set occurred, the median of the occurrences in % and the maximum.

Set	Issues seen	% of files with issues from set	Median %	Max %
Type resolution	4/4	26.04	3.96	20.1
Optimization	12/12	91.75	2.71	84.2
Unused code	5/5	26.86	2.50	16.2
Code duplication	3/3	4.99	2.28	5.0
Code size	13/13	13.69	1.40	8.2
Controversial	21/22	65.10	1.37	38.6
Import statements	6/6	10.61	1.02	8.5
Design	54/57	81.73	0.32	38.0
Unnecessary	8/8	10.25	0.11	9.6
Empty code	10/11	5.18	0.08	2.2
Coupling	3/5	41.98	0.04	39.7
Basic	23/24	2.52	0.02	1.3

Table 4: Top 10 issues

Set	Issue	In % of files
Optimization	MethodArgumentCouldBeFinal	84.2
Optimization	LocalVariableCouldBeFinal	61.3
Coupling	LawOfDemeter	39.7
Controversial	DataflowAnomalyAnalysis	38.6
Design	UseVarargs	38.0
Design	UseUtilityClass	36.2
Design	ImmutableField	27.8
Type Res.	UnusedImports	20.1
Unused Code	UnusedLocalVariable	16.2
Controversial	AvoidLiteralsInIfCondition	14.0

might be false positives. We therefore decided to omit this issue in the remainder of this study.

It is expected that SingularField occurs quite often with 8.2%, because most of the snapshots in our data set are unfinished programs. CyclomaticComplexity and the more lenient ModifiedCyclomaticComplexity version occur quite often with 7.7% and 5.2% respectively, which could point to serious problems, but that depends on the type of code. LooseCoupling occurs in 6.7% of the files implying that students do not always have knowledge of the use of interfaces. Duplicate50 occurs much more often than Duplicate100 with 4.7% against 1.3%. We argue that the lower threshold of 50 tokens is more suitable for novice programmers, whose programs are relatively short, so duplicates can be spotted more easily.

Figure 1 shows the occurrence of issues by the month in which they appeared, grouped by category. In the week of September the number of issues is quite low, probably because most courses had just started and only a limited set of topics would have been introduced. For the other three months we cannot see major differences, other than an increase in decomposition issues. In March we see a slight decrease in issues mainly in the flow and expressions category, but towards the end of the academic year the values slightly increase.

Table 5: Per issue, column I shows the percentage (%) of unique files in which the issue occurs, column II shows the average number of occurrences per KLOC

Cat	Issue	I	II
M	LawOfDemeter	38.7	42.6
D	SingularField	8.2	3.8
F	CyclomaticComplexity	7.7	1.5
M	LooseCoupling	6.7	2.1
I	AvoidInstantiatingObjectsInLoops	6.3	1.6
E	AvoidReassigningParameters	5.7	1.7
F	ModifiedCyclomaticComplexity	5.2	0.8
M	TooManyMethods	5.0	0.3
D	Duplicate50	4.7	0.7
E	ConfusingTernary	4.4	0.7
D	NcssMethodCount50	3.9	0.3
E	PositionLiteralsFirstInComparisons	3.5	1.6
F	NPathComplexity	3.3	0.3
E	SimplifyBooleanExpressions	3.1	0.8
F	PrematureDeclaration	2.6	0.4
M	GodClass	2.1	0.1
F	EmptyIfStmt	2.0	0.3
E	SimplifyBooleanReturns	1.9	0.4
I	SwitchStmtsShouldHaveDefault	1.7	0.3
I	MissingBreakInSwitch	1.4	0.2
D	Duplicate100	1.3	0.1
E	CollapsibleIfStatements	1.3	0.2
M	TooManyFields	1.2	0.1
D	NcssMethodCount100	1.0	0.0

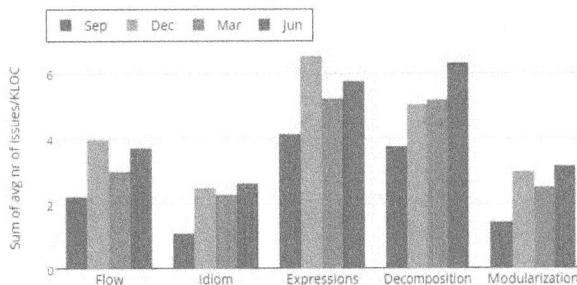

Figure 1: Issues over time

4.3 Fixing (RQ2)

Table 6 shows our fix metrics for each issue. EmptyIfStmt is solved in almost half of the cases, which can be expected because an if-statement with no code in it is probably not finished. The same can be said for SingularField: a student might start with defining the field of a class that is needed for methods that will be added later. On the bottom of the list we find four issues from the modularization category (GodClass, LooseCoupling, TooManyFields, TooManyMethods) that are fixed in fewer than 5% of the appearances.

Overall the rate of fixing issues is low. Either students do not recognise these issues in their code, or do not care to fix them. It should be noted that our data set was not cleaned of source files that continued to be fixed beyond the weeks (Monday to Sunday) we investigated, missing some possible fixes.

Table 6: Issue fixes

Cat	Issue	Appeared	Fixed	%
F	EmptyIfStmt	18,460	9,064	49.1
D	SingularField	103,004	30,152	29.3
F	PrematureDeclaration	21,008	5,891	28.0
D	Duplicate100	35,033	7,388	21.1
E	CollapsibleIfStatements	15,087	2,579	17.1
D	Duplicate50	91,951	15,520	16.9
E	AvoidReassigningParameters	76,359	10,023	13.1
I	MissingBreakInSwitch	9,594	1,033	10.8
F	NPathComplexity	20,549	2,129	10.4
E	ConfusingTernary	36,391	3,558	9.8
E	SimplifyBooleanReturns	12,612	1,162	9.2
E	SimplifyBooleanExpressions	48,965	4,347	8.9
F	ModifiedCyclomaticComplexity	56,822	4,475	7.9
I	AvoidInstantiatingObjectsInLoops	78,588	6,167	7.8
I	SwitchStmtsShouldHaveDefault	12,507	961	7.7
D	NcssMethodCount50	23,569	1,790	7.6
F	CyclomaticComplexity	85,426	6,240	7.3
D	NcssMethodCount100	6,178	410	6.6
E	PositionLiteralsFirstInComparisons	86,536	4,833	5.6
M	GodClass	9,575	437	4.6
M	LooseCoupling	57,039	2,056	3.6
M	TooManyFields	5,539	175	3.2
M	TooManyMethods	23,003	515	2.2

4.4 Extensions (RQ3)

Table 7 shows general information on the use of extensions. Figure 2 shows the differences in occurrence of issues between source files for which extensions were and were not active. The figure shows that there is only a small difference between the use of a tool compared to using no tool. Students using no tool even have a slightly smaller number of issues with 18.2 issues on average per KLOC versus 19.7 for students that use some tool.

Table 7: Extension use

Name	Snapshots	KLOCs	Unique source files
Checkstyle	73,553	7,756	10,833
PMD	26,126	1,840	4,299
PatternCoder	2,433	113	609

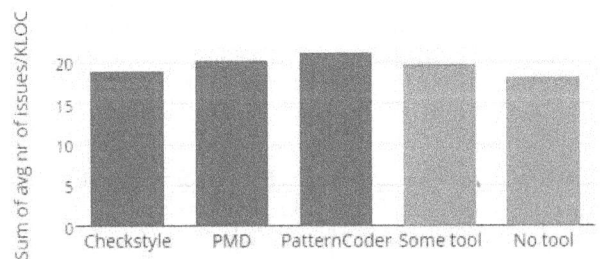

Figure 2: Issues and extension use

5 DISCUSSION

One of our main findings is that most issues are rarely fixed, especially when they are related to modularization. Another finding is that the use of tools has little effect on issue occurrence. Compared to the study of Scratch projects by Aivaloglou and Hermans [1], we found lower percentages of files that contain duplicates, large classes and large methods. Some reasons might be that block-based code cannot be directly compared to statement-based code and that block-based programming is targeted at a younger audience. Another reason is that we investigated single source files instead of projects. Our study supports the work of Pettit et al. [10] by observing that quality issues are not often solved, although we cannot confirm the positive effect of restricting submission attempts, because our data set does not contain information on submissions.

From working with PMD as a source code analyser we have noticed some problems with regard to suitability for students. PMD integrates with many IDEs and also provides an extension for users of BlueJ. We found that many of the checks PMD can perform are not suitable for novice programmers, and may cause confusion with students that might result in neglecting the tool. We advise educators to customize the tool by selecting a small set of relevant checks and adjusting threshold values. Other recommendations for using PMD for assessing programming exercises have been proposed by Nutbrown and Higgins [9].

The main focus of the field of automated feedback and assessment of programming exercises has been on functional correctness of programs, although some tools incorporate feedback on quality aspects as well [8]. This is often done by integrating a lint-like tool or calculating metrics such as cyclomatic complexity and LOC (e.g. [2, 4]). Many professional IDEs detect code quality issues and offer refactorings, but these are often too advanced for novices and not intended to support learning. We argue that these tools need to be better suited to novices, and should be used at various moments during learning and not only for assessment.

5.1 Threats to validity

The designers of the Blackbox project mention some restrictions of their data set that also affect this study [6]. First, BlueJ is often used in courses that use an 'objects-first' approach. Second, it is unknown on what task the student is working, and what the requirements of this task are, such as using a particular language construct. Third, we know nothing about the users of BlueJ. We expect them to be novices, but some programs have probably been written by instructors or more experienced programmers.

We have a limited data set of four weeks in one year. We also cannot be sure that we have all snapshots, events might be missed because something went wrong (e.g. no internet connection) or a user continued to edit the code in another program. Because we store weeks, we miss some snapshots that were compiled just before or after the week. However, because of its size we believe our data set has enough information to answer our research questions. Only tracking single files and not complete BlueJ projects gives an incomplete view of the presence of duplicates.

Vihavainen et al. [13] have investigated the effect of storing student data of different granularity: submission-level, snapshot-level (e.g. compiling, saving), and keystroke-level (e.g. editing text), and found that data might be lost if only snapshot events are studied. Although the Blackbox data set also stores keystroke events, we believe that researching compile events provides us with sufficient

information. For a more detailed analysis, investigating keystrokes could provide more insight into how students fix quality issues.

Although this study focuses on Java programs, we believe that the findings may apply to other languages too. The issues we investigated are not Java specific and can also be seen in other modern object-oriented languages. For functional and logic languages some issues are not applicable or should be adjusted for the paradigm.

6 CONCLUSION AND FUTURE WORK

In this study we have explored quality issues in 2.6 million code snapshots written by novice programmers using the BlueJ IDE. We have composed a list of issues that are relevant for novices. We found that novice programmers develop programs with a substantial amount of code quality issues, and they do not seem to fix them, especially when they are related to modularization. The use of tools has little effect on the occurrence of issues. Educators should pay attention to code quality in their courses, and automated tools should be improved to better support students in understanding and solving code quality issues. Further research is required to better understand how students deal with quality issues, for example by investigating the changes made in snapshots. Also, it is of importance to examine the reasons why students produce low-quality code: they may be unaware of it, or they simply do not know how to fix their code. Paying attention to code quality in education is vital if we want to keep improving our software systems.

ACKNOWLEDGMENTS

This research is supported by the Netherlands Organisation for Scientific Research (NWO), grant number 023.005.063.

REFERENCES

[1] Efthimia Aivaloglou and Felienne Hermans. 2016. How Kids Code and How We Know: An Exploratory Study on the Scratch Repository. In *Proc. of ICER*. 53–61.
[2] Kirsti Ala-Mutka, Toni Uimonen, and Hannu-Matti Jarvinen. 2004. Supporting students in C++ programming courses with automatic program style assessment. *J. of Inf. Technol. Educ.* 3, 1 (2004), 245–262.
[3] Amjad Altadmri and Neil C. C. Brown. 2015. 37 Million Compilations: Investigating Novice Programming Mistakes in Large-Scale Student Data. In *Proc. of SIGCSE*. 522–527.
[4] Eliane Araujo, Dalton Serey, and Jorge Figueiredo. 2016. Qualitative aspects of students' programs: Can we make them measurable?. In *Proc. of FIE*. 1–8.
[5] Dennis Breuker, Jan Derriks, and Jacob Brunekreef. 2011. Measuring Static Quality of Student Code. In *Proceedings of ITiCSE*. 13–17.
[6] Neil C. C. Brown, Michael Kölling, Davin McCall, and Ian Utting. 2014. Blackbox: A Large Scale Repository of Novice Programmers' Activity. In *Proc. of SIGCSE*. 223–228.
[7] Martin Fowler. 1999. *Refactoring: improving the design of existing code*. Addison-Wesley Professional.
[8] Hieke Keuning, Johan Jeuring, and Bastiaan Heeren. 2016. Towards a Systematic Review of Automated Feedback Generation for Programming Exercises. In *Proceedings of ITiCSE*. 41–46.
[9] Stephen Nutbrown and Colin Higgins. 2016. Static analysis of programming exercises: Fairness, usefulness and a method for application. *Computer Science Education* 26, 2-3 (2016), 104–128.
[10] Raymond Pettit, John Homer, Roger Gee, Susan Mengel, and Adam Starbuck. 2015. An Empirical Study of Iterative Improvement in Programming Assignments. In *Proc. of SIGCSE*. 410–415.
[11] Martijn Stegeman, Erik Barendsen, and Sjaak Smetsers. 2016. Designing a Rubric for Feedback on Code Quality in Programming Courses. In *Proc. of Koli Calling*. 160–164.
[12] Michele Tufano, Fabio Palomba, Gabriele Bavota, Rocco Oliveto, Massimiliano Di Penta, Andrea De Lucia, and Denys Poshyvanyk. 2015. When and why your code starts to smell bad. In *Proc. of ICSE*. 403–414.
[13] Arto Vihavainen, Matti Luukkainen, and Petri Ihantola. 2014. Analysis of source code snapshot granularity levels. In *Proc. of SIGITE*. 21–26.

Experiences in Teaching and Learning Requirements Engineering on a Sound Didactical Basis

Yvonne Sedelmaier
Coburg University of Applied Sciences
Faculty of Electrical Engineering and Informatics
D-96450 Coburg, Germany
yvonne.sedelmaier@hs-coburg.de

Dieter Landes
Coburg University of Applied Sciences
Faculty of Electrical Engineering and Informatics
D-96450 Coburg, Germany
dieter.landes@hs-coburg.de

ABSTRACT

Requirements are of paramount importance for the quality of software systems. Yet, requirements engineering education at universities is surprisingly hard. University students encounter difficulties in understanding the role of requirements and applying relevant methods to deal with requirements appropriately. One potential cause may be a lack of authenticity, i.e. settings that are too artificial to mirror the complexity of real-world situations adequately.

This paper presents an innovative and integrated didactical approach for teaching requirements engineering that was devised in a goal- and competence-oriented manner to avoid some of these shortcomings, in particular by including requirements elicitation with real customers into an integrated didactic step-by-step approach. Obviously, requirements engineering education is far more than assembling technical knowledge. Rather, it involves many non-technical skills that obtain a specific flavor in requirements engineering. Our didactic approach also addresses these skills, while resting on a sound pedagogical underpinning. The paper also summarizes indications for the success of this approach, in particular by participants' self-evaluations.

Keywords

Requirements engineering education; competence-oriented didactics; higher education; student learning;

1. WHY BOTHER WITH REQUIREMENTS ENGINEERING EDUCATION?

It is commonly accepted that requirements are a top success factor in software engineering projects, but, conversely, also a major reason for project failures [1]. Therefore, providing IT students with solid requirements engineering (RE) skills is of paramount importance. In practice, however, teaching and learning requirements engineering is not too easy.

Part of the problem is the fact that good requirements are essential in complex real-life projects. Gaining hands-on experiences in such projects is difficult since time and resource restrictions prohibit instructors from running many such projects – typically, there is only one such project during university education. Often, such a

ITiCSE'17, July 3–5, 2017, Bologna, Italy.
Copyright is held by the owner/author(s). Publication rights licensed to ACM.
ACM ISBN 978-1-4503-4704-4/17/07...$15.00.
DOI: http://dx.doi.org/10.1145/3059009.3059011

project comes late as a capstone project that ties together everything that should have been learned before.

Unfortunately, learning requirements engineering only theoretically does not work well either. Students tend to view many important issues in RE as commonplace and fail to see their importance. Yet, some of the basics are a precondition to enable students to work on a project successfully.

Obviously, there is a dilemma: on the one hand, some issues in RE that are taught early cannot really be understood by students due to lack of practical experience, on the other hand postponing these issues to become part of a project increases the probability for failure.

Thus, instructors face the huge challenge to make requirements engineering education as descriptive and tangible as possible for students. To achieve this, the complexity of real-world problems should be mapped at least in part to a university context. This needs to be done in such a way that the associated problems become evident for the students.

This contribution presents experiences with a didactical approach for requirements engineering education. To a large part, this approach is based on competence-oriented didactics [2, 3]. The main emphasis of this course lies on elicitation and modelling of requirements in various shapes, and the use of requirements in methods for effort estimation.

The didactical approach for this course was devised and refined in several revision cycles. A main characteristic of the resulting didactical approach is the extensive active involvement of students in the learning process. In particular the latter aspect has a solid theoretical underpinning in constructivist didactics [4] and theories from general didactics [5–7]. An additional characteristic is a strong emphasis on non-technical skills which are particularly relevant for requirements engineering, but also gain a very specific, context-sensitive shape in this particular domain [8].

In the following, we first outline how the initial shape of the course. Then, we present the goals and the current didactical approach. We describe the rationale behind our didactical decisions before we discuss evaluation results that indicate that the didactical approach had a positive effect with respect to intended learning outcomes. A summary and outlook concludes the paper.

2. WHERE DID WE START OUT?

Requirements engineering is a core ingredient of our software engineering education. "Software Modelling" is an elective course in the second year of a bachelor program in informatics, comprising 2 contact hours per week over 15 weeks. Typically, between 20 and 35 students are enrolled in this course, which builds upon a general introductory course on software engineering in the preceding semester and paves the way for a software engineering project which serves as a capstone project in the spirit of, e.g., [9].

The first issue of the Software Modelling course took place in 2010 and remained largely constant until 2012. In this period, the focus was primarily on technical aspects of modelling requirements: after a general introduction to modelling, various notations for describing functional and non-functional requirements (e.g., use cases, user stories, misuse cases, PLanguage) were discussed as a first major topic. A second major building block consisted of process modelling approaches (event-driven process chains, BPMN, Petri nets) with the goal of using process models as a source for deriving requirements. Finally, software cost and effort estimation (function points and variants, COCOMO II) constituted the third major building block of the course.

Even though some examples already triggered discussions with students, the course's teaching style was predominantly instructive. Examples at this stage were taken from many different scenarios and applications in such a way as to expose the relevant aspect in focus most articulately. The course encompassed two moderately intricate practical assignments, namely building a process model for registering a thesis (individual assignment) and writing requirements specification for an online job exchange (group assignment).

Although course evaluations showed that students pretty much liked the course, student feedback also indicated that the syllabus did not really catch and thrill students. Likewise, it became obvious that students had considerable difficulties in getting a proper idea of requirements, processes, and functional size, arguably since the coverage of the topics was too abstract, in spite of the two practical assignments. In addition, the diversity of examples tended to be confusing since some students lost the big picture and the insight into how various issues interrelate.

3. WHERE DID WE WANT TO GO?

When we started working on the course from a didactical perspective we applied a goal-driven top-down approach which is called competence-oriented didactics [2, 3]. This underlying didactical theory follows the primacy of didactics [10]. It starts out with answering the core question, namely what the main ideas and goals of the course are, before choosing methods or media.

According to the concept of competence-oriented didactics, we first worked out intended learning outcomes of the course. It became apparent that instructors had some of the intended learning outcomes already implicitly in the back of their heads, but not stated them explicitly and systematically, i.e. referring to a software engineering competence profile. Therefore, they could not serve as a compass for choosing the right didactical approach. To put things right, the intended learning outcomes were stated as follows on a somewhat abstract level:

- Students shall acquire a more tangible impression of the term "requirements".

- Students shall understand the importance of requirements and shall be able to act accordingly.

- Students shall understand characteristic approaches to the specification of functional and non-functional requirements and their prioritization.

- Students shall understand the role of communication with other involved parties in requirements engineering.

- Students shall understand the role of business processes as a source of requirements.

- Students shall be able to apply appropriate methods and notations collaboratively in order to specify requirements for a sample software application. In particular, this encompasses the capability to write a requirements document, but also to understand a requirements document that the students did not write themselves.

- Students shall understand popular approaches to complexity and cost estimation for software systems.

These teaching goals primarily represent competencies to be fostered. Requirements, their elicitation, and their documentation in some type of model are the core issues of this course. To that end, the course addresses not only factual knowledge, but also competencies to cope with situations that may arise when dealing with requirements.

4. HOW DID WE PROCEED?

Unfortunately, students fell short of completely achieving these teaching goals. Rather, they had difficulties in really understanding the issues covered in the course. Course evaluations showed that they could not adequately value the role of requirements for their future professional career. In particular, they found writing requirements for small sample problems almost trivial. Furthermore, they were neither able to appreciate business models as input to requirements elicitation, nor could they properly understand the interrelationship between the course's various subjects. One reason might be the sequence in which the topics were taught, namely first specifying atomic functional requirements, non-functional requirements, requirements prioritization, and recommended contents of requirements documents, and then, in a second step, modelling business processes. Analyzing the course showed a somewhat incoherent collection of topics because business processes are a source for deriving initial requirements, but where taught near the end of the course. Methods for describing requirements without knowing where they come from are more difficult to learn.

5. WHERE DID WE END UP?

Due to the perceived shortcomings of the course, several changes were made in order to better achieve the intended learning outcomes. Refinements that have been made in the first revision of the course are discussed in detail in [11].

A major modification consisted in changing the sequence and basic structure of the course (Fig. 1). Now, the basic question is how to first elicit and then describe requirements instead of simply describing requirements. To that end, teaching requirements engineering starts out from business process models. From these models, requirements for a workflow application are derived and specified in a requirements document. In particular, we generally use applications for workflows that are somewhat familiar to our students.

Obviously, students hardly understand why they should learn specific things when they neither have place, nor time to apply them or when they do not know which purpose the knowledge is intended to serve. Therefore, another change consisted in moving from instructive teaching to activating forms of learning. Rather than teaching "stockpiling knowledge" we first expose students to a problem for which they need a solution [12]. Then, it is far easier for students to understand the necessity of the learning topics and figure out what knowledge is necessary for which purpose, i.e. students build their own mental constructs in the sense of constructivist didactics [13].

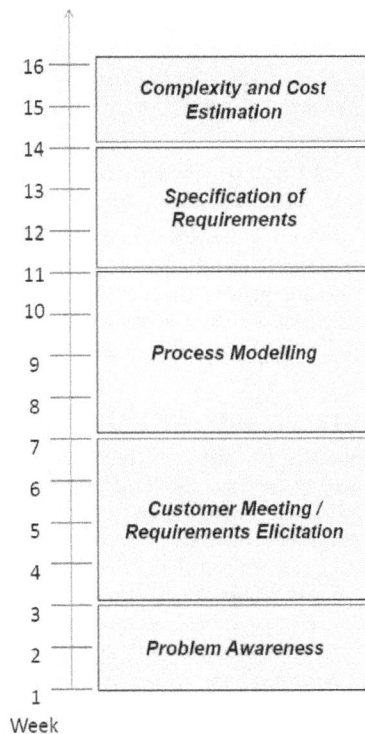

Figure 1 New Structure of Contents of the Software Modelling course

In particular, students are exposed to the complexity of an almost realistic workflow application that they have to specify. Being more realistic than a toy project, this setting makes them understand better why requirements should be described precisely. Furthermore, since teams of five students are in charge of writing a requirements document, non-technical competences become more important and can be exercised more extensively. Notably, self-organization and team collaboration became major issues.

Finally, all exercises and examples refer back to the same application scenario, e.g. a workflow system for managing business trips.

Generally, activating forms of learning were intensified. In order to motivate students to participate actively in several exercises, we allot micro-credits. As it turned out, micro-credits stimulate students to participate actively in the course to a surprisingly large degree.

5.1 Problem Awareness

Some students initially do not see the point of engaging themselves in inductive and activating methods. Thus, in the first lesson, students are informed about the new and, to their mind, unusual learning methods. Instructors explain the intended learning outcomes explicitly with an analogy. Learning software engineering, and requirements engineering in particular, may be compared with riding a push-bike. Riding a bike can only be learned by doing it, but not by looking at someone else riding a bike or, even less, by listening to someone explaining how to ride. The same holds true for software and requirements engineering. Consequently, instead of simple instructive ways of teaching, we rely on methods that foster competencies. Students need to take an active part in the course and are involved intensively by, e.g., exercises and discussions. In order

to state their commitment to this type of learning setting explicitly, each student is asked to sign a "contract" between her and the instructors. To do so, students should sign a flipchart with their name in order to enroll in the course.

Furthermore, instructors explain the rationale behind each exercise and the addressed competences. A short paragraph at the bottom of each worksheet clarifies the intended learning outcome for this specific exercise. This helps students to understand the goals and addressed competences.

For improving problem awareness with respect to the subject matter, the first exercise is centered around a scenario in which a customer demands an offer for developing a workflow-based software system. Students are requested to work out in groups which steps they would take next, how they would do this, what they think they need, and which problems might appear while preparing such an offer.

This exercise mainly aims at rising the awareness of requirements as an indispensable prerequisite for bidding for a software project. Students should arrive at this insight by themselves through working on this exercise. Referring to the results of this exercise, instructors explain the intended learning outcomes, the contents of the course, and the motivation for the methods.

5.2 Customer Meeting for Requirements Elicitation

Course evaluations indicate that students tend to take requirements for granted, i.e. they have no realistic idea of difficulties that may come along with eliciting requirements from a stakeholder.

In order to tackle this issue, students need to cope with a real external customer from whom they are supposed to elicit requirements. As an additional difficulty, the customer is a non-IT person, i.e. students have to overcome both, an unfamiliar domain and unknown terminology.

5.2.1 Preparing a Customer Meeting

Initially, students fell short of preparing, conducting, and reflecting the customer meeting. For this reason, instructors decided to support students at that point. Preparing a customer meeting is much easier when someone knows the customers' perspectives. Therefore, we make students change their perspective from a software engineer to a customer. Students are requested to assume they were the customer and figure out what they would expect from an IT company and from a successful meeting in general such that they would be willing to awarding a contract to this company. How should software engineers behave? What makes a meeting successful? What makes participants feel comfortable with the reached outcomes? In addition to that, students receive information about question types, strategies and methods, as well as simple communication theories as a framework for understanding complex communication situations. Topics of this lesson are - in addition to methodological aspects - communication skills, e.g. questioning, and self-organization, e.g. preparing a meeting.

5.2.2 Conducting a Customer Meeting

Then, student groups prepare the customer meeting offline and conduct it a week later. Each group of students has 5-6 members and stays constant for the remainder of the course. The customer meeting takes one hour at most and is recorded on video. Instructors observe the meeting, but do not interfere during the meeting.

5.2.3 Reflecting on a Customer Meeting

Students receive these videos and some guiding questions for reflecting on the meeting in a wrap-up session. Customers and instructors add their observations and help analyzing the customer meeting in some kind of a coaching.

5.3 Process Models

The customer meeting provides students with a lot of unstructured information on which they need to impose structure in order to derive requirements. For workflow systems, process models are a good tool for doing so. Thus, students are asked to build process models from the material they gained in the customer meeting.

To that end, general elements of process models are identified, e.g. who does what at what point in time, in a largely instructive manner. Then, students shall build a small process model as an event-driven process chain (EPC) on their own while in class. As background material, they receive a short text explaining the basic elements of the notation.

The resulting EPC is then "translated" by the instructor into an equivalent BPMN model, thus highlighting corresponding notational elements in the two notations.

As offline assignment, students are then requested to build additional process models in order to cover the material from the customer meeting completely. In a first step, each student works on this task individually, before the results are consolidated in the very same groups that conducted the customer meetings.

In a next step, each student group reviews another group's process models with respect to content as well as formal aspects. Findings are discussed in class, thus providing feedback to the process models' authors. Instructors also contribute to this feedback loop.

In order to familiarize students with yet another process notation, namely Petri nets, an additional exercise confronts students with a Petri net without prior explanation of the notation, and asks them to make sense of the model. This establishes a basis to explain the notational elements and their semantics.

In order to summarize and deepen the understanding of the various process notations, the final exercise aims at highlighting the particular strengths and weaknesses of the modelling notations. This exercise refers back to the general elements of process models that were identified to start off the topic of process modelling.

Taken together, this set of exercises constitutes an integrated didactical approach which fosters understanding of technical knowledge of process modelling as well as non-technical skills such as working techniques, self-organization, and teamwork [14].

5.4 Specification of Requirements

Process models serve as a basis to derive high-level requirements, namely use cases and use case specifications. Derivation rules are presented instructively, but students are requested to apply these rules and guidelines to their process models in an offline exercise.

A sample use case specification is then used to derive lower-level requirements. In an in-class exercise, students work in groups on a badly written low-level requirement that they shall analyze and express better and more precisely. The results of this exercise lead to quality criteria for requirements and templates for functional requirements, such as e.g. [15].

In this exercise, one student team works on a somewhat peculiar "bad" requirement. This requirement turns out to be a non-functional one and is used to explain the particular difficulties in specifying this type of requirement as well as to highlight possible approaches to do so, namely GQM [16], misuse cases, and PLanguage [17]. An additional in-class group exercise requires students to apply one of these techniques hands-on, i.e. specify another non-functional requirement precisely using GQM.

A final offline assignment puts all pieces together: writing a complete requirements document integrating all previous results such as process models, use cases, and non-functional requirements. Students work in the very same groups that conducted the customer meetings (5.2). The requirements document is not graded, but instructors as well as customers provide feedback to the students.

5.5 Complexity and Cost Estimation

In order to link back to the initial scenario of bidding for a development contract, students need to get insight into cost estimation. To this end, the last section of the course deals with complexity and cost estimation, in particular size estimation using function points, use case points, and algorithmic cost estimation using COCOMO [18]. This content is presented primarily in an instructive way, but includes a small exercise in which students calculate function points and use case points for a small part of their sample system.

6. HOW WELL DID IT WORK?

6.1 Evaluation

In principle, evaluation can be conducted quantitatively or qualitatively. Education research and social sciences have long realized that qualitative methods are better suited to understand human behavior such as learning. In particular, competences (in contrast to knowledge) can only be evaluated qualitatively, not quantitatively in traditional exams. Furthermore, only qualitative approaches can expose interrelationships between factors that influence learning. More than that, control groups are no viable approach in education since it is ethically unacceptable to deprive the members of the control group of didactical approaches that instructors believe to be effective and expose them knowingly to something inferior instead. The insight that qualitative evaluation methods may be equally valid as quantitative ones is gradually also being accepted in the software engineering field [19, 20].

Course evaluation is accomplished using the Software Engineering Competence Assessment Tool (SECAT) [21, 22]. This is a qualitative instrument to evaluate software engineering education by assessing students' increase of competencies. Most of the skills in software engineering are so-called multi-complex competences [23]. Due to their complex nature, this type of competences is hard to measure quantitatively in a reasonable manner.

In order to tackle the latter issue, SECAT uses a qualitative approach which builds upon a sophisticated competence model that consists of a functional, processual, and holistic shaping level. SECAT considers team achievements as well as individual ones, may integrate multiple perspectives from various groups of stakeholders, and pays attention to the outcome of a task as well as the process that was used to solve the task. In addition, it is worth mentioning that SECAT covers technical as well as non-technical competencies in an integrated framework.

Thus, SECAT may be used for assessing competence gains of individuals, but is primarily a tool that highlights shortcomings in didactical approaches in higher education that might be eliminated by changing didactical elements in a competence-oriented manner.

The intended learning outcomes for the software modelling course focus on problem awareness on the processual level, and context sensitivity, personal competences, and creativity on the holistic shaping level. A self-assessment on a 4-point Likert scale was chosen as evaluation perspective - the higher the value, the larger the increase of competence. Since 2014, intermediate evaluations after the customer meeting are conducted, plus a final evaluation at the end of the course. Course evaluations with SECAT regularly indicate an increase of students' competences in the addressed areas, as shown in Figure 2 for the 2015 issue of the course.

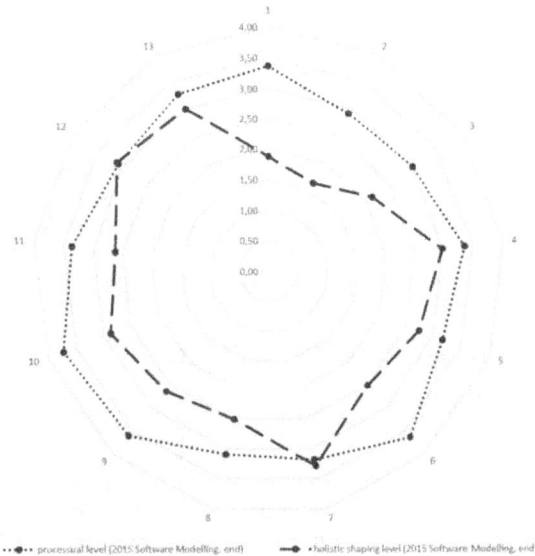

Figure 2: Evaluation results per student in 2015

All in all, evaluation with SECAT generally reveals a high increase in the addressed competences. This indicates that the developed didactical approach works well for this course and its intended learning outcomes.

6.2 Observations

The didactical approach works well. Since revising the didactical concept started in 2012, acceptance for the "new" methods of learning is increasing. Apart from student feedback, this also becomes apparent in the fact that fewer students drop out of the course and attendance in class is considerably higher than in other electives. Likewise, there is almost no decrease in attendance over time.

Yet, there is no such clear trend in some other aspects. While teams worked together quite well in earlier years, in 2016 some of them did not really act as a team, but rather as a collection of individuals. Still, they achieved the intended learning outcomes.

Likewise, there is no constantly high motivation across all the exercises. Apparently, students like some of the exercises better than others, but their favorites are different from year to year. In particular, in 2015 the Petri net exercise really thrilled the participants, but did not catch in 2016. In contrast, in 2015 students were not very interested in communication theory, while this topic gained momentum in 2016. In order to understand these phenomena and the underlying causes, we need to constantly fine-tune and extend our evaluation approach.

The role of micro-credits also seems to shift. In earlier issues of the course, students worked on voluntary assignments to earn a bonus in the first place. Recently, students seem to have understood that working on these assignments is beneficial for their learning anyway, and micro-credits are just a positive side effect.

7. WHERE ARE WE NOW AND WHAT´S LEFT TO BE DONE?

Quite a few publications deal with requirements engineering education in some way or the other. A series of international workshops, namely the International Workshop on Requirements Engineering Education and Training (REE&T) is devoted to the topic. A recent overview of activities in the field can be found in [24], up-to-date work is, e.g., reported by [25]. Many papers in requirements engineering education focus on describing learning approaches in a more or less anecdotal format, but lack a sound didactical underpinning. At best, a group of papers refers back to curricula such as SWEBOK or the IEEE/ACM Computer Science Curriculum. Likewise, a systematic evaluation is missing in a large portion of the reported work [24]. A curriculum with a didactical underpinning requires a clear goal [7] which is described in intended learning outcomes and is necessarily deduced from required competences in requirements engineering, namely the competence profile. Yet, there seems to be little work that mentions required competences explicitly. Usually, the focus of existing work is on methods that were used in requirements engineering classes, yet without referring to competences that would benefit from the proposed methods. Often, an underlying overall didactical concept or didactical foundation is completely missing.

Our work links requirements engineering and didactical aspects in a multidisciplinary experience. As a result, a university course in software engineering with focus on requirements and modelling issues was advanced in a competence-oriented way. It started out with an explicit formulation of the intended learning outcomes which lead to a restructuring of the contents of the course. Furthermore, active and inductive learning methods were introduced to foster students' competences in a goal-oriented way. The teaching and learning methods shifted from an instructive mode to an active way of learning. The number of exercises for the students increased from two large ones in 2012 to fifteen smaller ones in 2016, in part by turning earlier examples into exercises on which students work actively. Consequently, students can apply their theoretical knowledge immediately and transform it into usable action knowledge in small projects and team assignments.

A main characteristic of the new approach is the extensive active involvement of students in the learning process. In particular, the latter aspect has a solid theoretical underpinning in constructivist didactics. Furthermore, our approach is characterized by a strong emphasis on non-technical skills, which are particularly relevant for requirements engineering, but also gain a very specific, context-sensitive shape in this particular domain.

One continuous example across the whole course facilitates developing problem awareness and understanding the necessity of topics in requirements engineering.

Usually, students tended to take clear requirements for granted. Core ingredients of our approach are a realistic and integrated setting, which includes writing a requirements document for a complex application and eliciting requirements from real customers. After redesigning the course, students improved their problem awareness and, as a consequence, could better foster competences that are needed to cope with such situations.

Even if the new didactical approach consists of methods that our students initially find unusual, most of the students continuously took active part in the course. Only a small number of students dropped out during the course. This can be seen as an indication that students feel that the topics and the way they are taught are suitable with respect to intended learning outcomes.

In future iterations of the course, it would be interesting to collect and compare data from more cohorts of students. This would allow testing the hypothesis that this approach works well for similar groups of students.

8. ACKNOWLEDGEMENT

This work is part of the EVELIN project and funded by the German Ministry of Education and Research (Bundesministerium für Bildung und Forschung) under grants 01PL12022A and 01PL17022A.

9. REFERENCES

[1] The Standish Group International, "CHAOS: A Recipe for Success". Available: https://www4.informatik.tu-muenchen.de/lehre/vorlesungen/vse/WS2004/1999_Standish_Chaos.pdf (2014, May. 05).

[2] Y. Sedelmaier and D. Landes, "A Competence-Oriented Approach to Subject-Matter Didactics for Software Engineering," *International Journal of Engineering Pedagogy (iJEP)*, vol. 5, no. 3, pp. 34–44, 2015.

[3] Y. Sedelmaier and D. Landes, "Towards a Better Understanding of Learning Mechanisms in Information Systems Education," in Global Engineering Education Conference (EDUCON): IEEE, 2015, pp. 418–427.

[4] H. Siebert, *Didaktisches Handeln in der Erwachsenenbildung*, 2nd ed. Neuwied: Luchterhand, 1997.

[5] P. Heimann, *Unterricht*, 8th ed. Hannover: Schroedel, 1976.

[6] P. Heimann, G. Otto, and W. Schulz, Eds, *Unterricht*. Hannover: Schroedel, 1965.

[7] W. Klafki, "Didactic analysis as the core of preparation of instruction (Didaktische Analyse als Kern der Unterrichtsvorbereitung)," (en), *Journal of Curriculum Studies*, vol. 27, no. 1, pp. 13–30, 1995.

[8] Y. Sedelmaier and D. Landes, "Software Engineering Body of Skills," in Global Engineering Education Conference (EDUCON): IEEE, 2014, pp. 395–401.

[9] D. Monett and B. Kiehne, "Interdisziplinäres Projektlernen in der agilen Softwareentwicklung," *die hochschullehre*, vol. 2, no. 2, http://www.hochschullehre.org/wp-content/files/diehochschullehre-2016-2-Monett-Kiehne-Projektlernen.pdf, 2016.

[10] W. Klafki, "Didaktische Analyse als Kern der Unterrichtsvorbereitung," in Auswahl, Grundlegende Aufsätze aus der Zeitschrift Die deutsche Schule Reihe A, vol. 1, *Didaktische Analyse*, H. Roth and A. Blumenthal, Eds, Hannover: Schroedel, 1964, pp. 5–34.

[11] Y. Sedelmaier and D. Landes, "Using Business Process Models to Foster Competencies in Requirements Engineering," in 27th International Conference on Software Engineering Education and Training (CSEE&T), 2014, pp. 13–22.

[12] K. Holzkamp, "Wider den Lehr-Lern-Kurzschluß," in Grundlagen der Berufs- und Erwachsenenbildung, Bd. 5, *Lebendiges Lernen*, R. Arnold, Ed, Baltmannsweiler: Schneider, 1996, pp. 21–30.

[13] E. von Glasersfeld, "Radical constructivism and teaching," in Prospects: quarterly review of comparative education, XXXI, 2, *Constructivism and education*, C. Braslavsky, Ed.: UNESCO International Bureau of Education, 2001, pp. 161–174.

[14] Y. Sedelmaier and D. Landes, "A Multi-Level Didactical Approach to Build up Competencies in Requirements Engineering," in 8th Int. Workshop on Requirements Engineering Education & Training co-located with 22nd International Conference on Requirements Engineering (RE 2014): CEUR Workshop Proceedings, 2014, pp. 26–34.

[15] K. Pohl and C. Rupp, *Requirements engineering fundamentals*, 1st ed. Santa Barbara Calif: Rocky Nook, 2011.

[16] V. Basili, G. Caldiera, and D. Rombach, "Goal Question Metric Paradigm," in *Encyclopedia of software engineering*, J. J. Marciniak, Ed, New York: John Wiley, 1994, pp. 528–532.

[17] T. Gilb and L. Brodie, *Competitive engineering*. Burlington: Elsevier, 2005.

[18] B. W. Boehm, *Software cost estimation with Cocomo II*. Upper Saddle River: Prentice Hall, 2009.

[19] T. Dybå, R. Prikladnicki, K. Rönkkö, C. Seaman, and J. Sillito, "Qualitative research in software engineering," *Empir Software Eng*, vol. 16, no. 4, pp. 425–429, 2011.

[20] C. B. Seaman, "Qualitative methods in empirical studies of software engineering," *IIEEE Trans. Software Eng*, vol. 25, no. 4, pp. 557–572, 1999.

[21] Y. Sedelmaier and D. Landes, "A Multi-Perspective Framework for Evaluating Software Engineering Education by Assessing Students' Competencies," in 44th Frontiers in Education (FIE), 2014, pp. 2065–2072.

[22] Y. Sedelmaier and D. Landes, "Evaluating Didactical Approaches Based upon Students' Competences," in Global Engineering Education Conference (EDUCON): IEEE, 2016, pp. 527–536.

[23] W. Bender, S. Lerch, and M. Scheffel, "Interdisziplinäre Kompetenzen Studierender evaluieren. 2. Zwischenbericht der Wissenschaftlichen Begleitstudie zum Projekt "Der Coburger Weg" zum 31.05.2014," Hochschule Coburg, 2014.

[24] S. Ouhbi, A. Idri, J. L. Fernández-Alemán, and A. Toval, "Requirements engineering education," *Requirements Eng*, vol. 20, no. 2, pp. 119–138, 2015.

[25] R. L. Quintanilla Portugal, P. Engiel, J. Pivatelli, and J. C. S. do Prado Leite, "Facing the challenges of teaching requirements engineering," in ICSE 2016, [Los Alamitos, California], New York, New York: IEEE Computer Society; The Association for Computing Machinery, 2016, pp. 461–470.

About Programming Maturity in Finnish High Schools: A Comparison Between High School and University Students' Programming Skills

Erkki Kaila
Department of Future Technologies
20014 University of Turku, Finland
ertaka@utu.fi

Rolf Lindén
Department of Future Technologies
20014 University of Turku, Finland
rolind@utu.fi

Erno Lokkila
Department of Future Technologies
20014 University of Turku, Finland
eolokk@utu.fi

Mikko-Jussi Laakso
Department of Future Technologies
20014 University of Turku, Finland
milaak@utu.fi

ABSTRACT

In this study, we compare students' ability to learn and master a variety of computer programming concepts in two different student groups. The first group consists of 64 university level students with various backgrounds (adult control), and the second group consists of 40 Finnish junior high school students of age 15 (adolescent treatment group). Neither group had significant prior programming experience. Both groups were taught a similar semester-long introductory course on Python programming, using the same learning management system (LMS). We find that for almost all of the concepts, both groups perform equally well, but students in the adolescent treatment group perform significantly worse when learning the concepts of loop structures and repetition. The results are further compared to the lecture surveys that were collected from the junior high school course to further explain the causes of the findings. Based on the results and the teaching methods that are presented in this paper, we are able to show that adolescent junior high school students and adult university students have similar abilities to learn abstract computer science concepts using a fully functional programming environment.

Keywords

computer science education;maturity;adolescence;junior high school;Python;teaching methods;study habits

ITiCSE '17 July 3–5, 2017, Bologna, Italy

© 2017 ACM. ISBN 978-1-4503-4704-4/17/07. . . $15.00

DOI: http://dx.doi.org/10.1145/3059009.3059021

1. INTRODUCTION

There are several methodologies designed and proven to be effective for teaching programming to adults (or young adults). Most of the research conducted targets university level students, as most of the researchers in the area usually teach programming courses at universities (or at least have tight connections to such teachers) by themselves. However, according to popularity of graphical or visual programming environments, the current consensus seems to be that the methodologies used in the higher levels are not directly applicable to elementary schools or junior high schools. We argue that although the materials and exercises likely require adjusting, the same methods and technology we use successfully in university level programming courses can be perfectly well utilized in the lower level courses as well.

In this paper, we try to prove this claim by comparing two programming courses. The first one is a university level introductory course directed for students with non-computing background, and the second one a similar course taught at junior high school level to students aged 14 to 15. The methodologies and educational technologies used are similar enough to allow comparison, but the course content for the younger students is somewhat simplified. Still, the learning goals of the matched sections are similar: after passing the course the students should be able to understand the fundamentals of imperative paradigm (such as conditional execution, repetition and subprograms) and utilize it to write programs using Python.

2. LITERATURE REVIEW

An exact definition of what programming is seems to be transient and shifts over time (see [1]), and the book "Psychology of Programming" [4] devotes the first 77 pages for defining programming. Since programming is such a varied task, there are multiple cognitive skills involved in it. What these skills actually are, is under some debate. Regardless, many seem to agree on at least problem-solving, deductive reasoning and logical thinking (e.g. [4] pp.63–82, [13]).

Even if programming as a concept is elusive, the difficulties in learning it are not. Du Boulay [3] identifies five areas of difficulty when learning programming: 1) orientation; what benefits and possibilities learning programming offers 2) the notational machine; what is the computer and its capabilities 3) notation; the problems of syntax and semantics in programming languages 4) structures; the building blocks of programs and 5) pragmatics; the wider context of programming, such as debugging, designing and testing programs.

There should be no debate over the claim that novice programmers create more bugs and take more time to solve simple programming exercises. However, once students are able to write simple programs in one programming language, transitioning to other languages can be done with relative ease [5]. Learning to program, thus, is more than just learning a programming language. The five areas of difficulties identified by [3] support this statement: When learning to program, all five areas need to be focused on, whereas learning a new programming language allows the learner to focus on only the notational aspect. Building on this, visual programming languages such as Scratch are thus easier to learn initially, as the semantics layer can be mostly ignored. This can create problems later, when moving to a non-visual programming language. This is pointed out by both Weintrop & Wilensky [18] and DiSalvo [2]: the applicability of current visual programming languages is limited to learning the basics of programming and does not allow development of larger applications (web, mobile or games, to name a few). DiSalvo also found that student motivation and interest further influence students' views.

Adapting active learning strategies have been found to both improve learning results and motivation in students. (e.g. [8], [16], [11]). Active learning is heavily based on the currently widely adopted constructivist learning theories, which have their roots in the works of Piaget and Vygotsky. In active learning, the focus is on engaging the student in the current task and encouraging them to construct information that is meaningful to them. This is done by providing the students with mental scaffolds in the form of study material and instruction. This is in sharp contrast to the still-too-often used lecturing, in which students are expected to passively listen to facts told by the teacher, and at the end of the course produce the same facts during an exam. The methods vary by subject: program visualizations (e.g. [15]) are hardly useful for students of history, whereas role-playing exercises work well for teaching multiculturalism in America (as described in [12]), but are unlikely to produce significant results in teaching repetition in a CS1 course.

3. ABOUT THE LEARNING MANAGEMENT SYSTEM

Courses that are presented in this study rely heavily on the usage of a learning management system (LMS) called ViLLE. The LMS provides various general exercise types (such as quizzes or sorting and categorizing exercises) that can be used in programming education, as well as specialized programming exercise types that support several programming languages, including for example Python, Java, C#, C++ and JavaScript.

A complete description of the system can be found in [10]. Earlier experiences about using ViLLE to teach programming can be found for example in [6], [7] and [15].

4. PROGRAMMING COURSES OBSERVED IN THE STUDY

4.1 Programming Course at University Level

The first course observed (N = 61) is a Python programming course at university level (later UC). Unlike most programming courses at universities, the course is not directed for computer science or engineering students, but rather as a supplementary course for bioinformatics students and students with other majors interested in programming.

The course lasts for 14 weeks, with two weekly two-hour sessions. The first session is a teacher-driven lecture, with supplementary exercises done in the LMS right after the lecture part. The exercises are designed for students to actively engage into topics covered in the lecture. The other session is a demonstration session, where the students present their solutions to the programming tasks given to them a week earlier. Before the end of the course, the students complete a course project, which is a more extensive programming task. Typically, two final weeks of the course are reserved for completing the project, and additional guidance is offered to students who feel they might need it.

At the final week of the course, an electronic exam is taken. The exam is done using the LMS, and it typically consists of five to seven programming assignments accompanied with a quiz, a sorting or categorizing exercise, and one or two open questions (such as "What do we mean by saying that strings in Python are immutable" or "Describe the program code given in detail"). The essay type questions are evaluated by teacher, while all other exercises are automatically assessed. The principle behind using an electronic exam is to provide a coding experience that resembles real programming as closely as possible. This means that the code can be tested, debugged and refactored as many times as needed within a three-hour time limit.

The structure of the course is presented in Table 1. As seen in the table, the course is a rather typical programming course about the imperative paradigm. The weekly structure is not strict: only one two-hour session was used

Week #	Topic
1*	Course introduction
2	Variables and expressions
3	String operations
4	Conditional statements
5	Repetition
6	Procedures and functions
7	Lists
8	Lists (cont., including matrices) and tuples
9	Dictionaries, sets
10	File operations
11	Python's modules
12	Handling errors
13**	Course project

Table 1: The structure of the university course (UC). * = Only half a week, ** = one and a half weeks.

for course introduction, and the final two-hour session was spent on course project. Object-oriented programming is not discussed, although method calls and object creation are briefly referred to when introducing for example file or string operations.

The LMS was used quite extensively throughout the course. For each week (except for the two final rounds), a round consisting of seven to ten online exercises was offered. The LMS was also used for recording the attendances in the lectures, demonstration scores and the course project submissions and evaluation. There was a minimum limit for demonstrations (40%) and online exercises (50%) that needed to be completed to attend the final exam. If a student exceeded the limit, he or she could collect some bonus points for the final exam. There was no minimum requirement for attending the lectures, but the students who attended 10 or 11 of them (excluding the course project assistance sessions at weeks 12 or 13) also gained a few bonus points for the final exam.

The course was gradually developed between the years 2010 and 2014. A complete description of the development as well as the results can be found in [9].

4.2 Programming Course at Highschool Level

The second course observed (N = 41) is a programming course taught at junior high school level (JHSC) (in Finland, the participants are from grades eight and nine, being 14 to 15 year olds). It is an optional course for all students, and is also taught using Python as the programming language. The design is based on the same principles than in the university level programming course, but the methodology is developed further. Still, active learning is emphasized, and the LMS is used extensively throughout the course. The materials are designed to be a little lighter than in the university level, but the learning goals are still similar.

The course is divided into seven modules and into total of 17 two-hour sessions. The seventeenth session is reserved for the final exam. Typically, each module consists of three sections:

1. Lecture is similar to lectures in the university level programming course: a theoretical introduction to the topic followed by supplementary online exercises.

2. Tutorial consists of automatically assessed exercises accompanied with learning material (such as text, code examples, tables and images). The materials are typically a summary of lecture slides, presenting the most relevant topics needed to complete the exercises. The tutorials are answered in collaboration with other student, and discussion is encouraged.

3. Practical work consists of five to six programming tasks. This is the only section which is completed outside of the LMS, although the answers are still submitted into the system if the teacher wants to assess them. The practical work is completed in collaboration with another student.

An electronic exam, similar to one described in the previous section, was used in the high school course as well. The course structure is displayed in Table 2.

The course was modeled after the design principles and experiences collected from university level courses by the research group. A complete description of them can be found in [8] and [7].

4.3 Course Comparison

The course structures and methodologies resemble each other quite closely. Still, there are some methodological differences that need to be noted when the performance is compared. The methodology used in JHSC is a redesigned version of the one used in UC, and hence contains some research-based (see e.g. [8] and [7]) improvements. The most notable difference is the utilization of tutorial-based learning. In UC, online exercises were delivered without supplementary material attached (although the students could download the lecture slides right after the lecture), while in JHSC the exercises were accompanied with learning material. Another notable difference is the utilization of collaborative work in JHSC, which has been proven to be highly beneficial for learning results (see for example [14]). Finally, a formal feedback cycle was utilized in JHSC, while in the UC the students were required to fill only the opening and closing surveys. A comprehensive comparison of courses is displayed in Table 3.

5. RESEARCH SETUP

In order to find out whether the methodology previously proven effective at university level could be utilized with younger students as well, we compared an instance of the high school programming course (JHSC) to an instance of the university level course (UC). With this, we attempt to find answers to the following research problems:

1. Can the methodology be used effectively to teach all topics in the high school programming course?

2. If the learning performance is not similar throughout the courses, can we isolate individual topics where the differences occur?

3. If such topics can be isolated, can we find plausible reasons for the discovered differences?

The research was conducted with one instance of UC and one instance of JHSC. The instances, participants and the study methods are described in the following subsections.

5.1 Data Sets

For the JHSC, the data consisted of students' lecture survey answers for each of the lectures, as well as the assignment submission data for each of the assignments. There were a total of 12854 submissions to 129 assignments. The UC data set consisted of a similar set of assignment submissions as the JHSC, with 10710 submissions to 119 assignments. The assignments were grouped together to form lecture-sized rounds, and those rounds were grouped together form the

Module #	Topic
1	Introduction, variables and expressions
2	String operations
3	Conditional statements
4	Repetition
5	Functions
6	Lists
7	Python's module, file operations (briefly)

Table 2: The structure of the junior high school course (JHSC).

course itself. Each student could submit multiple submission to each of the assignments. On the university and JHS courses, there were eight and seven rounds with educational content, respectively.

6. RESULTS

6.1 About the Similarity of Student Scores Between the Two Courses

Each of the groups A–F that are listed in the Table 4 were tested for similarity using Kolmogorov–Smirnov test. The p-values of the tests are listed in the Table 5. The test results show that the students achieve similar performance on both of the programming courses. Only Group D (Loops) showed differing student performance between the two courses, so that the students on the JHSC receive worse scores for the content group D than the students on the UC.

While student populations show similar performance for most of the content groups, it might be possible that either of the student groups would consistently outperform the other group, but with so small a margin that it would remain undetected by the statistical tests. In order to account for this scenario, students' normalized score distributions from both courses were checked visually for all content groups, and examined for differences. Apart from the content group D, there is no systematic difference between the medians of the two courses.

6.2 About the Assignment Submission Counts Between the Two Courses

While submission scores are distributed quite similarly within the different content groups, the same does not apply for the average assigment submission counts within the same groups. By average, the students on the university course submit their assignments twice, regardles of the content groups (see Figure 1), whereas on the JHSC students tend to do more submissions, especially for the content groups E and F (see Figure 2). Groups E and F also have a much higher variance than the other content groups. Group D that displays differences between the two courses for the submission score distributions has similar median submission count as the earlier content groups A, B and C, but it has a higher variance than the preceding content groups do.

Round content	Group ID	Index 1 (UC)	Index 2 (JHSC)
Introduction	A	1, 2	1
Strings	B	3	2
Selection	C	4	3
Loops	D	5	4
Procedures	E	6	5
Lists	F	7	6

Table 4: The round mapping between the two courses. The rounds were ordered and taught in a similar order to omit any problems with the round ordering. On both courses, the students were taught some content after the mapped rounds, but these rounds were omitted from the analysis.

Round content	Group ID	K-S test p-value
Introduction	A	0.543
Strings	B	0.54
Selection	C	0.995
Loops	D	0
Procedures	E	0.637
Lists	F	0.238

Table 5: P-values for the Kolmogorov–Smirnov tests between the score distributions of the mapped parts of the university and junior high school courses. Only for the Group D the score distributions differ statistically from each other.

6.3 About the Student Activity on the Courses

Students have very different activity patterns on the two courses. Students on the UC remain active even after the course events and work on the course material outside the class room, while students on the JHSC work very little or not at all on their free time. The difference between the study habits can be seen from the Figures 3 and 4. The reasons behind these differences are discussed in the section 7.

7. DISCUSSION

Based on the analysis of the similarity of submission scores and times, it seems that the methodology worked equally well for JHS students in all topics, with the exception of repetition. In that round, the JHS group performed significantly worse (the difference was statistically significant with $p = 0.001$), while in all other rounds no statistically significant differences were found. The course methodologies were designed in similar fashion for most parts. The most notable differences are the introduction of tutorials and feedback in the JHS level, and the inclusion of a course project in the university level course.

There are some possible reasons for the JHS students' worse performance in the repetition round. First, to find out if the students reported any particular difficulties, the answers to feedback surveys in the repetition round were analyzed. Notably, there was only a single student reporting technical difficulties. However, when the submission counts to feedback surveys were analyzed, an anomaly was detected (see Table 6).

As seen in Table 6, the amount of feedback given in round 4 was much lower than in other rounds. When analyzing the

Element	UC	JHSC
Lectures	Yes	Yes
Supplementary online exercises	Yes	Yes
Main online exercises	As independent rounds	As tutorials
Practical work	Yes (as demonstrations)	Yes
Feedback cycle	Opening and closing surveys	Feedback after each section
Attendances recorded	Yes	No, attendance is mandatory
Final project	Yes	No
Electronic exam	Yes	Yes

Table 3: Comparison of the courses.

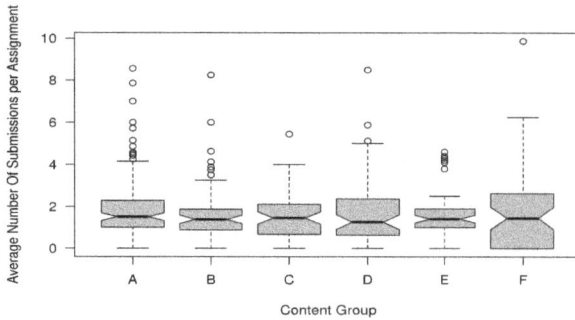

Figure 1: Boxplots of the average submission counts per assignment for the different content groups on the university course. The average submission counts remain fairly constant for all content groups. There were 3 cases where the student had by average more than ten submissions per assignment in an individual content group. These were removed from the figure to improve its readability.

Module #	Topic	Submissions to feedback surveys
1	Introduction, variables and expressions	31
2	String operations	32
3	Conditional statements	30
4	Repetition	19
5	Functions	27
6	Lists	36
7	Python's module, file operations	27

Table 6: Number of submission made into feedback surveys in each round of JHSC

feedback in more detail it seems that the amount of negative feedback given throughout the course was very low. It is hence possible that the low total amount of feedback indicates more negative experiences that just were not reported. The lower number of feedback could also indicate lower participation in the repetition round. However, since there is no drop in the total number of exercise submissions in that round (see Figure 2), this seems highly unlikely.

Both courses were taught by teachers that were experienced in teaching computer science and programming, and both courses were taught using the same sets of course material. While it is impossible to definitively prove that the reported differences are not caused by differences in the teaching, it remains unlikely that this is the case.

All in all, the younger students seem to work more to get the same results. The submission counts (as visualized in Figures 1 and 2) for all rounds are higher in all rounds of JHSC. It also notable that the submission counts in the university level course have a very little variation, while in the JHS level there are large differences between individual rounds. The very high number of submissions done in the 'Functions' round is particularly interesting. It seems that the students worked a lot harder on that round to compensate on the worse success in the previous round. The statis-

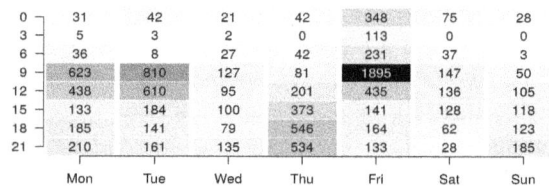

Figure 2: Average submission counts per assignment for the content groups on the junior high school course. The average submission counts vary significantly, and especially for the content groups E and F the variance of the submission counts increases when compared to the earlier content groups. There were 2 cases where the student had by average more than ten submissions per assignment in an individual content group. These were removed from the figure to improve its readability.

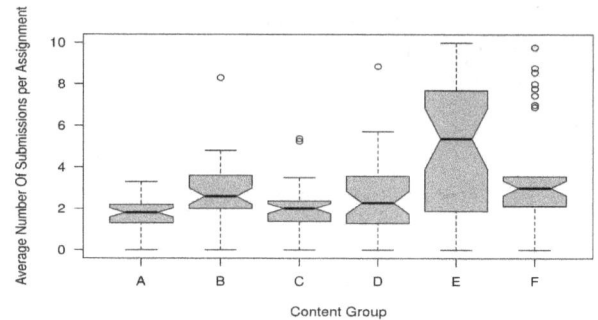

Figure 3: Student submission activity on the university course. Each cell in the figure shows the cumulative amount of submissions that were made on a specific weekday during a three hour time interval. The students are most active during the tutorials, but work also outside the lectures and tutorials, as well as in the evenings.

tical differences between JHS and university rounds seem to confirm this: the difference in the repetition vanished in the subsequent topic. Still, it should be noted that the standard deviation is a lot higher in the JHS course than it is in the university level course, so the submission counts vary a lot more among JHS students.

The submission behavior also seems to be highly different among the younger students, as seen in Figures 3 and 4. The students at the junior high school seem to submit almost exclusively during the class hours, while the students at university level submit evenly throughout the week. There are some obvious structural reasons for this: the students at JHS had dedicated tutorial sessions throughout the course where the majority of submissions seems to have been made. Still, it seems that the students in the JHS level work very little outside classroom. This might also be one of the reasons for the worse learning performance in the repetition round: it could be possible (though there is no obvious evidence

	Mon	Tue	Wed	Thu	Fri	Sat	Sun
0	0	0	0	0	0	0	0
3	0	0	0	0	0	0	0
6	0	0	0	0	7	0	0
9	7396	1	0	0	0	0	9
12	5103	1	0	2	0	0	31
15	18	0	66	2	9	0	38
18	40	3	30	0	0	20	34
21	1	0	0	0	13	0	30

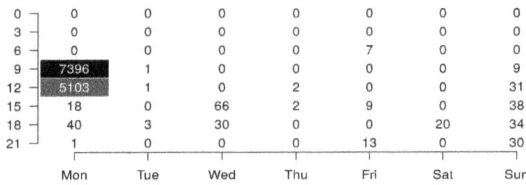

Figure 4: Student submission activity on the JHS course. The JHS students are active only during the tutorials, and spend little to no time on the assignments apart from the tutorials.

of this) that had the students kept on working outside the class hours, the difference could have been smaller. Based on the results, it might be possible that at least some of the students in the JHS level are mostly externally motivated, while in the university level the motivation is more internal. However, motivation is notoriously difficult to measure [17], and there is no direct evidence to support the assumption, especially as JHS students achieve as high scores as the university students.

All in all, it still seems that the same methodology we have applied successfully in the university level can be used effectively to teach programming in the junior high school level as well. There are differences in the learning performance, submission behavior and study habits, but in authors' opinion none of them are too dramatic. Still, the statistical differences provide valuable information which could be potentially used to fine-tune the methodologies used to teach programming for younger students. For example, the tendency to only perform course work during class hours is probably not a new issue for teachers at such levels, but it still drastically decreases the number of hours spent working during the course. The worse performance in the repetition round is also something that should be addressed, for example by dedicating more sessions to the topic.

8. REFERENCES

[1] A. F. Blackwell. What is programming. In *14th workshop of the Psychology of Programming Interest Group*, 2002.

[2] B. DiSalvo. Graphical qualities of educational technology: Using drag-and-drop and text-based programs for introductory computer science. *IEEE Computer Graphics and Applications*, 36(6):12–15, 2014.

[3] B. Du Boulay. Some difficulties of learning to program. In E. Soloway and J. Spohrer, editors, *Studying the Novice Programmer*, pages 283–299. Lawrence Erlbaum Associates, London, 1989.

[4] J.-M. Hoc, T. R. G. Green, R. Samurcay, and D. J. e. Gilmore. *Psychology of programming*. Academic Press, 2014.

[5] J. Holvitie, T. Rajala, R. Haavisto, E. Kaila, M.-J. Laakso, and T. Salakoski. Breaking the programming language barrier: Using program visualizations to transfer programming knowledge in one programming

language to another. In *12th International Conference on Advanced Learning Technologies (ICALT)*, 2012.

[6] E. Kaila, E. Kurvinen, E. Lokkila, M.-J. Laakso, and T. Salakoski. Enhancing student-teacher communication in programming courses: a case study using weekly surveys. In *Proceedings of ICEE 2015 - International Conference on Engineering Education*, 2015.

[7] E. Kaila, E. Kurvinen, E. Lokkila, M.-J. Laakso, and T. Salakoski. Redesigning an object-oriented programming course. *Accepted for publication in The ACM Transactions on Computing Education*, 2016.

[8] E. Kaila, T. Rajala, M.-J. Laakso, R. Lindén, E. Kurvinen, V. Karavirta, and S. T. Comparing student performance between traditional and technologically enhanced programming course. In *Proceedings of the Seventeenth Australasian Computing Education Conference (ACE2015), Sydney, Australia*, Sydney, Australia, 2015.

[9] E. Kaila, T. Rajala, M.-J. Laakso, R. Lindén, E. Kurvinen, and T. Salakoski. Utilizing an exercise-based learning tool effectively in computer science courses. *Olympiads in Informatics*, 8, 2014.

[10] M.-J. Laakso, E. Kaila, and T. Rajala. Ville – designing and implementing a collaborative education tool. *Submitted into British Journal of Educational Technology*, 2016.

[11] A. Matthíasdóttir. How to teach programming languages to novice students? lecturing or not. In *International Conference on Computer Systems and Technologies-CompSysTech*, volume 6, 2006.

[12] J. P. McCarthy and L. Anderson. Active learning techniques versus traditional teaching styles: two experiments from history and political science. *Innovative Higher Education*, 24(4):279–294, 2000.

[13] M. McCracken, V. Almstrum, D. Diaz, M. Guzdial, D. Hagan, Y. B. D. Kolikant, and T. Wilusz. A multi-national, multi-institutional study of assessment of programming skills of first-year cs students. *ACM SIGCSE Bulletin*, 33(4):125–180, 2001.

[14] T. Rajala, E. Kaila, J. Holvitie, R. Haavisto, M.-J. Laakso, and T. Salakoski. Comparing the collaborative and independent viewing of program visualizations. In *Frontiers in Education 2011 conference, October 12-15*, Rapid City, South Dakota, USA, 2011.

[15] T. Rajala, M.-J. Laakso, E. Kaila, and T. Salakoski. Effectiveness of program visualization: A case study with the ville tool. *Journal of Information Technology Education: Innovations in Practice*, 7:15–32, 2008.

[16] T. Rajala, E. Lokkila, R. Lindén, M.-J. Laakso, and T. Salakoski. Students' perceptions on collaborative work in introductory programming course. In *Proceedings of the EDULEARN15 Conference*, pages 2795–2800, 2015.

[17] M. Touré-Tillery and A. Fishbach. How to measure motivation: A guide for the experimental social psychologist. *Social and Personality Psychology Compass*, 8:328–341, 2014.

[18] D. Weintrop and U. Wilensky. To block or not to block, that is the question: Students' perceptions of blocks-based programming. In *Proceedings of IDC '15, June 21-25, 2015, Medford, MA, USA*. ACM, 2015.

Nailing the TA Interview: Using a Rubric to Hire Teaching Assistants

Dan Leyzberg
dl9@cs.princeton.edu

Jérémie Lumbroso
lumbroso@cs.princeton.edu

Christopher Moretti
cmoretti@cs.princeton.edu

Department of Computer Science
Princeton University

ABSTRACT

Where would we be without them? Teaching assistants (TAs) make it possible for us to deliver high-quality large-scale computer science courses with relatively few faculty. Though their responsibilities vary by institution, TAs often play a crucial role in student learning. The use of teaching assistants in computer science courses is a common and long-standing practice and, yet, little has been published about how to choose the best TAs among those interested in the job. This paper describes the development of an interview rubric in use by faculty teaching a large introductory computer science course to score applicant responses in a formal in-person 30-minute interview. We describe the motivation behind developing such a rubric, the initial development process, its refinement based on feedback provided by students about their TAs, and the preliminary results of implementing this hiring system.

CCS Concepts

•Social and professional topics → *Computer science education;*

Keywords

teaching assistants; hiring; hiring practices; hiring rubric; job interview; large courses; course management; course staff

1. BACKGROUND

Teaching assistants (TAs) serve a vital role in many college computer science departments. In some cases, their responsibilities can be quite extpensive. Typically, TAs perform one or more of the following functions: delivering course material, holding review sessions, offering one-on-one tutoring, running office hours, answering questions online, offering debugging support in a computer lab, or grading.

Teaching with large teams of TAs and the use of undergraduates as teaching assistants began in response to the surge of enrollment in computer science in the 1980's [11]

ITiCSE '17, July 3–5, 2017, Bologna, Italy.

© 2017 Copyright held by the owner/author(s). Publication rights licensed to ACM.
ISBN 978-1-4503-4704-4/17/07. . . $15.00

DOI: http://dx.doi.org/10.1145/3059009.3059057

and continues as a common practice at many institutions today.

TAs allow faculty to distribute an otherwise impossibly large workload among a big team and they allow for more students to discover and learn computer science than would be possible without their help. Despite this, formal discussion and research on hiring practices for teaching assistants in computer science is limited.

The implementation details of the undergraduate TA programs in various settings have been documented and evaluated, including TA programs at large research institutions such as Stanford [11, 12], the University of Arizona [10], and the University of Buffalo [2], as well as those at smaller liberal arts colleges like Hampshire College [3]. This body of work focuses on the responsibilities given to TAs and how they are supported and evaluated by the faculty and their peers, rather than how they are hired.

Another body of work on teaching assistants in computer science courses is that of training programs designed to train TAs to be more successful in the classroom [5, 10] or lab setting [8]. This work focuses on activities and lessons designed to improve the quality of teaching of TAs-in-training, but does not explicitly define the qualities that make for a good teaching assistant, nor how to interview potential TAs.

Decker *et al.* [2] describe hiring criteria (*i.e.*, scoring well on the final for the course, giving a good sample presentation/lecture) and an interview process (*i.e.*, evaluated by other TAs), but not the specific questions asked during the interview, nor how the candidates responses are scored.

Patitsas *et al.* [7] describe five desirable qualities of teaching assistants (*i.e.*, well prepared, helpful, considerate, easily understood, and effective instructor) but did not define those qualities in detail nor describe how to assess them in an interview setting.

The process of determining whether a prospective TA will be successful is susceptible to unconscious biases if not formalized. To minimize this bias, the authors advocate preparing a fixed set of interview questions and an associated scoring rubric in advance, as is done in other fields [9] and in the private sector (*e.g.*, see Bock's book [1] on hiring practices at Google). This formalization can make hiring practices more consistent and fairer to candidates, leading to a more diverse and more effective staff [6].

This paper outlines the authors' approach to formalizing the hiring process for graduate teaching assistants in a large first-semester course in computer science.

2. DEVELOPING A RUBRIC

It is widely considered a good pedagogical practice to use grading rubrics to ensure consistency between students and, where applicable, between graders. Using rubrics allows us to avoid unintentionally incorporating our unconscious biases into the scores and feedback we give students, ensuring that students' work is judged fairly by standards set in advance. Hiring rubrics, similarly, allow us to ensure consistency and equity in our hiring processes.

When interviewing candidates for teaching assistant positions, some interviewers and interviewees may have more in common and may form a stronger personal connection during the interview process than other pairs of interviewers and interviewees. This sort of personal association bias can be hard to separate from the evaluation of the prospective teaching assistant's readiness and talents [4]. By using a more structured interview process, one with standardized questions and procedures for scoring the candidate's responses, we can mitigate these biases.

Furthermore, when there are several interviewers, not all of which will attend every interview, rubrics are an easier and more systematic way to share the outcome of an interview.

Finally, although we have until now described a hiring process, an interview rubric may also prove helpful in the common situation where the choice of TAs is not up to the staff[1]. In this case, the rubric can help identify the strengths and weaknesses of a TA with some advanced notice, to the effect that it is possible to do something to compensate.

This practice of creating an interview rubric, listing desired qualities in a candidate in advance of meeting them, along with a standardized set of interview questions intended to assess these qualities, is common practice in industry, especially in technical interviews such as those conducted by Google [1, pp. 94-98].

The first step in developing an interview rubric is to compile a list of desirable characteristics in a teaching assistant. In doing so, it is important to recognize that the desirable characteristics of a teaching assistant for one course may vary from those desirable in another course. Desirable characteristics can also be influenced by the institution and the responsibilities the TA needs to take on, as well as the culture of the university or college at large. What we present in this paper is a sample of desirable characteristics, based on a rubric designed around graduate students who lead small-group sections two times per week in a large introductory course in computer science.

3. SAMPLE RUBRIC

The qualities described in this sample rubric (see Table 1) are defined and discussed in this paper, but are not intended to be universal. This section is intended to provide context for how we chose each of these desirable qualities for the TAs in our course and how we use the interview process to assess each of these qualities.

We include a sample rubric to motivate the choices we made in designing interview questions for one course at one university. In the future, we would like to extend this work to examine the hiring practices in other colleges, with different constraints than our own, but we believe this rubric to be an important first step for research in computer science education.

3.1 Clear and confident speaker

The first desirable quality in our sample rubric describes a teaching assistant's ability to speak clearly and confidently. While many communication skills are important for effective teaching, the ability to speak clearly and confidently is especially important for communicating in a technical field like computer science.

When potential TAs are weak in this skill, we find that they tend to exhibit one or more of the following behaviors during an interview:

(a) They speak too quickly, without checking whether the listener or audience is following.

(b) They frequently veer off topic in conversation, often without noticing.

(c) They display nervous body language or do not make eye contact.

(d) They frequently use hedge words and phrases such as "*like,*" "*sort of,*" or "*I think.*"

These communication problems can result in a loss of clarity. Students tend to form the impression, whether justified or not, that such TAs do not know the material or that their teaching methods are not effective. When TAs demonstrate these problems, the feedback students give on course evaluations tends to be varied and general, such as, "*His teaching is not very effective,*" or "*Engage the class more, actually teach us things.*" These two pieces of feedback come from an evaluation of a former TA who we know to be knowledgeable and committed to the job, but who struggled with confidence and clarity.

3.2 Active listener

We could not do our jobs as educators if we were not able to respond to our students' concerns and difficulties. Our listening skills play an important role, separate from our ability to speak clearly and confidently, in successfully addressing the potential misunderstandings of our students.

When TAs are weak in this skill, we find that they tend to exhibit one or more of the following behaviors during an interview:

(a) They frequently interrupt the interviewer mid-sentence. This behavior can deeply frustrate students, who often need more time than the interviewer to formulate their questions.

(b) They focus on their own ideas at the expense of the interviewer's. This can be a sign that the candidate is not willing to take on the perspective of his or her conversation partner—not an ideal situation for teaching.

(c) They do not answer the questions being asked of them, instead discussing a related subject or a previous subject.

---

[1]This can be the case, for instance, when the pool of applicants is too small; when teaching is a mandatory component of a student's tuition, and it is therefore not possible to fire a TA; when TAs have already been appointed to a course by an administrative process; etc.

	Unacceptable	Acceptable	Ideal
Clear and confident speaker	speaks too quickly or difficult to parse words	speaks clearly but lacks confidence	confident speaker, good communication skills
Active listener	frequently interrupts others mid-sentence	interested primarily in his/her own ideas	checks assumptions, asks clarifying questions
Will hold students' attention	sedate, unenthusiastic	enthusiastic but tempered personality	energetic, enthusiastic, has a "watchable quality"
Empathetic towards struggling students	not aware of struggling students or has a sink-or-swim mentality	shows concern about struggling students, but takes little action	seeks out struggling students, meets for review sessions
Interested in improving own teaching	does not acknowledge own teaching problems	open to new teaching methods, but reluctant	openly critical of his/her own teaching methods
Prefers interactive teaching methods	prefers to lecture at students	interested in active learning methods	developed hands-on activities for students
Sensitive to the freshman experience	prefers to teach "grown ups"	feels enthusiastic about teaching young people	has experience teaching young people
Proponent of CS as a major/discipline	little knowledge of CS courses/topics	excited about only one or a few CS topics	excited about a variety of CS topics
Familiar with Java programming	little or no experience in Java or C++	class assignments and other small programs	industry experience or taught course in Java
Familiar with data structures	"what is a linked list?"	took a data structures course	conversant in data structures
Familiar with CS theory topics	"what is a finite state machine?"	took a theory course	conversant in theory topics
Familiar with circuits & architecture	"what is a flip-flop?"	took a circuits or an architecture course	conversant in circuits or architecture topics

Table 1: Sample rubric used to interview the TAs that will be teaching in an introductory computer science, which incorporates some advanced concepts (such as circuits, architecture, automata, regular expressions, P vs. NP, etc.). The questions are organized roughly as follows: first they address general teaching abilities; then they focus on abilities which are especially pertinent for an introductory computer science course; finally we discuss some of the specific topics of the course's syllabus. In Section 3, some of these skills are discussed, and when appropriate, we illustrate, through student evaluations, how students experience a TA lacking any one of these skills.

The presence of active listening skills are sometimes expressed as pacing feedback in student evaluations, for example:

- *"[My TA] frequently asks the students if she is teaching too fast or too slow, and generally shows that she cares a lot about the students learning."*

- *"Instead of asking the students if everyone's clear on an important subject, it's usually a safe bet to assume someone did not understand it and explain it anyway."*

Active listening skill may also sometimes be described in student evaluations as patience: *"[My TA] is very good at explaining things in a clear, concise way. He is also extremely patient when going over concepts one-on-one in office hours."*

3.3 Holds students' attention

In addition to speaking and listening skills, showmanship and enthusiasm can be important skills in the classroom. This may be easier for extravert candidates, but a relatively quiet, introvert candidate can captivate students' attention with other qualities, such as dry humor or (mild) self-deprecation or otherwise being relatable to their peers.

When a TA lacks this quality, we find that in interviews they tend to:

(a) Talk very quietly or monotonously.

(b) Project a sedate, disinterested affect.

(c) Avoid making eye contact.

In course evaluations, students tend to address the absence of this quality directly, such as: *"Try to vary your tone of voice more," "smile more :)"* or, simply, *"More energy."*

3.4 Empathetic towards struggling students

Sometimes a potential TA may be an excellent student as well as being able to communicate about the material very proficiently with his or her peers, but not be able to understand the problems that novice or struggling students face in synthesizing the material in the course.

In an interview, when a potential TA is weak in this skill, they tend to:

(a) Lack awareness of the existence of struggling students around them or be dismissive towards the difficulty of the material.

(b) Demonstrate an overabundance of confidence in their abilities as a teacher. We are dubious when students claim they have never had a lesson or presentation not go as planned.

A lack of empathy can show up in student evaluations as unintended sarcasm or condescension:

- *"Sometimes answers to questions seem a bit condescending or patronizing."*

- *"Sometimes, he assumes that we know some things, but to a beginner it can be quite confusing."*

- *"Please answer all questions! Sometimes he can be a bit patronizing which is discouraging for new programmers like me."*

Although different educators will debate the relative importance of this point (perhaps even more so in a non introductory course), it bears remarking that most insidiously, unlike other skills discussed in this rubric, when TAs lack empathy, students have the potential to take it personally and get permanently discouraged: *"I was very confused for all but one [class] this semester. Every time I asked a question, I was made to feel stupid by [my TA's] reply. As a result, I stopped asking questions."*

3.5 Interested in improving own teaching

Some TAs, though outstanding in many other ways, are not able or willing to adapt to new teaching methods or exercises that are unfamiliar to them.

This rigidity, sometimes born of stubbornness, can be limiting, as it can make the planned exercises and lessons significantly less effective for this TA's students than how they are experienced by students who have other TAs. This typically comes up with overconfident TAs or ones who believe that their teaching methods are above reproach.

We find that TAs who demonstrate this behavior typically:

(a) Have had difficulties in previous courses for which they have TA'ed.

(b) Are unable to criticize or find fault in their own teaching methods and practice. For instance, when asked to describe a lesson or talk they gave that did not go as planned, they might answer, "All my lessons have been very good, I prepare for them very diligently." As interviewers, we typically give such a student a second chance to answer this question and continued insistence on their perfection can cause some concern among our staff.

3.6 Prefers interactive teaching methods

Related to, but not the same as the point above, some TAs have little experience or trust in interactive activities as means of pedagogy. Though this is not commonly a disqualifying characteristic for our interview process, this can be a warning sign about a TA's tendency towards a "sage on the stage" mentality. An ideal TA candidate for our course believes in active learning and has developed, or considered how to refine, worksheets or group activities in other courses.

3.7 Sensitive to the freshman experience

As a large introductory course, our enrollments are three-quarters first-year students. As a result, we are concerned if a potential TA dismisses such students' concerns or seems severely out of touch with the first-year experience.

First-year students have different needs than returning students and may require special attention (for instance, they are generally not as aware of the various ways they can get help, even if these have been advertised as incoming students generally have a lot to process). An ideal TA candidate is someone who will help a student who is lost on campus or reach out to a student that appears to be in trouble.

3.8 Proponent of CS as a major/discipline

When we are interviewing prospective TAs from the field for a course that is meant to survey computer science and support students who are considering CS as their major, we stress the importance of being an advocate for other courses in CS.

We find that prospective TAs who show little enthusiasm for other computer science courses are a poor fit for our course.

3.9 Familiarity with course material

Comprehensive content knowledge is very important for teaching assistants, but thorough testing for it is not a feature of the interview because it can be tested independent of an interview.

We do ask about content knowledge at a higher level, however, first as a means of checking with the potential TA that they have the background we expect, and second as an opportunity for them to demonstrate that they can describe their knowledge clearly and confidently.

4. INTERVIEW QUESTIONS

Standardizing a set of interview questions in advance is important for ensuring consistency and fairness in hiring practices. Below, we will describe a sample set of interview questions currently in use by faculty at a highly-selective university to interview teaching assistant candidates for a large introductory course in computer science. These questions are not meant to be exhaustive or definitive, but rather a demonstration of how to write interview questions for the sample rubric above.

Introduction of self and course. We find that the best way to start an interview is to introduce ourselves and discuss some significant details about the way our courses are run and the responsibilities of a TA. We pause for questions and establish a common ground upon which the remainder of the interview is based.

Trust-building. Following that, we invite the candidate to tell us more about themselves, by asking some of the following questions and allowing for follow-up questions:

- How long have you been in your academic program? How do you like it so far?

- Where were you before this program? What was that like?

- Where are you from? How do you like living in this town?

The goal of these questions is to establish trust for the remainder of the interview and assess the ability of the candidate to hold an audience's attention.

Teaching experience. After the trust-building and introductions, we ask about teaching experience:

- Do you have any classroom teaching experience? *(Most of our candidates do not.)*

- If not, have you ever done any tutoring, perhaps for family or as a teaching assistant in a previous course?

- Could you tell me about a time you felt particularly proud of a lesson/talk you gave? In particular, could you tell me what about this lesson/talk was particularly effective to facilitate the students' learning?

- Could you tell me about a time when you gave a lesson/talk that did not go as planned and what you would do differently next time?

- Could you tell me about any teaching materials that you created? This could be notes from class, slides for a presentation, etc.

The goal of these questions is to assess the potential TA's level of experience, as well as their empathy and openness to new teaching methods. The most important question of these is the second-to-last, where an ideal response reveals awareness of struggling students, interest in improving teaching, clear and confident speaking, active listening, and ability to hold an audience's attention.

Course-specific aptitude. Afterwards, we discuss the applicant's content knowledge relevant to our specific course's needs:

- How would you describe your experience with the Java programming language? If little or none, have you had any experience with C++?

- In this course we teach introductory programming and a survey of CS topics including data structures, theory, and circuits. Would you feel comfortable explaining what order of growth is (*i.e.*, Big-O notation)? Would you feel comfortable explaining what the concept of a "node" is in a linked list?

In the answers to these questions, we are looking for a confirmation of content knowledge, as well as the confidence and clarity of the candidates' explanations.

Responsibilities and questions. Lastly, we discuss the responsibilities of the course with the candidate. This includes the weekly time commitment we require of TAs, and what duties we typically expect, as well as an opportunity to customize a role to each student. The candidate's response is a key indicator of their general interest in the job as well as the specific responsibilities and curricular items that they find the most appealing. We can use this in developing our partage of the work in such a way as to maximize enthusiasm and engagement from our TAs.

5. DISCUSSION

First and foremost, the authors would like to emphasize that there is no one rubric or interview procedure that is appropriate for all courses or all institutions. The sample rubric we provide here and the interview procedure we describe are heavily influenced by the needs of our students, the curriculum of our course, and the resources and limitations of our university. We encourage the reader to develop his or her own rubric and formalized interview procedure using ours as a starting point.

We have found that creating interview scripts and rubrics is an inherently iterative process. As we train more TAs and see more student feedback and continue to use the script and rubric in our hiring, we arrive at more tweaks and additions, or perhaps consolidations to our materials. Perhaps there is no perfect rubric and interview script, but maintaining our best attempt encourages critical thinking about hiring practices that we find quite helpful.

Hiring via Rubric Leads to More "Excellent" TAs

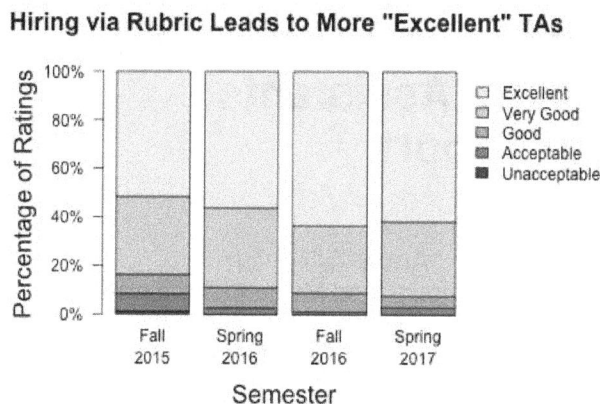

Figure 1: Student evaluations of TA performance in a large introductory course (N>200 each semester). This interview process was first used in Spring 2016.

We also find that, while having an interview script is important, it is sometimes quite valuable to ask off-script questions, or follow tangential topics as they arise naturally in conversation in order to best assess a candidate's readiness and talent. In addition, it is also sometimes necessary to ask the same questions over again in slightly different ways so candidates have a second chance to understand what is being asked. This is not necessary for all interviews, but is certainly something we encourage. Thus, a certain amount of flexibility is advised, even when using a script to conduct interviews.

Unfortunately, as we commented earlier, at some institutions, course staff members do not have the ability of choosing TAs. Instead, they may be assigned by a graduate or undergraduate coordinator or a peer. It may seem that this paper could be of little relevance to those situations, but we find that interviewing TAs, even if we do not have flexibility in hiring decisions, can lead to a better understanding of who is on our teaching teams and what each member's relative strengths and weaknesses may be. When we are in this situation, we use this information to tailor the responsibilities of the TAs to their strengths and to maximize the effectiveness of the staff as a whole.

It is also important to note the role that student evaluations can play in understanding what the strengths and weaknesses of your TAs may be. We recommend, where possible, conducting an anonymous mid-semester evaluation. We then recommend showing this feedback to your teaching staff. (See Figure 1 for data from such surveys.) The survey questions we have found particularly effective are:

- What aspects of your TA's teaching are particularly effective to facilitate your learning in this course?
- What specific advice would you give your TA to help him/her improve your learning in this course?

6. CONCLUSION

Teaching assistants serve an indispensable role in large computer science courses. Through conducting interviews, we found that most students who apply for a teaching assistantship position sincerely want to pass on their knowledge and excitement for computer science to their peers. A formalized interview process can serve to identify the applicants' relative strengths and weaknesses, allowing course staff to create an environment for them that best suits their strengths and gives them an opportunity to develop further as teachers and communicators. The authors strongly believe that interviewing TAs is critical to the success of a large computer science course. The authors also believe that conducting such interviews with a formalized procedure and scoring rubric, developed in advance, has gone a long way to encouraging fairer hiring practices, resulting in stronger and more effective course staffs.

7. REFERENCES

[1] L. Bock. *Work Rules!: Insights from Inside Google That Will Transform How You Live and Lead.* Grand Central Publishing, 2015.

[2] A. Decker, P. Ventura, and C. Egert. Through the looking glass: reflections on using undergraduate teaching assistants in CS1. *ACM SIGCSE Bulletin*, 38(1):46–50, Mar. 2006.

[3] P. E. Dickson. Using undergraduate teaching assistants in a small college environment. In *the 42nd ACM technical symposium*, pages 75–80, New York, New York, USA, Mar. 2011. ACM.

[4] L. P. Fried, C. A. Francomano, S. M. MacDonald, E. M. Wagner, E. J. Stokes, K. M. Carbone, W. B. Bias, M. M. Newman, and J. D. Stobo. Career development for women in academic medicine: multiple interventions in a department of medicine. *Jama*, 276(11):898–905, 1996.

[5] D. G. Kay. Training computer science teaching assistants: a seminar for new TAs. *ACM SIGCSE Bulletin*, 27(1):53–55, Mar. 1995.

[6] S. Lazos. Are student teaching evaluations holding back women and minorities. *Presumed Incompetent:. The Intersections of Race and Class for Women in Academia*, 2012.

[7] E. Patitsas and P. Belleville. What can we learn from quantitative teaching assistant evaluations? In *Proceedings of the Seventeenth Western Canadian Conference on Computing Education.* ACM, 2012.

[8] E. A. Patitsas and S. A. Wolfman. Effective closed labs in early CS courses: lessons from eight terms of action research. In *the 43rd ACM technical symposium*, pages 637–642, New York, New York, USA, Feb. 2012. ACM.

[9] P. K. Patrick and A. G. Yick. Standardizing the interview process and developing a faculty interview rubric: An effective method to recruit and retain online instructors. *The Internet and Higher Education*, 8(3):199 – 212, 2005.

[10] S. Reges. Using undergraduates as teaching assistants at a state university. In *ACM SIGCSE Bulletin*, volume 35, pages 103–107. ACM, 2003.

[11] S. Reges, J. McGrory, and J. Smith. The Effective Use of Undergraduates to Staff Large Introductory CS Courses. In *ACM SIGCSE Bulletin*, pages 22–25. ACM, Feb. 1988.

[12] E. Roberts, J. Lilly, and B. Rollins. Using Undergraduates as Teaching Assistants in Introductory Programming Courses: an Update on the Stanford Experience. *ACM SIGCSE Bulletin*, 27(1):48–52, Mar. 1995.

Bridging the Gap Between Desired and Actual Qualifications of Teaching Assistants: An Experience Report

Francisco J. Estrada
Dept. of Computer and Mathematical Sciences
University of Toronto Scarborough
festrada@utsc.utoronto.ca

Anya Tafliovich
Dept. of Computer and Mathematical Sciences
University of Toronto Scarborough
atafliovich@utsc.utoronto.ca

ABSTRACT

We report on our experience implementing a Teaching Assistant Training Program for Computer Science Teaching Assistants. The program is rooted in the well-established Instructional Skills Workshop's principles and methodologies. We describe the structure of the program, reflect on its successes, and discuss future expansion of, and improvements to the program.

Categories and Subject Descriptors

K.3.2 [**Computers and Education**]: Computer and Information Science Education—*Computer Science Education*

Keywords

Instructional Skills Workshop, training program, teaching assistants, TA, ISW, quality of teaching, teaching methodologies

1. INTRODUCTION

With ever growing enrolments in Computer Science programs [13], and the consequent rise in the size of Computer Science classes, large institutions become increasingly reliant on teaching assistants (TAs) to support undergraduate teaching. Furthermore, many departments are faced with the lack of graduate students to fill all available TA positions, and are now employing undergraduate students as TAs [18]. Moreover, many educators agree on certain benefits of having undergraduate rather than graduate teaching assistants, especially in introductory Computer Science courses.

Teaching assistants become essential members of a teaching team for a large course. Their duties typically include delivering tutorials, supervising computer labs, grading homework assignments and tests, and holding office hours. These activities require a TA who has mastered various teaching skills, such as delivering an effective presentation, selecting

appropriate examples, keeping the students engaged, asking and answering student questions, and many more.

An undergraduate student hired for their first TA position is hardly expected to possess the above skills. The important question for many departments is how to use a large number of inexperienced (undergraduate or graduate) students as teaching assistants without compromising the quality of teaching and of student experience in the course.

In this report we present a well-structured TA Training program that is rooted in the principles and methodologies of the well-established Instructional Skills Workshop (ISW) [10, 9]. We explain the modifications that were made to the original ISW format to serve a new purpose and new participants, and report on our experience with the program.

The gap between desired and actual qualifications of teaching assistants demands a bridge of great length. The TA Training program described here is an attempt to build a foundation for such a bridge.

This work is not a report on a research study, as we do not present any data on improvements of TAs' performance, nor quality of students' experience. We are sharing our experience in running an innovative TA Training Program, which, we believe, can greatly assist course instructors in scaling CS courses in the face of growing enrolment numbers.

The paper is organized as follows: Section 2 discusses previously published work on using undergraduate teaching assistants and on alternative approaches to TA training. Section 3 describes our institution, the courses that utilize teaching assistants, the teaching assistants' typical duties, and their typical background when hired for the first TA position. Section 4 is the heart of the report as it introduces the ISW model, provides details of the TA Training program, and discusses its costs and benefits to the department. Section 5 suggests ways to expand and improve the program. Sections 6 summarizes and concludes the report.

2. RELATED WORK

Many institutions [4, 3, 5, 2, 6, 8, 7, 1] help their novice teaching assistants by way of putting together informative booklets, constructing websites that contain advice on teaching, holding workshops on improving TAs' teaching practices, etc. Most of these are not specific to Computer Science nor, more generally, to the exact sciences, and in the majority of cases are not compulsory. As for published work, we note the following:

Stephenson *et al.* [19] report on the effects of creating a position of a Teaching Assistant in Residence — an experi-

ITiCSE '17, July 03 - 05, 2017, Bologna, Italy

© 2017 Copyright held by the owner/author(s). Publication rights licensed to ACM.
ISBN 978-1-4503-4704-4/17/07...$15.00

DOI: http://dx.doi.org/10.1145/3059009.3059023

enced five-star TA with the responsibilities of aiding novice teaching assistants, including visiting their tutorials and offering (unstructured) personalized feedback.

Kay [14] describes a course for graduate teaching assistants. The course covers various aspects of teaching assistants' duties, offers ways to improve the participants' teaching skills, and provides opportunities for practicing through in-class exercises. In their institution, each graduate student is required to TA at least once, so the TA training course is also a program requirement.

Roberts *et al.* [17] describe their success in the use of undergraduate students in various roles as part of teaching staff. Reges [16] and later Decker *et al.* [11] report on similar successful initiatives of involving undergraduate students in teaching introductory Computer Science courses. These reports pertain to large classes and, consequently, large numbers of TAs. In contrast, Dickson [12] describes the benefits of using undergraduate TAs in small Computer Science classes in a small college environment. While reporting on using novice teaching assistants, these works do not discuss their training.

Interestingly, Patitsas [15] discusses professional development of teaching assistants without the aid of any specialized programs, but rather through practice, teaching multiple courses, experience with team teaching, and feedback.

3. ENVIRONMENT

The TA Training program we describe here was implemented at the University of Toronto, a public, research-intensive Canadian university. The university accommodates three campuses. Computer Science graduate programs and research activities mainly take place on one of the three campuses, and all three campuses offer complete undergraduate programs. The TA Training program was carried out at the Scarborough campus where its host department is mainly concerned with undergraduate teaching.

3.1 Enrolments and TA Positions

The first year Computer Science courses are large. At the time of writing this report the enrolments were (1) 754 students in CS1 for majors, (2) 702 students in CS2 for majors, (3) 939 students in Intro to Discreet Mathematics, and (4) 368 students in CS1 for non-CS students. These enrolment figures resulted in a total of 89 TAs required just for first-year Computer Science courses.

In second year, the enrolments in the five required Computer Science courses vary between 160 and 307 per course, which creates a total of 35 TA positions. Third and fourth year courses are numerous; some are required and others are electives, depending on the program. With enrolments varying between 7 and 230 per course, they produce 55 TA positions.

3.2 Teaching Assistants' Duties

Teaching Assistant's duties vary greatly between the courses. In CS1 and CS2, the TAs are responsible for conducting traditional tutorials (the TAs are provided with tutorial materials in advance), supervising computer labs, holding office hours, and grading homework assignments and quizzes/tests. In theoretical CS courses the duties are similar, minus the computer labs. In second and later year courses that involve team projects, TAs are often tasked with supervising and advising student teams, observing and assessing their progress and development process, and advising on successful teamwork strategies. In some of these later year courses, the TAs need to develop their own tutorial materials.

3.3 Qualifications, If Any

Given the plethora of duties and the high standards of teaching Computer Science in the department, the TAs need to be fairly competent teachers.

To conduct a successful tutorial, a TA needs to effectively use a blackboard and/or a podium computer with an overhead projector. In programming courses, live coding during class has now become standard in the department, and so the TA needs to master this skill. To keep the students engaged, the TA needs to effectively ask and answer student questions, to be able to generate a group discussion and keep it on track, to monitor the audience's attention and involvement, and to be able to confidently make decisions on the spot.

Given the department's unfortunately scarce resources, supervising computer labs requires a TA to attend to the needs of up to 35 students in the lab. Identifying and addressing common questions, leading the class in carrying out a programming exercise, and helping and directing students as they develop code, without producing the code for them, are all fairly sophisticated teaching skills.

Holding office hours and, even more so, advising student teams requires considerable perceptiveness, good judgment, and communication and problem solving skills.

Developing tutorial material calls for careful planning, time management, selecting appropriate examples, and accurate coordination with contents of lectures and homework assignments.

An experienced educator at this point chuckles and notices that they can count on the fingers of one hand the number of their teaching assistants, past and present, who had all the qualifications listed above. If they are lucky.

3.4 Participants

Given that it is unrealistic to hire 180 TAs with such exemplary qualifications, the questions are: Whom does the department hire as teaching assistants? What are their qualifications?

As enrolment in undergraduate Computer Science programs grows much faster than the number of graduate students, and given the focus of the department on undergraduate teaching, the department relies more and more heavily on undergraduate TAs. Teaching Assistants in our first year Computer Science courses are now predominantly second year undergraduate students, who just took the course in the previous academic year. These students have no experience in teaching, limited experience in observing university level teaching, and are very often lacking in self-confidence, communication skills, presentation skills, and general maturity.

As we mentioned in the introduction, the gap between desired and actual qualifications of teaching assistants most certainly demands a bridge of great length. Building a foundation for such a bridge serves as our motivation for implementing the TA Training program.

So far the teaching assistants who participated in the program were all teaching CS1 or CS2 for CS majors. They numbered between 9 and 21 in each session, and were, for the most part, second year Computer Science students. In the future, we plan to extend this program to teaching assistants in other courses (see Section 5).

4. TA TRAINING PROGRAM

Our TA training program is based on the well established Instructional Skills Workshop approach [10], an intensive workshop designed for educators, based on micro-teaching, peer-feedback, and guided self-reflection, and whose goal is allowing participants to refine their teaching practice.

4.1 Instructional Skills Workshop

The ISW model involves a three- or four-full-days workshop, with 3 to 5 participants led by an experienced facilitator. Each day includes *topical sessions* on state-of-the-art teaching practices. These sessions are typically run by the facilitator who uses the sessions to demonstrate specific teaching ideas or to illustrate potential pitfalls common in higher-level teaching.

4.1.1 The BOPPPS Model

The first topical session introduces the BOPPPS model [9] which forms the basis of lesson planning within the ISW. BOPPPS stands for Bridge-in, Outcome, Pre-assessment, Participatory learning, Post-assessment, and Summary. Each component has an important role in a well-planned lesson. The facilitator demonstrates how these components were used to build their presentation for the group, and thereafter all participants are expected to follow the model closely when working on a lesson plan.

4.1.2 The Mini-Lesson Cycle

The core of the ISW is the mini-lesson cycle, during which the participants alternate between being *presenters* and being *learners*. Each day, participants in the workshop are expected to prepare and present a *complete 10-minute lesson* on a topic of their choice. During their presentation, the remaining participants take the role of active learners, not only focusing on the content of the lesson, but being careful to observe all aspects of the lesson implementation. The facilitator's job during this phase is to ensure a smooth process, helping participants set up their teaching environment, keeping questions on topic, and keeping track of time ensuring the presenter knows when their time is running out. Lessons are kept strictly to 10 minutes, and are *recorded on video*.

4.1.3 Self-Reflection and Personalized Feedback

After the presentation, the facilitator takes the presenter outside of the room and carefully guides them through the process of reflecting on their own presentation. The facilitator will ask questions that help focus the presenter's thoughts on specific aspects of their lesson, which may include delivery style, pacing, content, structure, audience engagement and participation, and whether or not the lesson went according to plan. While this is happening, the remaining workshop participants record their observations in writing. This is an important part of the cycle since it allows the learners to develop their skills as critical observers of teaching practice. This phase of the mini-lesson cycle lasts between 5 and 7 minutes.

The final part of the mini-lesson cycle involves the whole group. The presenter and facilitator return to the room,

whereby the facilitator guides a verbal-feedback session, allowing the learners to provide constructive feedback to the presenter. The facilitator may ask the learners specific questions to guide their feedback toward particularly relevant aspects of the presentation. The presenter is then handed the written feedback. The complete cycle lasts 40 minutes.

At the end of each day, every presenter is expected to review their feedback, to watch their lesson on video, and to make appropriate changes to their teaching in order to address any concerns raised during the session for their next-day mini-lesson. In this way, the participants complete the cycle of teaching, reflecting, and improving their teaching based on feedback.

4.2 TA Training

The ISW is quite demanding in terms of time and effort from the participants. Given the resources available and the number of TAs that require training, we have adapted the ISW model so that it scales to our group size while preserving its key components.

As our terms are 12 weeks long, our mentoring program consists of 11 one-hour sessions that are compulsory for first-time CS1 TAs. These are included in their contract, and paid for at the regular TA rate. The sessions are guided by two teaching faculty, both of whom have been through the ISW and one of whom is a trained ISW facilitator.

4.2.1 The First Session

The first session is used to introduce the facilitators and TAs to each other, to establish the process that will be followed during the remaining 10 sessions, to describe the mini-lesson cycle, and to introduce the BOPPPS model. A key objective for the facilitators during this session is to establish a *friendly and safe atmosphere* in which the TAs will be willing to provide each other with constructive feedback. This is achieved, among other things, by having the facilitators take a role one as a *presenter*, and the other as a *learner*. At the end of the topical session on the BOPPPS model, the learner provides constructive feedback to the presenter, demonstrating to the rest of the group that constructive yet friendly feedback can help identify areas of improvement, even for seasoned faculty.

4.2.2 Topical Sessions

The remaining sessions share the same format. We begin with a short (10 minute) topical session run by one of the facilitators illustrating a specific teaching technique. Here are some examples of past topical sessions from our program: (a) making effective use of blackboard, (b) creating an effective slides presentation, (c) advice on, and common pitfalls of live coding, (d) engaging the audience, (e) asking and answering questions effectively, (f) effective communication: verbal and non-verbal, (g) leading a discussion and keeping it on track, (h) providing help during office hours, and (i) time management.

4.2.3 Mini-Lessons

The topical session is followed by two mini-lesson cycles adapted to fit within our one hour mentoring session. That is, two TAs take the role of presenters in each session. We ensure that every TA presents at least once during the term.

For their mini-lesson, our TAs are asked to prepare a 7-

minute presentation on a topic chosen by the facilitators. The presentation must follow the BOPPPS model, and has to demonstrate the teaching idea discussed in the *previous* topical session. For example, if the previous week's session contained a topical presentation on effective use of blackboard, then the mini-lesson has to be blackboard based and their feedback will include observations on how well the board was used to aid the delivery of their lesson.

4.2.4 Self-Reflection and Personalized Feedback

After the mini-lesson, the facilitators take the presenter out of the room, and guide the TA in reflecting on their work. Unlike the ISW, the facilitators may provide feedback directly if they deem it necessary in order to help the TA through their upcoming tutorial. Meanwhile, the remaining TAs in their role as learners and critical observers record their feedback. This phase takes up to 5 minutes, after which the presenter and facilitators return to the room for a short discussion with the learners, focusing on aspects of the presentation that the facilitators deem particularly relevant.

The entire mini-lesson cycle takes between 15 and 20 minutes, including the set-up time for the participants. At the end of the mini-lesson, the facilitators retrieve the written feedback from all the observers, and produce a feedback summary that is sent, along with the original feedback from each learner, to the presenter. With the two mini-lessons and the short topical session, this makes for a very intense one hour training once per week.

In 10 weekly sessions, we are able to provide this teaching experience to up to 20 TAs. It is worth noting that while the participants' actual teaching time is relatively short, the weekly feedback that they must provide in part compensates for it. The continued expectation of critically observing another instructor's teaching, reflecting on its effectiveness, and providing constructive feedback are all extremely valuable. We expect that this habit of critical observation will help the participants improve their teaching long after they have completed their training. While we would like to have each TA present at least twice, so as to provide an opportunity to respond to the feedback, this has not been possible so far, due to department's limited resources.

4.3 Cost to the Department

As noted above, each TA is contracted to participate in training for 11 hours. Our typical TA appointment is 65 hours, so training takes up to 17% of the TA's time. This is a sizable commitment that leads to reduced resources allocated to tutorials, labs, and marking. Ideally, the training would be funded separately and added as a top-up to the TAs standard contract. However, given that we expect to see groups of 15 to 20 TAs in the training sessions, the total amount of hours devoted to training can be equivalent to over 3 full TA appointments. Given our current enrolment pressures, it is not possible to divert these resources exclusively into training.

In addition to the cost of TA contract hours, each of the two faculty facilitators is given teaching credit, which over the course of the academic year amounts to roughly the equivalent of teaching one-third of a course.

4.4 Benefits of the Program

Despite the cost to the department, we believe that the

benefits of the program have thus far greatly justified the effort. Although we have not conducted a formal study to measure success of the program, and, arguably, we rely solely on anecdotal evidence, we believe that in this case anecdotal evidence suffices to evaluate the results.

4.4.1 Positive Feedback from Course Instructors

Course instructors are naturally well-suited to evaluate the results of the training program, as they observe students' performance and receive students' comments throughout the term, as well as compare them from term to term. We have received feedback from the CS1 and CS2 course instructors, stating that the quality and usefulness of their tutorials has visibly increased since the training program was put in place. In particular, they have noted the lack of strongly negative student feedback related to TAs and tutorials, which used to be an expected part of the course. The same effect is observed on the end-of-term course evaluations.

4.4.2 Benefits to Higher-Level Courses

Our higher level courses have greatly benefited from an increasingly larger pool of trained qualified TAs who visibly outperform even graduate TAs that have not participated in our training sessions[1]. As the program participants move through the program, they become excellent TA candidates for second, third, and even fourth year courses.

4.4.3 Facilitators' Observations

As the sessions progress through the term, the program facilitators observe an increase in the quality of TAs' critical observations on various aspects of teaching, as well as in their effectiveness and assertiveness when asking and answering technical or teaching-related questions. Their reflections on the previous week's tutorials become more thoughtful, their course-related comments and suggestions more substantial. They invariably report increased student attendance and engagement during their tutorials.

Of course, these effects can, in part, be attributed to increasing teaching experience. The facilitators believe that, at the very least, the training sessions provide an enormous boost to these improvements, which would otherwise take multiple terms (if at all) to reach a similar level.

4.4.4 Strong Undergraduate Community

The facilitators and other members of the department also note that each group of TAs involved in the mentoring sessions winds up forming a tightly knit community of colleagues and friends. They continue to interact outside their roles as TAs, they support each other through higher-level courses, they help each other whenever unforeseen circumstances affect their ability to do their TA work.

For students not in the program, these groups of TAs become role models. This has been observed before in [17] and is indeed the case here. They help build a strong sense of community among our undergraduate students, and provide a source of advice and support for younger students.

4.4.5 Improved Faculty-Student Interactions

The close interaction between faculty and the TAs demanded by the program results in a much stronger bond between these undergraduates and the faculty. Thereafter

---

[1] Several faculty members, including the authors themselves, have experienced this benefit.

these undergraduate TAs actively look for opportunities to work with our faculty, for example by getting involved in guided research projects, by taking up part-time work related to course-software or project software development, or by informally bringing up matters related to their courses that they believe deserve faculty attention. The increased trust between these students and the faculty is an important benefit arising from the training program.

4.4.6 Considering Teaching as a Career

Finally, for many of our undergraduates, the TA mentoring program provides their first real exposure to the idea of pursuing teaching as a career. During the sessions they learn to observe their faculty as professionals at their craft, they learn to pay attention to what they do and how they do it, what works and what doesn't, and they get to spend a significant amount of time reflecting on their own teaching. During this process, some of them will discover that they love teaching, and will pursue this interest in their future careers.

4.4.7 Positive Participants' Feedback

TA feedback collected at the end of each term has been overwhelmingly positive in terms of the perceived usefulness of the sessions, with a significant number of TAs indicating that the sessions ended up being one of the most fun parts of their week. A few of the comments we have received from the participants are shown in the box below.

```
"The most valuable part was the presentation we
had to give, as it gave me experience explaining
concepts and helped me learn how to better
convey information"

"Helped my confidence, showed some creative ways
to make strong points"

"Watching how other people taught was useful to
see if I was doing anything not great or if
there was anything I could pick up"

"I learned to be more confident communicating
with my students, how to act when interacting
with students, and taught me that it is ok to say
'I don't know' and get back to the student with
the answer later or point them to someone who may
have the answer"

"Seeing different styles of presentation from the
other TAs, helped me to get more useful strate-
gies for doing my own tutorials."

"Listening to others present. It helped me come
up with new and interesting ways to teach a
certain topic."

"The interaction with other TAs helped my confi-
dence and improved my teaching style"
```

Overall, we report that the results of the program have been very positive, and the program itself has sparked interest beyond the training of CS1 and CS2 TAs, as well as outside our department.

5. DISCUSSION

The current mentoring program is the result of three years worth of work on determining the best format of the sessions and the right balance between discussing the upcoming tutorial content and focusing on techniques of effective teaching practise. We believe the current format is solid and adequately addresses the needs of our TAs, our course instructors, the students, and the department.

5.1 Future Improvements

Though the program is solid, there is plenty of room for improvement. Firstly, at present our mentoring sessions are designed to accommodate up to 22 – 24 TAs. In the academic year of writing this report, we were faced with a larger cohort, and, as a result, slightly adjusted the format. The initial topical sessions ran as usual, with all participants and facilitators present. Afterwards the group split in two for the mini-lesson cycle, with each group led by one of the facilitators. This allowed us to run up to 4 mini-lesson cycles per week, with the only downside being fewer learners and one less facilitator in each session to provide feedback. Overall, the change allowed us to *handle a larger TA cohort with minimal drawbacks*.

Given additional resources (more TA contract hours devoted to training), we would have each TA present at least twice. Not only will this give the presenters an *opportunity to respond to their feedback* from the first lesson, but also the learners will be able to observe the effects that incorporating constructive feedback can have on their teaching quality.

We are also considering whether or not to *video-record the presentations*. On one hand, it is clear from the ISW experience that watching oneself teach can be illuminating, and can help the instructor identify areas of improvement in their teaching style. On the other hand, it could have a negative effect on a TA's self-confidence, if they perceive themselves (whether justifiably or not!) not to be good at teaching. This is not a problem with the oral and written feedback since the facilitators work hard at making sure that all feedback is constructive (if critical) and delivered in a friendly, non-threatening manner. The video recording, on the other hand, would provide an unedited view of the session. When making this decision, one must keep in mind the differences in age, level of experience, social status, and maturity of the typical ISW attendee and of our first-time TA.

5.2 Program Expansion

The positive results of our mentoring program have sparked interest within the CS department to expand its reach to all first-time undergraduate TAs. While this would involve a larger commitment in TA contract time (and thus an increase in TA budget), additional faculty involvement, and a change to the topics of the mini-lessons (which would no longer be based exclusively on CS1/CS2 course material), we see no reason why the benefits would not justify the costs, as they already do in the existing program. Given the level of interest in the department, we expect an expansion of the mentoring program in the near future.

Our colleagues in Mathematics, who at the time of writing of this report employ 90 TAs in their first-year courses, have expressed a strong interest in starting a similar mentoring program for their undergraduate TAs. The plan is to keep the main features and structure of our sessions, and to adapt the topical sessions to highlight best practices in the teaching of Mathematics. Outside our department, the University's Centre for Teaching and Learning requested a workshop open to all University faculty to present the mentoring program and provide opportunities for discussion. Concurrently, we are looking at the possibility of adding a note to our students' transcripts stating their participation in the mentoring program. This will provide our trained TAs with a means to show they have received formal training, and will be useful to them should they choose to pursue a career in education at any level.

6. CONCLUSION

We have presented here a summary of our experience implementing a highly-structured TA Training program for first-time Computer Science undergraduate TAs. The program is rooted in the well-established Instructional Skills Workshop's principles and methodologies. We provided an overview of the ISW's structure, and described the amendments we implemented to suit our audience and to reach our goals.

We described the benefits of the program, which extend beyond increasing TA's competence and thereby improving course delivery and students' experience, to enhancing student-faculty interaction, creating a strong undergraduate community, and stimulating interest in teaching as a career.

The program has already produced a sizable cohort of trained TAs who have supported and continue to support both our junior- and senior-level courses. Finally, we discussed possible improvements to the program, as well as its future expansion to higher-level CS courses, Mathematics courses, and possibly beyond.

It is our hope that this program can serve as a foundation for that long bridge that is needed to overcome the vast gap between desired and actual qualifications of teaching assistants.

A formal evaluation of the impact of this training program is a subject for future work.

7. REFERENCES

[1] *Support for Graduate Students at the University of Waterloo.* https://uwaterloo.ca/centre-for-teaching-excellence/support-graduate-students.

[2] *TA Professional Development program at University of California Irvine.* http://cei.uci.edu/programs/tapdp.

[3] *TA Training program at Kent University.* https://www.kent.edu/graduatestudies/teaching-assistant-training-program.

[4] *TA Training program at University of British Columbia.* http://ctlt.ubc.ca/programs/all-our-programs/ta-training-program.

[5] *TA Training program at University of Southern California.* http://cet.usc.edu/resources/ta_resources/ta_training.

[6] *Teaching Assistants' Support at Carleton.* https://carleton.ca/tasupport.

[7] *Teaching Assistants' Support at Departments of Electrical and Systems Engineering and Computer and Information Science at University of Pennsylvania.* http://www.cis.upenn.edu/~introtas/resources.html.

[8] *Teaching Assistants Training Program at University of Western Ontario.* https://www.uwo.ca/tsc/graduate_student_programs/tatp.html.

[9] *Instructional Skills Workshop Manual.* https://www.iswnetwork.ca/wp-content/uploads/2014/02/ISW-Manual-2006PW.pdf, 2006.

[10] R. Day and the ISW International Advisory Committee. The instructional skills workshop: The heart of an educator learning community in British Columbia and beyond. In *Proceedings of the ISSoTL*, Vancouver, B.C., Canada, 2005.

[11] A. Decker, P. Ventura, and C. Egert. Through the looking glass: Reflections on using undergraduate teaching assistants in CS1. *SIGCSE Bull.*, 38(1):46–50, Mar. 2006.

[12] P. E. Dickson. Using undergraduate teaching assistants in a small college environment. In *Proceedings of the 42Nd ACM Technical Symposium on Computer Science Education*, SIGCSE '11, pages 75–80, New York, NY, USA, 2011. ACM.

[13] L. M. Fisher. Booming enrollments. *Communications of the ACM*, 59(7):17–18, 2016.

[14] D. G. Kay. Training computer science teaching assistants: A seminar for new TAs. *SIGCSE Bull.*, 27(1):53–55, Mar. 1995.

[15] E. Patitsas. A case study of the development of CS teaching assistants and their experiences with team teaching. In *Proceedings of the 13th Koli Calling International Conference on Computing Education Research*, Koli Calling '13, pages 115–124, New York, NY, USA, 2013. ACM.

[16] S. Reges. Using undergraduates as teaching assistants at a state university. *SIGCSE Bull.*, 35(1):103–107, Jan. 2003.

[17] E. Roberts, J. Lilly, and B. Rollins. Using undergraduates as teaching assistants in introductory programming courses: An update on the Stanford experience. *SIGCSE Bull.*, 27(1):48–52, Mar. 1995.

[18] R. Santa Maria and S. Banerjee. Using undergraduate teaching assistants in introductory computer courses. *J. Comput. Sci. Coll.*, 27(6):61–62, June 2012.

[19] B. Stephenson, A. Kuipers, R. K. Adl, and F. Stephenson. Teaching assistant in residence: A novel peer mentorship program for less experienced teaching assistants. *J. Comput. Sci. Coll.*, 29(4):183–190, Apr. 2014.

A Comparison of Online and Hybrid Professional Development for CS Principles Teachers

Jennifer Rosato
College of St. Scholastica
1200 Kenwood Ave
Duluth, MN
1 (218) 723-6000
jrosato@css.edu

Chery Lucarelli
College of St. Scholastica
1200 Kenwood Ave
Duluth, MN
1 (218) 723-6000
clucarelli@css.edu

Cassandra Beckworth
College of St. Scholastica
1200 Kenwood Ave
Duluth, MN
1 (218)723-6000
cbeckworth@css.edu

Ralph Morelli
Trinity College
300 Summit St
Hartford, CT
1 (860) 297-2220
ralph.morelli@
trinitycollege.edu

ABSTRACT

The College of St. Scholastica, in partnership with Trinity College, adapted the Mobile Computer Science Principles (CSP) curriculum and professional development (PD) for delivery online to reach high school teachers unable to attend traditional face-to-face PD. The Mobile CSP curriculum and PD were designed to increase the number of schools offering computer science (CS) courses and to broaden the participation of traditionally underrepresented students such as females and minorities. A deliberate and intentional process was used that incorporates evidence-based practices for the online environment and professional development. A comparison of student and teacher results suggests that online PD can be a successful strategy for scaling computer science professional development. This paper will discuss not only these results but also challenges from the first year of the project and how they are being addressed in subsequent years. This report focuses primarily on the activities and accomplishments of the online PD, although data and accomplishments are provided for the Mobile CSP project as a whole where appropriate.

CCS Concepts

Social and professional topics → Computing education; Computer science education; K-12 education

Keywords

Computer science principles; K-12 computer science; online professional development; community of practice

1. INTRODUCTION

The project is one of several CS10K projects funded by the National Science Foundation (NSF) in an effort to broaden participation of underrepresented groups in computing by increasing the number of computer science (CS) course offerings at the high school level in the United States [10]. Mobile CSP includes two main efforts to support broadening participation: (1) curriculum development for the College Board's Advanced Placement CS Principles (CSP) course, which will offer its first

Advanced Placement (AP) exam in May 2017; and (2) training and professional development (PD) for high school teachers. In addition to being funded by the NSF, Mobile CSP is one of several courses endorsed by the College Board. The PD is open to teachers from all academic disciplines, a necessity, due to the serious lack of teachers in the United States who are trained and certified to teach a high school computer science course [8].

There are a number of confounding factors that have created a lack of well-prepared CS teachers in the United States. Many educational leaders and government agencies have not recognized CS as a required content area, relegating this to an elective course in most high schools. Despite the fact that 9 out of 10 parents want their students to have exposure to CS courses, fewer than 25% of high schools offer CS [8]. The Computer Science Teachers Association [2], in its report on the status of teacher certification in CS, "Bugs in the System," highlights the United States confusing CS teacher certification process that varies widely from state to state. For example, in most states, teachers need to obtain a teaching license in another content area before they can gain certification in CS. Other states forego this process and do not require any CS certification requirement outside of the teacher holding a valid teaching license. The lack of well-prepared teachers and the lack of recognition for CS as a content area on par with other areas such as math and English has contributed to the shortage of certified and well-prepared CS teachers [2].

In addressing the teacher shortage, NSF has called out the need to scale up CS teacher PD, focusing in particular on the further development of online teacher PD. As Cuny [4] noted, the United States is far short of its original goal to train 10,000 teachers, yet there is growing interest in CS education. Online PD provides the scalability that is needed to address this challenge [4], offering not only cost saving measures, but also providing flexible options to meet the needs of teachers' personal lives. Additionally, teachers in rural locations may find that PD formats that require onsite attendance create accessibility barriers that cannot be overcome. Online PD can also address the isolation factor that many CS teachers face. According to the CS10K Common Data Elements Evaluation Working Group (EWG) Year 1 Project Report (R. Zarch & T, McKlin, personal communication, January 6, 2016), smaller and more rural schools are less likely to offer CS courses. Their teachers are more likely to be the only CS teacher and as such are eager for opportunities to discuss their courses and teaching with peers. Even teachers in larger schools that are just beginning to offer CS may suffer from the same sense of isolation. The CS Education Landscape study calls for CS PD that can address teachers who are isolated or difficult to reach as the majority of current PD offerings are in person with less than half of those providing online PD [1].

1.1 Professional Development

Effective teacher professional development includes several critical characteristics. Hardee's [9] meta-analysis of teacher PD as well as other effective practices suggested by the research have framed the Mobile CSP professional development. According to Hardee [9], the five guiding principles of effective PD include: 1) Long term and intensive professional development rather than short-term workshops; 2) Clear outcomes that prioritize the PD; 3) Collaborative and reflective learning communities; 4) PD that embraces online technology tools; 5) Five core features that include pedagogical content knowledge, incorporation of standards and policies, active learning, mentoring and individual learning (see Table 1). These guiding principles are also supported by the research of Darling-Hammond, Wei, Andree, Richardson, & Orphanos [5] who suggest in their meta-analysis that PD should be intensive, lasting at least 50 hours on a given topic, and ongoing, spanning six to 12 months. This critical component is also supported by the Landscape study [1] which recommends that CS PD include more contact over longer periods of time (e.g. ongoing support during the academic year). Additionally, Darling-Hammond et al. [5] noted that when teacher PD is part of a study group with mentoring, the potential for significant and positive change to teacher practices increases. The study also reports that effective PD should focus on the specific subject matter that is tied to classroom practices. Mobile CSP has worked to implement these guiding principles as shown in Table 1.

As stated earlier, the research on effective teacher PD calls out the importance of creating a sense of community with participants and to ultimately work towards a "community of practice". As defined by Wenger-Trayner, B., & Wenger-Trayner, T. [12] "Communities of practice are groups of people who share a concern or a passion for something they do and learn how to do it better as they interact regularly" (para. 5). Communities of practice have three critical components: 1) A commitment to the domain (a shared interest in the subject matter); 2) Community - individuals who engage in activities together, building relationships to learn together; 3) Practice - Communities of practice include practitioners who learn together to improve their practice [12]. Communities of practice support the goals of schools and educational professionals, and many schools have formal structures to support the learning goals of teachers called, professional learning communities (PLC) which focus on teaching practices and student learning goals [6].

1.2 Online Learning

The Mobile CSP project structures its PD around evidence-based principles that are grounded in research. Scaling the PD by offering the program online requires intentional and deliberate implementation choices to ensure that the critical components of the PD are incorporated. This approach to online learning is based on the Community of Inquiry Model or CoI [7], which reinforces the idea of establishing strong learning communities that include collaboration and reflection for improved understanding of course content. The model suggests that there are three elements in the online learning environment that need to be addressed: social presence, cognitive presence, and teaching presence.

Garrison et al. [7], note that social presence allows participants in the online environment to have a sense of self and belonging and to present themselves as "real people." Teaching presence is the

idea that teachers must do more than merely provide instructional materials; instead, teachers must facilitate social engagement so that students have opportunities to create real meaning from the material. Finally, cognitive presence is the process of constructing knowledge and meaning through collaborative reflection and inquiry.

The specific components of the Mobile CSP PD are described in the next section and outlined in Table 2. These components are aligned and supported by research in effective PD.

2. METHODOLOGY

The Mobile CSP course is one of several courses endorsed by the College Board and includes a complete off-the-shelf implementation of the CSP framework [3]. Mobile CSP has a unique focus on mobile app development: students learn the principles of computer science by creating "socially useful" mobile apps – apps, broadly speaking, that matter to them and their community in their everyday lives. In addition to programming and CS principles, the course is project-based and emphasizes writing, communication, collaboration, and creativity. The course content is hosted online on a Google Course Builder platform that consists of two branches: (1) a student-facing branch, designed to be used by teachers in the classroom; and (2) a parallel teacher-facing branch that contains lessons plans, assessments, and other resources used by teachers. In particular, it provides opportunities for critical reflection during the PD, background on evidence-based pedagogy, a focus on recruiting and retaining underrepresented populations, and other content to help support the teaching of Mobile CSP.

The project's PD is currently offered in a 4-week summer course that can be taken in two formats: completely online within cohorts of approximately ten teachers or in a hybrid format (part online and part in-person) within a regional cohort of other teachers.

Table 1. Implementation of Effective PD Practices

PD Practice	Implementation
Long-term and intensive	4-week summer course with ongoing academic year support
Outcomes clearly defined	Shared and reinforced with participants in application, webinars, master teacher training
Supports communities of teachers	10-12 teachers with a master teacher, who uses presentations, emails, and video conferences to provide support and encourage engagement
Online tools implemented	Video conferences, discussion forums, video recordings, and online portfolios
5 Core features: 1) pedagogy, 2) standards, 3) active learning, 4) mentoring, 5) individual learning	1) CSP framework and CSTA standards; 2) a review of CS education policy and reform efforts; 3) master teachers; 4) individual projects; and 5) active learning through discussions, Google Hangouts, and course materials

The professional development components, described in more detail below, support the CoI model by reinforcing teacher, social, and cognitive presence as follows.

Table 2. Community of Inquiry (COI) Model in Mobile CSP

	Teacher Presence	Social Presence	Cognitive Presence
Student Branch Lessons	X		X
Teach Branch Lessons	X		X
Discussion Forum		X	X
Master Teacher Hangouts		X	X
Project Support Websites	X		
Webinars	X	X	X
Video Reflection Task		X	X

2.1 Professional Development Components

2.1.1 Master Teachers

Master teachers aim to support, manage, motivate, and facilitate community amongst their assigned PLC. Master teachers have successfully taught Mobile CSP at least once, demonstrated an aptitude for online communication, and displayed a growth mindset towards those with little to no previous experience teaching CS. Before beginning their role, master teachers complete an in-person orientation that includes information on online learning, coaching, adult learners, stereotype threat, and cooperative learning. Master teachers also participate in a PLC throughout the PD and academic year. Master teachers are provided with an online discussion forum, resource website, and periodic video conferences that aim to discuss issues they may face when mentoring. Master teachers assist the project team in tracking teacher participation and completion of project requirements, especially during the summer PD.

2.1.2 Summer & Academic Year PD

During the summer PD, participating teachers complete a majority of the student lessons and assessments, review lesson plans, and reflect on the CSP concepts, practices, and pedagogical strategies. Following the requirements for the AP exam their students will undergo during the academic year, teachers complete the Create Performance Task (PT) and final exam, as well as review student samples for the Explore PT. The Create PT requires learners to work collaboratively to develop a mobile app. The Explore PT requires that learners work independently to research the societal impact of computing innovations related to mobile apps. Learners must complete a practice and final assignment for each PT. In addition to completing the PTs, teachers also complete a pre- and post-PD survey and meet with their PLC and master teacher via online video conferencing software once a week. While teachers are only required to attend one PLC meeting a week, they often attend two. In the academic year, participants teach the full curriculum, meet monthly with their PLC, complete pre- and post-academic year surveys, complete a video reflection task twice a year, and assist in collecting student data. Student data collected includes pre- and post-surveys, midterm, final exam, and PTs. Additional academic year support is provided to teachers in the form of a discussion forum, which is accessible to the entire Mobile CSP community, and optional monthly webinars hosted by Mobile CSP staff.

2.1.3 Project Support Websites

Three comprehensive support websites were created to provide support and communication avenues for participants and master teachers. The Master Teacher Resource website serves as a resource to aid master teachers in facilitating community with their assigned PLC. Teachers have access to a Teacher Resource and a Video Task Reflection website. Both serve to provide resources as well as tutorials to support project requirements.

2.1.4 Webinars

During the summer professional development, weekly webinars are hosted by the project team to provide a clear message on the project's goals and processes as well as provide an opportunity for reinforcement of key concepts. During the academic year, webinars are held less frequently on a quarterly to monthly basis but with a similar purpose - reinforcing project goals and processes and providing just-in-time professional development. Topics include active recruiting, PT overview, technical writing, and various pedagogical strategies.

2.1.5 Video Reflection Task

During the academic year, teachers are required to record video of their classroom, write a reflection, and discuss the videos of other PLC members. The video reflection task is supported by research in teacher professional development. Darling-Hammond et al. [5] noted that an important part of addressing isolation and improving teaching practice is to have teachers observe each other, providing ideas for improvement. The task provides teachers an opportunity to reflect on their teaching as well as conduct a virtual visit to another CS teacher's classroom. Darling-Hammond et al. [5] suggest that teachers may want to use videos of themselves teaching to share their practices and to watch other teachers teach and that by doing so are more likely to positively change their teaching practices. Tripp & Rich [11] emphasized the importance of guided reflection when teachers view and reflect on their own teaching through video. They also noted that teachers found the sharing of their reflections after watching themselves teach most meaningful when there was an opportunity to collaborate with other educational professionals. Most importantly, Tripp and Rich [11], shared that several studies support the positive impact on teacher change that may occur when teachers use video to reflect on their own teaching. In our project, teachers are sharing their videos of themselves teaching with their assigned PLC, connecting virtually from all areas of the United States.

2.2 Hybrid PD Model Differences

During the summer PD, the hybrid teachers met two of the four weeks face-to-face with the online weeks including daily check-ins using video conferencing. During the academic year, the hybrid and online teachers are provided similar supports, although hybrid teachers are not required to complete the video reflection task. Hybrid teachers did not have access to the teacher and master teacher resource websites, either. Finally, all of the hybrid locations included a pair of facilitators – a master teacher and a college or university CS professor.

3. RESULTS & DISCUSSION

Overall, the data show that the online PD has been successful and its students and teachers display similar results to those that participated in the hybrid PD. The Mobile CSP project offered online PD in summer 2015 and 2016, while the hybrid PD has been in place for two additional years (2013 and 2014). The hybrid and online PD used a common application form in which teachers could specify the format of the PD they were willing to attend. In 2015-16, teachers were required to select either hybrid or online. In 2016-17, almost half (49%, N=251) selected online PD, while another 29% (N=150) selected either online or hybrid.

Overwhelmingly, teachers are willing and interested in participating in online PD offerings.

Table 3 below illustrates the number of teachers who were trained in the online and hybrid programs. Stipends for completing the PD were available in all years. Hybrid teachers have received $1,000/week of PD each year, while online teachers received $1,000 for 2015-16 and up to $4,000 for 2016-17, a potential factor in PD completion rates.

Table 3. PD Completion Data

| | 2015-16 | | 2016-17 | |
	Hybrid	Online	Hybrid	Online
Accepted to participate in PD	N=12	N=42	N=98	N=117
Actual Trained (Completed PD)	100.00% N=12	45.24% N=19	96.94% N=95	88.03% N=103 *

* Note that 6 online participants dropped out before the program began, 5 dropped out during the PD, and 3 did not successfully complete PD requirements.

The online Mobile CSP PD serves teachers in more schools identified as rural than overall CS10K project statistics and national school data (Table 4). According to the CS10K Common Data Elements EWG Year 1 Project Report, online PD has also been able to reach teachers in states not served in other years, including Alaska and Hawaii (R. Zarch & T, McKlin, personal communication, January 6, 2016).

Table 4. "Urbanicity" of Schools Served

| | 2014-15 | | 2015-16* | 2016-17** |
	National***	CS10K Projects	Mobile CSP Online	Mobile CSP Online
City	27%	33%	22.73% N=5	31.96% N=31
Suburb	31%	41%	36.36% N=8	27.84% N=27
Town	14%	11%	9.09% N=2	12.37% N=12
Rural	28%	13%	31.82% N=7	27.84% N=27
Total			100% N=22	100% N=97

* Only 22 of the 42 total accepted 2015-16 participants' schools had National Center of Education (NCES) statistics available.
** Only 97 of the 117 total 2016-17 participants' schools had NCES statistics available.
*** National data on United States public school designation

3.1 Teacher Data

3.1.1 Teacher Demographics

Overall, the teachers in both the hybrid and online PD have similar backgrounds and experience levels in CS. Teachers in the hybrid PD have taught on average 9.42 years (2015-16) and 12.84 (2016-17), similar to teachers in the online PD, 10.63 years (2015-16) and 12.88 (2016-17). While teachers in both the hybrid and online PD are primarily STEM (science, technology, engineering,

and math) teachers, both formats include teachers from other backgrounds (see Table 5).

In 2016, 43% of teachers reported that they are currently teaching computer science, which represents an increase over previous years. Approximately 20% of this year's teachers reported that they had a degree in computer science and another 32% reported having taken CS courses in college. Regarding programming experience, 58% of teachers identified themselves as "beginners" (16%) or as having a little experience (42%).

Table 5. Teacher Certification and Subjects Taught

| | Certification | | Subjects Taught | |
	Hybrid	Online	Hybrid	Online
Science, Engineering, Math	63	62	53	49
Computer Science	21	44	77	87
Business/Career Tech Ed	35	71	35	64
All Other Subjects	14	24	4	8

3.1.2 Teacher CS Knowledge and Attitudes

Teachers in both the online and hybrid PD performed similarly on the common final exam. The final exam assessed CS content knowledge and mirrors the final assessment that students take at the end of the academic year. In the first year of the project, hybrid teachers on average received a score of 88% (N=12) whereas the online participants received a score of 90% (N=29). In the second year of the project, hybrid teachers received average scores of 82% (N=93) and online teachers of 83% (N=94). The overall lower score in Year 2 could be a result of the shortened PD (4 instead of 6 weeks), which did not cover some topics in the same depth and covered only a small portion of the data unit.

When asked to respond to the statement, "Teaching CS is highly appealing to me," 99% of online teachers (N=111) and 100% of hybrid teachers (N=87) replied strongly agree or agree on a standard 5 point Likert scale. Teacher attitudes towards CS, in general, were also positive and similar for both PD formats as shown Table 6.

Table 6. Computer Science Attitudes

| | Hybrid | | Online | |
	2015-16	2016-17	2015-16	2016-17
This course improved my understanding of computer science.	3.75	3.43	3.42	3.37
I learned that I have more programming talent than I was aware of.	3.09	2.80	2.84	2.80
I have become more interested in computer science.	3.75	3.40	3.11	3.26
Computer science is a socially beneficial discipline.	3.67	3.68	3.67	3.83
Four point scale 1-Not at all true; 2-Somewhat true; 3-Quite true; 4-Completely true				

3.1.3 Teacher PD Attitudes

Overall, in both years 1 and 2 of the project, teachers seemed to view the PD very positively. On average, teachers in both the hybrid and online projects tended to agree or strongly agree that they enjoyed the PD (see Table 7). Furthermore, in regards to year 2 data, 95.50% of online teachers (N=106) and 95.40% of hybrid teachers (N=82) identified that they felt generally to very confident that their Mobile CSP course would go well after participating in the 2016-17 PD.

In addition to enjoying the PD, teachers were also asked to evaluate whether or not they felt the training activities fostered a sense of community among participants. As noted in Table 7 below, hybrid teachers, on average, in both the 2015-16 and 2016-17 projects, tended to choose "agree" and "strongly agree" that the PD activities encouraged community among their cohort members. This figure is slightly less for online teachers who trend lower on the scale and tend to agree to this statement measuring community (see above). The higher average for the hybrid program aligns with expectations; those who have an opportunity to meet with others in their cohort face-to-face would be expected to feel a stronger sense of community among participants than those who do not have an opportunity to meet others in-person (online project). In Table 8 below the community component is explored further in the 2016-17 project as teachers were asked to identify the specific PD course activities that they felt fostered a sense of community.

Table 7. PD Attitudes

	Hybrid		Online	
	2015-16	2016-17	2015-16	2016-17
I have enjoyed this professional development course	4.67	4.58	4.37	4.51
Training activities fostered a sense of community among the participants	4.42	4.49	3.67	3.79
Five point scale 1-Strongly Disagree, 2-Disagree, 3-Neutral, 4-Agree, 5-Strongly Agree				

Table 8. Community Supporting Activities

	2016-17	
	Hybrid	Online
Narrated video content	3.14	3.05
Mentor Groups	3.42	3.13
Google Hangouts	2.85	3.12
Discussion Forums	2.60	2.43
Online Office Hours	2.85	2.75
In-person classroom sessions	3.71	3.29
Other	3.29	3.67
Averages are based on a 4 point Likert scale: 4-Very Helpful, 3-Somewhat Helpful, 2-Helpful, 1-Not at all Helpful.		

Overall, hybrid and online participants found the majority of the PD course activities to be somewhat to very helpful. However, there are some discrepancies that are important to note. Some of the PD course activities that are listed, such as an opportunity to meet in-person, were not offered to online participants. While those in the online project tended to identify "in-person classroom sessions" as being somewhat to very helpful (average of 3.29), this activity was unavailable to online participating teachers. We believe that teachers may have mistaken the "in-person sessions" for the required weekly virtual meetings with their mentors or personal one-on-one communications with project team members. Additionally, this section of questions did not offer a "Not Applicable" option. For the 2017-18 project, we have implemented changes to our surveys and assessments to ensure that all questions and categories are clearly defined as well as provide a "Not Applicable" option where appropriate.

3.2 Student Data

Table 9 summarizes student participation over the four years of the project. Only teachers and students who have shared student data with the project are included in the table. Table 10 provides an aggregate summary of student demographics over all four years of the project, including students served by both online and hybrid teachers. For the first time this year, the combined percentage of underrepresented minorities (URMs) and females has exceeded 50%. At the time of writing this paper, only student assessment data for 2015-16 was available. Students with teachers in the hybrid and online PD performed similarly on summative assessments (Table 11). Student attitudes towards the course and computer science were also positive (Table 12).

Table 9. Student Enrollments

	2013-14	2014-15	2015-16	2016-17*
Hybrid	330	648	554	2,280
Online	-	-	242	2,129
TOTALS	330	648	748	4,409
Does not account for courses with a spring semester start date.				

Table 10. Project-wide Student Demographics

	2013-14*	2014-15*	2015-16	2016-17
Males	77.16%	71.12%	78.05%	71.86%
Females	22.84%	28.88%	21.95%	28.14%
URM	31.69%	34.14%	21.62%	33.34%
URM or Female	43.61%	49.67%	38.77%	50.72%
*Hybrid only data				

Table 11. Student Summative Assessment Averages

	Hybrid		Online
	2014-15	2015-16	2015-16
Explore PT	70.5	78.1	82.7
Create PT	76.5	74.7	84.6
Final Exam	71.0	71.0	72.1

Table 12. Percent of students agreeing with statements about the course and CS (2015-16)

I enjoyed this class.	72%
I will probably take more CS courses after this one.	64%

I might major in Computer Science.	44%
Computer science is intellectually deep and challenging.	79%

3.3 Lessons Learned from Year 1

During the first year of the online PD, we encountered three significant challenges: 1) master teacher expectations for participant support; 2) consistent support from project staff; and 3) misunderstanding of program and curriculum requirements. Some of the challenges with master teachers were due to personal life events or lack of follow through on expectations. To better address expectations, in the second year of the project, a more detailed master teacher job description, application process, and two days of onsite orientation were implemented.

Secondly, during the first grant year, the project team hired a part-time staff member, who also had separate full-time employment. The part-time hours were not sufficient, making it difficult to address the communication and support needs of the participants. In the second year, the position was changed to full-time, providing consistent, high-quality support and communication. The staff member also conducted individual phone calls with each accepted participant and started a monthly newsletter.

Some participating teachers conveyed misunderstanding of program and curriculum requirements including technical difficulties. We believe that many of the difficulties were due to teachers not fully understanding the necessary technical components that were needed for the successful implementation of the curriculum (e.g. student access to Wi-Fi, student Google accounts, and availability of mobile Android devices).

To better address the technical issues in year 2, the project website was updated, a detailed technology checklist was created, and the memorandum of understanding was modified to include a principal signature and review of the IT checklist. Even with these new communication efforts, some of our online participants have experienced technical issues at higher rates than those in the hybrid format. We are continuing to examine this issue to resolve technical difficulties. For the third year of the project we have instituted further steps to help teachers seamlessly implement the Mobile CSP curriculum and ensure student success, such as technology questions on the application, an infographic on IT requirements and a project orientation for participants that reinforces the required technology.

4. CONCLUSION

Overall, the data from this project suggest that the online Mobile CSP format has been successful, providing comparable results to the hybrid Mobile CSP format. We continue to refine our PD model based on survey data and project staff and master teacher feedback. In many cases, the data show little to no difference, and the results are primarily very positive for both PD formats (online and hybrid). We believe that our results suggest that careful and deliberate planning of online PD, rooted in evidence-based practices, can be successful providing a viable, flexible and scalable option for teachers to receive PD.

5. ACKNOWLEDGMENTS

We would like to thank the Mobile CSP hybrid team members, Pauline Lake and Chinma Uche, our grant evaluator, Lawrence Baldwin, and all the master teachers and participant teachers. This material is based upon work supported by the National Science Foundation under Grant Nos. CNS-1240841, CNS-1440947, and CNS-1547051 and by Google's CS4HS program.

6. REFERENCES

[1] *Building an operating system for computer science: Landscape study.* Retrieved from http://outlier.uchicago.edu/computerscience/OS4CS/landscapestudy/

[2] Computer Science Teachers Association (CSTA), Association for Computing Machinery (ACM). (2013). Bugs in the system: Computer science teacher certification in the U.S. {Report}. Retrieved from http://csta.acm.org/ComputerScienceTeacherCertification/sub/CSTA_BugsInTheSystem.pdf

[3] College Board. (2016). Providers of CSP Curricula and Pedagogical Support. Retrieved from https://advancesinap.collegeboard.org/stem/computer-science-principles/curricula-pedagogical-support on January 15, 2017.

[4] Cuny, J. (2015). Transforming K-12 computing education: AP® computer science principles. *ACM Inroads* 6, 4 (November 2015), 58-59. DOI: https://doi.org/10.1145/2832916

[5] Darling-Hammond, L., Chung Wei, R., Andree, A., Richardson, N., & Orphanos, S. (2009). Professional Learning in the Learning Profession. *National Staff Development Council and The School Redesign Network at Stanford University.* Retrieved from https://edpolicy.stanford.edu/sites/default/files/publications/professional-learning-learning-profession-status-report-teacher-development-us-and-abroad_0.pdf

[6] DuFour, R. (2004). What is a professional learning community? *Educational Leadership 61* (8) 6-11 Retrieved from http://www.ascd.org/publications/educational-leadership/may04/vol61/num08/What-Is-a-Professional-Learning-Community%C2%A2.aspx

[7] Garrison, D. R., Anderson, T., & Archer, W. (2000). Critical inquiry in a text-based environment: Computer conferencing in higher education model. *The Internet and Higher Education,* 2(2-3), 87-105.

[8] Google Inc. & Gallup Inc. (2016). *Trends in the State of Computer Science in U.S. K-12 Schools.* Retrieved from http://goo.gl/j291E0

[9] Hardee, C., Duffin, M., & PEER Associates. (2013). Five (+) guiding principles for professional development: Summary report, professional development literature review. Project Learning Tree, Washington, DC.

[10] Morelli, R., Uche, C., Lake, P., & Baldwin, L. (2015). Analyzing Year One of a CS Principles PD Project. *SIGCSE-2105 Proceedings of the 46th ACM Technical Symposium on Computer Science Education,* pp 368-373. http://dl.acm.org/citation.cfm?doid=2676723.2677265.

[11] Tripp, T. and Rich, P. (2012). The influence of video analysis on the process of teacher change, *Teaching and Teacher Education,* Volume 28, Issue 5, July 2012, Pages 728-739, ISSN 0742-051X, http://dx.doi.org/10.1016/j.tate.2012.01.011.

[12] Wenger-Trayner, B., & Wenger-Trayner, T. (2015). *Introduction to communities of practice: A brief review of the concept and its uses.* Retrieved from http://wenger-trayner.com/introduction-to-communities-of-practice/ on January 14, 2015.

Examining a Student-Generated Question Activity Using Random Topic Assignment

Paul Denny, Ewan Tempero,
Dawn Garbett
University of Auckland
Auckland, New Zealand
{p.denny, e.tempero, d.garbett}
@auckland.ac.nz

Andrew Petersen
University of Toronto Mississauga
Mississauga, Canada
petersen@cs.toronto.edu

ABSTRACT

Students and instructors expend significant effort, respectively, preparing to be examined and preparing students for exams. This paper investigates *question authoring*, where students create practice questions as a preparation activity prior to an exam, in an introductory programming context. The key contribution of this study as compared to previous work is an improvement to the design of the experiment. Students were randomly assigned the *topics* that their questions should target, removing a selection bias that has been a limitation of earlier work. We conduct a large-scale between-subjects experiment ($n = 700$) and find that students exhibit superior performance on exam questions that relate to the topics they were assigned when compared to those students preparing questions on other assigned topics.

Keywords

question authoring; self-testing; study behaviours

1. INTRODUCTION

Assessment in many classrooms is dominated by tests and exams. As a result, students expend significant effort preparing to be tested. Without guidance, students often select the most obvious technique, reviewing or re-studying the material immediately before the test, but that method is less effective at promoting long term retention than methods that require repeated practice and retrieval of knowledge from memory. For example, *self-testing*, where students answer practice questions, is an effective strategy [9] based on the *testing-effect* [22] and the use of *spaced repetition*, where students recall and apply knowledge repeatedly at intervals spaced over days or weeks, is more effective than methods that rely on a single study session [21].

We examine the effectiveness of *question authoring*, where students generate practice questions prior to an exam, in a computer science context. This can be considered a comple-

mentary activity to self-testing, as the questions generated can be shared and utilised by others for practice.

The process of creating questions may help students reinforce their own knowledge, particularly if it involves reviewing related content and writing explanations to accompany their questions. The *generation effect* suggests that individuals tend to remember information better if they take an active role in its creation [10, 25]. This is a robust effect in the context of knowledge recall, however earlier work investigating question authoring in more natural settings did not find an effect [3, 13]. As a result, we may question its effectiveness in computer programming courses. When students are examined in a programming course, they will usually not encounter questions that are identical to examples they have studied. Instead, students must rely on skills in adaptation and generation [23, 24] to solve complex questions requiring synthesis of interrelated topics [7, 20].

Despite the complexity of assessments in computer programming courses, earlier work examining the effect of question authoring in computer science has demonstrated positive trends [4, 5, 15]. However, previous experimental setups have given students the freedom to select the topics that their questions will target, which introduces a potential topic-selection bias. Students may choose to author questions on topics they already understand well. Their subsequent performance may be explained by this bias, rather than being a result of learning through question authoring.

This paper presents the results of an experiment designed to control for this bias, and addresses whether question authoring is a useful exam preparation activity in introductory programming courses. Our specific research question is:

> *Do students who author questions on prescribed topics perform better on subsequent related exam questions compared with students who author questions on different topics?*

The experiment in this paper was performed in an introductory computer programming course using *PeerWise* [6], an online system that facilitates the question authoring process and hosts the generated questions so that they can be used for self-testing. As a pre-exam activity, students used the system to author a set number of questions. To remove self-selection and topic-selection bias, students were required to author questions and were randomly assigned the topics on which they were to generate their questions. To mitigate time-on-task issues, all students were asked to author an equivalent number of questions.

ITiCSE '17, July 03-05, 2017, Bologna, Italy
© 2017 ACM. ISBN 978-1-4503-4704-4/17/07...$15.00
DOI: http://dx.doi.org/10.1145/3059009.3059033

2. RELATED WORK

2.1 Study behaviours and self-testing

Students use a variety of study strategies. For example, Gurung found that the most commonly reported method of studying was "reading notes", with a much smaller fraction using "testing knowledge" [11]. However, testing knowledge has been shown to be more effective for long-term retention than restudying material (the *testing effect*) [22]. In many computer science courses, and specifically programming courses, students are given a variety of opportunities to self-test. Numerous tools reported in the computer science education literature allow students to practice solving programming exercises [1, 12, 17], test their understanding of algorithms through interactive simulations [16], and answer multiple-choice questions [19]. Multiple-choice questions (MCQs) are of particular relevance to the work reported here, and appear as a common format in studies of novice programming exams [14]. Students often prepare enthusiastically for exams by self-testing with questions and answers from previous semesters, and MCQs are commonly used to assess code comprehension [20].

2.2 Question authoring

Question authoring, where students *create* their own practice questions, is a less commonly used strategy and is the focus of the work we report here. Consider a student authoring a code-tracing MCQ in a computer science course. They may begin by reviewing similar examples and referring back to relevant information from a textbook or other instructional content. They may prepare one or more code fragments, and check their answer by executing this code. To generate a set of alternative answers, the student may try to predict the kinds of errors that their classmates would make. In addition, creating an explanation to accompany the answer to their question may help the student to reinforce the targeted concepts. By engaging in these creative processes, a student may develop a more robust understanding than if they simply attempt pre-prepared questions.

Question generation activities have previously been investigated in computer science courses. Luxton-Reilly et al. reported positive correlations between the number of free-response questions generated by students and their performance on subsequent exams [15]. Mishra and Iyer explored a question generation task that followed a summative quiz, reporting how quiz performance predicted the difficulty of the questions subsequently generated [18].

Other recent work on question authoring in computer science has examined MCQs [4] and programming exercises [5]. In these studies students have been given the freedom to select the topics that their questions target. As a result, while these studies demonstrated positive effects for authoring questions, the results may be biased by topic-selection as students could choose to target topics they already understood well. In addition, the experimental and control groups had different task requirements meaning not all students performed equal work, so the results may also be biased by time-on-task.

3. METHODOLOGY

In this experiment, students in a first-year, introductory C programming course for engineers were asked to author a set

number of questions as a homework exercise prior to an end of module exam. The questions were authored in *PeerWise* [6], an online system that supports both question authoring and self-testing. Each question consisted of a question stem, a set of answer options, and an explanation.

Every student in the course was required to author *three* questions in *PeerWise* in order to earn a small amount (2%) of course credit. Students were given one week to complete this task, and the end of module exam was conducted three days after the task deadline. Students were free to voluntarily answer questions in order to prepare for the exam, but no course credit was awarded for question answering.

3.1 Topic groups

Every student was randomly assigned to one of four *topic groups*. Students were informed that to earn the credit for the task the questions they authored must target the specific topics associated with the topic group to which they had been assigned. The four groups are "Variables, Arithmetic and Conditionals," "Functions and Parameter Passing," "Loops and Nested Loops," and "Arrays and Structures." For convenience, hereafter these groups will be referred to as "Variables," "Functions," "Loops," and "Arrays."

A set of instructions was distributed to all students that detailed the specific topics that should be targeted by these groups. For example, students in the "Variables" group were given instructions to create one question involving arithmetic expressions with integer operands, one involving expressions consisting of both integer and floating point variables, and one involving boolean expressions or conditional statements. The description below illustrates the outline provided to students regarding the third of these questions:

```
Question 3: Your third question must involve
boolean expressions or conditional statements
(e.g. if statements or if/else statements).
Examples here might include:
 - evaluating a boolean expression involving
   logical and relational operators
 - tracing through an if statement
 - tracing through an if/else statement
Topic: You must tag this question using the
topic tag "booleans_conditionals".
```

The last line of these instructions indicated that students must use the tag feature within *PeerWise* to associate a particular *topic tag* with their question. In this case, the topic tag was required to be "booleans_conditionals". Students could select the appropriate topic tag from a pre-populated list, and this provided an automated way to check that a student had satisfied the task requirements.

A total of 12 topic tags were defined, as each of the four topic groups included specifications for three questions and each question had a unique topic tag that students were required to use. Table 1 lists the topic groups, the specific topic tags that students used to classify their questions, and shortened summaries of the instructions given to students. For later reference, the table also includes three letter abbreviations of each of the topic tags defined.

3.2 Examination design

The end of module exam consisted of 17 MCQs. One of these questions, Question 5, targeted a specific concept involving random number generation and was not associated

Table 1: The four topic groups and the associated topic tags used to classify questions

Topic group	Abbr.	Topic tag name and summary of description provided to students
Variables	int	*int_arithmetic*: arithmetic operators applied to integer operands (either literals or variables)
	mix	*mixed_arithmetic*: arithmetic operators applied to operands of mixed types (including integers and doubles)
	boo	*booleans_conditionals*: boolean expressions or conditional statements using logical and relational operators
Functions	sin	*single_function*: a function, with declaration, that receives at least one input and may return an output
	mul	*multiple_functions*: multiple functions, where one calls the other or uses the output of the other
	inp	*input_array_function*: pass an array of integers to a function as an input, illustrating pass by reference, without the use of loops
Loops	for	*for_loops*: a single for loop, without the use of arrays
	whl	*while_loops*: a single while loop, without the use of arrays
	nes	*nested_loops*: one loop nested inside the body of another, without the use of arrays
Arrays	arr	*array_of_ints*: int array declarations and initializations, as well as basic operations applied to array elements
	str	*structures*: a structure definition and code that declares the defined structure
	alo	*arrays_and_loops*: a single loop used to process elements of an array

with any of the topic categories. The remaining 16 questions were designed so that the coverage of topics was reasonably well balanced across the four broad topic groups. To evaluate this, two authors independently classified all 16 questions using the 12 topic tags. There was full agreement on which topic groups were targeted by each of the exam questions. Table 4 includes the results of this topic classification.

In most cases, a single topic tag was sufficient to classify a question. For example, Question 3 (below) targeted the "booleans_conditionals" (boo) topic tag. Students were given a conditional statement and asked to determine the values for a, b and c that would produce the output "success":

```
if (a != b && a < b) {
  printf("failure");
} else if (a >= c) {
  printf("failure");
} else {
  printf("success");
}
```

Question 1, which was classified with the single topic tag "int_arithmetic" (int), was another example:

```
int x, y, z, a, b;
x = 10;
y = 6;
z = 4;
a = x + z % y;
b = x / (x % y);
```

Simple arithmetic operations featured in many of the exam questions. However, Question 1 was the only question that included both the integer division and remainder operators. Students assigned to the "Variables" group were explicitly encouraged to generate questions that targeted these operators. The detailed instructions for this group included the following description: "Examples you may like to consider include performing division (/) or remainder (%) using literals or variables of type int."

Some of the exam questions were classified by two different topic tags. For example, Question 6 presented students with one *for* loop and two *while* loops, and asked whether any pair of the three loops would generate identical output. In this case, both "for_loops" (for) and "while_loops" (whl) were targeted by the question, however both of these topic tags fall under the same broad topic group, which is "Loops."

In most cases it was simple to associate a topic group with each exam question. For questions classified using a single topic tag, or two topic tags from the same topic group, this was trivial. The exception was for exam questions that involved arrays, as each of these questions also involved loops. Loops were either used to systematically modify the elements of an array or to display the elements of an array. For example, Question 15 asked students to determine the values stored in each element of the *values* array after the code completed execution:

```
int values[5] = {1, 2, 3, 4, 5};
int i = 0;
while (i < 5) {
  values[(i+1)%5] = values[i];
  i++;
}
```

To answer this question successfully, an understanding of both array indexing and flow of control through *while* loops is required, and both concepts seem similarly important. In terms of classifying this question, both the "while_loops" (whl) tag and the "array_of_ints" (arr) tag appear relevant even though these tags are associated with different topic groups (namely "Loops" and "Arrays"). As a result, all exam questions involving arrays and loops (Questions 13, 15, 16 and 17) were classified with one topic tag from the "Arrays" group and one topic tag from the "Loops" group.

A post-hoc item analysis of the exam questions revealed that two questions, Questions 11 and 14, were problematic. These were the only two questions that failed to meet an acceptable threshold, as defined by Ding and Beichner [8], for both difficulty and discrimination. Both questions were answered correctly by 91% of students, and their mean discrimination index (0.19) was well below that of the other exam questions (0.44) as well as the level generally considered acceptable (0.3). As a result, both questions were removed, leaving a total of 14 exam questions for our analysis.

3.3 Threats to validity

Our experimental design addresses two major shortcomings of earlier studies on question authoring in computer science. Students were assigned the topics on which to author their questions at random, removing the bias of topic-selection, and all students were asked to complete the same activity, mitigating time-on-task differences. We now discuss other potential threats to the validity of our work.

Some students may not have complied with the provided instructions. For example, students may have authored questions that targeted topics that were not assigned to them or may have authored fewer than the required number of questions or no questions at all. Students in this latter category could not have benefited from the authoring activity, and moreover, students not participating may be less engaged with the course overall. To address this, our analysis includes only those students that correctly followed instructions and met the requirements for the task. To measure task compliance, we checked that students authored questions that targeted their required topics. This check was automated and based on the tags that students used to classify their questions during the authoring process. It is possible that students may have incorrectly tagged their questions or targeted additional topics in their questions that they were not assigned. However, this would lead to students performing relatively better on topics to which they were not assigned, thus we would expect any measured learning effects to diminish rather than be artificially inflated.

Our instructions to students were quite explicit so that their generated questions would closely target the exam questions. Had we instead only published the topic group names without further descriptions, we may have observed a more diverse range of questions created. If the generated questions poorly targeted the exam questions then we may expect to see smaller effects, however in terms of the analysis we present here no group is favoured over another.

A final threat to the validity of this work arose from the challenge of accurately classifying questions. The major difficulty in this regard was selecting the *most relevant* topic tags for questions that involved multiple topics. An example of this difficulty was highlighted earlier in the listing of Question 15 which included an array of integers, a while loop and use of the remainder operator. By limiting the classification of each question to the two most relevant topic tags, full agreement was achieved by two independent raters on the broad topic groups targeted by each exam question.

4. RESULTS

A total of 838 students took the end of module exam, and of these, 701 complied with the requirements of the question authoring task, generating 2130 questions in total. The percentage of students in each of the four groups that did not comply with instructions was very similar (between 15% and 19%), so it does not appear that the random topic assignments influenced whether or not students chose to comply with the task.

4.1 Overall performance by topic group

Table 2 gives a breakdown of the number of students in each of the four topic groups and, for each group, reports the average exam score and the average number of questions authored and answered. Overall, the groups performed similarly on the exam, and the differences are not statistically significant (Kruskal-Wallis rank sum test, $p = 0.724$). Table 3 shows two examples of student authored questions.

Time-on-task was identified as a threat in previous studies and we have attempted to address this by giving all students equivalent authoring requirements and by making question answering voluntary. This design was successful in eliminating the threat, as the distributions of both questions authored and answers submitted by students in each group

Table 2: Summary of activity, by topic group, for students complying with task requirements

	Variables	Functions	Loops	Arrays
n	176	176	177	172
exam	79.0%	80.6%	80.3%	79.3%
avg questions	3.05	3.05	3.03	3.03
avg answers	10.24	8.36	9.41	9.44

do not differ significantly (Kruskal-Wallis rank sum tests, $p = 0.6305$ and $p = 0.6252$ respectively). Since students do not appear to have been disadvantaged overall as a result of their topic group assignment and the topic groups each exhibited similar answering behaviour, we now turn our attention to the individual exam questions, the topics they target, and the related topics on which students authored their questions.

4.2 Question performance by topic group

Our hypothesis is that students assigned to a particular topic group, and thus authoring questions related to that topic, will perform better on the exam questions targeting that topic compared with all other students.

For each exam question, our analysis compares how well that question is answered by the students assigned to the same topic group as the question with the students assigned to different topics. Specifically, we compare the performance of students in the "Variables" group with the performance of all other students on exam questions 1, 2 and 3. Similarly, we compare the performance of students in the "Functions" group with the performance of all other students on exam questions 7, 10 and 12. Finally, we compare the performance of students in the "Loops" group with the performance of all other students on exam questions 4, 6, 8 and 9. The remaining exam questions involve both loop and array concepts, thus targeting two of the broad topic groups. We therefore compare the performance of all students in either the "Arrays" or the "Loops" group against the performance of students in the other two groups ("Variables" and "Functions") on exam questions 13, 15, 16 and 17.

Table 4 shows the results of these comparisons. For each exam question, students have been partitioned based on whether or not they were assigned to the topic group related to the question. The percentage of students answering the question correctly is shown, both for students in the topic group and for students not in the topic group. The *normalized difference* between the performance of students in these groups, expressed as a percentage, is also shown. The questions are organised according to the topic groups, and an average percentage difference is shown calculated across each group. All of the average percentage differences are positive, and only one of the individual question percentage differences (Question 9) is negative.

5. DISCUSSION

The performance differences shown in Table 4 are not significant for any individual question. Nonetheless, there is an interesting trend across all exam questions. Consider each question as an individual trial. If there was no learning impact for authoring questions, then in approximately half of the trials, we would expect students in the related topic group to outperform students in the other topic groups. The

Table 3: Examples of student-generated questions (formatting has been removed for space reasons)

Topic tag	Question (only stem shown)	Explanation
mix	What is printed? int a; int b; double c; a = 58; b = 10; c = a / b; printf ("%f", c);	Doing the arithmetic of c = a / b will give 58 divided by 10 which gives 5.8. Since a and b have both been predetermined to be int values, result is made an int value (5) but then because c is a double value, it gets changed to 5.000000. Therefore c is printed to be 5.000000.
arr	What values are stored in the array after this code? int nums[5] = { 0, 1, 2, 3, 4 }; nums[0] = nums[2] + 1; nums[nums[4] - nums[1]] = nums[2]; nums[1] = 3; nums[4] = nums[3];	The first line creates an array of five numbers [0,1,2,3,4]. The first line nums[0] = nums[2] + 1, changes the value at 0 to 3. The second line nums[nums[4] - nums[1]] = nums[2] changes the value at 3 in the array to 2. (number in position four is four and number in position one is one so four-one changes the third position value in the array to 2. nums[1] = 3 changes the value at 1 to three. nums[4] = nums[3] changes the value at 4 to 3.

Table 4: Exam performance by group (students complying with task requirements)

Group	n	Question	Tag(s)	In group	Not in group	% diff	avg. % diff
Variables	176	Q1	int	85.8%	84.8%	+1.2%	
		Q2	mix	73.3%	70.9%	+3.4%	+2.9%
		Q3	boo	90.3%	86.9%	+4.0%	
Functions	176	Q7	sin	86.9%	80.4%	+8.1%	
		Q10	mul	90.3%	87.0%	+3.8%	+5.8%
		Q12	inp	53.4%	50.7%	+5.4%	
Loops	177	Q4	for	66.1%	62.6%	+5.6%	
		Q6	for, whl	85.9%	81.9%	+4.9%	+1.7%
		Q8	nes	93.2%	89.9%	+3.7%	
		Q9	for, whl	76.8%	82.8%	-7.2%	
Arrays or Loops	349	Q13	arr, for	86.2%	84.1%	+2.6%	
		Q15	arr, whl	75.1%	73.3%	+2.4%	+2.5%
		Q16	alo, for	69.3%	68.5%	+1.3%	
		Q17	alo, for	75.1%	72.4%	+3.6%	

fact that students authoring on related topics performed better than students authoring on different topics on 13 of the 14 questions provides some evidence for authoring having a positive effect on learning (exact binomial test, $p = 0.0018$).

Group outcomes can also be examined by aggregating exam performance across *all* related questions. For example, we can calculate how many students correctly answered *all three* questions related to the "Variables" topic group. Of the 176 students randomly assigned to this topic group, 108 (61.4%) correctly answered Questions 1, 2 and 3. This compares with 309 (58.9%) of the 525 students not in the "Variables" group answering these three questions correctly. Table 5 gives similar performance comparisons for the other main topic groups. In all cases, students were more likely to answer all exam questions related to a particular topic correctly if they were authoring questions on that topic. If performance is measured as the percentage of students answering all related questions correctly, as shown in Table 5, effect sizes range from 4.2% to 13.4% and the greatest effect is seen for the "Functions" topic.

Question 9 was the only question for which students in the corresponding topic group ("Loops") underperformed compared with students in the other topic groups. The performance difference is not statistically significant (Wilcoxon rank sum test, $p = 0.078$) but is relatively large when compared with other exam questions. In Question 9 students were presented with a *while* loop and a collection of *for* loops, and were asked to identify which of the *for* loops produced the same output as the *while* loop. The provided *while* loop was constructed with the increment statement

at the *start* of the loop body rather than at the end as is more common. Therefore, students were required to realise that in an equivalent *for* loop, the increment and the loop body would be executed in the opposite order. Two-thirds of questions created by students that involved *while* loops placed the loop increment at the end of the loop body, and so the unusual construction seen in Question 9 may have been a source of confusion for students in the "Loops" group.

6. CONCLUSION

In this work, we investigated the impact of a question authoring activity on subsequent exam performance in an introductory programming course. We conducted a large-scale ($n = 700$) experiment, where each student was randomly assigned the topics that their questions should target. For 13 of the 14 exam questions, students that had authored questions on a related topic performed better than students who had authored questions on different topics.

Although we believe that question authoring has a positive effect on exam performance, we cannot claim that it is any more or less effective than other study strategies. It is possible that some combination of question generation and self-testing would be more effective than either strategy used on its own, and exploring this is future work. We also do not know if, like other strategies [2], the impact of question authoring fades over time. Nevertheless, we encourage instructors to add question authoring activities to the collection of exam preparation tasks they provide for students.

Table 5: Proportion of students answering all related questions correctly

Group	Questions	n (in group)	n (not in group)	% all correct (in group)	% all correct (not in group)	% difference (normalised)
Variables	1, 2, 3	176	525	61.4%	58.9%	+4.2%
Functions	7, 10, 12	176	525	44.9%	39.6%	+13.4%
Loops	4, 6, 8, 9	177	524	49.2%	46.4%	+6.0%
Arrays or Loops	13, 15, 16, 17	349	352	40.9%	38.9%	+5.1%

7. REFERENCES

[1] V. Barr and D. Trytten. Using Turing's Craft Codelab to support CS1 students as they learn to program. *ACM Inroads*, 7(2):67–75, May 2016.

[2] Y. Cao and L. Porter. Evaluating student learning from collaborative group tests in introductory computing. In *Proc. ACM Tech. Symp. on CS Ed (SIGCSE '17)*, pages 99–104. ACM, 2017.

[3] P. R. Denner and J. P. Rickards. A developmental comparison of the effects of provided and generated questions on text recall. *Contemporary Educational Psychology*, 12(2):135 – 146, 1987.

[4] P. Denny. Generating practice questions as a preparation strategy for introductory programming exams. In *Proc. ACM Tech. Symp. on CS Ed (SIGCSE '15)*, pages 278–283. ACM, 2015.

[5] P. Denny, D. Cukierman, and J. Bhaskar. Measuring the effect of inventing practice exercises on learning in an introductory programming course. In *Proceedings of the 15th Koli Calling Conference on Computing Education Research*, pages 13–22. ACM, 2015.

[6] P. Denny, A. Luxton-Reilly, and J. Hamer. The PeerWise system of student contributed assessment questions. In *Proceedings of the Tenth Conference on Australasian Computing Education - Volume 78*, pages 69–74. Australian Computer Society, Inc., 2008.

[7] P. Denny, A. Luxton-Reilly, J. Hamer, and H. Purchase. Coverage of course topics in a student generated MCQ repository. In *Proc. ACM Conf. on Innovation and Technology in CS Ed (ITiCSE '09)*, pages 11–15, 2009.

[8] L. Ding and R. Beichner. Approaches to data analysis of multiple-choice questions. *Phys. Rev. ST Phys. Educ. Res.*, 5:020103, Sep 2009.

[9] J. Dunlosky. Strengthening the student toolbox: Study strategies to boost learning. *American Educator*, 37(3):12–21, September 2013.

[10] P. W. Foos, J. J. Mora, and S. Tkacz. Student study techniques and the generation effect. *Journal of Educational Psychology*, 86(4):567–576, 1994.

[11] R. Gurung. How do students really study (and does it matter)? *Teaching of Psychology*, 32:238–240, 2005.

[12] D. Hovemeyer and J. Spacco. Cloudcoder: A web-based programming exercise system. *J. Comput. Sci. Coll.*, 28(3):30–30, Jan. 2013.

[13] J. R. Lehman and K. M. Lehman. The relative effects of experimenter and subject generated questions on learning from museum case exhibits. *Journal of Research in Science Teaching*, 21(9):931–935, 1984.

[14] R. Lister, E. S. Adams, S. Fitzgerald, W. Fone, J. Hamer, M. Lindholm, R. McCartney, J. E. Moström, K. Sanders, O. Seppälä, B. Simon, and L. Thomas. A multi-national study of reading and tracing skills in novice programmers. *SIGCSE Bull.*, 36(4):119–150, June 2004.

[15] A. Luxton-Reilly, D. Bertinshaw, P. Denny, B. Plimmer, and R. Sheehan. The impact of question generation activities on performance. In *Proceedings of the 43rd ACM Technical Symposium on Computer Science Education*, pages 391–396. ACM, 2012.

[16] L. Malmi, V. Karavirta, A. Korhonen, and J. Nikander. Experiences on automatically assessed algorithm simulation exercises with different resubmission policies. *J. Educ. Resour. Comput.*, 5(3), Sept. 2005.

[17] D. Marchena Parreira, A. Petersen, and M. Craig. PCRS-C: Helping students learn C. In *Proc. ACM Conf. on Innovation and Technology in CS Ed (ITiCSE '15)*, pages 347–347. ACM, 2015.

[18] S. Mishra and S. Iyer. An exploration of problem posing-based activities as an assessment tool and as an instructional strategy. *Research and Practice in Technology Enhanced Learning*, 10(1), 2015.

[19] A. Petersen, M. Craig, and P. Denny. Employing multiple-answer multiple choice questions. In *Proc. ACM Conf. on Innovation and Technology in CS Ed (ITiCSE '16)*, pages 252–253. ACM, 2016.

[20] A. Petersen, M. Craig, and D. Zingaro. Reviewing CS1 exam question content. In *Proceedings of the 42nd ACM Technical Symposium on Computer Science Education*, pages 631–636. ACM, 2011.

[21] H. L. Roediger and A. C. Butler. The critical role of retrieval practice in long-term retention. *Trends in Cognitive Sciences*, 15(1):20 – 27, 2011.

[22] H. L. Roediger and A. C. Butler. Retrieval practice (testing) effect. *In H. L. Pashler (Ed.), Encyclopedia of the Mind, Sage Publishing*, pages 660–661, 2013.

[23] J. Sheard, Simon, A. Carbone, D. Chinn, M.-J. Laakso, T. Clear, M. de Raadt, D. D'Souza, J. Harland, R. Lister, A. Philpott, and G. Warburton. Exploring programming assessment instruments: a classification scheme for examination questions. In *Proc. of the 7th International Workshop on Computing Education Research*, pages 33–38. ACM, 2011.

[24] Simon, D. Chinn, M. de Raadt, A. Philpott, J. Sheard, M.-J. Laakso, D. D'Souza, J. Skene, A. Carbone, T. Clear, R. Lister, and G. Warburton. Introductory programming: Examining the exams. In *Proceedings of the 14th Australasian Computing Education Conference*, pages 61–70, 2012.

[25] N. Slamecka and P. Graf. The generation effect: Delineation of a phenomenon. *Journal of Experimental Psychology*, 4:592–604, 1978.

Impact of Performance Level and Group Composition on Student Learning during Collaborative Exams

Yingjun Cao and Leo Porter
Department of Computer Science and Engineering
University of California, San Diego
La Jolla, CA, USA

ABSTRACT

Collaborative exams have shown promise for improving student learning in computing. Prior studies have focused on benefits for all students, whereas this study seeks to refine our understanding of which students benefit and how group composition impacts that benefit. Using a crossover experimental design, the study first investigates whether students from differing performance levels (low, medium, or high) benefit from the collaborative exam. We find that students in the middle of the class (neither high nor low performers) tend to benefit strongly from the collaborative exam. Second, we explore whether group composition based on performance levels impacts the performance of members of the group. The results suggest more homogeneous groups (i.e., students in the group are at similar performance levels) are beneficial whereas students in groups with high heterogeneity do not experience significant performance differences between the pre-test and post-test.

Categories and Subject Descriptors

K.3.2 [**Computer Science Education**]: Computer and Information Science Education

Keywords

Collaborative Exam; Group Composition; Performance Level; CS1

1. INTRODUCTION

Collaborative exams, especially two-stage exams, have shown promising results in improving student grades [10, 15] and promoting student learning [6, 12] outside of computing fields. Two-stage exams start with a normal individual exam which is then immediately followed by a group exam where students work in small groups to solve a set of problems [22, 28, 29]. Due to the high-stakes nature of an exam, students are expected to fully participate in the problem-solving process. As a novel hybrid form of summative and formative assessments, this exam format has been shown to statistically improve short-term student learning in computing through a recent controlled study [4].

Although collaborative exams have been shown to promote student learning in computing, it is unknown how the performance level of a student might impact their potential learning benefit from the exam. Moreover, it is unknown how group composition impacts learning given evidence that group composition can impact team effectiveness [1]. In prior studies on two-stage exams, students usually self-select team members [12, 27] or are randomly assigned to groups [4].

In this study, we investigate how collaborative exams affect student learning based on students' performance level, both individually and collaboratively in a group. We use students' normalized pre-test scores on specific topics as the metric for students' performance level. This is the first study in computing, to the best of our knowledge, to examine directly the impact of student performance levels on their learning and on group effectiveness during collaborative exams. To perform this study, we adopted a crossover design [4, 12] in order to measure students' performance differences between the pre-test and post-test. The crossover design modifies standard two-stage exams by placing students randomly into control or experimental conditions. All students take a normal individual exam for the first part of a midterm exam (i.e., a pre-test). Students in the control group for a topic then spend test time individually answering questions. Students in the experimental group for the same topic then answer those same questions but do so in small groups. In the end, all students complete a quiz a few weeks later (i.e., a post-test). The value of the crossover design is it enables all students to be in the control group for one topic and the experimental group for another topic (see Section 3 for details). Additionally, the format helps control for time-on-task by having a student spend time in the control group working individually.

Employing this study design, we find that mid-performing students show significant improvement in their post-test compared with their per-test after collaborative exams while low- and high-performing students tend to have insignificant performance differences. Using group members' performance levels in the pre-test to measure group heterogeneity, we find that low and moderate heterogeneity groups statistically benefit from collaborative exams. These results suggest the homogeneous grouping of students by performance when employing group exams.

ITiCSE '17 July 03-05, 2017, Bologna, Italy

© 2017 ACM. ISBN 978-1-4503-4704-4/17/07...$15.00

DOI: http://dx.doi.org/10.1145/3059009.3059024

2. BACKGROUND

Collaborative Exam Effectiveness: Although the primary purpose of formative assessments is to promote student learning, summative exams can also offer students the opportunity to learn. Studies on the "testing effect" [11, 23] have long shown that testing can improve knowledge retention. Tests and exams also promote learning indirectly as students usually only study on topics that they believe will appear in subsequent tests [3]. Given the prevalence of exams and tests in higher education, researchers have begun to examine how to additionally leverage testing as a learning tool [24]. In particular, two-stage exams, as a variant of collaborative exams [25], have been shown to improve student learning outside of the computing field [6, 12]. In computing, work by Yu et al. [27] has reported that students have positive attitudes towards this testing format. That study also examined student learning through the use of isomorphic questions on midterms and final exams to measure two-stage exam's effectiveness but did not find significant performance gains. In another recent work in computing, Cao and Porter employed a controlled study and found that the group portion of collaborative exams can provide short-term learning benefits for students overall [4].

Collaborative Exam Impact by Performance Level: Researchers outside of computer science have examined if collaborative exams benefit students with different performance levels. Students are categorized based on their exam or quiz scores before the collaborative test. Then performance difference between pre- and post-tests are further explored for each category of students. In the setting of a statistical methods course, Dahlstrom [7] uses pre-test scores of students to rank them into low (below 50% in the pretest) and high (above 50%) categories. Using a pre-post experimental design, the study shows low-performing students have significant performance gains in the post-test, both on repeated questions and new questions. No statistically significant results were observed for high-performing students. In another study in biology by Leight et. al. [17], the authors categorized students using their previous exam scores (A to F) and examined the impact of collaborative exams on knowledge retention. The conclusion was there was no difference in benefit by performance levels. In a study in geology [12], students were categorized into three quantiles based on their overall pre-test scores. The authors found that there is no statistical difference on performance among the three quantiles. To the best of our knowledge, no similar work exists in computing.

Collaborative Exam Impact by Group Heterogeneity: Collaborative exams use group work to promote learning. Research in organizational studies have shown that group performance is closely related to team members' characteristics [5, 16, 20, 26]. In the computing field, software engineering researchers have studied team members' attributes that impact team performance. For example, Faraj et. al. [9] found that communication and expertise are strongly correlated with team performance. Similarly, Gorla et. al. [13] incorporated personality into team productivity measure. While these studies inform this work, the group work during collaborative exams is different from common collaborative teamwork in software engineering in two key aspects: (1) the solutions to exam problems may require less creativity than those in software engineering projects; (2) students in the exam setting are time pressured—having little time to complete the task. These unique attributes of group work during collaborative exams may create interaction styles among team members which are different from those in prior studies. As such, this study examines if heterogeneity of performance levels in groups impacts student learning.

3. METHOD

Both sections of CS1.5 in Java offered in the Spring of 2016 at a large North American university were selected for this study. The total enrollment was 278 at the beginning of the term. At this institution, CS1.5 is a gateway course into the major and grades in the course impact students' ability to transfer into the computer science major. The lectures for these sections were held back-to-back. The course was structured to have two midterms and three quizzes. The pattern of the these assessments is quiz 1, midterm 1, quiz 2, midterm 2, and quiz 3. Each quiz and midterm are 2-week apart with the two-week window being a convenient choice for the flow of the course. Peer instruction [21] is used in this course. The instructor has taught this course twice using peer instruction and is one of the authors of this work.

For purposes of this study, both sections of CS1.5 are treated as one large section throughout the analysis. Using the consent form approved by the institutional review board, 247 students consented to participate in this research project by the time of the first midterm, and 228 of these students were present during the second midterm.

3.1 Experimental Design

The cross-over design from Cao et. al. [4] was used to measure potential performance differences with collaborative exam as the experimental condition. Figure 1 provides an overview of this design.

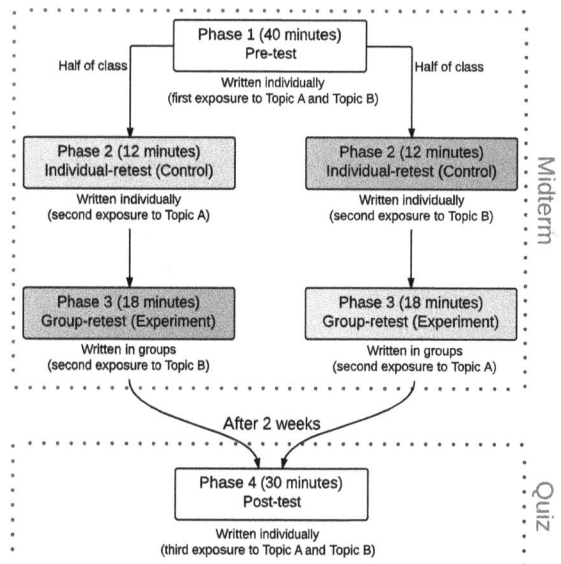

Figure 1: Experimental procedure. Students are randomly assigned to either the left path or the right path. The experimental phase and the control phase have the same questions per topic and students experience these questions either during the individual or group retest.

Two independent experiments were conducted with midterm 1 and quiz 2 forming an experiment and midterm 2 and quiz 3 forming the second experiment. The phases of the experiment are:

Phase 1 - Pre-test: The first portion of the midterm consists of students completing the individual exam (i.e. pre-test). The individual exam includes one problem on Topic A and one on Topic B. Individual exam papers are collected at the end of phase 1.

Phase 2 - Individual-Retest (control): Each student is given a retest paper with one in-depth problem on either Topic A or Topic B, depending on their path through Figure 1. Students are given 12 minutes to complete this task. The purpose of this phase is to help separate out the impact of spending more time on the topic alone during the retest (control condition) from spending more time on the topic in a collaborative setting described next (experimental condition).

Phase 3 - Group-Retest (experiment): The third phase is the experimental condition where students solve problems on the different topic from that they solved in the second phase (questions, per topic, are identical in the Individual- and Group-Retest phases). During this phase, students work together in groups of four to solve the problem with some rare cases of 3-person groups because of the number of student present during the midterm. This phase lasts 18 minutes which is slightly longer than the control phase to allow for students to fully engage in collaborative work. The group-retest is offered at the end of the midterm to avoid having to refocus students from group to individual work and to avoid groups hearing discussion of questions which they might later see during an individual-retest.

Phase 4 - Post-test: The 30-minute quiz, i.e. post-test, is given 2 weeks after the midterm. Similar questions to the pre-test for Topic A and Topic B are given in this phase. However question difficulty (and content) on each topic may vary between assessments.

To summarize, for an experiment, there are two assessment scores per student:

- **Individual pre-test**: Each student has a score for Topics A and B in the individual test (i.e. phase 1 in Figure 1) of the midterm. These scores also indicate the performance level of a student on these concepts.

- **post-test**: Again, each student will have a score for Topic A and another score for Topic B in the follow-up quiz (2 weeks after the midterm).

We compare scores between the post-test and pre-test to measure the performance difference for each student per topic. The performance difference (PD) can be thought of as the change in student performance on the topic between the pre- and post-test. For students in each of the control and experimental condition, we calculate this performance difference and examine differences between these groups. Note that because questions were not necessarily of equal difficulty, a negative performance difference does not imply students suffered a loss in understanding. A negative performance difference likely implies the post-test had simply more difficult questions.

The topics ("A" and "B") in each experiment were selected based on the normal flow of the course and the relationships between the topics. For the first experiment, the two topics were method overloading and overriding (Topic A) and

constructors (Topic B). Both topics are closely related to inheritance in Java. For the second experiment, the two topics were polymorphism (Topic A) and Recursion (Topic B). These two topics are not considered to be closely related. All exams and quizzes are closed book and closed notes. Due to space constraints, we omit sample questions here, and ask interested readers to examine sample questions from our prior work (Cao and Porter [4]).

3.2 Research Questions

This work explores two related research questions on the impact of collaborative exams on student learning categorized by students' performance level, both individually and collaboratively.

RQ1: How does the performance level of a student impact the learning benefit from collaborative exams?

RQ2: Does group composition affect student learning during collaborative exams?

3.3 Measurement Metric

To evaluate the effectiveness of the group portion of a two-stage exam, we compare performance differences of students exposed to the control or experimental condition. Between the pre-test and post-test, the only in-class difference among students' exposure to each topic is either via the individual-retest (control) or the group-retest (experiment). Every student experiences two performance differences from each experiment: one from the individual-retest, and one from the group-retest. Without losing generality, assume a student is exposed to Topic A in the individual retest and Topic B in the group retest (i.e., the left branch in Figure 1). Suppose the student's scores for Topics A and B in the pre-test are Pre_A and Pre_B. Similarly, the scores of the student in the post-test on the two topics are $Post_A$ and $Post_B$. The performance difference of this student from individual retest is $PD_{individual} = Post_A - Pre_A$, and that from group retest is $PD_{group} = Post_B - Pre_B$. We then calculate $PD_{diff} = PD_{group} - PD_{individual}$ which is the measurement of the relative effectiveness of collaborative exams compared to simply having extra time on the topics.

The metric above is the absolute performance difference. An alternative metric, normalized learning gain (or normalized performance difference here), was also explored [19]. However, we observed that this variant tends to exaggerate outcomes on easier topics/questions and because the overall conclusions were the same using normalized performance difference, we focus on absolute performance difference in presenting the results.

3.3.1 Student Performance Level

To measure the performance level of a student in each experiment, we used the average of z-scores on Topics A and B. The normalization process removes scaling effect (different difficulties and/or distributions) from two different problems before combining them together. This metric for performance level is different from previous studies [12, 18] which measured students' performance level with their overall pre-test scores. We believe that even though a student's scores on pre-selected topics are correlated with their overall pre-test scores (Pearson $r = .408, p < .001$ in our study), our proposed metric for performance measure may offer a more accurate measurement of performance level by focusing solely on the topics in question.

To rank students into commonly accepted categories of low, mid, and high performance level, we coded students who are within one standard deviation (SD) from the mean as mid-performing. Those who are below one SD from the mean is ranked as low-performing and those who are above one SD from the mean as high-performing. This strategy resulted in 22.3% of students binned to the low category (106 students in total), 65.5% to the mid category (311 students in total), and 12.2% to the high category (58 students in total). This ranking resulted in imbalanced groups of low, mid, and high performing students. However, simply binning by thirds produced questionable cutoffs whereas our categorization method yields more meaningful separation between student groups.

3.3.2 Group Categorization

Group heterogeneity is measured using the standard deviation of group members' performance. The larger the standard deviation, the more heterogeneous the group is with regard to group members' performance level. Each group's standard deviation is used to classify each group into three equal quantiles—low, mid, or high heterogeneity.

All categorization and rankings are performed within each experiment first. Then the results from both experiments are pooled together for analysis. For comparisons of PD, statistical significance is set at the $p \le 0.05$ level.

4. RESULTS

4.1 Experimental Results

For each experiment, we cross-tabulated student exam data with experimental conditions and pre-selected topics (individual-retest as control and group-retest as experimental). The differential PD is obtained for each student per experiment. Table 1 provides these results for the class overall.

Topic		Pre-test		Post-test		Ind. PD	Group PD	Diff. PD
		Ctrl	Exp	Ctrl	Exp			
Exp1	A	55.0	52.4	67.5	76.3	12.5	23.9	10.9
	B	71.1	69.8	70.3	77.4	-0.9	7.6	
Exp2	A	85.8	83.3	67.0	68.6	-18.8	-14.6	2.0
	B	89.1	87.8	79.7	77.2	-9.5	-10.6	

Table 1: Raw data from controlled experiments.

These results are provided for two reasons. The first is as a reminder that because questions on the Pre-test and Post-test may vary in difficulty, we may find students achieving lower scores on the post-test than the pre-test. The second reason is to show how these scores by topic and by experimental condition are combined into an individual PD and group PD. Concept B in the second experiment (recursion) shows that students in the experimental condition did worse than that from the control group. However, this study is focused on the benefit from the group exam over the individual retest, which is provided as the differential in group and individual PD. For both experiments, the differential PD was positive, showing a measurable benefit from the group exam. We pool data from both experiments after normalization for each experiment to remove potential scaling effects. For the remainder of the study, we focus on the differential PDs on the pooled dataset.

4.2 RQ1: How does the performance level of a student impact the learning benefit from collaborative exams?

For each student, the average performance level on the two pre-selected topics in the pre-test per experiment is calculated as discussed in Section 3.3.1. Student results are then binned based on their performance level into low, mid, or high performing students. Figure 2 provides the PD for students based on performance level. One-sample t-tests were used to calculate significance for differential PD. There are no statistically significant differences for both low-performing and high-performing students. However, for mid-performing students, collaborative exams statistically improve student learning with a small effect size (Cohen's d).

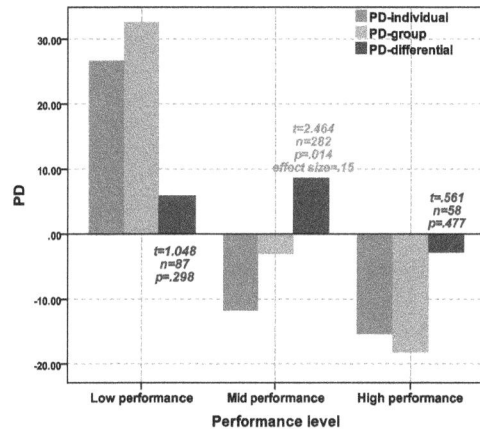

Figure 2: Student PD categorized by student performance level. Statistics for differential PD are provided; red font indicates statistical significance.

4.3 RQ2: Does group composition affect student learning during collaborative exams?

We next examine the benefit from the group exam based on the heterogeneity of performance levels among group members. The differential PD (PD of the experimental minus that of the control condition) for each binning of heterogeneity appears in Figure 3. One-sample t-tests are used to examine if differential PDs are zero. These results show

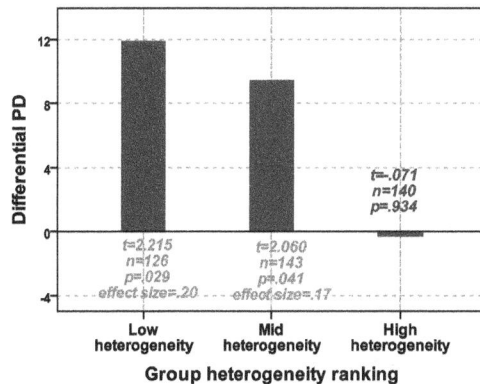

Figure 3: Differential PD categorized by group heterogeneity. Statistics for each category are provided; red fonts indicate statistical significance.

that groups with both low- and mid-levels of heterogeneity experience statistically significantly benefit from the group portion of the exam. High-heterogeneity groups do not.

The group composition within highly heterogeneous groups requires there be both high- and low-performing students. Homogeneous groups may consist of students from within any level of performance. Moreover, recall that the majority of students were classified as mid-performance, so a group of all low-performing students is less likely than one of all mid-performing. Figure 4 provides the number of students in each type of group based on their performance level.

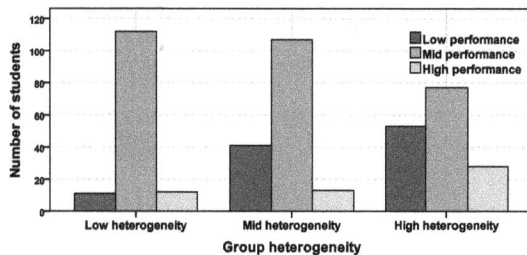

Figure 4: Composition of groups based on heterogeneity and student performance level.

These results show that high-heterogeneity groups have more low- and high-performing students than those with low heterogeneity. We also further stratified students for each heterogeneity group based on their performance level. It produces nine categories such as students with low-performance level in a low-heterogeneity group, students with mid-performance level in a high-heterogeneity group, etc. However, when dividing students into nine categories, the sample sizes in these grouping were small enough to limit our ability to draw reasonable conclusions or to perform meaningful statistical analysis. Also, no consistent pattern was observed from these sub-groupings.

5. DISCUSSION

RQ1 - Performance Level: For low-performing students, they experience positive learning benefit from both the individual retest and group exam. As a result, the additional benefit of the group exam lacks statistical significance. This may indicate that low-performers learn more simply by spending more time on the subject, either individually or collaboratively, or that they spend more time after the exam preparing for the next quiz.

The category which appears to benefit the most from collaborative exams is mid-performing students. Figure 2 showed that this group experienced negative PDs for both the control and experimental condition, likely due to differences in difficulty. Those students in the experimental condition experienced a much smaller drop in performance than those in the control condition. This difference, along with the larger sample size, causes the differential PD to be significant. These results confirm those from existing studies that collaborative exams tend to improve knowledge retention [6, 8]. For high-performing students, they have a similar amount of negative PDs from both the group-retest and individual-retest. Therefore, differential PD was minimum. This result partially confirms the conclusion by Dahlstrom [7] that high-performing students do not show significant improvements from collaborative tests.

RQ2 - Group Heterogeneity: The observation that low- and mid-level group heterogeneity tend to produce high levels of student PDs is quite intriguing as existing research in educational psychology indicates that a more diverse group tends to be more creative in solving problems [20]. We believe that the aforementioned unique characteristics of exams may be the cause. Students need to complete a set of challenging questions during a short period. We suspect this may limit the role of group creativity during brief, high-stakes summative exams [2].

In homogeneous groups, the smaller divide in performance between students may allow for easier communication in general which leads to the improved group learning. Specifically, we suspect homogeneous groups have more student engagement as the students may feel more comfortable interacting with peers with similar levels of understanding. We also believe that it takes less time for the students to explain their thinking to similarly knowledgeable students. In addition, homogeneous groups may also tend to reach a solution that is agreeable to most team members while a highly heterogeneous group's solution may simply be provided by the high-performing member of the group.

Figure 4 also shows that high heterogeneity groups tend to have more low- and high-performing students. As these students tend to have small PDs as shown in RQ1, it could also explain why high heterogeneity groups tend to have limited PDs. It is difficult to distinguish if the lower PDs for low- and high-performing students is the cause, or the effect, from the degree of group heterogeneity.

Overall, our results seem to indicate that homogeneous grouping strategies should be explored to maximize the impact of collaborative exams.

Threats to Validity
Defining Student Performance Level: Student performance level was ranked based on standard-deviation on scaled pre-test results. We selected this method as we believed it classified students more accurately as within one performance group than another. However, by using standard deviation, we invariably had a larger sample size for our mid-performers and smaller sample sizes for our low- and high-performers. The sample size differences may impact our results and certainly impact the p value for statistical tests. However, we attempted other ranking approaches, such as equal quantiles, for determining students' performance level and the same overall conclusions were found.

Lack of Isomorphic Questions: The questions given during the pre- and post-tests were similar but were not identical. We thoroughly examined the questions from the pre-tests and post-tests and believe they are quite similar in terms of content and associated concepts. However, because the questions were different the questions could unintentionally test different concepts or skills between the pre-test versus the post-test. Future work could examine using isomorphic questions to reduce this confound.

6. CONCLUSION

This study shows that the level of student performance impacts the benefit they receive from collaborative exams in computing. Mid-performing students are found to experience significant learning benefit from the collaborative exams whereas low- and high-performing students do not. Group heterogeneity, based on the difference between performance level of team members, also impacts the benefit offered from collaborative exams. Groups with low levels of heterogeneity experience significant learning benefit for students. These results suggest that student groups in collaborative exams should be formed to be homogeneous regarding student performance. Although there has been similar observations on group dynamics in pair programming [14], this result is contrary to results in other domains where more heterogeneous groupings are beneficial. Therefore, we recommend further study on this topic.

7. ACKNOWLEDGMENTS

This work was partially supported by NSF DEERS project (1525028, 1525173, 1525373). The authors want to thank Daniel Zingaro for his feedback on an early draft of this work, and also want to thank the anonymous reviewers for their helpful suggestions.

8. REFERENCES

[1] M. R. Barrick, G. L. Stewart, M. J. Neubert, and M. K. Mount. Relating member ability and personality to work-team processes and team effectiveness. *Journal of Applied Psychology*, 83(3):377–391, 1998.

[2] D. Baud. Reframing assessment as if learning were important. In *Rethinking assessment in higher education: learning for the longer term.*, pages 14–25. Oxford: Routledge, 2007.

[3] J. Biggs. Enhancing teaching through constructive alignment. *Higher Education*, 32(3):347–364, 1996.

[4] Y. Cao and L. Porter. Evaluating student learning from collaborative group tests in introductory computing. In *SIGCSE*, pages 99–104, 2017.

[5] M. A. Carpenter. The implications of strategy and social context for the relationship between top management team heterogeneity and firm performance. *Strategic Management Journal*, 23(3):275–284, 2002.

[6] R. N. Cortright, H. L. Collins, D. W. Rodenbaugh, and S. E. DiCarlo. Student retention of course content is improved by collaborative-group testing. *Advances in Physiology Education*, 27(3):102–108, 2003.

[7] Ö. Dahlström. Learning during a collaborative final exam. *Educational Research and Evaluation*, 18(4):321–332, 2012.

[8] M. L. Epstein, A. D. Lazarus, T. B. Calvano, K. A. Matthews, R. A. Hendel, B. B. Epstein, and G. M. Brosvic. Immediate feedback assessment technique promotes learning and corrects inaccurate first responses. *The Psychological Record*, 52:187–201, 2002.

[9] S. Faraj and L. Sproull. Coordinating expertise in software development teams. *Management Science*, 46(12):1554–1568, 2000.

[10] M. Fengler and P. M. Ostafichuk. Successes with two-stage exams in mechanical engineering. *CEEA*, pages 1–5, 2015.

[11] A. I. Gates. *Recitation as a factor in memorizing*. Number 40. Science Press, 1922.

[12] B. H. Gilley and B. Clarkston. Collaborative testing: Evidence of learning in a controlled in-class study of undergraduate students. *Journal of College Science Teaching*, 43(3):83–91, 2014.

[13] N. Gorla and Y. W. Lam. Who should work with whom? building effective software project teams. *Communications of the ACM*, 47(6):79–82, 2004.

[14] N. Katira, L. Williams, E. Wiebe, C. Miller, S. Balik, and E. Gehringer. On understanding compatibility of student pair programmers. In *SIGCSE*, pages 7–11, 2004.

[15] K. Knierim, H. Turner, and R. K. Davis. Two-stage exams improve student learning in an introductory geology course: Logistics, attendance, and grades. *Journal of Geoscience Education*, 63:157–164, 2015.

[16] R. A. Layton, M. L. Loughry, M. W. Ohland, and G. D. Ricco. Design and validation of a web-based system for assigning members to teams using instructor-specified criteria. *Advances in Engineering Education*, 2(1):1–28, 2010.

[17] H. Leight, C. Saunders, R. Calkins, and M. Withers. Collaborative testing improves performance but not content retention in a large-enrollment introductory biology class. *CBE Life Sciences Education*, 11(4):392–401, 2012.

[18] G. L. Macpherson, Y. J. Lee, and D. Steeples. Group-examination improves learning for low-achieving students. *Journal of Geoscience Education*, 59(1):41, 2011.

[19] J. D. Marx and K. Cummings. Normalized change. *American Journal of Physics*, 75(2007):87, 2007.

[20] B. A. Nijstad and C. K. W. De Dreu. Creativity and group innovation. *Applied Psychology*, 51(3):400–405, 2002.

[21] L. Porter, C. Bailey Lee, B. Simon, and D. Zingaro. Peer instruction: do students really learn from peer discussion in computing? *ICER*, pages 45–52, 2011.

[22] B. G. W. Rieger and C. E. Heiner. Examinations that support collaborative learning: The students' perspective. *Journal of College Science Teaching*, 43(4):41–48, 2014.

[23] H. L. Roediger and J. D. Karpicke. The power of testing memory basic research and implications for educational practice. *Perspectives on Psychological Science*, 1(3):181–210, 2006.

[24] H. L. Roediger III, P. K. Agarwal, M. A. McDaniel, and K. B. McDermott. Test-enhanced learning in the classroom: long-term improvements from quizzing. *Journal of Experimental Psychology: Applied*, 17(4):382, 2011.

[25] S. A. Stearns. Collaborative exams as learning tools. *College Teaching*, 44(3):111–112, 1996.

[26] M. A. West. Sparkling fountains or stagnant ponds: An integrative model of creativity and innovation implementation in work groups. *Applied Psychology: An International Review*, 51(3):355–424, 2002.

[27] B. Yu, G. Tsiknis, and M. Allen. Turning exams into a learning experience. In *SIGCSE*, pages 336–340, 2010.

[28] R. F. Yuretich, S. a. Khan, R. M. Leckie, and J. J. Clement. Active-learning methods to improve student performance and scientific interest in a large introductory oceanography course. *Journal of Geoscience Education*, 49:111–119, 2001.

[29] J. F. Zipp. Learning by exams : The impact of two-stage cooperative tests. *Teaching Sociology*, 35(1):62–76, 2007.

Study Habits, Exam Performance, and Confidence: How do Workflow Practices and Self-Efficacy Ratings Align?

Anthony Estey
University of Victoria
aestey@uvic.ca

Yvonne Coady
University of Victoria
ycoady@uvic.ca

ABSTRACT

Do students recognize the relationship between self-sufficient problem solving and exam performance? We explore this question based on log data and survey results collected over 3 semesters from 465 students who were split into cohorts based on final exam performance. Specifically, we consider three metrics: time on task, question difficulty, and self-efficacy ratings.

Our results show that, on average, median values for time on task between Low and High performing cohorts are within 16%. However, increased question difficulty revealed very different modes of spending time: when working through practice tool exercises, the High cohort regularly attempted to solve problems without assistance, whereas the Low cohort frequently requested hints during initial and subsequent attempts. Overall, when re-attempting a question that was previously attempted but incorrect, slightly over 20% of the Low cohort were able to complete the question without using hints, whereas roughly 50% of the High cohort were able to do so. Most strikingly, as the semester progressed, the average increase in confidence to solve a similar question after viewing hints was greatest for students in the Low cohort. It appears that students among the Low cohort, who went on to fail the final exam, believed that viewing solutions to problems, instead of solving the problem on their own, adequately prepared them to be able to solve similar problems without assistance in the future.

KEYWORDS

CS1; study behaviour; educational data mining

ACM Reference format:
Anthony Estey and Yvonne Coady. 2017. Study Habits, Exam Performance, and Confidence: How do Workflow Practices and Self-Efficacy Ratings Align? In *Proceedings of ITiCSE'17, July 03-05, 2017, Bologna, Italy,* , 6 pages.
DOI: http://dx.doi.org/10.1145/3059009.3059056

1 INTRODUCTION

Recent studies exploring predictors of success in CS1 have found ways to potentially identify students at risk of failure within the first few weeks of the course [1, 8]. Successful and unsuccessful students can be differentiated through patterns in log data with respect to debugging proficiency [11, 14, 20] and study behaviour [7, 18].

Often the data analysis is done after the current course has ended, to correlate log data with course grades [7, 15, 18, 19], allowing for vital information about the factors that correlate with success to be collected to support future students. This study compliments these recent studies by combining qualitative survey data with quantitative log data to attempt to better understand why unsuccessful students exhibit certain behaviour. Throughout the semester, students worked through practice exercises on a programming practice tool. Surveys were distributed to collect information about each student's perceived progress with respect to tool usage and course material. Using a mixed-methods approach, this study explores the following key research question: *do students understand whether or not their study habits are likely to lead to success on the final exam?* To answer this key research question, we consider the following intermediate research questions:

RQ1: How well does time-on-task differentiate between successful and unsuccessful students?

RQ2: How well does intended question difficulty differentiate between successful and unsuccessful students?

RQ3: Is there a difference in a student's reflection of self-efficacy between successful and unsuccessful students?

This paper presents the results of a four-semester study on interaction data collected from 465 students who voluntarily used a programming practice tool. This study was designed to help us better understand why students are not successful in our CS1 course. The main contributions of this paper are: (1) quantitative analysis of data collected over three semester showing consistent trends with respect to time on task and hint usage; (2) qualitative analysis of survey responses revealing student perception with respect to study behaviour and confidence; and (3) a mixed-methods approach correlating the quantitative and qualitative results to provide insight into the differences between real and perceived success.

The remainder of this paper is organized as follows. Section 2 discusses related works, Section 3 our methodology, and Section 4 the results. Section 5 provides an analysis and discussion, then Section 6 concludes the paper and discusses paths for future work.

2 BACKGROUND AND RELATED WORK

There have been a number of recent studies that have analyzed compilation and debugging behaviour [2, 8, 11, 12, 14, 20]. These studies have revealed the capabilities of detecting patterns in log data to predict overall student performance. Our work takes a more coarse-grained approach and looks at whether patterns in time on task and hint usage can also be used to differentiate between successful and unsuccessful students.

There have been a number of studies relating to time on task and study strategies, such as how and when students receive assistance.

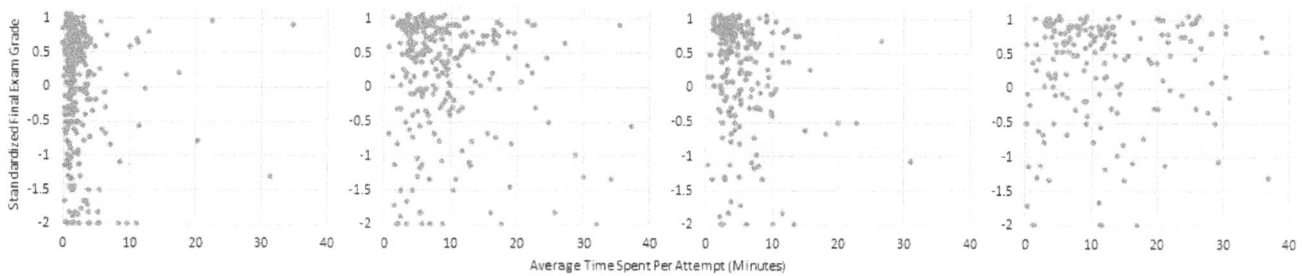

Figure 1: Time spent on task for students working on questions in the for-loop module, introduced in week 2. The graphs represent data collected from questions 1, 3, 5, and 7 from within this module. Final exam grades are standardized to account for possible changes in exam difficulty across semesters.

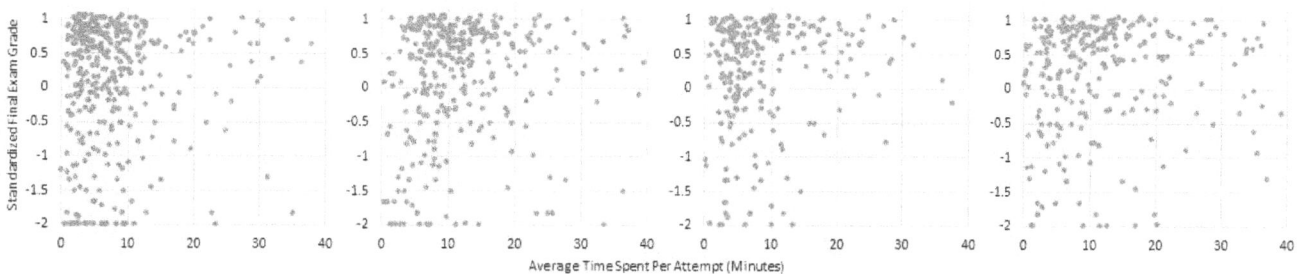

Figure 2: Time spent on task for questions 1, 3, 5, and 7 across all modules covered throughout each semester.

Arroyo et al. state that a student's goals and attitudes while interacting with a tutoring system are typically unseen and unknowable [3]. A study on student behaviour during lab periods found that confusion and boredom are two affective states associated with lower achievement [17]. Cocea and Weibelzahl have completed a number of very insightful studies on disengagement prediction [5]. They explain that engagement is an important aspect of effective learning, because time spent using an e-Learning system is not quality time if the learner is not engaged. Carter et al. found that most students wanted help that went beyond office hours and email, and that for the vast majority of them, their grades correlated positively with the amount of help they received for insurmountable difficulties, or those they could not progress through without assistance [4].

In a study exploring how to best support struggling students, Robins et al. speculate that the distinction between an effective and ineffective novice is more important than the one between a novice and expert programmer [16], and that the significant difference between effective and ineffective novices relate to learning strategies rather than knowledge. Fouh et al. explored student learning behaviour through an analysis of eTextbook data [10], and found that many students focus only on material they receive credit for, but do complete additional exercises prior to exams. Similarly, using a data-driven approach, Eagle and Barnes found that students with access to hints approach problems in statistically and practically different ways than those who do not [6].

The aforementioned studies inspired us to use a data driven approach to explore *how* students were spending time using the learning tool, in addition to submission correctness and time on task analysis. Previous studies highlight the importance of combining student perception data, which we collected through surveys, with learning tool log data to better understand student learning states.

3 METHODOLOGY

The data for this study was collected over three semesters from a 13-week CS1 course taught in Java. Topics covered include variables, control flow, methods, conditionals, loops, I/O, arrays, searching and sorting algorithms, and objects.

Interaction data was collected from an open-source[1] programming practice tool [9] introduced during the second week of the course. Tool use was completely voluntary, and did not affect student grades in any way. The tool was introduced as a supplemental practice resource offering exercises similar to those found on written exams. The tool also provided automatic feedback on submissions correctness. Buttons to compile code, run code, submit a solution, get a hint, and ask a question were all instrumented to collect student interaction patterns. As an optional feature, students could use a series of hints that progressively guided them through each question, and the final hint provided a full sample solution.

Data was collected from the 465 students who opted to take part in this study, out of the 656 enrolled in our course. Log data was linked to final exam scores, which were standardized to account for potential changes in difficulty between semesters. In the first Semester (S1), 53 out of 64 students attempted at least one question on the learning tool, and 41 (64%) students participated in the study. In the second Semester (S2), 319 out of 389 students attempted a question, and 269 (69%) participated in the study. In the third Semester (S3), 186 out of 196 students attempted a question, and 155 (79%) students participated in the study.

Final exam scores were standardized each semester, and students were split into three groups based on their standardized final exam score: students who were unable to pass the final exam (<-0.8

---

[1] http://www.github.com/aestey/phd

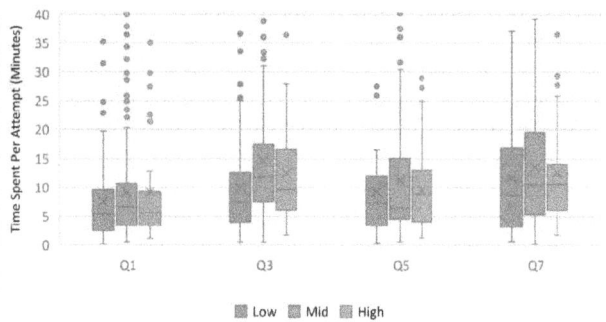

Figure 3: Time on task on Questions 1, 3, 5, and 7 across all modules, showing the range of the 25-75th percentile (box), min (vertical line, bottom), max (vertical line, top), average (X), median (horizontal line), and outliers for all cohorts.

standard deviations below the mean), identified as the *Low* cohort; students with an A letter grade on the final exam (>0.8 standard deviations above the mean), called the *High* cohort; and the remaining students were labeled as the *Mid* cohort. Overall for this study, 101 students were placed in the Low cohort, 274 in the Mid cohort, and 90 in the High cohort.

During the third semester, surveys were distributed during the 5th and 9th week of the semester. In total, 55 students filled out both surveys, 9 students from the Low cohort, 26 from the Mid cohort, and 20 from the High cohort. Similar to the learning tool, survey participation was completely voluntary, and participation and responses did not affect student grades. Survey questions were created to gather feedback based on the patterns in the learning tool log data found in the first two semesters of the study.

4 RESULTS

First, we explore common trends found across student groups throughout the three semesters the learning tool was used. We then explore whether survey responses about study habits align with collected log data during the third semester the tool was used.

Table 1: Aggregate usage trends recorded over all semesters

Cohort	Questions			Compiles			Hints		
	S1	S2	S3	S1	S2	S3	S1	S2	S3
Low	35.2	36.8	46.5	54	54	58	303	122	246
Mid	47.2	54.6	58.9	113	104	122	142	139	166
High	61.2	65.4	67.5	168	122	145	72	89	96

Table 1 shows the average number of unique questions attempted, compilations, and hints requested for the three semesters, labeled S1, S2, and S3. The data is split by cohort for each semester. Throughout all three semesters, higher performing students attempted more unique questions, compiled more often, but requested less hints. Table 1 shows aggregate data collected throughout the whole semester, explored in more detail in previous work [8], but does not show question-specific data. For instance, Table 1 shows the number of unique questions attempted, but does not show how many times a student revisited a question, or which question the hints were requested on. The following sub-sections expand on this analysis by delving deeper into the data, by looking at different modules and questions independently.

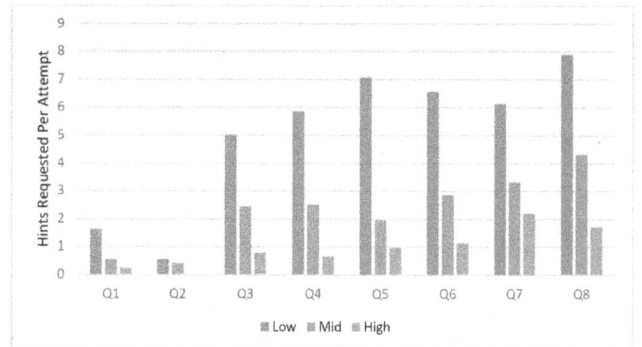

Figure 4: Hints requested per question number within the for-loop module.

4.1 Time on Task (RQ1)

To answer our first research question, we first explored whether patterns existed between student groups based on time spent on task working through exercises in the for-loop module (Figure 5), introduced during the second week of each semester. Figure 1 shows that on question 1 in the module, students across all semesters and grade ranges generally spent between 0 and 5 minutes working through the question. Although Figure 1 shows that time on task increased for all students when working through questions later in the module, time on task alone would not allow us to differentiate between successful and unsuccessful students in our study.

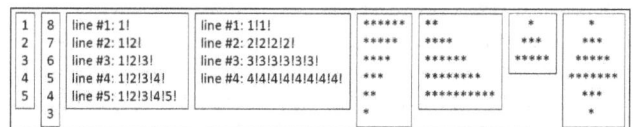

Figure 5: Each box outlines the output students were asked to generate in the for-loop module for Questions 1 to 8.

Figure 2 shows time on task for exercises covered in all modules throughout the semester. In comparison to Figure 1, the semester-long data trends show an increase the average time spent per question number, but it remains difficult to differentiate between unsuccessful and successful students using this metric. Figure 3 further illustrates that students cannot be identified by time on task across in this study.

It may be difficult to differentiate students based on time on task due to how the learning tool was used throughout our study. The learning tool was introduced as a supplemental ungraded *practice* tool, and students were under no pressure to complete an exercise within a certain amount of time. Students were also able to request hints, which provided step-by-step instructions and code snippets leading up to a complete solution of the problem. Figures 1 and 2 show how long students spent on each question, but fail to show *how* students spent their time working through each question. The following sub-section explores the study behaviour of students across the three cohorts, with a specific focus on hint usage in an attempt to better understand perceived question difficulty.

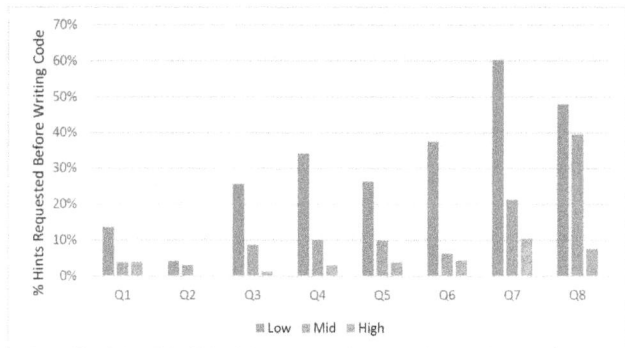

Figure 6: The percentage of times hints were requested before writing code within the for-loop module.

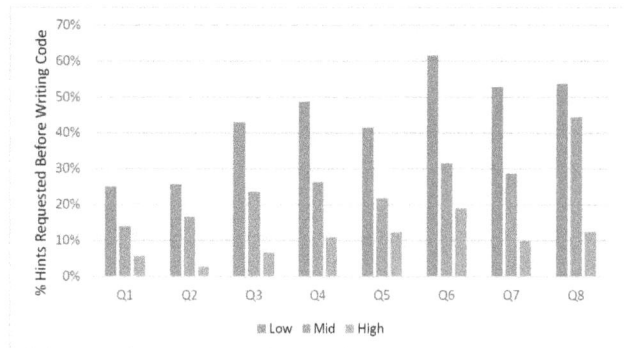

Figure 7: The percentage of times hints were requested before writing code across all modules.

4.2 Question Difficulty (RQ2)

The impact of question difficulty is considered from two perspectives. First, *intended* difficulty, designed to challenge the students as the questions within a module progressively build on newly acquired knowledge. Second, *perceived* difficulty, as established by student interaction with each problem within a topic module.

Within a given module, questions are designed to progressively become more challenging. Figure 5 shows questions 1 (Q1) through 8 (Q8) in the for-loop module. Figures 4 and 6 show hint data collected across the for-loop module on questions Q1 to Q8, which are ordered within the module by intended difficulty. These results show consistency with the trends established in Table 1 on the number of hints viewed among cohorts across all questions, independent of intended difficulty. Figure 4 shows that across all of the questions in the module, lower-performing students requested more hints on average when compared to higher performing students. In addition to this, Figure 6 shows that students in the Low cohort requested hints before attempting to write and compile code more often than the other cohorts.

Different questions in the module had a different number of total hints that could be requested, so Figure 4 alone may not effectively illustrate perceived difficulty. Figure 6 illustrates which questions students requested hints on before compiling any code on their own. Taken together, Figures 4 and 6 indicate that *perceived* difficultly does not necessarily increase linearly from question to question.

Expanding this analysis to all of the modules, similar trends were found. Figure 7 shows the frequency hints were requested before attempting to write and compile code across all modules. Throughout each semester, students in the Low cohort consistently requested hints before attempting to solve problems on their own more often than the Mid and High cohorts.

4.3 Self-Efficacy (RQ3)

To further explore hint usage behaviour, in the third semester, students were asked a number of questions about their hint usage. Surveys distributed during the fifth and ninth week of the course. In total, 55 students filled out both surveys, 9 students from the Low cohort, 26 from the Mid cohort, and 20 from the High cohort. The surveys asked students the following 5-point Likert scale questions:

- How difficult did you find the material over the [first/second] month of the semester?
- How often did you use the hints when working through the practice tool?
- In questions you did use hints, do you think in the future you could complete a similar question without hints?

Table 2 shows the results of the survey distributed during the 5th and 9th weeks of the semester. In the survey distributed during the 5th week, the Low cohort found the course material the most difficult, and reported using hints most often. The survey also shows that students in the Low cohort were also slightly less confident in their ability to complete questions they needed hints on without assistance in the future. The results from this survey align with the quantitative analysis results on tool log data.

Figure 8 shows the average changes in survey responses between the two surveys. Students from all 3 cohorts reported an increased change in difficulty, but it was students in the Mid cohort who had the highest jump in perceived difficulty between surveys. In terms of how often students felt like they used hints, the Mid cohort also had the biggest increase between surveys, while the High cohort's responses barely changed at all. The Mid cohort had the biggest decrease in confidence in being able to solve questions they used hints on without assistance in the future, whereas the Low cohort had the largest increase in confidence.

4.4 Connecting Survey Results with Log Data

When comparing Figures 6 and 7, it is apparent that as each semester progressed, students from all 3 cohorts increasingly resorted to viewing hints before attempting to solve the problem on their own. This trend aligns with the survey data, as students from all three cohorts perceived that the course material increased in difficulty as the semester progressed. Similarly, students from all 3 cohorts felt like they needed to use hints more often as the semester progressed.

Table 2: Survey results from the 5th and 9th week of the semester. Questions used a 5-point likert scale

Cohort	Q1: Difficulty		Q2: Hint Usage		Q3: Solve Alone	
	Wk5	Wk9	Wk5	Wk9	Wk5	Wk9
Low	3.3	3.9	3.1	3.3	3.9	4.2
Mid	2.9	3.5	2.9	3.4	4.0	3.8
High	2.3	2.7	2.4	2.4	4.1	4.1

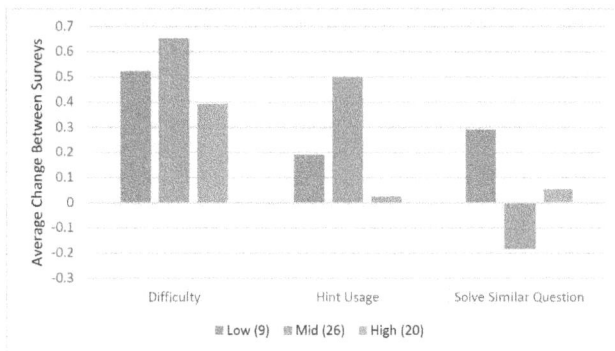

Figure 8: Average change in responses for each question between the surveys distributed in week 5 and 9.

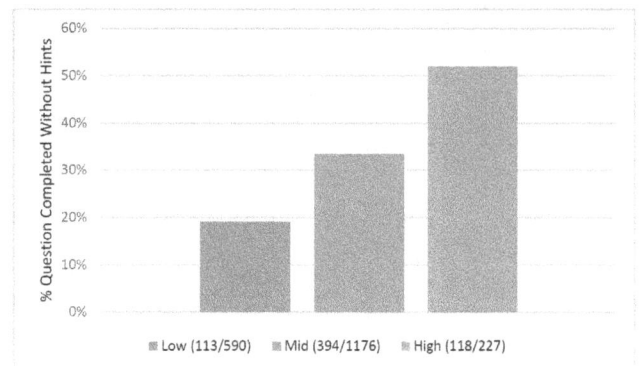

Figure 9: The percentage of times students were able to complete a question without hints when revisiting a question they were unable to complete previously.

As shown in Figure 8, the changes in survey responses are different among cohorts for the third question: *"In questions you did use hints, do you think in the future you could complete a similar question without hints?"* Students in the Low cohort reported an increased confidence in being able to solve questions in the future, whereas students in the Mid cohort decreased in confidence. Figure 9 shows how often students were able to answer questions without hints when revisiting questions they previously needed assistance on. Students in the Low cohort only answered questions without hints in follow-up attempts 19.1% of the time, compared to 33.5% for the Mid cohort, and 52.0% for the High cohort. Figure 9 fails to illustrate the difficulty of questions being revisited; remember from Figure 7 that students in the High cohort do not often request hints until later questions within a module, and yet still complete questions without hints in follow-up attempts more often than the other cohorts. Taken together, Figures 8 and 9 illustrate that survey responses from students in the Low cohort seem to most strongly contradict the study behaviour exhibited when working through exercises in the learning tool.

4.5 Threats to Validity

It is important to recognize the limitations and threats to validity of our study. Students were grouped into cohorts after the semester had ended based on final exam grades, and exam grades may not accurately represent overall student success in the course. Interaction data would be affected for students who studied in groups. Also, the analysis includes only the data from students who both chose to use the practice tool and also consented to take part in the study. Our analysis metrics penalize hint usage, but students may not view hints only when struggling to solve an exercise.

Time on task was evaluated as the difference between when a student loaded a question to when they last interacted with the question, but as the tool is browser-based, the calculated time might not accurately represent the actual time a user spent working on the exercise. Students may exhibit different behaviour when learning a new concept or when using the tool to study the night before an exam, but these types of things were not considered for this study.

Survey data was only collected during the most recent semester, and only 55 students completed both surveys. As more survey responses are collected in future semesters, further analysis will better establish confidence in the trends found in these initial findings.

5 ANALYSIS AND DISCUSSION

In this work, we explored whether the combination of interaction data and survey results can be used to differentiate successful from unsuccessful students. Our results complement recent studies that explore whether unsuccessful students can be identified based on an analysis of interaction data. Our work highlights the fact that although these students find the material difficult, students in the Low cohort, who went on to be unsuccessful on the final exam, actually reported an *increase* in confidence with respect to answering questions without hints as the semester progressed. This disconnect between student perception and performance requires further analysis, especially when comparing the change in survey responses between students in the Low cohort and those in the Mid cohort, who were able to pass the final exam. Figure 8 suggests that by week 9 students in the Mid cohort may have been able to identify that viewing hints was not an effective study practice, whereas students in the Low cohort were not. This is illustrated by the fact that students in the Mid cohort reported that they had to resort to viewing hints more often, but also that they felt less confident they could answer similar questions in the future after viewing hints.

It appears that students in the Low cohort might not understand that their study behaviour is not effective in learning the content in a CS1 course. In some disciplines, flash cards are used when students employ rote learning techniques to study for exams [13]. Students who have had positive experiences in other courses practicing this form of studying may feel like viewing solutions to programming exercises will also enable them to succeed in a computer science exam. It is unfortunate that many students in the Low cohort continued to study using the practice tool, and the survey results suggest believed they were learning effectively, but their efforts did not pay off. It may be interesting to compare our results with the results found by Robins et al. who reported that the difference between effective and ineffective novices relate to learning strategies rather than knowledge [16]. If study strategies turn out to be a significant factor in whether or not novices succeed in our course, with proper intervention we could potentially support a large population of students who enter the course unaware of which strategies will lead to success.

Our results also highlighted the difference between the intended difficulty and perceived difficulty of exercises. Within a given module, questions were designed to increase in difficulty, but the log data suggests that questions were not necessarily ordered in increasing difficulty. The for-loop module exercises are shown in Figure 5. Within this module, Figure 6 shows spikes on questions 3 and 7 with respect to how often students requested hints before attempting to solve the problem on their own. Question 3 was the first exercises a nested for-loop was required to solve the problem, whereas question 7 was the first exercises a series of for-loops were required nested inside an outer for-loop. Questions 4, 5, and 6 were intended to increase in difficulty, but each question required the same general design as question 3, but with different variable values. The disconnect between intended and perceived difficulty also requires further analysis, as it may affect the generation of lab work, assignments and exams.

6 CONCLUSIONS AND FUTURE WORK

This study presents a quantitative analysis of practice tool log data and a qualitative analysis of survey responses collected from 465 students over 3 semesters. Students were split into 3 cohorts, Low, Mid, and High, based on final exam grades. We found that unsuccessful students could not be differentiated from successful students based on time on task data. We identified differences across cohorts when looking into hint usage; students in the Low cohort requested more hints on average, and were much more likely to request hints before attempting to solve exercises on their own. Students in the Low cohort reported the biggest positive change between surveys distributed in weeks 5 and 9 regarding their confidence in solving similar questions in the future without hints. This increase in confidence did not align with their study behaviour, as when revisiting exercises this cohort used hints over 80% of the time.

We identified and described several issues that arise when trying to use practice tool log data for analysis. Despite these limitations, the results of this study have revealed a number of potentially important implications for CS1 instructors: (1) many students may not be aware of how to study CS1 material effectively; (2) an increase in student confidence does not necessarily mean a student is making progress understanding course material; and (3) learning aids such as hints and sample solutions may do more harm than good, depending on how and when they are used.

In future work, we plan to further investigate the disconnect between confidence and effectiveness of study behaviour by incorporating a wider variety of survey questions. It is still unclear why exactly students in the High cohort do better. It could be possible that they using hints differently, or are simply processing them in a more effective way. If we can better understand the study practices of successful students, we may be better able to guide struggling students towards more effective study practices.

REFERENCES

[1] Alireza Ahadi, Raymond Lister, Heikki Haapala, and Arto Vihavainen. 2015. Exploring Machine Learning Methods to Automatically Identify Students in Need of Assistance. In *Proc. of the Conference on International Computing Education Research (ICER)*. 121–130. DOI: http://dx.doi.org/10.1145/2787622.2787717

[2] Amjad Altadmri and Neil C.C. Brown. 2015. 37 Million Compilations: Investigating Novice Programming Mistakes in Large-Scale Student Data. In *Proc. of the ACM Technical Symposium on Computer Science Education (SIGCSE)*. 522–527. DOI: http://dx.doi.org/10.1145/2676723.2677258

[3] Ivon Arroyo and Beverly Park Woolf. 2005. Inferring Learning and Attitudes from a Bayesian Network of Log File Data. In *Proceedings of the 2005 Conference on Artificial Intelligence in Education: Supporting Learning Through Intelligent and Socially Informed Technology*. IOS Press, Amsterdam, The Netherlands, The Netherlands, 33–40. http://dl.acm.org/citation.cfm?id=1562524.1562535

[4] Jason Carter, Prasun Dewan, and Mauro Pichiliani. 2015. Towards Incremental Separation of Surmountable and Insurmountable Programming Difficulties. In *Proc. of the 46th ACM Technical Symposium on Computer Science Education (SIGCSE '15)*. ACM, New York, NY, USA, 241–246. DOI: http://dx.doi.org/10.1145/2676723.2677294

[5] Mihaela Cocea and Stephan Weibelzahl. 2007. Cross-system Validation of Engagement Prediction from Log Files. In *Proceedings of the Second European Conference on Technology Enhanced Learning: Creating New Learning Experiences on a Global Scale (EC-TEL'07)*. Springer-Verlag, Berlin, Heidelberg, 14–25. http://dl.acm.org/citation.cfm?id=2394166.2394169

[6] Michael Eagle and Tiffany Barnes. 2014. Exploring differences in problem solving with data-driven approach maps. In *Educational Data Mining 2014*.

[7] Stephen H. Edwards, Jason Snyder, Manuel A. Pérez-Quiñones, Anthony Allevato, Dongkwan Kim, and Betsy Tretola. 2009. Comparing Effective and Ineffective Behaviors of Student Programmers. In *Proc. of the Workshop on Computing Education Research (ICER)*. 3–14. DOI: http://dx.doi.org/10.1145/1584322.1584325

[8] Anthony Estey and Yvonne Coady. 2016. Can Interaction Patterns with Supplemental Study Tools Predict Outcomes in CS1?. In *Proc. of the ACM Conference on Innovation and Technology in Computer Science Education (ITiCSE)*. 236–241. DOI: http://dx.doi.org/10.1145/2899415.2899428

[9] Anthony Estey, Anna Russo Kennedy, and Yvonne Coady. 2016. BitFit: If You Build It, They Will Come!. In *Proceedings of the 21st Western Canadian Conference on Computing Education (WCCCE '16)*. ACM, New York, NY, USA, Article 3, 6 pages. DOI: http://dx.doi.org/10.1145/2910925.2910944

[10] Eric Fouh, Daniel A. Breakiron, Sally Hamouda, Mohammed F. Farghally, and Clifford A. Shaffer. 2014. Exploring students learning behavior with an interactive etextbook in computer science courses. *Computers in Human Behavior* 41 (2014), 478 – 485. DOI: http://dx.doi.org/10.1016/j.chb.2014.09.061

[11] Matthew C. Jadud. 2006. Methods and Tools for Exploring Novice Compilation Behaviour. In *Proc. of International Workshop on Computing Education Research (ICER)*. 73–84. DOI: http://dx.doi.org/10.1145/1151588.1151600

[12] Matthew C. Jadud and Brian Dorn. 2015. Aggregate Compilation Behavior: Findings and Implications from 27,698 Users. In *Proc. of the Eleventh Annual International Conference on International Computing Education Research (ICER '15)*. 131–139. DOI: http://dx.doi.org/10.1145/2787622.2787718

[13] Nate Kornell. 2009. Optimising learning using flashcards: Spacing is more effective than cramming. *Applied Cognitive Psychology* 23, 9 (2009), 1297–1317. DOI: http://dx.doi.org/10.1002/acp.1537

[14] Jonathan P. Munson and Elizabeth A. Schilling. 2016. Analyzing Novice Programmers' Response to Compiler Error Messages. *J. Comput. Sci. Coll.* 31, 3 (2016), 53–61. http://dl.acm.org.ezproxy.library.uvic.ca/citation.cfm?id=2835377.2835386

[15] Cindy Norris, Frank Barry, James B. Fenwick Jr., Kathryn Reid, and Josh Rountree. 2008. ClockIt: Collecting Quantitative Data on How Beginning Software Developers Really Work. In *Proc. of the 13th Annual Conference on Innovation and Technology in Computer Science Education (ITiCSE '08)*. 37–41. DOI: http://dx.doi.org/10.1145/1384271.1384284

[16] Anthony Robins, Janet Rountree, and Nathan Rountree. 2003. Learning and Teaching Programming: A Review and Discussion. *Computer Science Education* 13, 2 (2003), 137–172. DOI: http://dx.doi.org/10.1076/csed.13.2.137.14200 arXiv:http://www.tandfonline.com/doi/pdf/10.1076/csed.13.2.137.14200

[17] Ma. Mercedes T. Rodrigo, Ryan S. Baker, Matthew C. Jadud, Anna Christine M. Amarra, Thomas Dy, Maria Beatriz V. Espejo-Lahoz, Sheryl Ann L. Lim, Sheila A.M.S. Pascua, Jessica O. Sugay, and Emily S. Tabanao. 2009. Affective and Behavioral Predictors of Novice Programmer Achievement. In *Proceedings of the 14th Annual ACM SIGCSE Conference on Innovation and Technology in Computer Science Education (ITiCSE '09)*. ACM, New York, NY, USA, 156–160. DOI: http://dx.doi.org/10.1145/1562877.1562929

[18] Jaime Spacco, Paul Denny, Brad Richards, David Babcock, David Hovemeyer, James Moscola, and Robert Duvall. 2015. Analyzing Student Work Patterns Using Programming Exercise Data. In *Proc. of the 46th ACM Technical Symposium on Computer Science Education (SIGCSE '15)*. 18–23. DOI: http://dx.doi.org/10.1145/2676723.2677297

[19] Emily S. Tabanao, Ma. Mercedes T. Rodrigo, and Matthew C. Jadud. 2011. Predicting At-risk Novice Java Programmers Through the Analysis of Online Protocols. In *Proceedings of the Seventh International Workshop on Computing Education Research (ICER '11)*. ACM, New York, NY, USA, 85–92. DOI: http://dx.doi.org/10.1145/2016911.2016930

[20] Christopher Watson, Frederick W. B. Li, and Jamie L. Godwin. 2013. Predicting Performance in an Introductory Programming Course by Logging and Analyzing Student Programming Behavior. In *Proc. of the IEEE International Conference on Advanced Learning Technologies (ICALT)*. 319–323. DOI: http://dx.doi.org/10.1109/ICALT.2013.99

Application of the Delphi Method in Computer Science Principles Rubric Creation

Veronica Cateté
North Carolina State University
Raleigh, NC 27606
vmcatete@ncsu.edu

Tiffany Barnes
North Carolina State University
Raleigh, NC 27695
tmbarnes@ncsu.edu

ABSTRACT

Growing public demand for computer science (CS) education in K-12 schools requires an increase in well-qualified and well-supported computing teachers. To alleviate the lack of K-12 computing teachers, CS education researchers have focused on hosting professional development workshops to prepare in-service teachers from other disciplines to teach introductory level computing courses. In addition to the curriculum knowledge and pedagogical content knowledge taught in the professional development workshops, these new teachers need support in computer science subject matter knowledge throughout the school year. In particular, these new teachers find it difficult to grade programs and labs. This research study uses two variations of the Delphi Method to create learning-oriented rubrics for Computer Science Principles teachers using the Beauty and Joy of Computing curriculum. To perform this study we implemented (1) a heavy-weight, heterogeneous wide-net Delphi, and (2) a lower-weight, homogeneous Delphi composed of master teachers. These methods resulted in the creation of two systematically- and rigorously-created rubrics that produce consistent grading and very similar inter-rater reliabilities.

KEYWORDS

BJC, AP CS Principles, Rubrics, Evaluation, Delphi Method

ACM Reference format:
Veronica Cateté and Tiffany Barnes. 2017. Application of the Delphi Method in Computer Science Principles Rubric Creation. In *Proceedings of ITiCSE'17, July 03-05, 2017, Bologna, Italy, , 6 pages.*
DOI: http://dx.doi.org/10.1145/3059009.3059042

1 INTRODUCTION

This paper presents two variations of the Delphi Method used to develop well-defined, learning-oriented rubrics for programming labs taught by novice Computer Science Prinicples teachers using curriculum from *the Beauty and Joy of Computing* (BJC) [16].

First, we give a brief overview of the current state of teacher preparation for Advanced Placement Computer Science Principles (AP CS Principles), followed by examples of rubric development for introductory computer science. We then describe the Delphi process

or Delphi method, adapted from psychology, and its use in decision making. After a brief review of the Delphi process, we describe our application and evaluation of the Delphi in creating two separate well-defined rubrics. Finally, we compare the two Delphi process variations using inter-rater reliability, score distributions, and an overall cost-benefit analysis. We end our paper by discussing the merits of this methodology, and how to streamline the process for expanded use.

2 BACKGROUND

As public demand for computer science in K-12 classrooms continues to grow, there is a large shortcoming in the number of well-qualified Computer Science Education teachers. In the United States, few colleges offer teacher education directly in Computer Science. Many education departments offer Technology Education, however, this track often pertains to the use of technology in the classroom and engineering practices, rather than computational thinking and computing.

2.1 U.S. K-12 Computing Teachers

With the lack of infrastructure to quickly prepare new teachers directly for K-12 computing, researchers and universities are holding professional development (PD) seminars and training to convert existing K-12 teachers into computing teachers [2, 6, 7]. Attendees for this type of PD have diverse subject backgrounds ranging from Business to English and Language Arts [6, 9]. In order to be successful in teaching a course, Shulman suggests that teachers should have subject matter knowledge, curricular knowledge, and pedagogical content knowledge (PCK) [11]. Teachers in the CS oriented PD sessions are being trained in curricular knowledge and pedagogical content strategies [6, 9]. This support is a brief introduction and does not turn the novice computing teachers into content experts.

A 2016 study focused directly on measuring the computer science PCK of active K-12 computing teachers [17]. The study showed that teachers felt confident in transmitting the associated computer science knowledge and understandings, however, teachers demonstrated difficulty in addressing student problems relating to programming errors. This difficulty understanding and debugging student code directly relates to the teachers' lack in expert content knowledge.

A lack of content knowledge leaves teachers unprepared to understand and identify computational thinking in code [9], unprepared to assist students with programming errors [17], and unprepared to create instructional rubrics for students to learn programming assignment requirements [6].

2.2 Computational Thinking Rubrics

A summative review by Stegeman highlights that while many introductory CS rubrics focus on similar aspects of code quality, they are very diverse in form as well as content [3, 13]. Stegeman instead calls for a systematic approach to creating instructional rubrics that act as teaching tools to help students understand the requirements for an assignment to be successful. The instructional rubrics go beyond a summative scoring mechanism to also list verbal descriptions of the specific desired outcomes.

From the previously mentioned evidence, we believe that novice computing teachers need support in understanding and assessing student code through the use of learning-oriented rubrics. In order to systematically create these rubrics, we borrow the Delphi method from psychology and education.

2.3 Delphi Process

The Delphi process is a technique originating in the 1950s to obtain the most reliable consensus of opinion from a group of experts using intensive questionnaires interspersed with controlled-opinion feedback [5]. As emphasized by Adler, expertise is tied to having knowledge and practical engagement with issues under investigation [1]. As Delphi studies do not normally rely on random samples, these studies represent the best thinking and opinions of a group of people chosen for their special knowledge and experience [1, 8].

The Classical Delphi is characterized by four pillars: anonymity of participants, iteration for participants to refine their views, controlled feedback informing participants of other perspectives, and statistical aggregation of the group response to allow for quantitative analysis and interpretation of data [10]. As part of the Delphi Process, panelists complete a series of questionnaires which are analyzed and processed, with the results integrated into the next stage of survey rounds; Figure 1 outlines this process.

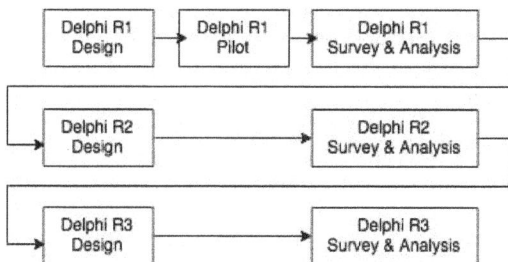

Figure 1: A simplified version of the Delphi Process.

As outlined by Skulmoski, the typical Delphi method can vary greatly in number of participants, with the number of rounds usually three or four [12]. As the number of rounds increases, so does participant drop off rate.

3 METHODS

In order to move towards well-defined learning rubrics with a structured foundation, we consulted expert panelists through the implementation of a modified Delphi process. Throughout 2015, we carried out two separate Delphi studies; the first (StudyA) was a national poll with a heterogeneous sample of CS Principle stakeholders, the second (StudyB) was local to a professional development

session with CS Principles Master Teachers (those who have taught 2+ years of CS Principles).

The subsections below describe how we systematically used the Delphi Process to solicit expert-chosen learning outcomes from the CS Principles Framework and applied them in the creation of learning-oriented rubrics for two popular BJC lab assignments. The final subsection 3.5, presents further details on how we evaluated the rubrics.

3.1 Lab Assignment Descriptions

Surveys show that most high school BJC teachers from 2012-2015 used the Brick Wall and Hangman Lab assignments in their classrooms, making these labs ideal candidates for our study.

BJC's Brick Wall lab was designed to demonstrate abstraction and the value of creating a function that can be called to perform the same task multiple times, and with different parameters. The main objective of the Brick Wall lab is to create a brick wall with an alternating pattern of bricks. In the assignment, two row types A and B are defined, where an A row is made up of whole bricks, and a B row starts and ends with half-bricks. Students are instructed to create one method that generates a brick wall, two separate methods that draw the two row types, and a method that draws an individual brick. These specific instructions are explained as levels of abstraction for solving the problem. The visual nature of the task and the clear and simple repetitive structure of a brick wall are affordances that should help make iteration and functions natural solutions to the problem.

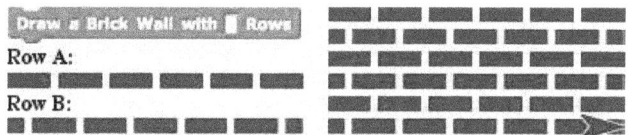

Figure 2: Levels of abstraction for the Brick Wall assignment

The Hangman Lab is part of the Lists and Higher Order Functions units in the BJC curriculum [14]. The lab was designed to combine tasks learned in exploring list operations such as 'map', 'keep', and 'combine.' This activity is more advanced than the Brick Wall lab and requires a better understanding of algorithms. The directions for completing the Hangman activity are in the text that follows.

> Imagine that you're writing a program to play Hangman. The program has thought of a secret word, and the user is trying to guess it. Write a display word block that takes two inputs, the secret word and a list of the letters guessed by the user so far. It should say the letters of the secret word, spaced out, with underscore characters replacing the letters not yet guessed. See Figure 3 below for an example.

Figure 3: Block displays a secret word 'Hangman' style.

Table 1: Summary of metrics used in Delphi Process implementation.

Delphi Process	# of Participants	Gender	Background	Study Rounds
StudyA: BrickWall	18 SIGCSE members	9 Female, 9 Male	4 Tenured Professors 2 Associate Professors 10 High School Teachers 2 Others	1 - Select and rank 2 - Rate agreement 3 - Importance and code samples
StudyB: Hangman	9 BJC Master Teachers	6 Female, 3 Male	All 2+ years teaching BJC	1 - Select and rank 2 - Rate agreement 3 - Importance and code samples

3.2 Panelists

In order to develop a rubric with well-determined learning objectives in StudyA, we recruited a heterogenous sample of 8 university Computer Science professors as well as 10 high school computing teachers through the SIGCSE mailing list. Participants were equally split 9 female and 9 male. Five participants indicated that they were involved in the development of either BJC or CS Principles and 9 participants had taught at least one year of CS Principles in their college or high school. These participants were considered expert panelists through their many years of teaching and researching computer science.

StudyB was comprised of 9 Master Teachers taking professional development to learn how to train new BJC teachers. Each participant was a current high school teacher with 2+ years of past experience teaching CS Principles; six female, three male. The primary courses taught by the panelists were: business management, mathematics, physical science, and computing. Two of the panelists have advanced degrees in teaching, two have Masters degrees in their subject field, and one of the teachers is National Board certified. Table 1 shows a summation of the Delphi metrics.

3.3 Survey Rounds

StudyA and StudyB followed a similar implementation of the Delphi Process when it came to study rounds. We implemented a three round survey requesting expert panelists to indicate which learning objectives from the CS Principles Framework [4] best applied to the given lab.

In Round 1, panelists were given a questionnaire containing each of the learning objectives related to Creativity, Abstraction, Algorithms and Programming listed in the AP CS Principles Framework. Data and Information, the Internet, and Global Impact learning objectives were not included due to their indirect relation with the selected programming labs. Panelists were instructed to select as many objectives as they thought applied to the particular lab, and were additionally required to indicate their top five choices for most relevant learning objectives. Once the surveys were completed, the research team compiled the lists keeping the top 80% of learning objectives indicated by frequency and any lesson objective that made a panelist's top five. The research team analyzed the survey results and proceeded to Round 2.

The Round 2 survey focused on rating the aforementioned highest ranked learning objectives. The survey was composed of Likert-based questions where each panelist had to rate how strongly they agreed that a particular learning objective pertained to the given lab assignment. The objectives were rated on a scale of 1 (Strongly Disagree) to 5 (Strongly Agree). Panelists then had the opportunity to indicate which Essential Knowledge components, discrete learning statements that make up each larger learning objective, were most relevant. Indicating essential knowledge components was important for broader learning objectives that had up to ten different sub-goals. The research team analyzed the results, carrying forward learning objectives and associated essential knowledge components rated 4.25 or above.

In the Round 3 survey, panelists were shown each objective rated 4.25 or above and given the option to contest any learning objectives they saw unfit. The uncontested learning objectives and associated essential knowledge components were thereby chosen by consensus from a panel of experts as being the most representative of the learning goals and objectives afforded by the given lab assignment.

The Delphi Process carried out by the research team differed from the Classical Delphi in that in the second half of Round 3, panelists were requested to submit their own demonstrations of the learning objectives in mock student coding samples. Panelists selected up to three learning objectives or related essential knowledge components and created a high, medium, and low level demonstration of that skill. Code samples could be submitted via Snap! source code [15], program screenshot images, or text explanations with varying degrees of student understanding and misconceptions. Additionally, panelists were given sample student programs and asked to select the top three learning goals demonstrated by that sample and explain why the code demonstrates those goals in short response form. The second half of Round 3 served to bridge the gap between computational thinking learning objectives applied to writing vs. to code.

3.4 Delphi Application

StudyA resulted in the selection of five learning objectives and eight essential knowledge components pertaining to the BJC Brick Wall lab assignment. StudyB resulted in the selection of five learning objectives and six essential knowledge components pertaining to the BJC Hangman lab. Each set of learning goals were then grouped by topic and split into five distinct rubric categories with one to two associated learning goals. Each category was given a simple name as well as the learning-based descriptions associated with them. See Table 2 below for an example.

The coding samples generated by the Delphi panelists were also paired with the rigorously developed rubrics to show novice BJC teachers the relation of written learning objectives to the learning objectives as seen in code. A sample of this pairing is as follows:

Table 2: Sample Parameters category on learning-based rubric for Hangman lab.

Category	4	3	2	1	0	Learning Goals
Parameters	Code blocks and abstract functions use parameters to increase usability and are easily changeable for testing.	Majority of abstractions utilize parameters to be used for testing.	Some functions and abstractions utilize parameters to allow greater functionality.	Few abstractions utilize parameters.	Abstractions do not utilize parameters.	EK 5.3.1F Parameters generalize a solution by allowing a procedure to be used instead of duplicated code. EK 5.3.1D Procedures have names and may have parameters and return values.

given Figure 4, a panelist has selected EK 5.5.1A *Numbers and Numerical concepts are fundamental to programming* as third in level of importance for relating to the code sample. Furthermore, the panelist explains, "The student has created algebraic expressions that generalize numerical concepts necessary to the problem's solution. S/he has clearly demonstrated knowledge of the concept."

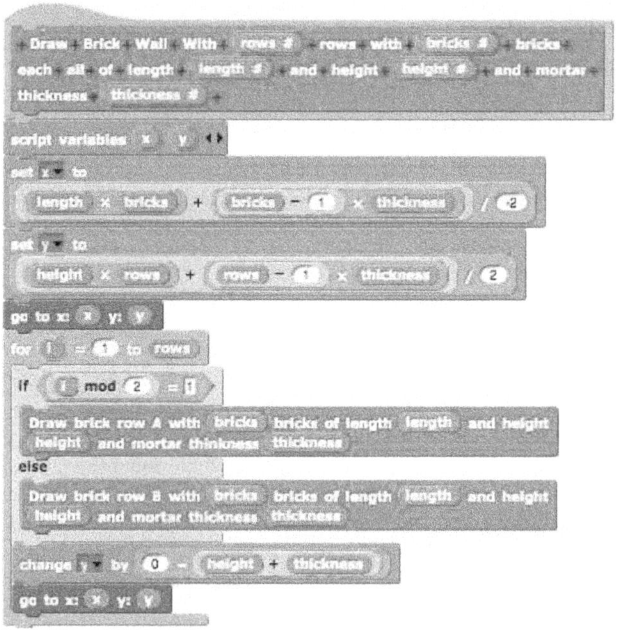

Figure 4: A portion of the code sample critiqued by Delphi Panelists in Round 3.

3.5 Rubric Evaluation

We tested the newly created rubrics with three university computing majors and two BJC Master Teachers. Participants were given from 60 to 103 coding samples and asked to grade each one using the same criteria.

3.5.1 Participants. The university student graders were comprised of one graduate student, one sophomore, and one freshman all majoring in computer science. The graduate student was selected for their expert content knowledge in computing, representing the ideally experienced CS teacher. The sophomore was a less experienced computing major and demonstrated modest programming

knowledge. The freshman had taken an introductory programming course in high school, but had not completed the first level computing class in university representing the novice CS Principles teacher.

The two BJC Master teachers were selected based on their past performance in professional development training as well as their willingness and eagerness to improve support materials for BJC. One teacher had successfully taught two sessions of BJC in their local high school, the other had taken the professional development course several summers in a row and now leads their own training sessions. The second master teacher, in addition to teaching at their local high school, was also enrolled in distance education computing courses to strengthen their content knowledge.

3.5.2 Data Corpus. We collected 103 Hangman programs and 94 Brick Wall programs from three BJC implementations in the 2013-2014 school year. Two of the implementations were completed as a high school CS Principles Honors class, the third as a university introduction to computing course for non-CS majors.

The two high school classes were taught by the same teacher, a seasoned computer science teacher with 15+ years of experience teaching computer programming and AP Computer Science A/AB. The teacher taught her CS Principles honors class using the BJC curriculum developed and shared by UC Berkeley. Students were given time in class to work on lab assignments collaboratively, any work not completed in the allotted time was assigned as homework. Thirty-nine Brick Wall assignments were collected between the two high school sections and forty-one Hangman assignments were collected. The difference in assignment counts is attributed to student absences.

In contrast to the two high school classes taught by an experienced AP Computer Science teacher, the college course had seven separate lab sections facilitated by five undergraduate teaching assistants (UTAs) under the tutelage of a tenured Computer Science professor leading the lectures. The five UTA majors were: computer science, civil engineering, materials science, paper science, and textile technology. The UTAs had minimal prior teaching experience and no similar computing course. The course professor led the UTAs through the labs the week before students did them, in much the same way that high school BJC teachers keep one step ahead of their students when they teach a new class for the first time. Fifty-five usable Brick Wall assignments were collected between the seven lab sections and sixty-two Hangman assignments were collected. Two Brick Wall assignments were unusable due to improper submission format.

Researchers noted the difference in background and teaching experience of the many class instructors and felt that the UTAs portrayed an accurate representation of the range of active BJC teachers. The level of teaching experience and quality would be reflected in the submitted student assignments, therefore representing a wide variety of program implementations and demonstrated learning outcomes. A compilation of submitted assignments and associated graders is shown in Table 3.

Hangman assignments ranged from fully animated and functional games to haphazardly organized and occasionally working single method implementations. The Brick Wall projects ranged from completely accurate walls with numerous parameters, to one brick telling a joke to a circle.

Table 3: A breakdown of rubric grading metrics.

	Brick Wall Lab	Hangman Lab
High School	39 projects	41 projects
College	55 projects	62 projects
Student Graders	Grad Student, Sophomore	Grad Student, Freshman
Master Teachers	N/A	A: 102 graded, B: 60 graded

3.5.3 Grading. In order to evaluate the effectiveness of the newly developed rubrics in supporting consistent and meaningful grading results, we had pairs of raters grade each assignment. A graduate-undergraduate pair graded both assignments and the master teacher pair graded the Hangman lab. Teacher B was only able to commit to grading half of the assignments due to heavy course load and ended up grading 60/103 of the Hangman projects.

In order to maintain more natural results, graders were given limited instructions on how to grade. They were instructed, however, to leave comments on the grading sheet whenever a particular program raised questions as to what grade value should be given. An example comment might be "Student A completed the task incorrectly, but utilized all of the desired list functions. Student A was given partial credit."

4 RESULTS

The aforementioned methods and research culminated in the creation of two rigorously developed learning-based rubrics hand-tested on a data set of 100 samples each by paired graders. When tested for inter-rater reliability the student-graders achieved a satisfactory .83 agreement on the Brick Wall lab assignment and .78 on the Hangman lab assignment. In the student-graded assignments, the grader acting as a computing expert remained consistent, the changing factor was the level of computing content known by the novice undergraduate student. When tested for inter-rater reliability the master teachers achieved a satisfactory .79 agreement on the Hangman lab assignment.

When broken down by course, Brick Wall projects submitted in the high school class averaged M=3.63 SD=0.78 and projects submitted in the college class averaged a composite score of M=3.06 SD=0.81. Table 4 shows average score by rubric category.

Table 4: Avg. Brick Wall project scores [0-4] using a learning-based rubric.

	Algo-rithms	Abstrac-tion	Parame-ters	Correct-ness	Mathe-matics
High School	3.53	3.80	3.60	3.75	3.50
College Class	3.10	3.25	3.45	3.00	2.50

When broken down by course, Hangman projects submitted in the high school class averaged M=3.71 SD=0.86 and projects submitted in the college class averaged a composite score of M=3.45 SD=0.82. Table 5 shows a breakdown of average score by rubric category.

Table 5: Avg. Hangman project scores [0-4] using a learning-based rubric.

	Algo-rithms	Abstrac-tion	Lists	Correct-ness	Mathe-matics
High School	3.80	3.92	3.63	3.51	3.70
College Class	3.56	3.52	3.26	3.34	3.60

5 DISCUSSION

In this discussion we examine the uses of the Delphi process, the effectiveness of the resulting rubrics, and strategies for streamlining the process for quicker and larger scale rubric creation.

5.1 Delphi Process

When reflecting on the dual implementations of the Delphi method, we find that the overall outcomes are the same. The main differences between the national poll and the PD group are the time needed to complete the study and the amount of participant attrition.

The national poll took 11 weeks to complete from the initial release of the first survey to the close of the final-round survey. Participants were given three-week intervals to complete each survey round interspersed with one week for the research team to analyze results and create the next survey. As the time and participation requirements increased, so did the attrition rates. Forty-nine participants started the first-round survey, but only fifteen completed the final-round survey. Since much of the SIGCSE mailing-list contains active university and high school teachers, we believe that time available to participate fluctuated with holidays and teaching schedules.

The second Delphi study took one week to complete from the initial release of the first survey to the close of the final round survey. As panelists in this group were selected from a professional development summer training session, they were given designated time throughout the week to complete each round of the survey. Additionally, none of the teachers were actively teaching summer classes, so the panel was less distracted. The homogeneous group of participants all had equal stakes in the outcomes this research, as these newly created rubrics would be added as support material to the BJC curriculum. Additionally, participants were committed to attending the PD so access and attrition were not an issue.

The attrition and commitment levels demonstrated by both panels is consistent with findings presented in Skulmoski [12].

5.2 Effectiveness of Rubrics

Although developed by separate groups, the reliability of the rubrics turned out to be similar and satisfactory. Each of the three paired graders were able to achieve a high level of inter-rater reliability (> .70). Additionally, the relationship in overall measured performance of the two data sets is as expected. The Honors CS Principles high school students, when measured by the rigorously developed rubric system, outperformed the sophomore and junior-based students taking an Introduction to Computers course for non-CS majors. As indicated previously, the Honors students were being taught by a highly-qualified teacher with years of experience in teaching computer science courses, where as the college students completed most of their assignments in lab sessions facilitated by novice computing undergraduate TAs.

5.3 Cost-Benefit Analysis of Methods

When looking through the lens of practicality, we are able to see a clear winner in regards to implementation of the Delphi. Polling the smaller more concentrated group of Master Teachers was much faster and just as effective as polling the larger heterogeneous SIGCSE-list. Less time was required on administrative part, as fewer reminders had to mailed out. Panelists also had designated time set aside to focus on the study.

Furthermore, when selecting graders to evaluate the rubrics, we found minimal difference in using early year computer science majors and BJC Master Teachers. Both groups measured similar results while using the rubrics. When looking at availability, we find that the student graders were more reliable and able to take on extra work.

6 CONCLUSIONS AND FUTURE WORK

The first goal of this study was to explore the use of the Delphi Method in creating a rigorously-vetted and systematic basis for learning-oriented rubrics. We focused our development on rubrics for two of the most popular BJC labs taught by first and second-year high school BJC teachers. Although these teachers may have many years of teaching experience in other subjects, their subject matter content knowledge in programming and ability to recognize computational thinking in code needs support.

As part of the Delphi process we surveyed two separate groups of expert panelists: members of the SIGCSE mailing list (both professors and K-12 teachers), and BJC Master Teachers. Both groups completed 3 rounds of consensus-building surveys and rating systems to determine the most-important and most-relevant learning goals associated with the respective lab assignments.Using these learning goals, we created two unique rubrics with five categories of learning goals comprised of Learning Objectives and Essential Knowledge from the AP CS Principles Framework [4].

The second goal of this study was to evaluate the use of the new learning-oriented rubrics by sample graders. There are two limitations to this study design. The first one is that the Delphi method uses experts and if different experts were surveyed we may have different outcomes. The second limitation is similar in that it depends on just a few raters and different raters may have different results. In this case, we found that each pair of graders was able to establish inter-rater reliability and the overall

measurements in student performance reflected the differences in student backgrounds and teacher proficiency.

When reflecting on this study, we find that a smaller Delphi panel with active BJC teachers shows minimal drawbacks when compared to a larger heterogeneous panel. Additionally, we find that when using the rubrics, lower classification CS majors perform comparably to Master BJC Teachers. Practically, there are still major drawbacks in holding a full Delphi Panel, such as locating proper stakeholders with time-availability, knowledge on the subject, and willingness to participate.

In future studies, we will replace the master teacher panel with upper classification computer science majors, in order to create comparably rigorous rubrics at a faster pace and at scale. It is our hypothesis that a small team of subject-literate computer science majors (comparable to BJC Master Teachers), when given the BJC curriculum and CS Principles Framework, will be able to draw comparable connections in learning goals for lab assignments. We also believe that using an expedited form of the Delphi Process as we did in study 2 ended up being very similar to the nominal group technique (NGT) [1]. As such, we will use NGT to continue to ensure an objective consensus by team members in future implementations.

REFERENCES

[1] Michael Adler and Erio Ziglio. 1996. *Gazing into the oracle: The Delphi method and its application to social policy and public health.* Jessica Kingsley Publishers.
[2] Tiffany Barnes, Jamie Payton, and Daniel D. Garcia. 2016. Scaling Up for CS10K: Teaching and Supporting New Computer Science High School Teachers. In *Proc. 47th ACM Tech. Symp. on CS Ed (SIGCSE '16).* ACM, 720–720.
[3] Veronica Cateté. 2016. Developing a Rubric for a Creative CS Principles Lab. In *Proceedings of the 2016 ACM Conference on Innovation and Technology in Computer Science Education (ITiCSE '16).* ACM, 290–295.
[4] College Board. 2014. AP CS Principles Curriculum Framework. *AP Program* (2014).
[5] Norman Dalkey and Olaf Helmer. 1963. An Experimental Application of the Delphi Method to the Use of Experts. *Management Science* 9, 3 (1963), 458–467.
[6] Barbara J. Ericson, Mark Guzdial, and Tom McKlin. 2014. Preparing Secondary Computer Science Teachers Through an Iterative Development Process. In *Proceedings of the 9th Workshop in Primary and Secondary Computing Education (WiPSCE '14).* ACM, New York, NY, USA, 116–119. DOI: http://dx.doi.org/10.1145/2670757.2670781
[7] Joanna Goode, Jane Margolis, and Gail Chapman. 2014. Curriculum is not enough: the educational theory and research foundation of the exploring computer science professional development model. In *Proc. 45th ACM Tech. Symp. on CS Ed.* ACM, 493–498.
[8] Gregory Lee Lecklitner. 1984. *Protecting the rights of mental patients: A view of the future.* Ph.D. Dissertation. Ohio State University.
[9] Thomas W. Price, Veronica Cateté, Jennifer Albert, Tiffany Barnes, and Daniel D. Garcia. 2016. Lessons Learned from "BJC" CS Principles Professional Development. In *Proc. 47th ACM Tech. Symp. on CS Ed (SIGCSE '16).* ACM, 467–472.
[10] Gene Rowe and George Wright. 1999. The Delphi technique as a forecasting tool: issues and analysis. *International Journal of forecasting* 15, 4 (1999), 353–375.
[11] Lee S. Shulman. 1986. Those Who Understand: Knowledge Growth in Teaching. *Educational Researcher* 15, 2 (1986), 4–14.
[12] Gregory J Skulmoski, Francis T Hartman, and Jennifer Krahn. 2007. The Delphi method for graduate research. *Journal of Inf. Tech. Ed* 6 (2007), 1.
[13] Martijn Stegeman, Erik Barendsen, and Sjaak Smetsers. 2016. Designing a Rubric for Feedback on Code Quality in Programming Courses. In *Proceedings of the 16th Koli Calling International Conference on Computing Education Research (Koli Calling '16).* ACM, New York, NY, USA, 160–164. DOI: http://dx.doi.org/10.1145/2999541.2999555
[14] University of California, Berkeley. 2014. Hangman Classic. (2014). web.
[15] University of California, Berkeley. 2017. Snap! Build Your Own Blocks. (2017).
[16] University of California, Berkeley and Education Development Center, Inc. 2017. Beauty and Joy of Computing. (2017). bjc.edc.org.
[17] Aman Yadav, Marc Berges, Phil Sands, and Jon Good. 2016. Measuring Computer Science Pedagogical Content Knowledge: An Exploratory Analysis of Teaching Vignettes to Measure Teacher Knowledge. In *Proceedings of the 11th Workshop in Primary and Secondary Computing Education (WiPSCE '16).* ACM, New York, NY, 92–95. DOI: http://dx.doi.org/10.1145/2978249.2978264

Educational Magic Tricks Based on Error-Detection Schemes

Ronald I. Greenberg
Loyola University
Department of Computer Science
820 N. Michigan Ave.
Chicago, Illinois 60611-2147, USA
rig@cs.luc.edu

ABSTRACT

Magic tricks based on computer science concepts help grab student attention and can motivate them to delve more deeply. Error detection ideas long used by computer scientists provide a rich basis for working magic; probably the most well known trick of this type is one included in the CS Unplugged activities. This paper shows that much more powerful variations of the trick can be performed, some in an unplugged environment and some with computer assistance. Some of the tricks also show off additional concepts in computer science and discrete mathematics.

KEYWORDS

computer science education; computational thinking; magic; outreach; public engagement; unplugged activities; discrete mathematics; error detection; error correction; parity checks; pigeonhole principle; permutations; counting principles; modular arithmetic; multidimensional representations; bijections; probability; analysis of algorithms

1 INTRODUCTION

Using magic[1] tricks for computer science education and outreach has been advocated by a number of previous authors. For example, Curzon and McOwan report on presenting 3-hour-long magic shows to gifted students [3]. A series of SIGCSE special sessions has also presented magic tricks that utilize computational thinking concepts and have strongly engaged large audiences of computer scientists [6, 7, 9]. A large pool of computing-related magic tricks also can be found at the "Computer Science For Fun" website, particularly through the "Magic of Computer Science" page [4]. Finally, the trick presented below as "Version 2a" was used by the author (and occasionally a student assistant) in some of the outreach presentations described in [15] that reached several thousand students. Students generally expressed great fascination with the trick and

typically wanted to repeat it if time permitted. In surveys of over 200 students, 79% rated the "magic tricks" portion as "Good" or "Very Good" (as opposed to "Poor" or "Fair").[2]

One trick that has become particularly well known through the CS Unplugged collection of activities is based on using parity checks for error detection [1, pp. 35–37]. This activity is recommended for ages 7 and up and may well amaze older students as well, but the trick is quite simple and might not impress sophisticated viewers. This paper shows that much more powerful variations of the trick can be performed, some in an unplugged environment and some with computer assistance. These tricks also show off additional computing concepts besides parity checking.

The remainder of this paper first explains the CS Unplugged error detection trick and then provides variations that are suggested to be performed (with an explanation each time) as an escalating series of tricks. (While the CS Unplugged trick is actually an error *correction* scheme, it is titled as error *detection* for the simple parity-check scheme on which it is based. The other tricks presented in this paper also perform *correction*.)

For all versions of the trick described below, a demo may be viewed at http://rig.cs.luc.edu/~rig/errdetectmagic/errdetect.html; simply append ?v=1, ?v=2a, etc. to select the desired version of the trick. Downloading the single source file will also provide a full HTML/JavaScript implementation that should run locally in any modern browser, and a copy of the file will be archived with a version of this paper under http://ecommons.luc.edu/cs_facpubs. (The demo does not perform the role of the magician but does provide all the other steps.)

2 VERSION 1: CS UNPLUGGED

The CS Unplugged setup works as follows, with a magnetic board and 36 magnetic tiles that are colored on one side only:

(1) A volunteer is asked to lay out a 5x5 grid of the magnetic tiles on the board with a "random" mixture of colored and uncolored sides showing.

(2) The magician casually adds a sixth row and column "to make it a bit harder". (This statement is actually untruthful, so it might be better to simply say "to make it a bit larger".)

(3) The volunteer flips a tile while the magician looks away.

(4) The magician looks back at the board and announces which tile was flipped.

The secret of this trick is that the magician adds an extra tile at the end of each row with the exposed side chosen so that the number

---

[1] The term magic in this paper does not refer to any supernatural effects or even sleight of hand. Nonetheless, use of this term is well within several dictionary definitions of "magic", and the tricks presented in this paper are not unlike many other "magic" tricks presented in the references and other sources that are based purely on mathematical or scientific phenomena. Furthermore, there are certain elements of showmanship involved that we might think of as constituting "sleight of mind".

ITiCSE '17, July 03-05, 2017, Bologna, Italy
© 2017 ACM. 978-1-4503-4704-4/17/07...$$15.00
DOI: http://dx.doi.org/10.1145/3059009.3059034

[2] Some of the presentations used instead, or additionally, the 1–125 number-guessing magic trick at [10]. Only a small portion of the total students reached were surveyed, due to the complicated requirements of research involving human subjects when interviewing students under age 18.

of colored tiles in the row is even. Then the magician adds an extra tile at the bottom of each column with the exposed side chosen so that the number of colored tiles in the column is even. In computer science terms, we would say that the magician is ensuring that each row and column has even parity. After the volunteer makes the flip that the magician does not see, the magician looks at the grid of tiles to see which row and column have odd parity, and the tile that was flipped is at the intersection of that row and column.

It is straightforward to extend this trick to a larger $n \times n$ grid, and, when the audience is not too large, I like to do it with an Othello™ set on a table, starting with a 7×7 arrangement of the black and white pieces and then extending to 8×8. Additionally, an interactive demonstration for arbitrary n is available at http://rig.cs.luc.edu/~rig/errdetectmagic/errdetect.html?v=1. (Make the appropriate addition to the query string for the desired value of n after the extension; e.g., the default is the same as appending &n=6.)

But the clever observer may recognize that addition of the extra full row and column of tiles is not making the trick harder but rather exploiting a simple rule, especially if the extra row and column are added by computer, or if the magician needs to proceed a bit slowly and deliberately to add the extra tiles.

Even this basic version of the trick can teach about parity checking and the XOR (exclusive or) operation as well as the common technique of identifying a cell in a 2D grid by specifying row and column number (for example to address memory cells). In successive versions of the trick, however, additional ideas will be introduced.

3 EASILY PERFORMED VERSIONS WITH LESS MAGICIAN INTERVENTION

A viewer who knows just a little bit about information theory may realize that the CS Unplugged version of the error detection trick is associating a lot of check bits with a modest amount of data. Specifically, the magician is placing $2n$ check bits on an array of n^2 bits. In principle, viewing the n^2 bits as a linear sequence (e.g., row-major order) and using a Hamming code [11], one would only need to add $\lg(n^2 + 1) \approx 2 \lg n$ bits (which can be shown to be optimal in the context of transmitting data with single-error correction), but this is not a very easy scheme for a human magician to use.[3] In Section 5, we will see a version of the error detection trick that is difficult to do without computer assistance, but, in this section, we will stick to schemes that are humanly manageable and are more impressive than the CS Unplugged version of the trick. (When we do proceed to a version that relies heavily on the computer, it will appear that we are violating the optimality of Hamming codes; the reality is that we can "beat" Hamming codes because there isn't actually any underlying data being transmitted that we need to retain as we create appropriate checks.)

3.1 Version 2a

The fancier version of the CS Unplugged trick that I have performed to the delight of many student groups may be explored interactively at http://rig.cs.luc.edu/~rig/errdetectmagic/errdetect.html?v=2a or

in its original home among other materials for high school outreach presentations [10]. Here, with the default 8×8 grid, the magician requests at most 3 flips in the grid generated by the audience volunteer and/or randomization. (Larger versions can be run by appending, e.g., &n=10 to the URL.)

The steps of the trick, most readily performed at a computer screen, are as follows:

(1) A random 8×8 grid of black and white tiles is generated, and a volunteer is asked to flip any desired tiles to make sure the pattern is complicated.
(2) The computer marks a set of at most three tiles that the volunteer is asked to flip. (A practiced magician could do this manually, but the computer assist makes it quicker and allows the magician to perform the trick without even looking at the grid at all until step 4.)
(3) The volunteer flips a tile while the magician looks away.
(4) The magician looks back at the board and announces which tile was flipped.

To explain this trick we need to explain how Steps 2 and 4 work. Step 2 is the much more complicated one, and the reader should remember it can be done quickly by the computer.

After Step 1, the computer (or magician) can determine the parities of the first seven rows (i.e., whether each row has an odd or even number of colored tiles). We are guaranteed to find that at least four of these rows have the same parity; let us call this the "majority" parity. (In explaining this to students we introduce a new concept, the generalized pigeonhole principle.) We now make note of the three or fewer rows among the first seven that have the other or "minority" parity; these are rows in which we would like to flip (change) the parity, and we will call them the "flip" rows. Next we apply the same process to the first seven columns, and we similarly find three or fewer "flip" columns.

We can achieve all the desired parity flips, by flipping the tile at the intersection of the first flip row and first flip column, the tile at the intersection of the second flip row and second flip column, etc. If there are actually fewer than three flip rows or fewer than three flip columns, we will run out of rows or columns to use in these pairings, but we can simply go to the last (eighth) row or column if we run out of flip rows or columns, respectively. In this way, we identify a set of at most three tiles that the volunteer is asked to flip, and the result then is that the first seven rows all have the same parity and the first seven columns all have the same parity. Figure 1 provides a screen shot from a sample run at the stage when the desired flips are presented to the volunteer.

Finally, it is straightforward (even mentally) for the magician to perform Step 4 by looking for the row and column among the first seven that has a different parity from the others. (If all seven have the same parity, he knows that the flip occurred in the eighth row; similar reasoning works with the columns.)

Everything described above for version 2a is readily generalized to an $n \times n$ grid, with the number of flips requested by the computer being at most $\lfloor (n - 1)/2 \rfloor$. While there is no conceptual change as n increases, the amount of work (mental juggling) for the magician does increase. (It is possible to reduce the work and increase the impressiveness a bit with the next variation.) While the number of flips the computer requests is at most $\lfloor (n - 1)/2 \rfloor$, it will sometimes

---

[3] The mechanics are actually similar to the workings of the previously mentioned number guessing trick (e.g., [10, 12]), but that trick imposes an organization on the relevant information that is not readily available from looking at just a 2D grid of bits.

The tiles with an X offend the wizard's sense of organization; please click them to flip.

Figure 1: A sample run for Version 2a at the stage where the subject is asked to flip at most three tiles, after which the magician can identify the next tile flipped.

be less, and Appendix A shows how to compute the probability distribution for the number of flips required given a random grid.

3.2 Version 2b

This version of the trick works for an $n \times n$ grid with $n \equiv 1 \pmod 3$. The basic idea here is for the magician to operate as in Version 2a but with Steps 2 and 4 performed in accordance with a grouping of all but the last row into sets of three (and similarly for the columns). By the pigeonhole principle, at least two of the first three rows have the same parity, so at most one of these rows becomes a flip row. There also is at most one flip row in the next three rows, and so on, for a total of at most $(n-1)/3$ flip rows. Similarly, there are at most $(n-1)/3$ flip columns. Pairing flip rows and columns as in Version 2a (and defaulting to the last row or column if we run out of flip rows or flip columns), the audience volunteer is asked to flip at most $(n-1)/3$ tiles to achieve the same parity within each group of three rows and the same parity within each group of three columns. Again, this calculation for Step 2 can be done with a computer assist.

The magician then can easily complete Step 4 by looking for a minority parity in one of the row groups (otherwise defaulting to the last row), and similarly for the columns.

In the case of $n = 7$, the volunteer is asked to flip at most two tiles. (The analysis of the probability distribution for the number of tiles needing to be flipped is again deferred to Appendix A.)

Note that when n is odd, greater care is required in computing the parity of each row and column. It is necessary to consistently count either the number of white tiles or consistently count the number of black tiles, whereas one can count either when n is even. For this reason, the magician may prefer to work with $n = 10$, while limiting the number of organizing flips to 3 as was the case in Version 2a that only worked with $n = 8$. (There also is an increased likelihood here relative to Version 2a of needing fewer than 3 flips, as shown in Appendix A.) An interactive demo for this version defaulting to a 10×10 grid may be explored at http://rig.cs.luc.

edu/~rig/errdetectmagic/errdetect.html?v=2b and different values of $n \equiv 1 \pmod 3$ may be utilized by appending, e.g., &n=7.

4 "CHEATING" TO ACHIEVE FEWER MAGICIAN-REQUESTED FLIPS

Garcia and Ginat have occasionally performed tricks involving a secret communication between the two of them, for example crafting a sentence so that the number of words conveys some information [8]. They refer to this as "cheating", and the same terminology is adopted here to describe secret communication from the computer or an assistant to the magician. The trick variations in Sections 3 do not involve any such cheating even though a computerized assistant provides a convenient way for the magician to quickly designate flips that he desires to organize the grid. (While a nimble magician could bypass the computerized assistant, I suggest using it to demonstrate that the magician does not even need to look at the grid until after the last flip and is certainly not memorizing anything about the grid arrangement or receiving any communications.) Having completed versions of the trick as in Section 3, however, the magician may magnify the feat performed by using a bit of subtle cheating as described below.

4.1 Version 3

An interactive demo for this version of the trick with a 10×10 grid can be explored at http://rig.cs.luc.edu/~rig/errdetectmagic/errdetect.html?v=3. In Version 2b, with $n = 10$, we can reveal one secret flip in the 10×10 grid after performing three organizing flips. Now we will explain how to reveal two flips, while staying at three organizing flips but using a bit of subtle communication of information from the computerized assistant.

The steps in this trick are as follows, with the magician not looking at the grid until Step 5:

(1) A random 10×10 grid of black and white tiles is generated, and a volunteer is asked to flip any desired tiles to make sure the pattern is complicated.

(2) The volunteer flips and remembers a tile.

(3) The computer presents at most three tiles, one at a time, that the volunteer is asked to announce and flip.

(4) The volunteer flips and remembers another tile.

(5) The computer prompts the audience to provide a "drumroll", and the magician looks back at the grid and announces the tile flipped at Step 4.

(6) The computer may prompt the audience to provide additional drumrolls (0, 1 or 2), and the magician announces the tile flipped at Step 2.

The reveal in Step 5 works just as in Version 2b, but one may observe that there is some flexibility in how the organizing flips are done, and that is the main source of communication to the magician. Specifically, there will typically be three flip rows and three flip columns, but we can use any ordering of the three flip rows and any ordering of the three flip columns before proceeding to pair them and proceed through the organizing flips. Since there are six possible orderings of the three flip rows and six possible orderings of the three flip columns, the computerized assistant can communicate enough information to discriminate between $6 \times 6 = 36$ possibilities. Here we are introducing the mathematical concept of how to count permutations as well as the multiplication principle for combining the information from the rows and the information from the columns.

(We can also communicate at least as much information if there are fewer than three flip rows or fewer than three flip columns. For example, if there are only two flip rows, we can use the last row as a third distinct flip row. If there is only one flip row, we can pick any other row to be used twice as a flip row, and by choosing an appropriate one from among the first six rows available we provide enough information to discriminate between six possibilities. Finally, if there is are no flip rows, we can use the last row as a flip row and use any other of the first six rows twice according to which of the six possibilities we wish to communicate.)

With the information communicated through the choice of organizing flips, we are nearly able to specify which of the 100 tiles in the grid was the last flip before the organizing flips. We can complete the cheating communication by communicating a number from one to three, which is sufficient to discriminate among $36 \times 3 = 108$ possibilities. Our subtle way to do this is through the number of drumrolls prompted at the beginning of Step 6. (The drumroll prompted at the beginning of Step 5 is just to get the audience to practice and to deflect attention from the true communication.)

In showing the way that we encode one of the 100 grid tiles by communicating three values with ranges of 6, 6, and 3 (not quite fully utilized), we can also introduce mathematical concepts such as encoding numbers using different choices of number base (radix) and construction of bijections.

4.2 Version 4

As a warmup for the final non-cheating trick in Section 5, we can reveal a flip in a very large grid with a single organizing flip but a heavy cheat. We can actually use an arbitrarily large n for this trick, but we will show it (http://rig.cs.luc.edu/~rig/errdetectmagic/errdetect.html?v=4) and explain it for $n = 11$. In this variation, we reveal a single secret flip after the computerized assistant requests the volunteer to announce and perform a single flip. There are actually a number of ways to do this easily (for example, request a flip to the tile that is in the mirror position across the diagonal of the grid from the secret flip), but a method that is reasonably subtle and likely to puzzle most audience members for a time is to use multiplicative inverses mod 11. Specifically, the computerized assistant can request a flip to tile (r, c) (row and column numbers starting at 0), such that the magician can then reveal the secret flip as being ($5r$ mod 11, $5c$ mod 11). Or to guard against the possible tendency of humans to pick $r = c$, one may want to increase the mystery by using two different values, at the expense of doing slightly more difficult arithmetic, for example, arrange that the secret flip will be ($5r$ mod 11, $7c$ mod 11); these are the details used in the referenced demo.

5 ORGANIZING ANY GRID WITH ONE FLIP

At this point, an audience that has been led through the above versions of the trick, has seen powerful variations with no "cheating" communication to the magician and extremely powerful tricks with such "cheating". We can now promise to go back to eliminating any opportunities for cheating communication but still increase the impressiveness of the trick. In fact, we will be able now to reveal a secret flip in an arbitrarily large grid by doing just one organizing flip beforehand and no cheating! The only wrinkle in this ultimate variation of the trick is that it is difficult for a human magician to complete it unaided. With practice, it should be manageable in an 8×8 grid, and I propose to create a smartphone app to perform the trick for larger grids. This smartphone app will photograph the grid after the secret flip occurs, but it will be operated by an audience volunteer who will first verify that the phone is in airplane mode so that it will be clear that no cheating communication is occurring. Following is a description of how this trick is performed in theory.

5.1 Version 5

In this version of the trick, we view the tiles as being arranged in a d-dimensional space with four positions in each dimension, i.e., 4^d total tiles. For smooth presentation, we will still display them in an $n \times n$ grid; the default size demonstrated in http://rig.cs.luc.edu/~rig/errdetectmagic/errdetect.html?v=5 is an 8×8 grid representing 4^3 tiles that can be thought of as comprising a 3-dimensional array of $4 \times 4 \times 4$ tiles. More generally, the demo can be run in higher dimensions by appending, e.g., &d=4 to the URL.

The idea in this version of the trick is a conceptually simple extension of Version 2b with $n = 4$. In each of the d dimensions, we consider the four possible indices and focus on the first three values. We compute the parity for the array slices with values 0, 1, and 2 and pick at most one slice in which a tile must be flipped so that all three slices will have the same parity; if no such flip is needed, we select the slice at value 3. After doing this for each of the d dimensions, we determine the single tile at the intersection of all d slices. This is the single tile we request the volunteer to flip. To reveal the secret flip, we check each of the dimensions for a slice among the first three that has different parity than the others or default to the last slice. That is, revealing the secret flip is done through essentially the same process as determining which single organizing flip is desired.

The difficulty for a human magician is that once we get up to at least three dimensions, the slices are large, and some mental gymnastics must be performed to view where they lie within a simple two-dimensional presentation. It is, however, quite straightforward mathematically to map between $d - dimensional$ coordinates of tiles and positions in a two-dimensional grid. Thus, it should be feasible to program a smartphone app to perform this trick.

6 CONCLUSION

Through the medium of magic tricks based on binary error detection/correction, we have shown that students can be entertained and taught about many concepts in discrete mathematics, such as parity checks, the pigeonhole principle, permutations, counting principles, modular arithmetic, multidimensional representations, and bijections. The smartphone app proposed in Section 5 also can provide an interesting programming assignment. Finally, the analyses in the Appendices motivate delving into probability and analysis of algorithms for more advanced students.

ACKNOWLEDGMENTS

The author is supported in part by National Science Foundation grants CNS-1543217 and CNS-1542971.

A PROBABILITIES FOR NUMBER OF MAGICIAN-REQUESTED FLIPS

For more advanced students, the versions of the trick in Section 3 motivate additional analyses regarding the number of organizing flips the magician must request. (The analysis for Version 2b will also be applicable to Version 3 in Section 4.) We already have established upper limits on the number of organizing flips, but sometimes fewer flips will suffice. Here we analyze the probabilities of needing differing numbers of organizing flips. Some of the analysis is common to Versions 2a and 2b, and we start with that portion of the analysis before proceeding in the two different directions.

In either version, let us denote by l the upper limit on the number of organizing flips, i.e., $l = \lfloor (n-1)/2 \rfloor$ for Version 2a and $l = (n-1)/3$ for Version 2b. Also denote by $F(n, f)$ the probability of having exactly f flip rows. The analysis is the same for columns, so that $F(n, f)$ will also denote the probability of having exactly f flip columns. Now the probability of having *at most* f flip rows is

$$S(n, f) = \Sigma_{i=0}^{f} F(n, i) .$$

Finally, the probability of needing f flip tiles, $\Pr(f)$ is the probability of having f flip columns and at most f flip rows or vice-versa, minus the intersection of these two events, i.e.,

$$\Pr(f) = 2F(n, f)S(n, f) - (F(n, f))^2 .$$

A simplified case is when $f = l$; in that case we see $S(n, l) = 1$, and the probability of needing l flip tiles is $\Pr(l) = 2F(n, l) - (F(n, l))^2$.

A.1 Version 2a

In Version 2a, we assume for simplicity that n is even (with only small modifications otherwise needed). To complete the analysis, we just need to note that

$$F(n, i) = 2\binom{n-1}{i}/2^{n-1} = \binom{n-1}{i}/2^{n-2} ,$$

Table 1: The probability $\Pr(f)$ that f is the minimum number of magician-requested flips in Version 2a for $n = 8$. (Exact fractional values are given; for uniformity, they are not necessarily in simplest terms.)

f	$F(n, f)$	$S(n, f)$	$\Pr(f)$
0	1/64	1/64	1/4096
1	7/64	8/64	63/4096
2	21/64	29/64	777/4096
3	35/64	64/64	3255/4096

Table 2: The probability $\Pr(f)$ that f is the minimum number of magician-requested flips in Version 2b for $n = 10$.

f	$F(n, f)$	$S(n, f)$	$\Pr(f)$
0	1/64	1/64	1/4096
1	9/64	10/64	99/4096
2	27/64	37/64	1269/4096
3	27/64	64/64	2727/4096

based on choosing exactly i of the first $n - 1$ rows to have even parity or choosing exactly i to have odd parity. It does not seem feasible to give simpler expressions for the probability of needing f flip tiles in general, but we note in Table 1 the values for $n = 8$.

A.2 Version 2b

In Version 2b, we complete the analysis by noting that

$$F(n, i) = \binom{l}{i} \left(\frac{3}{4}\right)^i \left(\frac{1}{4}\right)^{l-i} .$$

Again, it does not seem feasible to give simpler expressions for the probability of needing f flip tiles in general, but we note in Table 2 the values for $n = 10$.

Comparing Table 1 for Version 2a ($n = 8$) to Table 2 for Version 2b ($n = 10$), each with a maximum of 3 flip tiles, we see that the latter version improves the probability of getting by with fewer than 3 flips from about 1/5 to about 1/3.

B VERSION 5 COMPUTATIONAL EFFICIENCY

While all the trick versions presented in the paper illustrate computational concepts, most are actually computationally quite simple, such that they can be performed by a human. In the case of Version 5, however, a more involved computational organization is required, and the naive approach is not the most computationally efficient. This can motivate deeper analysis for advanced students, and we analyze here the required running time for a serial algorithm and even the required resources for a parallel algorithm. Recall that there are actually two computations, one to organize the array of tiles and one to reveal the secret flip performed by the audiene volunteer. But these two computations are the same, and we consider here the time to do it once. (Good references for fundamentals of algorithm analysis are [2, 13].)

Let us begin by defining some notation and determining the naive serial computation time. We have been working with tiles

displayed in an $n \times n$ square corresponding to a d-dimensional quaternary array. That is $n^2 = 4^d$ (i.e., $n = 2^d$), and each tile is addressed with a d-tuple of coordinates, $x_0, x_1, \ldots, x_{d-1}$, each coordinate having value 0, 1, 2, or 3. We denote by $P_d(C)$ the parity, i.e., XOR, of all the tiles in the d-dimensional quaternary array satisfying condition C. Our task then is to compute $P_d(x_i = v)$ for all $i \in \mathbb{Z}_d$ and $v \in \mathbb{Z}_3$ (with $\mathbb{Z}_m$ being the standard notation for the set $\{0, 1, \ldots, m-1\}$). Let $T(d)$ be the time to compute all these values. The naive approach is to compute each of these values independently as the XOR of $4^{d-1} = n^2/4$ bits, which involves a total of $3d(\frac{n^2}{4} - 1)$ XOR operations, which is $\Theta(n^2 \lg n)$, where, again, n^2 is the number of tiles.

B.1 Efficient Serial Computation

For more efficient computation, note that for $i \in \mathbb{Z}_{d-1}$,

$$P_d(x_i = v) = \bigoplus_{j=0}^{3} P_d(x_i = v \text{ and } x_{d-1} = j) . \qquad (1)$$

For any fixed value of j, finding $P_d(x_i = v \text{ and } x_{d-1} = j)$ for all $i \in \mathbb{Z}_{d-1}$ and $v \in \mathbb{Z}_3$ involves computing in a quaternary array of dimension $d-1$, so to complete that computation for all $j \in \mathbb{Z}_4$, time $4T(d-1)$ is sufficient. Once we have done that, the computations indicated in (1) for all $i \in \mathbb{Z}_{d-1}$ and $v \in \mathbb{Z}_3$ can be completed with $3 \cdot 3 \cdot (d-1)$ XOR operations. Finally, we need to compute $P_d(x_{d-1} = v)$ for each $v \in \mathbb{Z}_3$, which is easy to do using results already available in any of the dimensions, e.g.,

$$P_d(x_{d-1} = v) = \bigoplus_{j=0}^{3} P_d(x_1 = j \text{ and } x_{d-1} = v) . \qquad (2)$$

The computation of (2) for all $v \in \mathbb{Z}_3$ can be completed with just 9 XOR operations. Thus we obtain the following recurrence for the running time with initial condition $T(1) = 0$:

$$T(d) = 4T(d-1) + 9(d-1) + 9 = 4T(d-1) + 9d .$$

Rewriting in terms of $n = 2^d$ with $T'(n) = T(\lg n)$, we have

$$T'(n) = 4T'(n/2) + 9 \lg n$$

and $T'(2) = 0$, with solution $T'(n) = \Theta(n^2)$. Thus we shave a $\lg n$ factor off of the naive computation time, and we can see this is asymptotically optimal since we must inspect every one of the n^2 tiles except the one with all coordinates equal to 3.

B.2 Efficient Parallel Computation

For a parallel algorithm, we need some additional notation; let $x_{i,l}$ represent a tuple of l coordinates starting at x_i, i.e.,

$$x_{i,l} = (x_i, x_{i+1}, x_{i+2}, \ldots, x_{i+l-1}) .$$

Then for $v' \in \mathbb{Z}_4^{2l}$, let $S(v') \in \mathbb{Z}_4^l$ denote the starting half of the coordinates of v' and $E(v') \in \mathbb{Z}_4^l$ denote the ending half of the coordinates of v'. Further, let $T_l(d)$ and $W_l(d)$ be the time and work (total number of operations) to compute $P_d(x_{il,l} = v)$ for all $i \in \mathbb{Z}_{d/l}$ and $v \in \mathbb{Z}_4^l$, so that $T_1(d)$ time and $W_1(d)$ work suffice for the overall computation we need. Now the key relationships are

$$P_d(x_{il,l} = v) = \bigoplus_{\substack{v' \in \mathbb{Z}_4^{2l} \\ S(v')=v}} P_d(x_{il,2l} = v') \qquad (3)$$

and

$$P_d(x_{il+l,l} = v) = \bigoplus_{\substack{v' \in \mathbb{Z}_4^{2l} \\ E(v')=v}} P_d(x_{il,2l} = v') \qquad (4)$$

For fixed i and v, each of the computations in (3) and (4) is an XOR of 4^l values, which can be completed in $\Theta(\lg(4^l)) = \Theta(l)$ time with $\Theta(4^l)$ work. Thus, we can relate $T_l(d)$ and $W_l(d)$ to $T_{2l}(d)$ and $W_{2l}(d)$ by using (3) and then (4), each for i even. (Using the equations in sequence avoids a concurrent read to $P_d(x_{il,2l} = v')$ so that the results are valid even on an EREW PRAM.)

$$T_l(d) = T_{2l}(d) + \Theta(l) \qquad (5)$$

and

$$W_l(d) = W_{2l}(d) + \Theta((d/l)(4^l)^2) \qquad (6)$$

where (6) accounts for using (3) and (4) for d/l values of i and 4^l values of v.

Noting that $T_d(d) = W_d(d) = 0$, we can iterate (5) and (6):

$$T_1(d) = \sum_{j=1}^{\lg d-1} \Theta(2^j)$$

and

$$W_1(d) = \sum_{j=1}^{\lg d-1} \Theta\left((d/2^j)(4^{(2^j)})^2\right) .$$

In each case, the term with $j = \lg d - 1$ dominates, and we find $T_1(d) = \Theta(d)$ and $W_1(d) = \Theta(4^d)$, i.e., time $\Theta(\lg n)$ and work $\Theta(n^2)$ for n^2 tiles. This result matches the lower bound on work to compute even a single $P_d(x_i = v)$ as per the serial analysis, and it matches the lower bound on time for even a randomized CREW PRAM [5] and comes very close to the lower bound of $\Omega(\lg n/\lg \lg n)$ on the still more powerful randomized CRCW PRIORITY PRAM [14]

REFERENCES

[1] Tim Bell, Ian H. Witten, Mike Fellows, Robyn Adams, Jane McKenzie, and Sam Jarman. 2015. CS Unplugged: An enrichment and extension programme for primary-aged students. http://csunplugged.org/wp-content/uploads/2015/03/CSUnplugged_OS_2015_v3.1.pdf.
[2] Thomas H. Cormen, Charles E. Leiserson, Ronald L. Rivest, and Clifford Stein. 2009. Introduction to Algorithms (third ed.). MIT Press.
[3] Paul Curzon and Peter W. McOwan. 2008. Engaging with Computer Science Through Magic Shows. In 13th Annual SIGCSE Conference on Innovation and Technology in Computer Science Education. ACM SIGCSE, 179–183.
[4] Paul Curzon, Peter W. McOwan, and others. 2011. The Magic of Computer Science. http://www.cs4fun.org/magic. (2011). Accessed March 8, 2016.
[5] Martin Dietzfelbinger, Miroslaw Kutylowksi, and Rüdiger Reischuk. 1994. Exact Lower Bounds for Computing Boolean Functions on CREW PRAMs. J. Comput. System Sci. 48, 2 (1994), 231–254.
[6] Daniel D. Garcia and David Ginat. 2012. Demystifying Computing with Magic. In SIGCSE '12. Association for Computing Machinery, 83–84.
[7] Daniel D. Garcia and David Ginat. 2013. Demystifying Computing with Magic, continued. In SIGCSE '13. Association for Computing Machinery, 207–208.
[8] Daniel D. Garcia and David Ginat. 2016. Presentation associated with [9] of a trick not described in the written publication. (March 2016).
[9] Daniel D. Garcia and David Ginat. 2016. Demystifying Computing with Magic, part III. In SIGCSE '16. Association for Computing Machinery, 158–159.
[10] Ronald I. Greenberg. 2010. Activities (from high school presentation materials). http://www.illinoiscomputes.org/hspresent/what/activities. (Jan. 2010).
[11] R. W. Hamming. 1950. Error Detecting and Error Correcting Codes. Bell System Technical Journal 26, 2 (April 1950), 147–160.
[12] C. Heeren, T. Magliery, and L. Pitt. 1998. MATHmaniaCS Lesson 1: Binary Numbers. http://www.mathmaniacs.org/lessons/01-binary. (1998). Accessed 3/10/16.
[13] Joseph JáJá. 1992. An Introduction to Parallel Algorithms. Addison-Wesley.
[14] Miroslaw Kutylowski and Thomas Schwöppe. circa 1998. A lower bound for PARITY on randomized CRCW PRAMs. http://citeseerx.ist.psu.edu/viewdoc/versions?doi=10.1.1.46.5019 accessed 1/15/17. (circa 1998).
[15] Steven McGee, Ronald I. Greenberg, Dale F. Reed, and Jennifer Duck. 2013. Evaluation of the IMPACTS Computer Science Presentations. The Journal for Computing Teachers (Summer 2013), 26–40. International Society for Technology in Education. www.iste.org.

Playfully Coding: Embedding Computer Science Outreach in Schools

Hannah Dee
Aberystwyth University
Aberystwyth
UK, SY23 3DB
hmd1@aber.ac.uk

Xefi Cufi
Universitat de Girona
Escola Politècnica Superior
17003 Girona, Catalonia,
Spain
xcuf@silver.udg.edu

Alfredo Milani
University of Perugia
Via Vanvitelli, 1
06100 Perugia, Italy
milani@unipg.it

Marius Marian
University of Craiova
Decebal Blvd. 107
RO-200440, Craiova,
Romania
marius@cs.ucv.ro

Valentina Poggioni
University of Perugia
Via Vanvitelli, 1
06100 Perugia, Italy
poggioni@dmi.unipg.it

Olivier Aubreton
Université de Bourgogne
Franche Comté
IUT Le Creusot
71200 Le Creusot, France
olivier.aubreton@u-
bourgogne.fr

ABSTRACT

This paper describes a framework for successful interaction between universities and schools. It is common for computing academics interested in outreach (computer science *evangelism*) to work with local schools, particularly in countries where the computing curriculum in K-12 is new or underdeveloped. However it is rare for these collaborations to be ongoing, and for resources created through these school-university links to be shared beyond the immediate neighborhood. We have achieved this, through shared resources, careful evaluation, and cross-country collaboration. The activities themselves are inspired by ideas from the *Lifelong Kindergarten* group at MIT, emphasizing playful exploration of computational concepts and interdisciplinary working.

CCS Concepts

•Social and professional topics → Computing education; Computing literacy; *K-12 education;*

Keywords

School-University links; Computational Thinking; Playful coding

1. INTRODUCTION

This paper describes the development of a set of shared, ready-to-use activities which can be run in schools by teachers, or run by university staff in schools as *outreach* activ-

ITiCSE '17, July 03 - 05, 2017, Bologna, Italy

© 2017 Copyright held by the owner/author(s). Publication rights licensed to ACM.
ISBN 978-1-4503-4704-4/17/07...$ 15.00

DOI: http://dx.doi.org/10.1145/3059009.3059038

ities. These activities are designed to promote and engage children with Computational Thinking [11], in a playful and open-ended way. All of the activities we describe have been run by several teachers and/or academics, in several countries, and they are written up in such a way as to encourage and emphasize opportunities for re-use. This paper describes the context in which these activities were created, the content of the activities, and the process of refinement and editorial control that the activities have been subjected to. Through this process we have developed a means of resource reuse which has proved popular with teachers and academics alike. The aims of this paper are:

- **To share the process** which has enabled us to select playful workshops which engage school pupils in computational thinking activities, and then iteratively refine materials and content to maximize possible reuse

- **To encourage reuse of materials** and to offer our tried and tested workshops to the broader computing education community

We believe that a lot of excellent outreach work is locked inside institutions, and through sharing these workshops and providing a framework for activity representation, sharing and improvement, we can encourage colleagues to grow creative and engaging resources that involve K-12 students with computing at all levels.

Our process for creating re-usable materials and workshops is shown in Figure 1, and can be summarized as

1. Select workshops according to clear criteria

2. Write them up in draft form using a common structure

3. Perform a paper-based review of the draft

4. Test the workshop in schools independently

5. Test them in closely observed conditions

6. Release the workshop to the web

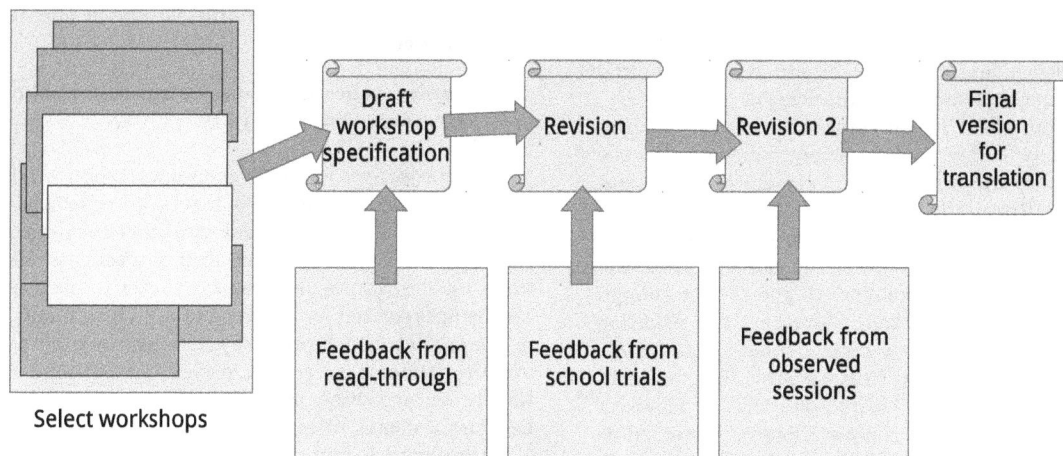

Figure 1: An overview of the workshop creation process

This results in a workshop that has been thoroughly tested in several situations – in the case of the project we describe here, several countries. This paper first briefly covers the local context for each of the participating countries, and then details what happens at each stage of our process, particularly stages 1, 4 and 5.

2. THE LOCAL CONTEXT

The project team come from different countries and cultural backgrounds; in particular, the relationship between computer science and the school curriculum is not uniform. These factors have required a flexibility about computational context, classroom resources and expected experience. In this section we provide a brief overview of the social and political background to school provision for each of the project partners. Note: two of the project partners are from minority nations (Wales, Catalonia) in which education policy is devolved.

Catalonia: Recently, the Catalan government has added coding to the curriculum in Primary and Secondary schools [1]. This should be a cross curricular subject, connected to different subjects or areas. Acquiring the skill of coding in a cross subject curriculum will help children develop knowledge in various areas. The government insists that teachers must awaken curiosity, challenge, and give enough time to investigate and reflect. Students also have to suggest improvements and expose their thoughts to others. This idea has been received as an improvement in the way of teaching, but unfortunately many public schools (administered by the government) have not got the economic resources to purchase the equipment required. This does not mean that public schools can't start to code, but it does introduce barriers.

France: For several years various plans for the development and implementation of digital technology have been set up by the French government [2]. These encourage the use of computational tools within schools (mainly primary schools and colleges). These "Plan d'Investissement d'Avenir" (investment plans for the future) concern the financing of digital equipment (computers for example), and also training

of teachers, digital resource banks and financing of learning-lab or "fablab" spaces. Today coding is present in secondary schools in the technology domain and in other fields such as mathematics and physics. In primary schools, the digital approach remains the responsibility of the teacher. The consequence is a great heterogeneity between primary schools on the practice of digital technology and coding.

Italy: In Italy we are witnessing a new, massive, national plan for the enhancement and the diffusion of computer science – both in primary and secondary schools [3]. This plan started in 2015 and will run until the end of 2020. During these years schools can ask for funds and resources for instruments, platforms, laboratories, high speed Internet connections and many other technical requirements. In particular schools will organize a broad programme of continuing education for teachers and technicians. New curricula for secondary schools are under study in the working groups at the Ministry of Education. The *Programma il futuro* program [5], an action promoting the spread of coding in schools, has been listed among 16 outstanding projects in the European Digital Skills Award 2016 [8]. Change is happening, but a lot of schools find keeping up with the national schedule difficult.

Romania: Romania uses a centralized model for the educational system. In 2011 a new national education enforced that the number of class hours dedicated to ICT and to Informatics should increase for primary and secondary education (both theoretical and vocational branches). The declared goal is to increase IT skills in a generation which is already born into the digital age.

Unfortunately, the adoption of this particular recommendation is rather slow, and sometimes almost absent for certain categories of education. The educational system in many areas provides two profiles: scientific and humanist (split into languages and social sciences). Only the scientific profile has classes for ICT or Informatics in the common core. The total number of classes per week (for all disciplines) may vary from 26 to 31 hours per week. Out of this, the number of classes for ICT/Informatics take a maximum of 4 hours, but more normally 1 or 2. Thus, whilst pupils enrolled in the theoretical scientific profiles are expected to encounter ICT and computer programming during their education, the need exists for further adoption of these disciplines at all levels and categories of education (including primary, humanist and vocational branches).

Wales: Within the UK the computing at school landscape is regionally varied, as Education is devolved to the Welsh government. As a result of a very active campaigning group and a Royal Society report[9], England has seen a massive upsurge in excellent school based provision[7] and a new curriculum which has shifted the problem from being one of "lack of technical content" to one of "not enough qualified teachers". Within Wales, however, the situation is less positive. There is a new digital competence framework[4] which goes some way towards providing for technological provision in schools beyond office skills. However it is not as far reaching or as computationally grounded as the English curriculum, and schools are just beginning to work through the implications. Thus whilst a schoolchild in England would expect to have encountered programming as part of the mainstream curriculum, a schoolchild in Wales may not have had this opportunity.

2.1 Summary

Across Europe change has been happening with regard to computing education, and the introduction of computational thinking, practical computer science, coding and informatics-type activities is becoming a widespread curricular move; there are challenges associated with this, however, and the transition is not completely smooth [6]. New subjects in the curriculum require new lesson plans, new teacher training, and new approaches to learning (as well as often needing new equipment). Whilst we come from different countries there are some commonalities, in particular we have all seen the computing curriculum change (or indeed, appear) recently. In this context, university outreach efforts can become key sources of additional support for schools and colleges trying to keep up with the pace of curricular change.

In short: IT is well-embedded across the curriculum in many of our participant countries. It is not unusual to see spreadsheets in History class, or word processing in English. Programming, however, is rarely seen outside of computing classes. In this project we propose innovative ways to foster creative and critical learning through programming and robotics; one of the slogans we adopted is *Learn2Code and Code2Learn*.

3. CONTENT AND CRITERIA

One of the core outputs of our project was a set of resources which could be easily used, re-used and re-mixed by both university staff engaged with outreach, and school teachers in search of inspiring lesson plans. The starting point for this was a long-list of ideas and half-tested activities, written by the project partners[1]. This long-list was cut down to a set of around 20, based upon inclusion criteria directly related to the main objectives of the project:

- **Explore new ways to promote the learning of programming in European schools.**

- **Help school children move from being digital consumers to digital creators.**

- **Make it easy for people to share the results of the project**

- **Inspire schools to use computer programming in a more interdisciplinary way**.

These objectives led us to choose workshop which encourage children and young people to stop being exclusively users or consumers of digital technologies and become creators and producers. Workshops which lead to products, like animations, movies, games or apps have this enabling aspect. This can be appreciated by the type of activities finally included in the project, which propose active learning methodologies, inviting students to create, design, modify and share. In the chosen activities, technology is not an end but instead becomes a means to express ourselves creatively.

With regard to the third objective there are some aspects of the overarching project which are vital in terms of sharing. Our outputs are accessible to the world, via a web platform [2]. Although the language of the platform is in English, the PDF teachers' guide and complementary material has been translated into all the official languages of the project, and some minority languages[3]. With regard to workshop selection, we chose those workshops with minimal setup cost, free software, and open/platform neutral environments. Within the project we have partners using Apple, Microsoft and Linux environments; it is important that we are able to support all platforms for maximum school applicability. Through encouraging reuse and adaptation of our materials we hope that teachers will see how computing can inspire across the curriculum, leading themselves to develop further resources.

The fourth objective led us to select examples of how to introduce programming and robotics into school curricula in the broadest sense. Workshops in the final selection have come from foreign language lessons, poetry lessons, geography lessons, art, and other subjects across the curriculum.

3.1 Scratch-related workshops

Many of the workshops are based upon the use of Scratch in combination with a multitude of other topics from the core curriculum. This interdisciplinary approach is useful to magnify the interest of both pupils and school teachers. This interdisciplinary connection could be seen as taking advantage of the entertaining nature of Scratch to learn specific topics from other subjects, but it could also be seen as taking advantage of students' interest in other subjects to encourage engagement with computing. We believe that both directions can benefit here: to quote Resnick, we can "learn to code and code to learn" [10].

Examples may include learning foreign languages, making and taking quizzes on topics from the core curriculum (maths, history, biology, etc.), and developing their creativity through programming.

3.2 Robotics and hardware related workshops

Robots are by their very nature motivating to some students. Students love seeing their program have an effect in the real world: they can literally move things around with their ideas. However, robots can be temperamental, and if they break down there can be catastrophic effects for

---

[1]Four universities, a start-up, and two schools

[2]http://playfulcoding.udg.edu/
[3]http://playfulcoding.udg.edu/teacher-guide/

How much time did it take you to prepare for the activity? [Numeric answer] Please give a global mark for how easy it was to understand the activity before implementing it [1-5] How much time did it take you to implement the activity with kids? [Numeric answer] Please give a global mark for how easy it was to implement the activity [1-5] Do you think the proposed age range is adequate? Would you recommend this coding activity to other teachers/schools? Is the goal of the activity clear enough? Did you achieve the goal of the activity? Did the activity reach your expectations? Did kids enjoy the activity?	Do you think kids have developed new skills while working on this activity? If yes, please, indicate which skills have they developed: Team Working Capabilities; Critical Thinking; Heuristic method (Trial-Error); Communication Skills; Computational Thinking; Skills related to the specific subject of the activity (maths, language, art, science, ...) ; Creative thinking; Problem solving What do you think kids like the most/least? [Free text] What would you change in terms of description of the activity? Free text Please give a final, overall mark for the activity [1-5]

Figure 2: A summary of the teacher feedback form from the distributed testing phase. Where not specified, questions were presented as Yes/No Questions with a "please comment" box. These questions were preceded by a series of questions about the school and the children in the classroom (age range, class size, public/private school, and so on).

a workshop experience. We believe that the motivational aspects far outweigh the risks. There is nothing more rewarding than seeing the sense of achievement on a student's face when they have finally managed to get the robot do what they wanted it to. We have tested and refined several workshops which involve robots, based upon three different hardware families (POB, Arduino-based robots, and Lego Mindstorms).

With robots, we found that schools will use what they have, as the cost of setup can be great. If schools have some other platform (you do not have Arduino, POB or lego robots) the key ideas and concepts can often be transferred to another wheeled robot. From a computational thinking perspective, the robot workshops deal with ideas of **control structures** (decisions, reacting to the environment), **iteration** (looping), **debugging** and other development related concepts, and perhaps most uniquely in child-focussed workshops, **precision** and imprecision. Dealing with feedback loops, noisy sensors and real-world robots is a great learning experience from a computational perspective.

3.2.1 Tips for a successful robot outing

- Power: Make sure you have spare batteries, chargers, or whatever else you need to make the robots go.

- Spares: If you can, take one more robot than you need in case of hardware failure.

- Unreliablility: One of the key lessons robots teach is that precision is hard. If you tell a robot to drive one meter, it will probably go 110cm. Or 90cm. If you are lucky, it will be consistent, but it might not be. Actuators and sensors suffer from noise. This is just the way robots are and it is one of the things we learn about through working with them. This has to be treated as a *feature*, not a *bug*.

When choosing a robot for use in the classroom one size does not fit all. A simplified programming environment can be very useful with younger pupils, but with older students, more traditional text-based programming (e.g. Arduino C)

can be an excellent and challenging route. Aim for one of robust *or* cheap: with the latter, you can have more spares. For primary aged children robust is the key feature: they will break things.

3.3 Other workshops

Whilst coding is clearly a core competence for computational thinking, computing is much more than just programming. For this reason we have some activities which do not involve so much coding, including a workshop (HTML-based) which looks at geolocation, mash-ups and other easy hands-on network-based activities, and a workshop on AI which considers more theoretical questions based around the Turing Test, and whether computers can think.

4. REFINEMENT OF WORKSHOPS

With our short-list of activities decided, we then embarked on testing. The refinement of the workshop proposals has been divided into three phases. The first was to capture the know-how of each partner through so called *raw materials* (initial proposals for inspirational workshops for teachers and children). The *raw materials* were tested in school trials and redesigned, in a second phase, generating the *draft products*. These proposals, already tested by several partners, were implemented in different countries during face-to-face observations and reassessed in order to generate the *final products* in the last phase. The result has been the generation of a catalog of inspiring playful coding activities, which has been growing, evolving and maturing.

4.1 Raw materials

Workshops were initially developed by each partner in close collaboration with their local community of teachers (as representatives for their schools). With this starting point, the first version of workshops naturally had a certain amount of imprint from local mentalities and also from the influence of national educational context. The first revision involved a paper-based review of the written workshop descriptions to clarify any ambiguities, and to smooth out any local quirks.

This was carried out by a partner from a different country

to the originating author; feedback was then acted upon to provide our first revision for in-school testing.

4.2 Distributed testing: school trials

The next stage of activity refinement involved testing by the partners within the consortium. Each and every partner was involved in organizing demonstrative workshops with classes from local schools in the region. We ensured as far as possible that each workshop was tested with classroom groups in at least two countries (as well as the originating country). In this way, workshop authors had feedback from outside of their social, national, economic and computational context. There were two workshops that were difficult to test outside the home environment in this way and these were both robotics workshops (due to equipment availability); the content of these workshops was approximated using alternative wheeled robots.

In this phase, project partners went into schools (not necessarily schools involved in the project), and ran lessons based upon workshops from other countries, or assisted classroom teachers with this task. During these sessions the classroom teachers were asked to take notes, and upon completion of the session they were asked to fill in a simple web form with feedback on the workshop.

A summary of the content of the web form is provided in Figure 3. As with many aspects of this project, the form passed through several iterations before settling on this format. Some teachers are very keen to assist with the project, and will fill in a lot of detail. But other teachers are very pressed for time and are less keen to provide detailed textual answers. Thus we arrived at a form design with predominantly yes/no questions, augmented with text boxes to enable the more voluble teachers to contribute fully. Teachers were asked to complete this feedback form soon after the workshop had occurred, and data was entered into the form directly using Google Forms.

In earlier iterations, we also asked for feedback from the children participating in the workshops; this was very positive and proved to us that the workshops were interesting to the children, but was not directly useful in the same way as teacher feedback (perhaps unsurprisingly). For example when asked *"what age would this activity be OK for?"* all children said something equivalent to "My age and up".

Feedback from these distributed school trials was passed back to the workshop originator, and the workshop description was then updated as required.

4.3 Face-to-face workshop observation

The final stage of workshop revision involved dedicated training events in which educators from different schools were asked to perform the activities with their own classes. These sessions were observed by project partners from different institutions, taking notes on various aspects of the activity. Verbal feedback was also solicited, from the observers and the observed instructor. Figure 4.2 shows the observation criteria for the written aspect of this face-to-face evaluation.

The feedback from these sessions was incorporated into the workshop description, to provide our final iteration of improvements. At the end of this phase, activities have been read through, amended, tried in two new environments, amended, observed in a new setting, and finally amended again.

This is a costly phase and we were fortunate enough to receive funding for travel, facilitating such intensive face-to-face evaluation. The feedback received from these sessions had much greater depth than that received from the earlier distributed in-school trials. This is perhaps because all of the participants were familiar with the aims of the project, but maybe also because they were familiar with each other, enabling robust comment in a way that is difficult in a "school visit" scenario.

5. PACKAGING WORKSHOPS FOR REUSE

The workshops form the heart of our project and the process just described has resulted in well-tested, standalone offerings for people outside our project to use. This took the form of a book, translated into all of the project languages.

Through the process of creating these workshop descriptions, testing them, and refining them we have learned and developed our ideas about computing, teaching, curriculum, classroom experiences and pedagogy. It is possible for someone to just pick up one of our packaged workshops and run it tomorrow, without looking at any of the surrounding materials. But there are links between the workshops, themes which have emerged, and we also wanted to capture these ideas. Thus the book contains sections on the learning environment, feedback (formative and summative), and assessment.

Within the book we use a restaurant metaphor to draw links between related activities, so if you want to have an extended series of activities around e.g. geography, there is a geographical menu featuring three workshops with activities surrounding the local situation (country, weather) using different technologies (HTML, Scratch). "Discover your country with Scratch" involves building an interactive map, "Talking about the weather with Scratch" involves discussing geographical concepts and implementing these in a Scratch-based animation and "Introduction to HTML: Hacking Google" involves embedding local APIs (e.g. weather, maps) in a webpage.

6. OUTCOME AND RESULTS

During the two year project, we have been able to accomplish both tangible and intangible results, briefly:

- We have been able to build a catalog of inspiring playful coding activities, which are integrated in the project web platform

- We have conceived, written, designed, edited and published a teacher's guide in book format (physical and digital), which has been translated into 6 languages. This includes the playful coding activities, and also the explanation of the pedagogical philosophy behind them, technical advice, ideas, suggestions and challenges, etc.

- We have established a procedure which will enable this resource of inspirational activities to live and grow over time. This procedure was built by the consortium and has been used during the creation and refinement of our activities.

Considering more intangible outputs, we have exchanged ideas and good practices and conducted a very deep intercultural dialogue. Firstly, at the internal level (consortium)

TASK: To observe and detect those aspects you consider important to take into account for the evaluation of the activity. Please take as a guideline the following items for the analysis:
Methodological Aspects: Introduction, presentation of the activity, rhythm of the work, timing, types of intervention during the activity, types of groups (individual, in pairs, in groups ...), time spent on the activity, reorientation of errors.
Interaction types: teacher-student, student-student, student-material.
Learning process: trial and error, planned strategy, collaborative work.
Evaluation: follow-up work, collection of evidence and results, observation guidelines.
Classroom environment: number of students, materials, space distribution, noise, orderliness, stimulus.

Figure 3: The classroom observation criteria for face-to-face testing sessions

through the close collaboration and involvement of all partners. The celebration of transnational meetings and face to face training activities have facilitated this, but we have also shared ideas and resources through online collaboration and video. This has been used to the maximum to share knowledge and generate new ideas. And secondly, externally, by working not only with schools who belong to the consortium but also schools outside of it. We have generated an exchange of good practice as well as an impact on them: there have been 45 talks, seminars, and training sessions communicating to educators outside of the project. We have also run activities in more than 80 schools, reaching more than 600 teachers and 4000 students.

7. CONCLUSIONS

In this paper we have presented a framework for transnational collaboration on teaching resources which has enabled us to produce a set of activities and a guidebook for engaging schools activities. Collaboration and resource sharing has been very productive thanks to this clear framework and process, despite the different computational, cultural, economic and financial contexts.

In particular, the three-phase workshop testing approach (paper-based review, practical activity review in the classroom, and then face-to-face observed activity) has required a certain amount of coordination and an openness to criticism from workshop authors, but has led to final activities with real robustness to situational variation.

Looking forwards, we have seen more than 1600 downloads of our teachers' guide so far but we are not stopping there. We are collecting feedback on the book as well as comments to improve it; it forms the final, tangible output of our two-year project but we are confident that it can be improved and extended. We are also designing and iteratively improving new activities, and invite others to join us by testing and submitting activities for schools to use. In this way we will build a living library of methods and tools for engaging young minds with creative computing.

8. ACKNOWLEDGMENTS

We would like to thank all of the academics and teachers who supported this project by writing, testing, and feeding into our activities and their evaluation: Amanda Clare, Anna Ferrarons, Anna Rhys Davies, Antoanela-Silva Dan, Caterina Lombardi, Cioaca Norica, Dan Antoanela, Dan Selisteanu, Delia Pirvu, Dorel Lupu, Eduard Muntaner, Elvira Popescu, Erin Good, Esther Villarroya, Eugen Ganea, Ferran Jambert, Guillaume Lemaitre, Gwenan Philips, Joan Massich, Jordi Freixenet, Laura Coravu, Mariona Niell, Mark Neal, Marta Peracaula, Martina Sabatini, Martin Nelmes, Meritxell Estebanell, Mireia Frigola, Mireia Pomar, Mitrea Maria, Nigel Hardy, Ouadi Beya, Samantha Roberts, Tegid Owen, and Wayne Aubrey. We would also like to thank all of the teachers and schoolchildren who tested and evaluated our workshops. This work was supported by **EU Erasmus+ 2014-1-ES01-KA201-004462**

9. ADDITIONAL AUTHORS

Additional authors: Anna Roura Rabionet (Escola Veïnat, Salt, Catalonia, Spain, email: aroura7@xtec.cat); Tomi Rowlands (Ysgol Bro Hyddgen, Machynlleth, Wales, UK, email: tr@brohyddgen.powys.sch.uk)

10. REFERENCES

[1] Competències bàsiques de l'àmbit digital. Technical report, Generalitat de Catalunya Departament d'Ensenyament, 2013. http://ensenyament.gencat.cat/web/.content/home/departament/publicacions/colleccions/competencies-basiques/primaria/prim-ambit-digital.pdf.

[2] Le plan numérique pour l'Éducation. Technical report, Ministère de l'Éducation Nationale, 2015. http://ecolenumerique.education.gouv.fr/plan-numerique-pour-l-education/.

[3] Piano Nazionale Scuola Digitale, 2015. http://www.istruzione.it/scuola_digitale/allegati/Materiali/pnsd-layout-30.10-WEB.pdf.

[4] Digital Competence Framework. In *Learning Wales*. 2016. http://learning.gov.wales/splash?orig=/resources/browse-all/digital-competence-framework/.

[5] Programma il futuro (version updated to Dec. 2016). Technical report, MIUR, Ministero dell'Istruzione, dell'Universita e della Ricerca, 2016. http://programmailfuturo.it/media/docs/Descrizione-progetto-Programma-il-Futuro.pdf.

[6] S. Bocconi, A. Chioccariello, G. Dettori, A. Ferrari, K. Engelhardt, P. Kampylis, and Y. Punie. Developing computational thinking in compulsory education. Technical report, European Union, 2016. http://dx.doi.org/10.2791/792158.

[7] N. C. C. Brown, S. Sentance, T. Crick, and S. Humphreys. Restart: The resurgence of computer science in uk schools. *Trans. Comput. Educ.*, 14(2):9:1–9:22, June 2014.

[8] EU. 16 outstanding projects in the European Digital Skills Award 2016. https://ec.europa.eu/digital-single-market/en/news/16-outstanding-projects-european-digital-skills-award-2016-final.

[9] S. Furber. Shut down or restart? The way forward for computing in UK schools. Technical report, The Royal Society, 2012. https://royalsociety.org/topics-policy/projects/computing-in-schools/report/.

[10] M. Resnick. Let's teach kids to code. In *TEDx*. 2012. https://www.ted.com/talks/mitch_resnick_let_s_teach_kids_to_code.

[11] J. M. Wing. Computational thinking and thinking about computing. *Philosophical transactions. Series A, Mathematical, physical, and engineering sciences*, 366(1881):3717–3725, 2008.

High-Coverage Hint Generation for Massive Courses

Do Automated Hints Help CS1 Students?

Phitchaya Mangpo Phothilimthana
University of California, Berkeley
mangpo@eecs.berkeley.edu

Sumukh Sridhara
University of California, Berkeley
sumukh@berkeley.edu

ABSTRACT

In massive programming courses, automated hint generation offers the promise of zero-cost, zero-latency assistance for students who are struggling to make progress on solving a program. While a more robust hint generation approach based on path construction requires tremendous engineering effort to build, another easier-to-build approach based on program mutations suffers from low coverage.

This paper describes a robust hint generation system that extends the coverage of the mutation-based approach using two complementary techniques. A syntax checker detects common syntax misconception errors in individual subexpressions to guide students to partial solutions that can be evaluated for the semantic correctness. A mutation-based approach is then used to generate hints for almost-correct programs. If the mutation-based approach fails, a case analyzer detects missing program branches to guide students to partial solutions with reasonable structures.

After analyzing over 75,000 program submissions and 8,789 hint requests, we found that using all three techniques together could offer hints for any program, no matter how far it was from a correct solution. Furthermore, our analysis shows that hints contributed to students' progress while still encouraging the students to solve problems by themselves.

Keywords
Computer-Aided Education; Program Synthesis; Program Analysis; Automated Tutor

1. INTRODUCTION

In an introductory programming course, there are many ways for students to receive help, such as going to office hours to ask in person and posting to the online course forum. However, as course enrollment increases, it becomes harder to scale these support mechanisms. An automated approach offers a scalable alternative.

Many intelligent systems have been developed to automatically provide guidance to students completing programming

exercises. Hint generation via path construction leverages existing student submissions to construct the most desirable path to a correct solution [1, 6, 4, 5, 7]. This approach can theoretically generate hints for any program, but in practice, it requires a tremendous amount of engineering effort for instructors to build a robust (high-coverage) hint generation system; the most robust system, ITAP, requires a large number of non-trivial program transformations to canonicalize students' programs and to undo the canonicalization [7].

Another popular approach, mutation-based, uses error models — or mutation rules, provided by the instructor — to mutate a student's incorrect program until it is semantically equivalent to a teacher's solution [8, 9]. Hints can then be naturally derived from the mutation rules that fix the program. While this approach requires far less engineering effort, it may fail to generate hints, especially when a student's program is not close to a correct solution.

This paper extends the mutation-base hint generation using complementary techniques to build a high-coverage hint generation system for Scheme assignments that:

- can provide hints for any program, no matter how far it is from a correct solution
- converts results from its internal algorithms to meaningful hints shown to students
- allows an instructor to add new problems and customize hint messages easily, and
- has been deployed and evaluated in a large introductory programming course with roughly 1,500 students and over 75,000 attempts on a single assignment.

2. OUR APPROACH

Our hint generation system was deployed in UC Berkeley's introductory computer science course. During the middle of the term, the course switched from using Python to Scheme. The course staff often complained that in Scheme office hours, they had to address the same question or similar syntax misconceptions repeatedly.

After reviewing student programs, we recognized three main categories of student errors. Instead of using a single approach to handle all kinds of errors, our system handles each kind differently.

The first category contains programs with semantic errors due to syntax misconceptions. Our observations revealed that this category covers a significant portion of incorrect programs because many students struggle with the placement of parenthesis in Scheme. For example, many students attempt to call a Scheme function with `f(x)` instead of the

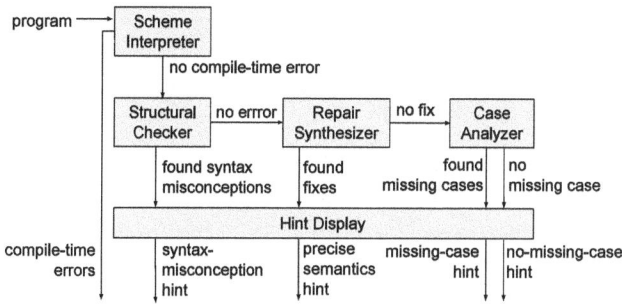

Figure 1: The workflow of the hint generator

The computer thinks that your program lacked or had extra pairs of parentheses.

(a) High-level syntax misconception hint

```
>> Syntax expert:
Check the syntax of the conditional clause
at line 95.

Example(s) of correct syntax:
(cond ((> a b) (* a b)) (else (func a b)))

Example(s) of bad syntax:
(cond ((> a b) * a b) (else func a b))
```

(b) Detailed syntax misconception hint

Figure 2: Examples of Scheme syntax misconception hints

correct way, (f x). To handle programs in this category, the system applies pattern matching on students' programs to check if there are common syntax misconception errors.

The second category contains programs that are almost correct. We handle this category by using the mutation-based hint generation approach. We improve upon the existing systems by introducing a more convenient way to encode error models for a new problem and allowing an instructor to customize a hint message associated with each error model.

The third category contains programs that are far from being correct. To handle programs in this category, we invent a case analysis technique to check if the student's solution contains all conditional checks (e.g. if/cond statements' conditions) appeared in the teacher's solution. Unlike the mutation-based technique, the case analysis technique does not know how to fix a student's program. Instead, it prompts the student to think about cases that he or she may have missed, thus, guiding the student toward a partial solution with a reasonable program structure.

Deploying all three different hint generation techniques together in a single system in a massive course showed that none of them alone would have been sufficient to generate helpful hints reliably.

3. HINT GENERATION

Figure 1 displays the workflow of our hint system, consisting of a Scheme interpreter and three hint generation components—the structural checker, the repair synthesizer (program mutator), and the case analyzer—corresponding to the three different types of programs described in Section 2. The system first checks a student's program with a Scheme interpreter to ensure there is no compile-time error before trying to generate:

1. a *syntax misconception hint* using the structural checker

2. a *precise semantics hint* using the repair synthesizer

3. a *missing-case hint* or *no-missing-case hint* using the case analyzer.

3.1 Structural Checker

The structural checker searches for an expression in a program that matches one of the invalid Scheme patterns described in Table 1. If the checker finds one or more invalid patterns, it displays a syntax misconception hint to the student. We designed the hint system to reveal details over time: it shows high-level hints within the first five attempts and then displays detailed hints after that. Most detailed

syntax misconception hints not only point out mistakes but also provide examples of correct syntax for a similar expression to the student's problematic expression. Figures 2a and 2b show an example of a high-level and a detailed syntax misconception hint respectively. Note that the Scheme interpreter will not detect this type of error during compile time but will instead display a more obscure runtime error.

3.2 Repair Synthesizer

The repair synthesizer is based on the mutation-based hint generation system used by the EdX MITx 6.00x programming course [9]. We implemented a similar system for Scheme instead of Python. Given a student program and error models (mutation rules), the system applies the error models on the student program to generate all possible mutations of the student program. If the synthesizer finds a correct mutated program — semantically equivalent to the instructor provided solution — it generates a hint based on the mutations applied. Figure 3 displays an example of a hint generated from our repair synthesizer when it fixes a program using two mutation rules; the first rule deletes one of the conditions in cond, and the second rule adds a base case. Although the system knows how to fix students' programs precisely, it does not tell the students exactly how to do so. Instead, the system guides them to reach the correct solution by themselves.

We utilize Rosette [11], a solver-aided language, as a constraint solver to prove an equivalence of two programs. Rosette is particularly suitable for building a repair synthesizer for Scheme programs because Rosette is an embedded language in Racket of which Scheme is a subset. Unlike the prior work, which converts a student's Python program into the Sketch language [10], we do not need to convert programs into another representation to synthesize fixes.

Adding New Error Models

To enable the repair synthesizer, an instructor must provide students' error models. An error model captures a com-

```
The computer thinks that:
1. One of the conditions in 'cond' at line 9 is
   unnecessary and causes an error.
2. You may have forgotten to specifically handle
   some of these following cases
   or handle them incorrectly in function (f s):
     (number? s)
```

Figure 3: An example of a precise semantics hint

Construct	Error	Example
cond	missing a test expression or a body	(cond ((> a b) #t) (#f))
cond	missing a pair of parentheses around a body	(cond ((> a b) * a b) (else func a b))
cond	missing a pair of parentheses around a test expression	(cond (> a b #t) (else #f))
cond	missing a pair of parentheses around a test expression, body pair	(cond (> a b) #t else #f)
if	not matching (if test-expr then-expr else-expr)	(if (< a b) #t)
define	no body	(define (min a b))
define	multiple bodies that return non-void values	(define (min a b) (if (<= a b) a) (if (<= b a) b))

Table 1: A list of invalid Scheme patterns used in the structural checker

```
context:  (cond ... (_ ?) ...)          [Rule A]
mutation: (cdr $x) => $x

context:  (define (f $arg) ?)           [Rule B]
mutation: $x => (cond ((= $arg 0) 1) (else $x))
hint: You may have forgotten to handle a base case
      when the argument is equal to 0.
```

Figure 4: Examples of mutation rules

mon mistake that students make, along with potential fixes. Some error models are applicable to most problems, such as an off-by-one error, using $\leq$ instead of $\geq$, and using *true* instead of *false*. Some error models are unique to a problem, such as missing base cases.

An improvement of our repair synthesizer over the prior work is a more convenient method to encode error models. In the prior work, instructors specify error models by overriding functions to mutate different types of AST nodes in students' programs. This method requires instructors to be familiar with the system's internals. Specifically, they must know about the mutation functions they need to override and the provided utility functions that can be used inside the mutation functions. A typical implementation of mutation functions for one question requires 300 lines of code.

In our system, instructors can conveniently encode error models by defining mutation rules without any knowledge of the system's internals. A rule consists of two parts: a context where a mutation can be applied and the mutation itself. Figure 4 shows examples of mutation rules.[1] The symbol ? identifies where in the context the mutation should be applied. For Rule A, the context indicates that the mutation can be applied only to a body expression inside cond; ? in (_ ?) indicates a body position; whereas _, which is a test expression, is ignored. Its mutation rule indicates that if a body matches (cdr $x), we can try to replace the body with just $x; the symbol $ informs the system that the term can match any expression. Rule B mutates a function *f* by adding a base case to return 1 if the argument to the function is 0. This rule is defined with a hint message, so if the repair synthesizer uses this rule to fix a solution, it will display this customized message.

3.3 Case Analyzer

When the repair synthesizer fails to provide hints, the program is passed on to the case analyzer, which reports the missing checks in the program with respect to all *conditional checks* extracted from the instructor's solution. Of course, there are multiple ways to implement a correct solution, and they may not use the same checks. However, we believe that if students are stuck, it may still be beneficial for them to think about scenarios that their programs have not handled.

To test if a conditional check from the instructor's pro-

---

[1]The syntax of mutation rules used in this paper has been modified from the actual syntax used in our working hint generation system for the purpose of explaining the concept.

```
1  (define (I x)
2    (cond
3      ((null? (cdr x)) #t)
4      ((<= (car x) (cadr x)) (I (cdr x)))
5      (else #f)))
```

(a) Instructor's program

```
check i1: (null? (cdr x))
check i2: (and (not (null? (cdr x)))
               (<= (car x) (cadr x)))
check i3: (and (not (null? (cdr x)))
               (not (<= (car x) (cadr x))))
```

(b) Conditional checks in the instructor's program

```
1  (define (S x)
2    (cond
3      ((< (car x) (cadr x)) (S (cdr x)))
4      ((null? (cdr x)) #t)))
```

(c) Student's program

```
check s1: (< (car x) (car (cdr x)))
check s2: (and (not (< (car x) (cadr x)))
               (null? (cdr x)))
```

(d) Conditional checks in the student's program

```
In your function (S x), what will happen if
the inputs to the (recursive) function meet
one of the following conditions? Does your
function handle these scenarios correctly?
  (null? (cdr x))
  (<= (car x) (cadr x))
  (and (not (null? (cdr x)))
       (not (<= (car x) (cadr x))))
```

(e) A missing-case hint generated for the student's program

Figure 5: How the case analyzer generates a hint

gram *I*, appears in a student's program *S*, we first collect all conditional checks in both *I* and *S*. We define a *conditional check* to be the test expression (e.g. if statement's condition) along with the path condition to the check. Consider programs in Figure 5: *I* in Figure 5a and *S* in Figure 5c contain the conditional checks shown in Figures 5b and 5d respectively. Notice that path conditions are included in the conditional checks. For example, the conditional check i2 in Figure 5b is a conjunction of the path condition (not (null? (cdr x))) and the test expression (<= (car x) (cadr x)) on line 4 of Figure 5a.

Then, we check if *S* has all the conditional checks that appear in *I*. Similar to the repair synthesizer, the case analyzer tests the equivalence of two conditional checks using Rosette. For this particular example, none of the conditional checks in *I* appear in *S*. Notice that although the check expression (null? (cdr x)) appears in both programs, their path conditions to the check are not the same. We consider a path condition as part of a conditional check because it captures the order of conditional checks, which matters for the correctness of a program. In our running example, we must make sure that (cdr x) is not empty before we call (cadr x); hence, (null? (cdr x)) must be checked first.

> The computer believes that your program has already covered all possible scenarios (different conditions on the inputs), but the logic to handle those scenarios are still incorrect.

Figure 6: No-missing-case generic hint

Furthermore, including path conditions reduces false alarms (reporting missing checks when there is no missing check) on programs with nested conditional statements and loops.

Once we have gathered all the missing conditional checks, we generate a hint accordingly. Figure 5e is the hint produced for the program in Figure 5c. We exclude most path conditions from a hint message to avoid complicating the hint. However, if the check expression alone is `#t` (such as `else`), we display the path condition. In the actual deployment, we set the system to print at most two missing cases in each hint so that we do not give away too much information.

In the scenario that there is no missing case, the system will print out a generic hint displayed in Figure 6.

4. SYSTEM DEPLOYMENT

We piloted our hint generation system for a Scheme assignment in UC Berkeley's introductory computer science course[2] in Spring, Summer, and Fall 2016. Students are graded on effort and completion in this assignment.

We integrated the hint system into the course autograder, called OK[3]. Students use OK through the command line to test their programs against instructor-provided tests. OK logs every time a student runs the autograder and sends the current copy of the program to the server [2]. To request a hint, students simply append `--hint` to the command for running the autograder. The system usually takes 1–10 seconds to generate a hint.

We used the Knowledge Integration framework to design the presentation of hints to the student [3]. Before providing hints, the system prompted the students to think about a particular comment from a list of instructor-selected prompts. The prompt encouraged students to reflect on their solutions before receiving new information via hints. Once the students had completed the problem, the system asked them to reflect on how the hint(s) changed their understanding of the solution.

The first deployment of the system in Spring 2016 revealed two major flaws of the system. First, the system was not able to provide hints for more than half of the requests due to the lack of the case analyzer. To resolve this, we developed the case analyzer. Second, we removed the requirement to respond to the Knowledge Integration pre-hint prompts so that we minimize the disruption to students. We deployed the improved system again in Summer and Fall 2016.

5. EVALUATION

We evaluated the effectiveness of the hint system by analyzing the data collected by OK in Fall 2016. In particular, we would like to answer two major questions:

1. Did hints help students complete the assignment?

2. Did students rely on hints in a way that may compromise learning?

[2]http://cs61a.org
[3]https://okpy.org

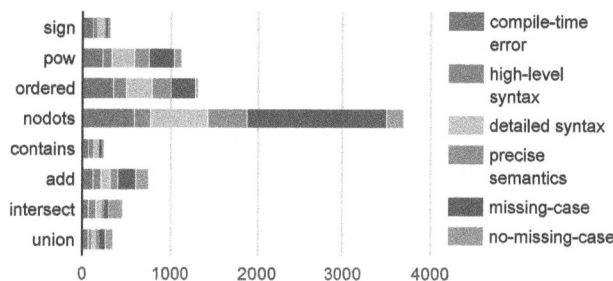

Figure 7: Number of hints per type per problem

The first question helps us determine if the system was helpful, while the second question determines if the system discouraged students from learning to solve problems by themselves. First, we start by presenting the general statistics on the hint usage in Section 5.1. Then, we answer the two central questions in Sections 5.2 and 5.3 respectively.

5.1 Hint Usage

A total of 1,485 students attempted the Scheme homework. The system logged approximately 75,000 student attempts as well as 8,789 hint requests.

918 students used the hint generation system at least once. The ratio of students asking for hints over all students range from 6.7%–41% across questions. Figure 7 displays the numbers of hints separated by question and types of hints. The order of the questions in the chart reflects the order presented to the students in the homework. As witnessed in the chart, `nodots` is the most difficult question and had the most number of hints requested. Also, notice that there are large portions of compile-time errors because most students in this course used the autograder not only to submit their programs but also to test and debug their programs. Apart from compile-time errors, 35% of hints were syntax misconception hints.

Among semantic hints, a majority of them were missing-case hints, which comprised 59% of all semantic hints, followed by precise semantic hints at 23%, and no-missing-case hints made up the remaining 18%.

The ability to generate precise semantic hints (23%) is far lower than that of the original work (64%) [9]. We hypothesize that the repair synthesizer performed worse in our real-world deployment because according to our survey, students requested hints mainly when they were stuck with solutions that were not close to being correct; as a result, these programs were harder to fix with a repair synthesizer.

5.2 Contribution Effect

To evaluate the overall contribution of the hint system, we compared the number of attempts students made on each problem in the assignment between Fall 2016 (with a hint system) and Fall 2015 (no hint system). An attempt is defined as an instance of a student locally running the autograder tests to determine if the current program is correct. Between the two offerings, the assignment as well as the instructor were identical, and the student population had similar demographics.

We found an 18.8% drop in the number of attempts made by students to get to a correct solution in Fall 2016, compared to that of Fall 2015. This reduction of the number of attempts was statistically significant ($p < 0.001$). The effect was particularly pronounced for students in the upper quartile of the number of attempts, demonstrating that the hint system helped students make progress.

In the rest of this section, we evaluate the contribution effects of the different categories of hints separately, using the data collected in Fall 2016.

5.2.1 Syntax Misconception Hints

Many students struggled with syntax misconceptions, making many attempts while trying to resolve their syntax errors. Students who used our hint system for syntax errors had been struggling with the same error for an average of 4.69 attempts before requesting a hint. After receiving a hint, the median amount of attempts to change the error was one attempt. This metric shows that while our hint system did not result in students immediately resolving all of their syntax errors, it helped students move past their current error and advance towards a correct submission.

5.2.2 Semantics Hints

To evaluate the semantics hints, we manually inspect students' programs from the log files collected by OK. A single log file contained a sequence of program snapshots of a student solving a single problem over time along with the hints seen by the student. Of the 1,218 log files that contained at least one semantics hint, we randomly selected 89 log files to analyze, giving us a 95% confidence level with 10% confidence interval. For each log file, we evaluated the *reaction effect* and the *contribution effect* of the hints.

The reaction effect measures how frequently the student modified the program according to hints whether or not the changes were toward the right direction. The reaction effect gives us an idea of how useful the hints were at the moment. It is computed by dividing the number of times the student reacted to hints by the total number of the hints received.

A contribution effect measures how much the hints contributed to the student's final solution. Its value ranges from 1 to 5: 1) no contribution, 2) neutral (unsure), 3) little contribution, 4) moderate contribution, or 5) significant contribution to the final solution of the student. Note that a contribution effect of 5 does not imply that the hints gave away the answer, rather that the hints influenced the student to arrive at the correct answer.

The two authors scored the reaction effect and the contribution effect of the hints of each log file. The average scores from the two authors were then used in this analysis.

We analyzed the reaction and contribution effects obtained from two groups of log files separately. The first group A (452 log files) received at least one precise semantics hint (and possibly other types of semantics hints). The second group B (766 log files) received only missing-case and/or non-missing-case hints. We separated the two groups because hints from the case analyzer (missing-case and non-missing-case hints) are less informative than hints from the repair synthesizer (precise semantics hints). Note that the students in both of the groups might have also received syntax misconception hints, but we ignore the effects from the syntax misconception hints in this section.

Figures 8 and 9 display histograms of the reaction and contribution effects on group A and B, respectively. According to the reaction effects histograms, most students in both groups made changes related to the hints. However, there is a significant number of students from group B (24%) who

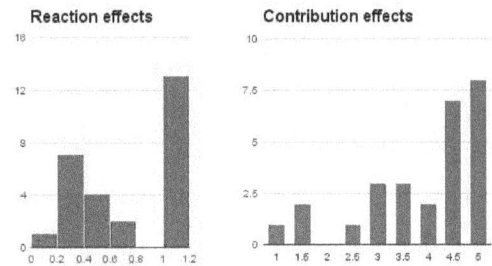

Figure 8: Histograms of effects from hints when students were receiving at least one precise semantics hint (group A). A reaction effect measures how often a student reacted to hints. A contribution effect measures how much hints contributed to a student's final solution.

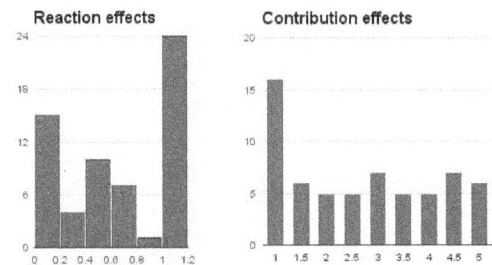

Figure 9: Histograms of effects from hints when students were receiving only missing-case and/or non-missing-case hints (group B)

rarely made changes related to hints (the first bin). Regarding the contribution effects, group A benefited from using hints 85% of the times, while only 48% for group B (bins 3-5). This result is not surprising because of two main reasons. First, hints from the case analyzer were more generic than hints from the repair synthesizer. Unlike the repair synthesizer, the case analyzer did not describe a specific fix for an incorrect program. Second, the case analyzer was only being evaluated on programs where the contribution of the mutation-based technique would have been zero because the mutation-based technique failed to generate a hint. Although the case analyzer did not appear to be as helpful as the repair synthesizer at first, it did help at least half of the students that the repair synthesizer could not help at all.

5.3 Dependence on Hints

The main concern with hints is that students may rely on hints too heavily and therefore avoid learning to solve problems by themselves. In this section, we show that students did not build dependence on the hint generation system.

5.3.1 Syntax Misconception Hints

Our hint system provided syntax misconception hints in the high-level form if a student made fewer than five attempts; otherwise, it displayed detailed information. We computed the ratio of high-level and detailed syntax misconception hints over all hints presented to students. Figure 10 shows that students who used the hint system received fewer detailed syntax hints over time, thus, more capable of fixing syntax misconceptions themselves.

5.3.2 Semantics Hints

We evaluated the rate at which students relied heavily on hints by analyzing a sample of the log files. Examining the

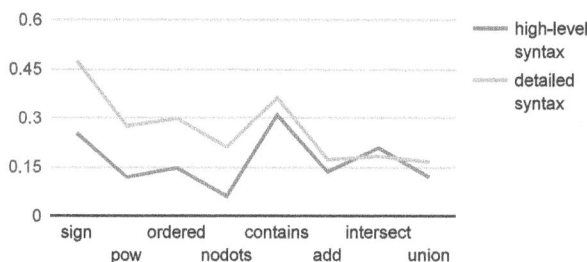

Figure 10: Ratios of high-level and detailed syntax misconception hints over all hints. The X axis is ordered from first to last problems in the assignment.

log files revealed that students who seemed to be mining the system for hints instead of trying to solve problems on their own obtained a large number of semantics hints (eight or more). There were a few students who did not rely on the hints heavily but received more than eight semantics hints. However, we took a conservative approach and categorized receiving eight or more semantic hints as relying too heavily on the system in a way that could compromise learning.

Out of students who received hints, the number of students who heavily relied on the system ranges from 0–3.8% across all problems except for `nodots`, which was 14%. Since `nodots` required many more attempts on average, it was more likely that these students actually needed more help and were not mining for more hints. Ignoring the outlier `nodots`, we conclude that only a small percentage of students misused the hint system and that the majority of students used the hint system as an assistant to help them learn.

6. DISCUSSION

The typical approach to individually helping students on programming assignments is difficult to scale to large courses. In this paper, we presented an automated hint generation system as a way to scale help to all students. We built on prior work to create a reliable hint system and deployed it in a massive CS1 course. The data collected from the deployment showed that applying different hint generation techniques enabled our system to provide hints reliably. Additionally, our hint system often helped students solving problems without having an adverse impact on learning.

According to the optional survey given to the students, there was a mix of both positive and negative responses. Many students expressed that the hint generation system was helpful: "it made the homework go faster, so I didn't have to wait for office hours or a response on [the online Q&A forum]." However, some students thought it was not: "it told me something I was already taking into account." Interestingly, some students expressed that they did not want any hint because "debugging the code on my own encourages more critical thinking and would help me learn more" and that hints would "diminish group collaboration."

Our experience suggests several ways that the system could be improved further. First, according to the survey, students expressed that some hints were not helpful because they contained Scheme expressions, which the students did not understand (e.g. hints in Figures 3 and 5e). To address this, we have customized hint messages in the repair synthesizer, and modified the case analyzer to output the missing cases in natural language and to suggest Scheme primitive functions that may be useful.

Secondly, instead of comparing a student's program to the instructor's solution (which may be very different), the case analyzer could compare the student's program to the most similar correct submission from all students. This way, the case analyzer can guide students toward more appropriate program structures for their current approaches.

Third, apart from providing more details for syntax misconception hints after five attempts, the hint system produces the same hint given the same student's program. Consequently, if students could not make any progress and ask for hints several times, they will receive exactly the same hint. Ideally, the system should detect this scenario and provide new information if possible or suggest students to review the material. As a step towards this, we have modified the system to provide a link to a Scheme tutorial when a student receives more than three syntax misconception hints on the same problem.

7. ACKNOWLEDGMENTS

We would like to thank Marcia Linn, Michael Clancy, and Eliane Wiese for their feedback on our system design; John DeNero and Andy Ko for their feedback on the paper.

8. REFERENCES

[1] T. Barnes and J. Stamper. *Toward Automatic Hint Generation for Logic Proof Tutoring Using Historical Student Data*, pages 373–382. Springer Berlin Heidelberg, Berlin, Heidelberg, 2008.

[2] S. Basu, A. Wu, B. Hou, and J. DeNero. Problems before solutions: Automated problem clarification at scale. In *L@S*, 2015.

[3] M. C. Linn, H.-S. Lee, R. Tinker, F. Husic, and J. L. Chiu. Teaching and assessing knowledge integration in science. *Science*, 313(5790):1049–1050, 2006.

[4] C. Piech, M. Sahami, J. Huang, and L. Guibas. Autonomously generating hints by inferring problem solving policies. In *L@S*, 2015.

[5] T. W. Price, Y. Dong, and T. Barnes. Generating data-driven hints for open-ended programming. In *EDM*, 2016.

[6] K. Rivers and K. R. Koedinger. *Automating Hint Generation with Solution Space Path Construction*, pages 329–339. Springer International Publishing, Cham, 2014.

[7] K. Rivers and K. R. Koedinger. Data-driven hint generation in vast solution spaces: a self-improving python programming tutor. *International Journal of Artificial Intelligence in Education*, 27(1):37–64, 2017.

[8] R. Rolim, G. Soares, L. D'Antoni, O. Polozov, S. Gulwani, R. Gheyi, R. Suzuki, and B. Hartmann. Learning syntactic program transformations from examples. In *ICSE*, 2017.

[9] R. Singh, S. Gulwani, and A. Solar-Lezama. Automated feedback generation for introductory programming assignments. In *PLDI*, 2013.

[10] A. Solar-Lezama, L. Tancau, R. Bodik, S. Seshia, and V. Saraswat. Combinatorial sketching for finite programs. In *ASPLOS*, 2006.

[11] E. Torlak and R. Bodik. A lightweight symbolic virtual machine for solver-aided host languages. In *PLDI*, 2014.

CodeWorkout: Short Programming Exercises with Built-in Data Collection

Stephen H. Edwards and Krishnan Panamalai Murali
Virginia Tech
Blacksburg, VA 24060
edwards@cs.vt.edu, pmk1433@vt.edu

ABSTRACT

Learning programming techniques can be challenging and frustrating for many students. Many instructors use drill-and-practice strategies to help students develop basic programming techniques and improve their confidence. Online systems that provide short programming exercises with immediate, automated feedback are often seen as a valuable approach to drill-and-practice. However, the relationship between practicing with short programming exercises and performance on larger programming assignments or exams is unclear. This paper describes CodeWorkout, an open-source drill-and-practice system that supports short programming exercises and multiple choice questions. CodeWorkout combines an open, gradual engagement model that allows any student to practice exercises, whether or not they have an account or are enrolled in a course, together with powerful course management features that support graded assignments, quizzes, and even practicum-style exams. It also provides a rich data collection and evaluation infrastructure for educational research purposes. We report on initial experiences using CodeWorkout in a CS1 course, including student perceptions of the tool and its benefits.

Keywords

CodeWorkout; homework; coding; skill development; practice; exam

1. INTRODUCTION

Rudimentary programming skills are essential to developing fundamental proficiency in computer science. But many computer science students lack effective resources to practice basic programming skills. Practicing manageably small programming exercises helps students gain confidence and hone their skills [3]. However, current programming practice systems provide minimal assistance to students struggling with exercises [3, 11]. Meanwhile, instructors would also benefit from a robust practice system that does not overburden them with heavy time and administrative demands.

ITiCSE '17, July 03-05, 2017, Bologna, Italy

© 2017 Copyright held by the owner/author(s). Publication rights licensed to ACM.
ISBN 978-1-4503-4704-4/17/07...15.00

DOI: http://dx.doi.org/10.1145/3059009.3059055

A number of drill-and-practice tools are emerging to help students develop basic programming techniques and improve their confidence. However, these tools continue to grapple with trade-offs between adding burdensome workload on instructors, and sacrificing content quality [5]. This paper describes CodeWorkout, a new drill-and-practice system designed to build on previous work and provide a more comprehensive solution to small-scale practice assignments in the contexts of both individual learning, and learning in the CS classroom. CodeWorkout provides open programming practice to anyone, without requiring an account, but also provides for more structured, course-based use by instructors and students working with graded assignments. It also offers the facility for instructors or students to write their own questions, and provides a rich data model for capturing all data regarding exercise attempts, errors, and feedback. In addition to providing a basis for educational research, this data model also offers the opportunity to develop analyses based on item response theory for evaluating questions and quantifying student understanding, both to track student progress and to refine and improve exercises. In this paper we report on our initial experiences using CodeWorkout for both homework and on-line exam questions in a CS1 course, and describe student perceptions of use of the system.

Section 2 discusses related work, while Section 3 describes CodeWorkout and its unique features. Section 4 follows by describing how CodeWorkout was used in our course, then presents a summary of results from a student survey intended to collect subjective views of using the tool. Finally, Section 5 summarizes the lessons learned and describes future directions for CodeWorkout.

2. RELATED WORK

Drill-and-practice is a long-established method for rehearsing and exercising new knowledge. It is widely considered an effective technique for learning and is best implemented when accompanied by indicators of progress made [1]. Intelligent Tutoring Systems (ITS) typically employ cognitive models to track student progress and have demonstrated some effectiveness by aiding students with an artificial tutor [8, 9]. However, the artificial intelligence (AI) infrastructure of an ITS is non-trivial and developing and maintaining an AI tutor to support course-wide material on programming would be particularly challenging. Furthermore, Weber and Brusilovsky found that teachers preferred versatility of instructional technology over other special features [15].

More versatility can be found in a variety of online practice systems. Practice systems generally categorize questions so that as students answer them, the system can track the students' progress within the category. However, there are practice systems with support for different types of questions and with other unique features. In the following sections, we highlight systems with notable approaches to learning.

2.1 Coding Systems

Coding systems have begun to emerge specifically to support practice at programming. Instead of questions, these systems ask students to solve problem descriptions through code. CodingBat (formerly JavaBat) offers a collection of small programming problems and now also supports instructor-contributed problems [11]. The accessibility of an open, online repository of practice exercises makes CodingBat a valuable resource for novice programmers. CodingBat takes advantage of test cases to evaluate the correctness of students' code. CodeWrite [3] similarly evaluates student code, but specifically holds students responsible for writing exercises and their respective test cases.

To explore the viability of a "student-sourced" approach to creating practice question banks, the 2015 study by Denny, Cukierman and Bhaskar [2] performed an empirical validation of the efficacy of student-created programming exercises in boosting learning. The study involved a set of randomly selected students who had to create a set of programming questions before a summative exam while the rest of the class did not have to. The study found that students who partake in the activity of creating viable practice programming questions achieve better grades. It was also shown that students were capable of producing exercises across a wide range of topics and difficulties.

WeBWork-JAG [5] is a practice system that uniquely extends a rich MCQ and FR system to also support coding exercises. Like several others, it allows students to provide questions. While they observed similar benefits of drill-and-practice as others, Gotel, et al. identified several challenges to practice systems. Most notably, they expressed concerns about the quality of student-provided content and the consequential demands of maintenance, exposing the need to address exercise quality in practice systems.

In addition to CodingBat, a related system that has also influenced CodeWorkout is CloudCoder [10], another open-source web-based system that is free to use for institutions. CloudCoder allows sharing of questions between instructors, and also supports the logging of keystroke-level data for research purposes. Unlike CodingBat, CloudCoder supports whole-program exercises, where the student code reads from the standard input and writes the computation result back into the standard output stream, in addition to simple function-based exercises, where the student completes a single method that returns a specific value.

Infandango [6] is a simple drill-and-practice system with a testing infrastructure that is similar to that of CodeWorkout. In this system, the final Java programs for an exercise are submitted by students through the web front-end after authentication. Then Infandango's JUnit daemon compiles the code, executes it in a sandboxed environment and runs the test cases against it. Students are then given feedback based on which cases passed and failed. The authors point out that the modularity of the system in the form of its authentication, web front-end and database are its unique selling points. However, Infandango relies on CoSign for authentication, an approach that is not used at many edu-

cational institutions, and one that makes it difficult to integrate with learning management systems. Infandango is also constrained by the fact that it works only for Java and not other programming languages.

2.2 Automated Grading Systems

Wilcox [16] provides a summary of the use of automation in undergraduate level CS courses, stating that are many benefits to using autograding, primarily resource savings. One benefit of automated approaches is that they enable instructors to assign multiple smaller questions, many more than would be practical with manual grading. Wilcox states that autograders impede neither the interest nor the academic performance of the students, but instead increase them if used appropriately.

Likewise, there are academic tools that take advantage of automated testing to assess program quality. Web-CAT [4] and Marmoset [13] are popular automated grading tools for computer science. Both use hidden unit tests—written by instructors—to test the correctness of students' programs. While automated graders may save instructors substantial time in grading programs, their strengths are in assessing student work. The design of CodeWorkout's infrastructure takes advantage of lessons learned from automated graders, but conversely focuses on facilitating learning over assessing larger-scale assignments.

3. CODEWORKOUT: A NEW DRILL-AND-PRACTICE SYSTEM

CodeWorkout is a completely online and open system for all those who are interested in teaching programming to their students. Thus, CodeWorkout is not limited to any particular institution. It provides a universal platform on which students from various backgrounds can practice programming and instructors can offer courses. CodeWorkout is not limited to short, single-method programming questions but is capable of supporting different kinds of questions, including multiple choice (both forced choice and multiple answer), coding by filling in the blanks, using arbitrary objects (lists, maps, or even instructor-defined classes) instead of only primitives, writing collections of methods or an entire class (instead of just single methods), multi-part questions that include multiple prompts, and "find and fix the bug" style questions where students are given a code implementation containing one or more errors to repair.

Figure 1 shows the view students use to enter answers for and receive feedback on exercises (video demo: http://code-workout.org/example.mp4). CodeWorkout uses an "exercising" metaphor to reinforce the idea that users are building their strengths (at programming). As a result, it uses terminology based in this metaphor, calling individual problems exercises, while collections of problems are called workouts, and the public practice area is known as the "gym". Students who practice on their own earn experience points instead of a grade, and practice counts towards the system's notion of topic mastery, whether conducted on one's own or as part of a class assignment.

CodeWorkout facilitates active learning through both its drill-and-practice approach and the facility for students to create their own questions that they share for the benefit of their peers. CodeWorkout also provides a facility for instructors to share their programming exercises with other

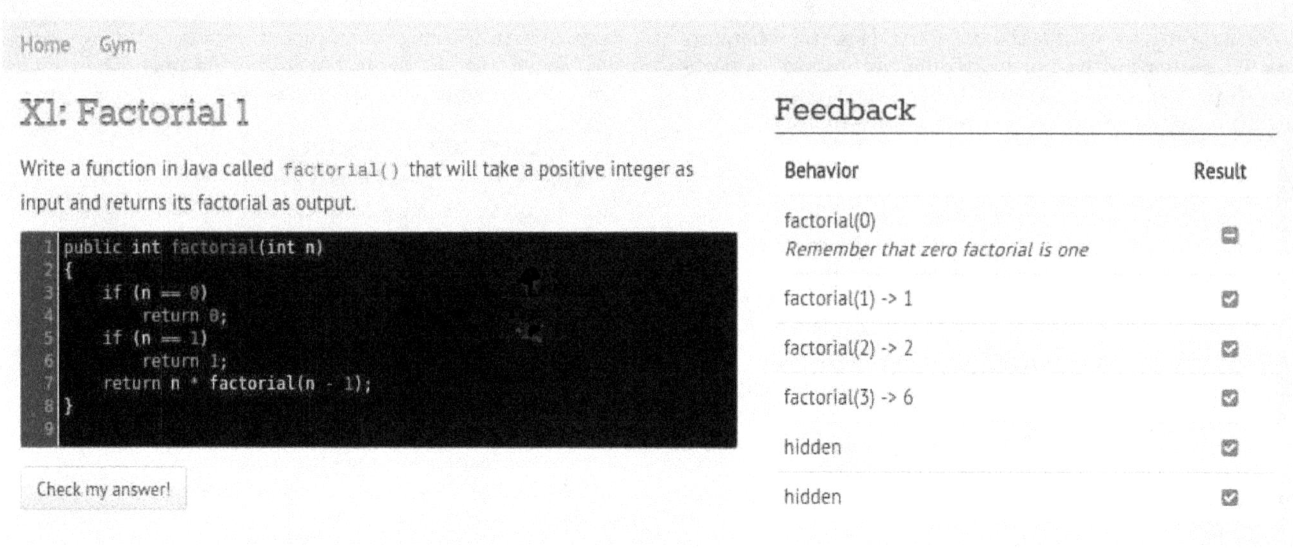

Home / Gym

X1: Factorial 1

Write a function in Java called `factorial()` that will take a positive integer as
input and returns its factorial as output.

```
1  public int factorial(int n)
2  {
3      if (n == 0)
4          return 0;
5      if (n == 1)
6          return 1;
7      return n * factorial(n - 1);
8  }
9
```

Check my answer!

Feedback

Behavior	Result
factorial(0) *Remember that zero factorial is one*	⊟
factorial(1) -> 1	☑
factorial(2) -> 2	☑
factorial(3) -> 6	☑
hidden	☑
hidden	☑

Figure 1: CodeWorkout's exercise interface.

instructors if they wish. It has the feature of tagging each
question/assignment with all the concepts involved in them.
In addition to supporting search features and an organic
classification scheme, this also allows the system to track
the scores of students on a concept-by-concept basis.

CodeWorkout aims to be a comprehensive system that
addresses many of the weaknesses of its predecessors while
meeting a wide variety of real classroom needs. As a result,
CodeWorkout's design targets the following objectives:

- **Simultaneously supporting courses and the gym:**
  CodeWorkout is designed to fully support classroom
  use by instructors who wish to use graded assignments.
  At the same time, CodeWorkout also provides a completely open "free practice" area where anyone, whether
  enrolled in a course or not, can browse and practice
  a large collection of publicly available exercises–a concept successfully pioneered by CodingBat. CodeWorkout provides full support for both uses. Classroom
  activities can include graded or optional homework,
  untimed or timed quizzes, or even live exams. Several
  workout policies are available so instructors can choose
  whether or not students can see scores or full feedback
  immediately (in homework) or not (during a test), and
  whether questions can be immediately reviewed, or review must wait until all students have completed. For
  timed quizzes and tests, CodeWorkout even allows instructors to set individual deadlines or allow extra time
  for specific students where necessary, to accommodate
  makeup work or students with special needs.

- **Gradual engagement:** CodeWorkout's open practice features are designed around the idea of *gradual
  engagement*–that is, users can use many of the site's
  features without an account, and they are not required
  to login or create an account until they reach the point
  where identifying information is required–such as enrolling in a course or needing to complete a course-
  specific assignment. Long-term sessions are used to
  track users, including anonymous users, so no data is

lost due to session timeouts or browser restarts. Once
users reach a point where an account is required, they
are prompted to provide the minimum necessary information: providing an e-mail address or logging in
using Gmail or Facebook, for example. By providing
a low effort login process that is delayed as much as
possible, new users have a smoother entry path into
the system. By using long-term sessions, once a user
logs in all of their anonymous activities can be carried
over into their account without loss of information.

- **Role-based permissions model:** CodeWorkout uses
  an egalitarian approach to security. Except for system
  administrators, all users are equal. Permissions are
  governed by one's role with respect to a specific piece
  of data. This idea is not novel, but is rare in many
  educational systems. Role-based permissions ensure
  that one who is listed as an instructor for a course has
  instructor-level access within that course, but nowhere
  else, for example. As a result, CodeWorkout is set up
  so that anyone can create a course, choosing to allow
  students to self-enroll or to upload a roster. Since self-
  proclaimed instructors only have access to their own
  courses, a more open and accommodating environment
  with lower barriers to entry can be maintained.

- **Exercise organization:** Exercises are the main focus of any drill-and-practice system and CodeWorkout
  aims to provide significant support features and facilities organized around it. Exercises are available to
  be either directly used in the gym or to be organized
  into workouts. The exercise model is truly polymor-
  phic in CodeWorkout: an exercise can be of different
  types like multiple-choice or coding; it can also consist of multiple parts, allowing for a richer variety of
  questions. Questions are automatically versioned in-
  ternally, so that the prompt a student is working on
  can be separated from edits being made concurrently
  by the question's author, and so that collected data
  on performance and answers can be tracked properly

through a question's edit history. Families of related questions are linked so that instructors can easily find alternative versions of a question, or avoid putting alternative versions of a question on a single assignment.

- **Collaborative and active learning**: CodeWorkout allows instructors to share exercises with one another. Its framework facilitates students who have mastered a particular topic to be able to create their own programming questions that they can share for the practice of their peers. Finally, it also tries to provide students with a facility to share hints for exercises and to participate in a Stack Overflow-like question forum associated with each question.

- **IRT statistics**: CodeWorkout aims to support the collection of statistics necessary to analyze questions and student performance using item response theory [14]. Using the workout scores as a basis for student skill level, CodeWorkout can determine the difficulty and discrimination values for student-created content like exercises and hints. As the system collects more and more data, these values can be used to filter out exercises and hints that are not as useful.

While CodeWorkout is still quite young, it aims to fill gaps in current support for small drill-and-practice coding problems. Providing classroom support that spans the range from open, unstructured (and even unenrolled) voluntary practice, all the way to in-class timed exam support, is an ambitious goal. It is also important to strive for supporting a broader audience of users. In their survey paper of automatic assessment systems, Ihantola et al. [7] note that most autograding systems have not been widely adopted because they were created solely for the sake of a thesis or a paper publication. They do not focus on building features that would make them a viable system for continuous use outside their parent institution. They point out significant barriers to wide-scale adoption. Vreda Pieterse also describes reasons that inhibit success of such systems [12]. She notes that setting up courses is problematic because they are not free, require extensive work for deployment on an institution's server, or suffer from significant usability issues. For these reasons, a robust solution targeted explicitly for external adoption is necessary.

4. STUDENT PERCEPTIONS

CodeWorkout has been used in two to three courses each semester at Virginia Tech during the 2015-2016 and 2016-2017 academic years, including use by 372 students in a CS1 course during Fall 2015, and 378 students in the same course in Spring 2016. CodeWorkout was used for graded homework assignments, for optional practice assignments, and for coding questions on in-class proctored and timed examinations. Students also had larger program assignments (graded using Web-CAT), as well as homework assignments that did not involve programming in this course. Finally, many students elected to voluntarily complete additional questions on CodeWorkout in a free practice mode, in order to study or prepare for exams.

While instructors reacted strongly positively to CodeWorkout as a classroom tool, we were also interested in how students reacted to the system. We distributed an opinion survey to 378 students in the spring 2016 CS1 course

just before students took Test 2. At that point, these students had already been using CodeWorkout for both voluntary and graded assignments, including in-class tests. The survey included nineteen questions, sixteen of which were five-point Likert scale questions rated from Strongly Agree to Strongly Disagree. In order to ascertain the consistency of results, these statements were both negatively and positively phrased. These statements deal with various topics pertaining to how well CodeWorkout was meeting its objectives, such as the usability of its interface, ease of access and usefulness of feedback. The final three questions were free-form text answer questions intended to gauge initial impressions, perceived drawbacks and overall usefulness of CodeWorkout. 173 students responded to the survey.

4.1 Likert-scale Question Results

Table 1 lists the mean scores and variances for the Likert-scale questions. Overall, students have a positive impression of CodeWorkout and see it as beneficial. The high means for questions 1, 2, 6, 8, 9, 10 and 15 were especially notable. These questions dealt with the usability and ease of access of CodeWorkout, two of its primary goals. Responses to two of the negative questions, Q3 and Q12, further support this, with low mean responses of 2.39 and 2.21 respectively. The high mean scores of 4.18 in Q8 (regarding the continuous availability of CodeWorkout) and 4.02 in Q15 (regarding ease of course enrollment) is an affirmation of this. The highest mean of all (4.31 in Q6) indicated that CodeWorkout was better than traditional paper-based settings for coding.

The only questions that were not as strongly supportive were Q4 and Q5. Q4 is a negatively phrased question asking how slow is CodeWorkout's feedback. The response to this has a mean of 2.85 (lower is better). While this certainly indicated that most students did not feel that the system was slow, a minority of students did feel that its speed can be improved. The positively phrased question with the lowest mean was Q5, which was directed towards a specific feature of CodeWorkout that allows students view their work in past assignments. While the mean of 3.57 indicates that the feature works, it also conveys that we could do more to improve it.

A majority of the respondents for Q1 (94.2%) said that they either agreed or strongly agreed to the statement that it was easy to submit exercise solutions in CodeWorkout. CodeWorkout's coding interface has received special praise: more than 85% of the respondents said that it was easy to write code with it.

Even though CodeWorkout is still very much under development, a majority of the students (63.9%) expressed their wish to use CodeWorkout in their next programming course. In Q9, 81.9% of students either agreed or strongly agreed that CodeWorkout is useful for learning introductory programming skills, its most important objective. Putting it a little differently, Q11 asks how much CodeWorkout has improved their programming skills. More than 76% of the responding students indicated that they either agreed or strongly agreed with this statement. Finally, with regard to usefulness in a traditional classroom setting, 78.6% of the respondents either agreed or strongly agreed that that the practice afforded by CodeWorkout will positively impact their performance in this course. These results present evidence that students see CodeWorkout as a viable drill-and-practice system in introductory programming settings.

Table 1: Student Survey Results

	Question	Mean	Variance
	Usefulness		
9	**CodeWorkout is helpful to use for learning introductory programming**	**3.99**	**0.92**
11	**The programming practice I get from CodeWorkout has improved my programming skills**	**3.83**	**0.88**
13	I believe that practicing on CodeWorkout will positively impact my performance on exams in this course, and on my grade in this course	3.85	0.8
14	I wish to use CodeWorkout in my next programming course	3.67	1.12
	Usability		
1	**It was easy for me to submit my solutions to exercises on CodeWorkout**	**4.29**	**0.47**
6	Practicing and submitting exercises on CodeWorkout is simpler as compared to paper-based systems	4.31	0.60
10	**I find CodeWorkout's coding interface easy to use**	**4.10**	**0.53**
12	I found it difficult to write my solutions for the exercises on CodeWorkout because of its interface‡	2.21	0.76
	Access and navigability		
2	It was simple for me to login to CodeWorkout for the first time	4.08	0.75
3	I was difficult for me to navigate to the exact course content that I was looking for on CodeWorkout‡	2.39	1.09
5	I was able to access my answers to previous assignments and exercises without complications	3.57	1.09
8	CodeWorkout is always available and accessible to me	4.00	0.50
15	The software made finding and opening my past programs easy.	4.02	0.59
	Feedback		
4	The automatic feedback generated by CodeWorkout was slow‡	2.85	0.96
7	The compilation error messages that CodeWorkout gives are useful for fixing syntax errors in my code	3.44	1.22

4.2 Free-form Question Results

The first free-form text question was: "What were your initial impressions about CodeWorkout as a programming practice system?" 168 of the total 174 respondents answered this question. From the student responses to this question, we can see that a majority of students had a positive first experience. The following are some of the sample responses:

- *It was helpful to see the tests ran against my code to see where I went wrong. The error messages also help me find the faults in my code*

- *Simple and gave feedback (which is invaluable).*

- *I like how it feels like an online game. Something that makes me want to achieve more and fill out the progress bar.*

- *It was fun to be given a problem, develop a solution, and immediately receive feedback about the task I completed, which was a welcome change from the needed practice in other formats in the course.*

The second free-form question was: "What were the aspects of CodeWorkout that you found to be an impediment to your learning?" Students complained about insufficient feedback when their solution did not work correctly. This is understandable because most of the students were first time Java programmers who may find compiler error messages to be cryptic. Also students sometimes were unable to figure out why their code was repeatedly failing some test cases. Unfortunately, this situation arose because hints and feedback at the test case level were not specified for the exercises used in this study due to lack of time, *even though CodeWorkout provides this capability.*

From the second free-form question, we understand that students had some difficulties in working out the computational logic for individual exercises and they were frustrated that CodeWorkout couldn't help them out when they were stuck. This was not an impediment *per se* to learning, but is an interesting direction to feedback that we did not consider before. Overall, the responses to this question were rather positive and this reinforces the inference made from the Likert-scale questions that CodeWorkout does not pose any barriers to student learning.

The final free-form question in the survey was: "Overall, how useful do you think CodeWorkout is to your learning and improvement of programming skills?" Of all three free-form text questions in the survey, the responses to this question were the most favorable. The few negative replies to this question pointed out the lack of certain features like more descriptive feedback or display of alternative working solutions. We would like to point out that these are features we are already building into CodeWorkout for next semester. The following are some of the sample responses:

- *Useful for studying.*

- *I think it's been quite useful for learning*

- *CodeWorkout hasn't helped me much in terms of improving my programming skills. It is good practice, and if hadn't had prior programming experience when using this website I would have benefited much more from it.*

- *It gives an opportunity to practice standard coding skills in a non graphical context. Personally I think that exposure to coding in this manner will be much more reflective of future/actual coding we will do.*

5. CONCLUSION

CodeWorkout is a new drill-and-practice system designed to provide a larger range of opportunities for students to practice basic coding skills. Inspired by predecessors, it design aims to combine the best strengths of prior work with new strategies for enhancing classroom support and supporting student practice. In the experiences reported in this paper, CodeWorkout was used quite successfully in an introductory course with a large number of students. Students reacted positively and appear to see clear benefits to using this style of exercise practice to develop their skills.

Nevertheless, there are still many research questions needing further exploration. In the future, we plan to continue refining CodeWorkout to support such investigations. An important part of this effort is the use of item response theory to characterize the performance of questions and the identification of questions that may need revision or editorial attention. At the same time, IRT offers a deeper, more data-driven way of estimating student ability. By modeling both student ability and question performance, it is possible to intelligently recommend new problems for practice that are closer to the student's zone of proximal development. The addition of social features and Stack Overflow-inspired Q&A discussions for questions offers a unique strategy to try to help students who get stuck. Similarly, prompting successful students to offer hints on how to tackle questions they have completed, together with analysis of when those hints help later students get unstuck, offer new strategies for engaging students in the community of users, instead of encouraging them to pursue individual practice in isolation. A consolidated approach to these issues is more likely to meet the needs of current and future educators.

6. ACKNOWLEDGEMENTS

This work is supported in part by the National Science Foundation under grant DUE-1245589. Any opinions, findings, conclusions, or recommendations expressed in this material are those of the authors and do not necessarily reflect the views of the National Science Foundation.

7. REFERENCES

[1] J. D. Bransford, A. L. Brown, R. R. Cocking, et al. How people learn, 2000.

[2] P. Denny, D. Cukierman, and J. Bhaskar. Measuring the effect of inventing practice exercises on learning in an introductory programming course. In *Proceedings of the 15th Koli Calling Conference on Computing Education Research*, Koli Calling '15, pages 13–22, New York, NY, USA, 2015. ACM.

[3] P. Denny, A. Luxton-Reilly, E. Tempero, and J. Hendrickx. Codewrite: Supporting student-driven practice of java. In *Proceedings of the 42Nd ACM Technical Symposium on Computer Science Education*, SIGCSE '11, pages 471–476, New York, NY, USA, 2011. ACM.

[4] S. Edwards. Web-CAT. http://web-cat.org. last accessed 04-07-2016.

[5] O. Gotel, C. Scharff, and A. Wildenberg. Extending and contributing to an open source web-based system for the assessment of programming problems. In *Proceedings of the 5th International Symposium on Principles and Practice of Programming in Java*, PPPJ '07, pages 3–12, New York, NY, USA, 2007. ACM.

[6] M. J. Hull, D. Powell, and E. Klein. Infandango: Automated grading for student programming. In *Proceedings of the 16th Annual Joint Conference on Innovation and Technology in Computer Science Education*, ITiCSE '11, pages 330–330, New York, NY, USA, 2011. ACM.

[7] P. Ihantola, T. Ahoniemi, V. Karavirta, and O. Seppälä. Review of recent systems for automatic assessment of programming assignments. In *Proceedings of the 10th Koli Calling International Conference on Computing Education Research*, Koli Calling '10, pages 86–93, New York, NY, USA, 2010. ACM.

[8] K. R. Koedinger and E. L. F. Sueker. Pat goes to college: Evaluating a cognitive tutor for developmental mathematics. In *Proceedings of the 1996 International Conference on Learning Sciences*, ICLS '96, pages 180–187. International Society of the Learning Sciences, 1996.

[9] P. D. Palma. Viewpoint: Why women avoid computer science. *Commun. ACM*, 44(6):27–30, June 2001.

[10] A. Papancea, J. Spacco, and D. Hovemeyer. An open platform for managing short programming exercises. In *Proceedings of the Ninth Annual International ACM Conference on International Computing Education Research*, ICER '13, pages 47–52, New York, NY, USA, 2013. ACM.

[11] N. Parlante. CodingBat. http://codingbat.com/. last accessed 04-06-2016.

[12] V. Pieterse. Automated assessment of programming assignments. In *Proceedings of the 3rd Computer Science Education Research Conference on Computer Science Education Research*, CSERC '13, pages 4:45–4:56, Open Univ., Heerlen, The Netherlands, The Netherlands, 2013. Open Universiteit, Heerlen.

[13] J. Spacco. Marmoset. http://marmoset.cs.umd.edu/. last accessed 04-16-2016.

[14] E. Thompson, A. Luxton-Reilly, J. L. Whalley, M. Hu, and P. Robbins. Bloom's taxonomy for cs assessment. In *Proceedings of the Tenth Conference on Australasian Computing Education - Volume 78*, ACE '08, pages 155–161, Darlinghurst, Australia, Australia, 2008. Australian Computer Society, Inc.

[15] G. Weber and P. Brusilovsky. Elm-art: An adaptive versatile system for web-based instruction. *International Journal of Artificial Intelligence in Education (IJAIED)*, 12:351–384, 2001.

[16] C. Wilcox. The role of automation in undergraduate computer science education. In *Proceedings of the 46th ACM Technical Symposium on Computer Science Education*, SIGCSE '15, pages 90–95, New York, NY, USA, 2015. ACM.

UNIXvisual: A Visualization Tool for Teaching UNIX Permissions

Man Wang,
Jean Mayo,
Ching-Kuang Shene
Dept. of Computer Science
Michigan Technological
University
Houghton, MI
{manw,jmayo,shene}
@mtu.edu

Steve Carr
Dept. of Computer Science
Western Michigan University
Kalamazoo, MI
steve.carr@wmich.edu

Chaoli Wang
Dept. of Computer Science
and Engineering
University of Notre Dame
Notre Dame, IN
chaoli.wang@nd.edu

ABSTRACT

UNIXvisual is a user-level visualization tool designed to facilitate the study and teaching of access control in UNIX. UNIXvisual is aimed at both novice users, who need only to control access to their own files, and students of computer security, who need a deeper and more comprehensive understanding. The system allows students to analyze permission settings in the underlying real file system, as well as in a combination of real and pseudo file systems defined through a specification file. It also allows a student to trace the value and effect of credentials within an executing process. UNIXvisual gives instructors flexibility in the allocation of lecture time by supporting self-study, lowers the overhead required for teaching access control by running under an ordinary user account, and enhances learning through the use of visualization.

We also present the results of an evaluation of UNIXvisual within a junior-level course on concurrent computing. The evaluation indicated that UNIXvisual helped students understand UNIX permissions and enhanced the course coverage of UNIX permissions, regardless of their prior UNIX experience.

Categories and Subject Descriptors

k.3.2 [**Computers and Education**]: Computer and Information Science Education—*Computer science education, information systems education*

Keywords

UNIX, Security, Visualization

1. INTRODUCTION

Increasing concern about the security of user data has led to the implementation of mandatory access control sys-

ITiCSE '17, July 3–5, 2017, Bologna, Italy.

© 2017 ACM. ISBN 978-1-4503-4704-4/17/07...$15.00

DOI: http://dx.doi.org/10.1145/3059009.3059031

tems with domain-specific models. Due to the complexity of policy development and maintenance, mandatory systems are often used together with the traditional discretionary UNIX permissions. The mandatory system is used to protect system data while user data continue to be protected with UNIX permissions. Additionally, many administrators choose to use only UNIX permissions, even for the protection of system data. Hence, it is critical that students understand traditional UNIX access control.

In our experience, many students believe that they understand UNIX permissions even though their understanding is incomplete. We believe that this is because of the difficulty of testing the effect of a particular permission bit setting, as it typically requires access to multiple user accounts. Additionally, through our graduate program, we have found that formal coverage appears to vary dramatically.

In order to address these concerns, we developed UNIXvisual, a tool to facilitate education on traditional UNIX access control. UNIXvisual runs from an ordinary user account. It provides several perspectives that help students explore the effect of permission bit settings. It also allows students to track process credentials in their running program. It supports a Query Mode in which students may test their understanding through standard questions. It also supports a Quiz Mode that allows instructors to conduct quizzes through the system outside of classrooms.

The remainder of this paper is organized as follows: Section 2 presents related work. Section 3 presents our tool, Section 4 has a detailed study of our findings from student evaluation, and Section 5 has our conclusions.

2. RELATED WORK

Tools have been developed to address the usability of access control models using a graphical interface. Eiciel [3], as a built-in component of the GNOME file manager, provides an interface that lists users and groups of an opened file and allows the direct click-and-check of ACL properties of that file. Intentional Access Management [1] also supports permission management through an interface and can automatically generate WebDAV policies from user input.

Some tools also leverage visualization to facilitate access control. Expandable Grids [4] shows effective access control using an interactive matrix given a policy. DTEedit and DTEView [2] by Hallyn and Kearns illustrate an input DTE policy as an interactive graph to help policy analysis. While visualization methods were used to help teaching many security fields and other access control models [5], we failed to find tools developed for the presentation and teaching of the UNIX permissions.

3. SOFTWARE DESCRIPTION

UNIXvisual requires a user-defined root directory to begin. The root directory defines the starting point at which the data from the underlying file system is extracted. The root directory can be specified directly in UNIXvisual or through the import of a specification file. A specification file allows the user to define a hypothetical file system (including permission settings) that overlays the underlying file system, users and groups.

The visualization illustrates the process of determining the access a user or group has to objects. UNIXvisual also uses visualization to help students monitor and control process credentials, e.g., for set-user-id and set-group-id programming within C programs. This part of visualization displays the executing sequence of system calls and shows the success and failure of the calls along with real and effective UIDs and GIDs. UNIXvisual also provides a query and quiz subsystem that leverages the visualizations. These features are described in more detail below.

3.1 Perspectives

UNIXvisual supports four main perspectives. The Decision Mode View illustrates a single decision by the access control system, excluding directory traversal. The Object View explores which users and groups have access to a selected object. The User View and Group View explore the set of objects accessible to a user (through the user bits) or to a group (through the group bits) respectively. Finally, the Program Trace View allows a student to trace the value and effect of process credentials within their running program.

3.1.1 Decision Mode

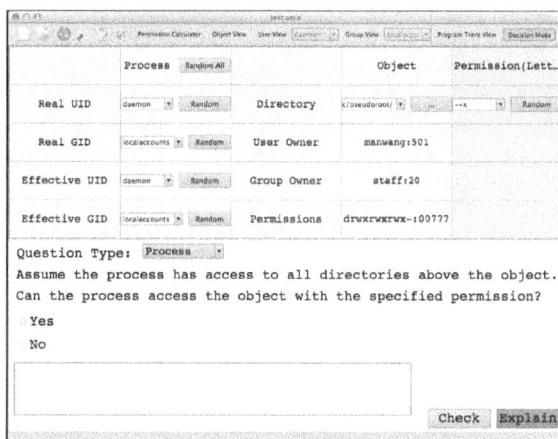

Figure 1: Decision Mode

The Decision Mode aims to provide obvious access to an interactive question system in order to encourage students to test their understanding. The interface has two parts (Figure 1). Parameters for the questions are configured in the top part. One of several questions can be chosen and the according choices are displayed in the bottom part. This mode provides two types of commonly asked questions: 1)

whether a process with certain credentials can access an object with a selected permission, and 2) conversion between the letter and octal permission notations. Students can answer the question and click on the "Check" button for the correct answer. If further explanation is needed, clicking on the "Explain" button will initiate an animation to guide students through the solution.

3.1.2 Object View

The Object View asks for an object of interest and illustrates the determination of which users have access to the object. Figure 2 shows a snapshot of the Object View. The top-left UI section asks for the necessary information such as the path of an object, a user and its group to perform the analysis. The visualization shows the analysis in a matrix form. On the left, paths from the root directory to the target object are represented as nodes with permission information at each directory level. This defines the rows of the matrix. On the right, the permission bit groupings, "Owner bits", "Group bits" and "Other bits", define the columns.

Figure 2: Object View

Students may choose an individual user or group, or they may use the (default) wildcard All option. In the case where all users are considered, results of multiple users' access are shown in the last row as color-coded user names. The columns in which a user name appears indicate the bits applied at the object level. Clicking on a user name enables an analysis of the user's access. Color-coded letters of "Y" and "N" are placed in the row which corresponds to object level, and the column which corresponds to the group of bits that are applied. In Figure 2, the user has selected lucy from the last row to obtain more information on the access lucy has to the object. Clicking on the letters of "Y" and "N" allows another level of detailed explanation of why these bits are applied and why the access is or is not allowed. This triple-layered analysis from color-coded user names to detailed explanation avoids showing complete explanation all at once, and thus encourages students to think about how the permissions work.

3.1.3 User and Group View

The User and Group View illustrates the access allowed by a user or group through the file permission bits to objects under a user-specified directory. An example of the User View is given in Figure 3. The visualization can be divided into two parts. The left part contains information about a user (above) or group. A user is represented as a node connected with three nodes to represent the owner, group and other permission bits. A group is represented as a node connected with all its member users (not shown). The right part has four sections. The top-left window is the **Permission Setting** section. In this section, students may choose the type of object access they want to investigate. The bottom-left window is the **Directory Tree** section. It shows the object structure in a standard directory tree hierarchy. Directories are clickable to expand and contract for one directory level.

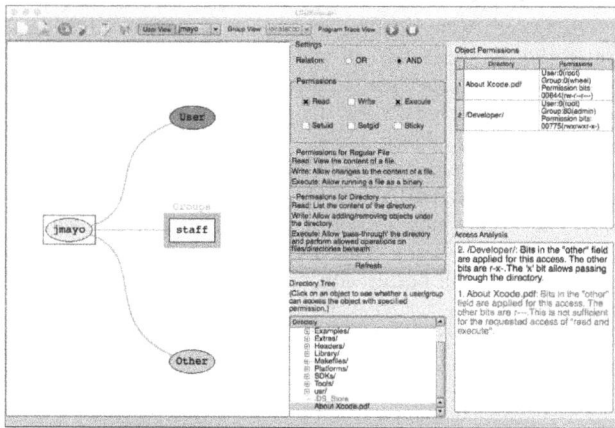

Figure 3: User and Group View

The two windows on the right are the **Object Permissions** and **Access Analysis** sections. They are blank initially. Once a user/group is selected, each object in the object hierarchy window is checked against the specified permission in the **Permission Setting** section. If an object can be accessed by the user with the specified permission, the object remains black. Otherwise, it is shown in red. Clicking on an object in the **Directory Tree** enables the **Object Permissions** and **Access Analysis** windows which show a detailed analysis. The permission information for the object selected from the **Directory Tree** and all directories up to the root directory is supplied in the **Object Permissions** section. An explanation of the access is given in the **Access Analysis** section. The analysis includes an explanation of which bits were applied and the access decision at the level.

3.1.4 Program Trace View

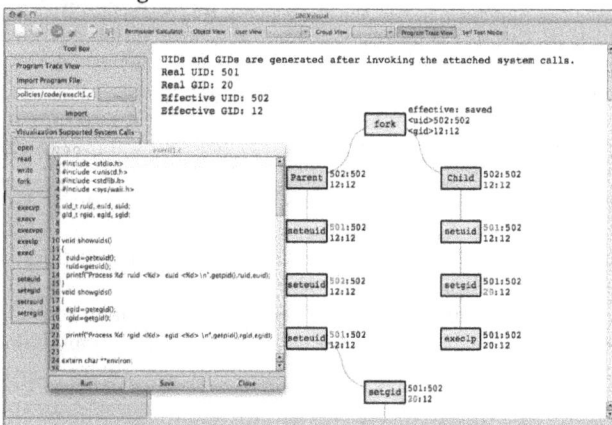

Figure 4: Program Trace View

The Program Trace View is designed to help students understand initial assignment of credentials to a process, dynamic modification of credentials, and the effect of these credentials on an access request. This view allows the import of a C program and tracks process credentials across

access control-related system calls, like open, fork, setresuid, read, write, etc. Figure 4 shows an example of the visualization. After loading a C source code or binary, the initial real and effective user/group IDs are shown in the top left corner. Invoked system calls are depicted sequentially as blocks with effective and saved user/group IDs. The success of a system call is reflected in its block color: green indicates success and red indicates failure. The credentials on the side use red highlighting to indicate changes in credential values after the system call.

3.2 Permission Calculator

Octal and letter notations are frequently used to specify UNIX permissions values through the command line. The conversion between these two notations can be tricky for beginners. The **Permission Calculator** is designed to help students learn different permission notations. Figure 5 (a) and (b) show the interface of the letter-to-octal and the octal-to-letter notation conversion. Both interfaces have three ways of expressing permissions: a matrix of checkboxes denoting permission bits, octal notation and letter notation. With the checkbox matrix and both notations side by side, it is easier to interpret the meaning of each bit and how each bit is expressed in different notations.

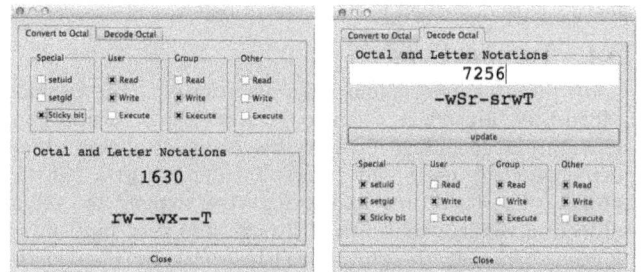

(a) Letter to Octal Notation   (b) Octal to Letter Notation

Figure 5: Permission Calculator

3.3 Query and Quiz

UNIXvisual also contains a **Query Mode** and a **Quiz Mode**. The Query Mode includes a list of commonly-asked questions on UNIX permissions. Question parameters are configurable through the interface and answers to the questions are presented through guided visualization. This mode provides the convenience of having problems clarified outside of the classroom at any time. The **Quiz Mode** provides an interactive environment for conducting quizzes. Text-based and visualization-based questions can be asked. All the questions are multiple-choice questions and can be configured to accommodate instructors' teaching goals. The questions that comprise a quiz are written through a text file that adheres to a prescribed format. Students can start the quiz by loading the question file distributed by the instructor. Each question will have to be answered before moving to the next one. At the end of the quiz, a dialog will show the location of the student's answer file and the student will be able to send the instructor an email which prevents manual changes.

4. EVALUATION

4.1 Environment, Procedure and Goals

The evaluation was conducted in a required junior-level Concurrent Computing course with a total of 55 students.

In a 75-minute session, students were asked to take a pre-test on UNIX permissions, followed by a 35-minute UNIX permissions lecture and a 15-minute demo of UNIXvisual. Students were allowed to use UNIXvisual in the following two weeks, and completed a post-test and an evaluation form. The pre-test and post-test plus evaluation are treated as quizzes. UNIX permissions is a standard topic in Concurrent Computing for the shared memory component, and there was no mechanism to enforce the use of the tool. Additionally, it is unfair to divide the students in this class to treatment and controlled groups so that one group of students would not use the tool. Therefore, we can only compare the performance between groups of students who only attended the lecture and who both attended the lecture and used the tool. The sample sizes of students who used the tool without attending the lecture and who neither used the tool nor attended the lecture are too small to be used for a meaningful statistical analysis.

We collected 40 valid pre-tests, 44 valid post-tests, and 44 valid evaluation forms. We also collected 51 final exam papers, and recorded grades of the UNIX permissions section. Of the 44 students who submitted the evaluation form, 21 used UNIXvisual, 40 attended the lecture, and 38 submitted the pre-test, post-test and final exam. The participants who used UNIXvisual majored in Computer Science (13 students), Software Engineering (5 students), and Computer Engineering (3 students).

4.2 Test Problems

The questions in the pre-test, post-test and final exam have the same form with the same level of difficulty. There are 10 questions in each test (1 point per question). Questions Q1 and Q2 (Group 1 or G_1) convert between the octal and letter notations of UNIX permissions. Questions Q3-Q6 (Group 2 or G_2) ask about access requests to an object without directory traversal. Questions Q7-Q10 (Group 3 or G_3) are about the access requests to an object with directory traversal. All these test problems are available through the link at the end of this paper.

Table 1: The Means (μ) and Standard Deviations (σ) of the Pre-test, Post-test, and Final Exam Questions

	Q1	Q2	Q3	Q4	Q5	Q6	Q7	Q8	Q9	Q10	Total
					Pre-test						
μ	0.80	0.78	0.98	0.88	0.88	0.80	0.34	0.88	0.37	0.44	7.05
σ	0.40	0.42	0.16	0.33	0.33	0.41	0.48	0.33	0.49	0.50	1.66
					Post-test						
μ	0.98	0.95	0.95	0.89	0.91	1.00	1.00	0.98	0.68	0.75	9.09
σ	0.15	0.21	0.21	0.32	0.29	0.00	0.00	0.15	0.47	0.44	1.29
					Final Exam						
μ	0.92	0.90	0.88	1.00	0.96	0.98	0.69	0.88	0.61	0.78	8.61
σ	0.27	0.30	0.33	0.00	0.20	0.14	0.47	0.33	0.49	0.42	1.60

Table 2: The Means (μ) and Standard Deviations (σ) of G_1, G_2 and G_3 in the Pre-test, Post-test and Final Exam

	Pre-test			Post-test			Final Exam		
	G_1	G_2	G_3	G_1	G_2	G_3	G_1	G_2	G_3
μ	0.79	0.88	0.51	0.97	0.94	0.85	0.91	0.96	0.74
σ	0.41	0.32	0.50	0.18	0.24	0.36	0.29	0.21	0.44

Table 1 and Table 2 have the mean and standard deviation of each question and question group in these tests. The correctness of questions in G_1 and G_2 are above 91% in the post-test and the final exam, and G_3 in all three tests has

the lowest means and the highest standard deviations. It is reasonable that G_3 received the lowest means as access request questions with directory traversal include more levels of permission checking and thus make the questions more challenging. Figure 6 depicts the group comparison of the three tests. It shows that 1) students' overall performance in all groups improved in the post-test and the final exam; and 2) students performed better in G_1 and G_3 in the post-test than in the final exam.

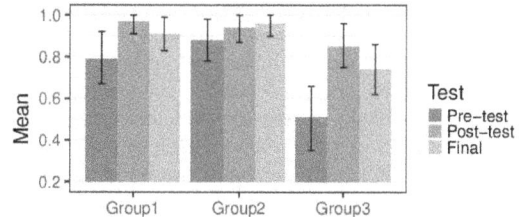

Figure 6: The Means with Confidence Intervals of G_1, G_2 and G_3 in the Pre-test, Post-test and Final Exam

Table 3 has the means and standard deviations of question scores of students who used UNIXvisual and who did not use UNIXvisual in all three tests. Students who used UNIXvisual received higher scores in all question groups in the post-test and the final exam than students who did not use UNIXvisual.

Table 3: The Means (μ) and Standard Deviations (σ) of G_1, G_2, G_3 and Total Scores of Students Who Used and Did Not Use UNIXvisual

			Students Who Used UNIXvisual									
	Pre-test				Post-test				Final			
	G_1	G_2	G_3	Total	G_1	G_2	G_3	Total	G_1	G_2	G_3	Total
μ	0.84	0.86	0.46	6.95	0.98	0.98	0.92	9.52	0.95	0.99	0.88	9.35
σ	0.37	0.35	0.50	1.58	0.15	0.15	0.28	0.81	0.22	0.11	0.33	1.23
			Students Who Did Not Use UNIXvisual									
	Pre-test				Post-test				Final			
	G_1	G_2	G_3	Total	G_1	G_2	G_3	Total	G_1	G_2	G_3	Total
μ	0.76	0.90	0.54	7.29	0.96	0.90	0.79	8.70	0.89	0.94	0.65	8.13
σ	0.43	0.30	0.50	1.65	0.21	0.30	0.41	1.49	0.32	0.25	0.48	1.65

4.3 Test Problems Analysis

In this part, significance tests were applied to find out 1) whether students' performance in the tests improved; and 2) whether UNIXvisual introduced the improvement. The significance tests include Student's t-test, ANOVA (parametric) and Kruskal-Wallis (KW) test (non-parametric), and repeated measures ANOVA (parametric) and Friedman test (non-parametric). We mainly used parametric methods with the non-parametric methods as backups. All significance tests were conducted at 95% significance level. The p-values below are from parametric tests and their non-parametric counterpart, and they agree on the test results.

To evaluate students' performance throughout the tests, we first compared the pre-test and post-test using Student's t-test and KW test. Only Q1, Q2, Q6, Q7, Q9, Q10 and the total score had p-value less than 0.05. With their increased means from the pre-test to the post-test (Table 1), this indicates that the students' performance on notation conversion, access requests with directory traversal, and the total score had significantly improved. We also applied Student's t-test and KW test to compare the pre-test and the final exam. The results show that students performed differently in only Q4, Q6, Q7, Q9, Q10 and the total score. As the means of these questions increased (Table 1), the performance significantly improved on questions of access request without and with directory traversal and the total score in the final exam. The scores of the post-test and the final exam were also compared using the same method. The results indicate significantly improved performance in Q4 and declined performance in Q7, which means that the performance in other questions and the total score did not differ significantly. Therefore, for the declined performance in G_1 and G_3 from the post-test to the final exam in Figure 6, we know that the performance decline in G_1 is insignificant, and that Q7 is the only question showed a declined performance in G_3. Note that G_3 has the most challenging questions in the tests. Since there was no homework or project on UNIX permissions between these two tests, the declined performance in Q7 was likely caused by students' less familiarity with the material over time due to a lack of practice.

To investigate the reason for the improvement throughout the tests, we looked into the students who submitted all three tests. As they participated in the UNIX permissions lecture and the UNIXvisual demo, and the use of UNIXvisual, this student group forms an important sample to assess the effect of the lecture with demo and the use of UNIXvisual on the scores of the tests. The repeated measures ANOVA and Friedman test were used, and the p-values of Q1, Q5-Q10, and the total score are less than 0.05. As the means of the total score of the post-test and the final exam are higher than that of the pre-test (Table 1), the lecture with demo and the use of UNIXvisual helped students perform better in the post-test and the final exam.

We further examined whether the use of UNIXvisual helped the improvement in the post-test and the final exam. We applied Students' t-test and KW test to the post-test question group scores of students who used UNIXvisual (21 students) and students who did not use the tool (23 students). The results show that G_2, G_3 and the total score had p-value less than 0.05. With their means in Table 3, the performance of students who used UNIXvisual is significantly better than those who did not use the tool. We also divided students who took the final exam into a group of 20 students who used UNIXvisual and a group of 31 students who did not use the tool, and compared their performance using the same tests. G_3 and the total score had p-value less than 0.05. Given their means in Table 3, students who used UNIXvisual performed significantly better than those who did not use the tool in G_3 and the total score. Lastly, we evaluated the background of students who used UNIXvisual and who did not use the tool by comparing their pre-test scores. The t-test and KW test show that the p-values for all question groups and the total score are greater than 0.05. Therefore, these two groups of students had similar background.

So far we have seen that UNIXvisual helped students improve significantly from the pre-test to the post-test, and that the improved performance continued in the final exam. Students who used UNIXvisual and those who did not use the tool had similar UNIX permissions background. But students who used UNIXvisual made significant improvement and received higher scores in all question groups in the post-test and the final exam than students who did not use the tool. More specifically, the use of UNIXvisual significantly increased the scores of G_3 in the post-test and the final exam. This suggests that UNIXvisual is very effective in helping students understand the access to objects with directory traversal, which forms the most difficult questions in the tests.

4.4 Evaluation Form

We used a set of questions (Table 4) to collect information on students' perception of the effectiveness of the tool. We also gathered information on the time spent on using the tool and the students' major. The first 12 rating questions study the effectiveness of UNIXvisual. Q1 and Q2 examine the overall effectiveness; Q3 and Q4 relate to the two views that show object permissions without and with directory traversal; Q5 and Q6 are about the views that interpret permissions from the perspective of a user or a group; Q7 and Q8 examine the Permission Calculator; Q9 is about the Query; Q10, Q11 and Q12 are about the interface design. The choices are: 1:strongly disagree, 2:disagree, 3:neutral, 4:agree, and 5:strongly agree. Q13 and Q14 study the time participants spent on the tool. The choices for Q13 are 1:once, 2:twice, 3:3-4 times, 4:5-10 times, and 5:more than 10 times. The choices for Q14 are 1:less than 5 mins, 2:5-14 mins, 3:15-29 mins, 4:30-60 mins, and 5:more than 1 hour.

Table 4: UNIXvisual Rating and Usage Questions

	Rating Questions
Q1	UNIXvisual helped to better understand UNIX permissions
Q2	UNIXvisual enhanced UNIX permissions course coverage
Q3	Decision View helped to understand which users have access to a certain object and why
Q4	Object View helped to understand which users have access to a certain object and why
Q5	User View helped to understand how decisions are made to the access request from a particular user
Q6	Group View helped to understand how decisions are made to the access request from a particular group
Q7	Permission Calculator was helpful for understanding the meaning of each bit in UNIX permissions
Q8	Permission Calculator was helpful for understanding how to specify permissions for an object
Q9	Query was helpful for understanding UNIX permissions
Q10	The use of colors in the visualization is effective
Q11	The size of items is reasonable and clear
Q12	The layout of items is reasonable and clear
	Usage Questions
Q13	How many times did you use UNIXvisual
Q14	How long did you use UNIXvisual in total

Table 5: The Means (μ), and Standard Deviations (σ) of UNIXvisual Evaluation Questions

	Q1	Q2	Q3	Q4	Q5	Q6	Q7	Q8	Q9	Q10	Q11	Q12
μ	3.81	4.05	4.00	3.81	3.85	4.10	4.43	4.29	3.89	3.81	3.71	3.29
σ	0.60	0.50	0.58	0.91	1.09	0.72	0.81	0.85	0.60	0.75	0.72	0.90

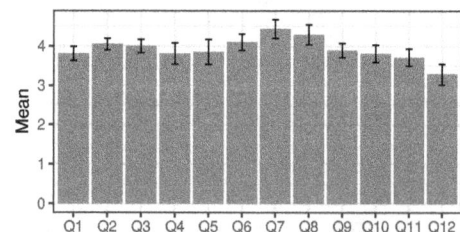

Figure 7: The Means with Confidence Intervals of UNIXvisual Rating and Usage Questions

Table 5 and Figure 7 have the means and standard deviations, and the means with confidence intervals of UNIXvisual rating and usage questions, respectively. All questions except Q12 received a mean greater than 3.7. Students generally believed that UNIXvisual helped the understanding of UNIX permissions and enhanced the course coverage. Permission Calculator received the highest rating (Q7, Q8). The layout received the lowest score (Q12). The reason may be, as mentioned in a student comment, due to the Object View not being scaled properly. Some text overlap was reported. The means of Q13 and Q14 are 1.95 and 2.43, indicating that students generally used UNIXvisual twice for 10 minutes in total. We used the middle point of a range for estimation.

4.5 Evaluation Form – Student Comments

The four write-in questions were used to collect information of the participants' major, their thoughts on the most and least useful features of the tool, features to add, and problems with installation.

Of the 21 students who used UNIXvisual, 15 students considered the Permission Calculator as the most useful feature. One student wrote that *"the permission calculator can be quite useful to ensure you know how the permissions will look for some file"*. Four students favored the User/Group View. Other two stated the overall features of *"being able to actually check access to a file and check different scenarios"* and *"the instant feedback of whether something works or not with quick explanation"* as the most useful. As for the least useful feature, 16 students did not state any, and three students answered the Permission Calculator. One student mentioned that *"I personally am familiar with permissions, so the calculator was not as helpful"*. Therefore, while 71% of the students considered Permission Calculator as the most useful feature, it is also considered as the least useful one due to the familiarity to the notation conversion on those students' part. Another student considered the Object View the least useful as the view did not scale properly and texts had some overlap.

All students did not encounter any installation problem. When asked to suggest features to add, students were content with the available features. They wrote *"I think it is very well designed. Nothing needs to be added"*, and *"the software was very friendly at aiding further learning and understanding of UNIX permissions the way it currently is"*. There are also some comments for further improvements. Students suggested to add *"something to detect if your files are visible by anyone else"*, and *"having a video tutorial on how to use the software"*.

4.6 Summary

UNIXvisual was evaluated in a classroom setting. Students were introduced the basic knowledge of UNIX permissions including the octal and letter notations, the access to an object with and without directory traversal. Students' average scores went from 7.05 in the pre-test, to 9.09 in the post-test, and 8.61 in the final exam. The final score calculation includes an additional of 11 students who did not attend the lecture and demo. We found significant improvement in students' performance in the post-test and the final exam. We also found that the use of UNIXvisual is very effective in helping to understand the more challenging permissions to an object with directory traversal.

The feedback to UNIXvisual was positive. The Permission Calculator was rated the highest, and was also considered as the most useful feature. The layout received the lowest rating. This may be due to the fact that the Object View could not scale properly on some monitors. No installation issue was reported. Most students believed that the software provides what is needed and is user-friendly. We plan to use the same materials in the following years and other classes so that UNIXvisual could be evaluated with more extensive and multi-year samples.

5. CONCLUSIONS

The paper presents UNIXvisual which is designed to facilitate the teaching and self-learning of UNIX permissions. Students can practice UNIX permissions configuration on the basis of a real as well as a hypothetical file system. They can examine the result of their permission bit setting through visualization, and evaluate their understanding of the model. Instructors can use the tool to teach the UNIX permissions, easily demonstrate steps to solve in-class questions and conduct quizzes. The tool can also demonstrate how process credentials are established and modified.

From the tests conducted in the evaluation process, students showed significant improvement in the tests taken after the use of UNIXvisual. UNIXvisual is very effective in helping to understand the more challenging permission to objects with directory traversal. Our evaluation showed that the feedback was positive. Students believed that UNIXvisual helped them understand the UNIX permissions better and enhanced the course coverage of UNIX permissions. We received suggestions on improving the tool and will incorporate them in the future.

UNIXvisual is a part of larger project to develop access control visualization tools that is supported by the National Science Foundation. In addition to UNIXvisual, DTEvisual for the Domain Type Enforcement access control model, and MLSvisual for the Multilevel Security, and RBACvisual for the Role-based Access Control have been developed. The tool, UNIX permissions slides, pre-test, post-test and final exam problems, and evaluation form can be downloaded at the following URL:

    http://acv.cs.mtu.edu/UNIXvisual.html

6. REFERENCES

[1] X. Cao and L. Iverson. Intentional access management: Making access control usable for end-users. In *Proceedings of the Second Symposium on Usable Privacy and Security*, SOUPS '06, pages 20–31, New York, NY, USA, 2006.

[2] S. Hallyn and P. Kearns. Tools to administer domain and type enforcement. In *Proceedings of USENIX Conference on System Administration*, pages 151–156, 2001.

[3] R. F. Ibáñez. Eiciel website, GNOME file ACL editor. http://rofi.roger-ferrer.org/eiciel, 2015.

[4] R. W. Reeder, L. Bauer, L. F. Cranor, M. K. Reiter, K. Bacon, K. How, and H. Strong. Expandable grids for visualizing and authoring computer security policies. In *Proceedings of the SIGCHI Conference on Human Factors in Computing Systems*, CHI '08, pages 1473–1482, New York, NY, USA, 2008.

[5] D. Schweitzer, M. Collins, L. Baird, U. States, and A. F. Academy. A visual approach to teaching formal access models in security. In *Proceedings of the 11th Colloquium for Information Systems Security Education*, CISS '07, pages 69–75, 2007.

Acknowledgements

This work was supported in part by the National Science Foundation under grants DUE-1140512, DUE-1245310, IIS-1456763, IIS-1455886, and DGE-1523017.

Understanding the Effects of Intervention on Computer Science Student Behaviour in On-line Forums

Daniel La Vista, Nickolas Falkner, and Claudia Szabo
University of Adelaide
nickolas.falkner@adelaide.edu.au, claudia.szabo@adelaide.edu.au

ABSTRACT

A key challenge for educators using online discussion forums is how to provide effective feedback and support to students, to ensure they are engaged with discussions on the forums, and do not disengage from the course. In addition, there is a significant problem of scale to address. Even relatively low population forums of less than a hundred students can generate thousands of posts, so it is infeasible for the lecturer to monitor every discussion to identify disengaging students. There is a need to understand the act of intervention, in order to provide automated tools to better assist teaching staff with this task. Measuring the impact of intervention can be challenging and requires us to, first, understand what "standard" behaviour looks like across different student groups and identify topics where intervention would be most effective. In this paper, we identify the impact of intervention on different groups of students, characterising their behaviour in terms of response time and activity, compare the different responses to programming-related questions and other questions, and identify the useful aspects of this study for computer science educators. We conduct an initial examination of the impact of the nature of the question on intervention effectiveness and propose an analysis method that can be applied to any computer science forum. we showcase the application of the method to three courses. Our results indicate that associating student activity with the number of forum posts is misleading, as students who are only reading the forums respond also to intervention.

Keywords

computing education; intervention; electronic forums

1. INTRODUCTION

Online discussion forums have considerable potential for creating an educational community of critical inquiry [Garrison et al. 1999]. At the same time, there still remain many questions about how to most effectively integrate them into courses, and how educators can best support student learning in this primarily text based medium. Interaction within forums has been suggested to benefit student-centred learning, encourage wider student participation, and produce more in-depth and reasoned discussion than counterpart face to face learning environments [Davies and Graff]. These factors can likely be attributed to the nature of forums themselves. Discussion forums are usually asynchronous, meaning that users contribute to the discussion at their own convenience, as opposed to a synchronous conversation, for example within the classroom, where timing is determined by the pace of the conversation. This allows users to take more time planning and considering responses, and overall results in greater consideration of the form and meaning of a discussion, thus supporting in-depth and reasoned discussion [Sotillo 2000]. There is wide consensus that active student participation in forums enhances student learning. For example, a combined quantitative and qualitative analysis of online discussion postings across distance education students in Australia found that the frequency of posting correlated to students' achievement, with students who posted more frequently achieving better grades [Palmer et al. 2008].

However, a significant portion of students act as 'invisible learners', posting infrequently (if at all) in the forums, and primarily lurking, engaging with the content through reading and other less visible means of interaction [Beaudoin 2002]. While these students would often be referred to as *passive*, as they do not post, this is misleading as any record of a student viewing content indicates that the student has chosen to download a resource, click a link, or otherwise engage with electronic content. However, from the earlier work, these students are theoretically at risk of achieving lower scores because they are posting less. However, it is not clear whether these invisible learners gain equivalent value from forum discussions as their more "active" counterparts.

Due to the lack of traditional social cues in an online discussion forum, it can be challenging for a lecturer to identify at-risk students unless they explicitly ask for help. If an invisible learner is struggling with course content, or disengaging from discussion, there are very few avenues for a lecturer to identify this and take action. Even when much more visible users start to disengage, behavioural changes can be hard to detect without performing detailed analysis of forum data. These problems increase with forum scale.

In this paper, we examine a range of student discussion forums across Level II and III Computer Science courses to identify student behaviour across the lifetime of the course, in order to determine if the presence and the action of lecturing staff affects the ways that students use and interact

DOI: http://dx.doi.org/10.1145/3059009.3059053

with the forum. We separate the groups based on whether they are actively posting or are reading through course materials and inspect activity, in terms of number and timing of actions, across the course and before and after lecturer intervention in individual threads.

2. RELATED WORK

Many studies have examined the role of the electronic discussion board in class discussions [Garrison et al. 1999, Davies and Graff , Beaudoin 2002]. When analysing these systems, the data of the system (post titles, content, student names) requires deeper and more complex analysis, where the metadata of the system (timing and linkages) can be extracted and processed mostly automatically. Studies incorporating metadata analysis typically investigate metrics such as post timing, user traffic and thread length, as well as other similar measures [Hewitt 2005, Hecking et al. 2016]. These measures are some of the simplest to analyse, but can reveal some very interesting and complex relationships within the discussion forums. Notable methods include investigating the effects of implementing threading and persistency and a post tagging system that aided users in classifying their posts [Guzdial and Turns 2000]. It was shown that the addition of these improved levels of sustained discussion and broadness of participation. However, this measured students who posted and, as many MOOC providers have discovered, presence in a forum does not require posting.

A study investigating the causes of thread death [Hewitt 2005] found that a large percentage of threads died within three days after the course changed topic. They also investigated student behaviour contributing to thread death and develop a simulation to investigate this effect, and assign probabilities to the chance of a user responding in general. However, certain students may have a much higher probabilities to write a response, or indeed may be responded to in general more often than others or may be considered to be key actors on forums, who may be likely to stimulate more discussion than an average student. Equally, there may be students who through a combination of factors tend to respond, or are responded to, with a lower likelihood.

A strong community is important from an educational perspective. Haig et al. attempted to identify at-risk students based on social network analysis, frequency of access analysis and a grouping based on grade bands [Haig et al. 2013] in order to identify similarities between student behaviours. They found that activity and engagement with the course correlated to students grade bands and that students accessing relevant materials at the appropriate times in some instances made the difference between a student achieving a Credit (over 65%) and a Pass (over 50%).

The results from this study corroborate the commonly held view that encouraging students to be more active on the forums is beneficial to their learning and results.

We focus on metadata and not on the textual content of the posts as there can be some serious issues related to the process of content analysis [De Wever et al. 2006]. Often simplifications in analysing student data need to be made to allow for feasible analysis, to simplify the discussions generated by a complex course structure, such as the work of [Oleksandra and Shane 2016]. Their goal was to investigate regular forum participants and characterise the type of content shared by them to determine if learner characteristics and types of conversation defined the formation of the

network. The concept of grouping students based on a measure of their behaviour is not a novel one, however it is crucial to the generalisability of results. It is much more likely that we will see common large scale behaviours be applicable across multiple datasets than very fine grained user-specific behaviours. Indeed it is reasonable that we will see many complex overlapping groups of users in a large forum, and understanding the factors that affect student engagement must take this into account.

Hecking et al. [Hecking et al. 2016] explore characteristics of structured information exchange in a MOOC forum, from a social (who is talking to whom?) perspective and a semantic (who is talking about what?) perspective in combination. They performed post classification in order to identify information seeking and information giving behaviour to construct a network that reflects these one way relationships. Chaturvedi et al. [Chaturvedi et al. 2014], looked at the prediction of where instructor intervention would take place within a forum, using a logistic regression model to predict whether a lecturer would intervene in a thread or not. The features used for training included thread metadata and aggregated post data, consisting of post metadata aggregated across each thread.

All of these methods focus on "active" participation in the course, rather than constructing a sequence of events that include student activities that change the environment (stateful changes such as posting) and student activities that make no changes (such as viewing a post, which enters an item in a log that is not visible to other students, or even staff unless they look for it. In our work, we will extend the previous studies by looking at all metadata and demonstrating that stateless interaction, which is effectively invisible, reflects engagement as much as stateful interaction does.

3. METHODOLOGY

The goal of this study is to characterise and identify changes in student behaviour in response to lecturer intervention, using only electronic forum metadata. In order to achieve this, student forum behaviour needs to be classified, taking into account that identifying behaviour will depend heavily upon the classification mechanism used. As the literature review has shown, measuring posting behaviour, the contribution of content to a course or topic, is one good measure but non-posting activities, reading and downloading, also correlate with indicators of student performance. The networks generated, and the social web we consider as the student's support group, will be very different shapes depending upon whether we regard the forum post as the prime activity or whether we consider viewing content to have significance.

From discussions of content analysis, we know that contextual analysis is hard and this correlates to the cognitive load implicit in long, detailed posts for both writers and readers. Posted questions that focus on programming language issues tend to use a more restricted syntax for expression, as programming languages are far less expressive than English. Such questions, often aligned with teaching materials and assignments, are on well-defined problems, have a clearer context and are thus notionally going to be easier for readers and writers. Given that discussions are immediately useful to Computer Science students, we would expect these posts to be more desirable in terms of benefit and in terms of ease of reading.

We define this analysis challenge with the following research questions:

RQ1 Can we see clear differences in behaviour between students who post and view, and students who only view content?

RQ2 Can we identify lecturer intervention by looking at user engagement metrics and does it apply across both student groups?

RQ3 Can we we legitimately separate programming language questions and other questions into two groups based on student behaviour?

We will be using three separate forum datasets in our investigation of these research questions. All three are Moodle 2 electronic discussion forums taken from separate courses run at the University of Adelaide over the period 2012-2015: we refer to them as Datasets 1, 2, and 3 respectively and also provide the course id, 528, 548, and 404 respectively. Students received no credit for participation or posting, although it was stated that all course information would be released through this channel. The instructional team was not the same for the three courses but all received the same instruction and course design notes, as well as the same learning management platform resources. The data has outlier removal for events that fell outside of the active course period but has undergone no other filtering.

3.1 Defining Key Metrics

We focus our analysis around seven identified metrics used to characterise aspects of a users "engagement" with forum discussion. As forum posting is not the only way to measure student engagement, we avoid classifying participants as "active" or "passive", based on whether they are posting in a forum. Where an electronic forum is for discussion, rather than assignment submission, a student could be just as engaged through reading actions alone, which are generally not measured as a proxy for activity. Therefore, we separate interactions with the forum into two groups, namely, those that make change and those that do not: stateful and stateless events.

Stateful events are events which modify the state of forum discussion. They are usually post events (or modifications to posts, for example edit or delete). Stateless events do not modify the state of the forum. They are usually view events (for example a user clicking on a discussion thread to read it). A stateless event itself does not directly contribute to discussion on the forum. The first four metrics from the list below are defined on a per-user basis in seconds and are recorded across the entire course. (Users with fewer than two interactions in either stateful or stateless mode are removed from that set as an average cannot be calculated.)

- Average Stateful Inter-Event Time: the average time between all stateful events for a user.

- Average Stateless Inter-Event Time: the average time between all stateless events for a user.

- First Stateful Event Δ Time: the time that the first stateful event took place for a user, measured from the first event in the course.

- First Stateless Event Δ Time: the time that the first stateless event took place for a user, measured from the first event in the course.

The next three measures describe stateful and stateless behaviour focused on engagement. There are many ways to measure engagement but many rely upon the user to make stateful change in the forum in order to be recognised as contributing. We define engagement as being measurable from the first measured point of contact with the forum, whether stateful or stateless. However, the time at which a student first connects will affect how we interpret the average time between events. A student who has one event every day but starts engagement in week 11 should not appear the same as a student who has been checking in daily all semester. We combine the inter-event time with the first event time (stateful or stateless) as an evenly weighted average to incorporate both aspects. Finally, we weight all measures against the "most" engaged student in either measure to normalise the result and to simplify comparison.

Stateful Engagement For the set of students S, we define stateful engagement (AE) as:

$$AE(S_i) = \frac{\text{MAW}(S) - \text{AW}(S_i)}{\text{MAW}(S)}$$

$$AW(S_i) = 0.5 \times \text{Mean Stateful Inter-Event Time} + 0.5 \times \text{First Stateful Event } \Delta\text{Time}$$

$$MAW(S) = max(\text{AW}(S))$$

A stateful engagement of 0 is considered to be the "worst" value, and a stateful engagement of 1 is considered the "best".

Stateless Engagement For the set of students S, we define stateless engagement (PE) as:

$$PE(S_i) = \frac{\text{MPW}(S) - \text{PW}(S_i)}{\text{MPW}(S)}$$

$$PW(S_i) = 0.5 \times \text{Mean Stateless Inter-Event Time} + 0.5 \times \text{First Stateless Event } \Delta\text{Time}$$

$$MPW(S) = max(\text{PW}(S))$$

A stateless engagement of 0 is considered to be the "worst" value, and a stateless engagement of 1 is considered the "best".

Overall Engagement For the set of students S, we define overall engagement (OE) as:

$$OE(S_i) = \frac{\text{MOW}(S) - \text{OW}(S_i)}{\text{MOW}(S)}$$

$$OW(S_i) = 0.5 \times \text{AW}(S_i) + 0.5 \times \text{PW}(S_i)$$

$$MOW(S) = 0.5 \times \text{MAW}(S) + 0.5 \times \text{MPW}(S)$$

An overall engagement of 0 is considered to be the "worst" value, and an overall engagement of 1 is considered the "best".

We observe several basic characteristics of the forum datasets, including the number of users in each, post and view count, and a simple statistical analysis of each forum according to our defined metrics, in order to get a baseline measure of the amount and type of activity we see in each.

3.2 Classifying Users

The next step focuses on identifying a small number of general behavioural patterns amongst the students. Student behaviour was not separated demographically, as existing work covers this in detail and we sought to investigate aggregate patterns. Ideally we want to characterise a behavioural measure for student types across the course, in terms of their engagement with the discussion on the forum, so that we can investigate when behaviour deviates from the baseline. Cluster analysis allows us to separate users and we use a k-means clustering approach to group users according to their overall engagement, and then investigate the assigned groups levels of stateful and stateless engagement, comparing the groups within each dataset, and then

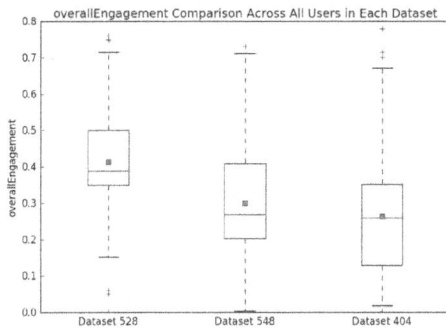

Figure 1: Overall Engagement Across All Users

comparing the groups across datasets to see what aspects the groups are similar and where they differ. K-means has been selected as it gives a clear group separation.

Once we have identified general behaviour patterns, we can see if users deviate from these behaviour patterns in response to intervention. If there is no change, then it is possible no intervention has taken place. To study the effect of intervention, we looked at each of the user groups engagement levels before and after each lecturer post, to see whether engagement changed. In addition, if there was a change we attempted to determine whether it was statistically significant.

Threads were manually classified into two groups: programming questions and any other type of enquiry, to investigate whether there is an engagement bias towards one type of discussion.

4. ANALYSIS

	Dataset 1 (528)	Dataset 2 (548)	Dataset 3 (404)
# Users	181	136	134
# Stateful Events	427	305	946
# Stateless Events	43772	14496	36226

Table 1: General Dataset Statistics

Dataset 1 had the largest number of users and generated the largest number of stateless events but dataset 3 had a far higher ratio of active events relative to the number of users, as shown in Table 1.

Examining the active engagement metrics, all of the quartiles except the first (25%) for dataset 3 are higher than the other two datasets, which indicates that users in dataset 3 were posting more frequently. However, all of the datasets maximum active engagement measures are very close, which indicates that, especially in dataset 1 and dataset 2, there were a number of outliers, whose measures were significantly higher than the 75% quartile. These represent the users with the most active posting behaviour in each dataset.

Despite dataset 1 and 2's relatively poor stateful engagement measures, both have much better stateless engagement and, at at the 25%, 50% and 75% quartiles and maximum, stateless engagement is higher in dataset 1 and 2 than dataset 3. Dataset 1 appears to have a majority of students with the highest stateless engagement measures.

When we look at overall engagement, shown in Figure 1, incorporating stateful and stateless engagement, we see that dataset 1 has the highest engagement levels of the three, which is unexpected given how dominant dataset 3's posting users were. The 1st, 2nd and 3rd quartiles of the data

(25%, 50% and 75%) are higher than dataset 1 and 2, and the max is only marginally lower than dataset 3. Importantly, dataset 2 is higher than dataset 3 in nearly all cases. It has a slightly lower min and max, however a significant portion of users have overall engagement higher than users in dataset 3. These results not only emphasise the importance of looking at more detailed metrics besides view and post count, but also the importance of considering both stateful and stateless students.

4.1 Grouping Users

We use k-means on the overall engagement metrics from each dataset to detect engagement groups. For all three datasets, the elbow method was used to determine that $k = 3$ was the optimum. Details of the division of users into groups are given in Table 2. We see that in all three datasets, the moderately engaged group makes up the majority of users. This group also generated the majority of posts and views for each dataset.

Engagement	Minimum	Moderate	Maximum
	Dataset 1 (528)		
#Users	32	93	54
#Posts	20	129	17
#Views	5800	23762	13278
	Dataset 2 (548)		
#Users	42	51	40
#Posts	20	189	68
#Views	3243	8420	2240
	Dataset 3 (404)		
#Users	56	70	8
#Posts	34	729	77
#Views	10154	24996	1075

Table 2: K-Means Clustering Divisions

The minimally engaged group generally has a smaller population than the moderately engaged group, and also much fewer posts. The minimally engaged group had significantly fewer posts than the moderately engaged group in all cases but the view count for this group was only around half of the moderately engaged group's view count for both dataset 2 and dataset 3. Despite their apparently low activity, these users are still monitoring the forum relatively frequently. The maximally engaged group represents the most stateful students in each dataset. Dataset 3 appears to have the fewest highly stateful students, however they have an extremely high ratio of posts/views per user. We show a comparison of the maximally engaged groups in Figure 2. These plots reinforce the differences between stateful and stateless participation: surprisingly, in terms of sheer volume of use of the forums, the students we habitually refer to as passive tend to be more engaged in reading posts.

4.2 Effects of Intervention

The event streams were analysed to identify the effects of lecturer intervention on both stateful and stateless activity. Given that students could not observe stateless activity from anyone else, lecturer intervention must be stateful, whether posting, editing, or deleting content (moderation activities). For statistical reasons, we identified that none of the inter-

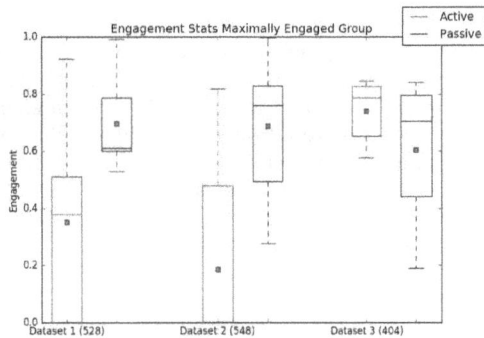

Figure 2: Comparison of Maximally Engaged Student Groups Across Courses

vention event datasets are normally distributed, according to both QQ plot and Shapiro-Wilk test. Also, all sets had different n, means and variances.

Table 3 shows the effect of lecturer intervention on posting activity across the three courses, counting all threads where lecturer intervention takes place. Results are given as change in Inter-Event time as seconds, where a negative number shows a reduction in the previously recorded time. We only show activities where there were at least five interventions, to reduce the disproportionate effects of a single intervention in a small group. As can be seen, a larger number of interventions correlates with reduced inter-posting time. Dataset 1, which had an overall engagement level higher than the others, also had the most noticeable effect in relation to lecturer intervention.

Table 4 shows the effect of lecturer intervention on viewing activity across the three courses, counting all threads where lecturer intervention takes place. Results are given as change in Inter-Event time as seconds, where a negative number shows a reduction in the previously recorded time. All of the viewing measures had enough events to be included. Viewing rates are much higher than posting rates throughout the course. There is no clear pattern at the aggregate level, due to the large number of interventions across many threads introducing averaging issues.

4.3 Detailed Analysis of Dataset 3

To reduce the confounding effects of analysing several threads, we examined Dataset 3 in detail, as it was neither the most nor least active forum, to attempt to identify lecturer intervention in stateless inter-Event times. 32 threads showed usable lecturer intervention and, of these, the inter-Event times did not show any clear patterns but the *number* of views rose after lecturer intervention in 22 of these. User behaviour, in terms of how often reading took place, did not appear to change but students appeared to refocus their reading on to the identified threads.

The forum thread topics were manually classified into two groups: programming questions and others, where a programming question was defined as containing elements of a programming language and a specific question that could be answered within that context. Questions on assignment work, which featured programming, would only be included if code was present. Algorithmic questions were not included. Coding was carried out by staff familiar with the course. Of the 140 threads, 37 were identified as being programming questions.

Neither inter-post or inter-view time differences were statistically significant according to a Wilcoxon Signed-Rank test. To reduce confounding effects, cluster analysis was used to identify any clear separation over the metrics of inter-event time for posts and views, and the number of posts and views, across each thread. Cluster analysis was applied to the dataset, resulting in an optimal $k = 2$ separation. This extracted data approximated a normal distribution and a confidence interval was generated for each variable based on the ratio of Programming posts in each cluster. Of 30 topics in the high inter-Event view time, only 4 were programming questions, compared with 34/110 in the shorter inter-Event group. 34/110 is outside of the 95% Adjusted Wald confidence interval for 4/30 and is considered to be significant. Within the two clusters, the number of measurable lecturer interventions are similar, 10/37 (0.27) and 27/103 (0.262) for the high inter-Event view time and low inter-Event view time respectively.

5. DISCUSSION

The data collected in this study shows that there is a difference in behaviour between students who regularly post to the fora and those students who tend to read, which answers RQ1: in the majority of cases, the key difference between the two groups is that the viewing students are viewing more content, more often. To address RQ2, measuring responses to teacher intervention is challenging but there is a correlation between the level of engagement in a course and the response to intervention, which is to be expected, where we would expect to be able to identify teacher intervention by looking at periods where inter-post times reduce, in the absence of other causal factors. More interventions generally correlate with increased reduction in inter-post time. However, dataset 3, where we had identified an existing core of frequently posting high engagement users, increased inter-post time when the lecturer participated. While this initially appears to be counter-productive, our in-depth analysis of dataset 3 shows that it contained panicking and dominating students and that intervention had interrupted a toxic loop of non-productive activity. Increasing the inter-post time in this case is a positive intervention but also highlights the importance of augmenting metadata analysis with context and content. Inter-view time does not change as consistently in response to intervention. In the most engaged course group, there is some small reduction but the students are already viewing so frequently that there is little capacity to view more. This is seen as a valuable area to investigate for future work. Finally, for RQ3, we identified that students seek out programming questions to view more quickly. The cause of this is part of our future research but we conjecture that the simple syntactic burden of an assignment-related coding question was perceived as being valuable and thus attracted readers who sought insight into solving their own problems. As noted, these programming questions had a similar level of lecturer intervention, thus reducing any confounding influence due to perceived value through lecturer presence.

6. CONCLUSIONS

Students have finite time to devote to forum discussion activities. Reading takes less time and effort than writing and we would expect students who devote their time to reading to be able to view more content. Lecturer intervention is perceived in different ways by students and it may take a lecturer many interventions to increase posting

Change	Dataset 1 (528)		Dataset 2 (548)	Dataset 3 (404)	
	Group 2 (Mod)	Group 3 (Max)	Group 2 (Mod)	Group 2 (Mod)	Group 3 (Max)
#Intervention Events	9	10	5	27	5
Mean Change (s)	-20187	-39201	49658	-2040	101997
Min Change (s)	-5183	7125	712	-377	12810
Max Change (s)	-205066	-317576	307725	-61794	441575

Table 3: Inter-Post Time Changes Over Intervention

Change	Dataset 1 (528)			Dataset 2 (548)			Dataset 3 (404)		
	Group 1 (Min)	Group 2 (Mod)	Group 3 (Max)	Group 1 (Min)	Group 2 (Mod)	Group 3 (Max)	Group 1 (Min)	Group 2 (Mod)	Group 3 (Max)
# Intervention Events	28	37	31	9	10	10	33	36	14
Mean Change (s)	1130	-206	0	2727	990	-10301	93	484	8221
Min Change (s)	30	0	0	-240	0	60	0	-15	255
Max Change (s)	34890	6450	17775	21075	22230	-82620	9435	7320	69615

Table 4: Inter-View Time Changes Over Intervention

levels. This study provides additional evidence to support the practice frequent and timely intervention in electronic fora as the majority of users will benefit, even if activity is not immediately observed. We have provided evidence that decreasing inter-activity time alone is not an ideal measure, as small inter-post intervals may be indicative of students who are reacting without reading; in at least one part of our study, they were panicking. Changes in inter-activity interval times are a clear indication that intervention has had some effect, although the raw numbers may not tell us everything. The distribution of events is also telling as, for example, programming language threads are not posted in or viewed more frequently, but the number of views that they accumulate occur in a shorter time.

Users who do not post are not disengaged just because they are not creating content. Stateless users make up the majority of engagement activity in forums and respond to intervention, as well as to thread topic. By considering stateful and stateless interactions with electronic fora, we can gain a true indication of the relative engagement of our students and thus the health of our teaching environment.

7. REFERENCES

[Beaudoin 2002] Michael F Beaudoin. 2002. Learning or lurking?: Tracking the "invisible" online student. *The internet and higher education* 5, 2 (2002), 147–155.

[Chaturvedi et al. 2014] Snigdha Chaturvedi, Dan Goldwasser, and Hal Daumé III. 2014. Predicting Instructor's Intervention in MOOC forums.. In *ACL (1)*. 1501–1511.

[Davies and Graff] Jo Davies and Martin Graff. Performance in e-learning: online participation and student grades. *British Journal of Educational Technology* 36, 4 (????), 657–663.

[De Wever et al. 2006] Bram De Wever, Tammy Schellens, Martin Valcke, and Hilde Van Keer. 2006. Content analysis schemes to analyze transcripts of online asynchronous discussion groups: A review. *Computers & Education* 46, 1 (2006), 6–28.

[Garrison et al. 1999] D Randy Garrison, Terry Anderson, and Walter Archer. 1999. Critical inquiry in a text-based environment: Computer conferencing in higher education. *The internet and higher education* 2, 2 (1999), 87–105.

[Guzdial and Turns 2000] Mark Guzdial and Jennifer Turns. 2000. Effective discussion through a computer-mediated anchored forum. *The journal of the learning sciences* 9, 4 (2000), 437–469.

[Haig et al. 2013] Thomas Haig, Katrina Falkner, and Nickolas Falkner. 2013. Visualisation of learning management system usage for detecting student behaviour patterns. In *Proceedings of the Fifteenth Australasian Computing Education Conference-Volume 136*. Australian Computer Society, Inc., 107–115.

[Hecking et al. 2016] Tobias Hecking, Irene-Angelica Chounta, and H. Ulrich Hoppe. 2016. Investigating Social and Semantic User Roles in MOOC Discussion Forums. In *Proceedings of the Sixth International Conference on Learning Analytics & Knowledge*. 198–207.

[Hewitt 2005] Jim Hewitt. 2005. Towards an understanding of how threads die in asynchronous computer conferences. *The journal of the learning sciences* 14, 4 (2005), 567–589.

[Oleksandra and Shane 2016] Poquet Oleksandra and Dawson Shane. 2016. Untangling MOOC Learner Networks. In *Proceedings of the Sixth International Conference on Learning Analytics & Knowledge (LAK '16)*. ACM, 208–212.

[Palmer et al. 2008] Stuart Palmer, Dale Holt, and Sharyn Bray. 2008. Does the discussion help? The impact of a formally assessed online discussion on final student results. *British Journal of Educational Technology* 39, 5 (2008), 847–858.

[Sotillo 2000] Susana M Sotillo. 2000. Discourse functions and syntactic complexity in synchronous and asynchronous communication. *Language Learning & Technology* 4, 1 (2000), 82–119.

Identifying Domain-Specific Cognitive Strategies for Software Engineering

Shifa-e-Zehra Haidry
shifa.haidry@adelaide
.edu.au

Katrina Falkner
katrina.falkner@adelaide
.edu.au

Claudia Szabo
claudia.szabo@adelaide
.edu.au

School of Computer Science,
The University of Adelaide,
Adelaide, South Australia 5005, Australia.

ABSTRACT

Due to the rapidly changing nature of today's work environment, software engineering (SE) students are required to have self-regulated learning (SRL) and problem solving skills. Previous research suggests that training students in the use of domain-specific cognitive strategies and using scaffolded instruction for strategy training improves students' SRL and problem solving task performance. In order to identify SE-specific cognitive strategies, we conducted a survey of advanced-level SE students. We then conducted a pre-test and post-test experiment with one control and two treatment groups, to analyze the effectiveness of identified strategies in improving students' task performance. The control group was not exposed to any strategies, while one treatment group was instructed verbally in the use of strategies and the other was trained using a newly developed scaffolded strategy training module. The results of the experiment demonstrate significant improvement in post-test task performance for both treatment groups, with a further increase in performance for those undertaking the training module.

CCS Concepts

•Social and professional topics → Software engineering education;

Keywords

Software Engineering; Learning and Education; Problem Solving; Self-Regulated Learning; Instructional Scaffolding

1. INTRODUCTION

Today's working environment is characterized by rapid change. Due to the evolving requirements within the IT market, it is crucial for software engineers to develop skills that allow them to acquire new knowledge, apply previously learned knowledge in unexpected situations, and to solve dynamic problems. In order to provide effective learning opportunities, educational institutions should not only facilitate the development of content expertise but also foster the development of problem solving and self-regulated learning (SRL) skills. This need is not only evidenced by reports from industry companies [17] but also by the fact that developing problem solving and SRL skills is a major educational objective in several countries [16].

Problem solving and SRL skills are effective cognitive tools that are widely applicable and involve the ability of acquiring and using new knowledge, or using pre-existing knowledge to solve unique problems [23]. The development of problem solving and SRL skills is important for students to progress from novice to experts within specific domains. The level of problem solving and SRL proficiency depends on domain-specific knowledge and strategies and how students adapt different strategies over time [14, 20]. Previous studies show that strategy training has had a positive impact on students' task performance [13]. Moreover, using instructional scaffolding further improves students' task performance and problem solving skills [8]. This underscores the fact that students should be trained to develop and use discipline-specific strategies to successfully solve problems and tasks related to a discipline and specifically designed and targeted educational interventions can be offered to develop and improve strategy use and problem solving skills within a domain.

Despite extensive focus on the structure of software engineering (SE) degrees [12] and on experiences on designing and teaching SE courses [24], previous research lacks, to the best of our knowledge, the identification of learning strategies that are specific to SE. There is a need for SE-specific strategies to be identified and articulated in order to assist students in developing effective problem solving skills.

This paper aims to identify SE-related strategies used by advanced software engineering students and to analyse how these strategies fit with various software development tasks. Howard-Rose & Winne [9] suggest that the nature of the tasks that students are asked to complete can influence the strategies learners use to achieve a solution. As different phases of the software development life cycle (SDLC) may require different cognitive and meta-cognitive skills, we align identified strategies according to the phases in software development process to identify task-based SE-specific strategies. The identified strategies can then be incorporated in the design of introductory and advanced level SE courses

ITiCSE '17, July 03-05, 2017, Bologna, Italy.

© 2017 ACM. ISBN 978-1-4503-4704-4/17/07...$15.00

DOI: http://dx.doi.org/10.1145/3059009.3059032

to support students' early and successful transition from novices to experts in SE domain. In addition, we will also examine if there is a significant difference in the performance of students who were taught to use the identified strategies and those who were not. For this purpose we will use verbal and scaffolded instruction methods to impart strategy knowledge. This will help us in analyzing the effects of these instructional methods on students' task performance.

The main contributions of this work are (a) identification of task based SE-specific strategies, which may in turn guide the design of SE curricula to assist students in developing problem solving and SRL skills, (b) development of a prototype tool for scaffolding the teaching of SE strategies related to requirement analysis, and (c) analysis of effectiveness of scaffolded strategy instruction in order to improve students' academic task performance.

2. RELATED WORK

Research has shown that training students on the use of cognitive and meta-cognitive skills and strategies results in significant gains in performance in a variety of content domains [5, 11, 13, 19]. Locke et al. studied the effect of strategy training on performance in a management course. As per the study results, strategy training had positive effect on students' task performance [13]. Çalışkan et al. investigated the effects of strategy instruction on students' physics problem solving performance. Students were provided domain specific strategy instruction and the results of the experiment revealed that the strategy instruction had positive effects on students' performance and strategy use [5]. Labouvie-Vief & Gonda compared task performance of the elderly when trained to use strategies on a training and a different but related transfer task. Results showed significant improvement in task performance of elderly after strategy training on both the tasks [11].

Further, studies have shown the effectiveness of scaffolding strategy instruction in improving problem solving skills. For example, Ge & Land demonstrate the use of scaffolding in improving problem solving for ill-structured problems [8]. Rittle-Johnson & Koedinger demonstrated that students' mathematical problem solving was improved when contextual, conceptual and procedural knowledge was scaffolded [21].

To be able to assist SE student in developing domain-specific cognitive skills, we first need to determine SE-specific strategies. Although some authors have discussed the cognitive processes involved in different aspects of software development such as in design [10] and requirements analysis [1], but no domain-specific cognitive strategies were cited. The closest study is by Falkner et al. (2014), who identified successful and unsuccessful learning strategies specific to the discipline of computer science and aligned these strategies with Zimmerman's learning model [7]. Another study by Falkner et al. (2015) compared reflections provided by students in software development courses, with the aim of analysing the evolution of learning strategies from novice first year students to expert final year students. Results showed that discipline-specific learning strategies evolve over course years, but that scaffolding is required in different areas to help students in strategy development [6]. Both these papers are focused on learning strategies for computer science domain as a whole but not specifically on SE.

3. RESEARCH QUESTIONS

Our research design is driven by the following research questions (RQ):

- **RQ1** What are the SE-specific cognitive strategies according to the key tasks in software development process?

- **RQ2** Is there a difference in task performance of students who were trained to use SE-specific cognitive strategies and those who were not?

- **RQ3** Is there a difference in task performance when students were trained using scaffolded strategy instruction and when students were trained using verbal instruction?

4. RESEARCH METHODS

To answer our research questions, we divided our research study into two phases.

In **phase A**, we conducted a survey as the primary data collection instrument to identify SE-specific cognitive strategies. The research survey was aimed at students who had completed an advanced level project-based SE course at a university. The survey questionnaire was based on open-ended questions, aimed at soliciting information about students' strategy use when performing various SE tasks during the project. Participation in the survey was voluntary and anonymous and we performed both qualitative and quantitative analysis on the survey responses.

To answer RQ1, the data collected from the survey was subjected to the inductive way of thematic analysis [4], where a coding framework and the design for analysis was developed based on the data itself. We first performed open coding and then proceeded to axial coding, subsequently aligning our coding framework in order to compare identified strategies with the SDLC phases.

During the open coding process, we read through the textual responses to the survey and selected a block of text representing an idea or a concept e.g. one student mentioned that they compared meeting notes to ensure that requirements are not changed. Similarly another student mentioned that keeping meeting records helped them in identifying requirements conflict. We mapped both these textual references to the same concept i.e. 'comparing meeting notes to identify requirements conflict'. Then in axial coding process we mapped this identified cognitive strategy to requirements analysis task in SDLC as making sure that there are no requirements conflict is part of requirements analysis phase.

In **phase B** of our research, we invited students at different level of SE courses to voluntarily participate in an experiment activity. We used pre-test and post-test research design and performed quantitative analysis on collected data to answer RQ2 and RQ3. In both pre-test and post-test, students were required to perform the task of extracting system requirements from a given textual description of real-world processes 'initiating requisition request to HR' and 'daily listing for newspaper delivery' respectively.

Students were randomly assigned to three separate groups of 10 students each that we labeled as NS (No Strategy), TS (Textual Strategies) and SS (Scaffolded Strategies). NS was not exposed to any cognitive strategies. TS was explained the concept of cognitive strategies; how to use cognitive strategies to extract requirements and was provided with

Figure 1: Computer-Based Animated Strategy Training Module - Illustration

Figure 2: Computer-Based Animated Strategy Training Module - Exercise

only the textual list of strategies to use during the task. SS was exposed to the scaffolded cognitive strategies. We created a computer-based animated strategy training module, where students viewed an animated tutorial guiding them in the use of strategies to extract system requirements from text. See subsection 4.1 for details. Both TS and SS were exposed to the same list of strategies, (1) list all the system objects (2) list corresponding functions and attributes for each system object (3) determine all the system interactions (4) list all the data input/output (5) map specific verb phrases in text with functions or events.

Both pre-test and post-test descriptions were created in a way that total 25 system requirements could be identified using the strategies. Same number of requirements for both tasks gave us uniformity in difficulty level and assessment process. Students' task performance for both pre-test and post-test was assessed on the basis of software requirements assessment criteria (SRAC) developed by the researchers. SRAC has 5 items based on the above strategies and each item can have maximum score of 5 based on the number of correct requirements identified using each strategy, hence the maximum score can be 25. SRAC items are, (1) requirements for each object have been extracted (2) requirements for each function of each object have been extracted (3) requirements for each system interaction have been extracted (4) requirements for each data input/output have been extracted (5) requirements for each verb have been extracted.

4.1 Strategy Training Module

Previous research suggests that animations can be useful when delivering complex conceptual, procedural, contextual and problem solving knowledge [15, 25]. To provide strategy training to the students, we developed a computer-based animated strategy training module using Udutu. Please see Figures 1 and 2. The design of our training module is in line with the guidelines provided by Weiss et al. [25] and Ploetzner & Lowe [18], and includes following characteristics:

Subject Matter Classification: It helps students in information organization. We first explained the concept of learning strategies; then we explained the purpose or benefit of using learning strategies and then provided animated illustration of each strategy to show students how to apply given strategies to extract requirements.

Segmented Dynamic Visualizations: Each strategy illustration was segmented over 2 or 3 slides and after each strategy learners had to go through a strategy exercise providing students with an opportunity to practice the strategy just learned.

User Control: In order to provide an opportunity to the learner to pace their own learning; we gave animation controls to the user such as pausing illustration; and option to watch the illustration in one go or walk through it step by step.

Temporal Navigation: After each strategy section, students had the option to repeat strategy illustration or go to next strategy. We also used cues like 'click to start strategy illustration' and 'click to move to next strategy'. Students also had the option of going back and forth between the strategy illustrations; or jumping to any strategy at any time during the training.

Representation and Abstraction: We employed iconic visual representations such as schematic pictures visually describing the strategy 'determine system interactions' through concept mapping; formal notations; and written text. Second, narrations explaining the animated subject matter were also used.

Visual Cues: As per attention-guiding principle [3], we used visual cues to emphasize or lead user to the important information such as using arrows; highlighting and underlining the text; changing font color; circling the text; making words zoom in and zoom out; and directional text movement. Using cues also helped us in reducing cognitive load required to comprehend animation.

In order to avoid burdening working memory and to reduce the cognitive load and attentional requirements in comprehending the animation, we consciously tried restricting the non-topic elements and seductive details to the minimum, and used animations only to illustrate strategies.

5. ANALYSIS AND DISCUSSION

PHASE A: A total of 29 students participated in the survey. Although a medium sample size, 29 participants is sufficient as Bertaux [2, p.35] mentions that 15 is the minimum acceptable sample size for qualitative research and the average sample size for qualitative research is 22 [22].

The identified strategies with corresponding number and

Table 1: SE-Specific Cognitive Strategies Mapped To Software Development Tasks (Total Responses: 29)

Strategies	Responses	% Responses
Requirements Analysis	15	51.7
List Objects, Data Inputs and Outputs	11	37.9
List Corresponding Object Functions And Attributes	9	31.0
Determine User And System Interactions	8	27.5
Map Specific Verb Phrases With Functions	4	13.7
Design	12	41.3
Development	17	58.6
Testing	13	44.8
Project Management	20	68.9

percentage of responses are provided in Table 1, detailing the requirements analysis strategies used in the training module[1]. The table also provides grouping of strategies according to the phases in SDLC. Please note that as one strategy was mentioned by more than one student and one student mentioned more than one strategy, therefore the cumulative percentage of responses is not equal to 100%. We also realize that the list in Table 1 is not an exhaustive list of SE-specific cognitive strategies and can be further improved.

During our analysis we noticed that besides articulating strategies that were developed specifically for SE, students also mentioned several strategies that were adapted to fit in SE context, which is consistent with the research by Falkner et al [7]. For example concept mapping is a general information visualization strategy, but here it was mentioned in SE context as 'conceptually mapping interactions among system entities and class objects to clarify design'. Ability to select relevant strategies and adapt them according to a specific context are useful skills to have. Design for SE courses should incorporate teaching students about general strategies and how these strategies can be adapted to specific discipline tasks. The strategies provided in the list can be used as an example.

Maximum number of students mentioned strategies belonging to project management phase, which shows that students mostly focused on the project management task. As project management involves all aspects of software development and spans all phases of SDLC, it can be a possible reason for students' focus on project management. An interesting observation is that though most students used project management strategies, highest number i.e. 12 strategies were identified for requirements analysis and most of these strategies are adapted. As for this course students were required to extract and elicit requirements from textual project description and client, it appears that students found it easier to adapt general strategies for requirements analysis task such as comprehension and organization strategies.

Least number of students mentioned design strategies. Also, lowest number of strategies were identified for design along with testing phase. Less focus on design and testing suggests that students might have struggled with these tasks and instruction on these areas should be supported

with carefully designed scaffolded learning activities in order to promote strategic action in these units. Moreover, over all there are several strategies that are mentioned by only 1 student. By incorporating these strategies in SE course instruction, more students can be made aware of them, which in turn can assist students in improving their meta-cognitive and cognitive skills.

The most popular strategy cited by students is 'using online forums to learn coding solutions', which was mentioned by more than half of the participants.

> Whenever I got stuck while coding I asked my peers or searched different forums. It is easy and it is fast. (Q3, Student 11)

It emphasizes the importance of virtual learning spaces and online sources as an important learning resource. On online forums, students can quickly find worked solutions for recurring coding and technical problems. This calls for the need for instructional mechanisms in SE courses, where quick and targeted guidance should be provided when students most need it.

Phase wise analysis reveals that there are many areas within each development phase, which were not mentioned at all. For example, in requirements analysis most strategies belong to requirements gathering or requirements discovery but areas like requirements management or how to specify requirements were not covered. Similarly, in design the focus was on visual representation or system modeling but strategies regarding how to come up with multiple design solutions or how to devise good design were not mentioned. In development, managing and debugging code; in testing, test planning and management; and in project management, risk management and resource planning were not covered. Some students mentioned facing difficulties related to some of these areas such as one student mentioned that responsibilities among group members were not properly defined, and students worked on different tasks on 'as needed' basis.

> There was no role assignment and accordingly no responsibility division. So the plan, tracking and evaluation was ineffective. (Q5, Student 4)

Some students mentioned that they faced difficulty in managing requirements early on and thus encountered difficulties in managing the schedule.

> Trying to identify all the requirements up front was quite difficult, so we kept adding requirements as we thought of them all throughout the project and that affected our timeline. (Q1, Student 9)

To overcome the difficulties mentioned above i.e. effective requirements gathering; controlling timeline; and team management, adaptive scaffolding should be used in SE content and strategy instruction, where personalized guidance and feedback should be provided to the students. Moreover, SE courses should incorporate varied tasks and assignments so that students can get exposure to strategy use in all areas of SE.

Although, several students mentioned using reviews to detect bugs before implementation, which is a good proactive strategy but one student quoted using peer reviews as a reactive testing strategy only.

---

[1]Space constraints prevent us from showing the full dataset here. Please refer to https://se-srl.github.io/se-specific/SE-Specific-Strategies.pdf for the full list of identified strategies.

We mainly used peer reviews to find issues as things that we developed did not work as intended. (Q3, Student 16)

This emphasizes the importance of informing students about not only which strategies to use but also when, where and how to effectively use those strategies.

PHASE B: The NS, TS and SS students' responses to the pre-test and post-test were analyzed using SPSS v23. Descriptive statistics and mixed between-within subjects analysis of variance (two-way mixed ANOVA) were performed to compare pre-test and post-test scores on the SRAC (task performance) within each group and between NS, TS and SS. We used an alpha level of .05 for all statistical tests. Descriptive statistics including mean and standard deviation for pre-test and post-test of each group are provided in Table 2. There were no outliers. The data was normally distributed, as assessed by Shapiro-Wilk's test of normality $(p > .05)$. There was homogeneity of variances $(p > .05)$ and covariances $(p > .05)$, as assessed by Levene's test of homogeneity of variances and Box's M test, respectively.

Table 2: Descriptive Statistics For The Groups

Measurements	Groups	n	M	SD
Pre-Test	NS	10	11.50	1.780
	TS	10	11.50	2.173
	SS	10	12.20	1.814
Post-Test	NS	10	11.90	1.792
	TS	10	15.50	2.550
	SS	10	19.90	2.079

When Table 2 is examined in the pre-test measurement of the SRAC, it can be seen that the mean of the NS (M=11.50) and TS (M=11.50) groups is equal but mean of the SS group is slightly higher (M=12.20). According to the results of the two-way mixed ANOVA, the difference between the NS, TS and SS pre-test means was not statistically significant $(p > .05)$ $[F(2, 27) = .438, p = .650, \text{partial } \eta^2 = .031]$. These results indicate that the task performance of the students before they started in the experimental study was very similar in all three groups.

When Table 2 is studied in the post-test measurement of the SRAC, the mean of the SS (M=19.90) is highest and the mean of TS(M=15.50) is higher than the mean of NS (M=11.90). When two-way mixed ANOVA was conducted to test the treatment main effect on the post-test means of the TS and SS, it was determined that for TS (4.000 ± 1.125 mmol/L, p = .006) and SS (7.700 ± 1.00 mmol/L, p < .001) both, task performance was statistically significantly greater in post-test than pre-test (P < .05). But there was no statistically significant difference in task performance of non-treated NS (.400 ± .221 mmol/L, p = .104) within pre-test and post-test (P > .05). See Table 3.

Table 3: Comparison Within Pre-Test And Post-Test For Each Group

Groups	Mean Diff.	Std. Error	P-Value
NS	-.400*	.221	.104
TS	-4.000*	1.125	.006
SS	-7.700*	1.001	<.001

*The mean difference is significant at the 0.05 level.

Table 4: Comparison Between Groups For Post-Test

Groups		Mean Diff.	Std. Error	P-Value
NS	TS	-3.60*	.967	.003
	SS	-8.00*	.967	<.001
TS	NS	3.60*	.967	.003
	SS	-4.40*	.967	<.001
SS	NS	8.00*	.967	<.001
	TS	4.40*	.967	<.001

*The mean difference is significant at the 0.05 level.

Furthermore, there was statistically significant difference in post-test task performance at p < .05 level between groups $[F(2, 27) = 34.318, p < .001, \text{partial } \eta^2 = .718]$. Post hoc comparisons using the Tukey HSD test indicated that post-test task performance was statistically significantly greater in SS (8.00 ± .97 mmol/L, p < .001) and TS (3.60 ± .97 mmol/L, p = .003) compared to NS. Task performance in TS was statistically significantly lower than SS (4.40 ± .97 mmol/L, p < .001). See Table 4. Therefore, the results can be seen to be in favour of the SS group.

In our experiment we trained students on relevant SE-specific strategies to extract requirements from a textual description. In light of the data analysis, it has been determined that use of the identified cognitive strategies has had positive effect on SE students' task performance. This is consistent with the results of previous research that examined the effects of strategy training on task performance [13]. Moreover, students' task performance was further improved when use of strategies was taught using scaffolded instruction as compared to the verbal explanation only, which is again in accordance with the previous research [8]. These findings have many implications for SE pedagogy. First and foremost, students should be taught domain-specific as well as general cognitive strategies. Second, to improve students' ability to transfer strategic action and cognitive skills to different tasks and problems, scaffolding should be used to teach how and when to use these strategies effectively i.e. declarative and procedural strategic knowledge should be followed by conditional knowledge, which is about when and where to apply these strategies.

6. CONCLUSIONS

Pressley & Hilden argued that students should develop strategies according to the contextual influences in a particular discipline [20]. In this paper we present cognitive strategies that are adapted or specific to SE context. Identified strategies can help guide the design of SE courses in order to provide awareness about strategies and enable students to become effective problem solvers and self-regulated learners. When students are more aware of their cognitive strategic action, their meta-cognitive skills can also improve, which enable them to better monitor and reflect on their learning and performance and develop and adapt strategies accordingly.

Mayer (1992) suggested that students' problem solving proficiency depends on the development of domain-specific strategies [14]. Our study found that students used general cognitive strategies such as mapping and questioning, and articulated them in SE context. The identified strategies can help guide the identification and adaptation of more strategies specific to SE domain. Moreover, our experiment shows that training students to use identified strategies improves students' SE task performance, which is in line with previous research on effect of strategy instruction on performance [13]. Another important aspect of strategic action is transfer. By training students on the use of strategies, students' transfer of cognitive skills can be improved, allowing them to apply strategies on other complex problems and tasks.

As suggested by Ge & Land, our experiment also shows that using scaffolding to teach strategy use is effective. Therefore, instructional scaffolding for strategy training, especially adaptive scaffolding providing personalized instructional experience should be used in SE courses to assist students in improving their cognitive and meta-cognitive skills [8].

To deliver strategy instruction, we created an animated training module according to the guidelines provided in [15, 25]. Our experiment results suggest that exposure to the module improved students' understanding of the strategies and hence task performance. We plan to further improve our training module by incorporating more attributes for good animated instructional scaffolding design, and including more strategies for various SE tasks. We hope that our animated module will contribute in furthering SE-specific strategy training and research.

The identified list of SE-specific cognitive strategies is not complete and additional research is warranted to identify more strategies. We suggest creating a knowledge base of adapted and SE-specific strategies; and example applications of various strategies in order to assist SE students, instructors and researchers in learning, designing curricula, and research.

7. REFERENCES

[1] R. Agarwal, A. P. Sinha, and M. Tanniru. Cognitive fit in requirements modeling: A study of object and process methodologies. *Journal of Management Information Systems*, 13(2):137–162, 1996.

[2] D. Bertaux. From the life-history approach to the transformation of sociological practice. *Biography and society: The life history approach in the social sciences*, pages 29–45, 1981.

[3] M. Betrancourt. The animation and interactivity principles in multimedia learning. *The Cambridge handbook of multimedia learning*, pages 287–296, 2005.

[4] V. Braun and V. Clarke. Using thematic analysis in psychology. *Qualitative research in psychology*, 3(2):77–101, 2006.

[5] S. Caliskan, G. S. Selcuk, and M. Erol. Effects of the problem solving strategies instruction on the students' physics problem solving performances and strategy usage. *Procedia-Social and Behavioral Sciences*, 2(2):2239–2243, 2010.

[6] K. Falkner, C. Szabo, R. Vivian, and N. Falkner. Evolution of software development strategies. In *37th International Conference on Software Engineering (ICSE)*, volume 2, pages 243–252. IEEE, 2015.

[7] K. Falkner, R. Vivian, and N. J. Falkner. Identifying computer science self-regulated learning strategies. In *Innovation & technology in computer science education (ITiCSE)*, pages 291–296. ACM, 2014.

[8] X. Ge and S. M. Land. Scaffolding students' problem-solving processes in an ill-structured task using question prompts and peer interactions. *Educational Technology Research and Development*, 51(1):21–38, 2003.

[9] D. Howard-Rose and P. H. Winne. Measuring component and sets of cognitive processes in self-regulated learning. *Journal of Educational Psychology*, 85(4):591–604, 1993.

[10] R. Jeffries, A. A. Turner, P. G. Polson, and M. E. Atwood. The processes involved in designing software. *Cognitive skills and their acquisition*, 255:283, 1981.

[11] G. Labouvie-Vief and J. N. Gonda. Cognitive strategy training and intellectual performance in the elderly. *Journal of Gerontology*, 31(3):327–332, 1976.

[12] L. Laird. Strengthening the "engineering" in software engineering education: A software engineering bachelor of engineering program for the 21st century. In *29th International Conference on Software Engineering Education and Training (CSEET)*, pages 128–131. IEEE, 2016.

[13] E. A. Locke, E. Frederick, C. Lee, and P. Bobko. Effect of self-efficacy, goals, and task strategies on task performance. *Journal of applied psychology*, 69(2):241, 1984.

[14] R. E. Mayer. *Thinking, problem solving, cognition*. New York : W.H. Freeman, 2nd edition, 1992.

[15] R. E. Mayer and R. Moreno. Animation as an aid to multimedia learning. *Educational psychology review*, 14(1):87–99, 2002.

[16] OECD. Pisa 2012 assessment and analytical framework. mathematics, reading, science, problem solving and financial literacy. 2012.

[17] C. Patrick, D. Peach, C. Pocknee, F. Webb, M. Fletcher, and G. Pretto. The wil report: A national scoping study. *Final Report to the Australian Council for Teaching and Learning, ACEN*, 2009.

[18] R. Ploetzner and R. Lowe. A systematic characterisation of expository animations. *Computers in Human Behavior*, 28(3):781–794, 2012.

[19] M. Pressley. *Cognitive strategy instruction that really improves children's academic performance*. Brookline Books, 1990.

[20] M. Pressley and K. Hilden. Cognitive strategies. *Handbook of child psychology*.

[21] B. Rittle-Johnson and K. R. Koedinger. Designing knowledge scaffolds to support mathematical problem solving. *Cognition and Instruction*, 23(3):313–349, 2005.

[22] M. Sandelowski. Sample size in qualitative research. *Research in nursing & health*, 18(2):179–183, 1995.

[23] R. J. Sternberg. *Thinking and Problem Solving*, volume 2. Academic Press, 2013.

[24] C. Thomas and K. Berkling. Redesign of a gamified software engineering course. In *International Conference on Interactive Collaborative Learning (ICL)*, pages 778–786. IEEE, 2013.

[25] R. E. Weiss, D. S. Knowlton, and G. R. Morrison. Principles for using animation in computer-based instruction: Theoretical heuristics for effective design. *Computers in Human Behavior*, 18(4):465–477, 2002.

Specification By Example for Educational Purposes

Isabelle Blasquez
Limoges University
33 rue François Mitterrand
Limoges, France
isabelle.blasquez@unilim.fr

Hervé Leblanc
IRIT
118 Route de Narbonne
Toulouse, France
leblanc@irit.fr

ABSTRACT

The Specification By Example (SBE) is a guideline for building the *right software*, a software that meets customer requirements. It is based on seven process patterns and enhances communication and collaboration and it usually is used in agile software development. The connection between education and agile software development sounds actually as an emergent topic. In this paper, we propose to structure a teaching approach in analogy to an agile software development by transposing each process pattern of SBE to a corresponding one in the teaching domain. Moreover, we show that thanks to the emergence of a collective intelligence process, the students are more confident and more responsible. Such a course offers the opportunity to learn not only technical skills, but also some values in a new mindset.

Keywords

Agile Software Development; Specification by Example; Agile Teaching

1. INTRODUCTION

"Building the product right and building the right product are two different things. We need both in order to succeed". From this observation, Godjko Adzick builds a collective knowledge by studying over 50 software projects [1]. The related process consists of gathering examples to clarify requirements, deriving tests and automating them. Specification By Example (SBE) is also defined as an approach of software development based on seven process patterns that help teams to build the right software product by writing just enough documentation to facilitate change effectively in short iterations or in flow-based development [1]. It also enhances communication and collaboration and it usually is used in agile software development.

The connection between agile software development and education sounds actually as an emergent topic. Some trans-

positions are developped concerning agile manifesto[1], agile values[2], the Scrum framework[3] and more generally agile approaches[4]. These propositions suggest the idea that education today needs a "refactoring". While the agile manifesto proposes to evolve from a traditional plan-driven paradigm to a value-driven paradigm, the agile school manifesto suggests an evolution from traditional teaching-approaches to new learning approaches.

We propose a teaching approach in analogy to an agile software developement by transposing each process pattern of SBE to a corresponding one in the teaching domain. The result of the transposition is a guideline usable by teachers to produce the *right course* as the agile methodologies are used to produce the *right software*.

As example, we use a software product methods course that we gave to eighty two-year french undergraduates. This course is a part of French National Pedagogical Program (PPN), a common program to all technical colleges specialized in Computer Technology. The objective of this course is to present software development processes. We have chosen to teach agile software development.

This paper presents a transposition of the seven process patterns of Specification By Example to improve the design of a course. This is one section per process pattern with three paragraphs each: an overview of the original pattern in SBE, the corresponding pattern in teaching-domain, and an example on the software development processes course. The next section gives some considerations about the concept of right course and gives a toolkit of our proposal.

2. BACKGROUND AND CONTEXT

Traditional teaching approach is teacher-centered and often relies only on lectures and small exercises. Nowadays, we remark that students become more quickly bored and inattentive due to mismatches between students learning and teaching styles [8]. To improve the quality of courses and to help both teacher and students for a better alignment, we have designed a guideline based on SBE.

A definition of quality in the context of educational game is suggested in [21] as *if it provides a positive learning effect, motivates students to study and provides a pleasant and engaging learning experience*. We choose to use this definition to the *right* course whose the expectations in terms of

---

[1]https://www.infoq.com/articles/agile-schools-education
[2]https://pedagogieagile.com/2012/05/12/les-valeurs
[3]http://eduscrum.nl/en
[4]http://approchealpes.info

ACM acknowledges that this contribution was authored or co-authored by an employee, contractor or affiliate of a national government. As such, the Government retains a nonexclusive, royalty-free right to publish or reproduce this article, or to allow others to do so, for Government purposes only.

ITiCSE '17, July 3-5, 2017, Bologna, Italy.

© 2017 ACM. ISBN 978-1-4503-4704-4/17/07...$15.00

DOI: http://dx.doi.org/10.1145/3059009.3059039

learning, collaboration, commitment and happiness to work are similar. The purpose of the *right* course is to enhance the individual student's capability to participate in and contribute to collaborative learning process based on collective intelligence process. According to Lévy, Collective Intelligence (CI) is the capacity of human collectives to engage in intellectual cooperation in order to create, innovate and invent [15].

The guideline is presented in the table 1. The first column provides original patterns of SBE. The second column provides corresponding teaching-domain patterns. And the last column provides practices used to implement the patterns. Teachers could design the right course by determining the right teaching resources as well as posssible. For students, this guideline gives the opportunity to learn not only technical skills, but also some values in a new mindset.

Throughout this paper, we propose an analogy between the agile software development terminology and the teaching terminology. As we have already suggested to translate *product* into *course*, we also suggest to translate *Product Manager* into *Course designer* and *requirements* into *syllabus* of the course. *Examples* from SBE will be transposed to *teaching resources*.

3. DERIVING SCOPE FROM GOALS

Original pattern.
A best practice for this pattern is to start with a customer's business goal and then to collaborate with the business to derive the scope. This pattern also first focuses on *why* something is needed and *who* needs it. For effectively collaborating, it recommends to ask *how* something would be useful before *what* you need to build it. "Impact Mapping" is a technique for deriving scope from goals which propose to build a minmap around four aspects of the software: goal (why), actors (who), impacts (how), and deliverables (what). [2]

Corresponding teaching-domain pattern.
This process pattern focuses on the course's vision by answering *why*, *who*, *how*, and *what*. The *why* helps to define the objective of the course also called learning goals. The *who* depicts actors, usually students. The *how* identifies impacts to help actors to achieve the objective. The impacts of the teaching domain are learning outcomes (knowledge and competencies acquired or improved by students). The *what* helps to outline deliverables needed to support the impacts. For teaching, they are *topics* which are the transposition from *features*.

Example.
Our objective is to propose an introduction to agile software development in an agile mindset: *Doing agile* and *Being agile* with respect to the first levels of Bloom's taxonomy suitable to undergradates (knowledge, comprehension and application) [3]. The actors are students. There are three learning outcomes relative to agile practices: delivering the right product, delivering the product right, and delivering fast and regularly. There is one learning outcome relative to agile values and principles. The scope is also determined by higher-level topics which are: introduction to agile software development, overview of collaborative tools, introduction to Scrum, from traditional to agile software development, business model, agile requirements, user story, Scrum in practice, tests, and retrospective.

As the students were novices, this course's vision has been suggested by the teacher. But in another context such as an advanced course, the course's vision could be defined collaboratively by an open backlog and a collective vote.

4. SPECIFYING COLLABORATIVELY

Original pattern.
Specifying collaboratively enables to harness the knowledge and the experience of the whole team. It also creates a collective ownership of specifications, making everyone more engaged in the delivery process [1]. No document should be written in isolation. To collaborate effectively, most popular models are introduced: workshops (all-team or smaller), pair-writing, and even informal conversations. All-team workshops are useful to discover and learn about the business model. They are a good way to build a shared understanding of the requirements and produce a set of examples that illustrate a feature. The smaller workshops help to clarify or complete the specification. Pairing to write specifications allows to mature products by getting several different perspectives on a example. Mostly, collaboration needs a preparation phase to be efficient. It is easier to initiate a collective discussion if some examples have been prepared before.

Corresponding teaching-domain pattern.
Specifying collaboratively transposes to Teaching collaboratively. In SBE, collaboration models are classified according to the size of the team. In teaching domain, collaboration models will be classified according to the teaching approach.

We propose two kinds of collaboration models: inductive and deductive workshops. Induction is a reasoning progression that proceeds from particulars (observations, measurements, data) to generalities (governing rules, laws, theories). Deduction proceeds in the opposite direction [8]. Traditional teaching approach is deductive. The inductive approach includes problem-based learning, discovery learning, inquiry learning, or some variation on those themes which are characterized by [19] as constructivist based approaches. These approaches impose more responsibility on students for their own learning. They almost always involve students discussing questions and solving problems (active learning) and the work is done in groups (collaborative or cooperative learning).

The Participatory Action Research (PAR) is a collaborative process of research, education and action explicitly oriented towards social transformation [12]. To promote the emergence of a collective intelligence process, we propose to structure the workshops around a AAA-PAR strategy that consists in three ordered steps. The first step is the Arrangement time: the preparation phase where teacher prepares materials provided to the students to start the workshop. The second step is the Action time: the core of the workshop. During this step, the students collaborate to achieve the required learning goals. The self-organized *development team* of an agile software development also transposes to an autonomous *student team*. The behavior of the stakeholders is a crucial factor for the success of these workshop. The main teacher's responsibility is to engage students in learn-

Table 1: Guideline for delivering the right course

Process Patterns	Teaching Patterns	Practices
Deriving scope from goals	Course's vision	goal, skateholders, skills, main topics
Specifying collaboratively	Teaching collaboratively	inductive workshop, deductive workshop structure of the workshop
Illustrating using examples	Illustrating with teaching resources (teaching resources support)	learning style teaching style
Refining the specification	Refining teaching resources (teaching resources details)	competency, timeboxing, application domain outcome, starter kit
Automating validation without changing specification	Teaching resources management	schedule, repetition
Validating frequently	Knowledge evaluation process	with or without grades, individual or collective material, frequency, ...
Evolving a documentation system	Evolving a documentation academic	access, material, architecture

ing: he becomes the facilitator of the workshop [19]. He must ensure trust behaviors. Thirteen trust behaviors have been identified by [5], some of them are: demonstrate respect, create transparency, listen first, keep commitments, and extend trust. The third step is the Assertion time: a kind of workshop review. The teachers also encourages students to explicitly reflect on the events of the Action time and to examine the lessons learned about the workshop. An agile retrospective [6] is well-adapted at this time and the three following questions could be asked: What did you learn in this workshop ? What is amazing in this workshop ? Why will you reuse or not the workshop later ?

Example.
Both inductive and deductive workshops are used in our course. Inductive workshops was preferred to respect the CI process and to promote the emergence of agile values. The teams are composed by six or seven students to respect the ideal size of an agile team.

5. ILLUSTRATING USING EXAMPLES

Original pattern.
Examples are used to clarify meaning in everyday conversation: they are concrete and less unambiguous. Illustrating requirements using examples is a way to specify with enough details that we can be checked by assertion. Using examples will ensure that the delivery teams focus on the right product and that they have a shared understandings of what the business users expect out of the system [1]. To be used from requirement analysis to testing, examples should be small, precise, realistic and easy to understand.

Corresponding teaching-domain pattern.
Illustrating with examples tranposes to illustrating with teaching resources. We define a *teaching resource* as an activity used by a teacher to engage students in learning to achieve required learning goals.

Learning is presented as a two-step process involving the reception and processing of information [8]. The processing step may involve different learning's models: simple memorization, inductive or deductive reasoning, reflection, action, and introspection or interaction with others. As students learn in many ways and as teaching methods are also various, learning styles and teaching styles are identified by [8]. A learning style should consider: perception (sensory or intuitive), input (visual or auditory), organization (inductive or deductive), processing (active or reactive), and understanding (sequential or global). A teaching style should con-

sider: content (concrete or abstract), presentation (visual or verbal), organization (inductive or deductive), student participation (active or passive), and perspective (sequential or global).

When mismatches exist between learning and teaching styles, students become bored and inattentive in class, do poorly on tests, and get discouraged about the courses [8]. To engage students in learning, a best practice is to choose the right teaching resources support by finding the better alignment between learning and teaching style. Sometimes, lectures are necessary to introduce or clarify a concept. For a better alignment of the right course, we suggest two others potential teaching resources.

Gamification is the process of using game-based mechanics, aesthetics and game thinking to engage people, motivate action, promote learning, and solve problems [11]. Game can also offer some moment of serendipity. The Assertion time is crucial to have benefits from games. A link between games, culture, happiness, learning, and productivity is shown in [16] and studied on an educational game in [20]. Innovation Games [10] or Game storming [9] give usefull examples of gamification.

Project Based Learning (PBL) is perceived to be a student-centered approach to learn [4, 18]. The students need to produce a solution to solve a problem and an outcome in the form of a report. PBL focuses on large, open-ended problems, like many real-world problems [17]. It is based on five principles: students work together in groups; a real world problem that affects the life of the students is presented for investigation; students discuss findings and consult the teacher for guidance, input, and feedback; the maturity level of students skills determines the degree of guidance provided by the teacher; resulting products can be shared with the community.

Example.
Various teaching resources have been used : traditional lectures, games (lego-based approaches as Lego4Scrum or TDDLego[14]), collaborative workshops (story-writing workshop and Coding dojo). A PBL approach has also been adopted including collaborative workshops (product vision statements, story mapping, impact mapping) and innovation games (Product Box, Speed Boat). Gamification has been preferred to introduce concepts whenever possible. Videos from professionnal conferences have been watched in some lectures. To introduce the visual management, visual information has often been used with pictures, animations and sketchnotes.

6. REFINING THE SPECIFICATION

Original pattern.

This pattern brings further informations about the specification. To be unambiguous, a good specification should be precise and testable, and concerns only business functionality. To be useful as long-term documentation, it should be self-explanatory, focused, and in domain language.

Corresponding teaching-domain pattern.

This pattern focuses on teaching resources details. It helps the teacher to refine the teaching resources and to improve it. A teaching resource should be focused about a specific competency and be well time-boxed to respect the duration of the workshop. To be precise, the application domain must be carefully chosen to promote the commitment of students. To be testable, an outcome must be defined. An outcome describes a way to verify and validate that the required learning goals are well-achieved. The *tests* in software development transposes to the *outcome* in teaching domain. Collective discussions induced by the teaching resource will be efficient only if everyone has a common understanding of it. A starter kit could prevent misunderstanding and promote self-organization of the activities.

Example.

Each teaching resource has been focused on a specific competency and time-boxed to respect the duration of a session. Each student team has choosen by collective vote his own application domain for the project used for the PBL workshops. At least, two major benefits can be highlighted with this kind of project. First, the product manager (a student) is always avalaible. Then most of students feel involved because they could be quickly become the users of this application. A starter kit has been provided for each new teaching resources. It includes a roadmap, a brief summary of the concept taught, a description of required deliverable, a glossary, and bibliographical references. The outcome have been various as oral feedback, photos, and specific artifact or summary.

7. AUTOMATING VALIDATION WITHOUT CHANGING SPECIFICATIONS

Original pattern.

After refining the specification, the examples can be used as a target for the implementation and the validation of the software. The tests should often be run during the development to ensure quality of the product and to reduce delays of the feedback. This pattern focuses on automation, as a solution of a quick feedback. The automation has long-term benefits: having an objective measurement of when the job is finished, checking more frequently, and getting a living documentation [1].

Corresponding teaching-domain pattern.

Thinking about automation is asking about repetition of a learning resource. The repetition is a well-known best practice in teaching. By using different types of teaching resources on a same competency, we prevent the disalignment between teaching and learning styles, we respect the learning time of each student, and we offer different opportunities to apply the competency. This pattern focuses on teaching resources management. It helps to select suitable teaching

resources by considering learning goals, learning styles and competency. A first sequence of teaching resources can be scheduled according to the sequence of topics. To ensure repetition of some competencies, new teaching resources can be introduced. During the course, a sequence can be changed by the teacher according to the feedback on student behaviors and feelings (motivation, comprehension, outcome validation, ...). The teacher should also apply some values to his behavior, as responding to change in his course's design.

Example.

The course run over a period of 10 weeks with two 2-hours sessions per week. Lectures, games, collaborative workshops and PBL have been alternatively used. As students have a mentored software development project to lead at the same time, some workshop of PBL have been repeated in this context to help students to find user-stories from the vision. These workshops were self-organized by the student teams.

8. VALIDATING FREQUENTLY

Original pattern.

A continuous integration system builds the product and runs the tests. It ensures that once the product is built right, it stays right. To satisfy this point, this pattern suggests to validate executable specifications frequently to keep them reliable. The best practices insist on reducing unreliability and on looking for ways to get faster feedback.

Corresponding teaching-domain pattern.

Mostly, the actors build their own knowledge during the right course. The teacher is responsible for the reliability of the knowledge. The students are responsible to get faster feedback. This pattern suggests to determine the knowledge evaluation process. This process must be defined by considering some questions as: is it an individual or collective evaluation ? What is the material for the evaluation ? How often should we evaluate ? Are grades really required as a measure of academic performance ? and so on.

Example.

An evaluation has been planned at the end of each workshop. This evaluation has taken place during the Assertion time with an oral presentation of the outcomes. No grade is attributed for this. For each workshop of the PBL, a summary has been required per team as material for the evaluation. This summary was based on a template provided by the teacher: presentation of the workshop, deliverables, comments, and retrospective. It allows to detail knowledge, comprehension, and application of the competency taught. Such a summary could also be used as a cookbook to apply easily the competency again. At the end of the course, a report including a presentation of the PBL project and all the summaries has been delivered by each team. These reports have been graded by one grade by team to respect the collective intelligence process.

9. EVOLVING A DOCUMENTATION SYSTEM

Original pattern.

Living documentation is an artifact and the end-product of SBE. It is a reliable and authoritative source of information on system functionality, which anyone can easily ac-

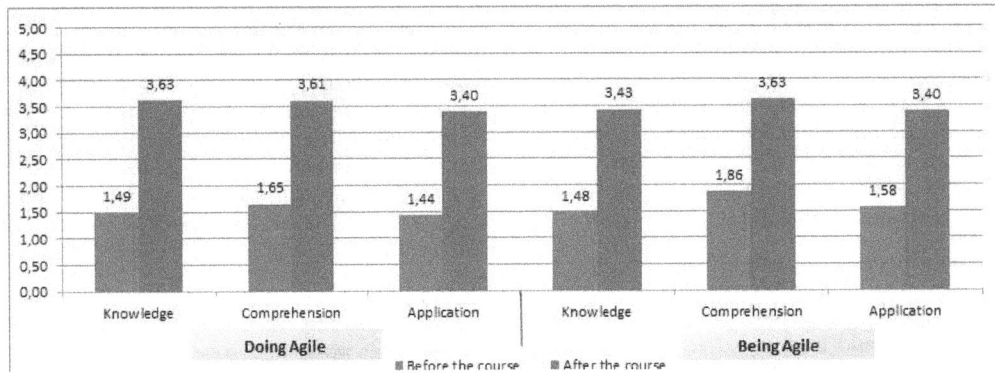

Figure 1: Frequency diagram of answers with respect to the feedback on learning.

cess [1]. Best practices dedicated to living documentation are: easy to access, easy to understand, and each change in the system needs to be reflected.

Corresponding teaching-domain pattern.

System documentation transposes to academic documentation in teaching domain. To easily access to the documentation, material courses (lectures, exercices, tutorials, references) can be deposit in repositories managed by a version control system. Each stakeholder (teacher and students) can consult or tell about changes to update material courses. The role of the teacher is to encourage students to share and update the materials to have more understable course notes. The documentation can be alive by setting up an automatic notification system to alert all the stakeholder when a new document is added or updated.

Example.

Github is used to share on-line public material courses[5]. It provides collaboration features such as pull request or wikis. A Slack[6] team has been created for this course to facilitate discussions between skateholders. The web-service IFTTT[7] connects Github with Slack to automatically notify all the stakeholder when a change in the documentation is pushed.

10. VALIDATION

We focus now on the evaluation of the *quality* (as defined in section 2) of the agile software project management course presented as the example. This course has been designed in 2015 and delivered in the fall 2015 and 2016.

The validation has been adapted from a specific framework [20] which is based on two questionnaries related to Bloom's taxonomy of educational objectives [3] and Kirkpatrick's levels of evaluation [13]. It has already been applied for educational games and coding dojo session [7, 21]. We adapted the terminology from game to course and we deleted some items from original questionnaires to only focus a set of teaching resources. Moreover, the evaluation is concerned by student perception in terms of motivation, user experience, and learning process. Questionnaries are given to the 80 students at the end of the course.

Results of the first questionnaire are presented in Fig. 1. It is based on [3] and evaluates the perception of the evolution of learning in the competencies taught before and after the

course. It focuses on the learning goals (*doing agile* and *being agile*) with respect to the perceived impacts rated on a scale from 1 to 5. The perception of the Agile Software Development (the heart of the course) was multiplied by more than two. It is the same for the *being agile* posture that students can reused for other courses.

Results of the second questionnaire are presented in Fig. 2. It is based on [13] consists in 21 items asking motivation, user experience, and learning on a Likert scale with response alternatives ranging from strongly disagree (-2) to strongly agree (2). The majority of the students agreed strongly that the course promotes moments of cooperation. They also confirmed that they had fun while interacting with other students. The social interaction has also been the highest rated dimension. Overall, results are positive in terms of fun, challenge, and social interactions.

11. CONCLUSION

This paper presents a guideline for delivering a *right* course by structuring a teaching approach as an agile software development. We defend a new teaching way based on collective intelligence process which aims to align a course with the needs of students by designing the right teaching resources. The role of the teacher as a facilitator has also been presented as a key of success. By maintaining trust behaviors and by encouraging the communication, he helps students to collaborate efficiently and to be more commitment, more creative and more responsible. In agile software development, the most popular methodologies used are: Scrum and eXtreme Programming. We showed that SBE can be transposed to specify teaching resources. Scrum has already been transposed to manage learning experience where the responsibility for the learning process is delegated to students. No transposition has already been proposed for eXtreme Programming. We plan to study their principles, especially the transposition from a user story to a teaching story.

12. ACKNOWLEDGMENTS

This same transposition was used for a specific course during 3 days on agile requirements at the University of Toulouse for a professional Bachelor dedicated to Development and Software Quality.

---

[5]https://github.com/iblasquez
[6]https://slack.com: a cloud-based team collaboration tool
[7]https://ifttt.com: *If This Then That*

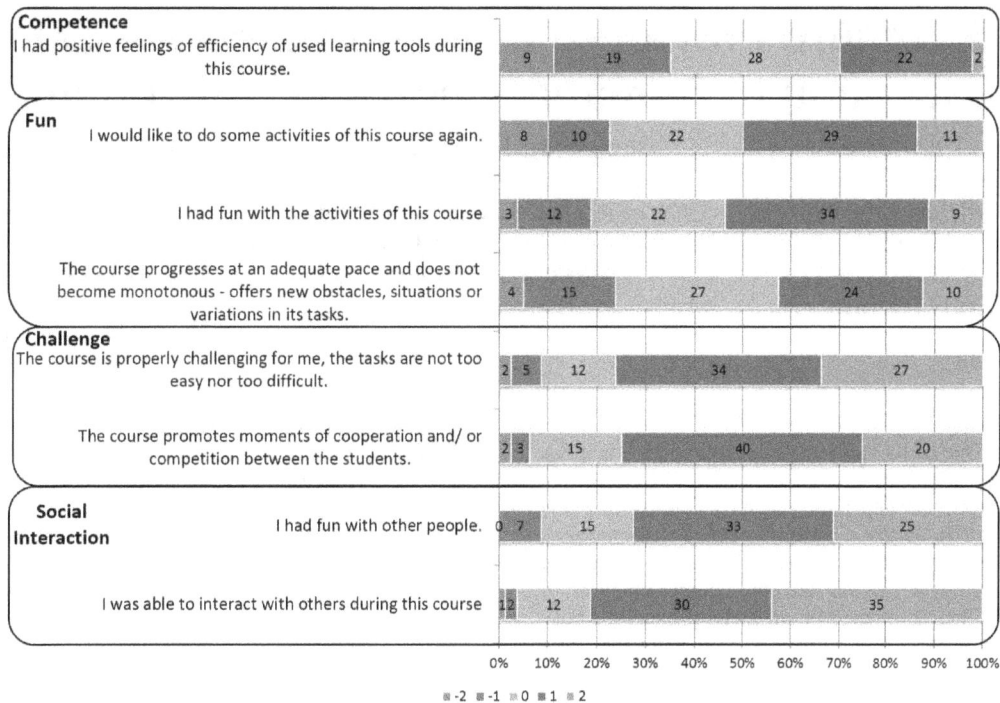

Figure 2: Frequency diagram of answers with respect to the sub-component user experience.

13. REFERENCES

[1] G. Adzic. *Specification by Example: How Successful Teams Deliver the Right Software*. Manning Publications Co., Greenwich, CT, USA, 2011.

[2] G. Adzic and M. Bisset. *Impact Mapping*. Provoking Thoughts, 2012.

[3] B. S. Bloom, M. B. Engelhart, E. J. Furst, W. H. Hill, and D. R. Krathwohl. *Taxonomy of educational objectives. The classification of educational goals*. Longmans Green, 1956.

[4] S. Chandrasekaran, A. Stojcevski, G. Littlefair, and M. Joordens. Learning through projects in engineering education. In *Proceedings of SEFI Conference*, 2012.

[5] S. Covey and R. Merrill. *The SPEED of Trust: The One Thing that Changes Everything*. Free Press, 2008.

[6] E. Derby and D. Larsen. *Agile Retrospectives: Making Good Teams Great*. Pragmatic Bookshelf, 2006.

[7] B. Estácio, N. Valentim, L. Rivero, T. Conte, and R. Prikladnicki. Evaluating the use of pair programming and coding dojo in teaching mockups development: An empirical study. In *HICSS*, pages 5084–5093. IEEE Computer Society, 2015.

[8] R. M. Felder and L. K. Silverman. Learning and teaching styles in engineering education. *engineering education*, 78(7):674–681, 1988.

[9] D. Gray, S. Brown, and J. Macanufo. *Gamestorming: A Playbook for Innovators, Rulebreakers, and Changemakers*. O'Reilly Media, 2010.

[10] L. Hohmann. *Innovation Games*. Pearson Education, 2006.

[11] K. Kapp. *The Gamification of Learning and Instruction: Game-based Methods and Strategies for Training and Education*. Wiley, 2012.

[12] S. Kindon, R. Pain, and M. Kesby. *Participatory Action Research Approaches and Methods: Connecting People, Participation and Place*. Routledge Studies in Human Geography. Taylor & Francis, 2007.

[13] D. L. Kirkpatrick and J. D. Kirkpatrick. *Evaluating training programs : the four levels*. Berrett-Koehler Publishers, 2006.

[14] S. Kurkovsky. A lego-based approach to introducing test-driven development. In *ACM Conference on ITiCSE*, pages 246–247, New York, NY, USA, 2016.

[15] P. Lévy. From social computing to reflexive collective intelligence: The ieml research program. *Information Sciences*, 180(1):71–94, 2010.

[16] D. Mezick. *The Culture Game: Tools for the Agile Manager*. FreeStanding Press, 2012.

[17] E. D. Ragan, S. Frezza, and J. Cannell. Product-based learning in software engineering education. In *IEEE Frontiers in Education Conference*, pages 1–6, 2009.

[18] J. R. Savery. Overview of problem-based learning: definition and distinctions, the interdisciplinary. *Journal of Problem-based Learning*, pages 9–20, 2006.

[19] K. Smith, S. Sheppard, D. Johnson, and R. Johnson. Pedagogies of engagement: Classroom-based practices. *Journal of Engineering Education*, 94(1):87–100, 2005.

[20] C. G. von Wangenheim, R. Savi, and A. F. Borgatto. Deliver! - an educational game for teaching earned value management in computing courses. *Inf. Softw. Technol.*, 54(3):286–298, 2012.

[21] C. G. von Wangenheim, R. Savi, and A. F. Borgatto. Scrumia : An educational game for teaching scrum in computing courses. *Journal of Systems and Software*, 86(10):2675–2687, 2013.

The Solothurn Project — Bringing Computer Science Education to Primary Schools in Switzerland

Anna Lamprou
School of Education
Univ. of Applied Sciences and Arts,
Northwestern Switzerland (FHNW)
Windisch, Switzerland
anna.lamprou@fhnw.ch

Alexander Repenning
School of Education
Univ. of Applied Sciences and Arts,
Northwestern Switzerland (FHNW)
Windisch, Switzerland
alexander.repenning@fhnw.ch

Nora A. Escherle
School of Education
Univ. of Applied Sciences and Arts,
Northwestern Switzerland (FHNW)
Windisch, Switzerland
nora.escherle@fhnw.ch

ABSTRACT

Currently Switzerland is going through a major reform in its education system. One of its most ambitious and important goals is the inclusion of Computer Science Education already on the primary school level, an important measure in achieving the establishment of an information society. Such a reform raises questions about the appropriate types of approaches to be developed and employed for an effective implementation of Computer Science Education concepts in Swiss primary schools. To this end, the project "Scalable Game Design Solothurn" was developed and evaluated. This project both trained teachers and exposed students to Computational Thinking concepts through the two Computational Thinking Tools AgentSheets and AgentCubes online. Results show that teaching Computational Thinking through Scalable Game Design is not only feasible on the primary school level but also enjoyable, with AgentSheets and AgentCubes online proving to be sustainable and effective tools for the implementation of Computer Science Education on this school level. Further analysis of the data enables us to make recommendations regarding optimal ways of implementation for the Swiss reality and point towards new research directions.

Keywords
Computer science education, Computational Thinking, primary schools, professional teacher development, experience report.

1. INTRODUCTION
The omnipresence of information and communication technologies (ICT) in our everyday lives and the continuously increasing demand for an ICT-skilled workforce [8,4] arguably require the introduction of ICT education in schools. And yet, Computer Science (CS) is not a mandatory subject at any school level in Switzerland. The Swiss education system is challenged to improve this situation. To that end, the Swiss Federal Council has adopted the "Digital Switzerland" strategy and proclaimed the promotion of Computer Science Education (CSE) as an important measure to achieve the goal of establishing an information society in Switzerland [6,7].

A first important step towards that goal is the *Lehrplan 21* (LP 21),[1] the new common curriculum for compulsory education in the 21 German-speaking cantons. LP 21 was developed in order to implement article 62 of the Federal Constitution of the Swiss Confederation, which states that the compulsory school system should be harmonized.[2] Apart from shifting the focus away from pure content onto the learning of competences, LP 21 importantly introduces CSE on the primary school level by way of the module "Medien und Informatik".[3] The important next step is to find ways to successfully implement the rather abstract and vague module descriptions of LP 21 in practice, and bring CSE to primary schools in Switzerland. This paper is an experience report describing the CSE project "Scalable Game Design Solothurn." This project aimed at integrating the field of CSE into selected classes using the two Computational Thinking Tools AgentSheets and AgentCubes online in the canton of Solothurn. This paper discusses the project's successful impact and based on the assessment of the data gathered, makes recommendations about an effective CSE inclusion in the Swiss education system.

1.1 Swiss K-12 Computer Science Education
Currently, ICT education in Swiss schools mainly stands for learning to use applications like Microsoft Office. While there are many innovative teachers that teach topics beyond that, most of them do this all on their own initiative. If a student is exposed to CS throughout his or her school career, it is simply by chance. There are a number of organizations that have been aiming at improving CSE in primary and secondary school (K-12) education for many years. Most initiatives that aim at introducing CS in K-12 education in Switzerland are funded and conducted by associations, foundations or even companies. The largest and most renowned one is the *Hasler foundation*. However, most of these programs and initiatives are focused primarily on secondary schools, and some even target only talented students.

Activities organized on a more regular, usually yearly, basis include project weeks in selected schools and competitions like the *Informatik-Biber*[4] or the *Swiss Olympiad in Informatics*,[5] or

ITiCSE '17, July 03-05, 2017, Bologna, Italy
© 2017 ACM. ISBN 978-1-4503-4704-4/17/07...$15.00
DOI: http://dx.doi.org/10.1145/3059009.3059017

---

[1] For details see http://v-ef.lehrplan.ch/index.php

[2] For details see http://www.lehrplan21.ch/rechtliche-grundlagen

[3] For details see http://v-ef.lehrplan.ch/index.php?code=b|10|0&la =yes

[4] For details see http://informatik-biber.ch/

[5] For details see https://soi.ch/

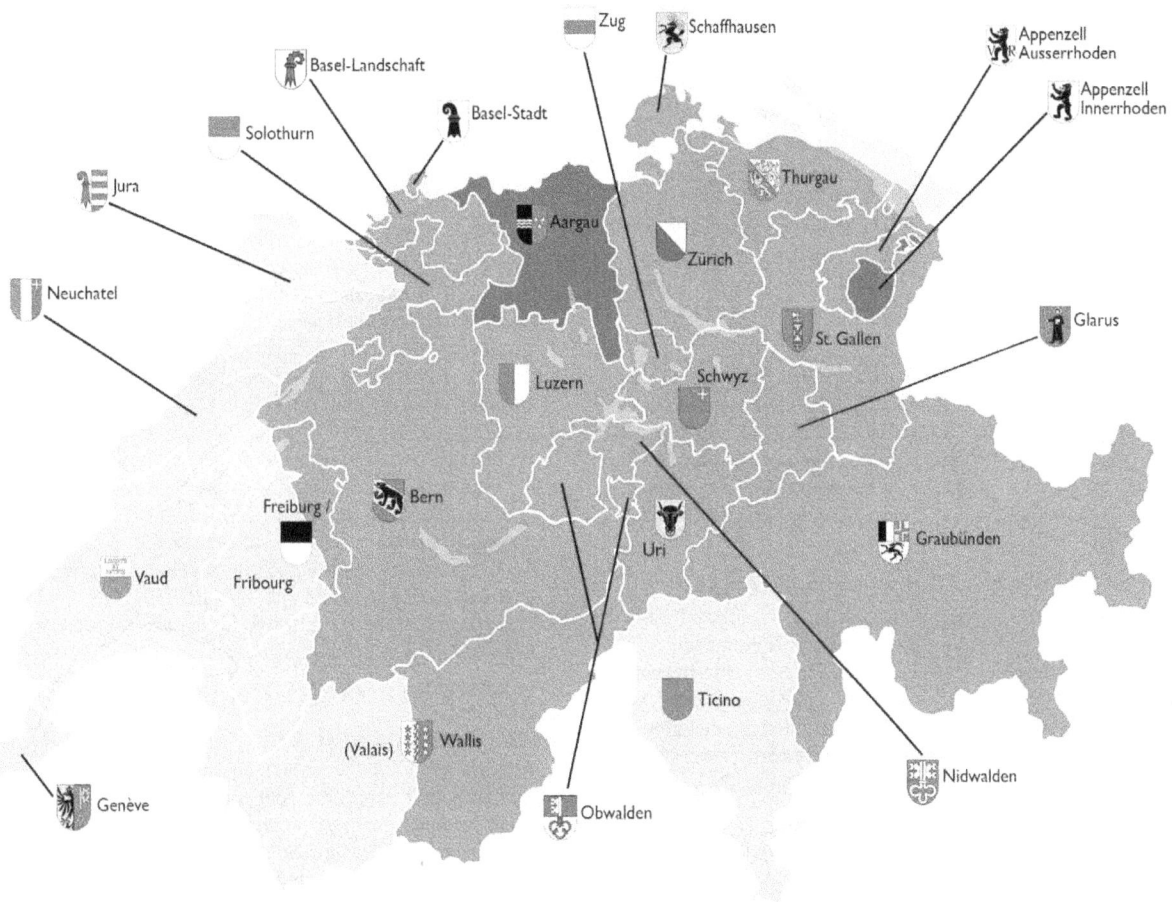

Figure 1. Cantons that will introduce LP 21. Green: Cantons that decreed the introduction of LP 21. Dark grey: Cantons where the decision is pending. Light grey: Cantons and francophone parts of cantons where LP 21 is not applicable.

offer teacher training. Among the few exceptions to date is the project "Primalogo-Programmieren an Primarschulen",[6] which was funded by the *Hasler foundation* as part of their *Fit in Informatik*-initiative. According to the project's website, it has exposed approximately 4'000 children and 100 teachers to programming with Logo[7] and thereby successfully introduced Computational Thinking (CT) and CSE in the primary school level. [14]

Regarding CSE initiatives on the level of the Swiss state, the implementation of the new LP 21 promises to have the greatest scope and impact and is therefore of the greatest importance for the comprehensive introduction of CSE in Swiss primary schools. The actual implementation of LP 21 proves to be highly difficult, however. Switzerland, with a population of eight million and located in the center of Europe is unique in many ways that bring about both great opportunities and challenges. It is a federal republic consisting of 26 cantons[8] and having four social national languages: German, French, Italian and Romansh (native speakers of this language are extremely few, and they all learn to speak German). The direct democracy and the state's highly federalist character are deeply rooted in the society and influence all aspects of life. All cantons' education systems differ considerably from one another, especially regarding compulsory education, which includes kindergarten, primary, and lower secondary school (total duration of approx. 11 years). Regarding the implementation of LP 21, each canton decides individually, if, when and how exactly it will implement it. To date, 19 of the 21 German-speaking cantons have agreed to implement at least some form of the new curriculum (see Figure 1).

One of the cantons that has already agreed to introduce a version of LP 21 in their schools and to change their curricula in order to include the elements of the module "Medien und Informatik", starting in the school year 2018/19, is the canton of Solothurn.[9]

---

[6] For details see http://primalogo.ch/

[7] For details see http://primalogo.ch/programmieren-primarschulen

[8] The 26 cantons are the member states of the Swiss Confederation. Each canton has its own constitution, legislature, government and courts. They are sovereign to the extent that

their sovereignty is not limited by federal law. The cantons also retain all powers and competencies not delegated to the Confederation by the constitution. Most significantly, the cantons are responsible for healthcare, welfare, law enforcement and public education; they also retain the power of taxation.

[9] For details see https://www.so.ch/verwaltung/departement-fuer-bildung-und-kultur/volksschulamt/lehrplan-21/

Conversely, in the two cantons of Aargau and Appenzell Innerrhoden the decision is still pending due to significant popular opposition against it.

While ICT topics such as Microsoft Office, which are currently taught in schools, are commonly seen as useful for a professional career, programming and other CS topics are often perceived as subjects that should only be taught at university. A related argument is that less than 30% of all students in Switzerland will pursue a tertiary education after school anyways [4], so why should something academic like CS be taught to everyone? When being informed about the role of CSE or specifically introductions to programming in schools, a common type of reaction encountered in teachers is "well, that's definitely something interesting to foster gifted students."

To summarize, in a federalist country like Switzerland it is difficult to achieve school reforms with a top-down approach, i.e. by introducing bills. Each canton is autonomous, and the final decision is often made by a popular vote. We need to consider the culture of the parents, students, and teachers. CS is commonly perceived as something academic or suitable for gifted students only.

1.2 Scalable Game Design in Switzerland

Scalable Game Design (SGD) Switzerland is located at the Institute of Primary Education at the school of education of the University of Applied Sciences and Arts Northwestern Switzerland (FHNW). This school of education, with approximately 3,000 students, is the institution responsible for certified teacher training in the four northwestern Swiss cantons of Aargau, Basel-Stadt, Basel-Land and Solothurn.

SGD Switzerland draws on the comprehensive research results and extensive experiences of the U.S. SGD project, which has successfully broadened computer science participation in the United States through engaging teachers and students in game and simulation design [1,11]. This research builds upon previous SGD work on engaging students in CSE with reference to cyberlearning [10] and CT. CT has a pivotal role in the SGD project. In its understanding and application of the concept of CT, the SGD project follows the both famous and widely acknowledged definition by Jeannette Wing who describes CT as the "cognitive processes involved in the formulation of a problem as well as in the representation of solutions, which can be carried out equally effectively by humans and machines" [16]. In line with Wing's definition, the SGD project considers CT a combination of mathematical-analytical thinking with natural sciences, engineering and other disciplines. In short, CT is conceptualized as *thinking with the computer*. It is regarded and employed as a way of thinking that uses the computer as an instrument to support the human thought process, to visualize the consequences of this thought process, and to formulate a problem so that a computer-supported solution can be introduced.

The didactic approach of SGD is based on a theory entitled the Zones of Proximal Flow [2], which combines Vygotsky's Zone of Proximal Development [15] with Csíkszentmihályi's theories on Flow [3]. The approach's central aim is to keep students motivated through simulation and game design and thereby optimize their learning success. SGD's comprehensive didactic approach with its focus on CT has resulted in the development, evaluation and providing of

- desktop and online programming environments that are specifically designed to teach and support CT and have been described as CT tools [13],

- tools for cyber learning,
- real time classroom management [1],
- implementation and evaluation of computational thinking [11],
- teacher professional development [11], and
- resources supporting low threshold/high ceiling curricula [2,9].

In the U.S., the SGD project has already helped over 20,000 students create their first games and simulations [11]. After over 20 years of research and teaching experience in the U.S., SGD extended its scope to Switzerland in 2014, when it was brought to the school of education at the FHNW. SGD Switzerland aims at adapting both contents and methods from the U.S. project to the specific affordances in Switzerland in order to expose Swiss teachers and students to STEM and CT through motivating game and simulation design activities. To this end, SGD Switzerland organizes the Swiss Computer Science Education Week [5,12], conducts teacher-training workshops and holds project workshops for students on different school levels. Supporting the implementation of the LP 21 in all its efforts and entertaining a long-term perspective that necessitates a sustainable strategy, SGD Switzerland also currently develops a curriculum for pre-service teacher training at the PH FHNW, which will be implemented in the form of two obligatory courses for all students of the Institute of Primary Education in 2017.

2. THE SOLOTHURN PROJECT

2.1 Concept and Aim

In preparation for the implementation of LP21, in the canton of Solothurn, and in order to find solutions about how to successfully accommodate the new curriculum needs, the CSE project "Scalable Game Design Solothurn" was developed. The project was designed and conducted by SGD Switzerland in collaboration with the office of compulsory education (Volksschulamt) of the canton of Solothurn. After learning about the SGD project and its multi-faceted, pedagogically thought-out curriculum of programming projects, the members of the Volksschulamt Solothurn decided that SGD would be an ideal method to introduce and teach CT on the primary school level. Choosing SGD's research-based and practice-oriented approach that exposes students to CT through the two CT Tools AgentSheets and AgentCubes online, the project's primary aim was to implement CSE in the primary schools of the canton of Solothurn.

2.2 Organization and Implementation

The project consisted of two parts: A continuing education training for the teachers followed by the introduction of the project and its techniques (i.e. teaching CT using SGD) by the teachers to their own students. The project's implementation started in the spring of 2014 and lasted until the autumn of 2016. According to the original planning, two groups were created, resulting from two recruitment efforts: group 1, with five teachers, all having classes on the primary level and group 2, with two teachers, one with a class in secondary school and the other on the primary school level.

The continuing education training consisted of seven meetings with each group. In the course of the first three to four meetings, the participating teachers went through an intensive training course on CT. Apart from a general introduction to the concept of CT, this training included a project-oriented introduction to the software (i.e., the CT tools AgentSheets and AgentCubes online) and didactic strategies for teaching CT. The participants were provided with extensive teaching resources both online and in the form of printouts. These included, among other things, detailed teacher guidelines for the introduction of coding activities in their classrooms, programming tutorials in step with actual teaching practice and easily adjustable according to individual students' skills, handouts for students and a set of debugging exercises. The training was intended to provide the participating teachers with sufficient knowledge, competences and self-confidence regarding the new contents and prepared them for teaching it to their students in their own classroom settings shortly afterwards. The teachers of group 1 used only AgentSheets both in their training and subsequently in their own classrooms with their students. In group 2, the teachers were additionally introduced to AgentCubes online, which they used as their tool to teach CT to their own classes.

The pedagogical concepts ensured that the majority of the students were highly motivated during classes, were able to work in teams as well as independently. The teaching methods introduced in the training were diverse and they were continuously revised in cooperation with the teachers and adapted to the local conditions. In parallel to their own training, the participating teachers began introducing the contents of the project to their classes. The focus of the subsequent meetings was more on exchanging experiences and receiving feedback from project leaders and the other participating teachers, regarding their own teaching activity.

2.3 Methods and Evaluation

In order to assess the success of the project and its suitability for a long-term inclusion of CSE in the educational curriculum of the primary school in the canton of Solothurn, a comprehensive evaluation was carried out. To this end, three questionnaires were developed and seven teachers, 133 students and 67 parents were surveyed. Of the students surveyed, 96 were from the primary school and 37 were from the secondary school. The quantitative questions were analyzed statistically, using the SPSS software for data analysis. The qualitative data were analyzed using a thematic analysis. Since the focus of the workshops differed not only amongst the teachers but also amongst the subsequent applications in the classroom, the data relating to workshop 1 (group 1) were analyzed in the presence of different trends separately from the data relating to workshop 2 (group 2). In addition, differences within group 2 between primary and secondary levels were observed. The latter differentiation was not relevant to group 1 since all students in that group were from the primary school level.

3. RESULTS

The project has proved to be successful in that, as expected, most students and especially the ones from the primary school level, showed great enthusiasm and motivation for programming. SGD is often associated with freedom in making your own decisions and working independently. The results are presented and discussed according to the three types of direct and indirect participants involved, i.e. teachers, students and parents.

3.1 Teachers

Most of the participating teachers and their students were, according to their own statements, highly motivated and profited very much from the continuing education, more specifically from the SGD teaching units. The analysis of the results paints a very positive picture of the project. After the training sessions, all seven surveyed teachers felt well to very well prepared for holding lessons in their own classes.

The participating teachers assessed the learning potential of SGD to be high (71.4 %) or even very high (28.6%). Also, all teachers thought that the lessons with SGD were received well (71.4%) or even very well (28.6%) by their students, which is in turn consistent with the statements of the students as well as of those of the parents. All seven teachers stated that game programming using AgentSheets / AgentCubes online promotes children's creativity and that they would recommend Scalable Game Design to their colleagues. The teachers also felt that the amount of time and effort required for the preparation of the actual lesson was low because of the quantity and quality of the teaching material provided. However, they would have liked to receive more practical examples of how to apply the material in special settings.

3.2 Students

The analysis of the results shows an equally positive picture among students. The vast majority of them (72.9%) said that they liked working with AgentSheets / AgentCubes online. Likewise, a large proportion (78.9%) of all students felt they had learned something new. These results vary according to age and school level and from teacher to teacher. For example, while only 56.8% of the secondary school students said they learned something new, 87.5% of the primary school students expressed that opinion. Looking only at the primary school students within group 2, the percentage of those saying they learned something new even goes up to 100% (see Figure 2).

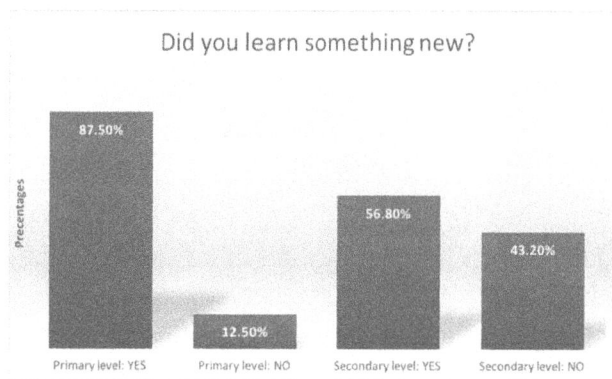

Figure 2: Did you learn something new? Percentages of the students' answer according to school level and type of response (yes or no).

Asked to describe what it was that they had learned, almost all students gave answers that can be related to learning programming and CT. Many students gave statements like "I learned programming" (66 mentions), "I can give/write a command" (4 mentions) and "I learned that you really have to program everything and that it does not work if you make a mistake" (5 mentions). Other answers were more directly related to the kind of project they were programming, i.e. versions of the 1980s Arcade Frogger or Pacman games. Those students said things like "I learned how to make/build a game" (11 mentions) and "I learned how to make something appear/disappear" (6 mentions).

The results also show that cooperation between the students was encouraged. Not only did almost all teachers testify to this, but also the statements of the students. A quarter of all students stated that they often sought help from other students when they encountered a problem. When asked if other children were able to help them when they needed assistance with the programming, a huge majority said yes (in group 1: 78.7% of all students; in group 2: 95,2% of all primary school students and 73.7% of all secondary school students). In a similar vein, most students expressed a high level of confidence in their ability to help other students in case they were asked for assistance. 73.3% of all students in group 1 confirmed that they were able to help others. The same is true for 71.4% of all primary school students and 73% of all secondary school students in group 2. Apart from proving a high level of co-operation between students during the programming classes, these answers also illustrate that students were very confident concerning the things they had only recently learned and are proof of the high learning potential of SGD.

The findings furthermore indicate that the students' motivation to continue working with AgentSheets/ AgentCubes online was generally rather high. This applies especially to the younger children who show the highest motivation. In order to determine the differences between the group mean values of the pupils' motivation for continuing working with AgentSheets/ AgentCubes online, we conducted a variance analysis with the dependent variable of motivation and the independent variable of teacher. The analysis showed a significant difference between the mean values. The post hoc tests (Scheffé) show that the class of teacher 1 in group 1 contains by far the most motivated students and significantly differs from all other teachers' classes. There are no significant differences between the other classes, however, partly because the motivation variance within the classes is relatively high (see Figure 3).

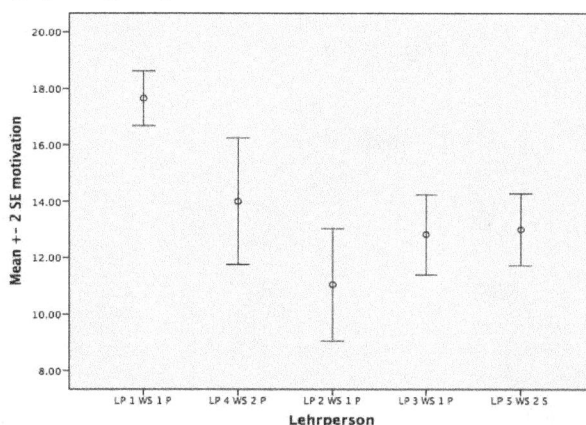

Figure 3. Motivation averages for continuing working with AgentSheets / AgentCubes online of the groups as defined by their teachers

When asked what they liked best about programming a game, the great majority of answers show that students appreciated the opportunity to freely use their imagination, be creative and work independently on their own projects/games. These results also coincide with the information given by the parents. The vast majority of parents of primary school students confirmed that their children were talking about SGD at home, saying that they had programmed a computer game (11 mentions) and had fun (13 mentions). This is an impressive argument for the special suitability of this project for primary schools.

3.3 Parents
The analysis of the data showed that parents have a very heterogeneous understanding of the term "Computer Science Education", expressing very different ideas about what their child had learned in the context of the project. Most parents assumed that their children learned general CS concepts and basic computer applications. 32% of the parents of students in the secondary level assessed the teaching of CS on that level as rather

not useful. This percentage is much higher than the one of the parents of students on the primary level, where only 11% from group 1 and 19% from group 2 made the same assessment. In that case more than 80% of the parents assessed CSE as useful to very useful and important for their children's future.

4. DISCUSSION
The analysis of the data clearly shows that CS taught with SGD is welcomed by teachers, students and parents on both primary and secondary levels. With regards to the continuing education for the teachers, the results indicate that teachers can easily learn to teach the subject of CS even if they do not have previous knowledge. Much depends upon the teacher's attitude and motivation as well as upon the provided educational material, didactic techniques and teaching tools. Even though the teachers who participated in the Solothurn project were enthusiastic for the most part, more research should focus on how we can make CS appealing to teachers so the latter can develop a more positive attitude. As for making the training more effective much attention should be given to the suggestions made and the needs expressed by the teachers who participated in the Solothurn training. For example making sure that in addition to theory the training provides more practical examples of how to apply the material in special settings. The more the content of the training is developed in cooperation with the teachers the more effective it will be.

Regarding the data from the students, even though all students expressed positive opinions, it is interesting that the primary level students were generally more motivated and more enthusiastic about the project. According to many teachers' comments, age can explain part of this differentiation because students after primary school level are generally more skeptical and less easily enthused by new things. However, still the fact remains: Primary level students are more likely to embark on CSE adventures. Introducing CSE on the secondary level might be too late. These are very important findings because they strongly suggest the necessity of introducing CT and CS as early as possible in a student's career, promising a both effective and sustainable interest in CT, CS and CS related fields. When children are familiarized with CSE already in their primary school years, they can be taught more advanced and more exciting CS subjects in secondary school, topics that are more in accordance with their interests and age. Following up on that, future research should be focusing on the further refinement of Computational Thinking tools that successfully capture the interests and affordances of secondary level students. When looking selectively at the data obtained only from the primary school students of both groups, it is striking that the students of teacher 1 in group 1 (left-most bar in figure 3) were by far the most motivated when asked if they wanted to continue working with AgentSheets/ AgentCubes online. We argue that this statistically significant variance can be explained by the specificities of the teacher and that the teacher's attitude towards the new subject plays a key role in raising (or lowering) the motivation levels of students.

Another factor that we think heavily influenced students' CSE experience was the kind of CT tool they used. A vast majority of the primary school students of group 2 expressed extremely positive opinions about their CSE learning experience. We argue that their exclusive usage of AgentCubes online was a significant factor towards their positive attitudes. More research is needed in order to investigate exactly what motivates students when using the various SGD tools as well as to understand the interactions between students and their teachers and their importance in the successful implementation of new educational subjects.

Finally, data analysis from the parents indicates that their lack of understanding of the concept of CT, may inhibit their children's interest and motivation and also may pose obstacles to the introduction of CSE into the Swiss school curriculum. More efforts should be made towards informing the parents about the benefits of CT. The fact that the majority of the parents of the primary level students showed a more positive attitude towards the importance of the subject might be an additional reason why the students were so positive towards it and vice versa. It also further supports our recommendation that CSE introduction should take place on the primary school level.

5. CONCLUSION

Even though CS is not an obligatory subject at any level in the Swiss education system yet, ICT knowledge is increasingly necessary not only for everyday activities but, more importantly, for building a successful future workforce. The Swiss education system is challenged to improve this situation. To this end, the aim of the CSE project "Scalable Game Design Solothurn" was to use a research-based and practice-oriented approach for introducing the field of CSE into selected classes using the two CT Tools AgentSheets and AgentCubes online. The project's main aim was to implement CT and CSE using SGD in the primary schools of the canton of Solothurn. The project succeeded in sufficiently training the teachers to teach CT to their students, who in turn learned basic concepts of CT. Analysis of the data shows that teaching CT through Scalable Game Design is not only feasible on the primary school level but also enjoyable. Our research also suggests that introducing CT concepts at the secondary level might be too late, recommending that instead, the key school level to a successful implementation of CSE to the Swiss education system is the primary school level. Improving the content of the continuing education training according to the teachers' requests and exploring further how to motivate more teachers, students, and parents and how to design age appropriate tools and teaching concepts are subjects to further research.

6. ACKNOWLEDGMENTS

This research has been funded by Swiss Hasler foundation and the National Science Foundation (G.No: 1138526, 0833612, 1312129). Any opinions, findings, and conclusions or recommendations expressed are those of the author(s) and do not necessarily reflect the views of the NSF.

7. REFERENCES

[1] Basawapatna, A. R., Repenning, A., and Koh, K. H. 2015. Closing the Cyberlearning Loop: Enabling Teachers to Formatively Assess Student Programming Projects. In *Proceedings of 46th ACM Technical Symposium on Computer Science Education*, SIGCSE '15: 12-17, New York, NY, USA.

[2] Basawapatna, A. R., Repenning, et al., 2013. The Zones of Proximal Flow: Guiding Students through a Space of Computational Thinking Skills and Challenges. In *Proceedings of 9th Annual International ACM Conference on International Computing Education Research*, ICER '13: 67-74.

[3] Csíkszentmihályi, M. 1977. *Beyond Boredom and Anxiety*. San Francisco: Jossey-Bass.

[4] Econlab (Braun, N. and Gmünder, M.). 2012. *Ict-Fachkräftesituation. Bildungsbedarfsprognose 2020. Schlussbericht*. ICT Berufsbildung Schweiz, Bern.

[5] Escherle, N. A., Assaf, D., Basawapatna, A. R., et al. 2015. Launching Swiss Computer Science Education Week. In *Proceedings of the 10th Workshop in Primary and Secondary Computing Education*, WIPSCE '15: 11-16.

[6] Federal Office of Communications (OFCOM). 2016. "Digital Switzerland" Strategy. Retrieved November 2, 2016, from https://www.bakom.admin.ch/dam/bakom/en/dokumente/ informationsgesellschaft/strategie/strategie_digitale_schweiz. pdf.download.pdf/strategie_digitale_schweiz_EN.pdf

[7] Federal Office of Communications (OFCOM). 2016. "Digital Switzerland" Action Plan. Retrieved November 2, 2016, from https://www.bakom.admin.ch/dam/bakom/en/ dokumente/informationsgesellschaft/strategie/aktionsplan_di gitale_schweiz.pdf.download.pdf/aktionsplan_digitale_schw eiz_EN.pdf

[8] Gehrig, M., Gardiol, L. & Schaerrer, M. 2010. Der MINT-Fachkräftemangel in der Schweiz. Ausmass, Prognose, konjunkturelle Abhängigkeit, Ursachen und Auswirkungen des Fachkräftemangels in den Bereichen Mathematik, Informatik, Naturwissenschaften, Technik. Büro Bass, Bern. Retrieved November 3, 2016, from http://www.buerobass.ch/ pdf/2010/SBF_2010_MINT_Schlussbericht.pdf

[9] Koh, K. H, Nickerson H., Basawapatna, A. R., and Repenning, A., 2014. Early Validation of Computational Thinking Pattern Analysis. In *Proceedings of the 2014 conference on Innovation & Technology in Computer Science Education*, ITICSE '14: 213-218.

[10] Pea, R. D. 2007. A Time for Collective Intelligence and Action: Grand Challenge Problems for Cyberlearning. In *NSF Cyberinfrastructure Team Workshop*, Washington, D.C.

[11] Repenning, A., Webb, D. C. , Koh, K. H. & al. 2015. Scalable Game Design: A Strategy to Bring Systemic Computer Science Education to Schools through Game Design and Simulation Creation. *ACM Transactions on Computing Education*, TOCE '15(2): 1-31.

[12] Repenning, A., Assaf, D., Basawapatna, A. R., et al. 2016. Retention of Flow: Evaluating a Computer Science Education Week Activity. In *Proceedings of the 47th ACM Technical Symposium on Computing Science Education*, SIGCSE '16: 631-638.

[13] Repenning, A., Basawapatna, A. R. and Escherle, N. A. 2016. Computational Thinking Tools. In *Proceedings of the IEEE Symposium on Visual Languages and Human-Centric Computing*, VL/HCC '16: 218-222.

[14] Serafini, Giovanni. 2011. Teaching Programming at Primary Schools: Visions, Experiences, and Long-Term Research Prospects. In *Proceedings of the 4th International Conference on Informatics in Schools: Situation, Evolution and Perspectives*, ISSEP '11: 143–154.

[15] Vygotsky, L.S. 1980. Mind in Society: The Development of Higher Psychological Processes. Harvard University Press.

[16] Wing, Jeannette M. 2006. Computational Thinking. In *Commun. ACM* 49(3): 33-35.

Computational Thinking in Italian Schools: Quantitative Data and Teachers' Sentiment Analysis after Two Years of "Programma il Futuro" Project

Isabella Corradini
Themis Research Centre
Rome, Italy
isabellacorradini@themiscrime.com

Michael Lodi
University of Bologna
Dep. of Comp. Science and Eng.
Bologna, Italy
michael.lodi2@unibo.it

Enrico Nardelli
University of Roma "Tor Vergata"
Department of Mathematics
Rome, Italy
nardelli@mat.uniroma2.it

ABSTRACT

In this paper the first two years of activities of "Programma il Futuro" project are described. Its goal is to disseminate among teachers in Italian primary and secondary schools a better awareness of informatics as the scientific basis of digital technologies. The project has adapted Code.org learning material and has introduced it to Italian schools with the support of a dedicated web site. Response has been enthusiastic in terms of participation: in two years more than one million students have been engaged and have completed a total of 10 million hours of informatics in schools. Almost all students found the material useful and were interested, teachers have reported. They have also declared to have experienced high satisfaction and a low level of difficulty. A detailed analysis of quantitative and qualitative data about the project is presented and areas for improvement are identified. One of the most interesting observations appears to corroborate the hypothesis that an exposure to informatics since the early age is important to attract students independently from their gender.

KEYWORDS

Computational thinking; Informatics education; Experience report

ACM Reference format:
Isabella Corradini, Michael Lodi, and Enrico Nardelli. 2017. Computational Thinking in Italian Schools: Quantitative Data and Teachers' Sentiment Analysis after Two Years of "Programma il Futuro" Project. In *Proceedings of ITiCSE'17, July 03-05, 2017, Bologna, Italy,*, 6 pages.
DOI: http://dx.doi.org/10.1145/3059009.3059040

1 INTRODUCTION

Digital technology pervades all aspects of human life and is based on an independent and recognized science: informatics ("computer science" in USA, "computing" in UK). Moreover, concepts and practices of informatics are used by researchers in a lot of fields, from other sciences to humanities. This approach to understand the world and solve complex problems is called *computational thinking* [11]: thinking like a computer scientist to solve problems. In the last decade, the awareness that computational thinking is a valuable skill for every human being has increased, and the introduction of informatics as a standard school subject is more and more discussed.

At school one learns Physics, Biology, History, Literature not (necessarily) to become a scientist, a writer, and so on, but to understand the world one lives in. Finding out what's behind technologies allows students to become informed citizens, and to better debate and decide on crucial issues like genetics, privacy, e-vote and so on. Moreover, a lot of the so-called "digital jobs" are unfilled because of the lack of prepared workforce. To cover this vacancy, a broad education in computing is mandatory. More specifically, to increase the number of students (and in particular underrepresented categories such as women) who choose to graduate in Computing disciplines, an early exposition during K-12 to the basis of informatics is required so as they can fully understand and - if the case - appreciate it.

Informatics is a powerful way to describe and comprehend the world: Denning and Rosenbloom have coined the expression "the fourth great domain", putting computing on par with physical, life, and social sciences as a way to grasp what is so about the world [1]. It is also a good learning tool: to "teach" the computer how to solve a problem, you have to fully understand problem domain, issues and strategies to solve it. Knuth wrote *"It has often been said that a person does not really understand something until he can teach it to someone else. Actually, a person does not really understand something until he can teach it to a computer"* [5]. Moreover, informatics offers a constructive strategy for problem solving.

Currently, the most widespread methodology to teach computational thinking is teaching to program, often with languages and environments suitable for learner's age and experience (for example, for young children and beginners, environments where instruction are not textual code but visual elements that must be combined together to create a videogame or an animation). Another widespread methodology involves the so called *unplugged activities* (the most famous is New Zealand CS Unplugged[1]) where students are taught computer science concepts like algorithms, information encoding, cryptography and so on through traditional games that don't need technology but material like pen and paper or simply student's own bodies. Particularly interesting for computational thinking are games where one child embodies the programmer and another one the programmed agent. Lastly, the use of educational robots that must be programmed is also dramatically increasing.

---

[1] http://csunplugged.org/

In recent years, no-profit organizations, volunteer movements and also private initiatives aiming at spreading computational thinking to young people flourished. Most of them are of high quality and have helped to gain institutions and media attention on computational thinking. But they can't afford to provide informatics education to all: K-12 public educational system has to take in charge this ambitious target.

Having recognized the importance of a broad informatics education [3], many countries are making efforts to introduce it at all school levels. Some example are United States [4], United Kingdom [10], France [2] and many other countries.

In Italy, the Ministry of University, Education and Research (MIUR) and the National Interuniversity Consortium for Informatics (CINI – a consortium made up of all Italian research universities active in Informatics) agreed, in March 2014, to launch the three-years project "Programma il Futuro" ("Program the Future") [7] to change the way informatics is taught in Italian schools. The objective to introduce computational thinking in primary and secondary school is explicitly stated in the school reform approved by the Italian Parliament in 2015 [8] whose operational plan for what concerns digital technology is defined in the subsequent Italian National Plan for Digital Education (Piano Nazionale Scuola Digitale — PNSD): "a policy launched [...] for setting up a comprehensive innovation strategy across Italy's school system and bringing it into the digital age"[2]. It was therefore important to stress that all digital technologies are rooted in a scientific discipline, informatics, independent from other sciences. "Programma il Futuro" was set up mainly to address this goal and to bring teachers and students closer to the fundamental concepts of informatics.

The project "Programma il Futuro" is explored in detail in Section 3. It is based on materials from Code.org organization, which is briefly outlined in Section 2.

2 CODE.ORG

Unlike UK, where computer science is a mandatory subject for all primary and secondary schools, until 2013 very few USA states had computer science in school curricula, in spite of being probably the most advanced country in IT technology. To counter this situation, the no-profit organization Code.org[3] launched in the same year the "Hour of Code" project, with the initial goal of having each student in the world do at least one hour of programming and, in perspective, the final goal of having for each student a proper education in computer science.

Code.org developed teaching material made up of online interactive web tutorials, featuring famous video games and cartoons characters, highly attractive for students. To define a program you have to combine visual blocks, based on Blockly library[4], much like it happens in Scratch [6] and in other visual programming environments. But differently from Scratch, where a student is exposed since the beginning to the entire set of instructions and has complete freedom in the artifact to realize, here the student is given specific tasks. The initial exercises are very trivial (e.g. have a bird move straight of 3 steps) and the set of available instructions

is very small (e.g. "move forward", "turn left/right"). Then, the difficulty degree increases very slowly from one exercise to the next, and instructions and programming structures are progressively added to the set. If the student is not able to successfully complete an exercise, the system provides some feedback, useful for self-correction. Students are thus increasingly exposed to the basic concepts of informatics (gradually introduced while reinforcing the previous ones) without being distracted by technical or syntactical details. A teacher is therefore able to follow her students during these tutorials with little specific training in informatics. Moreover, since students may have their own accounts to execute activities, they are able to learn keeping the pace better matching their needs.

Web tutorial are interspersed with *unplugged* activities that teach or reinforce important informatics concepts. Printable material and a detailed lesson plans are provided.

Teaching material and curriculum progression have been defined keeping in mind the K-12 Computer Science Framework[5], developed by ACM, CSTA, CIC, NMSI and Code.org itself.

Code.org tries to provide the first elements of a basic education in computer science to all students while an adequate number of teachers trained in that topic is not available. Its action addresses every classroom in a school, every children – both males and females – regardless their ability, family means or cognitive status.

Code.org had, in its first school-year alone, more than 40 million students doing their first hour of coding all around the world, and each year the participation doubled.

3 THE "PROGRAMMA IL FUTURO" PROJECT

3.1 The Project

The project "Programma il Futuro" (PIF, from now on) has a lifespan of three school-years, starting from 2014-15.

The initiative has been framed and presented in term of learning *computational thinking* as a key competence for modern education, so as to stress the importance of the cultural value of informatics more than its technical and technological aspects. Bear in mind that before this initiative, informatics teaching in primary school in Italy was mainly based on learning how to use word processors and spreadsheets.

PIF project is based on the teaching material developed by Code.org, described in Section 2. All Italian teachers are invited at the beginning of each school-year to use it in their classes, at least for one hour. Participation is optional and any teacher is encouraged to do the experience, whichever is her own teaching subject. This approach was chosen due to its scalability characteristics. By leveraging on-site teachers and well suited online teaching material it is possible to faster bring to action a much larger number of students.

In perspective, the project aims to facilitate the establishment of an adequate informatics education in all school levels in Italy.

While targeting primarily teachers and students, initiative has also addressed adult population, according to the principle that education in fundamental concepts in informatics has both an intrinsic intellectual value and a practical role in understanding the IT basis of today's societal mechanisms. The project material is used also in adults' training centres, out-of-school education initiatives and for self-learning, even by the elderlies.

[2]http://www.istruzione.it/scuola_digitale/allegati/2016/pnsd_en.pdf
[3]https://code.org/
[4]https://developers.google.com/blockly/
[5]https://k12cs.org/

3.2 Material

PIF translated the textual material of all the tutorials (both online exercises and unplugged activities), paying particular attention to scientific precision and consistency.

PIF implemented a support website[6] referred to by the Italian subdomain of Code.org[7] to allow teachers building an Italian community of users. Following a carefully designed communication plan and an iterated development approach, the site provides a comprehensive guide for teachers.

There are six main sections in the website: *Il progetto* ("The project"), with a general description of the project, of its background and motivations, of its theoretical foundations; *Chi* ("Who"), with specific information for the participation of different kind of users (teachers, students, others); *Percorsi* ("Paths"), with a description of available courses and teaching materials; *La comunità* ("The Community"), where users can find useful information to connect each others and share experiences; *Notizie* ("News") where press material and news about institutional events related to the project is collected; *Aiuto* ("Help") where users can ask for technical or educational support, interact in a forum, find tips to guide an activity with students.

In particular, in the *Percorsi* section, for each course and lesson of the courses proposed by Code.org a detailed webpage (in Italian) explains concepts taught in that lesson and its general and specific learning objectives. Additionally, for each lesson, a video tutorial in Italian has been realized to provide a step-by-step guidance to any user towards a successful completion of the activities. All video tutorials and other communication material is available on the project's YouTube channel.

The forum is structured in a set of threads, some of general nature (e.g., how to manage a class), others focused on the various available courses.

Teachers have the possibility of organizing, through the website, local meetings to discuss among themselves problems and solutions to teach informatics to students.

3.3 Organization

PIF operations are entirely supported by a set of companies financing it with different amounts of money and providing also volunteers that donate part of their working time to help schools in moving the first steps in a territory which is new and unknown for many of their teachers.

MIUR has given its endorsement to the project and at the beginning of each school-year officially invites all schools to participate by sending them a ministerial circular. This has been essential for a country where school organization and curricula are defined mostly at the state level.

Also important has been the constant support of a bipartisan group of Members of the Italian Parliament (Intergruppo Innovazione – Intergroup for Innovation), some of whom have even recorded a video where they code together with kids.

In 2016, the project has been recognized as a European outstanding initiative for digital education and awarded with one of the European Digital Skills Awards[8].

Many communication events have been held during the life of the project, which have been essential to increase its knowledge among teachers and parents. A prestigious one has been the opening of the second year, held at the Italian Chamber of Deputies, hosting as special guest Hadi Partovi, CEO and founder of Code.org. Moreover, since the beginning of the third school-year PIF has won the support of an international basketball star, Marco Belinelli, playing in NBA.

The project constantly interacts with end users through its social channelsand teachers can report and publish their first-hand experiences related to coding in theirs classes.

4 PARTICIPATION DATA

Since the first year (school-year 2014-15), Italian teachers have been highly reactive to the initiative, making Italy the most active non-english speaking country for what regards informatics education in school, at least in terms of participation to the CSEd week[9].At the end of school-year 2015-16 about 14,000 teachers in more than 4,000 schools had involved more than 1 million students (about one eighth of Italian students) in the activities. Project participation has tripled from the first to the second school-year and a similar trend for the current school-year is expected.

Considering both the two school-years, students have collectively done about 10 million hours of coding. In particular, during school-year 2014-15 students worked for a total of 1,657,101 hours (avg 5.4 hours per student), while during the next year (2015-16) students worked for 8,654,100 hours (8.5 per student), a more than five-fold increase.

Details of participation are described by the four charts in Figure 1, showing trends for schools, teachers, classes, and students.

5 PROJECT MONITORING

5.1 Data Collection

The project monitors progresses two times a year through a questionnaire sent to all teachers, first in December, right after the CSEd week, and then in May, a few weeks before the end of school year[10].

The questionnaire collects descriptive data about teachers and their classes/schools, quantitative data about students participation to coding activities, and qualitative feedback. A few optional questions are open and are intended to investigate both positive and negative sentiments of teachers with respect to the project.

The percentage of answers received has always been high (15% to 17% for 2014-15; 21% to 24% for 2015-16; number of recipients for each of the four questionnaires is shown in graph "teachers" in figure 1), providing a good confidence that values and comments received are reasonably representative of the situation of the entire population.

---

[6]http://www.programmailfuturo.it/
[7]https://italia.code.org/

[8]https://ec.europa.eu/digital-single-market/en/news/16-outstanding-projects-european-digital-skills-award-2016-final
[9]https://hourofcode.com
[10]http://programmailfuturo.it/progetto/monitoraggio-del-progetto

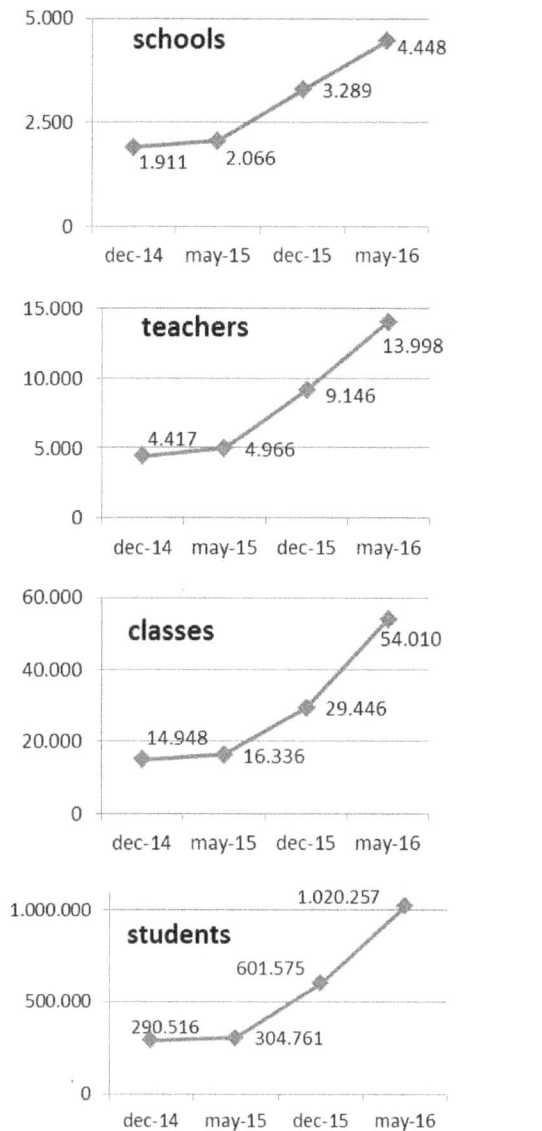

Figure 1: Students, teachers, classes and students participation.

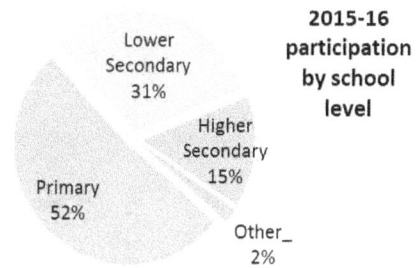

Figure 2: Participation by school level.

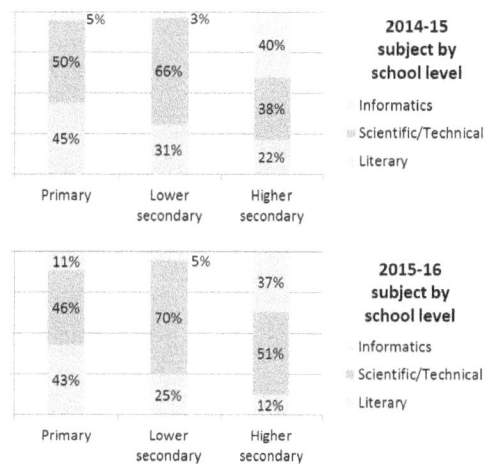

Figure 3: Teachers' subject distribution by school level.

5.2 Quantitative Data Analysis

In school-year 2015-16, more than half of teachers was in primary school, and almost a third in lower secondary (see Fig. 2) while in the previous year there was a higher percentage of primary school teachers (56%) at the expense of lower secondary one (27%).

It is interesting to observe the different distribution of subjects taught by the teachers involved in the project according to the different level of school. Subjects have been classified in two large groups: literary and scientific/technical, while informatics has been considered on its own. Please note that both in primary and lower secondary school generally informatics is not an independent subject. The distribution (shown in the two charts in Fig. 3) does not significantly change between the two school-years. It is a highly

positive element the fact that also teachers of literary subjects have involved themselves in bringing computational thinking to the attention of their students.

It was asked to teachers to evaluate how useful was the activity for their students on a 4-point Likert scale: 98% of them answered "useful" or "very useful". It was also asked them to evaluate how interested were their students during activities: 98% of them answered "interested" or "very interested". These outcomes are essentially the same in the two school-years.

Teachers were asked to evaluate whether in their classes students were equally interested by the activities irrespective of their gender, or females/males were more interested. Results, shown in the chart in Fig. 4, are similar across the two school-years and exhibit an increasing polarization when students grow up.

Similarly, teachers were asked to evaluate effectiveness of students in executing activities with respect to their gender. Also in this case the results, shown in the chart in Fig. 5, are similar across the two school-years: the older the students are, the higher is the polarization.

We think both results, hinting that informatics acceptance has a higher independence from gender when pupils are younger, provide some support for the importance of exposing students to it at an early age.

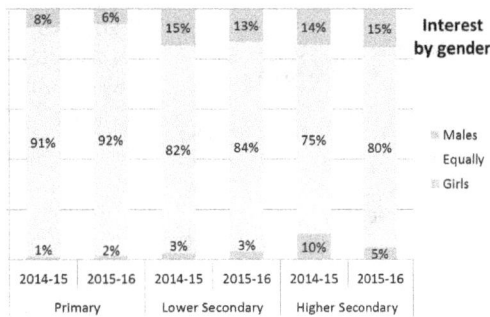

Figure 4: Interest by gender.

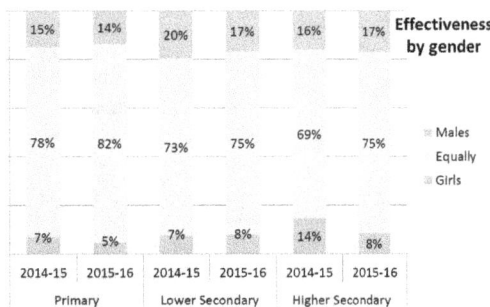

Figure 5: Effectiveness by gender.

5.3 Qualitative Data Analysis

We now discuss the sentiment analysis regarding teachers' answers to open questions.

Positive sentiments were explored by two open questions: "Describe the most positive factors in the project" and "Provide a reason to suggest participation to a colleague". A total of 1,342 (resp. 1,313) answers, across the two school-years, have been provided to the first (resp. second) question.

In a first phase, all answers were processed by the authors and divided if they contained more than one concept. We thus obtained a total of 1,523 (resp. 1,551) single concept sentences. All sentences were analysed again by the authors to identify recurring themes, that were found to be common to both groups of answers. These became the clusters used to classify sentences. Finally, each single concept sentence was manually assigned to one of the clusters. Here is the short name and description of the most relevant ones:

- *Cognitive stimulation and cognitive development* (promotion of awareness and comprehension of: computational thinking, problem solving, logical thinking, creativity, attention, planning ability, ...)
- *Motivation and participation* (motivation for learning, students interest, students and teachers involvement, cooperation between students)
- *Methodological aspects* (effective outcomes, ludic learning, innovative approach for teaching informatics, inclusive didactics)
- *Quality of instructional material* (well prepared, attractive, structured for gradual learning)

Table 1: Cluster distribution of positive sentiment answers

	Positive factors	Reasons to suggest
Cognitive	20%	26%
Motivation	32%	26%
Methodological	20%	26%
Quality	18%	9%

In both groups (see Table 1) *Motivation and participation* is the most frequent cluster, while also *Cognitive stimulation and cognitive development* and *Methodological aspects* play an important role. Cluster *Quality of instructional material* is perceived more as a "positive factor" then as a "reason to suggest", which is a viewpoint coherent with teachers' pedagogical perspective.

Other interesting answers by teachers, not included in the most relevant clusters, warrant deeper consideration and analysis in further works. For example, some teachers stressed the positive consequences in terms of attention improvement for students with concentration difficulties.

Negative sentiments were first explored by means of a follow-up open question to a yes/no question: "Have you experienced difficulties?". Furthermore, a yes/partly/no question: "Has the project matched your expectations?" is followed with an open question asking for clarifications, in case of partly or total mismatch. A total of 334 (resp. 275) answers, across the two school-years, have been provided to the first (resp. second) question.

The lower number of answers to these questions (roughly speaking, the total number of negative remarks is about one quarter of the total number of positive ones) is a clear indication of the general satisfaction of teachers with project activities. Indeed, 91% of teachers did not report any difficulty during school-year 2015-16 (it was 88% in 2014-15), and 84% of teachers were fully satisfied in 2015-16 (82% in 2014-15).

A first analysis of answers to the two open questions investigating negative sentiments showed that the kind of remarks were similar. It was therefore decided to merge the two sets and carry out a cluster analysis on the whole set, using the same methodological approach used for positive sentiment analysis. Multiple concept answers were simplified in 786 single concept sentences, that were manually partitioned in disjoint clusters.

We now list the most relevant topics resulting from this analysis, with a short name, a description and its ratio in the overall distribution:

- *Technical problems* (34%) (Obsolete or too few devices, absent or very slow Internet connection, ...)
- *Teacher training* (18%) (Lack of personal knowledge to solve the exercises or to prepare an adequate lesson plan with specific computational thinking learning objectives, too little time to self-train, absence of specific training courses, difficulties with English-written material, ...)
- *Organizational and logistic problems* (16%) (Mainly lack of time to teach the material during lessons due to an already crowded school schedule)

All these clusters point to infrastructural problems, that are independent from scientific issues concerning informatics education.

Other clusters, with a lower ratio, can provide useful hints for actions aiming at introducing informatics education at all school levels in Italy. In particular we found other four main topics:

- *Limitations of platform and support site* (11%) (Both technical problems or lack of features of Code.org and problems with the support site, sometimes stated as not clear or too verbose)
- *Quality/level of teaching material* (10%) (Material too easy or too difficult - and so not engaging - for the specific age level of the students)
- *Curriculum and didactics* (6%) (Teaching effects not clear or visible, difficulties in integration with standard curriculum, lack of creativity in activities - often compared to Scratch)
- *Colleagues/parents involvement and support* (5%) (Lack of support from colleagues during the activities or from parents at home)

Issues related to *Curriculum and didactics* are the most relevant ones to move from a stimulus action phase to a full operational one.

A final open optional question asked for "Observations and suggestions": most of its answers have been positive, stressing the importance of computational thinking education in Italian schools and showing willingness to continue activities, even proceeding in autonomy. The main request for improvement has been to provide the italian dubbing of videos accompanying the courses.

We finally provide a few literal quotations from teachers, highlighting some of the discussed positive outcomes:

- *"The ludic nature of activities has been able to create unexpected interest and motivation in students"*
- *"Students have been able to better understand what computers can do: there is more in information technology beyond game consoles"*
- *"I have observed improvement in observation and reflection skills: students have been able to find alternative solutions"*
- *"Students felt themselves in the spotlight of activities and were gratified by the immediate feedback"*
- *"Parents have appreciated the possibility of continuing activities at home"*

6 CONCLUSIONS AND FUTURE PERSPECTIVES

Outcomes of project monitoring show that informatics education is a highly interesting theme for both teachers and students and that in a short time span the proposed teaching material has been adopted, used, and appreciated in a significant number of classes. We therefore think that appropriateness of teaching material is a key factor to bring informatics education in schools.

Hence the project is on track to meet the goal of spreading among school teachers more awareness of the principles, concepts and methods of informatics.

Concerning competence acquisition by students, we do not have a formal measure of their progresses in the project, since the Code.org material does not include a set of assessment tools. Clearly, since learning material is partitioned into very small chunks and later exercises require having learned previous concepts and skills, progressing in courses is a good proxy indication of actual competence acquisition. How to carry out in schools the measurement of the acquisition of the various informatics competences is an open problem, to be tackled by joint efforts by computer scientists and pedagogists.

Another important issue, raised by some teachers, is how to merge the "closed" teaching paths provided by Code.org material with the need of providing more "open" venues, where both teachers and students are able to give space to their creativity. This issue, and the more general one whether it is better a "puzzle based" or a "project based" approach to informatics education, is also highly debated in the research community [9].

Finally, two issues of systemic and institutional nature are informatics curricula for different school levels and teachers training. They are clearly intertwined, since for each school level teachers have to be prepared to teach what students should learn at that level. Computer scientists can cooperate toward this goal, but the final responsibility is under the power of governmental institutions.

ACKNOWLEDGMENTS

We greatly thank teachers and students involved in our project and Code.org for its cooperation.

We acknowledge the financial support of TIM; Engineering; CA Technologies, Cisco, De Agostini Scuola; Andinf, ANP, SeeWeb. Other companies have financially supported the project during the first two school-years only: Samsung Italia; Microsoft Italia; Hewlett-Packard; Oracle; Facebook.

Rai Cultura, the culture department of Italian national public broadcasting company, is a media partner of the project since February 2017.

REFERENCES

[1] Peter J. Denning and Paul S. Rosenbloom. 2009. Computing: The Fourth Great Domain of Science. *Commun. ACM* 52, 9 (Sep 2009), 27. DOI : http://dx.doi.org/10.1145/1562164.1562176
[2] Académie des Sciences. 2013. L'enseignement de l'informatique en France: Il est urgent de ne plus attendre. http://www.academie-sciences.fr/pdf/rapport/rads_0513.pdf
[3] Informatics Europe and ACM Europe. 2013. Informatics education: Europe cannot afford to miss the boat. http://europe.acm.org/iereport/ACMandIEreport.pdf
[4] National Science Foundation. 2016. Initiative "Computer Science For All". http://www.nsf.gov/csforall
[5] Donald E. Knuth. 1974. Computer Science and Its Relation to Mathematics. *The American Mathematical Monthly* 81, 4 (Apr 1974), 323. DOI : http://dx.doi.org/10.2307/2318994
[6] John Maloney, Mitchel Resnick, Natalie Rusk, Brian Silverman, and Evelyn Eastmond. 2010. The Scratch Programming Language and Environment. *Trans. Comput. Educ.* 10, 4, Article 16 (Nov. 2010), 15 pages. DOI : http://dx.doi.org/10.1145/1868358.1868363
[7] Enrico Nardelli and Giorgio Ventre. 2015. Introducing Computational Thinking inn Italian Schools: A First Report on "Programma Il Futuro" Project. In *INTED2015 Proceedings (9th International Technology, Education and Development Conference)*. IATED, 7414–7421.
[8] Italian Parliament. 2015. Reform of the national system of education and training (Law n.107, July 13th, 2015).
[9] Mitchel Resnick and David Siegel. 2015. A Different Approach to Coding. *Bright/Medium* (2015).
[10] The Royal Society. 2012. Shut Down or Restart? The Way Forward for Computing in UK Schools. https://royalsociety.org/~/media/education/computing-in-schools/2012-01-12-computing-in-schools.pdf
[11] Jeannette M. Wing. 2006. Computational Thinking. *Commun. ACM* 49, 3 (March 2006), 33–35. DOI : http://dx.doi.org/10.1145/1118178.1118215

Computing Curriculum in Middle Schools
- An Experience Report

Samah Al Sabbagh
Computer Science
Carnegie Mellon University
Doha, Qatar
ssabbagh@cmu.edu

Huda Gedawy
Computer Science
Carnegie Mellon University
Doha, Qatar
hgedawy@cmu.edu

Hanan Alshikhabobakr
Computer Science
Carnegie Mellon University
Doha, Qatar
halshikh@cmu.edu

Saquib Razak
Computer Science
Carnegie Mellon University
Doha, Qatar
srazak@cmu.edu

ABSTRACT

This paper explores the results of a piloting and field-testing of Alice in the Middle East (Alice ME), a computing curriculum for students in Middle Schools in Qatar. Alice ME is a project aimed at designing and delivering a Qatari context appropriate computing curriculum using Alice software. Curricular materials and professional development were created to help participating teachers deliver the course. An evaluation of the effectiveness of the implementation was carried out during all stages of the project. Results show that students who studied computing through Alice ME showed an improvement in their critical thinking and problem solving skills. Moreover, students and teachers became more motivated to learn programing as a result. This paper suggests best practices in teacher training and CS teaching in K-12 schools in Qatar in addition to sharing lessons learned from the process.

CCS Concepts

• Social and professional topics~K-12 education

Keywords

Alice; Curriculum Evaluation; K-12; Computational Thinking.

1. INTRODUCTION

Rapid advancement in technology, including big data and data analytics, has caused a major shift in industry. Uber for example, is one of the biggest taxi companies but yet do not own a single taxicab. It makes millions of drives per day while functioning on a completely digital business model [1]. Due to this trend, business opportunities is becoming extremely reliable on the feasibility of digitizing services. In order to fulfil the technical expertise requirement, some countries started strengthening their education system in the area of computing education. In the US for instance, the National Science Foundation started the CS 10K program aimed at training 10 thousand high school teachers to teach CS. Moreover, various school systems around the world are shifting their curriculum from Information and Communication Technology (ICT) applications to computing. In England for example, they recently reintroduced CS as a mandatory subject at the secondary school level whilst the Singaporean government also directed their Ministry of Education to create CS curriculum for schools. In addition, research groups had put some effort in CS education, like ISSEP conference, ACM CSTA work, Koli group, etc.

ITiCSE '17, July 03-05, 2017, Bologna, Italy
© 2017 ACM. ISBN 978-1-4503-4704-4/17/07…$15.00
DOI: http://dx.doi.org/10.1145/3059009.3059012

Until very recently, the focus on preparing a computer science educated generation has been largely for tertiary education, while computing education in K-12 was limited. Hence, we know very little on teaching methods, curriculum, and teacher training required to teach the subject to a general student population. Qatar is a single-state nation having a ministry of education and higher education (MOE&HE) that manages the educational system of the entire country. In an effort to promote computing education in younger generations, we needed to work with the ministry to provide us with the opportunity to influence CS educational standards at a national level. The Qatari government recognized the importance of computing "know-how" and aims to become a leader in educational innovation in the Middle East. Qatar's vision for a knowledge-based society was the driver that brought this project to life.

In this project, we created a computing curriculum for middle school students in Qatari schools that was focused on introducing computing, logic and communication skills in the context of animations and games using Alice which is a 3D programming environment [2]. Alice showed promising results with novice programmers in the middle school level, especially females [3]. Our curriculum was piloted in one private school where English was the medium of instruction, as well as two public schools that used Arabic. A successful piloting resulted in our project proceeding to the field testing stage on a wider scale to include eleven different schools. Two years of successful implementation of this curriculum has resulted in MOE&HE adapting Alice based computing curriculum as the standard ICT curriculum in public schools. For the next academic year, MOE&HE will implement the curriculum in all of its 40 high schools as an elective. It is expected that 4000 students will be signing up to study this curriculum. We also extended the curriculum allowing the use of textual programming after learning the fundamental concepts using Alice. Our initial results indicated a successful transition to textual programming for middle school students. We refer the readers to our earlier papers for details about the curriculum [4] [5] [6]. A large part of our previous work included an effort to localize the Alice tool to better fit the Middle Eastern context. Adaptation efforts were focused on making the tool culturally suitable and more conservative in nature [6]. Incorporating Middle Eastern adaptations in the tool yielded positive results during the earlier pilot studies.

This paper presents our experience in implementing the Alice-based computing curriculum in local schools in Qatar. In an effort to make the learning experience more comprehensive, we trained ICT teachers on the new curriculum and created instructional materials. We discuss the challenges faced in teacher training. We also present our findings outlining our overall experience in the project. As computing education is taking root all over the world, we hope that researchers and educational specialists looking for means to implement a curriculum suitable for their local environment can learn from our experience.

2. TEACHER TRAINING

While the goal of all education reforms should be student improvement, a successful reform initiative must begin with recognizing the importance of teachers in raising student performance [7]. Thus there is a global consensus that an effective professional development is one that focuses on developing the essential traits of an effective teacher [8]. A pre-requisite to running a successful professional development is the administration and teachers' belief that this particular professional development will make a difference in their practice. Harwell called this step the 'buy-in', which refers to believing in the successful outcomes of the professional development offered [9]. In essence professional development coupled with strong administrative buy-in, aims at enhancing teachers' understanding of the content area they teach. It should provide teachers with a range of strategies that enables them to deliver knowledge to their students. In our study we needed to guarantee buy-in from the MOE&HE and so to begin our process we approached them with strong evidence about the advantages of running the Alice ME program. We wanted to gain access to schools as well as ensure that our participating teachers are properly equipped with the skills and knowledge in the content area of computer programming.

2.1 What Research Says

Research show that a good professional development is one that provides teachers with the skills necessary to teach and assess students' deeper understanding and develop them in a particular area of study. Although developing student skills is important, it is not sufficient to run an effective professional development program. There are factors that are consistent amongst most research studies contributing to conducting an effective professional development program. The most important factors as summarized by Darling-Hammond and her colleagues dictate that there are three aspects to running a successful professional development [8]. The first is that professional development should be intensive, ongoing, and connected to practice. This means that professional development that entails applications of knowledge to teachers' planning and instruction is a strong influencer of teaching practices and will lead to better student learning. The second indicates that professional development should focus on student learning and address the teaching of specific curriculum. In many ways research shows that concentrating on addressing the concrete, everyday challenges involved in teaching and learning, is more important than focusing on teaching methods taken out of context. The final aspect that needs to be considered is building strong working relationships among teachers. They stressed that professional learning can have a powerful effect on teacher skills and knowledge and will in turn have a positive effect on student learning if it is sustained over time, focused on important content, and embedded in the work of professional learning communities [8].

Higgens also described what needs to be considered when delivering any professional development. He identifies factors contributing to the success of any training session and explained that successful facilitators are ones who [10]: 1) introduce new knowledge and skills, 2) help participants access the theory and evidence underlying the relevant pedagogy, 3) help participants believe better outcomes are possible, 4) make the link between professional learning and pupil learning explicit through discussion of pupil progress, 5) support teachers through modelling, 6) providing observation and feedback and coaching.

Many professional development trainings around the world are conducted in the form of workshops. This traditional way of training has proven to be least successful in delivering trainings. Courses, and conferences are other traditional forms of professional development that share many of the features of workshops. They take place outside of the teacher's school and involve a leader with special expertise and participants attending at scheduled times [11].

2.2 Our Experience

In our initial evaluation of teachers, we found that most ICT teachers in Qatar in both public and private schools are trained ICT professionals who were mostly teaching computer applications. We found that although teachers did not have experience in teaching programming, they had to have studied most of the programming topics in the past. Teachers whom we worked with have never taught fundamental programming concepts to their students and therefore were not given the opportunity to develop this knowledge further in their field of work. We needed to refresh participating teachers' programming knowledge and help them understand how to use it in Alice. For example, we covered topics such as variables and loops in which teachers were familiar with but needed to access it through their prior knowledge and see the relevance of its application using Alice. Subsequently we perceived a need for professional development workshops aimed at preparing teachers to deliver programming knowledge and skills to students.

In an effort to carry out an effective professional development, we conducted several workshops to prepare teachers for using Alice during the pilot phase of the study. We offered 45 teachers from 15 different schools two workshops (three days in length each) to equip them with the necessary skills to be able to use the tool and deliver the curriculum. The first workshop was an introduction to Alice tool and the textbook. After the first training participating teachers were given a period of two months to get more familiar with using Alice and to learn more about its features and capabilities. Same teachers were then offered a second workshop at the start of the implementation phase to discuss topics and techniques that allowed them to understand how to teach computing and problem solving strategies to students using Alice.

2.3 Accomplishments

The first phase in implementing a highly effective professional development training in our case was achieving buy-in from the MOE&HE since it has a direct authority over public schools in Qatar. As described by research mentioned earlier, the process of "buy-in" is an important first step [9]. We presented the MOE&HE with a study done at the university level showcasing an increase in student performance by two grade levels after studying computing through Alice. The MOE&HE selected two schools for piloting the program. The success of the program in these two schools resulted in us getting access to more schools in the following academic year.

Although we resorted to the workshop model of training, we were successful in covering many of the factors contributing to successful professional development. If we measure our professional development training against Higgens' measures of successful facilitators, we find that although our training focused mainly on the first three conditions, it also covered most of the measures to some extent. For example, introducing new knowledge underpinned by theory, strong evidence and clear rational was accomplished through carrying out teacher discussions on the importance of computing education during our training sessions. Some teachers emphasized how they were only teaching students computer application skills and recognized that this does not provoke critical thinking among students. Our training led teachers to the realization that they need to unpack some of those programming skills learned in college and teaching them to students. Another success indicator we covered to some extent was building strong relationships between participating teachers which Darling-Hammond and his colleagues believe to be an important aspect of running an effective training. Although we didn't completely fulfil their definition of building strong relationships we did however, help build some sense of working relationships among participants. A good working relationship was evident from the level of teacher interaction and engagement with one another during the training as well as after the training. The fact that teachers were communicating with one another even after the training to provide each other with support and exchange experiences was a very good indication of a good working relationship amongst them. Bringing teachers from different schools together for the workshop also allowed them the opportunity to meet peers from the same profession. In addition, we provided teachers with lunch and a comfortable environment where they were able to sit, chat and share their ideas and experiences. We believe that this helped built a professional relationship among participants. It is important to point out that the working environment in Qatar in general does not support collaborative work among same discipline teachers in the different schools and this is perhaps related to work load and lack of time to meet. Hence setting up a professional network amongst ICT teachers in difference schools is considered a difficult task.

Throughout the training we identified the importance of introducing and building students' computing knowledge earlier in their lives (middle to high school). This allowed teachers to give students the opportunity to explore this field of study early enough to help shape their intention for further study at the college level.

2.4 Suggestions

Comparing the summary of research done with the method we used to administer professional development for our teachers, we found that there are some factors that could have paved the way to a more sustainable improvement in our professional development training. Factors such as, ongoing training based on teacher feedback and classroom practices, motivating teachers to learn, as well as creating a platform for teachers are what we need to consider in order to ensure a more effective professional development training is in place. The following are some suggested consideration to be taken into account when administering this professional development again in the future.

2.4.1 Intensive Ongoing Training

Intensifying the duration of our training to ensure longer ongoing professional development is definitely an important consideration for future work. Teachers in general believed that simple training was not sufficient, what they really needed is classroom support to help overcome potential problems faced while teaching. This ongoing training will provide teachers with the opportunity to teach the course work and come back to reflect and discuss their classroom experiences.

A stronger method of training to be considered is the lesson study approach. This approach will assist teachers in preparing lesson plans and developing a deeper understanding of how students will learn the lesson. The idea is to form a group of teachers and allow them the time to meet regularly to plan, design, implement, evaluate and consider modifications to refine a lesson. After the planning and designing phases are accomplished, a member of the team will teach the lesson while other members observe. The team should then meet to discuss their observations and reflect on the lesson and proper modifications are considered when teaching this lesson again. The idea is to promote a process whereby teachers experience gradual professional growth through developing a lesson in collaboration with peers [12]. This process will need to take place using collaboration among a team of teachers with the support and supervision of the trainer.

2.4.2 Motivating Teachers

This aspect is an imperative part of carrying out a successful professional development because lack of motivation on the teacher's part will result in limited learning of the concepts and objectives of the training taking place. Teachers recruited for the training were skeptical at the start and complained about the load of work and recommended not to introduce new topics because students are already struggling with the tools currently being used. What we would suggest doing is invite a teacher from the pilot stage who undergone the implementation stage to share his/her engagement in teaching the curriculum and report on own experiences with the training. Teachers have seen a major improvement in student perception and we need to use their positive attitude to train new teachers. This will illustrate the benefits of the training and help other teachers see the implications that this training will have on student achievement in computing.

2.4.3 Creating a Platform for Teachers

In general, collaboration is central to having not only a successful professional development but also better student achievements. "Research shows that when schools are strategic in creating time and productive working relationships within academic departments or grade levels, across them, or among teachers school wide, the benefits can include greater consistency in instruction, more willingness to share practices and try new ways of teaching, and more success in solving problems of practice" [8]. Teachers receiving training requested providing them with a means to share their experiences and help them exchange ideas and resources. Thus, we believe that an effective professional development is one that creates a support system for teachers that will result in an ongoing collaboration, which will consequently foster positive professional learning communities. Creating groups whether online or face-to-face is crucial in sustaining collaboration over time.

3. CURRICULUM IMPLEMENTATION

We began by making Alice a good fit for the Middle Eastern culture. We created 3D models of creatures, objects, vehicles, buildings and tools based on the local culture. Those models helped make students' learning experience more customized and enabled them to bridge what they learned in the schools' settings with their home culture. We then initiated the process by developing an Alice based computing curriculum that supported the delivery of the computing education required while preserving the local traditions. The curriculum materials focused on imperative concepts of programming, analytic, logical thinking, and problem solving skills in the context of creating animations as well as enabling creativity and innovation. The curriculum was designed to build a computing foundation for students and therefore upon completion of the course students were expected to understand and develop algorithms. Students were also expected to develop programs using different building blocks like sequence, selection, repetition and Boolean expressions, use decomposition and create modular programs and model physical systems.

3.1 Pilot Stage

In the academic year 2014/15, we collaborated with three schools, two of which were public (assigned by MOE&HE) and one private school in an effort to teach computing using Alice. More than 320 grade 8 students (13-14 years old) were taking Alice throughout the whole academic year. At this stage, teachers were provided with instructional materials such as year and term plans, lecture notes, lesson plans, class activities, short quizzes and assessments. These materials were used as a guidance for the teachers on how to teach and use Alice effectively.

Students were taught the program in 2 terms each 15 weeks in length. Classes usually met twice a week for 45 minutes. The lecture notes included explanation of the new concept, example for students to work out with teachers and an individual activity to be implemented using Alice. The lesson plans were developed for teachers to direct them on how the structure, management and flow of the lesson should be as well as how to address students' outcomes during the lessons.

In order to evaluate the effectiveness of this phase, we administered pre- and post-tests with targeted students for the purpose of assessing progress. Furthermore, we asked teachers and students for their feedback on the general experience, the tool, and the curriculum materials. During the evaluation of the pilot stage, we conducted some general visits to schools to get first-hand impressions of the progress. We attended classes to understand students' overall attainment in a classroom setting and to learn the extent of the usability of the support materials provided to teachers. School visits also involved support for students as well as providing continuous support to teachers, throughout the academic year.

3.2 Field Study Stage

Following the successful piloting of Alice and the curriculum materials in the three schools, the MOE&HE assigned six public schools for us to work with, in the next Academic year 2015/16. In addition to those, we reached out to five private schools to join this phase. More than 800 students in grades 8 and 11 (16-17 years old) were benefiting from the new curriculum. In this phase, we designed and developed textbooks in Arabic and English for students to use. Teachers, on the other hand, were provided with more training and were supported with more instructional materials and teaching resources.

The feedback and data collected from teachers and students during the evaluation of the pilot stage helped in assessing the quality and appropriateness of the curriculum and therefore helped in modifying the curriculum as required. Officials in the MOE&HE and teachers in Qatar indicated a real need to provide students with learning resources that they can take home and study. The intention was to support and facilitate students' learning and enable them to have a more successful experience. The tailored textbooks were developed because of the lack of resources available in the medium of instruction at schools. There was also a lack of availability of computing materials that suited our target learners. When developing the textbooks, we had to consider many factors, such as: culture, vocabulary selection, and age appropriate restrictions. Please refer to our earlier papers for details about the curriculum [4] [5] [6].

3.3 Analysis of Field Testing

During the implementation of the two phases of the program, we were able to collect data to help us measure the effectiveness of the tool and the curriculum from the teachers' and students' perspectives. The local 3D environment of Alice also gained acceptance in the local classrooms and students displayed interest in programming using it. Alice allowed students the opportunity to discover their abilities and improve their skills by using their imaginations while programming.

Teachers also succeeded in teaching computing for the first time to middle school students. This achievement was evident from the improvement in students' assessment results. This implied a development in teachers' knowledge and experience in teaching computing and programming through Alice, the first 3D visual programming language taught in Qatar. We present our findings in the results and discussion sections below.

4. RESULTS AND DISCUSSION

To confirm the success of the project we evaluated its effectiveness and the impact it had on participating schools. The result will always be higher student achievement in computing and this is what we looked at measuring. We collected data to assist us in examining the quality and appropriateness of their general experience, teacher training, curriculum materials, and Alice tool from the perspectives of teachers and students.

Data collected from teachers were in the form of focus group interviews (approximately one hour per school) and anonymous surveys collected from individual teachers reporting on their experience in teaching Alice. We felt it was important to hear from each teacher individually as to illuminate factors such as group pressure encountered during focus groups interviews.

A major stakeholder considered to be the primary beneficiary of the program is the student. Students completed surveys illustrating their opinion about their overall experience with the program in addition to completing assessments in the form of diagnostic tests. Two groups of randomly selected students were assessed: 1) An experimental group, students who took Alice, 2) A control group, students who took MOE&HE's pre-existing curriculum (Introductory Robotics and/or French). Student assessment comparisons were done on two levels. The first was a comparison between the pre and post assessments administered on the experimental group to measure the growth in student levels. The second was a comparison between the experimental and control groups to measure the contribution Alice made on the experimental group compared to the control group.

Data collected (except for student assessments) was compiled, analyzed and coded by three of the research team members to ensure consistency and reliability. The team examined data collected from teachers' and students' feedback about their general experience, Alice tool and workshop. We used the following coding in order to classify and use the qualitative data collected and report on it:

- Positive: A general positive comment about any aspect of the program of study (e.g. Alice is useful)
- Negative: A shortcoming on the part of the program that can be avoided in the future (e.g. Tutorials were more advanced than students' level)
- Challenge: A shortcoming that is beyond the scope of the program (e.g. when working with Alice, it takes students time to setup the scene)

4.1 Focus Groups Feedback

In the focus group interviews, we asked teachers from each school about their overall experience with teaching Alice as well as their perceived students' experience with the course in general. After analyzing the data, we found that 50% of their comments about Alice were positive while 35% of them were negative. Negative comments were mostly related to students' abilities, for example:

"When introduced to advanced topics and heavy programming they were taking two or three lectures to finish one exercise."

To evaluate the tool, we asked questions like; what worked well and what didn't work well, how would you compare it to other tools, and how engaged were students in their classes. The majority of teachers (67%) had positive impressions. On average 11% of the comments reflected challenges while 22% of them were categorized as negative impressions, for example:

"It was targeting students in higher grades, so it was more positive for higher ability students and challenging for average students".

Another key part in completing our evaluation process was assessing the usefulness of the teachers' training sessions. Half of the focus groups (50%) had positive while the others had negative impressions about the training. We had more negative comments about the second workshop that took place three months after the first. The main complaint about the second workshop was the redundancy of the materials being presented. We then redesigned workshops to include more reflective exercises, so teachers can reflect on methodologies being used in the curriculum.

4.2 Students' Feedback

A total of 167 students completed surveys about their overall experience with the program. Answers were then coded and classified into two categories; positive (very satisfied and satisfied) and negative (not satisfied and not satisfied at all). Survey questions focused on looking at students' satisfaction with the program. Only 97 students answered this question and 85% of their answers on their overall experience with Alice were positive while 15% were negative. An example of a positive experience was *"Alice was interesting and easy for me, I only faced few difficulties"*, another student stated that *"Alice was fun"*.

We also collected data on their experience with Alice tool by using answers from the survey question asking students to list other challenges they faced in the program. Only 52% of the students answered this question out of which 18% identified the English language as a barrier to learning.

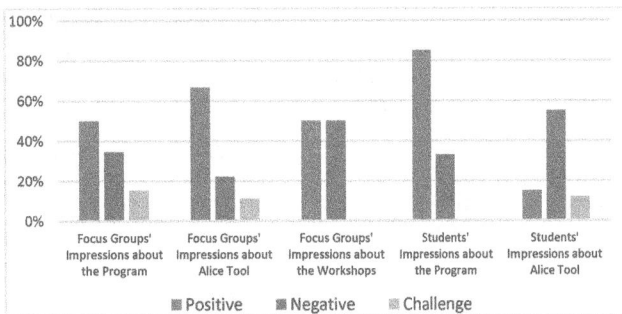

Figure 1: Focus Groups' Versus Students' Ratings of their experience with the overall program.

4.3 Teachers' Feedback

Survey questions focused on the teachers' individual perspectives about the program. We asked each teacher to rate their experience with respects to indicators such as overall program, perceived students' experience, Alice tool, Alice compared to other tools, using the book, appropriateness of the topics, suitability of exercises and questions, students' ability to produce projects, students' motivation etc. Teachers were given two rating scales ranging from 1-4 (1=poor/not at all, 2=good/somewhat, 3=very good/mostly, and 4=excellent/very much). We categorized anything above 2 as positive. All teachers gave a rating of above 2 when asked about their experience with Alice. For example, some teachers rated their overall experience with teaching Alice as excellent and felt that students were mostly able to produce projects independently.

4.4 Students' Assessments

In order to show the effect Alice had on students' skills, we compared two sets of data, one within the experimental group by comparing students' pre and post assessments and the other with the control group by comparing them to the experimental group. The assessment administered consisted of 15-20 multiple-choice questions that required thinking but no previous knowledge. Students were asked to use computational thinking concepts and skills to solve a list of problems they might encounter in their everyday lives. Some questions required students to analyze situations, think logically in sequence and/or algorithmic and drive conclusions. Other questions asked students to use their creative thinking and imagination abilities. Both assessments were done to help us measure the improvement in students' computational thinking and problem solving skills after taking Alice.

4.4.1 Pre vs. post Alice students' performance

We administered two student assessments with the experimental group. A pre-assessment was completed before starting the program to measure students' current critical thinking and problem solving abilities. We then required students to do another post assessment to measure improvements in their skills and knowledge after completing Alice. We had more students' responses in post Alice than we did in pre Alice.

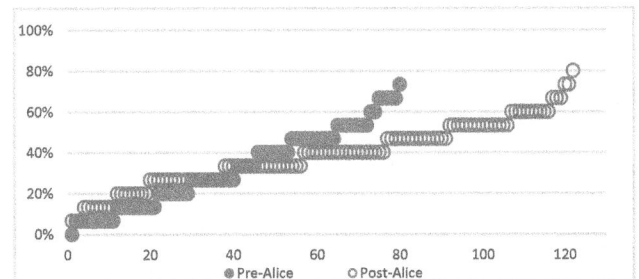

Figure 2: Pre-assessments Versus Post-Assessment Results among students who have completed the program.

In general, there was a 6.1% improvement between pre and post Alice which is considered an improvement taken into consideration that this increase was after only four months' exposure to the program which is normally not sufficient to see real improvements. It would have been useful if we were able to measure the progress of the same students over time by administering the pre and post-assessments to the same students. Due to confidentiality issues and restrictions on the research part, we were not able to that.

4.4.2 Alice vs. non-Alice students' performance

When we collected data to compare Alice to non-Alice, we only had 65 non-Alice students who completed the assessment while 122 Alice students completed the same assessment. In an effort to make meaningful comparisons between the two groups of students we decided to select a random sample of 65 students out of the 122 students who studied Alice to use in our data analysis. We found that Alice students scored 7.5% higher on average than non-Alice students. It is important also to emphasize that two Alice students scored above 70% on this assessment while no students from the control group scored above 60%.

Throughout our pre and post student assessments, we were able to display improvement in students' results and an incline in experimental students' scores suggesting that Alice students acquired more skills and knowledge in computing, critical thinking, and problem solving than the control group.

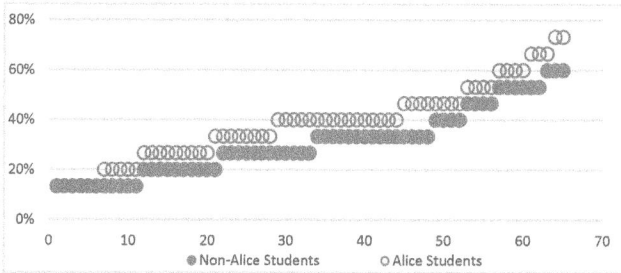

Figure 3: Assessment scores comparing results of students who studied Alice against Student who did not study Alice.

4.5 Alice Competition

After the successful implementation of Alice curriculum and using the newly Alice skilled students, we decided to carry out a national competition to motivate more students and highlight some of the work done. We hosted an Alice programming competition where 36 teams consisting of 148 students competed in presenting their Alice animations. Each group got a chance to present their project to a team of judges from different sectors in Qatar. This was a great chance for the students as it increased their confidence in their abilities and their newly learned skills.

Students were asked to create and present their own Alice animations and games. Projects were scored based on criteria such as creativity of the idea, oral presentation, visual and smooth motion, etc. In addition to allowing students the opportunity to demonstrate their innovations, we also attracted more schools as the event was hosted in a prestigious university and was well covered in the media. By the end of the event, students were already asking about the next Alice competition.

Motivating teachers was also critical to ensure success; hence, this competition was a good reward as they were honored by attending officials from MOE&HE, local universities and research centers. Teachers emailed us expressing their gratitude for hosting this competition. One of the teachers wrote: *"Thank you so much for the Alice Competition it was a great success"*.

5. CONCLUSION AND FUTURE WORK

In this paper, we presented our experience in bringing Alice ME to schools in Qatar. The results highlighted the positive impact the program had on students' knowledge, skills and performance as well as the positive impact it had on teachers using Alice.

We found that the 3D animation nature of Alice facilitated students' learning in fundamental programming concepts. This made Alice ME a more attractive and fun experience for students. In addition to its contribution to students' learning experience, Alice also enabled teachers to have a better approach to teaching computing in a more learners' motivated driven environment.

To improve the implementation of Alice ME in the future and to ensure better teachers' experience and students' results, we plan to provide more intensive training that fosters a culture of sharing and reflective practices as well as using more rigorous evaluation tools to help make more meaningful comparisons. We also plan to develop a 3-years computing curriculum that includes a textual-based programming language (e.g. python) to enrich the computing knowledge and experience of students in middle schools.

6. ACKNOWLEDGMENTS

This paper was made possible by NPRP grant # 5-1070-2-451 from the Qatar National Research Fund (a member of Qatar Foundation). The statements made herein are solely the responsibility of the authors.

7. REFERENCES

[1] R. M. Goldman, "Future Predictions," Linkedin, 4 June 2016. [Online]. Available: https://www.linkedin.com/pulse/future-predictions-robert-m-goldman-md-phd-do-faasp-len-eagles-pgce. [Accessed 29 June 2016].

[2] S. Cooper, W. Dann and R. Pausch, "Alice: a 3-D tool for introductory programming concepts," *Journal of Computing Sciences in Colleges,* vol. 15, no. 5, pp. 107-116, 2000.

[3] J. C. Adams, "Alice, middle schoolers & the imaginary worlds camps," in *ACM SIGCSE*, Covington, 2007.

[4] S. Razak, H. Gedawy, N. Tabet, W. Dann and D. Slater, "Alice in UK An Alice Based Implementation of UK National Computing Curriculum," in *International Conference on Computer Science Education Innovation & Technology (CSEIT)*, Singapore, 2015.

[5] N. Tabet, H. Gedawy, H. Alshikhabobakr and S. Razak, "From Alice to Python. Introducing Text-based Programming in Middle Schools," in *Proceedings of the 2016 ACM Conference on Innovation and Technology in Computer Science Education (ITICSE)*, 2016.

[6] S. Razak, H. Gedawy, W. P. Dann and D. J. Slater, "Alice in the Middle East: An Experience Report from the Formative Phase," in *In Proceedings of the 47th ACM Technical Symposium on Computing Science Education (SIGCSE)*, 2016.

[7] E. Armour-Thomas, C. Clay, R. Domanico, K. Bruno and B. Allen, "An outlier study of elementary and middle schools in New York City: Final report," in *New York city board of education*, New York, 1989.

[8] L. Darling-Hammond, C. Wei Ruth, A. Andree, N. Richardson and S. Orphanos, "Professional Learning in the Learning Profession: A Status Report on Teacher Development in the United States and Abroad," National Staff Development Council, California, 2009.

[9] S. H. Harwell, "Teacher Professional Development: It's Not an Event, It's a Process," CORD, Texas, 2003.

[10] S. Higgins, P. Cordingley, T. Greany and R. Coe, "Developing Great Teaching: Lessons from the international reveiws into effective professional development," The Teacher Development Trust, London, 2015.

[11] M. S. Garet, A. C. Porter, L. Desimone, B. F. Birman and K. S. Yoon, "What Makes Professional Development Effictive? Results From a National Sample of Teachers," *American Educational Research Journal,* vol. 38, no. 4, pp. 915-945, 2001.

[12] "Professional Learning in Effective Schools: The Seven Principles of Highly Effective Professional Learning," Leadership and Teacher Development Branch, Melbourne, 2005.

International Perspectives on CS Teacher Formation and Professional Development

Francesco Maiorana
Università di Catania
IISS G.B. Vaccarini
Italy
fmaioran@gmail.com

Miles Berry
University of Roehampton United Kingdom
m.berry@roehampton.ac.uk

Mark Nelson
Computer Science Teachers Association
USA
m.nelson@csteachers.org

Chery Lucarelli
College of St. Scholastica
USA
clucarelli@css.edu

Margot Phillips
ACG Sunderland College
New Zealand
margot.phillipps@gmail.com

Shitanshu Mishra
Indian Institute of Technology
India
shitanshu@iitb.ac.in

Andrea Benassi
INDIRE, Offices of Naples, Florence, Turin, Italy
a.benassi@indire.it

SUMMARY

Drawing on Mishra and Koehler's 'TPACK' model [1], we recognize that great Computer Science (CS) teaching demands great pedagogy, great technology skills and great subject knowledge. The main challenge facing any jurisdiction in implementing a CS curriculum within schools is the shortage of new teachers being trained in CS1 and to meet the demand many countries have focused on professional development (PD) for existing teachers across a diverse range of subjects. Some initial PD efforts in CS were often brief, with little follow-on support, and supported through external grant funding. As the need for CS at the K-12 level continues to grow, approaches should be sustainable and scalable. This includes preparing teachers at all levels, pre k-12 and some funding initiatives have included preservice teacher support as part of this [2]. Inside the European Union (EU) the Scientix project [3] represents a focus European Commission (EC) funded projects and is a repository for PD with resources for pedagogy, technology and subject knowledge[1]. Besides this effort, spreading CS knowledge has been supported by volunteers led movements like CoderDojo[2].

The panelists will discuss the following main topics: 1) Pre-service vs in-service, where do teachers come from? 2) Interdisciplinary ways of infusing CS. 3) Ways of replicatingacross countries CS teacher training initiatives aimed at sustaining and growing the number and quality of both in-service and pre-service teachers able to teach CS effectively. 4) Effective approaches to help teachers to build confidence in their ability to teach CS.

---

[1] www.scientix.eu/
[2] https://coderdojo.com/

ITiCSE'17, July 3–5, 2017, Bologna, Italy.
ACM. ISBN 978-1-4503-4704-4/17/07.
DOI: http://dx.doi.org/10.1145/3059009.3059067

Panelist Position Statements

Miles Berry

Faced with the challenge and opportunity of implementing a new national curriculum computing, with a significant emphasis on programming and other elements of computer science, the UK's Computing At School (CAS) group has emphasised the development of teachers' subject knowledge as a priority in continuing professional development (CPD). CPD through CAS has emphasised a geographically distributed peer-to-peer model. A network of nearly 450 'master teachers' has been established [4], supported by over 230 local hubs and ten universities as regional centres. A number of training programmes that could be used by these master teachers (and others) have been developed, and made freely available through financial support from industry and central government. Other initiatives have included Barefoot Computing, the BCS certificate in computer science teaching, Code Club Pro, PiCademy and a number of MOOCs. Despite this provision, many teachers report that it has been difficult to find the time to engage in meaningful professional development, due to the normal demands made on class teachers.

Mark Nelson

Approaches that enable teachers to integrate CS and computational thinking concepts and practices into their existing classes may be an effective approach to helping teachers build confidence in their ability to teach CS. In the US we estimate that there are more than 150 different professional development providers for CS. This can create a confusing environment for teachers new to the subject area. The Computer Science Teachers Association (CSTA) is working on an initiative called the Continuing Professional Development Pipeline. By working with PD providers, this project will support teacher professional development through micro-credentialing, developmental assessments, common communities, and customized professional development pathways. Via this model we aim to help teachers find the professional development best suited to their needs and interests. This project is supported by the Infosys Foundation USA.

Chery Lucarelli

The College of Scholastica, through a unique partnership between a Computer Science faculty member and an Education faculty member, has been able to offer professional development in computer science since 2011. Efforts at The College of St. Scholastica, include offering an online graduate Certificate in CS Education to practicing teachers. The teacher preparation programs are being revised to infuse computational thinking across a number of courses and it will include an optional minor in computer science education for preservice teachers. Ultimately, all of our teachers will have a basic computational thinking competency and awareness and an opportunity to dive deeper into CS[1].

Margot Phillipps

New Zealand is on the brink of introducing Computational Thinking into the compulsory national curriculum for years one to ten. Since 2011 there have been formal standards to assess elements of Computer Science in the Senior years of high school. These standards were introduced with a minimum of government supported professional development for teachers. For Computer Science, and to some extent Programming, this deficit has been met by CS4HS events and a website set up by Professor Tim Bell and post-graduate students at Canterbury University. Another program has been funded by a local IT company, Datacom, to train teachers in programming with support of a local teacher and volunteers from the company. The subject association, NZACDITT, has had a vibrant online group with teachers sharing resources and the burden of assessment moderation. Other universities have developed and plan further development of resources to aid the teaching of Programming. CodeAvengers have developed online learning resources for students. This approach has been ad hoc, dependent on the motivation and good will of many volunteers. It is hoped that the planned changes to the compulsory curriculum will be better planned and resourced centrally.

Shitanshu Mishra

The research focus of the interdisciplinary program in Educational Technology (IDP-ET) are two-pronged: 1) design based implementation research to refine the design of tertiary level, in-service teacher professional development (TPD) programs; 2) educational design research on developing pedagogies and technology-based learning environments for learning-teaching of pan-domain thinking skills. IDP-ET conducts various outreach programs which range from a single day workshop to full-length online teachers' training course. The longer outreach activities, utilize the design-based implementation research methodology to ensure scalability, sustainability of the efforts and feeds back to research by assisting in action research by participating teachers. The most recent outreach activity was a Teacher PD MOOC using IIT Bombay's Edx platform (IITBx). The MOOC was based on the design considerations of immersivity and pertinency to increase the learner perseverance in the course. For the second goal of thinking skills education, our primary research objective is to evolve a pedagogical framework to design effective learning environments for learning-teaching of thinking skills. Thinking skills are regarded as abilities and processes that human beings apply for sense-making, reasoning and problem-solving, and thinking skills in engineering and science include system design, computational thinking, troubleshooting, question-posing, hypotheticodeductive reasoning, etc. We envision the merging of the two approaches once we develop a community of teachers performing action research on the development of student thinking skills (Computational Thinking (CT) in the case of CS Education).

Andrea Benassi

A first reflection drawn by the fact that in England, Computer Science is embedded in the curriculum starting at the age of five. This choice is quite distant from the Italian way, where CS is not a discipline hitherto been considered but rather a "tool at the service" or a "transversal competencies" with respect to one or more disciplines. The idea of "computational thinking" as a fourth core competency (next to reading, writing, and numeracy) would seem to push a comprehensive application, but it poses at the same time a question: who are, in school, the teachers "owners" of this competency? If all teachers would be "responsible" for this competence, and no one would be in charge of it in an outstanding way, it is very likely that we would develop the same equity in the students. How could we go beyond? One could argue that the conceptual node lays in teacher training. If so, however, would it be enough to train teachers in diverse range of subjects to CS content and methods to get different results? What we argue, as a reflection from initiatives carried out in the Italian Digital School Plan, is that this is nor the main neither the only way. As well as math teacher is not only a teacher "trained to teach mathematics" but also and above all a bearer of a certain attitude, a certain way of approaching the real experience embodying passion and love for one type of organized mathematical knowledge and leads pupils along this path, the same has to be supported as for teaching computational thinking and computer science. We would like to engage and stimulate a deeper reflection about a specific teacher's profile capable to embody a true CT attitude, passion and love to involve students in a deep learning experience.

[1]ACKNOWLEDGMENTS

This material is based upon work supported by the National Science Foundation under Grant Nos. CNS-1240841, CNS-1440947, and CNS-1547051 and by multiple Google research programs.

REFERENCES

[1] Mishra, P. and Koehler, M.J., 2006. Technological pedagogical content knowledge: A framework for teacher knowledge. Teachers college record, 108(6), p.10-17.
[2] National Science Foundation (NSF) (2016), Computer science for all (CS for All: RPP). Retrieved from https://www.nsf.gov/pubs/2017/nsf17525/nsf17525.htm.
[3] European Schoolnet (EUN) Scientix 2 results. How Scientix adds value to STEM education Authors: Róbert Hlynur Baldursson and Michael John Stone Contributors: Àgueda Gras-Velázquez, Marina Jiménez Iglesias, Radostina Karageorgieva, Valentina Garoia, Victor J. Pérez Rubio.
[4] Sue Sentance, Simon Humphreys, and Mark Dorling. 2014. The network of teaching excellence in computer science and master teachers. In Proceedings of the 9th Workshop in Primary and Secondary Computing Education (WiPSCE '14). ACM, New York, NY, USA, 80-88. DOI=http://dx.doi.org/10.1145/2670757.2670789.

Plagiarism in Take-home Exams: Help-seeking, Collaboration, and Systematic Cheating

Arto Hellas
University of Helsinki
Department of Computer Science
Helsinki, Finland
arto.hellas@cs.helsinki.fi

Juho Leinonen
University of Helsinki
Department of Computer Science
Helsinki, Finland
juho.leinonen@helsinki.fi

Petri Ihantola
Tampere University of Technology
Department of Pervasive Computing
Tampere, Finland
petri.ihantola@tut.fi

ABSTRACT

Due to the increased enrollments in Computer Science education programs, institutions have sought ways to automate and streamline parts of course assessment in order to be able to invest more time in guiding students' work.

This article presents a study of plagiarism behavior in an introductory programming course, where a traditional pen-and-paper exam was replaced with multiple take-home exams. The students who took the take-home exam enabled a software plugin that recorded their programming process. During an analysis of the students' submissions, potential plagiarism cases were highlighted, and students were invited to interviews.

The interviews with the candidates for plagiarism highlighted three types of plagiarism behaviors: help-seeking, collaboration, and systematic cheating. Analysis of programming process traces indicates that parts of such behavior are detectable directly from programming process data.

KEYWORDS

plagiarism, programming process data, educational data mining

ACM Reference format:
Arto Hellas, Juho Leinonen, and Petri Ihantola. 2017. Plagiarism in Take-home Exams: Help-seeking, Collaboration, and Systematic Cheating. In *Proceedings of ITiCSE'17, July 03-05, 2017, Bologna, Italy,*, 6 pages.
DOI: http://dx.doi.org/10.1145/3059009.3059065

1 INTRODUCTION

Universities and other institutions are facing increased enrollments into their Computing programs. It is no surprise that teaching and learning is moving online at increased speed: there has been a push towards improving the feedback cycle that is associated with coursework and examinations. First, feedback should be available faster, and second, the costs should reduce. This is partially due to the instructional quality, but also due to the price of traditional

education. As a downside of this online learning movement, academic dishonesty such as plagiarism has become easier and even more common [11].

Merriam-Webster online dictionary defines **plagiarism** as *an act of copying the ideas or words of another person without giving credit to that person* [15]. This is a significant problem especially in computing education [5, 6], where students actually see copying and pasting source code somehow more acceptable than doing the same with natural language and essays [1].

Because of the wide impact and importance of the topic, source code plagiarism has been studied for nearly three decades [12]. Much of the research has revolved around tools for detecting plagiarism (e.g., JPlag [17] or MOSS [4]) or students' attitudes towards plagiarism [23]. Tools and methods for detecting plagiarism are typically based on comparing similarities between code segments [14, 19]. Although modern learning environments provide rich log information on how students solve programming assignments [10], this knowledge is rarely applied in plagiarism detection.

In this work, we study plagiarism in take-home exams of an introductory programming course. As a part of take-home exams, students were expected to use a custom tool for downloading the take-home exam questions and answer templates so that the exam questions could be answered on a schedule that best fits the student. In addition, the tool recorded and sent the typing level changes made to the downloaded answer templates.

Our research questions for this study are as follows:

(1) What types of plagiarism happen in take-home exams?
(2) How can these different plagiarism types be identified from programming process data?

We answer these questions by using a mixed method approach. First, we checked all the exam answers using JPlag[1] and manually reviewed the results to identify suspicious cases. Next, we interviewed all the related students from where different motivations and trends explaining students' behavior emerged. Finally, we compared programming traces to these verified plagiarism cases in order to find whether different behaviors could be identified directly from the traces.

The rest of the article is structured as follows. Next, in Section 2, we outline the related research on source code plagiarism. This is followed by a description of our data and context in Section 3. Section 4 outlines the study methodology and the results, which are then discussed in Section 5. Section 6 concludes the article and provides directions for future work.

---

[1]The tool was selected based on the comparison of multiple plagiarism detection tools supporting Java [7]

2 PLAGIARISM IN PROGRAMMING

Many studies have been conducted on plagiarism in programming [1, 5, 11, 22, 23]. Especially, the attitudes of students [1, 11, 22] and academics [5] on what constitutes plagiarism in programming, which is quite different from traditional plagiarism as reusing code is often encouraged on introductory courses [5]. This can lead into a situation where the fine line between plagiarism and normal course practice becomes unclear to students [11]. Cosma and Joy [5] propose a definition of plagiarism based on survey answers from computer science educators based in the U.K. Based on the survey results, they define plagiarism as reusing code segments without properly citing the original author of the code. They also include obtaining the source code in their definition. They suggest that the main reason behind plagiarism in programming assignments might be that students are confused as to what constitutes plagiarism.

Joy et al. [11] studied students' understanding of plagiarism in a programming context. Similar to Cosma and Joy [5], they believe that students' confusion about plagiarism can lead to accidental plagiarism. They found that students are especially confused about reusing code from previous assignments, how accurately references should be cited, to what extent can the students collaborate on assignments, and that existing code should also be referenced when it is converted from one programming language to another.

Students may also perceive some forms of cheating as less severe than others [22]. For example, students view collaborating on assignments to not be as serious an offense as cheating in the exam. Students can be reluctant to report the cheating of fellow students if they observe it, which suggests that automatic ways of identifying cheating would be beneficial [22].

From the technical point of view, source code clone detection methods can be divided between text based (e.g. hashing of code lines), token based (i.e. similar to tokenization in compilers), tree based (e.g. normalized AST comparison), metrics based (i.e. combining multiple simple characteristics), graph based (e.g. depency graphs), and mixed approaches [19]. Although all approaches aim at coping with simple refactoring such as editing names or changing the order interchangeable code blocks, many tools are still insensitive to such edits – especially if multiple refactorings are combined to hide the origin of the work [7]. To alleviate these challenges, it has been recently proposed to incorporate edit history more closely into plagiarism detection process [8, 21]. These previous experiments on utilizing the history, however, deal with more coarse-grained edit data than what is available to us.

3 CONTEXT AND DATA

This study took place in an introductory programming course organized during fall 2016 at University of Helsinki, a research university in Europe. The course is organized in Java, and the contents of the course are similar to many other introductory programming courses offered at universities: variables, input/output, selection, objects, lists, maps, inheritance and so on.

Students who enroll to the BSc program as CS majors take the course during their first semester. Students with other majors take the course when it fits their schedule, given that they wish to take it. It is only mandatory to the CS majors. From the course population,

roughly one third are CS majors, and two thirds potentially consider CS as a minor subject.

The grading of the course was based on a set of individual programming assignments and pair-programming assignments that correspond to 55% of the overall course mark, and three take-home programming exams that correspond to 45% of the overall course mark. The students had to gain at least half of the available points from the final take-home programming exam that covered the whole course in order to pass. The students in the course also had the option of participating in a traditional exam at the University facilities instead of the take-home exams.

All the programming assignments were administered using Test My Code [25]. Test My Code (TMC) provides a plugin for programming environments that makes it convenient to download, assess and return assignments. Over 95% of the participants used TMC with NetBeans, but some opted for Eclipse and IntelliJ IDEA.

Each take-home exam had three to five separate questions, and the students had four hours to complete the exam. Any kind of collaboration or help-seeking was strictly forbidden in the take-home exams, but the students were allowed to use the course materials and their own solutions to the course assignments while working on the take-home exam. Each take-home exam handout reminded the students of the rules. The university takes strict policy on plagiarism: plagiarism leads to a failed course mark and recurring offense leads to temporary expulsion from the university.

When a take-home exam was administered, the students could pick a suitable time from a set of days for the exam. In order to participate in the take-home exam, the students were expected to enable the logging of programming process in TMC and to download the assignment templates used in the exam. Downloading the templates, which also included the handouts, started the exam. The logs that TMC gathers includes every subsequent source code state as well as typical programming environment events such as running, debugging and testing the program.

In the course, 233 students participated in at least one take-home exam, and 204 participated in the final take-home exam from which the students had to gather at least half of the points to pass the course. For the analysis, data from all the students was used.

4 METHODOLOGY AND RESULTS

4.1 Identifying candidates

A preliminary list of candidates who potentially plagiarized in the take-home exams were identified using four separate methods:

(1) The JPlag-system [17] and a custom edit-distance metric was used to assess the similarity of students' solutions to the take-home exam questions. Students with very similar solutions to other students were suspect.

(2) Students' course mark from the programming assignments were contrasted with the take-home exam scores. Outliers, i.e. students with poor assignment scores and high take-home exam scores, were suspect.

(3) Pair-wise comparison of take-home exam start and end times as well as the submission times of the take-home exam questions. Students with similar start times, end times, and submission times were suspect.

239

(4) Pair-wise comparison of IP address spaces and IP addresses from which the submissions were made. Students with very similar IP addresses (outside known campus networks with roaming) were suspect.

The preliminary list was manually studied in order to remove false positives. False positives came mainly from JPlag and the custom edit-distance metric as some of the exam questions were highly structured.

After constructing a list of candidates approximately 15% of the participants were contacted for further interviews.

4.2 Contacting and interviewing the candidates

The students were contacted through email that informed them that they had been highlighted by a system that is used to detect plagiarism. The students were asked whether the information provided by the system makes any sense to them, and if they could recall of instances where they may have acted against the university policy. Finally, interview times were scheduled.

The interviews were scheduled so that students who were likely to have worked together were interviewed in successive time slots. The interview process was planned to consist of multiple steps, first showing the student a similarity matrix with one of the numbers being highlighted and telling them that their submission was similar to another student (or other students), then proceeding by showing the actual source codes, and finally asking for a potential explanation. Depending on the flow of the discussion, similar but not identical problems to those in the take-home exam were prepared for analysis.

As the students were contacted, a first type of plagiarism behavior – **help-seeking** – emerged. Multiple students responded to the initial email that another student in the course that they knew, typically a friend, had insisted for help, and that they could eventually no longer say no. These students were typically doing the exam in the same shared study space nearly at the same time, or, the student who was seeking help deliberately sought the other student out. In these cases, the students who were asked for help were typically performing well in the course, and the student who was asking for help knew of their performance. Students who had asked for help admitted their behavior.

The second plagiarism behavior – **collaboration** – emerged both through the data and through student interviews. Likely collaboration partners were identified through submission and programming process similarity, take-home exam start and end times, as well as possible previous collaboration in e.g. pair programming assignments. After contacting the students, some asked if they could come to talk either alone or together already before the assigned slot. Most of the students who were suspected for collaboration admitted doing so during the discussion, a typical approach was working on the exam in the same study space and discussing the problem with one another. Some initially denied any collaboration, but confessed afterwards.

The third plagiarism behavior – **systematic cheating** – emerged through individuals who did not respond to the contact request at all, and through students who did not have a clear colleague from whom they would have copied the solution. These typically emerged from abnormal correlations between the programming

assignment scores and the take-home exam scores, as well as the analysis of the sources from which the exam questions were downloaded and from which the submissions were made to the assessment system. Here, typically, the students had acquired the exam questions before taking the exam, and had practiced the tasks beforehand. Such behavior was rather rare, and students who were suspected of such behavior admitted to their behavior.

Finally, a number of the students were acquitted during the interview. Such students were often high-performing, and could either easily explain the design decisions in the program, or explain how they would solve another problem, or both.

4.3 Analysis of Log Traces

To understand how these different plagiarism behaviors could be identified from the data, two methods were applied. First, we used an edit distance algorithm [24] to study how each student's distance to their final solution changed during the programming process. Then, we used a global alignment algorithm [16] to align each student's programming process with the programming process of other students.

The alignment algorithm creates a matrix of size $m * n$ for each student pair, where m is the event count for one student, and n is the event count for another student, and calculates the edit distance between all possible states. It then proceeds to identify the best alignment by constructing a path in the $m * n$ matrix that minimizes the path cost (edit distance) over the subsequent events from start to end. When the best alignment has been identified, the path cost is normalized by the number of events in the programming process to account for solutions of different length. Finally, the best alignment (here, average edit distance) for each student-pair is reported.

Note that as the calculation of the alignment is time-consuming when conducted on fine-grained data that contains each keystroke, only a subset of the events was used for constructing the alignments.

4.3.1 Help-seeking behavior and Systematic cheating. Two abnormal behaviors emerged during the analysis of the changes to the students' edit distances to their final solutions. There were students who had copy-pasted content to reach a solution, see Fig. 1, and there were programming processes that were very linear, see Fig. 2.

The first case (Fig. 1) is an example of a student who first attempted to construct a solution to the question alone, but could not do it. The student then proceeded to ask for help from an another student, who eventually provided code that the help-seeker could use. The second case (Fig. 2) is an example of a student who had struggled with the course beforehand, and had acquired a solution to the question. The student does not copy-paste the code, but it is obvious that the student is copying it from another source.

The first case is typical to help-seeking behavior, and the second case was seen in both behaviors (those students who had sought out for help, and those students who had acquired the question and worked out a solution beforehand). Figure 3 shows a pattern which was more typical to those students who worked on the assignment in a normal fashion – we will look into this in further detail next.

4.3.2 Collaboration. The alignment of students' programming process data resulted in pair-wise alignment scores for each student.

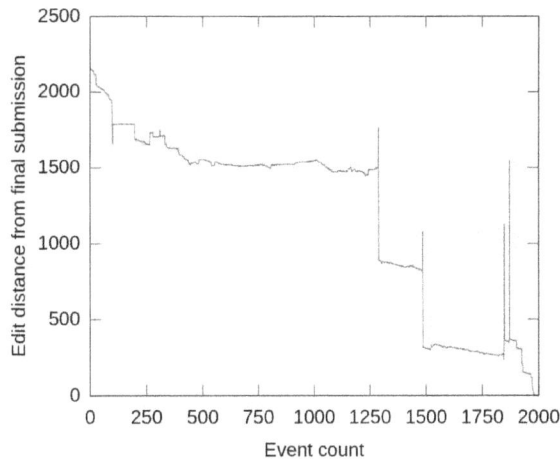

Figure 1: A student who first worked on a problem alone (events 0-1250). After being stuck for a while, the student asked for a solution from a peer. Parts of the received solution was pasted into the student's project to reach a final solution.

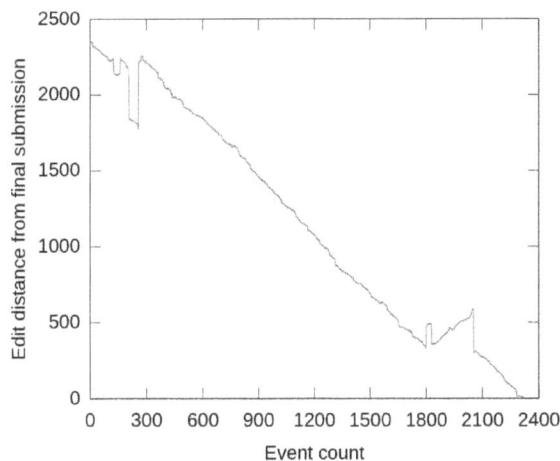

Figure 2: A student had previously asked and received a solution for the problem from a peer. The student mimicked the solution, but did not copy-paste it. At the end, the student modified the variable and method names, and somewhat reorganized the project.

Upon analysis, it became evident that the alignment of those students who have collaborated to reach a solution was significantly better than the alignment of random students. Such students could be detected using an outlier test [18].

A visual analysis of the alignments supported the finding. Figure 4 illustrates the average edit distance of two sample students to all other students in the class. In the Figure, the whiskers extend from each end of the box for a range equal to 1.5 times the interquartile range, and the box spans the range of values from the

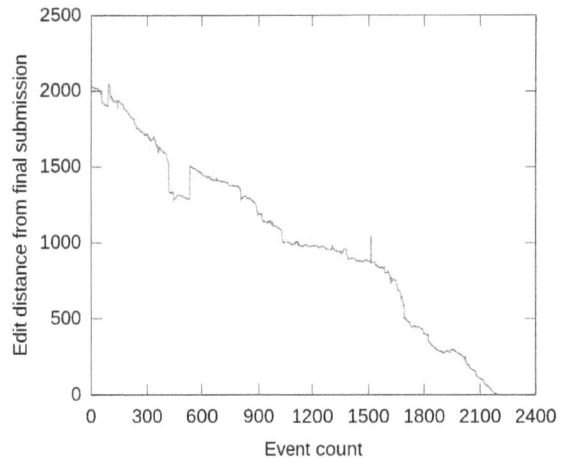

Figure 3: A student who had worked on the problem and eventually reached a solution. The behavior did not indicate copy-pasting or mimicking.

first quartile to the third quartile of the data. Outliers (detected by Gnuplot) are marked as dots.

The student on the left hand side, i.e. "Candidate", had collaborated with another student; the collaboration partner was the one with the smallest average edit distance. The student on the right hand side, i.e. "Random", is a randomly picked student who was not suspected of plagiarism, no outliers were detected for the student. Rosner's Extreme Studentized Deviate test [18] confirmed the existence of two outliers for the candidate when the strictness (probability) was set as $p = 0.05$. When the strictness was increased ($p = 0.00001$), one outlier was identified. After removing the outlier, Kolmogorov-Smirnov test indicated that the data was normally distributed ($p > 0.15$).

5 DISCUSSION

5.1 Behavior traits

Multiple behavior traits were detected during the analysis. Help-seeking students were typically struggling in the course and sought to pass by begging for answers from their peers. These students did not always simply copy and paste the solutions that they received, but for example, mimicked the solutions by typing them in keypress by keypress; it was also typical to modify the variable names and method names in order to mask obvious copy-pasting.

Collaborators had planned out meeting together with other students to work on the take-home exams. They worked together to reach a solution. The programming process often contains missteps and rethinking the solution, and copy-paste behavior or mimicking code received from others is almost absent. Collaboration can be detected from the process logs if the student is collaborating with a peer who is also taking the exam. Their solutions and problem solving processes were typically very similar, and they had started the exam nearly at the same time.

Systematic cheating was related to e.g. harvesting solutions using a separate account. However, the students typically stated that it

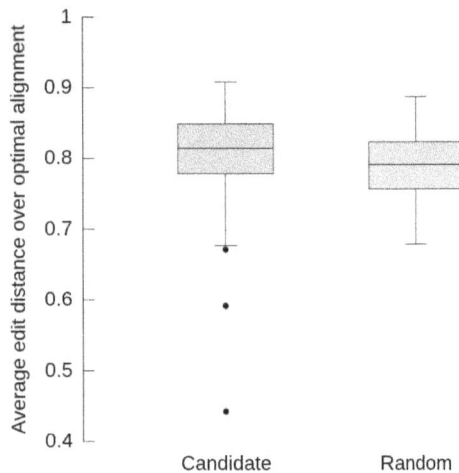

Figure 4: Two sample students and their alignment scores with every other student who worked on the assignment plotted using a box plot. The student labeled "Candidate" had collaborated with another student (the lowest point), whilst the student labeled "Random" had not.

was a "bad idea that they had in the middle of the night". Such behavior where students create multiple accounts in order to gain access to course content that is used for assessment purposes has recently been also identified in MOOCs [20].

When considering these behaviors, distinguishing between them is not easy, and it is possible that the same student shows multiple behaviors. For example, if a student had asked for a solution for a problem from a peer long before he or she started to work on the exam, it is a good question whether it should be considered systematic cheating. Similarly, collaboration was always planned and in that sense systematic.

5.2 Process data and course assignments

There has been an increase in the use of students' programming process data in research [10]. Such data shows plenty of promise in e.g. learning how students learn. However, as we have observed here, it is possible that the data that we gather is not an accurate representation of the students' knowledge.

When analyzing the students' programming process data, we observed that systems such as JPlag [17] are rather poor in detecting plagiarism from problems that are highly structured. If the assignment outline contains cues on class names, method names, variable names, etc., the solutions that students create are very similar. On the other hand, more variance is included in open-ended assignments. Both have also benefits and downsides in how easy they are to assess, and what types of tests one can write for them [9].

The use of process data as a part of the assessment and detection of plagiarism has multiple benefits. We could, for example, detect copy-paste events as well as programming behavior that shows that a student is mimicking a previously acquired solution.

5.3 Take-home exams

Our observations come from a set of take-home exams that have been used to assess students' programming competence. Take-home exams in the Computer Science education context have been previously studied by Leinonen et al. [13], who had access to data that was recorded from both the exam and normal course assigments. Their work has been more focused on identifying who is typing the code, whilst our work focuses on whether the student is doing the work on his or her own without help from others.

The take-home exam setup is an alternative version of the lab exam by Bennedsen and Caspersen, who note that such an exam *provides a valid and accurate evaluation of the student's programming capabilities, evaluates the process as well as the product, and encourages the students to practice programming throughout the course* [3]. Whilst in their context the students come to a specific time slot and lab for the exam, the approach is limited in terms of the number of students who can attend the exam. As a benefit, plagiarism is harder. In our context, on the other hand, there is no upper bound to the number of participants, and less resources and TAs are needed, but there are also more opportunities for plagiarism.

In an ideal setup, however, there would be no need for an exam. Currently, the line that separates the take-home exams and the course assignments from each other is the way that we expect the students work on them. Course assignments can be worked on with peers, but take-home exams should be completed individually. In addition, each take-home exam must be completed within four hours from the start of the exam, while the students have one week to complete each course assignment set.

One way to reduce the need for the take-home exam could – for example – be making it mandatory for the students to allow recording their programming process in the course. As a consequence, one could use algorithms such as the ones proposed by Ahadi et al. [2] to identify students who handle the course content well, and focus on only those students who struggle. This would have downsides though; some could plagiarize, and it is a good question whether the students would see such an approach as fair or ethical.

5.4 Limitations of study

Our study has multiple limitations, which we acknowledge next. First, as the exams were taken at home and other premises that the students chose to use, we do not know if we were able to reach all the students who did plagiarize. It is possible that, for example, a student had help from someone who is not on the course. It is also possible that we only caught those students who did not mask their plagiarism well enough.

Second, our setup has likely increased the tendency to plagiarize. It is likely that some of the students who participated in the take-home exam would not have attended a normal pen-and-paper exam at all. That is, the take-home exam opportunity can increase the tendency to plagiarize. Such behavior has been previously observed, for example, in business studies [26].

Third, a part of the students who we invited to the interviews were acquitted, and the final set of students who did plagiarize in the course is smaller than the interviewed population – we cannot claim that the behaviors that were identified during the interviews are a representative sample. Further studies, also from other contexts, are needed.

Fourth, we do not know whether the students plagiarized during the normal programming assignments as recording the programming process from the normal assignments was not mandatory. It is likely that information from such behavior would bring additional insight to those students who chose to plagiarize during the exams.

6 CONCLUSIONS AND FUTURE WORK

In this work we studied how students plagiarize in take-home exams. During the interview process with students who were suspected of plagiarism, three behavior types stood out: (1) help-seeking, (2) collaboration, and (3) systematic cheating. Students who were seeking for help were typically struggling on the course or in the exam, and insisted on help from their peers. Students who were collaborating worked on the exam together, and the students who were systematically cheating had e.g. created fake accounts to gain access to the exam questions in the submission system.

Furthermore, we analyzed the logs that were recorded as the students were working on the take-home exams, and found patterns that have the potential for identifying students who have plagiarized. A linear solution process in an assignment that is known to be challenging for students indicates plagiarism as does pasting parts of the solution. Collaboration where students in the same course are working together to solve the exam can potentially be detected through alignment of the programming process. At the same time, our approach is not a panacea, as we cannot – for example – identify students who have collaborated with external parties.

These results provide further means to detect plagiarism for instructors and researchers, and can be used as a discussion starter if an institution is considering the use of take-home exams. Furthermore, the recent ITiCSE working group on Educational Data Mining and Learning Analytics in Programming [10] indicated that more and more institutions are starting to gather such data. Researchers who are interested in, for example, building models of the student as a learner [27] or automatically identifying students who are struggling [2, 10] are likely to benefit from introducing plagiarism-related metrics to their models.

As a part of our future work, we are looking into incorporating data gathering into the whole introductory programming course in order to see to what extent the students plagiarize within the course assignments, and whether that behavior is linked with the plagiarism behavior in the take-home exams. We are also looking into additional means of reducing plagiarism on the courses, and considering the opportunity of removing exams completely.

REFERENCES

[1] Cheryl L Aasheim, Paige S Rutner, Lixin Li, and Susan R Williams. 2012. Plagiarism and programming: A survey of student attitudes. *Journal of Information Systems Education* 23, 3 (2012), 297.
[2] Alireza Ahadi, Raymond Lister, Heikki Haapala, and Arto Vihavainen. 2015. Exploring machine learning methods to automatically identify students in need of assistance. In *Proceedings of the eleventh annual International Conference on International Computing Education Research*. ACM, 121–130.
[3] Jens Bennedsen and Michael E. Caspersen. 2007. Assessing Process and Product. *Innovation in Teaching and Learning in Information and Computer Sciences* 6, 4 (2007), 183–202. DOI:http://dx.doi.org/10.11120/ital.2007.06040183
[4] Kevin W Bowyer and Lawrence O Hall. 1999. Experience using" MOSS" to detect cheating on programming assignments. In *Frontiers in Education Conference, 1999. FIE'99. 29th Annual*, Vol. 3. IEEE, 13B3–18.

[5] Georgina Cosma and Mike Joy. 2008. Towards a definition of source-code plagiarism. *IEEE Transactions on Education* 51, 2 (2008), 195–200.
[6] Fintan Culwin, Anna MacLeod, and Thomas Lancaster. 2001. Source code plagiarism in UK HE computing schools. *Issues, Attitudes and Tools, South Bank University Technical Report SBU-CISM-01-02* (2001).
[7] Jurriaan Hage, Peter Rademaker, and Nikè van Vugt. 2011. Plagiarism Detection for Java: A Tool Comparison. In *Computer Science Education Research Conference (CSERC '11)*. Open Universiteit, Heerlen, Open Univ., Heerlen, The Netherlands, The Netherlands, 33–46.
[8] Frederik Hattingh, Albertus AK Buitendag, and Jacobus S Van Der Walt. 2013. Presenting an alternative source code plagiarism detection framework for improving the teaching and learning of programming. *Journal of Information Technology Education* 12 (2013), 45–58.
[9] Petri Ihantola, Tuukka Ahoniemi, Ville Karavirta, and Otto Seppälä. 2010. Review of recent systems for automatic assessment of programming assignments. In *Proceedings of the 10th Koli Calling International Conference on Computing Education Research*. ACM, 86–93.
[10] Petri Ihantola, Arto Vihavainen, Alireza Ahadi, Matthew Butler, Jürgen Börstler, Stephen H Edwards, Essi Isohanni, Ari Korhonen, Andrew Petersen, Kelly Rivers, and others. 2015. Educational data mining and learning analytics in programming: Literature review and case studies. In *Proceedings of the 2015 ITiCSE on Working Group Reports*. ACM, 41–63.
[11] Mike Joy, Georgina Cosma, Jane Yin-Kim Yau, and Jane Sinclair. 2011. Source code plagiarism—a student perspective. *IEEE Transactions on Education* 54, 1 (2011), 125–132.
[12] Thomas Lancaster and Fintan Culwin. 2004. A comparison of source code plagiarism detection engines. *Computer Science Education* 14, 2 (2004), 101–112.
[13] Juho Leinonen, Krista Longi, Arto Klami, Alireza Ahadi, and Arto Vihavainen. 2016. Typing Patterns and Authentication in Practical Programming Exams. In *Proceedings of the 2016 ACM Conference on Innovation and Technology in Computer Science Education (ITiCSE '16)*. ACM, New York, NY, USA, 160–165. DOI:http://dx.doi.org/10.1145/2899415.2899472
[14] Vítor T Martins, Daniela Fonte, Pedro Rangel Henriques, and Daniela da Cruz. 2014. Plagiarism detection: A tool survey and comparison. In *OASIcs-OpenAccess Series in Informatics*, Vol. 38. Schloss Dagstuhl-Leibniz-Zentrum fuer Informatik.
[15] Merriam-Webster Online. 2016. Merriam-Webster Online Dictionary. (2016). http://www.merriam-webster.com
[16] Saul B Needleman and Christian D Wunsch. 1970. A general method applicable to the search for similarities in the amino acid sequence of two proteins. *Journal of molecular biology* 48, 3 (1970), 443–453.
[17] Lutz Prechelt, Guido Malpohl, and Michael Philippsen. 2002. Finding plagiarisms among a set of programs with JPlag. *J. UCS* 8, 11 (2002), 1016.
[18] Bernard Rosner. 1975. On the detection of many outliers. *Technometrics* 17, 2 (1975), 221–227.
[19] Chanchal K Roy, James R Cordy, and Rainer Koschke. 2009. Comparison and evaluation of code clone detection techniques and tools: A qualitative approach. *Science of Computer Programming* 74, 7 (2009), 470–495.
[20] Jose A Ruiperez-Valiente, Giora Alexandron, Zhongzhou Chen, and David E. Pritchard. 2016. Using Multiple Accounts for Harvesting Solutions in MOOCs. In *Proceedings of the Third (2016) ACM Conference on Learning @ Scale (L@S '16)*. ACM, New York, NY, USA, 63–70. DOI:http://dx.doi.org/10.1145/2876034.2876037
[21] Johannes Schneider, Avi Bernstein, Jan Vom Brocke, Kostadin Damevski, and David C Shepherd. 2016. Detecting Plagiarism based on the Creation Process. *arXiv preprint arXiv:1612.09183* (2016).
[22] Judy Sheard, Martin Dick, Selby Markham, Ian Macdonald, and Meaghan Walsh. 2002. Cheating and Plagiarism: Perceptions and Practices of First Year IT Students. In *Proceedings of the 7th Annual Conference on Innovation and Technology in Computer Science Education (ITiCSE '02)*. ACM, New York, NY, USA, 183–187. DOI:http://dx.doi.org/10.1145/544414.544468
[23] Simon and Judy Sheard. 2016. Academic Integrity and Computing Assessments. In *Proceedings of the Australasian Computer Science Week Multiconference (ACSW '16)*. ACM, New York, NY, USA, Article 3, 8 pages. DOI:http://dx.doi.org/10.1145/2843043.2843060
[24] Esko Ukkonen. 1985. Algorithms for approximate string matching. *Information and control* 64, 1-3 (1985), 100–118.
[25] Arto Vihavainen, Thomas Vikberg, Matti Luukkainen, and Martin Pärtel. 2013. Scaffolding Students' Learning Using Test My Code. In *Proceedings of the 18th ACM Conference on Innovation and Technology in Computer Science Education (ITiCSE '13)*. ACM, New York, NY, USA, 117–122. DOI:http://dx.doi.org/10.1145/2462476.2462501
[26] Tim West, Sue Ravenscroft, and Charles Shrader. 2004. Cheating and moral judgment in the college classroom: A natural experiment. *Journal of Business Ethics* 54, 2 (2004), 173–183.
[27] Michael Yudelson, Roya Hosseini, Arto Vihavainen, and Peter Brusilovsky. 2014. Investigating automated student modeling in a Java MOOC. In *Educational Data Mining 2014*.

Strategies for Maintaining Academic Integrity in First-Year Computing Courses

Judy Sheard
Faculty of Information Technology
Monash University, Australia
+61 3 9903 2701
judy.sheard@monash.edu

Simon
Electrical Engineering & Computing
University of Newcastle, Australia
+61 2 4348 4666
simon@newcastle.edu.au

Matthew Butler
Faculty of Information Technology
Monash University, Australia
+61 3 9903 1911
matthew.butler@monash.edu

Katrina Falkner
School of Computer Science
University of Adelaide, Australia
+61 8 8313 6178
katrina.falkner@adelaide.edu.au

Michael Morgan
Faculty of Information Technology
Monash University, Australia
+61 3 9903 1066
michael.morgan@monash.edu

Amali Weerasinghe
School of Computer Science
University of Adelaide, Australia
+61 8 8313 4626
amali.weerasinghe@adelaide.edu.au

ABSTRACT

Safeguarding academic integrity is an issue of concern to all computing academics due to high and rising levels of plagiarism and other cheating in computing courses. There have been many studies of the cheating and plagiarism practices of computing students and the factors that can influence these practices, and a variety of strategies for reducing cheating have been proposed. This national study of first-year computing programs provides insights into what strategies computing academics use to discourage or prevent their students from cheating. Having interviewed 30 academics from 25 universities we found 21 different types of strategy, which we classified into five themes: education; discouraging cheating; reducing the benefits of cheating; making cheating difficult; and empowerment. We also found that academics often employ strategies across all of these themes.

Keywords

CS1; assessment; academic integrity; cheating; plagiarism

1. INTRODUCTION

There is widespread concern about violations of academic integrity in university courses, with many reports of high levels of cheating in exams and in coursework. Furthermore, the incidence of these practices appears to be rising [2,12]. With the Internet facilitating access to resources and assistance, it is increasingly easy for students to find materials and even personal assistance with assessment tasks [7,9]. Problems arise when such resources or assistance are used inappropriately or without proper attribution.

Violation of academic integrity is a critical issue for universities to address. Cheating can damage the reputation of a course, an

ITiCSE '17, July 03-05, 2017, Bologna, Italy
© 2017 ACM. ISBN 978-1-4503-4704-4/17/07...$15.00
DOI: http://dx.doi.org/10.1145/3059009.3059064

institution, and a discipline. Not only does the cheating student miss out on an expected learning experience, but the cheating can also degrade the educational environment, ultimately affecting learning for all students [4].

Some studies have shown that violation of academic integrity is disproportionately high in computing courses [6,14], although there is some conjecture as to whether the reported higher levels are simply due to greater use of detection tools by computing academics [10]. Regardless, the levels of cheating in computing courses are certainly high [15].

This extensive national research project has provided the opportunity to gain insights into what computing academics do to discourage or prevent their students from cheating and plagiarising. The aim of this report is to identify and categorise the strategies used by computing academics to safeguard academic integrity in their introductory computing courses.

2. ACADEMIC INTEGRITY IN COMPUTING COURSES

Any strategy employed to safeguard academic integrity requires knowledge of student cheating practices. There is a corpus of research about this topic in regard to computing students, with research studies investigating what types of cheating computing students practice, why they cheat, and what would discourage them from cheating [6,16]. Over a range of practices the main influences on cheating in a couple of large studies were found to be time pressure and concerns about failing, while the main countering influences were students' desire to learn and to know what they have learnt [16,17].

Some computing courses have particular characteristics that can influence students' understanding of academic integrity and consequently their behaviour. In programming courses, the standard practice of code reuse can cause confusion about the appropriate use and attribution of code written by others [13]. At the same time, university-level information resources and policies about academic integrity typically focus on written prose and are usually not adequate to inform students about appropriate use and citation of others' code [19,21]. Likewise, many institutions mandate the use of text-based similarity detection tools, unaware that these are useless in the detection of program similarity. While there are many tools available for the detection of code similarity, most computing academics appear not to use them [21]. Finally, although not specific to computing courses, the requirement for group work in many courses can cause issues with attribution of work and with students' understanding of the difference between collaboration and collusion [6,20,22]. If strategies to address cheating among computing students are to be effective, they should take these factors into account.

Safeguarding academic integrity entails reducing the incidence of cheating. A previous study of academic integrity in computing courses proposed that the process of addressing cheating could be considered from four perspectives: education, prevention, detection, and consequence [5]. Education and prevention are proposed as the key considerations for strategies to stop cheating from occurring, while detection and consequence focus more on dealing with cheating after it has occurred.

The literature reports many ideas for reducing cheating in computing courses. Some strategies have focused on educating students about what constitutes cheating, the problems associated with cheating, and possible consequences. These strategies take various forms, including information material, education programs, and educative tools. For example, Stepp and Simon [22] required their students to devise and then discuss scenarios describing inappropriate collaboration practices. Joy et al [8] describe a resource to assess computing students' understanding of plagiarism and to help the students learn how to avoid it.

Investigating the cheating phenomenon through student focus groups, Dick et al [5] concluded that students were in need of education about cheating and plagiarism. They proposed a comprehensive list of 12 characteristics for such an education program; however, the students in their study maintained that education on its own would not be effective. Simon et al [19] described different ways that academics in their study informed their students about academic integrity. An interesting response from some students in this study was that they received little appropriate instruction about academic integrity.

A number of strategies have focused on preventing cheating through various means ranging from reasoned discouragement to making cheating difficult. The strategies proposed by Dick et al [5] in their focus group study include individualised assignments, continuous assessment, monitored assessment, peer assessment, and interviewing students about their assignment work. Although interviews are typically intended to detect cheating, students saw them as being highly effective in reducing cheating. Student presentations were also seen as effective, although to a lesser extent. The study by Simon et al [19] found that academics commonly used a number of these strategies except for interviews and peer assessment.

Other strategies have focused on helping students not to cheat through building a strong and supportive culture of academic integrity. This approach is championed by McCabe [11], who reports success with honor codes in the US. Dick et al [5] point out that honor codes are not possible or appropriate in all contexts, but some of their proposed strategies take a similar approach. For example, they suggest that caring about students and ensuring a high level of student interaction in the classroom would reduce the level of cheating.

The deterrent effectiveness of detection and punishment remain unclear. Fraser [6] argues that high rates of detection and prosecution will deter cheats, and conversely that students are more likely to cheat if they believe cheating is commonplace. An empirical study by Bennett [1] found that punishment was a deterrent to major forms of plagiarism but not necessarily to minor forms. However, Sheard and Dick [16] found that fear of consequences did not appear to have any influence on the level of cheating.

These studies indicate that there are many effective strategies that can be used to safeguard academic integrity in the computing education environment. In our study we investigated what strategies are actually used by academics in their important role as the designers and providers of the learning environment and the assessment tasks. The findings reported in this paper give insights into the focus of the academics' attention in ensuring academic integrity in the assessment strategies that they employ.

3. RESEARCH APPROACH

This study draws upon data collected in 2014 for a report on teaching practices in first-year computing courses in Australia [18]. The purpose of the report was to document information about teaching practices and factors influencing the first-year experience of computing students in the Australian higher education context.

For the report we interviewed 30 academics from 25 universities, all of whom were involved in teaching and/or coordination of first-year computing courses. Participants were recruited mainly by contacting computing departments to identify the staff involved with delivery of first-year computing programs. The recorded telephone interviews, which ranged in length from 45 to 60 minutes, were all conducted by a single researcher.

The semi-structured interview script addressed six themes designed to investigate different aspects of the first-year experience: what we teach; where we teach; how we teach; how we assess; how we strengthen the learning environment; and how we support our students. The interview questions pertinent to the current analysis are:

- What types of assessment are used in first-year courses?

- How are the students educated about academic integrity in the context of computing courses?

- How much of the assessment is more or less guaranteed to be the work of the individual?

- For work not done in supervised conditions, what techniques are used to verify that the work is the student's own work?

The responses to the first interview question were analysed to give an overview of the forms of assessment used in first-year computing courses, as reported in section 4.1.

The responses to the other three questions were coded using a thematic analysis [3]. Each code represented a particular type of strategy that was used to reduce cheating in a first-year computing course. The data was coded by one of the authors, then the codes were reviewed by two other authors, discussed, and refined as appropriate. The types of strategy were organised into four themes and again discussed and refined. The themes and strategies found are reported in section 4.2.

4. FINDINGS

We begin with an overview of the types of assessment used in the introductory programming courses in this study, then report the strategies used by the academics to reduce the occurrence of cheating in their courses.

4.1 Forms of Assessment

Overall there was a mixture of invigilated and non-invigilated assessment. An end-of-semester written exam was the typical form of summative assessment in first-year computing courses. Most exams were weighted between 40% and 60% of the overall mark for the course, with 50% the most common weighting. The lowest weighting was 20% and the highest was 70% of the overall mark.

In combination with an end-of-semester exam there were a variety of other forms of assessment. The most common was assignment work, done individually or sometimes in a group. Often more than one assignment was set during the semester or the assignment was set in stages. Tests held during semester were another common form of assessment. These were either mid-semester tests worth 10% to 20% or a series of smaller tests, typically conducted online. Tasks performed in tutorial or lab classes were also often used as low-stakes assessment worth 1% to 2% for each task.

Less common forms of assessment mentioned were portfolio assessment, presentations, and submitted homework tasks. One interviewee gave students a mark if they visited the lecturer to ask a question. There were indications of a growing use of social media, such as blogs and wikis, for assessment tasks.

4.2 How Computing Academics Safeguard Academic Integrity

Computing academics employ many different strategies in their attempts to uphold academic integrity in their courses. The analysis found 21 different types of strategy which were organised into four overarching themes: *education* (raising awareness and understanding of what constitutes cheating and its consequences); *discouraging cheating*; *making cheating difficult*; *reducing the benefits gained from cheating;* and *empowerment* (supporting students and helping them understand the benefits of behaving with integrity). The themes and strategies are shown in **Table 1** and further explained in the following sections.

4.2.1 Education

A number of strategies used to safeguard academic integrity involve educating students about the acceptability of different practices in the use of resources and assistance. The aim is to help students understand what practices constitute cheating and plagiarism, and the consequences of engaging in these practices. Strategies classified as education involve instruction, provision of information resources, and using instructional tools.

The interviewees described different approaches to educating first year computing students about academic integrity, ranging from *"a little bit ad hoc" (I-11)* to *"academic integrity is in every session that I [teach]" (I-7)*.

In more than half of the universities, academic integrity was taught by a central unit, either as a dedicated course or as part of a study skills course. In the other universities it was covered within individual courses. A few interviewees seemed to take a 'hands-off' approach, just pointing students to resources or

Table 1: Strategies to reduce cheating

Theme	Type of Strategy
Education	Instruction about academic integrity
	Information resources
	Instructional tools
Discouraging cheating	Heightening awareness of the consequences of cheating (e.g. punishment)
	Requiring students to commit to abide by academic integrity policies
	Observing students working
	Monitoring work
	Setting staged assignments
	Making work visible
	Requiring students to work in groups
	Oral presentations
	Interviewing students
	Making it too risky to cheat (e.g. detection)
Reducing the benefits of cheating	Low stakes assessment
	Setting hurdle assessments
	Verification of assignment work in exams
Making cheating difficult	Invigilating assessment
	Individualising assessment
Empowering students	Supporting students
	Building relationships with students
	Focusing on learning gained through doing the assessment tasks

relying on the university courses; however, most discussed and related academic integrity issues to their own courses.

> *[Academic integrity] is something that I discuss with them because the [course] that I do is generally one of the first they are likely to do. I talk about some of the specific traps that people could fall into; working together or ending up with someone's code and submitting that as your own and that sort of thing. So I discuss it specifically in the lecture as to what can happen and how they can protect themselves against getting into that situation. (I-12)*

Instruction about academic integrity typically begins early, usually during orientation week or the first lecture.

> *I start off very early talking about what they can steal online and how they can do it. Basically, I say 'I'm happy with you finding code online as long as you tell me where you got it from'. As long as it's not the entire program. If you bought the program you won't get the marks. (I-5)*

A particular concern in academic integrity is helping first-year students distinguish between acceptable collaboration and collusion:

> *Often in first year, because they are working together ... we have a chat with them about collaboration and when it's appropriate and when it's not. .... We tell them it's OK to work in collaboration in the sessions but when it comes to the practical we want them to work independently and we tell them what that means. (I-9)*

Most interviewees mentioned providing links to university plagiarism policies in course websites and in documents such as course outlines and assignment specifications. Many universities have created online resources, including instructional tools, to inform students about academic integrity.

A few interviewees mentioned ploys to ensure that their students access these resources. For example, at one university students were expected to complete a quiz on academic integrity in their first year of study. This quiz is worth 5% of a student's grade. At another university academic integrity is taught with an online module that can also be used as a contract with the student.

A number of interviewees mentioned a combination of activities forming multifaceted and integrated approaches to educating students about academic integrity. For example:

Lecturers provide information and discuss (in class) academic integrity policies, why academic integrity is important and consequences of breaches, etc. There are a couple of sessions with the [special unit] leaders that are devoted to academic integrity. ... This is reinforced through the study desk. Forums are used to discuss academic integrity and what is acceptable. ... There is a link to library resources on academic integrity as well. (I-3)

However, one interviewee suggested that the educational approaches are not entirely necessary:

... possibly more could be done ... but the majority of students who [cheat] are the ones who keep doing it time and time again. We don't get too many students who say they didn't understand that and honestly mean that. We do have a few issues with international students with things being a little bit different in their culture but for the majority of domestic students they learn that stuff in high school. (I-16)

4.2.2 Discouraging cheating

Interviewees described a number of approaches they had used to discourage students from cheating. Ten different strategies were identified and most of these related to in-semester assignment work.

To heighten awareness of the consequences of cheating, some interviewees sent or posted reminder messages to their students. In one case a letter was sent from the head of the school:

...every semester the Head of School sends an email to all students saying there were X number of students found guilty of plagiarism this semester and you should all be taking this seriously. He gives feedback about what students have been caught plagiarising to show them that we're actually catching them and doing something about it. (I-13)

A common practice is to require a commitment from students that they will abide by academic integrity policies:

... in the first introductory lecture we talk about academic integrity and then whenever they log in to the environment, first they have to read about this academic honesty policy and agree to those terms and conditions". (I-9)

Alternatively, when submitting an assignment students make a declaration that the work is their own *"They sign their life away physically or electronically when they submit things." (I-1)*

Taking a different approach, as a deterrent to cheating some interviewees mentioned observing their students working in class and actively monitoring their progress:

With the lab work generally most of that work is done in class so you have a fair idea based upon how they're progressing ... You also have the opportunity to ask them questions about 'what does that bit mean' or 'why did you do it this way'. If there's any question about whether the work is their own – sometimes someone will turn up at the start of the lab and has already done all the work – ... the tutor can ask them about it to get some reassurances about whether they understood it and therefore were likely to have done it themselves. It's not supervised in the same way as an exam but it's some kind of reassurance. (I-12)

Some interviewees used staged assignment work, with marks allocated at specific checkpoints, to enable monitoring of progress. This strategy helped students avoid pressures to cheat by encouraging them to start their assignments early and giving them more time to seek legitimate help if needed.

Observation and monitoring of student work is also possible electronically with the use of social media. An added advantage is that a student's work is visible to other students, which discourages them from using work that is not their own.

... we get students to collaborate on assignments or content on a Wikipedia-style server that they can all edit simultaneously. That's been successful. .... Because it's online the students see an evolving project and can see the group members' work. As staff members we ... can see who's doing work and who's not. (I-12)

There was no consensus about whether students should be required to work individually or permitted to work with others on their assignments. A number of interviewees required their students to work individually; however, one required students to work on their assignments in pairs as he considered *"... this makes it much less likely that they will seek outside help" (I-14)*.

Another strategy was to interview students or require them to give presentations as part of the assessment process.

Interviews are quite popular in the programming type subjects ... You can ask them a few pointed questions about their motivation for the design they made, why they did it that way, and you can start to poke them a bit and say 'if we were to change this what would happen; if you wanted to do this feature how would you do it'. I've used the interview and they tend to be pretty good at picking up students who mightn't [have done] all their work (I-1)

Although some interviewees saw interviewing as an effective strategy to discourage cheating, not many used it as it was seen as too time-consuming.

A common strategy to discourage cheating was to increase the risk of getting caught. A number of interviewees said that their use of similarity detection tools was a deterrent to plagiarism as the students were made fully aware that the tools would be used and they received the reports generated.

4.2.3 Reducing the benefits of cheating

A strategy used to deter cheating was to reduce the benefits gained from cheating. Several interviewees used low-stakes assessments, for example, in-semester tasks worth 1% to 2%, believing that students would not find it worthwhile to cheat for so few marks.

To reduce the chance of students passing entirely on other people's work, at many universities students are required to gain a minimum exam mark, typically 40% or 50%, to pass a course. That is, they reduce the benefit of cheating on one assessment item by establishing another item as a hurdle that must be cleared. A couple of interviewees observed that they used exams to verify that the students had done their own assignment work. One advised *"we kind of design the final exam to make sure that* the students have done their work" (I-10). However, another mentioned his university's policy that "exams are not to be for the purpose of ensuring that people haven't cheated" (I-8).

4.2.4 Making cheating difficult
Moving beyond discouragement, a number of strategies were used to greatly reduce the opportunity to cheat.

Interviewees agreed that the incidence of cheating is greatly reduced in invigilated situations. As one interviewee noted, "the only thing you can absolutely guarantee are the moderated parts, which are the exams" (I-4). All universities had invigilated assessment in at least the exam component, although a number of interviewees expressed their dissatisfaction with a closed-book written exam as a means of assessing students' learning of programming. In an attempt to make invigilated exams a more valid form of assessment a couple of interviewees had moved towards open-book exams in computer labs.

> ... we have decided to have open-book exams. .... That reduces the stress for the exam supervisors. When it is closed-book they are really frightened about what type of software the students are using; can they go online, etc. .... But if it is open book then they can use any software. ... we had to create the exam so they can't simply find the answer from the internet – a small case study or scenario. (I-10)

Interviewees mentioned different techniques to reduce cheating through individualising assessment; for example, using randomly generated questions in tests, tailoring assignment work to individual students, and allowing students to negotiate their own assignment.

> ... every student or group is doing a different task. That doesn't stop them getting help from people inside or outside the class. But it does diminish the prospect of people colluding on the same piece of work and each of them handing it in as their own. (I-14)

Cheating on assignment work was mentioned as problematic by most interviewees. However, this was not easily resolved, as one interviewee observed:

> The only other option I can think of [to having a programming assignment] is to have programming problems on the exam paper but the exam is not the place where you can do any thinking. (I-13)

4.2.5 Empowering students
From another perspective, a number of interviewees described their strategies to empower students so as to reduce the likelihood that they would resort to cheating or would want to cheat. These strategies entailed supporting students, building relationships with students, and focusing on the learning gained through doing the assessment tasks.

Recognising that cheating can occur when students are under time pressure or are afraid of failing, a number of strategies were used to support students in their learning outside the classroom or online teaching environment. For example, a couple of interviewees mentioned Peer Assisted Student Support (PASS) schemes, student-led sessions that provide supplementary support for students within a course. One interviewee offered personal support:

> I would send an email to students normally around the time the assignment is due because I think most plagiarism occurs when students get behind and the assignment is due and they

> quickly find a friend to copy from. I tell them if they have fallen behind to ask me, not their mate. (I-15)

A couple of interviewees were in a position to build a relationship with each of their students. This helped them better understand their students' needs and respond more promptly.

> We teach smaller numbers ... There is more interaction with students on a one-to-one basis ... They can consult when there are issues, able to respond quickly if they need help ... Students just about always come to class ... you're in a better position to build up relationships with them. That has an impact on a whole range of things including assessment. (I-6)

A number of interviewees mentioned the importance of encouraging students to work for their own learning. One interviewee had designed a curriculum based on portfolio assessment for that purpose.

> One of the big changes with the portfolio assessment was creating that really positive environment where everything was focused on learning and the assessment became secondary. If you do the learning you'll get good marks because you can show that you can do this stuff. (I-2)

Some interviewees stress to their students that writing code is important for them to learn to work on their own, and will help them to prepare for their exam.

> We see the assignments as learning opportunities as much as assessment. As long as the students haven't copied verbatim we're willing to accept that. (I-6)

5. DISCUSSION AND FUTURE WORK
From our study there appear to be two main philosophical approaches to safeguarding academic integrity. In one approach, the educator designs the learning environment and assessment so that cheating opportunities are reduced or cheating is very risky for the student. In this approach the strategies directly address the particular cheating practice. The strategies in the 'making cheating difficult' theme are aligned with this approach. Some practices in the 'discouraging cheating' theme, such as monitoring the students while they work and using plagiarism detection tools, are also related to this approach.

The other approach is to design the learning environment so that the desire and need to cheat are reduced. This is achieved by building an informed, inclusive, connected, and supportive learning environment where the students' learning needs are understood and addressed. The strategies in the 'education' and 'empowerment' themes are aligned with this approach, along with some practices in the 'discouraging cheating' theme such as raising awareness of the consequences of cheating.

A key difference between the two approaches is that in the first approach the educator tends to take responsibility for stopping cheating, whereas in the second approach the educator takes responsibility for informing the students, but the students take responsibility for not cheating. Another important difference is that the first approach, using policing and scaring students to stop cheating behavior, tends to be reactive; whereas the second approach, using education and empowerment to reinforce the students' decisions to behave with integrity, has a positive focus.

An educator's personal philosophy will guide the approach they take to safeguarding integrity. For example, I-8 remarked "We prefer to adopt a positive approach and encourage them to see us if we're stuck, rather than a punitive approach." We found in our study that most academics employed multiple strategies that straddled both philosophies, and it was acknowledged that no single strategy was effective in all contexts. Most acknowledged that it was necessary to put direct measures in place to make cheating difficult. For example, exams still formed a substantial proportion of the assessment and in many cases this was seen as necessary for ensuring academic integrity, particularly if a hurdle requirement was implemented. We propose that smart design of learning environments and assessments can be educationally very strong and have the added bonus of making cheating difficult.

Our work has led to ideas for future research. We have identified 21 strategies for reducing cheating but further work is needed to determine their effectiveness and how widely they are used. Further, while empowering students is an approach that academics tended to support, and anecdotally supported with the hypothesis that students tend to cheat when they are out of other options, there appears as yet to be very little research to support this as a strategy.

6. CONCLUSION

In summary, it is important that the students have trust in the academic integrity of the learning environment and that they are educated and empowered to comply with policy in this area. This study has highlighted the range of strategies and approaches that have been adopted by computing academics. It seems that it is wise to combine strategies that will discourage and prevent students from cheating with strategies that will reduce their interest in cheating.

7. ACKNOWLEDGMENTS

This project was undertaken with the support of the Australian Council of Deans of ICT through the ALTA Good Practice Reports Commissioned for the 2013–2014 grant scheme (http://www.acdict.edu.au/ALTA.htm). The authors would like to acknowledge the work of Dr Beth Cook who conducted the interviews and prepared the detailed interview notes.

8. REFERENCES

[1] Bennett, R., 2005. Factors associated with student plagiarism in a post-1992 university. *Assessment & Evaluation in Higher Education, 30* (2), 137-162.

[2] Brady, B. and Dutta, K., 2012. 45,000 caught cheating at Britain's universities. In *The Independent*. http://www.independent.co.uk/news/education/education-news/45000-caught-cheating-at-britains-universities-7555109.html Accessed: 15 Jan 2017.

[3] Braun, V. and Clarke, V., 2006. Using thematic analysis in psychology. *Qualitative research in psychology, 3* (2), 77-101.

[4] Dick, M., Sheard, J., Bareiss, C., Carter, J., Joyce, D., Harding, T., and Laxer, C., 2003. Addressing student cheating: Definitions and solutions. *ACM SIGCSE Bulletin, 35* (2), 172-184.

[5] Dick, M., Sheard, J., and Hasen, M., 2008. Prevention is better than cure: Addressing cheating and plaiarism based on the IT student perspective. In *Student Plagiarism in an Online World: Problems and Solutions*, T.S. Roberts Ed. Information Science Reference, Hershey, PA, USA, 160-182.

[6] Fraser, R., 2014. Collaboration, Collusion and Plagiarism in Computer Science Coursework. *Informatics in Education-An International Journal, 13* (2), 179-195.

[7] Jones, M. and Sheridan, L., 2014. Back translation: an emerging sophisticated cyber strategy to subvert advances in 'digital age' plagiarism detection and prevention. *Assessment & Evaluation in Higher Education, 40* (5).

[8] Joy, M., Cosma, G., Sinclair, J., and Yau, J.Y.-K., 2009. A taxonomy of plagiarism in computer science. *In Proceedings of the EDULEARN09* (Barcelona, Spain), 3372-3379.

[9] Lancaster, T. and Clarke, R., 2016. Contract cheating: The outsourcing of assessed student work. In *Handbook of Academic Integrity*, T. Bretag Ed. Springer, Netherlands.

[10] Marsan, C.D., 2010. Why computer science students cheat. In *Network World* International Data Group. http://www.networkworld.com/article/2207189/infrastructure-management/why-computer-science-students-cheat.html Accessed: 15 Jan 2017.

[11] McCabe, D., 2016. Cheating and Honor: Lessons from a Long-Term Research Project. In *Handbook of Academic Integrity*, T. Bretag Ed. Springer, Singapore, 187-198.

[12] O'Malley, M. and Roberts, T., 2012. Plagiarism on the rise? Combating contract cheating in science courses. *International Journal of Innovation in Science and Mathematics Education, 20* (4), 16-24.

[13] Petre, M., 2012. Academic integrity in a changing environment. *ACM Inroads, 3* (2), 15-16.

[14] Roberts, E., 2002. Strategies for promoting academic integrity in CS courses. *In Proceedings of the 32rd Annual Frontiers in Education Conference*, IEEE, F3G-14.

[15] Sheard, J. and Dick, M., 2011. Computing student practices of cheating and plagiarism: A decade of change. *In Proceedings of the 16th Annual conference on Innovation and Technology in Computer Science Education* (Darmstadt, Germany), ACM, 233-237.

[16] Sheard, J. and Dick, M., 2012. Directions and dimensions in managing cheating and plagiarism of IT students. *In Proceedings of the 14th Australasian Computing Education Conference* (Melbourne, Australia), Australian Computer Society, 177-185.

[17] Sheard, J., Markham, S., and Dick, M., 2003. Investigating differences in cheating behaviours of IT undergraduate and graduate students: The maturity and motivation factors. *Journal of Higher Education Research and Development, 22* (1), 91-108.

[18] Sheard, J., Morgan, M., Butler, M., Falkner, K., Weerasinghe, A., Simon, and Cook, B., 2014. *Experiences of first-year students in ICT courses: Good teaching practices*. Commissioned Report. Australian Council of Deans of ICT.

[19] Simon, Cook, B., Sheard, J., Carbone, A., and Johnson, C., 2013. Academic Integrity: Differences between Computing Assessments and Essays. *In Proceedings of the 12th Koli Calling International Conference on Computing Education Research* (Finland).

[20] Simon, Cook, B., Sheard, J., Carbone, A., and Johnson, C., 2014. Academic integrity perceptions regarding computing assessments and essays. *In Proceedings of the 10th Annual Conference on International Computing Education Research*, 107-114.

[21] Simon and Sheard, J., 2016. Academic integrity and computing assessments. *In Proceedings of the Australasian Computer Science Week Multiconference (ACSW '16)* (Canberra, Australia), ACM, New York, Article 3.

[22] Stepp, M. and Simon, B., 2010. Introductory computing students' conceptions of illegal student-student collaboration. *In Proceedings of the SIGCSE'10* (Milwaukee, Wisconsin, USA), 295-299.

Academic-Industry Collaborations:
Effective Measures for Successful Engagement

Irene Polycarpou
UCLan Cyprus
University Ave 12-14, Pyla 7080, Cyprus
ipolycarpou@uclan.ac.uk

Cary Laxer
Rose-Hulman Institute of Technology
5500 Wabash Ave, Terre Haute, IN 47803, USA
laxer@rose-hulman.edu

Panayiotis Andreou
InSPIRE Research Center
University Ave 12-14, Pyla 7080, Cyprus
pgandreou@inspirecenter.org

Stan Kurkovsky
Central Connecticut State University
1615 Stanley Street, New Britain, CT 06050, USA
kurkovsky@ccsu.edu

ABSTRACT
Academic-Industry collaborations have always been important to universities for generating high-value socio-economic impact. The need for developing strong, long lasting relationships with industry has been intensified during the last years, as universities seek alternative means for funding than traditional research projects. This led universities to seek both, conventional and unconventional forms of engagement at a much higher rate than ever before, leading to the transformation of modern universities into multi-channel knowledge transfer hubs. At the same time, this enabled companies to remain competitive in the global economy and stimulated economic growth and development in their regions. Despite the obvious benefits, fostering this change does not come without challenges. It requires each side to recognize the benefits, cultivate the appropriate innovation and enterprise-driven culture and in parallel, overcome the barriers of traditional processes and communications.

This panel will discuss different forms of effective measures for successful academic-industry engagement. Its main topics are:

- Cultivating an innovation and enterprise-driven culture within universities: What measures are effective?

- Industry informed curricula design and outcomes assessment: What are the challenges?

- Undergraduate/postgraduate internships and placements: How can they be integrated?

Keywords
Academic-industry collaborations; industry engagement; industry informed curriculum; student internships.

ITiCSE '17, July 03-05, 2017, Bologna, Italy
© 2017 Copyright is held by the owner/author(s).
ACM ISBN 978-1-4503-4704-4/17/07.
http://dx.doi.org/10.1145/3059009.3095098

PANELIST POSITION STATEMENTS

Irene Polycarpou
Promoting academic-industry engagement requires disruptive changes across all levels of an academic institution. Starting from the highest level, university leadership is perhaps the most vital aspect where changes should be integrated. Strategic partnerships should be formed with shared visions and goals, clearly highlighting the benefits of the partnership to both academic and industry organizations. Short-term targets (e.g., small scale projects and easy to implement activities) can be utilized to quickly forecast the longevity of the partnership, allowing the academic institution to focus on a smaller set of partnerships that will last longer and will increasingly provide wealthier benefits. However, the whole process depends on another vital component: the academic. Not all academics are up to the challenge; developing and most importantly, maintaining partnerships requires a special breed of academic, who has the ability and skills to know when to build bridges and when to challenge preconceptions and propose new ideas. Consequently, universities need to invest in the establishment of processes and mechanisms for training and developing faculty to acquire such project management and communication skills. Additionally, given the academics' busy schedules with scholarly and administration activities, attractive motivation mechanisms (e.g., remuneration and promotion schemes) are essential to "oil the wheel" and promote engagement.

Panayiotis Andreou
Internships and placements have always been extremely valuable for the students' personal and professional development, and of significant value to the industry, by allowing access to higher level skills, bringing new ideas and perspectives and many others. The Center of INterdisciplinary Science Promotion & Innovative Research Exploration (InSPIRE) has established a culture of innovative partnerships between academia, industry, community-based organizations and policy makers that allows students to receive quality internships and placements for developing small-scale research and industry projects. InSPIRE's innovative approach can be summarized in two words: open innovation. Any academic, student, or industry partner can share ideas and visions with InSPIRE members. Ideas are disseminated in the forms of calls to students and faculty that share the common vision and want to be involved in its design and development, leading to the formation

of small agile multi-cultural teams that work under the supervision of a collaborative group of coaches and mentors from both the academia and industry, for the fulfilment of the project requirements. This approach has proven so far to greatly enrich the student learning experience, cultivate citizenship and improve employability.

Cary Laxer

High impact research and innovation usually comes from the adoption of an interdisciplinary approach, combining science, technology and business. Promoting and facilitating interdisciplinary degrees is an effective way for the university to move towards this direction. However, the establishment of such complex degrees requires the engagement of the industry, typically by forming Industrial Advisory Boards, which allow industry partners to influence curricula design according to market needs. Through this process, new innovative partnerships and collaborative projects emerge, as on the one hand the university is informed about organizational requirements and seeks ways to engage in targeted research to address these needs, and on the other hand, the industry partner is exposed to the latest research breakthroughs and seeks ways to exploit it to become more competitive and increase economic growth.

Stan Kurkovsky

A substantial number of computing programs are accredited by external agencies, such as ABET (Accreditation Board for Engineering and Technology). ABET accreditation requires an academic program and/or department to have an established advisory board representing the program constituents. In many cases, these are comprised of the members of the industry. Although the advisory boards cannot 'dictate' what courses a program should offer and which courses to teach, they play a very important role in forming the overall direction for the evolution of each academic program, including program assessment and curricular changes. Additionally, members of the advisory boards may help build stronger connections between the universities and the industry by providing internship opportunities, student projects, and hiring the graduates of the program.

Broadening Participation in Computing: Examining Experiences of Girls of Color

Allison Scott	Alexis Martin	Frieda McAlear	Sonia Koshy
Kapor Center	Kapor Center	Kapor Center	Kapor Center
2148 Broadway	2148 Broadway	2148 Broadway	2148 Broadway
Oakland, CA 94612	Oakland, CA 94612	Oakland, CA 94612	Oakland, CA 94612
1-415-946-3057	1-415-946-3057	1-415-946-3057	1-415-946-3057
Allison@kaporcenter.org	Alexis@kaporcenter.org	Friedam@kaporcenter.org	Sonia@kaporcenter.org

ABSTRACT

In order to enhance participation in computer science for girls of color, this study examines the outcomes of a rigorous out-of-school culturally relevant computer science intervention designed to engage underrepresented students in computing. Findings demonstrated that within-race gender differences exist in early interest in computing. Female students of color demonstrated significantly lower engagement and interest in computing, suggesting that being a member of a marginalized gender group plays a unique role and has a multiplying (negative) effect. Further, there were still significant gender differences in computing engagement after participation in one summer of the computer science intervention. Promising outcomes were revealed among a group of students who chose to enroll in the optional Advanced Placement CS A preparatory course; there were no gender differences in enrollment and completion of the course. In examining longitudinal outcomes, gender is a significant predictor of majoring in computer science in college, with male students much more likely to major in computer science than female students. These findings have important implications for addressing the gender gap in computing, including understanding how the intersection of race and gender presents unique barriers and challenges for women of color in computing, and that interventions to broaden participation in computing must address the unique experiences of women of color.

Keywords

Computing; Culturally Relevant; Disparities; Efficacy; High School; Intersectionality; Underrepresented

1 INTRODUCTION

Addressing disparities in the participation of women and girls in computing and technology remains an economic imperative for countries across the globe [9,19]. Given the increasing demand

for highly skilled technology workers to contribute to economic growth and development among both OECD countries and non-OECD countries with emerging economies [19], the lack of participation of women and girls represents a loss of potential talent. Women comprise just 25% of the global computing workforce and roughly 30% of the computing workforce in Europe [6]. Rates of participation in computing among women in computing has been as low as 10% in some countries [9]. On average, gender disparities in computing are considerably wider in countries without substantive technology infrastructure, however sizeable gender disparities also exist in countries with high technology adoption rates [11]. In the United States, which has the largest technology market in the world, women comprise just 25% of the technology and computing workforce [2]. Therefore, parity of representation of women in the global computing workforce could drive economic growth in industrializing countries while satisfying demand for computing workers in the technology sector and spurring innovation in the expanding number of global labor market sectors which depend upon computing skills.

While global participation rates are low for all women in computing, women of non-European descent tend to be even more underrepresented in the global technology workforce than their peers of European descent. Using the United States as an example, women from racial/ethnic groups underrepresented in computing and technology (African American, Latinx, Native American, Native Hawaiian, and Pacific Islander) comprise 20% of the general population and just 4% of the computing workforce [23]. Further, they account for 39% of the female population and only 26% of the Bachelor's degrees awarded to women in computer science [1]. While data sources are difficult to obtain and standardize across contexts [12], research suggests that women of color in nearly all national contexts face a number of specific cultural, psychological and economic barriers to technology access, education, and career opportunities at the intersection of race and gender (18, 19). Examining the barriers, experiences, and outcomes of women of color in computing in the largest technology markets may inform programming for women and girls in other regions and countries, and provide evidence and opportunities to address disparities in the participation of all women in computing across contexts. This research builds upon existing research about the double-bind facing women of color in STEM fields [18], by examining gender differences in computing interest, participation, and outcomes among a sample of underrepresented high school students in the United States.

2 THEORETICAL FRAMEWORK

In order to examine gender differences in the experiences and outcomes within computer science, this research draws upon theories of intersectionality and critical race theory. Crenshaw's theory of intersectionality (1991) posits that individuals have multiple identities, and that individuals already marginalized by their racial/ethnic identities may be further marginalized by their other identities, including gender, sexual orientation, socioeconomic status, and (dis)ability. These identities are experienced collectively and are inseparable from one another [8]. Thus, for women of color in computing, it follows that there are unique barriers resulting from the intersection of race and gender, which differ from the barriers experienced by individuals with just one of those marginalized identities [18]. Critical race theory has been used to conceptualize racial disparities in educational contexts as a function of structural and institutional racism manifested in schools and society [14]. In the computing education pipeline, structural disparities detrimentally affecting students of color can be seen in a lack of access to school funding and resources [7], computer science courses [5,16], and access to relevant and engaging curriculum [10]. Additional social and psychological barriers emerge as a reaction to being from a marginalized group [15], affecting students of color and women in computing. These barriers include stereotypes about ability [21], a lack of diverse role models [22], stereotype threat and disidentification within a domain associated with being a member of a marginalized group [21], and stereotypical cues within computer science environments [3]. While these barriers affect students of color and women, it follows that women of color face unique barriers as a result of having dual marginalized identities.

3 METHODOLOGY

3.1 Research Questions

To examine whether there is evidence of a double-bind affecting the outcomes of women of color in computing, this study explores the following research questions: (1) Among underrepresented high school students participating in a rigorous summer intervention program, do gender differences exist in computer science interest and aspirations? and (2) Do existing gender differences persist in participation in AP CS A courses in high school and the pursuit and completion of computer science degrees?

3.2 Program Context

This study took place within a 5-week, 3-summer science, technology, engineering and mathematics (STEM) program serving underrepresented high school students across four sites in Northern and Southern California. Students are admitted to the program in the summer between 9th and 10th grade, and attend for three consecutive summers. The academic programming includes: math, science, and computer science core courses, an engineering design course, and college preparation activities in addition to a youth development-focused residential program with lessons and activities related to social, emotional, and leadership development. This research specifically examines the impact of the computer science intervention components on student outcomes. The computer science intervention includes a three-sequence computer science course, taken by all students, with

BARRIERS	Culturally Relevant and Responsive Pedagogical Framework	SHORT-TERM OUTCOMES	LONG-TERM OUTCOMES
• Lack of access to rigorous CS courses • Lack of access to diverse peers and role models in CS • Social/psychological barriers (identification, belonging, stereotypes)	**INTERVENTIONS** • Multi-year CS course sequence • Culturally responsive pedagogy and curriculum • Exposure to diverse CS role models, peers, and instructors • Leadership growth opportunities inside and outside of the CS classroom	• Computer science knowledge • Attitudes toward CS • Identification with CS • Belonging in STEM • Decreased racial stereotypes • Decreased gender stereotypes • Access to diverse CS role models • Network of STEM/CS peers • Leadership skills • CS college and career aspirations	• Declare CS major • Persist in CS • Graduate with CS degree • Community impact via changed CS industry demographics

Figure 1: Conceptual Model for STEM Program CS Initiatives

This research will build upon the theoretical frameworks of intersectionality and critical race theory to further explore whether there are unique barriers faced by women of color that affect their interest, participation, and persistence in computer science. This research will go beyond examinations of experiences of girls of color [20], and look comparatively at experiences and outcomes of both gender groups to further explore the double-bind facing women and girls of color in computing. Given the underrepresentation of women in computing across the globe, this research can contribute to understanding of unique experiences of women of color and has implications for informing interventions to increase participation of women of color in computing.

curriculum adapted from Exploring Computer Science (CS1), Beauty and Joy of Computing (CS2), and AP Computer Science A (CS3; College Board, 2016; UC Berkeley and Education Development Center, 2012; GSEIS, Center X, 2004). Each course provides 37.5 total hours of instruction per summer, for a total of 112.5 hours. Students have the option of participating in an additional AP CS preparatory course during their senior year which prepares students to take the AP CS A exam. All of the computer science programming and activities are situated within a culturally relevant and responsive pedagogical framework and provide exposure to diverse computer science role models, diverse instructors, and support networks of diverse peers (Figure 1).

3.3 Participants

Three samples were included in this study: (1) a sample of current high school students who participated in the program during the summer of 2016, (2) a sample of participants in 2014 and 2015 who enrolled in the optional AP CS A preparatory course, and (3) a sample of current college students who previously participated in the program in 2014 and 2015. In Sample 1, participants were recruited for this research study through a verbal invitation given during the program orientation meeting attended by students and their parents. A total of n=205 students consented to participate in the research study and completed both the pre and post-survey (80% participation rate). All participants were members of racial/ethnic groups underrepresented in STEM fields, relative to their percentage of the United States population. The majority of participants were Hispanic/Latinx (52%), Black/African American (34%) and Southeast Asian (8%), with participants classified as "other" or "multiracial" comprising the remaining 6%. The sample consisted of slightly more females (53%) than males (47%). Tenth graders were 43% of the sample, with 11th and 12th graders comprising 30% and 27%, respectively. The majority of students came from low-income households, as determined by federal qualification for Free/Reduced Price Lunch (78%). Seventy-six percent of the students will be the first in their family to complete college. All students attended high schools in California, in the San Francisco Bay Area and Los Angeles Area; with 92% attending public schools.

In Sample 2 and Sample 3, demographic data and program participation data were collected from program records of participants from 2014 and 2015. A total of 183 students participated in the program during that time, and of those participants, 71 (39%) chose to enroll in the optional AP CS A preparatory course during their senior academic year. 58% were male and 42% were female; 28% were African American and 62% were Latinx, with the remaining 10% from other underrepresented backgrounds. In Sample 3, students who had previously participated in the program were contacted by email and invited to complete a follow-up survey. A total of 129 students who participated in 2014 and 2015 completed the survey. In addition, educational data of 6 students from the 2014 and 2015 cohorts were captured from their recently updated LinkedIn profiles for an aggregated total of 135. Eighty-seven percent of those were enrolled in four-year universities (n=117). Forty-nine percent of the participants were male, and 51% female.

3.4 Data Collection Instruments, Procedures, and Analysis

Survey instruments, reviews of program records, and focus groups were used to examine computer science engagement and participation by gender. A pre- and post-program online survey containing demographic questions and 9 scales including a computer science engagement scale, was administered to all participants in Sample 1. The computer science engagement scale was the only scale utilized within this study and consisted of 6 items (α=.90) assessing interest in computer science and interest in pursuing computer science as a major in college and as a career. Items included, "I think computer science is interesting," and "I am likely to major in computer science in college." All items were measured on a 5-point Likert scale with higher values indicative of higher levels of agreement. Advanced Placement CS

A course enrollment and participation of students within Sample 2 was assessed using program records of student enrollment, participation, and completion of the AP CS A preparatory course in 2014-15 and 2015-16.

An alumni survey was used to collect demographic data and student current major/field of study (in addition to other variables not analyzed in this study) with Sample 3 participants in the fall of 2016. Current enrollment in a computing major was measured with one open-ended item asking students to "indicate your current undergraduate major." Responses that included computer science, computer engineering, computer programming, and electrical engineering were coded as computing majors. To collect qualitative data on experiences with computer science in the program, two focus groups were held during the summer of 2016 with 11 female and 6 male students. For the purposes of this study, only the female responses were utilized. A focus group protocol consisting of nine questions focusing on engagement, learning, and interest, was utilized, including items such as "How, if at all, did your [program name] computer science class affect how you feel about computer science?" and "What have you learned in computer science that really stands out to you?"

Descriptive analyses were used to examine the frequency of student participation, course completion, and test-taking rates, by gender. Descriptive analyses were also used to examine post-secondary outcomes by gender. Independent-samples t-tests and regression analyses were used to examine whether male and female participants differed significantly in CS engagement and whether gender was a significant predictor of post-program CS engagement levels, AP CS A participation, and college CS major. Focus group notes and transcripts were analyzed utilizing qualitative analysis software, and qualitative and quantitative data were triangulated to synthesize findings.

4 FINDINGS

4.1 Computer Science Interest and Engagement by Gender

Prior to entering the program, male students had significantly higher levels of engagement than female participants (M_{DIFF} = 0.33, 95% CI [0.13, 0.54], $t(203)$ = 3.183, p = .002.), demonstrating initial gender differences even among racially underrepresented populations (M_M=3.82, SD=.66 vs M_F=3.49, SD=.83). Computer science engagement from pre- to post-program was then analyzed to determine whether the intervention resulted in significant increases in computer science engagement. While there were no significant increases in CS engagement from pre- to post-program overall, $t(200)$ = -.68, p = n.s (M_{PRE}=3.66, SD=.76 to M_{POST}=3.69, SD=.86), regression analyses showed several demographics, including gender to be a significant predictor of post-program CS engagement scores. This finding revealed female participants were less likely to be engaged in CS than male participants ($β$ = -.33, p<.001). Qualitative data from surveys confirmed quantitative findings that disparities by gender exist in student perceptions of their "favorite course." Although girls represent 53% of participants, just 23% listed computer science as their "favorite," compared to 39% of male participants (Figure 2). Of the girls who chose computer science as their favorite course, 21% had just completed their first computer science course in the program. However, 50% of girls who listed computer science as their favorite class were in their second year of the program, suggesting that taking multiple CS courses may increase interest in computer science among girls of color. This indicates two important findings: (1) girls of color started out with less interest in computer science, but this interest grew over time, and (2) the intervention had differential effects on males versus females, with the intervention unable to close the gender gap in interests and aspirations in computer science, even though students received the same intervention and were from otherwise similar demographic backgrounds.

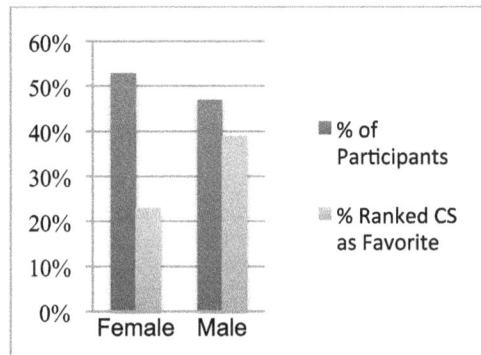

Figure 2. CS As Favorite Course, by Gender

Additional qualitative data from girls who listed computer science as their favorite course revealed promising practices and interventions that could be implemented to address barriers to participation among girls of color. Among girls who were highly engaged in computer science, themes of seeing CS as "fun and interesting" and "challenging" and seeing its relevance to their other interests (e.g. music, video games) were described. They also described the lack of exposure to CS in their high school and how exposure to the program's CS courses made them aware and interested in pursuing CS in college and career. Girls also indicated that teachers played a critical role in making the content engaging and in having high expectations of them.

4.2 Advanced Placement Computer Science Participation and Completion by Gender

To examine whether gender disparities in interest persist, the participation and completion rates in the optional AP Computer Science A preparatory course in 2014 and 2015 were examined. Seventy-one students chose to enroll in the optional course. Of these, 58% were male and 42% were female, demonstrating slight gender differences in enrollment rates. Of those who enrolled in the course, 41 (58%) of participants completed the course. Course completion rates and AP CS A exam completion rates were relatively equal by gender, with 60% of female students completing the course compared to 58% of males, demonstrating no gender disparities in persistence through the course. Regression analyses further reveal gender is not a significant predictor of AP CS A course participation (β = .04, p=ns) or completion (β = .10, p=ns). This is an important finding, demonstrating that of the group of students who self-select into the AP CS A prep course, there are no gender disparities in exam completion, which appears to counter the disparities seen broadly across the nation in AP CS A test-taking by gender [5].

4.3 Post-Secondary Computer Science Outcomes by Gender

This study also aimed to examine longitudinal outcomes and whether gender differences in initial interest in majoring in CS persisted into post-secondary education, among students who participated in the program in 2014 and 2015. Among the 117 program alumni currently attending 4-year colleges/universities, 24% of were declared CS majors. Males comprised the overwhelming majority of the CS majors (79%), while females comprised just 21%. Regression analyses demonstrated that gender is a significant predictor of majoring in CS in college, with female participants less likely to be CS majors than males (β = -.35, p=.00). This finding provides further evidence of the persistence and prevalence of female underrepresentation in the CS in post-secondary education, despite early interventions. Further, participation in the AP CS A course was a significant predictor of majoring in CS for male students (β = -.26, p=.05), but not for female students (β = -.03, p=ns). This is an interesting finding, suggesting that although previous research has demonstrated that participation in advanced computing courses are strong predictors of majoring in computer science in college [16], in this sample, taking a course did not increase the likelihood of majoring in CS for female students, further suggesting unique disparities among young women of color in computing.

5 CONCLUSIONS AND IMPLICATIONS

In computing and technology, there are vast disparities in participation by gender, with women underrepresented in computing worldwide. Within the United States context, where both women and people of color are underrepresented in computing, evidence suggests there are additional barriers affecting women of color who are marginalized by both race and gender [17,18]. Expanding upon this body of theoretical and empirical evidence, this study examined short and long-term outcomes of a sample of underrepresented high school students of color who participated in computing courses, and found that within-race gender differences exist in early interest in computing. Despite having similar racial and socioeconomic backgrounds, female students of color demonstrated significantly lower engagement and interest in computing, suggesting that being a member of a marginalized gender group plays a unique role and has a multiplying (negative) effect. Further, participation in the computing intervention alone did not close the gender gap; there were still significant gender differences in computing engagement after participation in one summer of the CS intervention. Promising findings were revealed among a small and self-selected group of students, who chose to enroll in the optional AP CS A preparatory course; there were no gender differences in enrollment and completion of the AP CS A course. In examining longitudinal outcomes however, gender is a significant predictor of majoring in computer science in college, with male students much more likely to major in computer science than female students. Participation in AP CS A in high school was only a significant predictor of majoring in computing in college for male students, but not female students. These findings have important implications for addressing the gender gap in computing, including understanding how the intersection of race and gender presents unique barriers and challenges for women of color in computing, and that interventions to broaden participation in computing must address the unique experiences of women of color. Interventions that provide short-term engagement and exposure to computer science may not be sufficient to address race and gender barriers to computing. Additional research is needed to understand initial barriers and experiences which affect early engagement and interest in computing for women of color and promising practices that increase and promote engagement in computing throughout high school, and thus increase participation and persistence in computing in college. Research within same-gender and different race context can also provide further evidence about effective intervention strategies. Expanding this body of research will have implications for broadening participation among women in computing in nations across the globe.

ACKNOWLEDGMENTS

This work is supported by the National Science Foundation under Grant Number 1339424.

REFERENCES

[1] Bartels, A. 2016. Global tech market will continue to grow at 4%-5% rates in 2016 and 2017. Retrieved from http://blogs.forrester.com/andrew_bartels/16-01-05-global_tech_market_will_continue_to_grow_at_4_5_rates_in_20 16_and_2017

[2] Bureau of Labor Statistics. 2013. Occupational Projections through 2022.

[3] Cheryan, S., Davies, P.G., Plaut, V.C., and Steele, C.M. 2009. Ambient belonging: How stereotypical cues impact gender participation in computer science. *J. Pers and Social Psych*. 97,6, 1045-1060.

[4] Crenshaw, K. (1991). Mapping the margins: Intersectionality, identity politics, and violence against women of color. *Stanford Law Review*. 43, 6, 1241-1299.

[5] College Board. 2016. Report to the nation.

[6] Economic Commission for Latin America and the Caribbean (ECLAC). 2014. *The software and information technology services industry in the United States: An opportunity for the economic autonomy of women in Latin America*. Santiago, Chile. Retrieved from http://selectusa.commerce.gov/industry-snapshots/software-and-information-technology-services-industry-united-states

[7] EdTrust. 2015. Funding Gaps. Retrieved from https://edtrust.org/wp-content/uploads/2014/09/FundingGaps2015_TheEducationTrust1.pdf

[8] Essed, P. 2001. Understanding everyday racism: An interdisciplinary theory. Sage Publications.

[9] Galpin, V. 2002. Women in computing around the world. *SIGSCE Bulletin*. 34, 2, 94-100.

[10] Goode, J. and Margolis, J. 2011. Exploring computer science: A case study of school reform. *ACM Trans on Comput Educ*. 11, 2.

[11] Hafkin, N. J., and Huyer, S. 2007. Women and gender in ICT statistics and indicators for development. *Information Technologies and International Development*. 4,2, 25–41. http://doi.org/10.1162/itid.2008.00006

[12] Hilbert, M. 2011. Digital gender divide or technologically empowered women in developing countries? A typical case of lies, damned lies, and statistics. *Women's Studies Intl Forum*. 34, 6, 479–489. http://doi.org/10.1016/j.wsif.2011.07.001

[13] Huyer, S. 2015. Is the gender gap narrowing in science and engineering? *UNESCO Global Science Report: Towards 2030*. Retrieved from http://unesdoc.unesco.org/images/0023/002354/235406e.pdf%5Cn

[14] Ladson-Billings, G., and Tate, W. F. 1995. Toward a critical race theory of education. *Teachers College Record*. 97,1, 47-67.

[15] Major, B., and O'Brien, L.T. 2005. The social psychology of stigma, *Ann Rev of Psych*. 56, 393-421.

[16] Martin, A., McAlear, F. and Scott, A. 2015. Path not found: Disparities in access to computer science courses in California high schools. Retrieved from: www.lpfi.org/pnf

[17] National Science Foundation. 2015. Survey of graduate students and postdoctorates in science and engineering. Retrieved from: https://www.nsf.gov/statistics/2015/nsf15311/tables/pdf/tab3-1-updated-2016-06.pdf

[18] Ong, M., Wright, C., Espinosa, L.L., and Orfield, G. 2011. Inside the double bind: A synthesis of empirical research on undergraduate and graduate women of color in Science, Technology, Engineering, and Mathematics. *Harvard Educ Review*. 81,2, 172-208.

[19] Powell, C., and Chang, A. M. 2016. *Women in Tech as a Driver for Growth in Emerging Economies*. Council on Foreign Relations.

[20] Scott, A, Martin, A., and McAlear, F. 2016. Computer science in California's schools: 2016 AP CS results and implications. Retrieved from: http://access-ca.org/wp-content/uploads/sites/4/2017/01/KC16017_Report-Final.pdf

[21] Steele, C. M., and Aronson, J. 1995. Stereotype threat and the intellectual test performance of African Americans. *J. Pers. and Social Psych*. 69,5, 797–811.

[22] Stout, J. G., Dasgupta, N., Hunsinger, M., and McManus, M. 2011. STEMing the tide: Using ingroup experts to inoculate women's self-concept and professional goals in science, technology, engineering, and mathematics (STEM). *J. Pers. and Social Psych*. 100, 255–270.

[23] U.S. Census Bureau, Population Division. 2015. *Annual Estimates of the Resident Population by Sex, Race, and Hispanic Origin for the United States*.

Out from the Shadows: Encouraging Girls in New Zealand into IT Careers

Alison Hunter
Manukau Institute of Technology
Auckland, New Zealand
ahunter@manukau.ac.nz

Raewyn Boersen
Designertech
Auckland, New Zealand
raewynb@designertech.co.nz

ABSTRACT

Shadow IT is a New Zealand intervention in which high school girls observe a day in the life of a woman working in IT. The effectiveness of Shadow IT in influencing girls to consider a career in IT was the subject of this research. Surveys conducted before and soon after Shadow IT showed that the girls participated in the event with an open mind and a positive attitude, and that the girls' levels of interest in an IT career had increased. In addition, the girls' perceptions of an IT workplace had become more realistic, with positive aspects better understood and earlier concerns allayed. However another survey one year later indicated that the influence of the event had not persisted for some of the girls. Girls intent on an IT career were studying IT subjects and had specific IT roles in mind, whereas girls who were now planning careers in other fields were not studying IT subjects. All the girls stated that Shadow IT had influenced their subject and career choices.

Keywords

Girls; Careers; IT; Interventions; High school; Education

1. INTRODUCTION

New Zealand is similar to many other Western countries in having a significant underrepresentation of women working in IT. In 2013, for example, only 25% of professional IT roles were occupied by women [20]. There is also noticeable horizontal and vertical segregation within the industry [14] as well as pay inequities for women working in IT [1]. These are not new phenomena; women's marginalisation in New Zealand's IT industry has been evident since at least the early 1980s [14]. In order to help address this shortage of women working in IT, many different interventions have been instigated around the world, many of them targeting teenage girls.

This paper reports on a pilot study which investigated the effectiveness of a New Zealand based intervention offered to high school girls.

2. BACKGROUND

2.1 Reasons for the Underrepresentation

Our understanding of the reasons for women's choices regarding a career in IT can be informed by considering factors that influence young girls' career choices. Studies (e.g., [12, 13, 22]) have shown

ITiCSE '17, July 03-05, 2017, Bologna, Italy
© 2017 ACM. ISBN 978-1-4503-4704-4/17/07...$15.00
DOI: http://dx.doi.org/10.1145/3059009.3059010

that teenage girls' career choices are influenced by many factors and these have been represented in a variety of career choice models.

One widely cited model proposed by Adya and Kaiser [2] identifies a range of social and structural factors influencing girls' career choices. Social factors comprising family, peer group, media, role models, and gender stereotypes [2] are most relevant to this study as these affect the perceptions teenage girls have of IT work. Many researchers have identified negative perceptions common to teenage girls, for example that IT work is uncool, nerdy, boring, technically oriented, male dominated, involves long work hours, and more suited to males [3, 12, 21]. These perceptions are exacerbated by other social factors such as stereotypical media representations of suitable work for females [18] and a lack of exposure to female IT role models [21]. Such negative perceptions all serve to put girls off an IT career. As Morton [17] found, very few high school girls in New Zealand intend to pursue an IT career despite perceiving IT work to be interesting, well paid, and secure.

2.2 Interventions

Interventions generally seek to overturn any negative influences associated with the social factors identified by Adya and Kaiser [2]; for example they may seek to challenge gender stereotypes or they may showcase successful female role models. By using a variety of techniques to engage girls with IT, interventions offer the encouragement and exposure identified by Wang, Hong, Ravitz and Ivory [22] as having the greatest influence on girls' career choices.

One of the first interventions in New Zealand was the Young Women's Programming Contest (YWPC), introduced in 1989. The YWPC ran for 11 years, giving a hands-on programming experience to girls so that they might choose a programming career [4]. A small study of YWPC participants indicated that the event was effective in encouraging some girls to enter the IT industry [7]. In 2008 the originators of the YWPC introduced the Programming Challenge 4 Girls (PC4G), again a one-day event aiming to influence high school girls towards a programming career. The PC4G was also a popular event which eventually expanded to include girls from six countries. Several other interventions have recently been introduced in New Zealand, e.g. Girl Code (girlcode.co.nz) and #GirlsInnov8 (girlsinnov8.weebly.com).

As Craig [8] and Craig, Lang, and Fisher [9] have pointed out, the effectiveness of interventions has often not been rigorously investigated. We may hypothesise that this was because intervention organisers often ran their events on a voluntary basis with minimal resources, and therefore gathered only informal feedback from participants. This was the case for the PC4G until 2013, when the first formal research was undertaken to investigate the effectiveness of that particular intervention – see Hunter and Boersen [15].

A few interventions have been evaluated. For example, the effectiveness of computing summer camps was evaluated by

Ericson and McKlin [11] however the focus of this work was on engaging students in computing rather than on the influence of the intervention on career choice. An intervention that did focus on career choice, Gr8 Designs for Gr8 Girls, was conducted and evaluated by Craig and Horton [10]. Immediately after the intervention girls' interest in choosing a computer science career rose considerably. A follow-up survey three months later showed that although the interest level had dropped, it remained higher than the pre-intervention level.

The intervention discussed in this paper, Shadow IT, began in 2014 as the brainchild of Manukau Institute of Technology (MIT), a large polytechnic in South Auckland. MIT is one of eighteen polytechnics or institutes of technology in New Zealand, all of which offer undergraduate degrees to local and international students, with some also offering post-graduate qualifications. Since the mid-1990s MIT has offered a bachelor degree in computing, and in 2016 became the first institution in New Zealand to have its degree accredited by the professional body, IT Professional New Zealand (https://itp.nz/). In 2014 and 2015 MIT ran the Shadow IT event with around 45 girls from the region participating each year. As is explained later, the event has since expanded to include other parts of New Zealand.

Shadow IT takes a different approach to the PC4G. It exposes high school girls to the wide range of roles available in the IT industry, rather than focusing only on programming. Organisers aim to "change perceptions that IT people work in dark rooms behind a computer all day" [19]. Its approach is to pair each girl with a female IT professional who the girl then 'shadows' for a day in the workplace – giving girls an observational opportunity rather than a practical experience, and a first-hand insight into the rewards and challenges for women working in IT. Each year girls have provided informal feedback to the event organisers and this data is used for planning purposes in the following year. In 2015 the research reported in this paper was instigated to determine the event's impact – did Shadow IT influence girls towards choosing an IT career or not.

3. RESEARCH QUESTIONS

The primary aim of this study was to measure the influence Shadow IT has on girls' intentions regarding a career in IT. Given that any influence detected immediately after the event may not be long-lasting, we took this into account in our methodology. We also investigated two assumptions underpinning the investigation: firstly, that attending Shadow IT would positively change any negative perceptions the girls might have of IT work, and secondly, that the event would be more successful if the girls' affective responses beforehand were positive. This second assumption was based on the experience of Boyle and colleagues [5] who found that student motivation, perceptions, and learning improved when students had positive feelings and emotions about their learning experiences. Consequently our assumption was that positive affective responses would mean we could expect the girls to enjoy the event and be highly motivated to learn from the experience.

Our specific research questions were therefore:

1. What evidence is there that attending Shadow IT positively influences girls' interest in an IT career?
2. What influence does attending Shadow IT have on the girls' perceptions of IT work?
3. What were the girls' emotional responses to Shadow IT, before and after the event?
4. What longstanding influence of attending Shadow IT is evident one year after the event?

4. RESEARCH METHODOLOGY

The primary method used to investigate these questions was survey research. Three surveys were required and are explained in the following section.

4.1 Survey Instruments

In order to investigate the immediate effectiveness of Shadow IT, we needed to survey participants before and after the event; these two surveys are referred to hereafter as the Before Survey and the After Survey. These surveys, constructed by the researchers, were based on a review of relevant literature (for example [12, 13]) and the researchers' previous research findings [15, 16] and included both closed-ended and open-ended questions covering matters relevant to Questions 1 to 3. The Before and After Surveys were made available to participants through Survey Monkey one week before the Shadow IT event and up to one week afterwards, respectively.

A third survey was required to investigate the long-term effect of Shadow IT (Question 4), and this was also constructed by the researchers. This survey was emailed to participants one year after the Shadow IT event and consisted of six closed-ended questions. A few further follow-up open-ended questions were then emailed to some girls, tailored to their individual responses to this survey.

4.2 Participants and Ethical Permissions

Participants in this study were recruited from the population of girls who attended Shadow IT in 2015. Because our participants were high school students aged 15 or 16, gaining consent required several steps. We first asked school principals to give permission for their students to be invited to participate and for their teachers to provide support, with confidentiality assured. We then provided girls from consenting schools with information about the research and an invitation to participate. Girls could participate only if their parents/guardians also consented. Teachers assisted by giving girls the information to take home and girls returned their consent forms to their teachers. Prior to the event, teachers returned to us all consent forms and a week before Shadow IT took place, they gave students details on how and when to access the Before and After Surveys. All girls, 44 from 12 high schools, were eligible to participate. Of the 12 schools, 10 principals gave permission for their schools to be involved, reducing the pool of possible participants to 36. Altogether, 21 girls from the 10 schools agreed to participate. Seventeen of these 21 girls also gave consent to be contacted again one year later.

4.3 Data Collection

From the pool of 21 participants, we received 17 completed Before and After Surveys (some incomplete surveys were discarded). The response rate for these surveys was therefore approximately 80%. Data from the surveys were downloaded from Survey Monkey.

One year after the event, we emailed the third survey to the 17 girls who had agreed to be contacted in this manner. This process proved to be rather unsatisfactory. Four emails immediately 'bounced' (these girls had probably changed their email addresses) and only seven girls supplied answers to the third survey. Further emails were exchanged with six of the seven girls and these provided a small amount of qualitative data. Our experience regarding the collection of follow-up data matched that of Craig and Horton [10] who reported having a similar problem when collecting data some months after their intervention.

We also obtained secondary data from the Industry and Community Engagement Manager at MIT, who sent us a copy of the *Shadow IT Student Feedback Report 2015*. This report summarised informal feedback obtained from girls by event organisers at the end of the event, as noted in section 2.2.

5. ANALYSIS

To analyse the quantitative data from the Before and After Surveys, we calculated frequency distributions of responses in order to facilitate comparison of before and after data. This analysis provided findings relating to Questions 1 and 3.

To analyse the qualitative data relating to Question 2, we undertook an inductive thematic analysis of responses, based on the process outlined by Braun and Clarke [6]. First we independently examined the data sets and generated initial themes, and then compared and adjusted these by mutual agreement. Because the girls' responses tended to be quite short, we found that there was usually no need for interpretation and we could identify themes semantically. For example, we agreed that a response *"the best thing about working in IT would be you get to work with technical things"* reflected this girl's passion for technology, as did similar responses such as *"the best thing [about] working in IT will be different things to learn about computers and spending more time on computers"*. The relevant theme, we agreed, was TECHNOLOGY. Using this process we identified five themes relating to the girls' perceptions of the best things about working in IT and five themes relating to the girls' perceptions of the worst things about working in IT.

The follow-up emails in 2016 provided a small amount of data which we treated as individual case studies.

6. RESULTS AND DISCUSSION

The *Shadow IT Student Feedback Report 2015*, our secondary data source, indicated that the event was a positive experience for the girls. All 44 girls (100%) reported that they "enjoyed the experience", 82% of the girls stated they had "learned a lot about the IT industry", and 87% agreed that they "now have a better understanding about careers in IT". No negative responses were received.

Findings from this study relating to each of our four research questions are reported and discussed in the following sections.

6.1 Emotional (Affective) Responses

Before the event, the girls were presented with a list of emotional states and were asked to select up to three of these which best described how they felt about attending Shadow IT. Table 1 lists the emotional states and the frequencies for each of these.

Table 1: Before Survey - Emotional Response – Girls' Feelings Before Attending Shadow IT

Emotional State	Frequency
Interested	12
Excited	11
Enthusiastic	6
Confident	3
Receptive	2
Neutral	2
Anxious	3
Uncertain	2
Cautious	1

Table 1 shows that a large majority of the girls reported anticipating the event with interest, excitement, and/or enthusiasm (most girls selected at least two of these options). A few of the girls also reported feeling confident and/or receptive, indicating that they would approach the event in an open-minded manner, with little apprehension. These positive affective responses suggest that the girls had high expectations that Shadow IT would be a fun and rewarding experience. Some negative affective responses were reported by a few girls, i.e. they were feeling anxious, uncertain, or cautious, as might be expected. However, as no girl selected more than one of these negative responses, it would appear that any unease the girls felt was minor and not likely to impact greatly on their enthusiasm for the event. No girl who reported feeling confident selected any of the negative responses.

After the event, the girls were asked to respond to four different statements related to the affective domain. These statements and the frequency of responses are presented in Table 2.

Table 2: After Survey - Emotional Response - How Girls Felt After Attending Shadow

Statement	Yes	No
I am excited and buzzy about IT career possibilities	16	1
I feel enthusiastic about IT and I am keen to tell others	16	1
I will choose IT related subjects next year	13	4
I feel uncertain about how to find out more about IT careers	7	10

The data in Table 2 show that after the event, all except one girl reported positive feelings about the IT industry and its career opportunities – they were excited, buzzy, and enthusiastic. In other words, their expectations before the event of a rewarding experience were met. These findings are consistent with similar data reported in the *Shadow IT Student Feedback Report 2015* noted earlier. In keeping with these positive feelings about IT careers, thirteen of the seventeen girls reported that they would choose to study IT subjects in the following year. These are encouraging findings for the event organisers, and the industry role model participants and their companies.

It is concerning, however, that seven of the girls (40%) felt uncertain about how they could find out more about IT careers. This suggests that Shadow IT organisers should provide career information to build on the girls' interest. The urgent need to make IT career information more readily available to high school girls is a matter raised previously by Hunter and Boersen [16].

6.2 Interest in an IT Career

Our first research question investigated whether attendance at Shadow IT changed the girls' interest in pursuing an IT career. These findings are shown in Table 3.

Table 3: Comparison of Girls' Interest in an IT Career Before and After Shadow IT

Level of Interest	Before Survey	After Survey
Strongly interested	5	9
Somewhat interested	12	8
Not really interested	0	0

These data indicate that Shadow IT has a positive effect on girls' interest in an IT career. Almost 25% more girls reported being 'strongly interested' in an IT career after the event than before, with a corresponding drop in the percentage of girls who were 'somewhat interested' before the event than after. This finding suggests that participation in the event strengthened the girls' interest in a career in IT.

6.3 Perceptions of IT Work

Our second research question was based on an assumption that attendance at Shadow IT would change the perceptions girls may have of working in IT, whether the perceptions are positive or negative. These findings are reported in Tables 4 and 5.

Table 4: Comparison of Perceptions: Best Things about Working in an IT Career Before and After Shadow IT

Themes	Before Survey	After Survey
Technology: An IT career allows you to pursue your passion for technology	8	11
Opportunity: An IT career allows you to explore many different fields and pathways	5	3
People: In IT you will be working with many like-minded people and will meet many different people	3	7
Contribution: An IT career allows you to help people and improve their lives	3	2
Fun: Working in IT would be enjoyable and fun	3	1

Using Table 4 we can see that before the event, the girls' perceptions were that an IT career would enable them to work with the technology they are passionate about, alongside people with similar interests, while also being fun and giving them opportunities to contribute and experience different pathways. Two example comments were "*if you're passionate about IT you will have a lot of fun; you'll be doing what you love day in and day out!*" and "*you get to work with people who have the same interest as you and you get to work with technical things which are fun*".

After the event, the girls' perceptions that an IT career would enable them to pursue their passion for technology and also involve working with many different people both increased. Comments such as "*it seems like a really friendly environment where you have to work in a team a lot*" and "*working in a friendly environment with a team*" suggest that the girls also became more aware of the importance of teamwork in the IT industry. These positive perceptions are in accord with girls' career preferences reported in Hunter and Boersen [16].

It is not clear why the incidence of some positive perceptions decreased after the event. Given that the girls' open-ended responses were rather brief, we might assume that once the girls had reported their most significant perception, they did not add others. We should not assume that the girls no longer perceived IT work to be enjoyable and providing opportunity to contribute or explore different fields.

Table 5: Comparison of Perceptions - Worst things about Working in an IT Career Before and After Shadow IT

Themes	Before Survey	After Survey
Gender discrimination: Being a woman among mainly men in IT will be problematic	7	3
Monotony: The office-bound and routine aspects of IT work are unappealing	7	5
Constant change: In IT you always have to keep up with new technologies	1	1
Long hours: IT work often involves working long hours	1	0
None/not sure: There are no negative things about working in IT	1	8

Before the event, the most commonly reported negative perceptions were that the IT industry is unsupportive of women and that the work can be monotonous. Comments such as "*I think the worst thing about working in an IT career is that females are usually looked down upon*" and "*we'll have to work around a lot of men and I know I'm quite nervous around guys, so it could be a bit of trouble*" indicate that the girls were aware of the underrepresentation of women in IT and that this is a concern to them. However, after the event this perception was not so prominent, and the related comments were more mild, for example, "*the lack of women, mainly*". This suggests that by spending the day with a female IT professional, the girls' concerns about gender discrimination were reduced. The perception before the event that IT work can be monotonous reduced slightly but remained a significant concern for some girls, as demonstrated by comments such as "*working on the same thing for a few days would be kind of boring*". However, the prospect of some monotony does not appear to have put girls off an IT career when we consider the data in Table 3. The most marked change in perception of the worst thing about working in IT was in the girls' responses of "*none*" or "*not sure*". After the event far more girls could not identify any negative aspect of IT work than before. These data give support to the proposition that Shadow IT positively influences girls' perceptions of an IT career.

6.4 One Year Later

One year after the event we were able to make contact with seven girls. Our purpose was to investigate whether any positive influence of the intervention was ongoing. Results from our third survey and follow-up emails are discussed below. In accord with our decision to treat these seven participants as individual case studies, we assigned each girl a pseudonym.

Of the seven girls, three (Yvonne, Helen, Karen) responded that they were "Strongly interested" in an IT career, one (Anna) said she was "Somewhat interested" and three (Ina, Cici, Linda) stated they were "Not really interested". All seven girls agreed that attending Shadow IT helped clarify their level of interest in an IT career.

For Yvonne, Helen, and Karen, Shadow IT appeared to strengthen their prior interest in an IT career (rather than awaken them to the idea). Karen said "*I'm really into computers and technology as a whole and it just interests me how such small machines can be so powerful and control so much*", and Yvonne stated "*I really enjoy using computers and the idea of coding my own programs and* games. I'd consider myself a gamer, not hard core but a gamer none the less. And being able to create my own games was really what made me interested in IT". These girls all reported having a specific role in mind: software engineer (Karen), programmer or game designer (Yvonne), and web designer (Helen). All three girls plan to study IT at tertiary level after they leave school.

In contrast, Ina, Cici, and Linda are now "Not really interested" in an IT career, despite having reported soon after the event that they were "Somewhat interested". Linda is "not a fan of routine and office-oriented jobs" and is thinking of a career in "either engineering, medicine or the film industry". Ina is "more interested in other subjects" and would like a career in "something relating to chemistry". We asked both these girls whether Shadow IT had put them off working in IT, and although Ina replied "no", Linda did express some disappointment with the event: "Seeing the structure and office-like nature of the job did put me off... I was assigned to a company which showed very little actual IT work. We came from a programming class and were looking into that sort of field but instead received an insight into clerical jobs that are mainly based around management rather than IT". It appears that attending Shadow IT may have influenced Linda away from an IT career (even though she did not state that at the time), given that at the time she was studying programming. Her comment is relevant to Shadow IT organisers when planning the event as it emphasises the importance of aligning girls' expectations with appropriate experiences on the day.

We also asked the girls to list the subjects they are currently studying. As expected, all girls who are strongly interested in an IT career are currently studying digital technologies, whereas those girls who are not really interested in an IT career have not chosen this subject. All the girls agreed that Shadow IT influenced their subject choice in the year following the event.

Our final question for the girls concerned their level of knowledge about IT careers. All the girls felt that they were well informed about IT careers and knew where to get more career information if necessary. This finding contradicts the data in Table 2 which revealed considerable uncertainty about IT career information. It may be that because the girls were now one year older, they were more informed generally about careers and sources of career information. We did note that Linda and Cici, two of the three girls who now stated they were not really interested in a career in IT, had reported one year earlier that they were not feeling uncertain about how to find out more about IT careers, whereas Ina, the third girl, had reported feeling uncertain. Thus it appeared that Linda and Cici had responded consistently with regards career information and that their decision not to pursue an IT career was not related to uncertainty about IT careers.

7. LIMITATIONS AND FUTURE WORK
A significant limitation of this pilot study was its small number of participants; our findings plainly cannot be extrapolated. Conducting research with underage participants was challenging. Firstly, we were dependent on principals' approval – one principal told us he refuses all research within his school. Secondly, we were vulnerable to the capriciousness of teenage girls, many of whom did not complete all phases of the research. These factors may partly explain why we recruited only 21 participants from a population of 44. We were not able to determine any factors that differentiated the girls who opted to participate from those who did not. It is possible that teachers in some schools were more supportive of the research than others.

In 2016, MIT handed the event over to the New Zealand Technology Industry Association (NZ Tech), the primary industry association for New Zealand IT companies, who rebranded the event as Shadow Tech Day. This allowed the event to be expanded to include a greater number of girls from other New Zealand cities. In 2016 the event was run in New Zealand's three largest cities, Auckland, Christchurch, and Wellington, with 300 girls participating in total, 120 in Auckland. This will allow for an enhanced study with revised surveys and procedures, and an increased sample size to take place in 2017. We also plan to ask girls to identify the role they are interested in and the role they shadowed, in order to correlate these to their level of interest in an IT career. To reduce the problem of locating participants one year later, we will request more than one method of communication.

We will also communicate to organisers the need to provide girls with access to IT career information as well as the possibility of matching girls' interest areas to appropriate role models.

8. CONCLUSIONS
Findings from this pilot study based on data collected before and soon after the event indicate that Shadow IT is an effective intervention in many respects. Over time, however, the positive effects of the intervention diminish and some girls become interested in careers in other fields.

The girls participated in the event with an open mind and a positive attitude; they were interested, excited, and ready to be engaged. After Shadow IT, 16 of the 17 participants who completed the surveys before and after the event (94%) confirmed their enthusiasm for IT work and 13 (76%) said that they would choose to study IT subjects the following year. The interest levels in an IT career also increased with almost 25% more girls stating after the event that they were strongly interested in an IT career than before. Shadow IT also provided the girls with a more realistic perspective of IT work in that they realised that there is a high level of teamwork and people interaction involved and that their prior concerns regarding gender discrimination had been overstated. Despite recognising these positive aspects of a career in IT, a perception among the girls that IT work can be monotonous remained fairly common.

Findings regarding the on-going influence of Shadow IT one year after the event indicated that Shadow IT strengthened the interest of girls previously inclined towards a career in IT, but for other girls, Shadow IT did not have a lasting influence. A positive finding was that the girls who reported being strongly interested in an IT career were not only studying IT, they had specific IT career roles in mind. The uncertainty girls had at the time of the event about where to find more information about an IT career was no longer a concern one year later.

Given that Shadow IT is a one day event, it would be unrealistic to expect it to have any major enduring influence on girls' career choices. But by partnering girls with female IT role models and effecting change in the girls' perceptions of IT work, Shadow IT aligns well with the career influencing social factors identified by Adya and Kaiser [2].

9. REFERENCES
[1] Absolute IT. 2015. Is NZ's gender gap in tech as bad as we think? Retrieved from https://www.absoluteit.co.nz/2015/07/nzs-gender-gap-in-tech-bad-as-we-think/

[2] Adya, M. and Kaiser, K. 2005. Early determinants of women in the IT workforce: A model of girls' career choices.

Information Technology & People 18, 3, 230-259.
DOI:http://dx.doi.org/10.1108/09593840510615860

[3] Appiaining, J. and Van Eck, R. 2015. Gender differences in college students' perceptions of technology-related jobs in computer science. *International Journal of Gender, Science and Technology* 7, 1, 28-56.

[4] Boersen, R. and Phillipps, M. 2006. *Programming contests: Two innovative models from New Zealand.* Paper presented at Perspectives on Computer Science Competitions for (High School) Students, Dagstuhl, Germany.

[5] Boyle, A., Maguire, S., Martin, A., Milsom, C., Nash, R., Rawlinson, S., Turner, A., Wurthmann, S. and Conchie, S. 2007. Field work is good: The student perception and the affective domain. *Journal of Geography in Higher Education* 31, 2, 299-317.
DOI:http://dx.doi.org/10.1080/03098260601063628

[6] Braun, V. and Clarke, V. 2006. Using thematic analysis in psychology. *Qualitative Research in Psychology* 3, 77-101.
DOI:http://dx.doi.org/10.1191/1478088706qp063oa

[7] Costain, G. 1999. *Benefits of holding young women's programming contests?* Paper presented at Living Science Conference 1999: A Conference for Women in Science, Dunedin, New Zealand.

[8] Craig, A. 2014. Australian interventions for women in computing: Are we evaluating? *Australasian Journal of Information Systems* 18, 2, 91-109.
DOI:http://dx.doi.org/10.3127/ajis.v18i2.849

[9] Craig, A., Lang, C. and Fisher, J. 2008. Twenty years of girls into Computing Days: Has it been worth the effort? *Journal of Information Technology Education* 7, 339-352.

[10] Craig, M., & Horton, D. 2009. Gr8 designs for Gr8 girls: A middle-school program and its evaluation. In *Proceedings of the 40th SIGSCE technical symposium on computer science education,* Chattanooga, TN, USA, 221-225.
DOI:http://dx.doi.org/10.1145/1539024.1508949

[11] Ericson, B., & McKlin, T. 2012. Effective and sustainable computing summer camps. In *Proceedings of the 43rd SIGSCE technical symposium on Computer Science Education,* Raleigh, NC, USA, 289-294.
http://dx.doi.org/10.1145/2157136.2157223

[12] Genrich, R., Toleman, M. and Roberts, D. 2014. Impacting IT enrolments: What factors most influence student career decisions. In *Proceedings of the 25th Australasian Conference on Information Systems*, Auckland, New Zealand.

[13] Gorbacheva, E., Craig, A., Beekhuyzen, J. and Coldwell, J. 2014. ICT interventions for girls: Factors influencing ICT career intentions. *Australasian Journal of Information Systems* 18, 3, 289-302.

[14] Hunter, A. 2012. *The professionalisation of computing work in New Zealand, 1960 to 2010: A feminist analysis.* Doctoral Thesis. University of Auckland, Auckland, New Zealand.

[15] Hunter, A. and Boersen, R. 2014. Short and sharp: Challenging girls to become programmers. In *EDULEARN 14 Proceedings*, Bareclona, Spain, 6857-6866.

[16] Hunter, A. and Boersen, R. 2016. Attracting Girls to a Career in Programming: A New Zealand Investigation. *International Journal of Gender, Science and Technology,* 8, 3, 338-359.

[17] Morton, S. 2013. The odd one out: Gender imbalance in tertiary ICT education. In *Proceedings of the 4th Annual Conference of Computing and Information Technology Research and Education in New Zealand*, Hamilton, New Zealand, 73-81.

[18] National Advisory Council on the Employment of Women. 2012. *Employment choices for young women - The influence of gender representation in New Zealand produced television watched by children.* Retrieved from http://www.womenatwork.org.nz/assets/Uploads/Files-PDFs-Docs/gender-representation-television-children.pdf.

[19] Paredes, D. 2016. Shadow Tech Day: Millennials investigate an IT future. *CIO.* Retrieved from CIO website: http://www.cio.co.nz/article/606086/shadow-tech-day-millennials-investigate-an-it-future/

[20] Statistics New Zealand. 2014. *2013 Census of population and dwellings: Occupation (ANZSCO) by sex.* Wellington, New Zealand: Customised report and licensed by Statistics New Zealand for re-use under the Creative Commons Attribution 3.0 licence.

[21] Thomas, T. and Allen, A. 2006. Gender differences in students' perceptions of Information Technology as a career. *Journal of Information Technology Education* 2, 165-177.

[22] Wang, J., Hong, H., Ravitz, J., & Ivory, M. (2015). Gender differences in factors influencing pursuit of computer science and related fields. In *Proceedings of the 2015 ACM Conference on Innovation and Technology in Computer Science Education*, Vilnius, Lithuania, 117-122.
DOI:http://dx.doi.org/10.1145/2729094.2742611

Insights on Gender Differences in CS1: A Multi-institutional, Multi-variate Study.

Keith Quille
Maynooth University
Maynooth, Co Kildare, Ireland.
keith.quille@nuim.ie

Natalie Culligan
Maynooth University
Maynooth, Co Kildare, Ireland.
natalie.culligan@nuim.ie

Susan Bergin
Maynooth University
Maynooth, Co Kildare, Ireland.
susan.bergin@nuim.ie

ABSTRACT

This paper describes a multivariate, multi-institutional study conducted in the academic year 2015-16. Six hundred and ninety-three students participated from 11 institutions, (ten institutions in Ireland and one in Denmark). The goal of the study was to compare the profile of male and female students enrolled on introductory programming modules (CS1), to determine if any significant differences could be identified by gender. The gender split was ~79:21, male to female respectively. The study took place early in the CS1 module with three instruments used to capture data: a background survey, a survey on programming self-efficacy, comfort and anxiety, and a short programming test. At the end of the module, the overall result for each participant was gathered. Of importance, the study was conducted across multiple levels of Computer Science education, from Level 5 Certificate up to and including Honors Bachelor Degree and Higher Diploma, (which are based on the Irish National Framework of Qualifications NFQ). This paper describes the approach taken and the detailed analysis performed. Several significant differences between male and female students were identified early in CS1, some of which did not hold true at the end of the module. A gender comparison between the two participating countries and the different institution types was also performed and discussed. The findings could be used to positively influence teaching practice and to the development of gender focused retention and recruitment strategies.

Keywords

Computer Science Education; Gender; Female; programming self-efficacy; Programming; CS1.

1. INTRODUCTION

In the western world, it is well acknowledged that Computer Science (CS) is a male dominated discipline, with declining female enrolments [9, 11, 28]. In Ireland, CS has the highest dropout rate of any third level discipline [15], which is mirrored in many other countries around the world [3]. In the late 1970's and early 1980's female enrolment increased but subsequently declined again [9]. On average Irish enrolment of female students in CS courses is currently around 20% [15] and this can be seen in many other western regions with the US seeing a significant decline from 28.3% in 1993 to 18.2% in 2012 [11]. Given the growing need for CS graduates increasing the number of female students is vital. Research leading to a better understanding of the factors that influence female students studying CS is timely, necessary and valuable.

ITiCSE '17, July 03-05, 2017, Bologna, Italy
© 2017 ACM. ISBN 978-1-4503-4704-4/17/07…$15.00
DOI: http://dx.doi.org/10.1145/3059009.3059048

2. MOTIVATION

The authors of this paper are part of a Computer Science education research group with over 100 years collective teaching and research experience. Initially, predicting student success at an early stage in an introductory programming module was the group's principal project. This was started in 2002 and led to the successful development of a prediction model named PreSS (Predict Student Success) [5]. During the initial development of PreSS, gender differences were identified as prominent predictors either of performance or in some way significant in CS education. This expanded the group's research to include gender and gender differences in the majority of research conducted since.

A plethora of studies have been conducted repeatedly validating the PreSS model and the research group has collected a substantial corpus of data on factors that influence programming success [5, 6, 21, 22]. A fully automated web-based version named PreSS# was subsequently developed [4–6, 21]. In the recent academic year (2015-16), the group conducted their most substantial study, recording responses from 693 students in 11 institutions. Using this large data set, the authors have carried out a substantial investigation on gender differences amongst CS students as described in this paper.

3. RELATED LITERATURE

Several studies are documented in the literature on gender differences in CS with arguably the most prominent repeated finding being the lower programming self-efficacy of female students. It should be noted that there are several related terms used within this space and their boundaries are sometimes unclear. These terms have included programming self-esteem, CS confidence, programming self-efficacy, and programming self-confidence.

Considerable evidence exists that female students have significantly lower confidence / programming self-efficacy in CS than their male counterparts [2, 8, 14, 24, 26]. Programming self-efficacy has been shown in multiple studies to significantly correlate to success [2, 5, 6, 21]. The effect of self-efficacy is not just prominent in CS, but also in mathematics where male student's self-reported self-efficacy was significantly higher than that of females [24, 26]. A noteworthy finding was that female and male students did not differ in science self-efficacy [10]. This may be due to the male to female ratio in CS courses, with many studies reporting that female students feel out of place, or that they are minorities within their CS classes [24], which can lead to female students experiencing stereotype-threat [8, 16, 24]. Furthermore female students have been shown to have far less confidence when it comes to asking questions in a CS class [24]. Social media for the student's personal use and as an educational tool has been a much-debated topic in education for many years. There have been several studies, which reported correlations between time spent on social media (such as Facebook) and self-esteem, some focusing on gender specific correlations [1], but were not in the CS or CS1 domain. A recent study examined the time spent on social media early in CS1, and found the time in hours negatively correlated to success in introductory programming [22]. Some studies have found that male students outperform female students during early stage programming tasks/ exams [13, 24]. The early difference in performance could be directly related to programming self-efficacy: female students have been shown to take longer on programming tasks, thus possibly inhibiting a true reflective result on programming ability [12, 25]. This may also contribute to the longer time required to complete programming tasks.

While examining the literature it became apparent that it is difficult to generalize on the findings. The studies were predominantly based on a single institution (with a single programming language and teaching and assessment methodology). In addition, several of the studies had small sample sizes. Where sample sizes were large and/ or included multiple institutions, the studies were conducted after the completion of CS1 or after the bachelor's degree was awarded. Timely data is required (early on in CS1) if uptake and attrition rates are to be addressed so that appropriate recruitment strategies and early interventions can be developed. This is particularly important given that some studies have found that gender differences are less temporally stable than expected [7].

To the author's knowledge there has been no such study completed on gender during the early stages in an introductory programming module that used a large multi-institutional student cohort, while simultaneously examining multiple gender differences. The study presented in this paper makes two significant contributions to the CS education community. First, the study examines a multitude of gender differences, early in CS1, across 11 institutions (consisting of universities, institutes of technology and community colleges), with a substantial student cohort (693 students). Secondly, it allows educators to generalize on the findings, as they are largely; institution; academic level; programming language; and teaching / assessment methodology independent.

4. RESEARCH QUESTIONS
Drawing on the findings of the related literature, combined with the group's previous research and practice, three research questions are presented and examined in this paper.

Q1. Are there differences in the set of examined background factors between male and female students, which may inhibit female students from succeeding as well as their male counterparts in CS?

Q2. Are there differences in self-efficacy, comfort-level and anxiety in relation to CS and specifically introductory programming, between male and female students?

Q3. Are there differences in performance between male and female students, at the beginning and the end of an introductory programming module?

These questions not only have a stereotypical and a gender biased origin, but need to be directly addressed for CS as a community to move forward and remove the prevalent male dominated stigma associated with the discipline.

5. DATA COLLECTION
During the academic years 2015-16, a large-scale multi-institutional study took place in Ireland and Denmark (two universities, five institutes of technology (comparable in academic level to colleges in the US) and four community colleges), which used the PreSS# system as the data collection method [23]. Ethical approval was sought and granted for the study. The main study was completed at approximately 4-6 hours into the introductory programming module (this is approximately, when students are 10% of the way through the module). There was an additional data collection when students completed the module, where the student's final year grade was recorded. In total, 693 complete student data sets were collected in the study, with a male to female ratio of ~79:21 respectively. This ratio seems to be in-line with Ireland, the US and many other countries [15, 25]. The study captured the solutions to three programming questions via PreSS#, where multiple different programming languages were used (across the institutions). The six languages included Java ($n=554$), C# ($n=75$), Python ($n=33$), Processing ($n=24$), Visual Basic ($n=4$) and C++ ($n=3$). In total 45 attributes were recorded which can be categorized under three main headings: background and student data survey, psychological questionnaire and a programming test. Each category will be described in detail in Section 6 along with the findings presented in Section 7.

6. INSTRUMENTS
6.1. Background and Student Data Survey (BS)
This instrument gathered general background, previous academic and related information. The factors recorded were selected based on the findings from the authors previous research [4, 5, 21, 22]. PreSS# also recorded additional data such as time taken to complete each instrument. Data on the following factors were collected: (i) student's age, (ii) the level of mathematics the student had before the module, (iii) the amount of hours a student spent playing computer games before the module, (iv) the amount of hours a student spent playing computer games during the module, (v) the amount of hours spent per day on social media, (vi) the amount of hours per week spent at a part time job. The study also gathered data at the end of the module, which was collected directly from each institution.

6.2. Psychological Questionnaire (PQ)
This instrument collected data on several psychological measures, numerically rated by each student. The measures selected for use in the PQ, resulted from the findings from the authors previous research [4, 5, 21, 22]. The measures were: (i) programming self-efficacy, (ii) a student's perception of their programming comfort-level under three headings (understanding programming concepts, designing the logic of a program without help and completing lab assignments [29]), (iii) a student's intrinsic goal orientation (beliefs about the importance of, interest in and utility value of the task [18]), (iv) a student's self-reported test anxiety (perception of the degree of fear or anxiety they have towards and during examinations [17]) and (v) the students self-reported expected result at the end of the module. Further details on these measures are provided in section 7.3.

6.3. Programming Test (PT)
The PT was designed to align with the completed CS1 learning outcomes at the time the test was administered. The PT was an online test consisting of three questions, designed to be of increasing difficulty and was administered without prior notice. Q1 was a single print statement, Q2 was a similar print statement that executed n-times (iteration) and Q3 was similar to Q2 but had a conditional statement for each iteration. It was envisioned that all students would complete Q1, most Q2 and few Q3 as the PT had an overall time limit, which was five minutes. This was selected for two reasons. First, to mimic time constraints that are typically part of tests and laboratory work, and second, only a short amount of time was available for this study, as it was usually conducted during laboratory times. A student could repeatedly compile their solutions without constraints, with compile errors or successful output

presented to the student and saved for analysis. If the student ran out of time, their current work was automatically submitted. Due to the large volume of submitted answers, which had to be manually graded by the authors, only one institution is reported on here. Future work will involve all of the institutions being examined in the same way. The institution selected for this initial examination had 36% of the student cohort, with a male to female ratio of ~73:27 respectively. The grounds for the selection of this institution was the large number of students. The PT recorded the time it took for a student to answer each question, the percentage of students who actually completed a question (by completion it is implied that a student submitted work, not that the work was correct), the percentage of students who ran out of time, and which question that they ran out of time on, and finally a manual grading of the code submitted, that was dichotomously recorded, as a correct or incorrect answer.

7. ANALYSIS

7.1. Approach

Statistical analysis was used to examine the three-research questions, and to examine if any significant differences between male and female students existed. A Welch's t-test was used to test the research questions. This is more suitable than a Student's t-test as the male and female data sets may have unequal variance. The p value was recorded for each of the Welch's t-tests where the confidence level was 95%. Thus, a p value of < 0.05 was considered a significant difference in means for the two data sets. If the p value was significantly less than 0.0001 then this was recorded as $p < 0.0001$ and was considered extremely significantly different.

7.2. Background Survey and Student Data (BS)

7.2.1 Age Profile

No significant difference was found in the age profile between male and female students, opposing some literature where female students were found to enter the field at a later stage [7].

7.2.2 Mathematical Ability

Mathematical ability prior to entering CS1 was normalized to incorporate all levels and types of mathematical examinations recorded in this study using an appropriate method as described in detail elsewhere by the authors [21]. Female students reported a significantly higher previous achievement in mathematics, in line with other research [8]. A significantly higher percentage of female students also reported that they took the highest level of mathematics in Ireland.

7.2.3 Time spent on social media and computer games

During the development of PreSS, the amount of hours spent playing computer games was a significant indicator of success and correlated inversely to performance for male students. A more recent study conducted also showed that the hours spent on social media may inversely correlate to programming self-efficacy that is, the less time spent on social media the higher one's programming self-efficacy [22], with research indicating that the time spent on social media is inversely correlated to self-esteem [1]. The study presented here, found male students spend significantly more time playing computer games than female students do, while when it comes to social media, the trend inverts where female students spend significantly longer on social media.

7.2.4 Hours spent working in a part time job

Previous research examined the hours spent working in a part time job as a predictor of success [5, 6], this study found no significant

difference between male and female students. That said this factor could warrant further analysis given a standard deviation of 7.26 and 7.11 hours respectively. This could suggest that many CS students do not have a part time job, while many others work up to 13 hours a week. This high commitment elsewhere in the latter instance could be contributing to the high attrition rates in the discipline and may require further research.

7.2.5 Time taken to complete the BS

No significant difference was found in the time it took to complete the survey section of this study. The recorded time included both the background survey and the psychological questionnaire, but not the programming test as this was timed separately.

7.2.6 BS Results summary

Table 1. BS results with Welch's t-test p values.

Data point	Male	Female	p value
Average age	22.37	21.32	*0.0902*
Average Mathematics grade prior to CS1 (normalized)	7.67	8.32	***0.0030***
Students who took the higher level mathematics before entry to the course	25.41%	38.36%	***<0.0001***
Student overall pass rate	70.75%	76.71%	***<0.0001***
Average hours spent a day playing computer games	1.68	0.66	***<0.0001***
Average hours spent a day on social media	2.57	4.19	***<0.0001***
Average hours per week spent working at a part time job	5.16	5.63	*0.4806*
Average time it took to take survey section of study	06:10	06:25	*0.3053*
Percentage of students who dropped out during the year	6.95%	4.11%	***<0.0001***

7.3. Psychological Questionnaire (PQ)

7.3.1 Programming self-efficacy

Programming self-efficacy is a common theme among modern CS education research. Bergin showed that a modified Rosenberg Self Esteem questionnaire where the questions were re-drawn to relate to a student's belief in their own programming ability, was the highest factor in predicting programming success and was therefore a key factor in the PreSS model [5, 6]. The recorded values ranged from -3.6 up to +4.6. A student with high programming self-efficacy was in the negative region, while the students with low programming self-efficacy was in the positive region, in both cases approaching the upper and lower ranges suggested the highest or lowest programming self-efficacy respectively. Not only did these results show that there is a significant difference between male and female self-reported programming self-efficacy, but that male students rate their programming self-efficacy positively whereas female rate their programming self-efficacy in a negative light, this is also echoed in a large body of literature [2, 7, 8, 10, 12, 19, 24].

7.3.2 Concepts, Design and completion of a program

This measurement recorded how students felt about the level of difficulty that they associated with three programming areas: understanding programming concepts, designing the logic of a program without help and completing lab assignments. This measure used a normalized 5-point Likert scale, which ranked each area: concepts, design and completion ranging from very difficult (1), to very easy (5), and was summated to give an overall value. Male students reported a significantly larger value than females. This measure could be related to other measurements recorded in this study, such as programming self-efficacy.

7.3.3 Intrinsic goal orientation

Intrinsic Goal Orientation is a component self-regulated learning [20] which measures the curiosity, desire for challenge or an ambition to master a task rather than just getting by. A student with a higher intrinsic goal orientation is likely to promote a higher level of persistence toward learning a subject, in both the short term and long term [27]. The questions used in this instrument were based on the motivated strategies for learning questionnaire (MSQL) using a seven point Likert scale [20]. Males reported a significantly higher average intrinsic goal orientation value than females.

7.3.4 Test anxiety

Test anxiety is a self-reported measure of one or a combination of tension, fear, worry, nervousness or unease that may occur on or before test situations, based upon the MSQL using a seven point Likert scale. Female students returned values significantly higher than that of males. Section 7.5.2 examines test anxiety across the three institution types, which may have value in future research if one institution type has lower test anxiety than another.

7.3.5 Predicted overall result vs actual overall result

Previous research by the authors determined that the grade a student expects to receive in CS1 (after minimal exposure) strongly correlates to success [22]. In the current study male students predicted, that they will achieve significantly higher results compared to their female counterparts. Male students have been found to perceive programming to be easier than females do [19], which could be related to general lower programming self-efficacy of female students, in turn contributing to the lower expected result early on. Contrary to this factor, when the end of year pass rates were examined, female students had a significantly higher pass rate than their male counterparts, as presented in Table 2. This may align with other research where findings show at least an equal par on performance at the end of the course compared to a male dominated initial period [13, 16].

7.3.6 PQ Results summary

Table 2. PQ analysis with Welch's t-test

Data point	Male	Female	p value
Programming self-efficacy	-0.1956	+0.7328	*<0.0001*
Concepts, Design and Completion	9.48	8.5	*<0.0001*
Intrinsic Goal Orientation	20.83	20	*0.0211*
Test Anxiety	21.14	25.33	*<0.0001*
Average expected end of year grade	76.89%	71.95%	*0.0007*

7.4.Programming Test (PT)
7.4.1 Programming timing analysis

The average time it took male students to answer Q1 compared to female students was not significantly different, but it is very noteworthy to examine the actual difference in average time. This was 18 seconds, or in other words, it took female students just over 10% longer on average to complete the question. The time

difference was substantially less in Q2. Although a significant difference was found in Q3, this must be interpreted with caution as the number of students that attempted Q3 was comparatively small, thus bringing into question its value. The percentage of students who attempted (at least attempted, but not necessarily completed) a question revealed a trend. Other than Q1 (which all students attempted), a significantly higher proportion of male students attempted Q2 and Q3. The percentage of female students who either ran out of time on Q1 or overall was significantly higher than that of their male counterparts.

7.4.2 Programming performance

The submitted code of each student for each submission was corrected. This was in dichotomous form, either correct or incorrect. The statistical analysis was completed using a binomial distribution and a Welch's *t*-test. Male students performed significantly better than female students did, even when individual questions are examined. There could be a strong link in this finding to that of time taken to answer the questions, which anecdotally could correlate to programming self-efficacy at this very early stage of tuition. At this point, it is noteworthy to consider that although female students may be performing weaker than males in early programming tests, they perform as good if not better at the end of year examinations, which is very positive for female students who may have low programming self-efficacy early on in the module.

7.4.3 PT Results summary

Table 3. PT results with Welch's t-test p values.

Data point	Male (n=180)	Female (n=68)	p value
Average time to complete: Q1	02:44	03:02	*0.1346*
Average time to complete: Q2	02:09	02:05	*0.6682*
Average time to complete: Q3	00:56	00:38	*0.0023*
Percentage who attempted: Q1	100%	100%	*NA*
Percentage who attempted: Q2	77.78%	76.47%	*0.0285*
Percentage who attempted: Q3	30.56%	16.18%	*<0.0001*
Percentage who ran out of time overall	84.44%	88.24%	*<0.0001*
Percentage who ran out of time on Q1	17.22%	19.12%	*0.0006*
Percentage who answered Q1 correctly	64.44%	61.76%	*0.00011*
Percentage who answered Q2 correctly	27.86%	19.23%	*<0.0001*
Percentage who answered Q3 correctly	1.82%	9.09%	*<0.0001*

7.5.Additional Analysis

Using the same instruments and recorded data, the authors examined differences in the genders, across the two countries and then over each of the three types of institutions. This novel analysis examined if male and female students exhibit the same characteristics as found in section 7.1 to 7.4, when examined in independent countries or academic institutions.

7.5.1 Country Specific differences

When each of the factors for both female and male students in Ireland and Denmark were compared, only one significant difference was found. This was the average hours spent per week working on a part time job, where Irish male and female students worked significantly longer hours. While this is interesting, it is important to note that in this comparison 95% of students were from

Ireland with only 5% of the students from a single institution in Denmark. Further work is required to determine if this finding would hold true on a large sample with other countries or institutions in Denmark.

7.5.2 Institution Specific differences

The 693 students were compared based on the three institution types in this study, which included two universities, five institutes of technology and four community colleges. First gender specific measurements that were not significantly different across all three of the institution types were examined. These included, the hours spent on social media per day, concepts, design and completion of a program, test anxiety, and intrinsic goal orientation. These findings are of value as they can be used for the development of gender focused retention and recruitment strategies while being institution and academic level independent. Secondly, gender specific measurements that differed across the three institutions were examined. Differences were expected in some measurements, for example, prior mathematical ability, which may be due institution entry requirements. A finding, which was identical for both male and female students, was the average expected end of year grade recorded in the BS. University students had the lowest average expected end of year grade, followed by the institutes of technology with community colleges reporting the highest average expected grade. A similar result was found when programming self-efficacy was examined across the three institution types, with university students reporting the lowest value (for both male and female students). For female students community colleges reported the highest average programming self-efficacy whereas for male students it was the institute of technology. This finding may be of value when developing institution specific strategies or methodologies. Future work should try to examine the underlying phenomenon resulting in self-efficacy and expected grade differences across institution types.

7.6.Research Questions

Q1 examined several background factors (presented in section 7.2) and found significant gender differences between male and female students. Female students reported higher mathematical ability prior to entry to the course; higher overall pass rates, lower dropout rates and spent less time spent playing computer games than their male counterparts. Female students however spent a significantly longer amount of time on social media.

Q2 examined psychological factors (presented in section 7.3) with the most notable difference; that female students have not only significantly less programming self-efficacy than male students but that males rate their own programming self-efficacy in a positive manor whereas female students rate theirs in a negative light. This is concerning and also may be the root cause of other PQ differences found, such as females have a higher test anxiety compared to male students, that female students rate their understanding of programming concepts, design and completion, lower than that of their male counterparts and the lower early-expected end of year grade exhibited by female students.

Q3 examined performance differences (presented in section 7.4) between male and female students. Significant differences were reported; with some opposing in nature depending on the stage within the course, they were recorded. Male students outperformed female students, when the early PT was administered. However, the reverse of this difference was found at the end of the module, where female students significantly outperformed male students in overall pass rates. A possible cause or contributing factor to female students performing lower than males in earlier in class

programming examinations could be the finding that female students have a lower programming self-efficacy than males.

8. CONCLUSIONS AND FUTURE WORK

This study has found that female students have multiple positive factors in an introductory programming module, such as higher mathematical grade prior to CS1, higher end of year pass rates and lower dropout rates compared to their male counterparts. This bodes very well for female students who undertake CS1. This holds true, even though female students not only have significantly less programming self-efficacy than males, but that female students have a less than neutral, negative programming self-efficacy, whereas their male counterparts have a positive programming self-efficacy. This is to say that female students underrate their programming self-efficacy compared to their end of year grade. This early, low programming self-efficacy is compounded by several measurements recorded: female students have a significantly lower end of year grade expectation, a significantly lower self-rating on programming concepts, program design and completion and a greater level of anxiety for tests or test situations all at the beginning of CS1 compared to their male counterparts.

This low programming self-efficacy and higher test anxiety of female students compared to their male counterparts may be a disadvantage early in the introductory programming module (where female students do not perform as well on average as their male counterparts in early programming tests) but could be advantageous in the later stages. These negative factors combined, may be the catalyst which could result in additional programming practice or study towards the end of the module. Thus resulting in the observed higher performance than their male counterparts in the overall module. The reverse may also be true for males, as their higher self-efficacy and lower test anxiety may result in less study effort towards the end of the module. Future work should include measurements from the BS and PQ along with the time spent studying at both the start and towards the end of the module to examine this hypothesis. Future work should also investigate, the underlying cause in the gender specific differences found in programming self-efficacy and expected end of year result, as these differences are not the same for male and female students across the three institution types. Finally considerations for the measurements that are not significantly different across the three institution types, such as test anxiety, should be given in the future development of interventions and methodologies that are institution and academic level independent.

A prominent concern in CS education is the lower uptake in CS by female students. This paper makes a valuable contribution to the CS education community. Multi-variate and multi-institutional studies like this one are valuable and timely as they allow educators and researchers to generalize on findings, such as self-efficacy, programming performance, grade expectation, time spent on social media and many others which are presented in this paper. These generalizations can be made without any doubt, across institution type, academic level or even programming language. The findings can then be used in the development of gender focused retention and recruitment strategies with the overall goal of increasing the number of female CS students, and as a result help alleviate the short fall expected in CS graduates.

9. ACKNOWLEDGEMENTS

The authors would like to extend their gratitude to all 11 institutions and 693 students who participated in this study.

10. REFERENCES

[1] Attrill, A. 2015. *Cyberpsychology.* Oxford University Press, Impression 1.

[2] Başer, M. 2013. Attitude , Gender and Achievement in Computer Programming. *Middle-East Journal of Scientific Researc.* 14, 2 (2013), 248–255.

[3] Bennedsen, J. and Caspersen, M.E. 2007. Failure rates in introductory programming. *ACM SIGCSE Bulletin.* 39, 2 (2007), 32.

[4] Bergin, S., Mooney, A., Ghent, J. and Quille, K. 2015. Using Machine Learning Techniques to Predict Introductory Programming Performance. *International Journal of Computer Science and Software Engineering.* 4, 12 (2015), 323–328.

[5] Bergin, S. and Reilly, R. 2006. Predicting introductory programming performance: A multi-institutional multivariate study. *Computer Science Education.* 16, February 2015 (2006), 303–323.

[6] Bergin, S. and Reilly, R. 2005. Programming: factors that influence success. *ACM SIGCSE Bulletin* (2005), 411–416.

[7] Beyer, S., DeKeuster, M., Walter, K., Colar, M. and Holcomb, C. 2005. Changes in CS students' sttitudes towards CS over time. *ACM SIGCSE Bulletin.* 37, 1 (2005), 392.

[8] Beyer, S., Rynes, K., Perrault, J., Hay, K. and Haller, S. 2003. Gender differences in computer science students. *ACM SIGCSE Bulletin.* 35, (2003), 49.

[9] Camp, T. 1997. The incredible shrinking pipeline. *Communications of the ACM.* 40, 10 (1997), 103–110.

[10] Dempsey, J., Snodgrass, R.T. and Kishi, I. 2015. The Emerging Role of Self-Perception in Student Intentions Categories and Subject Descriptors. *Proceedings of the 46th ACM Technical Symposium on Computer Science Education (SIGCSE '15).* (2015), 108–113.

[11] Field of Degree: Women - US National Science Foundation (NSF): 2012. *https://www.nsf.gov/statistics/2015/nsf15311/digest/theme2.cfm# psychology.* Accessed: 2016-12-28.

[12] Funke, A., Berges, M., Mühling, A. and Hubwieser, P. 2015. Gender Differences in Programming : Research Results and Teachers ' Perception. *Koli Calling Conference on Computing Education Research.* (2015), 161–162.

[13] Grande, V. and Parrow, J. 2014. Motivation and Grade Gap Related to Gender in a Programming Course. (2014), 2014.

[14] Lishinski, A., Yadav, A., Good, J. and Enbody, R. 2016. Introductory Programming : Gender Differences and Interactive Effects of Students ' Motivation , Goals and Self-Efficacy on Performance. *Proceedings of the 12th International Computing Education Research Conference.* (2016), 211–220.

[15] Liston, M., Frawley, D. and Patterson, V. 2016. *A Study of Progression in Irish Higher Education. A report by the Higher Education Authority, Ireland.*

[16] Murphy, L., Richards, B., McCauley, R., Morrison, B.B., Westbrook, S. and Fossum, T. 2006. Women catch up: gender differences in learning programming concepts. *Technical Symposium on Computer Science Education.* 38, (2006), 17.

[17] Nolan, K. and Bergin, S. 2016. The role of anxiety when learning to program : A Systematic review of the literature. (2016).

[18] Patrick, H., Ryan, A.M. and Pintrich, P.R. 1999. The differential impact of extrinsic and mastery goal orientations on males' and females' self-regulated learning. *Learning and Individual Differences.* 11, 2 (1999), 153–171.

[19] Pau, R., Hall, W., Grace, M. and Woollard, J. 2011. Female Students ' Experiences of Programming : It ' s Not All Bad ! *16th annual joint conference on Innovation and technology in computer science education.* (2011), 323–327.

[20] Pintrich, P.R. and De Groot, E. V. 1990. Motivational and Self-Regulated Learning Components of Classroom Academic Performance. *Journal of Educational Psychology.* 82, 1 (1990), 33–40.

[21] Quille, K. and Bergin, S. 2015. Programming: Factors that Influence Success Revisited and Expanded. *International Conference on Enguaging Pedagogy (ICEP)* (2015).

[22] Quille, K. and Bergin, S. 2016. Programming: Further Factors that Influence Success. *Psychology of Programming Interest Group (PPIG), 7th to 10th Spetember, University of Cambridge.* (University of Cambridge, 2016).

[23] Quille, K., Bergin, S. and Mooney, A. 2015. PreSS #, A Web-Based Educational System to Predict Programming Performance. 4, 7 (2015), 178–189.

[24] Redmond, K., Evans, S. and Sahami, M. 2013. A large-scale quantitative study of women in computer science at Stanford University. *Proceeding of the 44th ACM technical symposium on Computer science education - SIGCSE '13.* (2013), 439–444.

[25] Saulsberry, D. 2012. Dwindling Numbers of Female Computer Students : What are We Missing ? *SIGITE'12, Calgary, Alberta, Canada.* (2012), 221–226.

[26] Sinclair, J. and Kalvala, S. 2015. Exploring Societal Factors Affecting the Experience and Engagement of First Year Female Computer Science Undergraduates. *Proceedings of the 15th Koli Calling Conference on Computing Education Research.* (2015), 107–116.

[27] Vansteenkiste, M., Lens, W. and Deci, E.L. 2006. Intrinsic Versus Extrinsic Goal Contents in Self-Determination Theory: Another Look at the Quality of Academic Motivation. *Educational Psychologist.* 41, 1 (2006), 19–31.

[28] Watson, C., Li, F.W.B. and Godwin, J.L. 2014. No tests required: comparing traditional and dynamic predictors of programming success. *Proceedings of the 45th ACM technical symposium on Computer science education - SIGCSE '14.* (2014), 469–474.

[29] Wilson, B. 2008. Improving Comfort Level of Females in the First Computer Programming Course: Suggestions for CS Faculty. *J. Comput. Sci. Coll.* 23, 4 (2008), 28–34.

Linking Language & Thinking with Code: Computing within a Writing-Intensive Introduction to the Liberal Arts

Keith J. O'Hara, Kathleen Burke, Diana Ruggiero, and Sven Anderson

Computer Science Program, Bard College

Annandale-on-Hudson, New York 12504

kohara@bard.edu

ABSTRACT

This paper describes the design, implementation and preliminary evaluation of a computing component for a three-week writing-intensive introductory program at a liberal arts college. Specific curricular recommendations are presented that could have a direct, positive impact if adopted in similar courses. A two-pronged approach involving a faculty-led HTML workshop, along with student-led contextualized coding studios, was employed. Computing Unplugged activities were used, including a novel Page Rank Unplugged networking activity. An analysis of attitude surveys shows the program positively changed students attitudes about enjoyment solving CS problems, but potentially reinforced the misconception that CS is just learning programming languages.

KEYWORDS

computing in liberal arts; computing unplugged; attitudes

ACM Reference format:

Keith J. O'Hara, Kathleen Burke, Diana Ruggiero, and Sven Anderson. 2017. Linking Language & Thinking with Code: Computing within a Writing-Intensive Introduction to the Liberal Arts. In *Proceedings of ITiCSE '17, Bologna, Italy, July 03-05, 2017,* 6 pages.

DOI: http://dx.doi.org/10.1145/3059009.3059018

1 INTRODUCTION

In 2015, 48,994 students took the AP Computer Science Exam in the 4,310 schools that offer it. For comparison, over 500,000 students took the English Language and Composition AP Exam in over 12,000 schools [1]. In addition to efforts that look to mathematics as a way to bootstrap the study of computer science [14], why not appeal to students of language and literature as well?

Finding a place in the liberal arts for computing has a long and successful history [2, 8, 10, 11, 17]. Bard College has applied many of these lessons-learned to its computer science curriculum, for example, by developing contextualized introductory courses (e.g., robotics, graphics, digital humanities, web informatics) that satisfy the college's math and computing general education requirement. But as student interest grows, and the applicability of computing

Figure 1: Wooden nickels used in a Page-Rank-Unplugged activity and its D3 animation.

becomes ever more pervasive, exposing all students to the power of computing early and broadly becomes paramount.

Bard has two mandatory three-week programs in which all first-year students partake: **Language & Thinking (L&T)**, a writing-intensive program before the first semester; and **Citizen Science**, an immersive science experience for all first-year students between their first and second semesters. This paper describes the design, implementation and preliminary evaluation of a computing component for L&T. The majority (59.8%) of the 391 students surveyed did not self-report any computer science education prior to arriving at Bard College. Moreover, of those with a prospective major, only five students had computer science in mind.

First-year students at Bard College start their college experience with a three week course entitled "Language & Thinking" (L&T) which has been part of the curriculum for 35 years. Taught largely by humanities professors from other institutions, this program introduces students to critical thinking using writing as the primary tool. In sections of about fourteen members, students write informed responses to challenging academic material. The readings are collected in a printed anthology of short works and students are required to write in a paper *dialogical* notebook every day in which students create a dialogue by writing notes and responses on readings on the left half of a page and later comment on those notes using the right side of the page. The course's theme changes every few years; the current theme is "Change: What needs to be the case for things to be otherwise?"

The Language & Thinking program is a unique point in the liberal arts college curriculum for introducing computing because it:

- includes all students;
- celebrates creative acts of expression;
- is not explicitly linked to math or science; and
- occurs at a point of transition to college.

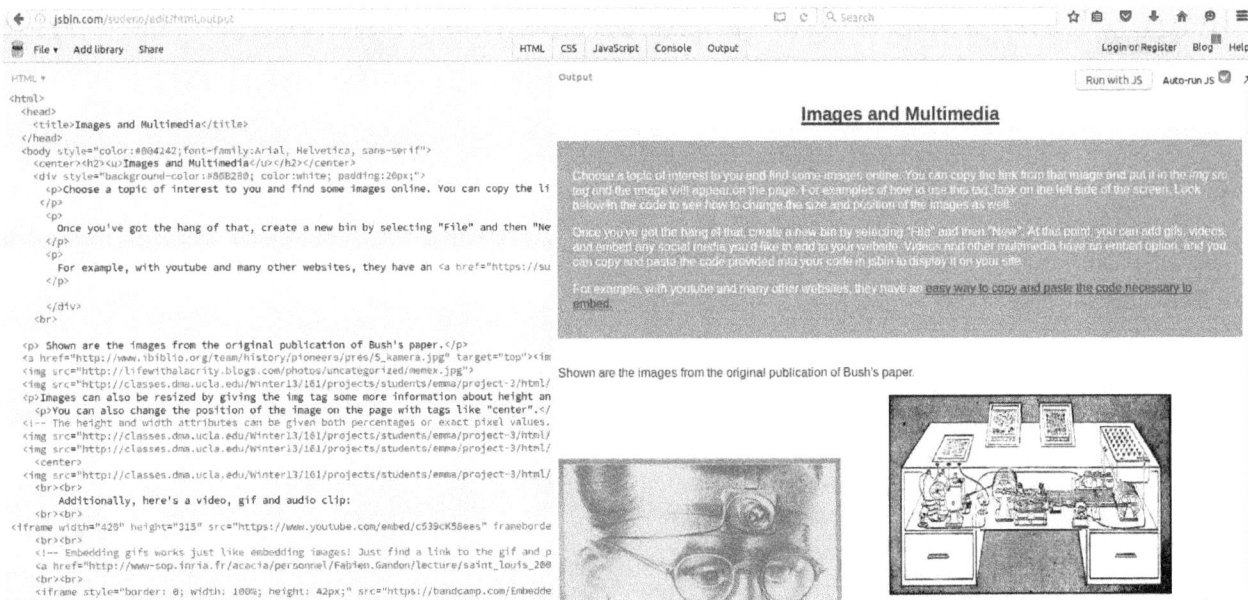

Figure 2: The images & multimedia `jsbin` tutorial from the Web Workshop; the source code on the left.

Believing that the L&T course was uniquely positioned to effect changes in student attitudes to computing, we adopted a two-pronged approach involving a faculty-led workshop on reading and writing the web using HTML and student-led contextualized coding studios focused on more algorithmic elements. In the following sections we outline the design of the computing module and perform an analysis of computing attitude surveys completed by the class of approximately 500 incoming students.

2 DESIGN

The computing components were designed around a few practical constraints imposed by its inclusion in the limited three-week duration of the L&T course:

- **limited time**: only 2 sessions, each approximately two hours long;
- **lack of smart classrooms**: not all 37 classrooms had digital projection systems;
- **not led by CS faculty**: we lacked the personnel for CS professors to instruct the computing module for all 35 sections;
- **anthology**: the coding materials should connect to the standard set of L&T readings.

As computer scientists at a liberal arts college, our goal is to help students express themselves using computing in a context relevant to their individual interests. The L&T Program emphasizes the use of writing as a means for communication and thought, and we advocate a similar role for the computational component. The severe time limitation caused us to carefully reconsider achievable outcomes, since we did not expect students would master even simple programming in so little time. Therefore, the primary objective of the component was to expose all first-year students to the power of code as language and computational thinking, and

positively change their attitudes about such matters. We identified an approach consistent with these constraints:

- **non-expert-led instruction**: Rather than being lectured to by computer scientists, the students would be led by, and hopefully identify with, instructors of all disciplines. L&T Faculty and current Bard undergraduates would be responsible for facilitating the workshops.
- **computing unplugged**: To emphasize the generality of algorithmic thinking, every activity would include a kinesthetic, computing "unplugged" activity.
- **quick start & rapid feedback**: Students should not be bogged down by tedious software installations, long write-compile-test, or write-upload-reload loops.
- **context**: Involve choice and specialization: students should explore specific media of interest vis-a-vis computing, whether it be textual, graphical or physical.
- **close reading**: The coding material should be consistent with the culture of the L&T program which is based on close reading of texts.

2.1 Anthology

The computing component connected directly with two readings in the L&T anthology. All students arrived on campus having read "Garden of Forking Paths" by Jorge Luis Borges [3] over the summer in preparation for the program. Later, some time over the three weeks, students also read "As We May Think" by Vannevar Bush [4]. The ideas of multiple realities from Borges and the hyper-media and associative linking of knowledge of Bush segued into the first coding Web Workshop centered on HTML.

2.2 Reading & Writing the Web

2.2.1 Web Workshop. In the first, 90-minute, workshop a set of exercises[1] was designed around the idea of the Memex and HTML — reading and writing the web. We had prior success introducing HTML through a computing module in an *Introduction to Media* course taken almost exclusively by humanities majors. Although HTML is not a complete programming language, it does introduce students to computing concepts such as syntax and semantics of formal languages, structured data, meta-data, protocols, and debugging. The algorithmic aspects lacking in the HTML workshop were reinforced in the coding studios.

Students used the website jsbin, similar to other sites like jsfiddle and codepen.io, to quickly learn and prototype HTML pages. Jsbin was chosen because it presents a simple editing interface in which the web page and its source code were presented side by side and with immediate update of the page as changes were made to the source code (See Figure 2). In addition, the pages are immediately publicly available (i.e., no need to upload files) including the source edits in real-time. This last feature provided a way for all students in a class to follow a common page without the need for a digital projector. Finally, jsbin is a web application, so no software installation was necessary.

A series of self-paced tutorials focused on:

1. EMPHASIS & FORMATTING
2. HYPERLINKS
3. IMAGES & MULTIMEDIA
4. DEBUGGING
5. FREE-WRITE WITH HYPER MEDIA

Instructors, who had worked through the materials at least once during training, led students through the tutorials, pausing between the stages above to deal with questions. Students shared their work and commented on the work of others, also helping one another out when questions and errors arose.

2.2.2 Networks Unplugged. At the end of the web workshop, students participated in a novel networking unplugged activity that showcased the power of the link as a knowledge discovery and power attribution mechanism. It involved visualizing the link structure of the web and simulating Google's Page-Rank algorithm. First, each student wrote the jsbin URL of their free-write, the last HTML exercise, on a slip of paper and added it to a hat—jsbin conveniently provides short human readable URLs for all the pages. Then each student drew a URL from the hat and linked to that random page. These links among student pages generate a small network over the web pages in that class.

Students visualized the class's network by throwing a ball of yarn around to map out the network of pages. Starting at some arbitrary student, that student passed the ball of yarn to the student they had linked to, who passed it to the student they had linked to, and so on. Occasionally, scissors were needed to break up the components of the network. When completed, this algorithm resulted in a very concrete visualization of how the web pages were connected.

Once the network had been mapped physically, the students were invited to move around and find a better layout of the network. The class could modify the network structure. For example, if there were some students (or a group of students) that weren't connected to the larger network, the class might decide to establish new links or perhaps dissolve existing ones.

After visualizing the network of the class, the next task was to run a simulation of Google's Page Rank. Page Rank is the way Google and other search engines rank websites based on the link structure of the web. By linking to another page, a page is implicitly voting or endorsing another page [6], and in doing so, is passing along authority.

Page Rank Unplugged Activity

At the start, each student receives 12 wooden nickels (see Figure 1). The wooden nickels act as currency for power or authority; the exchange of these nickels simulated how power is distributed and accumulated in the network. The number of wooden nickels at any point is essentially the PageRank score. The simulation works in rounds. In each round, the following steps are executed:

(1) Each student gives all of their nickels to the person whose page they linked to.
(2) Each student in the network gives 25% of their nickels to the "tax collector" (typically the instructor). If the number of nickels in a student's pile doesn't divide equally into 4, just round up. A convenient way to figure out 25% of any number of nickels without counting them was to break them up by sight into 4 stacks of as equal height as possible, giving one of the larger piles to the tax collector.
(3) The tax collector distributes the collected tax nickels equally among the students. If the number of nickels does not divide equally, distribute the remaining nickels arbitrarily.
(4) Repeat steps 1-3 for several rounds and notice the behavior of the network—where do the nickels tend to accumulate and how does it relate the shape and structure of the network connections?

Finally, a JavaScript program was developed to spider the student jsbin pages and visualize the Page Rank algorithm using d3.js (Figure 1, right panel).

2.3 Coding Studios

After the *Reading and Writing the Web* workshop, students were required to sign up for one or more coding studios. Each coding studio ran for two hours in the late afternoon and early evening after regular class meetings. In these coding studios, students were exposed to how computing can be the ultimate medium — the meta-medium [9] — allowing us to express ourselves in new ways with motion, sound, graphics and text. The three coding studios were led by a total of eight Bard computer science undergraduates, and were more algorithmic in nature than the web workshop. They comprised:

- **The Textual** — Students used IPython [12] notebooks to read and write algorithms that generate poetry and prose. Specifically they worked with an early Madlib-style, *Love Letter* Generator due to Turing and Strachey [15] (Figure 3).
- **The Visual** — Students used Processing [13] to read and write algorithms to create virtual fish and software mirrors. The students' fish were collected and added to a collective virtual fish tank.

---

[1]http://bard.jsbin.com/

```
FANCIFUL HONEYSUCKLE,

YOU ARE MY AMOROUS APPETITE. MY EAGER DEVOTION
ARDENTLY HOLDS DEAR YOUR BREATHLESS AFFECTION.
MY PASSIONATE AFFECTION BURNINGLY PINES FOR YOUR
PASSIONATE ADORATION. YOU ARE MY CRAVING
ENTHUSIASM.  YOU ARE MY CRAVING FELLOW FEELING.

YOURS FERVENTLY,

M.U.C
```

Figure 3: A Love Letter generated in the Textual Coding Studio (thanks to Strachey & Turing).

- **The Physical** — Students used IPRE scribbler robots [16] and Python to read and write algorithms that made robots sing and dance.

Each coding studio followed a similar structure. The workshop kicked off with a computing unplugged (e.g., collaborative whiteboard Madlib in the digital literature studio). Then the students were led through some provided code that was functional, and interesting, but written for clarity and understanding more than features or technical sophistication. Next, the students were asked to customize the code in some way (e.g., modify the appearance or behavior of their fish in the graphics studio). Finally, the students shared their work (e.g., demonstrate their robot dance routine).

3 IMPLEMENTATION

The workshop materials were implemented by two undergraduate CS majors, and introduced as an addition to the existing L&T curriculum. In a two-hour faculty training session, two CS professors modeled the web workshop. Coding studios were scheduled after regular teaching hours in the evenings and were lead by 2-3 CS undergraduates. Students signed up for the studio on a topic and at a time according to their interests and schedule. Approximately, 400 students participated in the coding studios: 143 students attended the graphics workshop, 125 attended the digital literature workshop, and 116 attended the robotics workshop. Online and telephone hotlines were maintained for faculty and students who needed additional support.

4 EVALUATION OF ATTITUDES

We evaluated whether student attitudes toward computing were affected by administering an abbreviated version of the computing attitudes survey (CAS) [5] before and after the L&T Program. Developed and validated on semester-long computing courses, the CAS contains numerous questions about programming and problem solving that are not part of the computing modules. We therefore reduced the 26 questions of the CAS to the eight questions (Figure 4) that are relevant to this program. Responses ranged from Strongly Disagree (1) to Neutral (3) to Strongly Agree (5). There were 391 responses for the entry (pre-program) surveys and 368 responses for the exit (post-program) surveys. Due to errors in the recording of participant codes, we were able to match pre-program and post-program surveys for a subset of 263 students, limiting subsequent paired analysis to this subset of the surveys.

Figure 4 shows the results of paired non-parametric Wilcoxon signed rank test on the each of the eight questions. Significant changes ($p < 0.05$ after Bonferroni correction) are apparent for four of the questions indicated in boldface font; effects for significant questions were approximately 10-30% of response deviation (Cohen's D). Increased agreement with Questions 3 and 4 suggests a greater interest in solving computer science problems. The broader interdisciplinary use of computation is undercut by the decrease in agreement with Question 2, that computer science is helpful to the study of other disciplines, as well as the increased agreement with Question 6, which equates computer science with programming. The magnitude of attitude change is indicated by the changes, both positive and negative, in individual paired responses shown in the third and fourth columns. For those questions with attitude changes that reach significance, we see a approximately twice as many changes in one direction when compared with the other (magnitude of change is ignored): for example, 30% of respondents have an increase in their agreement with Question 3 compared with 16% who have a decrease in agreement on that question. Mean attitudes, both before and after the program are near the value 3 (*neutral*), except for Question 2. We interpret these results in the Discussion.

Disaggregation of responses by gender suggests that the decline in agreement with Question 2 (*Computing is useful in other disciplines*) is most strongly affected by responses of male respondents, whereas the increase in agreement with Questions 3 (*Computer science problems are motivating*) and 6 (*Computer science is just programming*) is most strongly affected by responses of female students. Disaggregation by intended major into the arts ($N = 65$), humanities ($N = 38$), social sciences ($N = 63$), sciences ($N = 33$), and undecided ($N = 45$) revealed slight, but significant, changes only for Questions 3, 4, and 6 for social sciences majors, Question 4 for science majors, and Question 8 for students undecided about their major.

We also explored the extent to which student attitude changes indicate a transition from novice to expert attitudes (cf. [5, 7]). As in that analysis, participant responses were scored by determining the fraction of the responses to eight survey questions that are consistent with expected attitudes of computer scientists. That is, we assumed that computer scientists would agree with Questions 1, 2, 3, 4, 5, and 8, but disagree with Questions 6 and 7. This yields collapsed scores ranging from 0% to 100% that indicate the degree to which a participant's opinion matches that of an expert in the field. Data collapsed in this manner shows 55.0% mean agreement with expert opinion in both the pre-program and post-program surveys with no significant difference.

Interestingly, when disaggregated by gender for all but 2% of participants who did not self-report "female" or "male," we found a significant difference in pre-program attitudes (unpaired Wilcoxon $p < 0.0003, N = 389$). The average agreement with experts of female participants was significantly lower than that of males (52% vs. 59%). This pre-program difference is apparent in the histograms of respondent agreement with expert opinion shown in Figure 5. Post-program surveys do not indicate a significant difference between the average agreement for female versus male respondents

	question	% increase	% decrease		p-value	pre mean	post mean
1	I think about the computer science I experience in everyday life.	25	24	↑	5.48	2.58	2.61
2	**Tools and techniques from computer science can be useful in the study of other disciplines (e.g., biology, art, business).**	13	24	↓	0.008	4.13	3.98
3	**I find the challenge of solving computer science problems motivating.**	30	16	↑	0.024	2.65	2.82
4	**I enjoy solving computer science problems.**	36	14	↑	0.000	2.49	2.77
5	Reasoning skills used to understand computer science can be helpful to me in my everyday life.	17	27	↓	0.168	3.60	3.48
6	**Learning computer science is just learning how to program in different languages.**	28	16	↑	0.048	3.06	3.22
7	The subject of computer science has little relation to what I experience in the real world.	29	19	↑	0.136	2.55	2.70
8	I am interested in learning more about computer science.	19	26	↓	0.520	3.17	3.07

Figure 4: Paired comparison (Wilcoxon signed rank test) of the Likert-scale (1 – 5) survey questions before and after participation in the program (N = 264). Boldface indicates questions for which $p < 0.05$ after Bonferroni correction. Arrows indicate direction of change from pre-program to post-program. The magnitude of attitude change is indicated by the percentage of individual question responses that increased (decreased) from pre-program to post-program.

($p = 0.246$, means 54% vs. 56%). That is, after completing the program, the agreement with experts rose for female students, making their responses more similar to those of the male students. This gender difference is smaller in magnitude, but agrees with findings based on a full CAS study in a semester-long CS1 course ([5], p. 23).

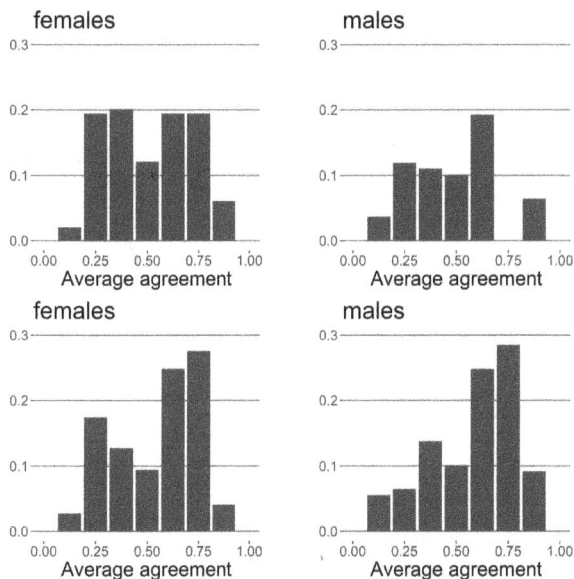

Figure 5: Histograms of pre-program (top) and post-program agreement (bottom) with experts for female and male participants.

5 DISCUSSION

The inclusion of a 3-4 hour computing component during the first step in an entering student's college experience was intended to reach all students at a transitional moment and, therefore, point of maximum potential impact on nascent attitudes toward college. The program was deemed a measured success and, as will be reported in a future paper, was repeated the following year. In this section we discuss what was learned from the attitude surveys and then turn to observations about the overall successes and failures of the program.

5.1 Attitudes Toward Computer Science

The survey responses suggest modest changes in attitudes that we interpret as positive outcomes and some which are negative. Increased agreement with Questions 3 and 4, as well as the attitude shift of female students toward greater appreciation of computation (Figure 5), both suggest a significant shift towards a more positive view of computer science as an enjoyable activity. On the other hand, the significant changes in Questions 2 and 6, taken together with insignificant changes on Questions 5 and 7, suggest that the computing program did not help students see a relationship between computer science and their own interests. We believe that the increased identification of computer science with programming may have been an unintended consequence of holding coding sessions outside the normal class period. This may have reinforced the opinion that the coding activities, however interesting they might be, were not an organic part of Language & Thinking coursework. This brief exposure to computing seemed to deepen understanding, but it did not significantly help students view computation as a personally useful tool.

The instrument used to measure attitude changes in this much shorter program was a subset of one developed and validated for semester-long courses. The subset of questions we employed may be insensitive to the attitude changes we seek to measure, and therefore demand a different instrument.

Of course, the effect of a program of such short duration, even at this propitious point in a student's education, may be inherently limited. The constraint on program duration is externally imposed by our placement of the program within L&T. We might have added the program to an existing Citizen Science Program, however we were mindful of linking computer science to all disciplines and most particularly those in the arts and humanities with which it is often held apart. To include it in Citizen Science would be to reinforce the stereotypes we wanted this computing program to belie. In addition, the Citizen Science program already includes a computing module focused on modeling infectious disease.

5.2 Broader Reflection

The content of the web workshop was selected to be most relevant to students and faculty from a broad array of disciplines. It was also important that it could be learned in less than two hours. The coding studios were designed to deepen this exposure to include ideas of algorithms more often viewed by the computing professionals as core elements of computer science.

Reports from student teachers and a small number of faculty indicate that the coding studios were well-received. One feature of the computing studio activities points to an approach we expect to implement—the use of current students as peer instructors. Incoming students respond positively to peer teachers, and these instructors are very comfortable teaching the basics of markup languages and programming. The most successful studio was the one in which students used Processing to create virtual fish that were included in a collective "fishtank."

The web workshops were successful in some sections and less so in others. In post-program questions, average student responses to the computing module readings and activities were fairly tepid (mean values of 2.59 and 2.86, respectively). We found that the reliance on instructors who do not generally have a familiarity with, or any particular interest in, writing hypermedia (i.e., HTML) led to some resistance for instructors to act as non-expert teachers in the classroom.

5.3 Revising the Program for a Language-Centered Context

Based on the findings above we proposed modifications to the computing component for the next incoming class (2016). The computing module was made more integral to the L&T Curriculum by having it directly address how web-based expression might differ from the written page. We increased the relevance of the computing module to L&T by making the entire lesson one in which students directly modified web pages in support of their final L&T project. The extra-curricular coding studios were eliminated and a basic introduction to algorithms was added to the web workshop materials taught during regular sessions. All web workshops were taught by small teams of two or three well-trained computer science students.

Readings chosen for the second class meeting were chosen by instructors from a collection of readings related to the relationship between coding, information, and communication. This class was taught in the traditional manner and independently constructed by L&T instructors. Results of this second iteration are being collected and will be discussed in a future report.

6 CONCLUSION

First impressions are critical, and we expect that this brief exposure to computer science will have its most significant effect on students when they make decisions about whether to engage computing in courses and employment opportunities. An increased familiarity with computing may allow them to entertain it as part of a viable pathway for their future.

ACKNOWLEDGMENTS

The authors thank Bard College's Language and Thinking faculty, staff, and directors, Thomas Bartscherer, Bill Dixon, Matt Longabucco, and Rebecca Smylie.

REFERENCES

[1] 2015. *AP Program Participation and Performance Data 2015: Program Summary Report.* http://research.collegeboard.org/programs/ap/data/participation/ap-2015.
[2] Valerie Barr. 2016. Disciplinary thinking, computational doing: promoting interdisciplinary computing while transforming computer science enrollments. *Inroads* 7, 2 (2016), 48–57. http://dl.acm.org/citation.cfm?id=2891414
[3] Jorge Luis Borges. 1964. The Garden of Forking Paths. In *Labyrinths: Selected Stories & Other Writings*, Donald A. Yates and James E. Irby (Eds.). New Directions.
[4] Vannevar Bush. 1945. As We May Think. *The Atlantic* (July 1945).
[5] Brian Dorn and Allison E. Tew. 2015. Empirical Validation and Application of the Computing Attitudes Survey. *Computer Science Education* 25, 1 (2015), 1–36.
[6] David Easley and Jon Kleinberg. 2010. *Networks, Crowds, and Markets: Reasoning About a Highly Connected World.* Cambridge University Press.
[7] Allison Elliott Tew, Brian Dorn, and Oliver Schneider. 2012. Toward a validated computing attitudes survey. In *Proceedings of the 8th of ACM International Workshop on Computing Education Research.* 135–142.
[8] Mark Guzdial. 2003. A Media Computation Course for Non-majors. In *Proceedings of the 8th ACM Conference on Innovation and Technology in Computer Science Education (ITiCSE '03)*. ACM, 104–108. DOI: http://dx.doi.org/10.1145/961511.961542
[9] A. Kay and A. Goldberg. 1977. Personal Dynamic Media. *Computer* 10, 3 (March 1977), 31–41. DOI: http://dx.doi.org/10.1109/C-M.1977.217672
[10] Charles Van Loan. 1980. Computer Science and the Liberal Arts Student. *Educational Forum, XLV* (1980), 29–42.
[11] Dave Mason, Irfan Khan, and Vadim Farafontov. 2016. Computational Thinking As a Liberal Study. In *Proceedings of the 47th ACM Technical Symposium on Computing Science Education (SIGCSE '16)*. ACM, 24–29. DOI: http://dx.doi.org/10.1145/2839509.2844655
[12] Fernando Pérez and Brian E. Granger. 2007. IPython: a System for Interactive Scientific Computing. *Computing in Science and Engineering* 9, 3 (May 2007), 21–29. DOI: http://dx.doi.org/10.1109/MCSE.2007.53
[13] Casey Reas, Ben Fry, and John Maeda. 2007. *Processing: A Programming Handbook for Visual Designers and Artists.* The MIT Press.
[14] Emmanuel Schanzer and Kathi Fisler. 2015. Teaching Algebra and Computing Through Bootstrap and Program by Design. In *Proceedings of the 46th ACM Technical Symposium on Computer Science Education (SIGCSE '15)*. ACM, 695–695. DOI: http://dx.doi.org/10.1145/2676723.2691860
[15] C. Strachey. 1954. The 'Thinking' Machine. *Encounter* III, 4 (1954), 25–31.
[16] Jay Summet, Deepak Kumar, Keith O'Hara, Daniel Walker, Lijun Ni, Doug Blank, and Tucker Balch. 2009. Personalizing CS1 with Robots. In *Proceedings of the 40th ACM Technical Symposium on Computer Science Education (SIGCSE '09)*. ACM, 433–437. DOI: http://dx.doi.org/10.1145/1508865.1509018
[17] Henry M. Walker and Charles Kelemen. 2010. Computer Science and the Liberal Arts: A Philosophical Examination. *Trans. Comput. Educ.* 10, 1, Article 2 (March 2010), 10 pages. DOI: http://dx.doi.org/10.1145/1731041.1731043

A First Look at the Year in Computing

Sebastian Dziallas
School of Computing
University of Kent
Canterbury, CT2 7NF, England
+44 1227 827684
sd485@kent.ac.uk

Sally Fincher
School of Computing
University of Kent
Canterbury, CT2 7NF, England
+44 1227 824061
s.a.fincher@kent.ac.uk

Colin G. Johnson
School of Computing
University of Kent
Canterbury, CT2 7NF, England
+44 1227 762811
c.g.johnson@kent.ac.uk

Ian Utting
School of Computing
University of Kent
Canterbury, CT2 7NF, England
+44 1227 823811
i.a.utting@kent.ac.uk

ABSTRACT

In this paper, we discuss students' expectations and experiences in the first term of the *Year in Computing*, a new programme for non-computing majors at the University of Kent, a public research university in the UK. We focus on the effect of students' home discipline on their experiences in the programme and situate this work within the context of wider efforts to make the study of computing accessible to a broader range of students.

CCS Concepts

• **Social and professional topics~Computer science education**

Keywords

non-majors; curriculum; qualitative research; student experience

1. INTRODUCTION

In recent years, a push to broaden the base of students studying computing has taken place. These efforts are not merely limited to undergraduate students. Jeannette Wing argued in 2006 that "computational thinking" is a skill everyone should possess [21]. Furthermore, in 2016, President Barack Obama announced the *Computer Science for All* initiative in the United States with the goal of providing opportunities for all students from kindergarten through secondary education to learn computer science [5].

Computing has also moved to embrace a more inclusive view of what is part of the discipline, particularly in relation to other fields. The authors of the 2013 ACM/IEEE curriculum report called this the "big tent view" of computing. They wrote:

> As CS expands to include more cross-disciplinary
> work and new programs of the form

> "Computational Biology," "Computational Engineering," and "Computational X" are developed, it is important to embrace an outward-looking view that sees CS as a discipline actively seeking to work with and integrate into other disciplines. [12]

Programmes for non-majors in computing can be roughly separated into three categories: those looking to broaden the student base in computing; to provide or increase the skills of students in their home discipline ("upskilling"); and to convert students into computing graduates.

An example for broadening the student base is the course for non-STEM students on media computation that Guzdial and Forte describe in their work. As part of their process of creating the course, they decided to maintain similar curricular goals as other introductory courses, while changing its context to motivate students [9, 10]. In the resulting course, students create and manipulate media, but still learn to program.

Other efforts are more concerned with providing students with a set of specific set of computing skills they can use in conjunction with their own subject area. For instance, *software carpentry* is a formal programme that stands outside of traditional institutional boundaries and brings together students from STEM backgrounds. It is designed to specifically address "small-scale and immediately practical issues" in software development using tools and techniques, such as version control and debugging [20]. Another example in this area is the work of DeJongh and LeBlanc, who intended to bring computer science concepts and tools to bioinformatics students [3].

At the university level, course offerings for non-majors have increasingly attracted interest, including from mainstream news organisations [18]. There is a wide range of courses: some are intended to introduce students to wide range of different concepts and applications (such as problem solving [13], algorithms and computational thinking [6], internet applications and web programming [8, 14]), others form the basis of a sequence of courses (and have adopted the have adopted the CS0 terminology [1, 11, 17]). At liberal arts institutions, mainly in the US, students may elect to complete a minor degree in computer science in addition to their major degree [4]. And in the UK, students can enrol in joint honours programmes that allow them to study two subjects during their time at university.

Finally, in terms of "converting" students who have already completed a degree in another subject, universities in the UK offer conversion MSc programmes which are open to all students with good results in their first degree.

In this paper, we examine the newly launched *Year in Computing* at the School of Computing at the University of Kent. The Year in Computing is currently in its first year and provides an opportunity for students from other disciplines to study computing. The programme is similar to MSc conversion programmes; however, those are taught at a postgraduate level and are intended to cover a large fraction of the core of Computer Science, whilst the Year in Computing is an undergraduate programme with a distinctive curriculum and a focus on web technologies. It is also an effort to both broaden the student base in computing at the University and to help students develop computing skills they can use in their home discipline or more generally in their future careers.

2. CONTEXT OF THE YEAR IN COMPUTING

Undergraduate degrees in the United Kingdom generally take three years to complete, although there are opportunities for an additional *Year in Industry* or a *Year Abroad*. Students declare their intended major upon application to university. Some students choose to enrol in so-called joint honours programmes that allow them to study two subjects (that do not necessarily have to be closely related) over the normal duration of an undergraduate degree. In a joint honours programme, each department is responsible for delivering their own respective courses, so students generally take existing courses together with undergraduates who are in single degree programmes. As a result, joint honours programmes often do not facilitate cohort formation among students. They also lack a coherent curriculum structure, while requiring that students complete the course requirements for both subject areas in a limited time, and often suffer from hidden pre-requisites in the courses they do take.

In contrast, the Year in Computing is a free-standing, self-contained additional year, offered to undergraduate students doing any degree in the University that does not contain computing. Students may take the Year in Computing in between the second and third year of their degree, or after year three. During the year, students work exclusively in the School of Computing. The programme operates as a stand-alone year of study in which students are taught as a single cohort; all students in the programme take the same courses at the same time as part of a coherent curriculum, instead of individual courses with other undergraduates. This allows for cohort identity formation and obviates issues of timetabling and pre-requisites that otherwise plague joint honours programmes.

The Year in Computing as a whole is "pass / fail". Successful students ultimately graduate with their degree title augmented with the designation "with a Year in Computing". If a student fails their Year in Computing, they return to their home discipline and graduate without the additional designation. So whilst the grades they receive in the courses appear on their transcript, they do not affect the classification of their degree which remains wholly dependent on their performance in their home discipline. Degree classification is a significant (although rather crude) measure of overall student achievement in the UK, used as a gateway to further study and employment, which does not reflect potentially

wide disparities between performance when students are studying more than one subject, as in a traditional joint honours programme.

3. CURRICULAR CONTENT

The Year in Computing is aimed both at students who want to "convert" into computing for vocational reasons, and for students who want to integrate computing with their home degree studies. The latter could include students who plan to integrate computing into a scientific discipline (e.g. in bioinformatics), to use data science skills in a social science area (e.g. in analysis of data from social networks), or to use computing technologies as part of an artistic practice.

Students in the programme follow a curriculum specifically developed for this context. The courses were designed from the ground up (or, in the case of HCI and web technologies adapted versions of the modules that undergraduate students in computer science take). This allows us to focus on the aspects most relevant to the students in the programme.

Courses for non-majors traditionally focus either on a breadth of computing topics or depth in terms of programming [17]. Whilst the introductory courses in the BSc in Computer Science at the University of Kent rely on Java as a first programming language and include a large component of logic and discrete mathematics, we decided to focus instead on web technologies. This allows us to introduce a wide range of computing topics in the context of the web (providing breadth) while exposing students to an entire stack of software (addressing depth).

Table 1. Courses in the Year in Computing

Autumn Term	Spring Term
An Introduction to Computer Systems: From the desktop to the global Internet. (7.5 ECTS credits)	**Solving Problems with Data**: Collecting, analysing and portraying data from specific domains, businesses, and the world. (7.5 credits)
Human Computer Interaction and User Experience: Designing information and applications for their users and their purpose (7.5 credits)	**Web Development**: Building and managing large scale, dynamic, web applications. (7.5 credits)
An Introduction to Programming and Web Technologies (15 credits): <ul><li>Presenting information (HTML and CSS)</li><li>A general introduction to programming, through coding in Javascript</li><li>Storing information (databases and SQL).</li><li>Dynamically generating content for web pages from stored data (PHP).</li></ul>	**Year in Computing Project** (15 credits): Putting learning into practice in a larger piece of work, perhaps related to a domain in the home discipline.

The curriculum for the Year in Computing (Table 1) then covers "back-end" topics such as understanding computer operating systems and networks, learning programming (through JavaScript), storing and manipulating data, and integrating with a Web server. At the "front-end" it includes producing web pages using HTML, CSS and JavaScript that work well, look good and are easy to interact with.

We also wanted to include explicit opportunities for students to work in the context of their home discipline. Both the Solving Problems with Data course and (particularly) the Project component encourage students to use data and address problems from their own disciplines.

Performance in the programme is assessed by means of practical coursework and a small number of written examinations.

By the end of the programme, regardless of whether they intend to continue to work in computing or plan to return to their home discipline, we expect students to be able to:

- Understand the role of technology and how it is used in the contemporary world.
- Have a good foundational knowledge of coding that is focused on the ideas of programming, not just learning a specific language.
- Build dynamic, modern web-based systems.
- Understand how data can be used to tackle complex problems.
- Have a practical grasp of methods for presenting data and designing interactions with computer-based systems.

4. CHARACTERISTICS OF THE STUDENT BODY

The University of Kent is a medium-size university with approximately 15,000 undergraduate students. Within this student body, only those students in their second or third year who are not pursuing a degree in Computing are eligible to apply to the Year in Computing. There are currently 34 students enrolled in the programme.

One pre-requisite for admission to the Year in Computing is success as a student at the University to date, not any given subject knowledge about computing. (The Year in Computing is not for students who are unsatisfied with their performance in their home discipline and looking to switch into computing.) A side-effect of only recruiting students from the same university is that they are already familiar with the campus, the institutional processes and (to an extent) University systems, thus significantly reducing their initial familiarisation difficulties compared to incoming undergraduate students. This familiarity can also be a "false friend" however, highlighted in the differences in expectations (of how and where to study) between the Year in Computing and students' home subjects.

The application process for the programme is also deliberately light-weight: Students submit a formless application statement expressing why they are interested in the Year in Computing and take part in an interview designed to assess their enthusiasm about engaging with computing. The student body resulting from this process consists of students from a great variety of different backgrounds.

As well as disparity of academic background, they also have a wide variety of previous experience of computers and coding, either as part of their prior academic experience in secondary or tertiary education, or as "hobbyists". Although this was captured

in the application process, and students who had (effectively) already covered the syllabus were excluded, judgements at the lower end of the experience range have been less robust.

Undergraduate students in Computing at most institutions are traditionally relatively homogenous: they are predominantly male and technology-focussed. For example, only 15% of the students in the BSc in Computer Science at the University of Kent are women. In contrast, 40% of the students in the Year in Computing are women. Furthermore, 47% of the 34 students in the programme are completing non-STEM degrees at the University.[1]

Studying this first Year in Computing will enrich our understanding and inform our approach to making computing attractive as a destination subject for students from a wider range of backgrounds and with a wider range of personal characteristics than those who typically choose this subject area.

5. THIS WORK

In this paper, we provide a 'first look' at the first term of the programme. We specifically focus on the role of students' home discipline, as well as their experiences in the programme to date.

We reviewed both students' application statements and their responses to an end-of-term survey conducted after the first semester in the course. (This was not the generic module evaluation form used for all courses, although some students took the opportunity to use it to provide feedback.) The survey asked students about their expectations for the course, their previous learning experiences at University, the amount of time they spent on the different modules, their own personal and professional goals, their assessment of the skills they developed, and the effect the Year in Computing on them to date. Out of 34 students in the programme, 12 responded to the end-of-term survey (35%).

6. THEMES

6.1 Why Students Chose to Apply

Students expressed different motivations in their application statements. Some of them were looking to enhance their employability within the context of their home discipline, particularly in STEM fields, such as chemistry and physics.

> "Throughout my course, we have been taught that the ability to collect and analyse data is a central skill for forensic scientists and I believe that adding this additional qualification will be very useful for my future job prospects in this field."

> "I became interested in computing after my first year module in 'computing skills' where I learnt some basics in coding. This interest propelled me to my project in computational chemistry. [It] has made me want to learn more about computing ... that would give me an edge when applying for jobs around chemistry and computational chemistry."

> "This is something I've done as an amateur for quite a while and having some proper grounding would allow me to do computing on a more professional basis. It would also give me skills that would apply to almost any area of physics work."

---

[1] We are not providing a full list of disciplines as students might otherwise be identifiable due to the small number of participants.

But the home discipline did not play a decisive role for all students. One anthropology student was interested in the subject matter and felt that facility with technical systems was important regardless of discipline.

> "I am self-taught, and being formally taught computing would allow me to polish my skills and develop new ones. Although computing is less applicable to my degree than others, I think that technical knowledge and web-related development is important regardless of academic background."

And for one student, who was unable to find a joint honours programme that offered their subjects of interest, the Year in Computing provided them a chance they never had:

> "Unfortunately, while applying for University, I had to choose only one subject and could not find any proper combinations with architecture and computing. However, with this new 'Year in Computing' being launched by the University, I feel that I have an exceptional opportunity to study a combination that I truly want."

Not all students who were offered spaces in the Year in Computing ended up enrolling. In fact, the reasons why students did not choose to do a Year in Computing matched common reasons why students do not take part in a placement year: they could not arrange accommodation in time or did not want to miss graduating with their cohort in their home discipline [7].

6.2 Expectations & Reality

When we surveyed students at the end of their first term, 8 out of 12 (67%) expressed that the course had met their expectations, particularly with regards to both breadth and depth of the curriculum.

> "I expected a general overview of aspects of computing, which for the most part I got."

> "I did expect to learn programming skills and the course is what I expected it to be."

However, some students indicated that certain aspects were different than they had expected. Their comments focussed particularly on the individual modules—Introduction to Computer Systems, HCI/UX, and Programing and Web Technologies (which students commonly referred to as "the programming module"). This was not entirely surprising to us, as the curriculum structures material into the three distinct courses which each have their own a set of teaching staff.

> "I expected to get an introduction into the world of computing, starting with some basic programming and understanding of computer systems. I don't really understand Computer Systems, but I'm getting better at programming, which is great!"

> "It's what I expected, apart from [the HCI module]. I was expecting some kind of design element to the course but it [the HCI module] went beyond what I had expected."

> "[The programming module] definitely makes it very clear when you've made progress and really makes you feel like you are learning and understanding and that the work you're putting in is actually producing something which is very motivating and encouraging especially in

> comparison to [the Computer Systems module] which can feel like swimming in quicksand at times."

Of course, not all of the students' learning experiences were positive and for some students the course has been harder than expected.

> "I believe some of the tasks have been too tricky for a beginner."

> "I expected the course to be for someone who is a complete novice [...]."

It is not immediately clear whether this student was expecting a course on computer literacy or computational thinking, rather than one with significant programming elements. Some of the students who expressed difficulty with the course included a different kind of reflection.

> "It's made me feel intimidated to go into computing-based jobs, and question my ability to handle next term."

> "I was quite disheartened by finding JavaScript a particularly difficult topic to study - it made me feel like maybe going into bioinformatics wouldn't be the best idea [...]."

We take both these expressions – of the current challenge of the course and of an imagined future with regard to computing – as expressions of self-efficacy. According to Bandura, self-efficacy is defined as the belief in one's ability to accomplish a task [2]. These comments then appear to reflect the students' own perceived ability to succeed in the Year in Computing as a result of their experiences in the first term. Wiedenbeck analysed factors affecting non-majors' experiences when learning to program and found that self-efficacy, as well as knowledge organisation, played a central role in their experiences [19]. Lishinski et al. showed for students in a CS1 course that students' motivation affects their self-efficacy, which affects their performance in the course, which in turn affects their self-efficacy in a virtuous (or vicious) cycle [15].

For our students there are two, related, aspects to increased self-efficacy. One is mastery of the taught material, being able to complete the assessments, write required programs and design interfaces. In this they work by themselves and with others in the cohort, invoking three of Bandura's elements of self-efficacy—individual achievement, observation of achievement of peers and verbal encouragement of others. However, there is a second element, more fleeting in this data, which is one of general familiarity with computational environments and systems—not something that is explicitly included in the course. Thus we read hints that the less "literacy" experience a Year in Computing student has, the lower their belief in their own self-efficacy which becomes a barrier for their further learning. "I expected [it] to be for a complete novice" suggests the lack of an entirely separate set of skills.

This presents an opportunity for future work for us and we intend to follow up with these students in the future to explore their expectations and experiences further. Additionally, it has prompted us to add a more explicit exploration of an applicant's familiarity with technology at interview.

6.3 Contrast to previous experience

Because we are ultimately interested in how metacognitive skills of "being a good student" transfer between disciplines, students were also asked to identify contrasts to their previous learning experiences in their home discipline at University. One of the students who found the course harder than expected was surprised to find that they were falling behind despite attending all of the scheduled class sessions.

> "I did feel lost by the wayside for most of the term and easily left behind in terms of understanding the course content even when I was attending my lectures/classes."

Thus suggesting that "attending all lectures/classes" was sufficient to this student's previous academic success, perhaps generally sufficient to academic success in their home discipline.

Conversely, one student arrived at the first Lab session for the programming course having already completed all the exercises, and being prepared to discuss their thinking (as, presumably, in seminars in their home discipline), but was surprised to find that they were expected to do it all (again) in the Lab.

Students were also surprised by the accessibility of staff in the programme.

> "The coding [in the programming module] is exactly what I expected and I have really enjoyed that section the most. There are more complicated Computer Systems than I thought there would be, but there is far more support than I could have dreamt of."

> "The support offered far supersedes expectations and the approachability of the staff is fantastic."

When we asked students what kind of advice they would offer to incoming students, they focussed on *practicing* both ahead of and during the term, rather than asking for help, in their responses: half of the students who responded to the survey said that they would tell their fellow students to "keep practicing". This advice was often focussed on the programming language used in the course, JavaScript:

> "Mess around with JavaScript beforehand, really try and get to grips with it, ask for plenty of help when stuck."

> "Do a lot more outside work for programming than is given, i.e. on Codecademy / w3schools etc."

Other differences in contrast to students' previous experiences at university concerned assessments, particularly in contrast how they are set in the humanities.

> "In my previous degree, there were 4 big essays all due in the last two weeks of term. I really like the way there is smaller continuous assessments, though there are more exams than I thought there would be."

> "The spread of assignments is generally better than multiple essays due at the end of week 6 and end of week 12, and the variety is refreshing."

> "The assignments are much more involved and the coursework is more work-oriented rather than test-oriented."

One student observed that the assessment criteria were also different:

> "I would say the standard of assessment is different though however, in my home discipline of biochemistry, assessments given are expected to be as perfect as possible however for this course, mainly for programming, the code can not work and still be marked reasonably high."

6.4 Goals & Changes

We were also interested in the effect of the Year in Computing. We asked students about their personal and professional goals and whether their experiences this term had changed what they intended to do in the future. Two students indicated that they were uncertain about their future goals. For others, the *Year in Computing* seemed intended to augment any kind of work they might do in the future.

> "To be successful in any career I go into."

> "[To] secure a job before graduating, not having to move home after graduation situation permitting."

But it also served as a way for students to expand on their home discipline.

> "I would like to eventually go on and study a bioinformatics masters and then either stay in academia looking at protein structure and function prediction programs [...] or going into industry and using bioinformatics as a skill for investigating possible pharmaceutical drug targets."

Again others had specific ideas about the work they planned to do after graduating, with a specific focus on computing.

> "I want to focus on Web Development or Data Control as a profession within a technology focussed business."

> "Simulation, data handling, software development."

> "I hope to do the MSc conversion course and go into software development, data management or marketing."

For these three students, the *Year in Computing* reinforced their confidence in choosing a career in a computing-related field.

> "It has made me more certain that I want to go into computer based careers in the future and assured my passion for it that I was unsure of at the beginning."

> "I feel better equipped for creating applications and may go more down that route"

> "Rather than a specific focus on marketing my experiences have massively opened my eyes to other options and piqued my interest in computer science fields and showed how related marketing can be to design and other things we have done this term."

For these students, achievement in course to date has increased their self-efficacy and confirmed their choice to study an additional year of Computing. The course also marked a significant change for other students, although not such a directly confirmatory one.

> "I have chosen to go into teaching, which is a career I never thought of much before this course."

"This course did make me consider becoming a web designer."

Indeed, one student went so far as to indicate they *"cannot imagine having to go back to my home degree now"* and advised future students to take the *Year in Computing* after their third (and not the second) year as a result. In the future, we plan to follow up with students to conduct in-depth interviews to understand what experiences led to these changes for them.

7. CONCLUSION

The Year in Computing provides an opportunity for non-computing majors at the University of Kent to extend their degree programmes by studying computing. It also provides work-related skills to support students in their future study, research, or careers.

For us, as teachers and researchers, the Year in Computing provides a rare chance to teach and study a stable and coherent group of non-traditional students (who did not intend to become Computing majors when entering University) over an extended period, and affords us insights not only into their development in computing, but also into the hidden assumptions in our own discipline and practices.

On an institutional level, the Year in Computing broadens the School of Computing's student base and provides resilience against fluctuation in undergraduate or taught postgraduate numbers. It also provides other Schools in the University with a model to offer an intercalated year in their own discipline (e.g. the *Year in Business* or the *Year in Quantitative Methods* proposed as part of the UK national Q-Step programme [16]).

8. FUTURE WORK

This work provided a first look at the Year in Computing at the University of Kent, with a particular focus on the effect of students' home discipline on their experience studying computing. In the future, we also plan to use both narrative and traditional qualitative methods to examine the transfer of metacognitive skills (of being a "good student") across disciplinary contexts, the curricular and pedagogical adaptations made by staff in respect of students' diverse disciplinary backgrounds, and the longitudinal effect of the programme on students' experience after graduation.

We intend to follow up with this first cohort of students at the end of their second term to conduct in-depth interviews and to explore the effect of both their home discipline and self-efficacy further. And eventually, we would like to follow them back to their home disciplines and out to work.

9. REFERENCES

[1]   Bailey, T. and Forbes, J. 2005. Just-in-time Teaching for CS0. *Proceedings of the 36th SIGCSE Technical Symposium on Computer Science Education* (New York, NY, USA, 2005), 366–370.

[2]   Bandura, A. 1977. Self-efficacy: Toward a unifying theory of behavioral change. *Psychological Review*. 84, 2 (1977), 191–215.

[3]   Bioinformatics in the Computer Science Curriculum: *http://www.cs.hope.edu/~dejongh/bioinformatics/sigcse/*. Accessed: 2017-01-13.

[4]   Cliburn, D.C. 2006. A CS0 Course for the Liberal Arts. *Proceedings of the 37th SIGCSE Technical Symposium on Computer Science Education* (New York, NY, USA, 2006), 77–81.

[5]   Computer Science For All: 2016. *https://www.whitehouse.gov/blog/2016/01/30/computer-science-all*. Accessed: 2017-01-09.

[6]   Cortina, T.J. 2007. An Introduction to Computer Science for Non-majors Using Principles of Computation. *Proceedings of the 38th SIGCSE Technical Symposium on Computer Science Education* (New York, NY, USA, 2007), 218–222.

[7]   Fincher, S. and Finlay, J. 2016. *Computing Graduate Employability: Sharing Practice*. Council of Professors and Heads of Computing.

[8]   Gousie, M.B. 2006. A Robust Web Programming and Graphics Course for Non-majors. *Proceedings of the 37th SIGCSE Technical Symposium on Computer Science Education* (New York, NY, USA, 2006), 72–76.

[9]   Guzdial, M. 2003. A Media Computation Course for Non-majors. *Proceedings of the 8th Annual Conference on Innovation and Technology in Computer Science Education* (New York, NY, USA, 2003), 104–108.

[10]   Guzdial, M. and Forte, A. 2005. Design Process for a Non-majors Computing Course. *Proceedings of the 36th SIGCSE Technical Symposium on Computer Science Education* (New York, NY, USA, 2005), 361–365.

[11]   Hickey, T.J. 2004. Scheme-based Web Programming As a Basis for a CS0 Curriculum. *Proceedings of the 35th SIGCSE Technical Symposium on Computer Science Education* (New York, NY, USA, 2004), 353–357.

[12]   Joint Task Force on Computing Curricula 2013. *Computer Science Curricula 2013: Curriculum Guidelines for Undergraduate Degree Programs in Computer Science*. ACM.

[13]   Joyce, D. 1998. The Computer As a Problem Solving Tool: A Unifying View for a Non-majors Course. *Proceedings of the Twenty-ninth SIGCSE Technical Symposium on Computer Science Education* (New York, NY, USA, 1998), 63–67.

[14]   Kurkovsky, S. 2007. Making Computing Attractive for Non-majors: A Course Design. *J. Comput. Sci. Coll.* 22, 3 (Jan. 2007), 90–97.

[15]   Lishinski, A. et al. 2016. Learning to Program: Gender Differences and Interactive Effects of Students' Motivation, Goals, and Self-Efficacy on Performance. *Proceedings of the 2016 ACM Conference on International Computing Education Research* (New York, NY, USA, 2016), 211–220.

[16]   Q-Step | Nuffield Foundation: *http://www.nuffieldfoundation.org/q-step*. Accessed: 2017-01-15.

[17]   Reed, D. 2001. Rethinking CS0 with JavaScript. *Proceedings of the Thirty-second SIGCSE Technical Symposium on Computer Science Education* (New York, NY, USA, 2001), 100–104.

[18]   Stross, R. 2012. Computer Science for Non-Majors Takes Many Forms. *The New York Times*.

[19]   Wiedenbeck, S. 2005. Factors Affecting the Success of Non-majors in Learning to Program. *Proceedings of the First International Workshop on Computing Education Research* (New York, NY, USA, 2005), 13–24.

[20]   Wilson, G. 2006. Software Carpentry: Getting Scientists to Write Better Code by Making Them More Productive. *Computing in Science Engineering*. 8, 6 (Nov. 2006), 66–69.

[21]   Wing, J.M. 2006. Computational Thinking. *Commun. ACM*. 49, 3 (Mar. 2006), 33–35.

Computing for Medicine: An Experience Report

Jennifer Campbell
Department of Computer Science
University of Toronto
campbell@cs.toronto.edu

Michelle Craig
Department of Computer Science
University of Toronto
mcraig@cs.toronto.edu

Marcus Law
Faculty of Medicine
University of Toronto
marcus.law@utoronto.ca

ABSTRACT

We report our experience developing and teaching a computing elective course for students enrolled in a Doctor of Medicine (MD) program. Students participated in a series of workshops to learn and practice programming, and gained additional experience by completing programming assignments. Students then participated in a novel seminar series delivered by experts who each discussed one application of computing to medicine. Each seminar included a corresponding programming project where students worked with the ideas introduced in the seminar and practiced their newly-acquired programming skills. We found that by streaming the students into levels based on prior experience, carefully scaffolding project handouts, and having each seminar co-led by a faculty member, we are able to support students — even beginners — to succeed. Students report that the topics are relevant, they appreciate the medical context of the programming exercises, and they would recommend the program to others.

KEYWORDS

non-majors, novice programming, medicine

ACM Reference format:
Jennifer Campbell, Michelle Craig, and Marcus Law. 2017. Computing for Medicine: An Experience Report. In *Proceedings of ITiCSE'17, July 03-05, 2017, Bologna, Italy,* 6 pages.
DOI: http://dx.doi.org/10.1145/3059009.3059027

1 INTRODUCTION

The University of Toronto Faculty of Medicine MD Program conducted an extensive consultative process between 2013 and 2015 in order to redesign the first two years of their curriculum. The resulting Foundations Curriculum includes a weekly self-learning day designed to enable students to explore non-traditional learning experiences that will distinguish the program graduates from their peers. Through regular meetings with students, the Dean of Medicine identified a strong student interest in learning about computing in medicine. No other Canadian medical school offered similar learning experiences.

At the same time, hackathons, software-development bootcamps and learning-to-code initiatives such as Hour of Code by Code.org [3],

Canada Learning Code [2], and others were gaining media coverage. Perhaps influenced by this trend, the medical students meeting with the Dean wanted more than to simply learn to be sophisticated users of medical technology — they wanted to learn to code.

The Dean of Medicine and the CS Department Chair together initiated a collaboration where faculty members from both areas would design and deliver a program to medical students. They envisioned an opportunity to expose these students to the exciting leading-edge collaborative research projects already happening at our institution, while at the same time giving the students some hands-on experience with basic computing skills including programming. They wanted it accessible and achievable for busy students including those with no prior programming experience.

2 RELATED PROGRAMS

In the last few years, a number of medical schools have redesigned their curricula to add competencies and learning objectives around the sophisticated use of information technology. These topics are labeled in a variety of ways, including health informatics [15], biomedical informatics [17], and medical informatics [11]. A survey of 557 students from four American medical schools found that 30% were interested in a clinical informatics career and 58% were interested in the opportunity to take an elective in this area [10]. While the varying terminology can be confusing, one commonality in all these programs is that they teach medical students about the use of technology in their future practices, but not how to write computer programs.

Other programs exist in computational biology [1, 9] that have much more computer science content, but these are typically designed for training researchers (who may also be physicians but not necessarily) and seem to include a precondition that students already know how to code in some programming language. In the research we did before designing our program, we found no learn-to-code programs for medical schools.

There is a large body of work on the design of computing education for different learner populations (learner-centered design) summarized recently by Guzdial [14] who argues that effective computing educators need to develop the learning goals for their materials by considering the eventual communities of practice and motivations of the learners. Another network that informed the design of our program was the well-established series of Software Carpentry Workshops [19], which focus on teaching computing skills, including introductory programming, to scientific researchers.

3 PROGRAM DEVELOPMENT

During initial exploratory meetings, we discussed the vision for the program, held a focus group to better understand the students' interests and expectations in this area, and interviewed researchers and medical practitioners about the most useful topics to include.

3.1 Should every student learn to code?

The creation of our computing program was prompted by a complete redesign of the first two years of the MD program. In this new Foundations curriculum, the materials for each week are designed to connect to a single medical case. The case motivates the students to explore related concepts and the learning goals across the entire curriculum are carefully tied to one or more of the cases. The first proposal was to integrate CS materials into a subset of these medical cases. To do this would have been challenging, but it would have demonstrated clearly how computer programming can be connected to clinical practice. To integrate computing into the cases, however, would have meant that every student in the MD program would be required to learn to program. Although we are in favour of providing everyone with an opportunity to learn to program, we did not want to require it of all medical school students. Instead, we decided to run the program as an elective.

3.2 Establishing Learning Objectives

Although it was clear that the learning objectives would include learning to read, write, and debug code and that the students should be exposed to the current research work performed in collaborations between medical and computer science researchers, other specific learning objectives were less obvious. As is almost always the case when one develops course syllabi, there were too many good topics to fit into too little time.

We tried to make learner-centred choices [14], taking into consideration what would cause less irrelevant overhead in the learning experience and what would connect most directly to students' prior experience. We also considered what the students might find useful in their future practices and more immediately, if they worked as summer research assistants.

A critical decision was whether to teach Python or R. Although arguments were made for each language, we deemed it more important to get a deeper grounding in one language than a shallow introduction to both and selected Python because of its more general applicability. In particular, library support for machine learning, data visualization, statistical analysis, databases, and other tools relevant to the application of computing to medicine, make Python a desirable choice.

Another choice was whether to expose students to the Unix command line, which is a topic typically included in Software Carpentry [8] workshops. Given that we wanted students to experience using a debugging tool, we decided not to teach command line tools and instead have students use a Python IDE.

One other topic strongly recommended by those we consulted from the medicine/CS research community was SQL. Several people advocated for teaching basic query syntax so that students could in the future use a database (rather than a spreadsheet) to store their own data. Rather than teach SQL as one of the fundamental topics, we introduced it through one of the later seminars.

3.3 Seminars: The Design Gem

The cornerstone of the design is a seminar series. Each seminar not only exposes the students to an exciting research area, but also includes a homework project based on the topic. This gives students something practical to implement after each seminar, so that they work with the material, rather than just attend a high-level research presentation, which is often soon forgotten. The projects connect with the corresponding research topic and help the students to understand the neat ideas, while reinforcing their developing coding skills.

4 COMPUTING FOR MEDICINE PROGRAM

The Computing for Medicine (C4M) program has four progressive phases. At present, we are finishing up Phase III of a pilot offering (with an atypical timeline and incoming students from both first and second year), and Phase II of a regular offering (with a standard September start date and incoming students from only first year). For the remainder of the paper, unless stated otherwise, all results referring to Phase I are for the regular offering and results for Phases II and III are for the pilot offering.

In September 2016, 43 of 259 first-year medical students (17%) opted to participate in the first regular offering of C4M. Participants were assigned to different levels based on their self-reported prior programming experience.

For all phases of the program, assignments are graded as pass or fail, and there are no exams or course grades. The course will not appear on the students' academic transcripts, but students can choose to include it in their curriculum vitae as a co-curricular activity.

Since C4M is an optional elective in a challenging and intensive medical program with demanding time constraints, some attrition is to be expected. For the first regular cohort, 88% successfully completed Phase I, with 91% of those carrying on to Phase II.

4.1 Phase I: Principles of Programming

In Phase I, students participate in a series of programming workshops. Courses involving active learning generally have higher exam scores and lower failure rates than traditional lecture-based courses [13]. With this in mind, we alternated between teaching new topics through instructor lectures and demos, and having the students apply what they have learned by solving problems. To promote active learning throughout the workshops, including the instructional portions, we require students to bring a laptop to each session and encourage them to type along during the demos. After each session, homework is assigned and is due the day before the next session. The sessions are held at least two weeks apart.

4.2 Phase II: Consolidation

In Phase II of the program, the students again attend workshops. At the beginning of this phase, the workshops provide additional instruction and practice similar to Phase I. However, over time, the focus shifts towards consolidation. The majority of the homework centers on the completion of two larger Python projects, which exercise almost all the programming concepts learned to date and are framed in a medical domain. The difficulty level and size of each project is fairly comparable to that of a large CS1 assignment.

	Score (out of 5) $n = 64$
Through this seminar, I gained a better understanding of how to apply computing to the field of medicine.	4.3
The seminar topic was appropriate for the Computing for Medicine curriculum.	4.5
The session format was enjoyable.	4.2
The amount of information I was expected to learn was reasonable.	4.2
The speaker was engaging.	4.3

Table 1: Phase III mean survey responses (for six seminars)

Considerable scaffolding was provided in the form of starter code and carefully-crafted guidance in an attempt to maximize the time students spend on the intellectually-interesting programming concepts, make the programs achievable in a reasonable amount of time, and prevent students from feeling overwhelmed and unable to begin. We also designed auto-tested exercises that had students develop individual functions needed to complete the project. The exercises were grouped into problem sets and assigned in the weeks leading up to the project due dates.

4.2.1 Medical Document Retrieval. The first project involved selecting appropriate documents based on relative frequencies of search terms from a corpus of related documents. This concept, referred to in some circles as Term Frequency/Inverse Document Frequency (TF/IDF), is not unique to medical applications. In order to contextualize it for the C4M audience, we used the infectious diseases web pages from Wikipedia [6] as the source for our corpus. The final programs asked the user to enter a list of symptoms and then selected a most-likely candidate infectious disease.

In an anonymous survey, students reported investing hugely varying amounts of time on this project. A few claimed they spent more than 25 hours and others reported only a few hours but then clarified that this was just to put together the final solution after doing the lead-up exercises. Surprisingly, it was the students assigned to the non-beginner levels who reported investing the most time. We suspect that this reflects the interest level of these students – the same keen interest that led them to pursue more computing before medical school.

4.2.2 Human Mobility and Epidemic Modeling. The second project involved first implementing Dijkstra's algorithm, framed as a program to find the shortest route between cities by which a disease could travel. Then, once the between-city distances were known, they were used to implement a time-driven simulation of an epidemic. Again, significant scaffolding was provided both in the form of lead-up exercises and step-by-step instructions for combining the functions into a working program. This structure allowed students — including beginners — to cope with the full project and the majority of students who attempted the project submitted a more or less complete solution.

4.3 Phase III: Enrichment

After students gain experience solving Python programming problems in Phases I and II, we aim to enhance their understanding of how computing can be applied to medicine. In six two-hour Phase III seminars, an expert in an area of computing related to medicine

gives an overview of their research. The speaker, in consultation with the CS faculty member teaching the C4M program, also develops a project to give students an opportunity to apply what they have learned in the seminar. During the second part of the seminar, the CS faculty teaches any additional programming or computer science concepts needed to solve the program. Students are required to attend five of the six seminars and complete three of the corresponding projects.

Student feedback is shown in Table 1, which contains mean survey scores for the six Phase III sessions. Overall, the sessions were quite well received and 94% (n=63) responded yes to the question "Would you recommend this session to others?"

Here are descriptions of some Phase III projects:

4.3.1 Natural Language Processing in Clinical Medicine. Based on work by Fraser et al. [12], students performed simple machine learning on a corpora to determine whether utterances were spoken by people with dementia. A significant amount of starter code was provided, but students wrote the code to extract features and classify feature vectors. The program relied on Python's numpy (numerical python), nltk (natural language toolkit), scipy (scientific computing), and sklearn (machine learning) modules. In addition, the provided data were pre-processed using the Stanford parts of speech (PoS) tagger. The students were introduced to numpy's array type and used it multiple times to complete the project.

4.3.2 Data Visualization. For this project, the students were introduced to the JSON data format and were provided with a set of nutritional-label data in that format. Their task was to visualize the data in a variety of ways, including normalizing nutritional-label data for two different products so that they could be visualized together. This project relied on Python's numpy and matplotlib modules. The students also learned about importing modules for the purpose of code reuse and using Python's main block.

4.3.3 Portable DNA Sequencing. In this project, students were provided with DNA sequencing data collected using portable DNA sequencing devices during the 2013 Ebola outbreak in Guinea [16]. The students were tasked with using the sequencing data to reconstruct Ebola genomes, finding mutations relative to a reference strain, and identifying related cases. They were also required to used an online tool [5] from the European Bioinformatics Institute to build a phylogenetic tree. This project relied on Python's biopython module. Students were also taught about Python's glob module and used it to write code to find and open files with particular names.

4.3.4 Medical Image Analysis. In this project, the students worked with a set of colon cancer histology data [18]. They wrote code to automatically detect Nuclei centres from these histology images and to detect features and classify the images. Although this project relied on several modules, most had been used in at least one of the other projects. The dependencies were `skiimage` (image processing) and `joblib` (a parallel computing package used in the starter code to speed up processing), as well as `numpy`, `pylab`, `scipy`, `matplotlib`, and `sklearn`. In terms of new Python topics, students were introduced to functions used to manipulate multidimensional arrays using `numpy`.

4.4 Phase IV: Practicum (Optional)

In the planned final phase of the program, selected students will work with faculty and researchers on projects applying computing to medicine. This phase of the program is optional and is dependent on the availability of projects and capacity of qualified and interested supervisors.

5 LESSONS LEARNED

5.1 Application process

The MD program sent an email announcement inviting students to apply. The application form included questions about why the student would like to enroll, the outcomes they hoped to achieve, and their prior programming experience. For the pilot offering, the students were under the impression that there were a limited number of spots and some overstated their programming experience in order to impress and gain entry into the program. This led to students being placed in a level that was too challenging for them and instructors overestimating the pace at which students could process the material.

In the next application cycle, when we asked students about their experience, we explained that we needed this information only to determine in which level they belonged. By making our intentions clear, students understood that they did not need to oversell their prior experience and instead gave us the information we needed to assign students to appropriate levels and better pace the workshops.

5.2 Levels

Streaming students into different levels, based on their previous programming experience, allows us to teach different sections at difference paces. The beginner section has an extra class meeting and moves more slowly but eventually covers the same material. However, even with multiple levels, it is still challenging to find the appropriate pace. Table 2 shows that in the beginner section, the majority of students found the pace either just right or too fast. Others with some prior programming experience found that the pace was either just right or a little too slow. Since the type of prior programming experience and programming language differs, the instructors need to spend time on the fundamentals to normalize the knowledge of the participants. Although the pace of delivery for non-beginners could be sped up slightly, the instructors do not believe it should be sped up significantly, since that may leave students lacking the solid foundation needed to tackle the Phase III projects.

	Beginners (n=8)	Others (n=10)
Way too slow		
A little too slow	1	5
Just right	3	5
A little too fast	1	
Way too fast	1	

Table 2: Survey responses regarding Phase I pace

5.3 Deadlines, grades, and time spent

Although the course is not for credit, we still need to evaluate student participation and motivate students to complete their coursework. We set deadlines for the homework exercises and projects, and although we were quite willing to be flexible and grant extensions, these deadlines were generally very effective for keeping students on track and ensuring that they were progressing through the course material. The instructors observed that many students did not start on the homework until very shortly before the deadlines. Given the many competing demands for students' time, we believe the deadlines are necessary in order to motivate students to complete the coursework.

The homework assigned through the PCRS online exercise submission system [20] was automatically marked and the projects were marked by the instructors or TAs. This feedback helped students to evaluate their progress, but no course grades were recorded.

Table 3 shows the students' estimates of hours spent on homework by level. The beginners are generally spending more time than the more experienced students. They also spend more time attending the sessions with 12 hours of instructional time for beginners and only 9 hours for others. All tolled, students spent from 12 to 36 hours on Phase I.

	Beginners (n=9)	Others (n=10)
up to 1 hour	1	3
2-3 hours	1	5
4-5 hours	4	2
6 hours	3	0

Table 3: Time spent on homework after each Phase I session

5.4 Scheduling

Although C4M is designed so that students enrol in the first year of their MD program, the pilot offering also admitted students in second year to Phase I. This made scheduling quite challenging, since the first and second year students have different schedules, and led to the pilot offering's Phase I sessions being offered in 4.5 hour blocks on Saturday or Sunday evenings. Although we tried hard to make this work by providing a dinner and a break, and structuring workshops to include lots of hands-on coding frequently interspersed with bits of instructive presentations, it was still not ideal. It was challenging for students to maintain focus near the end of each session because of physical burnout and mental overload.

For the pilot offering, some of the Phase III participants were third year students doing their clerkships. This presented a major challenge for scheduling the Phase III seminars and also for the students to find time to attend and to complete the projects.

If planning a similar program, we recommend having the students complete it at a time when their schedules are more predictable. With the newly designed curriculum, we have taken advantage of the one day per week of unscheduled self-learning time and have moved the Phase I and II sessions to the daytime. Phase III sessions are currently on weeknight evenings and we may need to continue with that schedule to accommodate the guest speakers.

5.5 Materials with a Medical Context

Once the learning goals of the program were established and we determined that the students would learn introductory programming in Python, a significant amount of development time was spent framing the instructional materials and the hands-on activities in a medical context. Although we believed that the MD students would be capable of learning with examples from any domain (e.g., looping over lists of random nouns or writing if statements about the weather), we wanted to vicariously demonstrate the usefulness of programming to medical applications through each example. The workshop materials included examples about body mass indices, heart rates, and DNA strings. Students wrote code to search for a specific drug in a list of prescribed medications or find a patient with certain values for various characteristics. Homework assignments framed questions in terms of medical calculations (return the appropriate dosage for a patient of this weight and age for this drug), patient management (return the average length of stay for patients in some ward), or medical research studies (return the list of smokers over age 65 who have consented to participate.)

Although there was insufficient time to convert every example to a medical domain, we tried to take existing introductory programming materials and find a simple medical context for each. This task was not easy because the CS faculty did not have medical expertise but they solicited help wherever they could find it, including the Medicine faculty member responsible for the program (a clinical practitioner himself), computational biology graduate students from the CS department, their own networks of medically-knowledgeable colleagues, and the internet. One source of useful inspiration was MDCalc [7], a website that contains small programs for a number of medical calculations and explanations about the equations behind them.

We asked the students from both offerings to comment anonymously on our attempts to frame examples in a medical context. We tried to word the prompt in a way that gave the students license to tell us that the context did not matter without feeling that this was not what we wanted to hear. The exact wording of our question was as follows:

> We tried to incorporate some medical situations into the examples to demonstrate how programming could be relevant to you. How successful was this? Did it matter at all to you that the programs were about diseases or biology or research subjects or would it have been just as motivating

> to see problems about mathematics or music or any other domain?

We categorized the 32 free text responses and found that while the vast majority of the students noted that they appreciated the medical context, almost half of them also indicated that it was not crucial for their experience. Table 4 summarizes the answers. Since 78% of the students said that the medical context contributed positively to their learning experience, we feel that the effort spent contextualizing the material was time well spent.

5.6 Session Format

The Phase I sessions involved a mix of instruction and hands on exercises. On the anonymous surveys, we asked students about the format of those sessions:

> Please comment on the format of the sessions (some teaching and then some programming on your laptops.) Did this work for you or would you have preferred something different such as more traditional lectures, videos, or step-by-step written instructions and no presentation?

Overall, students gave positive feedback on the session format and they enjoyed the mix of teaching and active learning:

> I loved the interactivity of everything and the fact that we were able to apply what we learned immediately during class; it allowed us to solidify our understanding of the concept independently, yet ask for and receive immediate help if needed.

Some students reported that they would have liked more step-by-step instructions or supplementary videos. A couple of students said it would have been helpful to have more time to solve the problems, while another requested more complex problems. The students' opposing views on the difficulty of problems shows the variation in their skill levels.

5.7 Software Tools

For Phases I and II, students completed the coursework on their own computers, which required them to install Python and an IDE. We discovered that all the students had laptops, installation was not a problem, and only one student's older machine had hardware limitations that made it too slow to use the full data set for the Infectious Disease project. For Phase III, multiple software packages were needed (e.g., numpy, matplotlib) and datasets were larger. Students were given the option of working on their own machines or via a remote connection to a university network on which all of the required software was installed.

Many of the homework exercises for Phases I and II were completed using the PCRS online exercise submission system. This system allows students to submit multiple times and their submissions are immediately graded.

For Phases I and II, the workshops summaries were generated using Jupyter Notebooks and posted on the course website [4]. 95% of students reported referring to the lecture notes at least once, with 63% reporting that they used them a lot. We will continue these practices, including using Jupyter Notebooks, which we recommend to colleagues who haven't explored them in a teaching context.

Category	Count	Representative Sample quotations
very positive	9	"Very motivating to see how programming is interconnected within the field of healthcare." "I liked that it was relevant to medicine. I don't think I would have appreciated it as much if it was about unrelated topics."
positive	8	"I liked the medical relevance of some of the examples; showed me how concepts can be applied to medical domain" " enjoyed the medical aspect - made it more relevant personally"
positive, but qualified	8	"It made it somewhat more interesting / engaging to have examples using medicine, but it wouldn't make a big difference if examples were non-medical"
indifferent	5	"It didn't matter very much to me. It was sort of nice to be able to see medical applications, but I would have been engaged either way."
other	2	"I would have liked seeing both types of problems, to gain appreciation when applications in medical and mathematical problems are juxtaposed."

Table 4: Summary of Student Comments on Medical Context for Materials

5.8 Resources

In the first academic year, planning, development and delivery costs for Phases I and II for faculty were roughly equivalent to teaching four 12-week courses. Additionally, 100 hours of graduate student TA help was used. In the second academic year, teaching credit equivalent to two 12-week courses and a further 200 TA hours were budgeted to rework and deliver Phases I and II, and to organize and deliver Phase III. In addition, honorariums (roughly equivalent to 1/5 of the amount paid for teaching a course) were given to each Phase III speaker for developing and delivering the seminar and corresponding project.

6 CONCLUSIONS

C4M is a novel program that provides medical students with a unique opportunity to learn about programming and the application of computing to medicine. Although the program is not mandatory, one-sixth of medical students opted to enroll. This participation is remarkable, given that the program is 20 months long and involves an estimated 100 hours of sessions and course work, on top of typical medical program commitments.

Given the demands of the medical program, some C4M program attrition was expected and occurred, but many students still benefited from completing some or all of the program. Among those participating and succeeding in the third phase of the program are students who entered the program with no prior programming experience. In addition to this student success, student feedback about the program was generally positive.

Adding computing to a medicine program is an ambitious and challenging goal, but we believe that we have achieved that through the C4M program. This program gives medical students the chance to broaden and enhance their medical education by incorporating computing in it, strengthening the education of future researchers and clinicians.

Although C4M is unique, we expect that its success and the increased presence of computing in medicine will lead to similar programs at other medical schools. We find our C4M experience intellectually stimulating and the students a joy to teach. We enthusiastically encourage others to embrace the opportunity to lead similar programs and take advantage of the lessons we have learned.

REFERENCES

[1] Bioinformatics computing: Introduction to scientific computing. http://cmb.path. uab.edu/training/cb2-101.html. Accessed: 2016-12-06.
[2] Canada learning code. http://www.canadalearningcode.ca. Accessed: 2016-12-08.
[3] code.org anybody can learn. https://code.org. Accessed: 2016-12-08.
[4] Computing For Medicine course website. http://c4m.toronto.edu/. Accessed: 2016-12-09.
[5] The european bioinformatics institute: Simple phylogeny. http://www.ebi.ac.uk/ Tools/phylogeny/simple_phylogeny/. Accessed: 2016-12-08.
[6] List of infectious diseases - Wikipedia. https://en.wikipedia.org/wiki/List_of_ infectious_diseases. Accessed: 2016-12-07.
[7] MDCalc - medical calculators, equations, algorithms and scores. http://www. mdcalc.com. Accessed: 2016-12-07.
[8] Software carpentry. https://software-carpentry.org. Accessed: 2016-12-08.
[9] This is your brain on informatics. http://www.uab.edu/medicine/pathology/ news-and-announcements/147-this-is-your-brain-on-informatics. Accessed: 2016-12-06.
[10] R. Banerjee, P. George, C. Priebe, and E. Alper. Medical student awareness of and interest in clinical informatics. *Journal of the American Medical Informatics Association*, 22(e1):e42–e47, 2015.
[11] M. H. Burnette, S. L. De Groote, and J. L. Dorsch. Medical informatics in the curriculum: development and delivery of an online elective. *Journal of the Medical Library Association: JMLA*, 100(1):61, 2012.
[12] K. C. Fraser, J. A. Meltzer, and F. Rudzicz. Linguistic features identify alzheimer's disease in narrative speech. 49(2), 2015.
[13] S. Freeman, S. L. Eddy, M. McDonough, M. K. Smith, N. Okoroafor, H. Jordt, and M. P. Wenderoth. Active learning increases student performance in science, engineering, and mathematics. *Proceedings of the National Academy of Sciences*, 111(23):8410–8415, 2014.
[14] M. Guzdial. Learner-centered design of computing education: Research on computing for everyone. *Synthesis Lectures on Human-Centered Informatics*, 8(6):1–165, 2015.
[15] W. R. Hersh, P. N. Gorman, F. E. Biagioli, V. Mohan, J. A. Gold, and G. C. Mejicano. Beyond information retrieval and electronic health record use: competencies in clinical informatics for medical education. *Advances in medical education and practice*, 5:205, 2014.
[16] J. Quick, N. J. Loman, S. Duraffour, J. T. Simpson, E. Severi, L. Cowley, J. A. Bore, R. Koundouno, G. Dudas, A. Mikhail, et al. Real-time, portable genome sequencing for ebola surveillance. *Nature*, 530(7589):228–232, 2016.
[17] H. Silverman, T. Cohen, and D. Fridsma. The evolution of a novel biomedical informatics curriculum for medical students. *Academic Medicine*, 87(1):84–90, 2012.
[18] K. Sirinukunwattana, S. E. A. Raza, Y.-W. Tsang, D. R. Snead, I. A. Cree, and N. M. Rajpoot. Locality sensitive deep learning for detection and classification of nuclei in routine colon cancer histology images. *IEEE transactions on medical imaging*, 35(5):1196–1206, 2016.
[19] G. Wilson. Software carpentry: lessons learned. *arXiv preprint arXiv:1307.5448*, 2013.
[20] D. Zingaro, Y. Cherenkova, O. Karpova, and A. Petersen. Facilitating code-writing in PI classes. In *Proceeding of the 44th ACM Technical Symposium on Computer Science Education*, SIGCSE '13, pages 585–590, 2013.

On the Educational Impact of Lecture Recording Reduction: Evidence from a Randomised Trial

Michael James Scott
michael.scott@falmouth.ac.uk
Falmouth University
Games Academy
Penryn, Cornwall, United Kingdom

Gheorghita Ghinea
george.ghinea@brunel.ac.uk
Brunel University
Department of Computer Science
Uxbridge, Middlesex, United Kingdom

ABSTRACT

Students often use lecture recordings to learn and revise. This approach, however, demands time to locate and review relevant topics. The automatic reduction and indexing of lecture recordings, then, could focus students' attention on the most relevant content. This article investigates whether lecture recording reduction leads to improved learning outcomes on an undergraduate computer networking module. Students participated in a randomised trial which compared lightly edited full lecture recordings to those that had been significantly reduced in duration and indexed. A pre-test conducted after the initial lecture series was followed up with a post-test after several weeks of using the recordings. The results show a statistically significant difference between the groups in terms of perceived effort. However, only the students with little prior knowledge showed a statistically significant difference in learning outcome in favour of the reduced lecture recordings. Moderating factors, such as prior knowledge, warrant further research to help elicit guidelines to inform the design and deployment of future lecture video reduction approaches.

CCS CONCEPTS

• **Applied computing** → **E-learning**; • **Human-centered computing** → *Empirical studies in HCI*; • **Information systems** → Multimedia information systems;

KEYWORDS

lecture; video; recording; summaries; reduction; learning; revision; randomised trial; human factors; experiment

ACM Reference format:
Michael James Scott and Gheorghita Ghinea. 2017. On the Educational Impact of Lecture Recording Reduction: Evidence from a Randomised Trial. In *Proceedings of the 22nd Annual ACM Conference on Innovation and Technology in Computer Science Education, Bologna, Italy, July 03–05, 2017 (ITiCSE'17)*, 6 pages.
DOI: https://doi.org/10.1145/3059009.3059037

1 INTRODUCTION

Producing archives of lecture recordings for the purpose of student revision can be well received by students [5, 6, 12, 16, 20] and has been shown to support their learning [9, 22]. However, many students do not always watch lecture recordings for their full duration, often taking a more strategic approach during sessions of revision [1, 7, 16, 18]. As such, manually navigating lecture recordings to find particular content may not represent a productive use of their revision time. In order to minimise this limitation, the content of lecture recordings could be reorganised. More specifically, the topics could be indexed into segments and prioritised. Furthermore, unnecessary content could be removed, in accordance with the learning objectives. Such changes might help to focus students' attention on the most relevant content and therefore lead to enhanced learning outcomes.

Judgements must be made regarding what content to include and what content to discard. This often requires substantial human input. An approach that aims to minimise the time needed to provide such input is using metadata associated with the presentation slides as a framework for reduction. Prior work shows that such meta-data can be mined from slides, notes, and audio from the lectures themselves [23], minimising the preparation required to edit the recordings. However, the implications of using this technique for revision purposes are not clear. Therefore, prior to investing time and resources into developing a high fidelity toolset, this research acts as a feasibility study, exploring the educational impact of lecture recording reduction.

The following section of the article provides some background on the use of lecture recordings and the pedagogical theories that could inform efforts to modify lecture videos to enhance student learning. The proposed approach to reducing the lecture recordings is then described. The research questions and the expected outcomes, in the form of hypotheses, are then made clear. The following sections then describe the methodology of the experiment, the results, and a discussion of the findings.

2 BACKGROUND

A literature review on the use of podcasts in education highlights that the use of lecture recordings is associated with a range of benefits, including: positive attitudes; sense of control over learning; improved study habits; and increased learning performance [10]. As such, there is considerable evidence supporting the use of lecture recordings to help students understand and revise lecture content. However, there are several open questions with respect to how lecture recordings should be presented. The review makes a number of suggestions regarding avenues for future research, including: a focus on the quality and design of videos; their relationship with pedagogical strategies; viewing strategies; and their impact on learning effectiveness. This perspective is extended in a further review [17] which points out that a number of studies have not applied appropriate measurement approaches, often using self-report measures for variables such as learning.

It is, therefore, important to further investigate whether different styles and presentations of videos will have different impacts on key variables of interest, such as student learning, using appropriate measurement approaches. Students have demonstrated a range of different approaches to interacting with videos, sometimes leading to only surface-level learning [11], and so lecture recordings are often considered to be complementary to existing teaching methods. Given that the recordings, therefore, make effective revision tools, it is then possible that designing them with revision in mind could enhance their effectiveness.

Such a strategy could be realised through the utilisation of a number of pedagogical strategies. The principle of constructive alignment [2] emphasises that only material that will be tested should be formally covered. It is likely that questions and points raised in lecture discussions, although useful for students' deeper and future learning, will not be tested on. As such, this unnecessary material can be cut from the lecture recording. Similarly, the principle of scaffolding [4], which emphasises that students receive additional support when first introduced to a topic (in line with their zone of proximal development [21]), can be used to ensure that material is ordered such that topics build upon each-other and enable students to easily identify related topics. Another key concept is cognitive load [19]. This theory contends that the amount of information that can be processed in working memory is finite and so presenting too much information simultaneously can overload working memory and subsequently impede learning. It is not unusual to find that lecture slides are over-crowded with information. Such content can be re-organised in post-production to reduce cognitive load and consequently focus students' attention more effectively [3].

3 EXPERIMENTAL TOOL

The proposed system aims to apply the concepts of constructive alignment [2], scaffolding [4], and cognitive load theory [3, 19] to the reduction of lecture recordings. Using this approach, data about the slides is applied in three ways: assigning topic importance; indicating dependencies to previous slides; and coding the purpose of a slide (e.g. presenting information, questioning the audience, etc.). Additionally, further data about each slide is captured, including: slide duration; and slide-associated audio.

The proposed work-flow, shown above in Figure 1, is a semi-automatic process for reducing the duration of lecture recordings. Firstly, the recording is segmented based on the structure of the slide show that accompanies the lecture. Secondly, segments of the lecture are removed based on a back-propagation technique using the data provided. Slides associated with a low importance topics and their supporting slides are removed, while slides that do not present new information are also removed. Existing content analysis techniques (see [13] for a review) are then applied to further eliminate interruptions within each segment. Such techniques also

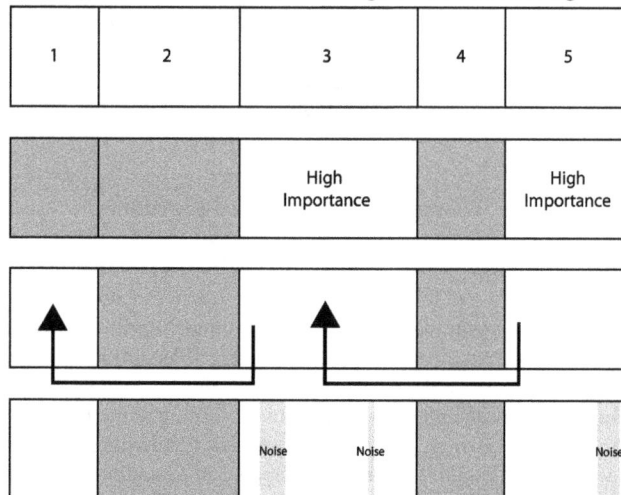

Figure 1: Workflow for Editing Lecture Recordings

highlight segments that potentially present a high cognitive load, for final manual editing in the post-production stage.

4 RESEARCH QUESTIONS & HYPOTHESES

In the educational context, "impact" can have different meanings. This article investigates educational impact in terms of the following research questions:

RQ1. Do students use full lecture recordings in the same way as reduced lecture recordings?

RQ2. Does the use of reduced lecture recordings lead to different learning outcomes compared to full lecture recordings?

RQ3. Do students hold different perceptions of full lecture recordings and reduced lecture recordings?

The first research question examines one hypothesis: there will be no significant difference between the number of minutes that students spend watching either type of video (H_1). The second research question also examines one hypothesis: students watching the reduced lecture recordings will score higher on a test of the intended learning outcomes (H_2). The third research question examines five hypotheses: students will find reduced lecture recordings more useful (H_3); students will perceive reduced lecture recordings to be of higher quality (H_4); students will perceive the full lecture videos as being too long (H_5); students will perceive the full lecture videos as requiring too much effort to watch (H_6); the students will perceive an increase in their performance after watching the reduced lecture video (H_7).

5 METHOD

A short series on four lectures on an introductory computer networking course (designed and performed by the second author) were recorded (by the first author)[1]. Edited lecture videos were then prepared and created (by the first author) according to recommendations generated by a low-fidelity prototype based on the

---

[1]Both authors were at the same institution at the time of the study.

Table 1: Content of the Lecture Videos

#	Lecture Topics	Slides	Video Duration	
			Full	*Reduced*
1	Course Intro, General Definitions, Operating System History, Networks and Operating Systems	42	47.06	19.02
2	Internet History, Internet Protocols, Layers, Physical Media, Switching, Network Throughput, Security	83	67.35	36.23
3	Application Layer Protocols, HTTP, FTP, SMTP, POP3, IMAP, DNS	48	80.11	52.40
4	Client-Server, Peer-to-Peer, TCP and UDP Protocols, Socket Programming	66	81.31	35.38

slide meta-data (provided by the second author). Two videos for each lecture in the lecture series were then produced: one that had been lightly edited; and one that had been heavily edited, and thereby reduced. The prototype did not manipulate the lecture recordings directly, but instead generated recommendations which were manually applied using Sony Vegas 10.0.

These were uploaded to YouTube and were selectively made available to participants through the BlackBoard virtual learning environment. The impact of each recording on student learning was compared using an experimental approach. YouTube analytics (such as minutes watched) and a post-study questionnaire were used to evaluate student perceptions of the videos, while learning was examined through an online test taken by each participant before and after the experiment.

5.1 Experimental Design

The experiment used a between-participant design because practice and preference effects could have biased the evaluation if each participant was exposed to both experimental conditions. The experimental design itself consisted of a parallel-group double-blind randomised trial, incorporating balanced allocation between two groups (1:1).

Two versions of each lecture recording were compared, one edited using the recommendations produced by the prototype implementing the proposed method (experimental group) and the lightly edited version, that included the full lecture (control group) as listed above in Table 1. A pre-test is conducted to establish whether the groups are equal before the experiment and a post-test is conducted after the students have used the videos to examine differences between the groups.

5.2 Recruitment

Participants were recruited from an introductory computer networking course within the undergraduate computer science degree programme at the authors' institution. The study was promoted via: institutional email; notices on the relevant BlackBoard module; and a course-related FaceBook group. Participation was voluntary in accordance with ethics guidelines.

5.3 Data Collection

A pre-test was deployed on BlackBoard six weeks into the course, after the first five lectures had been delivered (four, of which, were recorded for the study). The pre-test was available for 10 working days after which, in the ninth week, the relevant videos were released to students in accordance with their group allocation. The

Table 2: Participant Characteristics

Characteristic	Sample (%)	HESA (%)	χ^2	p
Male	83.3	82.3		
Female	16.7	17.7	0.36	.848
Traditional Student	87.0	88.9		
Mature Student	13.0	11.1	.170	.679

post-test was then made available on BlackBoard in the eleventh week, alongside a post-survey that was emailed to eligible students via SurveyMonkey. This was also made available to participants for 10 working days.

5.4 Sample Size

Hattie suggests an appropriate effect size for educational relevance is: $d > .40$ [8]. Thus, an *a priori* power analysis was conducted using the statistics software G*Power 3.1.3 to determine an appropriate sample size ($\alpha = .05, 1 - \beta = .80$). Based on conducting an ANCOVA analysis, a minimum of 52 cases is suggested. A sample of 60 was obtained and included in the analysis for this study.

6 DATA ANALYSIS

The data was analysed in PASW 18.0.3 for Windows. There were no cases with missing data. All reported p-values are two-tailed and significance has been determined at the conventional .05 level.

6.1 Participant Characteristics

All participants were students enrolled on a second-year undergraduate computer networking module, having passed CS1 and CS2. Note that these students also typically required at least 300 points on the University and College Admission System (UCAS) to enrol on the course (see [omitted for review] for details). For ethical reasons, all participants were volunteers. So, although all of the students in the cohort were invited to participate in the study, the initial response rate was ~50% (75 of 151 students), but with an attrition rate of 20%, resulted in only ~40% (60 of 151 students). Thus, self-selection bias is a possibility. Table 2 contrasts the descriptive statistics of the sample with known population proportions in the 2011-2012 dataset available from the United Kingdom's Higher Education Statistics Agency (HESA). As there are no statistically significant differences, in terms of age or gender, the sample is assumed to be adequately representative of a typical computer science cohort in the UK.

Table 3: T-Tests Comparing Length and Amount Watched for the Experimental and Control Videos (Full Sample)

Measurement	$\bar{x}$	σ	t	df	p
Minutes Watched					
Experiment	323.50	109.70			
Control	389.00	117.30	-1.169	3	.189
Minutes Duration					
Experiment	35.92	13.73			
Control	69.09	15.95	-7.685	3	.005

Table 4: T-Tests Comparing Learning Outcomes (Low Pre-Test Scores Only, N = 40)

Measurement	$\bar{x}$	σ	t	df	p	d
Pre-Test Score						
Experiment	-7.41	5.65				
Control	-9.94	8.05	-1.167	38	.250	—
Post-Test Score						
Experiment	3.13	10.51				
Control	-4.77	11.69	-2.252	38	.030	-0.73

6.2 Measurement Validity and Reliability

The measurement used in the pre-test and post-test was created for the purpose of this study, based on the content of the first four lectures. Five learning objectives were identified, and a pool of 30 items was created (six questions for each learning objective). As this test was created for the study, prior to the analysis, the test was reviewed for appropriate validity and reliability.

Firstly, the pool was reviewed for content validity by the three teaching assistants assigned to the unit. No items were removed at this stage. Secondly, validity was then further assessed through a pilot study using a difficulty metric, based on avoiding extreme proportions of student success on an item, and an appropriate discrimination metric, ensuring success on an item is related to success on the test overall. Items were included based on the following criteria: $(10\% < difficulty < 90\%) AND (discrimination > 0.1)$. Four items were eliminated at this stage. Thirdly, the reliability of the remaining items for each learning objective was assessed using Cronbatch's α. Each group of items, based on the five learning objectives, exceeded the 0.7 threshold proposed in [15]. Therefore, validity and reliability can be considered adequate.

6.3 Video Usage (RQ1)

In order to examine H$_1$, the duration of each video was examined and the estimated total minutes watched was captured from the available YouTube analytics. This data is summarized in Table 3.

The table shows that the duration of the experimental reduced lecture videos was statistically significantly shorter than the lightly edited lecture videos (p = .005), with the prototype tool achieving a typical 49% reduction, based on the four example cases ($\bar{x} = -33.16 minutes$, $\sigma = 8.63 minutes$). However, of the 2850 minutes that participants in the study watched the videos for, the overall amount of time that students spent watching the different types of video was not statistically significantly different ($\delta\bar{x} = 65.5 minutes$, $p = .189$). This supports the notion that students engaged with the videos in a similar way, in terms of allocating time to watch them, despite their substantially different durations.

6.4 Impact on Learning Outcomes (RQ2)

Analysis of statistical assumptions suggested that an ANCOVA may not be appropriate due to the heteroskedasticity assumption. There was considerable variance in pre-test scores and the regression predicting post-test score did not appear to be equal across the

range of scores. Consequently, the sample was segmented into two sub-samples based on pre-test score: high performing; and low performing. Thus, two independent sample t-tests were conducted on these sub-samples to examine H$_2$ and shown in Figure 2.

The data in Table 4 only shows data for the low performing students. The table shows no statistically significant difference in the pre-test ($\delta\bar{x} = 2.54, p = .250$). However, a statistically significant difference was found between the two groups in the post-test ($\delta\bar{x} = 7.90, p = .032$). Thus, although the groups were equal at the start of the experiment, those students who had been assigned the reduced lecture videos to watch received a higher score on the test compared to those students who had been assigned lightly edited full lecture videos to watch by the end of the experiment ($d = 0.73$).

On the other hand, there was no statistically significant difference between pre-test and post-test scores for students in the high performance sub-sample (t[19] = -1.210, p = .241), this suggests that the lecture video reduction had no measurable impact on the intended learning outcomes. This is unlikely to be due to a ceiling effect as the maximum possible score on the measurement was not achieved. However, as there were only 20 students in this sub-sample, a lack of statistical power should be noted. A *post hoc* power analysis indicates that the sensitivity of the statistical test ($\alpha = .05, 1 - \beta = .80$), in this case, is $d > .66$, rather than the $d > .40$ criterion suggest by Hattie [8].

6.5 Difference in Perceptions (RQ3)

In order to examine H4-8, the data from the post-survey was analysed using a series of Mann-Whitney U Tests because Likert-type items were used and the data did not appear to follow a normal distribution. These items and their analyses are shown in Table 5.

Based on a maximum score of six, with higher scores denoting agreement, the results indicate that students tended to endorse the usefulness of the revision videos. They tended to disagree that the videos were poor. They also tended to endorse the notion that their performance increased. There was little consensus about whether the videos were too long, although there was no statistically significant difference between the groups. However, there was a statistically significant difference with respect to effort required to watch the video. Although students allocated to watch either type of video both tended to disagree with the statement, those allocated to watch the reduced lecture videos seemed to perceive much less effort being required ($\delta\bar{x} = 0.88, p = .024$).

Figure 2: Box-Plot Illustrating Gain Scores Between Sub-Samples and Experimental Allocation

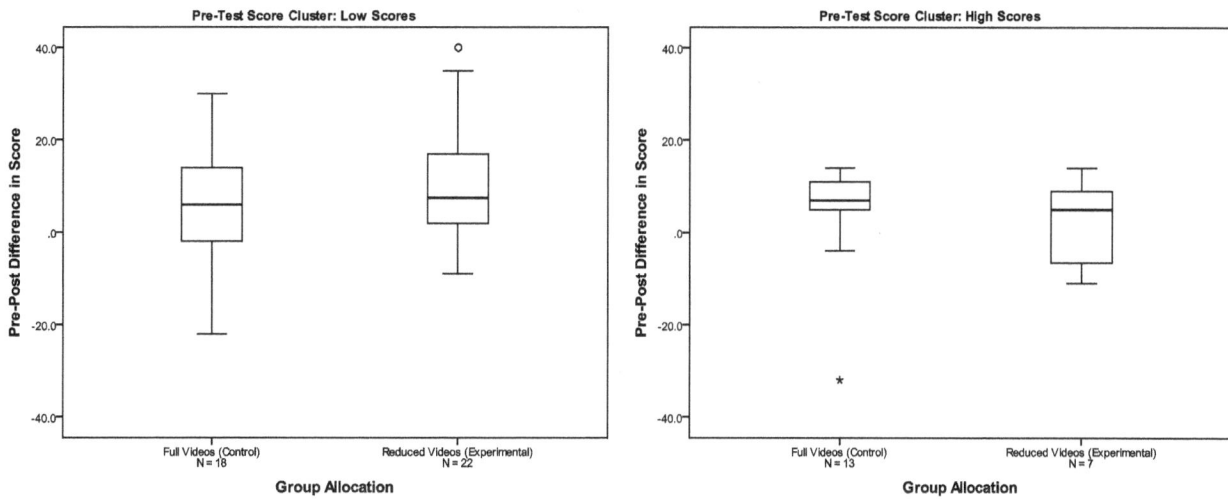

Table 5: Mann-Whitney U Tests Comparing Student Attitudes Between the Experimental and Control Conditions

Measurement	$\bar{x}$	σ	U	p
These revision videos were useful				
Experiment	5.00	0.92		
Control	4.47	1.34	204.0	.243
I believe the quality of the revision videos was poor				
Experiment	3.18	1.29		
Control	2.86	1.35	211.5	.461
The revision videos were too long				
Experiment	3.86	1.20		
Control	4.17	1.26	202.5	.238
Watching the revisision videos required too much effort				
Experiment	2.59	1.14		
Control	3.47	1.30	156.5	.024
I believe I increased my performance on the tests using revision videos				
Experiment	4.95	0.95		
Control	4.47	1.41	211.5	.321

7 DISCUSSION

7.1 Findings

Few studies evaluate lecture recordings in the computing context. Fewer still explore the educational impact of content reduction. This paper contributes to this literature by showing, through the use of a low-fidelity proof-of-concept prototype, the efficacy of lecture recording reduction in an undergraduate computer networking module. The experiment reveals mixed impacts on learning outcomes. Some positive and some questionable. This may be because many students do not allocate study time based on the nature of the available material. This notion is supported by the number of minutes spent watching videos being the same for both groups; despite the videos provided to one of the groups having substantially longer durations. This presents an opportunity to improve lecture recordings based on constructive alignment [2], scaffolding [4], and cognitive-load theory [3, 19].

Reducing the duration of the lecture videos and indexing their content facilitates search and review, permitting greater focus on the most pertinent material. This notion is supported through the learning demonstrated by those students with low pre-test scores. Although both groups improved, the post-test scores reveal a statistically significant and educationally relevant improvement for those students viewing reduced lecture videos. Additionally, there was a statistically significant difference in perceived effort required to watch the reduced lecture videos, which may have aided engagement.

However, it is important to note the lack of a difference for those students who performed well on the pre-test. This is indicative, perhaps, of an interaction between the type of video and prior knowledge. One potential hypothesis can be found in research on science videos: when students feel they already know a topic, they only perceive that the content of videos reinforces their existing misconceptions (irrespective of the actual content) [14]. Given that participants were not made aware of their pre-test scores during the study, students with prior knowledge of the topic may have encountered such a phenomenon. Another hypothesis is that depth of learning is a factor (see Biggs and Tang [2]). The reduced lecture videos only focus attention on surface-level material, denying the depth of discourse needed to promote learning enough to achieve the higher scores.

It would also be interesting to see how lecture recording reduction impacts absentees. The approach seems effective for students with low pre-test scores (such as absentees) and may be suited to help students achieve the most important learning objectives.

Table 6: Summary of Findings and P-Values

RQ	H_n	Hypothesis	Observation	p	Conclusion
1	H_1	$\Delta Usage = 0$	$t = -1.169$	.189	*Supported*
2	H_{2a}	$\Delta Learning \neq 0$	$t = -2.228$	.032	*Supported*
	H_{2b}	$\Delta Learning \neq 0$	$t = -1.210$	.241	—
3	H_3	$\Delta ATT1 \neq 0$	$U = 204.0$	.243	—
	H_4	$\Delta ATT2 \neq 0$	$U = 211.5$	.461	—
	H_5	$\Delta ATT3 \neq 0$	$U = 202.5$	.238	—
	H_6	$\Delta ATT4 \neq 0$	$U = 156.5$	.024	*Supported*
	H_7	$\Delta ATT5 \neq 0$	$U = 211.5$	.321	—

7.2 Limitations

It is important to note the sample size as a limitation in this study. As statistical assumptions did not hold, the sample had to be divided into two sub-samples at the data analysis stage. This not only has implications for the representativeness of theses sub-samples and the generalizability of the results. In particular, as there were a relatively small number of students receiving high scores on the pre-test (N = 20), statistical power for the analysis of this group was low. Therefore, the risk of Type-II error for H_{2b} is increased, with a noted sensitivity of $d > .66$. Further research with a larger sample size and an experimental design that accounts for a possible interaction effect is therefore needed.

It is also important to note that it was not possible to explore and differentiate between individual students' video usage behaviour based on the data provided by YouTube analytics. As such, neither the different ways in which the participants potentially used the lecture recordings, nor whether either version of the videos were an important revision tool could be established. The use of qualitative research methods and an additional no-video control group may be necessary to establish this.

8 CONCLUSION

This article presents a proof-of-concept, demonstrating the impact of lecture video reduction using slide meta-data. It was hypothesized that the time students spend watching lecture videos would not depend on their duration. Thus, editing lecture videos would encourage students to spend a greater proportion of their time focusing on relevant content; thereby, enhancing performance on the intended learning outcomes. The results of the trial, summarized in Table 6, support several of these hypotheses. However, a possible interaction effect is revealed: those who performed poorly on the pre-test only benefited from watching the reduced lecture videos (H_{2a}), while those who performed well on the pre-test did not seem receive any benefit (H_{2b}). This suggests that reducing lecture videos can be worthwhile when compared to lightly edited full lecture videos, but only for those students with little prior knowledge. Further work is needed to explore this interaction in more detail and to elicit guidelines to support the development of future lecture video reduction approaches.

REFERENCES

[1] Jack Barokas, Markus Ketterl, and Christopher Brooks. 2010. Lecture capture: Student perceptions, expectations, and behaviors. In *World Conference on E-Learning in Corporate, Government, Healthcare, and Higher Education*, Vol. 2010. 424–431.

[2] John Biggs and Catherine Tang. 2011. *Teaching for quality learning at university*. McGraw-Hill International.

[3] Michael E Caspersen and Jens Bennedsen. 2007. Instructional design of a programming course: a learning theoretic approach. In *Proceedings of the third international workshop on Computing education research*. ACM, 111–122.

[4] Michael Cole, Vera John-Steiner, Sylvia Scribner, and Ellen Souberman. 1978. Mind in society. *Mind in society the development of higher psychological processes*. Cambridge, MA: Harvard University Press (1978).

[5] Lyn Collie, Viral Shah, and Don Sheridan. 2009. An end-user evaluation of a lecture archiving system. In *Proceedings of the 10th international Conference NZ Chapter of the Acm's Special interest Group on Human-Computer interaction*. ACM, 77–80.

[6] Paul E Dickson, David I Warshow, Alec C Goebel, Colin C Roache, and W Richards Adrion. 2012. Student reactions to classroom lecture capture. In *Proceedings of the 17th ACM annual conference on Innovation and technology in computer science education*. ACM, 144–149.

[7] Susan M Engstrand and Suzanne Hall. 2011. The use of streamed lecture recordings: patterns of use, student experience and effects on learning outcomes. *Practitioner Research in Higher Education* 5, 1 (2011), 9–15.

[8] John Hattie. 2013. *Visible learning: A synthesis of over 800 meta-analyses relating to achievement*. Routledge.

[9] Wen-Jung Hsin and John Cigas. 2013. Short videos improve student learning in online education. *Journal of Computing Sciences in Colleges* 28, 5 (2013), 253–259.

[10] Robin H Kay. 2012. Exploring the use of video podcasts in education: A comprehensive review of the literature. *Computers in Human Behavior* 28, 3 (2012), 820–831.

[11] Ada Le, Steve Joordens, Sophie Chrysostomou, and Raymond Grinnell. 2010. Online lecture accessibility and its influence on performance in skills-based courses. *Computers & Education* 55, 1 (2010), 313–319.

[12] Kam K Leang. 2012. Short Online Videos to Excite and Engage Students About Control [Focus on Education]. *Control Systems, IEEE* 32, 2 (2012), 70–71.

[13] Ying Li, Shih-Hung Lee, Chia-Hung Yeh, and C-CJ Kuo. 2006. Techniques for movie content analysis and skimming: tutorial and overview on video abstraction techniques. *Signal Processing Magazine, IEEE* 23, 2 (2006), 79–89.

[14] Derek A Muller, J Bewes, Manjula D Sharma, and Peter Reimann. 2008. Saying the wrong thing: Improving learning with multimedia by including misconceptions. *Journal of Computer Assisted Learning* 24, 2 (2008), 144–155.

[15] Jum C Nunnally, Ira H Bernstein, and Jos MF ten Berge. 1967. *Psychometric theory*. Vol. 226. McGraw-Hill New York.

[16] Ron Owston, Denys Lupshenyuk, and Herb Wideman. 2011. Lecture capture in large undergraduate classes: Student perceptions and academic performance. *The Internet and Higher Education* 14, 4 (2011), 262–268.

[17] B Pursel and H Fang. 2011. Lecture Capture: Current Research and Future Directions. *Available on line at http://www. psu. edu/dept/site/pursel_lecture_capture_2012v1. pd f* (2011).

[18] Amber Settle, Lucia Dettori, and Mary Jo Davidson. 2011. Does lecture capture make a difference for students in traditional classrooms. In *Proceedings of the 16th annual joint conference on Innovation and technology in computer science education*. ACM, 78–82.

[19] John Sweller. 1994. Cognitive load theory, learning difficulty, and instructional design. *Learning and instruction* 4, 4 (1994), 295–312.

[20] Ross H Taplin, Lee Hun Low, and Alistair M Brown. 2011. Students' satisfaction and valuation of web-based lecture recording technologies. *Australasian Journal of Educational Technology* 27, 2 (2011), 175–191.

[21] Lev Semenovich Vygotsky. 1980. *Mind in society: The development of higher psychological processes*. Harvard university press.

[22] Janice Whatley and Amrey Ahmad. 2007. Using video to record summary lectures to aid students' revision. *Interdisciplinary Journal of E-Learning and Learning Objects* 3, 1 (2007), 185–196.

[23] H Yang and C Meinel. 2014. Content Based Lecture Video Retrieval Using Speech and Video Text Information. *IEEE Transactions on Learning Technology* 7, 2 (2014), 142–154.

Silence, Words, or Grades: The Effects of Lecturer Feedback in Multi-Revision Assignments

Claudia Szabo
The University of Adelaide
claudia.szabo@adelaide.edu.au

Nickolas Falkner
The University of Adelaide
nickolas.falkner@adelaide.edu.au

ABSTRACT

Detailed in-depth feedback on programming assignments is beneficial because it identifies specific software design and development aspects that students can improve on. For the feedback to be effective, it is important that students are given the opportunity to address the feedback in a timely manner. However, detailed in-depth feedback often needs to be manually written by the lecturer or marker, especially for large and complex final year assignments where automated test suites are difficult to implement, introducing potential delay in providing the feedback. Following existing work, we propose a two-stage assignment design where students receive feedback on their final submission and are then given the opportunity to address the feedback. We analyse 147 assignment submissions and show that this assignment design improves assignment marks when compared to a single-stage submission, with failure rates dropping by up to 30%. To determine the impact of in-depth detailed feedback, we compare the learning outcomes across two years where students taking the two-stage assignment were given either detailed feedback or simple feedback consisting of component marks at the initial stage. We show the benefits of both approaches and analyse the potential advantages of providing more costly, manual feedback.

KEYWORDS

Feedback, Revision assignment

ACM Reference format:
Claudia Szabo and Nickolas Falkner. 2017. Silence, Words, or Grades: The Effects of Lecturer Feedback in Multi-Revision Assignments. In *Proceedings of ITiCSE'17, July 03-05, 2017, Bologna, Italy,* , 6 pages.
DOI: http://dx.doi.org/10.1145/3059009.3059030

1 INTRODUCTION

Giving and receiving feedback for submitted work is a fundamental act of teaching and learning. Receiving feedback on submitted assignments is a critical activity in computer science, through which students improve their programming practices as well as their software design and development skills, as well as providing a valuable channel for educators to foster skill development within a cognitive apprenticeship model [10], [11], [12],[3]. Several works

present automated systems that give students feedback on their submitted code based on failed test cases or more costly manual feedback [2, 7, 14]. However, in most cases, feedback is given after the final submission of the assignment, and students are not given the opportunity to immediately address the feedback, despite studies reporting their frustration on not being able to do so [13].

The quality of received feedback matters as well, with reports showing that feedback containing only specific failed test cases can lead students to running re-submission cycles with small, incremental changes, focused only on passing test cases and not on the software product as a whole [1, 7]. However, detailed, manual feedback becomes harder to provide in large-scale classrooms or when the lecturer's resources are limited. In addition, there can be cases where specific assignment aspects can only be assessed manually and as such the feedback offered must be manual. This is the case complex final year assignments, where the design and implementation of some considerations such as, e.g., fault tolerance considerations in a large distributed systems assignment, cannot be analyzed only through automated test-cases.

Two-stage submission approaches, where students submit what they consider to be their final assignment, receive feedback on it, and then address that feedback in a revision cycle followed by a final re-submission has been proposed before [2, 14]. We follow a similar approach in the design of a large assignment for a final year course and compare the assignment outcomes across three years of the course being offered. In the first year, the assignment followed a traditional design with a single submission point returning a mark, with linked feedback that the students could not subsequently address to improve their code. A two-stage submission was introduced in the second year, with students submitting a final version of their code, receiving feedback but no marks for their submission, and subsequently addressing the feedback and receiving their final mark. The feedback received by students was detailed and was manually written by the marking staff. In the third year, the assignment followed the same design but only very simple feedback was given at the earlier stage, in the form of marks for various components of the assignment, due to a change in lecturing staff and marking budget.

In this paper, we aim to quantify the benefits of the two stage submission design and to understand the quantifiable benefits, if any, of students receiving the detailed, more costly, assignment feedback. To achieve this, we compare the assignment outcomes across the three years. We analyze the feedback points received and addressed by students in the detailed and simple feedback cases to discover if any particular assignment aspects would benefit from detailed feedback, or whether simple feedback, in the form of a grade, is sufficient.

2 RELATED WORK

The importance of feedback on assignments has been recognised in numerous works [10], [11], [12] and approaches have been proposed for giving feedback on programming assignments, either manual [2] or automated [7]. Automated feedback by a computer-based toolset is returned to the student usually in the form of a description of failed test-cases and is an extremely useful tool for handling large-scale classes. Ihantola et al. [7] present a systematic literature review of automated assessment tools as an extension to the detailed review presented in [4], highlighting that automated assessment tools are inherently used iteratively, where students perform multiple re-submissions in attempts to meet the requirements of the testing harness. This can lead to overuse of the assessment tools and to the tool not meeting the desired learning outcome, i.e., students learning to program, as students hack their code to meet a submission requirement rather than thinking through the problem. Timely feedback is crucial [5, 13] but most automated assessment tools run the risk of students changing their code to match testcases [1, 7]. Karavirta et al. [9] studied students' re-submission mechanisms and determined that it was possible for students to iteratively and semi-randomly change code to solve a problem, without necessary understanding the solution. Both non-iterative and iterative students used resubmission with similar frequencies, but only non-iterative students who focused on the overall code had improvements in their final grades.

This leads to the insight frequently observed in classrooms but also shown in [14], that intervention and feedback during an assignment have a different effect from post-submission feedback. Constructive feedback improves students' ability to correct their mistakes. [8] shows that programming assignments benefit from in-progress feedback and from re-submission. The construction of multiple stages of automated feedback can lead to changes in student behaviour with increased activity before and after assignment deadlines [6]. Students who can resubmit their work following feedback improve for subsequent assignments in the course. Moreover, students can be frustrated when they receive feedback after the point at which it can be acted upon [13]. This highlights the importance of receiving timely feedback, which then leads to the trade-off between manual and detailed, but inherently costly and automated and less descriptive, but less costly feedback.

This is addressed by recent work by Blaheta [2] who introduced a revision cycle in the assignment submission, allowing the students to use instructor feedback to improve their solution. Specifically, once an assignment was submitted, the students initially received only the instructors' comments, without grades. The students were then given the opportunity to respond to the instructor comments through a revision cycle, and then finally received their mark without any more feedback. To keep the marking load low, a limited scale was used for grading. The number of students was too small to draw a correlation between the use of this assignment structure and exam grades but students reported enjoying the assignment structure. No analysis was performed about the benefits of a two-stage submission over a single-stage submission assignment. We employ a similar assignment structure in this study and perform a quantitative and qualitative analysis of student submissions and responses to feedback across three years.

3 RESEARCH METHODOLOGY

Timely feedback on programming assignments is critical but so is offering students the opportunity to address the received feedback, and there is a potential trade-off between the cost and timeliness of manual, in-depth feedback. In this work, we aim to study the effectiveness of a multi-stage submission and feedback assignment with respect to improving the learning outcomes of the assignment. At the same time, we wish to analyse the impact of manual, detailed feedback when compared to more cost-effective automated feedback. Towards this, our research questions are:

- **RQ1** What are the benefits of a multi-stage assignment where students are given the opportunity to address received feedback?
- **RQ2** Do student marks improve from the first submission to the final submission *when feedback is used without associated grade*?
- **RQ3** Does the depth and detail of the received feedback affect learning outcomes?

3.1 Assignment Structure

The assignment under study is a final year assignment in the topic area of Distributed Systems given to students at the University of Adelaide, from 2013 to 2015. Distributed Systems concepts are delivered through a Level 3 face-to-face course in a single semester and is taken mostly by students who are close to graduation or in the final year of study. The assignment was offered across three consecutive years and requires students to implement a news aggregation system comprising of a news aggregation server, news generation servers and news requesting clients. Students were given a detailed specification of how the system should work but were asked to design the class structure themselves and to design and implement solutions for fault tolerance, synchronisation and persistence. Students prepared for the assignment with teaching materials that extensively discussed the relevant topics in the form of lectures, tutorials, and collaborative discussion sessions.

The assignment was part of summative assessment, although it contained formative elements, and was worth 10% of the final mark for the course in every offering. The assessment components were basic functionality (XML parsing, server-client connections, GET/PUT operations) - 18 %, full functionality (heartbeat, Lamport clocks, multiple content servers) - 24%, fault tolerance - 10%, testing - 30%, design - 10% and code quality - 8% of the assignment mark.

In all years, the assignment was manually marked by an external marker following a rubric provided by the lecturers. In 2013, the assignment setup followed a traditional structure where students received a mark and feedback after submission. Following student feedback highlighting the need of intermediate check-in points during the assignment, the assignment structure was changed in the following years.

In 2014, the assignment structure followed that proposed by Blaheta [2], namely:

(1) Students submitted an assignment design sketch and received high-level feedback.
(2) Students submitted their assignment.
(3) Students received feedback in six areas: basic functionality, advanced functionality, design, testing, fault tolerance,

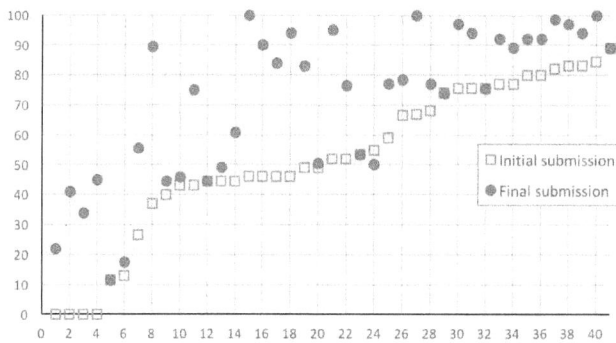

(a) Assignment $S-detailed$

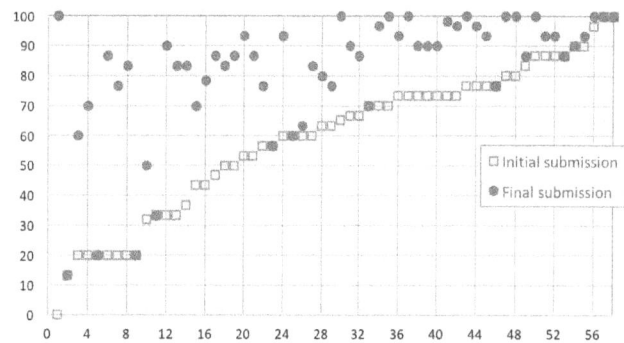

(b) Assignment $S-simple$

Figure 1: Variation of student marks between submission and revised submission

and code quality, **without grades**. Each main feedback point included discussion of several key implementation or design points within that area.

(4) Students resubmitted the assignment, including a document discussing how they had addressed feedback. Students were aware that if they chose not to re-submit, they would be awarded the initial submission grade.

(5) Students received final grade.

In 2015, the assignment followed a similar structure to that from 2014, except that in step 3 students received their marks before the revision cycle and no additional written feedback beyond these marks. The marks received by students after the first submission are for code quality, architecture, basic functionality, full functionality, and testing. We still consider this as an assignment with feedback, albeit limited, as students are able to determine that they need to improve particular aspects of their submission. In the following, we refer to the 2013 assignment as $\mathcal{T}$, to the scaffolded, detailed feedback assignment from 2014 as $S-detailed$ and to the simple feedback assignment from 2015 as $S-simple$. For both $S-detailed$ and $S-simple$ students were given six weeks to complete the assignment, namely, four weeks for the initial submission, with a break of one week for teacher marking and feedback, and two weeks to address feedback. The assignment was the same across all three years, and code analyzers were run across all three cohorts to check for collusion (no collusion across years found).

4 ANALYSIS

Submissions and marks were analysed for a total of 147 students, separated across the three years as 47 for $\mathcal{T}$, 41 for $S-detailed$, and 58 for $S-simple$. All assignment marks are out of 100 points. In this analysis, we only consider students who have submitted the assignment. 11.32% of students (6 of 53) did not submit the assignment in 2013, in contrast to 4.65% (2 of 43) and 3.44% (2 of 60) for 2014 and 2015 respectively, but the reasons behind this are not explored in this paper.

4.1 Impact of Revised Final Submissions

We show in Table 1 the average marks and standard deviation for all assignments and their stages where applicable. We can see that the final average marks for both $S-detailed$ and $S-simple$ were significantly higher than those for $\mathcal{T}$.

We can see that for both $S-detailed$ and $S-simple$ the marks increased from the first to the final submission. On average, for $S-detailed$, each assignment mark increased by 35.58%, whereas for $S-simple$, each student mark increased by 55.12% (not including students whose initial mark was 0). We show the mark variations in Figure 1 (a) and (b) for $S-detailed$ and $S-simple$ respectively, ordered by the values of the mark in the initial submission.

All students who submitted an assignment for revision in $S-detailed$ chose to submit a final version. In contrast, 25.86% of the students who submitted an assignment for revision in $S-simple$ chose not to resubmit, either because they had obtained full marks (5.17%) or because they were satisfied with the received marks[1] (17.24%). Students final marks were significantly better in the final submission for both $S-detailed$ and $S-simple$ than in the initial submission (two-way mixed ANOVA $p = 0.00003$ and $p = 0.00001$ respectively).

To understand whether the revised submission affected students differently, we perform additional tests. Student results over a sufficiently large group of students may be expected to follow a normal distribution, however, this is not guaranteed and the small number of students in both cases might lead to skew. An F-test would usually be used to compare two distributions which are normally distributed, however a Levene's test can be used based on the distance from the mean, without requiring both distributions to be normal, as shown in Tables 2 and 3.

From these results, it appears that the variance of the 2014 cohort does not change between the first and the final, revised submission, which can be interpreted as the treatment, i.e., the multi-stage assignment, applying in an equivalent way to all students. However, Levene's test is susceptible to the influence of outliers and outliers within the final marks can be clearly seen in Figure 1. We run a Brown-Forsythe test to further confirm our hypothesis that the 2014 data has no variance, showing that the initial and final submission groups in $S-detailed$ have no variance ($p - value = 0.9014$). When looking at individual students, in the initial submission for $S-detailed$, 48.78% were failing, 21.95% had marks between 50 and 75, and %29.27 had marks between 75 and 100. In the final submission, 24.39% were failing, 17/07% had marks between 50 and 75, and 58.53% had marks between 75 and 100, with 50% of the students who were failing now passing or obtaining high marks.

---

[1] Students specifically mentioned that they were satisfied with the marks, hence not re-submitting.

Table 1: Assignment Mark Summary

Assignment	Failure Rate Stage 1	Avg. Stage 1 Mark	Std. Dev	Failure Rate Final	Avg. Final Mark	Std. Dev
$\mathcal{T}$	-	-	-	36.18	57.93	22.98
$S-detailed$	48.78	51.69	21.59	24.39	71.43	23.83
$S-simple$	29.31	59.26	23.60	6.90	82.01	20.62

Table 2: Levene's Test Comparing Initial and Final Submissions in $S-detailed$

Anova Single Factor					
SUMMARY					
Groups	Count	Sum	Ave	Var	
Initial to Mean	41	827.976	20.195	243.129	
Final to Mean	41	829.171	21.760	158.331	
ANOVA					
Variation Source	SS	df	MS	F	P-value
Between Groups Fcrit=3.96	50.256	1	50.256	0.2504	0.618
Within Groups	16058.373	80	200.730		
Total	16108.629	81			

In 2015, the variances are different at p=0.05, indicating that the treatment has changed the behaviour of the class from what it was before treatment. Specifically, 65.51% of students changed their mark with more than 20% from initial submission to the final submission. When looking at individual students, in the initial submission 29.31% were failing, 43.10% with marks between 50 and 75 (inclusive), and 27.58% with marks between 75 and 100. In the final submission, only 6.90% were failing, 13.79% with marks between 50 and 75 (inclusive), and 79.31% with marks between 75 and 100, with 76.47% of the students who were failing now passing or obtaining high marks. In contrast, in 2013 36.18% failed the assignment (mark smaller than 50), 46.80% had marks between 50 and 75 (inclusive), and 23.40% had marks greater than 75.

Table 3: Levene's Test Comparing Initial and Final Submissions in $S-simple$

Anova Single Factor					
SUMMARY					
Groups	Count	Sum	Average	Variance	
Initial to Mean	58	1175.4943	20.2671	192.2307	
Final to Mean	58	849.0805	14.6393	207.1507	
ANOVA					
Variation Source	SS	df	MS	F	P-value
Between Groups Fcrit=3.9243305	918.4997	1	918.4996	4.5997	0.03410
Within Groups	22764.737	114	199.6907		
Total	23683.2367	115			

As it can be seen, not only are the failure rates and average significantly marks better in $S-detailed$ and $S-simple$ compared to $\mathcal{T}$, but also the percentage of high marks (greater than 75) is significantly higher in $S-detailed$ and $S-simple$ than in $\mathcal{T}$, with 58.53% and 79.31% compared to 23.40% respectively. This shows the benefits of the revision cycle addressing feedback, when compared to a traditional assignment design. To answer RQ1, we observe indeed that marks significantly increase between the initial and final submissions in $S-detailed$ even though students have

not been given marks as incentive to re-submit, which is the case in $S-simple$. We also observe that the average marks in the final submission of $S-simple$ increase more than in the case of $S-detailed$, but our data does not allow us to draw more in-depth conclusions. From our statistical analysis, we can hypothesise that the $S-simple$ increase is larger because fewer students chose to resubmit and only those who sought grade improvement thus went on, which would present a selection bias for students who were more likely to have the belief that they could improve their marks.

4.2 Impact of Detailed Feedback

In the following, we compare between the detailed feedback received in $S-detailed$ and the simple, template feedback received in $S-simple$ to determine the effect of detailed feedback. We first analyse the kind of detailed feedback received by students and what they chose to address in $S-detailed$. We then look at the student responses to the feedback and compare between the responses of students who received detailed feedback and those who received template feedback.

For assignment $S-detailed$, students received six main points of text feedback about their assignments: basic functionality, advanced functionality, design, testing, fault tolerance, and code quality. The average size of the total feedback was 1257.95 characters, with the average size of feedback points being 239.43 characters, roughly the length of the last two sentences in this paragraph. For the basic and advanced functionality, the feedback contained discussions about the various solutions provided by the student to the basic and advanced functionalities. We counted the in-depth feedback received by students. An example feedback received for a solution's fault tolerance is:

You did a good job in general. However, the content server should have some timeout / retry mechanism in case something goes wrong! Also, remember to close all sockets and buffers in a finally block.

Example feedback received for a solution's code quality is:

It is a (sic) good code in general. Methods are short and have a comment above their header. However, avoid utilizing a variable several times within a method to store different stuff. Especially if that variable is a parameter (see serverSocket.processRequest). Finally, remember that in Java, as a best-practice, class names start with a capital letter :)

while an example feedback for a solution's testing is:

I liked that you did a file comparator. However, tests should be automated, and remember to try all possible scenarios and failure cases (servers crashing, malformed XMLs, etc.).

Table 4 shows the percentage of students who received feedback as well as the percentage of students who addressed the suggested feedback. We remove the four students who did not make an initial submission (as shown in Figure 1 (a)) and thus did not receive feedback. To determine whether the students reflected on received feedback, we read through their submitted change summary document to see if they refer to the received piece of feedback and subsequently their code to verify that the implementation was in accordance with what the students had reflected on changing. We found no disparities between what the students mentioned as having changed in their code and what they had actually changed.

Table 4: Received and Addressed Feedback in $S-detailed$

Feedback point	Received (% of total students)	Addressed (% of received)
Basic functionality	89.18	87.87
Advanced functionality	81.08	93.33
Design	70.20	**32.13**
Fault tolerance	91.89	85.30
Testing	91.89	**64.70**
Code quality	91.89	**41.17**

As it can be seen in Table 4, the majority of students received feedback with respect to their basic functionality as well as the fault tolerance of their solution, the quality of their testing and the quality of their code. The design received the smallest quantity of feedback. We believe this to be because the design and structure of the code had inherently been addressed through the hurdle submission at the beginning of the assignment.

We observe that the most addressed feedback points were related to basic and advanced functionality, and fault tolerance. The least addressed feedback is that related to testing, code quality, and design. This is surprising considering that they, together, constituted nearly 50% of the final mark, namely, 30 % for testing, 8% for code quality and 10% for design. This suggests that students are very focused on achieving and improving on functionality, and least focused on what they perceive as cosmetic changes [15] such as providing a testing infrastructure and maintaining good code.

The results in Table 4 also raise questions about how to better scaffold the feedback to ensure that students feel confident to address it. With respect to testing, an approach could be to include more specific examples of what and how they could test and perhaps links to online tutorials or other external resources. As final year students previously have reported their inability to test and maintain large, complicated codebases [15] and since there are many variables and scenarios that need to considered when testing this particular assignment, having a skeleton testing framework that students could perhaps modify or employ to test their own assignment specifically can be beneficial.

We analyzed the feedback received by students in $S-simple$, which was in the following format, followed in some cases with brief comments about the entire assignment:
Code Quality: **mark/max_mark**
Architecture design decisions: **mark/max_mark**
Support for basic functionality: **mark/max_mark**
Support for full functionality: **mark/max_mark**

Support for fault tolerance: **mark/max_mark**
Testing: **mark/max_mark**
We believe this to be useful feedback as it provided the students with an indication of the specific areas where they needed to improve in their final submission and we have clear evidence that indications of partial progress can be meaningful as feedback, even in an automated sense [6]. Table 5 shows the percentage of students who received feedback as well as the percentage of students who addressed the suggested feedback. In some cases, students followed up with the lecturer to obtain more specific information as to what needed to be improved in their solution, and addressed that specific information in their change summary.

Table 5: Received and Addressed Feedback in $S-simple$

Feedback point	Received (% of total students)	Addressed (% of received)
Basic functionality	100	**41.37**
Advanced functionality	100	79.31
Design	100	**5.17**
Fault tolerance	100	72.41
Testing	100	**60.34**
Code quality	100	**5.17**

As in $S-detailed$, code quality and design were the feedback points that students addressed the least. However, in this case we hypothesize the cause to be different. The average mark obtained by students is 97.58 and 96.12 of 100 maximum points for code quality and design respectively, so, in the absence of text to describe what could be improved, there was no need for students to address these points. This is not the case for basic functionality, where the average mark is 68.10. We hypothesize that in the case of the basic functionality, students spent their remaining time improving full functionality and fault tolerance. This would explain the overall increase in marks and the higher percentage of addressed feedback in these categories.

4.2.1 Student responses to feedback. In the following, we aim to analyse the responses to the feedback provided by students in both $S-detailed$ and $S-simple$. In both cases, in their change summary response, students were asked to list which point of feedback they have addressed. Our observation of the responses submitted in $S-detailed$ is that most students not only listed the feedback points they addressed, but also provided ample details about how they addressed the feedback. Table 6 compares between the feedback responses submitted by the students. We consider a feedback response to be "in-depth" if the student discusses specific implementations, design details, or alternative designs or implementation choices of their solution in response to the feedback received. An example in-depth response to a testing feedback point is:

It was suggested that testing be improved particularly in order to test failures and concurrency. I have now tested failure conditions of many individual components using unit tests. I've also added integration tests written in Bash which run the programs in different configurations and comp are the output. Added More Unit Tests in FuncTester.java Added new tests to exercise the functionality below: HttpRequest parsing, Invalid HttpResponse parsing, XML parsing [...]

To determine if a change summary was in-depth, the researchers analyzed the change summaries submitted by students and coded them as in-depth or otherwise (inter-rater reliability 100%). As it

Table 6: In-depth Discussions in Change Summaries

Assignment	Change Summary (% of total students)	In-depth Discussion (% of summaries)
$S-detailed$	87.80	61.11
$S-simple$	65.51	39.47

can be seen in Table 6, a smaller percentage of students submitted a change summary in $S-simple$. This is to be expected as 22.41% of students either received the maximum mark or chose not to re-submit after the first submission was graded in $S-simple$. We observe though that in $S-detailed$, in contrast to $S-simple$, a much larger percentage of students submitted detailed, in-depth discussions of how they fixed the code following the feedback received. This could be a direct consequence of the detailed received feedback which could result in increased student engagement or an indication of the impact of cognitive apprenticeship in how such feedback should be given, however further studies using controlled experiments are needed to confirm this hypothesis.

5 DISCUSSION & CONCLUSION

Our analysis highlights several key points. Firstly, that a two-stage submission assignment where students are given the opportunity to revise their code leads to significantly better learning outcomes (average assignment mark of 71.43) when compared to a single-stage submission assignment (average assignment mark of 57.93). Failure rates were also significantly smaller in the two-stage assignments than in the traditional assignment design. In addition, student marks increased from the first to the final submission and failure rates dropped in both $S-detailed$ and $S-simple$. One confounding factor could be that students use the initial submission simply as a mechanism to extend the assignment deadline. But this was generally not the case, with all assignments having submitted code that attempted to implement almost the entire assignments[2].

Secondly, we observe that even simple feedback, in the form of grades for specific components, can lead the students towards specific areas of improvement and thus increase assignment outcomes.

Our second research question focused on understanding the benefits, if any, of providing detailed written feedback for a large number of aspects of the submitted student code. In both cases (with or without detailed feedback) we noticed that there are some assignment aspects that students will not address or are less likely to address, regardless of the level of feedback received. These are testing, design, and code quality. The causes of students not addressing these areas are subject for future analysis, however one cause could be that they were considered less important than meeting specific functionality goals, despite being given a large percentage of the marks.

However, when looking at the student submissions that received detailed feedback but no marks, we noticed that students tended to improve all (but the three above) areas of the code where they

received detailed feedback. For example there is a significant difference between students addressing basic functionality feedback in $S-detailed$ (87.87%) and $S-simple$ (41.37%), despite the average marks for this component being similar (71.71 in $S-detailed$ and 68.10 in $S-simple$). This is the case across all other feedback components. We can conclude that detailed feedback, together with the lack of actual marks, encourages students to attempt to improve their code. Moreover, our analysis of the discussions submitted by students shows more in-depth, detailed discussions submitted by students receiving detailed feedback, however we cannot prove that this is a direct consequence of the detailed feedback itself or other confounding factors. Confounding factors include differences in lecturing styles between the two lecturers of 2014 and 2015, as well as the presence of the mark itself in the simple feedback of $S-simple$. Our future work will look at analyzing the effect of detailed feedback beyond a single assignment, either for the following assignments in the course or when looking at the effect of exam marks. This study was not possible for this course as the next and last assignment in the sequence was a report, and the exam was mainly focused on theoretical, high level concepts that would not have necessarily been addressed by the detailed feedback.

REFERENCES

[1] M. Ben-Ari. Constructivism in computer science education. In *Acm sigcse bulletin*, volume 30, pages 257–261. ACM, 1998.
[2] D. Blaheta. Reinventing homework as cooperative, formative assessment. In *Proceedings of the 45th ACM technical symposium on Computer science education*, pages 301–306. ACM, 2014.
[3] A. Collins, J. S. Brown, and S. E. Newman. Cognitive apprenticeship. *Thinking: The Journal of Philosophy for Children*, 8(1):2–10, 1988.
[4] C. Douce, D. Livingstone, and J. Orwell. Automatic test-based assessment of programming: A review. *Journal on Educational Resources in Computing (JERIC)*, 5(3):4, 2005.
[5] S. H. Edwards, J. Snyder, M. A. Pérez-Quiñones, A. Allevato, D. Kim, and B. Tretola. Comparing effective and ineffective behaviors of student programmers. In *Proceedings of the fifth international workshop on Computing education research workshop*, pages 3–14. ACM, 2009.
[6] N. Falkner, R. Vivian, D. Piper, and K. Falkner. Increasing the effectiveness of automated assessment by increasing marking granularity and feedback units. In *Proceedings of the 45th ACM Technical Symposium on Computer Science Education*, SIGCSE '14, pages 9–14, New York, NY, USA, 2014. ACM.
[7] P. Ihantola, T. Ahoniemi, V. Karavirta, and O. Seppälä. Review of recent systems for automatic assessment of programming assignments. In *Proceedings of the 10th Koli Calling International Conference on Computing Education Research*, pages 86–93. ACM, 2010.
[8] N. Kalogeropoulos, I. Tzigounakis, E. Pavlatou, and A. Boudouvis. Computer-based assessment of student performance in programing courses. *Computer Applications in Engineering Education*, 21(4):671–683, 2013.
[9] V. Karavirta, A. Korhonen, and L. Malmi. On the use of resubmissions in automatic assessment systems. *Computer science education*, 16(3):229–240, 2006.
[10] P. Kinnunen and B. Simon. Experiencing programming assignments in cs1: the emotional toll. In *Proceedings of the Sixth international workshop on Computing education research*, pages 77–86. ACM, 2010.
[11] A. J. Ko, B. A. Myers, and H. H. Aung. Six learning barriers in end-user programming systems. In *Visual Languages and Human Centric Computing, 2004 IEEE Symposium on*, pages 199–206. IEEE, 2004.
[12] B. A. Linderbaum and P. E. Levy. The development and validation of the feedback orientation scale (fos). *Journal of Management*, 36(6):1372–1405, 2010.
[13] U. Nikula, O. Gotel, and J. Kasurinen. A motivation guided holistic rehabilitation of the first programming course. *ACM Transactions on Computing Education (TOCE)*, 11(4):24, 2011.
[14] E. Panadero, J. A. Tapia, and J. A. Huertas. Rubrics and self-assessment scripts effects on self-regulation, learning and self-efficacy in secondary education. *Learning and individual differences*, 22(6):806–813, 2012.
[15] C. Szabo. Student projects are not throwaways: Teaching practical software maintenance in a software engineering course. In *Proceedings of the 45th ACM Technical Symposium on Computer Science Education*, SIGCSE '14, pages 55–60, New York, NY, USA, 2014. ACM.

---

[2]In some cases, the code did not run at all, hence the zero marks awarded.

Learning Dimensions: Lessons from Field Studies

Chris Martin
Life Sciences - CITR
University of Dundee
Dundee, UK
+44 1382 385828
c.j.martin@dundee.ac.uk

Janet Hughes
School of Computing and
Communications
The Open University, UK
+44 131 549 7118
janet.hughes@open.ac.uk

John Richards
IBM T.J. Watson Research
Center USA &
University of Dundee, UK
+1 914 945 2632
ajtr@us.ibm.com

ABSTRACT

In this paper, we describe work to investigate the creation of engaging programming learning experiences. Background research informed the design of four fieldwork studies involving a range of age groups to explore how programming tasks could best be framed to motivate learners. Our empirical findings from these four studies, described here, contributed to the design of a set of programming 'Learning Dimensions' (LDs). The LDs provide educators with insights to support key design decisions for the creation of engaging programming learning experiences. This paper describes the background to the identification of these LDs and how they could address the design and delivery of highly engaging programming learning tasks. A web application has been authored to support educators in the application of the LDs to their lesson design.

Keywords
Learning dimensions; motivation; programming.

1. INTRODUCTION

A substantial literature going back several decades (e.g. [25]) has explored various aspects of learning computer programming. [19] provide a detailed review and discussion of the literature pertaining to novice programmers. [22] review and discuss issues relating to development of CS1 courses. All of these authors note that programming is a multi-faceted task with many interrelated skills, and there is recognition that the transition from novice to expert is challenging. One result of this growing understanding is the major improvement in the educational technology developed to support learners [13]. Environments in themselves cannot provide the entirety of support for the different needs of novice learners, however. Educators also have awareness that whilst novices may apparently be making progress, their knowledge may be fragile and/or their lack of confidence can lead to 'stopper' behaviour. [20] suggest that knowledge in novice programmers is more complex than just 'knowing'. They describe the presence of 'fragile knowledge', which is categorised as missing, inert (learned but not used), or misplaced. They further observe that there can be different types of novice programmers: stoppers, movers and super movers [20].

A 'stopper' is characterised as person who is halted abruptly by an error or difficulty and does not have the inclination to tackle the problem independently. In contrast, a 'mover' is a learner with enthusiasm who views an error as a challenge rather than an

obstacle. Perkins describes a third category of novice as a 'super mover': "tinkerers who are able to respond to errors but are unable to modify their program effectively and lose track of edits" [19]. Consequently, we judge that emotional response and enthusiasm are valid factors to consider in the process of learning to program. Our work takes an alternative approach to that of tool or IDE development, by considering the *context* in which learning takes place and the efficacy of learner motivation.

A recurring theme that emerges from the literature is that learning is fruitful in experiences that are personally meaningful for the learner. Aspects that increase personal motivation include personal, social, and contextual elements in addition to purely technical elements such as programming language and environment. Examples include the capacity to tap into and contribute to a community of like-minded learners, and the ability rapidly to make a thing that the learner values. The next section will introduce a set of field studies that explored learner-motivated programming.

2. FIELD STUDIES

Four field studies were performed with participants who were relative novices to programming, ranging in age from pre-school to university students. A range of qualitative and quantitative methods was used to gather data across the set of studies. An overview of each study is given next, together with the main conclusions reached from the observations and data collected.

2.1 Robot Dance

This study [15] was designed to explore how working with Arduino robots can support introductory programming learning. Arduino-based differential drive robots [1] were programmed for 1 to 2 hours by a total of 135 middle-school students (51% female), ranging in age from 12 to 16 years. The increased understanding of programming concepts by these learners, as measured by the difference in a pre- and post-test, was impressive: in a short space of time, learners were all able to use a textual language (C-style, rather than block-based) to create a simple program and demonstrably improve their knowledge in the areas of sequence, syntax and programming variables.

Further analysis suggested that a key aspect of this successful outcome was having a 'time to first task' of only around 10 minutes. This offered sufficient time to cover all the required knowledge to subsequently get a minimum viable robot program written and uploaded. Another important factor was the performance element of Robot Dance, enhanced as the workshops progressed by the inclusion of powerful external speakers, a wood-effect dance floor and a stage light served to increase the motivational effect of the end performance. Robot Dance delivered small pieces of skill and knowledge, giving the learners space to explore and experiment 'hands on' with the new material. The delivery of a new concept followed by space to explore the example was repeated several times. This cycle

ITiCSE '17, July 03-05, 2017, Bologna, Italy
© 2017 ACM. ISBN 978-1-4503-4704-4/17/07…$15.00
DOI: http://dx.doi.org/10.1145/3059009.3059046

supported a gradual increase in learner independence and task complexity. The next study reduced the degree of structure offered to learners.

2.2 Robot Dance in the Community

Here, the learners of introductory programming skills were given a greater degree of independence. Rather than a tight cycle of skill delivery and learning consolidation, learners were given a brief introduction and left to develop their Robot Dance, asking for assistance if and when they required it. The learning experience was organised to be drop-in, situated in a public shopping centre. Learners (members of the public) started at different times and could work as long as they wanted. Learners were also free to self-organise, which resulted in individuals, pairs, parent and child pairs, and larger groups. Following a brief introduction to Arduino, learners were given a very basic skeleton Arduino program to extend. To make this introduction concrete, learners were "walked-through" the program required to make the robot move forward a short distance. Once learners had successfully completed this task, the challenge of creating 20 seconds of dance moves was presented. The learners observed comprised a group of six parents and 35 children. Parents were considered where they performed an active role as opposed to passive observation. The children's ages ranged from five to 15 with the majority around seven. Four different groupings were observed: single child, child pairs, child parent pairs and multiple children and parents. All learners demonstrated an observable emotional response to the performance they had programmed. Learners exhibited pride in their creation, even though the audience was small. Observations from this study confirm that different learners require different degrees and types of support: freedom to experiment and self-direction worked well for some learners but was more challenging for others. It highlighted the extent to which programming has an emotional dimension. The next study investigated this further.

2.3 Whack-a-Mole

Robot Dance [15] demonstrated the extent to which the physical artefact mattered. The Whack-a-Mole study was designed to capture more insights into the emotions experienced by learners of programming, particularly when programming with different interfaces: a physical interface or a screen-based equivalent. The essence of the Whack-a-Mole game is simple: a stimulus occurs in one of several locations and the player reacts to it as quickly as possible. In the simplest version, a light comes on at random and stays on until the corresponding button is pressed. Using Arduino to give a physical interface, each of four LEDs has a corresponding button. When the light comes on, the player must press the corresponding physical button to progress through the game. The screen-based equivalent shows buttons on screen and the keyboard is used to press 'buttons'.

2.3.1 Capturing emotional responses

The Whack-a-Mole study involved 38 students (24% female) of a first level undergraduate computing module. In the first phase, learners were taught via three specific worked examples relating to programming with arrays and fixed loops. In the second phase, learners were required to demonstrate their understanding by applying the taught material to a novel problem. Learners were allocated at random into small practical groups of three or four. One set of groups used the physical Arduino interface whilst the other set used the screen-based equivalent. Emotional responses to programming were gathered at task completion by the Reflective Emotion Inventory (REI) derived from the HUMAINE

project [22]. The REI questionnaire asks users to identify emotions they have experienced, to note the degree of intensity for each using a four-part Likert scale (0 indicated no emotion; 3 indicated that the emotion occurred intensely). They were asked also to offer some contextual information to describe why they experienced the given emotion. An example response is: annoyance, 3, "Getting the wires in the correct place".

2.3.2 Comparing responses to interfaces

When the physical set and screen-based sets of students' REI data responses were compared, the physical set was found to report greater intensity in all bar one of the emotional sub-categories (Figure 1). This matched the rich contextual data offered by the physical set. Where students worked with the physical artefact, they had a strongly positive experience.

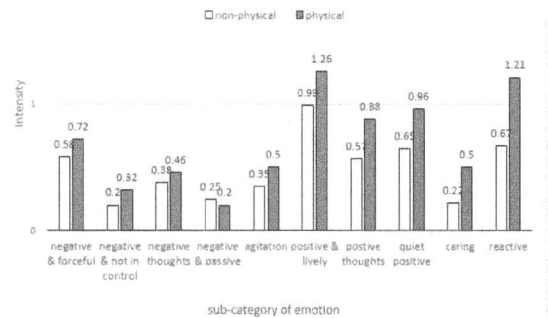

Figure 1: Whack-a-Mole emotional responses

Two of the positive emotions reported by the physical set were notably greater than that of the screen-based set: *positive & lively* and *reactive*. The Whack-a-Mole study uncovered a notable difference in emotional response to the learning experience for the students using a physical device compared to the students using a screen-based equivalent. Both sets of students described a range of negative emotions with similar levels of strength and for similar reasons, and a similar range of positive emotions. However, the physical set noted a greater strength of positive emotions associated with the learning experience. The next section describes a final field study, which was designed to further empower learners to create programs for problems they define and personally identify with.

2.4 Digital Makers

Additional aspects here were included to increase ownership, personalisation, and purpose. In previous studies, learners were tasked with solving challenges devised by the educator. Here, design decisions were less constrained for the learners, who could apply their newly acquired programming skills to solve a problem of their own. The study was part of One Day Digital, a series of digital making events for young people organised by [16]. Four events ran on consecutive weekends in different cities, engaging 48 young volunteer learners (17% female) from across the UK.

2.4.1 Programming set tasks with Arduino

In the morning, learners were walked through the process of wiring and programming some components with Arduino; for this stage learners worked as individuals. Following this, the programming of the component was demonstrated and then carried out by the learners. In three iterations of short demonstration followed by enactment by learners, three tasks were tackled: making an LED blink, using a potentiometer to control the blink rate and using a button to make the LED blink when pressed. To introduce a creative disruption to the flow of tuition, an idea-generation session was used to gather ideas posted together on a wall serving as an information radiator [24] for use later in the day. The learners were then guided through some additional Arduino output devices: servo, speaker and red green blue (RGB) LED. This gave the opportunity to show examples built into the Arduino IDE and the use of an external library for the servo. The final example they constructed was a red, green and blue colour mixer in which the colour of the LED was specified by three parameters passed to a user-defined function. Using the `random` function and bringing in sound (with loudspeakers playing beeps of a program-specified tone), the learners extended this to create a light and sound show.

2.4.2 Programming user-designed tasks
In the second stage, learners were given the chance to self-select groupings and build a physical app utilising the morning's teaching. Groups were given three hours to build a physical app based on one of the ideas they had selected from those they generated earlier. Before the workshop ended, participants were asked to complete the REI emotional response questionnaire.

The most striking result was the reporting of positive emotions as being far more intensely experienced than negative emotions (Figure 2). The physical apps session evoked a rich emotional response from the participants. Negative emotions experienced tied into problems reported in the literature about novice programming. Many of the error-prone features of coding match with those of physical prototyping, with bread boarding being particularly error-prone. Nonetheless, the minor irritations of an error-prone medium were outweighed by the strength of the positive emotions reported. Many positive emotions stemmed from a sense of overcoming challenges to produce something that worked.

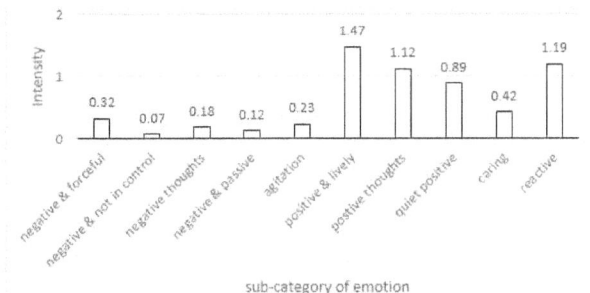

Figure 2: Digital Makers emotional responses

In summary, the Digital Makers study used ownership, personalisation, and purpose to create a highly engaging learning experience that resulted in strong positive emotional responses from learners. The next section describes how insights generated from these four studies were synthesised as a set of Learning Dimensions (LDs). The LDs follow the style that [9] proposed in their 'Cognitive Dimensions of Notations' framework, in which they outline a common vocabulary and reference point for the design and discussion of notations. It has served as a successful nucleus for a great deal of research relating to notations of many forms including code, sketching, algorithm visualization and musical staff notation. Cognitive Dimensions provided a common vocabulary that enabled researches to discuss insights. It is hoped that the LDs fulfil a similar role for educators making design decisions for motivating programming experiences.

3. LEARNING DIMENSIONS
3.1 Introduction
The aim of the Learning Dimensions is to provide a resource for computer science educators that can be used either in the design of new learning experiences or as a reflective toolkit for the review and improvement of existing learning experiences. The eight LDs address high-level aspects of learning experiences, particularly relating to practicalities of the design and delivery of a learning task. Each LD is described in its fullest form in [14], that is with (i) a detailed description; (ii) links to relevant literature; (iii) a summary of its rationale; (iv) examples from fieldwork; and (v) how it can be applied. Space constrains the description of each that can be provided here.

The first three dimensions relate to the design of activities to be particularly motivating and engaging. *Closed versus Open* describes the relative merits of designing learning tasks with or without a lot of detail and structure. *Cultural Relevance* describes the affordances presented by locating learning tasks within the learner's culture. *Recognition* describes opportunities arising from enabling learners to share their work. The next five LDs deal with the extent to which the programming experience can be learner-centred. *Space to Play* describes the impact of designing learning tasks that encourage iterative experimentation, for example with peers, and self-directed discovery of knowledge and skills. *Driver Shifting* describes the affordances of transferring the role of driving the learning experience from the educator to the learner, vice-versa, or via a collaboration of both. *Risk Reward* describes how the duration of tasks and the frequency of feedback can be adjusted to suit different learning experience needs. *Grouping* describes the possible arrangements of learners. *Session Shape* describes the affordance of the physical environment and how this may enhance or impede the learning experience.

3.2 Motivating programming
3.2.1 Closed versus open
This dimension encapsulates the extent to which activities have a well-defined structure, route, and end point. A good example of a closed problem is programming a robot to follow a line. There is little scope for the learner to take ownership. Towards the open end of the dimension would be a free choice activity where learners are able to demonstrate competency in a given skill through the creation of a piece of work that is not fully constrained by the educator. An example is creating a robot dance. In the fieldwork reported in section 2, Robot Dance in the Community and Digital Makers both exemplified the motivating effects of open programming tasks. Similar examples can be found in the literature. For instance, [21] conducted interviews with teams taking part in a RoboCup Junior (RCJ) event which invited teams of schoolchildren to compete using robots almost exclusively developed using LEGO Mindstorms [12]. Interviews were followed up by a detailed case study with one team. Two important factors that arose from the analysis were motivation and evidence of learning. One frequently reported reason for being motivated was the 'openness' of the task.

3.2.2 Cultural relevance
Often part of a learning experience involves creating a product of some kind, such as code or a sketch. The *Cultural Relevance* dimension considers where this product sits within the learner's culture. It prompts consideration of whether or not the tasks they are asked to perform are authentic and relevant to their daily life

experience. If the learning experience is divorced from the world the learner inhabits, the cultural relevance will be low. Digital Makers, described in section 2, showed that ownership, personalisation, and purpose were related to strong positive emotional responses to programming. Personalisation and choice have been highlighted in the literature as important for increasing intrinsic motivation in learners. In one study of 72 fifth grade learners (10 to 11 year olds), [7] observed a powerful learning benefit in the personalised choice condition. Learners were observed to have not only increased motivation but also displayed a deeper engagement in the task.

3.2.3 Recognition

The *Recognition* dimension considers the potential for the learner to share the product of their learning. As early as nursery school, learners seek recognition from their teachers, peers, and parents. A good example of this is pleasure gained from the displaying of work on the walls of the learning environment for all to see. In section 2, *Recognition* was an important dimension in Robot Dance and Digital Makers when learners demonstrated their products in an end-of-workshop performance. *Recognition* is also possible via many educational programming tools which allow individuals to contribute to online communities of learners [7]. Learners can be inspired and informed by the work of others and in equal measure provide the inspiration and support for those who follow them. Considerable motivational affordances can come from sharing work and observing it being valued by others. [21] noted that a number of participants also identified placing the task in a social context as a factor contributing to motivation; the opportunity to share ideas and the pride associated with demonstrating expertise was reported to be important.

In LDs, the authors acknowledge that discussion is a richer mode of interaction than simply viewing work or broadcast-style presentation. With a discussion, a conversation about the product of the learning can take place between the learner and the audience. Learners gaining recognition through discussion are not just exposing a product, presenting an idea or artefact but they are also engaging in rich discourse about the artefact and process. This should ensure the audience and the learner reach a shared understanding of the idea or knowledge being presented. Where a deep interaction takes place, the learner's engagement and motivation will be affected by the amount of time, effort and interest the observers have invested in the interaction.

3.2.4 Space to play

The *Space to Play* dimension seeks to break down the traditional view of a teacher-learner relationship. It encapsulates the extent to which a learning experience offers and encourages learners to explore independently. *Space to Play* addresses the fact that space and independence may be intimidating for certain learners. It suggests a flexible structure to learning experiences, with frequent opportunities for learners to iterate over a concept that has just been introduced. This empowers individual learners to approach exploration on their own terms and take ownership of the learning experience. In [10], the teacher assumes the role of a facilitator rather than a gatekeeper to knowledge. This sets up a more progressive learning experience in which learners have a degree of influence on the direction of their learning.

In the Digital Maker study, *Space to Play* was integral to the design of the learning experience. The majority of the morning was spent learning about Arduino programing and electronics. Programming is a high precision error-prone activity; electronics prototyping has similar characteristics. To support this, the session was designed around frequent short *Spaces to Play*. A piece of programing and electronics was demonstrated and learners were given a time-boxed opportunity to try the task for themselves and experiment.

3.2.5 Driver Shift

This dimension attempts to capture who is driving the learning experience, i.e. controlling it at a given point in time. For example, a classic higher education style lecture where the lecturer projects content to the learners for a sustained period would have a low degree of *Driver Shift*. In contrast, a guided practical session with a tight cycle, in which learners are shown a brief example and then given space to try it, would have a high degree of *Driver Shift*. The concept emerged particularly from the Digital Makers study. As the day progressed and competence with newly acquired skills and knowledge grew, the length of the learner-driven blocks was increased and the scope of the task opened out. This offered more opportunity for creativity. Throughout the session, the role of driver switched between learner and facilitator with a gradual progression towards the learners working autonomously under their own direction, seeking advice rather than direction from the facilitator. This dimension is proposed to encourage the creation of learning experiences in which learners become active participants rather than passive recipients. When applied to programming in particular, a session with high *Driver Shift* offers an opportunity for learners to consolidate code comprehension with code generation [22].

3.2.6 Risk Reward

The *Risk Reward* dimension considers the relationship between the investment of effort or risk that a learner undertakes and the reward when feedback is received. Investment of effort without confirmation that the correct actions have been taken by the learner is considered a risk. This is because it may result in wasted effort or even worse, confirming an incorrect understanding or application of a skill. For a language such as Java, the amount of effort investment required from the learner to get the payback or reward of some text being displayed is considerable, so high risk. In a language like Processing, the effort investment made by the learner before observable outcome is much less; it is possible to render output in one line of code, so there is lower risk. A special case of this dimension is the time to start the first task. In Robot Dance, this was an important consideration for establishing teacher-student relationships. In all the studies conducted, the *Risk Reward* cycles were extended from initially very tight cycles of around 10 minutes per example to a larger and longer open-ended task that reflected the learners' confidence with skills being taught. One of the key decisions for the design of creative tools put forward by [13] was that they must possess a 'low floor' or enable a quick win for learners. The *Risk Reward* dimension takes this a step further than purely identifying difficulties. It encourages thought around the relationship between challenging aspects of work and the reward learners receive. An advantage of this dimension is that it encourages reflection on how much autonomy learners are given, for example arranging a looser risk reward if a learner is a 'mover' rather than a 'stopper'.

3.2.7 Grouping

The *Grouping* dimension draws attention to the different arrangements of learners that are possible. Throughout the studies conducted, three natural groupings of learners were noted: individuals, pairs, and groups of more than two people. In addition, there have been situations where there have been asymmetric groups in which learners worked with parents or with learners of different abilities, as in Robot Dance in the Community. There is a substantial body of literature exploring various approaches to group learning, including collaborative learning (e.g. [2]), team based learning (e.g. [11]), cooperative learning (e.g. [4]) and peer learning (e.g. [27]). It is beneficial for learners to experience the social complexity that working in a group brings. This needs to be balanced against the desire to support individual focus on a particular learning point. Switching groups can be a good way to reach a compromise, as achieved in Digital Makers. The duration of the session is an important consideration, however, as switching groups is potentially disruptive, which could be useful or harmful. As with the other LDs, *Grouping* highlights and provokes reflection around the merits and shortcomings of a particular design decision

3.2.8 Session Shape

A strong theme throughout [18] is the relationship between the physical environment and its affordance for better educational practices. The physical environment encapsulates all elements of the space in which learning takes place, including aspects such as the arrangement of tables and location of supporting visuals such as white boards or projectors. The physical environments involved in the studies here were classroom (Robot Dance), public space (Robot Dance in the Community), computing lab (Whack-A-Mole) and informal learning space (Digital Makers). The *Session Shape* dimension serves as a placeholder to consider what constraints and affordances are offered by the space that you inhabit with your learners. Flexibility is the most desirable attribute for a learning space. In an ideal situation, a room will have enough space to allow movement of learners as the session requires, as was seen in Digital Makers.

3.3 Working with Learning Dimensions

Learning Dimensions are intended to be a lightweight tool that can aid the design and refinement of learning experiences in programming. A web application has been written to help educators use the LDs [26]. It comprises two screens: a view screen presents information about the LDs; a notes screen gives a mechanism for educators to make relevant notes. This view screen of the application was designed to focus upon each LD. When an LD is selected, its title and brief description are presented as an aide memoire. In addition, there is a check box to indicate whether the educator has control over this aspect of the learning experience and a text box for relevant information (Figure 3). Below the description is a set of bullet points that describe different aspects of the LDs and how they may affect the learning experience being designed. This is intended to aid the educator in reflecting about how they might apply LDs to their learning experience. Underneath this description box is a text area where notes can be made. Finally, a button enables navigation to the notes screen that presents all the LD notes together. This alternative notes screen shifts the focus from the description of individual LDs to the educator's notes and those LDs over which they have control. This view allows one to see an overview of the entire learning experience and to think about how decisions relate to each other.

An example use of the application was to reflect on the design of a further workshop that allowed learners to gain an understanding of some other elementary computing concepts in a tactile learning experience using Bare Conductive Electric Paint [3]. The web application identified that three of the LDs were constrained by the nature of the task and the event, and thus could not be emphasised in the workshop design.

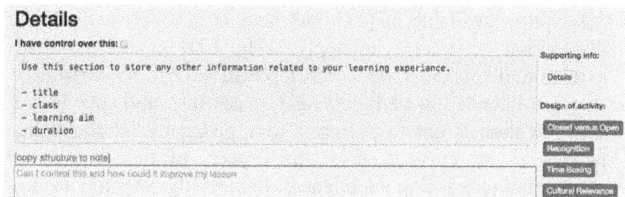

Figure 3: example edit view from web application

The remaining dimensions, in contrast, were sufficiently open that they could be tailored to influence the design of the session. Examples of notes recorded in the web application by the first author are given next.

Closed versus Open:
"Elements that were closed were chosen to support learners' lack of experience with the task. To offset the closed element, a softer open element was included to allow learners to have some control over an aspect of the learning experience.
Open elements: part of this activity involves the design of a face that incorporates flashing LEDs. This is very open as learners can design anything they wish.
Closed elements: the circuit the learners use is screen-printed and thus pre-defined. This constraint limits creativity but enables the workshop to be delivered to a wide range of learners, as the challenge is understanding a 'thing that is' rather than creating something new which is a higher order task."

Space to Play:
"The workshop naturally split into two activities that learners could perform independently, firstly designing their artwork and secondly hooking up the electronics. This aspect of *Space to Play* is valuable when encouraging a group of learners to diverge after the launch and then converge, sharing findings at the landing.

launch: introduce activity, choose which LED to include.
activity: make holes for LEDs and draw and colour picture.
landing: review and reinforce what has been created.
launch: describe how to use the conductive paint to form connection between the printed circuit and the components.
activity: hook up components.
landing: confirm it is working."

4. CONCLUSIONS

For a learning experience to be successful, it is crucial that learners are as engaged as possible. [10] described the Contributing Student Pedagogy, which aims to achieve this by enabling learners to have a prominent role in their learning experiences. CARSS is a framework for learner-centred design of educational software [8]. It offers a comprehensive set of issues associated with the design and development of educational technologies, identifying five important areas: context, roles, stakeholders, activities and skills. Creating an engaging learning experience is not a mechanical process governed by a set of rules to be followed dutifully to guarantee consistent results. It requires reflection and consideration not just of what is to be learned but also of who is learning and how they can best succeed. [17] continues to gather and share successful ideas for CS assignments and their materials. [6] likewise addresses the sharing of materials relating to assessment, also in the context of creative computing.

This paper is more general: it describes four studies of novel learning experiences which generated insights aligned with the literature and which informed the creation of a set of Learning Dimensions. The work reported here is a summary of a larger description available at [14], and here is intended to focus on things that educators can apply. The LDs have been made available to educators via a web application [26]. As a resource, they are intended to be lightweight, accessible, and easy to use. The intention is not to present a new pedagogy or theory that tackles all or even most of the aspects of the creation of programming learning experiences. Instead, the LDs are a set of important factors from which educators can select to add value and to make informed decisions about their practice. They should provoke thought about areas of opportunity in the design of an engaging learning experience and as a source of inspiration and information for educators who are critically evaluating a learning experience. Furthermore, the LDs unify published conclusions from other authors with new insights from the four field studies into a single suite. It is an inexact categorisation of some of the finer aspects of learning to program but should provide a useful background against which to assess the totality of the experience to maximise each learner's motivation and engagement.

5.   ACKNOWLEDGMENTS

Nesta; University of Dundee, for funding the first study.

6.   REFERENCES

[1]   Arduino [Online]. Available: http://www.arduino.cc [Accessed 2014]

[2]   Bagley, C.A. and Chou, C.C., 2007, June. Collaboration and the importance for novices in learning java computer programming. *ACM SIGCSE Bulletin*, 39 (3), pp. 211-215).

[3]   Bare Conductive, 2014. *Creative electronic tools – Bare Conductive* [Online]. Available: http://www.bareconductive.com [Accessed 2014].

[4]   Beck, L.L., Chizhik, A.W. and McElroy, A.C., 2005, February. Cooperative learning techniques in CS1: design and experimental evaluation. *ACM SIGCSE Bulletin*, 37(1), pp. 470-474.

[5]   Brennan, K., Monroy-Hernández, A. and Resnick, M. 2010. Making projects, making friends: Online community as catalyst for interactive media creation. *New directions for youth development*, 2010(128), pp.75-83.

[6]   Cateté, V., Snider, E. and Barnes, T. 2016. Developing a Rubric for a Creative CS Principles Lab. *Proceedings of the 2016 ACM Conference on Innovation and Technology in Computer Science Education*. ACM, New York, NY, USA, pp. 290-295.

[7]   Cordova, D. I. and Lepper, M. R. 1996. Intrinsic motivation and the process of learning: Beneficial effects of contextualization, personalization, and choice. *Journal of Educational Psychology*, 88(4), pp.715-730.

[8]   Good, J. and Robertson, J. 2006. CARSS: A framework for learner-centred design with children. *International Journal of Artificial Intelligence in Education*, 16(4), pp.381-413.

[9]   Green, T.R.G. and Petre, M., 1996. Usability analysis of visual programming environments: a 'cognitive dimensions' framework. *Journal of Visual Languages & Computing*, 7(2), pp.131-174.

[10]   Hamer, J., Cutts, Q., Jackova, J., Luxton-Reilly, A., McCartney, R., Purchase, H., Riedesel, C., Saeli, M., Sanders, K. and Sheard, J. 2008. Contributing learner pedagogy. *ACM SIGCSE Bulletin*, 40(4), pp.194-212.

[11]   Lasserre, P. and Szostak, C., 2011. Effects of team-based learning on a CS1 course. *ACM Conference on Innovation and Technology in Computer Science Education*. ACM, New York, NY, USA, pp. 133-137.

[12]   Lego. 2010. *LEGO Mindstorms* [Online]. Available: http://mindstorms.lego.com/en-us/default.aspx [Accessed 2010].

[13]   Maloney, J., Resnick, M., Rusk, N., Silverman, B. and Eastmond, E. 2010. The Scratch Programming Language and Environment. *ACM Transactions on Computing Education (TOCE)*, 10(4), p.16.

[14]   Martin, C. 2017, PhD Thesis, University of Dundee.

[15]   Martin, C. and Hughes, J., 2011. Robot dance: Edutainment or engaging learning. In *Proceedings of the 23rd Annual Psychology of Programming Interest Group Conference*.

[16]   Nesta. 2014. *Nesta* [Online]. Available: http://www.nesta.org.uk [Accessed 2014].

[17]   Nifty Assignments [Online]. Available: http://nifty.stanford.edu/ [Accessed 2016]

[18]   Oblinger, D. 2006. *Learning spaces,* EDUCAUSE Washington, DC

[19]   Pane, J.F. and Myers, B. A., 1996. Usability Issues in the Design of Novice Programming Systems. *Human-Computer Interaction Institute Technical Report CMU-HCII-96-101.*

[20]   Perkins, D.N. and Martin, F. 1989. Fragile knowledge and neglected strategies in novice programmers. In *first workshop on empirical studies of programmers on Empirical studies of programmers* (pp. 213-229).

[21]   Petre, M. and Price, B. 2004. Using robotics to motivate 'back door' learning. *Education and Information Technologies*, 9(2), pp.147-158.

[22]   Petta, P., Pelachaud, C. and Cowie, R. 2011. Emotion-Oriented Systems. *The Humaine Handbook, ISBN*, pp.978-3.

[23]   Robins, A., Rountree, J. and Rountree, N. 2003. Learning and teaching programming: A review and discussion. *Computer Science Education*, 13(2), pp.137-172.

[24]   Sharp, H., Robinson, H. and Petre, M. 2009. The role of physical artefacts in agile software development: Two complementary perspectives. *Interactive. Computing*, 21, 108-116.

[25]   Soloway, E. and Spohrer, J.C 1989. *Studying the Novice Programmer*, Hillsdale, NJ, USA, L. Erlbaum Associates

[26]   http://sspog1.github.io/ LD web page [Online].

[27]   Topping, K., 1998. Peer assessment between learners in colleges and universities. *Review of educational Research*, 68(3), pp.249-276.

How Tool Support and Peer Scoring Improved Our Students' Attitudes Toward Peer Reviews

Daniel Toll
Dept. of Computer Science
Linnaeus University
Kalmar, Sweden
daniel.toll@lnu.se

Anna Wingkvist
Dept. of Computer Science
Linnaeus University
Växjö, Sweden
anna.wingkvist@lnu.se

ABSTRACT

We wanted to introduce peer reviews for the final report in a course on Software Testing. The students however had experienced issues with peer reviews in a previous course which made this a challenge. To get a better understanding of the situation, we distributed a pre-questionnaire to the students and 48 of the 83 students provided their expectations on peer reviews. To deal with some of the perceived issues, we developed a peer review tool where we introduce anonymity, grading of reviews, teacher interventions, as well as let students score and comment on the reviews they receive. In total, 67 reports were submitted by 83 students and 325 reviews were completed. We also distributed a post-questionnaire and this was answered by 48 students. Results from our study show that 27 students expected incorrect feedback but only 13 students agreed to have got incorrect feedback. The students also reported that they found the feedback from their peers more valuable (+15%) than expected, and 88% of the students think they learned from doing peer reviews. There are still some issues with peer reviews but overall we find that the students' attitudes toward peer reviews have improved.

KEYWORDS

Peer Review, Peer Grading, Software Testing, Courseware

ACM Reference format:
Daniel Toll and Anna Wingkvist. 2017. How Tool Support and Peer Scoring Improved Our Students' Attitudes Toward Peer Reviews. In *Proceedings of ITiCSE'17, Bologna, Italy, July 03-05, 2017*, 6 pages.
DOI: http://dx.doi.org/10.1145/3059009.3059059

1 INTRODUCTION

The original idea was that we were interested in using peer review in a Software Testing course (7.5 ECTS). The course was run on 50% study pace over ten weeks during late autumn 2016. Our Computer Science students write test plan reports as a final assignment and these reports have in previous iterations of the course been read and graded by teachers. However, with more than 80 students, we felt that reviewing these reports will be too costly with respect to

time. Since we knew that the students had experienced peer reviews in a previous course and expressed some issues related to this, we needed to investigate further before implementation. They mentioned, for example, issues related to lack of anonymity, feedback, and motivation, but also fears of getting misleading feedback.

The aim to use peer review for this particular course is that students will receive feedback from each other while we as teachers can focus on the introduction of a tool, support the review process, resolve potential disputes, and deal with final grading. We also think the students would benefit from reviewing each other's work. They will learn to be independent and apply critical thinking since they need to judge the quality of other students test plan reports and motivate their standpoint.

Initially, we see two issues with letting students provide feedback. First, it can be argued that students do not have enough knowledge to review each other's work. Second, students may not want to put in the required effort to review, i.e., what Hamer et al. [3] call "rogue" reviewers. We handle the first issue by providing an assignment that is specific and well defined, so anyone who had the knowledge to complete the assignment should be able to review reports. We address the second issue by providing an incentive; reviewing other students' reports can result in a higher grade. This, in combination with multiple reviewers per report, should increase the chance that a report gets properly reviewed and that the overall feedback provided is relevant.

Additionally, students can respond to, and score, reviews they receive. They can rate a review as "Not even an attempt", "Failed", "Sufficient", "Good", and "Excellent". If a review is scored as "Failed" by a student, a teacher should intervene and resolve the dispute between the student and the reviewer. Note that the final *grading* is done by teachers, which is why we refer to the activity done by students as *scoring*.[1]

We present how we introduced a tool for peer review that supports anonymous scoring of reports, the possibility for students to score received reviews, teacher intervention when disputes occur, and teacher grading of both reviews and reports. Knowing that the students had experience with peer review from a previous course and expressed concerns made us cautious and curious. So, to understand the situation better, we wanted to know the students' expectations before the introduction of our tool. We also want to compare these expectations to their experiences after they tried the tool-supported peer review to see if the issues remained, and if so, to what extent.

We pose two research questions (RQ).

---

[1]In other papers this can be called marking, peer grading, etc

RQ1. What are the students' expectations of receiving feedback from their peers before and experiences with receiving feedback from their peers after tool-supported peer reviews?

RQ2. Are the students less worried about getting scored by their peers after they have used the peer review tool in a new course?

2 TOOL-SUPPORTED PEER REVIEW

We introduced a tool-supported peer review in a Software Testing course given during the second year of several computer science study programs at our university. The students were presented with a requirement specification and source code for a web server software, and their assignment was to test to what extent the provided requirements were implemented. The test effort is planned, executed, and documented in a report.

When the assignment started, the students formed groups of up to four students. The students then had four weeks to complete the testing and writing up the report. At the end of the four weeks, they submitted the report describing their work including a test strategy, a test plan, manual test cases that should cover the requirements, and the results of their test efforts. 55 of the 83 students who submitted a report decided to work alone and the rest of the students worked in groups.

A total of 67 documents were uploaded by the students, which were all peer reviewed using our tool. The peer review process is described below.

2.1 Review Instruction

Before the reviews could start, the teacher described how these were to be done, wrote an instruction, and decided scoring criteria. The review form was divided into three different scoring criteria. Each of the criteria had a description, a free text input field and a scoring rubric. The scoring rubrics had five different levels: "Not even an attempt", "Failed", "Sufficient", "Good", and "Excellent", and each level was described with a set of characteristics.

The first scoring criterion focused on the documents clarity, language, disposition, use of tables, headings, and images. The second scoring criterion focused on the completeness of the report, and the third and final scoring criterion focused on the thoroughness of the test effort. Further, to better explain the review, scoring, and grading process to the students, we recorded a short video on "How to be a helpful reviewer". The video was released a few days before the review phase, and described the overall process as well as how to review. During the review phase, the teachers supported the students by answering questions and participating in discussions on how to score through the messaging system Slack[2].

2.2 Uploading and Revising

The students were given individual access to the peer review tool from the course web page. Once they were logged in, they could upload their report, preview how it would appear to the reviewers, and revise it until the upload deadline had passed. We decided to use Markdown[3] for the reports, since students had previously used it

to document their source code repositories on GitHub[4]. We wanted an option for the students to create reports with headlines, anchor links, pictures, and tables that could easily be viewed within the tool.

2.3 Peer Reviews

The students began to review each other's work after the deadline had passed. When a student started the task of doing a new review, the peer review tool selected a random report from the set of reports that currently had the least amount of reviews, excluding the reviewers own report.

To get a passing grade, a student had to review at least two reports, but could review more to increase their chance of getting a higher grade. To get the highest grade, they needed to write at least four reviews. If they wrote more than four reviews, only the four highest graded reviews determined their grade. To remind students at risk of not getting a grade, we emailed all students that had not completed the two reviews one day before the review deadline.

2.4 Review Response

After the review deadline, students were given access to the reviews of their report. They should respond to each review with free text input and score how useful, correct, and thorough each review was. If a report has multiple authors, each of them should respond individually. The students were told to motivate their scoring of the review and that this information was helpful for the teacher that would grade the review.

2.5 Teacher Interventions and Grading

The teachers are responsible for grading and the general quality of the students' learning experience, so this should be supported by the peer review tool. The tool allows the teachers to browse through the submitted reports, reviews, and review responses. Since several students review each report, the teacher gets an overview of how each report was scored as well as how each of the report's reviews was scored.

We wanted to make it easy for the teachers to detect and handle potential disputes, so we introduced a number indicator that a teacher can use to decide if an intervention is needed or not. First, if a reviewer decides on a failing grade for a report or if an author marks a review as failed, this is clearly indicated (marked with red in the tool). The teacher can view the review as well as the author's response and determine if any of the students failed in their effort or if both are deemed to be adequate. A free text input is also provided.

Second, since several students review each report, the teachers' interface shows the minimum, median, and maximum score for each of the three grading criteria. This allows the teacher to investigate if any review significantly diverges from the median score, and if so, the reasons for the spread. Likewise, when several students collaborated on a report, their views of a review might also diverge.

The teacher sets two grades for each student; one for the report and one for the reviews. These are weighted into a final grade for the complete assignment.

---

[2]https://slack.com/
[3]https://daringfireball.net/projects/markdown/

---

[4]https://github.com

3 CAPTURE STUDENTS' EXPECTATIONS AND EXPERIENCE

We distributed a pre-questionnaire (to be answered anonymously) to capture the students' expectations of peer reviews. Furthermore, to investigate the students' experiences from using our tool-supported review process, we distributed a post-questionnaire (also to be answered anonymously). The students had completed their reviews when they answered the post-questionnaire, but no teacher interventions or grading had taken place.

We posed six statements in the pre-questionnaire and eight in the post-questionnaire. Answers were given on a five-grade Likert-scale: Strongly agree, Agree, Neutral, Disagree, and Strongly disagree. Statements that investigate before and after opinions are identified with .a in the pre-questionnaire and .b in the post-questionnaire.

- S1.a I think my peers can give me valuable feedback on my report.
- S2.a I'm afraid my peers will give me "incorrect" feedback on my report.
- S3.a I'm afraid my peers will give me "incorrect" scores on my report.
- S4.a I'm afraid I will give "incorrect" scores on another student's report.
- S5.a I think the teacher's feedback is more useful than my peer's feedback.
- S6 I look forward to reviewing other student's reports.

We also provided a free text option "Please share your view on peer reviews" to let students share their opinions on the use of peer reviews.

For the post-questionnaire we adjusted statements 1 to 5 from the pre-questionnaire to capture the students' experience after the peer review ended. We also added the same free text option for this questionnaire.

- S1.b I have received valuable feedback on my report by my peers.
- S2.b I have received "incorrect" feedback on my report by my peers.
- S3.b I have received "incorrect" scores on my report by my peers.
- S4.b I'm afraid I have scored other student's report incorrectly.
- S5.b I think the teacher's feedback is more useful than my peer's feedback.
- S7 It was fun to score other student's reports.
- S8 I learned from reading other students reports.

Statements S6 in the pre-questionnaire, and S7 and S8 in the post-questionnaire were adopted from Turner and Pérez-Quiñones [8], but reformulated to fit the assignment context.

4 RESULTS

The pre-questionnaire attracted 48 responses. In total, 325 reviews were written for 67 reports by 83 students. On average, a student wrote 4 reviews and received 5 reviews. One student completed 22 reviews! The post-questionnaire was distributed to the students after they responded to their reviews but before the teachers had graded their work. It was distributed to all students that had submitted a report. The number of students that responded was also 48. Note that this is not necessarily the same 48 students, since the questionnaires were answered anonymously. All responses to the statements can be seen in Table 1.

4.1 Received Valuable Feedback from Peers (S1)

In the pre-questionnaire, 28 students (58%) agreed or strongly agreed with that their peers can give valuable feedback (S1.a). 17 students were neutral and only three students disagreed.

In the post-questionnaire responses to S1.b, the number of students that agree to have received useful feedback rose to 35 (73%). Three students mentioned they got better reviews than they expected, and one wrote: "After receiving mostly good and honest feedback my attitude changed to be more positive".

4.2 Receive Incorrect Feedback from Peers (S2)

In the pre-questionnaire, seven students commented in the free text section that they had experienced getting poor feedback from peers and getting feedback that was contradictory. This is visible in S2.a, where 27 students (56%) agree that they are afraid of getting incorrect feedback. Only five students (10%) disagree. One student remarked that the motivation to do good reviews had dropped since they received poor quality reviews in a previous course.

In the post-questionnaire 13 (27%) students agree that they have received incorrect feedback while 24 (50%) students disagreed or strongly disagreed with this statement (S2.b).

4.3 Receive Incorrect Scores from Peers (S3)

More than half of the students (52%) in the pre-questionnaire feared receiving incorrect scores. One student even expressed that only teachers should score and grade students. In total, 15 (31%) students in the post-questionnaire agreed that they had experienced scoring that did not match their expectations. However, the number of students that disagreed improved from 5 (10%) in the pre-questionnaire to 24 (50%) after experiencing getting scores by their peers.

When it comes to students scoring students, the post-questionnaire revealed in the free text option that students experienced variation in the scores that they got from the reviewers and in one case the student wrote "got correct scores but for the wrong reasons".

4.4 Give Incorrect Scores to Peers (S4)

22 (46%) students worried about scoring other students incorrectly in the pre-questionnaire. This was reduced to 9 (19%) in the post-questionnaire. Two students mention concerns that their grading depends on how lucky they are to receive good reviews themselves and/or easy reports to review.

4.5 Teachers Feedback is More Valuable (S5)

The number of students that think the teacher's feedback is more valuable was comparable between the pre-questionnaire (30) and post-questionnaire (27) and thus remained around 60%. Two students mentioned the need for teachers to take a strong role in grading in the post-questionnaire; one of them wrote that he/she has confidence that it will happen in this case.

Table 1: Responses to the pre- and post- questionnaire. N=48

	S1.a	S1.b	S2.a	S2.b	S3.a	S3.b	S4.a	S4.b	S5.a	S5.b	S6	S7	S8
Strongly agree	7	5	4	1	4	2	2	2	5	4	12	12	17
Agree	21	30	23	12	21	13	20	7	18	20	18	15	25
Neutral	17	11	16	11	14	17	19	18	12	15	13	17	2
Disagree	3	2	4	22	7	15	5	18	7	5	3	4	2
Strongly disagree	0	0	1	2	2	1	2	3	6	4	2	0	2

4.6 Attitudes to Peer Review (S6) & Scoring (S7)

According to the pre-questionnaire, students generally liked peer reviews and considered reading each other's reports to be good for learning. Three students indicated that peer reviews increased their motivation to do a good job writing the report and that it is fun to do reviews since they get to share their expertise. 23 respondents (48%) looked forward to writing reviews while 13 respondents (27%) disagreed. Nearly identical numbers of students, i.e., 24 of the respondents (50%) thought scoring other students was fun in the post-questionnaire, while 9 students (19%) disagreed or strongly disagreed.

A student in the pre-questionnaire explained that their reason for poor motivation came from the need to invest a lot of time reading and reviewing other's reports. Since the reviews are taking place around Christmas, one student reported that they felt even less motivated to invest effort during this time of the year.

In the post-questionnaire three students mention that the process did require a lot of work, and one student suggested that they should not be required to do more than two reviews to get a good grade. One student wrote he/she felt motivated by the possibility of getting a better grade by writing more reviews.

4.7 Learned from Reviewing (S8)

In the post-questionnaire, 17 of the students strongly agreed and 25 students agreed to have learned from the process. Thus, in total 88% of the students state they learned from reviewing other students' reports. Three of the students also emphasized this in their free text responses.

5 VALIDITY

There are three main validity issues related to the way we collect information from our students.

First, in order to track actual changes in attitude for individual students, we need to pair responses from the pre- and post-questionnaires. Our anonymous questionnaire only allows us to study changes for the entire group, and not for individual students. Consequently, since the same students occur in both groups, the samples cannot be considered independent. Statistical tests for ordinal numbers with independent samples can however be used, but with less power to detect significant results. We use Mann-Whitney U test[5] to check for statistical significance.

Second, the populations sampled are not exactly the same, since we only distributed the post-questionnaire to students that submitted a report. So, any attitude changes might result from students

[5]This can also be called a Wilcoxon rank-sum test

who were most against peer reviews dropped out before trying the tool. However, we have seen no such indication and students that dropped out cited other reasons.

Third, in the pre-questionnaire, we ask about the students' fear of something and in the post-questionnaire we ask about their experience of it occurring. Thus, it can be argued that if a student fears something and it did not occur during the peer review, they might still fear it. The free text responses show several attitude changes for the better, but one student wrote that this experience had not changed his or her (negative) view.

6 DISCUSSION

Bauer et al. [1], Hamer et al. [3], Orsmond et al. [5], Sondergaard [7] have all investigated the drawbacks and benefits of peer reviews in the context of computer science education. These all investigate students' attitude *after* the review process. We also investigate whether the students' attitudes toward the peer review process were changed.

Sondergaard [7] used online peer reviews in a course on compiler construction, where students had to review source code written by other students. He reports that students found the peer review task very valuable and that it particularly helped them to better understand their own progress in the course. 79% felt that other students' feedback was useful. His students had the non-mandatory option of commenting on the reviewer's reviews, similar to what we do in our study. The student's view of this option was however not investigated in detail. In our study, only two students disagreed to have received valuable feedback (S1) while 72% of the students agreed or strongly agreed. This is an increase of 15% compared to the pre-questionnaire. Therefore, we think our students found value in each other's feedback. This is close to the findings of Bauer et al., where students expressed that they found their peers competent, thorough, and helpful. Bauer et al. [1] investigated how students perceived online peer reviews in a computer science course on scientific writing. In a questionnaire, the students reported that online peer reviews were a very positive experience, that reading other students' work changed their perception of their own work, and that they became more confident in the quality of their own work. Similarly, our students reported that they felt it useful to see how other solved the same problem as they had been working on.

Smith et al. [6] used peer reviews as part of a testing course. Their students, like ours, submitted double-blind reviews and wrote a report on what they learned from the review process and from evaluating the received peer reviews. However, in their case, the teachers were grading the reviews without peer scoring. Smith et al. found that 90% of their students reported to have learned from doing peer reviews. Similar values were reported by Sondergaard, and in our study (S8), we found that 88% students agreed or strongly agreed to have learned from the experience. We think the outcome is similar since the act of reviewing is somewhat universal, albeit a difference of assignment, process, and tools.

Our results and the other studies cited above clearly suggests that there are benefits of using online peer reviews. There are however a number of problems that needs to be addressed, especially when the students are also scoring each other's as pointed out by Hamer et al. [3]:

(1) Assignments and reviews have to be distributed and collected in an efficient way.
(2) Anonymity must be ensured.
(3) Validity and reliability of the scoring must be ensured.
(4) Scoring disputes must be dealt with.
(5) The students must be motivated to take the review task seriously.
(6) The effect of rogue reviewers, i.e., reviewers who do not take the task seriously and submit bad and misleading reviews, must be minimized.
(7) Plagiarism must be detected and handled.

Problem 1 is addressed by our online tool for distributing and submitting reviews. Regarding anonymity (problem 2), 13% of the respondents of the questionnaire used by Bauer et al. [1] would have judged differently if they were absolutely anonymous. We ensure double-blind anonymity in our tool and think it allows the students to write what they think.

According to Moskal et al. [4], scoring validity (problem 3) can be achieved using scoring rubrics. Scoring rubrics means that instead of giving one total score on what is reviewed, the reviewers rate their level of agreement on a number of aspects using, e.g., a Likert-scale. Moskal et al. [4] point out several benefits of using scoring rubrics:

- Students know how they will be scored before submitting their assignment, typically resulting in higher quality submissions.
- It can help teachers track the knowledge development of students over time.
- The total score on a submission differed only slightly between different reviewers, increasing the reliability of the peer review task.

Falchikov [2] argues that peer scoring with marks has little meaning if the peer who scores has no knowledge about the standards. Using scoring rubrics helps the students know what standard is expected of their submissions.

We used scoring rubrics to addresses problem 3. We also used statistical tests to analyze if the use of our rubrics was adequate. In the pre-questionnaire, 25 students (52%) expected to receive incorrect scores (S3), however only 15 students (31%) experienced it. In Figure 1, we see that more students disagree to have received incorrect scores than expected it in the pre-questionnaire. A Mann-Whitney U Test suggests a statistically significant difference in that fewer students experienced incorrect scoring than expected it ($U = 673, p < 0.01$). We investigated the students free text answers, and they state that receiving variation in scores lowers their confidence for using peer reviews, which we interpret as the

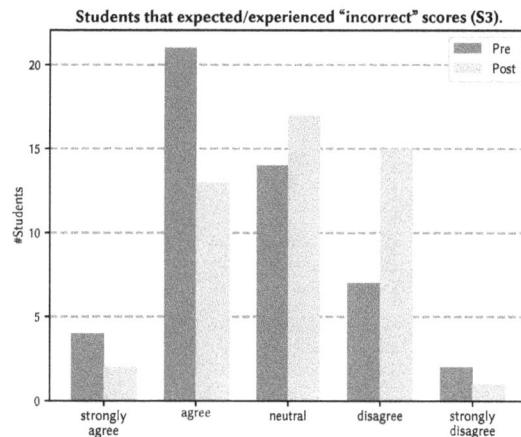

Figure 1: More students expected to receive incorrect scores from their peers (pre) than experienced it (post).

scores given were either not properly motivated or students simply did not agree with the motivations. Orsmond et al. [5] studied peer scoring and found that clear scoring criteria is very important to get consistent results. Therefore, we think that our scoring rubrics could be made more specific and with better instructions to increase the reliability of the peer scoring. However, it was noted that our students gained confidence in giving scores and fewer students experienced problems scoring other students than expected it (S4). A Mann-Whitney U Test suggests a statistically significant change ($U = 489.5, p < 0.01$).

Note that teacher interventions, i.e., where incorrect scores were removed, happened after the post-questionnaire was completed. We expect that the students' experience concerning scoring will improve when scoring disputes are resolved by the teachers.

To motivate the students (problem 5), the peer review task (minimum of doing two reviews) was mandatory to pass the assignment and students could increase their chances of getting a higher grade by doing more reviews.

Our strategy to minimize the effect of rogue reviewers (problem 6) is to let the authors of a report score each review. This score guides the teacher to investigate the review. A bad review can be disqualified and this can be seen by both author and reviewer. With this transparency we hope to ensure the validity and reliability of the review process (problem 3) to the students. This strategy also addresses the problem of scoring disputes (problem 4). If scores differ much for a submission, the teachers can investigate the reasons for this and suggest a consensus.

The expectations of receiving incorrect feedback was high (S2) with five students disagreeing and 27 students agreeing to this in the pre-questionnaire. The number of students who agreed with having received incorrect feedback in the post-questionnaire was 13. A Mann-Whitney U Test suggests that fewer students experienced incorrect feedback than expected it ($U = 462, p < 0.01$). Half of the post-questionnaire respondents disagree with having experienced incorrect feedback. This can also be seen in Figure 2, where a shift towards disagreement is evident. Therefore, we think that the

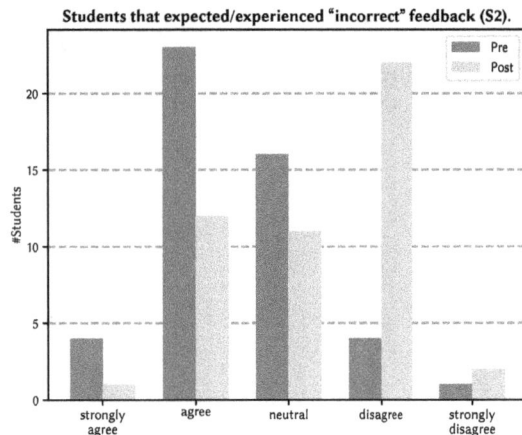

Figure 2: More students expected to receive incorrect feedback from their peers (pre) than experienced it (post).

scoring of reviews motivated our students to spend more time and to write better reviews.

The total number of students that agreed with having experienced either a bad review or an incorrect score (or both) from one of their peers was 20 (41%). This shows that these problems are still widespread and that a large number of students experience them. The teachers resolved conflicts between authors and reviewers 19 times (28%) on 17 different documents. In total, the teachers detected, inspected, and resolved 78 feedback and grading issues for 40 (60%) of the submitted reports. Therefore, we hope that the impact of those bad reviews were minimized. When we compare the students responses on "if the teachers feedback is more valuable" (S5), we can see no significant difference. However, this is to be expected since the teachers had not given any feedback when the post-questionnaire data was collected.

When we investigate the students' attitude towards peer review (S6) and scoring (S7), only 50% were positive. Considering the tool and our efforts, we expected better numbers. But, as one student mentioned, the reviews took place over Christmas and involved a lot of work therefore we think this could be the reason why only 50% were positive.

Plagiarism (problem 7) is currently not dealt within our review tool. We do however have plans of considering it in the future.

7 CONCLUSIONS

From prior knowledge, answers, and analysis of statements S1, S2, S5, S6, and S8 as well as from the free text we find that the student group had experienced problems with peer reviews before taking part of the tool-supported peer review process. It was clear that many students expected problems with bad feedback (RQ1). A third of the students experienced at least one bad review. However, all students got a minimum of three reviews and on average five reviews, so it is unlikely that a student got only bad reviews.

The responses to statements S3, S4, and S7 showed that students had concerns on giving and receiving scores from their peers. The

post-questionnaire results indicate that fewer students actually experienced problems (RQ2). However, students experienced a variation in their scores, and a third of the students reported that they got at least one incorrect score. We therefore conclude that we need to improve our instructions and scoring rubrics.

We find that the overall attitude toward peer reviews did improve and students experienced fewer issues than they expected.

8 FUTURE WORK

While scoring reviews seemed to motivate our students, we are concerned that students thought it was easier to get a high grade on their reviews if the report they reviewed had obvious flaws. We plan to investigate the factors that affected the students' grades in more detail using data collected with the tool. We also want to investigate different means of improving the review process, such as adding a checklist to the review instructions. This was suggested by one student in the post-questionnaire.

We aim to improve our research method in three ways for our next study. First, we want to make sure the pre- and post-questionnaires are comparable. Second, we aim to make sure the questionnaire respondents can be tracked anonymously between the pre- and post-questionnaire, perhaps with a unidirectional code. Third, we want to separate questions into tool-, process-, and learning benefit-statements. Since many students reported that peer reviews stimulated their learning it would be interesting to investigate more in detail what learning benefits students actually perceived.

Finally, to improve the peer review system itself we plan to include handling plagiarism and support more languages and formats.

ACKNOWLEDGMENTS

We want to express our appreciation to Johan Hagelbäck who provided valuable feedback to the research. We are also grateful to Morgan Ericsson who moderated this paper and in that line improved the text significantly.

REFERENCES

[1] Christine Bauer, Kathrin Figl, Michael Derntl, Peter Paul Beran, and Sonja Kabicher. 2009. The Student View on Online Peer Reviews. In *Proceedings of the 14th Annual ACM SIGCSE Conference on Innovation and Technology in Computer Science Education (ITiCSE '09)*. 26–30.
[2] N. Falchikov. 2007. *The place of peers in learning and assessment. In D. Boud and N. Falchikov, editors, Rethinking Assessment in Higher Education: Learning for the Longer Term*. Routledge.
[3] John Hamer, Kenneth T. K. Ma, and Hugh H. F. Kwong. 2005. A Method of Automatic Grade Calibration in Peer Assessment. In *Proceedings of the 7th Australasian Conference on Computing Education - Volume 42 (ACE '05)*. 67–72.
[4] Barbara Moskal, Keith Miller, and Laurie A. Smith King. 2002. Grading Essays in Computer Ethics: Rubrics Considered Helpful. In *Proceedings of the 33rd SIGCSE technical symposium on Computer science education (SIGCSE '02)*. 101–105.
[5] Paul Orsmond, Stephen Merry, and Kevin Reiling. 1996. The Importance of Marking Criteria in the Use of Peer Assessment. *Assessment & Evaluation in Higher Education* 21, 3 (1996), 239–250.
[6] Joanna Smith, Joe Tessler, Elliot Kramer, and Calvin Lin. 2012. Using Peer Review to Teach Software Testing. In *Proceedings of the Ninth Annual International Conference on International Computing Education Research (ICER '12)*. 93–98.
[7] Harald Sondergaard. 2009. Learning from and with Peers: The Different Roles of Student Peer Reviewing. In *Proceedings of the 14th Annual ACM SIGCSE Conference on Innovation and Technology in Computer Science Education (ITiCSE '09)*. 31–35.
[8] Scott A. Turner and Manuel A. Pérez-Quiñones. 2009. Exploring Peer Review in the Computer Science Classroom. *ArXiv e-prints* (July 2009). arXiv:cs.CY/0907.3456

Evaluating Test Suite Effectiveness and Assessing Student Code via Constraint Logic Programming

Kyle Dewey
UC Santa Barbara
kyledewey@cs.ucsb.edu

Phill Conrad
UC Santa Barbara
pconrad@cs.ucsb.edu

Michelle Craig
University of Toronto
mcraig@cs.toronto.edu

Elena Morozova
UC Santa Barbara
emorozova@umail.ucsb.edu

ABSTRACT

A good suite of test inputs is an indispensable tool both for manual and automated assessment of student submissions to programming assignments. Yet, without a way to evaluate our test suites, it is difficult to know how well we are doing, much less improve our practice. We present a technique for evaluating a hand-generated test suite by comparing its ability to find defects against that of a test suite generated automatically using Constraint Logic Programming (CLP). We describe our technique and present a case study using student submissions for an assignment from a second-year programming course. Our results show that a CLP-generated test suite was able to identify significant defects that the instructor-generated suite missed, despite having similar code coverage.

ACM Reference format:
Kyle Dewey, Phill Conrad, Michelle Craig, and Elena Morozova. 2017. Evaluating Test Suite Effectiveness and Assessing Student Code via Constraint Logic Programming. In *Proceedings of ITiCSE'17, July 03-05, 2017, Bologna, Italy,*, 6 pages.
DOI: http://dx.doi.org/10.1145/3059009.3059051

1 INTRODUCTION

To evaluate student submissions to programming assignments, we need a good set of test cases. This is certainly true when assessing student code by hand, and even more crucial when assessment is automated. As course enrollments grow, so has the use of automated assessment tools, sometimes called *autograders* [8, 20]. An ideal test suite for either manual or automated grading would be able to (a) provide helpful information on in-progress student work to detect and diagnose defects, and (b) differentiate between student solutions in a way that maps to student learning so that instructors can assign an appropriate distribution of grades.

In practice, however, instructors have limited time to devote to developing test suites for their course assignments. Moreover, instructors often update assignments over time, be it for improving

the assignment, altering learning objectives, preventing previous solutions from being dishonestly proliferated, or otherwise. The end result is that gaps can be easily introduced in a test suite, leading to overlooked edge cases and untested behaviors. By their very nature, these gaps are elusive and difficult to pinpoint, as tests fundamentally can only spot problems one is looking for.

We observe that the problem of developing better test suites and testing techniques is well-studied in Software Engineering, with a variety of automated techniques being employed. These approaches have found several thousand bugs in popular software like gcc, clang, and Mozilla FireFox [6, 11–13, 21]. Most importantly, these bugs have been found in software which has been heavily tested manually with extensive handwritten test suites. As such, these sort of automated testing techniques are well-suited to our problem of finding gaps in a traditional handcrafted test suite.

Building on this research, we applied an automated testing technique based on *Constraint Logic Programming* (CLP [9], explained in Section 3) to the automated generation of a test suite for a programming assignment (described in Section 4) from a Sophomore-level Java course. The assignment is complex, requiring students to implement non-trivial modifications to the tokenization, parsing, and evaluation components of an interpreter for infix arithmetic expressions. Moreover, the assignment has a history of modification and it features a large handwritten test suite authored jointly by two course instructors. For these reasons, it serves as an excellent case study in seeing where the gaps lie in its existing tests.

This case study (described in Section 5) has revealed a number of deficiencies in the handwritten tests, with a multitude of defects being found by the automated tests which were not spotted by the manual tests. We confirmed via manual code inspection that these defects can be tied to real bugs in student code which were missed by the handwritten test suite. We also found that the tests passed and failed by the automated test suite were instrumental in grouping student solutions with similar behaviors.

The contributions of this paper are (1) a description of how to apply CLP to automatically produce a test suite for an interpreter's tokenizer, parser, and evaluator components (2) a technique for evaluating a handwritten test suite's defect-finding effectiveness by comparison against an automatically-generated test suite (3) a case study of this technique for a non-trivial sophomore-level Java assignment, demonstrating its effectiveness.

This work was supported by NSF CCF-1319060.

2 RELATED WORK

At many campuses, Computer Science course enrollments are increasing faster than resources available to instructors; we are being asked to evaluate more student work in the same amount of time. Wilcox et al. [20] argues that "carefully designed and managed automation can improve student performance while realizing a significant savings of scarce teaching resources."

Tillmann et al. [17] created Pex4Fun, which is a non-traditional solution to grading in Massive Open Online Courses. Pex4Fun incorporates automated grading based on symbolic execution. Gulwani et al. [5] attempt to address the tedious process of manually creating tests by developing a tool that generates feedback on the performance of student programs. The tool is a light-weight programming language extension that uses dynamic analysis. Singh et al. [15] devised a new method for giving feedback to incorrect student solutions. They created a language which describes correction rules for a specific student solution. Their method requires that the instructor provide a reference implementation of the assignment solution. Ihantola [7] applied an automatic test data generation tool named *Java Pathfinder* [18] to automatic assessment and found that symbolic execution with lazy initialization can be used to generate test data directly from student programs.

CLP was first introduced in Jaffar et al. [9], as a general framework encompassing logic programming languages such as Prolog [16]. For the purposes of this paper, CLP is viewable fundamentally as Prolog with some convenient extensions. The work of Dewey et al. [1–3] discusses how CLP can be applied to generating test suites for a variety of domains, including language interpreters [2], data structure APIs [1], and typecheckers [3]. While Dewey et al. uses CLP for the purposes of testing, a significant amount of CLP code must be written for the particular domain which is to be tested. While CLP has shown itself to be effective for testing large industrial applications, we are not aware of any work describing its application to evaluating student code, nor has it specifically been applied to testing tokenizers or parsers.

3 TEST SUITE GENERATION VIA CLP

This section discusses why and how we use CLP for generating test suites for language tokenizers, parsers, and evaluators. We start first with some background on CLP-based test suite generation.

3.1 Background on CLP-Based Testing

Programming languages allow one to use code to specify how outputs should be derived from inputs, and in this respect, CLP is no different from more traditional languages.

What makes CLP interesting for our purposes is that, intuitively, this same derivation process can be run in *reverse*, as well as being run with no initial inputs or outputs whatsoever. That is, CLP can be used *both* to derive the inputs corresponding to some given outputs, as well as derive entire valid input/output pairs. From a high level, this is possible with CLP because CLP code describes a series of logical constraints relating inputs to outputs. These constraints can be efficiently explored via a multitude of existing CLP engines (e.g., SWI-PL [19] and GNU Prolog [4]), allowing for the generation of whole input/output pairs which satisfy the constraints. The technical details behind how this is possible is

$$Exp ::= AddExp$$
$$AddExp ::= PrimExp \mid PrimExp \text{ '-' } AddExp$$
$$PrimExp ::= \text{ '0' } \mid \text{ '1' } \mid \text{ '(' } Exp \text{ ')' } \mid \text{ '-' } PrimExp$$

Figure 1: Small grammar used for running CLP example.

beyond the scope of this discussion, but it has been well-described elsewhere (e.g., [9, 16]).

This capability of CLP to derive valid input/output pairs of a program lies at the heart of CLP-based testing (e.g., [1–3]). For our specific purposes, from a high level this entails first implementing a *reference solution* in CLP, which only differs from a traditional reference solution in the fact that CLP is used as the implementation language. The CLP-based reference solution can then be used to derive valid input/output pairs which will stress different parts of the solution. In a straightforward manner, these input/output pairs can then be applied to testing student solutions, where the input in a pair specifies a test input, and the output of a pair specifies the expected test result. A specific example of how this is done for a tokenizer is presented in Section 3.2.

The aforementioned strategy has one weakness, however: we will never produce a test with no output, as when an invalid input has been passed to the program. It is not possible to derive invalid inputs via this mechanism, as by definition there is no way to relate them to valid outputs. For our purposes, this is unfortunate, as invalid inputs are useful for testing that student error-checking routines exist and behave as intended; therefore a different approach is needed for generating invalid inputs.

To this end, we employ *mutation-based fuzz testing* (e.g, [6]), which starts with arbitrary valid inputs. These valid inputs are then *mutated* in some way by intentionally injecting something which is guaranteed to make it invalid. The invalid inputs produced are suitable for testing, and all should trigger error-checking routines in the student solutions. While more sophisticated approaches are possible (e.g., generating invalid inputs by construction [3]), the approach used here is both simple and effective for finding faults in student solutions. Further discussion of how this is done for a tokenizer and a parser is presented in Section 3.3.

3.2 Generating Valid Inputs

This subsection discusses how we use CLP to test language tokenizers, parsers, and evaluators. Throughout this subsection, we use a running example based on the grammar shown in Figure 1, with the corresponding tokens 0 (zero), 1 (one), - (minus), ((left parentheses) and) (right parentheses). While this grammar is admittedly simple, it serves to illustrate all the applicable core concepts, and it forms a subset of the grammar used in the case study.

An executable CLP-based tokenizer applicable to tokenizing the grammar in Figure 1 is presented in Figure 2. The charToToken helper procedure simply maps characters to their token representations. The tokenize procedure in Figure 2 consists of two *rules*. The first rule states that if there are no characters to tokenize, then there are no tokens produced. The second rule states that if the

```
% charToToken: Character, Token
charToToken('0', token_zero).
charToToken('1', token_one).
charToToken('-', token_minus).
charToToken('(', token_lparen).
charToToken(')', token_rparen).

% tokenize: Characters, Tokens
tokenize([], []).              % tokenize rule 1
tokenize([SingleChar|Chars],   % tokenize rule 2
        [SingleToken|Tokens]) :-
    charToToken(SingleChar, SingleToken),
    tokenize(Chars, Tokens).
```

Notation: % indicates end of line comments. [] is empty list. [A|B]
  is a list, with head A and rest of list B. tokenize takes two
  parameters: a list of characters, and a list of tokens produced.

Figure 2: CLP-based tokenizer for language of Figure 1.

character input begins with a single character, then the tokens produced begin with a single token, where the token is derived from the charToToken helper procedure. Furthermore, the second rule recursively calls tokenize to process the rest of the input. While we have kept this illustrative example as simple as possible, it is straightforward to add CLP code to allow for whitespace, integers with multiple digits, and multiple-character tokens, all of which appear in the actual assignment used in our case study.

When given a valid input list of characters, the tokenize routine behaves as follows (where lines starting with ?- indicate something typed by the user at a prompt for a typical CLP engine):

```
?- tokenize(['1', '-', '0'], Tokens).
Tokens = [token_one, token_minus, token_zero].
?- tokenize(['(', '-', '1', ')'], Tokens).
Tokens = [token_lparen, token_minus, token_one,
          token_rparen].
```

With an invalid input, the engine instead returns false, indicating the input could not be successfully tokenized. For example, the engine cannot tokenize the input below, because + is not a valid token according to the language in Figure 1:

```
?- tokenize(['1', '+', '1'], Tokens).
false.
```

As previously discussed, this CLP-based solution can be used to generate input/output pairs. For example, the code below will derive all inputs of length 4, along with their corresponding lists of tokens:

```
?- length(Input, 4), tokenize(Input, Tokens).
Input = ['0', '0', '0', '0'],
Tokens = [token_zero, token_zero, token_zero,
          token_zero] ... % many more elided
```

This capability to automatically generate valid inputs lies at the heart of CLP's power for test case generation.

The parser for these tokens using a standard recursive-descent style can similarly be implemented in CLP, as well as a typical pre-order-based recursive expression evaluator. Because these components do not significantly differ in style from the aforementioned tokenizer example, they have been omitted for space reasons.

3.3 Generating Invalid Inputs

For generating invalid inputs for the tokenizer, we insert characters which will never yield valid tokens into an otherwise tokenizable stream of characters. Specifically, we insert $, = (ensuring it does not follow either > or <), =>, and =<. The character $ was chosen arbitrarily as a representative of an unconditionally invalid character, and the rest of the characters were chosen as they intuitively seem more likely to trigger faults in a buggy tokenizer. For generating invalid inputs for the parser, we first produce a valid list of tokens which can be parsed to form a valid expression. We then insert an arbitrary valid token into the list, either an integer 0 or 2 (arbitrarily chosen), or any other one of a finite list of remaining valid tokens. Because this process may still yield a parsable list of tokens (as when negating a subexpression), we run the CLP-based parser on the newly generated input to ensure that it **fails**, thus ensuring the input is invalid. While these approaches to generating invalid inputs for the tokenizer and parser are simplistic, we have nonetheless found them to be effective at finding faults in student code.

As for the evaluator, relatively few things act as invalid inputs. By construction, the AST definition in both the Java and CLP reference solutions does not allow for the construction of ASTs which are in any way invalid. With this in mind, the only significant edge case which can be safely deemed "invalid" is that of cases which trigger division by zero, which is supposed to be checked beforehand by student solutions. We observed that a significant number of the generated valid parser outputs (ASTs produced as described in Section 3.2) would attempt to perform division by zero. As such, if we simply re-used these ASTs as inputs to the evaluator, along with a record of what the AST should evaluate to (be it a number or a trigger for division by zero).

4 THE PROGRAMMING ASSIGNMENT

The programming assignment used as a case study was given in a second-year programming course in advanced application programming. Students were given code for a working interpreter of infix arithmetic expressions, with separate Java classes for (1) a finite-state-automaton based tokenizer (and classes for various kinds of tokens), (2) a recursive descent parser that corresponded exactly to the grammar given and produced an Abstract Syntax Tree (AST) (and classes for various AST nodes) (3) a straightforward interpreter based on a pre-order traversal of the AST.

To simplify the assignment, it was assumed that all constants and expressions would be of type integer. The given code was capable of interpreting expressions involving addition (+), subtraction (-), multiplication (*), integer division (/), unary minus (-), and parentheses (()). The students were also given a grammar in EBNF for the language supported by the interpreter, shown in Figure 3. The students were then required to add support for six relational operators, (<, <=, >, >=, ==, !=) (each of which returns either 0 or 1 based on the truth value of the comparison), as well as exponentiation (**), as reflected in the modified grammar of Figure 4.

```
expr     ::= add-expr
add-expr ::= mult-expr ( ( '+' | '-' ) mult-expr ) *
mult-expr ::= primary ( ( '*' | '/' ) primary ) *
primary  ::= '(' expr ')' | INTEGER | '-' primary
```

Figure 3: Given EBNF grammar

```
expr     ::= comp-expr
comp-op  ::= '==' | '!=' | '<' | '<=' | '>' | '>='
comp-expr ::= add-expr ( comp-op add-expr ) *
add-expr ::= mult-expr ( ( '+' | '-' ) mult-expr ) *
mult-expr ::= exp-expr ( ( '*' | '/' ) exp-expr ) *
exp-expr ::= primary '**' exp-expr | primary
primary  ::= '(' expr ')' | INTEGER | '-' primary
```

Figure 4: Modified EBNF grammar

The intent of requiring students to add this particular set of new features was that they necessitated the students to be able to handle two cases that are not in the starting code: (1) tokens involving multiple characters—especially tokens where one valid token is a prefix of another valid token (e.g. < prefix of <=, * prefix of **), (2) a right-associative binary operator (exponentiation); all binary operators in the starting code are left-associative.

5 THE CASE STUDY

During Fall 2016, students submitted solutions which were then autograded via a traditional handcrafted test suite composed of 230 tests. The assignment had an option for either individual or pair submission. The study is based on 48 submissions where either the sole author or both partners gave informed consent.

We then used the CLP-based technique described in Section 3 to generate a test suite composed of 7,291,812 tests, specifically tests focused on the tokenizer, parser, and evaluator for the grammar from Figure 4. Where possible, the same test input was reused to test multiple components. For example, consider the following test input:

$$1 - 1$$

This input should tokenize, parse, and evaluate successfully down to the value 0. As such, it can be used to test each component individually; that is, the characters serve as a tokenizer test, the tokens corresponding to it serve as a parser test, and the expression produced by the parser serves as an evaluator test. If a solution failed part of the tokenizer to parser to evaluator chain, a correct intermediate form was substituted so the remaining components could be individually tested.

We first ran both test suites on the instructor's own Java reference solution. The CLP code corresponding to the Java reference solution was intentionally **not** coded by the same individual, to reduce the likelihood of the Java and CLP reference solutions sharing common bugs. The instructor's solution passed 100% of both the hand-crafted tests and the CLP-generated tests, indicating that the CLP solution was correct and not marking any outputs incorrectly as valid or invalid.

We then ran both the hand-crafted and the CLP-generated tests against the student solutions. Our raw data, therefore, consisted

of results for 230 hand-crafted tests and just over seven million CLP-generated tests for each of the 48 student solutions. Looking at the data, the following conclusions were immediately reached:

- There was no case where a solution passed all of the CLP-based tests, but failed at least one of the handcrafted tests.
- Of the 40 solutions that passed all of the 230 handcrafted tests, only 30 of those passed all 7,291,812 of the CLP-based tests. This alone was a clear indication that the CLP-based suite detected at least one defect that the handcrafted tests did not.

Eight of the solutions failed tests on both the handcrafted test suite and the CLP-based test suite. Because failures occurred on both test suites for these solutions, a more sophisticated approach was necessary in order to draw any meaningful conclusions.

5.1 Test Suite Comparison via Equivalence Classes

We observe that solutions can be separated into equivalence classes based on the tests they fail. That is, it is common for multiple solutions to fail the exact same set of tests, suggesting that different solutions share the same underlying defects.

We first partitioned the 48 solutions on the basis of which tests were failed on the handcrafted tests, which yielded only six equivalence classes. These six classes are shown visually in the top half of Figure 5. There were:

- three singleton classes
- one class of two solutions
- one class of three solutions
- one class of 40 solutions—these are the solution that failed none of the hand-crafted tests

While the small number of equivalence classes may raise the question of plagiarism, follow-up with MOSS [14] showed that plagiarism alone cannot account for this effect.

Partitioning the 48 solutions based on which tests were failed by the CLP-based test suite resulted in a a further refinement of these six equivalence classes were further refined into thirteen classes, as shown in the bottom half of Figure 5. The partitions produced via the CLP-based test suite are represented visually by the arrows in Figure 5. Each division represents a case where the CLP-based tests are potentially revealing something that the manual test suite missed.

The set of solutions that passes all of the CLP tests contains only 30 solutions; ten of the solutions from the original equivalence class of 40 failed some of the CLP-based tests, resulting in four additional equivalence classes. The original classes of two and three were also further split into singletons. Each of these splits represents a case where the CLP-based tests were able to more distinguish among solutions with finer granularity, thus potentially revealing additional defects missed by the manual test suite.

5.2 Code Inspection

We did a manual code inspection of representative solutions from both sides of each equivalence class split to learn more about what these splits signified. It is tempting to assume that each such split indicates a new bug or set of bugs. Our explorations show that

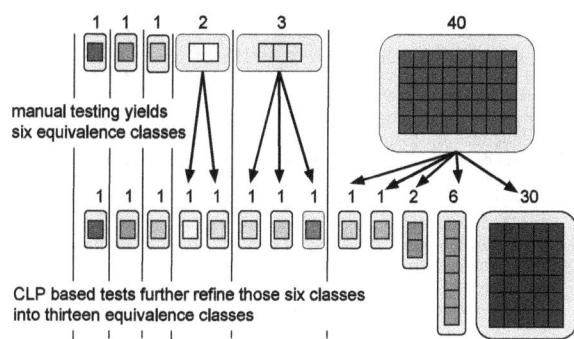

Figure 5: Equivalence classes of student submissions, based on which tests they failed.

this is often, though not always the case. The other possibility is that the solutions have made similar errors but errors that differ enough in the particular way they are incorrect, such that they pass different numbers of tests. However, each division did offer some insight into ways in which students approached the problem, and the types of mistakes they made in their code.

The original large equivalence class of 40 students is broken up five ways, overall revealing that 10 students who passed all the handcrafted tests nonetheless still had bugs in their code (an indication that if the test suite had been more powerful, there may have been more rigor and fairness in the grades assigned). These 10 were divided into two singletons, a pair, and a group of 6. One of the singletons was a solution that, although it was correct from the standpoint of an end user, failed many parser tests because the testing code relied on the .equals() method of one of the student-defined AST classes to work properly (when comparing actual vs. expected results), however the student failed to override this method. This was a case where the handcrafted test suite was deficient. The three remaining classes were all characterized by various errors involving negative exponents, bringing to light the fact that the instructors had completely overlooked testing for the cases of zero and negative exponents (focusing the manual tests instead on the right-associativity of the operator).

Students that correctly handled the exponent operator used a variety of approaches. Some students computed a value using Java's Math.pow() method and then cast the result to an integer value. Others used loops that did repeated multiplication for non-negative exponents, and repeated division for negative exponents. With these loops, some handled x^0 as a special case while others initialized a product value to 1, and then used a loop to repeatedly multiply by the base of the exponent (so that zero iterations of the loop naturally returns the correct value).

Figures 6, 7, and 8 show three incorrect approaches to computing exponents with loops all taken from the group of 40, each passing a different number of CLP-based tests. Figure 6 correctly computes positive and zero exponents, and has an incorrect attempt at negative exponents. Figure 7 correctly calculates positive and zero exponents, but has no code for negative exponents. Figure 8 calculates only positive exponents correctly.

There were two other equivalence classes that were further partitioned by the CLP-based testing: an equivalence class of two,

```
// calculate left ** right
int result = left;
if (right == 0) {
  return 1;
}
else if (right < 0) {
  for (int i = 0; i < (right * -1)-1; i++) {
    result = result / left;
  }
  return result;
} else {
  for (int i = 0; i < right-1; i++) {
    result = result * left;
  }
  return result;
}
```

Figure 6: Incorrect approach to negative exponents

```
// calculate base**exp
int result = 1;
for (int i=0; i<exp; i++)
  result *= base;
return result;
```

Figure 7: Does not handle negative exp

```
// calculate left ** right
int x = left;
for(int i = 1; i < right; i++) {
  x = x * left;
}
return x;
```

Figure 8: Handles neither 0 nor negative exponents

and one of three, each of which was refined into singletons by the CLP-based testing. Code inspection of the class of two solutions revealed that both of the solutions failed the hand-written tests for both the new comparison operators and the exponentiation operator. What distinguished one solution was an error in the finite state automaton; it failed to recognize that the * token was a prefix of the ** token, and did not set up a state transition from the state for the multiplication operator to the state for the exponentiation operator.

The equivalence class of three solutions was refined further by CLP-generated tests into three singletons. All three solutions shared a common bug related to an improperly structured if/else. The first of these had a bug not found in the other two, related to an issue of == vs. .equals() for objects. All three had problems related to calculation of exponents, but the third solution handled an exponent of 0 correctly, in contrast to the first two solutions.

Our overall conclusion is that while each division between equivalence classes is an interesting place to look for defects, it is not necessarily the case that each corresponds to a particular discrete bug. This sort of difficulty in defining exactly what "bug" means is a known problem in Software Engineering research (e.g., [10]), and this work makes this apparent in the context of educational assessment.

5.3 Test Suite Code Coverage

While the CLP-based test suite exposed clear deficiencies in the handcrafted test suite, we wondered as to whether or not these deficiencies could have been discovered ahead of time with a more traditional approach. To this end, we measured average code coverage across all students for the two test suites. For the handcrafted test suite, we observed an average line coverage of 77%, an average method coverage of 74%, and an average branch coverage of 62%. For the CLP-based test suite, we observed an improvement of three percentage points for average line coverage (80%), an improvement of nine percentage points for average method coverage (83%), and no improvement in average branch coverage (62%). For all coverage metrics, the relatively low values can be uniformly explained by the presence of debugging-oriented code, as well as methods which are good practice to implement but not directly under test (e.g., hashCode(), toString(), and equals()). It is difficult to fairly prune out such code, because some students did nonetheless use it during testing.

As shown, while the CLP-based test suite tended to get better code coverage than the handcrafted test suite, the improvements are often marginal at best. This leads us to conclude that code coverage can be a misleading measure of a test suite's effectiveness. This motivates the direct measurement of the defect-finding power of a test suite, as can be done through our CLP-based approach.

6 CONCLUSIONS AND FUTURE WORK

Our case study shows that a CLP-based approach that generates millions of test cases can be used to expose weaknesses in a hand-crafted test suite for a programming assignment. Sifting through the millions of test cases results might seem daunting, but we have shown that by focusing on the differences among representative solutions from different equivalence classes, considerable insight can be gained into test-suite deficiencies, and student errors.

There are two major limitations to this work which we seek to address in future work: unfamiliarity with CLP programming and scalability. To address the first of these, we propose to develop a targeted Prolog/CLP tutorial for instructors who want to apply the technique, or even a domain-specific language which compiles to CLP, allowing instructors to bypass using CLP directly. As for scalability, the fact that our technique entails generating millions of test cases raises research, engineering, and deployment concerns. In our study, we bypassed these concerns by performing an offline analysis after the course was over. We are working towards an open source software framework for managing the computational requirements of applying this technique at scale, enabling its use for online formative and summative assessment.

REFERENCES

[1] Kyle Dewey, Lawton Nichols, and Ben Hardekopf. 2015. Automated Data Structure Generation: Refuting Common Wisdom. In *Proceedings of the 37th International Conference on Software Engineering - Volume 1 (ICSE '15)*. IEEE Press, Piscataway, NJ, USA, 32–43. http://dl.acm.org/citation.cfm?id=2818754.2818761
[2] Kyle Dewey, Jared Roesch, and Ben Hardekopf. 2014. Language Fuzzing Using Constraint Logic Programming. In *Proceedings of the 29th ACM/IEEE International Conference on Automated Software Engineering (ASE '14)*. ACM, New York, NY, USA, 725–730. DOI:http://dx.doi.org/10.1145/2642937.2642963
[3] Kyle Dewey, Jared Roesch, and Ben Hardekopf. 2015. Fuzzing the Rust Typechecker Using CLP. In *Proceedings of the 2015 30th IEEE/ACM International Conference on Automated Software Engineering (ASE) (ASE '15)*. IEEE Computer Society, Washington, DC, USA, 482–493. DOI:http://dx.doi.org/10.1109/ASE.2015.65
[4] Daniel Diaz and Philippe Codognet. 2000. The GNU Prolog System and Its Implementation. In *Proceedings of the 2000 ACM Symposium on Applied Computing - Volume 2 (SAC '00)*. ACM, New York, NY, USA, 728–732. DOI:http://dx.doi.org/10.1145/338407.338553
[5] Sumit Gulwani, Ivan Radiček, and Florian Zuleger. 2014. Feedback Generation for Performance Problems in Introductory Programming Assignments. In *Proceedings of the 22Nd ACM SIGSOFT International Symposium on Foundations of Software Engineering (FSE 2014)*. ACM, New York, NY, USA, 41–51. DOI:http://dx.doi.org/10.1145/2635868.2635912
[6] Christian Holler, Kim Herzig, and Andreas Zeller. 2012. Fuzzing with code fragments. In *Proceedings of the 21st USENIX conference on Security symposium (Security'12)*. USENIX Association, Berkeley, CA, USA, 38–38.
[7] Petri Ihantola. 2006. Test Data Generation for Programming Exercises with Symbolic Execution in Java PathFinder. In *Proceedings of the 6th Baltic Sea Conference on Computing Education Research: Koli Calling 2006 (Baltic Sea '06)*. ACM, New York, NY, USA, 87–94. DOI:http://dx.doi.org/10.1145/1315803.1315819
[8] Petri Ihantola, Tuukka Ahoniemi, Ville Karavirta, and Otto Seppälä. 2010. Review of Recent Systems for Automatic Assessment of Programming Assignments. In *Proceedings of the 10th Koli Calling International Conference on Computing Education Research (Koli Calling '10)*. ACM, New York, NY, USA, 86–93. DOI:http://dx.doi.org/10.1145/1930464.1930480
[9] J. Jaffar and J.-L. Lassez. 1987. Constraint logic programming. In *Proceedings of the 14th ACM SIGACT-SIGPLAN symposium on Principles of programming languages (POPL '87)*. ACM, New York, NY, USA, 111–119. DOI:http://dx.doi.org/10.1145/41625.41635
[10] René Just, Darioush Jalali, and Michael D. Ernst. 2014. Defects4J: A Database of Existing Faults to Enable Controlled Testing Studies for Java Programs. In *Proceedings of the 2014 International Symposium on Software Testing and Analysis (ISSTA 2014)*. ACM, New York, NY, USA, 437–440. DOI:http://dx.doi.org/10.1145/2610384.2628055
[11] [meta] Bugs Found by jsfunfuzz 2006. [meta] Bugs Found by jsfunfuzz. (2006). https://bugzilla.mozilla.org/show_bug.cgi?id=349611
[12] [meta] LangFuzz (Grammar-based Mutation Fuzzer) - JS shell bugs 2011. [meta] LangFuzz (Grammar-based Mutation Fuzzer) - JS shell bugs. (2011). https://bugzilla.mozilla.org/show_bug.cgi?id=676763
[13] Jesse Ruderman. 2007. Introducing jsfunfuzz. (2007). http://www.squarefree.com/2007/08/02/introducing-jsfunfuzz/
[14] Saul Schleimer, Daniel S. Wilkerson, and Alex Aiken. 2003. Winnowing: Local Algorithms for Document Fingerprinting. In *Proceedings of the 2003 ACM SIGMOD International Conference on Management of Data (SIGMOD '03)*. ACM, New York, NY, USA, 76–85. DOI:http://dx.doi.org/10.1145/872757.872770
[15] Rishabh Singh, Sumit Gulwani, and Armando Solar-Lezama. 2013. Automated Feedback Generation for Introductory Programming Assignments. *SIGPLAN Not.* 48, 6 (June 2013), 15–26. DOI:http://dx.doi.org/10.1145/2499370.2462195
[16] Leon Sterling and Ehud Shapiro. 1994. *The Art of Prolog (2Nd Ed.): Advanced Programming Techniques*. MIT Press, Cambridge, MA, USA.
[17] Nikolai Tillmann, Jonathan De Halleux, Tao Xie, Sumit Gulwani, and Judith Bishop. 2013. Teaching and Learning Programming and Software Engineering via Interactive Gaming. In *Proceedings of the 2013 International Conference on Software Engineering (ICSE '13)*. IEEE Press, Piscataway, NJ, USA, 1117–1126. http://dl.acm.org/citation.cfm?id=2486788.2486941
[18] Willem Visser, Klaus Havelund, Guillaume Brat, Seungjoon Park, and Flavio Lerda. 2003. Model Checking Programs. *Automated Software Engg.* 10, 2 (April 2003), 203–232. DOI:http://dx.doi.org/10.1023/A:1022920129859
[19] Jan Wielemaker, Tom Schrijvers, Markus Triska, and Torbjörn Lager. 2012. SWI-Prolog. *Theory and Practice of Logic Programming* 12, 1-2 (2012), 67–96.
[20] Chris Wilcox. 2015. The Role of Automation in Undergraduate Computer Science Education. In *Proceedings of the 46th ACM Technical Symposium on Computer Science Education (SIGCSE '15)*. ACM, New York, NY, USA, 90–95. DOI:http://dx.doi.org/10.1145/2676723.2677226
[21] Xuejun Yang, Yang Chen, Eric Eide, and John Regehr. 2011. Finding and understanding bugs in C compilers. In *Proceedings of the 32nd ACM SIGPLAN conference on Programming language design and implementation (PLDI '11)*. ACM, New York, NY, USA, 283–294. DOI:http://dx.doi.org/10.1145/1993498.1993532

Use of Gamification to Teach Agile Values and Collaboration
A multi-week Scrum simulation project in an undergraduate software engineering course

Sonja Hof
Baloise Insurance Ltd
Aeschengraben 21
4002, Basel, BS, Switzerland
sonja.hof@baloise.ch

Martin Kropp
University of Applied Sciences
Northwestern Switzerland
Bahnhofstrasse 6
5120, Windisch, AG, Switzerland
martin.kropp@fhnw.ch

Marla Landolt
University of Applied Sciences
Northwestern Switzerland
Bahnhofstrasse 6
5120, Windisch, AG, Switzerland
marla.landolt@fhnw.ch

ABSTRACT

Collaboration and communication are key to successful agile software development. Respect, openness, transparency and trust are core Agile values. However studies show, that there is a shortage of software developers with these skills. How can we teach these skills to software engineering students? This paper presents the approach of using a multi-week Scrum Paper City simulation game. The course execution was accompanied by a thorough evaluation to find out how effective this approach is compared to traditional ex-cathedra teaching. While the evaluation shows some aspects to be improved, it clearly shows that students like to experience the Agile approach directly in a project, that they enjoy more fun, and the collaboration in the team.

KEYWORDS

Agile; Collaboration; Values; Software Engineering; Education; Gamification

1 INTRODUCTION

Agile methods like Scrum, XP and, more recently, Kanban, have become mainstream approaches in software project development, with Scrum being by far the most followed approach as recent studies like [4, 6, 14] show. Subsequently, in the meantime, teaching Agile methods, and especially Scrum, has also found the way into the Software Engineering curricula of many universities ([1, 3, 8, 9]).

Many courses typically apply the Scrum development process on an appropriately scaled software project. In these projects, students typically focus on programming tasks which they like most.

However, more recent studies show that the hard part of adopting Agile seems to be the collaboration practices and living the Agile mindset [7], as it seems to take very long until these practices are applied (>5 years). Only by applying all Agile practices, organizations seem to gain major improvements in their software development [7].

The study seems to indicate two important issues:

- software engineers do not only need to have excellent (technical) competences in programming, but also need excellent competences in communication and collaboration, and should have adopted the so called Agile values.
- today's engineers seem to lack the needed competences and learn them only over a long time by doing on the job.

So it appears that there is a high demand for well-educated software engineers in the Agile domain, and that there is especially a significant lack of knowledge in Agile collaboration and in living the Agile mindset.

However, the question is: How can these competences be taught to students in an engineering course on undergraduate level?

Based on our experience in teaching software engineering and Agile methods for more than a decade now, we developed a course which provides an introduction into Agile methods which focuses on Agile collaboration and values through a multi-week Scrum simulation game by adapting the Scrum City Lego game [1] to our needs. The goal of this course is that students experience *the Agile way* by applying and living the Agile values and collaboration in a simulation project over several weeks.

We accompanied this year's course with 67 students with a series of questionnaires to evaluate the chosen approach compared to ex-cathedra teaching with exercises. Our evaluation goals (EG) were to find out:

EG1. Do the students like this approach better than traditional ex-cathedra learning approaches?
EG2. Does the game approach better help to learn the *Agile way*?
EG3. What are the concrete learnings of the students?
EG4. What are they lacking?

The rest of the paper is structured as follows: Section 2 presents related work in this area. Section 3 explains the course educational concept, its organization and execution in detail, showing how collaboration and Agile values are taught and practised in the classroom. Section 4 presents the results of the course evaluation, made through online surveys and retrospectives. Section 5 discusses the findings and lessons learned, followed by final conclusions.

2 RELATED WORK

Though it took quite a while until Agile development methods were noticed by the academia, there are now many courses offered at universities all over the world that teach the Agile approach.

ITiCSE'17, July 03-05, 2017, Bologna, Italy
© 2017 ACM. ACM ISBN 978-1-4503-4704-4/17/07...$15.00
DOI: http://dx.doi.org/10.1145/3059009.3059043

---

[1]https://www.lego4scrum.com/

In a panel at SGICSE 2016 [2] Campbell et al report about their experiences on teaching Agile methods and raised issues for teaching Agile, like why we should teach Agile, who should take the Scrum Master and Product Owner roles, and what is most difficult to teach. In [13] Steghöfer et al. report about the problem that in software projects students focus too much about product delivery, and not about learning the Agile process itself. They introduced the Lego game to improve their course.

Schroeder et al. [12] report on the setup of two software development labs specifically designed so that the social interaction 'how to deal with collaborative software development processes and their need for self-organization, motivation and work coordination' is taken into conscious consideration. Scharf and Koch [11] present the design of a Scrum-based undergraduate software engineering course, which is based on role-playing. To ensure that their students understand 'Agile' thoroughly, they designed the complete course as realistically as possible. For instance, they make research assistants play customers and a student play the Scrum master.

In [1] and Anslow report about their experiences teaching a group-based Agile software development project course. They report that students enjoy the interactive exercises and the self-organized teams, but also that it is challenging to get the right customer involvement. In [10] Rico and Sayani report about their results about teaching student teams Agile methods in their final year. They report that proper coaching and tutoring of the teams is a key factor for the project success.

In [5] Kropp et al. describe the importance of advanced collaboration skills in Agile development and make suggestions on how to integrate them in undergraduate courses.

Little work has been done specifically addressing the issue of teaching Agile collaboration and Agile values using gamification in graduate and undergraduate courses. Our work reports about experiences teaching students the Agile process focussing on Agile collaboration and living the Agile values in a multi-week Scrum simulation game.

3 COURSE DESCRIPTION

3.1 Educational Concept

The entire Software Development Process course aims to give a practical introduction into various modern software development processes and user experience design processes. The learning objectives are that students can apply appropriate methods and techniques to organize, plan, estimate and execute software projects. The software development part of the course is based on mixing traditional ex-cathedra teaching with team-based Agile game-play, playing the Scrum City simulation game, giving the students practice in not only using the methods, but being able to experience collaboration and live out embracing Agile values. User experience design basics combines theory with mandatory group work of a case study.

In this paper we focus on the experiences we made teaching the Agile approach playing the Scrum City simulation game within the first seven weeks of the course.

The course is one of eight courses in the Software Engineering track spanning various topics of software engineering (see Figure 1). There is a separate track focussing on teaching programming

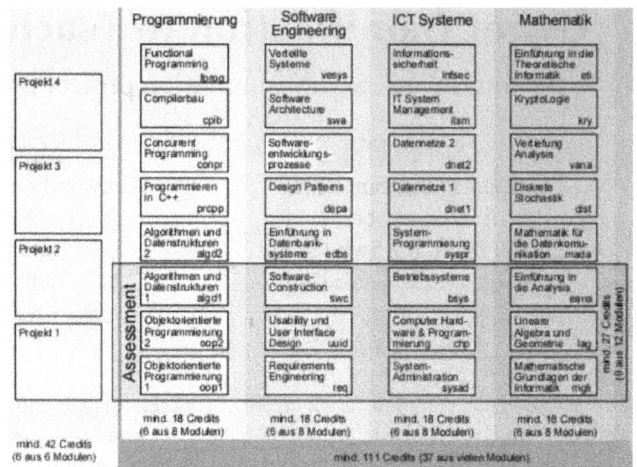

Figure 1: The Computer Science undergraduate schedule

languages. A central element of our practice-oriented curriculum is the so-called project-track (shown on the left of Figure 1)), whereby the students work in independent teams with real customers from the local industry, economics or research. The project-track is a required subject in each semester of the bachelor studies in Computer Science at FHNW, allowing students early exposure to the industry and building future-oriented solutions.

3.2 Scrum Paper City Simulation

The original Scrum Lego City game is a widely used game approach in industry courses to teach Scrum in a one day course. Product vision and User Stories are already given. The team focuses on sprint planing and sprinting.

In our course we wanted the team to experience the complete Agile project process. So we adapted the Scrum Lego City game in various aspects: starting with building the teams, creating the product vision, writing and estimating user stories, planning the sprint and finally constructing the city in several sprints.

For a more versatile and collaborative construction phase, we decided that teams construct the city not just by putting Lego bricks together, but rather by constructing their city with construction paper. This requires different activities during the sprint like cutting, glueing and drawing for example. We believe that this approach enforces more coordination and interaction among the team members.

A complete sprint cycle was designed to last 30 minutes, consisting of sprint planning (10'), sprinting (10'), demo (3') and retrospective (7').

All construction material (scissors, thick and thin paper cards of different colors, glue, colored pencils) was provided to the students by the lecturers. The instruction document "Scrum Paper City Guide" which described the Scrum Paper City simulation game was handed out to the students in the first lesson and discussed with them.

Table 1: Course Schedule

CW[2]	Topic	Scrum Game
1	Agile Manifesto & Scrum Intro	Team building and Product vision
2	Agile Requirements Management	User Stories, Product Backlog
3	Estimation and Planning	Estimate User Stories, plan first Sprint
4	-	Build the city in Sprints
5	Debriefing	-

3.3 Schedule

The whole course runs over 15 weeks. There is one weekly class comprised of one block of three consecutive units at 45 minutes each. The Scrum Paper City simulation ran over the first 5 weeks. After the mid-term exam on software engineering processes, the second half of the semester contained a block dedicated to usability topics in software development. Furthermore, the final week's class was given by a guest lecturer who were selected by us based on the actuality of their work/or specialty, in order to share an industry case study with the students.

Each weekly class was typically divided into three sections: The class starts with the presentation of new theory, followed by small exercises to clarify and deepen the new theory (typically 30' each). The major part of the class, the team was playing a part of the Scrum simulation game-play (60') to apply the theory in practice. The class finished with a voluntary retrospective which was conducted as an online survey. Each week we handed out an optional worksheet as homework containing questions related to the week's lesson topic to repeat and further deepen the theoretical knowledge. We offered to review the answers, whereby the students had to contact us if desired. Table 1 shows the complete schedule for the Scrum simulation game executed over 5 weeks.

3.4 Class Setup

We had a total of 67 students split up into three classes. Class A had 29 student, class B had 28 students, and class C had 10 students. Class A and B were taught on Tuesday, class C on Friday morning. Each class was taught by another lecturer. Classes A and C were taught in German, whereas class B was taught in English. All classes were visited by German speaking students.

The following sections describe each week's content, structure, goals and the Scrum Paper City simulation in detail.

3.5 Team Building and Vision

Theory. While introducing agile software development in the first week, our goals were that students:

- understand the objectives and concepts of Agility
- understand the key values and principles of the Agile Manifesto and their impact on software development
- relate Scrum to the values and principles of the Agile Manifesto

We started with elaborating the basic of Scrum. We imparted upon the class the self-organizing team spirit while talking about the rights and duties of the different roles, the Scrum events and artefacts. In addition, we clarified some misunderstandings which we regularly observe e.g., that the Daily is not for the Scrum Master or the Product Owner to give a status, but to encourage and promote the team spirit and the collaboration aspects. To complete the picture, certain Scrum Concepts, e.g., Time-boxing were also explained. Also in the first lesson, the Scrum Paper City simulation guide was presented to the students and discussed with them.

Scrum Game. The first task of the students was to build teams consisting of a Product Owner, Scrum Master and up to 4 developers. As every product starts with a vision, the first exercise for each team was to generate a vision for their city. Based on the vision the students formulated in a later session user stories. The teams were completely free about what kind of city, ranging from a classical city, to leisure parks, or a science fiction "city in the cloud". To avoid that the developers write their own product vision, we re-arranged the teams for this task and the following User Story week's class slightly. The developers of team 1 became the end users of team 2, those from team 2 became the end users of team 3, and so on.

3.6 Agile Requirements Management

Theory. We based the section "Agile Requirements Management" on the challenge to find an appropriate way between the business owners and the developers as to who dominates the requirement specification. The focus in this part is to make it clear what User Stories are and who is writing them. As a concise written description of a single piece of functionality that will be valuable to a user, the focus is clearly set on the needs of the customers. It should combine the strengths of written and verbal communication, find the right balance and respond to change. During the lesson, we started writing User Stories for our paper city with each group focusing on their city. To get more focus on the customer's needs, we exchanged team members to represent the customer within the other group. After this lesson, the students better understood the problems related to requirement specifications and could explain better what User Stories actually are. They were able to write User Stories more efficiently as well as to explain the pros and cons of User Stories.

Scrum Game. The teams elaborated User Stories for their paper city. They discussed the stories and prioritized them based on the input of the Product Owner. Furthermore, the students started preparing a physical board per team for their User Stories. This board was later used as a task board.

3.7 Estimation And Planning

Theory. Focus of this lesson was the estimation and planning aspect as such, i.e., not the actual plan. One needs to find a balance between the effort in planning compared to the knowledge that the plan will be revised repeatedly during the actual project. Working on the product to gain more knowledge, reduce uncertainty as well as embrace change is key to a successful project, as it leads to more knowledge and increased accuracy.

Besides teaching agile techniques for user story estimation and being able to make release plans for agile projects, we taught the students how to derive effort and cost for an agile project.

Figure 2: A team in a Planning Poker session

Figure 3: A team in a Sprint building the city

Scrum Game. Each development team used Planning Poker for effort estimation (see Figure 2). The planning preparation was completed by creating and discussing their respective Sprint Backlogs for the paper city game, in order to be ready for the final building/construction sprints. In addition, a burn down chart was added to the board to track the team's progress after each sprint.

3.8 Building And Demo

In this week there was no theory input. The whole three lessons were used to run four Sprint cycles to construct the city.

The class started with a Sprint Planning session to review the user stories prepared in the last lesson and to negotiate with the Product Owner the User Stories to be worked on during the upcoming sprint. After the planning session (10 minutes), the teams did a Sprint (10 minutes), in which they tried to achieve all promised items. Once the Sprint is over, the teams presented in a Review (3 minutes) the result of their working phase. During the Sprint execution the physical board as well as a Burn-down chart were regularly updated. The team closed the sprint with a Retrospective (7 minutes) to reflect on where they had difficulties or were not as efficient as they expected themselves to be. We displayed a stopwatch with a projector to show the remaining time for each timeboxed activity. Figure 3 shows a team during a Sprint building a city.

3.9 Debriefing

Debriefing is very important, else there is no feedback and hence no insight to what was learned and liked. In order to meet our main objective that the students reflected on the teaching format and the game-play learnings, we prepared a set of questions to be answered by each team. The week after completion of the Scrum Paper City game, we devoted one lesson to the debriefing. It is important to note here that during the Sprint we also asked the students questions about their motives. For example, normally after the first Sprint not all work items were done so the natural question to ask was why the Sprint was not successful. Or if the Product Owner challenged the results at the Review, a question about negotiating or exchanging with the customer's representative is helpful and makes implicit assumption explicit.

4 EVALUATION

4.1 Evaluation Method

We used several tools to evaluate the course in the three classes to get answers to our four evaluation goals. We conducted a weekly online survey questionnaire as well as a final retrospective and debriefing session in the week after game-play was completed.

Online Survey. The online survey was conducted with the web tool SurveyMonkey [3] allowing students to participate anonymously. After each weekly lesson we asked the following six questions, where three of them were based on a five-level symmetric Likert Scale, and three of them were free-form questions for written feedback:

(1) How much did you like today's lesson?
(2) How balanced was the mix of theory and practice?
(3) How did you like today's Scrum City Game part compared to traditional teaching?
(4) What are your three most important learnings from the Scrum City Game for today?
(5) What did you like most of today's Scrum City game part?
(6) What could be improved of today's Scrum City game part?

Retrospective. One week after the end of the Scrum simulation game we executed a 4L-Retrospective in which asked for feedback using Post-it's concerning the following aspects:

(1) What did you like?
(2) What did you least-liked?
(3) What did you learn?
(4) What did you lack?

Debriefing. In the debriefing, which was executed together with the retrospective we asked the students to rate the overall Scrum simulation game approach vs the traditional ex-cathedra teaching with respect to the aspects "Learning Effect", "Fun factor, "Team Building", and "Transferability to practice". We asked the question: *How would you rate the following aspects compared to ﬁtraditionalﬁ teaching (meaning presentation and isolated/standalone exercises), on a scale: much worse, worse, the same, better, much better*

---

[3]https://www.surveymonkey.com/

Table 2: Participation rate in the online survey

Week/class	3iCa	3IEng	3Ia
class size	29	28	10
1. Vision	20	14	9
2. User Stories	22	17	7
3. Planning	21	17	9
4. Sprints	19	8	8
Total	82	56	32
Overall Total			170

4.2 Results

In the following sections we report about the results of the various evaluations we conducted.

4.2.1 Online Survey. Across all four weeks we received a total 170 responses from all three classes. Table 2 shows the participation distribution over all four weeks. Table 3 lists the summarized results over all four weeks.

The data show that the simulation and gamification approach is preferred over traditional ex-cathedra by 76% of the students, and liked or liked very much by 58% percent. Most of the students also like the balance between theory and practice (71%). For reasons of limited space we cannot list all the answers of the open-ended questions. Concerning the major learnings, the students typically mentioned issues related to the corresponding week's topic. For the last week, when doing the sprints, they mentioned especially the importance of the planning before the sprint, and communication within the team. Concerning what they liked most about the game part, again especially in the last week, students mentioned working in the team,i.e., "doing" Scrum. The most cited comments about improvements were "nothing", more time for the practical part, and in some lessons reducing the theory part in favour of the practical part.

4.2.2 Debriefing. The debriefing session with the rating was executed only in two classes with a participation number of 30 students in total . Table 4 shows the results. There was one student who did not like the game approach at all. Otherwise the learning effect, team building aspects and the fun factor were rated better or much better by the majority of the students. The transferability of the learnings are estimated similarly to traditional teaching.

4.2.3 Retrospective. Table 5 shows the total number of responses for each aspect of the 4L-Retrospective. It shows that the students posted 13 "liked" feedbacks, but only 5 "least liked".

Among the most often named liked issues were teamwork, application of the theory in practice and living the process. They least liked the tough time schedule for the practical parts (not enough time), too big teams (about 7 people), simulation game took too long and coordination. Their feedback about what they lacked was a glossary, a real software project, concrete examples from industry practice and enough time for practice. The learning feedback included: the complete process, how Scrum team members collaborate with each other, importance of coordination of work, many new terms, the requirements are typically much more extensive than the given time to realize them.

In the discussion, the feedback was overall good and the only point of discussion was how possible it will be to achieve a know-how transfer to other areas of their work. Some participants of the course were not sure how to put their experience into practice.

5 DISCUSSION

Of the three different classes, it was interesting to observe that one class had a different approach to the game and the building of the city. Firstly, they were more doubtful and questioning of the method. Secondly, before they actually started building the city they asked for a more traditional exercise to do like programming. But, as soon as they started building the city this experience encouraged them to be very creative. This more programming-focused class even brought their own materials along, e.g., hot glue, string, etc.

The overall feedback for the simulation approach was very positive. They especially liked applying the process in a concrete scenario. Some wished to rather use a real software project. The available time for the practical parts in the Scrum City simulation was a major issue. It was too tight, so that students didn't have time to reflect properly about it, and we as lecturers couldn't provide thorough feedback. It was also interesting to observe how certain students really thrived in their role e.g. as Product Owner or Scrum Master. Some promoted quite well the collaboration and interaction that are underlying Agile values.

Additionally, the discussions among the students while doing the Sprint were very focused. Without realizing it, they improved communication, interaction and craftsmanship very quickly. The roles and tasks of the Product Owner and Scrum Master became clearer while playing (actually doing). compared to while teaching theory. Nonetheless some students had difficulties in playing the Scrum Master role, which might be a problem of missing experience. This came out by questions of the students like "What should I do during Sprint Planning?", "May I also write User Stories?", "What should I do during a Sprint", for example. Furthermore, the role of the instructor is not just timeboxing, but coaching the teams during each step of the game. Trigger actions through asking questions was very powerful as well as observing how the groups did generate insights while constructing and at the same time learning was very impressive.

With respect to our evaluation goals EG1 to EG4, the results show that students like this approach much more than traditional ex-cathedra learning approaches (EG1). If the students learned the Agile process better with the gamification approach (EG2) could not be evaluated with our surveys. For this one class should have been taught the traditional way. But even then, it would be doubtful, if not other aspects would influence the performance more (teacher, level of students, for example). Also the marks of students are in a similar range as in former courses. In the final retrospective we asked about the concrete learnings of the students (EG3). They especially mentioned "how the team members and roles work with each other", "importance of division of work", and "the complete process", "a real project process", "experience the challenges", "the Scrum process". A very encouraging feedback, since they mention core aspects of the Agile mindset. The students mentioned that they lacked especially a real software project (3 times), and a glossary with terms and more time for the practical part. The latter two

Table 3: Online survey results

(a) How much did you like today's lesson?

level	%
Very much	18%
much	40%
same	40%
not like	2%
not like at all	0%

(b) How was the mix of theory and practice balanced?

level	%
exactly right	15%
right	56%
ok	21%
unbalanced	8%
totally unbalanced	1%

(c) How did you like the Scrum City Game today compared to traditional teaching?

level	%
much better	27%
better	51%
same	20%
worse	2%
much worse	0%

Table 4: Comparison to traditional ex-cathedra teaching

aspect	-2^4	-1	0	+1	+2
Learning effect	0%	7%	28%	48%	17%
Fun factor	3%	0%	13%	50%	34%
Team building	0%	13%	16%	42%	29%
Transfer to practice	0%	14%	57%	21%	7%

Table 5: Number of responses in the 4L-Retrospective

Aspect	#
liked	13
least liked	5
lacked	5
learned	6

aspects can be solved within the course; the first issue could be solved by applying the Agile methods in the projects of our project track.

Overall, we got very positive feedback about the course, despite some doubts at the beginning - and it adds a lot of fun to teaching to an otherwise rather dry subject.

6 CONCLUSION

In this paper, we report how we changed teaching software development processes by combining traditional didactics with game-play going hand-in-hand. We (again) realized that having fun while working is one of the biggest motivators of all and that specially young people have no fear or preconception moving forward with a game-oriented way of teaching.

The results presented here suggest that we should continue to combine teaching software development processes theory together hand-in-hand with team-based Scrum game-play. As a result one can experience the benefits of Agile values collaboration and communication. As a next step we plan to enrich our lessons with a Kanban game to widen the horizon of Agile Software Processes even more. Generally we encourage all lecturers to think of a more playful, more collaborative and more interactive way of teaching their subject.

ACKNOWLEDGMENTS

The authors would like to thank the students of our three courses, who were patiently participating in the weekly surveys and provided most valuable feedback for further improvement of the course.

REFERENCES

[1] Craig Anslow and Frank Maurer. 2015. An Experience Report at Teaching a Group Based Agile Software Development Project Course. In *Proceedings of the 46th ACM Technical Symposium on Computer Science Education (SIGCSE '15)*. ACM, New York, NY, USA, 500–505. DOI: http://dx.doi.org/10.1145/2676723.2677284

[2] Jennifer Campbell, Stan Kurkovsky, Chun Wai Liew, and Anya Tafliovich. 2016. Scrum and Agile Methods in Software Engineering Courses. In *Proceedings of the 47th ACM Technical Symposium on Computing Science Education (SIGCSE '16)*. ACM, New York, NY, USA, 319–320. DOI: http://dx.doi.org/10.1145/2839509.2844664

[3] Vladan Devedžić and Saša R. Milenković. 2011. Teaching Agile Software Development: A Case Study. *IEEE Trans. on Educ.* 54, 2 (May 2011), 273–278. DOI: http://dx.doi.org/10.1109/TE.2010.2052104

[4] Torgeir Dingsøyr, Sridhar Nerur, VenuGopal Balijepally, and Nils Brede Moe. 2012. A Decade of Agile Methodologies. *J. Syst. Softw.* 85, 6 (June 2012), 1213–1221. DOI: http://dx.doi.org/10.1016/j.jss.2012.02.033

[5] Martin Kropp and Andreas Meier. 2013. Teaching Agile Software Development Competences - The Agile Competence Pyramid. In *European Computer Science Summit (ECSS), 2013 9th*.

[6] Martin Kropp and Andreas Meier. 2014. *Swiss Agile Study 2014*. Technical Report ISSN: 2296-2476.

[7] Martin Kropp, Andreas Meier, and Robert Biddle. 2016. *Agile Practices, Collaboration and Experience*. Springer International Publishing, Cham, 416–431. DOI: http://dx.doi.org/10.1007/978-3-319-49094-6_28

[8] Martin Kropp, Andreas Meier, and Robert Biddle. 2016. Teaching Agile Collaboration Skills in the Classroom. In *Software Engineering Education and Training (CSEE&T), 2016 IEEE 29th Conference on*. IEEE, 118–127. DOI: http://dx.doi.org/10.1109/CSEET.2016.27

[9] Viljan Mahnic. 2012. A Capstone Course on Agile Software Development Using Scrum. *IEEE Trans. on Educ.* 55, 1 (Feb. 2012), 99–106. DOI: http://dx.doi.org/10.1109/TE.2011.2142311

[10] David F. Rico and Hasan H. Sayani. 2009. Use of agile methods in software engineering education. In *In Proceedings of the International Conference on Agile, pages 172-179, 2009. (AGILE '09)*. IEEE, 174 – 179. DOI: http://dx.doi.org/10.1109/AGILE.2009.13

[11] Andreas Scharf and Andreas Koch. 2013. Scrum in a Software Engineering Course: An In-Depth Praxis Report. In *Software Engineering Education and Training (CSEE&T), 2013 IEEE 26th Conference on*. IEEE, 159 – 168. DOI: http://dx.doi.org/10.1109/CSEET.2013.6595247

[12] Andreas Schroeder, Annabelle Klarl, Philip Mayer, and Christian Kroi. 2012. Teaching agile software development through lab courses. In *Global Engineering Education Conference (EDUCON), 2012 IEEE*. 10. DOI: http://dx.doi.org/10.1109/EDUCON.2012.6201194

[13] Jan-Philipp Steghöfer, Eric Knauss, Emil Alégroth, Imed Hammouda, Håkan Burden, and Morgan Ericsson. 2016. Teaching Agile: Addressing the Conflict Between Project Delivery and Application of Agile Methods. In *Proceedings of the 38th International Conference on Software Engineering Companion (ICSE '16)*. ACM, New York, NY, USA, 303–312. DOI: http://dx.doi.org/10.1145/2889160.2889181

[14] VersionOne. 2015. *10th State of Agile Survey*. Technical Report. VersionOne, Inc.

Practical Robotics in Computer Science Using the LEGO NXT

An Experience Report

Francisco J. Estrada
University of Toronto at Scarborough
1265 Military Trail
M1C 1A4, Toronto, On., CANADA
festrada@utsc.utoronto.ca

ABSTRACT

We report on our experience building and implementing a robotics course for Computer Science based on the LEGO NXT. The goal of the course is to provide students with an opportunity to learn the fundamental principles involved in designing, programming, and operating mobile robots in a completely experiential setting, while abstracting away the hardware complexity of typical robotics platforms. To this end, we built the course around the LEGO NXT robot kits. We have developed a software framework that allows the NXT to be used in conjunction with a laptop computer and a webcam to enable our students to learn in the context of a robotics soccer game. We describe the process of designing the robotics soccer project so that it is tightly coupled with course learning goals, and report on our experience running the course over the past three years. The software platform is freely available, and allows anyone with a webcam-equipped laptop and an NXT set to implement their own soccer playing bot.

Categories and Subject Descriptors

K.3.2 [**Computers and Education**]: Computer and Information Science Education—*Computer Science Education*

Keywords

Robotics in Computer Science, LEGO NXT, Experiential Learning, Course Curriculum, Robotic Soccer

1. INTRODUCTION

Robotics applications have become ubiquitous in recent years, and have taken an important place in our day-to-day lives. Modern households already contain various forms of automation, and robotics is transforming entire industries such as transportation and manufacturing. Autonomous systems rely on specially written software to carry out their

ITiCSE '17, July 03 - 05, 2017, Bologna, Italy

© 2017 Copyright held by the owner/author(s). Publication rights licensed to ACM.
ISBN 978-1-4503-4704-4/17/07...$15.00

DOI: http://dx.doi.org/10.1145/3059009.3059025

work, it is therefore of critical importance to provide Computer Science students with a solid background and a well rounded education in how these systems work, with robotics being one of the main areas of application.

Teaching robotics within a computer science program can be challenging. It is important to abstract away the complexities of hardware design and operation and instead focus on the computational foundations of automation. At the same time, for students to truly learn the computational principles, they have to be given the experience of designing and programming a real world robot, with actual sensors and actuators that behave in unexpected ways. The robot has to be acting within a realistic environment where unexpected events and variables outside of the students' control are at play. Finally, it is expensive. Equipping a lab with robots such as the NAO [3] that are sophisticated enough to allow students to implement interesting algorithms would be prohibitively expensive for most institutions.

In order to address these issues, we developed a robotics curriculum based on the LEGO NXT robot kits. It is designed to allow students to apply, experiment, and gain a solid understanding of a wide range of topics in mobile robotics. It requires no custom, overly complex hardware, and is realistically affordable, easy to maintain, and easy to extend. LEGO NXTs have proven successful in the past for improving learning at many levels of CS education. At the undergraduate level many interesting proposals have been brought forth: [13] proposes bringing NXTs into senior-level courses, using a maze-solving task to engage students, and reporting increased engagement. A report in [8] discusses the use of NXTs in introductory level courses, also noting greatly increased student engagement; [6] goes further, showing via a comparative study of learning outcomes that the introduction of NXTs not only increases student engagement but also significantly improves learning outcomes at the introductory level. More specific applications include [14] which suggests using NXTs to teach concurrency, [10] which employs LEGO bots to introduce students to test-driven development, [9] which employs NXTs to teach automata theory, and [12] and [7] which propose different visual interfaces for facilitating the learning of programming concepts on robotic platforms.

Despite all the interest in bringing robotic hardware to the classroom, most of the interest so far has been geared either toward intro-level courses or toward specific topics in CS. A prior proposal in [11] had looked at the feasibility of implementing robotics algorithms such as particle filtering, but did not attempt to use the NXT as a platform for building an entire robotics course. To our knowledge, this is the first attempt at setting up a complete robotics course appropriate for a computer science program, designed and built around the NXT platform. The rest of this paper describes our experience designing and bringing this course to life over the past three years.

2. INSTITUTIONAL CONTEXT AND COURSE OVERVIEW

The course we describe was put together and implemented at the University of Toronto at Scarborough. Our computer science program has seen significant enrollment increases over the past few years. For the current school year, we have close to 800 students in CS1, 700 in CS2, and around 550 students taking courses in the second- through-fourth years. Computer science specialists are required to take two Calculus courses, two Linear Algebra courses, and a probability and statistics course. At the time the robotics course was designed, students had access to a variety of senior-level courses on machine learning and artificial intelligence, but there was no course dedicated to mobile robotics and autonomous systems.

To address this gap in our program, we set out to design a course that would cover the following fundamental topics in mobile robotics:

- Components of an autonomous robotics system
- Sensors and measurement
- Signals and signal processing
- Actuators and control systems
- Localization and navigation
- Simple A.I.s for robot control
- Real-time systems

These topics were selected so that: a) They cover the basic building blocks that would enable students to design, implement, and operate a fully-functional mobile robot; b) they have little overlap with existing machine learning and A.I. courses; c) they do not require the more advanced calculus and linear algebra courses; and d) there is a direct mapping from lecture content to tasks the students have to explore with their NXT kits. By the end of the course, students are able to design, build, and program a simple robot able to play soccer against another robotic opponent.

We currently have 23 NXT v2.0 kits acquired directly from LEGO Education. Students work in small groups (at most 3 people), which means our current set up can accommodate up to 66 students. This is a medium sized class for upper-level computer science courses at our institution. The course consists of 2 hours of lecture and 2 hours of tutorial time each week, plus one hour per week of consulting time with the instructor and/or TAs. While there is a dedicated hardware lab that students use during tutorials, consulting sessions, and project reviews, student teams are allowed to check-out a robot kit at the start of each project, and to take it home to work at their discretion. This has created quite an atmosphere of friendly excitement around the building as teams of students testing their robotic creations attract the attention of passers-by.

3. JUST HOW MUCH CAN WE DO WITH AN NXT?

Our NXT kits contain a computer brick equipped with an Atmel 32-bit processor, with 64Kb of RAM and 256 Kb of program memory (flash RAM). The brick has 4 ports for sensors (the kit includes one colour sensor, an ultrasound sensor, and two touch sensors), and 3 ports for servo-motors.

At first glance, the specs of the computer brick may look unimpressive given the computing power available in a contemporary smartphone. However, these limited specs are more than sufficient for implementing projects that cover each component of the curriculum detailed above. In fact, we find that exposing students to a platform that has very limited resources available for their use is a valuable learning experience - students are required to think carefully about what resources they will need to solve a task, and they have to put more thought into their software design. There are two major projects during the 12-week term, and each of them has an important role to play in the students' learning.

3.1 Robot Localization

The first project consists of solving a carefully set up robot localization task. The project is designed to directly support the learning of sensor management, signal processing and filtering, basic motion control and navigation, and one of the most widely used robot localization algorithms known as particle filtering [15]. In a nutshell, a particle filter works as follows:

```
Given a map of the environment the robot is moving
in, the robot will -

1.0 Generate a list of locations where it could
    possibly be. Initially, these hypotheses
    must cover the whole map.

(Particle Filtering Loop)
2.0 Use its sensors to look for identifiable
    landmarks.

    2.1 Score each hypothesis in the list by how
        well it agrees with the observable
        landmarks.

    2.2 Create a new list of possible locations,
        where previous hypotheses with better
        scores have a higher chance of making it
        into the new list.

    2.3 Move to a new location and go back to 2.0.

Eventually, one of the hypotheses in the list will
have a significantly higher score than all the
others. At this point the robot has found its
location.
```

As an analogy, this is similar to guessing our location in an unknown city by looking for landmarks and matching them to a city map. The more we walks, and the more landmarks we observes, the more certain our guess becomes about our location in the map.

The student's are given the map shown in Figure 1. It contains of a set of roads (black), intersections (yellow), and buildings (blue and green). Students then have to write an NXT program that will implement the particle filtering pro-

Figure 1: The map used in our project. One of the teams' robot is scanning the building colours around the intersection.

ces described above. For this particular problem, students will need to deal with:

- Writing code to enable the robot to travel reliably along streets

- Detecting intersections

- Scanning the colours of the buildings around the intersection, which requires fine motion control

- Checking measurements against the map, factoring-in the possibility of a sensor read error

- Processing the particle filter loop until localization has been achieved

The robot has access to the map as an array listing the building colours around each of the intersections starting at the top-left. Initially, the robot is placed at a random intersection, with a random heading. Once the algorithm is started, the robot has to complete the task without intervention.

Students are given freedom in designing their robot, and have to decide where to place their colour sensor so as to obtain reliable readings on the map. This is not a simple task: The map is printed on standard colour printer white paper, and is carefully stitched together from multiple pages. The paper can be slippery so control software is needed to allow the robot to accurately follow streets and scan intersections despite slips and variations in motor performance due to changing battery charge. The NXT's colour sensor can be noisy, and the values read from the map change depending on the illumination conditions of the room. Students have to figure out how to handle these sources of variation in order to solve the task reliably.

Once students have mastered sensor management, and have a working prototype of a robot that can follow streets and scan intersections, they still have to write the localization software. They work in a C-like language called NXC [2] which includes an API for controlling the robot's motors and reading from the robot's sensors. Programming is done on a laptop computer, and compiled executables are uploaded to the NXT brick via USB for testing.

A good solution to the localization task requires a significant amount of work and care, as well as a solid understand-

ing of the course material related to sensors, signal processing, control, and localization. The NXT is perfectly suited to the task and we have used its limitations as a teaching tool. Despite the apparent simplicity of the platform, students are solving the same task, using the same particle filtering technique that has been applied with success on self-driving vehicles.

The robot localization project already challenges students to implement a fully autonomous bot capable of solving a non-trivial task. However, we have something far more ambitions in mind for the final project.

3.2 Robots Playing Soccer

Having learned the basic low-level components of robotic applications, the students are ready to take on a project that brings together the material they have mastered through the robot localization process, and the topics covered in the second half of the course. This project directly supports the learning of advanced navigation, state-based A.I. techniques for planning and decision making, and integrating high-level behaviours with the lower-level processing modules that handle sensors and motion in order to implement an autonomous robot that solves a non-trivial task. They have to do so under the constraint that the robot has to respond in real time to events in the environment.

The project requires students to design, build, and program an autonomous soccer-playing robot. This is not a new idea, an international robotics soccer competition, the RoboCup [4], has been held annually since 1997 and has evolved to contain multiple different events. Each event is focused on specific aspects of robotics: The small-robot league focuses on multi-agent cooperation problems. The middle-size league focuses on aspects of mechanical design and control as well as multi-agent cooperation. There are two large-size leagues, one that requires all teams to use the same robot platform (the NAO robots [3]), and one that allows teams to design and build their own humanoid bots.

To participate in any of these leagues, serious knowledge of hardware design, control theory, and techniques in A.I. and machine learning are required. It is also expensive: The NAO robots are several thousand dollars each. Designing and building a complex humanoid robot is well beyond the level of skill we can expect at the undergraduate level, would require much more time and effort than a single course project would accommodate, and would be at least equally expensive. Our goal here is to allow our students to experience the excitement and fun of a robotics soccer competition, to do so in a way that is realistically affordable for our institution, and to avoid the need for knowledge about hardware design or advanced control theory. The NXT platform provides an excellent solution for these problems.

In order to play soccer, the robots need to be able to see the soccer field, their opponent, and the ball. Unfortunately the NXT bots do not support a camera attachment. Even if they did, the limited amount of computing power on the NXT brick would mean only very low level image processing could be carried out, and the response of the bot would not happen in real-time. In order to be able to play soccer with NXT bots, we turned instead to the NXT's ability to communicate with a laptop computer via bluetooth.

For the soccer task, we use an augmented NXT kit which includes a laptop computer and a webcam. Our setup is shown in Fig. 2. The NXT is linked to the laptop via blue-

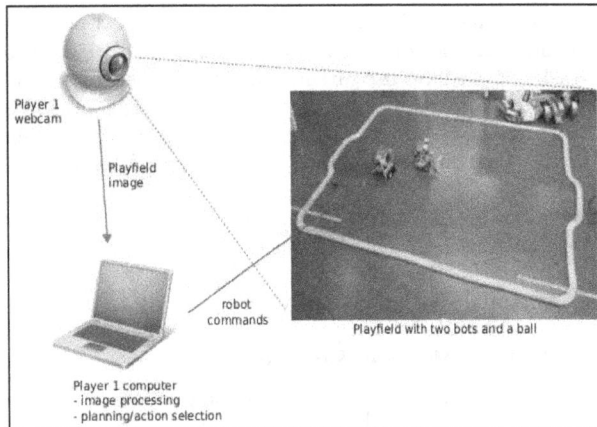

Figure 2: Setup for robotic soccer. A playing field contains two opposing robots and a ball. Each robot is controlled by a (separate) laptop computer via bluetooth, and a webcam overlooking the field provides the input used by the software on the laptop to determine the robot's next action.

tooth. The laptop receives visual input from the webcam overlooking the play field, processes the image to identify the robots and the ball, and determines what the robot needs to do. Then it issues motion commands to the robot over bluetooth. In this configuration, the NXT is a mobile extension of the laptop, with the NXTs sensors serving as an extension to the webcam.

For this project the students task is as follows:

- Design a mobile robot with the goal of playing soccer

- Write the basic software routines allowing the bot to move toward the ball

- Write the basic software routines that will allow the bot to kick the ball

- Write a simple, state-based A.I. to determine the bot's actions in a game

- Test and refine their A.I. so the bot plays well

Each of these tasks is defined in careful detail in the project handout. Students are given a starter code package that

- Handles bluetooth communication with the NXT bot

- Contains a simple, C-based API for robot control

- Handles the webcam, and performs all the image processing

- Contains a skeleton of the A.I. for students to extend

The starter package was carefully designed so that students will be able to focus only on the parts of the code that support the learning of the course material. Students will not be distracted by having to deal with low-level communications with the NXT, by having to learn computer vision to process and use the webcam input, or by having to worry about how to design and embed their A.I. routines so that they work with the rest of the code.

Figure 3: The image processing software takes the camera input and produces an image in which the background is removed, the robots and ball are clearly identified as solid-coloured blobs, and lines indicate motion and velocity vectors. All measurable quantities are updated in real-time by the starter code, and are available for the students to use as they deem appropriate.

The starter code provides students with a list of values that include the robot's position, heading, direction and speed of motion (if the robot is moving), as well as the same variables for the opponent robot. It also provides the position, direction, and speed of motion for the ball. Figure 3 shows the view of the field after the starter code has processed the webcam's input and extracted all the information needed for the bots to plan their actions. The usefulness of the framework we have built is that it isolates students from distracting complexities and allows them to get to work immediately.

The students take these inputs and use them to implement their soccer playing routines. They start with seemingly simple tasks such as moving toward the ball and kicking. They soon find that the quantities reported are noisy and unstable, and that they have to apply the signal processing techniques and motion control methods they learned earlier in the course. From that point, they work on their A.I. in the form of an FSM which controls whether the bot is defending or attacking, and determines how the bot will respond to changes in the position of the opponent as well as the ball. Everything must work in real-time.

The project lasts four weeks, with weekly progress checks at which the TAs and course instructor review pre-specified implementation goals each team must meet to stay on track, offer help and advice with design or implementation problems, and help struggling teams stay on course. The progress check sessions are open, so every team can see and learn from what other teams are doing. Often teams will offer each other advice for dealing with common problems, and suggest improvements to the robot designs of their peers. This happens outside of lectures and tutorials as students work on their bots at the computer lab. The atmosphere is one of friendly cooperation, and of figuring out how to solve the challenging task at hand.

The final day of the course consists of the soccer competition. There is an all-teams round where each team plays two others. Teams that win the most matches (there is a procedure for breaking ties fairly) move on to the elimination round. Pairs of bots face each other, and match winners move on until the final round. Tied games are resolved by penalty shootouts. The atmosphere during competition day is one of excitement and fun. Students get excited about their robot's performance, and they watch and cheer even when their bot is not at play. The elimination rounds are met with enthusiasm as well as the expected dose of elation for the victors and bittersweet feelings for the teams that are eliminated. The end result has been the same over the past three years of competitions: Students feel at the end of the day like they have been a part of something special.

It is worth noting that in three years of running this competition, all the student teams that arrived at competition day had managed to put together a robot capable of following and kicking the ball, kicking a penalty shot (though not necessarily scoring one), and handling the basic tasks that were given out. However, there is clearly a large difference in performance between the teams that were eliminated at the all-teams stage, and those that have made it to the final.

4. WHAT WE HAVE LEARNED

The course has been running for three years now, each year between 60 and 66 students enroll, and between 50 and 55 complete the course. It is an elective course, and compared to other electives at our CS program, it enjoys large enrollment. The attrition rate is fairly low given the demands the course places on students; indeed, in course evaluations the course is typically rated as having a high work load compared to other CS courses at our institution. Evaluation is heavily based on project work, with 75% of the course grade being assigned to projects and labs (of which there are 4, helping students with individual concepts that will later be applied in their projects). The rest of the grade is earned on the final exam.

What sets the course apart, is the work produced by the students during the term. The localization project has produced a number of creative and even surprising robot designs. While designing a cool robot is not part of the rubric for the project, students become very invested in building something exciting, and it can count for bonus marks. A video showing a sample solution from one of our student teams can be found here [5].

The particle filtering algorithm has to be adapted from the general discussion in the lecture to the specific configuration of the NXT. This requires understanding of the algorithm, understanding of the hardware platform, and a bit of ingenuity. Only about half the teams complete the localization task, the remaining half hit snags with either their sensor management, or with the motion control. As a result of this, each year we add to the project handout specific advice intended to help students avoid pitfalls that previous teams have stumbled on. The project review session is always crowded, students arrive early and stay late, regardless of when their own project is being showcased. Teams openly discuss the technical issues they found, how they addressed them, and those who solved the task completely share their expertise with teams who did not succeed for some reason.

The amount of cooperation is encouraging, but it raises the concern of plagiarism. However, because each student

Figure 4: This is what our students feel like on competition day.

team produces a unique robot design, it is difficult to share code and the interaction between teams has taken on the shape of healthy discussion and peer-supported learning. We have not found a single case of plagiarized code in the three years the project has run.

The robotic soccer project has produced even more exciting results. All the teams that show up on competition day have a robot that is at least capable of driving toward the ball, and kicking a penalty shot. Beyond that, there is wide variability in how well their robots perform, with the most capable teams showcasing bots that clearly outperform the average design in speed, accuracy, and decision making ability. The competition itself is an event full of student energy. Teams are excited to play, students get very invested in what is happening on the field of play even when their own robot is not in the game, and they typically forget that behind the competition, their work is being evaluated by the TAs and the course instructor. Figure 4 shows a picture taken during the competition. The expressions on the students' faces illustrates what the course is all about. A video of the final match of the robotic soccer competition can be found here [5].

To excel at robotic soccer, students must have mastered all the main topics covered in the course. The input provided by the webcam and the image processing software is quite noisy and can be unstable. Software has to be able to handle uncertainty and variability, and must be able to adapt to the actions of an opponent trying to win the match. Students must have mastered fine robot control, and have written a good A.I. able to determine the best course of action given the positions of the two robots and the ball. For evaluation purposes, the TAs ask students technical questions about their implementation, delving into sensor usage and noise management, how the robot turns and moves, and what the A.I. is doing at every step of the match. For competitive teams, it is very clear talking to the students that they have indeed mastered the course material. Whereas for teams whose project did not completely solve the problem, it presents one final opportunity for the TA and course instructor to clarify concepts and algorithms before the final exam, having a working practical example right there for the students to see and touch.

The complete starter code and project handouts for both

the robotic soccer project, and the localization project, are available here [5]. They will allow anyone with an NXT kit, a laptop, and a webcam to set up both the localization and the robotic soccer projects with little effort. It is our hope that the framework the code for these projects provide will be of use to other educators interested in practical robotics within their computer science curriculum. We will be delighted to receive and answer to any inquiries related to these projects or the starter code provided for them. We will also be delighted to hear from any instructors currently embarked on, or planning to undertake their own robotics projects.

5. CONCLUSION AND FUTURE PLANS

Our experience running the course has been very positive. The use of NXT bots has definitely enriched the course experience for our students, and their learning of course topics is directly evidenced by their robots at work. Overall, the feedback from students has been very positive despite their uniform impression that the amount of work is quite high. We are very pleased with the learning results observed in the final projects turned in by each team, as well as by the interest that the course generates for related courses in the CS program, including machine learning and artificial intelligence. The level of engagement and excitement generated by the robotic soccer competition is unique among other CS courses, and from students' feedback, is clearly a memorable experience.

Looking forward, and considering the increased enrollment in computer science at our home department, we are looking at possibilities for scaling up the course. The current set of robot kits limits our enrollment to 66 students, adding NXT kits is slightly complicated by the fact that the NXT v2.0 has now been discontinued. Fortunately, the current LEGO robot kits (the EV3) are compatible with sensors and components from the NXT, so they are inter operable. Each EV3 kit is about 400 dollars (US), so equipping a lab with 20 kits would cost about 8000 dollars not counting shipping and taxes. This is still less thank it would cost to acquire 2 NAO robots. Another option is to replace the NXT computer bricks altogether and only use the LEGO building blocks, sensors, and motors. Dexter Industries offers what they call a Brick Pi [1] kit that includes a Raspberry-Pi with custom software and a casing that contains compatible ports for the NXT's sensors and motors. Each Brick Pi sells for 180 USD so acquiring 20 of these would cost about 3600 dollars. An institution looking to use Brick Pi units would need to acquire sensors, motors, and LEGO pieces for building the robots. However it is realistic to expect the total cost of setting up a complement of 20 fully operational robot kits to be less than 10,000 dollars. This will support 60 students working with a robot for the duration of a term.

We hope that this paper will provide a few concrete ideas for educators looking to start, or to expand on, their own robotics courses. We will be happy to provide any assistance, advice, or technical help that we can with the software base we have developed. Robotics is an exciting field, it should provide plenty of space for students to experiment and, as far as it is possible, should happen outside the computer screen.

6. REFERENCES

[1] Dexter Industries Brick Pi. https://www.dexterindustries.com/brickpi/.

[2] Not eXactly C at Sourceforge. http://bricxcc.sourceforge.net/nbc/.

[3] NOW Robots from Aldebaran Robotics. https://www.ald.softbankrobotics.com/en/cool-robots/nao.

[4] The RoboCup Federation. http://www.robocup.org/.

[5] Videos, Project Handouts, and Source Code. http://www.cs.utoronto.ca/~strider/Robotics/.

[6] M. Anderson and C. Gavan. Engaging undergraduate programming students: Experiences using lego mindstorms nxt. In Intl. Conf. on Information Technology Education, 2012.

[7] P. Feijóo and F. de la Rosa. Roblock: Programming learning with mobile robotics. In ACM Conf. on Innovation and Technology in Computer Science Education, 2016.

[8] T. S. Hall and W. Munger. Integrating robotics into first-year experience courses. In American Society for Engineering Education Annual Meeting, 2011.

[9] M. Hamada and S. Sato. Lego nxt as a learning tool. In ACM Conf. on Innovation and Technology in Computer Science Education, 2010.

[10] S. Kurkovsky. A lego-based approach to introducing test-driven development. In ACM Conf. on Innovation and Technology in Computer Science Education, 2016.

[11] M. F. Mcnally and F. Klassner. Demonstrating the capabilities of mindstorms nxt for the ai curriculum. In Robots and Robot Venies: Resources for AI Education, AAAI Spring Symposyum, 2007.

[12] M. Meyer and D. T. Burns. Robotran: A programming environment for novices using lego mindstorms robots. In Intl. Florida Artificial Intelligence Research Society Conference, 2007.

[13] Simon. Using a primary-school challenge in a third-year it course. In Australasian Conference on Computer Education, 2010.

[14] L. Szweda, D. Wilusz, and J. Flotynski. Application of nxt based robots for teaching java-based concurrency. In Intl. Conf. on E-learning and Games for Trainig, Education, Health, and Sports, 2012.

[15] S. Thrun. Particle filters in robotics. In Uncertainty in AI, 2012.

Teaching Operating Systems Concepts with SystemTap

Darragh O'Brien
School of Computing
Dublin City University
Glasnevin
Dublin 9, Ireland
dobrien@computing.dcu.ie

ABSTRACT

The study of operating systems is a fundamental component of all undergraduate computer science degree programmes. Making operating system concepts concrete typically entails large programming projects. Such projects traditionally involve enhancing an existing module in a real-world operating system or extending a pedagogical operating system. The latter programming projects represent the gold standard in the teaching of operating systems and their value is undoubted. However, there is room in introductory operating systems courses for supplementary approaches and tools that support the demonstration of operating system concepts in the context of a live, real-world operating system. This paper describes an approach where the Linux monitoring tool SystemTap is used to capture kernel-level events in order to illustrate, with concrete examples, operating system concepts in the areas of scheduling, file system implementation and memory management. For instructors and students (where often for the latter seeing is believing) this approach offers an additional simple and valuable resource for solidifying understanding of concepts that might otherwise remain purely theoretical.

KEYWORDS

SystemTap, operating system, scheduling, file system, memory management

ACM Reference format:
Darragh O'Brien. 2017. Teaching Operating Systems Concepts with SystemTap. In *Proceedings of ITiCSE '17, Bologna, Italy, July 3-5, 2017,* 6 pages.
DOI: http://dx.doi.org/10.1145/3059009.3059045

1 INTRODUCTION

The study of operating systems plays a key role in undergraduate computer science degree programmes. Essential learning outcomes are delivered by operating systems related projects. The latter traditionally involve programming extensions in the areas of process management, file system support and memory management to a pedagogical operating system [2, 7]. Such programming projects represent the gold standard in the teaching of operating systems

and their value is undoubted. However, there is room in introductory operating systems courses for supplementary approaches and tools that support the demonstration of operating system concepts in the context of a live, real-world operating system.

This paper describes how SystemTap [3, 4] can be applied to both demonstrate and explore low-level behaviour across a range of system modules in the context of a real-world operating system. SystemTap scripts allow the straightforward interception of kernel-level events thereby providing instructor and students alike with concrete examples of operating system concepts that might otherwise remain theoretical. The simplicity of such scripts makes them suitable for inclusion in lectures and live demonstrations in introductory operating systems courses.

This paper is structured as follows: In Section 2 SystemTap and its capabilities are briefly introduced. In Section 3 we apply SystemTap to capture scheduling-related events and to demonstrate context switching and multitasking. In Section 4 we employ SystemTap to intercept and record I/O events across a selection of file system implementations. An explanation of such events necessitates an understanding of the underlying file systems and the differences between them. In Section 5 we use SystemTap to explore page table allocation under Linux's memory manager. Early informal evaluation results are reported in Section 6 and Section 7 concludes the paper.

2 SYSTEMTAP

SystemTap allows the dynamic monitoring of Linux kernel events. A SystemTap script is compiled to a module that is loaded into the kernel where it gathers data that is fed back to the user. Scripts typically consist of a set of handlers that fire when kernel events of interest occur. For example, the script presented in Listing 1 monitors the return status of each invocation of the open system call and, for each successfully opened file, displays both the name of the file and the name of executable that opened it.

```
# Listing 1
probe syscall.open.return {
    if ($return == -1) next
    printf("%s opened %s\n", execname(),
        kernel_string($filename))
}
```

The combination of an event plus handler is known as a *probe*. Several event types and filtering options exist to allow a script to be tailored to a fine-grained set of events of specific interest to the user. SystemTap comes with an extensive collection of examples as well as reusable components (known as *tapsets*) for inclusion in user-defined scripts.

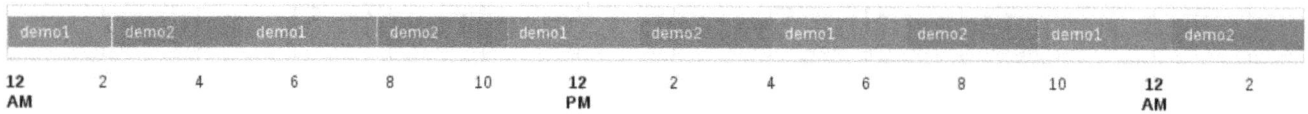

Figure 1: CPU bound processes

3 SCHEDULING

Every introductory operating systems module touches on the areas of process management, scheduling, multitasking, multithreading, etc. With SystemTap it is a straightforward task to monitor CPU on/off events i.e. the reassignment of the CPU from one schedulable entity (process or thread) to another. For example, the script excerpt presented in Listing 2 intercepts and timestamps (in microseconds) every CPU reassignment involving a process of interest (defined by the user in target_names). After a predefined number of recordings (MAX_SAMPLES) the script exits.

```
# Listing 2
probe scheduler.cpu_on
{
 prev_task_name = task_execname(task_prev)
 next_task_name = task_execname(task_current())

 # Only record target processes
 if (!(prev_task_name in target_names ||
       next_task_name in target_names)) {
           next
 }

 # Record process coming off CPU
 if (prev_task_name == currently_on) {
   timestamps[num_samples, prev_task_name] =
     gettimeofday_us()
   num_samples++
 }

 # Record process coming on CPU
 if (next_task_name in target_names) {
   timestamps[num_samples, next_task_name] =
     gettimeofday_us()
   currently_on = next_task_name
   num_samples++
 }

 # Collect MAX_SAMPLES samples
 if (num_samples >= MAX_SAMPLES) {
   exit()
 }
}
```

3.1 CPU bound processes

In a first experiment the above script is executed while concurrently running two instances (*demo1* and *demo2*) of a CPU bound process (each process simply spins in an infinite loop). An excerpt of the script output (simply a dump of the contents of the timestamps associative array) is presented below (the number on the right is

the normalised time (in microseconds) at which the corresponding process came on/off the CPU):

```
demo1, 0
demo1, 7809
demo2, 7937
demo2, 17764
demo1, 17767
demo1, 27766
demo2, 27828
demo2, 37765
```

Translating the above data into a format suitable for Google Charts (with microseconds translated to seconds) yields the timeline presented in Figure 1. As is evident from the timeline the two CPU bound processes dominate CPU usage and are allocated roughly equal time on the CPU. (Those periods in the timeline when neither process is executing are too short to be visible in the figure.)

Although a simple exercise the above example illustrates graphically and *with real data* the concept of preemptive multitasking (preemptive because each process must be forcefully evicted from the CPU since it is *always* in a runnable state). In this case the script was executed on a virtual machine with a single CPU. This simple script could be extended to produce scheduling timelines for a (virtual) machine with multiple CPUs thereby demonstrating the concept of *parallel* execution.

3.2 I/O bound processes

In a second experiment a slight variation on the script presented in Listing 2 is executed where scheduling data on *all* processes is collected (rather than only on a predefined set). An excerpt of sample output is presented below:

```
systemd-journal, 0
systemd-journal, 256
rcu_sched, 257
rcu_sched, 260
ksoftirqd/0, 261
ksoftirqd/0, 264
vlc, 264
vlc, 312
```

Translating the above data into a format suitable for Google Charts (again with microseconds translated to seconds) yields the timeline presented in Figure 2. As is evident from the timeline the period an I/O bound process spends on the CPU before blocking is shorter than that of a CPU bound process. We also see the swapper process make an appearance. This is Linux's *idle task* i.e. a process that is executed when there are no other runnable processes (as may happen on a lightly loaded machine). Although not arising in this example, occasionally Linux *appears* to take the CPU from a process only to immediately reassign it to the same process. This is rather the successive scheduling of *threads* within the same process.

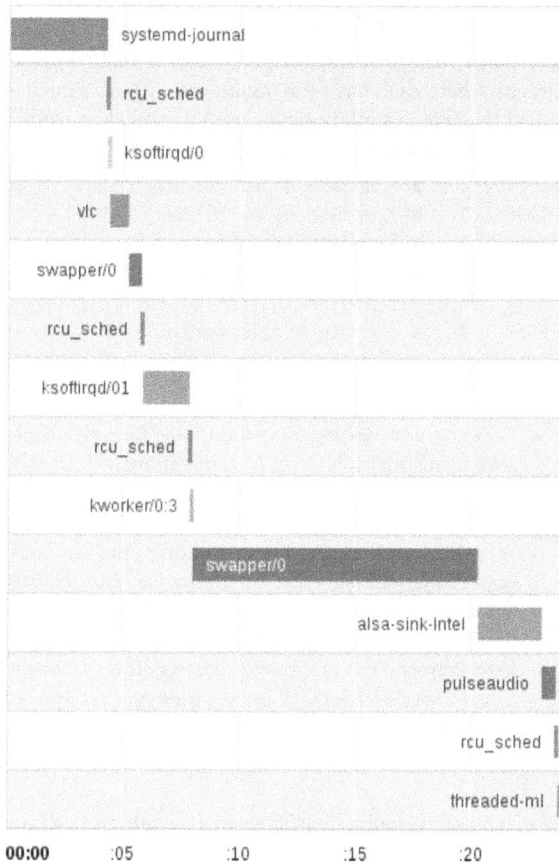

Figure 2: I/O bound processes

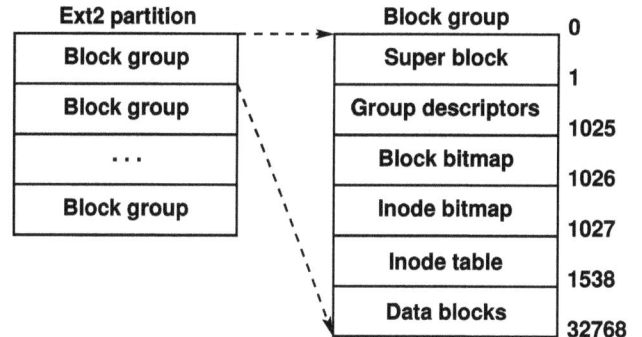

Figure 3: Ext2 partition

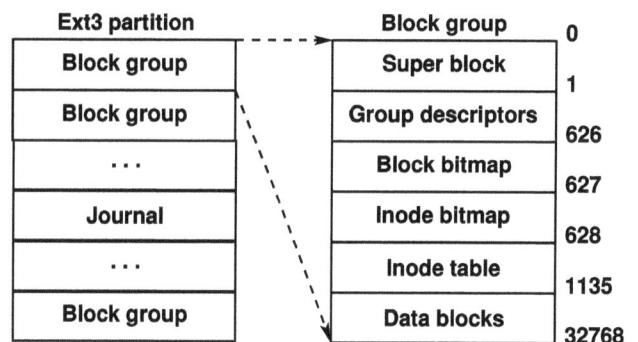

Figure 4: Ext3 partition

Extending the script to differentiate between threads of the same process would serve to demonstrate the concept of *multithreading*.

4 FILE SYSTEMS

In Section 4.1 the experimental setup is described. Subsequent sections present SystemTap scripts and example experiments for demonstrating file system concepts. In Section 4.2 prefetching is demonstrated. In Sections 4.3 and 4.4 two widely deployed file systems are compared: Ext2 [1] and its journalled successor Ext3 [9]. In Section 4.5 the functioning of log-structured file system NilFS [5] is briefly examined.

4.1 Setup

SystemTap monitors system-wide Linux kernel events. To facilitate straightforward filtering on events of interest the file systems under investigation, namely Ext2, Ext3 and NilFS, are installed to dedicated spare partitions. The physical layout (i.e. block offsets from the start of the partition to each of its logical regions) of each of the Ext2/3 partitions is extracted using dumpe2fs. Ext2/3 layouts are respectively depicted in Figures 3 and 4. As can be seen, the essential difference between Ext2 and Ext3 is the journal maintained by the latter in order to efficiently restore file system consistency in the event of a crash.

In the experiments described below we are interested in observing file system reads and writes. The SystemTap script presented in Listing 3 uses two probes to intercept all I/O request creation and completion events. Sectors are converted to blocks in order to allow straightforward mapping of the script's output to the partition structures presented in Figures 3 and 4. The file systems to be monitored have been installed in partitions sda6-8.

4.2 Prefetching

Prefetching [6] is a common I/O technique for improving sequential file access performance. The idea is a simple one: while fetching block N from the disk, prefetch blocks $N+R$, where R is a read-ahead value specified in blocks. The assumption is that prefetched blocks will be requested in the near future. Those requests can be satisfied from the block cache and costly I/O operations are thus reduced.

While the SystemTap script presented in Section 4.1 is running, a Python program is executed that uses the following code excerpt to issue one hundred read requests for each of one hundred contiguous blocks in a file on the Ext3 file system:

```
with open('/ext3/4mb.img', 'r') as f:
    for i in range (0, 100):
        f.read(4096)
```

In response the SystemTap script reports the following eight I/O operations where each has been annotated with the total number of blocks read after its completion:

```
C : 3360 : 1 : R : 1
```

```
# Listing 3
probe ioblock.request {
  if (!size) next
  if (devname != "sda6" &&
      devname != "sda7" &&
      devname != "sda8") next

  # Convert from sectors to blocks
  sblock = sector / 8
  eblock = (sector + size / 512 - 1) / 8
  blocks = eblock - sblock + 1

  # Note request for matching with completion
  sector += lbas[devname] + size / 512
  queued[sector] = 1
  line = sprintf("%u : %u : %s",
    sblock, blocks, bio_rw_str(rw))
  bios[sector] = line
}

probe ioblock.end {
  if (!queued[sector]) next

  # Report completion
  printf("C : %s\n", bios[sector])
  delete queued[sector]
  delete bios[sector]
}


C : 3361 : 4  : R : 5
C : 3365 : 8  : R : 13
C : 3373 : 16 : R : 29
C : 3389 : 32 : R : 61
C : 3421 : 32 : R : 93
C : 3453 : 32 : R : 125
C : 3485 : 32 : R : 157
```

Several file system concepts are demonstrated by this simple exercise:

- One hundred read requests, each for a single block of size 4096 bytes, thanks to prefetching translates to far fewer I/O operations, eight in this case.
- As the Linux I/O subsystem grows increasingly confident that a file is being processed sequentially it steadily increases the read-ahead value from 1 to a maximum value of 32 blocks.
- Linux implements asynchronous read-ahead i.e. blocks 126-157 are prefetched despite the fact that block 126 is never requested by the program.
- Running the same Python program immediately after completion of the first run results in zero reported I/O operations: all reads are satisfied from the block cache.

4.3   Ext2

While the SystemTap script presented in Section 4.1 is running, the following commands are executed (where sync forces changed blocks to be written to disk):

```
$ echo "Hello world!" > /ext2/hello.txt ; sync
```

In response the SystemTap script reports the following six I/O operations where each has been annotated with an explanation (note that the debugfs utility can be used to map blocks 1538 and 6152 to the files to which they belong):

```
C :    1 : 1 : W : update group descriptor
C : 1025 : 1 : W : update block bitmap
C : 1026 : 1 : W : update inode bitmap
C : 1027 : 1 : W : update inode table
C : 1538 : 1 : W : add new dirent to root dir
C : 6152 : 1 : W : write "Hello world!"
```

Several file system concepts are demonstrated by this simple exercise:

- Creating and writing to a file under Ext2 translates to several distinct low-level I/O operations across various locations in the file system as both new data and metadata must be written to disk.
- A system crash during the execution of the required I/O operations will leave the file system in an inconsistent state.
- Omitting the call to sync results in an observable delay before SystemTap reports I/O activity. This demonstrates Linux's write-back block cache strategy: changed blocks are periodically rather than synchronously written to disk.

4.4   Ext3

A key advantage of a journalling file system is its ability to efficiently restore a file system to a consistent state after a system crash. To this end, before committing file system changes to disk they are written as a contiguous transaction to a journal. During reboot any intact journal transactions that were not successfully committed to disk are replayed. Any half-written journal transactions are simply ignored.

Ext3 supports several journalling strategies. The default (and the one studied below) is metadata-only journalling (known as *ordered mode* journalling) in which data blocks are written to disk before metadata changes are journalled.

While the SystemTap script presented in Section 4.1 is running, the following commands are executed:

```
$ echo "Hello world!" > /ext3/hello.txt ; sync
```

In response the SystemTap script reports the following 13 I/O operations where each has been annotated with an explanation (note again that the debugfs utility can be used to map blocks 1539, 1245783-1245789 and 1135 to the files to which they belong):

```
C :    1539 : 1 : W : write "Hello world!"
C : 1245783 : 1 : W : update journal
C : 1245784 : 1 : W : update journal
C : 1245785 : 1 : W : update journal
C : 1245786 : 1 : W : update journal
C : 1245787 : 1 : W : update journal
C : 1245788 : 1 : W : update journal
C : 1245789 : 1 : W : update journal
C :       1 : 1 : W : update group descriptor
C :     626 : 1 : W : update block bitmap
C :     627 : 1 : W : update inode bitmap
```

```
C :      628 : 1 : W : update inode table
C :      1135 : 1 : W : add new dirent to root dir
```

Several file system concepts are demonstrated by this simple exercise:

- Creating and writing to a file under Ext3 translates to several distinct low-level I/O operations across various locations in the file system as new data, journal entries and metadata must be written to disk.
- Although writes to a journal are contiguous, maintaining a journal incurs an observable overhead.
- Ext3's default journalling strategy journals only metadata updates.
- A system crash during the execution of journal updates means metadata changes are never committed to disk as incomplete journal transactions will be ignored at boot time and, although some data is lost, the file system remains consistent.
- A system crash during the execution of metadata updates is recoverable: at boot time the journal entries are replayed and the file system is restored to a consistent state.

4.5 NilFS

In a final experiment a third partition was installed with log-structured file system NilFS [5]. A log-structured file system aims to optimise file system writes [8]. To this end, all writes, whether data or metadata, are simply appended to a log that expands across the disk. The assumption is that as system memory capacities increase most reads will in future be satisfied from the block cache and thus file systems should target performance-hurting writes.

While the SystemTap script presented in Section 4.1 is running, the following commands are executed:

```
$ echo "Hello world!" > /nilfs/hello.txt ; sync
```

In response the SystemTap script reports the following single I/O operation:

```
C : 269566 : 15 : W : append data and metadata to log
```

Creating and writing to a file under NilFS translates to a single, multi-block contiguous write to the head of the log on the disk.

5 MEMORY MANAGEMENT

The Linux process address space structure is depicted in Figure 5. From the bottom up: The text section holds machine executable code, global data resides in the data section, runtime memory requirements are served from the heap and the stack supports procedure call and return. Assuming a 32-bit architecture the size of the address space is 4GB (2^{32} bytes) with the top quarter (1GB) reserved for the kernel (not shown in Figure 5). Under virtual memory the size of the process address space is independent of the size of the physical address space (i.e. the quantity of physical RAM installed on the machine). Virtual addresses are 32 bits wide and run from 0x00000000 to 0xFFFFFFFF.

The Linux memory manager is responsible for translating virtual to physical addresses. In the simplest case this translation is managed by a hierarchical structure consisting of a single page directory which points to a set of page tables with each of the latter pointing to physical page frames. (A hierarchical structure that

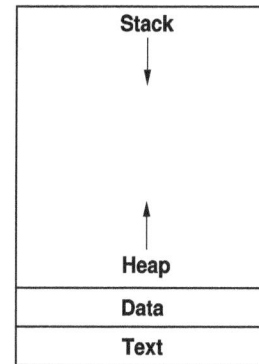

Figure 5: Process address space

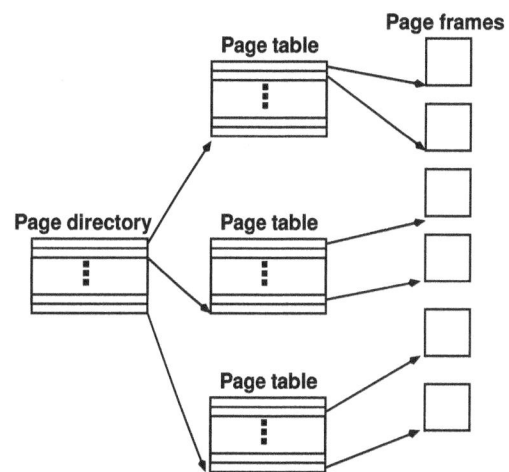

Figure 6: Page directory, page table, page frame hierarchy

expands in response to demand is more memory-efficient than a single flat structure.) This structure is depicted in Figure 6.

There are 1024 entries in a page directory and in each page table. Each page frame is 4096 bytes in size. Thus the described hierarchical structure is capable of mapping the full 4GB ($1024 * 1024 * 4096 = 4GB$) address space. Each page table is capable of mapping 4MB ($1024 * 4096 = 4MB$) of the process address space.

For a "small" process the low end of the address space (text, data and heap sections) can be expected to be mapped by a single page table. Similarly, the high end of the address space (stack) is assumed to be mapped by another page table. Thus we would expect the entire process address space of a "small" process to be mapped by a total of two page tables. Below we use a SystemTap script to confirm that this is indeed the case.

The script presented in Listing 5 hooks the return from the __pte_alloc() function in order to intercept all page tables created in the context of the *hello* process whose source code is presented in Listing 4.

```
# Listing 4
int main() {
 printf("Hello world!\n");
}
```

```
# Listing 5
probe kernel.function("__pte_alloc").return
{
  if (execname() != "hello") next

  printf("Faulting address: 0x%08x\n", $address)
  task = task_current()
  mm = task->mm
  nr_ptes = atomic_long_read(&mm->nr_ptes)
  printf("Page tables now: %d\n", nr_ptes)
}
# stap -g alloc.stp -c "./hello"
Hello world!
Faulting address: 0x080f4f88
Page tables now: 2
```

The above output confirms that two page tables are indeed sufficient to map the process address space of the *hello* process. Interestingly we see that although two page tables are required, only a single call to __pte_alloc is intercepted. The first call to __pte_alloc occurs in the context of the parent process (it is the parent process that initialises a child process's stack) and is thus missed by our script. In a second experiment, we add a 4MB global array to our process address space's data section as follows:

```
# Listing 6
char x[1024*4096];
int main() {
  printf("Hello world!\n");
}
```

Running the SystemTap script in the context of the "larger" process confirms that one additional page table is now required to map the enlarged address space:

```
# stap -g alloc.stp -c "./hello"
Hello world!
Faulting address: 0x080f4f88
Page tables now: 2
Faulting address: 0x084f5c54
Page tables now: 3
```

6 EVALUATION

The effectiveness of the proposed SystemTap-enhanced approach to demonstrating operating systems concepts has yet to be formally and quantitatively compared to other approaches. However, feedback from annual anonymous student surveys is consistently positive. Student comments indicate the module rates among the most popular of the degree programme. Of particular note is the high level of student engagement with the module. In class presentation of material and demonstrations are described as "interactive", "fun", "engaging" and "interesting". Students commented positively on the "beneath the bonnet" treatment of the subject. Students also indicated the module motivated them to carry out further research in the area of operating systems in their own time.

7 CONCLUSIONS

The study of operating systems plays a critical role in undergraduate computer science degree programmes. Operating systems concepts covered in lectures are traditionally made concrete through the undertaking of significant programming projects. While such programming projects are invaluable and remain the gold standard in delivering the desired operating system learning outcomes, there is room for supplementary approaches and tools that support the classroom-/lab-based demonstration of operating system concepts in the context of a live, real-world operating system.

SystemTap is a Linux monitoring tool. This paper has demonstrated how simple SystemTap scripts can be used to intercept kernel events which can then be mapped to operating system concepts which might otherwise have remained purely theoretical. Examples in the paper covered topics traditionally covered in a module on operating systems: scheduling, file system implementation, and memory management.

To date the SystemTap scripts described in this paper have been used primarily for demonstration purposes only. Possible extensions were suggested to a selection of the SystemTap scripts presented. It would be interesting to create and evaluate the effectiveness of a series of SystemTap programming exercises for students. Requiring students to write SystemTap scripts and explain their output would yield valuable learning outcomes:

- Selecting appropriate events to hook demonstrates an understanding of the Linux kernel,
- explaining SystemTap output demonstrates an understanding of operating system concepts,
- as a general purpose Linux monitoring tool with a vast array of applications beyond those considered in this paper, SystemTap programming skills are valuable in their own right.

For instructors and students (and particularly for the latter group for whom, often, seeing is believing) SystemTap demonstrations, whether in a classroom or laboratory setting, have a valuable role to play in solidifying understanding of operating system concepts.

REFERENCES

[1] Remy Card, Theodore Ts'o, and Stephen Tweedie. 1994. Design and Implementation of the Second Extended Filesystem. In *Proceedings of the First Dutch International Symposium on Linux*. State University of Groningen, Netherlands, 1–6.

[2] Wayne A. Christopher, Steven J. Procter, and Thomas E. Anderson. 1993. The Nachos Instructional Operating System. In *Proceedings of the USENIX Winter 1993 Conference Proceedings on USENIX Winter 1993 Conference Proceedings (USENIX'93)*. USENIX Association, Berkeley, CA, USA, 4–4. http://dl.acm.org/citation.cfm?id=1267303.1267307

[3] Frank Ch. Eigler. 2006. Problem Solving with SystemTap. In *Proceedings of the Ottawa Linux Symposium*. 261–268.

[4] Frank Ch. Eigler. 2015. SystemTap Tutorial. (2015). https://sourceware.org/systemtap/tutorial.pdf

[5] Ryusuke Konishi, Yoshiji Amagai, Koji Sato, Hisashi Hifumi, Seiji Kihara, and Satoshi Moriai. 2006. The Linux Implementation of a Log-Structured File System. *ACM SIGOPS Operating Systems Review* 40, 3 (2006), 102–107.

[6] R. H. Patterson, G. A. Gibson, E. Ginting, D. Stodolsky, and J. Zelenka. 1995. Informed Prefetching and Caching. *SIGOPS Oper. Syst. Rev.* 29, 5 (Dec. 1995), 79–95. DOI: http://dx.doi.org/10.1145/224057.224064

[7] Ben Pfaff, Anthony Romano, and Godmar Back. 2009. The Pintos Instructional Operating System Kernel. *SIGCSE Bull.* 41, 1 (March 2009), 453–457. DOI: http://dx.doi.org/10.1145/1539024.1509023

[8] Mendel Rosenblum and John K Ousterhout. 1992. The design and implementation of a log-structured file system. *ACM Transactions on Computer Systems (TOCS)* 10, 1 (1992), 26–52.

[9] Theodore Y. Ts'o and Stephen Tweedie. 2002. Planned Extensions to the Linux Ext2/Ext3 Filesystem. In *Proceedings of the FREENIX Track: 2002 USENIX Annual Technical Conference*. USENIX Association, Berkeley, CA, USA, 235–243. http://dl.acm.org/citation.cfm?id=647056.715922

Improved Mobile Robot Programming Performance through Real-time Program Assessment

Rémy Siegfried
LSRO, EPFL
Lausanne, Switzerland
remy.siegfried@alumni.epfl.ch

Severin Klingler
Dept. of Computer Science, ETH
Zurich, Switzerland
kseverin@inf.ethz.ch

Markus Gross
Dept. of Computer Science, ETH
Zurich, Switzerland
grossm@inf.ethz.ch

Robert W. Sumner
Dept. of Computer Science, ETH
Zurich, Switzerland
robert.sumner@inf.ethz.ch

Francesco Mondada
LSRO, EPFL
Lausanne, Switzerland
francesco.mondada@epfl.ch

Stéphane Magnenat
Dept. of Computer Science, ETH
Zurich, Switzerland
stephane@magnenat.net

ABSTRACT

The strong interest children show for mobile robots makes these devices potentially powerful to teach programming. Moreover, the tangibility of physical objects and the sociability of interacting with them are added benefits. A key skill that novices in programming have to acquire is the ability to mentally trace program execution. However, because of their embodied and real-time nature, robots make the mental tracing of program execution difficult.

To address this difficulty, in this paper we propose an automatic program evaluation framework based on a robot simulator. We describe a real-time implementation providing feedback and gamified hints to students.

In a user study, we demonstrate that our hint system increases the percentage of students writing correct programs from 50 % to 96 %, and decreases the average time to write a correct program by 30 %. However, we could not show any correlation between the use of the system and the performance of students on a questionnaire testing concept acquisition. This suggests that programming skills and concept understanding are different abilities.

Overall, the clear performance gain shows the value of our approach for programming education using robots.

KEYWORDS

robotics in education; Thymio; automatic program evaluation; gamified hint system; simulation

ACM Reference format:
Rémy Siegfried, Severin Klingler, Markus Gross, Robert W. Sumner, Francesco Mondada, and Stéphane Magnenat. 2017. Improved Mobile Robot Programming Performance through Real-time Program Assessment. In *Proceedings of ITiCSE'17, July 03-05, 2017, Bologna, Italy., , 6 pages.*
DOI: http://dx.doi.org/10.1145/3059009.3059044

1 INTRODUCTION

The last decade has seen a large number of initiatives and products aiming at teaching programming and computer science to children using robots. They do so by providing a simplified programming environment, typically visual, inside which children define the behavior of the robot. The main motivations are the strong interest robots raise in children, the tangibility of programming physical objects, and the sociability of interacting with them. These elements are important for the healthy physical, intellectual and social development of children. Moreover, several studies have shown that robots can be effective to teach certain computer science and software engineering notions to beginners [1, 8]. In addition, with young children, robots can do so without a strong gender bias [7]. Furthermore, robots show how information processing can be embodied within the physical world.

However, it is not known whether robots are effective at teaching computer science and software engineering in general, especially compared to a traditional software programming course. The fact that robots allow children to quickly write programs that do something indicates neither deep learning nor the acquisition of transferable skills. Moreover, a key skill that novices in programming have to acquire is the ability to mentally trace program execution [13]. We argue that programming robots poses challenges, that combined, render tracing programs difficult:

(1) **Not steppable.** Programs cannot be executed step by step, as robots are physical real-time systems.
(2) **Not trivially inspectable.** As the program is not steppable, the internals of execution is not easily visible.
(3) **Not deterministic.** As robots operate in the continuous real world, having sampled and noisy sensors and imperfect motors, the execution of a program might be hard to predict from the code itself.
(4) **Bad source code locality.** As most programming paradigms for mobile robots are concurrent, modifying a part of a program might affect other parts.

Therefore, as observed by previous work [8], both students and teachers face difficulties identifying bugs in their code, and progressing beyond trivial exercises is problematic.

Hence, to leverage the advantages of robots for programming education, one must overcome the aforementioned challenges. One way is to improve the programming tools to make the internals of program execution more visible. Previous work has, for example, explored the use of visual feedback and augmented reality [5]. A complementary way to technical tools is to train the tracing skills of the students, by guiding them through problems of increasing difficulty.

A common way of providing adaptive guidance is to employ an intelligent hint generation system. In the context of programming education, hint systems have been successful at providing hints for code correctness [12] and coding style [2], but have not yet been applied to robot programming.

A necessary brick to provide hints and feedback to students is the ability to assess a given code regarding a set of metrics [4]. While there are well-established methods for software programming [3], evaluating the quality of a robot program and providing meaningful feedback to the student are open research questions. In this paper, we address these questions. In particular, we provide the following contributions:

(1) an automatic evaluation framework for robot programs based on running simulations in background,
(2) a real-time implementation on a mobile device, providing feedback and gamified hints to the student,
(3) a user study and its analysis, evaluating the effects of this system on learning.

2 ROBOT PROGRAM EVALUATION

Static evaluation is difficult for robot programs, because a slight change in a parameter might lead to a completely different behavior. An obvious way to dynamically evaluate a robot program is to run it on a real robot in a physical environment and check whether the robot performs its task. This is not practical for automatic program evaluation, as instrumentalizing such tests would require a lot of resources and result in slow results. Another way is to execute the program within a virtual robot in a simulated environment. That is significantly faster and can be fully automatized. A potential drawback is that the quality of the program evaluation depends on the accuracy of the simulation. However, typical educative programming tasks do not rely on advanced physical phenomena, so a simple simulator providing collision and kinematic support would suffice.

2.1 Simulation-based performance evaluation

Figure 1 shows the overall structure of the robot program evaluation system. It is similar to software-only approaches [10], but with all tests taking place within the simulator. However, robot programs are difficult to separate into functional units, so the breadth of a test varies in function of its simulation conditions. For example, imagine a task in which the student must program the robot to navigate a labyrinth. A very specific case, such as following a straight corridor, could be

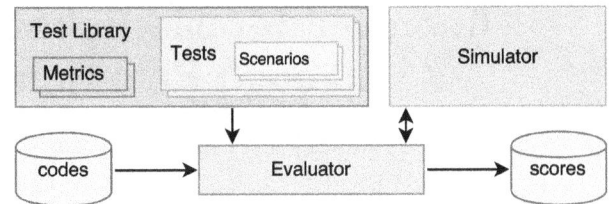

Figure 1: The automatic robot program evaluation system.

considered a unit test, and a complete task, such as navigating a given labyrinth, could be considered an end-to-end test. Hence, we use the term *test* broadly, to refer to any kind of simulation-based evaluation.

The robot program evaluation system is composed of a test library, an evaluator, and a simulator. The test library provides, for a given task, a set of tests. Each test consists of one or more *scenarios*, and a function to compose the *scenario scores* into a *test score*. A scenario is the unit of simulation, it contains

- a description of the environment (walls, obstacles),
- a script describing the actions to perform during the simulation, such as pressing a button on the robot or moving an object in the environment,
- the name of a metric to compute the scenario score.

The *metric* evaluates the performance of the robot in a given scenario; it is a function, over time, of the robot's sensor and motor values and its relation with its environment. The evaluator simulates each scenario and computes test scores using simulation results and the metrics from the library.

2.2 Didactic sequencing through gamified hints

Building on our program evaluation framework, we propose a gamified hint system. A key decision is what amount of information about the program quality to report to the student and when. If too little is provided, the system brings no benefit. If too much is provided, it would be detrimental to learning, as students could superficially solve the problem by following the hints rather than reasoning by themselves. Moreover, they could also experience cognitive overload.

For a given task, such as navigating a labyrinth, our system progressively displays hints indicating test results. A hint is an image representing one test, with its background color changing in function of the test outcome (see Figure 5). Hints can be in three states: locked, unlocked or active.

- Active hints display how well the current program performs at the corresponding tests. The background can take 3 different colors: green, orange and red corresponding to good, mediocre or bad test scores.
- Unlocked hints do not show the performance of the tests, to push students to think by themselves.
- Locked hints are invisible, and the tests are not run.

A task is split into a list of levels, each containing one or more hints, unlocked in order. The system maintains a current level. Hints for higher levels are locked, hints for the current level are unlocked, and hints for the lower levels are active.

Hints are updated each time the student runs the program on the real robot. A student passes to the next level when her or his program is good at all tests (their scores are above a threshold) up to and including the current level. Moreover, after a given time, the next level is automatically unlocked, regardless of the results of the tests.

3 IMPLEMENTATION

3.1 Thymio II, Aseba and VPL

We have implemented our robot program evaluation system on the Thymio II robot and its visual programming environment. The Thymio II robot [11] and its Aseba software were created at the EPFL, ETH Zürich, and ECAL. Both the hardware design and the software are open-source.

The robot is small ($11 \times 11 \times 5$ cm), self-contained and robust with two independently-driven wheels for differential drive. It has five proximity sensors on the front and two on the back, and two color intensity sensors on the bottom. There are five buttons on the top, a three-axis accelerometer, a microphone, an infrared sensor for receiving signals from a remote control and a thermometer. For output, there are RGB LEDs at the top and bottom of the robot, as well as mono-colored LEDs next to the sensors, and a sound synthesizer.

The Aseba programming environment [6] uses the construct **onevent** to create event handlers for the sensors. VPL is a component of Aseba for visual programming[1]. This work branches from the development version of the tablet implementation, and runs on an Android tablet Nvidia Shield K1. Figure 2 shows a VPL program for following a line of black tape on a white floor. On the left is a column of *event blocks* (buttons, proximity, ground color intensity, accelerometer, microphone) and on the right is a column of *action blocks* (motors, colors of the robot). By dragging and dropping one event block and one or more action blocks to the center pane, an *event-actions pair* is created. Both event and action blocks are parametrized, enabling the user to create many programs from a small number of blocks.

The VPL tablet prototype is implemented in Qt Quick[2]. This allows writing the test library in a comfortable declarative language, and the evaluator in JavaScript. The evaluation itself is performed using the Enki simulator[3]. This simulator is simple and fast yet accurate enough, and already supports the Thymio robot. Moreover, Aseba provides a library for embedding its virtual machine into Enki, allowing a seamless simulation of a valid Thymio program inside Enki. The software used in the experiment is available on github[4].

3.2 Gamified hints for labyrinth navigation

To evaluate our system, we have implemented hints for a task in which students must program a robot to navigate inside a labyrinth. The task consists in programming the robot such that it traverses as much of the labyrinth as possible in 10

[1]https://www.thymio.org/en:visualprogramming.
[2]https://www.qt.io/qt-quick/
[3]https://github.com/enki-community/enki
[4]https://github.com/aseba-community/thymio-vpl2/releases/tag/iticse2017

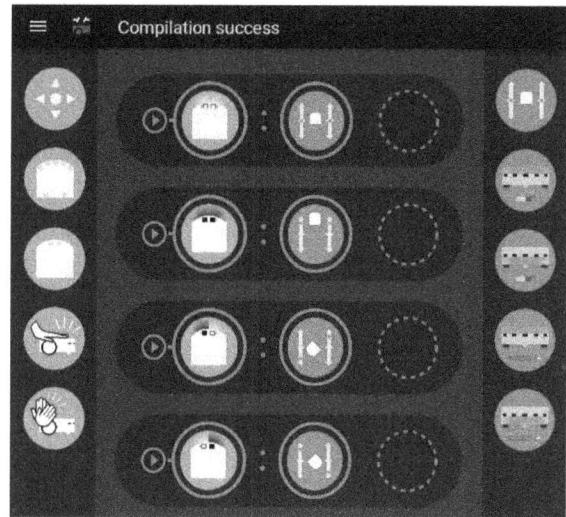

Figure 2: The Thymio VPL tablet environment.

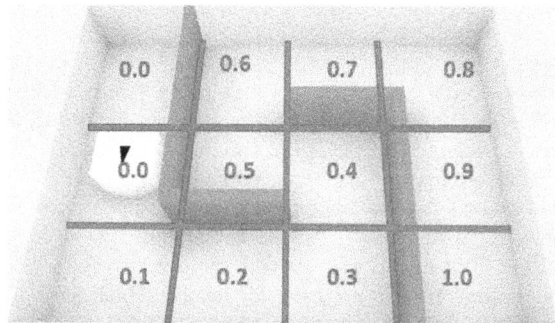

Figure 3: Labyrinth split into tiles of increasing score.

seconds. Figure 4f shows a picture of the labyrinth, which consists of a tortuous corridor with a width of 20 cm.

To compute a score of a scenario, the labyrinth is split into small tiles as shown in Figure 3. The score is given by the furthest reached tile, with the distance of the robot to the next tile taken into account to provide sub-tile precision. To test the program in different environments of increasing complexity, we create different tests and scenarios, starting with simplified versions of the labyrinth. Each scenario is simulated for a certain duration. If the robot has a high score, it indicates that the program is correct for that scenario. Only the score is available to the user through hints, the simulation itself is hidden. There are 8 scenarios, organized in 5 tests/hints, and unlockables in 4 different levels:

 Hint 1: empty area, level 1   see Figure 4a
- **scenario 1**: going straight forward in an empty arena, for 5 seconds.

As there is no tile in an empty area, this test computes the score using the traveled distance.

Hint 2: corridor, level 2   see Figure 4b
- **scenario 2.1**: following a corridor, starting aligned to it, for 5 seconds.
- **scenario 2.2**: following a corridor, starting unaligned to it, for 5 seconds.

Hint 3: left turn, level 3   see Figure 4c
- **scenario 3.1**: passing a left turn, starting oriented to the left, for 7 seconds.
- **scenario 3.2**: passing a left turn, starting oriented to the right, for 7 seconds.

Hint 4: right turn, level 3   see Figure 4d
- **scenario 4.1**: passing a right turn, starting oriented to the right, for 7 seconds.
- **scenario 4.2**: passing a right turn, starting oriented to the left, for 7 seconds.

Hint 5: labyrinth, level 4   see Figure 4e
- **scenario 5**: navigating in the complete labyrinth, for 10 seconds.

Some hints have more than one scenario, to capture the different conditions of the corresponding test. For example, in the case of the left turn, a robot going straight forward will achieve a different score between the two scenarios, as it is initially oriented to the left in the first one. The score of a hint is the average of the scores of all its scenarios.

We give the user a maximal duration to complete each level, after which the system automatically passes to the next one. This duration is set to 5 minutes, except for level 3 which lasts 10 minutes, and for level 5 which lasts until the activity finishes. Figure 5 shows the system in action: the user is currently at level 4 (*labyrinth*) and the last run program obtained a mediocre score to the *empty*, *left turn* and *right turn* tests and a bad score to the *corridor* test.

4 EXPERIMENT AND RESULTS

To measure the efficiency of gamified hints on performance and learning, we ran a set of programming workshops for two days over a week-end. Seven sessions of 75 minutes each were proposed. Each session was composed of:
(1) Introduction (10 minutes): the robot and the tablet software were introduced by a small demonstration.
(2) Discovery activities (10 minutes): four easy tasks were given to the children.
(3) Labyrinth activity (30 minutes): children were asked to program the robot to navigate in the labyrinth, like shown in the Figure 4.
(4) Hand following activity (15 minutes): children were asked to program the robot to follow their hand.
(5) Questionnaire (10 minutes): children were asked to fill a questionnaire, similar to Magnenat et al. [8].

The workshops were attended by 43 children including 7 girls between 9 and 12 years, with 4 to 10 children per session (average 6). No previous programming or robotics experience was required, but 22 children had already used the Thymio

robot and 15 reported previous programming knowledge, of which 11 had already used the robot. Children were provided one tablet and one robot each and shared four labyrinths. For the labyrinth activity, children were split into two groups, each given a different configuration of the software:
- The *Hints* group (24 children, 12 previous Thymio users, 8 with programming knowledge, 5 girls, ages: 9: 12, 10: 4, 11: 2, 12: 3) used the full system.
- The *Control* group (19 children, 10 previous Thymio users, 7 with programming knowledge, 2 girls, ages: 9: 10, 10:1, 11: 6, 12: 2) used a restricted version in which the levels were shown without indication of program quality, and were passed only at the end of their maximal duration.

Sessions Hints and Control were alternated during the weekend to avoid any bias due to the different assistant teams, their tiredness or their growing experience of the setup. Other activities were done with the bare VPL software for both groups, without providing any didactic sequence. We had no control on which child joined which session.

One of the authors and five university students provided assistance. The author was always present and the assistants were distributed over the two days, such that there were always two of them available. To avoid biases, the assistants were combined into three different configurations, which all supervised both types of sessions. Their role was to answer questions, and, when a child was blocked, ask her or him a related question to help progression and avoid frustration.

4.1 Research questions and results

Based on this experiment, we address 5 research questions on the effects of providing hints:

Is it feasible to perform a real-time evaluation considering the number of tests to run? We measure the time used to run the simulations of all tests. On an Android Nvidia Shield K1 tablet, the 8 scenarios, whose real-time durations add up to 53 seconds, are simulated within ≈1 second, including the computation of scores. Although the app freezes during this second, it is acceptable as students are often looking at the robot after clicking the run button. Therefore, we demonstrated the concrete feasibility of our approach.

Does feedback allow students to write programs faster? During the labyrinth activity, we measure the duration students took to successfully solve each level (1 to 4). As the Control group students could not pass levels before the end of the maximal test duration, the time at which they reached a level was recomputed offline during data analysis, using the algorithm as used online for the Hints group. Children in the Hints group took significantly less time than the ones in the Control group to reach the different levels (Table 1a). Yet one must be cautious as this result could be biased: children in the Hints group were more pushed toward completing each level, due to the fact that they could pass to the next level if they succeeded at the test of the current level, which was not the case for the Control group.

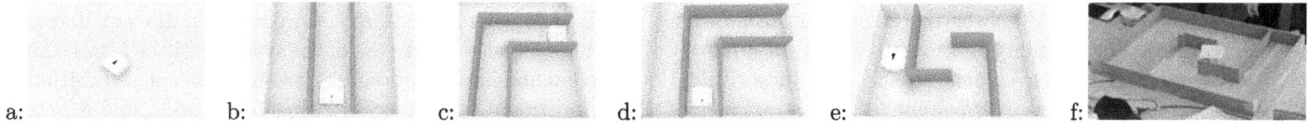

Figure 4: Different virtual environments used to test the labyrinth task (a to e); Real environment (f).

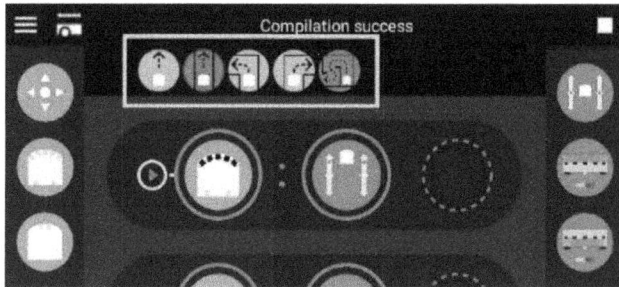

Figure 5: Hints in the Thymio VPL environment.

Does feedback allow more students to create better programs? During the labyrinth activity, we measure the best achieved score for each level (1 to 5) separately. In the Hints group, 95.65 % of children achieved all tests, against 52.36 % for the Control group, a statistically significant difference (Table 1b, p-value = 0.001).

Does feedback improve the building of transferable skills? During the hand following activity, we measure the duration students took to solve the task and the number of times they run a program. We observe no significant differences between the two groups (Table 1c). Therefore, we cannot answer this question with this study, but it seems unlikely that there is an improvement in transfer due to the hint system.

Does feedback improve the understanding of computer-science concepts? The answers to the questionnaire are converted into a grade, giving one point per correct answer. We see that the error rate is similar for both groups (Table 1d), so we cannot answer this question with this study. However, it seems that the hint system has no significant effect on the acquisition of computer-science concepts overall.

5 DISCUSSION AND LIMITATIONS

Our results might indicate that the scores obtained from the robot programming task and the grades in the questionnaire measure two distinct competencies. Thus, we believe that crossing the information from questionnaire assessment and performance metrics can help to better understand and assess the different programming abilities of students. Furthermore, by combining our system with human tutoring that focuses on theoretical and methodological foundations of computer science, our system could provide a motivating and stimulating playground to develop programming skills.

The proposed simulation framework is able to capture extensive statistics about the development of a program, including the evolution of program performance, the best program achieved or the frequency of program production.

Level	Hints	Control	p-value
Level 2	171	141	0.398
Level 3	336	553	**0.014**
Level 4	680	927	**0.045**
Level 5	961	1364	**0.002**

a. The mean level reaching time in seconds for the labyrinth activity, and the p-value of Student's t-test (H0: means are equal), between the two groups.

Test	Hints	Control	p-value
empty area	0.89	0.70	0.065
corridor	0.72	0.74	0.498
left turn	0.88	0.55	**0.003**
right turn	0.94	0.60	**0.003**
labyrinth	0.96	0.57	**0.001**

b. The mean best scores for each test of the labyrinth activity, and the p-value of Student's t-test (H0: means are equal), between the two groups.

Metric	Hints	Control	p-value
Number of runs	14.8	13.3	0.347
Task completion time	742	604	0.681

c. The mean number of runs and task completion time for the hand following activity, and the p-value of Student's t-test (H0: means are equal), between the two groups.

	Q1	Q2	Q3	Q4	Q5	Q6	Q7	Q8
Hints	0.42	0.00	0.05	0.32	0.00	0.63	0.32	0.11
Control	0.29	0.00	0.00	0.46	0.08	0.63	0.21	0.04
p-value	0.85	0.99	0.73	0.83	0.65	1.00	0.89	0.88

d. The error rate for Hints and Control groups; p-values of Pearson's chi-square test (H0: both conditions follow the same distribution). n = Hints: 24, Control: 19.

Table 1: Quantitative results of the user study.

These statistics are useful for many different applications that go beyond a hint system. A distinct advantage of our solution over direct source code analysis is that our approach is agnostic to the underlying programming language as all metrics are based on the simulated behaviour of the robot.

From our qualitative observations during the experiments, the gamified hint system seemed to increase the students involvement in the task. We observed that the performance feedback provided by the hints prompted students for a more critical assessment of their current solutions as they could directly observe which previously passing tests were no longer correct with their new solution attempt.

We have explored potential effects of factors such as gender, previous programming knowledge or previous exposition to Thymio, but could not draw relationships of similar importance as the use of Hints. The only statistically significant one is that children with previous programming knowledge completed the labyrinth significantly faster than the ones without (average 15 min 55 s against 21 min 32 s, p=0.026).

The main limitations of our work are the limited number of participants (43), the simplicity of the hand following task used to test transfer, and the short duration of the workshop. All these factors must be improved to find an answer to the unresolved questions of this paper. Moreover, the current implementation of the simulator only simulates a 2-D environment and its physics engine is simplistic. As such, it is not applicable to flying robots, for example.

6 FUTURE WORK

A direct extension of our work would be to combine the results obtained from the simulation with other data extracted from the programming environment. For instance, we could count the number of times a program is run on the robot or directly analyze its source code. We believe that, with enough data, it would be possible to automatically identify students who are struggling with a given task.

We plan to investigate the effect of directly providing the feedback from the hint system to teachers. Indeed, during an informal survey after the experiment, several assistants reported that it was easier to aid students when using the hint system, as it gives a high-level overview of the capabilities of their program. In addition, the progress made visible by the hint system allowed assistants to quickly identify students in need of guidance. Directly providing this feedback to educators through a tablet computer similar to the work of Maldonado et al. [9] has the potential to facilitate personalized interventions and improve learning.

7 CONCLUSION

In this paper, we presented an innovative way to guide students learning to program using robots. We demonstrated a gamified hint system based on the automatic assessment of robot programs. Our system is able to evaluate programs in real-time on a tablet device. By running the program in a virtual machine inside a fast robot simulator, it can be tested in different scenarios without affecting the user experience.

We ran a user study in which students had to program a robot to navigate a labyrinth. We demonstrated that our hint system increases the percentage of students writing correct programs from 50 % to 96 %, and decreases the average time to write a correct program by 30 %. However, our findings on the effect on the learning outcome are inconclusive. We could not show any transfer of programming skills to the new

task of following the hand. Moreover, we did not find any correlation between the use of the system and the performance of students on a questionnaire testing concept acquisition.

Additional studies considering more tasks and a longer exposition to the system are needed to further investigate the relationship between the user guidance and the acquisition of computer science concepts. Nevertheless, the clear performance improvement in the task where students were guided shows the value of this approach for programming education using robots.

8 ACKNOWLEDGEMENTS

This work was supported by ETH Research Grant ETH-23 13-2, by Mobsya, by the Swiss NCCR "Robotics", and by the Swiss CTI grant 17479.2 PFES-ES. The authors thank Moti Ben-Ari and the anonymous reviewers for their feedback.

REFERENCES

[1] Marina Umaschi Bers, Louise Flannery, Elizabeth R. Kazakoff, and Amanda Sullivan. 2014. Computational Thinking and Tinkering: Exploration of an Early Childhood Robotics Curriculum. *Computers & Education* 72 (2014), 145–157.

[2] Rohan Roy Choudhury, Hezhengm Yin, and Armando Fox. 2016. Scale-Driven Automatic Hint Generation for Coding Style. In *Intelligent Tutoring Systems*. Springer, 122–132.

[3] Petri Ihantola, Tuukka Ahoniemi, Ville Karavirta, and Otto Seppälä. 2010. Review of recent systems for automatic assessment of programming assignments. In *10th Koli Calling International Conference on Computing Education Research*. ACM, 86–93.

[4] Hieke Keuning, Johan Jeuring, and Bastiaan Heeren. 2016. Towards a Systematic Review of Automated Feedback Generation for Programming Exercises. In *21st Conference on Innovation and Technology in Computer Science Education*. ACM, 41–46.

[5] Stéphane Magnenat, Morderchai Ben-Ari, Severin Klinger, and Robert W. Sumner. 2015. Enhancing Robot Programming with Visual Feedback and Augmented Reality. In *20th Conference on Innovation and Technology in Computer Science Education*. ACM, 153–158.

[6] Stéphane Magnenat, Philippe Rétornaz, Michael Bonani, Valentin Longchamp, and Francesco Mondada. 2010. ASEBA: A Modular Architecture for Event-Based Control of Complex Robots. *IEEE/ASME Transactions on Mechatronics* PP, 99 (2010), 1–9.

[7] Stéphane Magnenat, Fanny Riedo, Michael Bonani, and Francesco Mondada. 2012. A Programming Workshop using the Robot "Thymio II": The Effect on the Understanding by Children. In *Advanced Robotics and its Social Impacts (ARSO)*. IEEE.

[8] Stéphane Magnenat, Jiwon Shin, Fanny Riedo, Roland Siegwart, and Morderchai Ben-Ari. 2014. Teaching a Core CS Concept Through Robotics. In *19th Conference on Innovation & Technology in Computer Science Education*. ACM, 315–320.

[9] Roberto Martinez Maldonado, Judy Kay, Kalina Yacef, and Beat Schwendimann. 2012. An interactive teacher's dashboard for monitoring groups in a multi-tabletop learning environment. In *International Conference on Intelligent Tutoring Systems*. Springer, 482–492.

[10] Amit Kumar Mandal, Chittaranjan Mandal, and Christopher MP Reade. 2006. Architecture of an Automatic program evaluation system. *CSIE Proceedings* (2006).

[11] Francesco Mondada, Michael Bonani, Fanny Riedo, Manon Briod, Léa Pereyre, Philippe Rétornaz, and Stéphane Magnenat. 2017. Bringing robotics into formal education using the Thymio open source hardware robot. *IEEE Robotics and Automation Magazine* (2017). Accepted.

[12] Kelly Rivers and Kenneth R Koedinger. 2015. Data-driven hint generation in vast solution spaces: a self-improving python programming tutor. *International Journal of Artificial Intelligence in Education* (2015), 1–28.

[13] Juha Sorva. 2013. Notional Machines and Introductory Programming Education. *Transactions on Computing Education* 13, 2 (2013), 8:1–8:31.

TrAcademic: Improving Participation and Engagement in CS1/CS2 with Gamified Practicals

Brian Harrington
Dept. of Computer & Mathematical Sciences
University of Toronto Scarborough
brian.harrington@utsc.utoronto.ca

Ayaan Chaudhry
Dept. of Computer & Mathematical Sciences
University of Toronto Scarborough
ayaan.chaudhry@mail.utoronto.ca

ABSTRACT

Practice is an important part of introductory CS courses, and practical sessions are a student's best opportunity for hands-on experience with the material covered in the course in a supervised, supportive environment. However, finding a balance between challenging more experienced students and alienating newcomers can be difficult and frustrating. One possible solution is to let the students self-select the problems they wish to attempt. The difficulty then becomes one of motivation and administration.

This paper details our experiences with implementing a gamified system for practicals whereby students in CS1 and CS2 level courses receive points for various activities, including attendance, attempting basic problems, completing challenge problems and aiding fellow students with their work. These points have no bearing on final grades, but are displayed on a public leaderboard.

In our experience, this gamified system dramatically improved attendance at practical sessions, was well received by students and TAs alike, improved retention rates, and offered students the opportunity and motivation to overcome poor performance early in the course and improve their results.

CCS Concepts

•Social and professional topics → Computing education; Computer science education; CS1;

Keywords

Computer Science Education, CS1, CS2, Practicals, Gamification, Engagement

1. INTRODUCTION

Introductory CS courses regularly suffer from an "experience gap". Some students enter the course knowing nothing about computer science/programming, while others have extensive experience either from high-school, or by being self-taught. The challenge for instructors is to design a course which challenges and interests the latter group, without alienating the former, while still teaching the fundamentals of computer science necessary for upper year courses. One solution to this problem is to offer à la carte practical sessions, where students can choose the number and difficulty of the practice problems they complete. This solution relies on students choosing to attend these sessions, and having the discipline and maturity to participate to the full extent of their ability.

Prior iterations of our courses had made course marks contingent on participation in these practical sessions. This ensured attendance, and added a measure of accountability, but we found this system to be time consuming, frustrating, and not particularly beneficial to either experienced or novice students. Experienced students felt the sessions were a waste of their time, while newcomers were intimidated and felt lost. Teaching assistants felt they spent all of their time dealing with administrative duties rather than actually helping students with the material.

Making the practical sessions entirely optional alleviated several of these problems: experienced students didn't waste their time, novice students didn't feel intimidated, and TAs were relieved of their administrative burden. The one problem: no one showed up.

The ultimate goal of this project was to develop a practical system that offered the flexibility and administrative simplicity of optional sessions, but with the engagement and accountability of the mandatory sessions. Our attempts at finding this balance eventually led us to the solution of gamification. We developed the TrAcademic system, a public leaderboard of points that could be awarded by TAs during the practical session for a number of engagement related activities. The goal was to reward students for not just attendance, but participation and peer assistance, in a way that is public and enjoyable, without being intimidating or administratively prohibitive.

The TrAcademic system for gamified practicals was implemented in CSCA08 and CSCA48, a CS1 and CS2 level course pairing with enrolments 850 and 525 students respectively. We found that the gamified practical sessions vastly increased attendance at the practical sessions and improved the experience subjectively for both the students and the teaching assistants. We further discovered that participation in the system appears to correlate well with student performance and that the inclusion of gamified practicals appears to have improved student retention. There is even data to indicate that the gamified practicals are helping struggling students get back on track. Overall, the gamified practicals were a huge success, improving all aspects of the course, and helping to develop a much more convivial atmosphere among the student population.

2. BACKGROUND

2.1 Game mechanics and Gamification in Education

The use of games to enhance education has a wide assortment of benefits, and there are several game design mechanics that have shown success in different education environments [18][7]. Games allow a "player" to restart or play again when they fail a task. This ability to recover from failure allows players to experiment without fear of severe repercussions and will thereby enhance students' engagement [15]. Feedback for students in the normal education setting are often limited: In class, teachers can often only interact with and provide feedback to one student at a time, while feedback on assignments can be more extensive but usually involves an associated mark, which can prevent students from feeling comfortable learning from mistakes.

Thus, incorporating the frequent and immediate feedback found in game design, without the usual association of grades, may be even more beneficial [13]. Furthermore, instructors usually use scaffolded instruction, where information is presented to the class in categories that scale by difficulty. This technique does not allow for accommodation to each individual student's level of understanding and experience. Games, on the other hand, can be adjusted for progression through different difficulties on an individual basis, keeping student's at a specific level until they can show mastery of the skills to move onto the next level [1]. In addition, other elements of game design commonly applied to gamification might be helpful: leaderboards encourage engagement through competition, and differentiating between types of points can offer a visual display of mastery [4][13].

Despite considerable speculation about the benefits of introducing gamification to courses [16][9], there has been limited empirical research on the effectiveness of gamification. The few studies conducted on the inclusion of various components of gamification into educational setting are mixed. One study found that students who were given feedback about performance in the course through the use of a competitive game enjoyed the experience more, learned more, and had lower rates of failure than previous classes [5]. A second study reported higher student interest and engagement after gamifying a course using competition, leaderboards, and multiple serious games intended to teach course concepts [2]. DeMarcos et al[7] used a gamification system that gave students rewards and trophies, and used a leaderboard to encourage competition. They compared this and a traditional platform with a social networking learning platform where students could comment, blog, and interact with each other. The authors found that students in both the gamification group and the social networking group outperformed the control group on skill based assignments, however the control group did better on the final written examination designed to assess course knowledge. Additionally, students tended to have very low participation rates with the gamified (24%) and social networking platforms (38%). These findings are similar to those that study gamification in non-education contexts. Hamari et al[10] conducted a com-

prehensive review of empirical studies of gamification across different contexts (e.g., marketing, entrepreneurial, education), but were only able to identify a handful of studies. Of the studies identified, only 2 were found to report entirely positive effects. Most studies found some positive aspects of gamification, such as increased engagement and enjoyment, but these outcomes were often dependent on the context of the gamified system (e.g., computer science, educational) and the characteristics of the player. The authors also found major methodological problems with the studies; of the 24 reviewed, only a few were found to actually compare gamified and non-gamified experiences [10]. Thus, it is uncertain whether the effects found can be attributed to gamification or other factors.

Some studies have indicated that providing too strong an emphasis on gamification, in particular courses having final marks heavily tied to the gamified elements, can negatively impact students satisfaction with the course by promoting a competitive and anti-collegial atmosphere [11].

2.2 Social comparison and leaderboards

By nature, humans make judgments about their own abilities and those of others through comparison, since it is difficult to make an assessment of a person's ability without a reference point [12]. Theories on social comparison predict that an individual compares himself to other people in order to reduce uncertainty, make judgments, and validate opinions [8]. Typically, individuals would compare themselves with those that are equal on a desired trait, but research shows comparisons often occur with others who are worse (downward comparison, which are meant to invoke positive affect and a feelings of superiority) or better (upward comparison, which invoke a negative affect and can be used as a form of motivation) than the individual making the comparison [3]. Gamification of a course typically involves the addition of a leaderboard, where players' scores on given tasks or points accumulated are displayed for everyone to see. Depending on a given person's position, a leaderboard can offer both the opportunities for upward and downward comparisons, dependant on the fields displayed [6]. Although individuals high on the leaderboard may have a sense of superiority and positive affect, they may also feel greater pressure to maintain their higher position [19]. This increased pressure from social comparisons may influence students' academic performance [6]. Social comparison fits almost naturally into the classroom setting, where objective evaluation and exposure to peer performance and ability are constantly provided [19], and the addition of leaderboards might provide a visible, objective reminder of their performance relative to others. The effects of a digital leaderboard may be even more substantial when compared to other traditional methods (e.g., a sticker chart posted in a classroom). Traditional leaderboards are only accessible to students in one location whereas digital leaderboards are accessible to students anywhere using the internet. Since digital leaderboards can be accessed outside of the classroom at any time, students can spend as much time as they like evaluating the class or comparing their achievements with others. Furthermore, students are able to compare themselves to other students on multiple dimensions, and customize the leaderboard by sorting according to different criteria.

3. THE TRACADEMIC SYSTEM

In this section we detail the decisions that led to the inclusion of gamified practicals, and the automated system we developed for managing/tracking the sessions.

3.1 Mandatory Labs: 2013 – 2014

For multiple years, our CS1 and CS2 courses had used weekly 2 hour lab sessions, with paired programming to complete a specific task. Students had 10% of their mark allocated to these labs (1% per lab for 10 weeks). To receive the mark for the week, students had to demonstrate a working completed program to the TA by the end of the session.

Post course surveys showed students to be unhappy with these labs. 55.7% of students rated the labs as unhelpful, compared to only 26.8% rating them as helpful. All other course components (Lectures, Assignments, Readings, Office Hours) had positive response rates of at least 50%. Student complaints tended to cluster into those saying the labs were a waste of time (e.g., "I would normally be done the labs in the first 20 minutes, but would have to sit around waiting forever for the TAs to sign me out"), and those saying the labs were too difficult (e.g., "My partner and I would get stuck all the time, and not know what to do next. The TA would help, but then 5 minutes later we would be stuck again and have to wait"). Overall, the major complaint seemed to stem from the fact that the TAs had to spend large portions of their time taking attendance and validating the work of all of the students, and had little time remaining to actually help the students understand the material.

3.2 Optional Practicals: 2014 – 2015

For the 2014 – 2015 academic year, the labs were changed to be entirely optional (with marks re-distributed to weekly quizzes and auto-marked exercises). Rather than a single lab exercise to complete in a set period of time, a variety of exercises of varying difficulty were made available. Students were not assigned to specific times/rooms, but instead a full schedule was posted, and students were told they could "drop-in" for as many or as few hours as they felt they required. Rather than taking attendance, TAs were free to offer help to whomever required during the session.

In informal surveys, the TAs responded positively to these changes, saying they felt their time was better utilized in this new system (e.g., "Last year I spent most of my time running from group to group checking things off a list, this year I actually feel like I got to help students"). And the student surveys seemed to agree, with only 10.6% of students rating the practical sessions as "unhelpful", and 23.3% who rated them as "helpful". Unfortunately, 66.1% of students chose "No opinion/I did not use this resource" (up from only 17.5% the previous year).

While we did not take formal attendance during the practical sessions, TAs were asked to keep track of the number of students in each session. The average attendance rate was 4 students/hour (26 students/week). The maximum attendance was 15 students (on a session just before the second term test). Some sessions had no students attend at all. In a course of 500+ students, this paints an even worse picture of attendance than the surveys, and indicates that only approximately 5% of students are attending practical sessions in any given week.

3.3 Gamified Practicals: 2015 – 2016

For the 2015 – 2016 academic year, the practical sessions themselves were left unchanged . The schedule, rooms, rules and exercises were identical to the previous year (with the exception of a few questions being updated to fix minor errors or to provide better emphasis). However, this time, we introduced gamified elements to the practical sessions. The goal was to provide a simple, unobtrusive, publicly viewable leaderboard to reward students for participation and engagement. TAs were provided with a tablet outfitted with a magnetic card reader and specially designed app that allowed them to swipe a student card to pull up the record of an individual student (a search feature was also implemented for students who did not bring their card). TAs could award a student 3 different types of points:

- Experience Points: 1 point for attendance at practical session (students could swipe their own cards at a kiosk for this point) and 1 point for completion of a minimum number of exercises (awarded by TAs).

- Challenge Points: 1-3 points for weekly "challenge questions". Usually designed to require reading beyond the core course material or group work (awarded by TAs).

- Teaching Points: 1-3 points for aiding other students in their learning (awarded by TAs). Activities which could earn teaching points included: assisting with front-of-class demonstrations, explaining concepts to other students (whether at the request of a TA or by a student's own volition), or aiding other students with debugging or coding efforts.

The swipe-based app meant that awarding a point took on average 1-2 seconds (5-7 seconds if the student did not have their ID present and the TA had to use the search feature). It was made clear to the students that these points had no bearing on their grade in any way, and existed purely for fun [1]. This policy of not connecting grades directly to points was done partially due to the author's dislike of paternalistic approaches, but also to avoid adding any extra stress to the students and risking the development of an overly competitive and adversarial atmosphere. The decision was also made to limit the gamification to this simple leaderboard in order to properly evaluate the impact of a minimally invasive, low-cost approach.

A public leaderboard displayed the students point totals and individual category points as shown in Figure 1

4. RESULTS

The gamified practicals were used for the 2015–2016 academic year in the CS1 and CS2 courses (627 and 456 students respectively). In this section we review the data collected during that time. Our primary goal was to increase attendance and engagement in the practical sessions. To this end, we estimated attendance by analyzing the usage data of the TrAcademic system. We also wanted to see how this affected the student and TA perception of the course. For this purpose we analyzed the standard end-of-year surveys, as well as a separate survey given to teaching assistants

---

[1] In the interest of full disclosure, it should be noted that the instructor did mention that points, particularly teaching points, could be used as a selection criterion in future TA hiring.

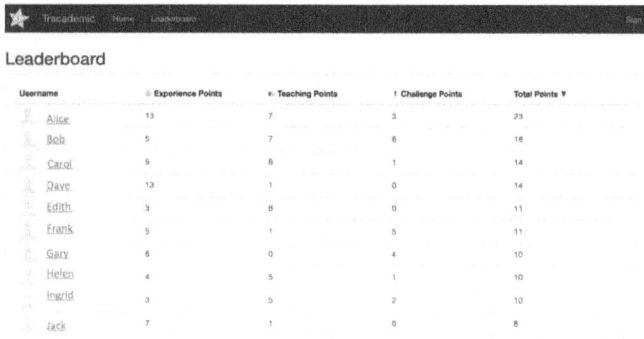

Figure 1: The TrAcademic Leaderboard

	Non-Gamified	Gamified
Min Attendance/hour	0	18
Max Attendance/hour	15	50
Avg Attendance/hour	4	27
Avg Attendance/Week	26	243

Table 1: Attendance in gamified vs non-gamified practical sessions.

specifically targeting the gamified practicals. Finally, we analyzed the performance of the students based on their usage/attendance patterns in the gamified practicals to obtain quantitative data of the relationship between participating in the practicals and course outcome.

4.1 Attendance/Usage

In the 2014–2015 academic year, attendance was not formally taken, but the TAs were asked to report on the total number of students in each practical session. Attendance was skewed greatly to sessions immediately prior to assignment deadlines and term tests. The maximum attendance for any single hour of practical session was 15 students, and several sessions had no students attend at all. The average across the entire term was 4 students/hour or 26 students/week.

In the 2015–2016 academic year, with the addition of the gamified practicals, attendance improved dramatically. Several sessions had to turn students away (the room had a maximum capacity of 50 students), and the lowest attendance was 18 students in an hour (3 more than the maximum attendance a year previous). The average across the term was 27 students/hour, or 243 students/week (an increase of over 500%). Full details are shown in Table 1.

It should be noted that the course enrolment did increase between the two years (20% for CS1 and 18% for CS2), but this is unlikely to account for the dramatic increase in attendance.

Prior to using the TrAcademic system, it was not possible to accurately monitor how many questions were attempted/completed by a student, but the attendance numbers show that even if no students were double counted (a very un-likely scenario), less than 6% of students attended practical sessions regularly.

In the gamified practicals, we were able to more accurately track individual students (though it should be noted that participation in the TrAcademic system was entirely

optional, and many students attended the practicals, but did not bother to record their points). 57% of students enrolled in the course received at least one experience point for attendance, 18% solved at least one challenge question, and 13% received at least one teaching point.

4.2 Surveys

In the end of term survey 45% of respondents rated the practicals as "helpful" as opposed to 20.6% which rated them as "unhelpful". While the ratio of helpful to unhelpful respondents was similar to previous years, the response rate was almost double. Results of the surveys are summarized in Table 2

The teaching assistants completed a short survey at the end of the course specifically targeting the gamified practicals. All 21 TAs (all upper year undergraduate CS students) completed the survey, 7 of whom had TAed the course in the previous academic year. All of the TAs agreed or strongly agreed with the statements: "The practical sessions were helpful for the students", "The TrAcademic system encouraged students to attend practicals", and "The TrAcademic system encouraged students to help one-another".

Of the 7 returning TAs, 100% strongly agreed with the statement: "The new gamified practical system is an improvement over last year's practicals".

	Helpful	Unhelpful	No Opinion /Did Not Use
2013–2014 (mandatory)	26.8%	55.7%	17.5%
2014–2015 (optional)	23.3%	10.6%	66.1%
2015–2016 (gamified)	45.0%	20.6%	34.4%

Table 2: Results of student surveys rating helpfulness of practicals

4.3 Performance

After collecting data on usage, we decided to compare the number of points gained by students against several other metrics to determine whether there was a relationship between system usage and performance.

Points vs Performance

Simply opting into the system seemed to have a high correlation with success in the course. We divided the class into 3 groups, non-users (those who never opted into the system, or received 0 points), users (those with at least 1 attendance point), and 'heavy-users' (those with at least 5 attendance points). The heavy users performed better than the regular user group, which in turn performed better than the non-users. This pattern was evident in all course components (except weekly quizzes and exercises, for which the average was very high among all groups), as can be seen in Table 3. Differences were found to be significant in all course elements (using Kruskal-Wallis one-way analysis of variance, with $p < 0.01$) with the exception of the CS2 project mark, where there was little difference between users and heavy users.

A similar pattern can be found for the various types of points. Students with at least one challenge point or at least

!

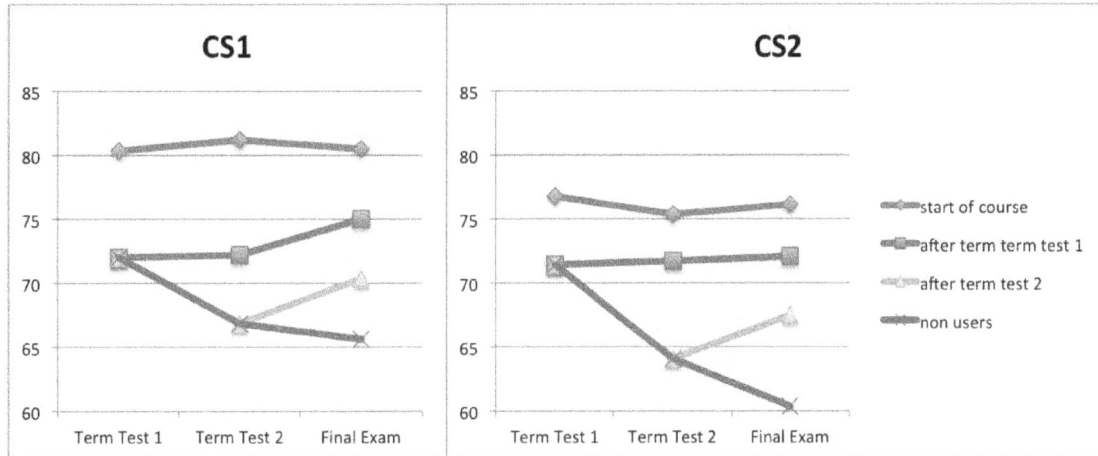

Figure 2: Comparison of average student results on major course components based when they started using the TrAcademic system

		Projects	Midterms	Exam	Final
	Non-Users	58.22	58.22	58.91	60.94
CS1	Users	68.27	66.28	65.89	69.26
	Heavy-Users	69.39	69.87	67.80	71.68
	Non-Users	53.03	64.18	63.38	62.39
CS2	Users	60.43	72.41	70.66	70.24
	Heavy-Users	60.84	75.64	72.08	72.15

Table 3: Average grade received vs degree of use

		mark < 50	mark ≥ 80
	Non-Users	20.97	18.98
CS1	Users	7.60	29.23
	Heavy-Users	5.88	35.29
	Non-Users	16.39	17.86
CS2	Users	8.05	29.88
	Heavy-Users	5.00	35.00

Table 5: Percentage of students failing the course and receiving a final grade of A for users vs non-users of the TrAcademic system

one teaching point had final grades significantly higher than users who only had experience points, as can be seen in Table 4. All differences were statistically significant (Kruskal-Wallis, $p < 0.01$). There was a positive, but not statistically significant correlation between the number of challenge/teaching points and final course grade.

	CS1 Final	CS2 Final
Users with 1+ challenge point	76.64	75.34
Users with 0 challenge points	67.30	67.27
Users with 1+ teaching point	75.11	75.12
Users with 0 teaching points	68.17	69.25
Non-users	60.94	62.39

Table 4: Average grade received vs presence/absence of challenge/teaching points

The relationship between usage and marks seemed to affect the entire grade spectrum, as seen in Table 5. There was a strong relationship between system use and a lower fail rate, as well as a higher rate of achieving a grade over 80%. All differences were statistically significant (Kruskal-Wallis, $p < 0.01$)

Starting Stage vs Outcome

Obviously correlation does not imply causation. So comparing points and performance does not tell us whether the system was actually directly benefiting students, or the better students were using the system more. In order to better analyze the effect that the system had on users, we divided user groups based on when they actually began using the system, in order to see if there was a temporal relationship between the direction of marks over time and usage of the system. We hoped to see that students who are performing poorly and begin to use the system part way through the term would see an improvement in their marks.

Usage of the system tended to jump in between the major course milestones, with a steady (percentage) increase throughout the year. We analyzed the results of students on the 3 major components of the courses (two term tests and a final exam) and plotted them against whether the students started at the beginning of the term, after the first term test, or after the second term test. As can be seen in Figure 2, it is clear that even when students started later in the term, they were able to improve their outcome.

Once again, it should be noted that there are many confounding variables here, and we would naturally expect students who begin to take their studies more seriously part way through the term to be more likely to take advantage of available resources. However, this trend is promising.

Retention

Introductory CS courses have notoriously low retention rates [17] for a variety of reasons [14]. One of the initial goals of the gamified practicals was to improve engagement among struggling students, which would hopefully result in a lower drop rate. With this in mind, we compared the retention rates (percentage of students who signed up for the course who wrote the final exam) in the 2015–2016 year with those of the previous year, where the only significant difference in the courses was the introduction of the gamified practicals. We found that there was a marked improvement in retention for both CS1 and CS2, with the retention rising by 3% in CS1 and 6% in CS2. The results for both CS1 and CS2 were found to be significant (using Chi-Squared test, $\chi = 4.2946, 6.7926$ respectively, p<0.05). The results can be found in Table 6.

	CS1	CS2
2013–2014	0.72	0.79
2014–2015	0.73	0.81
2015–2016	0.76	0.87

Table 6: Retention (percentage of enrolled students who wrote final exam) in CS1 and CS2 for 2014–2105 (non-gamified practicals) vs 2015–2016 (gamified practicals)

5. FUTURE WORK

The implementation of gamified practicals has been a huge success. We have every intention of continuing to use the gamified practical model and the TrAcademic system in the future. One major aspect of the system that we were not able to cover here is the social effect that it had on the course. From instructor feedback and TA reports it was clear that the gamified practicals lead to a much more dynamic, convivial and social atmosphere. Not just in the practical sessions themselves, but across the entire course. We hope to study this aspect with a series of surveys and interviews, and also to continue to monitor the effect that the gamified practicals have on the course more generally. For example, evaluating the effect based on gender, prior programming experience, intended major, and other personal data could provide very interesting insights into how to make these practicals more effective for specific target groups. Inclusion of the TrAcademic system into our CS1/CS2 courses will not only improve student engagement and provide an additional avenue for students to gain programming experience, but will also provide us with a valuable resource to track trends in student development, which can be used for future pedagogical improvement. We intend to release the TrAcademic system under an academic license for public use.

The authors would like to thank the students and TAs of CSCA08 and CSCA48. None of this would have been possible without their participation and feedback.

6. REFERENCES

[1] P. L. Beed, E. M. Hawkins, and C. M. Roller. Moving learners toward independence: The power of scaffolded instruction. *The Reading Teacher*, 44(9):648–655, 1991.

[2] F. Bellotti, R. Berta, A. D. Gloria, E. Lavagnino, A. Antonaci, F. M. Dagnino, and M. Ott. A gamified short course for promoting entrepreneurship among ICT engineering students. pages 31–32. 2013 IEEE 13th International Conference on Advanced Learning Technologies, Beijing, 2013.

[3] B. P. Buunk and F. X. Gibbons. *Toward an Enlightenment in Social Comparison Theory*. The Springer Series in Social Clinical Psychology. Springer US, 2000.

[4] V. Camilleri, L. Busuttil, and M. Montebello. *Social Interactive Learning in Multiplayer Games*. Springer London, London, 2011.

[5] D. Charles, T. Charles, M. McNeill, D. Bustard, and M. Black. Game-based feedback for educational multi-user virtual environments: Game-based feedback for educational MUVEs. *British Journal of Educational Technology*, 42(4):638–654, 2011.

[6] K. R. Christy and J. Fox. Leaderboards in a virtual classroom: A test of stereotype threat and social comparison explanations for women's math performance. *Computers & Education*, 78(5):66–77, 2014.

[7] L. de Marcos, A. Dominguez, J. S. de Navarrete, and C. Pages. An empirical study comparing gamification and social networking on e-learning. *Computers & Education*, 75(2):82–91, 2014.

[8] L. Festinger. A theory of social comparison processes. *Human Relations*, 7(2):117–140, 1954.

[9] C. Ganzalez and M. Area. *Breaking the Rules: Gamification of Learning and Educational Materials:*. SciTePress - Science and and Technology Publications, 2013.

[10] J. Hamari, J. Koivisto, and H. Sarsa. Does gamification work? – a literature review of empirical studies on gamification. pages 3025–3034. 2014 47th Hawaii International Conference on System Sciences, Waikoloa, HI, 2014.

[11] M. D. Hanus and J. Fox. Assessing the effects of gamification in the classroom: A longitudinal study on intrinsic motivation, social comparison, satisfaction, effort, and academic performance. *Computers & Education*, 80:152–161, 2015.

[12] V. Hoorens and C. V. Damme. What do people infer from social comparisons? bridges between social comparison and person perception: Inferences from social comparison. *Social and Personality Psychology Compass*, 6(8):607–618, 2012.

[13] K. M. Kapp. *The Gamification of Learning and Instruction: Game-based Methods and Strategies for Training and Education*. Pfeiffer, 1 edition, 2012.

[14] P. Kinnunen and L. Malmi. Why students drop out cs1 course? In *Proceedings of the Second International Workshop on Computing Education Research*, ICER '06, pages 97–108, New York, NY, USA, 2006. ACM.

[15] J. J. Lee and J. Hammer. Gamification in education: What, how, why bother? *Academic Exchange Quarterly*, 15(2):71–76, 2011.

[16] J. McGonigal. *Reality is Broken: Why Games Make Us Better and How They Can Change the World*. Penguin Group US, 2011. OCLC: 898986343.

[17] L. Porter and B. Simon. Retaining nearly one-third more majors with a trio of instructional best practices in cs1. In *Proceeding of the 44th ACM Technical Symposium on Computer Science Education*, SIGCSE '13, pages 165–170, New York, NY, USA, 2013. ACM.

[18] A. Stott and C. Neustaedter. Analysis of gamification in education. Technical report, Connections Lab, Simon Fraser University, Surrey, BC, Canada, 2013.

[19] B. M. Wells and J. J. Skowronski. Evidence of choking under pressure on the PGA tour. *Basic and Applied Social Psychology*, 34(2):175–182, 2012.

Programming as a Performance – Live-streaming and Its Implications for Computer Science Education

Lassi Haaranen
Department of Computer Science
Aalto University, School of Science
Espoo, Finland
lassi.haaranen@aalto.fi

ABSTRACT

This article discusses an emerging phenomenon of streaming programming to a live audience who in turn can interact with the streamer. In essence, this means broadcasting the programming environment and typically a web camera feed of the streamer to viewers. Streaming programming bears many similarities with live-streaming playing of video games, which has become extremely popular among gamers over the recent years. In fact, streaming programming often use the same web services as streaming gaming, and the audiences overlap.

In this article, we describe this novel approach to programming and situate it in the broader context of computer science education. To gain a deeper insight into this phenomena, we analyzed viewer discussions during a particular programming stream broadcasted during a game programming competition. Finally, we discuss the benefits this approach could offer to computer science education.

Keywords

computer science education, streaming, game-based learning, online communities

1. INTRODUCTION

In recent years, the desire to include programming and computational thinking into elementary school curricula has increased. Programming and computational thinking are increasingly seen as competencies which would benefit every member of the modern society. In 2014, European Schoolnet surveyed 20 European Ministries of Education regarding the inclusion of computing or coding in their current or planned initiatives [1]. All participating countries, apart from one, either already had included coding in their curricula (12 countries) or had plans to do so in the future (7 countries).

The interest in learning to program is also reflected in the number of tools designed specifically to aid in this ac-

tivity. Tools and technical innovations are being developed and research that is specific to computing education is being conducted, such as program visualization [14], automated assessment of program code [7], incorporating professional tools to course environments [5]. Naturally, research and development of more general tools also benefits computing education, such as learning management systems [3] and interoperability protocols (e.g., Learning Tools Interoperability [8]).

With this article, we wish to present to the computing education research community a novel approach to disseminating programming and computer science knowledge: the live streaming of programming. Live streaming, or simply streaming, has roots in the gaming community, where it has become a major phenomenon over the past few years. Streaming with games usually consists of a person (the streamer) broadcasting live footage from a particular game, as well as usually a webcam feed of his face. The streamer narrates the action and entertains the audience, which may include tens of thousands live viewers.

As the streaming community has grown, some of the streamers have started to stream the act of programming (often a game) to a live audience. In essence, they aim to entertain as they create a new piece of software. As far as we know, this phenomenon has gone completely unnoticed by the computer science education research community. In general, learning to program in informal contexts has received relatively little attention from researchers.

One aspect that makes streaming novel and different, for example, from recording programming lectures is the audience participation. Since the streamer is "performing" live, he or she can interact with the audience. The live interaction, either in programming or gaming contexts, has so far received little research interest, but new research projects will further investigate this emerging phenomenon (e.g., [13]).

Streaming programming allows the audience to join the programming process, for example, by doing a code review, suggesting alternative approaches, and spotting bugs that the streamer might have missed. Naturally, the live streams can be made available online afterwards as recordings known as VODs (Video On Demand).

As the main contribution, this paper introduces the phenomena of streaming programming, especially focusing on its potential relevance to computer science education. We approach this phenomenon by first describing the history of streaming in general and how streaming has become a popular form of entertainment. After this, we focus on a specific

ITiCSE '17, July 03 - 05, 2017, Bologna, Italy

© 2017 Copyright held by the owner/author(s). Publication rights licensed to ACM.
ISBN 978-1-4503-4704-4/17/07...$15.00

DOI: http://dx.doi.org/10.1145/3059009.3059035

case example of streaming programming by examining the discussion that the viewers had during a stream.

The rest of this article is organized as follows. In Section 2, we review the history of streaming and programming streams in general. In Section 3, we present a specific case of streaming programming during a game development event. Additionally, we analyze the discussion in which viewers participated in during the stream. In Section 4, we consider the implications of streaming programming to computer science education and outreach. Finally, Section 5 concludes the article and considers directions future research.

2. BACKGROUND

In this section, we first provide background to the birth of streaming in the gaming community. After this, we look at how computer science education and games have been connected to each other in the past. Finally, we investigate the phenomenon of streaming programming.

2.1 Live Streaming

Streaming, whether in games or something else, takes place through a web service where different streamers have channels, typically focused on particular themes. These channels allow viewers to discover new material as well as follow the streamers that they like. One of the leading services in streaming is called Twitch.tv (https://www.twitch.tv/). Already in 2012, the number of viewers and streamers was considerable on Twitch.tv, reaching daily tens of thousands of viewers [9]. The phenomenon of streaming has continued to grow, alongside with e-sports (playing computer games competitively); for example, Witkowski et al. report that popular e-sports tournaments reach millions of viewers [16].

The first major event that introduced Twitch.tv to the gaming community was "Twitch Plays Pokemon" in February 2014. In this event, the viewers were also players and collaboratively gave commands through IRC protocol to play the game Pokemon Red. Overall, it attracted 1.6 million players who participated among 55 million viewers [17]. The size of the community and the scale of the phenomena is reflected by the fact that Amazon decided to purchase Twitch.tv for nearly one billion dollars later in 2014 [10].

2.2 Relating Games and Computer Science Education

Games in various forms have been used in computer science courses as a context for learning to program. There are many ways in which games can be used in CS courses. Wallace et al. [15] categorized different approaches into four distinct types:

- Programming a game (designing and programming a full game as a part of a course project)

- Programming a part of a game (implementing missing parts of an existing game project)

- Programming an agent that acts within a game world

- Playing a (serious) game that has been created to teach particular programming context during the gameplay

Generally, there has been increasing interest, especially in STEM (Science, Technology, Engineering, and Mathematics) fields, to incorporate games into education. Based on systematic literature reviews, positive effects of games and serious games in STEM education has increased in the recent years [2].

Games and game-like themes can be incorporated into individual assignments, project and group work, or even used as the underlying theme for a whole course, as did Leutenegger and Edgington [11]. They argued that basing a course on a game theme is motivating for most new programmers, and gained good results teaching introductory programming concepts through games.

One game-related approach that has also gained popularity in recent years is gamification, which refers to the use of game-like elements in non-game contexts, such as education [4]. Computer science education has also been a fertile testing ground for gamification as well, with many experiments set up on computer science courses (see e.g. [6]).

2.3 Streaming Programming

Although Twitch.tv and streamers using it still mainly focus on games, Twitch.tv has recently opened up its terms and conditions to allow also other types of content. In 2015, it was announced that Twitch.tv would introduce support for creative content:

"All along, the Twitch community has included a determined community of artists, crafters and builders, who have been using Twitch to broadcast their creative processes. These creative broadcasters share many of the same characteristics as all Twitch broadcasters: passion, engagement, and a community-centric worldview." [12]

One of these creative areas now available for streaming is programming (https://www.twitch.tv/directory/game/ Creative/programming). This allows programmers and developers perform programming as a form of entertainment. The streamer typically has a project, commonly some form of game development, which he develops while the audience can simultaneously participate in the process via chat. The developer's desktop is streamed live to the audience, allowing them to see the process. Figure 2 illustrates this process.

3. CASE LUDUM DARE 37

This section first describes Ludum Dare – a game development event, describing its history and purpose. After this, we discuss a single programming stream and analyze discussions that the viewers of this stream had over a weekend.

3.1 Ludum Dare – "A Regular, Theme-based, Accelerated Game Development Event"

Ludum Dare (http://ludumdare.com/compo/) is a game development competition where the contestants create a game from scratch over a weekend. It is held three times a year. At the beginning of the competition, a theme specific to that competition is announced. Starting from the announcement of the theme, the participants have 48 hours to create a game alone. Alongside this competition, the event also includes a 'jam', a category in which the participants can work in teams and have 72 hours to complete a game. The event is held completely online, and after the competition ends, participants can vote on the submitted entries. Although there are no tangible prizes, the best voted entries receive significant attention – and even some commercial games have started as Ludum Dare entries[1].

Ludum Dare itself has existed before live streaming, and the next event in spring 2017 marks the 15th anniversary of the competition. In addition, participants have a tradition of releasing time-lapse videos of the game development process[2]. Naturally, since streaming programming is gaining popularity, many participants create the entire game while streaming it live to an audience, which may include several thousands of viewers in popular streams. The increased popularity of Ludum Dare streams can partly be explained by the fact that Ludum Dare itself has grown to be more popular over the years, as can be seen in Figure 1. During the weekends when Ludum Dares are arranged, more people are exposed to streaming programming. This is because some people who normally stream playing a game and have an established audience, switch to programming in order to participate in Ludum Dare.

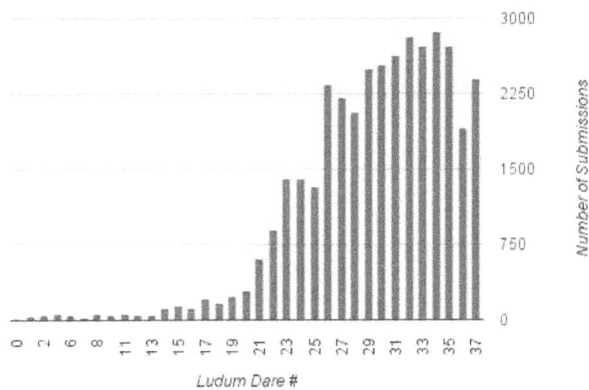

Figure 1: Number of submissions for each Ludum Dare. Data from https://en.wikipedia.org/wiki/Ludum_Dare

For this particular case study, we recorded the discussions in a chat of one streamer participating in Ludum Dare 37 (themed 'One Room') during December 9th-11th, 2016. During the event weekend, the streamer held live streams on three occasions (taking breaks to sleep in between). The streams lasted for approximately 6 hours, 12 hours, and 14 hours. During the weekend, all chat activity was logged for later analysis, including the chat when the stream was offline. The over thirty hours of streaming detail the creation of a game from initial ideas to the finished product submitted to the competition, partial screenshots in Figure 2 illustrate how the stream appeared to viewers.

The streams gathered approximately 3600, 1700, and 1100 views (in the order of appearance). Overall, the chat included 183 unique participants that commented at least once. Approximately 39 000 comments were typed into the chat window during the Ludum Dare weekend.

---

[1]http://store.steampowered.com/curator/537829-Ludum-Dare/

[2]Ludum Dare 18 Timelapse Videos: http://www.indiegames.com/2010/08/ludum_dare_18_timelapse_videos.html

Since the amount of text in the chat was so vast, it was filtered to include only comments that pertained to computer science or programming in some way. This was detected by keywords that were found on the particular comment, the keywords by no means provide an exhaustive list, but they include different programming languages (C#, Java, etc.), programming constructs (loops, recursion, etc.), and programming concepts (debug, bug, stack trace, etc.). The list was created based on our initial observations on the data with some common programming languages with additional concepts. This limited the data set down to approximately 1300 comments, which were then read through to gain insight into the types of discussed themes.

Naturally, filtering the chat with preselected keywords also means that some of the relevant comments will be lost, and the remaining comments depend on the used keywords. However, this was deemed acceptable, since the purpose was to gain an initial understanding of what types of discussions, if any, related to computer science took place in the discussions.

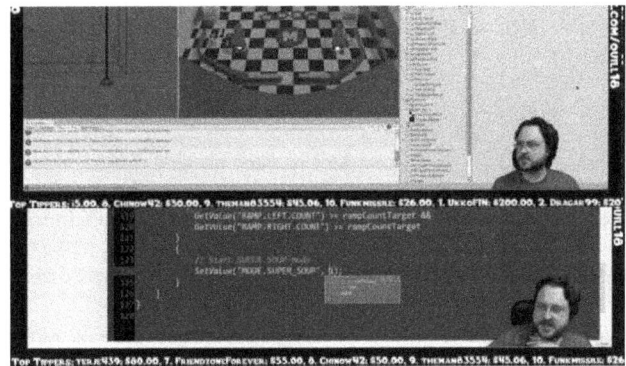

Figure 2: Partial screenshots captured from the Ludum Dare stream where the chat was recorded. The screenshot at the top shows the game inside the development environment, and the lower screenshot shows some code from the game.

3.2 Discussion During The Streams

To gain further insight to the phenomena of streaming, we analyzed the discussions collected from the chat logs during the streams. The goal was not to conduct a comprehensive discussion analysis but rather to gain an insight into the themes present in the discussions. More importantly, our goal was to understand in which way topics related to computer science and programming were present.

During the analysis, we read through the comments and grouped them based on their similarity. Based on the grouping, broader themes were identified within the comments. The following sections discuss the themes and provide concrete examples from the comments.

Interest in Programming

At first glance, it might seem plausible that only those who already know programming would follow a programming stream. However, there is evidence in the discussions that this is not the case. For example, one viewer lamented that he or she did not how to program: *"Wish I knew programming. I think doing this even would be something fun."* It is also worth noting that the streamer had portrayed programming in such a way that the the commenter thought of it as something fun.

The common perception that programming is a particularly difficult activity and that only some people are able to do it was also reflected on in the comments. For example, one viewer stated: *"Sorry. I have no idea about coding. And seeing [the streamer] I think I never would understand it. I think it [sic] great but don't think I can ever do it."*

Questions and Answers

One of the particularly relevant themes that emerged from the discussion was the questions and answers related to computer science and programming. Overall, this theme highlights the collaborative and community-oriented nature of streaming. The questions ranged from very broad questions to specific ones. Broad questions included *" Question: How hard is it to implement multiplayer into a game? Is it easier to make a multiplier[sic] game only (against implementing it)?"* and *"Any tips for someone that is pretty new to game dev (will be using unity) and never took part in a LDJAM [Ludum Dare Jam]?"* Similarly, some of the very specific questions included [chatter1]: *"Hey [streamer]. A really really dumb question, but do you know how to keep an idle thread alive? Like I have a while(isRunning) loop and I'm trying to pause the loop, but if I set isRunning to false, the thread instantly dies... so how would I go about keeping it alive?".* Although some of the questions were addressed to the streamer, other viewers provided answers when possible: *@["chatter1] I'm not sure exactly why you need this, but if you want to keep threads idle so they can quickly be reused consider using a ThreadPool if you are using c#".*

Interaction With Streamer

Perhaps one of the reasons that streaming is so engaging lies in the possible to interact with the streamer. Accordingly, many of the comments in the chat were indeed addressed to the streamer, such as *"Hey [streamer], I really enjoyed watching your hell wars game from ludum dare 33, I learned a lot about c# delegates through it."*

The interaction with the streamer is not just limited to commenting or asking questions, but it can be more collaborative in nature. For example, when trying to solve a particular bug, the audience can notice details that the streamer misses, or propose alternative approaches: *"try removing your clamp code that moves the model downward"*

General Computer Science Discussion

Naturally, there was also a plenty of general discussion regarding computer science and programming. Comments in this category were generally clearly posted by someone who is already fairly familiar with computer science and programming. Many of the comments in this category were devoted to discussion about programming languages and their features, with comments such as *"yep python was the first language i learned and is a great one to start with"* and *"@[other chatter] Long is guaranteed to be a 64-bit integer in c#.'.*

4. RELEVANCE TO COMPUTER SCIENCE EDUCATION

So far this article has focused on describing the phenomena of streaming programming and analyzing discourse during a streaming event. This section observes streaming programming from an educational point of view and argues its relevance to computing educators as well as researchers working in the field.

4.1 Outreach

One of the more interesting aspects of streaming programming is that it allows anyone to see the *process of creating programs*. This can act as an introduction to the field of software development, and notably, one that is very easily accessible. Through streaming, anyone with internet access is able to see what a development process looks like, typically with live commentary of the development. While there are many videos (e.g., on YouTube) describing what working as a software developer is like, watching a developer work live gives an unedited point of view to the profession.

Particularly in the case of game programming streams, the subject matter might attract viewers who may have played games before but have no prior experience in programming. Considering the comments in the previous section regarding the expression of interest in programming, this type of interaction might prove to be a very valuable way to do outreach.

4.2 As a Teaching Method

Much like streaming, Massive Open Online Courses (MOOC) have become highly popular in recent years. Live streaming programming could be adopted on programming MOOCs to facilitate live interaction. As opposed to watching recorded videos, live streams offer the ability to interact and ask questions regarding the code as they arise. Given the vast number of participants receive by some MOOCs, it might not be feasible for the streamer to answer all the questions, but in an open chat environment, other participants could provide an answer as well, as happened in the case study.

One interesting prospect for streaming would be to utilize this approach in more advanced computer science classes. The code demonstrations often given during lectures must remain fairly shallow for practical reasons. With streaming, perhaps outside normal lecture hours, it would be possible to focus on a larger software project and talk about slightly more abstract topics such as program composition.

4.3 Extra-Curricular Material

One related phenomenon which could prove to be an interesting supplementary resource to computing education is Video On Demand (VODs). These are recordings of streams that are made available either in their raw form or in a more edited manner. For example, Twitch.tv enables streamers to publish their streams automatically be available after the live event. This allows someone to watch the stream again, and in the particular case of Twitch.tv, they can also see the chat unfold during the live stream. Streams and VODs can be used as supplementary materials for various courses, thus showcasing the creation of more complex programs.

5. DISCUSSION

In this article, we have described the phenomenon of live-streaming programming in relation to computer science education as a whole. It creates a performance out of the act of developing software and programming in general. Streaming allows those interested in the art of crafting programs to see in first-hand what it is like, and furthermore, allows interaction with seasoned programmers.

Perhaps one of the most interesting possibilities of streaming programming is its ability to reach a wider audience, and more specifically, an audience which might not have considered a programming interesting otherwise. Furthermore, based on the discussions during the streams, it seems that there are a number of people who do not know how to program that are watching these streams. In some ways, streaming programming already works as an outreach program, although it is difficult to estimate or investigate its true impact. It is also worth noting that the group of people that gamers are the most likely group to be exposed to streaming programming without explicitly seeking it. In addition, although the group of people who play games and watch gaming streams is heterogeneous, they are not representative of the whole population.

The phenomenon of live streaming programming is relatively new and so far has not been researched. Nevertheless, it has the potential to impact formal education as outreach in computer science in a significant way.

5.1 Future work

Due to a preliminary and descriptive nature of this research, more research is needed to understand the potential applications and implications of streaming programming. It would be beneficial to understand the demographics of the people watching programming streams since this would give information regarding its effectiveness as an outreach.

Currently, we are not aware of any courses, whether in a university or in a MOOC, which have utilized streaming programming. This type of teaching method could be particularly well-suited for MOOCs. For this reason, research into an authentic setting would be particularly interesting.

6. REFERENCES

[1] A. Balanskat and K. Engelhardt. *Computing our future: Computer programming and coding-Priorities, school curricula and initiatives across Europe*. European Schoolnet, 2014.

[2] E. A. Boyle, T. Hainey, T. M. Connolly, G. Gray, J. Earp, M. Ott, T. Lim, M. Ninaus, C. Ribeiro, and J. Pereira. An update to the systematic literature review of empirical evidence of the impacts and outcomes of computer games and serious games. *Computers & Education*, 94:178–192, 2016.

[3] D. Dagger, A. O'Connor, S. Lawless, E. Walsh, and V. P. Wade. Service-oriented e-learning platforms: From monolithic systems to flexible services. *IEEE Internet Computing*, 11(3):28–35, 2007.

[4] S. Deterding, D. Dixon, R. Khaled, and L. Nacke. From game design elements to gamefulness: defining gamification. In *Proceedings of the 15th international academic MindTrek conference: Envisioning future media environments*, pages 9–15. ACM, 2011.

[5] L. Haaranen and T. Lehtinen. Teaching git on the side: Version control system as a course platform. In *Proceedings of the 2015 ACM Conference on Innovation and Technology in Computer Science Education*, ITiCSE '15, pages 87–92, New York, NY, USA, 2015. ACM.

[6] J. Hamari, J. Koivisto, and H. Sarsa. Does gamification work?–a literature review of empirical studies on gamification. In *2014 47th Hawaii International Conference on System Sciences*, pages 3025–3034. IEEE, 2014.

[7] P. Ihantola, T. Ahoniemi, V. Karavirta, and O. Seppälä. Review of recent systems for automatic assessment of programming assignments. In *Proceedings of the 10th Koli Calling International Conference on Computing Education Research*, pages 86–93. ACM, 2010.

[8] IMS Global Learning Consortium. Learning tools interoperability, 2010. http://www.imsglobal.org/toolsinteroperability2.cfm. Accessed 2017-01-10.

[9] M. Kaytoue, A. Silva, L. Cerf, W. Meira, Jr., and C. Raïssi. Watch me playing, i am a professional: A first study on video game live streaming. In *Proceedings of the 21st International Conference on World Wide Web*, WWW '12 Companion, pages 1181–1188, New York, NY, USA, 2012. ACM.

[10] E. Kim. Amazon buys twitch for $970 million in cash. *Business Insider*, 2014. Available online: http://www.businessinsider.com/amazon-buys-twitch-2014-8.

[11] S. Leutenegger and J. Edgington. A games first approach to teaching introductory programming. *SIGCSE Bull.*, 39(1):115–118, Mar. 2007.

[12] B. Moorier. Introducing twitch creative. *Twitch Blog*, 2015. Available online: https://blog.twitch.tv/introducing-twitch-creative-fbfe23b4a114.

[13] A. Pellicone. Performing play: Cultural production on twitch. tv. In *Proceedings of the 2016 CHI Conference Extended Abstracts on Human Factors in Computing Systems*, pages 244–248. ACM, 2016.

[14] J. Sorva, V. Karavirta, and L. Malmi. A review of generic program visualization systems for introductory programming education. *ACM Transactions on Computing Education (TOCE)*, 13(4):15, 2013.

[15] S. A. Wallace, R. McCartney, and I. Russell. Games and machine learning: a powerful combination in an artificial intelligence course. *Computer Science Education*, 20(1):17–36, 2010.

[16] E. Witkowski, B. Hutchins, and M. Carter. E-sports on the rise?: Critical considerations on the growth and erosion of organized digital gaming competitions. In *Proceedings of The 9th Australasian Conference on Interactive Entertainment: Matters of Life and Death*, IE '13, pages 43:1–43:2, New York, NY, USA, 2013. ACM.

[17] C. Zhang and J. Liu. On crowdsourced interactive live streaming: a twitch. tv-based measurement study. In *Proceedings of the 25th ACM Workshop on Network and Operating Systems Support for Digital Audio and Video*, pages 55–60. ACM, 2015.

Teaching Computational Thinking To 8-Year-Olds Through ScratchJr

Hylke H. Faber
Hanzehogeschool Groningen
Zernikeplein 9 9747 AS
Groningen, The Netherlands
h.h.faber@pl.hanze.nl

Jan Salvador van der Ven
Groningen Programmeert
de Waard 100 9734 CS
Groningen, The Netherlands
mail@jansalvador.nl

Menno D. M. Wierdsma
Hanzehogeschool Groningen
Zernikeplein 9 9747 AS
Groningen, The Netherlands
m.d.m.wierdsma@pl.hanze.nl

ABSTRACT

This synopsis presents the preliminary results of a larger study that aims to uncover design principles for teaching computational thinking to primary school children. This research focuses on teaching computational thinking to 8-year-olds through ScratchJr. By engaging in a cyclic process in which we create lesson materials and use evaluation data to improve them, we formulate design principles and provide teachers with sample course materials.

Keywords

computational thinking; primary education; ScratchJr

1. BACKGROUND

Computational thinking (CT) can be understood as thinking like a computer scientist in order to solve problems. Some researchers agree that *abstraction* is an essential aspect of CT [1].

The main outcome of an *Educational Design Research* (EDR) study is expanding the body of knowledge surrounding a particular subject [3]. By creating and improving an educational design, through a cyclic process of gathering evaluation data and using that data to improve the design, design principles can be revealed These can be used to guide future educational designs.

2. RESEARCH METHOD

ScrathJr is a tool developed to teach programming to children aged 5-7. Research has shown that programming may be used to address all concepts of CT [2]. This led to the conclusion that ScratchJr could potentially be used to teach CT to 8-year-olds. To compensate for the age discrepancy, more complex and unplugged assignments were added, focussing on teaching abstraction.

We designed a short course, consisting of five 90 minute lessons. The first lesson focused on introducing the graphical programming environment of ScratchJr, while the other lessons focused on the various aspects of CT.

During a period of 5 months the lesson materials were implemented in 6 classrooms with a total of 163 students. We reflected on each of the sessions to uncover which elements had a positive effect on the desired learning outcomes and used these to improve the course. Even though the study is in an early stage, the evaluation data can help guide the next phase in the EDR process.

3. EARLY RESULTS

Evaluation of the first design cycle of the course has revealed the following preliminary results:

- Story-assignments can be useful for students to develop the concept of abstraction. During this activity students are required to design a program to tell an original story. Students first create a pen-and-paper model of their story, consisting of drawings indicating what happens in the story. This model acts as an abstraction of the story, highlighting the most important aspects of the story and guiding the coding process.

- Reconceptualizing conditionals, a complex aspect of programming, in an unplugged environment seems to clarify the concept. Students take on the role of robots and have to react only to certain stimuli, caused either by the environment or by other students.

In the coming months, we will focus on gathering more evaluation data, to culminate in the next version of the intervention. By continuing this cyclic approach, in the future, design principles can be revealed.

4. REFERENCES

[1] S. Grover and R. D. Pea. Computational Thinking in K-12: A Review of the State of the Field. *Educational Researcher*, 42(1):38–43, 2013.

[2] L. Mannila, V. Dagiene, B. Demo, N. Grgurina, C. Mirolo, L. Rolandsson, and A. Settle. Computational Thinking in K-9 Education. In *Proceedings of the Working Group Reports of the 2014 on Innovation & Technology in Computer Science Education Conference*, pages 1–29, New York, New York, USA, 2014. ACM Press.

[3] J. van den Akker. Principles and Methods of Development Research. In J. Van den Akker, R. M. Branch, K. Gustafson, N. Nieveen, and T. Plomp, editors, *Design Approaches and Tools in Education and Training*, chapter 1, pages 1–14. Springer Science+Business Media, Dordrecht, 1999.

ACM ISBN 978-1-4503-4704-4/17/07.
DOI: http://dx.doi.org/10.1145/3059009.3072986

K-12 Teachers Experiences with Computing: A Case Study

Steve Cooper*
University Nebraska Lincoln
Lincoln, NE 68588, United States
stephen.cooper@unl.edu

Susan H. Rodger
Duke University
Durham, NC 27708, United States
rodger@cs.duke.edu

Kathy Isbister
SF Unified School District
San Francisco, CA 94110 United States
isbisterk@sfusd.edu

Madeleine Schep
Columbia College
Columbia, SC 29203, United States
mschep@columbiasc.edu

RoxAnn Stalvey
College of Charleston
Charleston, SC 29424, United States
StalveyR@cofc.edu

Lance Perez
University Nebraska Lincoln
Lincoln, NE 68588, United States
lcperez@unl.edu

ABSTRACT

We offered professional development to in-service K-12 teachers. Teachers learned programming, and how to teach programming. During the subsequent academic year, they taught programming in their schools. We interviewed the teachers to better understand their experiences. This poster describes case studies of K-12 teachers as they teach programming for the first time. As this study is qualitative, it does not attempt to measure findings. Rather, in exploring individual teachers' experiences, we hope to benefit both future teachers who will need to teach computing as well as those who will be helping those teachers.

KEYWORDS

Alice; Teacher professional development; K-12; case study

ACM Reference format:
Steve Cooper, Susan H. Rodger, Kathy Isbister, Madeleine Schep, RoxAnn Stalvey, and Lance Perez. 2017. K-12 Teachers Experiences with Computing: A Case Study. In *Proceedings of ITiCSE'17, July 03-05, 2017, Bologna, Italy., ,* 2 pages.
DOI: http://dx.doi.org/10.1145/3059009.3072989

1 BACKGROUND

We have been working with several hundred K-12 teachers in the United States, helping to provide them with sufficient pedagogic and content knowledge to enable them to teach programming to their students. Most of the teachers teach in public schools, where information technology (IT) resources are fewer and administrative support lower than in private schools. The majority of these teachers teach at the middle (grades 6-8, student ages 11-14) or high (grades 9-12, student ages 14-18) school level. Some teachers are primarily STEM teachers teaching required courses and meeting state-specified student learning standards. Others teach elective courses, typically as part of career and technical education (CTE)

*For the first five authors, this material is based upon work supported by the National Science Foundation under Grants NSF ITEST 1031351, 1031029, and 1031356.

programs. We have also worked with several individuals who were employed by their schools in other capacities, most commonly as librarians and technology coordinators.

We typically spend a couple of weeks working with the teachers in the summer, as part of one or two workshops. We spend a week teaching the teachers to program in Alice, as most teachers have little to no previous programming experience. We then spend a week focusing on how to teach programming. Using selections from our curricular materials together with their own materials (as appropriate), teachers are expected to develop and deliver curricular modules for their class(es) the subsequent academic year. During the academic year, we support the teachers with their teaching. Our website containing information about our program, our curriculum materials, and teacher lesson plans are at www.cs.duke.edu/csed/alice/aliceInSchools.

Our poster presents interviews of seven of the teachers detailing their experiences with their attempts in teaching computing.

2 OBSERVATIONS AND RECOMMENDATIONS

We list several observations and recommendations from our experiences and the interviews with the select teachers. It is important to note that nearly all of these teachers introduced computing to students who would not otherwise had gotten this experience.

1) Incorporating computing into a non-programming course (whether a core or elective) can be challenging. 2) The administration can be supportive, indifferent or obstructive to a teacher. 3) IT can be challenging for teachers. 4) In the US, in many states, there is a tension between CTE and STEM education (particularly at the secondary level). 5) A professional development workshop provides teachers with the confidence to teach computing. 6) It is very important for teachers to develop a sense of a community. 7) There are significant differences between private and public schools. 8) Getting K-12 teachers involved in teaching computing offers them amazing leadership opportunities. 9) Teachers need ideas for advertising courses. 10) There is an opportunity to get the technology coordinator involved as a teacher of computing. 11) State standards can be challenging for teachers wishing to get computing introduced as modules into other courses. 12) Replacing teachers who can teach computing can be very challenging. 13) It can be challenging for workshop presenters to keep their teaching support materials up to date. 14) It is important for professional development to provide materials "in a box" at the lesson-plan level. 15) It is very important to select the "right" teachers for a workshop.

Designing an Undergraduate Minor Program in E-Discovery

Milton Luoma[1]　　　Jigang Liu[1]　　　Kai Qian[2]

[1] Metropolitan State University, St. Paul, Minnesota 55106, USA {Milt.Luoma, Jigang.Liu}@metrostate.edu
[2] Kennesaw State University, Atlanta, Georgia12345, USA kqian@kennesaw.edu

Abstract

While the market for the E-Discovery (Electronic Discovery) is predicted to grow rapidly in coming years, the anticipated shortage of electronic discovery professionals is a result of the lack of education programs in this emerging field. In this paper, an undergraduate minor program in electronic discovery is proposed based on the experience and accomplishment of an established computer forensics program at a public university. Not only will the new program meet the demand of a booming job market, it is also an inspiring practice in expanding computer science education to a non-programming-centric field.

Key words: *Electronic Discovery, eDiscovery, Curriculum Design*

1. Introduction

According to the Amendments to the Federal Rules of Civil Procedure originally published in 2006 [4] and most recently amended in 2015, electronic discovery (also called E-Discovery or eDiscovery) is an integral part of civil procedure in which each party to a lawsuit can request and obtain Electronically Stored Information (ESI) created by the other party or parties. As the rapid development of the technology in cloud computing and big data for handling huge amounts of ESI continues unabated, the electronic discovery market will grow from $7.89 billion in 2016 to $22.62 billion by 2021 [3].

Although eDiscovery and Computer Forensics are both essential aspects of litigation, eDiscovery primarily involves ESI provided by the adverse party in a lawsuit, while Computer Forensics is more focused on investigating digital equipment for finding and preserving digital evidence. In addition, typical tasks and issues in eDiscovery include litigation holds, early case assessment, data processing, technology assisted review, proportionality, and data production, while computer forensics is more concerned with locating hidden information associated with deleted files, unallocated or slack disk space, or encrypted files. While many concepts and tools used for computer forensics can be applied to eDiscovery, eDiscovery still carries its unique characteristics and tasks illustrated by EDRM (http://www.edrm.net) and Gartner as shown in Figure 1 below, where the four out of nine phases are defined as information technology (IT) centric.

2. The New Curriculum

Since we have been running a baccalaureate program in Computer Forensics for more than 10 years [2] and have developed the faculty expertise in eDiscovery, the new curriculum can be well constructed based on what we have accomplished. The new minor

program will require 24 credits of course work, where there are four required courses for 16 credits and two elective courses for 8 credits. The four required courses are "CFS 280 Introduction to Computer Forensics," "CFS 345 Electronic Discovery I," "CFS 445 Electronic Discovery II," and "CFS 484 Computer Laws." All of the required courses are existing courses and the sequence for taking those required courses is shown in Figure 2 below.

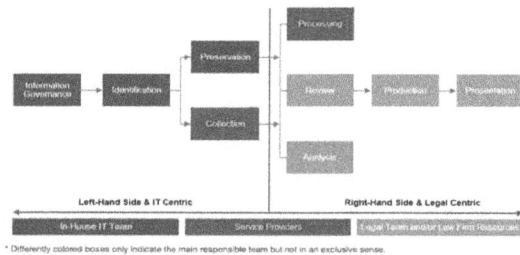

Figure 1. The EDRM eDiscovery process enriched by Gartner [5]

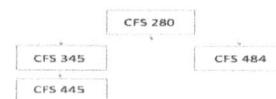

Figure 2 The study sequence of the required courses

The two elective courses can be taken from all related subjects in criminal justice, para-legal, law enforcement, accounting, statistics, information technology, and computer science, etc.

3. Conclusion

For a computer science department to offer an academic program that is not programming centric is often debatable due to the way the faculty have been trained. However, since there are 17 areas of computing technology besides programming that are included in the well-respected computer science curriculum 2013 (https://www.acm.org/education/CS2013-final-report.pdf), and it is also identified in [1] as one of the misconceptions that computer science is equivalent to programming, to have an undergraduate minor program in eDiscovery will definitely present our students, as well as our potential students, a more inclusive and marketable area to expand their skill sets. Ultimately, computer science is about new ideas and innovative ways to solve problems using computer and information technology.

References

[1] Denning, P. J., Tedre, M., and Yongpradit, P., "*Misconceptions about Computer Science,*" Communications of the ACM, Vol.60, No.03, March, 2017, pp.31-33

[2] Liu, J., "*Ten-Year Synthesis Review: A Baccalaureate Program in Computer Forensics,*" the proceedings of the 17th ACM Annual Conference on Information Technology Education (SIGITE2016), Boston, MA, Sept. 28 to Oct. 1, 2016, pp.121-126

[3] Marketsandmarkets.com., "*E-Discovery Market worth 22.62 Billion USD by 2021,*" Press Release on November 2016

[4] The Committee on the Judiciary House of Representatives, "Federal Rules of Civil Procedure," Dec. 1, 2006

[5] Zhang, J. and Landers, G., "*Market Guide for E-Discovery Solutions,*" Gartner Report, June 30, 2016

Alignment of Undergraduate Curriculum for Learning IoT in a Computer Science Faculty

Jorge Guerra Guerra
Universidad Nacional Mayor de San Marcos
Facultad de Ingeniería de Sistemas e Informática
Departamento de Ciencias de la Computación
Calle Germán Amézaga 375, Lima 1, Perú
jguerrag@unmsm.edu.pe

Armando Fermín Pérez
Universidad Nacional Mayor de San Marcos
Facultad de Ingeniería de Sistemas e Informática
Departamento de Ciencias de la Computación
Calle Germán Amézaga 375, Lima 1, Perú
fferminp@unmsm.edu.pe

ABSTRACT

This poster present the alignment of the undergraduate curriculum of Computer Science Faculty at National University of San Marcos, so that students can learn IoT topics, in accordance with Peruvian industry needs for well-trained graduates in the developing of IoT applications.

Categories and Subject Descriptors

• **Social and professional topics**→**Computer science education**

Keywords

IoT Education; Computer Science Education; Arduino.

1. INTRODUCTION

In 2014, the undergraduate curriculum of the Faculty was improved including the student´s competency in the developing of embedded applications, using open hardware, to provide customized applications for the Peruvian industry needs. So here it is shown how is being improved the actual curriculum, following also the main ACM Computing Curricula.

2. INTERNET OF THINGS IN COMPUTER SCIENCE CURRICULA

Internet of Things (IoT) [1] presents opportunities for novel applications in many industries such as healthcare, transportation among others, that is why, it must be considered the educational needs of a well-trained workforce that develop IoT products and services [2]. So, last 2014, in Computer Science Faculty at National University of San Marcos (UNMSM) was approved a new curriculum [3] in alignment with the Knowledge Body by ACM Computer Science Curricula [4], and including main topics about IoT Architecture [5] as shown later.

3. PROPOSAL IMPLEMENTATION

Courses as Digital Principles (IV semester), Computer Organization (VI semester) and Control Engineering (Elective) provide topics about sensor networks. Data Networks (VIII) and Cloud Computing (Elective) introduce topics about network layer. Distributed System (IX semester) see topics about middleware management layer. And at last, in Software Engineering (IX semester) and Intelligent Systems (VIII semester), students learn about the developing of products in the application layer.

4. ACHIEVED RESULTS

In this process of alignment with new curricula, a first main result was the implementation of an IoT research lab [6], a second result was the increase of the number of student's team projects about IoT applications, and the third one is about the increase of the relationships between the faculty and several Peruvian companies.

4.1 Participation in academic events

Last November, 2016, a team of undergraduate students has attended a national science fair called "Peru with Science", by National Council for Science and Technology (Concytec), where they have showcased two projects, one about the environmental monitoring with Arduino and managing data in the cloud; and another project about a brain computer interface to control a car for disabled persons, among others.

4.2 Projects between academia and industry

Several companies from diverse industries has increased their relationships with the IoT Research Lab looking for helping them to improve their applications including Internet of Things, and hiring undergraduate students, too. Also, the Faculty is signing agreements with some companies to develop projects funded by them.

5. CONCLUSIONS

With the including of Internet of Things topics in the curricula of Computer Science Faculty at UNMSM, the undergraduate students have more opportunities to improve their professional career and their performance developing novel applications, involving Internet of Things and the traditional knowledge suggested by ACM Computing Curricula, so, helping the Peruvian industries to resolve hard problems of actual society.

6. REFERENCES

[1] Mattern F. and Floerkemeier C. 2010. From the Internet of Computers to the Internet of Things. Springer LNCS. volume 6462, 242–259.

[2] Voas J. and Laplante P. 2017. Curriculum Considerations for the Internet of Things. IEEE Computer. 50, 1. 72-75. doi: 10.1109/MC.2017.27

[3] EAPIS FISI UNMSM. Plan de estudios 2014. Escuela de Ingeniería de Sistemas, Universidad Nacional Mayor de San Marcos. http://sistemas.unmsm.edu.pe/sistemas/eap/plan-2014

[4] Joint Task Force on Computing Curricula, ACM and IEEE Computer Society. 2013. Computer Science Curricula 2013: Curriculum Guidelines for Undergraduate Degree Programs in Computer Science.

[5] Hua-Dong M. 2011. Internet of things: Objectives and scientific challenges. Journal of Computer Science and Technology. 26, 6. 919–924.

[6] Guerra J. and Fermin A. 2016. Implementation of a Robotics and IoT Laboratory for Undergraduate Research in Computer Science Courses. In Proceedings of the 2016 ACM Conference on Innovation and Technology in Computer Science Education (ITiCSE '16). ACM, New York, NY, USA, 369-3691.

Using Common Problem Sets to increase Student Engagement and Retention in CS2

Aparna Mahadev (CS)
Elena Braynova (CS)
Worcester State University
Worcester, Massachusetts, USA
+1(508) 929-8715
{amahadev,
ebraynova}@worcester.edu

ABSTRACT

Data Structures ranks as one of the most challenging courses in our program core curriculum. It has the steepest learning curve for our students, and the lowest retention rate. A persistent problem we face in teaching data structures is finding time and a mechanism to cover the mathematical concepts that are necessary for understanding the important aspects of the course. The authors addressed the challenge with various approaches over several years including: reorganization of the discrete mathematics I (MA220) and discrete mathematics II (MA290); reordering coverage of topics in courses, changing pre-requisites, changing credit hours, requiring students to submit weekly blogs, developing common problem sets to be used in both the MA220 and CS242, and providing peer-assisted learning sessions. In this poster presentation, we share our integrated pedagogical approach, and the benefits and shortcomings of various approaches we tried over the years. We share the results of a student survey we developed to assess our latest approach of using common problem sets in both courses. The survey results show that by using common problem sets, students had the opportunity to make connections not only between these two courses, but also between how what is being learned in the classroom fits into a broader scope of learning.

Keywords

Student Engagement; Student Retention; Curriculum Issues; Pedagogy; Instruction; CS2

1. MOTIVATION

All departments on our campus go through a program review on a 5 year cycle. During our program review in 2012, we realized that our Data Structures course was in trouble. Our first course CS101 (Basics of Computer Science), offered in the fall semester is a gateway course open to all students across campus and involves no programming. CS140 (Introduction to Programming) offered in the spring semester has a closed lab each week. CS242 (Data Structures) follows CS 140 and is offered in the fall semester. Assessment data showed that there is a 0.29 actual point drop in grades from CS 101 to CS 140 and a 1.66 point drop in grades from CS 140 to CS 242 (on a scale of $0.0 - 4.0$). Additionally, 24% of the students improved their grades from CS 101 to CS 140 while

only 12% of the students shown an improvement in their grades rom CS 140 to CS 242. The withdrawal rate in CS 242 was also higher.

2. METHODOLOGY

To address this problem, the department undertook many initiatives. We understood two reasons why CS 242 is a stumbling block for our students: (a) Summer break between CS 140 and CS 242; (b) CS 140 has a closed lab that provides a good scaffolding that CS 242 lacks. Though we could not do anything about (a) and (b), we realized that we could increase retention by taking several measures. These included: revamping course topics and changing the pre-requisite and requiring students to write weekly reflective blogs in CS 242 [1][2]. These blogs were helpful in identifying the frustrations students faced with mathematical concepts. All CS majors are required to take MA 220 and MA 290 with MA 290 being a pre-requisite for CS 242. Since CS 242 relies heavily on the concepts from MA 220, the department made MA 220 a co-requisite for CS 242. Since fall 2013 the authors linked CS 242 and MA 220 by covering the topics in both courses in a specific sequence. Additionally, with the help of a student who took CS 242 previously, we developed common problem sets to be given in both CS 242 and MA 220. As corroborated by a student survey, this approach shows a lot of promise as students see the connection between the two courses and are able to perform better in both courses.

3. FUTURE DIRECTIONS

We realize that we are not the only department facing issues students ability connect mathematical concepts in their CS courses [3]. We hope that our approach help students see the relevance of proof techniques, set theory, formal logic and complexity analysis in computer science curriculum.

4. REFERENCES

1. Jeffrey Stone, Using Reflective Blogs for Pedagogical Feedback in CS1, in *Proceedings of the SIGCSE technical Symposium on Computer Science Education (SIGCSE '12),* ACM, USA, 259 – 264.
2. Fekete, A., Kay, J., Kingston, J. and Wimalaratne, K. 2000. Supporting reflection in introductory computer science. In *Proceedings of the thirty-first SIGCSE technical symposium on Computer science education (SIGCSE '00),* Susan Haller (Ed.). ACM, New York, NY, USA, 144-148.
3. Parker, A. 2014. What makes Big-O analysis difficult: understanding how students understand runtime analysis. In Journal of Computing Sciences in Colleges, Volume 29, Number 4, 164-174

New Trends in Teaching Programming in Secondary Education in Slovakia

Janka Majherova
Catholic University in Ruzomberok
Hrabovska cesta 1, 03401 Ruzomberok, Slovakia
janka.majherova@ku.sk

Jana Jackova
Matej Bel University in Banska Bystrica
Tajovskeho 40, 974 01 Banska Bystrica, Slovakia
jana.jackova@umb.sk

ABSTRACT

We describe a pilot research study within the project "Innovative methods in teaching Informatics in secondary education". We introduce some results of a survey regarding the content of the school subject Informatics in lower and upper secondary education in Slovakia. We plan to develop some new educational materials for further education of informatics teachers.

CCS Concepts

• **Social and professional topics** → **Computing education**; *K-12 education*

Keywords

Teaching programming; Secondary education; Innovative methodology; Educational materials; Informatics; Curriculum

ACM Reference format:

J. Majherova, J. Jackova. 2017. New Trends in Teaching Programming in Secondary Education in Slovakia. In *Proceedings of ACM ITiCSE conference, Bologna,Italy, July 2017 (ITiCSE'17)*, 1 page.
DOI: 10.1145/3059009.3072997

1 INTRODUCTION

Hubwieser et al. [1] analysed 14 extensive case studies about the various situations of Computer Science Education in K-12 schools in 12 states. Situation in Slovakia was not analysed there.

A research team consisting of computer science teachers from two Slovak universities solves a grant project called "Innovative methods in teaching Informatics in secondary education". This project aims to raise the level of teaching programming in lower secondary and upper secondary schools (ISCED 2, ISCED 3) in Slovakia. The objective of this project is to develop innovative methods for teaching Informatics with a focus on algorithmization and programming in conjunction with the current trends in use of digital technologies.

2 CURRENT SITUATION

Slovakia has seen the introduction of the Innovated National Education Programme (INEP) for primary and secondary education. Main thematic areas of the subject Informatics are [2]: Representations and structures (Application software); Communication by web; Algorithmic problem solving; Software and hardware; Information Society. A great emphasis in the INEP within the subject Informatics is given to algorithmization and programming. For a long period of time we have followed

development of learning algorithmization and programming at schools (as a part of teacher practice of our students in the study programmes Teacher Training in the subject Informatics). In 2014-2016 we analyzed teaching records of our students in lower secondary schools (L) and upper secondary schools (U) again. The highest number of teaching hours was devoted to teaching the theme Application software (see Graph 1): 52% in L, 47% in U. Results for algorithmization and programming hours were: 13% in L and 32% in U. According to the INEP curriculum it is recommended to increase the proportion of programming hours of instruction to 25%.

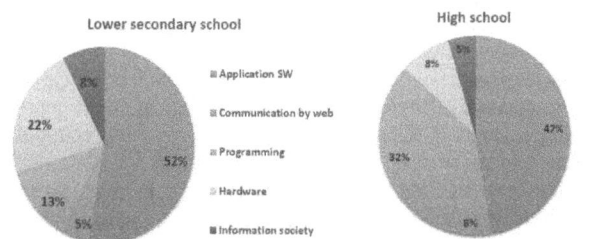

Graph 1: Informatics in Slovak schools in 2014-2016

3 FUTURE WORK

In collaboration with qualified teachers of Informatics at partner schools, we carry out an applied research within seminars for teachers and future teachers of Informatics.

Video tutorials will be created on specific topics for use in further teacher training. We will show created methodology materials for ScratchJr [3] and Scratch language teaching at a conference. Furthermore, we plan to create materials for learning Python and programming of robotic models.

Our project outputs will be available to all teachers of Informatics at the project website. They will be accessible for next use in further education of teachers.

Acknowledgments

This work is supported by the Cultural and Educational Grant Agency of the Slovak Republic under grant No. KEGA 009KU-4/2017.

4 REFERENCES

[1] P. Hubwieser, M.N. Giannakos, M. Berges, T. Brinda, I. Diethelm, J. Magenheim, Y. Pal, J. Jackova, and E. Jasute. 2015. A Global Snapshot of Computer Science Education in K-12 Schools. In *Proceedings of the 2015 ITiCSE on Working Group Reports* (ITICSE-WGR '15). ACM, New York, NY, 65-83. DOI=http://dx.doi.org/10.1145/2858796.2858799

[2] *Inovovaný Štátny vzdelávací program* [Innovated National Education Programme]. Retrieved March 11, 2017 from http://www.statpedu.sk/clanky/inovovany-statny-vzdelavaci-program

[3] http://tablet.jecool.net

A Graph-based Approach to Analyze and Compare Computer Science Curricula for Primary and Lower Secondary Education

Stefan Pasterk
Alpen-Adria-Universität Klagenfurt
Universitätsstraße 65-67
9020 Klagenfurt, Austria
stefan.pasterk@aau.at

Andreas Bollin
Alpen-Adria-Universität Klagenfurt
Universitätsstraße 65-67
9020 Klagenfurt, Austria
stefan.pasterk@aau.at

ABSTRACT

A growing number of countries start to introduce computer science related topics in primary education, but their curricula or educational standards significantly differ in various aspects. This contribution introduces a way to analyze and compare curricula, education standards and competency models, using a graph-based representation form and several graph-theoretical metrics.

CCS Concepts

•Social and professional topics → Computer science education; K-12 education; *Model curricula;*

Keywords

Curricula; primary education; graph-based; comparison

1. INTRODUCTION

As information technology (and computer science) deeply affects everyday life, more and more countries start to teach topics of computer science in kindergarten or primary schools. For this purpose, curricula, educational standards and/or competency models were developed and in some countries, like Switzerland or Australia, already established. These models show differences with regard to focus, content, structure and number of skills or competencies which makes a comparison a complex task. This contribution introduces a technique and framework to comprehensibly evaluate different curricula, standards and competency models for computer science education in primary and lower secondary schools.

2. A GRAPH-BASED APPROACH

The idea behind this new methodology is to establish 'requires' or 'expands' relations between individual knowledge elements within a curriculum, educational standards

or competency model for computer science. The knowledge elements are represented as vertices of a graph and the relations as the connections between them. Similar approaches were used [1, 2], but focus on curricula in higher education and do not consider different types for vertices or relations. Our approach uses a graph database for analyzing the data via simple queries. We consider graph-theoretic measures like vertices with the highest degree, the number of vertices without dependencies, the overall number of relations of one model, the amount of different relations within a curriculum, or the number of cross-theme dependencies in an analysis.

3. RESULTS

First results show that our graph-based representation clearly illustrates the main focus of different curricula. In one study that took place end of February 2017, experts categorized the knowledge elements of different curricula into 'digital literacy' and 'computer science' and the results were mapped to our graph representation. The analysis clearly depicted that the Australian curriculum for the subject 'Digital Technologies' has a very balanced distribution of the topics concerning *computer science* and *digital literacy*, whereas the curriculum from Switzerland for 'Media and Informatics' strongly focuses on *digital literacy*. Further descriptions and results can be found on the project-homepage[1].

4. CONCLUSION AND FUTURE WORK

This approach gives an interesting overview of structural components and offers the possibility to analyze and compare them. As further steps the content of the curricula, educational standards and competency models will be broken down to their basic competencies and knowledge items and they will be categorized into knowledge areas.

5. REFERENCES

[1] J. M. Lightfoot. A Graph-Theoretic Approach to Improved Curriculum Structure and Assessment Placement. *Comm. of the IIMA*, 10(2):59–73, 2010.
[2] L. Marshall. A comparison of the core aspects of the acm/ieee computer science curriculum 2013 strawman report with the specified core of cc2001 and cs2008 review. In *Proceedings of Second Computer Science Education Research Conference*, CSERC '12, pages 29–34, New York, NY, USA, 2012. ACM.

ITiCSE '17 July 03-05, 2017, Bologna, Italy
© 2017 Copyright held by the owner/author(s).
ACM ISBN 978-1-4503-4704-4/17/07.
DOI: http://dx.doi.org/10.1145/3059009.3072985

[1]See IT-SG project at iid.aau.at/bin/view/Main/Projects

Bebras as a Teaching Resource: Classifying the Tasks Corpus Using Computational Thinking Skills

Violetta Lonati, Dario Malchiodi, Mattia Monga, Anna Morpurgo
Dept. of Computer Science, Università degli Studi di Milano, Milan, Italy
{lonati, malchiodi, monga, morpurgo}@di.unimi.it

ABSTRACT

We present a new classification method for Bebras tasks based on the ISTE/CSTA operational definition of computational thinking. The classification can be appreciated by teachers without a formal education in informatics and it helps in detecting the cognitive skills involved by tasks, and makes their educational potential more explicit.

1. THINKING COMPUTATIONALLY WITH BEBRAS TASKS

The Bebras "International Challenge on Informatics and Computational Thinking" (http://bebras.org/) [4] had about one and a half million participants from more than 50 countries in the last edition. Bebras tasks can be the starting point for further educational activities (a recent proposal is [2]), provided they are categorized to make them easier to retrieve and to use during curricular activities. Indeed, tasks categorization is an issue in the Bebras community since the beginning [3]. A survey we conducted in Italy after the Bebras' last edition (2016) confirms the need by teachers for such a classification: we propose to base it on the operational definition of computational thinking [1] developed by ISTE (International Society for Technology in Education) and CSTA (Computer Science Teachers Association). To decide whether a task belongs to a class ot not, one should answer the question "Would you choose this task to promote or teach this Computational Thinking skill?".

Logically organizing data. Typical tasks in this class deal with: organization of data according to given criteria (*i.e.*, database), use of data structures to make data easier to process, organization of data so that they enjoy relevant properties as in cryptography or compression.

Logically analyzing data. Beside "logical problems" that require logical inference, deductive reasoning, and drawing conclusions about the data presented in the task, in this class we find tasks that require accurate observations (*e.g.*, recognizing patterns), or a systematic approach to establish whether the data of the problem satisfy certain properties.

Representing information. Typical tasks in this class deal with the digital representation of data, or their visual representation with diagrams like histograms or charts. Other tasks refer to data structures to represent relevant properties (*e.g.*, graphs for binary relations).

Algorithmic thinking. Tasks in this class require to go beyond generic intuitive approaches, towards settings that enable automatic processing, for instance by: decomposing a problem into components; combining primitive operations; understanding some formal procedure (*e.g.*, execute it or compute/recognize its output); applying some transition rules to a system in a given configuration; and so on.

Identifying strategies. Problem solving and in particular finding a non-trivial algorithmic strategy to tackle a problem is the theme of this class of tasks.

Analyzing algorithmic solutions. This class contains tasks concerning global characteristics of the considered algorithm, like correctness or complexity. Other typical tasks in this class are those inspired by optimization problems.

Implementing algorithmic solutions. Tasks in this class may be referred to as programming or coding tasks since the focus is on the implementation of algorithms according to a formal syntax defined in the task.

2. REFERENCES

[1] Computational thinking for K-12 education. https://csta.acm.org/Curriculum/sub/CurrFiles/CompThinkingFlyer.pdf, 2011.

[2] V. Dagienė and S. Sentance. It's computational thinking! Bebras tasks in the curriculum. In *ISSEP 2016*, vol. 9973 of *LNCS*, p. 28–39, 2016.

[3] V. Dagienė and G. Futschek. Bebras international contest on informatics and computer literacy: Criteria for good tasks. In *LNCS*, vol. 5090, p. 19–30, 2008.

[4] V. Dagienė and G. Stupuriene. Informatics education based on solving attractive tasks through a contest. *IFIP–KEYCIT 2014*, p. 51–62, 2014.

Tasks for Assessing Skills of Computational Thinking

Tauno Palts
University of Tartu,
Tartu Ülikool, Ülikooli 18, 50090 TARTU,
+(372) 737 5445
tauno.palts@ut.ee

Margus Pedaste
University of Tartu,
Tartu Ülikool, Ülikooli 18, 50090 TARTU,
+(372) 737 5957
margus.pedaste@ut.ee

ABSTRACT

Thinking computationally has become an important part of many disciplines. In creating lesson plans for teaching computational thinking (CT), an instrument can be used to assess the development of CT. This poster presents the Bebras Challenge tasks for assessing two skills of CT: exploring and developing algorithms, and finding patterns.

Keywords
Computational thinking; assessing; school

1. INTRODUCTION
In today's innovative world, computer science has become an important part of many disciplines and thinking computationally has come to be an essential skill for everyone. Recent years have seen a rise of interest in developing CT already at comprehensive school level.

2. COMPUTATIONAL THINKING
Wing has defined CT as "the thought processes involved in formulating problems and their solutions so that the solutions are represented in a form that can be effectively carried out by an information processing agent" [1].

Selby and Woollard develop this definition further by describing the core CT skills: abstraction, algorithmic thinking, decomposition, evaluation, and generalization [2]. As there are no tasks to assess these skills, Dagiene and Sentance have categorized the tasks of international informatics competition Bebras into the aforementioned five categories to create several tasks for developing and assessing the development of CT [3].

Google has approached teaching CT differently by creating a course for developing CT, which focuses mainly on two skills of CT: exploring and developing algorithms, and finding patterns (https://computationalthinkingcourse.withgoogle.com/).

3. INSTRUMENT FOR ASSESSING COMPUTATIONAL THINKING
As the Bebras Challenge tasks have been categorized to assess core CT skills [3], the tasks were used in Bebras Challenge 2015 in many countries. This study focused on the results of students in the benjamin age group (12–14 years of age) from Estonia (n=2595) and Lithuania (n=7100).

ITiCSE'17, July 3–5, 2017, Bologna, Italy.
ACM. ISBN 978-1-4503-4704-4/17/07.
DOI: http://dx.doi.org/10.1145/3059009.3072999

Although five factors were expected to describe five aspects of CT from the original skills assessed in the Bebras Challenge, the confirmatory factor analysis did not support this theory. Therefore, exploratory factor analysis with principal axis factoring was used with the Varimax with Kaiser normalization and two factors were found. Five tasks describing the factors, factor loadings and original skills assessed were compared (see Table 1).

Table 1. Two factors of the results of Bebras tasks in 2015.

Task name	Factor 1	Factor 2	Original skill assessed
Crane operating	.50		Algorithmic
Mushrooms	.42		Algorithmic
Biber Hotel	.37		Algorithmic
Animal Competition		.44	Evaluation
Walnut Animals		.40	Abstraction

The factors found in the study can be described as follows:

Factor 1 – exploring and developing algorithmic thinking. Tasks that needed step-by-step solutions for various situations.

Factor 2 – finding patterns. Tasks that needed skills of abstraction, evaluation and decomposition to recognize patterns.

Although the factor loadings are not very high, the Bebras tasks can be used to assess two skills of CT when creating lesson scenarios to develop CT. The tasks are rather complex, which leads to the idea for the future of breaking the tasks into smaller, more specific tasks more distinctly assessing the five skills of CT. The tasks still need to be analyzed thoroughly and tested empirically in a school environment, considering the possibility of having factors other than skills of CT influencing the results.

REFERENCES

[1] Wing, J.M. Computational thinking. In *VL/HCC*, 2011, 3.
[2] Selby, C., and Woollard, J. Computational thinking: the developing definition, 2013.
[3] Dagienė, V., and Sentance, S. It's Computational Thinking! Bebras Tasks in the Curriculum. In *International Conference on Informatics in Schools: Situation, Evolution, and Perspectives*, 2016, 28-39.

CodeAdventure: Learning Introductory Programming

Giorgos Nicou
UCLan Cyprus & InSPIRE
Larnaka, 7080
(+357) 24694048

gnicou@uclan.ac.uk

Panayiotis Andreou
UCLan Cyprus & InSPIRE
Larnaka, 7080
(+357) 24694085

pgandreou@uclan.ac.uk

Irene Polycarpou
UCLan Cyprus & InSPIRE
Larnaka, 7080
(+357) 24694085

ipolycarpou@uclan.ac.uk

ABSTRACT

This paper describes the design and implementation of an educational game, called CodeAdventure, which is an adventure game for learning introductory programming concepts. CodeAdventure adopts an integrated design approach that employs various mechanisms and techniques to achieve an immersive learning experience in a fun and engaging way. CodeAdventure incorporates different learning techniques that have been shown to be effective for students' learning, such as providing hints and clues on how to solve puzzles, referencing instructional material, and providing immediate feedback on students' performance.

Keywords

Educational Games; Programming; Educational Technologies; Adventure Games for Education.

1. INTRODUCTION

Introductory programming is one of the most fundamental concepts of computer science education, yet, it is well known that students have difficulties understanding basic programming concepts. As a result, students show poor performance with course assessments, which in turn, can lead to dropping out of their studies after their first experience with programming. Through the years, a number of approaches have been proposed to mend the situation, including effective approaches to teaching programming to novice learners. One such approach is the utilization of educational games which can motivate, stimulate interest and engage students to a greater extent than conventional approaches [1].

2. CODE ADVENTURE

2.1 The Game

In CodeAdventure the player assumes the role of the protagonist, exploring the game environment, and in the process, solving puzzles and overcoming challenges, in order to discover and acquire certain items. In particular, the game has an attractive storyline and offers a highly interactive 3D environment that allows the user to explore different levels, which are composed of multiple rooms, each one containing a diverse set of puzzles. Some examples of challenges used in the game include: solving multiple choice questions; turning wheel(s) to solve a puzzle; and rotating boxes with operators to validate a statement.

Each room has specific objectives and includes various encyclopaedic interactive elements that convey the required knowledge to meet the objectives as well assessment methods that allow the user to reflect on his/her current status and progress. Moreover, achievements, rewards and secret items provide a feeling of accomplishment and increase overall engagement.

2.2 Prototype

CodeAdventure was implemented with Unity 5.5 using C# scripts. It uses unity libraries and in order to facilitate access into the scene, the majority of the developed scripts extend monoBehavior class, so they can have access to the models in the scene. The monoBehavior class includes easy to use functions that facilitate seamless interaction in each frame. In order to allow for modularity, every object (e.g., lever, wheel) that interacts with the player has its own dedicated script. For the overlaid questions and information, we have utilized XML manipulation and IO libraries from the .NET framework. Finally, all room configurations, including all room objects, are loaded from XML files to allow for maintainability and expandability. The current prototype implementation includes full development of level 1 (Introduction to the JAVA programming language), which covers the following topics: Data Types, Casting, Operators and their Precedence, Expressions, Conditional Statements, and Loop Structures.

2.3 Level Design

Code Adventure is designed to accommodate four distinct levels representing different "subject areas" of introductory programming. In particular, the following four levels will be incorporated in the final version of the game: (i) Introduction to the JAVA programming language; (ii) Object-oriented Programming; (iii) Data Structures and Algorithms; and (iv) Advanced Topics. Each level is composed of multiple rooms with one or more doors (e.g., traditional doors, automatic doors, and electric fences), each one posing unique challenges (e.g., quizzes and puzzles) that must be met in order to allow the user to continue to the next room. Each room has a specific theme that represents one or more related programming topics (e.g., introduction to data types, operators, conditional statements, etc.).

3. REFERENCE

[1] Prensky, M. 2001. *Digital game-based Learning*. McGraw-Hill, NY.

Build Your Future: Guiding Student Employability

Bruce Scharlau
University of Aberdeen
Computing Science, Meston Building.
Aberdeen, AB24 3UE, UK
+44 (0)1224 272193
b.scharlau@abdn.ac.uk

ABSTRACT
Students need to be told how to make the most of their time at university to best aid their future career. We need to remind them that the 'degree' is more than the sum of the diverse classes they take as part of their degree curriculum. We developed a guide for students to contextualize their degree, and 'build their future' to develop their university time to suit their career aspirations.

Keywords
Curriculum; Co-curriculum; Placements; Employability; Work-related learning.

1. INTRODUCTION
Students are often focused on the courses of their discipline without much thought about the non-discipline subjects they take as part of their degree. The University of Aberdeen moved to a Melbourne Model type degree in 2010 [1] with students required to take almost a quarter of their credits from non-discipline subjects. Since then, students regularly miss opportunities to develop a degree to suit their career aspirations.

2. BACKGROUND
Computing students regularly expressed opinions at staff-student liaison committee meetings that they found the options available for their non-CS options difficult to choose from. Students aiming for joint degrees with Philosophy or Mathematics were fine, as they knew what to take. Others, have been less sure about their options. The weight of choice is with the students, who sometimes lack the patience to explore their options.

3. THE 'BUILD YOUR FUTURE' GUIDE
We created a diagram illustrating opportunities for students to work alongside professionals during their degree. There are four components to this: CS degree requirements; breadth degree requirements for non-computing components, which can work well with the CS components; placement and other work opportunities; co-curriculum activities that regularly occur on campus and offer places where students can work with professionals.

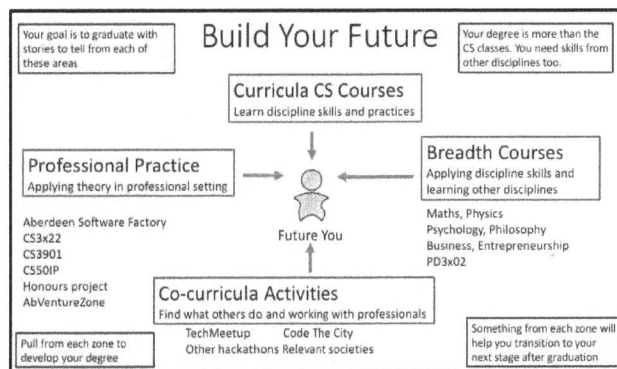

The students should see that although they might take the same, or similar courses as their classmates, that they can tailor their degree to suit them.

4. DISCUSSION AND CONCLUSIONS
We are still in early days with the diagram. We expect it to form a discussion point with students and their personal tutors when talking about career aspirations.

While this is focused on CS degree options, we will also trial it with other disciplines too. This will either be a generic format, or tailored to specific disciplines.

5. ACKNOWLEDGMENTS
Thanks to the 'Building a Graduate Employability Community in Computing' workshops for providing the impetuous for this project. [2]

6. REFERENCES
[1] Anon. *Curriculum Reform*. University of Aberdeen. http://www.abdn.ac.uk/staffnet/teaching/curriculum-reform-and-enhanced-study-2760.php Accessed 12 March 2017

[2] Council of Professors and Heads of Computing. *GECCO Workshops*, https://employability.disciplinarycommons.org Accessed 12 March 2017

Addressing the Paradox of Fun and Rigor in Learning Programming

Mohsen Dorodchi
University of North Carolina at Charlotte (UNCC)
Charlotte, NC, USA
Mohsen.Dorodchi@uncc.edu

Nasrin Dehbozorgi
University of North Carolina at Charlotte (UNCC)
Charlotte, NC, USA
Ndehbozo@uncc.edu

ABSTRACT

Course withdrawal and failure rates are known problems in introductory computer science programming courses (CS1). In turn, these problematic performance rates contribute to declines in retention rates between introductory programming courses and subsequent CS courses. In a bit of a twist, however, retention rates are also influenced by successful student performance. Some students frequently leave the computer science major due to unpleasant experiences and lack of satisfaction, despite earning good grades [1]. These competing retention factors create a paradox to provide a fun learning experience that makes students want to stay in the CS major while simultaneously emphasizing the rigor and discipline needed to advance in the CS major.

Categories and Subject Descriptors

K.3.2 [**Computer Science Education**]: Computer and Information Science Education

Keywords

Experiential learning, teamwork activities, collaborative learning, introductory programming, CS1

1. INTRODUCTION

Lack of continuous disciplined practice by students, has been claimed to be the reason students perform poorly in programming courses [2]. Infusing such rigor, however, is a challenging task in CS1 lecture models, due to diversity of topics and lack of time for students to practice the concepts in class. Experiential Learning Theory (ELT) has been recommended as a mechanism to improve the learning process by involving students into practicing and experiencing the concepts [3]. Team-based active learning methods have also been widely applied in CS1 to provide a support model to increase students' enrollment and satisfaction while making programming a fun experience for them [4, 5]. ELT, however, goes a step further with a semi-structured approach that engages students in hands-on and minds-on activities, both individually and in teams while the instructor facilitates the learning process by structuring the tasks [3]. This aspect of ELT fits the concept of team-based learning in which students are supposed to cooperate, learn from each other, and be involved during the class time [3].

ITiCSE'17, July 3–5, 2017, Bologna, Italy.
ACM. ISBN 978-1-4503-4704-4/17/07.
DOI: http://dx.doi.org/10.1145/3059009.3073004

2. METHODOLOGY

In this work, we combined the concept of Kolb's theory of experiential learning (ELT) [3] with team-based learning [4] to propose a set of course activities for CS1. The goal is to improve students' performance and satisfaction during the course. ELT entails three phases of "do", "reflect", and "apply" to learn the concepts [3]. We mapped these phases onto our proposed set of activities in CS1: pre-lab/class, in lab/class, and post-lab/class activities. In our proposed activities, the "do" phase is partially completed by every student during pre-lab/class in preparation for the upcoming lab/class activities. During the lab/class, students "do" more in-depth practices and discussions in teams. Then, at the end of the lab/class activities, they "reflect" on what they have learned, which correlates to the second phase of ELT. In addition, students often "do" more challenging problems at the end of the lab/class. Eventually, during the third phase of ELT, the "apply" phase, students do more comprehensive activities outside class (i.e., assignment) and lab (i.e., post-lab), imitating real-world problems so that they are able to individually "apply" the knowledge they just gained. We discovered that the continuation of the activities and their sequential correlation are crucial factors in the design of the course activities and any isolated practices should be avoided.

3. FINDINGS

The primary study of our proposed activity patterns confirms their effectiveness on improving student performance. Samples of the activities as well as corresponding statistical analysis would be presented to indicate how the activities support students' learning by improving their problem-solving skills which leads to higher performance.

4. REFERENCES

[1] Biggers, M., et. al. 2008. Student Perceptions of Computer Science: A Retention Study Comparing Graduating Seniors with CS Leavers, ACM SIGCSE Bulletin, 402-406.

[2] Balid, W., et. al. 2015. The Impact of Different Pre-Lab Preparation Modes on Embedded Systems Hands-on Lab. The 9th Annual ASEE Global Colloquium on Eng. Education.

[3] Northern Illinois University. 2010. Experiential Learning. http://www.niu.edu/facdev/_pdf/guide/strategies/experiential_learning.pdf

[4] Latulipe, C., Long, N. B., & Seminario, C. E. 2015. Structuring Flipped Classes with Lightweight Teams and Gamification. Proc. 46th ACM SIGCSE, 392–397.

[5] Huss-Lederman, S., Chinn, D., & Skrentny, J. 2008. Serious fun. ACM SIGCSE Bulletin, 40(1), 33.

Building a Secure Hacking Lab in a Small University

Nadimpalli Mahadev
Department of Computer Science
Fitchburg State University
Fitchburg, Massachusetts, USA
+1(978) 665-3270
nmahadev@fitchburgstate.edu

ABSTRACT

Ethical Hacking is an important course in any cyber security program. The objective of ethical hacking is to test a given network for possible vulnerabilities through authorized hacking and report the findings. The course requires a hacking lab where students can learn through hands on experience various tools and techniques used for hacking and gain insight into security fundamentals. The challenge is to ensure that the students have access to Internet in some stages of hacking but are prevented from accidentally hacking into unauthorized systems. In a small university like ours, the lab must also be cost-effective. We present here our approach to setting up such a lab.

Keywords

Ethical Hacking; Cyber Security; Curriculum Issues

1. MOTIVATION

The demand for trained ethical hackers is out-pacing the supply [2]. Many universities are introducing courses in ethical hacking to meet this demand. Many universities, including ours, are nervous about legal and security issues if a student were to hack into unauthorized systems using university resources. They prefer that the course be taught using only a hacking lab consisting of a closed network of computers with no external access to Internet. While it is possible to set up such a network, an important phase of hacking called passive reconnaissance [1] is a skill best practiced on real world targets. And this step is harmless and legal since no unauthorized access to any system is gained. An expensive alternative will be to set up a closed network that resembles a typical real-world network with firewalls, services and multitude of servers. That is not an option in budget-constrained universities like ours. After considering different options, we have come up with an alternative that might serve our purpose.

2. METHODOLOGY

The approach we considered involves 20 PCs connected to a single switch. The only Internet access they have is through this switch. We use Virtual Box on each of the 20 PCs to install the attacker along with 2 servers and 2 clients as the targets inside the virtual box. The Virtual Box is configured to be the DHCP server that creates an internal network with no Internet access. We then configured the servers to include various Internet services. Students can individually fix the vulnerabilities they find in their own setup and test further. At the end of the course, the networks can easily be reset to the original configuration.

The course begins with a brief review of network security concepts covering the network architecture and the potential attacks at various layers. We then allow students to conduct reconnaissance on a target site on the web and discuss the information gathered. This phase does allow students to use the Internet. Since they will not be using virtual box, they do not have access to the hacking tools. For the rest of the course, students are limited to using virtual box with no Internet access. Students will be hacking the servers and clients inside the virtual box. They will attempt to fix any vulnerabilities that they unearth and then retest. Students are graded for the reports they generate in various stages of this process and also for the classroom discussions on the reports.

3. FUTURE DIRECTIONS

The closed network sandboxed inside a virtual box provides a safe environment for testing various hacking tools. But the network inside a sandbox we have does not match the complexities of real-world networks. We are looking at two approaches to remedy this situation. One is to employ student researchers to create a more sophisticated network inside the virtual box. Another approach is to seek out private cloud-based hacking labs that are leased to academic institutions.

4. REFERENCES

[1] P. Engebretson. *The Basics of Hacking and Penetration Testing.* Syngress, 2013.

[2] M. Libicki, D. Senty, and J. Pollak. Hackers wanted. An examination of the cybersecurity labor market. *https://www.rand.org*, 2017.

Visualization for Secure Coding in C

Extended Abstract

James Walker, Jean Mayo,
Ching-Kuang Shene
Michigan Technological University
Houghton, MI
jwwalker,jmayo,shene@mtu.edu

Steve Carr
Western Michigan University
Kalamazoo, MI
steve.carr@wmich.edu

ABSTRACT

This paper describes a pedagogical system to visualize program execution.[1] The visualization is designed to help students understand how to develop more secure and robust C programs. The system provides several perspectives on the execution including: the values of registers and the logical address space, a call graph, the file descriptor and inode tables, and the handling of sensitive data like passwords and keys. These visualizations are designed to help students understand fundamental concepts such as: buffer overflows, integer overflows, proper handling of sensitive data and application of the principle of least privilege in several contexts including file operations, secure SUID programming, and use and management of the process environment.

Keywords

Security Education; Program Execution; Visualization

1. OVERVIEW

Many program vulnerabilities are introduced into C programs through poor understanding of the program's layout in memory and its execution. We have developed a visualization system to help students make the connection between their C code and its execution. The system was designed to teach secure coding in C, but can be useful in many courses including courses on C, systems programming, concurrent computing, and operating systems.

2. VISUALIZATIONS

The system currently provides four perspectives: Program Address Space (PA), Call Graph (CG), File Operations (FO) and Sensitive Data (SD). The system takes input from dynamic analysis using Pintool[1]. The analysis produces a sequence of events that are processed by the visualizations. A student can step through an execution and view one or multiple visualizations at once. Source code is displayed and events are linked to the corresponding line of source code.

The PA visualization depicts the values of registers and the program address space. Students may expand and collapse individual activation records. A user may choose among multiple levels of detail. For example, data related to the use of shared libraries can be hidden. The PA visualization clearly depicts buffer overflows, integer overflows and other memory errors.

The CG visualization depicts the sequence of function calls made during an execution. In its least complex form, the hierarchy of processes created using fork() is displayed. The user can freely expand and collapse the sequence of calls. This visualization intends to help students understand and identify sequences of actions that affect program security. This includes execution with unnecessary privileges and improper handling of sensitive data.

The FO visualization shows kernel structures commonly used to maintain the UNIX file abstraction. This helps students to understand the impact of parameters to the open() system call and to understand how parent and child interact through the file system following a call to fork() or exec().

The SD visualization teaches students how to protect sensitive data so that it never appears unencrypted on secondary storage. The visualization compares related actions in a student's program to a sequence of actions required to keep the data secure. The PA visualization can be used with the SD visualization to show students the correspondence between their code and the appearance of sensitive data in memory.

3. CONCLUSIONS AND FUTURE WORK

The system will be evaluated in classroom use in courses at several levels within our undergraduate curriculum. The visualization will be integrated into an IDE that identifies and explains security vulnerabilities as a student edits her C program. A module for visualizing the output from a taint analysis of C programs is under development.

4. REFERENCES

[1] Intel Software. Pin - a dynamic binary instrumentation tool. https://software.intel.com/en-us/articles/pin-a-dynamic-binary-instrumentation-tool, 2017. [Online; accessed 10-Mar-2017].

[1]This work has been supported by the National Science Foundation under grants DUE-1245310, DGE-1523017, IIS-1456763, and IIS-1455886.

ITiCSE '17 July 03-05, 2017, Bologna, Italy
© 2017 Copyright held by the owner/author(s).
ACM ISBN 978-1-4503-4704-4/17/07.
DOI: http://dx.doi.org/10.1145/3059009.3072990

E-Assessment and Bring Your Own Device

Bastian Küppers
IT Center, RWTH Aachen University
Seffenter Weg 23
D-52074 Aachen, Germany
kueppers@itc.rwth-aachen.de

Ulrik Schroeder
Learning Technologies Research Group, RWTH
Aachen University
Ahornstraße 55
D-52074 Aachen, Germany
schroeder@cs.rwth-aachen.de

ABSTRACT

Following the trend of digitalization in university education, lectures and accompanying exercises and tutorials incorporate more and more digital components. These digital components spread from the usage of computers and tablets in tutorials to incorporating online learning management systems into the lectures. Despite e-Assessment being a valuable component in form of self-tests and formative assessment, the trend of digitalization has not yet been transferred on examinations. That is among other things caused by financial reasons, because maintaining a suitable IT-infrastructure for e-Assessment is expensive in terms of money as well as administrative effort. Bring Your Own Device is a potential solution to this issue, but also poses new challenges regarding the integrity of examinations. Therefore, we propose a framework for e-Assessment that tackles these challenges.

CCS Concepts

•Applied computing → Education;

Keywords

E-Assessment; BYOD; Bring Your Own Device; Computer based Examinations; Computer aided Examinations

1. STATEMENT OF THE PROBLEM

Despite e-Assessment being a valuable component in form of self-tests and formative assessment, the trend of digitization has not yet been transferred on examinations in Germany [1]. Similar trends can be observed also in other countries, e.g. the UK [5] or the USA [3].

Retaining examinations on paper is mainly caused by two reasons. First, reservations against e-Assessment, which concern for example the fairness or reliability of e-Assessment [4]. Second, financial reasons, because implementing and maintaining a suitable IT infrastructure is expensive [2].

ITiCSE '17 July 03-05, 2017, Bologna, Italy

© 2017 Copyright held by the owner/author(s).

ACM ISBN 978-1-4503-4704-4/17/07.

DOI: http://dx.doi.org/10.1145/3059009.3072994

Since most students already possess devices, which are suitable for e-Assessment, Bring Your Own Device (BYOD) is a potential solution. BYOD, however, poses also new challenges regarding the fairness and reliability of e-Assessment. Thus, BYOD potentially boosts the mentioned reservations. Hence, it is crucially important to have these issues solved in a transparent and comprehensible way.

This paper presents the design of an e-Assessment framework that takes into account the specialties of BYOD and presents solutions to them.

2. SOLUTION

The framework is based on a client-server architecture. The client is designed to need very few resources, thus smoothing the differences between the students' devices. Having more resources than the minimum requirements does not bring an advantage. To prevent cheating, security functionality comes with the client, which prevents certain actions on the students' devices and logs everything to the server, thus making a student's workflow comprehensible, if in doubt about the integrity of the solution.

The server provides needed information to the client and collects the students' results. These are stored safely during and after the examination. Thus, it is possible to switch devices in the examination without loss of data in case a device breaks down.

Data and communication are secured with asymmetric cryptography, which ensures integrity of the students' results after the examination and also allows to identify a particular student.

3. REFERENCES

[1] Hochschulforum Digitalisierung. The Digital Turn: Hochschulbildung im digitalen Zeitalter, 2016.

[2] B. Küppers and U. Schroeder. Bring Your Own Device for e-Assessment - a Review. In *International Conference on Education and New Learning Technologies*, EDULEARN proceedings, pages 8770–8776. IATED, 2016.

[3] R. M. Luecht and S. G. Sireci. A Review of Models for Computer-Based Testing: Research Report 2011-2012, 2011.

[4] M. Vogt and S. Schneider. E-Klausuren an Hochschulen: Didaktik - Technik - Systeme - Recht - Praxis, 2009.

[5] R. Walker and Z. Handley. Designing for learner engagement with computer-based testing. *Research in Learning Technology*, 24(0):88, 2016.

Discovering Indicators of Commitment in Computer-Supported Collaborative Student Teams

Antti Knutas[1], Jouni Ikonen[1], Laura Ripamonti[2], Dario Maggiorini[2], Jari Porras[1]

[1] Lappeenranta University of Technology
P.O. Box 20
FIN-53850 Lappeenranta, Finland
+358-0294-462-111
firstname.lastname@lut.fi

[2] Università di Milano
via Comelico 39/41
I-20135 Milano MI, Italy
+39-02-503-16212
firstname.lastname@unimi.it

ABSTRACT

In this paper, an approach and a rubric for measuring commitment to computer-supported collaboration in student teams is presented.

Categories and Subject Descriptors

• Human-centered computing~Collaborative and social computing theory, concepts and paradigms
• Applied computing~Collaborative learning

Keywords

Collaborative learning, computer science education, computer supported collaborative learning, metrics

1. INTRODUCTION

There has been extensive research on the benefits and drawbacks of collaborative learning approaches in higher education [1]. However, there has been less research on evaluating how the individual aspects of teamwork affect collaborative outcomes [1]. A link between student attitudes to teamwork, team cohesion and collaborative learning outcomes has been established [2, 4]. In this study, we are interested if there are more factors that affect teamwork outcomes. More specifically, we want to identify and measure factors that affect commitment to team collaboration, communication and shared decision-making process.

Our research questions in this study are:

1. Which factors affect individual commitment to shared team goals and team collaboration?
2. How can these factors be expressed as a rubric for comparing student teams' collaboration?

In order to develop the metric, we studied three engineering courses, two of which were longer in duration (28 and 13 weeks) and one was a weeklong intensive course. Two of the courses involved a software project, one course arranged in Italy and the second one in Finland. The third course, arranged in Finland, was multidisciplinary with electrical engineers, mechanical engineers, industrial management and business science students.

2. RESEARCH PROCESS

The main data source for the study was team interviews. The interviews were coded and analyzed by using a limited version of the Strauss-Corbin version of the Grounded Theory (GT) method [3]. We chose a mixed method approach, where we identify and describe the phenomena using the first two steps of GT. We built an evaluation rubric[1] from the data extracted from the interviews.

3. CONCLUSIONS

In this study, we identified several factors that affect commitment to team goals and collaboration, and present a metric for measuring them. The factors are cooperative goal setting processes, goal tracking, effective communication, and the level of collaboration. They do not have direct causality with individual commitment, but are indirect indicators of it. For example, having a successful cooperative goal setting process requires a certain level of organization and effort from the team.

The presented metric extends measuring student commitment to collaboration beyond direct inquiry about student motivation. It does so by using several indicators that were detected in the qualitative study. The metric uses an observation-based approach and qualitative observations as a data source. It can for example be used to compare team approaches or used as an average measure to evaluate different versions of course arrangements.

4. REFERENCES

[1] Resta, P. and Laferrière, T. 2007. Technology in support of collaborative learning. *Educational Psychology Review*. 19, 1 (2007), 65–83.

[2] Serrano-Cámara, L.M., Paredes-Velasco, M., Alcover, C.-M. and Velazquez-Iturbide, J.Á. 2014. An evaluation of students' motivation in computer-supported collaborative learning of programming concepts. *Computers in Human Behavior*. 31, (Feb. 2014), 499–508.

[3] Strauss, A. and Corbin, J.M. 1990. *Basics of qualitative research: Grounded theory procedures and techniques*. Sage Publications, Inc.

[4] Williams, E.A., Duray, R. and Reddy, V. 2006. Teamwork Orientation, Group Cohesiveness, and Student Learning: A Study of the Use of Teams in Online Distance Education. *Journal of Management Education*. 30, 4 (Aug. 2006), 592–616.

---

[1] http://dx.doi.org/10.5281/zenodo.546087

Labware for Secure Mobile Software Development (SMSD) Education

Kai Qian,
Hossain Shahriar
Dept. of Computer Science
Kennesaw State University
1100 South Marietta Pkwy SE
Marietta, GA, USA 30060
001-678-915-3717
{kqian,hshahria}@kennesaw .edu

Fan Wu
Dept. of Computer Science
Tuskegee University
1200 W. Montgomery Rd.
Tuskegee, AL, USA 36088
001-334-727-8362
wuf@mytu.tuskegee.edu

Lixin Tao
Dept. of Computer Science
Pace University
861 Bedford Rd
Pleasantville, NY, USA 10570
001-914-773-3449
ltao@pace.edu

Prabir Bhattacharya
Dept. of Computer Science
Morgan State University
205 Calloway Hall
Baltimore, MD, USA 21251
001-443-885-3963.
prabir.bhattacharya@morgan.edu

ABSTRACT

This poster addresses the needs of pedagogical learning materials for Secure Mobile Software Development(SMSD) education and challenges of building SMSD capacity. In this poster, we present an innovative authentic learning approach for SMSD through real-world-scenario case studies. The primary goal of this learning approach is to create an engaging and motivating learning environment that encourages students in learning emerging security concepts and practices such as mobile software developments. It provides students with hands-on laboratory practices on real-world mobile app developments and security. Each module consists of a series of progressive sub-labs: a pre-lab, lab activities, and a student add-on post-lab. The preliminary feedback from students is positive. Students have gained hands-on real world experiences on mobile security with Android mobile devices, which also greatly promoted students' self-efficacy and confidences in their mobile security learning.

Keywords
Secure Mobile Software Development, Android, Labware

1. INTRODUCTION

As mobile computing is becoming more and more popular, the security threats to mobile application are also growing explosively. Mobile app flaws and security defects could open doors for hackers to break into them and access sensitive information. Defensive secure coding needs to be an integral part of coding practices to improve the Security of our code. We need to consider data protections early, to verify security early in the development lifecycle rather than fixing the security holes after attacking and data leaks take place. Early eliminating known security vulnerability will help us increase the security of our software and reduce vulnerabilities in the programs, and militate the consequence of damages of data loss caused by potential malicious attacking.

However, many software developer professionals lack awareness of the importance of security vulnerability and the necessary security knowledge and skills at the development stage. Many schools offer mobile app development courses in computing curriculum, however, secure software development is not yet well represented in most schools' computing curriculum. There is a need to promote mobile security education and meet the emerging industry and education needs. We need effective mobile-security learning materials and hands-on laboratory platform and resources for SMSD.

2. LEARNING MODULE DESIGN

The labware organizes the learning materials into a sequence of reusable and self-contained integratable laboratory learning modules based on based on the OWASP recommendations. They are Data Sanitization for Input Validation and Output Encoding, Data Storage Protection, Secure Inter-Process Communication (IPC) and Inter-Application Communication(IAC), Secure Mobile Database, Unintended Data Leakage, Identity and Authentication Controls, Access Control Checks. The labware not only introduces to mobile software security principles but also addresses on mobile app vulnerabilities and exploits such that each module can be easily integrated into other courses for a security learning component. Each module consists of pre-activities which presents learning concepts and tutorials on the subject to prepare students with fundamental background knowledge on the subject; hands-on activities (hands-on step-by-step laboratory practices) which provides students with step-by-step interactive hands-on activities, engages and motivates students in building secure mobile apps; and post-activities (student add-on labs) that encourage students to work on their own to analyze and assess new mobile vulnerabilities and risks and to develop and integrate defensive tools for risk prevention and mitigation. This post-lab can help students to build self-efficacy by observing a successful task from their peers and strengthen confidence in their own abilities through vicarious experience.

Although the SMSD has many special mobile security issues but the principals behind are same for all secure software development. These learning modules can be easily incorporated into various computing courses such as networking, database, Web development, mobile software development to enhance the security education.

testSQL: Learn SQL the Interactive Way

Joshua License

Sheffield Hallam University

Howard Street

Sheffield, S1 1WB (UK)

Joshua.License@gmail.com

ABSTRACT

Students learning Structured Query Language (SQL) at higher education often involves solving problems on paper, often viewed as a sub-optimal and non-interactive method in facilitating the learning of SQL, as witnessed first-hand.

This poster will summarize an alternative learning method in the form of an interactive web application which was developed to not suffer from the shortcomings seen in paper-based learning. The application presents each user a personalized set of dynamically constructed problems each focusing on a certain aspect of SQL standard, to which the user can attempt to solve receiving detailed feedback for incorrect attempts.

1. INTRODUCTION

This poster gives an overview of a web application that will provide an alternate method to learn SQL, a programming language that is taught in many higher educational institutions who regularly utilize non-interactive learning methods as a means of teaching SQL to its students, often argued to hinder learning partly due to the disadvantages listed below:

- Delayed feedback – Students usually must wait several days to receive feedback from their work, often waiting until the subsequent tutorial which was identified to have a negative impact while learning [1].

- No visual outcome – It's agreed that it's particularly difficult to correctly construct a complex query without using the result set of the prior incorrect query [2].

A tutor can also come under immense pressure when marking solutions from an entire class, frequently allocating significant resources which could be better spent elsewhere.

The main aim of this project was to develop a web application that doesn't suffer from the inadequacies identified previously. This was achieved by creating an application, seen in Figure 1, that presents its users a wide range of dynamically created problems, purposely constructed so that the solution requires the incursion of specific SQL keywords, returning detailed feedback to the user for incorrect attempts.

ITiCSE '17, July 03-05, 2017, Bologna, Italy

© 2017 Copyright is held by the owner/author(s).

ACM ISBN 978-1-4503-4704-4/17/07.

http://dx.doi.org/10.1145/3059009.3072991

2. CONSTRUCTING THE QUESTIONS

The application generates a set of dynamic questions relating to the current database in-use, be it imported or the default database. For instance, question 19 focuses on the LEFT JOIN keyword and proceeds to display the user a problem that requires the joining of two linked columns from different tables targeting the specific incursion of the LEFT JOIN keyword.

At the time of question construction various information such as the problem text, the model solution and any keywords that require incursion in the user's input are stored locally to allow persistency and improve load times.

3. VALIDATING THE INPUT

The validation process involves running the user's input through several steps each further validating the user's answer to ensure a valid solution to the problem is submitted. The main steps are listed below in order of execution:

1. Firstly, a check for the incursion of specific keywords in the user's input, provided the keywords were set while constructing the question.

Both queries, the model answer and the user's input are then executed in the database and the results are stored.

2. The result sets proceed to be run through a series of comparisons comparing the total number of rows and columns in each result set to ensure similarity and provide an early indication of an incorrect solution.

At this stage, more thorough checks are required to determine if a correct solution was supplied.

3. Both result sets are split into their respective columns and each of the column rows are individually compared to confirm an exact match in both sets.

4. REFERENCES

[1] Mehta, S. & Schlecht, N. (1998). Computerized Assessment Technique for Large Classes. Journal Of Engineering Education, 87(2), 167-172.

[2] Prior, J. (2003). Online assessment of SQL query formulation skills. ACE '03 Proceedings Of The Fifth Australasian Conference On Computing Education, 20, 247-256.

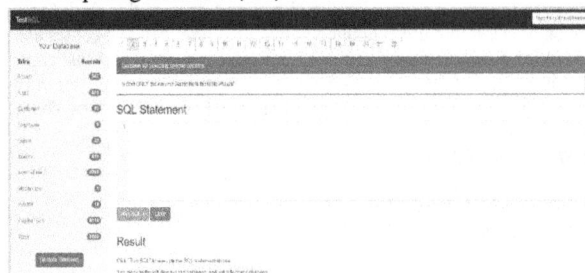

Figure 1 TestSQL's user interface

Yellow and Red Cards to Deal with Hitchhiking in Groups

Herman Koppelman
University of Twente
PO BOX 217
7500 AE Enschede, The Netherlands
Tel. +310610833037

H.Koppelman@utwente.nl

ABSTRACT

The idea is to give the students of a group some control over the behavior of fellow members, by providing them with a standard way to handle non-performance. Being given a yellow card results for the involved student in a known penalty, which can be cancelled after improved performance.

Keywords

Group work; cooperative learning; pedagogy.

1. INTRODUCTION

In group work it happens that not all students contribute satisfactorily. Sometimes this phenomenon of hitchhiking becomes clear, but in many cases it remains unnoticed by staff. Of course, this is undesirable, from the point of view of both the students and the supervisors. The objective of the system of cards is to make hitchhiking more visible, and to handle it, by giving the group itself the opportunity to deal with non-performance of group members.

2. THE IDEA

The basic idea is discussed by Fincher et al. [1]. Students are allowed to give fellow members of their group a yellow card, and in exceptional cases, a red card. A yellow card is given to a student who is not making full contribution to the group, for example because he/she is deficient in effort or not showing up. A yellow card can only be given if the majority of the group wishes to do so, and is registered by the supervisor. A yellow card results in a penalty. In our case, the penalty consists of a loss of one point (on a 10-pt scale) of the mark for the project. A yellow card can be cancelled, if the performance of the involved student improves.

After two yellow cards the group can give a red card to a student, which means exclusion from the project. There is no recovery from a red card. A red card can only be given after involving the supervisor, who usually invites the whole group to discuss the matter.

Our main objective is to stimulate a group to deal with problems of hitchhiking during the project, not to stimulate a group to

punish a student afterwards. Because of that reason, we do not allow groups to give a card by the end of the project.

In our course we added a green card: a group can give at most one member a green card, in case of outstanding efforts for the project. A green card results in a bonus of one point. In this way we give groups not only the possibility to 'punish', but also to 'reward'.

3. OUR EXPERIENCES

We have been working with this system of cards for more than 10 years. Some groups don't like the idea and don't consider giving cards. But in practice, several groups actually do give cards to members of the groups. If a student receives a yellow card, usually two things can happen: the card is retracted after some time, because of increased effort, or the student leaves the group and the course, sometimes after receiving another yellow card or a red card.

We have never seen any frivolous use of the cards. Sometimes we notice that groups were reluctant to give a yellow card, out of compassion with a member. But at least, they told the staff.

The main advantage is that it is much easier to discuss the level of involvement of individual members. Of course, without the system of cards, groups can notify the supervisor about the behavior of students. But many students don't like the idea to complain about a fellow student. The consequence of a yellow card is well-known and rather mild, which lowers the threshold to handle non-performance of a group member. The system of cards makes it also easier for groups to bring up this topic in interaction with their supervisors. We have the idea to be better informed about the involvement of team members.

The system of cards is not the definite solution to the phenomenon of hitchhiking, but it certainly helps to make it more visible and manageable.

4. REFERENCES

[1] Fincher, S., Petre, M. & Clark M. (Eds). (2001). *Computer Science Project Work: Principles and Pragmatics.* Springer-Verlag, London, UK.

ITiCSE '17, July 03-05, 2017, Bologna, Italy
© 2017 Copyright is held by the owner/author(s).
ACM ISBN 978-1-4503-4704-4/17/07.
http://dx.doi.org/10.1145/3059009.3072992

A Course Based on Open Organization Principles

Heidi J. C. Ellis
Western New England University
Springfield, MA, USA
ellis@wne.edu

Gregory W. Hislop
Drexel University
Philadelphia, PA, USA
hislop@drexel.edu

ABSTRACT

This poster presents a plan for a first-semester freshman computing course based on Open Organization principles using humanitarian organizations as the context. The goal of the course is to instill engagement with learning in students from the beginning of their academic careers when they are psychologically invested in their learning and more likely to internalize the learning. The anticipated outcome is students who are motivated, engaged, and able to handle the rapid rate of computing change in today's society.

CCS CONCEPTS

• **Applied computing** → *Collaborative learning*;

KEYWORDS

Open Organization, Humanitarian Computing, Computing education

ACM Reference format:
Heidi J. C. Ellis and Gregory W. Hislop. 2017. A Course Based on Open Organization Principles. In *Proceedings of ITiCSE'17, July 3–5, 2017, Bologna, Italy,* , 1 pages.
DOI: http://dx.doi.org/10.1145/3059009.3072998

1 INTRODUCTION

Computing is advancing at an exponential rate, resulting in a vast array of new technologies and ideas that are transforming the world dramatically. We must prepare motivated, engaged and empowered students who are able to contribute to the businesses that develop and support these new technologies and ideas.

An open organization is one that "engages participative communities both inside and out ... and inspires, motivates, and empowers people at all levels to act with accountability [2]." The open organization applied to education provides students and faculty with a high degree of choice and flexibility in an environment of trust, allowing students to learn at their own pace and according to their own styles. Students and faculty work together in community to transparently adopt new ideas and technologies.

2 COMPUTATIONAL CULTURES

Two sections of a first-semester freshman course titled "Computational Cultures" will be offered in fall 2017 at Western New England

University. Expected enrollment is 20 or fewer students per section with the majority of students being in the CS & IT programs.

Course Description: This course explores the social, cultural, political, and economic forces surrounding the pervasiveness of computers and computational practices in everyday life, with emphasis on the rapidly expanding number of contexts in which familiarity of the computational is imperative today. Principles of Open Organization will be practiced in this course.

The course will utilize humanitarian projects as the domain for course deliverables. Students will collaborate to answer the question of how they can impact the world for the better through the project. Forms could take advocacy, marketing and community building, in addition to technical efforts. By setting their own purpose, it is hoped that students will create meaning and excitement in their work. Key principles of Open Organizations include:

Empowerment: Students decide about their learning directions including how to approach topics and course structure such as policies for attendance, late arrival, cell phone use, etc.

Manage by Example: The instructor will be transparent about the constraints on the course (timing, course goals, etc.) and work along with students to solve problems, modeling problem-solving behavior.

Fast Innovation: Assignments will involve a creative component where students can push the boundaries of their learning and take risks.

Incremental Improvement: An incremental approach will be taken in the course where students will learn that the first innovation will not be perfect and that an incremental process can be used to refine and ensure ongoing improvement to ideas.

Collaboration: All discussions will happen in public when possible, and all course decisions will be made in public.

In order to understand the impact of the course, engagement in the course will be assessed at the beginning and end using a known instrument such as [1].

ACKNOWLEDGMENTS

This material is based on work supported by the National Science Foundation under Grant Nos. DUE-1525039, DUE-1524877, and DUE-1524898. Any opinions, findings and conclusions or recommendations expressed in this material are those of the author(s) and do not necessarily reflect the views of the National Science Foundation (NSF).

REFERENCES

[1] James J. Appleton. 2006. Measuring cognitive and psychological engagement: Validation of the Student Engagement Instrument. *Journal of School Psychology* 44, 5 (2006), 427–445.
[2] Jim Whitehurst. 2015. *The Open Organization: Ignighting Passion and Performance.* Harvard Business Review Press, Cambridge, Massachusetts.

Self-Assess Competency as Yes/No - A Preliminary Study

Malcolm Hutchison
Queen's University Belfast
18 Malone Road, Belfast
Northern Ireland
m.hutchison@qub.ac.uk

ABSTRACT
Some modules in computing degrees have problems with the wide variation in students' prior experiences and risk losing good students who are bored with the initial elementary topics. One possible solution is to specify in detail what the student should be capable of at the end of the module and allow them to decide how to arrange their studies. This study compares the accuracy of student self-assessments of capability against the learning outcomes on a binary Yes/No scale with their exam performance. Predicted marks from their responses were found to have a weak correlation to the student performance. Higher level learning outcomes and responses by female students generated lower reliability scores.

Keywords
Outcome based learning; resource based learning; systems administration; gender differences; self-regulated learning

1. INTRODUCTION
There have been increasing enrolments on computing courses with the students having a diverse range of computing experiences. Attempting to "teach to the middle" can lead to even good students dropping out [1]. In addition to their studies, students having to balance time between family and work commitments [2] are unable to attend all classes, and instead adopting either surface or deep approaches to different subjects, concentrating on what will improve their marks in assessments.

One possible way of tackling this diversity is to combine outcome based education with resources and self-regulated learning, however this requires students to assess themselves correctly. This preliminary study examines how accurately students can assesses whether they can or cannot do something with no guidance except the learning outcome text.

2. DATA GATHERED
Students (46M, 20F) on a systems administration module completed a web-based questionnaire (optimized for mobile devices). They recorded their capability against 205 different fine grained learning outcomes (divided into 17 topic areas) as either:

1. *Yes* – student can already do it (i.e. knew prior t o course)
2. *Learnt* – student can now do it (i.e. learnt on the course)
3. *No* – student knows that they cannot do it
4. *Don't know* – student not certain what a learning outcome is

ITiCSE '17, July 03-05, 2017, Bologna, Italy
© 2017 Copyright is held by the owner/author(s).
ACM ISBN 978-1-4503-4704-4/17/07.
http://dx.doi.org/10.1145/3059009.3073003

Yes and *Learnt* are positive states (i.e. the student believes they have the capability), whereas *No* and *Don't know* are negatives (i.e. the student does not believe they can do it or do not recognize it).

Students could update their current competence at any time or place, dipping in and out of the system as they saw fit (i.e. they did not have to answer all "questions" in a single sitting and could change responses at a later date).

For the preliminary analysis, the components of one exam question were mapped to the learning outcomes, giving 15 question-learning outcome pairs.

3. ANALYSIS
A predicted mark was calculated for each student by awarding the full marks for those components where students recorded a positive answer (i.e. *Yes* or *Learnt*) in the matching learning outcome. A weak relationship between predicted and actual marks was found (Pearson r=0.39).

The reliability of each learning outcome was calculated as the fraction of how often the students' recorded capabilities matched their performances in the matching exam question (i.e. positive and scored some marks, or negative and scored no marks), excluding students who left the learning outcome blank.

The average reliability of the learning outcomes for the male students (0.65) was slightly higher compared to the females (0.59), but not significant (t-test, p> 0.05).

To help identify the source of unreliability, the positive and negative capabilities recorded by students are further divided into true-positives, false-positives, true-negatives and false-negatives by comparing the statement with the mark obtained in the exam component. The unreliability for the female results came from the false-negatives (i.e. saying they cannot do something, but in the exam demonstrating that they do know).

4. FUTURE WORK
The next stage of the study is to investigate whether having resources associated with each of the learning outcomes affects the accuracy of the self-assessment and how the student self-assessment changes over the semester and in relation to engagement with the resources.

5. REFERENCES
[1] Bruce, K.B. 1994. Attracting (& Keeping) the Best and the Brightest: An Entry-level Course for Experienced Introductory Students. In *Proceedings of the Twenty-fifth SIGCSE Symposium on Computer Science Education,* Phoenix, Arizona, USA, Anonymous ACM, New York, NY, USA, 243-247.

[2] Jonas, G.A. And Norman, C.S. 2011. Textbook websites: User technology acceptance behaviour. *Behaviour and Information Technology* 30, 147-159.

Students' Feedback in Using GitHub in a Project Development for a Software Engineering Course

Francesca Arcelli Fontana
Università degli Studi di Milano-Bicocca
Dip. di Informatica, Sistemistica e Comunicazione
Viale Sarca 336, Ed. U14, 20126, Milan
arcelli@disco.unimib.it

Claudia Raibulet
Università degli Studi di Milano-Bicocca
Dip. di Informatica, Sistemistica e Comunicazione
Viale Sarca 336, Ed. U14, 20126, Milan
raibulet@disco.unimib.it

ABSTRACT
GitHub is a platform used for the development of software projects. It provides a traceable project repository and a social meeting place for communities of practices. This poster presents the students' feedback on using GitHub as a development platform for software projects counting as an exam for a 3rd-year undergraduate software engineering course on software design. Students worked in teams and their feedback is positive overall.

CCS Concepts
• **Software and its engineering → Software creation and management.**

Keywords
GitHub; students' feedback; software engineering course.

1. INTRODUCTION
GitHub has gained the attention of the industrial and academic worlds. In the academic context, GitHub is used as a development platform for software projects and as a social meeting platform for courses [2, 3]. Based on our interest in GitHub concerning the quality of software projects and the use of GitHub for their development [1], in this paper we investigate the students' feedback in exploiting GitHub for the development of different software Web application projects assigned to students teams of 3 to 5 members. We evaluate how each team use a Git repository to manage the code and the communication among the team members. All the students used GitHub during the course labs.

2. RESULTS AND DISCUSSION
We asked 30 students questions grouped in 3 categories: general (e.g., their knowledge about the existence and previous usage of GitHub), technical skills (e.g., about GitHub functionality - pull request or shared repository model), communication and teamwork skills (e.g., communication with the team members, tasks distribution). Here we discuss some of the answers.

Concerning the general category of questions, 19 students heard about GitHub before this course, while only 4 have used it. 27 students had basic knowledge about GitHub before starting the project development.

ITiCSE'17, July 03–05, 2017, Bologna, Italy.
© 2017 Copyright is held by the owner/author(s).
ACM ISBN 978-1-4503-4704-4/17/07.
DOI: http://dx.doi.org/10.1145/3059009.3072984

Except 1 student, all the others have improved their skills in using GitHub during the project development for the software engineering course. All the students acknowledged that GitHub was useful for the project development. Except 1, all students plan to use GitHub for future projects.

Concerning the technical skills category of questions, 19 students have exploited the notification and pull request mechanism of GitHub, 12 students the shared repository model, and 27 found the history and version control facility very useful.

Concerning the communication and teamwork skills, all students read the code written by the other team members and they do not have any concern about having their code read by others. 18 confirm that GitHub helped the communication among the team members. 7 students consider that GitHub is not useful enough for the management of the tasks distribution inside the team. The motivation for these results may be due to the usage of chats, skype, whatsup by students for communication and tasks distribution. Moreover, they know each other and they also met physically at university. 7 students declared that they met their team members daily, 11 students met 2 or 3 times a week, 9 students met once a week. 3 students met only 3 times during the entire project development.

3. CONCLUSIONS
To summarize, after the project development, the students have a good knowledge on using GitHub. Not all the students have used all the functionality provided by GitHub as the notification and pull request mechanisms. Hence, we aim in future projects to encourage and motivate students to use these functionality. While most of them were able to capture the advantages provided by GitHub concerning the history and version control mechanisms.

4. REFERENCES
[1] Arcelli Fontana, F., Roveda, R., Raibulet, C. and Zanoni. M. 2017. Does the Migration to GitHub Relate to Internal Software Quality? In *Proceedings of the 12th Conference on Evaluation of Novel Approaches to Software Engineering (ENASE'17)* (Porto, Portugal, April, 28th-29th, 2017)

[2] Feliciano, J., Storey, M.-A., and Zagalsky, A. 2016. Student Experiences Using GitHub in Software Engineering Courses: A Case Study. In *Proc. of the IEEE/ACM 38th International Conference on Software Engineering Companion)*, 422-431

[3] Zagalsky, A., Feliciano, J., Storey, M.-A., Zhan, Y. and Wang, W. The Emergence of GitHub as a Collaborative Platform for Education. In *Proc. of the 18th ACM Conference on Computer-Supported Cooperative Work*, 1906-1917

Cross Cultural Project Based Learning & Soft Skills Practice

Alexandra Badets
CESI
1 rue G. Marconi
76130 Mont-Saint-Aignan, France
+33 235 593 173
abadets@cesi.fr

Becky Grasser
Lakeland Community College
7700 Clocktower Drive
Kirtland, OH 44094
+001 440.525.7282
bgrasser@lakelandcc.edu

Stefan Peltier
CESI
1 rue G. Marconi
76130 Mont-Saint-Aignan, France
+33 235 593 658
speltier@cesi.fr

ABSTRACT

This poster presents an ongoing experience carried out by two international higher education institutions, Lakeland Community College, Ohio and CESI, France. Based on the introduction of a PBL cross-cultural cooperative project, this classroom innovation aims at introducing soft skills practice and self-reflection into the curriculum of computer science students. This poster explains our approach, the results of the first step of this project, perspectives to replicate cooperative workshops on a larger scale, and give students and academics tools to monitor soft skills development.

CCS Concepts

•Social and professional topics -> Computing education; Applied Computing -> Education -> Collaborative learning

Keywords

PBL; soft skills; collaboration; cross-cultural; communication

1. BACKGROUND

CESI Rouen in France and Lakeland Community College, Ohio have run a collaboration for five years. Second year students from both institutions are learning the basics of web programming from April to June 2017. The two groups are a heterogeneous set of students: the French group is made up of 35 20-year old students enrolled in a 5-year curriculum to become IT engineers, while the American group is made up of 13 16-to-60-year-old students enrolled in a web content developer concentration in an Associate of Applied Business degree program. However, both groups have common professional goals: become IT professionals.

Literature [1], accreditation boards, and reference books insist on non-technical skills, i.e. "soft skills" such as collective thinking, learning how to learn, being adaptive, as key elements to the success of a project. To help both groups of students take a step back from technical skills and have a more holistic view of their future position in companies, we decided to have them work together from a distance on a PBL collaborative project.

2. CURRENT WORK

The first step was to introduce into CESI and LCC's curricula a cooperative short module, where students designed a website from scratch. The design and graphic part was sub-contracted to the US students by the French students, who designed the specs of the

ITiCSE '17, July 03-05, 2017, Bologna, Italy
© 2017 Copyright is held by the owner/author(s).
ACM ISBN 978-1-4503-4704-4/17/07.
http://dx.doi.org/10.1145/3059009.3072988.

website so the US-based group could implement them. Working with peers from a different culture, at a distance, on an actual project answering client requirements meant dealing with requirement ambiguity, issues with communication, time management, and cross-cultural differences. All students were asked to assess their soft skills before the project, using a scale inspired by the University of Exeter [2], and to provide a ranking of the soft skills they expected to develop with this project. The aim was to develop their self-reflexivity and soft-skills awareness, and to provide us with data on self-perceived soft skills development before and after the project, that ends in June 2017.

3. FINDINGS

The results will allow us to compare differences between the two cohorts, as well as differences before and after the project. Before the project, cultural differences were already noticeable (Table 1).

Table 1. Self-evaluation results before the project

	Average rating	Top skills	Weakest skills	Expected development
US students	74,60%	Respect views and values others	Analysis, synthesis, evaluation, argument	Cooperation; working and planning with others
FR students	70,90%	Use data as tool in support of argument	Manage time effectively : meet deadlines	Communication

4. FUTURE WORK

Once we have collected the results of the second self-evaluation, we shall be able to measure evolutions, discuss them with students, look for ways of improving the project, and to monitor soft skills development. In step two of the project we will focus on the main soft skills identified as key for them, as well as the main soft skills developed during the first step, so as to design a more accurate evaluation scale that will include tutors, clients, and peers in addition to the self-evaluation of these key skills [3].

5. REFERENCES

[1] Stevens, M., & Norman, R. (2016, February). Industry expectations of soft skills in IT graduates: a regional survey. In *Proceedings of the Australasian Computer Science Week Multi conference* (p. 13). ACM.

[2] http://urlz.fr/4UwL

[3] Zheng, G., Zhang, C., & Li, L. (2015, September). Practicing and Evaluating Soft Skills in IT Capstone Projects. In *Proceedings of the 16th Annual Conference on Information Technology Education* (pp. 109-113). ACM

Data Science for All: A Tale of Two Cities

Lillian Cassel
Villanova University
Department of Computing Sciences
Villanova PA 19085 USA
1 610 519 7341
Lillian.Cassel@villanova.edu

Don Goelman
Villanova University
Department of Computing Sciences
Villanova PA 19085 USA
1 610 519 7310
Don.Goelman@villanova.edu

Michael Posner
Villanova University
Dept. of Mathematics & Statistics
Villanova PA 19085 USA
1 610 519 3016
Michael.Posner@villanova.edu

Darina Dicheva
Department of Computer Science
Winston Salem State University
Winston Salem, NC USA
1 336 750-2484
dichevad@wssu.edu

Christo Dichev
Department of Computer Science
Winston Salem State University
Winston Salem, NC USA
1 336 750-2477
dichevc@wssu.edu

ABSTRACT

In this poster the authors report on experiences in teaching an introductory course in Data Science at two different institutions. Their approaches were informed by the aims of their NSF-funded project: to provide insight on learning goals, central data science topics, content modules, and a framework for implementing a flipped classroom approach to introduce data science to students with various technical backgrounds. The authors, investigators on the grant mentioned above, are a collaborative team of computer scientists and a statistician working to create flipped material for an introductory data science class. After ITiCSE the materials described in the poster will continue to be available in Ensemble, at http://computingportal.org/datascienceflipped

Keywords
Data Science, flipped classroom, computer science education

INTRODUCTION
Data Science programs of various granularities are emerging in many areas and are related to many disciplines, including any field dealing with massive amounts of data. This project looks at core concepts to provide resources for faculty teaching computing and statistics topics in the context of data science. The poster will review an overview of topics from both the computer science and statistics perspective, along with consideration of requirements related to domains. Its emphasis will be a description of, reflection on, and lessons learned from our experiences in delivering such a course at two institutions. Since we committed to producing learning materials, we chose to use the flipped classroom approach in the design of the materials. We believe that lack of suitable materials severely constrains the adoption of the flipped classroom approach, and we set out to address that in the context of the data science modules we produce.

Confirmation of the significance and relevance of this project was evident in well-attended (indeed overflowing) Birds of a Feather sessions at the SIGCSE Symposia in 2016 and 2017.

A mailing list of people interested in data science education now resides on a Villanova server. People who visit the poster will have an opportunity to join the mailing list and to use it for communication with the ever growing group.

The poster will include details on the pilot offerings by the authors, together with their reflection and recommendations. They will be described along various axes: the differences between the two institutions (Villanova University and Winston Salem State University); the relative roles of computing and statistics; student backgrounds; and the degree to which the flipped format was used.

A significant number of programs in data science now exist, and the poster will consequently include as well a representative sample of the program types, together with comparisons with our own experiences. There are several projects currently exploring curriculum issues related to data science. One of these is sponsored by the United States National Academies. Another project brings together a number of societies with interest in data science, including the Association for Computing Machinery (ACM), the American Statistical Association (ASA), the Association for Information Systems, The Association for Computers and the Humanities, The Business Higher Education Forum, the iCaucus, INFORMS, IEEE-CS, and others. Information about the meetings and conclusions of these groups are included in the poster.

ACKNOWLEDGEMENTS
This work is supported by NSF-DUE IUSE grants 1432256 and 1432438. In addition, we gratefully acknowledge the support of the graduate assistants who have worked on the project, including Dheeraj Kumar Reddy Kurla, Sai Vishwa Teja Mitta, Yamini Praveena Tella and LeelaRajesh Sayana.

Understanding International Benchmarks on Student Engagement - Awareness, Research Alignment and Response from a Computer Science Perspective

Michael Morgan
Monash University
Melbourne, Australia
michael.morgan@monash.edu

Matthew Butler
Monash University
Melbourne, Australia
matthew.butler@monash.edu

Jane Sinclair
University of Warwick
Coventry, UK
j.e.sinclair@warwick.ac.uk

Gerry Cross
Mount Royal University
Calgary, Canada
gcross@mtroyal.ca

Janet Fraser
Monash University
Melbourne, Australia
janet.fraser@monash.edu

Jana Jackova
Matej Bel University
Bystrica, Slovakia
jana.jackova@umb.sk

Neena Thota
University of Massachusetts
Amherst, USA
nthota@cs.umass.edu

ABSTRACT

There is an increasing trend to use national benchmarks to measure student engagement, with instruments such as North American National Survey of Student Engagement (NSSE) in the USA and Canada, Student Experience Survey (SES) in Australia and NZ (previously known as the University Experience Survey UES), and Student Engagement Survey (SES) in the UK. Unfortunately, Computer Science (CS) rates fairly poorly on a number of measures in these surveys, even when compared to related STEM disciplines. Initial research suggests there may be several reasons for this poor performance: i) the suitability of the instruments to the CS context, ii) a lack of awareness of CS academics of these instruments and the student engagement measures they are based on, and iii) a misalignment between these instruments and the research focus of computing educators, leading to misdirected efforts in research and teaching practice. This working group focused on the last two aspects of this issue. We carried out an in-depth analysis of international student engagement instruments to facilitate a greater awareness of the international benchmarks and what aspects of student engagement they measure. The working group also examined the focus of current computing education research and its alignment to student engagement measures on which these instruments are based. Armed with this knowledge, the computing education community can make informed decisions on how best to respond to these measures and consider ways to improve our performance in

relation to other disciplines. In particular it is important to understand why certain measures of student engagement are built into these instruments and how these align to our current research practice.

Given the global nature of these benchmarks, an ITiCSE working group was needed to obtain the perspectives needed to address these challenges. This ITiCSE working group facilitated international input to the following activities:

Stage 1 - A study examining the trends and variations in the data for the computing discipline from several international student engagement instruments (NSSE, SES, UKSES) over the past decade, including:

- A longitudinal study of the data, comparing the results from the various instruments.

- Benchmarking of the performance of CS, with a focus on comparisons to other STEM disciplines

- A summary of the published data and the perceptions this may generate of CS for perspective students and university administrators.

Stage 2 - Analysis of the instrument design and the student engagement measures they use. This is examined through:

- A comparative analysis of the various survey instruments of student engagement.

- An analysis of the engagement measures used in the instruments (this analyse was contrasted with the focus of current computing education research).

- A survey of research literature used to justify the use of these student engagement measures.

Stage 3 - Meta-analysis of current CS research literature related to computing education with specific focus on any initiatives to promote student engagement, including:

- A survey of current topics in computing education research literature to establish the current research focus of the discipline.

- A focus on any research and teaching initiatives to promote student engagement.

- An analysis of the alignment of current CS research to student engagement measures used in international survey instruments.

Stage 4 - Interviews on the perceptions of CS academics to the various survey instrument student engagement measures/questions, focusing on:

- Interviews with academics to examine how they respond to specific questions extracted from current survey instruments, how they interpret the question in the context of CS and how the questions relate to their teaching practice.

- Analysis of the response of academics to international student engagement survey instruments and the engagement measures used.

Stage 5 - Responding to findings by:

- Providing suggestions for adapting the focus of future computing education research to maximise outcomes from existing international benchmarks on student engagement.

- Presenting ways of increasing staff awareness of international benchmarks and student engagement measures.

Since these student engagement measures are widely publicised, and are used by students to make course selection decisions and by administrators to assess courses, it is important for the computing education discipline to have a greater awareness of these instruments and their design. We need to better understand how current computing education research relates to these instruments and the engagement measures they use. A better understanding of the engagement measures used in these instruments, why they are considered important, and how they align to our teaching and research practice, is crucial if we are to improve the performance of the computing discipline in these national benchmarks. Finally, we must investigate ways in which we might respond as a discipline in order to improve the performance of CS on these student engagement measures.

CCS Concepts

•**Social and professional topics** → **Computer science education;**

Keywords

Student Engagement; Computer Science; International Benchmarks

1. ACKNOWLEDGMENTS

Support for this project has been provided by the Monash Education Academy and also by KEGA, The Ministry of Education, Science, Research and Sport of the Slovak Republic (KEGA 009KU-4/2017).

Working Group: Game Development for Computer Science Education

Monica McGill
(co-leader)
Bradley University
mmcgill@bradley.edu

Chris Johnson
(co-leader)
Univ. of Wisconsin, Eau Claire
johnch@uwec.edu

James Atlas
University of Delaware
jatlas@udel.edu

Durell Bouchard
Roanoke College
bouchard@roanoke.edu

Laurence D. Merkle
Air Force Institute of
Technology
xphileprof@gmail.com

Chris Messom
Monash University
christopher.messom@monash.edu

Ian Pollock
California State University,
East Bay
ian.pollock@csueastbay.edu

Michael James Scott
Falmouth University
adrir@adrir.com

1. BACKGROUND

Educators have long used digital games as platforms for teaching. Games tend to have several qualities that aren't typically found in homework: they often situate problems within a compelling alternate reality that unfolds through intriguing narrative, they often draw more upon a player's intrinsic motivations than extrinsic ones, they can facilitate deliberate low intensity practice, and they often emphasize a spirit of play instead of work.

At ITiCSE 2016, this working group convened to survey the landscape of existing digital games that have been used to teach and learn computer science concepts. Our group discovered that these games lacked explicitly defined learning goals and even less evaluation of whether or not the games achieved these goals. As part of this process, we identified and played over 120 games that have been released or described in literature as means for learning computer science concepts. In our report, we classified how these games support the learning objectives outlined in the ACM/IEEE Computer Science Curricula 2013.

While we found more games than we expected, few games explicitly stated their learning goals and even fewer were evaluated for their capacity to meet these goals. Most of the games we surveyed fell into two categories: short-lived proof-of-concept projects built by academics or closed-source games built by professional developers. Gathering adequate learning data is challenging in either situation. Our original intent for the second year of our working group was to prepare a comprehensive framework for collecting and analyzing learning data from computer science learning games.

Upon further discussion, however, we decided that a better next step is to validate the design and development guidelines that we put forth in our final report for ITiCSE 2016.

We extend this working group to a second year—with a mission to collaboratively develop a game with clearly defined learning objectives and define a methodology for evaluating its capacity to meet its goals.

2. OBJECTIVE

In this second year of the working group, we plan to collaboratively define a target learning area in computing education and design and develop a game for this learning area. We will define explicit and measurable learning goals and propose evaluation measures than can be followed and modified as desired by the general computing education community. The process of building a game as an international group of educators—and playtesting it with and releasing it to the computer science education community—is a necessary first step in forming a broader understanding of how these games might be used to facilitate learning.

To avoid the trap of creating polished but unevaluated games that have been published, the group will develop its game using the format of a game jam to take place during ITiCSE 2017. Prior to the conference, the group will decide on learning objectives and prototype game concepts. During the conference itself, the team will implement an alpha version of the game, recruiting conference attendances to play and give their feedback. After the conference, the release version of the game will be published online, with an additional goal of incorporating analytics to help educators understand their student-players' learning.

We intend for our game to be non-monolithic, with no pretense to serve as a standalone learning resource. Rather, we intend for it to have challenges or levels that are episodic in nature and will be embeddable as supplementary exercises distributed throughout a larger course. We will seek input from fellow computer science educators by incorporating them early in the development process through playtesting.

ITiCSE '17, July 3–5, 2017, Bologna, Italy.

© 2017 Copyright held by the owner/author(s).

ACM ISBN 978-1-4503-4704-4/17/07.

DOI: http://dx.doi.org/10.1145/3059009.3081325

Integrating International Students into Computer Science Programs: Challenges and Strategies for Success

Michael J. Oudshoorn (leader)
Northwest Missouri State University
Maryville, MO, USA
+1 660 562 1764
oudshoorn@nwmissouri.edu

Alison Clear (co-leader)
Eastern Institute of Technology
Auckland, New Zealand
+64 9 300 7410
aclear@eit.ac.nz

Janet Carter (co-leader)
University of Kent
Canterbury, Kent, United Kingdom
+44 1227 827978
j.e.carter@kent.ac.uk

Joseph A. Abandoh-Sam
Valley View University
Oyibi, Ghana
+233 27 745 5565
abandoh@vvu.edu.gh

Christabel Gonsalvez
Monash University
Clayton, VIC, Australia
+61 3 9905 5806
chris.gonsalvez@monash.edu

Leo Hitchcock
Auckland University of Technology
Auckland, New Zealand
+64 9 921 9999
leo.hitchcock@aut.ac.nz

Shoba Ittyipe
Mount Royal University
Calgary, Alberta, Canada
+1 403 440 6787
sittyipe@mtroyal.ca

Aparna Mahadev
Worcester State University
Worcester, MA, USA
+1 508 929 8715
amahadev@worcester.edu

Janice L. Pearce
Berea College
Berea, KY, USA
+1 859 985 3569
jan_pearce@berea.edu

ABSTRACT

International students are an important and desirable constituent in most computer science programs. These students help to enrich the programs, bring new perspectives into the classroom, diversify the student population, globalize the curriculum, broaden the perspective of domestic students, and generate revenue for the host institution. Each of these characteristics is desirable and increasingly important in today's highly connected world and job market. Most institutions invest resources in attracting international students and provide orientation sessions for them on arrival to help acclimate them to the new environment and to introduce them to other students. There are often clubs to provide support groups and social functions to help them meet and make friends with domestic students. However, challenges for international students, and for the faculty teaching them, persist at many institutions despite these efforts to help international students deal with culture shock, differing academic expectations and teaching methods, and different attitudes toward issues such as plagiarism.

CCS Concepts

• **Social and Professional topics→Adult education, computing education programs**

ITiCSE'17, July 3–5, 2017, Bologna, Italy.
ACM ISBN 978-1-4503-4704-4/17/07.
DOI: http://dx.doi.org/10.1145/3059009.3081326

Keywords

International students; computer science education; computing; information systems; information technology; information and communication technology.

1. INTRODUCTION

The goal of this working group is to bring together of international faculty to discuss the challenges faced at various institutions and to explore those challenges and identify strategies to ameliorate them.

Participants in the working group come from diverse institutions with diverse missions. Several of the participants have been international students themselves. Each institution, however, attracts international students into their graduate and/or undergraduate programs, and must face and address the challenges presented as a result. These challenges are faced by the students who travel to the host country in order to pursue a degree, but also by the faculty and administration at these institutions. These challenges persist despite the resources invested by institutions to create and provide an inclusive and supporting environment for the international students. Support comes in many forms including clubs, social events, orientation sessions, and regular meetings with support staff in an attempt to acclimate the students in their new environment.

Faculty at many institutions are not provided any training on the challenges facing international students, or on their cultural backgrounds or norms. As a result, classroom challenges arise. Often these are born from a cultural misunderstanding, or simply a lack of knowledge of the student's home countries educational system.

2. THREE SAMPLE INSTITUTIONS
2.1 Northwest Missouri State University, USA

Northwest Missouri State University (NWMSU) is a regional university located in Maryville, MO. It services 6,530 students of which 10% are international students. The School of Computer Science and Information Systems offers a number of degrees at the undergraduate and graduate level. These include degrees in Computer Science, Information Systems, Information Technology, and Data Science. Programs are offered at the main campus or at regional offices in St. Joseph and Kansas City.

The undergraduate Computer Science program attracts a number of international students primarily from Nepal, while the graduate degrees in Applied Computer Science, and Information Systems are almost entirely international students almost exclusively from India. Each of these programs presents its own challenges in terms of attracting, and retaining international students. However, the challenge of integrating the students into the classes, and into the academic community, is common across the programs and the locations where they are offered. Several initiatives have been tried over the years including regular, required advising sessions for students where topics ranging from exam study habits to plagiarism to expectations in a US academic environment are covered. Despite such efforts, challenges persist.

2.2 Eastern Institute of Technology, New Zealand

Eastern Institute of Technology (EIT) has three campuses in New Zealand. One of the campuses, based in Auckland, is exclusively for international students studying in the areas of Business, Applied Management and Information Technology. To gain entry to the programs the students must have a degree from their home country and meet an English language requirement. International students can also study the same Business, Applied Management and IT programs on the main campus in Napier where they are integrated with the domestic students.

There are many challenges for these new students and the faculty have implemented different strategies to support the students however they have not all been as successful as they would have liked. A new strategy will be implemented in semester 1, 2017 and this will be compared to the previous three strategies to gauge the success. Focus groups and surveys will be held with graduating students to better understand the issues and then design interventions that will be of interest and importance to the wider Computer Science education community.

International education is the fourth largest export earner in New Zealand and the country has an impressive international reputation in providing education for these students. Investigating comparative educational institutions and different countries strategies will be of significant importance for the support and guidance for these students.

2.3 University of Kent

The University of Kent (UoK) is based in Kent, England. The main campus is situated in Canterbury and overlooks the historic city. It services over 15,800 students. The Medway campus presents professionally focused programs for 4,000 students in renovated listed buildings on Chatham's Historic Dockyard. Overall 149 nationalities are represented. There are also a number of smaller satellite postgraduate campuses throughout Europe: Athens, Brussels, Paris and Rome. 27% of our student population are international with 11% from the EU. Also, 37% of our teaching and research staff come from outside the UK.

Kent is consistently voted one of the top UK universities in international student satisfaction surveys and has established a number of support services to benefit its international population, with academic help, personal support and social events tailored to those studying away from their home country. More still needs to be done to help attract and retain these students.

Students whose first language is not English are required to have an appropriate grade/score in an approved English language examination for entry to the undergraduate degree programs we offer. Students whose English is below the required standard, or whose school leaving qualifications are insufficient for direct entry are encouraged to register for the International Foundation Program (IFP), which facilitates degree-level entry into almost all of our undergraduate programs. It provides a year's preparation in academic subjects, study skills and English language.

The School of Computing offers postgraduate research degrees and undergraduate taught courses at both UK campuses with more business focused courses based at the Medway campus. The undergraduate Computer Science (CS) program runs at the Canterbury campus and has recently begun offering a module on the IFP as a means to improve international recruitment levels. A taught Masters CS course at the same campus attracts students from around the world but particularly French students, who comprise approximately half the cohort.

3. CONCLUSION

While these three sample institutions are given here just as example, they give an overview of the current situation. The three examples also show that the challenges are not unique to one host country, or one source country, but rather are a shared challenge faces by computing programs with significant international populations. It is envisaged that with many other working group participants a wider perspective on international students will be gained. The challenges that these students faced will be addressed and different strategies will be developed to help universities support and integrate their international students into their computer science programs. This will be a valuable resource of importance to the computer science educators worldwide.

Developing Assessments to Determine Mastery of Programming Fundamentals

Andrew Luxton-Reilly
(co-leader)
University of Auckland
New Zealand
andrew@cs.auckland.ac.nz

Brett A. Becker (co-leader)
University College Dublin
Ireland
brett.becker@ucd.ie

Yingjun Cao
University of California, San Diego
USA
yic242@eng.ucsd.edu

Roger McDermott
Robert Gordon University
Scotland, UK
roger.mcdermott@rgu.ac.uk

Claudio Mirolo
University of Udine
Italy
claudio.mirolo@uniud.it

Andreas Mühling
Kiel University
Germany
andreas.muehling@informatik.
uni-kiel.de

Andrew Petersen
University of Toronto Mississauga
Canada
andrew.petersen@utoronto.ca

Kate Sanders
Rhode Island College
USA
ksanders@ric.edu

Simon
University of Newcastle
Australia
simon@newcastle.edu.au

Jacqueline Whalley
Auckland University of Technology
New Zealand
jacqueline.whalley@aut.ac.nz

ABSTRACT

Current CS1 learning outcomes are relatively general, specifying tasks such as designing, implementing, testing and debugging programs that use some fundamental programming constructs. These outcomes impact what we teach, our expectations, and our assessments. Although prior work has demonstrated the utility of single concept assessments, most assessments used in formal examinations combine numerous heterogeneous concepts, resulting in complex and difficult tasks.

The exclusive use of these traditional assessments results in two major problems. Firstly, teachers who are administering the assessments find it difficult to quantify what students are struggling with. A program that fails to compile or fails to pass test cases provides little information about what a student can successfully achieve. Secondly, it deprives the students of feedback about what they do know and what they can achieve, which we know is one of the most significant factors that influence student learning. Our traditional compound assessment tasks limit the nature and quality of feedback to teachers and students alike, and may contribute to the perceived difficulty and high drop out rates observed in introductory programming courses.

This working group aims to decompose existing CS1 learning outcomes into their component parts, and develop assessment items focused on these individual components. We aim to create exemplar assessments that may be used for formative or summative feedback on student understanding of specific components of programming knowledge. Focusing on independent components of programming increases opportunities for students to demonstrate what they can achieve, and may improve diagnosis of student difficulties.

It is likely that this project would be of particular relevance to teachers and researchers interested in mastery learning, or those who wish to demonstrate tight coupling between learning outcomes and assessment tasks. It may also be of relevance to teachers and researchers interested in promoting a more positive mindset in the classroom, focusing on what students *do know* and what they *can achieve* during a typical CS1 course.

KEYWORDS

ITiCSE working group; CS1; learning outcomes; assessment; exam; questions; mastery; learning; computer science education; novice programming

Developing a Holistic Understanding of Systems and Algorithms Through Research Papers

Ali Erkan
Ithaca College
953 Danby Rd
Ithaca, New York 14850
aerkan@ithaca.edu

John Barr
Ithaca College
953 Danby Rd
Ithaca, New York 14850
barr@ithaca.edu

Tony Clear
Te Ara Auaha,
Faculty of Design & Creative
Technologies
Auckland University of
Technology
Private Bag 92006
Auckland 1010
btony.clear@aut.ac.nz

Cruz Izu
The University of Adelaide
Level 4, Ingkarni Wardli
Adelaide SA 5005
cruz@cs.adelaide.edu.au

Cristian Jose Lopez del Alamo
Universidad La Salle -
Arequipa
Av. Alfonso Ugarte 517,
Cercado
Arequipa - Perú
clopez@ulasalle.edu.pe

Hanan Mohammed
Carnegie Mellon University
in Qatar
Education City
PO Box 24866
Doha, Qatar
skymohammed@gmail.com

Mahadev Nadimpalli
Fitchburg State University
160 Pearl St.
Fitchburg MA 01420-2697
nmahadev@gmail.com

Even though a computer science or computing-oriented degree is unavoidably broken into semesters and courses, we always hope that our students form a holistic picture of the discipline by the time they graduate. Yet we do not have too many opportunities to make this point in a convincing manner. The goal of this working group will be to address a well-defined portion of this problem: revealing the significant connections between algorithmic courses (such as Discrete Math, Data Structures, Algorithms) and systems oriented courses (such as Organization, Computer Networks, Operating Systems, and Hardware) that may be missed by students. In particular, we will explore how *research papers* can be used as the glue for this purpose.

The objectives of this working group are to identify crucial systems topics, locate papers of the appropriate nature, and categorize algorithmic concepts necessary to master the papers. Most importantly, we will create a framework to design combined systems/algorithm courses that hinge on the selected papers. Consequently, instead of using papers in the conventional manner to expose students to research, we will focus on how papers can be used to express the holistic structure of a conventional computer science or computing-oriented degree.

Particular outcomes of the working group will include

1. Development of a rubric that can be used to vet systems papers that present or test algorithms.

2. Identification and classification of relevant papers.

3. Identification of foundational algorithmic topics that are a prerequisite to each paper.

4. Identification of foundational and secondary system topics that can be covered in a course using this approach

5. Development of *exemplar courses* for this approach and identification of the algorithmic and system concepts in each course and the papers used in the course.

6. Development of a generic syllabus for combined algorithm-system courses.

7. Creation of assessments that can be used to evaluate the efficacy of this approach

ITiCSE '17 July 03-05, 2017, Bologna, Italy

© 2017 Copyright held by the owner/author(s).

ACM ISBN 978-1-4503-4704-4/17/07.

DOI: http://dx.doi.org/10.1145/3059009.3081329

Keywords

Education, Operating Systems, Networks, Algorithms

Developing a Holistic Understanding of Systems and Algorithms Through Research Papers

Ali Erkan
Ithaca College
953 Danby Rd
Ithaca, New York 14850
aerkan@ithaca.edu

John Barr
Ithaca College
953 Danby Rd
Ithaca, New York 14850
barr@ithaca.edu

Tony Clear
Te Ara Auaha,
Faculty of Design & Creative
Technologies
Auckland University of
Technology
Private Bag 92006
Auckland 1010
btony.clear@aut.ac.nz

Cruz Izu
The University of Adelaide
Level 4, Ingkarni Wardli
Adelaide SA 5005
cruz@cs.adelaide.edu.au

Cristian Jose Lopez del Alamo
Universidad La Salle -
Arequipa
Av. Alfonso Ugarte 517,
Cercado
Arequipa - Perú
clopez@ulasalle.edu.pe

Hanan Mohammed
Carnegie Mellon University
in Qatar
Education City
PO Box 24866
Doha, Qatar
skymohammed@gmail.com

Mahadev Nadimpalli
Fitchburg State University
160 Pearl St.
Fitchburg MA 01420-2697
nmahadev@gmail.com

Even though a computer science or computing-oriented degree is unavoidably broken into semesters and courses, we always hope that our students form a holistic picture of the discipline by the time they graduate. Yet we do not have too many opportunities to make this point in a convincing manner. The goal of this working group will be to address a well-defined portion of this problem: revealing the significant connections between algorithmic courses (such as Discrete Math, Data Structures, Algorithms) and systems oriented courses (such as Organization, Computer Networks, Operating Systems, and Hardware) that may be missed by students. In particular, we will explore how *research papers* can be used as the glue for this purpose.

The objectives of this working group are to identify crucial systems topics, locate papers of the appropriate nature, and categorize algorithmic concepts necessary to master the papers. Most importantly, we will create a framework to design combined systems/algorithm courses that hinge on the selected papers. Consequently, instead of using papers in the conventional manner to expose students to research, we will focus on how papers can be used to express the holistic structure of a conventional computer science or computing-oriented degree.

Particular outcomes of the working group will include

1. Development of a rubric that can be used to vet systems papers that present or test algorithms.

2. Identification and classification of relevant papers.

3. Identification of foundational algorithmic topics that are a prerequisite to each paper.

4. Identification of foundational and secondary system topics that can be covered in a course using this approach

5. Development of *exemplar courses* for this approach and identification of the algorithmic and system concepts in each course and the papers used in the course.

6. Development of a generic syllabus for combined algorithm-system courses.

7. Creation of assessments that can be used to evaluate the efficacy of this approach

ITiCSE '17 July 03-05, 2017, Bologna, Italy

© 2017 Copyright held by the owner/author(s).

ACM ISBN 978-1-4503-4704-4/17/07.

DOI: http://dx.doi.org/10.1145/3059009.3081329

Keywords

Education, Operating Systems, Networks, Algorithms

Understanding the Effects of Lecturer Intervention on Computer Science Student Behaviour

Claudia Szabo
The University of Adelaide
Australia
claudia.szabo@adelaide.edu.au

Nickolas Falkner
The University of Adelaide
Australia
nickolas.falkner@adelaide.edu.au

Mohsen Dorodchi
University of North Carolina
USA
Mohsen.Dorodchi@uncc.edu

Antti Knutas
Lappeenranta University of
Technology
Finland
Antti.Knutas@lut.fi

Francesco Maiorana
University of Catania
Italy
fmaioran@gmail.com

ABSTRACT

A key challenge for computer science educators worldwide is providing effective feedback and support to students, to ensure they are engaged with the course. This includes online feedback on discussion forums as well as feedback on programming assignments. Due to the significant problems of scale that need to be addressed, effective lecturer intervention is difficult, and at the same time the effect of intervention in online discussion forums is challenging to measure accurately. The same problem occurs when marking programming assignments, where detailed, in-depth feedback is often replaced with output from failed testcases, which the students sometimes proceed to address without giving thought to the quality of their overall solutions.

The working group will (1) identify and survey existing literature on quantifying lecturer intervention in online discussion forums and on assignment feedback, (2) identify existing datasets that could be used to study intervention in depth, (3) identify key data characteristics and associated tools that can be used to effectively process the data, and (4) identify and outline key recommendations for effective lecturer intervention. The outcome of this working group will be a report but the working group will also bring together researchers focused on understanding effective lecturer intervention, thus contributing to the growth of the community.

KEYWORDS

Lecturer intervention, Feedback

ACM Reference format:
Claudia Szabo, Nickolas Falkner, Mohsen Dorodchi, Antti Knutas, and Francesco Maiorana. 2017. Understanding the Effects of Lecturer Intervention on Computer Science Student Behaviour. In *Proceedings of ITICSE 2017, July 3–5, 2017, Bologna, Italy.*, 2017, 1 pages.
DOI: http://dx.doi.org/10.1145/3059009.3081330

The Internet of Things in CS Education: Current Challenges and Future Potential

Barry Burd (leader)
Mathematics & Computer Science
Department, Drew University, USA
bburd@drew.edu

Lecia Barker
Department of Information Science,
University of Colorado Boulder, USA
barkerl@Colorado.edu

Monica Divitini
Department of Computer Science,
Norwegian University of Science
and Technology, Norway
divitini@idi.ntnu.no

Ata Elahi
Computer Science Department,
Southern Connecticut State
University, USA
elahia1@southernct.edu

Armando Fermín Pérez
Computer Science Department,
National University of San Marcos,
Perú
fferminp@unmsm.edu.pe

Alcwyn Parker
The Media Centre,
Falmouth University, UK
Alcwyn.parker@falmouth.ac.uk

Jorge Guerra Guerra
Computer Science Department,
National University of San Marcos,
Perú
jguerrag@unmsm.edu.pe

Ingrid Russell
Computer Science Department,
University of Hartford, USA
irussell@hartford.edu

Bill Siever
Department of Computer Science &
Engineering, Washington University
in St. Louis, USA
bsiever@wustl.edu

Liviana Tudor
Department of Informatics,
Information Technology,
Mathematics and Physics,
Petroleum-Gas University of Ploiesti,
Romania
LTudor@upg-ploiesti.ro

ABSTRACT

Smart devices are everywhere, and the Internet of Things (IoT) revolution is only in its infancy. In the Internet of Things, everyday objects share data over networks, with or without human intervention. Self-driving cars, sensing thermostats, door locks, pet feeders, light bulbs, wearables of all kinds, and smart materials for manufacturing all belong to the new Internet of Things, applying sensors and cloud computing to allow for object-to-object communication.

As computer science educators, we will soon be teaching students how to develop and maintain IoT technologies. This presents enormous challenges and even greater opportunities. How will we integrate IoT concepts and technologies into existing curricula? How will we handle the mix of software and hardware topics that most IoT projects involve? How will we deal with the legal, social, and ethical issues? How will we choose from the growing number of IoT industry standards? What kinds of equipment and lab spaces are optimal for small, medium, and large-scale programs, and how will we budget for all this? What are the opportunities for interdisciplinary studies? How will we leverage the enthusiasm students feel when they create projects that go beyond text, beyond graphics, beyond virtual reality, and into the tactile, three-dimensional, realm of moving real-world objects?

In this working group, we study and document the current state of IoT education and interview educators with IoT teaching experience. We will then make recommendations to help educators integrate IoT topics in computer science curricula.

CCS Concepts
Social and professional topics → Professional topics → Computing education → Computing education programs → Computer science education

Keywords
Internet of Things; IoT technologies; Computer Science Curricula

ITiCSE'17, July 3–5, 2017, Bologna, Italy.
ACM ISBN 978-1-4503-4704-4/17/07.
DOI: http://dx.doi.org/10.1145/3059009.3081331

Searching for Early Developmental Activities Leading to Computational Thinking Skills

Quintin Cutts (leader), Peter Donaldson (co-leader) and Elizabeth Cole (co-leader)
University of Glasgow
United Kingdom
{quintin.cutts, peter.donaldson.2}@glasgow.ac.uk, e.cole.2@research.gla.ac.uk

Bedour Alshaigy	Mirela Gutica	Arto Hellas
Oxford Brookes University	British Columbia Institute of Technology	University of Helsinki
United Kingdom	Canada	Finland
bedour.alshaigy-2012@brookes.ac.uk	mirela_gutica@bcit.ca	arto.hellas@cs.helsinki.fi

Edurne Larraza-Mendiluze	Robert McCartney	Elizabeth Patitsas
University of the Basque Country	University of Connecticut	University of Toronto
Spain	USA	Canada
edurne.larraza@ehu.eus	robert.mccartney@uconn.edu	patitsas@cs.toronto.edu

Charles Riedesel
University of Nebraska, Lincoln
USA
chuckr@unl.edu

Drawing on the long debate about whether computer science (CS) and computational thinking skills are innate or learnable, this working group is based on the following hypothesis:

The apparent innate ability of some CS learners who succeed in CS courses despite no prior exposure to computing is a manifestation of early childhood experiences and learning outside formal education.

The key elements here are *early experiences* which are *outside* formal education that may be leading to success in CS courses, as these aspects have not been previously studied in detail.

Example experiences and learning are the kinds of toys played with, the encouragement given to explore, particular hobbies, exposure to different kinds of languages, and so on. An informal exercise with 16 CS academics elicited the following potential pre-requisites from their own childhood experiences:

- Modelling, particularly when designing from scratch
- Autonomous devices from paper planes to steam engines
- Exposure to ad-hoc household fixing / repair processes
- Toys with discrete, not continuous, elements, e.g. Lego bricks, not smooth wooden blocks
- Interest in notations – music, languages (bi-lingual parents)

- Parental attitudes encouraging open exploration, with minimal limits and permission to fail
- Following instructions: knitting, cooking, origami, Lego
- Making games – a set of rules

Consideration of the hypothesis leads to the following research questions:

1. Can we find activities that are relatively more common to the childhood experiences of those with CS skills, e.g. successful CS students, academics and professionals, by comparison with other members of the population?
2. If such activities can be determined, what common understanding, skills or attitudes can be derived from them?
3. Can the common aspects of the activities be linked to CS skills and therefore seen as pre-requisites?
4. In what ways are these common aspects already present in formal early years or primary education, and where they are not, how could they be incorporated effectively?

Studies supporting this hypothesis would be beneficial as follows:

- Provide further evidence against the innate view of CS skills, encouraging study of CS specific pedagogy.
- Inform educational practices and research in the early years, a field recognised as being of increasing importance.
- Enable early years and primary teachers with no formal CS background to focus on educational activities with which they are familiar and confident while still developing essential foundations for CT skills.

The primary focus of this working group is the first research question above. If this is answered positively, then we will work on preliminary answers to the subsequent questions.

ITiCSE'17, July 03-05, 2017, Bologna, Italy
© 2017 Copyright is held by the owner/author(s).
ACM ISBN 978-1-4503-4704-4/17/07.
DOI: http://dx.doi.org/10.1145/3059009.3081332

Author Index

www.ingramcontent.com/pod-product-compliance
Lightning Source LLC
Chambersburg PA
CBHW082104220326

41598CB00066BA/5216